MASTER GUIDE

SECOND EDITION

Greetings Citizens of Azeroth,

Brady is pleased to present this fully-updated and revised Official Strategy Guide, now called the Master Guide.

We at Brady still play WoW and we have taken a second look at our Official Strategy Guide with a very critical eye. After 12 patches, much of the information in the original guide had become outdated. In addition to updating the meat of the guide, we wanted to make the book more manageable and easier to use. We are confident you will find it easier to navigate, packed with more information, and more attractive than before. It is also important to note that this guide, although smaller in page count, covers much more than the first. You need only compare the two to find that this Second Edition keeps the "1st day" chapters, intro to WoW, world maps, and classes. We have added a PvP chapter, an Instances and Raids chapter, and about 1500 quests.

We hope you enjoy using this guide as much as we enjoyed creating it. We didn't just create a book we hope you will use; we created the book we wanted to use ourselves.

Enjoy!

BradyGames

I AN INTRODUCTION TO WOW

II YOUR FIRST DAY

III LEARNING ABOUT THE WORLD

IV BEYOND THE BASICS

We Begin Anew

One of the greatest difficulties of strategy writing is that there is almost never the time, money, and ability to return to a beloved product and update the original material. With World of Warcraft, we've been given the opportunity to do just that: to update, improve, and expand on the original guide with no time or expense spared. It seemed like a rare luxury to spend over half a year in preparation for the release of the first World of Warcraft strategy guide. Yet, that is modest compared to the time placed on this guide. Players and writers who have been involved with World of Warcraft from Beta 1 forward have come together for this incredible task. And in case you can't tell, we're excited. This is an amazing chance to take a guide that we loved and bring it to life once again.

If you are wondering what has changed, the list is a bit daunting. Almost all text is entirely new; strategies have been broken apart and rebuilt from the ground up. We have new tables, data, and updated maps to handle the changes from the last year and a half of updates. Newer screenshots with greater character variety were taken while logging in thousands of hours between characters on all manner of servers. Searching for Rare or Epic items? We have them all in here. Planning equipment sets, trying out different PvP builds, looking for ways to excel in dungeons, raids, and in the battlegrounds? We have been too, and the results are in here.

Everything that could possibly fit between two covers is ready. New players: you are still going to receive the comfortable introduction to World of Warcraft that was present in the first guide (we'll take you through the early hours of play and explain everything to help you on your way). Experienced players fear not; there an amazing amount for you here as well. We've taken all of the resources from all over Azeroth and the real world and brought them into one place. Tired of keeping the Net up in the background or on another system to look up item drops in your favorite instances? Do you want to squeeze those last few percentage points of critical strike out of your character without losing precious Stamina or Attack Power? We found the best ways to do it. We'll help you level your second, third, and fourth characters to 60 in style. We'll get you to Exalted in all the battlegrounds. And, we promise that it's going to be fun this time too.

Glad to have you back.

Glossary

This Glossary gives you a good idea what the common terms mean in World of Warcraft. Gaming slang, internal statistics, and other such ideas are explained in enough detail to get complete novices and gaming veterans speaking the same language.

Term	Definition
Add	A creature that adds into an existing fight against you. As a verb, it is the act of having a creature add into a fight "That Ogre is going to add."
AFK	Away From Keyboard. This means that the person won't be available for a short time. There is also a specific /afk command to let others who message you know that you are AFK.
Aggro	Most often this is used to note that a creature is attacking you or your group "We've got aggro!" The term denotes the aggressive interests of a monster/npc. If a person says, "Go aggro that monster" if means to intentionally get the enemy to attack you.
Aggro Radius	This is the distance from which an enemy decides to attack a character. This radius is influenced by the level difference between the monster and the character (with relatively tougher monsters aggroing from farther away). This distance is also influenced by the type of creature involved, as a number of predators have a larger aggro radius to begin with.
Agility	Agility is an attribute in World of Warcraft. This attribute determines a character's ability to Dodge attacks, score Critical Hits (that deal at least twice the damage), and deal more damage in general with their attacks (though this is only true with certain classes).
AKA	Shorthand for Also Known As
Alt	A secondary character. This usually refers to a character that you put less time into or a character that is lower in level compared to your primary (Main) character.
Area of Effect	These are spells, abilities, and items that influence multiple targets over a given area. Sometimes these are based on a circle around a specific target person (the caster or an enemy off in the distance). These can also be based off of a selected area (these are called ground targeted AoEs).
Armor	This reflects the amount of protective armor your character is wearing. This statistic increases as you continue to find better equipment with higher levels. Your character's current armor is the primary factor in determining physical damage mitigation.
Artificial Intelligence	Or AI. NPCs of various sorts have a certain level of intelligence that determines their activities in and outside of battle.
Attack Power	This is a statistic that influences the physical Damage Per Second of your character. Having a higher melee Attack Power greatly helps in dealing more damage, especially with heavier weapons. Having a higher ranged Attack Power increases overall ranged damage.
Attack Skill	Each character has an Attack Skill with at least several weapon types. Your maximum Attack Skill is equal to five times your current level. Training with a weapon by attacking increases your Attack Skill towards this cap. During battle, Attack Skill (relative to your enemy's Defense) influences the chance to strike successfully and score Critical Hits.
Attribute	A major statistic for a character. Each attribute reflects on a major side of a character's capabilities (Strength for melee damage and blocking with shields, Agility for Dodging, Critical Hits, and some classes' Attack Power, Stamina for Hit Points, Intellect for Mana, and Spirit for recovery of Hit Points/Mana over time)
Auction House	Frequently shortened to AH. These areas allow characters to post many items for sale. The transactions have a modest fee, yet they allow your character to make sales and purchases without meeting other characters directly and investing major time in buying/selling.
Avatar	The visual representation of your character in World of Warcraft
Battleground	An instanced area for PvP conflict. Sign up today in the major cities or at specific instance portals. WSG is Warsong Gulch, AB is Arathi Basin, AV is Alterac Valley.
BBL	Be Back Later
Bind	To Bind to a certain inn with your Hearthstone (so that you can teleport there in the future). This can also be used to define when an item Binds to your character on pickup (BoP) or on first equip (BoE).
Bind on Equip	This means that a specific item will Bind to your character the first time it is equipped. After that point, it cannot be traded or put onto the Auction House. Before that time, normal trade is completely allowable.
Bind on Pickup	These items immediately Bind to a character when looted or crafted, and they can never be sold or traded for any reason. Most often, these items are of Rare quality (or higher) and are found from powerful enemies.
Boat/Zeppelin	Boats and Zeppelins are used for travel between the continents.
Boots	Not just an armor piece! This is also used to signify a power-up object in the Battlegrounds (Warsong Gulch) that increases run speed ("If you can make it to our base, the boots are up!").
BRB	Be Right Back
BRT	Be Right There
Buff	Using spells to increase the potential of your allies. This refers to both the act "Please buff me, good Priest" and to the actual spell effect "With this buff I have 4,240 Hit Points, woot!"
Bug	An in-game problem that causes something unexpected to happen. This may require Customer Service Representative/GM intervention (you will need to submit a ticket if the bug is dramatic).
Camp	To control a given area in the hopes of either getting all the monster spawns for yourself/your group, or for the purpose of stopping PvP enemies from having safety there. You can camp an area, a graveyard, the corpse of a fallen enemy, and so forth. This often involves multiple people to be done most effectively (the group fans out and watches for anything that will try to disrupt their activities).
Carebear	Somewhat derogatory name for a person who avoids PvP, plays on non-PvP servers, and so forth.
Cast	To use a spell. This may occur instantly with some spells (instant-cast spells have almost no delay of any sort) or require up to several seconds of time invested in the casting process during which interruptions may occur if the caster is struck.
Caster	A person who is capable of casting spells. Often used to refer to Mages, Warlocks, Priests, and Druids who stay in Caster Form. It is implied in the name that the person is a softer target who needs either protection or fast elimination, depending on their affiliations. "Kill their casters first, they are supporting the flag carrier!!!"
Chain Casting	Going from one spell directly into the next. "That Shaman Chain Casts Lesser Healing Wave every time she gets in trouble."
Cheese	A method of winning that isn't exploitive but appears to be unfair in one way or another. This may be quite inaccurate in some cases. This is a synonym for abuse.
Class	A set of abilities and statistics for your character that is chosen during creation. This greatly influences how you will play your character.
Combat Pet	Warlocks and Hunters have pets that can fight beside them and greatly affect the outcome of combat.
Con	Short for consider. This was used in many older MOGs to tell how powerful a creature was. In World of Warcraft, this is done with both a numeric level comparison and by the the background color of the mob's frame.
Corpse Camping	To stay near a slain enemy in world PvP in an attempt to prevent them from resurrecting at their body without being killed again. This is not griefing by definition. It is also not friendly and is considered a fair act of aggression against the party being camped.
Crash to Desktop	When the game kicks you back onto the desktop. In-game, people will likely refer to this as a DC (a disconnect).
Creep	Term for neutral creatures.
Crit	Short term for a Critical Hit (a blow that deals roughly twice normal damage).
Critters	Creatures out in the wild that have no combat capabilities (small snakes, rabbits, etc.). Killing these is absolutely necessary.
Crowd Control	Using spells or abilities to disable enemy targets for a substantial period. Sap, Polymorph, and Fear are major examples of POWERFUL Crowd Control (CC) that not only limits the enemies' options to act, but almost removes them entirely from combat. Lesser/limited Crowd Control may inhibit movement but still allow enemies a moderate amount of control; Frost Nova, roots, and Hamstring are good examples of limited control.
Customer Service Representative	The in-game staff that exist to help players with major problems. Often called GMs by the players.
Damage Mitigation	The Armor statistic is compared to a table of estimated Armor values for a given level. The result is your character's Damage Mitigation (found by highlighting the Armor stat on your character page). This value roughly explains the amount of damage absorbed by your armor when your character is struck by a creature of similar level. Abilities and Spells can influence both Armor and Damage Mitigation.
Damage Per Second	Base damage from a spell, weapon, or ability is only part of the story. Damage Per Second (DPS) is a way to figure out how effective, per unit time, a given action is. The higher the DPS, the more damage an activity can produce. This is often most important for attrition PvP or PvE situations. In short-term PvP, burst damage is more important than specific DPS.
Debuff	A debuff is any spell that goes on an enemy target and stays there for a period of time. Some deal damage; some reduce stats.
Defense	This stat determines how often your character is struck physically and how often such blows are Critical Hits. This stat has a cap of five times the character's level and increases toward that cap when your character is attacked.
Direct Damage	Spells, Abilities, or Items that deal damage immediately and directly to a target.
Dispel	To remove a Debuff from an ally or to remove a positive effect from a foe.
DMG	Shorthand for Damage.
DnD	Do Not Disturb
DOT	Shorthand for Damage Over Time. DOT abilities/spells are often very efficient but require slower tactics for the attrition to run its course. Warlocks are especially known for their cruel DOTs.
Duping	Creating multiple items from a single source. This is only possible through rare exploits (if at all during this stage of the game), and WILL lead to major penalties or banning of accounts.
Emote	An action (often with voice or animation) that is made by your character. Emotes are very useful for roleplaying and are covered in this guide.
Experience	Experience/XP measures your progress toward another level.
Exploit	Activities that are against the Terms of Use for World of Warcraft and capitalize on bugs to give players an unfair advantage over others.
Farm	To repeatedly kill a given target or type of target, often for desired drops of trade items or equipment
Flag	An object (target) in the Battlegrounds; these are right-clicked to pick up or activate. Also used to denote PvP activity, as in "That warrior is flagged for PvP! Get 'em!"
Flagged	To be PvP enabled. On PvE, Standard RP servers, and in the starter Zones, using /pvp is required before fighting against the other faction is possible. Once /pvp is used, your are Flagged.
Flight	Both factions use bats/gryphons/etc. to fly characters between cities and towns. People may refer to this as being "on the bird."
Free for All	This is a loot rule that allows any character to loot any body. Often reserved for VERY close friends and trusted allies.
Gank	Primarily a PvP server term and function. This is when characters of much higher level go after younger targets that have no hope of surviving or even escaping, or when people are unprepared due to combat with a mob. A person who does this activity is a "ganker."
GG	Short for "Good Game!" Spoken to buddies after the end of many battleground matches, even when on the losing side.
GJ	Short for "Good Job!" to signal approval or appreciation.

Term	Definition
Gimp	To Gimp means to take a course of action with Talents or equipment that makes your character ineffective. Being a Gimp is to be such a character. An example would be a full Intellect gear Warrior with a side dose of +Healing improvements.
GM	In-game Blizzard representatives that try to correct for bugs or deal with harassment issues.
Graveyard	A place where characters return after death. The spirits can run back to their bodies for life to begin anew, or they can Resurrect at the Spirit Healer nearby (this damages their equipment and causes a status debuff for a short time).
Graveyard Camping	Staying in areas where enemies are spawned in the Battlegrounds or use the Spirit Healer in the normal world. This is considered to be in very poor taste by many players and may (in some servers) be defined as griefing.
Grief	Making an active effort to harass another player that goes beyond the rules of the game. Graveyard Camping another player, Kill Stealing, and other malicious acts are included in this.
Grind	To specifically gain experience by attacking monsters (as opposed to questing for experience). Often repetitive and mindless.
Group Loot	A standard set of loot rules for groups in instances. Group Loot does a Round Robin system for standard items, letting each person loot a fair number of bodies. Then, when items of a chosen threshold drop, window appears that allows people roll Need, Greed, or Pass on the item.
Group/Party	A team of up to five characters that are invited (/inv) to complete common goals. This is great for questing and almost mandatory for doing instance dungeons at their appropriate level.
GUI	Graphical User Interface
Guild	Groups of players get together and form guilds. Initially, this takes nine signatures from unguilded characters on unique accounts. This starts off by getting a charter from one of the three major cities in your faction.
Hate List	Monsters keep an internal list of the character they WANT to kill the most. This is the Hate List. Damage done, healing, and other activities against the monster's interests determine who stays high on the Hate List.
Heal Over Time	In shorthand, used as HOT. A healing spell that helps another character in doses instead of in one instant chunk.
Hearthstone	An item given to all characters that allows you to Bind at Inns for instant teleportation (once per hour). The process of leaving an area using the Hearthstone is "Hearthing."
Hit Points	The stat to measure how tough your character is (how much damage they take before dying). Stamina bonuses, levels, and buffs affect Hit Points.
Honor	Points gained from kills against enemies of similar (or higher) level and from Battleground victories.
Hybrid	A class that fills several niches or rests in-between them. Shamans, Paladins, and Druids are very good examples of Hybrid classes because they can switch between some tanking, healing, and damage dealing roles.
IC	In-character (often used to let people know that you are speaking as your character, in a roleplaying sense).
IMO	In My Opinion (or IMHO for In My Humble Opinion)
Incoming	Or INC, used to let people know that enemies are on their way.
Instance	An area that is privately loaded for individual characters or groups (e.g. instance dungeons, battlegrounds)
IRC	Used to denote the use of outside communication channels (like voice chat or instant messaging programs).
Intellect	Stat that determines the amount of Mana your character has, the speed at which Defense and Weapon Skills are learned, and improves the spell Critical Chance.
j/k	Common internet term to signal that someone is "just kidding" and that they should not be taken seriously.
Kill on Sight	Often used as a PvP term for someone that receives no mercy at all. "That guy used /spit on my boyfriend, he is KOS now!"
Kill Steal	To Tap enemies that another player is setting up to fight. This prevents that player from being able to get experience for the monster. This can be griefing if done repeatedly, and it's very poor etiquette in any event.
Kite	To Kill in Time, also summons the image of stretching enemies behind you like a person flying a kite. This is a technique of killing enemies slowly by using DOTs and ranged attacks to wound them while evading/running away from the foes.
Lag	Delays caused by poor Internet latency. Lag jumping is when your computer corrects for this and jumps things around onscreen to get people into their proper positions.
Leech	To be in a group or raid and contribute nothing "They just sat there and leeched Reputation in Alterac Valley for two hours."
Leet Speak	Also known as 1337 speak. The use of numbers for replacing certain letters and generally idiosyncratic grammar to denote allegiance to the younger geek culture.
Level	A measure of your character's power and progression in Azeroth. This ranges from 1-60 before the game's first expansion arrives. In the future, this will extend from 1-70, and who knows what the future will hold!
Leveling	Gaining levels, and through them abilities and power for your characters. This is done by completing quests, killing monsters, exploring the world, and so forth.
Line of Sight	The direct line between one entity and their target. Many abilities require a direct Line of Sight, and when LOS is broken the spells/abilities will fail to go off.
Link	To post a item in a channel so that others may see its statistics. Holding down Shift while clicking on an item will do this for whispers and guild chat, but not for private chat channels.
LOL	Laugh Out Loud; common Internet usage for anything amusing. ROFL (rolling on the floor laughing) is also used.
LOM/OOM	Low on Mana and Out of Mana; these are statements made by casters to let the group know that fun time is almost over.
Looking For Group	Or LFG–used to let people know that you are trying to find a group to accomplish a task. Groups with open slots may yell LFM, or "Looking for more."
Loot	Loot itself is the treasure that is taken from monsters after they fall; To Loot means to actually bend over and right-click on bodies to take said items.
Lowbie	A person of low level for a given activity. This can mean someone in the first few levels of a PvP bracket, even if that person is level 50-52!
Mailbox	Many Inns or Bank areas have Mailboxes. Auction items and money are delivered here. Money can also be sent to other characters, as can items and letters! The fee for this is trivial, even at low levels.
Main	Your current primary characteras opposed to your alts.
Master Looter	A loot setting that only allows the group leader to handle treasure and its dispensation. This is time inefficient and is often used in DKP-type systems or when dealing with extremely valuable loot.
Med	To rest, eat/drink, and restore any fallen buffs while preparing for future fighting. This is often called by the group leader or a primary healer.
Melee	Direct physical combat at close range.
Mistell	Or MT. Done when you message the wrong person with a /tell or when you post to the wrong chat channel. Example: "Yeah, my guild sucks and I'm thinking of leaving them" said in guild chat. Response "YIKES, MT. I was talking about another guild!"
Mob	Short for Mobile. An old gaming term that persists. All of the world's monsters are Mobs.
MOG	Massive Online Game
Mount	A creature that your character can ride. At level 40, every character has the ability to learn to ride a mount and, for a fee, purchase one.
Need Before Greed	The honor system of loot in instance dungeons. This means that you do not try to roll NEED on items that your character doesn't actually want to equip. If you are going to equip something, you need it. If you want it to sell, or send it to one of your alts or friends, it's greed.
Nerf	When the game is patched and certain actions/abilities are reduced in effectiveness. "They finally stopped Nerfing Mortal Strike!"
Ninja	To loot an item that was up for discussion or to roll need on items that are quite clearly not ones that you need. This is akin to an act of stealing from a group. Don't do it if you want to have friends, good guilds, good groups. It is NOT worth the money.
NM	Nevermind. Sometimes used as NVM.
Noob/Newbie	An insult. This is often said when someone does something completely foolish that gets them or their group/team in trouble. "The Paladin bubbled while carrying the flag, NOOB!!!" It can also be used in a self-deprecating manner: "Even though I've been through Wailing Caverns 3 times, I still feel like a noob there."
NPC	Non-Player Character. The various people of Azeroth who give quests, offer services, and exist to support the backstory of World of Warcraft are all NPCs.
Offtank	Also known as Secondary Tanks. These are tough characters that back up the primary Tank by worrying about single targets that peel onto casters. When not needed for this role, Offtanks often attempt to deal high damage.
OMW	On My Way
OOC	Out Of Character. Sometimes signified on roleplaying servers with the use of parentheses, as in "The horn has sounded! I must leave this place! (gotta log guys)"
Own/Pwn	1337 speak for a major victory over someone or something.
PC	Player Character
Ping	To create a glowing yellow circle on the local map through right-clicking on an area; this indicates direct position of a target (especially useful in the Battlegrounds). This is also a specific Hunter ability that is used to uncover Stealthed targets.
Point Blank AoE	An area of effect ability that centers around the caster. Shortened to PBAoE.
Port	To Port or Portal is to immediately travel to a certain location. Mages do this by Porting to set locations, any player can use their Hearthstones to Port to an Inn that they have bound to, and Warlocks can Summon people to themselves.
Pot	Potions are often shortened to Pot in-game. Pot use is common in PvE and PvP for restoring Hit Points or Mana. Other important Potions include Free Action, Swiftness, and many stat-enhancing choices as well.
Powerlevel	To assist a lower-level character by helping them quest/grind at a much faster pace. Often more effective with slightly higher-level characters that stay out of group.
Proc	An item effect that goes off under certain conditions (on hit, when struck, etc.). These often occur somewhat randomly and are somewhat powerful when they do occur. Short for "P.rogrammed R.andom O.C.currence".
Profession	Trades for crafting and gathering. A character can only learn two normal Professions, as opposed to secondary skills.
PST	Please Send Tell, used with ads for items or requests for services. This lets people know that you want to be privately messaged with any offers.
Puller	The person designated to pull enemies back to a group (a task that is essential for safe play in tougher instance dungeons). Hunters are ideal pullers, but any class can take this role if they are skilled and cautious.
PvE	Player vs. Environment. Quests, dungeon delving, and monster grinding are considered to be PvE content.
PvP	Player vs. Player. Battlegrounds, world conflicts, and duels are examples of PvP content.
QFT	Quoted For Truth. Used to indicate an assenting opinion.
Queue	The waiting list for the Battlegrounds and log-in server.
Raid	Groups above five characters can form when a leader selects the Convert To Raid button. Although experience is reduced dramatically and quests are no longer completable (with several exceptions), the firepower (or camaraderie potential) of a large force can be quite beneficial, and necessary in late-game raid dungeons and battlegrounds.
Random	Used to figure out who gets certain items that many characters want. For instance, if there are several Miners in a group, they may /random for a Mithril Vein that they come across.
Rank	Gaining high Honor in a given week increases your Standing compared to other players of the same faction. Working hard allows you to increase in PvP Rank, allowing considerable rewards in your capital city.
Reputation	Different NPC groups can be courted in various ways. With increased Reputation you gain access to items, recipes, and resources. Or, if you go to war against a given faction, you can lose such opportunities and slaughter the masses of their people for fun and profit.
Res Sickness	When brought back to life by a Spirit Healer, there is a period of decreased combat effectiveness. This debuff cannot be cured by characters.
Resistance	Ability to negate or mitigate damage and effects from various magical or non-physical attacks. There are Resistances for Arcane, Fire, Nature, Frost, and Shadow.
Rested Bonus	Characters gain double the normal experience for kills while they are in a Rested state. This occrues while you are logged out or in an Inn/City. Note that Inn/City resting gives your character FOUR times the amount of Rested Bonus, so it REALLY helps to log off at such a location at the end of a day.
ROFL/ ROFLMAO	Common internet term used as response to something very entertaining: "Roll on the Floor Laughing/Roll on the Floor Laughing my [butt] Off."
Resurrection/ Rez	Being brought back to life. This is done by returning to a corpse, speaking to a Spirit Healer, or by having healing characters cast various types of Resurrection Spells.
Roleplaying	Staying in-character to promote a greater sense of depth to the world.
Root	To lock an enemy in place for a short time. They can fight, but they cannot move.
Run Speed	How fast your character moves across terrain. There are several ways to increase this, including potions or specific class Abilities.
Snare	To slow an enemy's movement. Hamstring, Wing Clip, Frost Spells of many types, and other such abilities Snare opponents. They can still move and fight, but it is much easier to Kite them during this time.
Spawn	Defeated enemies and gathered resources return to the world after a time. This event is called a Spawn (or a Pop).
Specialization	Often refers to Talent selections. This denotes a focus on playing your character in a specific way. Gear, Talents, and playstyle all come together to maximize a given Spec. Can refer to trade skills.
Spirit	Attribute that controls the rate of Hit Point/Mana regeneration for your character.
Stacking	Abilities that work in harmony instead of replacing each other are said to Stack. Snares often do NOT Stack. DOTs of almost all types absolutely DO Stack.
Stamina	Attribute that determines your character's Hit Point total.
Standing	A ladder for Honor gained in a week. You compete against your own faction for high Standing. Achieving extremely high Rank is impossible without consistently high Standing and a huge investment of time.
Stat	A Statistic that reflects on your gear, levels, Attributes, and current state. Your stats provide a general idea for your character's combat performance.
Stealth	An Ability that allows a character limited invisiblity at the cost of movement speed, available to only Rogues and Druids (as well as some mobs). Stealth is broken when the character takes specific actions or takes damage of any type.
Strength	Attribute that determines melee damage and potential for damage mitigation from shield blocking.
Stun	Any ability/effect that COMPLETELY halts an enemy. They cannot move or escape this effect until it wear off. No combat is possible for them at this time.
Talents	Talent Points are used to invest in one of three Talent Trees. Each character class has three major fields of Talents to choose from, and you can absolutely mix and match from two or even three Talent Trees. Talent Points are given from levels 10-60, adding up to 51 total TPs.
Tank	A tough character designed to grab enemy aggro and hold it while mitigating as much of the damage as possible. Warriors are often the best tanks, but Paladins and Druids are useful here as well. In lower levels, Shamans and both Hunter or Warlock Pets can also be reliable tanks.
Tap	The first point of damage against any target Taps it for you/your group. This designates the monster as yours, turning its status bar grey to all others. Only you can get experience or loot from your Tapped target.
Taunt	An ability that pushes your character much higher or to the top of a creature's Hate List. Great for Tanking!
Tell/Whisper	A private message, sent directly to a person by typing /tell or /whisper and their name. You can also click on a character's name on the screen and send a /tell from there.
Threat	The amount of influence on the Hate List that a given activity causes. High Threat is GREAT if you want aggro. High Threat is horrible if you are squishy.
Toon	Another term for your character in-game.
Train	A term used to denote the process of gaining new abilities (which can be done every even level), as in "I'll go train in Ironforge." It can also be used to denote the act of pulling enemies through another person/group and getting those people engaged in combat. The second definition can be taken as griefing if done repeatedly to people of the same faction.
Twink	A character (usually low-level) that possesses gear/enchantments greatly above their abilities/means.
Uber	Common slang usage means that a person/monster/item is extremely powerful if it is uber.
WTB/WTS	Want to Buy/Want to Sell
Zerg	To gather in a large group and rush forward. This is often a foolish or risky tactic in the battlegrounds because it leaves points undefended/unwatched. Supporting Allies is good; blind rushing is bad.
Zone	Common term for a region of Azeroth. Wetlands, Hillsbrad, Barrens, Durotar are all Zones.

Creating a Character

Choosing a name, race, and class for your character may seem like a simple start, but it's all about investment. You can pick the first class that comes to mind in any race and click on the button to give you a default name. Or, you can sit down and consider with full attention to detail what you want from a character, what each class provides, and which race fits you the best, then think about a name that reflects all of that. Though this is a very personal decision, there are still a few tips that might help along the way.

CLASS

Your intended class is the best thing to decide first. After all, you don't want to fall in love with a race and suddenly find that they don't have the class you were hoping to play. If you don't have a class in mind already, stop and think about yourself. Do you want to get up close and personal? Is ranged combat more your style? Is magic a way of life for characters in the games you love, and, if so, do you like to support/heal or go on the offensive with it?

If you don't have answers to those questions yet, perhaps because you are new to fantasy games, go deeper into your analysis. Do you lead well? Prefer to sit quietly and act suddenly, on your own? Is supporting others very important to you, or are you disinclined to be constantly involved with other people's needs and problems? There are no wrong answers here. It's better to be honest about what you want and seek the class that suits you.

The table below may help here. Though personality issues are extremely subjective, there is a tendency that you will notice in people that are happiest in a given class.

The Classes in a Nutshell

Class	Major Aspects of Play	Personality Leaning
Druid	Flexibility, Healing	People Who Crave Change
Hunter	Survival, Interception, Pulling	Those Who Hold Back From Direct Conflict
Mage	Crowd Control, Range, Fast Life/Fast Death	The Fearless
Paladin	Cannot Be Killed Easily, The Healer Who Won't Die	People Who Hate Losing
Priest	Massive Healing and Group Support	Supporters
Rogue	Sudden Damage, Many Stuns, High Preparation	Aggressive Players
Shaman	Specialization Can Lead to Strong Melee, Ranged Damage, or Healing, Many Paths to Succeed	All Types
Warlock	Tougher Than They Look, Major Utility Options, Gods of Attrition Warfare	Those Who Love to Win
Warrior	Grab Immense Aggro, Hamper Enemies, Requires Both Skill and Gear to Show Their Ultimate Beauty	Leaders

The people who end up being happiest in their classes almost always feel that way because the personality of the class matches their own. There are many folks who play a class for the "wrong" reasons and end up never quite clicking with it. This is because they chose the class based on stats instead of soul. Class X may be the flavor of the month, but nerfs/buffs come and go. Try everything, analyze what feels right, and run with that.

RACE

Though Racial Traits are discussed later and certainly have an influence in gameplay, it is still STRONGLY recommended that you choose a race based on feel. If you grow to love your character, you are going to spend hundreds of hours watching them fight, grow, and succeed. Don't pick a character that doesn't look or feel right to you; look at all of the races, try male and female versions of each, and see what clicks. Let no one influence your decision in this. Pick what you like. Love it, enjoy it, and mock anyone who doesn't understand. In World of Warcraft, all possible character/race combinations are fully viable for the endgame. Anyone can solo to level 60. Anyone can group up to 60. End of story.

NAME

You might be amazed to realize how much goes into a name and how much people assume about you based of this. Generic fantasy names are near-on impossible to remember, movie characters are almost despised, and comic names might not get you into all the best groups. Consider the following:

Naming Tips

The World of Warcraft Name Generator gives you random names to consider. You can click on this as many times as you like and keep what you want. At the minimum, this avoids many of the issues with offensive names.

Other fantasy name generators are found online as well. Search for these and see if there is anything you like.

Simple names are often much better than complex names. If people have trouble typing your name, they won't remember it either. This is bad! You want people to remember who you are and to enjoy typing in your direction (well, if you like grouping and roleplaying).

Strongly consider avoiding popular names from fiction. Almost no one is going to treat you well if your name is a variant on common characters. Drisst Entruri Pickkardd is not your friend. Seriously, there are already 50 Hunters on your server alone with the name xxLegolaxx. Nobody can remember which is which. Nobody wants them around. If you want to go for it, good luck! Enjoy. But, don't say we didn't warn you.

Real world names are right out too. Jaylow the Priest might be able to team with Bennnifer the Druid, but things just won't work out in the long run.

It also needs to be said that names of major religious figures may be taken as major insults by some of the playing community. Be considerate and try not to make major political/social statements with your World of Warcraft time. People are in-game to get away for a while and enjoy the beauty of Azeroth. Be kind to the folks out there; most of them are pretty good people and would be happy to be your friend. By the same token, racial slurs are right out, and, yes, GMs will change names without warning. If you see someone using a name that is offensive in these ways, have no guilt in reporting them to a GM. Odds are, you aren't the only person offended by such language.

You don't need to have the most creative or incredible name to get by. Just choose something that you like. Something that sounds good to you. Simple, concise, clear, and easy to type.

Etiquette in the World of Warcraft

Online games have their own systems of social rules; there are certainly more interactions in a game like World of Warcraft than with offline roleplaying games, where people are seldom able to compete or cooperate while playing. WoW creates an environment where both positive and negative interactions between players are intended to occur, but even the negative ones are set within certain guidelines. Behaviors that fall outside of normal etiquette can be considered rude or inappropriate or even as griefing. To make friends and have a smooth experience in game, it pays to learn the rules up front.

WHILE HUNTING

The environment is primarily cooperative in the open field (at least within your own faction), where players are aligned against the monsters that stalk Azeroth. Whether soloing or grouping to accomplish this, there are ways to keep from stepping on other peoples' toes. Beyond that, it's good to know when someone else is doing something that is genuinely disrespectful so that you can advise them (at first), avoid them if they continue, and ignore them if no change occurs.

You Took My Mobs!!!

Mob ownership is often a point of contention during PvE hunting. Soloists and groups run into situations where other characters will come through and kill some of the same targets in the area where they were already hunting. The first point here is to use a cool head; everyone has a right to go after monsters. Even when a higher level person is attacking a beast, they may be after trade items that are useful, doing a backlog of old quests, or just farming something for their allies.

Instead of reacting with a negative attitude, see what can be done for both sides from the beginning. If you are on a kill quest, offer to bring the other person/people into your group—everyone benefits from this. By the same logic, if you are on a collection quest and someone else is going after the same targets for different reasons, it is STILL faster to group together and hunt. Take the time to ask them first before immediately moving to invite them; players often respond more favorably and happily to a verbal request for a party than if you ambush them with an invitation box.

For whatever reason, an alliance may not be an option. This happens often enough. No problem; you can state what you are doing and see if the other players are willing to give you the space to continue with what you were already doing. If they can't outright help, at least they can give you enough mobs to maintain the same kill rate and excitement. Fair enough for everyone concerned.

By asking people nicely and making your needs clear, you have every chance to get more of what you want if the other people are nice. Also, acting politely is less likely to trigger their obnoxious side (the side that might get them to intentionally stay longer and be even more obtrusive).

How to Handle Hunting Conflicts
Try to Work Together With Newcomers for Mutual Benefit
Agree to Leave Each Other Enough Targets and Space
Find a Better Hunting Spot If Nothing Can Be Arranged
Avoid Aggressive Players and Report Any Griefing to a GM AFTER You Are Certain That It Is Intentional

Most groups and conflicts are settled by the first two options. However, there are times when another group doesn't want to join with yours and is not willing to share anything in the region. That doesn't make them griefers—it's still within their rights to kill as much as they can within the area (that is your right as well). If the other group refuses to have a comfortable attitude, you may try another camp of the same creature (this DOES NOT mean that you are backing down or acting like a coward); there are often several camps of important monsters in a given region. Rather, it shows that you are sensible enough to have a good time and keep from wasting your night, experience points, and energy fighting for meager kills on a single quest. You can always come back later. Your fun, experience, and treasure are more important than making sure someone else ISN'T getting those things.

Okay, so is there any griefing at all that occurs in regard to mob ownership? Well, yes. Even with the tapping system in place, there are ways for people to make life difficult for many other classes. Someone with a real chip on their shoulders can use fast abilities to tap a monster just before your anticipated pull. This negates the experience and treasure you receive from the kill, so it's a bad situation. If someone does this once, ignore it entirely (it was most likely an accident). However, a person who follows your party around and does this multiple times is absolutely trying to get in your way. Ask the person what they are doing, then report anything foul in their response to a GM. If they ignore you and keep doing it, find a new place to hunt and ditch the offenders. Even at this stage, they may simply be too young, inexperienced, or otherwise hindered to know what they are doing.

It is still useful to know how to combat the people who try to tap "your" monsters. Note that your DOTs and debuffs aren't useful for tapping. You need to deal damage to a target, and deal it quickly. Find your fastest ranged ability and use that for grabbing monsters. If you are a melee class, see what works the best out of your existing options. For a Rogue, a fast thrown weapon or missile attack may be ideal. With Warriors, a Charge and immediate Hamstring. Obviously, Hunters and magic classes have the edge in doing this, but any skilled player who knows their class can learn to tap quickly and get the monsters they want.

One very useful thing to be aware of is the ability of certain classes to immediately lose aggro. Rogues and Hunters especially are able to grab creatures and then get them onto you (whether they are members of your faction makes no difference in this). What happens is that these characters gather the aggro, move over to you, then use deaggro abilities, such as Vanish or Feign Death. This puts the aggro onto you even if you haven't touched the monsters. Yikes! Most often this happens by accident when someone gets too many mobs at once on them and needs to escape; you are now the closest target for monster aggression and in the wrong place at the wrong time. However, a few nastier players of the community make an art form of doing this on purpose—and they are not usually subtle about it. If you see a suspicious/aggressive person gathering mobs into a tight group and then making a direct line toward you, prepare yourself for escape or an attack of your own against the monsters. Report those of your faction who do this consistently for griefing.

Treasure Distribution

When hunting in a group, especially when that group is composed of strangers, it is very wise to establish loot rules ahead of time. The dominant form of drop rules is to makes a pledge of Need Before Greed. This means that any character in the group who needs an item is placed in priority above someone who would just sell the item to a vendor or give it to an alternate character/guildie. This keeps parties together in a better atmosphere of cooperation. By agreeing on this BEFORE any powerful items drop, people save minutes of wasted hunting time trying to figure out who gets what.

Even with good loot systems in place, the game cannot police each player and make sure they don't roll for items in an honorable way. Indeed, Group Loot and Need Before Greed can't see into a character's inventory and determine whether they are actually going to equip an item. Thus, honor and trust play a huge part of proper treasure distribution.

Though individual definitions vary, the standard idea is that Need means that you are going to equip and use an item as soon as you possibly can, either the moment you get it or as soon as you reach the proper level. This item is an actual upgrade for your character, has an important place for you, etc. Greed is frequently used for items that aren't needed or for Enchanters who pretty much want everything that drops for their trade. Passing is done for items that aren't needed at all or for cases where guild groups are supporting their Enchanters (e.g., Need if you really need an item, Greed for Enchanters, and Pass for other people).

It's good to know what the loot systems do and do not do. This is useful for seeing why some things are very bad form. With Master Looter, a group leader is going to distribute things in the first place, so you don't have to worry about anything (just do what you are told, /random if asked to, etc.). More often, though, groups stick with Group Loot or Need Before Greed. In any event, you frequently have the option to roll on items that you don't need. Technically, a Warrior can equip plate, mail, leather, and cloth armor pieces. There might even be some leather with greater +Str and +Stam bonuses than your current equipment, so you might feel that you need it. Hold on before you click that Need button, and think!

If there are Rogues in the group, they are likely to have some serious need for such gear. It is very important to realize that the Need button carries certain subjectivity. If an item isn't ideal/perfect/godly for you, wait and see if other people are rolling Need on it. Ask people "This is actually an upgrade for me, if no one else Needs, can I roll?" They can always say no. This way, you are working with your group and avoiding the cries of "Ninja" or "I really needed that item."

The muddiest waters come when several people can use an item AND it is an upgrade, but one class may need the upgrade far more than others. Consider a party with a Mage who uses swords, a Warrior (also specializing in blades), and a Rogue who likes having a sword as well. Who NEEDS the epic sword that those lovely elite trolls just dropped? Do all of them? Yes and no, of course.

The Warrior would use it a great deal. The Rogue would too. For the Mage, it would be an improvement, but that player wouldn't be using it nearly as often. In these cases, it's better if the Mage backs off, but it isn't required either. So, the "right" thing to do for the Mage is to let the primary melee characters roll for it while looking for lesser swords. The "right" thing for the Warrior and Rogue is to accept the Mage's request to roll if he does push forward. Either side has the ability to walk away looking respectable, even if they don't come away with a rare item!

You can gain a great deal of respect from other people just by stating that although something would be nice for you to have, you would like someone else to receive the item. This is particularly true if you have had good luck and previously gotten some good drops during the run. By the same token, if someone else receives an item that you both rolled for, be a good sport and congratulate them on their good fortune. Everyone gets a little disappointed when they don't get what they really wanted, but behaving in a mature fashion increases the entire party's enjoyment of the game—and increases the chance that you can get a good party for the next run.

If someone in your group consistently tries to get every item that falls, talk to them about it first. Point out that they are pushing other people out of the way equipment wise and that it isn't fair. If they don't listen well, don't group with them again. If they are outright rude or unresponsive, boot them immediately and get another person for the group. The last thing you want is to reach the end of a long dungeon, defeat the boss, and have the best items of the night plundered by some jerk who came in with the very intention of stealing people's hard-earned gear.

Fast Drop Guidelines

- Set Drop Rules Before Leaving Town
- Don't Spend Large Amounts of Time Determining Treasure Distribution (More Fighting=More Treasure Anyway!)
- If a Player Acts Poorly, You Don't Have to Group With Them Again, But Making a Scene Hurts the Rest of the Group
- If People Continue to Be Greedy Even After It's Pointed Out, Cut Your Losses And Get Rid of Them

WHAT DO YOU DO ABOUT NINJA LOOTERS?

Put them on your Ignore List and don't group with them again. These players aren't likely to be considerate of your group's needs in the future, and it certainly brings down everyone's mood when the best items of a long instance go up in smoke. Move on, keep finding your favorite allies, and don't worry about it. Instances are repeatable, and there are more evenings, more encounters, and plenty more treasure for you. As for the Ninja Looter, imagine how things are going to go when nobody wants to group with them later for end-game content a couple months in the future. Having a bad reputation isn't much fun, and a few good items aren't worth the trouble.

Some people try to call out Ninja Looters on the boards. "This guy rolled need on everything, or formed a group and made himself Master Looter before we fought the bosses, etc." This usually isn't worth the effort. Go ahead if you feel that this person was so foul that others outside your circle of friends need to know, but the more sensible path is to inform friends/guild members and leave it at that. You can't stop everyone on the server from dealing with the bad folks, so it's often a more stable course to take care of your own.

Dealing With Incompetent Players

Not everyone has the same level of skill in World of Warcraft. Indeed, there is a huge gradient between the most adept and experienced players and those who are new to MOGs, WoW, and cooperative play in general. As with many suggestions, the best default should be to allow for some mistakes and be patient with others. Yet, there are still times when a player is performing so badly that something must be done about it.

When someone in your group (most likely a person in a pickup group) is performing poorly and getting others killed, have the group leader take the first step. The group leader should stop for a short rest (area allowing) and explain how the party should be performing. If the new player is pulling extra monsters onto a party, advise them on who to [/assist] and where to stand. When they outright pull monsters that aren't desired, tell them that they aren't responsible for pulling and that a different player is already handling that.

Unless the player is outright rude in their response to your party's suggestions, keep them around at least for the quest/expedition that you invited them to join. Good etiquette dictates that the group should stay together until the task is done, even if the weakest link in the party does not improve. Cutting a player for performing poorly is rude. That said, no one is obliged to take unskilled players out for every quest and every raid. If you aren't interested in helping that player improve their skills, don't group with them in the future. That is absolutely your choice. And, it's probably a wise decision.

Spam Invitations

It is best to look for groups with the tools available (general chat, Meeting Stones, looking for group world chat channel, asking in guild if people want to run X instance/quest, etc.). Walking around an area inviting everyone you see into a group is not polite. Ask first and you will find that it is much easier to collect a better grade of players!

The same is true for duels. Practicing with your character in 1-on-1 PvP is exciting, and many other players are happy to join you in duels, especially near towns when they are not engaged with quests, other parties, etc. However, spamming a person with duel invites is quite obnoxious and will land you on an Ignore List some of the time. The best duels take time to set up, with fun talk, mutual bows, and a brief discussion for any rules that are desired. Duels do not simulate true PvP anyway, and out-of-the-blue ones aren't worth the breach in manners.

Asking for Help

As long as you don't demand help from anyone, it is perfectly polite to ask for assistance when going after difficult fights, quests, and such. This can be done on the general chat channel, from guildies, or from people in the area. If you see people fighting their way toward a quest mob that you need to fight, there is nothing wrong with asking to join them. When you can't get close enough for [/say] to work, whisper to one of the members in the group. People rarely mind grabbing an extra person for a few kills.

A side issue of practicing good manners is when your party is standing close to an important quest NPC, getting ready for the fight. Because some of these monsters are hard to find (because of wandering, spawn problems, etc.), it is polite to either yell or send a message over general to let people know that that enemy is not long for this world. By doing this, you give others the chance to ask for an invite if they are close.

Requesting Buffs from Strangers

When soloing, you find that certain buffs make a huge difference to your performance. A Warrior out by his lonesome is greatly improved by a Priest's Stamina Buff (Holy Word: Fortitude). Getting conjured food and water from Mages is another boost to soloers, because it is effectively free to both parties. However, no one is obligated to help a character with abilities that cost time and Mana to cast. The best way to get what you want here is to approach characters that are out in the field and ask politely for the buffs or spells that you desire.

Don't be afraid to help the person in question polish off a few monsters; because of the tap system you receive 0 experience and they get their kills substantially faster. Be aware, this reduces the experience a player receives. That is usually a good way to help out while waiting for a response (ask first, either way, "May I have some food, my Mage brother? I can help you kill monsters for a time or give you some coin for your trouble!"). Also, if you have buffs that are useful, throw those on the stranger while they make up their mind (it won't hurt your request, certainly).

If a Mage conjures a large quantity of food/water for you, throw a modest tip in there even if the Mage doesn't ask for it; that person is going to have a short bit of downtime for what they gave you, and a tip makes them feel better about being generous. Besides, the cost of buying vendor food and water is so much higher that you save entire gold pieces at the moderate levels just by getting Mage assistance; encourage them!

From the buffer's perspective, it is nice to receive tips. However, a kind "thank you" is what you should expect and require for future assistance. When people don't thank you for your time and effort, it's not worth helping them time and time again.

On the other side, if you do not demand a tip, don't expect one from every character you help (many may be too poor to make things sweet for you). Thus, if you aren't going to feel right about helping someone unless money is exchanged, TELL the other players up front. Selling your services is perfectly acceptable. Pretending to donate them and getting upset when people don't realize your expectations is a bit unfair.

Trains

Running through a region often causes a number of monsters to collect in your path, following behind. Even if you are high enough level to survive this, there are sometimes grave consequences to these trains (so called because it looks a tad like a train, with you as the engine and the monsters as cars following behind). When these monsters break off from the chase, they have a chance to aggro on various players during the trip home; this varies depending on the monsters and area, but it always has the potential for chaos. This can cause many deaths and problems to lower-level players in an area.

If you are running around with a train behind you, avoid other players by as wide a margin as possible. And, if your way is blocked by a group (at dungeon entrances or other such bottlenecks), be willing to move off to the side and wait until your train heads home before advancing. It's FAR better to die than to cause another group to wipeout. Besides, the characters you just protected may have a rezzer, offer you a group for future protection, etc. If you get them killed, they are not so likely to keep you on their friends list!

Jumping In

It is fairly common to see other players in trouble. A bad pull or just a poor turn of luck can place another character or entire group in a situation they cannot win. There is no hard and fast rule for what you are supposed to do at that point. If you believe your character would turn the tide of battle, feel free to jump in. When you KNOW the other group needs help, take a fresh target and pull that away (you get the experience and treasure, but they have one fewer problem to deal with). However, if you think the other group might be fine and are uncertain, jump onto a tapped mob; there is almost no way to give offense by doing that because the other party still gets their loot and experience.

All that said, people are strange. You can give offense to some people for things that don't hurt them in the least. They might be roleplaying or just misunderstand the system, but, whatever the case, don't always expect thanks for stepping in. If people don't ask for help directly, you assume a certain risk by charging forward. Shrug it off either way and do what you feel is right. In general, healing the people in trouble is least likely to upset folks, killing tapped monsters would be next, and snagging an untapped add is the most risky.

Perhaps the situation is entirely hopeless. When a dozen monsters get trained onto a small group, it is unlikely that they will evacuate safely. Don't jump in when the battle is hopeless (just get out of the way and hope for your own survival). Adding to a failing battle makes things even more chaotic and could even cause a fleeing group to stop and try to hold their ground.

If you are a Rezzer or your group has such a character that is willing, send one of the people in the doomed group a whisper and ask if they want a Rez (not everyone does if the map is small enough and the Graveyard is somewhat close by). It's worth a short moment to Resurrect the group if that is what they want. The good will is nice to have, and your group may need a Rez one day too. You never know who will be around when that time comes.

Staying in a Group

Groups may form for a single quest, an hour of play, or even a single battle. Proper manners here vary, but the basic key is to be honest about how long you intend to stay with a group and stick to your word. If you join someone for a quest, say that you are able to stay around for "X" amount of time and that is your limit. Work to get the quest done, then stay to make sure that it is done for everyone before leaving. In the event that you must leave unexpectedly, apologize, give at least some of the reason, and offer to make things up to people later.

When the task has been completed, make your intentions known then as well. If you like the party, ask them if they would like to continue grouping and see which quests you have in common. If you don't want to group any longer, thank them for the help and wish them luck (especially if the party wasn't very good; they'll need it). In any event, resist the urge to wander off and go back to your own business without saying anything to the group or suddenly separating from them after criticizing or demeaning them. Being polite and practicing good manners makes grouping more enjoyable for everyone.

By the same token, don't assume that everyone who leaves suddenly is being a jerk and ditching the group. Phone calls, family, lightning, penguin outbreaks, and other problems simply occur. If you group with someone a couple times and they consistently ditch after finishing their part of the quest, don't group with them in the future (at least, if that type of thing upsets you).

Grabbing Resources

Resources that spawn at static points (e.g., Metal and Herbs) are available to everyone, and it is another case where first come, first served is the rule. Yet, there are a few ways to keep from doing unfair things while collecting. Because many resource points have monsters nearby, groups and solo characters must fight to clear the area first, unless they are high enough level to simply sneak past and grab what they want. Regardless, if you see a person clearing the area near a resource point, do not rush past and steal that point. Whisper to the person or group and ask if they are going after the resource node; if they say "yes", move on and look for another (you should get to the next point first since that person is still going after the last one).

If you badly need points for your skills, you may ask a person for a chance to access the resource point without taking anything. With Mining and Herbalism, the point is given for using the resource node, not for taking what is inside it. Thus, a whack on a vein of ore or a moment looking through the herb patch gives you everything you need without costing another person anything (either their point or the materials). There is no harm in asking for a chance to do this, and most harvesters won't have a problem letting you try, especially after they find that you are good to your word.

Note that some gatherers are from the other faction (thus you can't talk to them). When that is the case, go ahead and get the point without worrying about things. Competing with the other faction is a good thing! The neutral route is to get your point and leave the node for others, even if they are jerks; if they were clearing a point, let them have it. You've got your point either way. But, if you want to detract from the competing faction, go for it. Be ready for a /slap or /spit though (on a PvP realm, never gather from a node without killing the enemy first)!

In groups, there may be several resource collectors of the same type (two Skinners, two Miners, etc.). As the group is moving into the area, discuss how you plan to tradeoff resources. For mines, it may be that everyone gets a hit for points, then the metal is split evenly. For Skinning it may be that just one person skins each monster, for time reasons, and the Skinners trade who is on duty.

BACK IN TOWN

Even in the somewhat relaxed state of standing in town, hawking wares and seeking various trainers, there are proper ways to conduct yourself.

Where Is Everything?

Some of the NPCs in cities can be hard to find. A system is in place that allows players to ask the guards of major cities where to find various NPCs. Right-click on the guards to bring up a list of the NPCs and locations they are aware of, then choose the person you seek (a red flag on the mini-map appears to help guide you there).

Sometimes, people in the General Chat Channel ask where different NPCs and stores are located. Try to provide an answer for difficult questions. If the players are asking for answers to simple questions that they have access to, direct them to the source they should be using ("The Quest description tells you where those monsters are" or "Ask a city guard in Stormwind; they will put a marker on your map").

If you are the one who has questions, ask in General and see if people are willing and able to help. There is nothing wrong with asking every now and then if you don't receive assistance and are still having trouble. This is an area where "Please," "Thank You," and general courtesy go a LONG way. The more polite you are the more often future questions are answered. Also, players tend to provide more information when they feel connected to the person asking the question. "Does anyone know if the Mo'Grosh Crystal is a shared drop? :)" will get more attention than "Is Mo'Grosh Crystal shared?"

The best tendency is to try and find things you need on your own at first, because many items, stores, NPCs, and quest targets are quite accessible. Asking where to go and what to do the moment you receive a quest frustrates other players on chat, and they won't be as likely to help after several rounds of queries. Instead, wait until the tools available to you are exhausted. Look around, reread quests or pertinent text, ask your guild or group, then go into General Chat. Also, feel free to whisper a personal "Thanks!" to anyone who helps you. Showing that you are genuinely appreciative of their help is a suitable payment for the time they spent typing an answer.

ON THE BATTLEFIELDS OF PVP

Many of the rules that govern play in PvE change when dealing with players of the opposite faction. This is a desired aspect of the game for many people, and it is best to choose a server that fits your view of etiquette from the beginning if you are worried about certain aspects of competitive play. PvP is one of the rare times when the server is what dictates etiquette more than common sense, disposition, or morality.

When to Attack

Going after enemies of the opposite faction is a matter of duty on the PvP servers, to a fair extent. Disrupting another player of your faction when they are fighting a monster would be griefing; doing the same thing to an opposing faction's player is acceptable (perhaps even desired depending on how bitter the rivalry is on the server currently).

Indeed, attacking other players in a PvP environment is anticipated and encouraged. Any civility that you want to put into such combat (waiting until enemies are fully healed, outside of combat, have seen you, etc.) is above and beyond what others expect from you. Much like in real life, indulging your enemies in this way is a risk that won't always be returned. Let roleplaying and your sense of enjoyment dictate these responses instead of standard etiquette. If you want to be a dirty, rotten, backstabbing fiend that leaps onto hapless foes at the worst of times...go ahead and do it!

Is it possible to grief members of the opposition? Yes, there could be griefing, but this would only be an issue if there was a bug that was exploited against members of one faction. Things that would normally be considered griefing are often allowable otherwise. Training monsters into enemies is not griefing; it's a viable strategy. Again, you may not choose to do it, but your enemies have every right and ability to do it against your party. Be prepared.

Ganking

Ganking is the process of going after helpless characters or characters of MUCH lower level. If ganking doesn't do anything for you and it makes other people's lives difficult, is it wrong? No. Some people on both sides of the war see ganking as a practice of griefers. However, this is not an act of griefing because it is a game dynamic that is mutually agreed upon by the parties involved (the targeted players chose to come to a server where non-instanced PvP is a reality). Thus, they knew the risks and consented to the attack simply by joining the server.

That said in defense of gankers, it still is not an act that earns you respect from the majority of players unless you accomplish your attacks in novel and exciting ways. Using stealth or invisibility to get into contested areas where relatively low-level enemies are questing and going after solo targets is fairly simple. Charging in with raiding parties, fighting out in the open, going after larger groups, etc. is the way to have more fun and truly challenge yourself.

Play as you wish. Those who want to avoid this style of gaming are absolutely free to join the servers where Faction-based combat is restricted to instances and opt-in combat (e.g., defending city NPCs that are being attacked or flagging for PvP).

Corpse Camping

When an enemy dies, their corpse becomes a respawn point (when their spirit returns). Only in dire circumstances do PvPers take Durability penalties for their deaths, so it is probable that the person who died will return to their corpse. Corpse Camping is the act of patrolling the region where an enemy has died while waiting for the person to return (the followup is to attack the recently Rezzed character and kill them a second time).

Again, this is not griefing. However, it is both obstructive to the other person's enjoyment (since they can't even get enough health to have a good fight with you) and it holds your group in place instead of getting you more experience, money, combat, etc. The camped person is free to log off and return at a later point when you are gone, and it's impossible to know if that is the case. So, it is often better to get your kills, move on, and know that the victim could be after you at any time (enjoy the rush).

As far as etiquette goes, people are FAR happier on both sides when corpse camping is minimal. Very few players enjoy being camped this way, and most classes simply don't have the ability to get away safely when five or six people are boxing them into a small area. The flipside of this is what happens when a ganker/corpse camper goes down. Suddenly, tons of people are ready to camp the offending party, and the hunter quickly becomes the hunted.

Battleground DOs and DON'Ts

The PvP Battlegrounds have rules of conduct all to themselves. Some things are entirely fair there that would be mean in other parts of the game, yet other aspects are surprisingly cordial. Note, these are moral issues. Killing players is one of the key means of acquiring Honor, so many people feel the need to kill any and all, no matter the circumstances.

GRAVEYARDS

Graveyard camping in the battlegrounds is the most complex issue to bring out. In Warsong Gulch and Arathi Basin, this action is highly reprehensible. Many players on both sides turn nasty toward you if you stay in the area where the other faction is brought back to life. Don't attack these people until they have left the safety of the Graveyard. Not only is this a nice thing to do; it keeps people coming back for more even after their side has suffered a defeat. When people camp, it causes the other side to feel more than just defeated; they feel broken and humiliated. Then they don't come back. No more easy wins for you—often no more BGs at all for a few hours. Ouch!

Yet, in Alterac Valley, camping is a standard part of fighting strategy. This is because Graveyards are an active part of Alterac Valley warfare (they can be captured). Thus, the game encourages you to go after these sites directly.

EMOTING

The use of [/spit] is extremely unpleasant. Though realistic for roleplayers and an allowed action by Blizzard, many players find spitting to be rude/insulting. Reserve this for enemies who are vile. Graveyard campers perhaps?

The flipside of emotes is that they can be used to show respect or friendship, toward allies and enemies alike. Try [/salute] to let people know that they are respected even if you are trying to kill them. Or, [/love] and [/hug] work well for friendship. A good [/dance] is another way to let people know that things aren't always about fighting. If one side of a battleground is vastly outnumbered, the other side may choose to play around while accomplishing their goals as a way of saying, "we're going to try to win this quickly, but we won't fight you directly unless you attack us." Giving the understaffed side the initiative in this way is very good form.

EXITING BATTLEGROUNDS

Leaving a Battleground can be a point of contention as well. Because the game allows you to queue for multiple Battlegrounds, it's not a rare occurrence for a Battleground to pop up while you are already fighting in another. If your team is in trouble or the fight is close, please don't leave unless you have a very good reason without telling your team first. Even if others take your place, the disruption might be enough to tip the other side toward victory. If you do have to leave, let people know and apologize, then leave the raid or [/afk] before logging out so a replacement can enter as soon as possible.

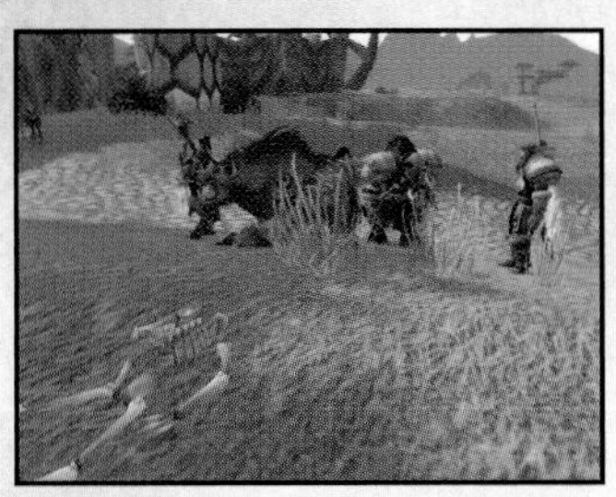

WHEN NOT TO ATTACK

In the Battlegrounds, don't attack enemies if they stop fighting entirely. When outnumbered or just outgunned, some people give up and pull back (this doesn't happen often, but it's worth knowing about). In these cases, the enemies want the match over as soon as possible so they can try to get more people into the next Battleground. Just win the match and don't attack them unless they attack you.

This also comes into play when other players are zoning into a Battleground that is already in progress. If you see someone standing absolutely still, despite combat going on around them, it's likely that they aren't being deceptive. They are probably just away from their keyboards or waiting for the area to load (especially if you see them doing this in their spawn-in points).

To be safe, go ahead and use crowd control or a snare on such targets, to make sure they can't quickly follow and attack you, but don't kill the poor people.

Eleven Things Worth Knowing

There are certain aspects of MOG play that are almost universal. Appropriately, these are present in World of Warcraft and should be explained for people who are new to the game, genre, or even to Blizzard games from the past.

PATIENCE IS THE KEY TO GLORY

It is invariably true that patience leads to greatness in many tasks. Most roleplaying games have a huge element of this, and MOGs are even more representative of the idea. It's impossible for players to sit down and see everything there is to World of Warcraft in one day (or week, or month, or...). Thus, no matter how hard you try there is no way to rush through the game world and get to the "end." In fact, though there is an end-game portion of content where players are capped in level, there is never going to be a heavy hand on your shoulder saying "The game is over now, you win."

Regardless of anyone else's view of how fast someone should play, level, and enjoy the game, there is no specific time to reach a quest or an area. Take a week hunting for Kodo Leather in Mulgore, or try exploring all of Kalimdor at level 20 if you are truly brave. Nothing that you enjoy in World of Warcraft is wasted time. The world is here for you to enjoy! Take it easy and play as you wish. Indeed, the levels are more exciting, the gameplay refreshing, and every group a bit better when you remember that fun is more important than getting the next skill, level, Wombat of Slaying, etc.

LEARN WHAT YOU CAN HANDLE

It's exciting to push your character to the very limits of survivability. This is good to try on a limited basis for several reasons. First off, it provides a nice rush (even if you eventually lose and have to do a short corpse run). Beyond that, this type of testing brings you closer to your characters; understanding how to get every last bit of power out of a class makes every difference when it comes to complex challenges such as Player Vs. Player combat and dungeon Instances.

Though you naturally cover the limits of your character over time, simply by playing the game and dealing with the troublesome situations that arise from large pulls, trains from other groups, and ambushes out in the wild, testing still has its place. The issue here is that intentionally testing your class makes the process more analytic; you can prepare new strategies, test them out, and really see the effects. It's MUCH harder to keep a keen eye out when you are surprised.

Try finding situations that push your character to the limit to see what things your race/class/style combo are best for countering. Try going against single targets of high level in solo encounters; engage entire groups of equal or slightly lower-level monsters; grab wide aggro from a huge range of enemies and try to flee successfully. These tests reveal a great deal about the strengths of a player and that person's chosen character.

FIND A CLASS THAT SUITS YOUR MENTALITY

A character's class defines what they are capable of doing in so many ways. Though every class is quite impressive in World of Warcraft, even in solo encounters, there are styles of fighting that are more effective for certain classes. For Instances, Warriors handle groups of enemies FAR better than most alternatives (they have high health, impressive armor, and a Rage bar that is easier to fill when there are more targets aggroing). Casters, on the other hand, have more options for crowd control or healing, but must be quite careful of burst damage from enemies; success for casters involves damage at range, frustrating enemy advances, and using mana efficiently.

Class Style Quicklist

Class Name	Dominant Traits
Warrior	Very High Survivability; Gather Aggro; Damage Mitigation; Versatile Melee
Paladin	Adequate Damage; Backup Healing; Resurrection; Strong Armor; Survival Abilities; Great Vs. Undead; Alliance-Only Class
Rogue	High and Sustained Damage; Many Stuns; Stealth; Low Armor; Light Hit Points, Lockpicking
Hunter	Powerful, Consistent Pets; Wonderful Sustained Damage, Traps, Tracking of Beasts and Sentient Enemies, Moderate Armor
Druid	Shapeshifting; Style Flexibility; Can Act as Substitute Tank, Rogue, or Healer; Damage at All Ranges; Great Roots; Backup Healing
Shaman	Totems for AoE Status Effects; Superb Group Support; Ranged Magic; Substantial Melee Damage; Moderate Armor; Resurrection; Horde-Only Class
Priest	Powerful, Fast, and Efficient Healing; Stamina Buff; Protective Shield Buff; Close-Range Fear on a Quick Timer; Anti-Undead Powers; Impressive Damage With Some Builds; Fragile Hit Points and Armor
Warlock	Multiple DOTs; Fear (LOTS of Fear); Extensive Pet Summoning; Many Channeling Spells; Blurred Line Between Hit Points and Mana (Can Use One to Gain the Other); Complex Class
Mage	High Ranged Damage; Snare Enemies With Cold or Root Them Briefly; Create Free Food/Water for Self and Others; Create Mana Gems for Personal Use; Many Instant Damage Options; In-Combat Crowd Control; Very Fragile Hit Points and Armor

Don't be afraid to message players of specific classes and ask them about their experiences. Use the WoW community site forums for the same purpose and see how actual players feel about their play experience. This avoids the path of reaching level 20-30 before realizing that a class is good but still not your style. Of course, it's good to try everything yourself in the long run, but that is a different issue.

CHOOSE A RACE THAT LOOKS AND FEELS RIGHT

Though class selection is dictated by logic, race is a decision based on aesthetics. Certainly, there are starting advantages to some race/class combinations (Tauren Warriors have higher starting damage per second and health, Gnomes have more mana to throw around than other races, etc.). Weigh the racial advantages against your aesthetic needs.

The choice of a character's race can be a great time to go with your heart. That character will charge about the screen for months to come, so pick a race that looks and feels right to you! This yields a starting location that suits your playstyle, since all of the starting areas are geared to the races that inhabit them. Also, it conveys an immediate sense of closeness between you and your character; the more you enjoy your character, the better each level seems.

Voice Emotes

Another fun thing to try is various voice emotes for the sex/race combination of your character. Create a character and try the [/flirt] and [/silly] commands five or six times each. If the humor of the combination works for you, the style of that race's quests are likely going to synch as well. Don't forget to sample the [/dance] of your choice as well, and know that there are male/female differences even within the races.

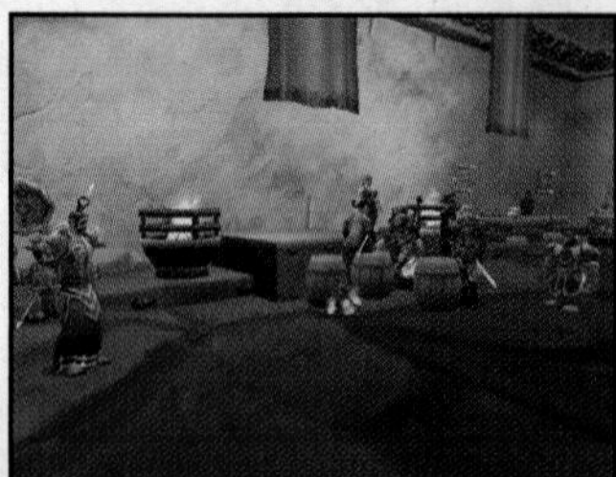

Don't let stats or racial traits decide race unless that is truly important to you! If you are interested in playing any combination, no matter how odd at first, go for it and have no regrets. In WoW, player skill and a good reputation gets you into high-quality groups far more often than race, class, etc.

INVEST IN FRIENDS AND SKILLED ALLIES

And speaking of good groups, there are a few tips to help with finding them. While you are playing, even at low level, try to see which people are active in General Chat in a helpful way. Make note of polite, informed players and how they are dealing with each other. Out in the field, see who is eager to buff ungrouped characters, jump in to help other characters when a pull goes poorly, etc. Don't be afraid to spend time getting to know the other players; the ones who stay involved with their characters into the higher levels may be your companions for months to come. And, the sooner you become friends with the more friendly and skilled players, the sooner pickup groups will be a thing of the past.

Ironically, to get away from pickup groups, people have to rush into many of them. The best times to do this are for kill quests, elite quests, and other activities where having more people around aids the process EVEN when they are strangers. Try to keep track of all the people you enjoy grouping with. Had a good time with Player A?—ask if you can put that person on your Friends list. They will most likely do the same for you. Continue this and there will be a cluster of a dozen or more people from other guilds that you know and like in no time (leading to faster groups with more familiarity, less down time, and more fun).

On the whole, the best players to choose for your list are the people who click with your personality and style of play. Even when some players are unskilled and make mistakes, they may be wonderful choices in the long run. You cannot train someone to be an exciting friend; skill in MOGs, on the other hand, is easily acquired over time by someone willing to learn. The vast majority of players who start off poorly but have the will to practice and learn end up being quite good by the time they reach high levels.

TRY EVERYTHING AT LEAST ONCE

There are many classes, races, and areas to explore. Even if one thing grabs you from the start, you become a better player by understanding where everyone else has been. Look into both factions even if you are sold on one of them. Playing a dedicated Alliance character, it is quite an eye opener to see the Barrens as a soldier of the Horde. Learning how the other side works together, quests, and levels aids in countering those tactics with your original character. Also, there is a chance that somewhere you haven't been will completely capture your heart. A player that immediately chooses to play as an orc may fall in love with Mulgore or even pine away for the beauty of Elwynn Forest.

For those with enough patience, try starting characters in each of the six initial regions to see if there is something special in one of them. Spending a couple hours on this your first day may pay off with a character you didn't even know you wanted to play.

In the same vein, be sure to experience world PvP, Battlegrounds, roleplaying, raids, and other such content several times, even if they don't seem to call to you. Some "carebear" players find that world PvP isn't their style at all, but Battlegrounds on a PvE or RP server are great for them. Or, you might discover that roleplaying is wonderful once you've met a few buddies and understand your character a tad better. Try it all!

IDENTIFY GOALS AND SUITABLE TARGETS

There are many goals for a player to seek in a given session. Sure, it is possible to play without more than an urge to beat monsters and have a good time (a goal unto itself, honestly). If that is all that you are looking for, recognize that and take a leisurely pace; fight the monsters you enjoy fighting even if there aren't any quests for that area. With a casual pace, it is entirely possible to group with a huge level range of friends and just do whatever you want!

When you have a more specific goal, do what you can to identify the best targets for accomplishing that. Indeed, someone looking for the best experience on a given evening should queue the most quests for an area, find a group that is willing to stay together for at least a few hours, and then plow through those quests with military efficiency. Or, when quests are dry for multiple areas, gather a high-kill rate party and grind elite mobs in an Instance (not entirely ideal for experience, but a fine way to work with others and increase your chance for higher-quality gear). By choosing the right group, activity, and monster type, you gain more money and experience without investing more time or energy.

Perhaps you want money instead. Taking professions to harvest resources is great for this. Mining, Herbalism, and Skinning are great ways to farm for cash. Sell the materials on the Auction House and watch the gold pieces roll into the mailbox. This will net your character far more money than grinding against even the best monsters for your class.

Another good money-farming technique is to hit instances that are far beneath you in level. Solo these and sell the green and blue items that drop (obviously only the Bind on Equip pieces can be sold, but instances drop far more of these). On many servers, items that are between 16-19 and 26-29 can be sold at painful buyout prices in the Auction House. This is because second-generation characters with heavy funding are buying such gear for use in the Battlegrounds.

The global point is to do what you like without worrying about experience per hour (unless experience per hour is your goal, of course). People love to explore, roleplay, dance around Ironforge with stray Gnomes, etc. Experiment, find your favorite activities, then indulge.

THE RIGHT PLACE AT THE RIGHT TIME

While leveling, there are certainly better places to get the job done at any given point. Because questing is such a major aspect of WoW, it is quite useful to know where the most quests are throughout the game. One of the keys to progressing smoothly comes in traveling back and forth between equivalent regions; when quests are depleted in one area, try another for a time then return to see if new things are available.

In Alliance lands, a person may be hunting in Loch Modan from levels 12-14, then suddenly find a few of the remaining quests to be a bit challenging (or they will simply wish for something new). For a change of pace and some easy experience, move down into Westfall and do all of the quests there for the early levels. By the time Westfall becomes old news for your budding adventurer, Loch Modan's "tougher" quests should be just right. Or, there is always a trip out to Darkshore for yet another batch of level-appropriate quests. Horde characters often bounce between The Barrens and Silverpine Forest for the exact same reasons.

To find out about quests areas and new regions, read this guide, talk to people around your level, and see what other people are doing. Another trick is to do a search for people around your level. Try a [/who] for characters within a level or so and look at their location. You might find that some people are in places that you didn't expect.

USE ALL RESOURCES

In game, using your resources means that it is important to keep in touch with other players via the chat channels and the guild you choose. Be confident in yourself and try to find answers through exploring and testing, but don't be hesitant to ask others for help when things become muddled or frustrating. Buy quality items from other players as well, and be fast to sell the good things you find but can't use (this will make more coin than vendoring the items, and it substantially helps others at the same time).

Outside WoW, there are web sites, strategy guides, guild pages, and forums waiting for you. Each of these offers a different aspect of assistance for mastering World of Warcraft. Guild pages offer social interaction, networking, and a feeling of playing a game outside the game. Open forums have tons of information on quest problems, upcoming game changes, and developments in the world. Obviously, strategy guides have a good place because they can go into the game with you; kept beside your computer, they offer fast information, data charts, etc. Also, guides can be taken around for perusal when a computer won't be available (commute by train, long trips, and such).

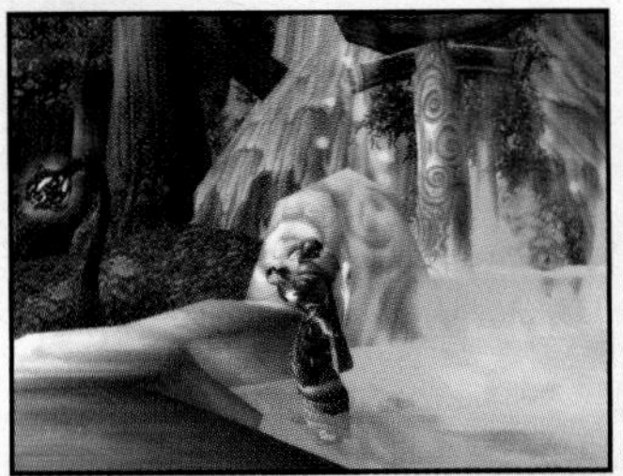

If you want to know everything there is to know about WoW, play long, play hard, and use ALL of these sources. No single one of them is going to replace the others. Even with this guide and a few major websites about general WoW data, you may find great joy on the forum for your specific server. This is covered more in the Community Site section.

TAKE BREAKS

Eating, sleeping, work, friends, and all of the other needs demand their own time, but there are also breaks in game that can be useful to you. For one, it is nice to have a few characters to play unless you are madly driven to reach the level cap in the least possible time. Having a few characters gives a player the breathing room to play according to a given mood instead of being forced into the same style each evening. It is nice to have a tank for slugging things out, a caster for ranged spell-work, a crafting and farming character for making money and finding special gear, and whatever else calls to you.

By switching around the characters you play, the game stays more vibrant and has fewer demands on you. Instead, you get to go with your mood each time you play. The only serious downside of having multiple characters is that friends on the same server may out-level you. That is one of the many perks of having a guild; there is often a cluster of people in every region, so you won't be left out by leveling at a different pace than the "average" player. For that matter, it is pretty darn hard to find an average player when it comes to leveling, since there is a huge range in terms of speed and style of play.

Try keeping a character on both the Alliance and Horde sides on some servers. This is especially worthwhile on servers with heavier roleplaying groups because you can play off of more people and come up with better organization for cross-faction events. Very fun! This provides for breaks from the grind even while staying in game.

USING THE COMMUNITY

Being on online game, World of Warcraft has a number of components in the online community that are very useful for players. The community site, at www.worldofwarcraft.com, has an extensive forum for all users of the game. It also has news updates, contests, basic game info, support information, patch notes, account management, and a wealth of others treats.

TOOLS ON THE LEFT SIDE OF THE SITE

Account Management is the most essential function of the community site. This is shown at the very front of the page (on the left side, where many of the major navigation points are found), and it allows users to control their payment type, cancel accounts, and so forth. Password use, paid characters transfers, and parental controls are all based from here as well. If you have played WoW for a few weeks and it is something that you will play for a while, consider changing your billing information.

Using the Workshop gives everyone the ability to see PvP rankings, calculate talent templates for any character combination, look forward to events and raid resets in the game, and view major armor types.

The Media page is a repository for movies, music, screenshots, wallpapers, and the Blizzard Store. The Gadgetzan Times is also based there. WoW is not just an in-game community, check it out and get involved.

The Forums are a frequent stop for many players of all skill levels. There are always new people asking questions, veterans answering and debating the future of classes, and a full range of odd folks in-between. Though sometimes the Forums are a bit too much to take in all at once, they are often a very early source for knowledge about added areas, upcoming changes, and strategies for difficult encounters. Any major changes to classes show up here first, and much debate ensues. There are also server forums. If you are new and want to get the feel for a server, this is often a good first stop.

The Community pages have comics, contests, important links to events and community elements, and fan artwork. Guild Relations also have links here (to general discussions and the specific Guild Relations forum).

Use the Support pages if you are having trouble with billing, game access, and other major issues that prevent the game from working.

QUICK LINKS (THE RIGHT SIDE)

Look on the right side of the main community page for Quick Links of various sorts. These are sometimes in flux, as new content is added or being focused on during patch times and such.

Learn about new items or areas of the game, recruit buddies to play with you in World of Warcraft using the Recruit a Friend program, or set the PvP Rankings to your favorite server to see who is staying on top of the battlefield.

Don't forget to click on the In Development link to check on future elements of the game. Patches are always in the works, and these unleash entirely new challenges on the players.

UNDERSTANDING EQUIPMENT, ENEMIES, AND LEVELS

Levels of NPCs, monsters, and equipment means a great deal to new and veteran players alike. Just because there are items of stunning power out there doesn't imply that you should be wielding them from the beginning. Indeed, the theory behind World of Warcraft is that you must build your character's skills and abilities to the point where they are able to wield the items of greatest power. The same is true for which enemies you are able to fight with any degree of safety; the bitter and hard-fought skirmishes your friends have against Defias Pillagers in Westfall will seem like a fond memory in a few weeks when you begin engaging the Trolls of Stranglethorn Vale! And these are but minor foes in retrospect once your character steps into the flames of Stratholme in an attempt to stop the Scourge and Scarlet Crusaders that war there.

SHADES OF QUALITY: THE EQUIPMENT SYSTEM

For almost all forms of equipment, there are ways to quickly judge their approximate power and usefulness to you. The minimum level of an item reveals when you can use it, and the color of said item provides a rough sense of how powerful that piece is at that level.

The table below lists the different equipment tiers.

Equipment Color Scheme
Poor (Grey)
Common (White)
Uncommon (Green)
Rare (Blue)
Epic (Purple)
Legendary (Orange)

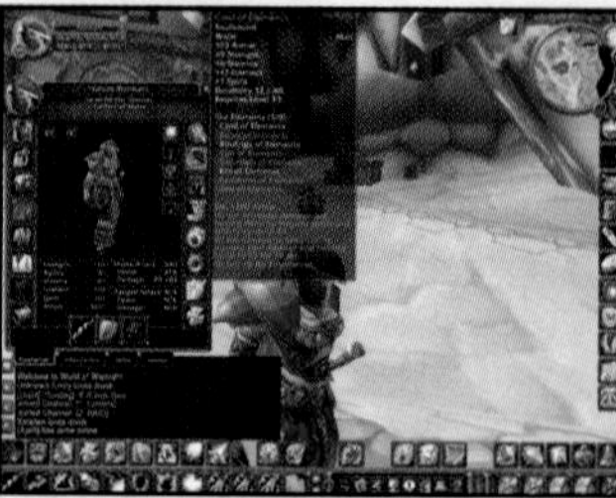

Items of Poor quality show up in an ugly grey color and are inferior to everything else; there are only useful when nothing else is available. This happens most often when you reach levels where new slots of equipment can be used (shoulderpads are the most common example beyond level one).

Common items are the standard ones for early trade/crafting or for crummy vendor equipment. Their color is a lifeless white. You won't use these items long at all, and only at the lowest levels is there much of a chance to intentionally equip such gear and care about it as an upgrade.

Uncommon items are frequently called "Greens" due to their color. Quite a large number of these pieces Bind on Equip and provide attribute bonuses to your character. This is the rank-and-file's base equipment. You can find green items from monsters all over the world, and the loot tables are very large. Sell or trade the pieces that you find and don't need while collecting the proper gear for your character from the Auction House.

Rare items start to get quite interesting. These appear in a wonderful shade of blue and offer bonuses that are substantially above what an Uncommon item would give at the same level. Some of these are Bind on Equip and can be found anywhere in the world (with a low drop rate), but a huge number are discovered in dungeons, where they are a Bind on Pickup drop from specific enemies. Thus, Rare items require more dangerous fighting to get, but they offer higher rewards and more specific character customization. Sell Bind on Equip blue items on the Auction House at a premium!

Everything from Epic gear onward is very difficult to get. These items require a massive investment in crafting, reputation quests that are repeatable and slow to complete, weeks of Battleground combat, or the farming of raid-level Instances. These items of the higher tiers are way above the power level of green and blue items. Anything that is purple, red, or orange is impressive! Some of these are only found once on an entire server.

NPCS, ALLIES, AND ENEMIES

Much like items, people and monsters you encounter in World of Warcraft are color coded. For both enemies and allies, there are color distinctions that are important to understand.

Other characters of your faction and NPCs will be either Blue or Green in appearance when you highlight their avatar. A bar appears that lists that person's name, class/job, and level. The color of that bar declares whether that person is flagged for PvP. A blue bar means that the target is not currently set for /PvP in that area. A green bar means that the person is a viable /PvP target for enemies from the opposing faction. NPCs are always viable targets.

Enemies and Beasts are different colors. Creatures out in the wilderness may be Yellow if they are passive. These neutral creatures do not attack anything on sight, regardless of proximity. You are free to walk up next to a Deer, Zhevra, or any other neutral creatures without fear of reprisal. If you attack these creatures, however, they will aggro on you and engage in battle just like any proper foe.

Aggroing Neutral Creatures

Even area-of-effect debuffs from your party can cause neutral creatures to aggro. To avoid this, use fire control and hold back on AoE activities when there are neutral creatures in the way.

Also note that many neutral creatures are shy and retreat from the area if there is a battle taking place. This prevents some problems with accidental aggro.

More aggressive creatures, such as various predators, undead beings, demons, members of the opposing faction that are PvP flagged and attacking, etc., appear with a Red bar when they are highlighted. Red stands for an aggressive creature; these foes aggro on you simply for stepping within a certain distance. That distance is determined by the difference between your level and the hostile creature's level.

Aggro Distance

Aggro distance, as stated, is computed by determining the difference in level between you and the enemy. Being lower level than the creature increases the distance at which it chooses to attack. Thus, very low-level characters for a given region have predators and enemies alike racing across fair distances for a chance at some fresh meat.

On the flipside, characters who are much higher level than the hostile monsters in an area won't aggro them without walking right next to them.

Finally, some enemies have a higher aggro range than others. Wolves, Coyotes, certain casters, and various additional foes aggro at a greater distance than your level difference dictates. It doesn't take long to learn which enemies do this for an area; you are then free to use greater caution when trying to avoid attacks from such targets.

Enemies from the other faction are a bit more complex, color wise. If you are on a PvE or RP server, the game doesn't assume that they are all red targets. If you aren't flagged for PvP yourself, the other team shows up as blue if they are also unflagged or as yellow if they are. When you flag and engage such targets, the coloring turns to red.

The Reputation System allows for more variety in certain NPCs. Regions with complex NPCs are given a faction of their own. Goblin towns, rogue elements of the Alliance and Horde, and fully independent groups feature this. If you improve relations with these groups, their mood changes to a Friendly one with your character. However, attacking NPCs of these factions turns them against your character.

NPCs just beneath Neutral are Unfriendly. Though they won't attack you outright, they don't offer to speak with your character, sell, or give quests to you.

Beneath Unfriendly is the Hostile Ranking; this turns previously passive NPCs into aggressive ones. Unless steps are taken to raise your faction with them dramatically, expect to be fighting these enemies for the rest of your days.

Be alert about attacking enemies from various factions. Fighting against the Bruisers in Booty Bay or the Timbermaw Furbolgs might seem like fun, but these actions hurt your reputation with certain factions by quite a margin. This can greatly hinder your interests in achieving quest goals, finding crafting recipes, or just reaching a safe haven. The general rule of thumb is that you should make as many friends as you can out in the world of Azeroth. You are likely to need them!

Reputation Quicklist

Condition	Effect
Exalted	Final Tier; Rewards Are Very Specific to the Faction Involved
Revered	Rewards Are Specific to Faction Involved
Honored	10% Discount on Items Purchased from Vendors
Friendly	Standard Reputation Level for Friends of Your Faction
Neutral	Standard Reputation Level for Factions That Aren't On Your Side (Goblins, Many Gnomes)
Unfriendly	Cannot Buy, Sell, or Interact Extensively, But This Faction Won't Attack You
Hostile	NPCs From This Faction Will Attack You on Sight
Hated	All Members of This Faction Are Enemies

Not Everyone Comes Alone

There are several ways for enemies to get help from other creatures in the region. First, some creatures try to bring allies from the moment they are pulled. Humanoid mobs are the most notable for this, but there are beasts that do this as well. This makes camps of enemies harder to fight because even ranged attacks may bring several foes.

Another method that some humanoids and beasts have (especially with foes like Raptors) is to call for help. These calls can even bring creatures that are from different races; for example, an NPC Druid may respond to the call of a wounded Raptor. There is little to be done about these calls for help because they occur instantly. The best thing to do is pull such foes back to areas where their calls won't grab anything that you aren't already interested in fighting. The range on calls for help will vary by both creature and location (the distance is farther outdoors).

There is a third way for certain enemies to seek aid. When badly wounded, a number of wise foes run away (some of them at very high speed). If the monsters bump into any allies along the way, they will return with friends. Using snare or stun abilities can help quite a bit to prevent this problem. For classes without such tools, try to save damage for the end of the fight (by saving mana, instant abilities, etc.) so that the creatures can be struck down when they try to run.

What Are Those Special Pictures by Certain Mobs?

Elite monsters have special icons that surround their pictures in the interface. Elite monsters have a Gold Dragon border around their portraits; these creatures have much higher health compared with normal mob of that level (they also have more powerful attacks and abilities in many cases). Be wary of these mobs, but know that they drop better treasure and are worth more experience, so hunting them in groups can be lucrative.

Often, the strategies for fighting Elite mobs are different from those used against normal creatures. The general changes are that long-term abilities are even more powerful when fighting Elites (DOTs, debuffs, and short-term buffs are wonderful in these fights). Instead of using the philosophy of "Bring it down quickly to stay alive," the characters are pushed more toward "Bring it down safely and with maximal control of the situation." Use snares to keep these monsters from rushing off to heal or get allies. Healing is more important than ever when facing Elites, as your tanks won't always have enough health to survive against even a single Elite foe without assistance.

Now and then you also see creatures with Grey Dragon borders around their names. These are specific creatures instead of a racial type. Each monster of this type has a name ("Murgos Pugnose" instead of a generic Defias). The power level of named monsters varies tremendously. Some of these are rare but aren't especially powerful. Others may have new attacks, abilities not normally given to their race, and deal far more damage than one might expect. This is all a matter of experience and cannot be predicted simply by looking at the creature. So, rare spawns are noted by their grey borders and may or may not be Elite. They are often referred to as Treasure Mobs, as they have specific loot.

The Basics of Group Dynamics

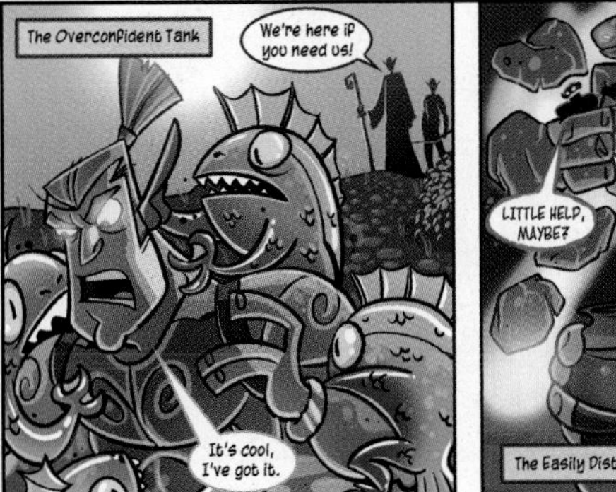

Grouping is such a central aspect of MOG play that it is discussed several times in this guide (each time with increased detail). Here in the Introduction, our examination of groups focuses primarily on the basic mechanics and reasons for getting into groups. Later on, we explain more about performing in high-level groups and in a wider variety of situations.

What Is a Group

Groups are formed when characters decide to work together. By sharing the duties in combat, far more monsters can be brought to defeat, and safety is dramatically improved. Normal groups can be as large as five characters.

To start a group, one character targets another person and types [/invite] or they can invite a person from far away by using the character's full name [/invite Serene]. Using character portraits is another way to interact with people nearby (right-click on the person's portrait and choose invite from the list of options that appears). You can even right-click on a person's name on the text bar at the bottom of the screen when they enter areas/come online/speak/etc. and invite them from there or [/whisper] to them.

People who are invited into a group have a query box that appears on their screen; it asks whether they wish to join the inviter's group. If they decline, the inviter is informed by both a sound and a text message. If they join, the new character's portrait is added in the upper-left side of the screen. You are able to see their health and mana (or Energy/Rage). Even that character's pets are shown under their portrait.

So, a group, at its core, is a joining of characters who are going to attempt their challenges together. With two to five people, groups can attempt all of the quests or hunting activities that are normally available to characters. The quicklist below explains some of the changes when doing tasks in a group.

Changes Between Soloing and Grouping

- Groups Share Their Experience From Kills
- Looted Money is Divided Evenly Between Participating Group Members
- Bodies Are Lootable for Items Based on a System Decided by the Group Leader (Master Looter, Round Robin, Group Loot, Need Before Greed, or Free-for-All)
- Quests Can Be Shared Between Members (So Long as the Prerequisites Are Completed by All Members)
- Enables the Group Chat Channel (used by typing [/p "Text"])
- Character Information Is Displayed for All Group Members

Ultimately, groups are able to accomplish more things than a solo player, especially in the later stages of the game. The quantity or type of loot you receive improves dramatically when going through Instance dungeons, Raid areas, and other group-related content. The Battlegrounds are also far more viable when working and communicating well with your raid and within your group.

Loot Systems Revisited

Group loot systems are very important to most players. Unless you only play with friends and guildmates, it is important to find a fair system that distributes loot in a way that keeps everyone content.

Which system is the best to use? As you have probably guessed, it depends on the group, its leader, and the needs of the current mission.

Loot Systems

Name	Best For	Description
Master Looter	Careful Distribution	Group Leader Distributes All Valuable Items
Round Robin	Not Ideal	Valuable Items Are Looted as if They Are Normal Treasure
Group Loot	Simplicity w/ Some Protection	Allows Everyone to Roll on Powerful Items
Need Before Greed	Raising the Fairness of Drops	Only Allows Characters Who Can Use an Item to Get It
Free-for-All	Pure Speed and Ease of Use	Everyone Can Loot Any Corpse

What is a Raiding Party

Raiding parties are basically groups of groups. For difficult Instances, large-scale Player vs. Player attacks, or actual raid areas, these large groups are welcome (or even needed).

To form a raid, wait until a group is started normally, then open the raid tab (this is the final tab from the character screen). Press "O" to bring these pages up and select the raid tab from the bottom. There is a button on the page that appears to "Convert to Raid."

The next stage of a raiding party is to gather several fully-independent groups. This isn't a situation where everyone just clumps together and it doesn't matter which person is in which group. Indeed, leadership and organization are either the beauty or bane of raid work. Without organization, it is extremely hard to succeed when there are so many people together in a tight area.

Thus, groups should have an experienced leader at their head. The raid leader/organizer should often be the person with the most experience and skill in commanding for the given task. That means a talented PvPer should be at the head of a raiding party against another faction. A person who has done Blackrock Spire 30 times should lead two groups into the Raid.

Raiding parties are discussed at much greater length later in the guide, primarily in the Advanced Player vs. Environment chapter. Raids aren't needed or often done by characters at the lower or even mid-tier levels, so knowing what they are is more than enough for now.

WHEN TO GROUP

Groups offer many things to both casual and hardcore players. But, that doesn't mean they are perfect for everything. It's good to know what you want before seeking a group; this makes it much easier to achieve your goals.

Groups are able to complete quests at a faster pace for Kill Quests, Escorts, and Exploration/Delivery Quests. However, groups are far slower when dealing with Collection Quests (especially if ground spawns are involved). If pure speed is an issue, it's wise to solo while collecting items, and group when attacking monsters, escorting, or exploring high-level areas.

When it comes to farming coin, the situation is quite complex. Solo characters get a fair bit of money if they go after the right targets (farming lower Instance dungeons for Bind on Equip blues, harvesting metal and herbs, etc.). If money is your goal, try these activities by yourself or with a partner. Avoid large groups for cash!

Duos

Many duos work quite well, but certain combinations are even better for specific tasks. Remember that everyone has weaknesses; if you choose a duo that accounts for these weaknesses, it makes life much easier. For example, Warriors hold aggro, making the fighting safer for low armor classes (Rogues, Mages, Priests).

Even beyond the class pairings, try to find someone who is willing to play to the duos strengths and minimize weaknesses. If a Priest and Mage group, it is obvious that tanking isn't a strongpoint of the pair. Instead, those two would succeed quickly by using their high DPS and lean heavily on burst damage to keep enemies from engaging for long periods.

Fun is a fine goal, and groups are easily the best target for having a good time. Making friends with good players and nice people makes the game better no matter what you enjoy. Even for quests when groups aren't needed, having buddies around keeps there from being any tedium to slaying entire bands of roving wolves and bears.

Good Reasons to Group

- Trying to Complete Red, Elite, or Dungeon Quests
- Dealing With Kill/Explore/Escort Quests
- Taking on Instances in Full Groups
- Forming Raids for High-End Content
- Safety in PvP-Intense Areas (e.g., Hillsbrad)
- To Play With Friends!

WHEN NOT TO GROUP

Okay, so you see the reasons to group and the times when it is desired/needed. Here is the other side of grouping; there are goals that make grouping a bad idea.

Gaining experience in a group can be slow at certain stages of the game. Unlike a number of MOGs, World of Warcraft is dedicated to making it easy to level even when you play as a solo character.

Indeed, leveling during solo play is fast if you keep your skills, gear, and items up to par. Take a great deal of food/water/bandages out with you and slash down the beasts of the open field. This pulls in experience at a very impressive clip, dwarfing just about any group that can't get into motion quickly. Find VERY target-rich areas, and stay focused the entire time.

During the low levels, quests are worth an even higher percentage of total experience gained. If you are trying to fly through the levels, jump into groups for the group-friendly quests (as listed above) but solo all of the collection quests. Grinding solo kills on the way to and from quests is also a major way to improve experience efficiency. These are efficient kills because you gain health and mana on the move, so your character is getting to fight without the same level of downtime.

It's not useful to group when the players you meet are unfriendly, uncooperative, or just don't match your style of play. If a group isn't enjoyable, it's not worth your time. Gold, experience, and levels mean so much more when you're having a good time, and players who enjoy the game have better characters. Even with a stat-specific view of things, happier players end up with more potent characters (these people play more because they are having a good time, and more hours equals more experience, treasure, and power).

WHAT COMPRISES A "GOOD" GROUP

This is certainly a subject for debate, but good groups are the ones that fulfill your goals without making game time stressful or obnoxious. You, as a player, get to decide what a good group is for your needs. If you want pure experience and money, simply look for the groups that are intense, dedicated to a high kill count, fast questing, and disciplined Instance running. If fun is your target, find players who relax a bit more, joke around, talk more, and explore.

There are so many players on each server that there are always people who share your interests and goals. Don't try to push other players into your mold; it takes less time and is better for everyone if you seek like-minded players from the beginning. Let the PvPers fight, let the roleplayers get into their roles, etc.

What Are Quests?

The World of Warcraft has a Quest system in place that not only helps you learn the history of the land but also gives experience points and treasure beyond those gained from any fighting. Experience earned from these quests does not count against your Rest State and automatically adjusts the experience needed until your State changes; this makes for very fast leveling when a player understands how to mix hard fighting with consistent questing.

There are many different types of quests players can take part in. This is designed to make leveling fun and interesting; the system also helps to guide players from one area to the next at appropriate times, making it easier to know where it's "safe" to continue adventuring.

TYPES OF QUESTS

There are many types of quests that are offered in World of Warcraft, from simple Kill Quests to the more involved Storyline Quests. They are designed to allow players to decide on the amount of time investment they want to make.

Kill Quests

Kill Quests ask you to go out and either kill a number of creatures or a named NPC. These types of quests are often best to do in a group if time is an issue. While the experience of the kills is spread out among the group, everyone gets credit for the kills. Often when killing an NPC for a quest you are required to bring back proof of the kill. These quests allow all the group members to loot the item off of the corpse and do not have to be repeated in order for all members to get the item. The few exceptions ask that you complete the quest alone.

Collection Quests

Collection Quests require that you go out and get a specific number of items either from a location or from creatures. These can be done in groups to accomplish the quest safely; note that only one of the item at a time is lootable from any creature. Unlike the Kill Quests requiring you to bring back a head or item, these are not shared quest items.

Collection Quests are often quite slow when done with other people. Even having competition in the same area for kills or ground spawns of the necessary type can be challenging. It is best to take care of Collection Quests when you are in the mood to solo and are playing during quieter server times. For example, if you log on during prime time, try to run instances or do Kill Quests, Battlegrounds, and those types of activities. Early in the day or late at night, Collection Quests become FAR more efficient.

Delivery Quests

These quests require that you deliver an item from one place to another. The risk isn't in facing any particular creature or killing anything on your way (generally speaking). The risk comes from traveling through hostile territory and making it through alive. As an additional challenge, some of these quests are timed. Packages must be delivered within that time in order to be successful.

Delivery Quests often have very poor rewards and are not enticing in the short run. Yet, it is useful to pick up such quests when you can and wait until you are in the right neighborhood before completing them. "Oh, I'm in Westfall tonight, I better drop off this letter." Keep such quests items in your bank to save bag space, and try to remember to take the goodies out before jumping on a flight.

The main reason to bother with Delivery Quests is that many lead into chains. Longer quest chain start in mundane ways at times, and the rewards at the end of the quests are sometimes quite nice.

Escort Quests

Escort Quests ask you to keep an NPC safe as you travel through dangerous territory. These are often difficult to solo, and an entire group can benefit from completing it together. Often you must defeat creatures that attempt to kill the person/creature you are escorting and keep the escort safe until they reach a designated location.

Stay close to the quest NPC at all times. Should you stray too far from the NPC, the quest fails and everything must be started again. When that happens, look in your quest log, abandon the quest, and talk to the escort NPC again when they respawn.

QUEST MODIFIERS

Not all quests play by the same rules. Some quests are race/class specific, and others are only given by certain factions. These quest modifiers are explained below.

Faction Quests

Faction quests involve gaining faction with an NPC or group of NPCs in order to complete the quest. This can involve killing opposing NPCs or by doing some task that they would like done. Because the Reputation System can rise and fall based on your actions toward certain factions, these quests are often repeatable. Thus, you have a means of staying in good graces with a faction even if there are occasional problems (Sorry I killed your Auntie, but here is a Troll Necklace!).

Note that repeatable quests are designated with blue symbols over an NPC's head instead of the normal gold symbols.

Class Quests

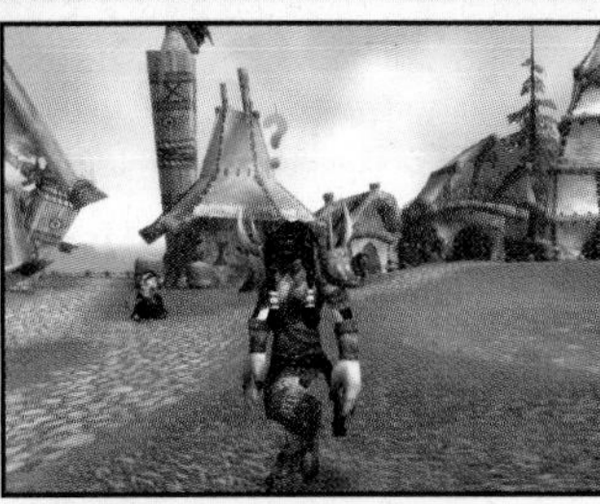

Class Quests are specific to one class. These quests grant new abilities or special items to the character that completes them. These can be done in a group or solo depending on your own abilities, but the group gains little unless they are of the same class. Find other characters entering the Class Quest or try to help others doing their own quests in return for assistance on yours.

Class Quests are most often found from class trainers or with NPCs who are near your class trainers. At landmark levels (10, 20, 30, etc.) you are most likely to gain something of this sort; they are not found randomly or at unimportant levels.

Quest Chains

Quest chains are part of a larger and evolving storyline. As players accomplish each part of the quest chain the line gets more difficult. The last quest is often a final encounter against a boss monster. Many of the major quests in Instances start off in a mild way, with a quest out in the world. Look into quest chains for greater rewards.

Elite Quests

Elite Quests pit you against NPCs that are indicated as being elite. These NPCs have more health than others of their level and are much tougher to kill. These are generally group-friendly quests and may take you and your group into Instances. Elite Quests often take the most time to complete.

Dungeon Quests

Quests that are specifically noted as Dungeon Quests are going to take your group into an Instanced Dungeon. These are major locations that many other players are likely to know. If you haven't been to such a place before, ask others to group with you and give you the full tour. Let people know ahead of time that you are new to the Instance so that they know to explain more complex aspects of the quest. Also try asking group members if there are sharable quests for the Instance that you don't have yet!

FINDING AND COMPLETING QUESTS

It's easy to find quests in many areas. Quest givers that have quests available in your level range have yellow exclamation points above their heads. NPCs that have a silver exclamation point above their head have a quest waiting for you in a couple of levels.

Once a quest giver has given you all the quests they can, no more exclamation marks hover over their head.

After right-clicking on a quest-giving NPC, a quest log appears to tell you what the quest is all about and what kind of reward you shall receive. Players have the option of either accepting the quest or turning down the request. Don't worry if you turn down a quest. It is possible to return to the NPC to get it once more. Just be careful about turning one down that may be a part of a series, because you might miss out of something fun later on.

Quests are stored in your log file on your hotbar and can be brought up by using the default 'L' hotkey. Twenty quests can be stored in your log at any time (any further quests are ignored until some of the current ones are completed or abandoned).

Your log file automatically organizes your quests for you and puts them into categories based on where the quest was received (or, in special cases, the log lists if the quest is a class or crafting quest). It also is color coded to indicate how difficult a quest is for you.

Clustering Quests

To save a lot of running time, cluster your quests by doing several in one area at a time rather than running around from place to place. For that matter, complete several quests in a specific section of a map before returning to town (this is very efficient and leads to faster leveling).

Grey indicates that the quest is easy and only gives a fraction of normal experience for having completed it at a lower level. Generally this is as little as 1/10th of the entire possible experience. Don't let fun or important quests fall to grey before they are turned in, and consider abandoning quests that are grey.

Green indicates that a quest is easy with a minimal amount of danger. The first level at which a quest becomes green does not reduce its reward. Afterward, you will receive slightly reduced rewards for quests that are completed after becoming green, but the ease of completing such tasks mostly negates this penalty.

Yellow indicates that the quest is within equal range of your level and has significant risk even with with proper preparedness. These can be accomplished either alone or with a minimal group. At this range experience is right on target for your level.

Orange indicates that the quest is difficult and will most likely need a group. Yet, with potions at the ready and a solid background in your class, most orange quests are doable.

Red indicates Danger! Danger! Danger! With a group you can certainly pull it off, but it's likely a good idea not to solo a red quest unless you already know it (by completing it with another character). Death may be the only thing you get out of going up against a quest that difficult so soon. Give it a level or two and watch to see when it changes to orange or yellow to make it more attainable.

Quest Colors

Color	Difficulty	Result
Grey	Trivial	Substantial Reduction of Quest Experience
Green	Easy	Almost Full Experience
Yellow	Standard	Full Quest Experience
Orange	May Require Group	High Quest Experience (Items of Higher Level)
Red	Requires Group	Very High Experience (Items of Considerable Power for Current Level)

It is as easy to find the end of a quest as it is the start of one. Ending quest NPCs have a yellow question mark over their heads. In addition, these NPCs appear on your mini-map, so guiding your character back to them is very easy. When returning to town, look for the golden dots that indicate a tracking target for the mini-map; quest NPCs show up when their quests are completed, and highlighting these dots will list the name of the NPC.

But wait, There's More?

Make sure to double check an NPC that you turn a quest in to. They may have another yellow exclamation point over their head indicating they have another quest or a follow-up quest for you. For that matter, an NPC that talks or starts an animation sequence is worth waiting around for; these NPCs sometimes have quests that won't appear until they are done with their song and dance about life, love, and growing up.

When finishing a quest, you are given a reward beyond experience. Rewards are often in the form of cash and/or a choice of objects. Even if you are unable to use an item, it is possible to sell it to a vendor. Quest items are soulbound and cannot be traded between players; sell unusable items to a vendor and enjoy the extra cash. Or, if you are an Enchanter, disenchant the item and use the ingredients to improve existing equipment.

Read through your combat log after completing quests. Notice that many major quests provide a healthy boost to your reputation with one faction or another. This is a great way to get various groups to like your character.

QUEST SHARING

An exciting feature of WoW is the ability to share quests. If your character is the only person in a forming group with a certain quest, it is easy to "give" the quest to everyone else in the party. In effect, you become the quest giver for the others, though they return to the normal NPC for their completion rewards.

You cannot share quests if there are prerequisites that the rest of the group members haven't accomplished (or if the quest is class/race related and they aren't of said class/race). You also cannot give them a quest that requires that a specific item given by the NPC (like a special Moonvial or package). A message lets you know if your quest has been successfully accepted or if the other person doesn't meet the requirements or has a full quest log.

You cannot receive quests again if you have already completed them. If your quest log is full, you have to abandon one of your quests and the other person will have to share it again.

To share a quest, open the quest log and click on the quest that you want to share. The option is there to abandon or share the quest; choose "Share" and your entire party is queried with that quest (if they accept it, you are good to go). When looking at the screen, it even says how many characters in your current group are also engaged in quests that you have. If a quest has a [3] to the left of it, three other people in your group have that quest as well.

ABANDONING QUESTS

At any time, you are free to abandon a quest. This clears the quest out of your log (making room for other quests). The original NPC that gave you the quest resets, thus enabling you to start the quest again at a later point. You can abandon quests for the quest log space, for convenience (if you know you won't do the quest again), or to make a second attempt at a quest you have failed. Timed Quests and Escort Quests are the most likely to fail; these should be abandoned and tried a second time.

Death and Rebirth

When returning to your body, make sure that all the spiders are gone.
Hey! Hey, I see you back there! There's like thirty of you guys!
I told you this wasn't going to work.
Just be cool!

The lives of adventurers would be short indeed if death were a permanent fixture in MOGs. Either that, or people would spend FAR more time inside inns, hoping that various abominations wouldn't burst through the door. To make the game world a bit more fun, and a lot more survivable, Blizzard has implemented a system without vicious death penalties. This section explains the various types of death that your character could face and how to respond to these problems.

WAYS TO DIE

Characters that are slain drop to the ground and are taken out of your control. It is impossible to move, cast spells, emote, speak normally, or do anything of importance to yourself or your group. Private and guild messages are allowed, so you can message nearby folks to let them know if you need a Rez.

Your character enters this state when his or her health drops to zero. Falling from too high a distance, being struck by physical or mystic forces too many times, or drowning can do this. There is no starvation in WoW, nor are their status effects that directly cause death (though poisons and damage over time abilities can and will kill you whether you are still in combat or not). Keep your health high and life goes on.

When a character is slain by monsters, there is a 10% hit to the durability of all currently-equipped items. This can be a fairly painful slap to your money when it comes to repairing the pieces (especially at high levels). If you are planning to intentionally get your character killed off (for fun, roleplaying, etc.), consider taking off especially pricey gear ahead of time. Those who use Spirit Healers to Rez normally lose 25% of their durability to ALL carried items, not just equipped ones. Very painful indeed.

Deaths in Instances

Instances won't allow characters to return to their corpses; this would make it too easy to regroup and continue fighting in difficult Instances. Though Resurrection spells and Soulstones work in the same manner inside and outside Instances, trying to Release and Return to your body fails. Instead, your character automatically revives when they enter the Instance.

The penalty here is simply that parties aren't able to survive losing a character during an Instance run without using either Resurrection or a Warlock Ritual of Summoning (once the person has revived normally). Of course, if the enemies of the Instance haven't respawned yet, the newly spawned character can run back to the group on their own without needing to clear anything.

Death on the Battlefield

Player versus Player deaths are the most trivial of all in terms of system penalties. Everyone is there is to fight honorably and die trying, so the game mechanics are extremely lenient on the characters. No durability hits are taken from PvP deaths. In fact, characters that are slain inside the Battlegrounds are brought back to life after a short delay; a nearby Spirit Healer does the work for them and returns the fallen fighters to full health and mana. Pets are even restored as well! Thus, hit release when your character falls in battle during the Battlegrounds and wait for the fun to start again.

THE PATH TO BETTER HEALTH

There are several ways to respond after your character dies. Each method of revival has different consequences, so it is wise to learn all three methods before stepping onto the field of battle.

Returning to Your Body (Release and Return)

The most common method of revival comes from Releasing and Returning to your corpse. Click on the Release button that appears once your character falls; this teleports you to the nearest Graveyard for your faction. As a spirit, you can see the world around you, but other characters and monsters are hidden from view. Only other spirits of your faction and the nearby Spirit Healer are visible.

A pointer on the mini-map appears to lead you toward your body; there is also a small gravestone to mark your corpse. Follow the pointer and don't worry about random monsters. Take a direct path and only avoid a fast route if the land prevents a direct run; as a spirit, you can even walk on water. Once you get near your body, the line between life and death blurs (this causes monsters to become visible to your spirit). Move within a radius of 40 or so yards and an option appears to revive. Click on this in a spot where you are safe from the aggro of nearby monsters or PvPers. If you died deep underwater, you have to fully submerge to get in range to revive.

Reviving in this manner has NO penalty toward your character's experience. Also, you are returned to your body with 50% of your maximum health and mana (these return normally after that point). There is no Resurrection Sickness, and you are free to adventure normally.

Resurrection (Rez)

If there is an allied person in the area where your body falls, Resurrection may be possible. Shamans, Paladins, Priests, Druids, and Warlocks have various powers to Resurrect characters in some way, shape, or form. In the first three cases, Shamans, Paladins, and Priests cast spells on corpses that call the spirit back to the body. The player in question receives an accept/decline button to let them know that Resurrection is being used on them. This works even if the person has already released and is heading back to their body as a sprit.

When Resurrected your character appears almost instantly in the area, alive, but not well. Depending on the spell used, your character may have as little as 1% of their health and mana.

There are no penalties to accepting a Resurrection. Your characters suffers no experience penalty or long-term attribute harm. Thus, the tradeoff with Resurrection over a release and corpse run is a matter of time only.

DRUID REBIRTH

Druids are able to use a spell called Rebirth to Resurrect a person. This spell has a 30-minute timer and is used in battle to bring someone back to life with a fair portion of their health and mana (it's a set quantity, based on the rank of Rebirth used). This spell allows Druids to save a primary Rezzer in the event that a group or raid is in very bad shape. In raid PvE content and the Battlegrounds, Rebirth is a tremendous advantage to everyone involved.

A Seed reagent is needed for Rebirth. These are purchased in major cities and carry a trivial price compared to their value for preventing catastrophic wipes.

WARLOCKS AND SOULSTONES

Warlocks are able to Resurrect as well, but it's a special case that merits an explanation. Warlocks turn Soul Shards (collected from enemies as the creatures die) into various stones. One of these items is a Soulstone. Warlocks use these on other characters.

If you have a Soulstone, the game immediately asks if you wish to revive when you die. Your character returns to life in the location where you fell. The Soulstone is destroyed in the process (though if you use a different method to Resurrect, the Soulstone is not used).

This power is quite good for use in Instances, where losing a character who has Resurrect might mean the end of a good expedition. Even a total party wipeout can be reversed with these items (almost always give the Soulstone to the group's primary Rezzer).

THE SHAMAN SELF-REZ

A wonderful ability of Shamans is the power to Resurrect themselves. This requires that they have Ankhs in their inventory (purchased from vendors in major cities at a trivial price), and Ankhs can only be used once an hour. This spell is learned at level 30, and after that point Shamans become an incredible tool for groups and raids against total wipeouts. If everyone goes down, the Shaman should wait and find out if anyone is using a Soulstone from a Warlock. If not, the Shaman pops back up and starts Rezzing the rest of the group as soon as they can. A self-Rezzing Rezzer! Who could ask for more? Note that this does not need to be cast ahead of time. Simply having an Ankh in your inventory after the spell is learned is enough to trigger the option after death.

GOBLIN JUMPER CABLES, FOR THE NON-REZZERS

Okay, so we saved one of the secret tricks for last. Even non-Rezzers have a chance to save their buddies if they are Engineers with 165 skill and have Goblin Jumper Cables. This item is used to attempt a Resurrection. There is a 30-minute timer on the Cables, so be sure to use them on a Rezzer. Also, remember that this is a fine piece of Goblin Engineering; that means you very well might end up dead just for trying to use them! They deal 100 damage to you when they fail.

Rogues with Goblin Jumper Cables are especially valued. In the event that a group or raid wipes multiple times and uses its full supply of tricks to Rez itself, the Rogues can run back to the dungeon, stealth past mobs that have respawned, and try to save a Rezzer. Sending several Rogues to do this may mean the difference between a brief wipe or losing an entire raid to bad luck and having to reclear a major raid dungeon.

The Spirit Healer

Okay, so there had to be a costly method somewhere. People who cannot retrieve their bodies, are too tired or frustrated to try, or who want a VERY fast Rez can choose to Resurrect at the Spirit Healer.

Every Graveyard has a Spirit Healer. These floating figures of death and rebirth return people to life where their spirit stands (thus, you appear at the Graveyard of the nearest allied faction). Even if you make the long run to a farther Graveyard and use their Spirit Healer, your body appears at the yard closest to your corpse.

Do you lose experience? Nope. That doesn't even happen here. However, you do lose more durability than you would for a normal death. Beyond that, Resurrection Sickness hits your character. This debuff lasts for a short time and prevents your character from fighting well. Thus, you take a financial hit in terms of repairs, and you are forced to fight very soft enemies for a while or run the risk of dying again.

Does this mean that the Spirit Healer is a bad deal for most players? Yes, most of the time it does, but in no way is the Spirit Healer a bad thing to consider in special cases. If you are so far away from your corpse that a run would cost major time and frustration, it might be worth a Rez at the Spirit Healer. Or, if you die way out in the ocean somewhere, or at a place that is almost unreachable anyway, it's worth avoiding the trouble.

COMMANDS AND MACROS

It's actually quite easy to start moving around and controlling your character in World of Warcraft; the system is quite intuitive. Still, there are always commands that you won't think of right off the bat. This section explains more about the command system and the macros that can be used during gameplay. Guild commands and aspects are discussed later in the guide.

GENERAL COMMANDS

General commands can be bound to keys or typed out fully. These control a wide array of speech and combat options.

/assist "Name"	Switches your target to that of the person named; If no name is used, your current target is selected as the default for the assist.
/cast	Used in macros to control spell use (automatically initiated when you click on spells or press their equivalent hotkey)
/em [message]	Creates a custom emote
/exit	Leaves the game
/follow	Follows the current character from your faction (great to bind to a hotkey)
/invite [player]	Invites "player" into your current group or starts a group with "player" as the second person
/logout	Exits your current character, cannot be done in combat; takes 20 secs. unless in a city
/party or /p [message]	Puts up text in a different color that is only heard by group members
/played	Displays the amount of time you have invested in your current character and the amount of time you have spent in your current level
/pvp	On PvE and RP servers, this flags your character for PvP combat; even if you toggle this by typing PvP again there is a five minute delay before you become unflagged
/r	Replies to the last person who whispered you
/random [X]	Rolls a random number with "X" being the maximum roll (100 is the default)
/say [message]	Speaks out loud; anyone nearby will hear you
/sit	Your character sits down
/stand	Your character stands back up (or move forward to automatically have your character move)
/tell or /t [player] [message]	Sends a private message to "player"
/whisper or /w [player] [message]	Sends a private message to "player"
/ignore "Name"	Places the person named onto a list of people that cannot message you; you also won't hear them /say,/yell, emote, invite, mail, etc.
/who	Used to search for specific people, to list characters of a given level range, or characters found in a specific area (Examples: /who 10-11 for a level search, /who Kayal to see if there are people with that type of name, /who Winterspring to see who is playing in Winterspring)
/yell [message]	Shouts a message that appears in a different color than /say and will be heard over a larger distance (don't spam these)

CHAT CHANNEL COMMANDS

Chat Channels are extremely useful for interactions with both public players and friends. There are default channels, like World Defense and General, that you cannot control (save to leave them or re-enter them), and there are also ones that you can create and moderate on your own.

Some ideas for Chat Channels: if you have close friends who aren't in a guild with you, make a private Chat Channel with a name that all of your buddies can remember. Type /join MidlandHigh (if your friends were from such a high school).

/# (#=Number of Chat Channel)	For channels that you are already in, speaking is a matter of typing /1, /2, etc. So /1 Hi everyone might say Hi everyone in General if that was the first channel in your list
/afk "X"	Lets anyone who messages you know that you are away from keyboard
/dnd "X"	"X" Creates an autoreply so that people who message you get X as a response (Example: We are raiding Molten Core, Talk Later)
/announcements, /ann	Toggles whether a channel displays people entering and leaving
/ban "X"	Bans player X from using the channel
/unban "X"	Unban character "X"
/chathelp	Lists and explains Chat Channel commands
/chatlist "Number" /chatwho "Number"	Lists the characters logged into the channel "Number"
/join "X" /channel "X" /chan "X"	Joins Channel "X"
/kick "Name"	Kicks character "Name" out of the channel
/leave, /chatleave, /chatexit [channel]	Takes you out of the listed channel (you can use the name or number of the channel to do this)
/mod "Name" /moderator "Name"	Makes the named person a moderator for the channel
/unmod "Name" /unmoderator "Name"	Stops the named person from being a moderator
/moderate "Number"	Toggles whether the channel can be moderated
/password, /pass [channel] [password]	Creates a password to protect the channel from unwanted visitors

MACROS

Macros are used to create automatic actions (sometimes entire groups of them) that are used with a single key press.

Creating a Macro

- Click on the text bubble by your chat bar and select Macros from the menu there; this brings up the Create Macros system
- Select whether a macro will be a general macro or a character-specific macro
- Select "New" then use one of the icons available and name your macro
- At the bottom of the screen, type in the text for your macro; any mix of standard commands can be used

Ideas for Macros

- Roleplaying while using abilities
- Used to shift equipment or use several abilities in tandem
- Alert other players to problems or dangers
- Inform people about rules or protocols

Macro Name: Assist

Macro Text Line 1: /assist "Name of Main Assist"

Macro Name: Sap (Rogue)

Macro Text Line 1: /cast Sap(Rank #)—# is the Proper Level of Your Sap Ability
Macro Text Line 2: /p Sapping %t

Macro Name: Bandaging You

Macro Text Line 1: /script SendChatMessage["Hold Still, Bandaging You","Whisper","Language To Be Used", UnitName("target")];—Language Would be Common in Many Cases
Macro Text Line 2: UseContainerItem(#,#);—Where #,# is the Bag You Are Using and Slot Within That Bag
* Bags are (0) Backpack through (4) Far Left and slots are (1) Upper Left to (n) Lower Right

Macro Name: Loot Rules

Macro Text Line 1: /say Group Loot for today will be used
Macro Text Line 2: /say Need can only be rolled for item upgrades that will be used
Macro Text Line 3: /say Greed is rolled for Bind on Equip items OR on Bind on Pickup Items if you are an Enchanter
Macro Text Line 4: /say Pass on Bind on Pickup items if you are not an Enchanter

Macro Name: Raid Conduct

Macro Text Line 1: /ra Do Not post in raid chat unless you are a group leader or the information is VITAL
Macro Text Line 2: /ra Keep chat to private channels or within your group
Macro Text Line 3: /ra Inform your group if/when you go /afk and put /follow on a healer
Macro Text Line 4: /ra Pay extra attention to all attack and cease fire orders

Keyboard Layouts

PC Keyboard

Movement

Key	Action
clear (Mac)	Auto Run
Num Lock (PC)	Auto Run
W	Move Forward
A	Turn Left
S	Move Backward
D	Turn Right
Q	Strafe Left
E	Strafe Right
Space Bar	Jump
X	Toggle Sit/Stand
Z	Sheathe/ Unsheathe Weapon
NumPad /	Toggle Run/Walk

Camera

Key	Action
Help (Mac)	Pitch Up
Insert (PC)	Pitch Up
Delete	Pitch Down
Home	Next Camera View
End	Previous Camera View
Y	Flip Camera
Keypad 2	Back
Keypad 4	Rotate Left
Keypad 8	Rotate Right
Right Mouse Button + A	Rotate Left
Right Mouse Button + D	Rotate Right

Hotbar

Key	Action
1-0, - and +	Hotbar Keys
Alt + Hotbar Key (PC)	Use ability on Self without changing Targets
CTRL + Hotbar Key	Secondary Action Button (Pet Bars)
CTRL + F1-F10	Special Action Button
ESC	Open/Close Game Menu
SHIFT + 1-6	Toggle through Hotbars 1-6
SHIFT + 7	Next Action Bar
SHIFT + 8	Previous Action Bar

Inventory

Key	Action
B	Open/Close Backpack
F8	Open/Close Bag 1
F9	Open/Close Bag 2
F10	Open/Close Bag 3
F11	Open/Close Bag 4
F12	Open/Close Bag 5 Close All Bags
SHIFT + B	Open/Close All Bags

Targeting

Key	Action
F1	Target Self
F2 - F5	Target Party Members 2 - 5
SHIFT + F1 - F5	Target Party Pets 1 - 5
TAB	Select Front Hostile Target Toggle Hostile Targets
G	Select Last Hostile Target
CTRL + TAB	Target Nearest Friend
CTRL + SHIFT + TAB	Target Previous Friend

Chat

Key	Action
ENTER	Initiate Chat
/	Initiate Chat Command
R	Reply to a /whisper or /tell
/em	Initiate Emote
/v	Initiate Voice Command
Shift +R	/whisper to last person whispered

Attacking

Key	Action
T	Attack Target
SHIFT + T	Pet Attack Target
F	Assist Target
Shift +F	Target Last Hostile

Character Info

Key	Action
C	Character Pane
SHIFT + C	Combat Log
I	Ability Pane
SHIFT + I	Pet Book
K	Skill Pane
L	Quest Log
N	Talent Pane
O	Social Pane
P	Spellbook
U	Reputation Pane
H	Honor Pane

Display

Key	Action
V	Show Name Plates
ALT + Z	Toggle HUD
F13 (Mac)	Capture Screenshot
Print Screen (PC)	Capture Screenshot
M	Opens Map

Sound

Key	Action
CTRL + M	Toggle Music
CTRL + S	Toggle Sound
CTRL + +	Master Volume Up
CTRL + -	Master Volume Down

Mac Keyboard

DUN MOROGH

Dwarves and gnomes have been part of the Alliance for quite some time. These industrious folk have also supported each other, and that shows in the way both races live in close proximity without savaging each other every few years. Yet, there are clear differences between these two cultures. The dwarves are strong, courageous, and proud. They produce blades, guns, armor, and great buildings of stone. Gnomes are more inquisitive, building gadgets that are not always of immediate use or even known purpose. Together, the two races make Dun Morogh a land of many trades.

Legend

1 Gnomeregan	5 The Grizzled Den	9 Coldridge Valley	13 Eastern Dun Morogh	17 Far Eastern Dun Morogh	21 South Gate Pass
2 Frostmane Hold	6 Kharanos	10 Anvilmar	14 Misty Pine Refuge	18 Helm's Bed Lake	22 Ironforge (Capital City)
3 Southwest Dun Morogh	7 Steelgrill's Depot	11 Iceflow Lake	15 Amberstill Ranch	19 North Gate Pass	
4 Chill Breeze Valley	8 Coldridge Pass	12 Shimmer Ridge	16 Gol'Bolar Quarry and Mine	20 North Gate Outpost	

Your First Day

Anyone who suddenly appears inside Ironforge or any number of Dwarven Strongholds might think that the land outside was blasted with heat and steam. Yet, Dun Morogh is a cold land, high in the mountains where a biting wind becomes one's frequent companion. Between the rocky crags and icy lakes, the Yetis, Trolls, and beasts find their niche, but there are rewards in this isolated land. Potent herbs find a way to poke through the snows, desperate for light, and metal seems to pour up through the earth as well. For the wary eye, Dun Morogh is a place of great riches!

ANVILMAR

Anvilmar is a place of rest in southern Dun Morogh. Mainly a dwarven site, the merchants, trainers, and travelers who come through are often on their way to more comfortable climates. Luckily, your first steps are quite safe. There is very little danger from the weaker troggs and wolves that dominate the hunting grounds nearby, and people are friendly in Anvilmar, offering many quests and services to those who are willing to work.

Sten Stoutarm has work for you (**Dwarven Outfitters**). He's willing to make you some gloves if you bring him eight pieces of Tough Wolf Meat. Accept his offer and head south to find the wolves. They are weak and do not pose a danger to you.

With the required meat in your backpack, return to Sten for your reward. Now that he knows he can count on you, he has more work for you, as do others in the area. He'll have a message for you from your class trainer and some mail he needs delivered. Accept **Coldridge Valley Mail Delivery** and speak with Balir Frosthammer for more work.

This local toughman is angry at the Troggs for their recent attacks; instead of ignoring the "buggers," he wants to bring them to heel. He asks you to slay five Rockjaw Troggs and five Burly Rockjaw Troggs (**A New Threat**). Both are found in the local fields, though more Burly Troggs can be found in camps west of Anvilmar.

The Spoils of War

Your backpack is nearly full. First, take the time to look through it and see if there is any usable equipment for you. If there is, equip it. Second, become familiar with any recovery items (potions, food, drink, etc.) you've accumulated. Everything else that can be sold to vendors should be.

Head up the path and into Anvilmar. Speak with your trainer to complete your first class quest and to learn your level two abilities. With everything in town accomplished, head south across the wolf fields and engage the Rockjaw Troggs.

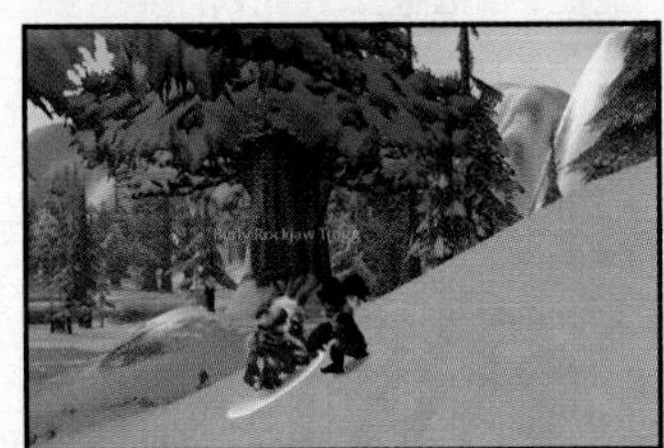

The Rockjaw Troggs are fairly easy fights, aren't aggressive, and won't double team you. At most you may need to rest a short while between fights to recover mana and health. There are a few Burly Rockjaw Troggs in the hills, but if they are scarce, head along the path west from Anvilmar.

Traveling the Bloody Way

As you're traveling, consider killing any enemies that are your level or lower. The enemies around Anvilmar are fairly weak and the additional experience and usable equipment make it worth your time.

Take the path west of Anvilmar to Talin Keeneye's camp. Talin is grateful for the mail and lets you know that not all the mail is for him. A letter is for Grelin (**Coldridge Valley Mail Delivery**). Talin makes a living by hunting the boars in the area. Recently, however, there are so many boars that it has become dangerous for him. He'll reward you if you can help him by killing 12 Small Crag Boars (**The Boar Hunter**).

The boars are everywhere around his camp. Head out and start killing. Watch your health and mana; rest between fights if either is low. The boars aren't terribly dangerous, but they're higher level than your targets thus far. Kill the required Small Crag Boars and return to Talin for your reward.

As you only have a single backpack, your inventory is getting full. Make a quick stop back at Anvilmar to sell, search for upgrades, train (if you've gained level 4), and speak with Balir once again for your reward.

Stopping inside Anvilmar reveals that Felix Whindlebolt would like to have a word with you. He tells a story that is common among the Gnomes. In his haste to escape the catastrophe in Gnomeregan, some of his belongings were lost. He's fairing better than most since he knows where they are. He saw trolls taking them to their camps in the southwest. Felix asks you to recover his belongs for him since he isn't an adventurer (**A Refugee's Quandary**).

Now it is time to deal with the letter to Grelin Whitebeard. If you are nosy, you can read it. Wow! It's signed by Magni Bronzebeard, the King of Ironforge. This must be really important and you shouldn't delay its delivery any longer. Head southeast across the snows to the end of the path and Grelin's camp.

Grelin is pleased to receive his mail and tips you for the service. He's also very eager to conscript you into the service of Ironforge. **The Troll Cave** to the south needs to be dealt with before it can become a real threat. He wants you to kill 14 Frostmane Troll Whelps for your reward. Nearby, Nori has a predicament. He's got a delivery of Scalding Mornbrew that needs to get to Anvilmar before it gets cold. He's got a fire to keep it hot and you're going the other way, so avoid the quest for now (it's a timed quest).

To the southwest is the troll cave and inside the trolls you need and Felix's belongings. The Frostmane Troll Whelps are much more aggressive than the enemies you've fought so far. They will attack you if you get close (called aggro) and they come to the aid of their friends if you're not careful. The outer trolls are spread out so this isn't as much of a worry. Keep the fights quick and pull back if reinforcements are nearby.

Felix's Bucket of Bolts is near the campfire at the entrance to the cave. Stick to killing the Frostmane Troll Whelps outside the cave as inside is more dangerous. If there are enough of the trolls outside, you won't even need to venture within the cave just yet. Once you've killed enough Frostmane Troll Whelps, don't delay in returning to Grelin.

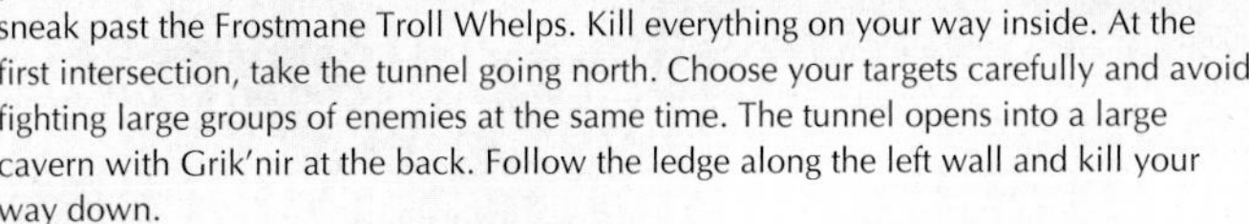

While you were attacking the cave, a group of trolls attacked Grelin's camp. Everyone's okay, but the trolls stole Grelin's journal and he wants it back. Grelin got a reasonable look at the troll that took it and wants you to kill Grik'nir the Cold to retrieve it (**The Stolen Journal**). Head back to the troll cave. This time you need to go inside.

While the constant fighting may cause you to rest more often, do not try to sneak past the Frostmane Troll Whelps. Kill everything on your way inside. At the first intersection, take the tunnel going north. Choose your targets carefully and avoid fighting large groups of enemies at the same time. The tunnel opens into a large cavern with Grik'nir at the back. Follow the ledge along the left wall and kill your way down.

Pull the enemies one at a time until Grik'nir stands alone. He's a tough fight and you don't want any of his friends helping. Without friends, kill Grik'nir and recover Grelin's Journal.

Inventory Full?

It's been a good while since you were near a merchant and your inventory shows it. Once your inventory is full you can't pick up any more items, including quest items. Take the time to destroy some of the less lucrative items in your inventory when you need room for quest items.

Less lucrative items are items of lowest quality and lowest armor (symbolized by the grey name). This means grey cloth items are often the first to be dropped. If you don't need the food or drink for recovery purposes, these are also prime candidates.

Exit the cave as quickly as caution allows. Don't try to run past any trolls that have respawned. Take the time to kill each one. Once out of the cave, head east to the next troll camp. You still need to collect Felix's belongings. Felix's Chest is sitting beside the fire at the first camp you come to. Exercise the same caution attacking this camp as you used in the cave. Kill the enemies one at a time until you get to the chest.

Grab Felix's Chest and head northeast to the final troll camp. Felix's Box is just inside the camp. Recover it and head back to Grelin's camp. Grelin rewards you for his journal and asks you to deliver a report to Mountaineer Thalos for him (**Senir's Observations**). As your next stop is Anvilmar, speak with Nori Pridedrift for the **Scalding Mornbrew Delivery**. This quest is timed, so don't delay much on your way to Anvilmar.

Durnan Furcutter is in the very back of Anvilmar awaiting his Scalding Mornbrew. He enjoys the mug of Mornbrew and, as a kind soul, asks if you would return to empty mug to Nori (**Bring Back the Mug**). Return Felix's items on your way out of Anvilmar. He's very pleased to have them back and rewards you with some coin. Sell any excess loot and make a quick run to return the mug to Nori.

The work for you in Coldridge Valley is finished. Stop by your trainer in Anvilmar if you've reached level six. Consider spending some time killing if you haven't reached level six yet. Follow the path east from Anvilmar when you're ready to make the trip to Kharanos.

The trail ascends to the tunnel entrance. Mountaineer Thalos warns you of the trogg infestation in the tunnel. At first, Thalos advises you to stay in Anvilmar until the tunnel is cleared, but when you show him Grelin's letter he realizes the import of your trip. He gives you directions to Kharanos and bids you a safe travel to Senir Whitebeard (**Senir's Observations**).

Stranded outside the tunnel entrance is Hands Springsprocket. He has a delivery to make to the inn at Kharanos, but can't get through the tunnel with the troggs in the way. He asks you to make the delivery for him as you're heading through the tunnel already (**Supplies to Tannok**).

Head into the tunnel with your weapon ready. The troggs are very aggressive and do not back down from the fight. Kill them as you move through the tunnel and to Dun Morogh proper. It's quite a hike to Kharanos, but follow the stone path and you can't miss it.

KHARANOS AND STEELGRILL'S DEPOT

Standing by a tent at the entrance to town is Senir Whitebeard. Deliver the report to him. He mentions that he'll have work for you later and rewards you for your work thus far. There are others who wish to speak with you, but first head to the inn on the east side of the road. Deliver the supplies to Tannok Frosthammer and speak with Innkeeper Belm. He can set your hearthstone to return you here if you ask him to make this inn your home. Do so.

Head outside and speak with Ragnar Thunderbrew. He's run into a bind. The trapper that used to supply him with crag boar ribs enlisted in the King's Army and was deployed elsewhere. He's willing to give you the recipe to cook **Beer Basted Boar Ribs** and even a sample if you collect six Crag Boar Ribs for him and buy a Rhapsody Malt from the inn. Accept the quest and head across the street.

Tharek Blackstone makes tools and is constantly supplying Steelgrill's Depot. The latest shipment is ready and he asks you to drop it off on your way out (**Tools for Steelgrill**). Head northeast over the hill to Steelgrill's Depot. Kill any boars you come across on the way.

The tanks and mechnostriders are a dead give-away for Steelgrill's. Speak with the pilots and mechanics on your way in. Pilot Bellowfiz needs help **Stocking Jetstream**, his tank. He asks you to get four Chunks of Boar Meat and two Thick Bear Furs. Pilot Stonegear wants to make a rug for the inside of Trollplow. Eight Wendigo Manes should be enough. You can get these from **The Grizzled Den**. Loslor Rudge needs you to recover a lost shipment of **Ammo for Rumbleshot**. The previous courier was frightened off by the wendigo west of Kharanos. Before heading out with all this work, remember to deliver the tools to Steelgrill.

Head southwest through Kharanos, to the Grizzled Den. The wendigo are very aggressive and dangerous. The Young Wendigo outside the cave can drop the manes and the ammo crate is in the camp, so there is little reason to enter the cave at this time.

Kill the boars and bears in the area while killing the wendigo near the cave entrance. Grab the ammo crate when you need a break from fighting to recover. Watch for the snow leopards in the south. They aren't terribly dangerous, but they are aggressive and run around a lot. With Kharanos so close, return to sell excess loot should your inventory fill up. As the boar meat is sellable, be careful about emptying your entire inventory. Keep the items needed for your quests.

Wendigo have it All

Wendigo can be skinned for their leather. In addition, they frequently drop coin and cloth. Add to that the supply of copper in their dungeon and herbs nearby and you have an area that is *perfect* for crafters, even in groups. Low-level characters interested in raising their new trades often find that the Wendigo offer much while demanding little.

With your quests finished, return to Kharanos. Stop at the distillery to purchase the Rhapsody Malt and bring it and the Crag Boar Ribs to Ragnar. Senir now has work for you. Speak with him about **Frostmane Hold**. The trolls near Brewnall Village have been more active of late and he needs you to poke around and kill a few to see what's going on. Accept the quest and head back to Steelgrill's Depot for more rewards.

Bellowfiz appreciates all the hunting you did for him. He pays you for your work, and asks another task of you. He needs something to drink on the road. **Evershine** is his favorite and can only be bought in Brewnall Village. Head back to Kharanos then follow the road south toward Coldridge Valley. Hegnar Rumbleshot is awaiting his ammo shipment along the road. Continue following the road toward Coldridge Valley, but head northwest before entering the tunnel. A short ways through the valley and you come across a trail at the base of Chill Breeze Valley.

Investing in Your Future

With so much time spent between towns and so much killing being done, your backpack tends to fill up quickly. Consider speaking with the General Supplies merchant in the Thunderbrew Distillery. He sells bags as well. These aren't inexpensive, but they allow you to carry more loot home. More loot sold means more money. The bag makes up its cost quickly.

CHILL BREEZE VALLEY

Head north up the valley. There are two caves along the valley; one on each side. Give the eastern cave a wide berth and head to the western cave. Follow the path up and speak with Tundra MacGrann. An elite wendigo has stolen his locker of dried meats. Old Icebeard can't open the locker, but Tundra still needs to eat.

Old Icebeard is very powerful and can't be killed alone. There are two ways to accomplish this rather daunting task. If you are alone, hide near the entrance to his cave and wait for him to wander off. When he does, rush in, get the meats from the locker, and run out. If you have a number of friends and feel up to a challenge, engage Old Icebeard directly. Either way, returning the meats to Tundra prompts his appreciation and a reward. Head to the southern end of the valley and follow the path west to Brewnall Village.

BREWNALL VILLAGE

Speak with Rejold to get the cask of **Evershine**. He will give it to you...if you do him a favor. The wildlife has been encroaching on Brewnall Village and the crafters are losing time dealing with them. If you kill eight Elder Crag Boars, eight Snow Leopards, and six Ice Claw Bears, the Evershine is yours (**A Favor for Evershine**). He also has a more personal favor to ask. Rejold wants to create **The Perfect Stout**. He's still searching for the right ingredients and would like to try Shimmerweed. The problem is the Frostmane Seers use it in their rituals. He wants you to swipe six of them for him.

No one has **Bitter Rivals** like crafters. Marleth Barleybrew wants you to swap her Barrel of Barleybrew Scalder with a barrel of Thunder Ale next time you're in Kharanos. Accept the quest and head back to Kharanos. Head east around Iceflow Lake and through Chill Breeze Valley this time. It's shorter and there is wildlife that needs to be thinned.

Stop at the small workshop just north of Kharanos. Inside, two gnomes are diligently working on the Gnomeregan problem. Razzle Sprysprocket would like your help with **Operation Recombobulation**. He needs you to collect eight Restabilization Cogs and eight Gyromechanic Gears from the leper gnomes near Gnomeregan. Grab the quest and continue into Kharanos.

Head into the Thunderbrew Distillery. In the lower levels sits the Guarded Thunder Ale Barrel. Jarven Thunderbrew is almost as vigilant a guard as he is a drinker. Buy some Thunder Ale from the Innkeeper and help Jarven quench his thirst. Once Jarven has one, he has to have another. Wait for him to get up the stairs before switching the barrels and making a hasty exit. While you're in the distillery, stop by your trainer and see if you can learn any new abilities.

It's time to return to Brewnall. Take the northern route and trim the wildlife on your way.

GNOMEREGAN, TROLLS, AND BREWNALL REVISITED

Marleth is grateful for the switch you pulled at the Thunderbrew Distillery and gives you some coin to show it. Repair your gear, sell excess loot and head northwest. It isn't far before you can see the green gases spewing from Gnomeregan.

Continue pruning the wildlife as you search for the parts Razzle needs. Whatever happened in Gnomeregan, it's driven the leper gnomes quite mad and they have no problem taking that anger out on you.

The leper gnomes are very dangerous. While clearly loony, they're still intelligent. If they're losing a fight, they run for help. Be ready to finish your enemies off quickly or stop their flight. Allowing one to run guarantees a long walk from the graveyard. They do a lot of damage, so be ready to fully rest after each engagement.

With the required parts and wildlife killed, return to Brewnall. Rejold rewards you for hunting the animals with the cask of Evershine for you to **Return to Bellowfiz**. Sell excess loot and head southwest to Frostmane Hold.

Anyone can sneak up to a camp and observe the enemy. Senir needs you to enter the cave and scout the area. Follow the tunnel west into a large cavern. Continue along the outer edge killing as you go and watching for the patrols. Once you've explored the cave to satisfaction (your quest log will show this), fight your way back out. Hunting the trolls outside is much safer.

Once the quest is complete, return to Brewnall. You don't have anything to turn in, but you should repair and sell excess loot before heading out again. Your next stop is Shimmer Ridge. Be aware, the trolls on Shimmer Ridge are quite dangerous and work together.

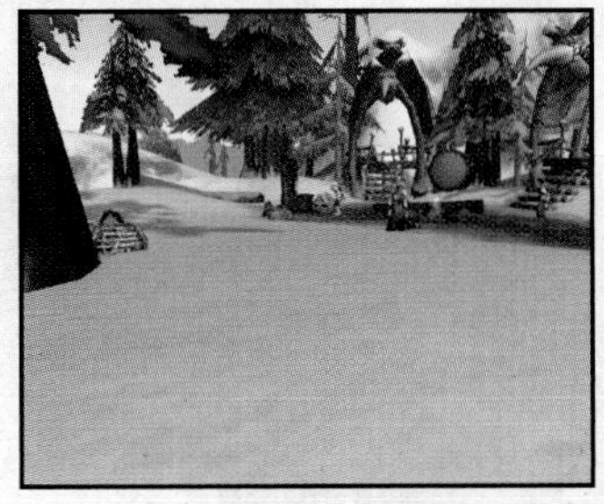

The path up to Shimmer Ridge is on the east side of Iceflow Lake. Look around for others heading up the path and join forces if they are willing. Shimmerweed can be obtained from both the Frostmane Seers and the baskets on the ground. If there are no baskets and all the Frostmane Seers are dead, sit and wait. The camp is very dangerous if it's allowed the spawn fully. Kill the trolls as soon as they spawn to keep the danger to a minimum.

First kill the Frostmane Seers around the edge of the camp. The center is a bit crowded and too much for a single person. The enemies are primarily casters and ranged attackers. This means they are very difficult to pull. Use a ranged attack and run away from them. When you get out of their casting range, they will be forced to come after you. As soon as they are clear of their friends, turn around and show them the mistake they just made.

A good technique for clearing the camp is to attack, kill one, and run away. The keys are being able to kill the first enemy quickly and being able to get away before his friends kill you. Using this technique over and over again slowly clears the camp and makes it much more manageable.

Now it's time for a bit of walking. Return to Brewnall and speak with Rejold for your reward. He asks you to deliver a barrel of the new **Shimmer Stout** to his brother. It'll be some time before you get there, but stout never goes bad, so pick up the quest. Next head back to Kharanos and the gnome house just north of it.

The recombobulator isn't quite working yet. You've collected everything you need for Razzle. Wish him luck in returning Leper Gnomes to sanity, and head to Kharanos to give your report to Senir. With the information you gathered, it's time to make a report to Ironforge. Senir asks you to deliver **The Reports**. Stop by Steelgrill's on your way north and speak with Bellowfiz.

IRONFORGE AND THE ROAD TO LOCH MODAN

Senir's mission is one of importance, but it also gives you a nice break from the constant work. Much of southern and eastern Dun Morogh is calming down (thanks to your good deeds). It's time to see the capital of the dwarves. Take the road north and climb the long ramp to the mighty Gates of Ironforge.

As all classes and professions are represented in Ironforge, it's a good place for training. If you're picking up crafting professions, seek out the trainers while you are delivering the letter for Senir. Senator Barin Redstone is in the High Seat, which sits on the southeast side of the Great Forge.

It's Big!

Ironforge is a rather impressive town. Exploring all of it would take quite a bit of effort, but you're not the first to get lost in this city. The guards are accustomed to newcomers needing directions and they give them freely. To find things in a hurry, ask a guard and they will plot it on your mini-map.

Ironforge Points of Interest

Location	Useful Stores/NPCs
Main Gate	Inn, Bank, Visitor's Center, General Goods, Auction House
Mystic Ward	Mage/Portal Trainer, Paladin Trainer, Priest Trainer
Forlorn Caverns	Rogue Trainer, Fishing Trainer, Warlock/Demon Trainer
Hall of Explorers	Quest Recipients
Tinker Town	Gnomeregan Quests, Engineering Trainer, Alchemy Trainer, Stormwind/Ironforge Tram
Military Ward	Inn, Warrior Trainer, Hunter Trainer
Great Forge	Griffon Master, Herbalism Trainer, First Aid Trainer, Enchanting Trainer, Mining Trainer, Blacksmith Trainer, Tailoring Trainer, Leatherworking Trainer, Skinning Trainer, Cooking Trainer, High Seat

Becoming More Talented

Every level (starting at level ten), you gain a Talent Point. These can be used to increase your abilities or learn new ones. Open your talent window (defaulted to 'n'). There are three panels in the window. Look at each talent carefully before choosing as once you spend your points, it costs gold to unlearn them. There is more about the benefits of each talent in the class section.

With the capital explored and many fine quests completed, it's appropriate for you to seek Loch Modan, the beautiful land east of Dun Morogh. There are still some exciting places to see before you leave your homeland, so start making your way east and look for some of the following hotspots.

There is a ranch just a minute or so east of Ironforge. Rudra Amberstill breeds rams there, yet she is beset by troubles caused by a monster named Vagash. She asks you to help her by **Protecting the Herd**. Vagash is found in a cave above the ranch. Climb west and around the bulk of the mountains and bring a friend or two unless you are greatly prepared for an ugly fight! Vagash is level 11 and is an elite wendigo, so take that into consideration before the fight starts. Offer the Fang of Vagash as proof to Rudra that the attacks will stop and claim your reward.

Further east sits the Gol'Bolar Quarry. Generally a mine dedicated to supplying Ironforge with stone, the quarry has become overridden with troggs. Senator Mehr Stonehallow is asking all adventurers to find **The Public Servant** inside themselves and help. He needs you to kill 10 Rockjaw Bonesnappers before the miners can return to work.

Foreman Stonebrow is standing on the edge of the quarry in frustration. He doesn't have the political power that Stonehallow does, but he wants the troggs dead all the same. He asks you to kill six Rockjaw Skullthumpers to help end the occupation of **Those Blasted Troggs!**

With a group, these two quests are frighteningly easy and fast. If alone, take the quarry very slowly and fight near the walls to avoid as many patrol issues as possible. Be careful of troggs that stand behind the pillars of ice near the cave entrance, and stay well rested in case sudden adds demand more from your hit points and mana.

A Crafter's Dream

The Wendigo Cave was good, but the Quarry is an even better location for crafters of all sorts. There is a wealth of copper inside the mine itself, but there are also veins outside of it (in the general Quarry). Beyond that, the troggs are a fine source of Linen and drop money as well. Herbalists will also be pleased with the high concentration of Earthroot, Silverleaf, and Peacebloom nearby.

In the far northeast is a short quest that you can finish to ease the mind of a troubled dwarf. Pilot Hammerfoot is guarding some engines in the area, but he won't leave the region until he's convinced that his friend Mori is either alive and well, or dead and lost. **The Lost Pilot** charged off into the hills some time back, and you can help out by discovering his fate. Move farther north along the road until you can break west. The body of Mori lies in a pile of bloody snow.

Though slain, Mori was able to account for his fate before his death. In his journal the dwarf wrote of a powerful bear named Mangeclaw. Vengeance was the pilot's final wish, and it would further aid his companion to know that this was done. Look slightly south and scour the area for the bear, then slay the beast. Tell Pilot Hammerfoot when the mission of vengeance is complete.

The road east leads directly through South Gate Outpost where Mountaineer Barleybrew works; give him his brother's barrel of Shimmer Stout. The dwarf also wants one of his friends to try the mixture, and he passes the brew along with a request that it be sent to Mountaineer Kadrell of Loch Modan (one of the Thelsamar guards). Because you were on your way to Loch Modan already, this offers no expense of time or energy.

Congratulations on your success in Dun Morogh. Rams are breeding happily, the dwarves have raised a fine toast in your name, and even the snow seems to have receded a bit because of such fine efforts. New challenges wait in Loch Modan and in lands such as Westfall to the south and Darkshore across the ocean, but those are adventures for another day.

Elwynn Forest

Elwynn Forest is the pleasant home of Stormwind City and the basket of human civilization in the east. Surrounded by settled farms, lumber mills, and mines, it's no wonder where the Humans get their grand ideas of a peaceful future.

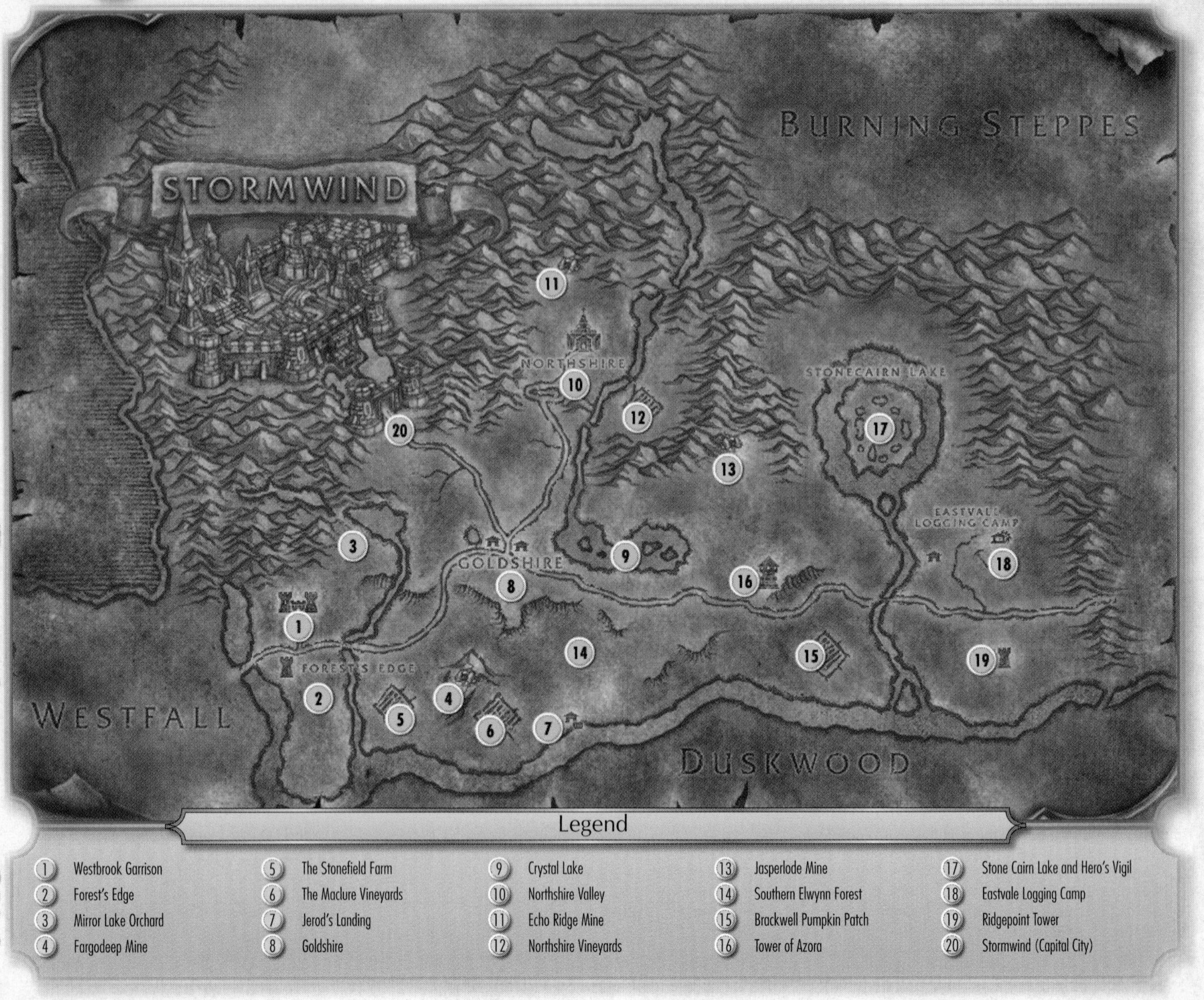

Burning Steppes
Stormwind
Northshire
Stonecairn Lake
Eastvale Logging Camp
Goldshire
Forest's Edge
Westfall
Duskwood
Legend
1 Westbrook Garrison
2 Forest's Edge
3 Mirror Lake Orchard
4 Fargodeep Mine
5 The Stonefield Farm
6 The Maclure Vineyards
7 Jerod's Landing
8 Goldshire
9 Crystal Lake
10 Northshire Valley
11 Echo Ridge Mine
12 Northshire Vineyards
13 Jasperlode Mine
14 Southern Elwynn Forest
15 Brackwell Pumpkin Patch
16 Tower of Azora
17 Stone Cairn Lake and Hero's Vigil
18 Eastvale Logging Camp
19 Ridgepoint Tower
20 Stormwind (Capital City)

Your First Day

A light breeze blows through the trees. The smells of freshly cut wood and baked goods drift from just through the woods. The sun is shining and it's just warm enough for a refreshing glass of water or lemonade. Such is life at the heart of the human lands where the guards patrol the roads and train daily.

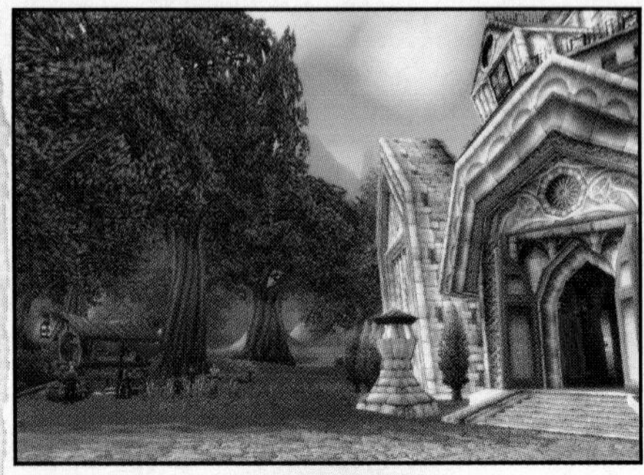

NORTHSHIRE

Northshire is one of the first places adventurers are sent to train. In the abbey are veterans of many trades and walks of life to help you grow. The merchants outside understand who they are dealing with and sell many weapons and armor designed for the newly enlisted. Few of the problems here are terribly dangerous and most make for good practice of skills that keep you alive elsewhere.

Report to Deputy Willem to begin your training. As you are here answering the call about **A Threat Within**, he directs you to Marshal McBride inside the abbey. McBride's first orders are for you to assist in a **Kobold Camp Cleanup**. He wants you to kill ten Kobold Vermin and return. The kobolds are just northwest of the abbey, but head around the right side of the building first.

Eagan Peltskinner has more work for the willing. With so many **Wolves Across the Border**, Eagan is hiring people to hunt them. He wants eight pieces of Tough Wolf Meat to cook. He rewards you for your time, so accept the quest and head north to hunt the wolves.

Young Wolf

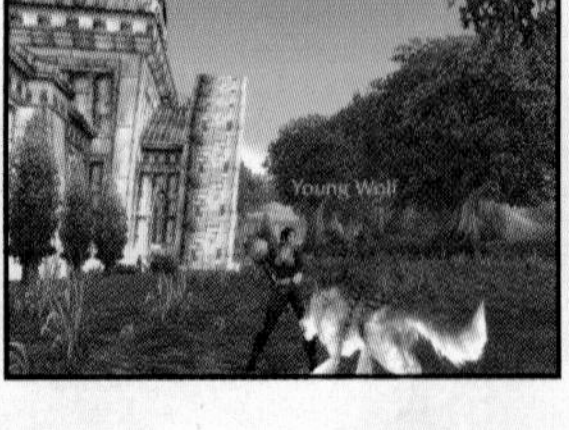

The kobolds aren't terribly bright and don't much like each other. You can kill them with impunity and those nearby do not assist. Avoid going into the mine as your targets are around the campfires outside and the enemies in the mine are more dangerous. With both quests done, return for your rewards.

The Spoils of War

Your backpack is nearly full. First, take the time to look through it and see if there is any usable equipment for you. If so, equip it. Second, become familiar with any recovery items (potions, food, drink, etc.) you've accumulated. Everything else that can be sold to vendors should be.

McBride has more work for you now that you've proven a willing hand. He has a message for you from your trainer and needs you to help **Investigate Echo Ridge**. To remove the kobold infestation, he wants ten Kobold Workers killed.

Take a moment to visit your trainer and learn any new abilities before heading out of the abbey. Deputy Willem has more work for you. The Defias Brotherhood has been seen in the area. This **Brotherhood of Thieves** must be put down before they can become a problem. He asks you to collect 12 Red Burlap Bandanas as proof of your commitment to the safety of Northshire.

First head north to the kobold camps. The Kobold workers are at the campfires with the Kobold Vermin. Do your part to aid in the investigation and return McBride for more work. McBride outranks Willem and thus his work comes first.

Your work has shown that the kobold infestation is worse than expected and a **Skirmish at Echo Ridge** may be unavoidable. McBride asks you to penetrate the kobold defenses around the mine and kill 12 Kobold Laborers to bring their digging to a halt. Head north and carry out his orders.

Traveling the Bloody Way

As you are traveling, consider killing any enemies that are your level or lower. The enemies in Northshire Valley are fairly weak and the additional experience and usable equipment make it worth your time.

McBride is pleased with your work and gives you leave to **Report to Goldshire**. Accept the documents, but don't head out of Northshire just yet. Deputy Willem needs your assistance and there is more to do. Visit your class trainer again to check for new abilities to learn.

When you are ready, head across the creek to the Northshire Vineyards. The thieves are everywhere and more intelligent than the wolves and kobolds you've fought so far. They will attack you on sight, and assist their friends.

With proof of your deeds, return to Willem for your reward. While you were killing the brigands, there have been other developments. There's a **Bounty on Garrick Padfoot** for harassing the farmers and leading the local thieves. Willem is authorized to pay well for Garrick's Head. **Milly Osworth**, a friend of Willem's, also needs a hand. Milly stands behind the abbey.

Milly was harvesting in the vineyards when the Defias moved in. **Milly's Harvest** was left in several crates. She's worried they'll either be stolen or damaged and wants you to recover eight of them. Head across the bridge again and kill the enemies around Milly's Harvest. When you've recovered all you need, head further east to find Garrick.

Milly is very pleased to have the harvest saved. While she still rewards you, someone else would like to reward hard work. Take the **Grape Manifest** to Brother Neals in the bell tower to show the work you've done.

Both Brother Neals and Deputy Willem reward you. With so much accomplished in Northshire, it's time to head to Goldshire.

GOLDSHIRE

The south road from Northshire takes you through a well-guarded set of walls. Falkhaan Isenstrider is relaxing at a beautiful fountain advertising the Lion's Pride Inn at Goldshire. His friend owns the establishment and Falkhaan suggests stopping by for some **Rest and Relaxation**.

Follow the road south to Goldshire. Make a quick stop at the Lion's Pride Inn for some free food or water. Speak with Innkeeper Farley about how to make this inn your home. This resets your hearthstone to this location and is a good habit to get into. William Pestle stands off to one side of the inn looking troubled. He's looking to gather wax, but the best source of it is **Kobold Candles**. He's no adventurer, so he'll pay if you bring him eight Large Candles.

Now that you've taken a moment to rest from your travels, deliver your papers to Marshal Dughan. He doesn't waste any time putting you to work and wants you to explore **The Fargodeep Mine** and report back on the kobold presence. Remy "Two Times" runs the local **Gold Dust Exchange**. Bring him ten Gold Dust from kobolds and he pays handsomely.

Pretty much everything people are asking of you so far involves the kobolds at Fargodeep Mine but it's a bit too dangerous to go in without having a better understanding of the area. Follow the road west until you can cut south to the Stonefield Farm. "Auntie" Bernice Stonefield is upset about a **Lost Necklace**. She believes Billy Maclure took it and wants it back. Find and question Billy Maclure at the Maclure Vineyards to the east.

Billy Maclure claims he knows who took it, but he's smarter than he looks and wants some pie for the information. Bernice makes a good Pork Belly Pie, but she needs four Chunks of Boar Meat to make the **Pie for Billy**. Luckily, the boars in the vineyards have the meat you need. Hunt them and return to Bernice.

Bernice isn't happy about being blackmailed to get her necklace back, but she'll do whatever it takes. Bernice makes the pie and asks you to take it **Back to Billy**. Ma Stonefield has work for you as well. The Brackwells have a prize-winning pig that has a habit of sneaking over and eating the veggies from the Stonefield Farm. Ma has decided that **Princess Must Die!** Bring Princess' collar to Ma and she rewards you.

With the pie in hand, return to the Maclure Vineyard and speak with Billy. Billy saw a kobold making off with Bernice's Necklace. The kobold ran into the Fargodeep Mine and had a huge **Goldtooth**. Before you run into the mine, speak with Maybell Maclure. She's having some real trouble as her one and true love is...a Stonefield. The rivalry between the two families is terrible, but these **Young Lovers** are determined to find a way to happiness. Take Maybell's Love Letter to Tommy Joe Stonefield, who is moping at the river west of Stonefield Farm.

Tommy Joe is so caught up in his love for Maybell that he can't think straight. He asks you to **Speak with Gramma** to find a way for the two to be together. Gramma has seen a number of things in her life and knows that a potion can fix anything. Take her **Note to William** in Goldshire next time you're in the area. For now, prepare to enter Fargodeep Mine.

The kobolds in the mine are very aggressive. Take it slow and kill everything near you. There are two entrances: one to the upper level and the other to the lower level. Goldtooth stands in the corridor that joins the levels, but you'll be in here long enough you're bound to see him.

The Marshals haven't been lax about recruiting people to clear the mine and you won't be alone. Consider joining forces with others already there. These quests take longer to do in a group, but your survivability is much higher with friends. Be extra careful to pull enemies to you when entering the larger chambers as several of the kobolds may attack from different sides.

Inventory Full?

It's been a good while since you were near a merchant and your inventory shows it. Once your inventory is full you can't pick up any more items, including quest items. Take the time to destroy some of the less lucrative items in your inventory when you need room for quest items.

Less lucrative items are items of lowest quality and lowest armor (they are grey in name). This means grey cloth items are often the first to be dropped. If you don't need the food or drink for recovery purposes, these are also prime candidates.

Keep your health and mana full as you clear out the mine. When you've finished with the quests, return to Bernice at the Stonefield Farm. She's very happy to have her necklace back and frees you to return to Goldshire. Use your hearthstone for a quick trip back or simply leg it.

William Pestle packages the candles and asks you to take the **Shipment to Stormwind**. This isn't a time sensitive quest and you can deliver them when you visit the capital. Accept the quest and give him the note from Gramma Stonefield. William has a way to help them, but he needs help **Collecting Kelp** for the potion. He needs four Crystal Kelp Fronds. Crystal Lake is patrolled by nasty Murlocs. They are VERY social, so adds are very common.

Report to Marshal Dughan next. He's very pleased with your exploration of the Fargodeep Mine. He's so pleased he asks you to explore **The Jasperlode Mine** as well. Accept his assignment and speak to Remy about your gold dust. True to his word, he pays you for the dust. He also asks you to speak with Dughan about **A Fishy Peril** elsewhere in Elwynn Forest.

Dughan has spoken with Remy before and his hands are tied until he gets an official call for aid to combat the murloc menace. He doesn't have the manpower to check the situation...you've been his eyes and ears already. If you have **Further Concerns** about the matter, he suggests you speak with Guard Thomas along the east road. Accept the quest and take a moment to visit your trainer before heading out.

Investing in Your Future

With so much time spent outside of town and so much killing being done, your backpack tends to fill up quickly. Consider speaking with the General Supplies merchant in the Lion's Pride Inn. He sells bags as well. These aren't inexpensive, but they allow you to carry more loot home. More loot sold means more money. The bag pays for itself quickly.

Head east following the lake. There are murlocs on the islands of the lake; they have the kelp you need. Pull them back and be ready to finish them off quickly. They're aggressive, don't like to fight alone, and run for help when wounded. Once you have the required kelp, retreat to the road and continue east.

THE EASTVALE LOGGING CAMP

Follow the road east until it crosses the river. Guard Thomas is standing here. Speak with him about the murloc threat in the area. Two guards were sent to investigate the matter further, but they haven't returned. Thomas needs you to **Find the Lost Guards** so he can complete his report. They were looking around where the river meets the lake.

Murlocs are not the only threat to the logging camp. The bears and wolves in the area are becoming more numerous and more brazen as the loggers become the only food source in the area. Thomas asks you to join in the effort to **Protect the Frontier** by killing eight Prowlers and five Young Forest Bears. Accept both his quests and follow the river north.

Watch for the bears as you move north to the lake. There aren't any Prowlers on the west side of the river, but the remains of Footman Malaki Stone are lying where the river drains from Stone Cairn Lake. This solves the fate of one soldier, but you still need to **Discover Rolf's Fate**. Webbed footprints lead east from the corpse and you can see a murloc village on the edge of the lake. Follow the lake edge east.

The murlocs are very aggressive and attack if they catch the slightest hint you are in the area. Look for others hunting the murlocs and join forces. If there is no one to join forces with, continue to Eastvale Logging Camp and speak with Supervisor Raelen. You'll be in the area for awhile and you can investigate the camp when it's safer.

Raelen is in **A Bundle of Trouble**. Because of all the attacks, her loggers haven't been able to gather the required lumber. They've felled the trees but the wood is in small piles. She needs you to bring eight Bundles of Wood back. Head out of the camp and search near the base of the nearby trees.

Watch for the Prowlers and Young Forest Bears. These are the reason the loggers had to flee. They need to be killed. As you hunt through the trees, keep an eye on the murloc camp. If someone else is hunting them or in the area, join together or sneak in before the murlocs respawn. Rolf's remains are easier to get to from a southern approach.

With the fate of both guards revealed, **Report to Thomas**. The murlocs are a greater threat than previously believed. **Deliver Thomas' Report** to Marshal Dughan. But first, head back to the logging camp. Sara Timberlain is a kind person and will make you clothes if you bring her the materials she needs. She prefers to work with **Red Linen Goods**. Bring six Red Linen Bandanas from gang members in Elwynn Forest.

Drop off your wood and sell excess loot before crossing the river west. Travel northwest to the Jasperlode Mine. Without even setting foot in the mine, the kobold presence can be seen. Marshal Dughan needs to know the strength of the infestation though.

The kobolds here are more dangerous than the ones in Fargodeep. They don't travel alone often, and the ones wearing blue shirts understand magic. The casting kobolds can do a lot of damage quickly, but don't last long in a fight. Target them first if you are engaged by more than one kobold.

Deeper in, the tunnel walls are covered with web, and kobolds hang from the ceiling in silky cocoons. You've seen what you needed and now it's time to get out. If your Hearthstone is ready, port back to Goldshire. Should your Hearthstone be on cooldown, exit the mine as quickly as caution allows and head back to town.

William uses the kelp to make an Invisibility Liquor that helps with **The Escape**. Hold onto it until you see Maybell Maclure next. Marshal Dughan is eager to hear your reports. He doesn't like what's happening, but he rewards you as promised. He gives you a Stormwind Armor Marker to give to Sara Timberlain. She'll craft **Cloth and Leather Armor** for you to use in the defense of Elwynn Forest.

As one of the commanding officers in charge of Elwynn's defense, Dughan always has more work for you. He asks you to **Report to Gryan Stoutmantle** in Westfall when Elwynn is under control, and alerts you that the **Westbrook Garrison Needs Help!**

Smith Argus has work for you if you're willing. He's been asked to send people to Grimand Elmore in Stormwind. **Elmore's Task** is one of several that are sending you to the capital.

STORMWIND CITY AND BACK TO EASTVALE LOGGING CAMP

Now is a good time to see the glorious city of Stormwind. Follow the northwest road to the city of light and the center of the human armies.

As all classes and professions are represented in Stormwind, it's a good place for training. If you're picking up crafting professions, seek out the trainers while you are delivering the shipment for William and speaking with Grimand. Morgan Pestle is in his apothecary just inside the gates while Grimand is in the Dwarven District.

Stop by and listen to Renato Gallina, who is standing on a large crate on the west side of the street. He's advertising the Gallina Winery and gives you a ticket to prove you were sent by the **Wine Shop Advert** and garner a free Bottle of Pinot Noir.

It's Big!

Stormwind is a rather impressive city. Exploring all of it would take quite a bit of effort, but you're not the first to get lost in this city. The guards are accustomed to newcomers needing directions and they give them freely. To find things in a hurry, ask a guard and they will plot it on your mini-map.

Stormwind Points of Interest

Location	Useful Stores/NPCs
Trade District	Griffon Master, Inn, Bank, Weapon Trainer, Auction House, Visitor's Center
Mage Quarter	Alchemy Trainer, Enchanting Trainer, Herbalism Trainer, Tailoring Trainer, Mage/Portal Trainer
Park	Hunter Trainer, Stable Master, Druid Trainer, Herbalism Trainer
Cathedral Square	Paladin Trainer, Priest Trainer
Dwarven District	Blacksmithing Trainer, Engineering Trainer, Mining Trainer, Forge, Anvil, Tram to Ironforge
Old Town	Cooking Trainer, Leatherworking Trainer, Skinning Trainer, Warrior Trainer, Rogue Trainer
Canal District	Fishing Trainer

Becoming More Talented

Every level (starting at level ten), you gain a Talent Point. These can be used to increase your abilities or learn new ones. Open your talent window (defaulted to 'n'). There are three panels in the window. Look at each talent carefully before choosing as once you spend your points, it costs gold to unlearn them. There is more about the benefits of each talent in the class section.

Stormpike's Delivery is given to you by Grimand. He wants the supplies sent to Loch Modan in the Dwarven Lands. These lands are far away, but accept the quest now so you have it when you venture there. If you've reached level ten, speak with your trainer for a class specific quest before heading back to Goldshire.

There's still more to do in the east. Take the road from Goldshire to the Eastvale Logging Camp. Guard Thomas has another mission for you. With the information you've brought, the Stormwind Army has placed a **Bounty on Murlocs**. Thomas is authorized to reward you if you bring eight Torn Murloc Fins as proof of the kills. Continue east to Eastvale Logging Camp.

Turn your armor marker in to Sara Timberlain for your armor, then head south across the road. East of Ridgepoint Tower is a small Defias camp. Kill them for their Red Linen Bandanas. When you've acquired enough for Sara, return to Eastvale. Sell your excess loot before heading north to the murloc camps.

Quests Falling From the Sky

A number of quests are started by items found on corpses. Keep your eyes open for the Westfall Deed and Gold Pickup Schedule as you fight the Defias and Gnolls in Elwynn Forest.

To activate a quest from these, open your inventory and right click on the item.

The murlocs are a bit easier now that you've gained a level or two. Do the lower level characters a favor and kill the enemies near Rolf's Remains first. Clear the murlocs slowly as they are still very aggressive. With the fins in hand, follow the river south to Guard Thomas and your reward.

Break off the road and head southwest to the Brackwall Pumpkin Patch. The outer edges are guarded by brigands, but between the pumpkins a beast moves. Princess and her entourage move about the patch with a royal bearing. To attack one is to gain the wrath of all three. Check for other players in the area that are willing to help you before attempting the kill.

Take the Brass Collar and return to the Maclure Vineyard to the west. Give the Invisibility Liquor to Maybell and help the two lovers break free of the oppression of the hate between their families. Your next stop is the Stonefield Farm. Ma Stonefield is rather pleased to have her veggies safe from the monster and rewards you accordingly. Sell any excess loot to Homer Stonefield and head north to the road, and west to the Westbrook Garrison.

WESTBROOK GARRISON

On the path from the road to the garrison is a large wanted poster. **Wanted: "Hogger"** doesn't leave much to the imagination. The Stormwind Army has placed a bounty on the savage gnoll and empowered Marshal Dughan to reward anyone bringing his Huge Gnoll Claw as proof of the deed.

Report to Deputy Rainer at the garrison for your assignment. The gnolls in to the south have grown in number to become a significant threat. The guard tower doesn't have the numbers to clear the vermin out, so adventurers are being recruited for the **Riverpaw Gnoll Bounty**. Bring back eight Painted Gnoll Armbands for your reward.

Head south across the road. Many of the gnolls stay in camps where their numbers offer protection. If you are in a larger group, attack these camps carefully. Solo adventurers should avoid these camps entirely as they are nothing more than a fast trip to the graveyard. Instead, look for the few gnolls that patrol between the camps alone. Ambush these for the armbands.

Keep a watchful eye for Hogger. He is very dangerous and can be the doom of you or your party if he attacks while you are engaged with other gnolls. When you see Hogger, rest to full and wait for him to be away from other gnolls. He is an elite enemy, shown by the gold dragon encircling his portrait, and has many more hitpoints and does much more damage than most enemies his level.

Collect the armbands and return to Deputy Rainer. As promised, he rewards your service to king and country. With little else to be done at Westbrook Garrison, hearthstone back to Goldshire and turn the Huge Gnoll Claw in to Dughan.

Congratulations on your success in Elwynn Forest. Farmers are back at work, the local merchants tell stories of you to customers, and the roads are just a little bit safer. The call for aid has come from the land of Westfall and the allies in the dwarven land of Loch Modan and the Elven land of Darkshore could certainly use a skilled hand, but those are adventures for another day.

TELDRASSIL

Teldrassil is the new home of the brave night elves, a people who have taken arms and magic to battle against demons and restore the balance of their spirits. With the former capital of Elven power nearly destroyed by the fighting against the demons, the refuge has grown in prominence. Those ancient and animated trees that remain to protect the forest have gathered here to stop any final advance from the evil remnants. Now the night elves are shaking off their suffering and readying themselves for the next chapter in their history.

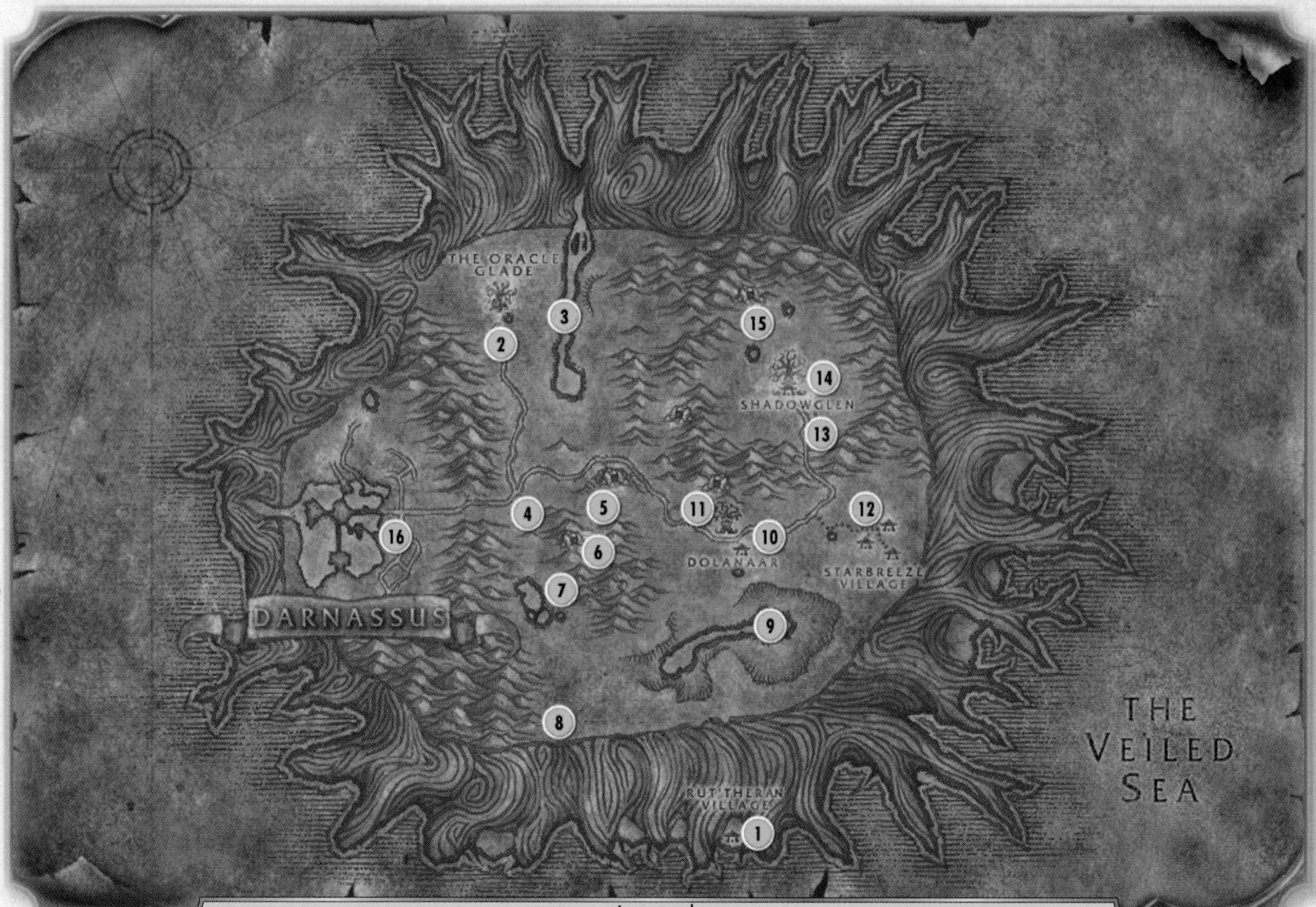

Legend

1	Rut'theran Village	5	Ban'ethil Hallow	9	Lake Al'Ameth	13	Shadowglen
2	The Oracle Glade	6	Ban'ethil Barrow Den	10	Dolanaar	14	Aldrassil
3	Wellspring River	7	Pools of Arlithrien	11	Fel Rock	15	Shadowthread Cave
4	Road to Darnassus	8	Gnarlpine Hold	12	Starbreeze Village	16	Darnassus (Capital City)

YOUR FIRST DAY

Teldrassil is a tree the size of a large island off the coast of Kalimdor. Isolated from the effects of many recent troubles, the land itself is free from some of the greater taint that plagues many of Kalimdor's forests. Yet even here, there are the stirrings of disease and corruption.

The greatest problems that exist in Teldrassil involve the tainting of natural creatures and beasts by a force of evil. Your duties often involve seeking out this taint in an attempt to isolate it, redeeming those corrupted, or, when all else fails, to destroy the creatures who are beyond salvation.

ALDRASSIL

Aldrassil is the starting town, in the north-east of Teldrassil, where your character begins the journey into greatness. As with all new character areas, the majority of the creatures are neutral and won't attack unless engaged directly. A single large building at the center of this forested valley holds trainers, vendors, and the leaders of Aldrassil.

Speak to a nearby night elf after watching the introduction to Teldrassil. Conservator Ilthalaine stands a few feet from you. He tells you of **The Balance of Nature** and how Shadowglen has become unbalanced with the rapid growth of the boar and nightsabre populations. He asks you to kill seven Young Nightsabres and four Young Thistle Boars to begin trimming the populations. Accept his quest and move east as you kill.

Night Elves Have Mettle, Not Metal

If you want to be a miner, be warned that Teldrassil is starved for metal. No one out here trains you in the hearty act of mining, and the problems don't end there. Copper is so rare here that you won't find any of it. If mining is of tremendous importance to you, create the night elf you want and head to the human lands (this is possible even at low levels).

On the flipside, Peacebloom and Silverleaf are in great abundance, so harvesters who prefer Herbalism are often quite happy here. Skinners, too, have abundant resources from which to gather, as many beasts in the area are skinnable.

At the entrance to the main building in Aldrassil is Melithar Staghelm. Tarindella, **The Woodland Protector**, has been seen in Shadowglen. Melithar asks you to find out why she is here and aid her in any work. Continue east into a field plentiful with Young Nightsabres and Young Thistle Boars. Kill them until your quest is complete and you've gained level two. On your way back to Conservator Ilthalaine, speak with Dirania Silvershine at the cooking pot. Iverron, **A Good Friend** of Dirania, hasn't been seen since he headed up to the spider cave. Dirania would like you to find him for her.

Speak with Ilthalaine and get the next step of restoring **The Balance of Nature**. Now you need to kill seven Mangy Nightsabres and the same amount of Thistle Boars. He also has a message from your class trainer. Accept both the quests and head to your trainer. Most of the trainers are inside the main hall of the building, but the nature-based class trainers (such as the Druid trainer) are in the higher branches of the building. Get your character any new skills, then find Tarindella just north of Ilthalaine.

Traveling the Bloody Way

As you're traveling, consider killing any enemies that are your level or lower. The enemies in Shadowglen are fairly weak; the additional experience and usable equipment make it worth your time.

Tarindella is in the area fighting the corruption. The Grells in the area are collecting Fel Moss (which spreads the corruption). She asks you to collect eight pieces of Fel Moss. The Grells have been driven quite made by the Fel Moss and won't give it up without a fight. Travel north to the Grell camps and kill them until you have the Fel Moss and have gained level three. If you finish the Fel Moss before gaining the next level, kill a few more…it's the only way to be sure.

Your bags are likely full by now. Return to Tarindella and give her the Fel Moss. With her gratitude stop at the merchants in Aldrassil and sell any excess loot. Remember to equip any extra bags you've found and head north once again. Gilshalan Windwalker stands at the bottom of the ramp nearby. He's studying the spiders in the area and needs ten **Webwood Venom** sacs from the spiders. As you have other quests near the spider cave, accept his and continue north to Shadowthread Cave.

Poison

All of the major breeds of spiders in Teldrassil are venomous. This makes fighting them a slow process due to the increased time spent resting after fights. They are also aggressive and attack anyone who ventures too close. Though needed for quests, the spiders are better avoided when hunting for money or basic experience.

Look to the west of Shadowthread Cave, in a small valley, a wounded night elf male named Iverron waits. He was bitten by the largest of the foul spiders and is too weak to return to Aldrassil. His condition is worsening as the poison runs its course. He asks you to help **A Friend in Need** by telling Dirania Silvershine of his plight. He's a strong man and can survive a bit longer, so finish your other quests before heading back.

When you've collected the venom sacs, head southeast. There are more Mangy Nightsabres and Thistle Boars if you return this route. With the animal populations successfully thinned, speak with Dirania about Iverron's situation. She can make **Iverron's Antidote**, but needs some ingredients. She needs seven Hyacinth Mushrooms which grow near the trees in the area but you must fight the grells that wander nearby. Look around the northern ponds for the four Moonpetal Lily, while the Webwood Ichor is easily obtained from the spiders you are already fighting.

Stop at the merchants to sell excess loot and speak to your trainer about learning new abilities before heading out again. Get your reward from Ilthalaine and give the venom sacs to Gilshalan. With the venom specimens, he has set his sights higher. He wants a live spider to observe. As capturing a full grown spider is a daunting task, he wants you instead to bring him a **Webwood Egg**. Accept his quest and head north to collect the ingredients for the antidote. With the ingredients collected, head into Shadowthread Cave.

Inventory Full?

It's been a good while since you were near a merchant and your inventory shows it. Once your inventory is full you can't pick up any more items, including quest items. Take the time to destroy some of the less lucrative items in your inventory when you need room for quest items.

Less lucrative items are items of lowest quality and lowest armor (grey named). This means grey cloth items are often the first to be dropped. If you don't need the food or drink for recovery purposes, these are also prime candidates.

There are said to be hundreds of the eggs inside Shadowthread Cave, so the only worry comes from fighting past all of the poisonous beasts. The eggs are on the top level of the cave. The center path takes you through a narrow passage as it climbs up to the eggs. Only one of the spiders is as high as fifth level, so even a solo character can move through the cave safely (just don't try to fight more than one enemy at a time). Grab the Webwood Egg and return to town triumphant. The spiders might have respawned by now. Fight your way out or use your Hearthstone for a fast trip back.

After you give Gilshalan the egg, he asks you to answer **Tenaron's Summons**. This accomplished night elf won't take much of your time. He merely asks that you fill a Crystal Phial with the waters of the Moonwell just north of town as payment for learning of the **Crown of the Earth**. Head down the tree and give the ingredients to Dirania to make the antidote. It won't stay potent for long (it is a timed quest), so immediately head north to the Moonwell.

Filling the Phial

To fill the Phial, stand in the Moonwell and open your inventory (defaulted to 'i'). Right click on the Empty Phial to get the Filled Crystal Phial.

With the Filled Crystal Phial, turn west and fight through the spiders to Iverron. He rewards you for giving him the antidote. With things just about done here, return to Tenaron atop Aldrassil for your reward.

Tenaron informs you that your time in Aldrassil is at an end and hands you a vessel with the Moonwell water to take to Dolanaar, a large town near the center of Teldrassil.

ENTERING DOLANAAR

Following Tenaron's bidding, it's time to seek the greater town of Dolanaar. Finish selling extra items to the vendors below, and make sure to train with the masters that specialize in your class. With that done, take the southern road away from Aldrassil and into the greater wilds of this majestic land.

At the entrance to Shadowglen, Porthannius stands. He has a **Dolanaar Delivery** he'd like you to help with. As you were already heading that way, it costs you nothing and is worth your while. Accept his quest and continue south.

Stick to the road, and fight creatures nearby if you wish. A lone Satyr, Zenn Foulhoof, stands on the right side of the path, by a tree. He seems friendly, and is willing to award you a simple quest. Return items from the Nightsabres, Strigid Owls, and Webwood Spiders to complete **Zenn's Bidding**. It takes a number of kills to collect everything, so this is best accomplished while you are busy with other quests.

Press on to Dolanaar and talk to everyone in town. Standing at the ramp to the north building is Syral Bladeleaf. She has a delivery she would like you to finish for her. She gives you **Denalan's Earth** and directions to find him at the lake to the south. At the entrance stands Athridas Bearmantle, who wants you to enter the Firbolg village to the east. Athridas feels **A Troubling Breeze** and there is another night elf there who he is worried about. Promise to help him and head to the top of the building.

Tallonkai Swiftroot is in the highest room and has a few problems you can help with. First, he lost **The Emerald Dreamcatcher**. It was held at Starbreeze Village to the east and he can't retrieve it himself. Accept this quest and ask him about his other problem. Tallonkai Swiftroot wants to see the head of Melenas, minus the body. Melenas is a dark Satyr who lives in a cave called Fel Rock, just north of Dolanaar. The **Twisted Hatred** Melenas feels toward all things healthy must be stopped.

There is yet more to do before heading out of town. Head into the building just south of the road and speak with Innkeeper Keldamyr.

Dolanaar, A Good Home

Talk to Innkeeper Kaldamyr in Dolanaar to set your home point. With all the running back and forth that needs to be done, especially for some of the later quests, it's nice to have the option of getting back quickly.

After getting your reward, continue south out of the building and deliver the Partially Filled Vessel to Corithras Moonrage. He accepts the delivery and asks you to continue working on the **Crown of the Earth** by collecting water from the Moonwell near Starbreeze Village. Accept his quest and look to the east.

Zarrin is a cook who works well with odd dishes. If you have taken Cooking as one of your secondary professions, seek this teacher for the quest to learn the **Recipe of the Kaldorei** (a fine piece of spider-cuisine).

With your quest log nearly bursting, head out of town. Run east, mostly following the road and kill any owls, nightsabres, or spiders nearby until you see the outskirts of Starbreeze Village and the Moonwell. Jump into the Moonwell and fill the phial.

Next, move slowly into the village but beware of the Furbolgs (they have become quite feral and attack almost anything they see). The first large building on the right has two floors, and Gaerolas Talvethren is on the top floor. Fight the few Firbolg in the way and head upstairs. Gaerolas isn't in great shape, but he tells you what has happened and asks you to tell Athridas in Dolanaar of the **Gnarlpine Corruption**. Before leaving, move to the south-eastern cottage of Starbreeze and search the dresser for the Emerald Dreamcatcher.

Return to Dolanaar, fighting the beasts for Zenn along the way, to turn in the quests you have completed. Corithras gives you another phial to fill, while Athridas asks you to collect the **Relics of Wakening**. After returning the dreamcatcher to Tallonkai, he realizes that part of it is missing. He asks you to get it from **Ferocitas the Dream Eater** and slay some of the Firbolg Mystics in the area. Take a companion or two if you are uncertain of victory. Tallonkai's Jewel isn't immediately apparent on the corpse of Ferocitas. Take the Gnarlpine Necklace and right click to reveal the jewel. Return to Zenn (if you have completed his quest) and to Tallonkai Swiftroot.

Investing in Your Future

With so much time spent outside of town and so much killing being done, your backpack tends to fill up quickly. Consider speaking with the General Supplies merchant in Dolanaar. He sells bags. These aren't inexpensive, but they allow you to carry more loot home. More loot sold means more money. The bag will pay for itself quick enough to warrant the purchase.

RECOVER AND CLEAR THE LAKE

By now, it's probably time to train again and sell a few things. Talk to any of the craft trainers in town if you want to learn Cooking, First Aid, Alchemy, or Herbalism (three are on the south side; look to the north to find the First Aid trainer). There are a fair number of quests to grab now. Talk to everyone but focus on getting **Seek Redemption** from Syral Bladeleaf. To make things right with her, leave town and walk south until you reach Lake Al'Ameth. First, speak with Denalan, on the eastern edge of the lake. Then, while walking around the Lake, collect the Fel Cones on the ground near the trees.

After putting the soil you brought him in a nearby planter, Denalan has two quests that can be completed while looking for more Fel Cones. He too wants to find out what is harming the land, but he's not a fighter. Collect the **Timberling Sprouts**, and **Timberling Seeds** for him. The sprouts are found all around the lake (and other bodies of water in Teldrassil). Right-click on these growing plants while moving around.

Fight the aggressive Timberlings you come across to gain the seeds. If your eyes are sharp and can spot the steaming Fel Cones, all three quests can be done in a single pass around the lake!

Turn in everything to Denalan and receive his shipment to Rellian Greenspyre. Rellian is in Darnassus (do not head out to Darnassus yet), the capital, and can be found on either the east side of town, just outside Warrior's Terrace, or north of the bridges (before reaching the Druid's Grove).

It's time to bring an end to Melenas. Seek a small group on the same quest. There are many aggressive Grells in the cave, and having a few friends can make a huge difference. Stop at Zenn on the way over to give him the Fel Cones and get a good laugh. Search the cave while killing the nasty monsters and look for the wandering Melenas; though he stands in the north-western corner atop a ledge, he also patrols from time to time. Target Melanas first and bring him down to make sure the quest is a success. Even if you die, return to the body and loot it for victory.

With that done, there are several quests west of town that can be done in a loop. If you still have a group, it is even easier, since one of the small dungeons is on the list and can be quite challenging.

WEST OF TOWN: HOME OF THE DRUIDS

Athridas Bearmantle has been patiently waiting for you to gather **The Relics of Wakening**. With a small group in tow, head out west of town. A Sentinel tells you **The Road to Darnassus** is dangerous to travel. Tell him you will help and move west, toward the mountains ahead. Look for the Gnarlpine Ambushers south of the road. The quest for these is very fast, as you only need to kill six. Follow the hill that rises to the south, beyond the Ambushers, and notice the slightly stronger Furbolgs.

At the top of the hill is Ban'ethil Barrow Den. Below are the relics that you are seeking, but dozens of Firbolg patrol the corridors and make life difficult for anyone who tries to enter. Move slowly with your group, taking on only one or two Firbolg at a time, and search the rooms of the dungeon for the four artifacts. They are held in grey chests (usually in alcoves). This is not your only goal in the dungeon. A restless spirit resides in a room on the second tier of the dungeon. Oben Rageclaw was trapped in slumber when the Firbolg found a way to separate his body and spirit. They now use it to attack people. Oben's spirit wants this to end. Slay the Shamans for **The Sleeping Druid** until you find the Shaman Voodoo Charm. Return this to Oben, then agree to slay his body. Seek the animated body at the lowest level of the dungeon, fight it, then use the Charm to give this druid a final, lasting rest.

Speak with Oben again, then return the artifacts to town. Athridas is ready to have you go after **Ursal the Mauler**, the very Firbolg who began this war against the Druids of Teldrassil. Move to Gnarlpine Hold in the south-west, at the very base of Teldrassil. While getting into position, fill your phial at the next Moonwell (completing another portion of **Crown of the Earth**), and steal a piece of fruit from the glowing tree south of the Moonwell. Denalan rewards you for bringing him the **Glowing Fruit**.

Ursal is somewhat easy to kill, yet the many Furbolgs around him offer moderate resistance. Hopefully you can carry the group from the last dungeon onward and plow through Ursal's allies without trouble. Be wary of the Avengers and casters, since these enemies pack a wicked punch.

Avengers are *EVIL!*

Avengers are a troublesome class of enemies. The Furbolgs are one of the races that have Avengers, and there are a number of them out in the forests of Teldrassil. When you slay another Firbolg near an Avenger, the Avenger bursts into a rage and starts to attack very quickly with devastating results. Try to slay the Avengers first.

If there are casters around, they need to be brought down quickly as well. To solve this conundrum, have one person attack a caster to interrupt their spells while the other party members beat on the Avenger. This way, both enemies are limited in their ability. It's not optimal, but fighting both casters and Avengers at the same time never is.

DARNASSUS AND THE NORTHERN QUESTS

Return to town and rejoice. All of the substantially challenging quests are done in Teldrassil, and the remaining ones are much easier with the skills you are already beginning to master. The next part for **Crown of the Earth** takes you up to the Oracle Glade, in the north-eastern section of Teldrassil. Sell, train, and grab that final quest before moving out.

The house on the side of the road as you head toward Darnassus has a Skinner and Leatherworking trainer. Stop there for a second if you are interested, then it's on to the capital. Before striking out to the Oracle Glade, complete Denalan's dropoff to Rellian; better late then never, eh? Rellian wants you to collect **Tumors** from the larger Timberlings that live along the Wellspring River, east of Oracle Glade. Accept that quest and visit the temple on the south side of town for **Tears of the Moon**. Priestess A'moora gives you that quest, and she is on the upper tier of the temple.

It's Big!

Darnassus is a rather impressive city. Exploring all of it would take quite a bit of effort, but you're not the first to get lost in this city. The guards are accustomed to newcomers needing directions and they give them freely. To find things in a hurry, ask a guard and they will plot it on your mini-map.

Darnassus Points of Interest

Location	Useful Stores/NPCs
Cenarion Enclave	Druid Trainer, Hunter Trainer, Rogue Trainers; Arch Druid Fandral Staghelm, Night Elf Mount Vendor
Craftsmen's Terrace	Alchemy Trainer, Tailoring Trainer, Leatherworking Trainer, Enchanting Trainer, Cooking Trainer, Inn
Warrior's Terrace	Warrior Trainer, Weapon Master
Tradesmen's Terrace	Auction House, Merchants
Temple Gardens	Bank, Mailbox, Teleporter to Ruth'theran Village
Temple of the Moon	Priest Trainer, Herbalism Trainer, Chief Archaeologist Greywisker, Priestess A'moora

Now that you are loaded up with quests for the northern area, head out from town and walk to the Wellspring River. Fight the Timberlings as you plod north along the banks, and keep your eyes peeled for a dark-colored Timbering named **Blackmoss the Fetid**. Kill him if you see him (his heart can be turned into Denalan for additional experience, and you soon shall see Denalan for other rewards, so it's win-win).

Once the tumors are yours, walk along the north side of the area and search for the spider, Lady Sathrah. This magnificent spider has been tainted, like so many things in the land, and you need to slay her. Take the Spinneretes from her body after the deed is done. Also, continue just west of her usual location to find a second glowing tree (another piece of fruit can be picked there). Denalan will reward you for bringing him **The Shimmering Frond**.

Steer toward the center of the region and talk to the night elves who live there and fill up your phial at the Moonwell. Recently, a messenger to Darnassus was murdered by the Harpies while carrying a report from **The Enchanted Glade**. Sentinel Arynia Cloudsbreak needs to see their numbers beaten back, and she asks you to take up the challenge. Agree. West and slightly to the north, between the western wall and the trees, is where you find the harpies. Not only do these kills help to rake in the Bloodfeather Belts, that you need but there is also a trapped tiger named Mist. Talk to the wounded beast and escort it back to the Glade safely. Turn in the belts and receive the reward for that and saving Mist. Return to Darnassus to receive rewards from the temple and from Rellian. Only one thing is left to do for Sathrah to rest. Place her silvery spinnerets in the fountain inside the temple to complete **Sathrah's Sacrifice**.

Becoming More Talented

Every level (starting at level ten), you gain a Talent Point. These can be used to increase your abilities or learn new ones. Open your talent window (defaulted to 'n'). There are three panels in the window. Look at each talent carefully before choosing as once you spend your points, it costs gold to unlearn them. There is more about the benefits of each talent in the class section.

With Teldrassil almost done, it's time to wrap up a few loose ends. Return to Dolanaar using your Hearthstone, if it's available, or your feet if it is not. Give the phial to Corithras. The next step of **Crown of the Earth** involves Darkshore, so tuck the Empty Phial into a bag and head south. Talk to Denalan and give him the final few goodies you found in the north. Take the time to examine the results of Denalan's experiments.

With the tumors to examine, he'll ask that you destroy the Timberling with the most Gargantuan Tumor that he has seen. This is certainly one that has the power to damage the land further because it has been tainted so badly. **Oakenscowl** is the Timberling's name, and he is undoubtedly the most powerful monster in the vicinity. Bring several allies to attack Oakenscowl, who lives south-west of the lake, just inside a small cave.

Bid Denalan farewell after receiving your reward, sell and train in Darnassus. The mists of Darkshore beckon. To reach the foreign coast, look for a glowing pagoda on the western end of Darnassus that teleports users to Rut'theran Village. Here a boat can send you across the seas. Once you arrive in Darkshore, be sure to speak to the Hippogriff Master to open up a flight path between Darkshore and Rut'theran.

Elune be praised!

DUROTAR

Durotar is the new homeland of the Orcs and Trolls on the continent of Kalimdor. It was Thrall who led the Orcs to this new desolate land and began to rebuild what his people had lost. Thrall rescued the Trolls as well and the remnants of the Darkspear tribe have also taken up residence in Durotar. Though chosen for its desolate and arid climate, enemies still lurk in the crags and caves of Durotar.

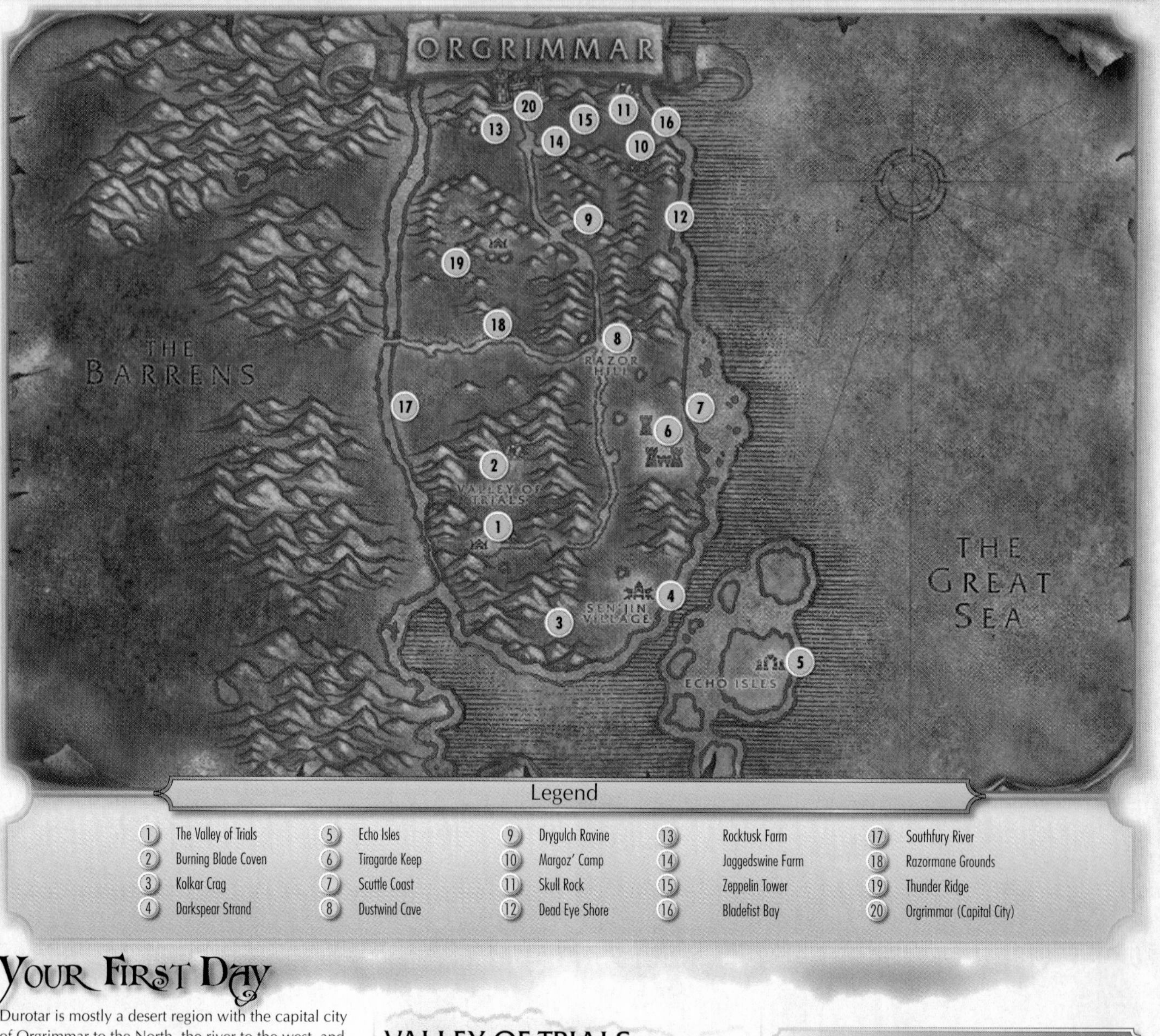

Legend

1	The Valley of Trials	5	Echo Isles	9	Drygulch Ravine	13	Rocktusk Farm	17	Southfury River
2	Burning Blade Coven	6	Tiragarde Keep	10	Margoz' Camp	14	Jaggedswine Farm	18	Razormane Grounds
3	Kolkar Crag	7	Scuttle Coast	11	Skull Rock	15	Zeppelin Tower	19	Thunder Ridge
4	Darkspear Strand	8	Dustwind Cave	12	Dead Eye Shore	16	Bladefist Bay	20	Orgrimmar (Capital City)

YOUR FIRST DAY

Durotar is mostly a desert region with the capital city of Orgrimmar to the North, the river to the west, and ocean to the east and south. Caverns and crags wind their way through the rocky terrain creating havens for those seeking to strike at the newcomers. Even the lush island chain to the southeast houses ill intent.

VALLEY OF TRIALS

Kaltunk has been assigned to greet all upcoming additions to the Horde armies. His primary duty is to set you on the path to finding **Your Place In The World**. He decides you should start by speaking with Gornek and working in the immediate area.

Gornek is just west in The Den. Gornek isn't terribly friendly or charismatic, but that isn't his duty. He's here **Cutting Teeth** with the new recruits. He wants you to kill ten Mottled Boars before he gives you a more difficult assignment. Head out of The Den and north.

You don't need to go far to find the troublesome creatures. There are many scavenging the arid grounds. Kill them, but don't stray too far from The Den as you return shortly.

The Spoils of War

Your backpack is nearly full. First, take the time to look through it and see if there is any usable equipment for you. If so, equip it. Second, become familiar with any recovery items (potions, food, drink, etc.) you've accumulated. Everything else that can be sold to vendors should be.

Return to Gornek for your next mission. The scorpids in the area have a nasty poison so the army keeps antidote on hand for accidents. Their supply is running low and the scorpids are a good way to prove yourself in battle. Bring ten Scorpid Worker Tails to Gornek to resupply antidote for the **Sting of the Scorpid**.

Gornek also has a message for you from your class trainer. Take the message to your trainer for a small amount of experience. Speak to them to train new abilities. Leave The Den and immediately turn north. Duokna is a General Goods merchant that buys any excess loot you have and Galgar will cook you some food if you bring him ten Cactus Apples. **Galgar's Cactus Apple Surprise** is very good...just don't ask what the surprise is!

South of the entrance to The Den, Zureetha Fargaze is recruiting aid. She has found a group of the Burning Blade residing in the Valley of Trials. These beasts must be brought to justice. The first step is to slay 12 of their **Vile Familiars**. Accept her quest and head to the east side of the valley (travel first north through the boars, then turn east).

Traveling the Bloody Way

As you're traveling, consider killing any enemies that are your level or lower. The enemies in the Valley of Trials are fairly weak and the additional experience and usable equipment make it worth your time.

The Cactus Apples can be found growing on many of the cacti in the valley. Gather these as you move east and keep an eye out for them as you harvest the scorpid tails. Lying in the shade of a tree is Hana'zua. He was stung badly by a particularly aggressive scorpid named **Sarkoth**. Before he can seek aid, his honor must be upheld. He asks you to find and slay this beast. Turn south hunting the scorpids as you climb the narrow slope.

Sarkoth is surrounded by other scorpids, but these beasts understand nothing of teamwork and do not aid him. If there are any other people in the area, recruit them to help you before bringing an end to this monster. Return to Hana'zua with Sarkoth's Mangled Claw as proof of its demise. With his honor protected, Hana'zua asks you to tell Gornek of the attack by **Sarkoth**. Report to Gornek of Hana'zua and to give him the scorpid stingers.

True to his word, Galgar gives you an entire stack of his Cactus Apple Surprise for your hard work. Gornek has no more work for you, but others do. Take a quick visit to your trainer before speaking with Foreman Thazz'ril to the east of The Den. He's having trouble keeping the Lazy Peons working. He gives you a Foreman's Blackjack to use on any peons you find sleeping. Between the two of you, the work will get done.

Follow the mountain edge north looking for sleeping peons and Vile Familiars. The familiars are aggressive and have some ranged capabilities, so engage them quickly. Return to The Den when the demon forces outside the cave are weakened and when your arm gets sore from blackjacking peons.

Thazz'ril appreciates your hard work and efficiency enough that he's willing to pay you for another task. **Thazz'ril's Pick** was left in the northern cave last time he was surveying and he'd like you to retrieve it for him. Visit Zureetha before heading out as she has sensed a leader in the cave to the north who possesses the **Burning Blade Medallion** that is calling the demons there.

The cave is filled with demons that are not only aggressive, but determined to end your life. Take the enemies one at a time and stick to the right tunnel as you ascend through the cave. Yarrog Baneshadow walks along a ledge at the back of the cave. Destroy this worshipper of dark magic and take the medallion from his corpse. Thazz'ril's Pick is in the center room by the waterfall. Grab it on your way out.

SOUTHERN DUROTAR

With your work in the Valley of Trials finished, Zureetha asks you to **Report to Sen'jin Village**. Sell you excess loot and head east past the gates and into greater Durotar.

Standing on the road is Ukor. He brought food to the valley without knowing they didn't need it and is afraid to take it back to Razor Hill. Though this delivery is **A Peon's Burden**, accept his quest. Razor Hill is to the north, but you have business in the south, so take the path off the road toward Sen'jin Village.

Watch for Lar Prowltusk south of the path. He doesn't stay in one place too long because he's watching the Kolkar. He's working hard, but he needs your help with **Thwarting Kolkar Aggression**. He snuck into their camp last night and found they are planning on an organized attack. He needs you to break into their camps and destroy the attack plans. Gather fellow warriors and head southeast toward Kolkar Crag to do your duty as a member of the Horde.

The male centaur are purely melee attackers and can be pulled to avoid fighting several at once. The female centaur use bows and do not move to you, so the fight must be taken to them. No matter who you're fighting, be ready to kill them quickly. They are not stupid and run for help when they get low on health. Find the attack plans in their three camps, destroy them, and return to Lar.

Now that you've gained level 6, it's time for a bit of walking. Only mages have a class trainer in Sen'jin Village, so follow the road north to Razor Hill. The fights on Echo Islands are tougher and you need all the abilities you can get. Speak with the Innkeeper to complete **A Peon's Burden**, but don't reset your hearthstone. Visit your class trainer and speak with Cook Torka at the east exit of town. He needs you to **Break a Few Eggs**. Accept his quest and use your hearthstone to return to Valley of Trials and walk to Sen'jin Village.

Report to Master Gadrin and collect the other quests before heading to the beach. Master Gadrin is in charge of the defense of Sen'jin and is recruiting adventurers to deal with **Zalazane.** Zalazane's Head must be brought back as along with the deaths of eight of the Hexed and Voodoo Trolls that have joined him. One of Zalazane's first victims was Gadrin's brother Mishina. **Mishina's Skull** has been enchanted by Zalazane to hold Mishina's spirit forever. Bring the skull back to Gadrin so it can be destroyed properly. Master Vornal needs four Intact Makura Eyes and eight Crawler Mucus for **A Solvent Spirit**. Vel'rin Fang asks you to hunt more **Practical Prey** for more practical reasons. He asks you to bring four Durotar Tiger Furs to stock his supplies.

There's a great deal to do. Start by hunting the crawlers and makura on your way to the islands. There will be plenty of time to get them, so don't worry about finishing it just yet. Head to the islands and search for the tigers and raptor nests. Stay on the smaller islands until you finish Practical Prey and Break a Few Eggs. This gives you time to get some experience and look for adventurers to join in attacking Zalazane's island.

Swimming With The Fishes

Crawlers and makura are underwater creatures. As such they have no need for air and can move much faster than you in the water. Pull them to the surface to avoid suffocating during a long fight and have ranged attacks ready if they run from you.

Once you have a couple adventurers with you, strike out to the largest island. On the southeast side, there is a camp near a small hill. Zalazane patrols this camp, protected by the Hexed and Voodoo Trolls. He guards the skulls on the hill. Pull the trolls one at a time until you can pull Zalazane to your party and his doom. Decapitate the monster and collect Mishina's Skull from the circle of power on the hill. Continue killing the trolls on the island until your quest is complete.

Inventory Full?

It's been a good while since you were near a merchant and your inventory shows it. Once your inventory is full you can't pick up any more items, including quest items. Take the time to destroy some of the less lucrative items in your inventory when you need room for quest items.

Less lucrative items are items of lowest quality and lowest armor (grey colored). This means grey cloth items are often the first to be dropped. If you don't need the food or drink for recovery purposes, these are also prime candidates.

Once the more difficult quests are complete, take the time to finish hunting the less intelligent enemies before returning to Sen'jin Village with swelled bags and pride. Gather the rewards for all your hard work and head north once again to **Report to Orgnil** in Razorhill.

CENTRAL DUROTAR

Razor Hill is built in the center of Durotar. The road north leads to Orgrimmar, the road west leads to The Barrens, the road south leads to The Valley of Trials, while east...well, there really isn't anything east.

Give the eggs to the cook, and report to Orgnil. Orgnil is rather upset and immediately orders the death of Fizzle, the one causing these **Dark Storms**. Gar'thok, on the second floor of the bunker, has quests for you. He asks you to **Vanquish the Betrayers**, and slow the quilboar **Encroachment**. Accept his quests, take care of in-town errands, and head out the south gates to Tiragarde Keep.

Investing in Your Future

With so much time spent between towns and so much killing being done, your backpack tends to fill up quickly. Consider speaking with the General Supplies merchant in the Razor Hill Barracks. He sells bags as well. These aren't inexpensive, but they allow you to carry more loot home. More loot sold means more money. The bag will more than make up the cost.

Show the Kul Tiras that their treachery will not go unpunished by slaying ten Sailors, eight Marines, and Lieutenant Benedict, their leader. Kill your way into the keep and climb the stairs. While in the open, the humans running is of little consequence, it can mean your death inside the keep. Reinforcements aren't far off and you must stop them quickly or face a fight against several opponents.

Once in the hallway atop the stairs, turn left and take the ramp up to the highest room. Lieutenant Benedict stands guarded by several marines. Pull the marines near the doorway one at a time before engaging Benedict and his final guard. Loot the body for his key and take the right path and head to the roof. Open Benedict's Chest and examine the aged envelope within. Take **The Admiral's Orders** to Gar'Thok.

With the leadership of Tiragarde Keep dead, it's time to pick up the pieces **From The Wreckage...** Garthok wants you to recover three Gnomish Tools from the shipwrecks off the coast of Tiragarde Keep and deliver **The Admiral's Orders** to Nazgrel in Orgrimmar. Sell your excess loot and head east to the ocean, gather the tools, then return.

Take the east road out of Razor Hill. To the south are camps of Razormane Quilboars and Scouts. To the north are Razormane Dustrunners and Battleguards. Kill four of each before returning to Gar'Thok for your reward.

NORTHERN DUROTAR

With work at Razor Hill done, continue north toward Orgrimmar. Follow the road through the canyons until you find a goblin on the side of the road beside a cart. Rezlak is upset with the harpies in the area. These **Winds of the Desert** keep attacking the caravans and stealing the supplies. He needs you to retrieve five Sacks of supplies from the harpies. Head southwest and visit the Tor'kren Farm. Misha's son Kron has been **Lost But Not Forgotten**. She asks you to look for some sign of him along the river. Assure her you will and travel directly west to the harpy canyon. Collect the sacks, then speak with Rezlak again.

With the supplies recovered, Rezlak employs you in **Securing the Lines**. He wants you to kill 12 Dustwind Savages and 8 Dustwind Storm Witches. Accept his quest and travel south to Drygulch Ravine. Travel through the tunnel and begin your killing spree. Return to Rezlak when the deed is done.

Gather a force and head to Thunder Ridge. It's time to stop Fizzle once and for all. Take your party to the southern entrance to Thunder Ridge. Fight your way past the lizards slowly until you are looking into the small alcove the Burning Blade have taken as their own. Pull Fizzle's guards one at a time and kill them outside the alcove. When Fizzle is alone, teach him the meaning of fear and take his claw from his dead body. Take the claw to Orgnil in Razor Hill and learn of **Margoz**.

ORGRIMMAR AND PREPARING FOR RAGEFIRE CHASM

Take the road north and complete your journey to Orgrimmar. Take the time to set your hearthstone here, visit your class trainer, and sell excess loot before heading to Thrall's Chambers in the Valley of Wisdom.

It's Big!

Orgrimmar is a rather impressive town. Exploring all of it would take quite a bit of effort, but you're not the first to get lost in this city. The guards are accustomed to newcomers needing directions and they give them freely. To find things in a hurry, ask a guard and they will plot it on your mini-map.

Orgrimmar Points of Interest

Location	Useful Stores/NPCs
Valley of Spirits	Mage/Portal Trainer, Priest Trainer, First Aid Trainer
Valley of Strength	Windrider Master, Reagent Vendor, Inn, Auction House, Mailbox
The Drag	Leatherworking Trainer, Skinning Trainer, Tailoring Trainer, Herbalism Trainer, Enchanting Trainer, Alchemy Trainer, Cooking Trainer, Mailbox
Cleft of Shadows	Rogue Trainer, Warlock Trainer, Demon Trainer, Poison Vendor, Reagent Vendor, Ragefire Chasm Entrance
Valley of Wisdom	Shaman Trainer, Thrall
Valley of Honor	Warrior Trainer, Hunter Trainer, Blacksmithing Trainer, Engineering Trainer, Mining Trainer, Fishing Trainer, Weaponmaster

Deliver the Admiral's Orders and speak with Thrall. He asks you to help him uncover **Hidden Enemies** within Orgrimmar itself. To begin, you need to get a Lieutenant's Insignia from Skull Rock. Accept the mission and leave Orgrimmar.

Travel southeast and speak with Margoz, who has work for you in **Skull Rock** as well. He wants you to gather six Searing Collars from the cultists inside and bring them to him. Travel to the northeast and enter the cave. If there are others around, recruit their assistance.

Becoming More Talented

Every level (starting at level ten), you gain a Talent Point. These can be used to increase your abilities or learn new ones. Open your talent window (defaulted to 'n'). There are three panels in the window. Look at each talent carefully before choosing as once you spend your points, it costs gold to unlearn them. There is more about the benefits of each talent in the class section.

Take the cave slowly and avoid fights with more than one enemy when you can. Many of the cultists have mastered the ability to control demons and have them at their beck and call. Kill the cultist before focusing on the pet. Work you way to the back collecting collars. A dark painted orc named Gazz'uz who has been leading the Burning Blade. Kill him and take the Burning Eye of Shadow from him. Take it to Neeru Fireblade in Orgrimmar who knows more about **Burning Shadows**.

Return to Thrall with the insignia to receive your next task. Thrall needs you to deceive Neeru Fireblade into believing you are a member of the Burning Blade. Gather as much information as you can about the **Hidden Enemies** before returning to Thrall.

Neeru takes the Eye of Burning Shadow from you and rewards you for its collection. Speak to him about **Slaying the Beast** within Ragefire Chasm. He wants you to bring him the heart of Taragaman the Hungerer. With all the formalities finished, tell Neeru that he may speak frankly and listen to him. Continue pumping him for information until you've found what Thrall wanted you to. High-tail it back to Thrall to squeal on Neeru.

With the new information, your role as a spy is at an end. Thrall tasks you with the destruction of the **Hidden Enemies** beneath Orgrimmar. He wants Bazzalan and Jergosh the Invoker dead.

Congratulations on your success in Durotar. Peons are taking fewer naps, the Trolls have some peace of mind returned to them, and even the glare of the sun seems less burdensome. There is still more to do to the west in The Barrens or across the seas in the Silverpine Forest. But what of the Burning Blade and the Shadow Council? Treachery directly beneath the capital of the Horde can not go unchallenged, but those are adventures for another day.

MULGORE

The Tauren, once a nomadic people hunted by the centaur, have taken up residence within the grassy meadows of Mulgore. They walk paths closely intertwined with the Earth Mother and the way of the hunt is a right of passage for all Tauren. Through hunting the beasts of the land and making a place for themselves in the cycle of life, the Tauren gain a greater understanding of the world around them. With the help of Thrall, the Tauren were able to drive the centaur out of Mulgore. The Tauren have gained a home where they can raise their children in safety and they seek to repay the favor.

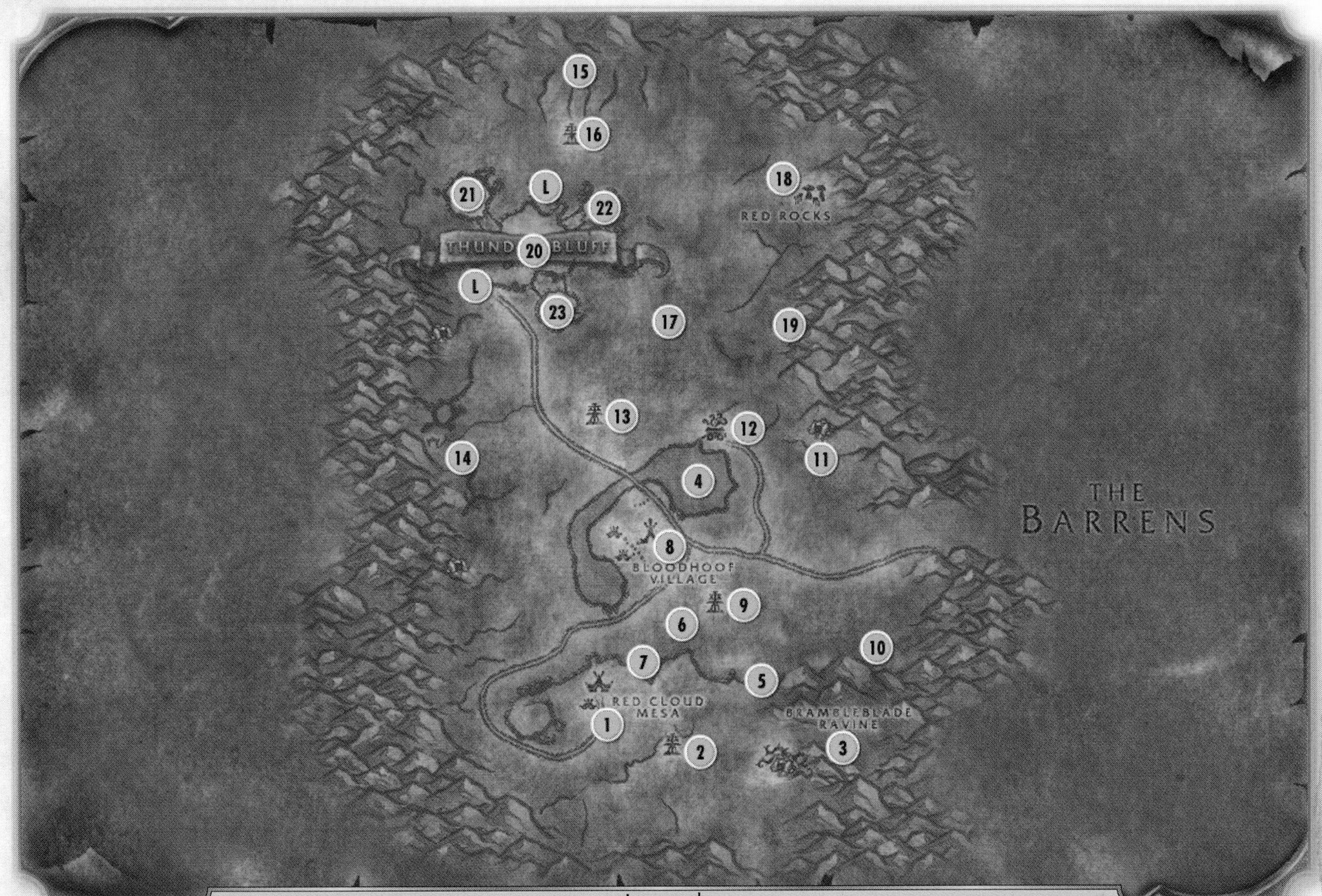

Legend

L	Lift	5	Stonebull Lake	10	Winterhoof Water Well	15	Wildmane Water Well	20	Spirit Rise
1	Camp Narache	6	Palemane Camps	11	The Venture Co. Mine	16	The Golden Plains	21	Elder Rise
2	Well	7	Palemane Rock	12	Ravaged Caravan	17	Windfury Ridge	22	Hunter Rise
3	Seer Graytongue	8	The Rolling Plains	13	Thunderhorn Water Well	18	Red Rocks		
4	Brambleblade Ravine	9	Bloodhoof Village	14	Bael'Dun Digsite	19	Thunder Bluff		

YOUR FIRST DAY

The Tauren have built their home in harmony with Mulgore. The gentle breeze make some think of paradise and relaxation, but the Tauren are constantly on a path of both betterment and enlightenment. The Tauren stewardship of this land can be seen in the lush fields of grass, prevalence of herbs, and the roaming herds of kodo, but there are those that seek to pillage this rich land. dwarves and Venture Company alike dig deep into the earth to steal the copper.

CAMP NARACHE AND THE RITE OF STRENGTH

Camp Narache is where all who seek citizenship in Thunder Bluff begin. The teachers help you take your first steps in the Rites of the Earthmother and teach you how to learn from the world around you.

Grull Hawkwind stands before you and wastes no time with meaningless chatter. As **The Hunt Begins**, Grull wants you to collect seven Plainstrider Feathers and Plainstrider meat. This begins your training and helps restock the village supplies. Accept his quest and move northwest to Chief Hawkwind's tent. Chief Hawkwind asks **A Humble Task** of you. His mother set out this morning to fetch water from the well, and he would like you to check on her. Assure him you will and leave the village to the southeast.

There are many Plainstriders on the way to the well and around it. Kill these as you move to speak with Greatmother Hawkwind.

The Greatmother has arrived safely at the well and even drawn the water, she is just resting before making the trip back up the hill to the village. She asks you to take a pitcher from the well and take it to her son. The pitchers are sitting on the edge of the well and can be picked up by right-clicking them.

Hunt the Plainstriders until you have enough meat and feathers. Avoid going far to the east as the Battle Boars are aggressive and attack you on sight. With the supplies collected, head back to the village.

The Spoils of War

Your backpack is nearly full. First, take the time to look through it and see if there is any usable equipment for you. If so, equip it. Second, become familiar with any recovery items (potions, food, drink, etc.) you've accumulated. Everything else that can be sold to vendors should be.

Grull is pleased with your prowess and **The Hunt Continues**. He wants you to hunt the Mountain Cougars to the south and collect ten of their pelts for clothing and tents. He also has a message from your class trainer. Accept both quests and take a moment to visit your trainer as you've gained level 2 and have new abilities waiting for you.

Chief Hawkwind is impressed with your kindness and begins the **Rites of the Earthmother**. First you must seek out Seer Graytongue to the south. Accept his quest and head south.

Hunt the Mountain Cougars as you move up the hill toward Seer Graytongue's camp. Graytongue sets you on the first rite, the **Rite of Strength**. To gain respect, you must slay the enemies of the tribe. Bring 12 Bristleback Belts to Chief Hawkwind from the quilboars in Brambleblade Ravine to the east. Accept the quest and finish hunting the cougars.

With the pelts received, Grull asks you to trim some of **The Battleboars** from the hunting grounds and bring back the parts for some food. Brave Windfeather patrols nearby and has a task for you. The quilboars have been waging a war against the Tauren for some time and Brave Windfeather wants it to end. She charges you with bringing her the head of their leader—she asks you to **Break Sharptusk!**

Traveling the Bloody Way

As you're traveling, consider killing any enemies that are your level or lower. The enemies around Camp Narache are fairly weak and the additional experience and usable equipment make it worth your time.

Prepare yourself, then travel east. Slay the Battleboars for their flanks and snouts as you enter the Brambleblade Ravine. Once inside, slay the quilboars and take their belts as proof. Fight your way east to the very heart of their land. Make them pay for the suffering they have caused. Heal this scar upon the land.

Most of the quilboars in the area know only how to attack with their fists and their weapons, but there are ones that are more intelligent. The Bristleback Shamans have learned the use of magic and attack from range, if allowed. These can be easily spotted by their blue robes and should be killed quickly as they can do quite a bit of damage.

Atop a rise in the heart of the Bristleback lands, stands a large tent. From here Chief Sharptusk Thornmantle leads the war against the Tauren. Slay first his guards, then remove his head. Much work has been done this day, but there is more to do. Leave the tent and head south to a cave in the mountain.

Inventory Full?

It's been a good while since you were near a merchant and your inventory shows it. Once your inventory is full you can't pick up any more items, including quest items. Take the time to destroy some of the less lucrative items in your inventory when you need room for quest items.

Less lucrative items are items of lowest quality and lowest armor (grey colored). This means grey cloth items are often the first to be dropped. If you don't need the food or drink for recovery purposes, these are also prime candidates.

Sharptusk's younger sibling, Squealer Thornmantle, sits in the cave guarding the plans his chief has drafted. Kill Squealer and take the plans from the floor. Continue hunting until all your quests are complete, then use your hearthstone to return to the village triumphant.

Speak with your teachers and be rewarded for your hard work. Once you have room in your inventory, right-click the Dirt-Stained Map and learn of the **Attack on Camp Narache**. Take your findings to Chief Hawkwind. He gives you a totem to take to Baine Bloodhoof so that you may continue the **Rites of the Earthmother**.

BLOODHOOF VILLAGE AND THE RITE OF VISION

Your time at Camp Narache is at an end. You have the Totem of Hawkwind to show your progress. Follow the path south and east until you come to the border of Red Cloud Mesa. Antur Fallow stands nervously. She has **A Task Unfinished** as she is working on the Rite of Strength. As you are already heading to Bloodhoof Village, take the Bundle of Furs there for her.

Deliver the furs to Innkeeper Kauth and ask him to make this inn your home. This sets your hearthstone to return you here. Next Speak with Baine Bloodhoof. He tells you of the **Rite of Vision** and asks you to help him deal with the gnolls in the area. The gnolls have moved into Mulgore, but have not respected the Tauren attempts at **Sharing the Land**. He asks you to kill ten Palemane Tanners, eight Palemane Skinners, and five Palemane Poachers.

There are many people with tasks for you. Wander the village and collect all the quests. Mull Thunderhorn asks you to help him with a **Poison Water** problem, Harken Windtotem speaks of **Swoop Hunting**, while Zarlman Two-Moons continues your **Rite of Vision**, Maur Raincaller was attacked and poisoned by **Mazzranache** and Ruul Eagletalon teaches of the **Dangers of the Windfury**.

Taking Up Skinning?

Only a few of the professions are represented in Bloodhoof Village. If you intend to become adept at the art of skinning, now is a good time to start. Speak with the Skinning Trainer and purchase a skinning knife.

Collect the plethora of quests and head south out of the village. Keep your eyes open for the Ambercorns as you move about. They are small pinecone-like objects usually found near trees.

The gnolls have their camps against the cliffs to the south. They are very aggressive and have many ranged attackers. Kill them one at a time and don't be afraid to rest between fights. Kill the gnolls at the first camp and move east to the next. You need parts from all the animals out here, so kill everything in your path.

With the required number of gnolls dead, move north to the Winterhoof Water Well. The Venture Company has taken residence around it, but you need two Wellstones. Kill the hirelings around the edge until you can reach the wellstones. Collect what you need and return to Bloodhoof Village killing everything along the way.

Visit your trainer and learn any new abilities possible and speak with Baine Bloodhoof about the gnoll situation. He rewards you and asks for additional assistance. A **Dwarven Digging** group has been recklessly harvesting metal in the west. Accept the quest and speak with Zarlman Two-Moons. He gives you the Water of the Seers to consume at the bonfire to produce a vision. Do so, but don't follow the visionary wolf. The wolf leads you to a cave in the north that you will be visiting soon enough to complete your **Rite of Vision**.

Investing in Your Future

With so much time spent between towns and so much killing being done, your backpack tends to fill up quickly. Consider speaking with the General Goods merchant in Bloodhoof Village. He sells bags as well. These aren't inexpensive, but they allow you to carry more loot home. More loot sold means more money. The bag pays for itself fast.

Sell any excess loot and head southeast toward the Windfury Harpies. As you complete the quests, keep track of which enemies you still need to kill. A good policy, however, is to kill everything in your path. You can always use the money and experience after all.

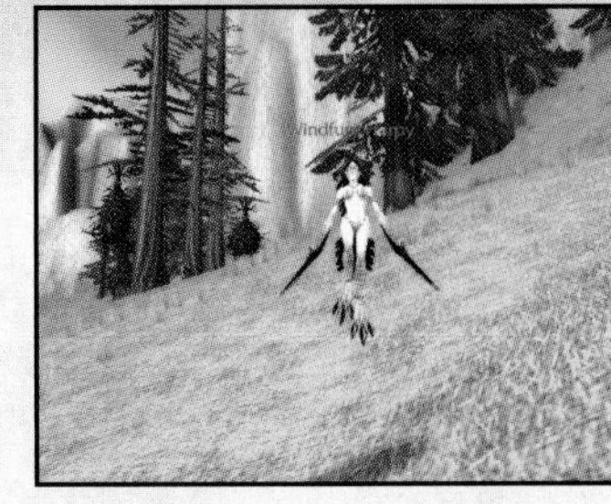

The enemies on the way to the harpies are higher level than any you've fought so far and most are aggressive. Take care to only engage them one at a time and only after you've recovered your health and mana.

Collect the Windfury Talons until you have all eight of them. Keep fighting on the edge of the cliffs as the wolves below are much higher level then the harpies. When the quest is complete, use your hearthstone to return to Bloodhoof Village and speak to Ruul and Mull.

With the items you've gathered, Mull creates a totem for the **Winterhoof Cleansing**. Take the totem and head to the water well to end the poisoning. Start by killing the hirelings around the edge, then slowly kill your way to the water well. Use the totem to cleanse the well and return to Mull. There are other water wells that need cleansing and he needs materials for each. He needs six Stalker and Cougar Claws to craft the **Thunderhorn Totem** next.

Your next target is the Bael'Dun Digsite. Cross the river and head northwest. Kill any targets you still need for quests (swoops are likely one) as you move to the cliffs. The dwarves present a new problem for you. While you've fought aggressive enemies that run for help before, the Bael'dun Appraisers are healers and can draw fights out. Pull the diggers away from the healers one at a time and dispatch them. When a healer is alone, throw everything you have at it as quickly as possible. If you have abilities that interrupt casting, be prepared to use them.

Watch for other adventurers in the area and group together as this quest is made easier with more hands. Gather the Prospector's Picks from the dwarves as you kill them. When you have five, move to the forge at the back of the camp. Use each of the tools to break them. Exit the camp and turn north.

Thunder Bluff can be seen in the distance, but that is not your current destination. Move north past another area of harpies and watch for a cave in the eastern cliffs. Seer Wiserunner has been waiting for you since the lupine vision arrived. He is here to set you upon the **Rite of Wisdom**. Accept his quest and travel east, across the road, to hunt the Prairie Stalkers and Flatland Cougars on your way back to Bloodhoof Village.

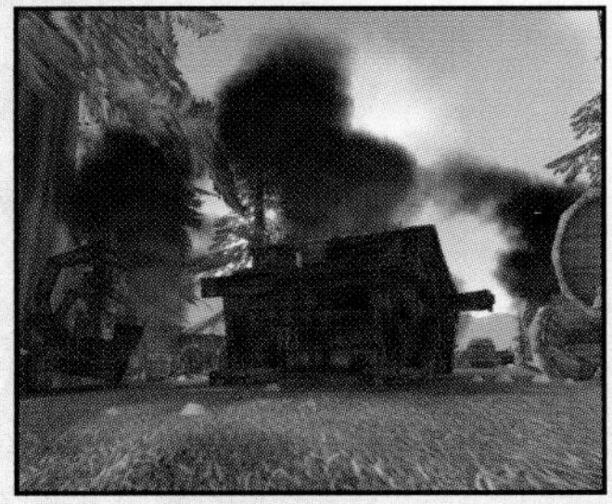

Turn in your quests, get your rewards, repair, sell excess loot, train if you need to, then follow the road east. Morin Cloudstalker patrols the road and has a task for you. He needs you to search **The Ravaged Caravan** near the lake and find why the Venture Company are trying to salvage it. The caravan sits smoldering on the northeast edge of Stonebull Lake. Kill any cougars and stalkers you need to finish **Thunderhorn Totem** while you're in the area.

Clear out the Venture Company workers and open the Sealed Supply Crate near the center fire. Return to Morin with what you've found. After examining the evidence you recovered, Morin has more work for you. **The Venture Co.** must be stopped and the best way to do that is to kill **Supervisor Fizsprocket** and many of the workers. Morin wants 14 Venture Co. Workers and 6 Venture Co. Supervisors killed and Fizsprocket's Clipboard pried from his cold, dead hands. Move to the Venture Co. Mine.

The enemies inside the mine are very dangerous as they are close together and it's difficult to get fights with only one enemy. Gather any adventurers you see in the area and venture in as a group. Make sure everyone in your party is rested before starting each engagement.

Becoming More Talented

Every level (starting at level ten), you gain a Talent Point. These can be used to increase your abilities or learn new ones. Open your talent window (defaulted to 'n'). There are three panels in the window. Look at each talent carefully before choosing as once you spend your points, it costs gold to unlearn them. There is more about the benefits of each talent in the class section.

When you have his clipboard and have killed the help, return to Morin for your rewards. Make a quick trip to Bloodhoof to sell, train, repair, and speak with Mull. With the totem complete the time for the **Thunderhorn Cleansing** is at hand. Skorn Whitecloud talks of **The Hunter's Way** and suggests you gather four Flatland Prowler Claws and present them to Melor Stonehoof as a gesture of willingness to learn.

Cross the river to the north and begin clearing the Thunderhorn Water Well. Kill the Venture Co. workers and cleanse the water well and return for your reward and a list of ingredients for the **Wildmane Totem**. Take care of any final errands and head north to Red Rock.

THUNDER BLUFF AND THE RITE OF WISDOM

Once you cross into the Golden Plains, begin hunting the Flatland Prowlers and Prairie Wolf Alphas as you move northeast. Lorekeeper Raintotem sits by a fire south of Red Rocks. He charges you with removing the interlopers from **A Sacred Burial**.

Move north and clear your way through the vagabonds to the Ancestral Spirit. Your Rites of the Earthmother are now complete. The spirit informs you that it is time to **Journey Into Thunder Bluff**. Return to Lorekeeper Raintotem south of here for your reward.

Turn downhill and head deeper into the Golden Plains. Hunt the wolves and cougars until you've finished **The Hunter's Way** and the **Wildmane Totem**. Once both quests are complete, hearthstone back to Bloodhoof Village and speak with Mull about the **Wildmane Cleansing**.

Take the road north to Thunder Bluff. The road ends at a set of lifts that take people far above the plains of Mulgore and to the majestic mesas of the Tauren capital.

As all Tauren classes and professions are represented in Thunder Bluff, it's a good place for training. If you're picking up crafting professions, seek out the trainers while you Speak with Cairn Bloodhoof and Melor Stonehoof. Cairn is on the highest level of the central rise and Melor is on Hunter Rise.

It's Big!

Thunder Bluff is a rather impressive town. Exploring all of it would take quite a bit of effort, but you're not the first to get lost in this city. The guards are accustomed to newcomers needing directions and they give them freely. To find things in a hurry, ask a guard and they will plot it on your mini-map.

Thunder Bluff Points of Interest

Location	Useful Stores/NPCs
Bottom Central Rise	Weaponmaster, Auction House, Bank, Mail Box, Blacksmithing Trainer, Mining Trainer, Inn
Middle Central Rise	Tailoring Trainer, Leatherworking Trainer, Skinning Trainer, Herbalism Trainer, Alchemy Trainer, Enchanting Trainer
Top Central Rise	Cairn Bloodhoof, Cooking Trainer, Fishing Trainer
Hunter Rise	Warrior Trainer, Hunter Trainer, Pet Trainer
Elder Rise	Druid Trainer, Magatha Grimtotem
Spirit Rise	Shaman Trainer, First Aid Trainer
Tower	Windrider Master

Eyahn Eagletalon stands at the lifts with a problem. He's behind in his **Preparation for Ceremony** and needs you to collect six Azure Feathers and six Bronze Feathers from the harpies northwest of Thunder Bluff. Accept his quest and continue on to speak with Melor and Cairn. Cairn has one last task for you to complete your **Rites of the Earthmother**. He wants you to hunt the mighty Arra'chea.

Take the western lifts down to Mulgore and head northwest to the harpies. Hunt them for their feathers before moving northeast to the Wildmane Well. All the harpies are casters, so have your interrupt abilities ready.

With the well cleansed, there are only a few things left to do. Travel east and hunt Arra'chea. She wanders a great deal, but is usually found within the Golden Plains. When you find her, clear any aggressive animals first or wait until she moves away from them. Engage Arra'chea and prove yourself to Cairn.

Take her horn and complete your **Rites of the Earthmother**. Return to Thunder Bluff to turn in your quests and pick up any you find before traveling to Bloodhoof. Tell Mull of the cleansing of the final well before following the road east to the Barrens.

Congratulations on your success in Mulgore. Kodo are breeding happily, the Tauren of Thunder Bluff recognize your name, and the spirits know you. New challenges wait in the Barrens and even in the Ragefire Chasm beneath Orgrimmar, but those are adventures for another day.

TIRISFAL GLADES

Tirisfal Glades has seen better days. The mighty city of Lordaeron has fallen, demons encroach, and the last vestige of humanity has declared war on anything that isn't part of the Scarlet Crusade. What keeps this land to succumbing to anarchy? From below the ruins of Lordaeron, the Banshee Queen commands the Forsaken. Though killed by the plague and never granted death, the Forsaken have rebelled. They have chosen to reclaim Tirisfal Glades and halt the advance of the Scourge.

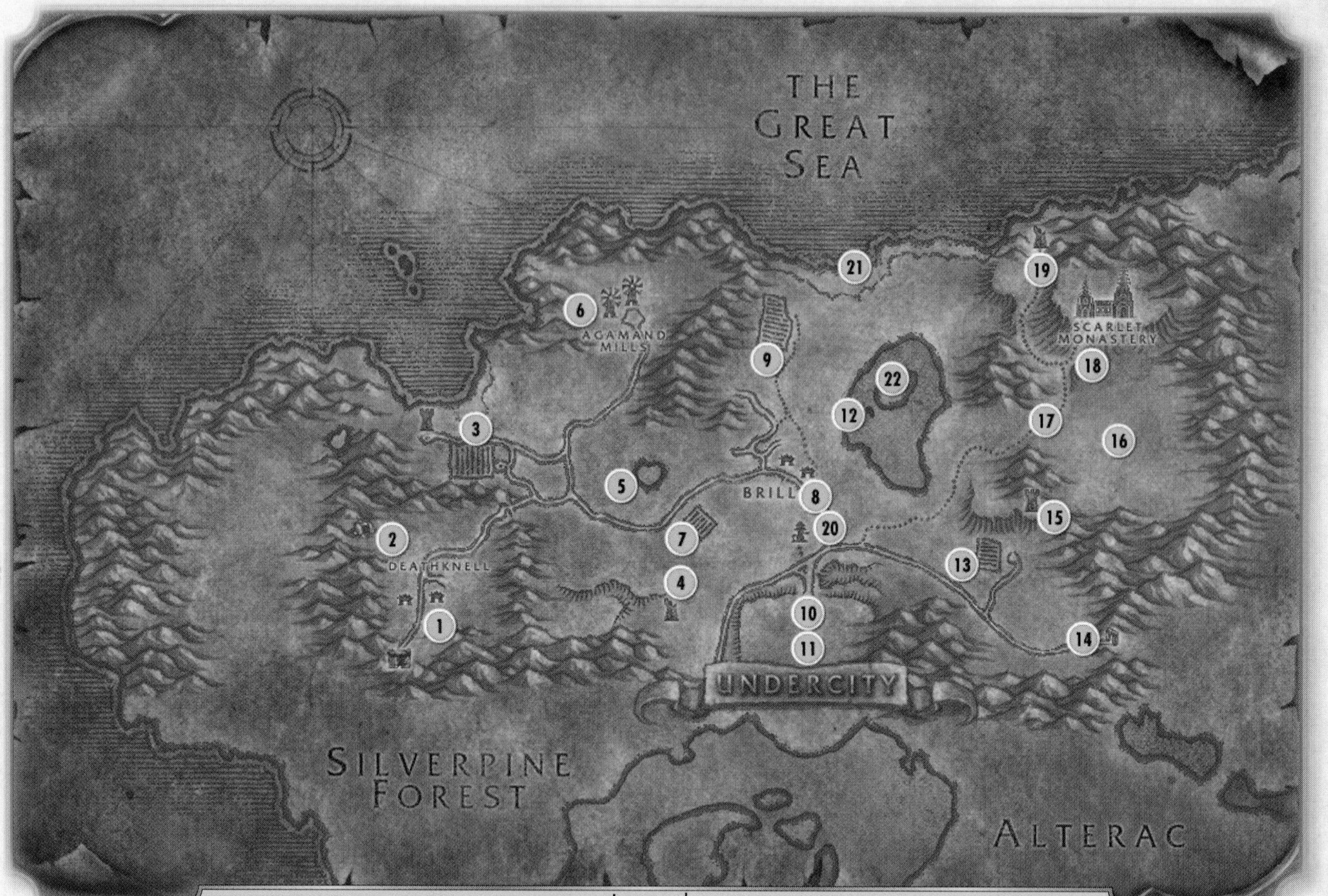

THE GREAT SEA

AGAMAND MILLS

SCARLET MONASTERY

BRILL

DEATHKNELL

UNDERCITY

SILVERPINE FOREST

ALTERAC

Legend

1 Deathknell	5 Stillwater Pond	9 Garren's Haunt	13 Balnir Farmstead	17 Faol's Rest	20 Zeppelin Tower
2 Night Web's Hollow	6 Agamand Mills	10 Ruins of Lordaeron	14 The Bulwark	18 Whispering Gardens-The Scarlet Monastery	21 The North Coast
3 Solliden Farmstead	7 Cold Hearth Manor	11 Undercity (Capital City)	15 Crusader Outpost	19 Scarlet Watch Post	22 Gunther's Retreat
4 Nightmare Vale	8 Brill	12 Brightwater Lake	16 Venomweb Vale		

YOUR FIRST DAY

Lordaeron and the other establishments within Tirisfal Glades had been sacked, burned, and forgotten. The land was assumed to be a stronghold of the Scourge, but the will of Sylvanas Windrunner shattered the plans of the Scourge and brought a major player to the table. The Forsaken have chosen to ally with the Horde in an attempt to stave off their destruction. While the Forsaken are a power to be reckoned with, there are many that wish them nothing short of a final rest.

The Bulwark holds the plagued wildlife and forces of the Scourge from seeping in from the Plaguelands, but the war with the living isn't far off. A bastion of the Scarlet Crusade has survived against the Scourge, and now survives against the Forsaken.

A COLD AWAKENING

You awaken much like all undead…in a crypt. You not only took ill, but you died and were buried. The flesh has rotted from parts of your body, but you are still mobile. Ascend the stairs and speak with Undertaker Mordo about your **Rude Awakening**.

Mordo stands at the opening to the crypt and directs the newly awakened to Shadow Priest Sarvis in Deathknell. Accept his quest and follow the stone path into what's left of town. Once through the gate, turn left, then enter the remains of the town church to find Sarvis.

Sarvis tells you more about what's happening. He relates how not everyone who was killed by the plagues awoke as Forsaken. Many became **Mindless Ones**. These poor souls have no will of their own and are merely tools of the Lich King. They must be destroyed. Sarvis tasks you with destroying eight Mindless Zombies and just as many Wretched Zombies.

Exit the building and turn north. Just down the street, guards are keeping the zombies at bay, but are terribly outnumbered by the shambling forces. There is so little left in the minds of these enemies that they do not attack you until you attack them. Engage and kill the zombies before returning to Sarvis for your reward.

Sarvis congratulates you on your decision to take up the banner of the Banshee Queen and fight for the Forsaken. There is more to do, however. He wants you to join the others **Rattling the Rattlecages**. The skeletons are tougher than the zombies, but need to be removed from Tirisfal all the same. Sarvis also has a message from your class trainer. Accept both of these quests and seek your trainer for new abilities and speak with Novice Elreth.

Elreth spends her unlife helping those enlisting in the military. She is willing to make you some armor if you bring her parts of **The Damned** in the area. Six Scavenger Paws and Duskbat Wings net you some experience and a piece of armor. The bats and dogs can be found in abundance to the northwest.

Traveling the Bloody Way

As you are traveling, consider killing any enemies that are your level or lower. The enemies around Deathknell are fairly weak and the additional experience and usable equipment make it worth your time.

Kill the skeletons as you exit town to the north, then hunt the dogs and bats. When you've harvested enough parts, return to town and finish killing the skeletons. With both quests complete and your bags full, return to the ruined church and speak with Sarvis and Elreth for your rewards.

Elreth had a friend named Marla who was murdered by her husband after he succumbed to the plague and joined the Lich King's forces. Though now Forsaken, Elreth wants help granting **Marla's Last Wish** which was to be buried beside her husband. She's buried in the cemetery, but her husband still roams as a slave to the Lich King. Elreth wants you to destroy him and bury his remains with Marla.

Inventory Full?

It's been a good while since you were near a merchant and your inventory shows it. Once your inventory is full you can't pick up any more items, including quest items. Take the time to destroy some of the less lucrative items in your inventory when you need room for quest items.

Less lucrative items are items of lowest quality and lowest armor (grey in color). This means grey cloth items are often the first to be dropped. If you don't need the food or drink for recovery purposes, these are also prime candidates.

Take a moment to stop at the merchant in the house across the street to sell your excess loot and speak with Executor Arren. He is recruiting aid in clearing the spiders from **Night Web's Hollow** so the gold mining can be restarted. He rewards you if you kill ten Young Night Web Spiders and eight Night Web Spiders. Remember to equip any extra bags you've found and head north to speak with Deathguard Saltain.

Saltain's attitude might be a bit rough, but his goals are in tune with the Banshee Queen's. He's organizing the recruits in **Scavenging Deathknell** for equipment for the newly risen. He wants you to collect six Scavenged Goods from the ruined town and return. With several quests in your log, it's time to head out. Search the buildings of Deathknell for the boxes as you head north.

Follow the road as it bends east. At a northern turn of the road, there is a ruined camp and several named skeletons and zombies shambling about. Find Samuel Fipps and give him the final rest so many have been denied by the Lich King. Carefully collect his remains and store them in your pack before turning northwest and traveling to Night Web's Hollow.

The Young Night Web Spiders are plentiful outside the mine and are still fairly docile. They won't attack you until you strike first. The Night Web Spiders, however, stay inside the mine and are quite aggressive. They attack without any provocation and care must be exercised as you move through the mine. At the very back of the cave sits the Night Web Matriarch. Though you have no specific quest to slay her, she has a cloak that would be very nice to have. With the spiders trimmed back, use your hearthstone to teleport back to the crypt.

Run back to Deathknell and speak to Arren and Saltain for your rewards. Directly behind Arren is the graveyard. In the first row is Marla's grave. Place Samuel's Remains there to fulfill Marla's Last Wish and speak with Elreth for your reward. Take a moment to speak with your trainer before Arren gives you more work.

With the mine being brought under control, it's time to use your talents elsewhere. **The Scarlet Crusade** has set up a camp to the southeast. There is little doubt in anyone's mind that they intend to attack Deathknell. Take the fight to them first by collecting 12 Scarlet Armbands from their corpses.

Leave town to the east and look for the tents. The Scarlet Crusade attack on sight, so be watchful as you approach the camp. Pull the enemies one at a time and avoid entering the camp as they also help each other. The Scarlet Initiates are mages and will be reluctant to come to you. Be ready to kill them quickly. With the required armbands, return to Arren for your reward and your next assignment.

The numbers at the Scarlet camp have been lessened. Now you have a chance to strike at **The Red Messenger**. Meven Korgal is in possession of the Scarlet Documents. While unsure of the contents of the documents, Arren knows that it's better to have them then allow Meven to keep them. Find Meven near the tent at the southern edge of the camp. Pry the documents from his cold, dead fingers.

After reading through the documents, Arren finds some **Vital Intelligence** that must be taken to Brill. He can find more work for you here, but getting this information to Brill is more important. Take a moment to visit your trainer and sell any excess loot before taking the road north.

GUARDING WHAT'S LEFT

Calvin Montague stands at the palisade along the road. He has a letter to be delivered to Brill. Accept his quest and continue along the road until you find Deathguard Simmer. Simmer wants you to steal ten pumpkins from a nearby farm. It sounds easy, but don't do it just yet. Accept the quest and continue to Brill. Watch for aggressive enemies near the road as you travel.

Gordo, an abomination, patrols the road. Accept **Gordo's Task**. He needs three Gloom Weeds picked up and taken to Brill. The weeds are near the road, so take the time to pick them before continuing to Brill. Watch for the aggressive demon dogs nearby and avoid venturing too far into the woods.

There are a number of people to speak with in Brill. Junior Apothecary Holland, in the graveyard, should be your first. It seems Gordo isn't very bright, Holland needs you to collect ten **Doom Weed**. Speak with Deathguard Dillinger to receive **A Putrid Task**. Inside the first building on your right, Apothecary Johaan has work for you as well. He's working on **A New Plague** and tells you to collect five Darkhound Blood. Continue speaking with people in Brill and collecting all the quests. The Wanted sign behind Executor Zygand shouldn't be ignored as it offers a reward for killing Maggot Eye.

Talk with Innkeeper Renee and have her make this inn your home. This allows you to teleport here using your hearthstone. If it is in your plan, pick up First Aid from the rather striking undead female near the entrance. With all your errands done and many quests in your log, leave town and head north toward Garren's Haunt.

Follow the fork in the road as it bends west. The **Graverobbers**, Rot Hide Gnolls, have been stealing the corpses from the mass graves to bolster the Scourge's armies. Kill eight Rot Hide Graverobbers, five Rot Hide Mongrels, and collect eight of their Embalming Ichor.

Once you've killed the graverobbers, continue north to Garren's Haunt. As you move through the woods, watch for **Doom Weed** near the bases of the trees. Patrolling the field are Rot Hide Gnolls and Mongrels. Enter the field carefully as the gnolls are very aggressive and attack at even the slightest hint of your presence. Kill the mongrels as you move north across the field. In a small building stands Maggot Eye. He is far too powerful for you to attack alone, so look for other adventurers in the area and form a group to kill him.

With Maggot Eye's Paw, the Embalming Ichor, and the Doom Weed, return to Brill. There are several people you should talk for your rewards. Sell any excess loot, pick up any new quests, and head west toward Solliden's Farmstead.

Investing in Your Future

With so much time spent outside of town and so much killing being done, your backpack tends to fill up quickly. Consider speaking with the General Supplies merchant in the Lion's Pride Inn. He sells bags as well. These aren't inexpensive, but they allow you to carry more loot home. More loot sold means more money. The bag pays for itself rather quickly.

At the bridge, some of the Scourge have made their way into Tirisfal Glades. Take a few moments to kill the Rotting Dead and Ravaged Corpses. It's **A Putrid Task**, but someone's got to do it. Collect seven Putrid Claws from the bodies before continuing to Solliden's Farmstead.

Farmers guard the field while soldiers patrol the road. Kill the farmers as you harvest the pumpkins. Turn the farmstead into **Fields of Grief** by stealing ten Tirisfal Pumpkins. Continue west and show that you are **At War With The Scarlet Crusade** by slaying ten Scarlet Warriors.

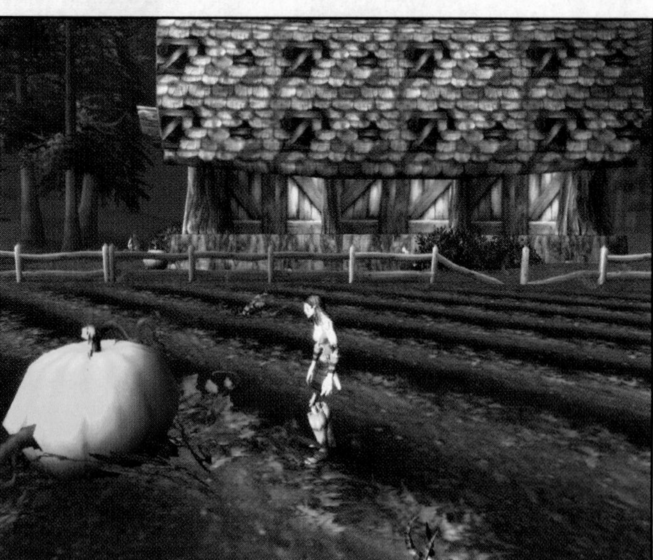

Use your hearthstone or your feet to return to Brill and turn in your quests. Pick up any quests that become available, and visit your trainer if you've gained a level. See a merchant before heading to the bottom floor of the inn and giving the pumpkin to the Scarlet Zealot.

With so much in town taken care of, head southwest toward the Nightmare Vale. Hunt the darkhounds for samples of **A New Plague** and the duskbats to stave off **The Chill of Death**. The darkhounds attack from a great distance, so be watchful of them and avoid fighting more than one enemy at a time.

The Scarlet Crusade have taken the ruined tower and turned it into a bastion of zealotry. This cannot go on. Slay the guards outside the tower one at a time as you make your way closer. Take ten Scarlet Insignia Rings from their corpses as **Proof of Demise**.

Captain Perrine stands inside the tower with a bodyguard. Slay them both to show them the Forsaken are, and will always be, **At War With The Scarlet Crusade**. Finish killing the humans around the tower before heading back to Brill. Take the time to collect the Darkhound Blood and Duskbat Pelts before returning.

Stop at Abigail Shiel, by the wagon, to buy a single Coarse Thread and sell loot before turning in all your quests.

BURYING THE PAST

A number of the dead in Tirisfal have risen as servants of the Scourge. **The Mills Overrun** with mindless undead. Head west to grant them final rest. Collect five Notched Ribs and three Blackened Skulls as you destroy the servants of the Scourge.

Watch for Devlin Agamand as you travel **The Haunted Mills**. He patrols near the road approaching the mill and is slightly higher level than the enemies around him. Grab his remains and continue north. Certainly everyone has **Deaths in the Family**, but you are about to be the Agamand's personal reaper. Nissa is just inside the first house on the right side of the road. Take your time pulling the enemies out front as they can all attack at the same time.

Thurman and Gregor wander the mills long the path to the northwest. Collect all their remains and hunt for the ribs and skulls. When all is collected, hearthstone or walk back to Brill.

A Letter to Yvette

As you loot all the skeletons, watch for A Letter to Yvette. Right-click on it to start a quest that sends you back to Brill. How convienent!

UNDERCITY AND BUILDING A NEW FUTURE

Follow the road southeast from Brill. At the intersection, take the east road far enough to speak with Deathguard Linnea. Accept her quests and continue south to Undercity. Bethor is in the Magic Quarter waiting for you.

It's Big!

Undercity is rather impressive. Exploring all of it would take quite a bit of effort, but you're not the first to get lost in this city. The abominations are accustomed to newcomers needing directions and they give them freely. To find things in a hurry, ask a guard and they will plot it on your mini-map.

Undercity Points of Interest

Location	Useful Stores/NPCs
Trade Quarter	Auction House, Bank, Inn, Mailbox, Merchants, Bat Handler
Magic Quarter	Tailoring Trainer, Reagent Vendor, Mage Trainer, Portal Trainer, Warlock Trainer, Demon Trainer, Fishing Trainer
Rogues' Quarter	Poison Vendor, First Aid Trainer, Skinning Trainer, Leatherworking Trainer, Engineering Trainer, Forge, Anvil, Rogue Trainer
Apothecarium	Alchemy Trainer, Herbalism Trainer, Enchanting Trainer
Royal Quarter	Varimathras, Lady Sylvanas Windrunner
War Quarter	Mining Trainer, Weapon Master, Blacksmithing Trainer, Forge, Anvil, Warrior Trainer, Priest Trainer

You have a number of quests for eastern and northern Tirisfal Glades. Take the elevators back to the surface and follow the road east toward the Balnir Farmstead.

The Bulwark stops most of the Scourge from entering Tirisfal, but some slip past. Destory eight Bleeding Horrors and eight Wandering Spirits for the **Rear Guard Patrol**. The horrors don't move much, but the spirits wander a good bit so watch your back to avoid having one attack when you're already engaged.

Becoming More Talented

Every level (starting at level ten), you gain a Talent Point. These can be used to increase your abilities or learn new ones. Open your talent window (defaulted to 'n'). There are three panels in the window. Look at each talent carefully before choosing as once you spend your points, it costs gold to unlearn them. There is more about the benefits of each talent in the class section.

Once you've done your part to keep the Scrouge from Tirisfal, climb the cliff to the north and engage the Scarlet Crusade. Until these religious zealots are destroyed, the Forsaken are **At War With The Scarlet Crusade** and you are their favorite soldier. Kill the friars as you make your way to the tower. Captain Vachon is inside and needs to be shown the error of his ways.

The Scarlet Friars heal themselves and their compatriots. They must be killed quickly or interrupted to avoid long fights. Watch for others in the area and form a party to make this quest easier. With the leadership of another Scarlet outpost dead, head northwest to Brightwater Lake.

The Prodigal Lich lives on an island in Brightwater Lake surrounded by his own mindless protectors. Search through Gunther's books until you find his spellbook. Now it's north to the coast to work on **A New Plague**.

If one had never been to Tirisfal Glades, you might expect the coastline to be in better shape. The ocean is very large and the waves always tearing away at the plague that is gripping the land. It's a nice thought, but the beach is just as diseased as the rest of the land. It appears that even the ocean is powerless against such terrible magic.

Tear the fins off the murlocs you find. Watch for the oracles as they have mastered lightning magic and make your time at the beach difficult.

You Can't Fight Just One

Murlocs are notorious for their ability to bring an army to a one-on-one fight. When engaged, they immediately call any of their nearby friends to aid them. Pull the murlocs carefully and be ready to kill them quickly. At the first sign of losing the fight, they make tracks back for help.

If you weren't able to get a group to kill Maggot Eye earlier, stop by his shack now. You've gained a number of levels while he hasn't. With the five Vile Fin Scale samples, walk or hearthstone back to Brill to turn in your quests.

Begin another circuit by heading to Undercity. Speak with Bethor Iceshard again, then take the road east to speak with Linnea. Follow the path north from Linnea toward the Scarlet Monastery. When the path turns north, break east. Do not approach the Monastery, as the seat of the Scarlet Crusade is beyond your reach for quite some time. Enter the Venomweb Vale to continue gathering reagents for **A New Plague**. You need four Vicious Night Web Spider Venom and the spiders aren't likely to give it freely.

Venom in hand, follow the path north until it forks. Take the west fork toward the Scarlet Watch Post. Watch for other adventurers to join as you approach the Scarlet Watch Post.

Kill the guards as you approach the tower. Watch for the caster that patrols around the tower. Wait for her to come into range and eliminate her before engaging Captain Melrache and the Scarlet Bodyguards. The bodyguards are much lower level and can be killed quickly while Melrache is held by a warrior or combat controlled. Finish this portion of **At War With The Scarlet Crusade** and head southwest to Gunther's Retreat.

Gunther is grateful when you **Return the Book**, but he doesn't fully trust you. He gives you the task of **Proving Allegiance**. Grab a candle from the box at his feet and head to the south edge of the island. On a smaller island sits Lillith's Dinner Table. Place the candle on the table to summon Lillith Nefara and slay her. Return to Gunther to show that you are an enemy of the Scourge just as you've been telling him.

Return to Brill and help Johaan test **A New Plague** by giving it to the Captured Mountaineer in the inn. There is little else to be done in Brill. Head west to Agamand Mills and **The Family Crypt.**

Follow the path past the mills and over the bridge. The crypt is on the north side of the area. Kill the Wailing and Rotting Ancestors as you approach the crypt and descend into the depths. Take the crypt slowly as there are many wandering enemies and not a lot of space. Fights of two are almost guaranteed with fights of three or more being possible if you get careless or unlucky.

At the lowest room, Dargol stands with several ancestors. Pull the ancestors one at a time until Dargol stands alone. Collect Dargol's Skull and rest a moment. There are likely to be enemies respawned behind you. If your hearthstone is up, teleport back to Brill. If not, fight your way out of the crypt and return by foot.

Congratulations on your success in Tirisfal Glades. The dead are waking safely, a new plague designed to threaten all life is in the works, and even the Scarlet Crusade seems to have receded a bit because of such fine efforts. New challenges wait in Silverpine Forest to the south, in the Ragefire Chasm beneath Orgrimmar, and in the Barrens across the ocean, but those are adventures for another day.

Learning About the World

A Glimpse of the World

Setting foot into unknown lands is a dangerous prospect. The lands of Azeroth have been ravaged by wars and plagues, but peace is finding footholds and the land is healing…in places.

This section gives a brief description of each of the areas. While role-players gain the greatest use, even general gamers will find the information useful as it influences quest lines, ongoing wars, and other matters of import.

THE EASTERN KINGDOMS

Long past are the days of Lordaeron standing proud and strong. Deadly plagues have divided the population into the infected and those who fear infection. Caught between religious zealotry, and mindless undead, the races living here do so only through constant vigilance.

Lordaeron

Based under the ruins of Lordaeron, the Forsaken have thrown off the shackles of the Scourge and retained their own will. The Forsaken have tossed their lot in with the Horde…for now. This gives them aid as Dwarves and Humans are constantly seeking to take Hillsbrad to the south. This war has seen many shifts in power and is unlikely to be resolved anytime soon.

A threat even closer to home shows itself in the Scarlet Crusade. Many of this religious order have declared war on anyone and anything that is not a member. While their methods are disdainful, their fear is echoed by the Forsaken. How does one defend themselves from the mindless undead legions of the Scourge?

With only the Bulwark outpost between Tirisfal Glades and the Plaguelands, Lordaeron is infested with wildlife that has succumbed to one plague or another. The previously gentle wildlife has turned bloodthirsty and violent. The constant threat of their surroundings makes it more difficult for the Forsaken to concentrate on malevolent intelligent dangers. The forces of Dalaran across the lake and the mage Arugal in Silverpine are threats far more dangerous than any set of poisoned fangs.

Khaz Modan

The Dwarves of Ironforge patrol the lands of Khaz Modan devoutly, but their numbers are spread thin. Incursions of Ogres and Troggs slip past and are allowed to fester while the army is busy elsewhere. Word of attacks comes from all over the Dwarven lands. Even the outpost of Dun Algaz has been attacked and communications have been lost.

Perhaps this is a fitting view of the Dwarves themselves. The Dark Iron Dwarves, having split off hundreds of years ago in an event known as the War of the Three Hammers, have become a considerable threat to Ironforge and the Alliance.

After fleeing from their home of Gnomeregan, the Gnomes have been taken in by the Dwarves. Release of dangerous toxins researched for the war against the Troggs have made Gnomeregan unlivable and any Gnomes unfortunate to be caught inside…quite insane. Though exiled from their home, the Gnomes continue to fight at the side of the Dwarves. An underground tram connecting Stormwind and Ironforge has been completed and makes movement between the cities much easier.

Azeroth

The glimmering white walls of Stormwind stand proud and tall, but its military is scattered and worn. The Defias Brotherhood, a group of thieves and brigands, has grown to such strength that many wonder why the king has been absent on the matter. Combined with the Orcs, Gnolls, and walking dead, the armies of Stormwind are kept from mobilizing due to Lady Katrana Prestor's influence.

The coast of Westfall has come under attack. Defias have taken Moonbrook while an army of Gnolls slowly threatens the common peoples. The local militia has pulled back to try and hold Sentinel Hill, but they are vastly outnumbered. Word has been sent to the capital, but no more troops have arrived.

The peaceful land of Elwynn Forest is no longer. The guards of Stormwind keep the road safe, but much of Westfall lacks adequate protection. The nuisances of Kobolds, Murloc, and brigands have become full dangers.

Signs of trouble are stirring in both Stormwind and Duskwood. With so many Defias thrown into the Stockades so quickly, the guards find themselves outnumbered and out-muscled. The guards that made it to the surface have erected a chokepoint at the exit, but the Stockades are in the hands of the Defias now.

Something stirs in Duskwood. The dead of Ravenhill Cemetery are no longer content to lie buried. The Worgen have taken several farms and attack any who draw near. The Night Watch is comprised of concerned citizens, but without the help of the Stormwind guards, can these warriors keep Darkshire safe?

KALIMDOR

Many races have made Kalimdor home. The Orcs, Trolls, and Tauren have carved a home from the rock, but peace escapes them still. Night Elves, Ogres, and Demons all threaten the homelands of the Horde.

Central Kalimdor

Most of the Horde have carved homes out of Central Kalimdor. Built within in the canyons on northern Durotar stands Orgrimmar. The Orcs and Darkspear Trolls have made a home in the red sands and thrived. Centaur infestations and even the cult of the Burning Blade are small dangers to the unity Orgrimmar symbolizes.

To the west lies Mulgore; a lush and rich land. Thrall helped the Tauren claim this land from the centaur and that aid will be repaid for generations to come. While still active in Thousand Needles and Desolace, the centaurs have no presence in Mulgore and only small camps in the Barrens.

At first sight, the Barrens seem a dangerous land and Crossroads a village about to be blown away by the wind. While the peace of Crossroads is fragile and often broken, it is permanent. The Barrens is a success story of the cooperation of the Horde. Once a land where only the most stalwart adventurer would go, the combined forces of the Horde are slowly bringing peace to the land.

The task is not yet done. Harpies and the Venture Company still terrorize the northern Barrens while the Quilboar are firmly entrenched in the south. Even the Dwarves are trying to carve out a piece of this potent land by excavating near the border to Dustwallow Marsh.

Southern Kalimdor

The wilderness is as varied and untamed as the races living there. Small outposts are the only glimpse of civilization and those are few and far between.

Thousand Needles is largely controlled by the centaur, but even they are kept in check by the harpies and other more dangerous creatures of the wild. The desolate silence of Thousand Needles is broken by the thunderous crashes from the Shimmering Flats. Though far from civilization, the salt flats provide the perfect track for the Gnomes and Goblins to race their most recent inventions. They pay good money for people to keep their track clear.

West of Thousand Needles the land is much more lush. The forest of Feralas is quite beautiful to behold. Were it not for the Ogres infesting the ancient ruins and the Gnolls camped throughout the valleys, this land would be quite a place to visit.

Venturing further south from Thousand Needles leads into the desert of Tanaris. Gadgetzan and Steamwheedle Port are the only signs of friendly civilization. The Goblins put a city anywhere there is profit to be had. The gates of Ahn'Qiraj have been opened in the far south, but their reach is ever expanding. The Silithid desert on the other side of the crater is a place of epic danger and glory untold.

Northern Kalimdor

Much of Northern Kalimdor shows the touch of the Night Elves. Though pushed to Teldrassil, the Elves have returned to repair the damage done to the land.

Just across the sea from Teldrassil, Auberdine has become a haven for crafters and those wishing to help heal the land. While the threat of Naga is strong and the spirits of the ruins in the north are angry, demonic corruption has tainted the Furbolg and wildlife populations.

South of Darkshore lays Ashenvale. The Horde have erected a camp on the beach just outside some ruins and deeper in the woods at Warsong Lumber Camp, but they are the least of the problems in the forest. Naga patrol the coastline and large tribes of aggressive Furbolg have taken residence in Ashenvale. The land is, for the most part, healthy. Felwood to the northeast is not so lucky. Corrupted animals and twisted trees are the hallmark of this terrible place.

A bridge across the Southfury River leads to Azshara. Though the land is beautiful, there are many powers at work. Naga and Satyr have claimed many of the ruins in central Azshara while Furbolg and Dragonkin roam the southeast.

Teldrassil

The Night Elves moved to Teldrassil in an attempt to unite the Night Elves in a single city. Teldrassil, created to restore the waning power of the Night Elves, is beginning to show signs of corruption.

Alterac Mountains

The Alterac Mountains are home to many powerful Ogres and to the Dalaran. While standing on the northwest shores of the area, a person can see over to the grim canopy of Silverpine Forest, a land filled with the walking dead. Yeti hold many of the high, snow-filled areas of Alterac, while the mages of Dalaran and the dangerous Syndicate control the lowlands.

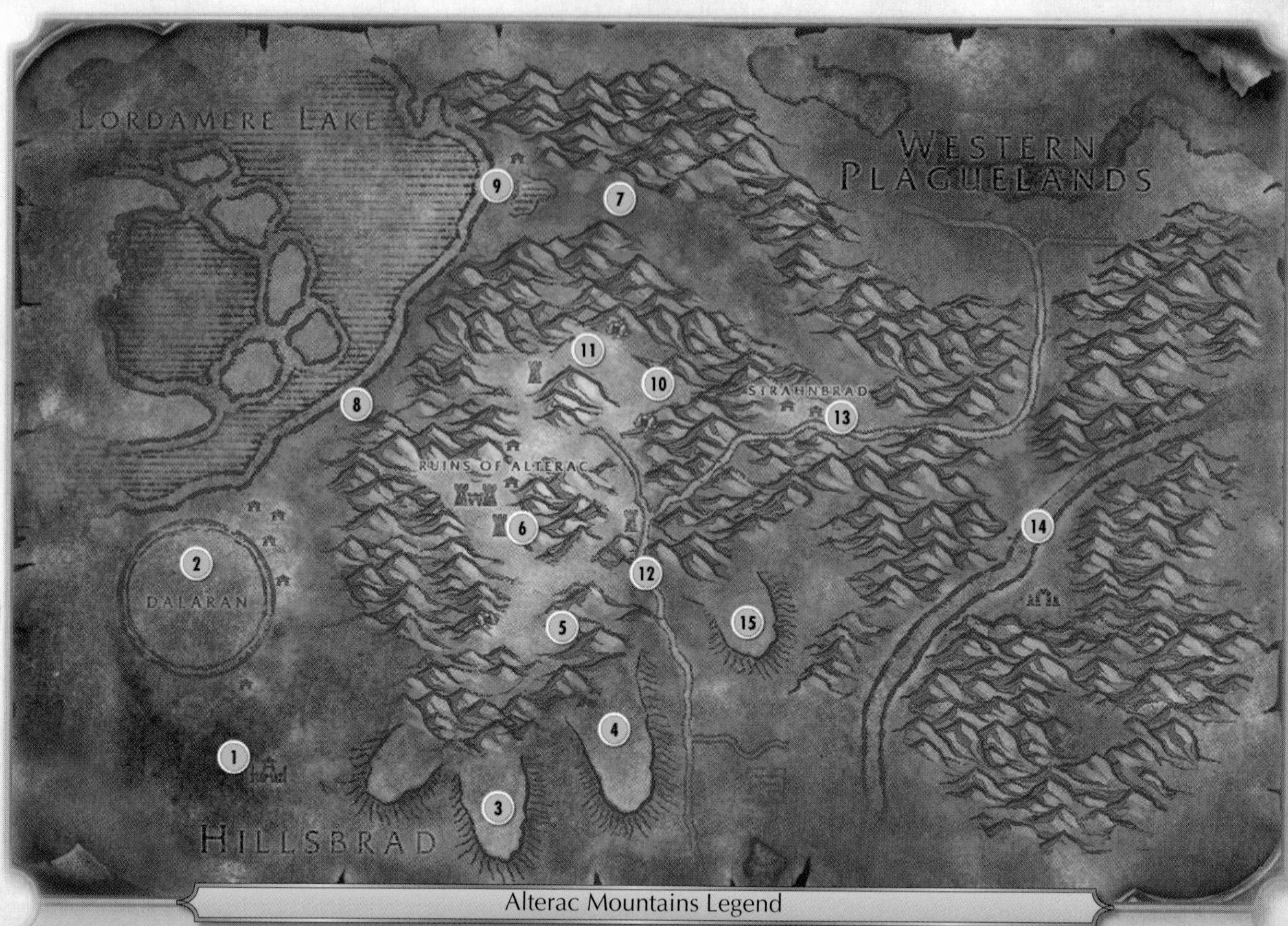

1 Lordamere Internment Camp

- Alina 33 Quest Target
- Dalaran Shield Guard 31-32
- Dalaran Theurgist 32-33
- Dermot 34 Quest Target
- Elder Gray Bear 25-26
- Giant Moss Creeper 24-25
- Mountain Lion 32-33
- Ricter 33 Quest Target

2 Dalaran

- Archmage Ansirem Runeweaver 40
- Dalaran Shield Guard 32
- Dalaran Summoner 34-35
- Dalaran Theurgist 33
- Dalaran Worker 33-34
- Elder Gray Bear 25-26
- Elemental Slave 33-34
- Gavin's Naze
- Giant Moss Creeper 25-26
- Giant Moss Creeper 25-26
- Hulking Mountain Lion 33-34
- Mountain Lion 32-33
- Snapjaw 30-31

3 The Headland

- Mountain Lion 32-33

4 Corrahn's Dagger

- Hulking Mountain Lion 33-34
- Mountain Lion 32-33
- Syndicate Footpad 33
- Syndicate Thief 33-34

5 Growless Cave

- Giant Yeti 33-34
- Mountion Yeti 32-33

6 Ruins of Alterac

- Bro'kin 49 Speciality Alchemist
- Crushridge Enforcer 38-39 Elite
- Crushridge Mage 37-38 Elite
- Crushridge Mauler 37-38 Elite
- Crushridge Warmonger 39-40 Elite
- Mudrake 40 Elite

7 The Uplands

- Argus Shadow Mage 36
- Giant Yeti 33-34
- Grandpa Vishas 34 Elite
- Hulking Mountain Lion 33-34
- Nancy Vishas 33 Elite
- Syndicate Saboteur 37-38
- Syndicate Sentry 36-37

8 Misty Shore

- Snapjaw 30-31

9 Dandred's Ford

- Hulking Mountain Lion 33-34
- Snapjaw 30-31
- Syndicate Assassin 38-39
- Syndicate Enforcer 39-40

10 Slaughter Hollow

- Crushridge Brute 35-36
- Crushridge Ogre 34-35

11 Crushridge Hold

- Crushridge Brute 35-36
- Crushridge Ogre 34-35

12 Gallows' Corner

- Crushridge Brute 35
- Crushridge Ogre 35

13 Strahnbad

- Syndicate Spy 35
- Syndicate Wizard 35

14 Chillwind Point

- Bath'rah the Windcatcher 35 Quest
- Hulking Mountain Lion 33-34
- Mountain Lion 32-33
- Snapjaw 30-31
- Stonefury 37

15 Sofera's Naze

- Henchman Valik 30
- Syndicate Footpad 32
- Syndicate Thief 33-34

Arathi Highlands

A fragrant wind of pollen, grass, and other living things blows over those who enter the Highlands of Arathi. People from both the Horde and Alliance settle here, trying to farm the arable land of the north and struggle against the many natural dangers of the land. Raptors walk across the flatlands, hunting for prey, and there are many aggressive Ogres and Trolls out in the wild as well. Beware the deadly elementals that spawn near old and forgotten shrines, for they have tremendous power. Seek Hammerfall in the northeast for safety (as the Horde), or walk into the small gorge of Refuge Pointe (as Alliance) in the center of the Highlands.

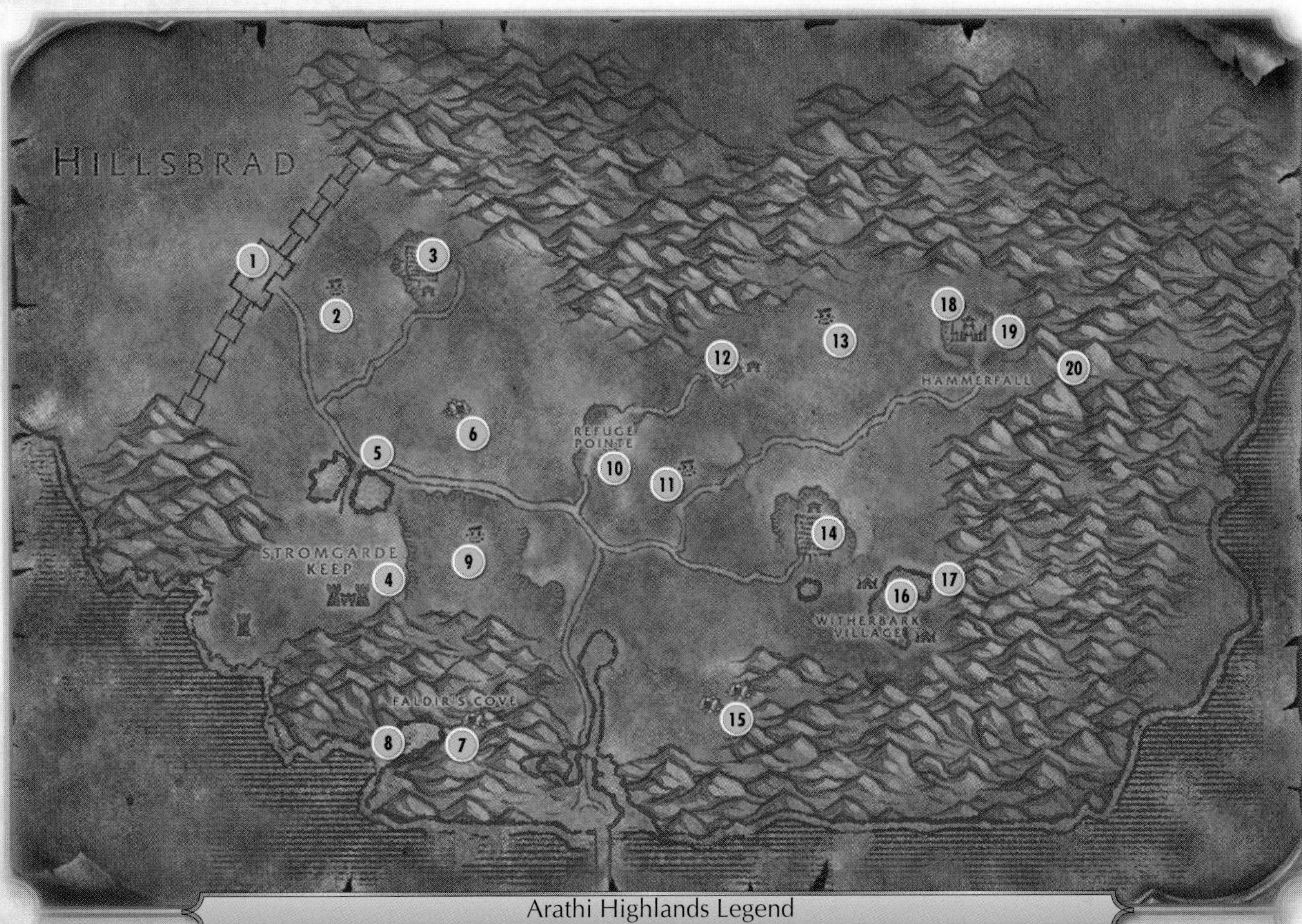

Arathi Highlands Legend

1 Thoradin's Wall
- Highland Strider 30-31
- Plains Creeper 32-33
- Young Mesa Buzzard 31-32

2 Circle of West Binding
- Burning Exile 38-39

3 Northfold Manor
- Plains Creeper 32-33
- Syndicate Highwayman 30-31
- Syndicate Mercenary 31-32
- Syndicate Pathstalker 32-33
- Young Mesa Buzzard 21-32

4 Stromgarde Keep
- Boulderfist Lord 39-40 Elite
- Boulderfist Mauler 37-38 Elite
- Boulderfist Shaman 38-39 Elite
- Lord Falconcrest 40 Elite
- Otto 38 Elite
- Prince Galen Trollbane 44 Elite
- Stromgarde Defender 38-39 Elite
- Stromgarde Troll Hunter 37-38 Elite
- Stromgarde Vindicator 40 Elite
- Syndicate Conjurer 36 Elite
- Syndicate Magus 38 Elite
- Syndicate Prowler 36 Elite

Arathi Highway
- 5 Forsaken Courier 35
- Forsaken Bodyguard 35
- Lieutenant Valorcall 38 Elite
- Stromgarde Cavalryman 37-38 Elite

Boulder'gor
- 5 Boulderfist Ogre 32-33
- Highland Thrasher 33-34
- Witherbark Troll 31-30

Boulderfist Outpost
- 6 Boulderfist Enforcer 33-34
- Witherbark Witch Doctor 33

Faldir's Cove
- 7 Lolo the Lookout 39 Quest
- Shakes O'Breen 40 Quest

8 The Drowned Reef
- Daggerspine Raider 38-39
- Daggerspine Sorceress 39-40

9 Circle of Inner Binding
- Highland Thrasher 33-34
- Mesa Buzzard 34-35
- Rumbling Exile 38-39

10 Refuge Pointe
- Apprentice Kryten 30 Quest
- Captain Nials 41 Quest
- Cedrick Prose 55 Gryphon Master
- Highland Strider 30-31
- Young Mesa Buzzard 31-32

11 Circle of Outer Binding
- Thundering Exile 38-39

12 Dabyrie's Farmstead
- Dabyrie Laborer 30-31
- Dabyrie's Militia 31-32
- Fardel Dabyrie 33 Quest Target
- Marcel Dabyrie 34 Quest Target

13 Circle of East Binding
- Shards of Myzrael
- Cresting Exiles 38-39

14 Go'Shek Farm
- Kinelory 38 Quest
- Quae 38 Quest
- Giant Plains Creeper 35-36
- Hammerfall Grunt 34-35
- Hammerfall Peon 33-34
- Mesa Buzzard 34-35

15 Boulderfist Hall
- Boulderfist Brute 35-36
- Boulderfist Magus 37
- Highland Fleshstalker 36-37
- Kor'gresh
- Mesa Buzzard 34-35
- Witherbark Berserker 36-37 Elite

16 Witherbark Village
- Giant Plains Creeper 35-36
- Witherbark Axe Thrower 32-33
- Witherbark Head Hunter 34-35
- Witherbark Witchdoctor 33-34

17 Witherbark Cave
- Witherbark Headhunter 34-35
- Witherbark Shadow Hunter 35-36

18 Hammerfall
- Drum Fel 30 Quest
- Gor'mul 40 Quest
- Innkeeper Adegwa 30 Innkeeper
- Slagg 38 Superior Butcher
- Tharlidun 30 Stable Master
- Tor'gan 40 Quest
- Urda 55 Wind Rider Master
- Zaruk 60 Quest
- Zengu 40 Quest
- Highland Strider 30-31

19 Drywhisker Gorge
- Drywhisker Kobold 35-36

20 Drywhisker Cave
- Drywhisker Digger 36-37
- Drywhisker Surveyor 37-38

Ashenvale is a lush and vibrant area of forests, meadows and lakes. Today Demons, Elementals, Furbolgs and many more supernatural creatures rule this land. The Night Elves, inherently attuned to nature, have started to cleanse this land, but it will take many years before it is safe for travelers to roam freely through this land.

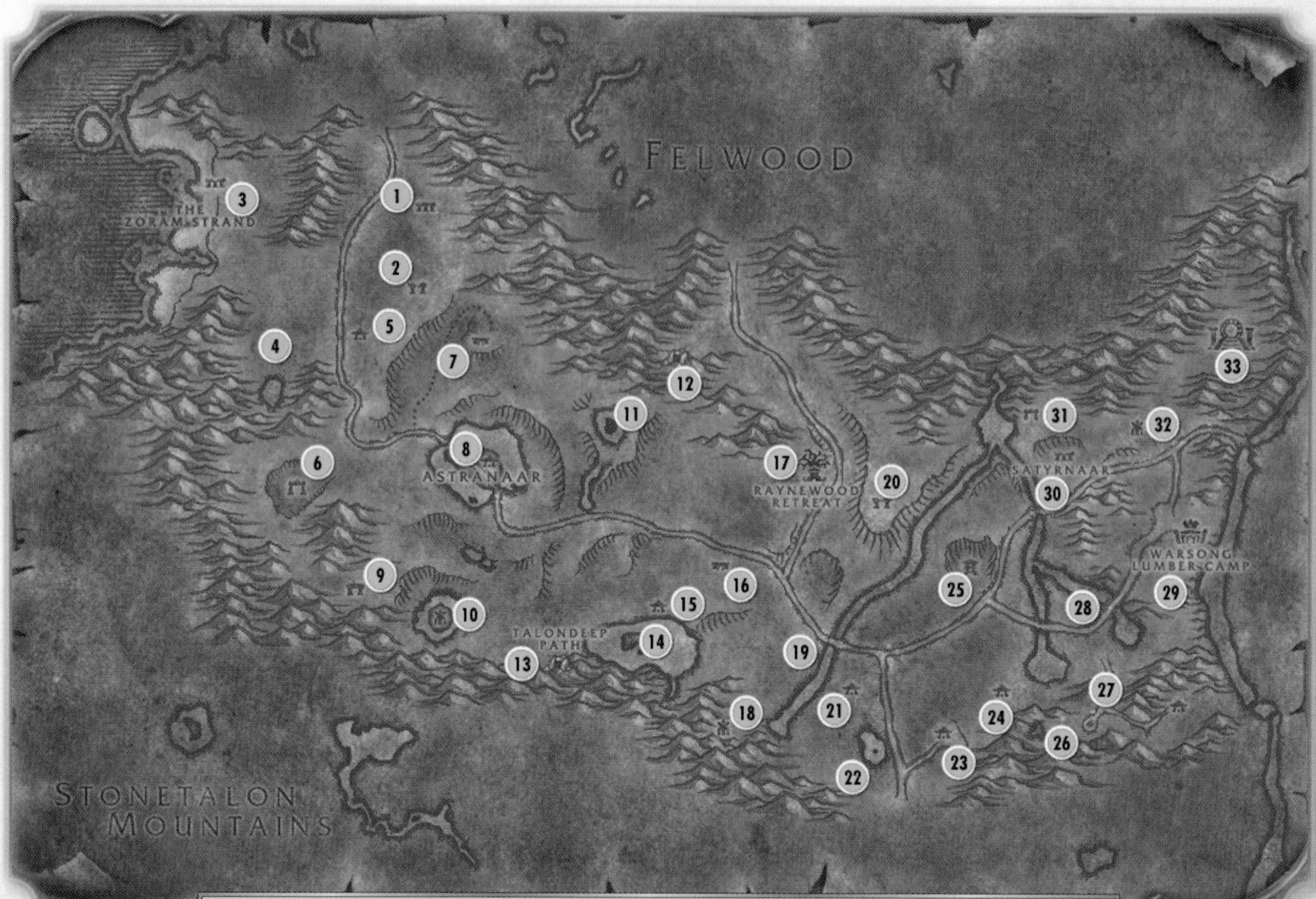

Ashenvale Legend

1 Bathran's Haunt
- Forsaken Seeker 18-19
- Forsaken Herbalist 18-19
- Forsaken Thug 20

2 The Ruins of Ordil'
- Dark Strand Cultist 18-19
- Imp (Minion) 18-19
- Dark Strand Adept 18-19
- Voidwalker Minion 18-19

3 The Zoram Strand
- Andruk 55 Wind Rider Master
- Clattering Crawler 19-20
- Mystlash Hydra 20
- Spined Crawler 20-21
- Wrathtail Sorceress 18-19
- Wrathtail WaveRider 18-19
- Ghostpaw Runner 19-20
- Wild Buck 18-19
- Entrance to Blackfathom Deeps World Dungeon

3A Fishing Village
- Talen 17 QuestAndruk 55 Elite Wind Rider Master

4 Lake Falathim
- Ghostpaw Runner 19-20
- Mugglefin 23+
- Saltspittle Muckdweller 20-21
- Saltspittle Oracle 20-21
- Saltspittle Puddlejumper 19-20
- Wild Buck 18-19

5 Maestra's Post
- Feero Ironhand 20 Quest
- Delgren the Purifier 19 Quest
- Orendil Broadleaf 27 Quest
- Liladris Moonriver 42 Quest
- Sentinel Onaeya 20 Quest
- Wild Buck 18-19

6 The Shrine of Aessina
- Illiyana 24 Quest
- Therysil 17 Quest
- Sentinel Melyria Frostshadow Quest
- Lilyn Darkriver Quest

7 Thistlefur Village
- Dal Bloodclaw 25
- Thistlefur Shaman 22-23
- Thistlefur Avenger 22-23
- Thistlefur Pathfinder 22-23

8 Astranaar
- Pelturas Whitemoon 21 Quest
- Nantar 21 Baker
- Maluressian 30 Stable Master
- Raene Wolfrunner 25 Quest
- Dagri 23 Raene Wolfrunner's Pet
- Fahran Silentblade 28 Tools and Supplies
- Maliynn 19 Grocer
- Korra 20 Tiger
- Haljan Oakheart 26 General Goods
- Kimlya 30 Innkeeper
- Dalria 24 Trade Goods
- Xai'ander 35 Weaponsmith
- Aayndia Floralwind 37 Leatherworker
- Faldreas Goeth'shael 19 Quest
- Sentinel Thenysil 23 Quest
- Shindrell Swiftfire 25
- Daelyshia 55 Hippogriff Master
- Lardan 25 Leatherworking
- Llana 25 Reageant Supplies
- Tandaan Lightmane 23 Leather Armor Merchant
- Aeolynn 22 Clothier
- Astranaar Sentinenl 40

9 Fire Scar Shrine
- Felslayer 22-23
- Burning Legionnaire 23-24

10 Ruins of Stardust
- Shadethicket Raincaller 23-24
- Shadethicket Woodshaper 23-24

11 Iris Lake
- Shadethicket Moss Eater 21-23

12 The Howling Vale
- Terrorwulf Fleshripper 28-29
- Terrorwulf Shadow Weaver 29-30

13 Talondeep Path
- Shadowhorn Stag 21-22
- Ashenvale Bear 21-22

14 Mystral Lake
- Befouled Water Elementals 23-25

15 Silverwind Refuge
- Harklan Moongrove 24 Alchemy Supplies
- Shandrina 24 Trade Goods
- Ulthaan 26 Butcher
- Danlaar Nightstride 35 Hunter Trainer
- Jayla 23 Skinner Trainer
- Bhaldaran Ravenshade 34 Bowyer
- Cylania Rootstalker 24 Herbalist
- Kylanna 31 Alchemist
- Sentinel Velene Starstrike 25 Quest

16 Greenpaw Village
- Foulweald Totemic 23-24
- Foulweald Ursa 23-24
- Foulweald Shaman 23-24
- Foulweald Warrior 23-24
- Foulweald Den Watcher 23-24
- Foulweald Pathfinder 23-24

17 Raynewood Retreat
- Keeper Ordanus 29
- Laughing Sister 24-25
- Cenarion Protector 25-26
- Cenarion Vindicator 26-27

18 Bloodtooth Camp
- Ran Bloodtooth 30
- Bloodtooth Guard 27-28
- Ghostpaw Runner 19-20
- Ashenvale Bear 21-22

19 Moonwell
- Blink Dragon 26
- Ghostpaw Howler 23
- Wildthorn Venomspitter 24

20 Night Run
- Wildthorn Venomspitter 24-25
- Elder Ashenvale Bear 24-25
- Felmusk Satyr 25-26
- Felmusk Rogue 26-27
- Felmusk Felsworn 27-28
- Felmusk Shadowstalker 26-27

21 Silverwing Outpost
- Ashenvale Sentinel 40
- Ashenvale Warrior 40

22 Fallen Sky Lake
- Shadethicket Stone Mover 25-26
- Shadethicket Bark Ripper 26-27
- Wildthorn Stalker 20-21

23 Nightsong Woods
- Wildthorn Stalker 20-21
- Warsong Shredder 27
- Rotting Slime 20-22
- Ghostpaw Runner 19-20
- Horde Shaman 28-29
- Horde Grunt 29-30

24 The Dor'Danil Barrow Den
- Uthil Mooncaller 32
- Rotting Slime (Outside) 21-22
- Forsaken Infiltrator 28-29
- Forsaken Intruder 28-29
- Forsaken Stalker 28-29
- Forsaken Assasin 28-29
- Severed Druid 28-29
- Severed Dreamer 29-30
- Severed Keeper 29-30
- Severed Sleeper 29-30

25 Splintertree Post

26 Monument to Grom Hellscream
- Felguard 29-31
- Legion Hound 29-31
- Searing Infernal 29-31

27 Demon Fall Canyon
- Legion Hound 29-30
- Mannoroc Lasher 29-30
- Searing Infernal 29-30
- Felguard 29-30

28 Felfire Hill
- Mannoroc Lasher 29-30
- Searing Infernal 29-30
- Felguard 29-30

29 Warsong Lumber Camp
- Loruk Foreststrider 44 Banker
- Horde Grunt 29-30
- Horde Shaman 28-29
- Warsong Shredder 27-28
- Horde Scout 26-27
- Horde Peon 26-27

30 Satyrnaar
- Bleakheart Trickster 26-28
- Bleakheart Shadowstalker 26-28
- Bleakheart Saytr 26-28
- Bleakheart Hellcaller 26-28

31 Xavian
- Galtharis 32
- Xavian Felsworn 28-30
- Xavian Betrayer 28-30
- Xavian Hellcaller 28-30
- Xavian Rogue 28-30

32 Forest Song
- Kayneth Stillwind 31 Quest
- Giant Ashenvale Bear 29-30
- Wildthorn Lurker 29-30

33 Bough Shadow
- Dreamstalker 62
- Emeraldon Tree Warders 60
- Emeraldon Oracles 61

Azshara

Azshara is located to the east of Ashenvale. Named after Queen Azshar, the Naga still roam this land. This zone has progressive level increases as you travel to the edges of the land.

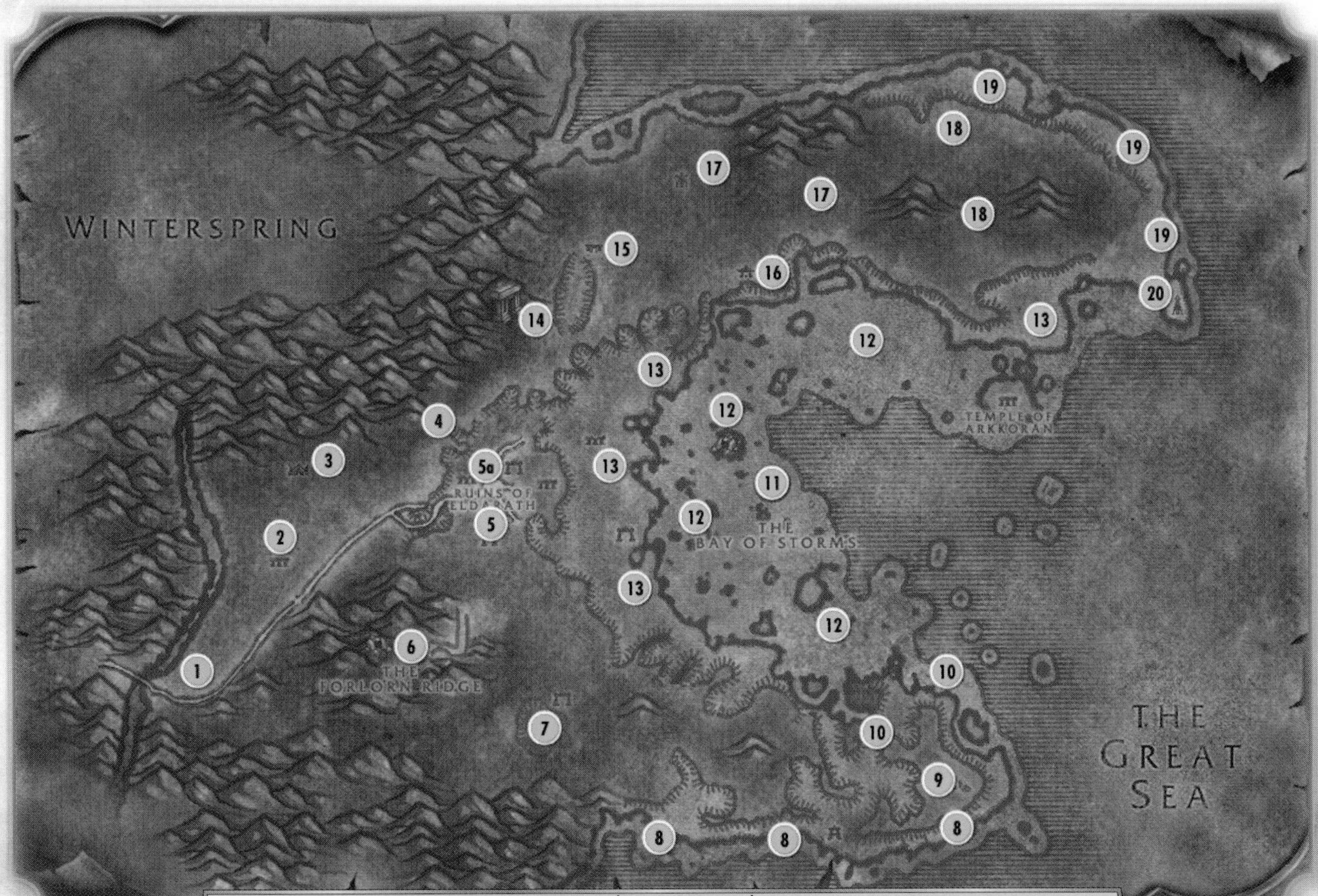

Azshara Legend

1 Shadowsong Shrine
Highborn Apparition 45-47
Highborn Lichling 45-57
Mosshoof Runner 45-46

2 Haldarr Encampment
Cliff Walker 53-54 Elite
Haldarr Felsworn 45-46
Haldar Satyr 45-46
Haldarr Trickster 45-46
Mosshoof Runner 45-47
Sentinel Keldara Sunblade 45
Thunderhead Hippogryph 46-48

3 Valormok
Ag'Tor Bloodfist 45 Quest
Haggrum Bloodfist 45
Jediga 49 Quest
Kroum 55 Elite Flight Master
Mosshoff Runner 45-46

4 Bear's Head
Cliff Walker 53 Elite
Timbermaw Pathfinder 47-48
Timberweb Recluse 47-48
Timbermaw Totemic 47-48
Timbermaw Warrior 47-48

5 Ruins of Eldarath
Lady Sesspira 51 Elite
Lingering Highborne 48-50
Spitelash Screamer 46-48
Spitelash Siren 51-52
Spitelash Serpent Guard 48-49
Spitelash Warrior 46-48
Thunderhead Stagwing 49-60
Timberweb Recluse 47-48

5a Temple of Zin-Malor
Spitelash Serpent Guard 48-49
Spitelash Siren 51-52
Warlord Krellian 55

6 Forlorn Ridge
Forest ooze 52-53
Mosshoof Courser 53-54

7 Lake Minnar
Blue Dragon Spawn 50-51
Blue Scalebane 52-53
Draconic Magelord 53-54
Draconic Mageweaver 51-52
Mosshoof Courser 52-53
Azuregos

8 The Ruined Reaches
Horizon Scout Crewman 42
Jubie GadgetSpring 44 Engineer Supplier, Rare Schematics
Coralshell Lurker 53-54
Great Wavethrasher 53-54
Makrinni Razorclaw 54-55
Storm Bay Oracle 54-55

9 Ravencrest Monument
Spitelash Battlemaster 53-54
Spitelash Enchantress 54-55

10 South Ridge Beach
Coralshell Lurker 53-54
Makrinni Razorclaw 54-55
Great Wavethrasher 53-54
Storm Bay Oracle 54-55

11 Hetaera's Clutch
Servant of Arkkoroc 53-55 Elite

12 Bay of Storms
Lormus Thalipedes 60 Quest
Rataf 50 Elite Lormus' pet
Shatllar 50 Elite Lormus' pet
Zaman 50 Elite Lormus' pet
Servant of Arkkoroc 53-55 Elite

13 The Shattered Strand
Coralshell Lurker 53-54
Great Wavethrasher 53-54
Makrinni Razorclaw 54-55
Spitelash Myrmidon 50-51
Spitelash Siren 51-52
Arkkoran Clacker 53-54
Arkkoran Muckdweller 53-54
Arkkoran Oracle 53-54

14 Timbermaw Hold
Cliff Walker 53-54Elite
Timberweb Recluse 47-48
Timbermaw Pathfinder 46-47
Timbermaw Shaman 50-51
Thunderhead Stagwing 49-50
Timbermaw Watcher 49-50
Timbermaw Warrior 47-48

15 Ursolan
Timbermaw Shaman 50-51
Thunderhead Skystormer 51-52
Timbermaw Ursa 51-52
Timbermaw Watcher 49-50

16 Thalassian Base Camp
Blood Elf Reclaimer 52-53
Blood Elf Surveyor 51-52
Thunderhead Skystormer 51-52

17 Legash Encampment
Cliff Breaker 54-55 Elite
Cliff Walker 52-53 Elite
Forest Ooze 52-53
Legashi Hellcaller 52-53
Legashi Rogue 52-53
Legashi Satyr 51-52
Mosshoof Courser 51-52
Thunderhead Consort 53-54
Thunderhead Skystormer 51-52

18 Bitter Reaches
Cliff Breaker 54-55 Elite
Cliff Thunderer 54-55 Elite
Cliff Walker 52-53 Elite
Forest Ooze 52-53
Mistwalker Ravager 52-53
Mosshoof Courser 51-52
Thunderhead Skystormer 51-52
Thunderhead Consort 53-54
Thunderhead Patriarch 54-55

19 Jagged Reaches
Coralshell Lurker 53-54
Makrinni Scrabbler 52-53
Storm Bay Warrior 51-52
Wavethrasher 52-53

20 Tower of Elpara
Coralshell Lurker 53-54
Makrinni Scrabbler 52-53
Storm Bay Warrior 51-52
Wavethrasher 52-53

21 Temple of Arkkoran
Arkkoran Clacker 53-54
Arkkoran Oracle 54-55
Arkkoran Pincer 54-55
Arkkoran Muckdweller 53-54
Lord Arkkoran 60 Elite

Badlands

South of Loch Modan is an area of open sand and rock known as the Badlands. Many natural predators hunt here, but there are also rare and fierce creatures as well. Dragon Whelps of considerable size grow in the eastern part of the region, near Uldaman (a place with quite a reputation for danger and adventure). To the west is a Horde town, barely more than a well-staffed building to show for itself, but offering what little civilization holds out in this rugged place.

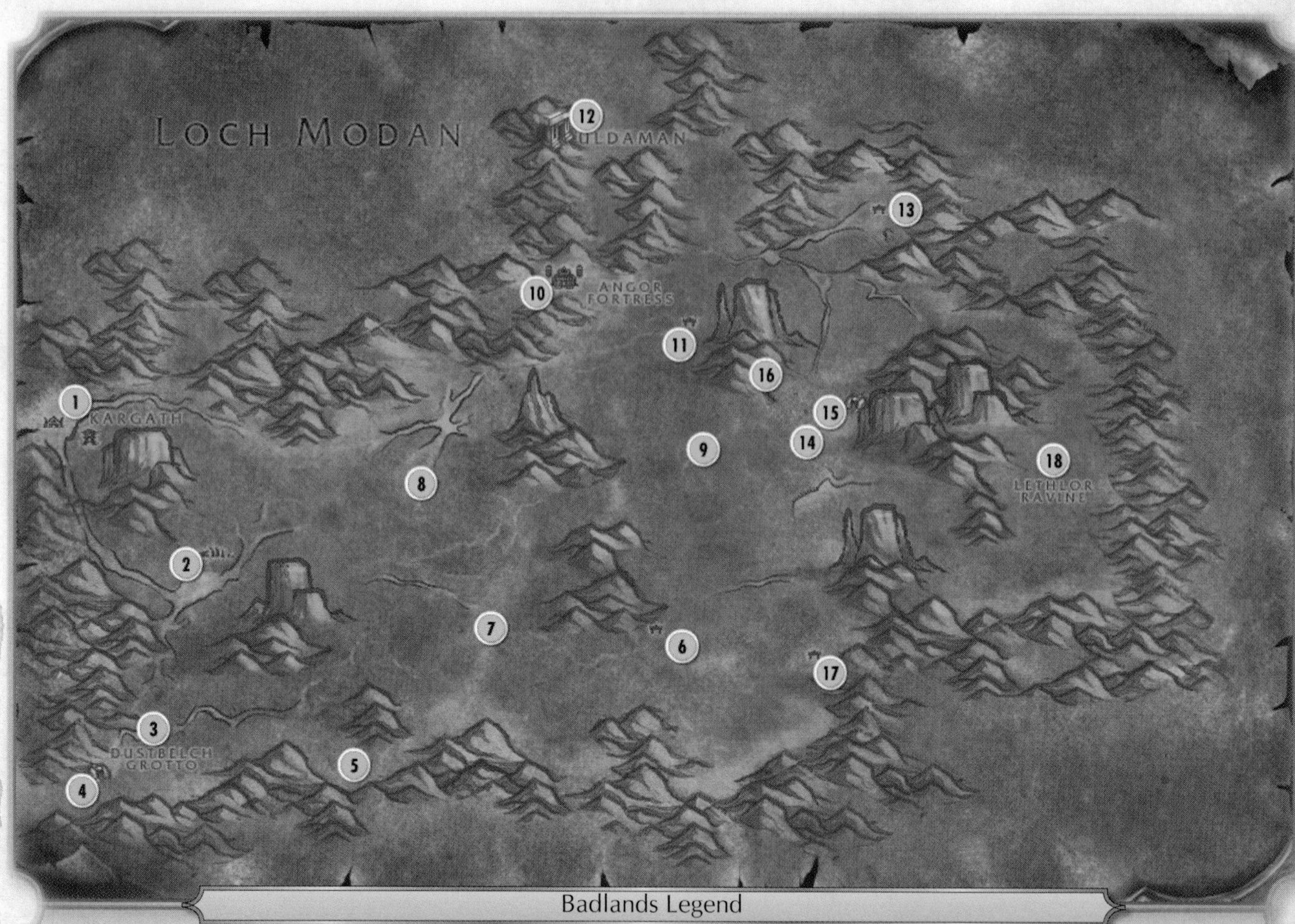

Badlands Legend

1 Kargath
- Gorrick 55 Wind Rider Master
- Greth 30 Stable Master
- Grunt Gargal 52 Quest
- Initiate Amakkar 52 Quest
- Innkeeper Shul'kar 30 Innkeeper
- Razal'blade 52 Quest
- Shadowmage Vivian Lagrave 60 Quest
- Thal'trak Proudtusk 55 Quest
- Thunderheart 52 Quest

2 Apocryphan's Rest
- Elder Crag Coyote 39-40
- Giant Buzzard 39-40
- Ridge Stalker Patriarch 40-41

3 Camp Cagg
- Boss Tho'grun 41 Quest Target
- Dustbelcher Mauler 41-42
- Dustbelcher Mystic 37
- Dustbelcher Shaman 41-42
- Dustbelcher Wyrmhunter 40-41
- Greater Rock Elemental 42-44

4 Dustbelch Grotto
- Dustbelcher Lord 44
- Dustbelcher Ogre Mage 44

5 Mirage Flats
- Elder Crag Coyote 39-40
- Giant Buzzard 39-40
- Ridge Stalker Patriach 40-41
- Zaricotl 55 Elite

6 Agmond's End
- Agmond's Body Quest
- Theldurin the Lost 30 Quest
- Buzzard 37-38
- Feral Crag Coyote 37-38
- Murdaloc 42 Quest Target
- Ridge Huntress 39
- Rock Elemental 39-40
- Stonevault Shaman 40-41
- Stonevault Stonesnapper 39-40

7 Camp Wurg
- Dustbelcher Brute 39
- Dustbelcher Ogre 38-39
- Elder Crag Coyote 39-40
- Ridge Stalker Patriarch 41

8 The Dustbowl
- Lotwil Veriatus 36 Quest
- Lucien Tosselwrench 31 Quest
- Elder Crag Coyote 39-40
- Giant Buzzard 39-40
- Lesser Rock Elementals 37-39
- Ridge Stalker Patriarch 41

9 Valley of Fangs
- Jazzrik 38 Vendor
- Martek the Exiled 42 Quest
- Rigglefuzz 37 Quest
- Crag Coyote 35-36
- Ridge Huntress 38-39

10 Angor Fortress
- Crag Coyote 35
- Ridge Stalker 36-37
- Shadowforge Chanter 38-39
- Shadowforge Warrior 38
- Stone Golem 38-39

11 Hammertoe's Digsite
- Prospector Ryedol 35 Quest
- Sigrun Ironhew 40 Quest
- Crag Coyote 35-36
- Ridge Stalker 35-36
- Shadowforge Darkweaver 36-37
- Shadowforge Tunneler 35-36
- Starving Buzzard 35-36

12 The Maker's Terrace
- Primary Entrance to Uldaman World Dungeon
- Shadowforge Digger 35-36 Elite
- Shadowforge Ruffian 36-37 Elite
- Shadowforge Surveyor 35-36 Elite

13 Camp Kosh
- Dustbelcher Mystic 37
- Dustbelcher Warrior 36-37

14 Dustwind Gulch
- Garek 50 Quest
- Thorkaf Dragoneye 50 Master Dragonscale Leatherworker
- Buzzard 37-38
- Feral Crag Coyote 37-38
- Ridge Stalker 35-36
- Starving Buzzard 35-36

15 Dustwind Gulch Cave
- Secondary Entrance to Uldaman World Dungeon
- Stonevault Basher 40 Elite
- Stonevault Seer 39-40 Elite

16 Crypt

17 Camp Boff
- Dustbelcher Brute 39-40
- Dustbelcher Ogre 38-39
- Feral Crag Coyote 37-38

18 Lethlor Ravine
- Large Gray Pillar
- Pillar of Amethyst
- Pillar of Diamond
- Blacklash 50 Elite
- Hematus 50 Elite
- Scalding Whelp 42-43
- Scorched Guardian 43-45 Elite

The Barrens

The Barrens are one of the largest zones and a central hub for travel between regions. Savannah Prowlers roam the land and remain hidden from younger adventurers, while Raptors, Centaurs, Harpies and all sorts of other wildlife can be seen hunting or foraging. This provides plenty of skinning opportunities. Ore and herbs are also all across the landscape. Three dungeons are within the zone: The Wailing Caverns, Razorfen Downs, and Razorfen Kraul. The Barrens offers access to many other zones including Stonetalon, Thousand Needles, Durotar, and Dustwallow Marsh; of course, that doesn't mention the Wyvern paths or the port town of Ratchet where adventurers can book passage on a ship.

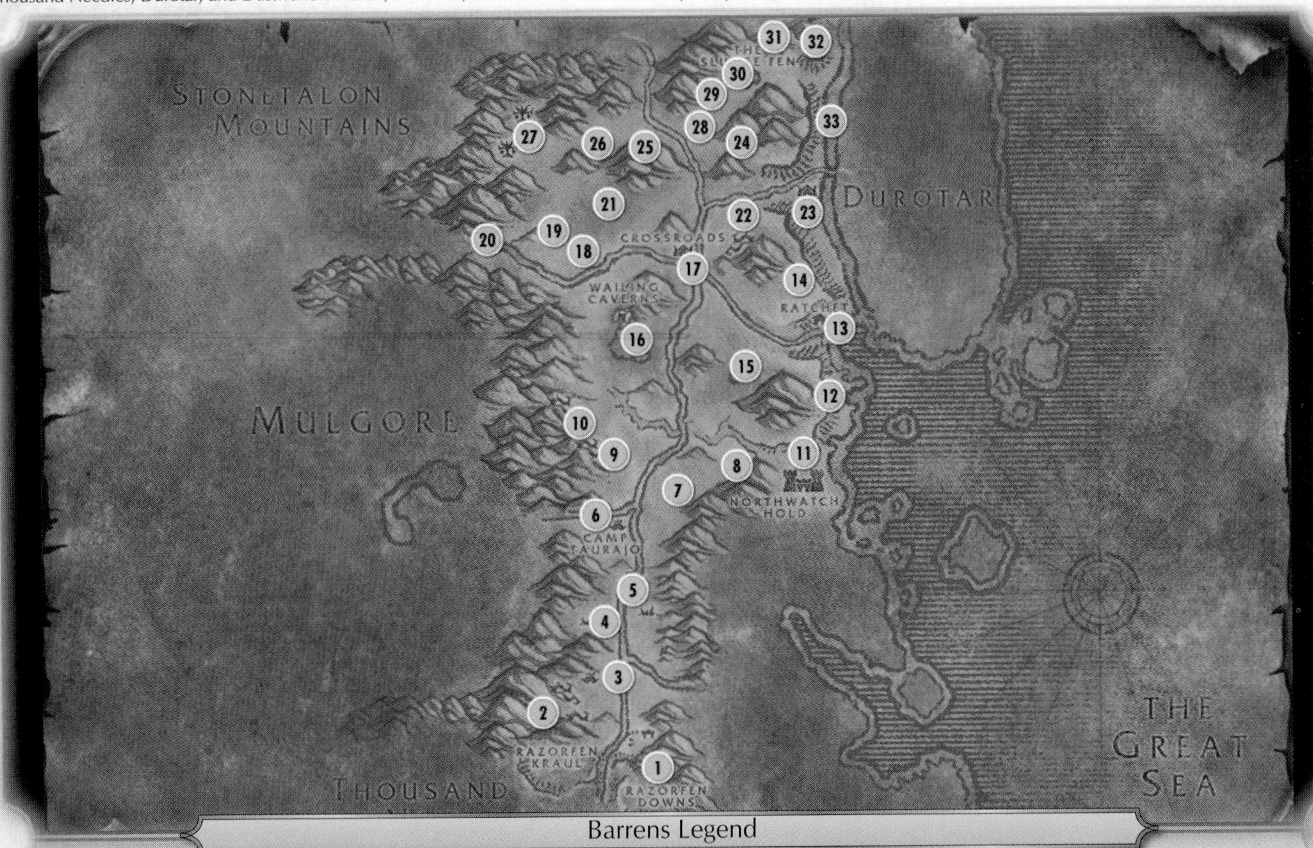

Barrens Legend

1 1 Bael Modan
Bael'dun Excavator 21-22
Bael'dun Foreman 22-23
Bael'dun Officer 26
Bael'dun Rifleman 24,25
Bael'dun Soldier 23,24
Digger Flameforge 24
General Twinbraid 30
Lord Cyrik Blackforge 23
Malgin Barleybrew 25
Prospector Khazgorm 26
Captain Gerogg Hammertoe 27 Elite

2 Blackthorn Ridge
Razormane Pathfinder 20,21
Razormane Seer 23,24
Razormane Stalker 22,23
Razormane Warfrenzy 24,25
Kuz Orcbane 21
Nak Orcbane 23
Lok Orcbane 25
Hagg Taurenbane 26 Elite

3 Southern Barrens
Gann Stonespire 18 Quest
Hannah Bladeleaf 24 Elite
Marcus Bel 24 Elite
Thora Feathermoon 25 Elite
Brontus 27 Elite
Barrens Kodo 19,20
Greater Barrens Kodo 24,25
Wooly Kodo 25,26
Greater Thunderhawk 23,24
Hecklefang Stalker 22,23
Stormhide 22,23
Thunderstomp 24
Washte Pawne 25

4 Silithid Mounds 18-24
Hannah Bladeleaf 24 Elite
Marcus Bel 24 Elite
Thora Feathermoon 25 Elite
Brontus 27 Elite
Silithid Creeper 20,21
Silithid Grub 20
Silithid Harvester 24
Silithid Protector 18,19
Silithid Swarmer 21,22
Barrens Kodo 19,20
Wooly Kodo 25,26
Greater Barrens Kodo 24,25

5 Field of Giants
Azzere the Skyblade 25
Owatanka 24
Brontus 27 Elite
Hannah Bladeleaf 24 Elite
Marcus Bel 24 Elite
Thora Feathermoon 25 Elite
Thunderhead 20-21
Wooly Kodo 25-26
Zhevra Courser 20-21
Thunderhawk Cloudscraper 20-21
Greater Barrens Kodo 24-25
Gazelle 2
Barrens Kodo 19120
Zhevra Courser 20-21

6 Camp Taurajo
Kelsuwa 30 Stablemaster
Innkeeper Byula 30 Innkeeper
Dranh 15 Skinner
Jorn Skyseer 32 Quest
Yonada 25 Tailoring & Leatherworking Supplies
Mahani 31 Expert Tailor
Krulmoo Fullmoon 42 Expert Leatherworker
Gahroot 25 Butcher
Ruga Ragetotem 30 Quest
Grunt Logmar 20 Quest
Grunt Dogran 20 Quest
Mangletooth 17 Quest
Kirge Sternhorn 22
Tatternack Steelforge 14
Takar the Seer 45 Quest

7 Bramblescar
Bristleback Geomancer 19-20
Bristleback Hunter 18-19
Bristleback Thornweaver 17-18

8 Raptor Grounds
Sunscale Scytheclaw 15-16
Sunscale Screecher 13-15
Sunscale Lashtail 11-13
Fleeting Plainstrider 12-13
Hecklefang Hyena 15-16
Ornery Plainstrider 16-17
Zhevra Charger 17-18

9 Middle Barrens
Hannah Bladeleaf- 24 Elite
Marcus Bel 24 Elite
Thora Feathermoon 25 Elite
Barrens Giraffe 15-16
Wandering Barrens Giraffe 18-19
Barrens Kodo 19-20
Hecklefang Snarler 18-19
Thunderhawk Hatchling 18-20
Gazelle 2
Stormsnout 18-19

10 Agama'gor
Bristleback Geomancer 19-20
Bristleback Hunter 18-19
Bristleback Thornweaver 17-18
Bristleback Water Seeker 16-17
Geopriest Gukk'rok 19
Swinegart Spearhide 22 Elite

11 Northwatch Hold
Gilthares Firebough 17 Quest
Theramore Marine 15-16
Theramore Preserver 16-17
Cannoneer Smythe 19
Cannoneer Whessan 19
Captain Fairmount 20

12 The Merchant Coast
Klannoc Macleod 65 The Islander, Quest
Islen Waterseer 37 Quest
Mahren Skyseer 32 Quest
Southsea Brigand 12-13
Southsea Cannoneer 13-14
Southsea Cutthroat 24-15
Southsea Privateer 14-15
Polly 18
Tazan 13
Baron Longshore 16
Slimeshell Makrura 18-19
Isha Awak 27

13 Ratchet
Brewmaster Drohn 9 Quest
Captain Thalo'thas Brightsun 25 Quest
Wrenix the Wretched 20 Quest
Vazario Linkgrease 40 Master Goblin Engineer, Quest Giver
Tinkerwiz 25 Journeyman Engineer
Gagsprocket 20 Engineering Goods
Gazlowe 60 Quest Giver
Sputtervalve 15 Tinkers' Union, Quest Giver
Crane Operator Bigglefuzz 18 Quest Giver
Zikkel 30 Banker
Fuzruckle 27 Banker
Mebok Mizzyrix 17 Quest Giver
Ironzar 23 Weaponsmith
Wharfmaster Dizzywig 15 Quest Giver
Shipmaster Grimble 45 Shipmaster
Kilxx 24 Fisherman
Liv Rizzlefix 17 Workshop Assistant
Grazlix 25 Armorer & Shieldcrafter
Vexspindle 24 Cloth & Leather Armor Merchant
Ranik 22 Trade Supplies
Jazzik 22 General Supplies
Zizzek 22 Fisherman
Reggifuz 35 Stablemaster
Innkeeper Wiley 35 Innkeeper
Menara Voidrender 50 Quest Giver
Strahad Farsan 60 Quest Giver
Acolyte Magaz 20 Quest Giver
Acolyte Fenrick 20 Quest Giver
Acolyte Wytula 20 Quest Giver

14 North Ratchet Plain
Thun'grim Firegaze 29 Quest
Ornery Plainstrider 16,17
Savannah Matriarch 17,18
Sunscale Scytheclaw 15,16
Zhevra Charger 17,18
Ishamuhale 19
Swiftmane 21 Elite
Humar the Pridelord 23 Elite

15 Stagnant Oasis
Kolkar Marauder 15-16
Kolkar Pack Runner 14-15
Kolkar Packhound 13
Kolkar Stormer 13-14
Kolkar Wrangler 12-13
Oasis Snapjaw 15-16
Brokespear 17
Verog the Dervish 18
Rocklance 17 Elite

16 Lushwater Oasis/ Wailing Caverns
Falla Sagewind 25 Quest
Kalldan Felmoon 27 Specialist Leatherworking Supplies
Nalpak 14 Disciple of Naralex, Quest
Ebru 14 Disciple of Naralex, Quest
Waldor 28 Journeyman Leatherworker
Deviate Coiler 15,16 Elite
Deviate Creeper 15,16 Elite
Deviate Lurker 16,17 Elite
Deviate Slayer 16,17 Elite
Deviate Stalker 15,16,17 Elite
Deviate Stinglash 17 Elite
Devouring Ectoplasm 16,17 Elite
Cloned Ectoplasm 16,17 Elite
Mad Magglish 18 Elite
Kolkar Marauder 15-16
Kolkar Pack Runner 14-15
Kolkar Packhound 13
Kolkar Stormer 13-14
Kolkar Wrangler 12-13
Oasis Snapjaw 15-16
Hezrul Bloodmark 19
Gesharahan 20 Elite

17 Crossroads
Innkeeper Boorand Plainswind 30 Innkeeper
Larhka 18 Beverage Merchant
Zargh 16 Butcher
Moorane Hearthgrain 18 Baker
Lizzarik 19 Weapon Dealer
Sergra Darkthorn 34 Quest Giver
Kil'hala 25 Journeyman Tailor
Wrahk 18 Tailoring Supplies
Halija Whitestrider 19 Clothier
Tonga Runetotem 22 Quest
Kaltimah Stormcloud 23 Bags and Sacks
Mankrik 15 Quest
Thork 42 Quest
Devrak 55 Wind Rider Master
Hula'mahi 30 Reagents and Herbs
Korran 12 Quest
Uthrok 16 Bowyer and Gunsmith
Jahan Hawkwing 21 Leather & Mail Armor Merchant
Nargal Deatheye 35 Weaponsmith
Traugh 31 Expert Blacksmith
Sikwa 30 Stable Master
Barg 14 General Goods Vendor
Tari'Qa 14 Trade Supplies
Gazrog 25 Quest
Apothecary Helbrim 22 Quest
Tarban Hearthgrain 22 Baker
Grub 13 Quest Giver
Duhng 18 Cook
Kranal Fiss 15 Quest Giver

18 Orc Rampart
Lanti'gah 4
Regthar Deathgate 28 Quest
Kolkar Invader 16-17
Kolkar Storm Seer 15-16
Warlord Krom'zar 20

19 Central Barrens
Barrens Giraffe 15-16
Gazelle 2
Hecklefang Hyena 15-16
Lost Barrens Kodo 14-15
Ornery Plainstrider 16-17
Savannah Prowler 14-15
Sunscale Screecher 13-15
Zhevra Charger 17-18
Snort the Heckler 17

20 Honor's Stand
Ornery Plainstrider 16-17
Sunscale Scytheclaw 15-16
Zhevra Charger 17-18

21 The Forgotten Pools
Kolkar Stormer 13,14
Kolkar Wrangler 12,13
Barak Kodobane 16
Stonearm 15

22 Thorn Hill
Razormane Defender 12,13
Razormane Geomancer 12,13
Razormane Hunter 11,12
Razormane Mystic 13,14
Razormane Thornweaver 10,11
Razormane Water Seeker 10,11
Kreenig Snarlsnout 15
Elder Mystic Razorsnout 15 Elite

23 Far Watch Post
Ak'Zeloth 22 Quest
Kargal Battlescar 15 Quest
Uzzek 20 Quest

24 Kodo Bones
Savannah Huntress 11-12
Savannah Prowler 14-15
Echeyakee 16

25 Dreadmist Peak
Burning Blade Acolyte 11-12
Burning Blade Bruiser 10-11
Rathorian 15

26 The Mor'shan Rampart
Vrang Wildgore 48 Weaponsmith & Armorcrafter
Wenikee Boltbucket 19
Ornery Plainstrider 16-17
Savannah Patriarch 15-16
Sunscale Scytheclaw 15-16
Zhevra Charger 17-18

27 The Dry Hills
Witchwing Ambusher 17,18
Witchwing Harpy 14,15
Witchwing Roguefeather 15,16
Witchwing Slayer 16,17
Witchwing Windcaller 17,18
Sister Rathtalon 19 Elite

28 Northern Barrens
Barrens Giraffe 15,16
Fleeting Plainstrider 12,13
Hecklefang Hyena 15,16
Lost Barrens Kodo 14,15
Savannah Prowler 14,15
Sunscale Screecher 13,14,15
Zhevra Runner 13,14
Gazelle 2

29 Venture Company Operations
Taskmaster Fizzule 35 Elite Quest
Venture Co. Peon 13-14
Venture Co. Drudger 14-15
Tinkerer Sniggles 16

30 Sludge Fens
Venture Co. Mercenary 15-16
Venture Co. Drudger 14-15
Engineer Whirleygig 19
Foreman Grills" 19
Formeman Silixiz 25
Overseer Glibby 16
Grand Foreman Puzik Gallywix 26 Elite

31 Northern Plain
Ornery Plainstrider 16-17
Sunscale Scytheclaw 15-16
Zhevra Charger 17-18
Takk the Leaper 19 Elite

32 Boulder Lode Mine
Venture Co. Enforcer 16-17
Venture Co. Overseer 17-18
Boss Copperplug 19

33 Southfury River
Dreadmaw Crocolisk 9-11

Blasted Lands

The Dark Portal sits here, ominous in its presence and guarded for unknown purposes. Ogres, cultists, and warped beasts walk through the Blasted Lands almost unchecked, save for an Alliance stronghold, Nethergarde Keep. Though well stocked with people and provisions, this outpost of Humans and their allies is scarcely enough to hold back the tide of danger from the rest of the southern lands. Who can say what would happen if enough Warlocks gathered at the portal one day?

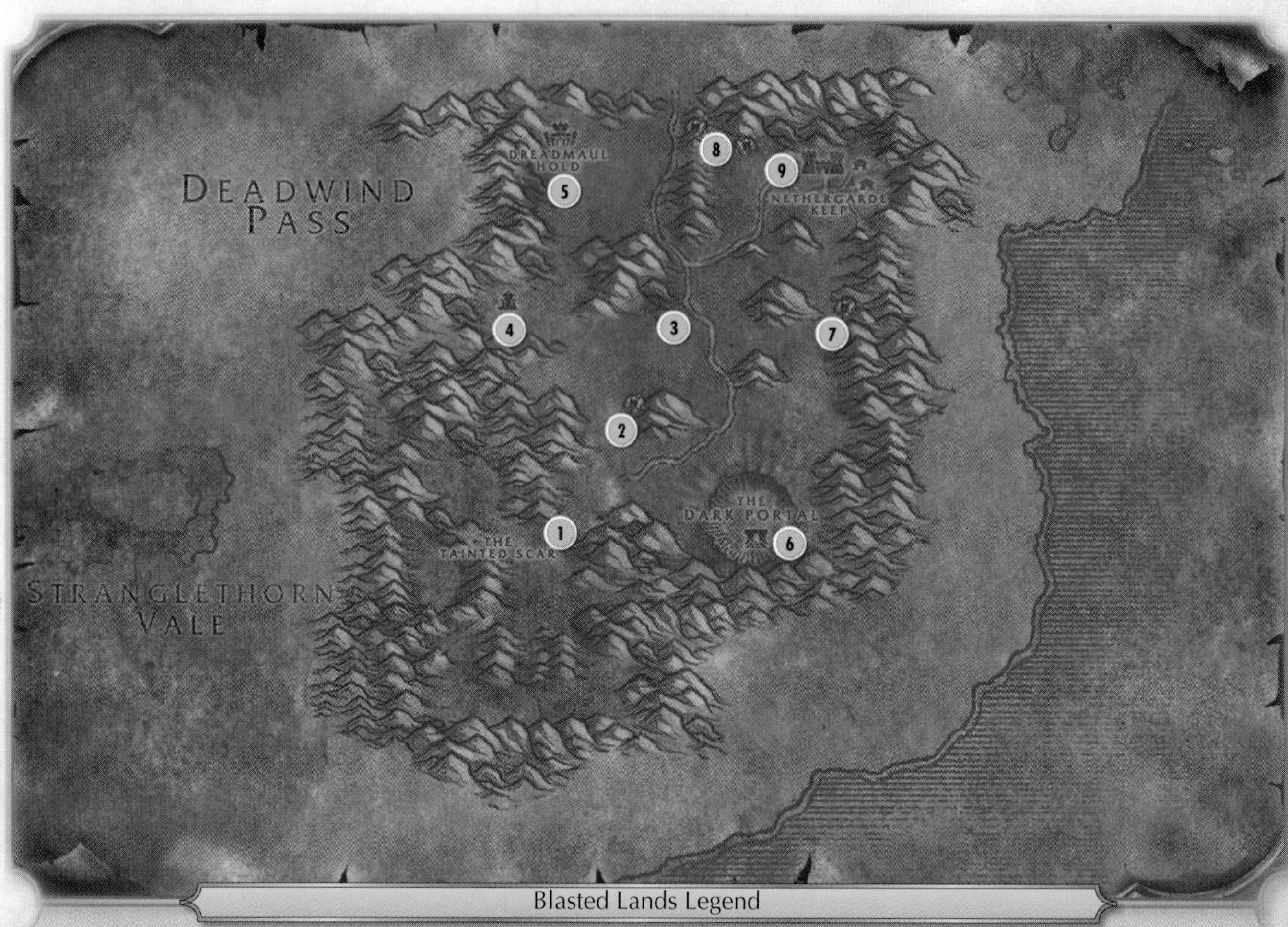

Blasted Lands Legend

1 The Tainted Scar
- Felguard Elite 60
- Doomguard Commander 61
- Manahound 60
- Lord Kazzak

2 Dreadmaul Post
- Dreadmaul Mauler 53-54
- Dreadmaul Warlock 53-54
- Servant of Grol 53-54

3 Rise of the Defiler/ Central Blasted Lands
- Kum'isha the Collector Quest
- Black Slayer 47-48
- Felbeast 50-51
- Hellboar 52-53
- Portal Seeker 52-53
- Redstone Basilisk 47-48
- Redstone Crystalhide 50-51
- Scorpok Stinger 51
- Starving Snickerfang 46

4 Altar of Storms
- Lady Sevine 59 Elite
- Servant of Sevine 56
- Shadowsworn Dreadweaver 53-55
- Shadowsworn Enforcer 54
- Shadowsworn Warlock 53-55

5 Dreadmaul Hold
- Dreadmaul Brute 46-47
- Dreadmaul Ogre Mage 46-47
- Grol the Destroyer 58 Quest Target
- Scorpok Stinger 50-51
- Servant of Grol 53
- Starving Snickerfang 45-46
- Wretched Lost One 46

6 The Dark Portal
- Felguard Elite 60 Elite
- Felguard Sentry 55
- Felhound 55
- Hellboar 52-53
- Manahound 60 Elite
- Redstone Crystalhide 51
- Scorpok Stinger 50-51
- Servant of Razelikh 57
- Razelikh the Defiler 60

7 Serpent's Coil
- Ashmane Boar 47-49
- Black Slayer 48
- Redstone Basilisk 47-48
- Servant of Allistarj 54
- Shadowsworn Adept 52-53
- Shadowsworn Cultist 52
- Shadowsworn Thug 52-53

8 Nethergarde Armory
- Nethergarde Engineer 47-48
- Nethergarde Forman 46-48
- Nethergarde Miner 47-48

9 Nethergarde Keep
- Alexandra Constantine 55 Elite Gryphon Master
- Ambassador Ardalan 55 Quest
- Enohar Thunderbrew 50 Quest
- Watcher Mahar Ba 45
- Nethergarde Analyst 50
- Nethergarde Cleric 49-51
- Nethergarde Elite 55 Elite
- Nethergarde Officer 50
- Nethergarde Riftwatcher 49-51
- Nethergarde Soldier 49-51
- Quartermaster Lungertz 54

Burning Steppes

The Burning Steppes are more dangerous than almost any realm in the east, save perhaps for the Plaguelands, where the Scourge is located. In the Burning Steppes, massive Drakes, Whelps, and Dragonkin thrive in the heat, ash, and shadow of Blackrock Mountain, and other great mountains that line the area's perimeter. Passage into the Steppes is mainly possible through the road up from Lakeshire, in Redridge, but the creatures are so terrible in this land that few dare to approach.

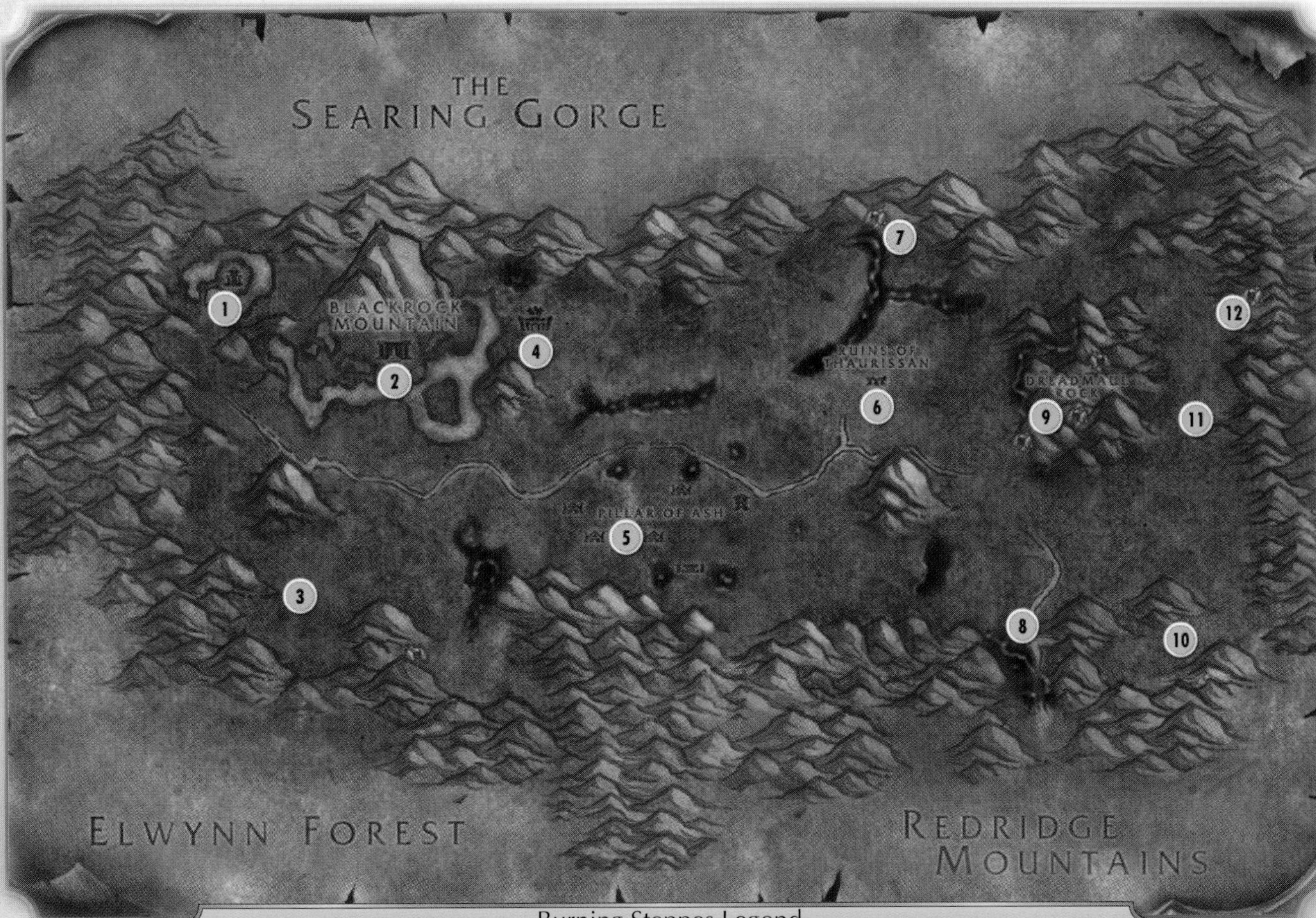

Burning Steppes Legend

1. **Altar of Storms**
   - Blackrock Warlock 55-57
2. **Blackrock Mountain**
   - Black Wyrmkin 51-54
3. **Draco'dar**
   - Firetail Scorpid 56-57
   - Flamescale Broodling 55-56
   - Flamescale Dragonspawn 56-57 Elite
   - Flamescale Wyrmkin 57-58 Elite
   - Giant Ember Worg 55-56
   - Scalding Broodling 51-54
   - Scalding Drake 52-55 Elite
   - Searscale Drake 55-58 Elite
4. **Blackrock Stronghold**
   - Grark Lorkrub 56 Elite Quest
   - Blackrock Slayer 54-57
   - Blackrock Soldier 53-56
   - Blackrock Sorcerer 53-56
   - Blackrock Warlock 55-57
5. **Pillar of Ash**
   - Blackrock Slayer 54-57
   - Blackrock Soldier 53-56
   - Blackrock Sorcerer 53-56
   - Blackrock Warlock 55–57
   - Deathlash Scorpid 53-55
   - Flamekin Rager 54-56
   - Flamekin Spitter 50-53
   - Flamekin Sprite 51-53
   - Flamekin Torcher 54-56
   - Greater Obsidian Elemental 55-57
   - Obsidian Elemental 50-53
   - Slavering Ember Worg 53-54
6. **Ruins of Thaurissan**
   - Black Broodling 48-52
   - Black Dragonspawn 50-53 Elite
   - Black Drake 48-52 Elite
   - Black Wyrmkin 51-54 Elite
   - Flamekin Rager 54-56
   - Flamekin Spitter 50-53
   - Flamekin Sprite 51-53
   - Flamekin Torcher 54-56
   - Greater Obsidian Elemental 55-57
   - Obsidian Elemental 50-53
   - Thaurisan Agent 54-55
   - Thaurisan Firewalker 53-55
   - Thaurisan Spy 53-54
   - War Reaver 53-55
7. **Flame Crest**
   - Kibler 56 Quest
   - Mathredis Firestar 60 Quest
   - Maxwort Umberglint 42 Quest
   - Ragged Jon 57 Quest
   - Tinkee Steamboil 53 Quest
   - Yuka Screwspigot 53 Quest
   - Deathlash Scorpid 53-55
8. **Blackrock Pass**
   - Venomtip Scorpid 50-53
9. **Dreadmaul Rock**
   - Remains of Sha'ni Proudtusks Quest
   - Firegut Brute 50-53
   - Firegut Ogre Mage 48-52
   - Firegut Ogre 48-51
10. **Morgan's Vigil**
    - Helendis Riverhorn 55 Quest
    - Marshal Maxwell 55 Quest
    - Mayara Brightwing 55 Quest
    - Oralius 55 Quest
11. **Terror Wing Path**
    - Ember Worg 49-52
    - Venomtip Scorpid 50-53
12. **Slither Rock**
    - Cyrus Therepantous 52 Quest
    - Flamescale Wyrmkin 57-58 Elite

Darkshore

Darkshore is the first port of call for Night Elves leaving their beloved Darnassus behind. This zone can easily support those characters wishing to create a home until they gain a bit of experience. As a zone on the sea, it has many beaches and the perils to go with them. While it's not as large a metropolis as Stormwind or Ironforge, Auberdine does a good job of supporting the adventurers and boasts a fine dock in which ships ferry travelers into more dangerous territories.

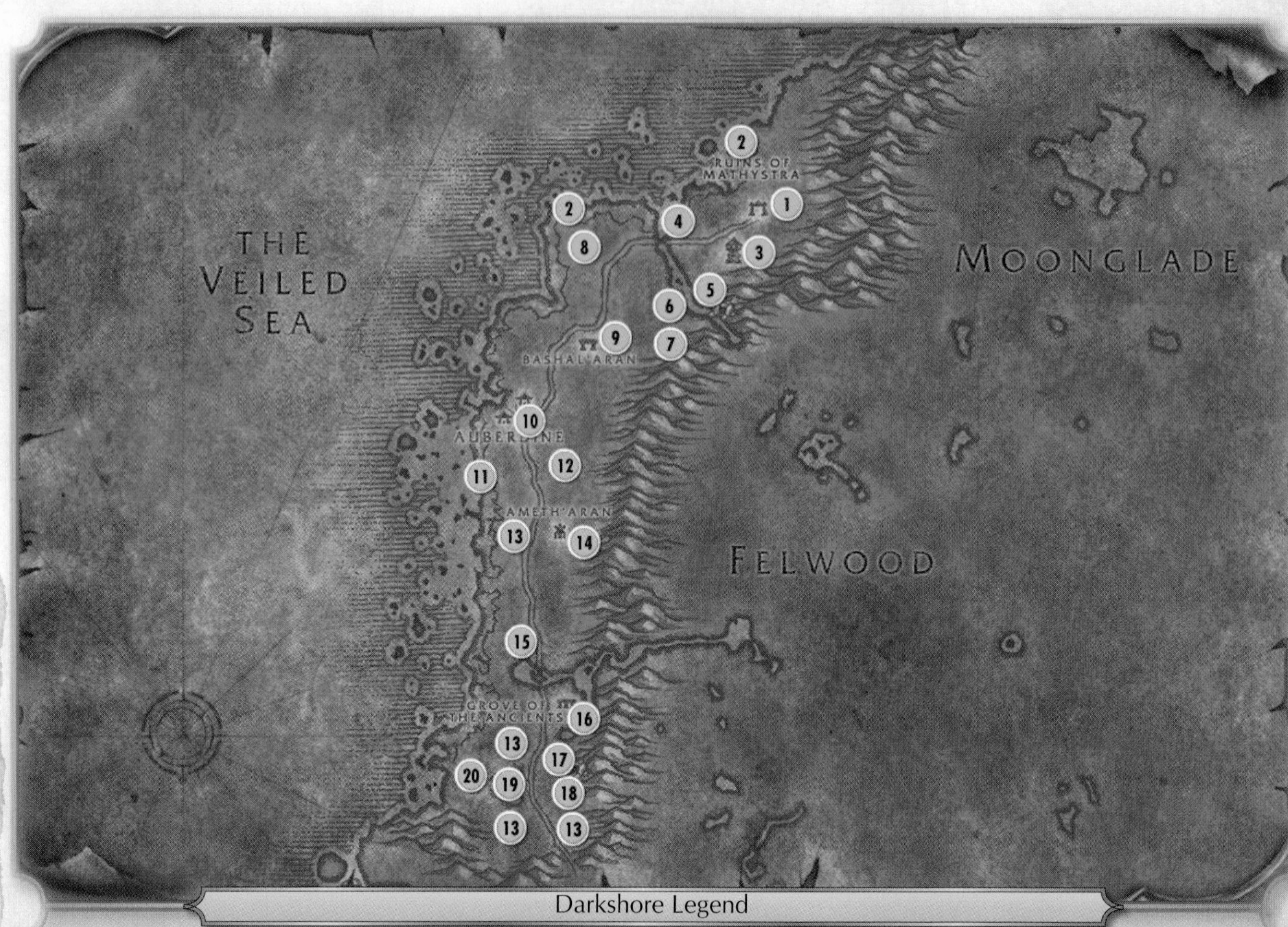

Darkshore Legend

1 Ruins of Mathystra
Giant Forestrider 17-19
Moonstalker Matriarch 19-20
Moonstalker Sire 18-19
Moonstalker Runt 16 Moonstalker Matriarch's Minion
Stormscale Myrmidon 18-19
Stormscale Sorceress 19-20
Stormscale Warrior 20-21

2 Mysts Edge
Gelkak Gyromist 18 Quest
Raging Reef Crawler 20-21
Greymist Tidehunter 19
Greymist Oracle 18-19
Elder Darkshore Thresher 16-17

3 Tower of Althalaxx
Dark Strand Fanatic 16-17
Delmanis the Hated 17
Dark Strand Voidcaller 28-29
Dark Strand Voidcaller's Minion 28-29
Balthule Shadowstrike 15

4 Cliffspring River
Encrusted Tide Crawler 18-20
Reef Crawler 15-17
Moonstalker 14-15
Rabid Thistle Bear 13-15
Forestrider 14-16

5 Cliffspring Falls
Stormscale Wave Rider 15-16
Stormscale Siren 16-17

6 Blackwood Village
Blackwood Warrior 16-17
Blackwood Totemic 18

7 Thistle Bear Den
Thistle Cub 10
Den Mother 18

8 Darkshore General
Thistle Bear 11-12
Rabid Thistle Bear 13-14
Moonstalker Runt 10-11
Moonstalker 14-15
Forestrider Fledgling 11-13

9 Bashal'Aran
Asterion 15 Quest
Vile Sprite 10-11
Wild Grell 11-12
Deth'ryll Satyr 12-13

10 Auberdine
Auberdine Sentinel 40
Tharnarian Treetender 18 Quest
Terenthis 15 Quest
Grimclaw 13 Quest
Sentinel Elissa Starbreeze 20 Quest
Gershala Nightwhisper 20 Quest
Thelgrum Stonehammer 30 Mining Supplier
Jenna Lemkenilli 26 Journeyman Engineer
Kurdram Stonehammer 35 Mining Trainer
Delfrum Flintbeard 25 Journeyman Blacksmith
Elisa Steelhand 30 Blacksmithing Supplier
Gorbold Steelhand 30 General Trade Supplier
Valdaron 14 Tailoring Supplies
Grondal Moonbreeze 29 Journeyman Tailor
Shaldyn 15 Clothier
Alanndarian 22
Dalmond 17 General Goods
Naram Longclaw 20 Weaponsmith
Thundris Windreaver 15
Mavralyn 18 Leather Armor and Leatherworking Supplies
Harlon Thornguard 25 Armorer & Shieldsmith
Archeologist Hollee 12 Explorer's League Quest
Sentinel Glynda Nal'Shea 45 Quest
Barithras Moonshade 14 Quest
Allyndia 15 Grocer
Taldan 16 Drink Vendor
Innkeeper Shaussiy 30 Innkeeper
Kyndri 13 Baker
Laird 14 Fish Vendor
Wizbang Cranktoggle 15 Quest
Cerellean Whiteclaw 15 Quest
Boats to Teldrassil and Menethil
Gwennyth Bly'Leggonde 21
Caylais Moonfeather 55 Elite Hippogryph Master
Yolda 51
Joelysa 30 Stable Master
Gubber Blump 15 Quest

11 The Long Wash
Pygmy Tide Crawler 9-10
Greymist Raider 11-12
Greymist Coast Runner 12-13
Young Reef Crawler 10-11
Darkshore Thresher 13

12 Moonkin Cave
Moonkin 12-13
Young Moonkin 11-12

13 Twilight Vale
Blackwood Windtalker 13-14
Blackwood Pathfinder 12-13
Moonstalker 14-15
Rabid Thistle Bear 13-14
Grizzled Thistle Bear 16-17
Foreststrider 15
Blackwood Warrior 16-17
Blackwood Totemic 17-18
Giant Foreststrider 17-19
Moonstalker Sire 18-19
Moonstalker Matriarch 19-20
Moonstalker Runt 16 Moonstalker Matriarch's Minion

14 Ameth'Aran
Anaya Dawnrunner 16 Quest
Cursed Highborn 10-11
Writhing Highborn 11-12
Wailing Highborn 12-13

15 Wildbend River

16 Grove of the Ancients
Onu 55 Ancient of Lore Quest
Tiyana 15 Grocer
Ullana 15 Trade Supplies

17 Grimclaw 13 Quest

18 Blackwood Den
Blackwood Ursa 18-19
Blackwood Shaman 19-20

19 The Master's Glaive
Twilight Disciple 16-17
Twilight Thug 17-18

20 Remtravel's Excavation
Prospector Remtravel 16 Explorer's League Quest
Cracked Golem 18-19
Sentinel Aynasha 20 Quest

Desolace

Appropriately named, Desolace is a land where there is little growth, joy, or hope. In the south, demons move about the hills, poisoning the territory and attacking anything that comes near. (They are thankfully lacking in greater demons or leadership.) Because the territory is so poorly held by any concentrated force, the Horde and Alliance both have a foothold here, with the Alliance in the north and the Horde farther down. Warring Centaur tribes stay of opposite sides of the lower central areas, east and west. It is possible to join with one of these and turn the tides against the other, improving relations with the first. In a land so unrelenting, perhaps war is the only means of survival.

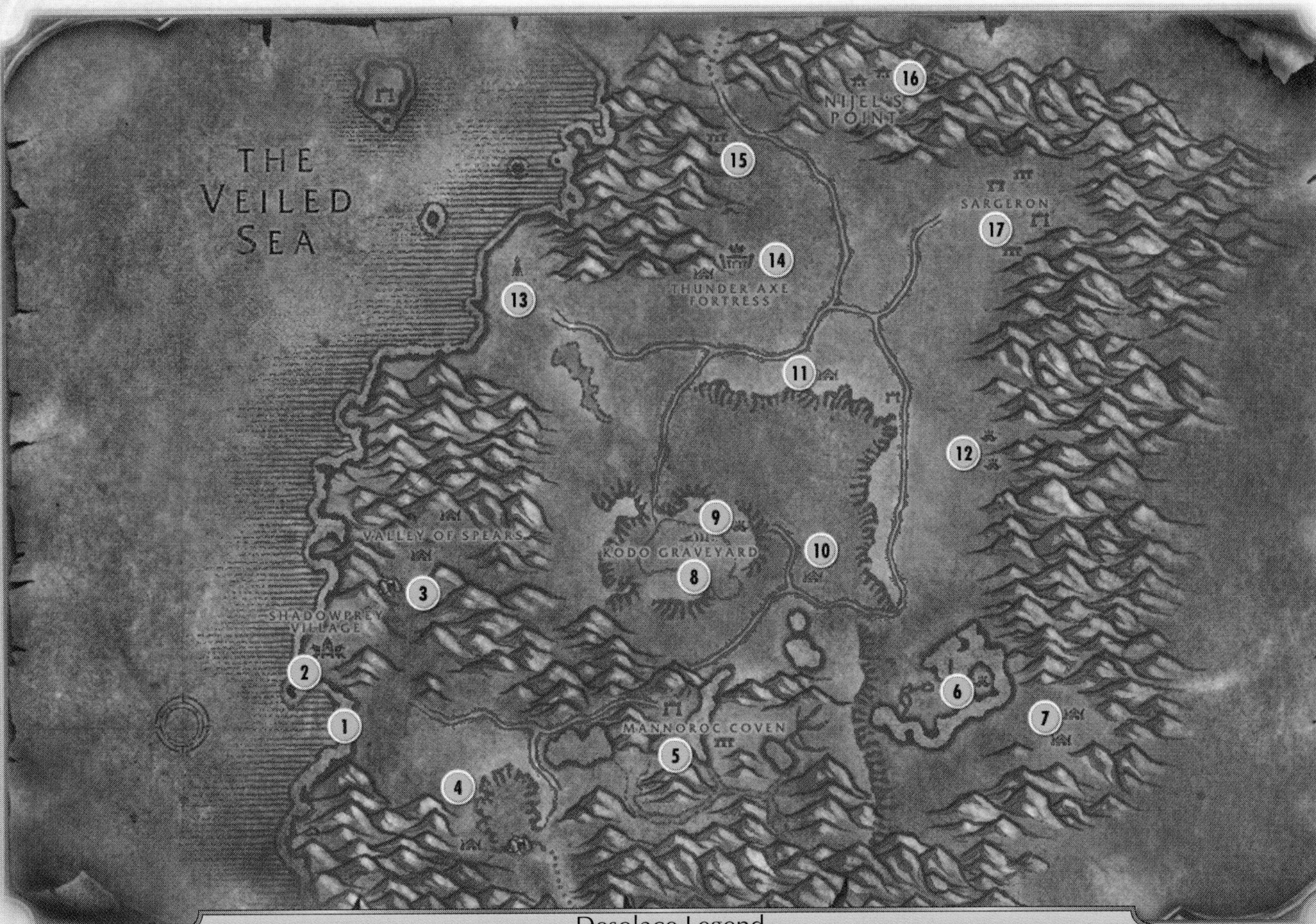

Desolace Legend

1 Sar'theris Strand
Drysnap Crawler 33-34
Drysnap Pincer 34-35
Elder Thunder Lizard 34-38
Dread Ripper 37-40
Scorpashi Lasher 34-35
Scorpashi Snapper 30-32

2 Shadowsprey Village
Thalon 55+ Wind Rider Master
Jinar'Zillen 40 Quest
Roon Wildmane 45 Quest
Inkeeper Sikewa 30 Innkeeper
Aboda 30 Stable Master
Taiga Wiseman 60 Quest

3 Valley of Spears
Maraudine Bonepaw 37-38+
Maraudine Khan Advisor 38-39+
Maraudine Khan Guard 39-40+
Maraudine Marauder 39-40+
Maraudine Mauler 38-39+
Maraudine Pack Runner 39+
Maraudine Scout 37-38
Maraudine Windchaser 38-39
Maraudine Wrangler 37-38

4 Gelkis Village
Gelkis Earthcaller 34-35
Gelkis Marauder 35-36
Gelkis Mauler 35-36
Gelkis Outrunner 32-33
Gelkis Scout 32-33
Gelkis Stamper 33-34
Gelkis Windchaser 33-34
Dread Ripper 37-40
Elder Thunder Lizard 34-38

5 Mannoroc Coven
Scorpashi Lasher 34-35
Scorpashi Snapper 30-32
Elder Thunder Lizard 34-38
Ley Hunter 39-40
Doomwarder 37-38
Doomwarder Captain 38-39
Doomwarder Lord 39-40
Lesser Infernal 36-37
Nether Maiden 37-38
Mage Hunter 38-39

6 Magram Village
Warug 44 Quest
Magram Bonepaw 37-38
Magram Marauder 35-36
Elder Thunder Lizard 34-38
Dread Ripper 37-40
Whirlwind Shredder 32-34

7 Shadowbreak Ravine
Burning Blade Invoker 40
Burning Blade Summoner 38-39
Ley Hunter 40
Imp Minion 38-39
Burning Blade Nightmare 40

8 Kodo Graveyard
Aged Kodo 33-35
Ancient Kodo 37-38
Dying Kodo 37
Carrion Horror 35-38

9 Ghost Walker Post
Gurda Wildmane 35 Quest
Felgur Twocuts 44 Quest
Superior Macecrafter 40
Nataka Longhorn 40 Quest
Narv Hidecrafter 42 Expert Leathercrafter
Takata Steelblade 40 Quest
Maurin Bonesplitter 35 Quest
Harnor 40 Food & Drink
Kireena 41 Trade Goods
Ghost Walker Brave 50

10 Scrabblescrews Camp
Smeed Scrabblescrews 45
Gizelton Caravan Kodo 35
Tamed Kodo 34-35

11 Kormek's Hut
Bibbly F'utzbuckle 45 Quest
Cork Gizelton 38 Quest
Rigger Gizelton 36 Quest
Gizelton Caravan Kodo 35
Hulking Gritjaw Basilisk 37-38
Elder Thunder Lizard 34-38
Bonepaw Hyena 30-32
Whirlwind Stormwalker 36-38
Dread Flyer 34-38
Scorpashi Lasher 34-35
Scorpashi Snapper 30-32

12 Kolkar Village
Elder Thunder Lizard 34-38
Raging Thunder Lizard 31-34
Dread Swoop 31-33
Kolkar Battle Lord 32-33
Kolkar Centaur 30-31
Kolkar Destroyer 32-33
Kolkar Mauler 31-32
Kolkar Scout 30-31
Kolkar Windchaser 31-32

13 Ethel Rethor
Azore Aldamort 60 Quest
Scorpashi Lasher 34-35
Scorpashi Snapper 30-32
Hulking Gritjaw Basilisk 37-38
Whirlwind Stormwalker 35-37
Whirlwind Ripper 32-34
Dread Swoop 30-33
Slitherblade Myrmidon 34-35
Slitherblade Naga 32-33
Slitherblade Oracle 34-35
Slitherblade Razortail 35-36
Slitherblade Sea Witch 35-36
Slitherblade Tidehunter 36-37
Slitherblade Warrior 33-34

14 Thunder Axe Fortress
Burning Blade Adept 31-32
Burning Blade Augur 30-31
Burning Blade Felsworn 31-32
Burning Blade Invoker 38-39
Burning Blade Reaver 30-31
Burning Blade Shadowmage 32-33
Burning Blade Summoner 38-39

15 Tethris Aran
Gritjaw Basilisk 32
Dread Swoop 32-33
Scorpashi Snapper 30-31

16 Nijel's Point
Vahlarriel Demonslayer 37 Quest
Corporal Melkins 39
Captain Pentigast 42
Kreldig Ungar 35 Reclaimers Inc. Quest
Innkeeper Lyshaera 30 Innkeeper
Janet Hommers 40 Food & Drink
Shelgrayn 30 Stable Master
Baritanas Skyriver 55 Hyppogryph Master
Nijel's Point Guard 45

17 Sargeron
Hatefury Betrayer 32-33
Hatefury Felsworn 30-32
Hatefury Hellcaller 31-33
Hatefury Rogue 30-32
Hatefury Shadowstalker 32-33
Hatefury Trickster 31-32

Dun Morogh

Dun Morogh rests in the highlands between the Wetlands and the Searing Gorge. Blocked from reaching either because of the impassable cliffs of stone and ice that surround it, Dun Morogh is only traversable over land via the route through Loch Modan. This is the home of the dwarven capitol, Ironforge. Though Wolves, Troggs, and a small pocket of resistance from Dark Iron Dwarves are found here, few greater threats exist. The most dangerous part of Dun Morogh is located in the north-west, where the Gnome capitol of Gnomeregan once bustled with activity. A failed experiment in weaponry has altered the capitol into a nightmare of disease and poison, avoided by many.

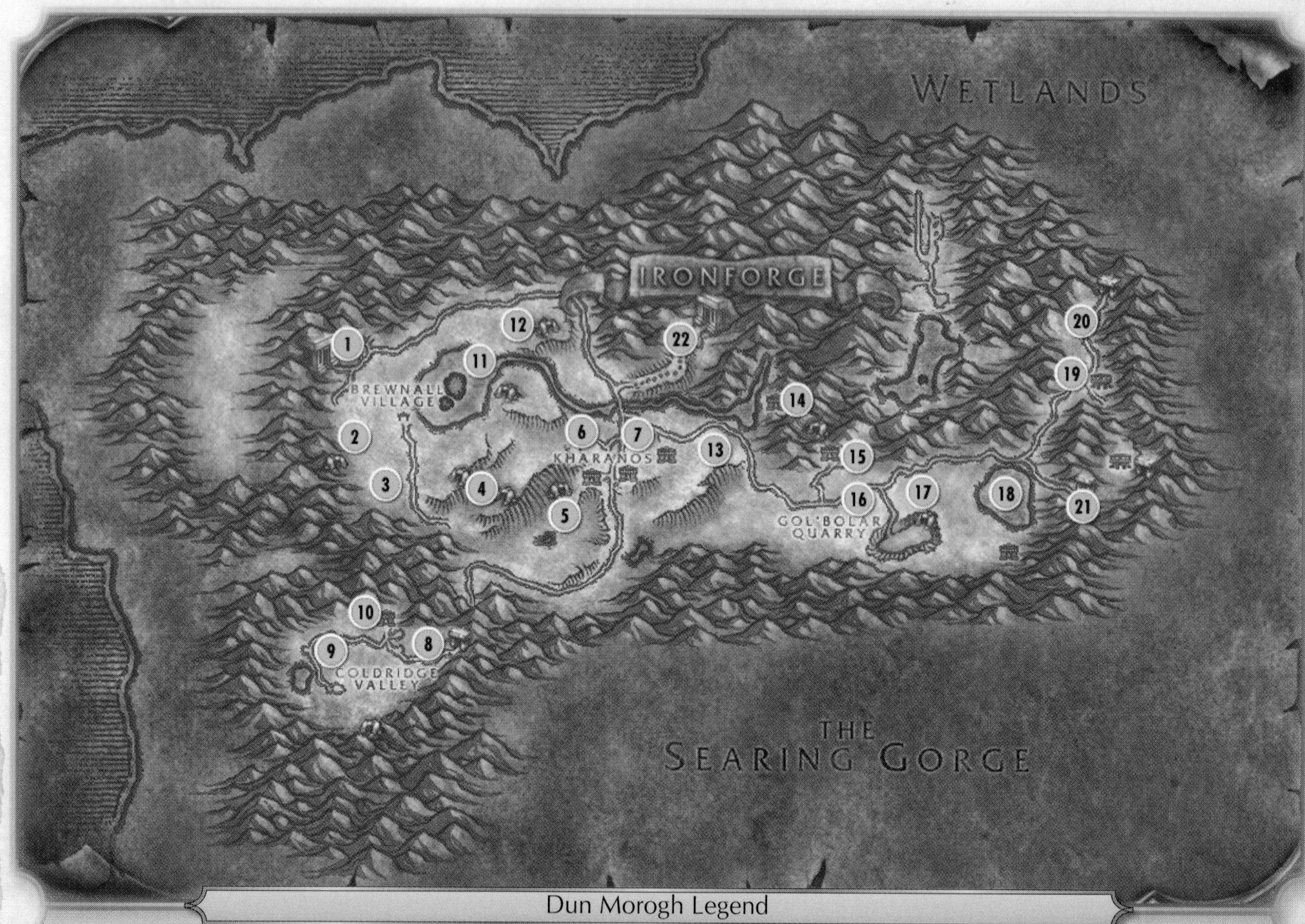

Dun Morogh Legend

1 Gnomeregan
- Entrance to Gnomeregan Instance
- Elder Crag Boars 7-8
- Ice Claw Bear 7-8
- Leper Gnome 8-10
- Snow Leopard 7-8

2 Frostmane Hold
- Elder Crag Boars 7-8
- Frostmane Headhunter 8-9
- Frostmane Snowstrider 8-9
- Frostmane Troll 7-8
- Ice Claw Bear 7-8
- Snow Leopard 7-8

3 Southwestern Dun Morogh
- Crag Boar 5-6
- Juvenile Snow Leopard 5-6
- Young Black Bear 5-6

4 Chill Breeze Valley
- Tundra MacGrann 20 Quest
- Large Crag Boar 6-7
- Old Icebeard 11+

5 The Grizzled Den
- Wendigo 6-7
- Young Wendigo 5

6 Kharanos
- Golorn Frostbeard 10 Vendor
- Gremlock Pilsnor 10 Cook
- Innkeeper Belm 30 Innkeeper
- Jarven Thunderbrew 15 Quest
- Ozzie Togglevolt 10 Quest
- Ragnar Thunderbrew 30 Quest
- Razzle Sprysprocket 20 Quest
- Senir Whitebeard 12 Quest
- Shelby Stoneflint 30 Stable Master
- Thammer Pol 11 Physician
- Tharek Blackstone 12 Quest
- Tognus Flintfire 30 Blacksmith

7 Steelgrill's Depot
- Beldin Steelgrill 12 Quest
- Bronk Guzzlegear 24 Engineer
- Milli Featherwhistle 50 Mechanostrider Merchant
- Pilot Bellowfiz 18 Quest
- Pilot Stonegear 20 Quest
- Yarr Hammerstone 10 Miner

8 Coldridge Pass
- Rockjaw Raider 3-4

9 Coldridge Valley
- Grelin Whitebeard 5 Quest
- Talin Keeneye 5 Quest
- Burly Rockjaw Trogg 2
- Frostmane Novice 3-4
- Frostmane Troll Whelps 3-4
- Grik'nir the Cold 5 Quest Target
- Ragged Young Wolf 1-2
- Rockjaw Troggs 1-2
- Small Crag Boar 3

10 Anvilmar
- Adlin Pridedrift 5 Quest
- Felix Whindlebolt 2 Quest
- Sten Stoutarm 5 Quest

11 Iceflow Lake
- Elder Crag Boars 7-8
- Ice Claw Bear 7-8
- Snow Leopard 7-8

12 Shimmer Ridge
- Frostmane Headhunter 8-9
- Frostmane Seer 8
- Frostmane Snowstrider 8-9
- Frostmane Troll 7-8

13 Eastern Dun Morogh
- Elder Crag Boar 7-8
- Snow Tracker Wolf 6-7

14 Misty Pine Refuge
- Father Gavin 15 Argent Dawn

15 Amberstill Ranch
- Rudra Amberstill 10 Quest
- Turuk Amberstill 10 Vendor
- Vagash 12+ Quest Target

16 Gol'Bolar Quarry and Mine
- Foreman Stonebrow 12 Quest
- Senator Mehr Stonehallow 50 Quest
- Rockjaw Bonesnapper 8-9
- Rockjaw Skullthumper 8-9

17 Far Eastern Dun Morogh
- Elder Crag Boars 8-9
- Rockjaw Ambusher 9-10
- Scarred Crag Boar 9-10

18 Helm's Bed Lake
- Captain Beld 11 Quest Target
- Dark Iron Spy 9-10
- Rockjaw Backbreaker 11-12
- Rockjaw Bonesnapper 8-9
- Scarred Crag Boar 9-10

19 North Gate Pass
- Elder Crag Boars 8-9
- Ice Claw Bears 8-9
- Scarred Crag Boar 9-10

20 North Gate Outpost
- Pilot Hammerfoot 17 Quest
- Snow Leopard 8
- Mangeclaw 11 Quest Target

21 South Gate Outpost

22 Ironforge

Durotar

Some of Azeroth's Orcs and Trolls call Durotar their home. The Valley of Trials begins to temper the characters with its rugged and demanding landscape. Sen'jin is to the south and Razor Hill lies to the north. Orgrimmar, the capitol city of the Orcs, is at the exteme northern edge of the region. A new dungeon was recently discovered within Orgrimmar itself and adventurers trying to prove themselves often venture there before even leaving Durotar for far off lands.

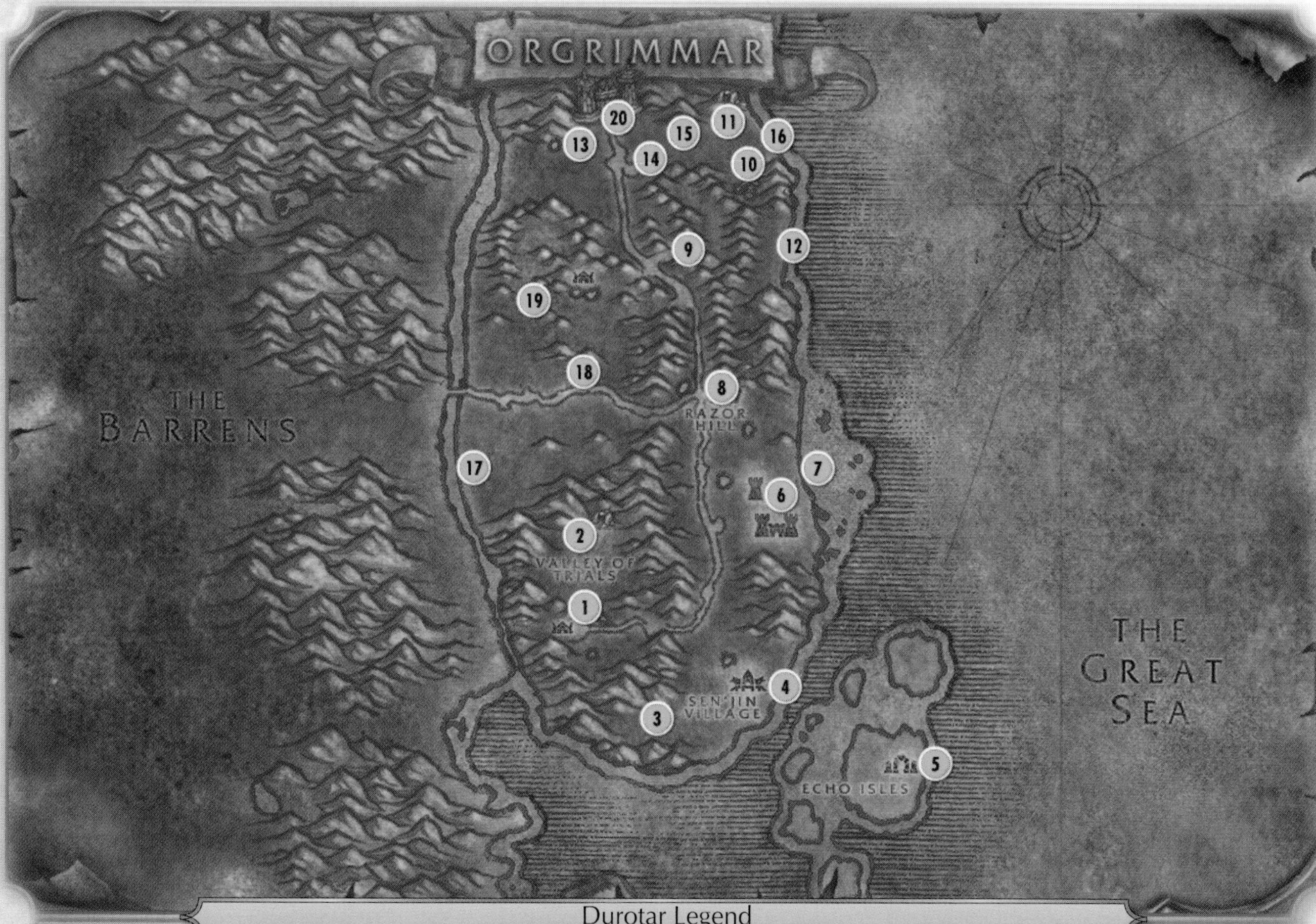

Durotar Legend

1 The Valley of Trials
- Kzan Thornslash 34 Weaponsmith
- Rarc 10 Armorer & Shieldcrafter
- Huklah 11 Cloth & Leather Armor
- Rwag 8 Rogue Trainer
- Gornek 5 Quest
- Den Grunt 75
- Ken'Jai 10 Priest Trainer
- Shikrik 10 Shaman Trainer
- Canaga Earthcaller 8 Quest
- Mai'ah 10 Mage Trainer
- Ruzan 10 Quest
- Zureetha Fargaze 12 Quest
- Jen'shan 8 Hunter Trainer
- Frang 11 Warrior Trainer
- Magga 5
- Duokna 10 General Goods
- Zlagk 9 Butcher
- Galgar 8
- Kaltunk 20
- Mottled Boar 1-2
- Sarkoth 4
- Scorpid Worker 3
- Vile Familiar 3-4
- Felstalker 3-4

2 Burning Blade Cove
- Yarrog Baneshadow 5
- Vile Familiar 3-4
- Felstalker 3-4

3 Kolkar Crag
- Kolkar Drudge 6-7
- Kolkar Outrunner 7-8

4 Sen'jin Village/ Darkspear Strand
- Ukor 4 Quest
- Sen'jin Watcher 25-30
- Miao'zan 25 Journeyman Alchemist
- Hai'zan 14 Butcher
- Vel'rin Fang 7 Quest
- Master Vornal 11 Quest
- Master Gadrin 12
- K'waii 11 General Goods
- Tai'tasi 12 Trade Supplies
- Xur'gyl 40 Axe Trainer
- Trayexir 40 Bow Trainer
- Zansoa 14 Fishing Supplies
- Xar'Ti 50 Raptor Rider Trainer
- Zjolnir 45 Raptor handler
- Un'Thuwa 14 Mage Trainer
- Bom'bay 8 Witch Doctor in Training
- Mishiki 14 Herbalist
- Clattering Scorpid 5-6
- Dire Mottled Boar 6-7
- Pygmy Surf Crawler 5-8
- Makura Clacker 6-7
- Makura Shellhide 6-7

5 Echo Isles
- Zalazane 10
- Durotar Tiger 5-8
- Bloodtalon Taillasher 6-8
- Makrura Clacker 5-8
- Surf Crawler 7-8
- Hexed Troll 8-9
- Voodoo Troll 8-9

6 Tiragarde Keep
- Lieutenant Benedict 8
- Kul Tiras Marine 6-7
- Kul Tiras Sailor 5-6

7 Scuttle Coast
- Pygmy Surf Crawler 5-6
- Makura Clacker 6-7
- Makura Shellhide 6-7

8 Razor Hill
- Razor Hill Grunt 28-32
- Orgnil Soulscar 18 Quest
- Thotar 16 Hunter Trainer
- Gar'Thok 10 Quest
- Kaplak 14 Rogue Trainer
- Takrin Pathseeker 30 Quest
- Grimtak 14 Butcher
- Cook Torka 6 Quest
- Showja'my 30 Stable Master
- Innkeeper Grosk 30 Innkeeper
- Yelnagi Blackarm 16
- Wuark 16 Armorer & Shieldcrafter
- Krunn 16 Miner
- Dwukk 27 Journeyman Blacksmith
- Uhgar 15 Weaponsmith
- Ghrawt 13 Bowyer
- Cutac 14 Cloth & Leather Armor Merchant
- Dhugru Gorelust 37 Warlock Trainer
- Ophek 10
- Kitha 17 Demon Trainer
- Voidwalker 17 Kitha's Minion
- Flakk 15 Trade Supplies
- Rawrk 15 First Aid Trainer
- Jark 14 General Goods
- Swart 15 Shaman Trainer
- Tai'jin 18 Priest Trainer
- Tarshaw Jaggedscar 43 Warrior Trainer
- Furl Scornbrow 6 Quest

9 Drygulch Ravine
- Dustwind Harpy 7-8
- Dustwind Pillager 7-8
- Dustwind Savage 9-10
- Dustwind Storm Witch 10-11

10 Margoz' Camp
- Margoz 18 Quest

11 Skull Rock
- Gazz'uz 14
- Burning Blade Thug 8-9
- Burning Blade Apprentice 10-11
- Rezlak 5 Tinker's Union

12 Dead Eye Shore
- Makrura Snapclaw 8-9
- Encrusted Surf Crawler 7-10
- Corrupted Surf Crawler 10-11
- Elder Mottled Boar 8-9
- Venomtail Scorpid 9-10
- Bloodtalon Scythemaw 8

13 Rocktusk Farm
- Swine 3
- Elder Mottled Boar 8-9
- Venomtail Scorpid 9-10
- Bloodtalon Scythemaw 8

14 Jaggedswine Farm
- Swine 3
- Elder Mottled Boar 8-9
- Venomtail Scorpid 9-10
- Bloodtalon Scythemaw 8-10

15 Zeppelin to Grom'gol Base camp and Undercity

16 Bladefist Bay
- Makrura Snapclaw 8-9
- Encrusted Surf Crawler 7-10
- Corrupted Surf Crawler 10-11
- Elder Mottled Boar 8-9
- Venomtail Scorpid 9-10
- Bloodtalon Scythemaw 8

17 Southfury River
- Bloodtalon Scythemaw 8-10
- Bloodtalon Taillasher 5-10
- Armored Scorpid 8-10
- Corrupted Bloodtalon Scythemaw 10-11
- Dreadmaw Crockilisk 9-11
- Elder Mottled Boar 8-9
- Misha Tor'kren 5 Quest

18 Razormane Grounds
- Dire Mottled Boar 6-7
- Razormane Dustrunner 8-9
- Razormane Battleguard 9-10
- Razormane Scout 7-8
- Razormane Quillboar 6-7
- Bloodtalon Taillasher 6-8
- Armored Scorpid 7

19 Thunder Ridge
- Fizzle Darkstorm 12
- Voidwalker Minion 10
- Lightning Hide 10-11
- Thunder Lizard 9-10
- Burning Blade Apprentice 10-11
- Burning Blade Fanatic 9-10

20 Orgimmar

Duskwood

Duskwood has become quiet; the silent dead now wander through this once tranquil forest, slaying the living and threatening to overwhelm the town of Darkshire. People of that town speak of Raven Hill, a western town whose people have all but disappeared. And through it all, a force of great power wanders the road to Darkshire, calling to the people of Duskwood, "I hunger!"

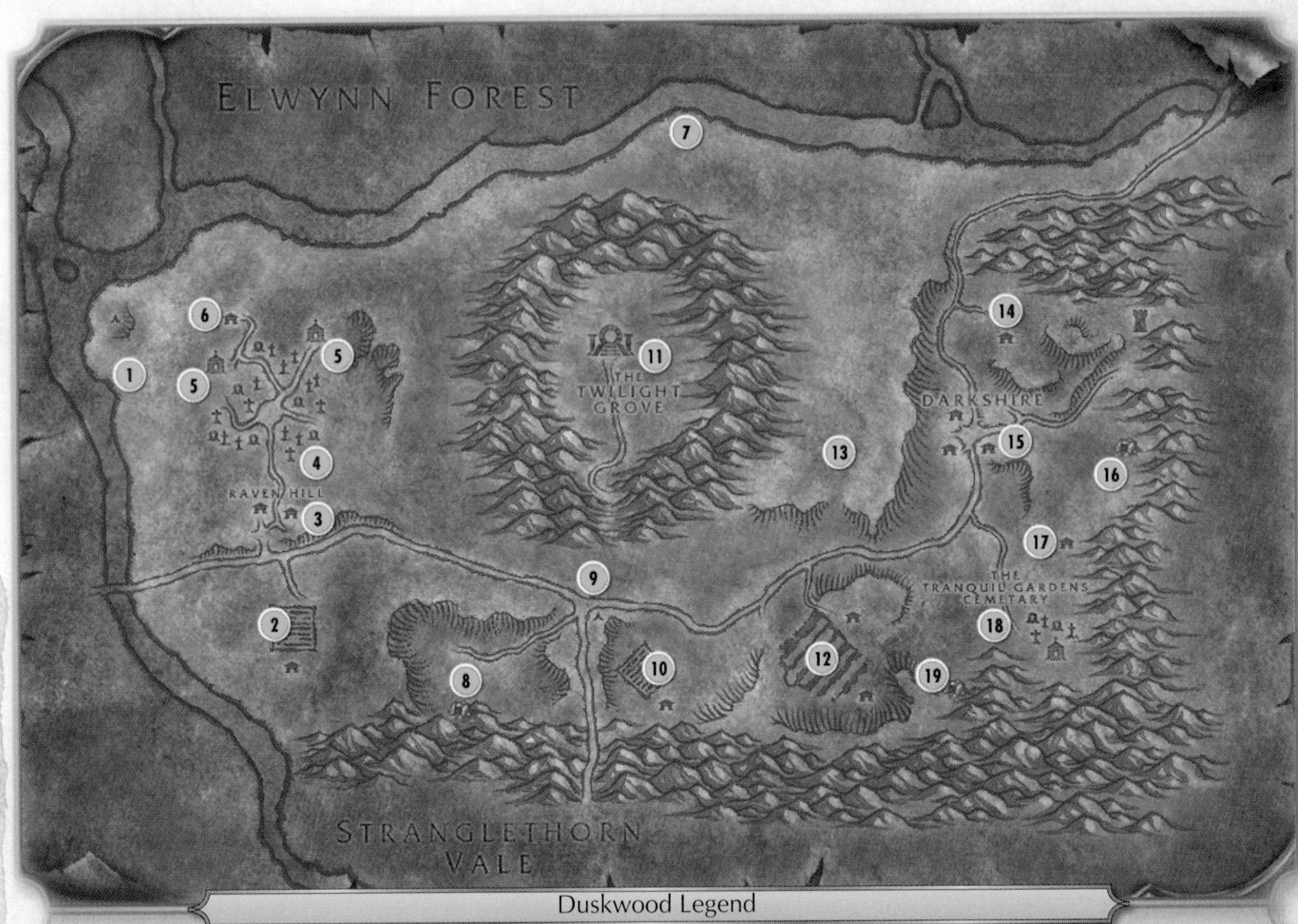

Duskwood Legend

1 The Hushed Bank
- Sven Yorgen 20 Quest
- Green Recluse 21-22
- Pygmy Venom Web Spider 18-19
- Rabid Dire Wolf 20-21
- Starving Dire Wolf 19-20
- Venom Web Spider 19-20

2 Addle's Stead
- Defias Enchanter 26-27
- Defias Night Blade 25-26
- Defias Night Runner 25-26
- Pygmy Venom Web Spider 18-19
- Rabid Dire Wolf 20-21
- Venom Web Spider 19-20

3 Raven Hill
- Jitters 25 Quest

4 Raven Hill Cemetery
- Abercrombie 35 Quest
- Bone Chewer 26-27
- Carrion Recluse 25-26
- Flesh Eater 24-25
- Mor'ladrim 35 Elite Quest Target
- Rotted One 25-26
- Skeletal Fiend 24-25
- Skeletal Raider 27-28

5 Dawning Woods Catacombs
- Brain Eater 28-29
- Plague Spreader 27-28
- Skeletal Warder 28-29

6 Forlorn Rowe
- Brain Eater 28-29
- Morbent Fel 35 Elite Quest Target
- Plague Spreader 28
- Skeletal Healer 26-27
- Skeletal Raider 27-28

7 The Darkened Bank
- Black Widow Hatchling 24-25
- Green Recluse 21-22
- Pygmy Venom Web Spider 18-19
- Rabid Dire Wolf 20-21
- Starving Dire Wolf 19-20

8 Vul'Gor Ogre Mound
- Splinter Fist Enslaver 30-31
- Splinter Fist Firemonger 28-29
- Splinter Fist Taskmaster 27-28
- Splinter Fist Warrior 29-30

9 Crossroad
- Watcher Dodds 29 Quest
- Black Ravager Mastiff 25-26
- Black Ravager 25-26
- Stitches 35 Elite
- Young Black Ravager 23-24

10 Yorgen Farmstead
- Defias Enchanter 26-27
- Defias Night Blade 25-26
- Defias Night Runner 24-25
- Young Black Ravager 23-24

11 Twilight Grove

12 The Rotting Orchard
- Nightbane Shadow Weaver 27-28
- Nightbane Dark Runner 28-29

13 Brightwood Grove
- Black Ravager Mastiff 25-26
- Black Ravager 25-26
- Nightbane Dark Runner 28-29
- Nightbane Shadow Weaver 27-28
- Nightbane Worgen 26-27
- Young Black Ravager 23-24

14 Manor Mistmantle
- Fetid Corpse 29-30
- Stalven Mistmantle 35 Elite Quest Target

15 Darkshire
- Ambassador Berrybuck 30 Quest
- Calor 20 Quest
- Chef Grual 30 Quest
- Clarise Gnarltree 31 Expert Blacksmith
- Clerk Daltry 31 Quest
- Commander Althea Ebonlocke 45 Quest
- Councilman Millstipe 28 Quest
- Danielle Zipstitch 27 Specialty Tailor
- Felicia Maline 55 Gryphon Master
- Finbus Geargrind 31 Expert Engineer
- Innkeeper Trelayne 30 Innkeeper
- Jonathon Carevin 25 Quest
- Lord Ello Ebonlocke 30 Quest
- Madame Eva 25 Quest
- Sirra Von'Indi 24 Quest
- Steven Black 30 Stable Master
- Tavernkeeper Smitts 22 Quest
- Viktori Prism'Antras 28 Quest
- Watcher Backus 42 Quest

16 Spider Cave
- Black Widow Hatchling 24-25

17 Blind Mary's Haunt
- Blind Mary 40 Quest
- Black Widow Hatchling 24-25
- Skeletal Horror 23-24

18 Tranquil Gardens Cemetery
- Insane Ghoul 26 Quest Target
- Skeletal Mage 22-23
- Skeletal Warrior 21-22

19 Roland's Doom
- Gutspill 32
- Nightbane Tainted One 30-31
- Nightbane Vile Fang 29-30

Dustwallow Marsh

Watery murky pools scattered among the land are the biggest indication that you're in Dustwallow Marsh. Theramore, an Alliance City, has a few trainers and vendors and there are many travel options including a flight path and a boat going to Menethil on the Eastern Kingdoms continent. This is a dangerous area and only adventurers reaching the mid to highest levels of their training can wander here in safety. There are plenty of quests for either faction to take part in, but be careful. The creatures in the marsh tend to attack in packs, so be cautious while you travel through.

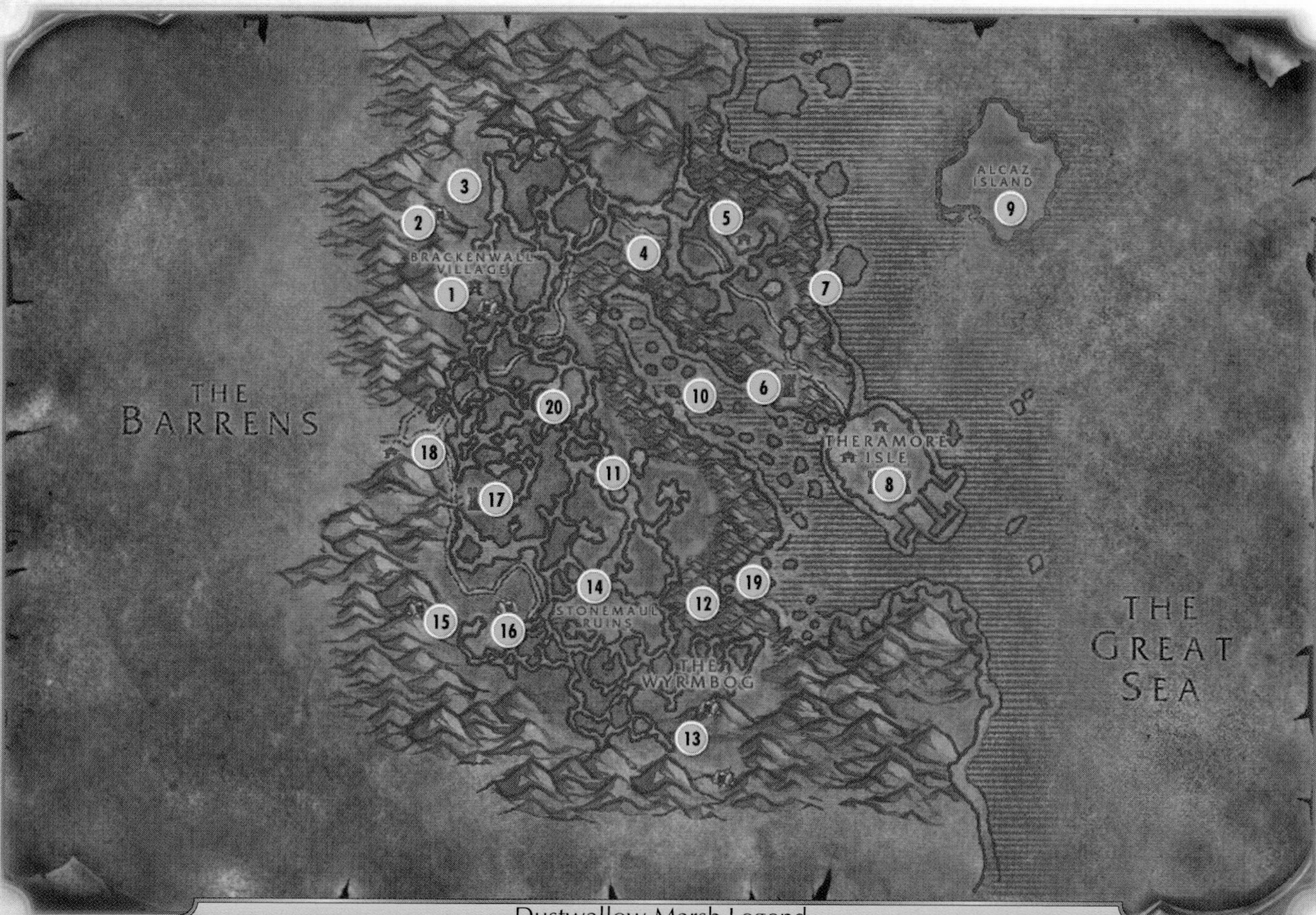

Dustwallow Marsh Legend

1 Brackenwall Village

Mudcrush Durtfeet 42 Quest
Brackenwall Enforcer 55
Nazeer Bloodpike 48 Quest
Ghok'ka 43 Tailoring Supplies
Shardi 55 Elite Wind Rider Master
Zanara 43 Bowyer
Zulrg 43 Weaponsmith
Overlord Mok'Morokk Quest
Krog 40 Quest
Krak 43 Armorer
Do'gol 30
Ogg'mar 40 Butcher
Draz'Zilb 40 Quest
Tharg 44 Quest

2 Dark Mist Cavern

Darkmist Recluse 36-37
Darkmist Spider 35-36

3 Bluefen

Drywallow Crocolisk 35-36
Bloodfen Raptor 35-36
Drywallow Vicejaw 36-37
Darkfang Spider 35-36
Darkfang Lurker 36
Withervine Bark Ripper 36-37 Elemental
Theramore Infiltrator 36
Withervine Creeper 35-36

4 North Sentry Point

Theramore Sentry 35-36

5 Witch Hill

'Swamp Eye' Jarl 42 Quest
Drywallow Crocolisk 35-36
Bloodfen Raptor 35-36
Bloodfen Screecher 36-37
Drywallow Vicejaw 36-37
Withervine Creeper 35-36

6 Sentry Point

Sentry Point Guard 32-33

7 Dreadmurk Shore

Mirefin Coastrunner 36-37
Mirefin Muckdweller 36-
Murdrock Spikeshell 37-38
Murdrock Tortoise 37

8 Theramore Isle

Theramore Guard 53-57
Theramore Lieutenant 52
Michael 30 Stable Master
Morgan Stern 36
Fiora Longears 26
Innkeeper Janene 30 Innkeeper
Bartender Lillian 45 Bartender
Craig Nollward 32 Cook
Ingo Woolybush 39 Explorer's League
Guard Byron 40
Medic Tamberlyn 51
Captain Thomas 53 Blue Team Captain
Guard Kahill 50
Guard Narrisha 50
Combat Master Szigeti 55
Combat Master Criton 55
Medic Helaina 51
Guard Jarad 50
Captain Andrews 53 Red Team Captain
Guard Tark 50
Spot 35
Theramore Practicing Guard 48-49
Brother Karman 45 Paladin Trainer
Dwane Wertle 28 Chef
Piter Verance 41 Weaponsmith & Armorer
Clerk Lendry 20
Captain Evencane 45 Warrior Trainer
Command Samaul 40
Captain Garran Vimes 50
Adjutant Tesoran 35
Alchemist Narett 37 Expert Alchemist
Uma Bartulm 37 Herbalism & Alchemy Supplies
Marie Holdston 37 Weaponsmith
Hans Weston 37 Armorer & Shieldsmith
Caz Twosprocket 35
Gregor MacVince 35 Horse Breeder
Helenia Olden 34 Trade Supplies
Timothy Worthington 51 Master Tailor
Baldruc 55 Elite Gryphon Master

9 Alcaz Island

Strashaz Hydra 59-60 Elite
Strashaz Siren 59 Elite
Strashaz Sorceress 61 Elite

10 Dust Wallow Bay

Mottled Drywallow Crocolisk 38-39
Drywallow Snapper 37
Drywallow Daggermaw 40-41 Elite

11 The Quagmire

Darkfang Creeper 38
Tabetha quest npc

12 The Dragonmurk

Mottled Drywallow Crocolisk 38-39
Drywallow Snapper 37
Drywallow Daggermaw 40-41 Elite
Searing Whelp 42

13 The Wyrmbog

Firemane Scalebane 43-44 Elite
Searing Hatchling 41-42
Firemane Flamecaller 44 Elite
Giant Darkfang Spider 41
Entrance to Onyxia's Lair World Dungeon

14 Stonemaul Ruins

Firemane Ashe Tail 42-43 Elite
Firemane Scout 41-42 Elite
Searing Hatchling 41-42

15 Bloodfen Burrow

Bloodfen Lashtail 40-41

16 The Den of Flame

Firemane Ash Tail 42-43 Elite
Firemane Scout 41-42 Elite

17 Lost Point

Theramore Deserter 37
Swamp Ooze 38
Bloodfen Scytheclaw 37
Darkfang Venomspitter 38
Mottled Drywallow Crocolisk 38-39

18 Shady Rest Inn

19 Tidefury Cove

Muckshell Pincer 42
Muckshell Scrabbler 42

20 Beezil's Wreck

Acidic Swamp Ooze 39-41
Corrosive Swamp Ooze 38

The Eastern Plaguelands

Beyond Darrowmere Lake are the Eastern Plaguelands, home of disease, sorrow, and some of the Scourge's greatest troops. Poison fills the air and the water is dangerous. Only the Scarlet Crusaders and the Argent Dawn are brave (or foolish) enough to stay here and fight against impossible odds. All wise adventurers avoid the Scarlet Crusade, who see the taint in everything, but the Argent Dawn camp, in the east, is a safe haven for the Alliance.

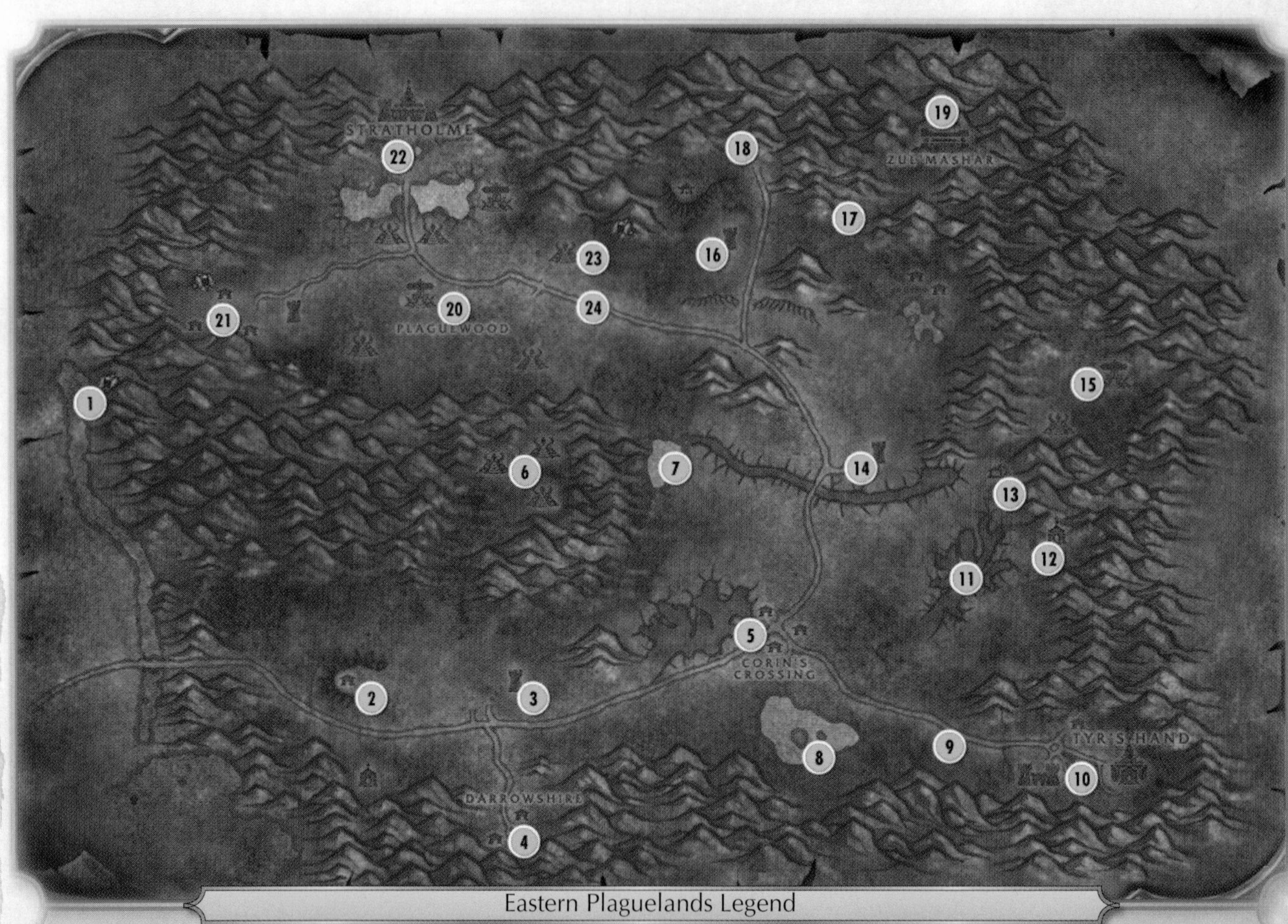

Eastern Plaguelands Legend

1 Thondroril River
Tirion Fordring 61 Quest
Carrion Grub 54-55
Plaguebat 54
Plaguehound Runt 53-54

2 The Marris Stead
Abomination 59-60
Death Singer 57-59
Diseased Flayer 59
Duskwing 60 Elite
Eyeless Watcher 58
Scourge Champion 60

3 Crown Guard Tower
Carrion Grub 55
Noxious Plaguebat 55-56
Plaguehound 55-56

4 Darrowshire
Carrion Grub 55
Plaguebat 53
Plaguehound Runt 53-54
Putrid Gargoyle 56

5 Corin's Crossing
Dark Caster 56
Gibbering Ghoul 57
Hate Shrieker 55-57
Scourge Warder 56
Stitched Horror 58
Unseen Servant 55
Vile Tutor 56-57

6 The Fungal Vale
Abomination 59-60
Crypt Slayer 58-59
Dark Adept 57
Death Singer 59
Diseased Flayer 59
Eyeless Watcher 58
Scourge Champion 59-60
Shadowmage 59-60

7 Blackwood Lake
Blighted Horror 56-57
Plague Monstrosity 58

8 Lake Mereldar
Plague Ravager 55-56

9 Scarlet Base Camp
Scarlet Cleric 54 Elite
Scarlet Enchanter 55 Elite
Scarlet Warder 53-54 Elite

10 Tyr's Hand
Scarlet Archmage 55-57 Elite
Scarlet Cleric 54-55 Elite
Scarlet Curate 55-56 Elite
Scarlet Enchanter 53-55 Elite
Scarlet Praetorian 56-57 Elite
Scarlet Warder 53-54 Elite

11 Pestilent Scar
Living Decay 55-56
Rotting Sludge 54-55

12 Light's Hope Chapel
Archmage Angela Dosantos 60
Argent Guard 55
Argent Medic 57
Argent Rider 60
Argent Sentry 60
Betina Bigglezink 57
Carlin Redpath 58
Commander Eligor Dawnbringer 60
Craftsman Wilhelm 57
Dispatch Commander Metz 60
Duke Nicholas Zuerenhoff 60
Emmisary Gormok 55
Emmissary Whitebeard 55
Father Inigo Montoy 60
Georgia 55 gryphon master
Huntsman Leopold 60
Jose Farlane 56
Jessica Chambers 52, Innkeeper
Khaelyn Steelwing 55 gryphon master
Korfax, Champion of the Light 60
Leonid Bartholomew the Revered 60
Lord Maxwell Tyrosus 62
Matous the Wrathcaster 60
Pack Mule 1-2
Packmaster Stonebruiser 59
Quartermaster Miranda Breechlock 60
Rimbalt Earthshatter 60
Rohan the Assassin 60
Smokey LaRue 55
Scarlet Commander Marjhan 60

13 Browman Mill
Death Singer 58-59
Diseased Flayer 58
Dread Weaver 58-59
Scourge Champion 59-60

14 Eastwall Tower
Borelgore 61 Elite
Carrion Grub 55
Crypt Horror 57-58
Diseased Flayer 59
Noxious Plaguebat 55-56
Plaguehound 55-56
Scourge Guard 57-58

15 The Noxious Glade
Crypt Slayer 58-59
Death Singer 59
Diseased Flayer 59
Dread Weaver 59
Scourge Champion 60

16 Northpass Tower
Aurora Skycaller 62
Kriss Goldenlight 60
Carrion Grub 55
Noxious Plaguebat 55-56
Plaguehound 55-56

17 Northdale
Death Singer 57-59
Eyeless Watcher 57-58
Frenzied Plaguehound 57
Plague Monstrosity 58

18 Quel'Lithien Lodge
Pathstrider 57-58
Ranger 59-60
Ranger Lord Hawkspear 60 Elite
Woodsman 58-59

19 Zul'Mashar
Mossflayer Cannibal 57-59
Mossflayer Scout 57-58
Mossflayer Shadowhunter 58-59

20 Plaguewood
Cannibal Ghoul 54
Cursed Mage 54-55
Putrid Gargoyle 56
Scourge Soldier 53-54
Scourge Warder 56
Stitched Horror 57

21 Terrordale
Carrion Devourer 56
Crypt Fiend 53-54
Crypt Walker 55-56
Dark Caster 56
Gibbering Ghoul 57
Hate Shrieker 55-57
Scourge Soldier 53
Scourge Warder 56
Stitched Horror 57-58
Stitched Horror 58
Torn Screamer 53-55
Unseen Servant 55
Vile Tutor 56-57

22 Stratholme
Entrance to Stratholme World Dungeon
Hate Shrieker 55-56
Necromancer 54
Stitched Horror 58
Torn Screamer 53-55

23 Stratholme
Secondary Entrance to Stratholme World Dungeon

24 Naxxramas

Elwynn Forest

Elwynn Forest has been a quiet land for some time, but pressing attacks from the Defias Brotherhood and nearby Gnolls have made the Humans here nervous. It seems that the times of peace are over, because only the mighty city of Stormwind seems immune to the presence of foul beasts and aggressive bandits. The once great copper mines of Elwynn are plagued with Kobolds now, and the people of Goldshire have had to arm themselves against the wild beasts of the valley.

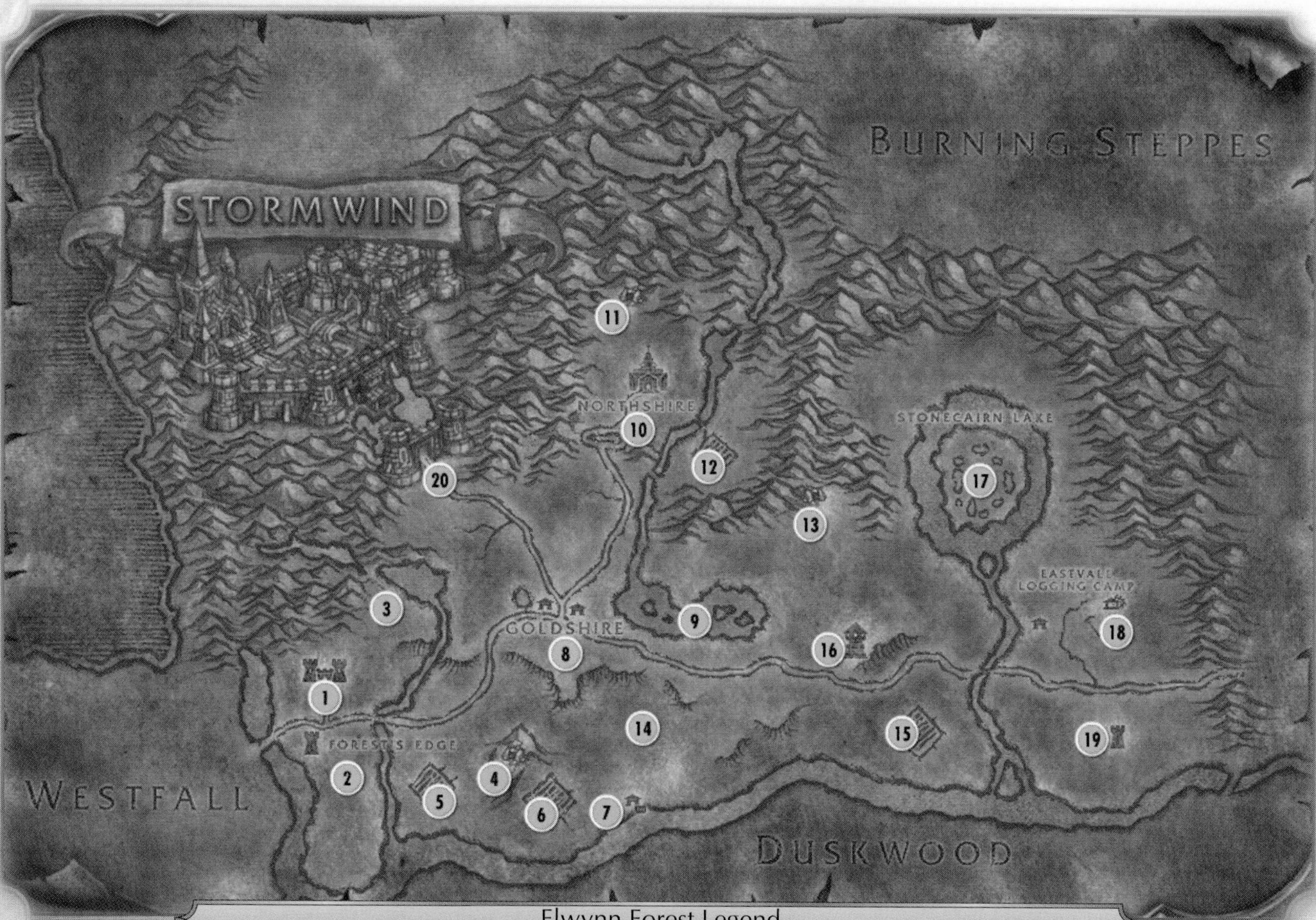

Elwynn Forest Legend

1 Westbrook Garrison
- Deputy Rainer 10 Quest

2 Forest's Edge
- Hogger 11+ Quest Target
- Longsnout 10-11
- Riverpaw Outrunner 9-10
- Riverpaw Runt 8-9
- Young Forest Bear 9

3 Mirror Lake Orchard
- Defias Bandit 8-9
- Defias Cutpurse 6
- Defias Rogue Wizard 9
- Mangy Wolf 5

4 Fargodeep Mine
- Goldtooth 8
- Kobold Miner 7
- Kobold Taskmaster 10 Rare
- Kobold Tunneler 5-6

5 The Stonefield Farm
- "Auntie" Bernice Stonefield 6 Quest
- Gramma Stonefield 3 Quest
- Ma Stonefield 3 Quest
- Tommy Joe Stonefield 2 Quest
- Stonetusk Boar 5-6
- Young Forest Bear 8-9

6 The Maclure Vineyards
- Billy Maclure 1 Quest
- Joshua Maclure 5 Vendor
- Maybell Maclure 2 Quest
- Stonetusk Boar 5-6
- Rockhide Boar 8

7 Jerod's Landing
- Defias Dockmaster 10
- Rockhide Boar 8

8 Goldshire
- Adele Fielder 22 Leatherworker
- Helene Peltskinner 12 Skinner
- Innkeeper Farley 30 Innkeeper
- Marshal Dughan 25 Quest
- Michelle Belle 11 Physician
- Remy "Two Times" 5 Quest
- Smith Argus 24 Blacksmith Quest
- Tomas 10 Cook
- William Pestle 6 Quest

9 Crystal Lake
- Lee Brown 8 Fisher
- Defias Bandit 8-9
- Grey Forest Wolf 7-8
- Mangy Wolf 5-6
- Murloc Steamrunner 6-7
- Murloc 7

10 Northshire Valley
- Deputy Willem 18 Quest
- Eagan Peltskinner 3 Quest
- Falkhaan Isenstrider 10 Quest
- Marshal McBride 20 Quest
- Milly Osworth 2 Quest
- Young Wolf 1-2

11 Echo Ridge Mine
- Kobold Laborer 4
- Kobold Vermin 1-2
- Kobold Worker 3

12 Northshire Vineyards
- Defias Thug 3-4
- Garrick Padfoot 5 Quest Target

13 Jasperlode Mine
- Kobold Geomancer 7-8
- Kobold Miner 6-7
- Mine Spider 9

14 Southern Elwynn Forest
- Rockhide Boar 7-8
- Young Forest Bear 8

15 Brackwell Pumpkin Patch
- Ripe Pumpkin (Ground Spawn)
- Defias Bandit 8-9
- Erlan Drudgemoor 8
- Morgan the Collector 10
- Porcine Entourage 7
- Princess 9
- Rockhide Boar 7-8
- Surena Caledon 9

16 Tower of Azora
- Dawn Brightstar 35 Arcane Goods
- Kitta Firewind 44 Enchanter
- Morley Eberlein 10 Vendor
- Servant of Azora 8-9
- Theocritus 24 Quest

17 Stone Cairn Lake and Hero's Vigil
- Defias Rogue Wizard 9-10
- Murloc Lurker 9-10

18 Eastvale Logging Camp
- Katie Hunter 10 Vendor
- Marshal Haggard 20 Quest
- Sara Timberlain 5 Quest
- Supervisor Raelen 15 Quest
- Terry Palin 11 Vendor
- Prowler 9-10

19 Ridgepoint Tower
- Dead-tooth Jack 11 Quest Target
- Defias Bandit 8-9
- Prowler 9-10
- Young Forest Bear 8-9

20 Stormwind

Felwood

Felwood is rife with corruption. The once green of the land is now filled predominantly with shades of ominous brown. The Emerald Circle works hard to push out the corruption that has taken over this land however, their efforts seem miniscule compared to the sheer devastation that surrounds them. This zone is located to the north of Ashenvale and serves as a passageway to both Moonglade and Winterspring. This area is a higher-level region best for those from Level 45 and up.

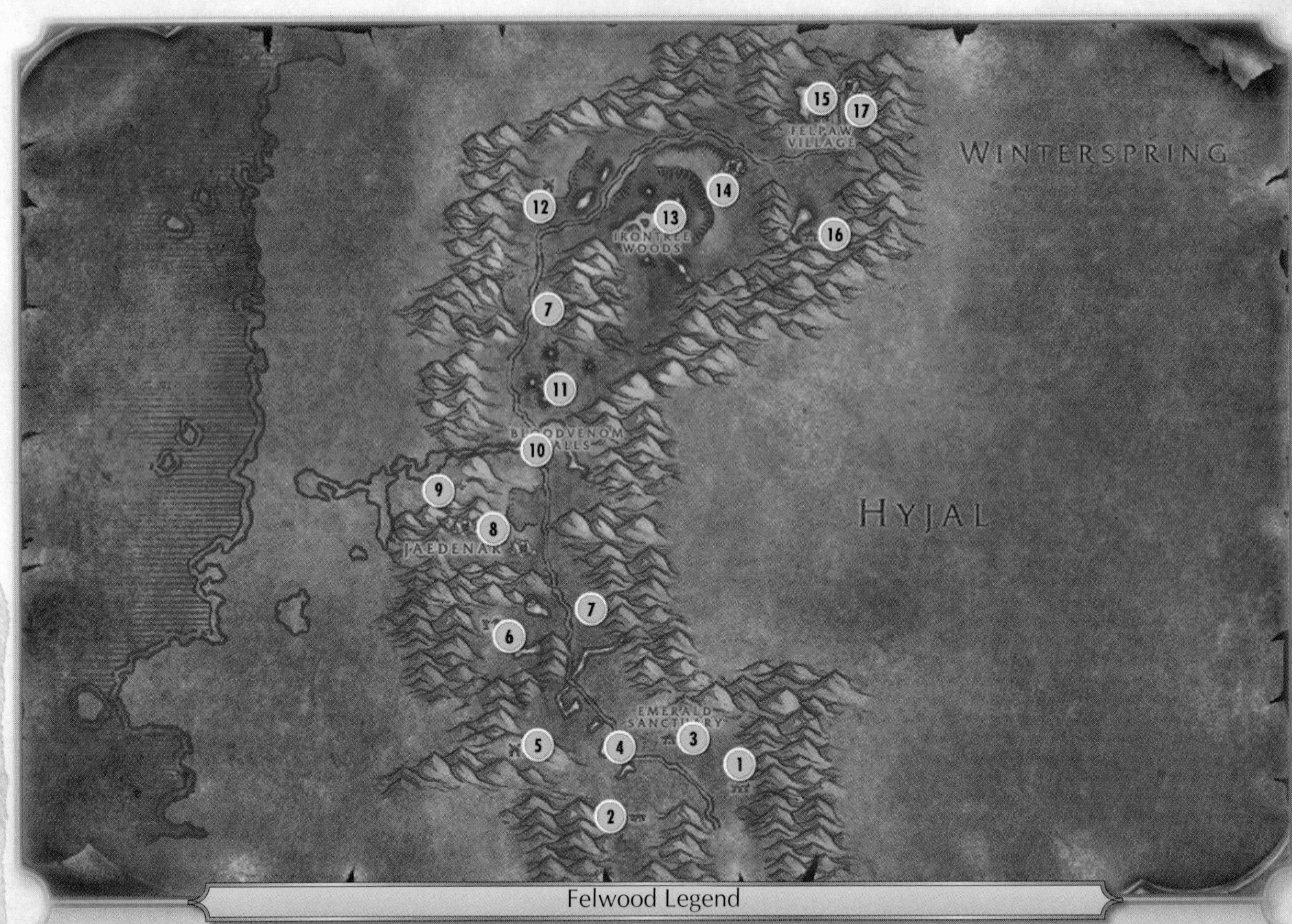

Felwood Legend

1 Morlos'Aran
- Arathandris Silversky 60 Emerald Circle
- Angerclaw Bear 47-48
- Ironbeak Owl 48-49
- Felpaw Wolf 47-48

2 Deadwood Village
- Felpaw Wolf 47-48
- Deadwood Warrior 48-49
- Deadwood Pathfinder 49-50
- Deadwood Gardener 48-49
- Ironbeak Owl 48-49

3 Emerald Circle
- Jessir Moonbow 50
- Della 49 Jessir's Pet
- Greta Mosshoof 59 Emerald Circle
- Tenell Leafrunner 62 Emerald Circle
- Kelek Skysweeper 57 Emerald Circle
- Eriden Bluewind 57 Emerald Circle
- Taronn Redfeather 50 Emerald Circle
- Ivy Leafrunner 63 Emerald Circle
- Ironbeak Owl 48-49
- Angerclaw Bear 47-48
- Felpaw Wolf 47-48

4 Maybess Riverbreeze 60 Emerald Circle

5 Jadefire Glen
- Jadefire Satyr 49-50
- Jadefire Felsworn 49-51
- Felpaw Wolf 47-48

6 Ruins of Constellas
- Xavathras 54
- Cursed Ooze 49-50
- Felpaw Wolf 47-48
- Angerclaw Bear 47-48
- Jadefire Shadowstalker 51-52
- Jadefire Rogue 50
- Jadefire Felsworn 50-51

7 Felwood (General)
- Felpaw Wolf 47-48
- Angerclaw Bear 47-48
- Angerclaw Mauler 49-50
- Ironbeak Hunter 50-51
- Felpaw Scavenger 49-50

8 Jaedenar
- Tainted Ooze 51-52
- Jaedenar Hound 50-51
- Jaedenar Guardian 50-51
- Jaedenar Adept 51-52
- Ironbeak Hunter 50-51
- Jaedenar Cultist 51-52

9 Bloodvenom Post
- Bloodvenom Post Brave 65
- Storm Shadowhoof 60 Quest
- Trull Failbane 55 Quest
- Bale 55 General Goods
- Brakkar 55 Elite Wind Rider Master

10 Bloodvenom Falls
- Tainted Ooze 51-52
- Angerclaw Mauler 49-50
- Ironbeak Hunter 50-51

11 Shatter Scar Vale
- Entropic Horror 54
- Entropic Beast 51-52
- Infernal Bodyguard 54 Elite
- Infernal Sentry 52-53 Elite

12 Jadefire Run
- Jadefire Trickster 52-53
- Jadefire Betrayer 52
- Jadefire Hellcaller 53-54
- Felpaw Scavenger 49-50
- Angerclaw Mauler 49-50

13 Irontree Woods
- Arei 56 Quest
- Irontree Stomper 52-53
- Toxic Horror 54

14 Irontree Cavern
- Warped Shredder 53
- Warpwood Moss Flayer 52-53

15 Felpaw Village
- Felpaw Ravager 51-53
- Deadwood Den Watcher 53-54
- Deadwood Shaman 53-54
- Deadwood Avenger 54-55
- Winterfall Runner 57
- Chieftain Bloodpaw 56

16 Talonbranch Glade
- Golhine the Hooded 60 Druid Trainer
- Kaerbrus 57 Hunter Trainer
- Shi'alune 56 Kaerbrus' Pet
- Malygen 55 General Goods
- Ironbeak Screecher 53

17 Timbermaw Hold/ Passage to Winterspring and Moonglade
- Grazle 55 Quest

Feralas

Feralas is a tropical region filled with plenty of vegetation where various creatures hide. It's located south of Desolace and west of Thousand Needles and is a contrast to their stark landscapes. This is a region for mid-level adventurers and has many great soloing opportunities within it as well as some great grouping regions. There are also Horde and Alliance towns within this region. Skinners find this region to offer abundant targets for their trade and, for those looking for good experience at relatively low risk, this could be the place for which you're looking.

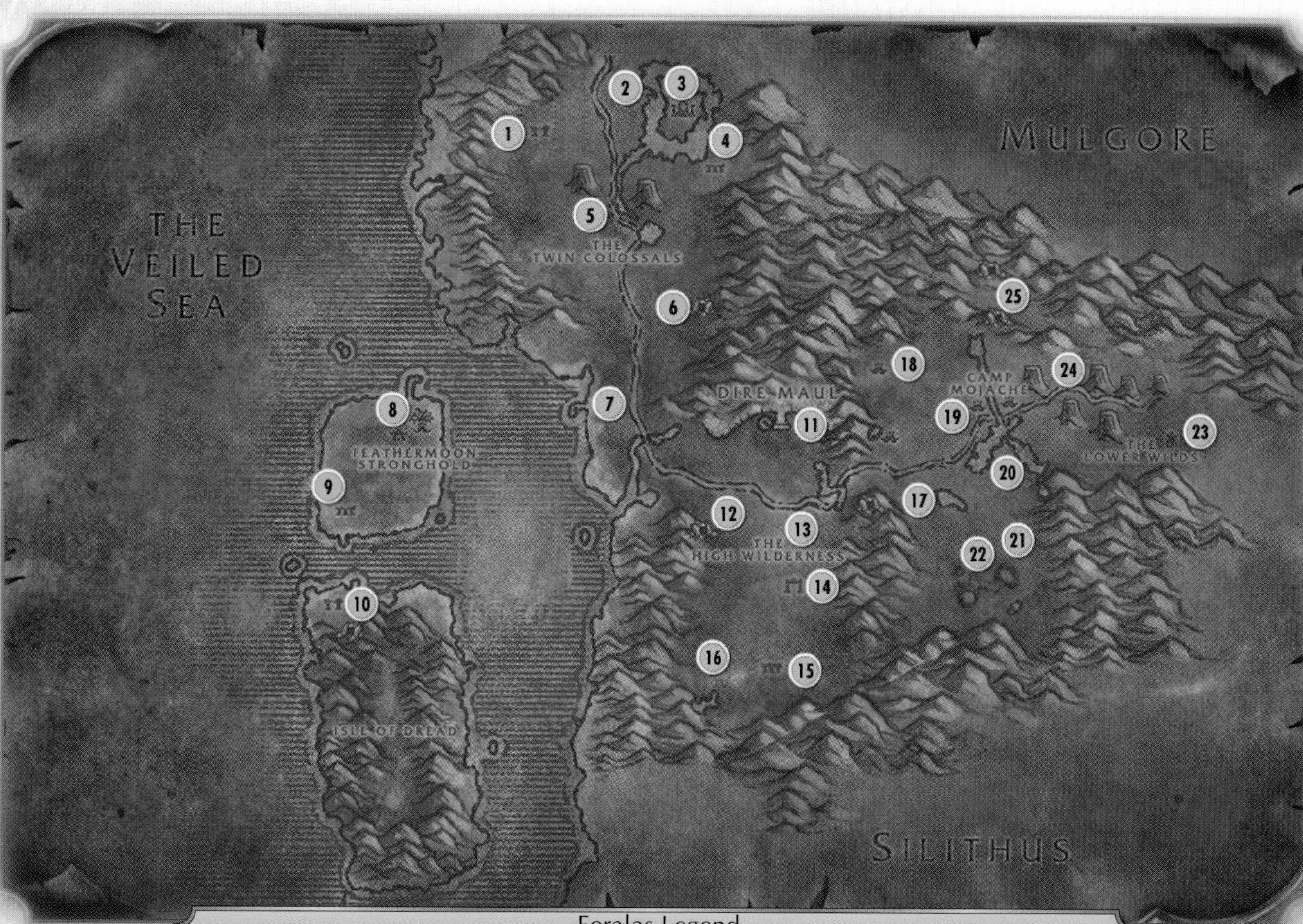

Feralas Legend

1. **Ruins of Ravenwind**
   - Northspring Roguefeather 48-49
   - Northspring Windcaller 49-50
   - Northspring Slayer 49-50
2. **Jademir lake**
   - Jademir Dragonspawn 60 elite
3. **Dream Bough**
   - Jademir Dragonspawn 60 elite
4. **Oneiros**
   - Jademir Dragonspawn 60 elite
5. **The Twin Colossals**
   - Milbon Snarltooth 50
   - Ironfur Patriarch 48-49
   - Rabid Longtooth 47-48
   - Groddoc Thunderer 49-50
   - Sprite Dragon 48-50
   - Rockbiter 45
   - Land Walker 48-49 elite
   - Cliff Giant 49-50 elite
   - Wandering Forest Walker 45 elite
6. **Rage Scar Hold**
   - Ferocious Rage Scar 47-48
   - Rage Scar yeti 46-47
   - Elder rage Scar 48-49
7. **The Forgotten Coast**
   - Rogue Vale Screecher 44-46
   - Sea Elemental 48-49
   - Deep Strider 47 elite
   - Shore Strider 48-48 elite
   - Wave Strider 48
   - Sea Spray 47-48
8. **Feathermoon Stronghold-Alliance camp (Sardor isle)**
   - Innkeeper Shyria 30
   - Feathermoon Sentinel 65
   - Fyldren Moonfeather 55 elite
   - Pratt McGrubben Leatherworker 55
   - Brannock 52 fisherman
   - Antarius 30 stablemaster
   - Logannas 52 alchemy supplier
   - Vivianna 52 trade supplies
   - Madrack Greenwell 54 food and drink
   - Faralorn 53 General supplies
9. **Ruins of Solarsal**
   - Hatecrest Warrior 42-43
   - Hatecrest Screamer 41-42
   - Hatecrest Siren 42
   - Hatecrest Wavenider 41-42
10. **Isle of Dread**
    - Hatecrest Myrmidon 43-44
    - Hatecrest Sorceress 43-44
    - Hatecrest Serpentguard 44-45
    - Lord Shalzaru 47
11. **Entrance to Dire Maul World Dungeon**
    - Arcane Chimaerok 61-62
    - Chimaerok 60-61
    - Gordok Brute 60 elite
    - Grizzled Ironfur Bear 44-45
    - Longtooth Howler 44
    - Lord Lakmaeran 63
    - Rogue vale Screecher 45
12. **Feral Scar Vale**
    - Feral Scar Yeti 43-44
    - Enraged Feral Scar 44-45
    - Hulking Feral Scar 46
    - Lurking Feral Scar 46
    - Vale Screecher 42
13. **High Wilderness**
    - Grizzled Ironfur Bear 44
    - Rogue Vale Screecher 46
    - Longtooth Howler 44
14. **Ruins of Isildien-North**
    - Gordunni Brute 42-43
    - Gordunni Mauler 43
    - Gordunni Warlock 43-44
    - Vale Screecher 41
    - Ironfur Bear 41-42
    - Groddoc Ape 42-43
15. **Ruins of Isildien-South**
    - Gordunni Mauler 43-44
    - Gordunni Warlock 43-44
    - Gordunni Shaman 45
    - Gordunni Mage-lord 45-46
    - Gordunni Warlord 46-47
    - Gordunni Battlemaster 45-45
16. **Frayfeather Highlands**
    - Frayfeather Stagwing 44-45
    - Frayfeather Hippogryph 43
    - Frayfeather Skystormer 45-46
    - Cursed Sycamore 45 elite
    - Frayfeather Patriarch 46-47
17. **Lower Wilds-west**
    - Grimtotem Shaman 43-44
    - Sprite Darter 44-45
    - Ironfur Bear 42
    - Grimtotem Naturalist 41-42
    - Grimtotem Raider 42-43
    - Longtooth Runner 40
18. **Grimtotem Compound**
    - Grimtotem Naturalist 41-42
    - Grimtotem Shaman 43-44
    - Grimtotem Raider 42-43
19. **Camp Mojache**
    - Rok Orhan 40
    - Witch Doctor Uzer'l 50
    - Shyrka Wolfrunner 30 stablemaster
    - Kulleg Stonehorn 41 skinning trainer
    - Hahrana Ironhide 55 Master Leatherworker
    - Worb Strongstitch 46 leatehrworking supplies
    - Sheendra Tallgrass 42 trade supplies
    - Hodoken Swiftstrider 45
    - Sage Palerunner 44
    - Ruw 44 herbalism trainer
    - Bronk 45 alchemy trainer
    - Jannos Lighthoof 43 druid trainer
    - Camp Mojache Brave 65
    - Orik'andi 42
    - Talo thornhoof 50
    - Loorana 43 food and drink
    - Orwin Gizzmick 50
    - Shyn 55 elite wind rider master
    - Blaise Montgomery 47
    - Innkeeper Gruel 30
    - Cawind Trueaim 46 gunsmith and Bowyer
20. **Wildwind Lake**
21. **Woodpaw Hills**
    - Woodpaw Brute 41-42
    - Woodpaw trapper 40-41
    - Woodpaw Mongrel lvl 40-41
    - Woodpaw Alpha 43-44
    - Woodpaw Reaver 42-43
    - Woodpaw Mystic 42-43
22. **The Writhing Deep**
    - Grizzled Ironfur Bear 44-45
    - Longtooth Howler 43-44
    - Zukk'ash Wasp 44-45
    - Zukk'ash Worker 44-45
23. **Lower Wilds**
    - Longtooth Howler 44
    - Groddoc Ape 41-43
    - Ironfur Bear 42
    - Longtooth runner 41
    - Woodpaw Trapper 41-42
    - Woodpaw Brute 41-42
    - Woodpaw Mongrel 40-41
24. **Lariss Pavilion**
    - Ironfur Bear 41-42
    - Longtooth Runner 41
25. **Gordunni Outpost**
    - Gordunni Brute 41-43
    - Gordunni Ogre 40-41
    - Gordunni Ogre-mage 41-42

Hillsbrad Foothills

The gentle foothills around Hillsbrad would have stayed peaceful if not for the fall of Lordaeron. Now, these farmlands have become the frontlines for the war between the Alliance and the Undead of the Forsaken. Tarren Mill is a Horde town in the northeast with strong connections to the Undercity. Southshore, loyal to the Alliance, is settled in the south, along the river. Tension is high in Hillsbrad itself, to the northwest, and its people are constantly under attack by Horde troops. There is no escape from this by land, and neither does the sea offer salvation (Sirens and Murlocs wander the strands, settling freely while their enemies fight amongst themselves).

Hillsbrad Foothills Legend

1 Southpoint Tower
Deathstalker Lesh 32
Elder Gray Bear 25-26
Forest Moss Creeper 20-21

2 Azurelode Mine
Elder Gray Bear 25-26
Giant Moss Creeper 25-26
Hillsbrad Foreman 28
Hillsbrad Miner 26-27
Hillsbrad Sentry 27-28
Miner Hackett 29 Quest target

3 Western Strand
Torn Fin Coastrunner 29-30
Torn Fin Muckdweller 28-29
Torn Fin Oracle 30-31
Torn Fin Tidehunter 31-32

4 Hillsbrad Fields
Hillsbrad Tailor 24 Tailor (Alliance)
Blacksmith Verrington 26 Quest TargetBlacksmith (Alliance)
Clerk Horace Whitesteed 26 Quest Target
Farmer Ray 23 Quest Target
Forest Moss Creeper 20-21
Gray Bear 21-22
Hillsbrad Apprentice Blacksmith 24-25
Hillsbrad Councilman 25-26
Hillsbrad Farmer 23-24
Hillsbrad Farmhand 22-23
Hillsbrad Footman 25-26
Hillsbrad Peasant 24-25
Magistrate Burnside 30
Starving Mountain Lion 23-24
Vicious Gray Bear 23-24

5 Darrow Hill
Cave Yeti 30-31
Starving Mountain Lion 23-24
Vicious Gray Bear 22-23

6 Yeti Cave
Cave Yeti 30-31

7 Southshore
Bartolo Ginsetti 32 Quest
Chef Jessen 35 Quest
Darren Malvew 30 Quest
Innkeeper Anderson 30 Innkeeper
Lieutenant Farren Orinelle 25 Quest
Loremaster Dibbs 30 Quest
Magistrate Henry Maleb 30 Quest
Marshal Redpath 41 Quest
Merideth Carlson 32 Horse Trainer
Phin Odelic 36 Quest
Wesley 30 Stable Master
Snapjaw 30-31
Starving Mountain Lion 23-24
Vicious Gray Bear 22-23

8 Tarren Mill
Apothecary Lydon 35 Quest
Arachne Venomblood 29 Herbalist
Daryl Stack 56 Master Tailor
Deathguard Humbert 32 Quest
Deathguard Samsa 32 Quest
High Executor Darthalia 50 Quest
Innkeeper Shay 30 Innkeeper
Kayren Soothsallow 30
Keeper Bel'varil 34 Quest
Krusk 25 Quest
Magus Wordeen Voidglare 42 Quest
Melisara 25 Quest
Novice Thaivand 30 Quest
Serge Hinnot 32 Expert Alchemist
Tallow 27 Quest
Theodore Mon Claire 30 Stable Master
Zarise 55 Bat Handler
Elder Gray Bear 25-26
Forest Moss Creeper 20-21
Giant Moss Creeper 24-25
Gray Bear 21-22
Snapjaw 30-31

9 Durnholde Keep
Elder Gray Bear 25-26
Forest Moss Creeper 20-21
Giant Moss Creeper 24-25
Syndicate Rogue 21-22
Syndicate Shadow Mage 21-22
Syndicate Watchman 20-21
Vicious Gray Bear 22-23

10 Thoradin's Wall
Elder Gray Bear 25-26
Elder Moss Creeper 26-27
Giant Moss Creeper 24-25

11 Nethander Stead
Elder Gray Bear 25-26
Elder Moss Creeper 26-27
Feral Mountain Lion 27-28
Giant Moss Creeper 24-25
Mudsnout Gnoll 26-28
Mudsnout Shaman 27-28
Snapjaw 30-31
Syndicate Rogue 21-22
Syndicate Shadow Mage 21-22
Syndicate Watchman 20-21

12 Dun Garok
Dun Garok Mountaineer 28-29 Elite
Dun Garok Priest 29-30 Elite
Dun Garok Rifleman 29-30 Elite
Elder Moss Creeper 26-27
Feral Mountain Lion 27-28

13 Eastern Strand
Daggerspine Screamer 29-30
Daggerspine Shorehunter 30-31
Daggerspine Shorestalker 29-30
Daggerspine Siren 30

14 Purgation Isle
Arados the Damned 35 Quest Target
Condemned Acolyte 57
Condemned Cleric 31-32
Condemned Cleric 59-60
Condemned Monk 31-32
Condemned Monk 58
Cursed Acolyte 30-31
Cursed Justicar 33
Cursed Justicar 59-60
Cursed Paladin 30-31
Cursed Paladin 57-58
Judge Thelgram 34 Friendly to Alliance
Writhing Mage 31-32
Writhing Mage 58-59

The Hinterlands

In the far northeast is a land that is almost forgotten by those who fight for survival throughout the Eastern Kingdoms. The Hinterlands is an expanse of trees and valleys where Wolves, Owlbeasts, and even Dragonkin live. On the southern ridgeline are many outposts of the Vilebranch and Witherbark Trolls, all powerful and very much steeped in a bloody philosophy that even divides them from the Horde's Trolls. Along the northwest end are Dwarves and Elves. Hunting up in Hinterlands is usually safe and quiet, making it a place beloved by crafters throughout the world.

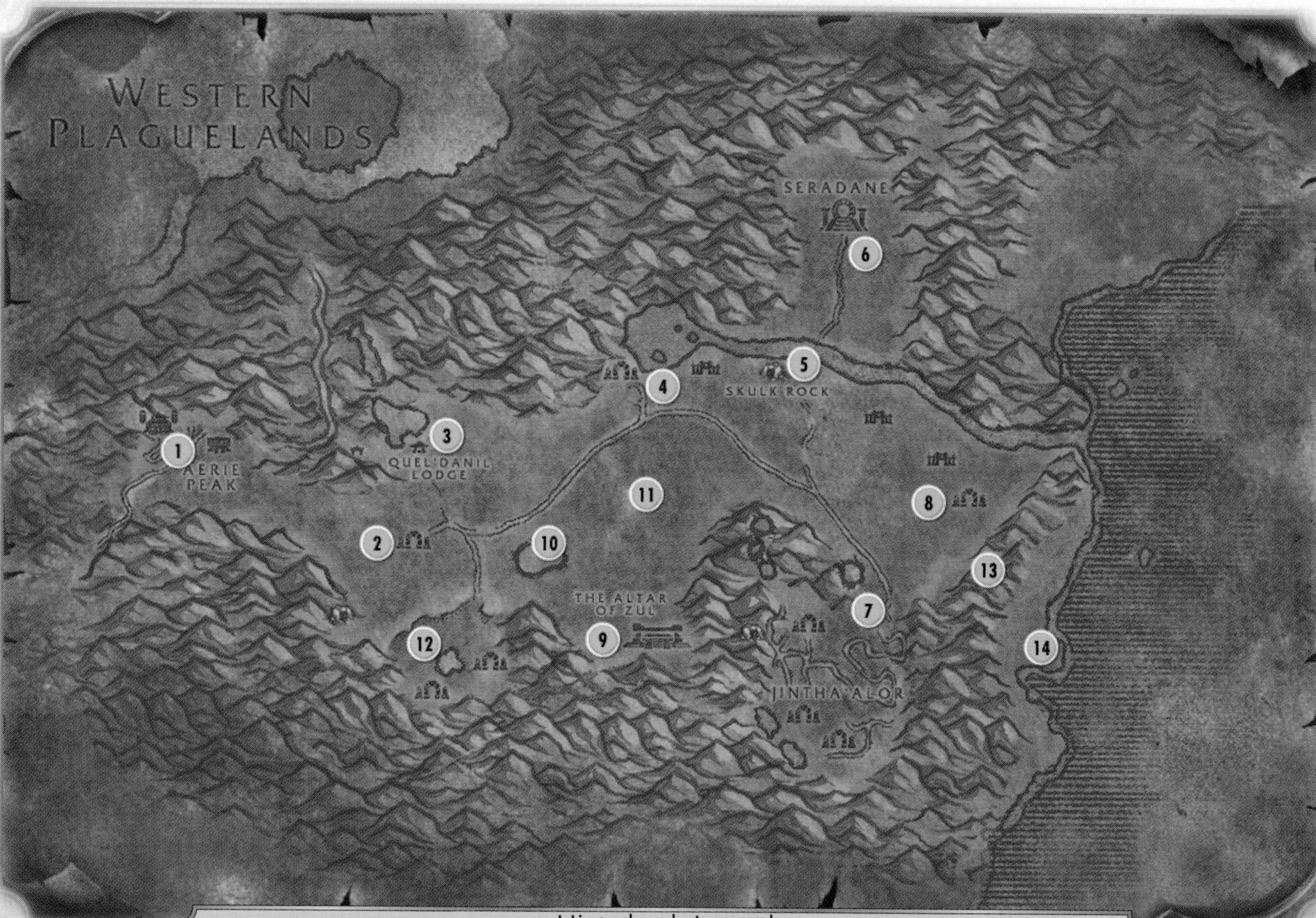

Hinterlands Legend

1 Aerie Peak
- High Thane Falstad Wildhammer 50
- Killium Bouldertug 50 Stable Master
- Wildhammer Sentry 55
- Mangy Silvermane 41-42
- Razorbeak Gryphon 45
- Trained Razorbeak 40-41

2 Hiri'watha
- Witherbark Hideskinner 42-43
- Witherbark Venomblood 43

3 Quel'Danil Lodge
- Highvale Marksman 45-46
- Highvale Outrunner 43-44
- Highvale Ranger 46-47
- Highvale Scout 44-45

4 Agol'watha
- Cerulean Dragonspawn 48-49
- Green Sludge 46-47
- Jade Ooze 48
- Primitive Owlbeast 44

5 Skulk Rock
- Green Sludge 46-47
- Jade Ooze 47-48
- Savage Owlbeast 46-47

6 Seradane
- Dreamtracker 62
- Verdantine Boughguard 62
- Verdantine Oracle 61
- Verdantine Tree Warder 60
- This is also one of the four spawn points of the Emerald Dragon world bosses.

7 Jintha'Alor
- Hitah'ya the Keeper 51
- Jade Sludge 47-48
- Silvermane Stalker 47-48
- Vile Priestess Hexx 51
- Vilebranch Aman'zasi Guard 50-51
- Vilebranch Berserker 47-48
- Vilebranch Blood Drinker 49-50
- Vilebranch Headhunter 46-47
- Vilebranch Hideskinner 48-49
- Voidwalker Minion 47-48
- Vilebranch Raiding Wolf 50-51
- Vilebranch Shadowcaster 47-48
- Vilebranch Shadowhunter 48-49
- Vilebranch Soul Eater 49-50
- Vilebranch Warrior 45-46
- Vilebranch Warrior 46 Elite
- Vilebranch Witch Doctor 46-47
- Vilebranch Witch Doctor 46-47 Elite
- Vilebranch Wolf Pup 46 Beast

8 Shaol'watha
- Silvermane Stalker 47-48

9 The Temple of Zul
- Morta'Gya The Keeper 50 Elite
- Qiaga The Keeper 52 Elite Quest Target
- Vilebranch Soothsayer 47
- Vilebranch Axe Thrower 46
- Vilebranch Scalper 47
- Vilebranch Wolf Pup 46-47

10 Valorwind lake
- Primitive Owlbeast 44-45
- Razorbeak Gryphon 45
- Silvermane Howler 46

11 The Creeping Ruin
- Green Sludge 46-47
- Jade Ooze 48

12 Shadra'Alor
- Atal'ai Exile 45 Quest
- Witherbark Broodguard 44-45
- Witherbark Caller 45-46
- Witherbark Sadist 44-45

13 The Overlook Cliffs
- Gammerita 48 Elite Quest Target
- Saltwater Snapjaw 49-50

14 Revantusk Village

Loch Modan

Loch Modan is a large lake, created by the presence of the Stonewrought Dam and large meltoffs from the surrounding cliffs. Offering a blast of color and warmer weather to the Dwarves coming from Dun Morogh, this is a place of comfort. Yet, the presence of many militant Troggs and the recent ingress of Orc tribes to the north has put things on edge in Loch Modan. The Dwarves have concentrated more of their efforts here, and hope to fight the good fight against these enemies (and perhaps the dangerous Ogres in the northeast as well), but setbacks occur at every angle. Could there be traitors in the ranks?

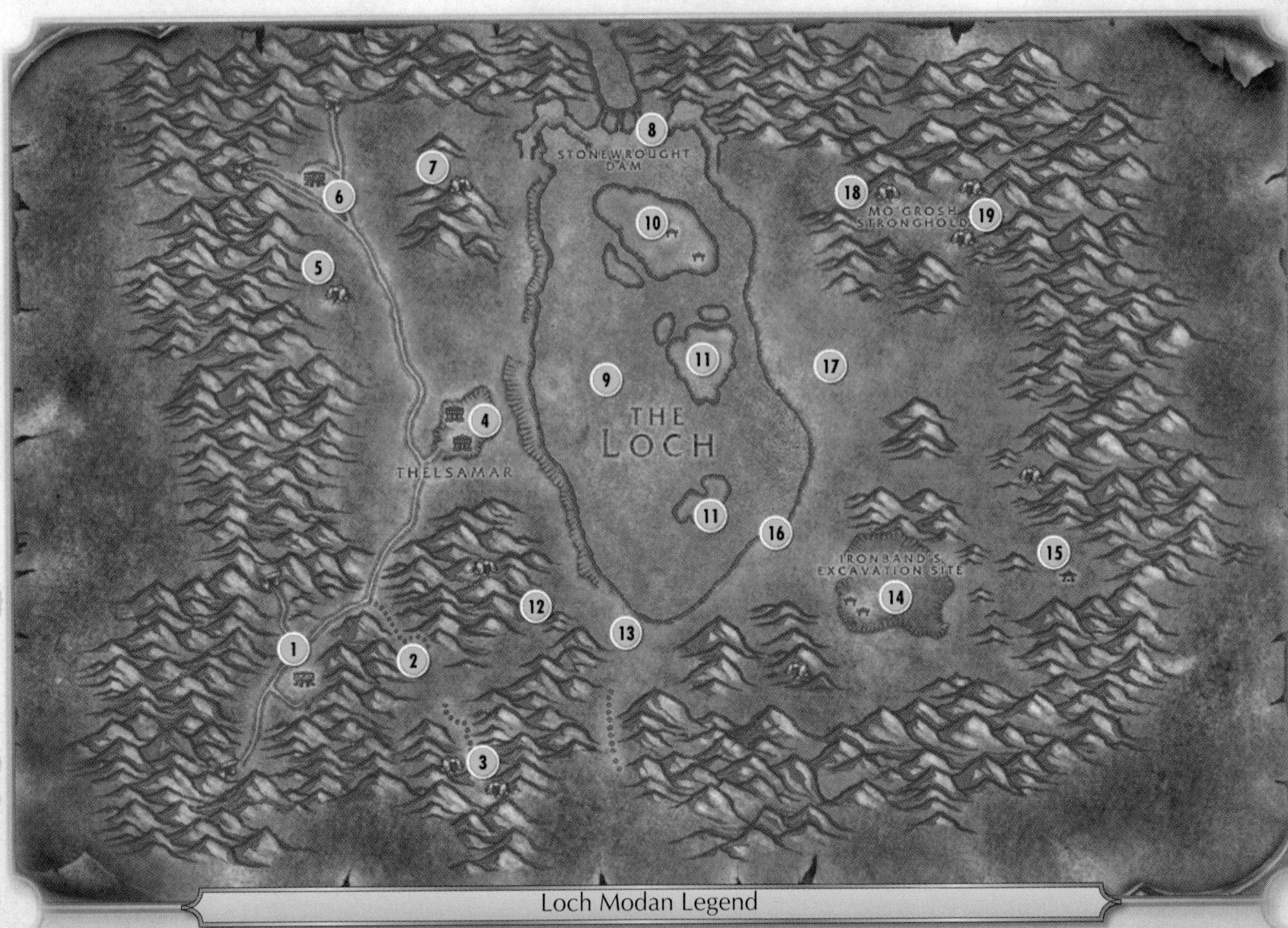

Loch Modan Legend

1 Valley of Kings
- Captain Rugelfuss 40 Quest
- Mountaineer Cobbleflint 30 Quest
- Mountaineer Gravelgaw 30 Quest
- Mountaineer Pebblebitty 44 Quest
- Elder Black Bear 11-12
- Forest Lurker 10-11

2 Stonesplinter Valley
- Stonesplinter Bonesnapper 15-16
- Stonesplinter Scout 11-12
- Stonesplinter Seer 13-14
- Stonesplinter Shaman 15-16
- Stonesplinter Skullthumper 13-14
- Stonesplinter Trogg 11-12

3 Stonesplinter Caves
- Brawler 16
- Gnasher 16
- Grawmug 17 Quest Target
- Stonesplinter Bonesnapper 15-16
- Stonesplinter Seer 13-14
- Stonesplinter Shaman 15-16
- Stonesplinter Skullthumper 13-14

4 Thelsamar
- Brock Stoneseeker 15 Mining Trainer
- Dakk Blunderblast 15 Quest
- Ghak Healtouch 25 Quest
- Innkeeper Hearthstove 30 Innkeeper
- Kali Healtouch 14 Herbalism Trainer
- Lina Hearthstove 30 Stable Master
- Magistrate Bluntnose 20 Quest
- Mountaineer Kadrell 30 Quest
- Mountaineer Langarr 30 Quest
- Mountaineer Stenn 30 Quest
- Thorgrum Borrelson 55 Gryphon Master
- Torren Squarejaw 15 Quest
- Vidra Hearthstove 10 Quest
- Elder Black Bear 11-12
- Forest Lurker 10-11
- Mountain Boar 10-11
- Stonesplinter Scout 11-12
- Stonesplinter Trogg 11-12

5 Tunnel Rat Cave
- Tunnel Rat Scout 10-11
- Tunnel Rat Vermin 10-11

6 Algaz Station
- Mountaineer Stormpike 30 Quest
- Elder Black Bear 11-12
- Forest Lurker 10-11
- Mountain Boar 10-11

7 Silver Stream Mine
- Elder Black Bear 11-12
- Forest Lurker 10-11
- Mountain Boar 10-11
- Tunnel Rat Digger 12-13
- Tunnel Rat Forager 11-12
- Tunnel Rat Geomancer 12-13
- Tunnel Rat Kobold 11-12
- Tunnel Rat Vermin 10-11

8 Stonewrought Dam
- Chief Enginneer Hinderweir VII 40 Quest
- Deek Fizzlebizz 27 Journeyman Engineer
- Dark Iron Insurgent 18
- Dark Iron Sapper 17

9 The Loch
- Cliff Lurker 13-14
- Loch Frenzy 12-13
- Mangy Mountain Boar 14-15
- Young Threshadon 19-20

10 Trogg Islands
- Bingles' Tools (Ground Spawn)
- Stonesplinter Bonesnapper 15-16
- Stonesplinter Bonesnapper 15-16
- Stonesplinter Seer 13-14
- Stonesplinter Shaman 15-16
- Stonesplinter Skullthumper 13-14

11 Crocolisk Islands
- Loch Crocolisk 14-15

12 Grizzlepaw Ridge
- Black Bear Patriarch 16-17
- Grizzled Black Bear 13-14
- Mangy Mountain Boar 14-15
- Ol' Sooty 20 Elite Quest Target

13 Caravan
- Huldar 15 Quest
- Miran 15 Quest
- Dark Iron Ambusher 10
- Saean 10

14 Ironband's Excavation Site
- Prospector Ironband 15 Quest
- Berserk Trogg 19-20
- Grizzled Black Bear 13-14
- Mangy Mountain Boar 14-15
- Stonesplinter Digger 18-19
- Stonesplinter Geomancer 18-19

15 Farstrider Lodge
- Daryl the Youngling 15 Quest
- Vyrin Swiftwind 15 Quest
- Cliff Hadin 15 Bowyer Vendor
- Irene Sureshot 15 Gunsmith Vendor
- Grizzled Black Bear 13-14
- Mangy Mountain Boar 14-15
- Mountain Buzzard 15-16

16 Bingles' Crash Site
- Bingles Blastenheimer 20 Quest

`7 Hunting Grounds
- Black Bear Patriarch 16-17
- Elder Mountain Boar 16-17
- Wood Lurker 17-18

18 Mo'grosh Stronghold
- Mo'grosh Enforcer 18-19 Elite
- Mo'grosh Orge 18-19 Elite
- Mo'grosh Shaman 18-19 Elite

19 Mo'grosh Cavern
- Chok'sul 22 Elite Quest Target
- Mo'grosh Brute 19-20 Elite
- Mo'grosh Mystic 19-20 Elite

Moonglade

Moonglade is a peaceful and serene setting with a small village named Nighthaven looking down on it. There isn't much here as of yet, but the way in is dangerous if you aren't friendly with the Timbermaws that guard the way in. The Lunar Festival takes place here. Brave souls can also find Malfurion Stormrage resting in the Stormrage Barrow Dens.

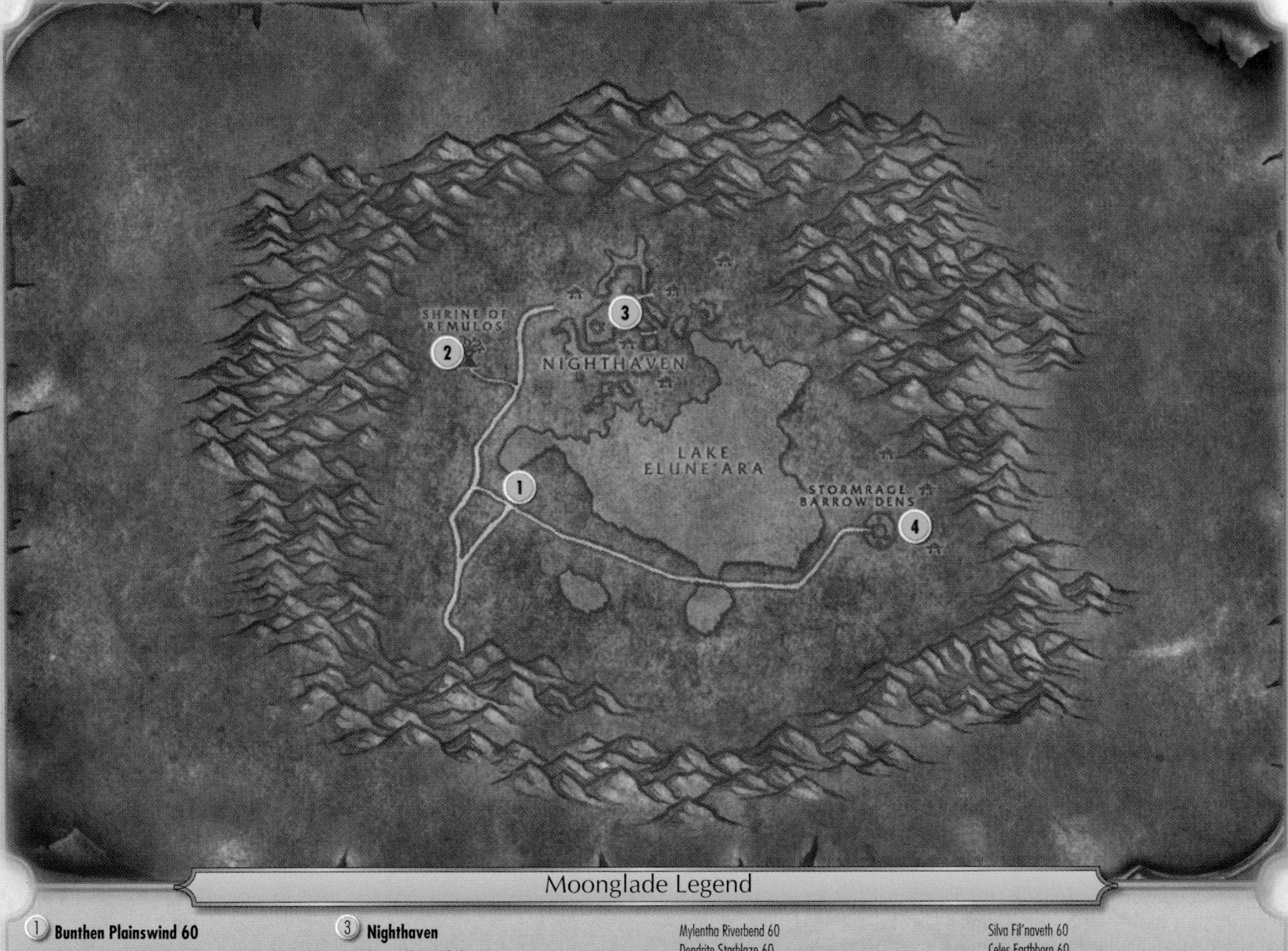

Moonglade Legend

1. **Bunthen Plainswind 60**
2. **Shrine of Remulos**
   - Keeper Remulos 62 Quest
3. **Nighthaven**
   - Bessany Plainswind 60
   - Genia Sunshadow 51 Specialty Dress Maker
   - Darnall 53 Tailoring Supplies
   - Mylentha Riverbend 60
   - Dendrite Starblaze 60
   - Moren Riverbend 60
   - Keeper Remulos 62
   - Rabine Saturna 60
   - Silva Fil'naveth 60
   - Celes Earthborn 60
   - Tajarri 60
4. **Stormrage Barrow Den**

Mulgore

Mulgore is the starting region for the Tauren. The largest portion of the land is made up of open plains ringed by mountains and the mesas that make up the capitol city of Thunder Bluff to the north. Wild Kodo Beasts roam the land and there is a rumor that a massive patriarch walks among them. Harpies have taken residence along the hillsides and the Venture Co. is trying to strip the land around Thunder Bluff and Bloodhoof Village. However, among even those dangerous adversaries, there are heroes. Cairne Bloodhoof sits in Thunder Bluff waiting for those willing to defend the land to join him.

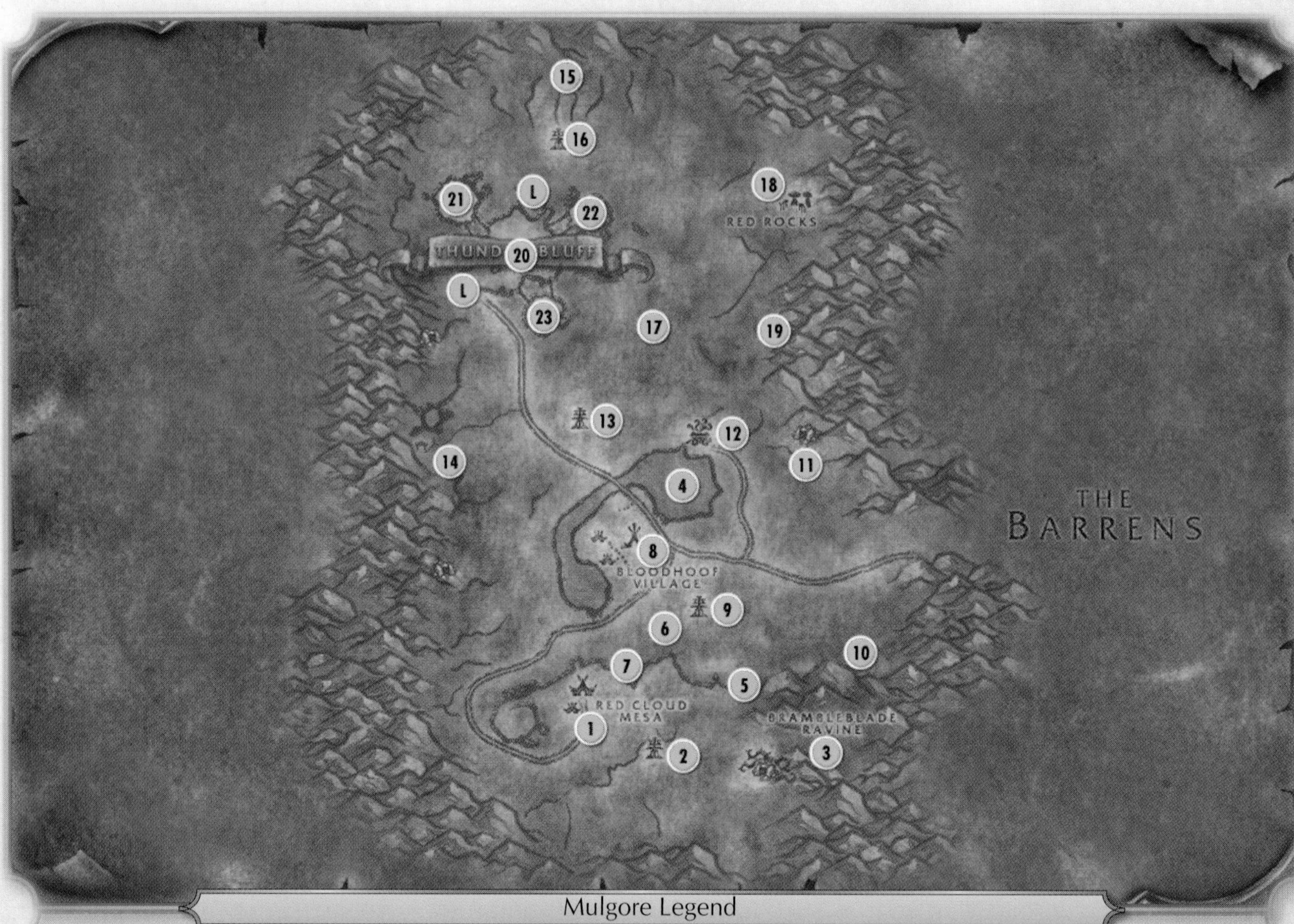

Mulgore Legend

(L) Lift

(1) Camp Narache

- Moodan Sungrain 11 Baker
- Brave Windfeather 13 Quest NPC
- Vorn Skyseer 5
- Bronk Stoolrage 10 Armorer and Shieldcrafter
- Marjak Keenblade 9 Weaponsmith
- Varia Hardhide 7 Leather Armor Merchant
- Grull Hawkwind 4 Quest
- Chief Hawkwind 36 Quest
- Harutt Thunderhorn 10 Warrior Trainer
- Lanka Farshot 11 Hunter Trainer
- Seer Ravenfeather 10
- Meela Dawnstrider 10 Shaman Trainer
- Gart Mistrunner 9 Druid Trainer
- Hawnie Softbreeze 8 General Goods
- Brave Lightning Horn 15
- Brave Proudsnout 16
- Brave Greathoof 13
- Brave Running Wolf 12

(2) Well/Red Cloud Mesa

- Antur Fallow 3 Quest
- GreatMother Hawkwind 9 Quest
- Mountain Cougar 3
- Plainstrider 1-2
- Battleboar 3-4
- Seer Graytongue 8 Quest

(3) Brambleblade Ravine

- Chief Sharptusk 5
- Bristleback Quilboar 3-4
- Bristleback Battleboar 4-5
- Bristleback Shaman 4

(4) Stonebull Lake

(5) Palemane Camps

- Palemane Tanner 5-6
- Palemane Skinner 6-7
- Palemane Poacher 7-8

(6) The Rolling Plains

- Prairie Wolf 5-10
- Taloned Swoop 8-9
- Elder Plainstrider 8- 9
- Galak Centaur 10
- Galak Outrunner 9
- Flatland Cougar 7-8
- Prairie Stalker 7-8
- Swoop 7-9
- Adult Plainstrider 6-7
- Flatland Prowler 9

(7) Palemane Rock

- Palemane Tanner 5-6
- Palemane Skinner 6-7
- Palemane Poacher 7-8

(8) Bloodhoof Village

- Brave Rainchaser 14
- Krang Stonehoof 14 Warrior Trainer
- Gennia Runetotem 12 Druid trainer
- Narm Skychaser 13 Shaman Trainer
- Harken Windtotem 21 Quest
- Zarlman Two-Moons 7
- Brave Wildrunner 14
- Brave Strongbash 14
- Brave Ironhorn 14
- Brave Cloudmane 14
- Brave Dawneagle 14
- Yaw Sharpmane 11 Hunter Trainer
- Harn Longcast 9 Fishing Supplies
- Wunna Darkmane 10 Trade Goods
- Moorat Longstride 12 General Goods
- Yonn Deepcut 8 Skinner Trainer
- Chaw Stronghide 23 Leatherworking Trainer
- Pyall Silenstride 12 Cooking Trainer
- Kennah Hawkeye 10 Gunsmith Supplier
- Mahnott Roughwound 11 Weaponsmith
- Harant Ironbrace 13 Armorer and Shieldcrafter
- Skorn Whitecloud 21 Story Teller
- Seikwa 30 Stable Master
- Magrin Rivermane 6
- Innkeeper Kauth 30
- Vira Younghoof 13 First Aid Trainer
- Varg Windwhisper 14 Leather Armor Merchant
- Ruul Eagletalon 9 Quest
- Jhawna Oatwind 13 Baker
- Morin Cloudstalker 10 Quest

(9) Winterhoof Waterwell

- Venture Co. Hireling 5-6
- Vencure Co. Laborer 6

(10) Windfury Harpies

- Windfury Harpy 7-8
- Windfury Wind Witch 9
- Windfury Matriarch 10-11
- Windfury Sorceress 9-10

(11) The Venture Co. Mine

- Venture Co. Worker 8-9
- Venture Co. Supervisor 9-10

(12) Ravaged Caravan

- Flatland Cougar 7-8
- Adult Plainstrider 6-7
- Prairie Stalker 7-8
- Venture Co. Laborer 7
- Venture Co. Taskmaster 7-8
- Swoop 7-9

(13) Thunderhorn Water Well

- Flatland Cougar 7-8
- Elder Plainstrider 8-9
- Adult Plainstrider 6-7
- Swoop 7-9
- Praire Stalker 7-8
- Venture Co. Laborer 6-7
- Venture Co. Taskmaster 8

(14) Bael'Dun Digsite

- Bael'dun Digger 7-8
- Bael'dun Appraiser 8-9

(15) Windfury Ridge

- Seer Wiserunner

(16) Wildmane Water Well

- Prairie Wolf Alpha 9-10
- Flatland Prowler 9
- Elder Plainstrider 8-9
- Venture Co. Worker 8-9
- Venture Co. Supervisor 9
- Windfury Matriarch 10-11
- Windfury Sorceress 9-10
- Taloned Swoop 8-10

(17) The Golden Plains

- Kodo Calf 7
- Kodo Bull 7-11
- Kodo Matriarch 11-12
- Prairie Stalker 7-8
- Swoop 7-9
- Taloned Swoop 8-10
- Adult Plainstrider 6-7
- Elder Plainstrider 8-9
- Flatland Prowler 9
- Prairie Wolf Alpha 9-10
- Flatland Cougar 7-8
- The Rake 10
- Windfury Matriarch 10-11
- Windfury Sorceress 9-10

(18) Red Rocks: Sacred Burial Ground

- Lorekeeper Raintotem 8 Quest
- Ancestral Spirit 9 Quest
- Flatland Prowler 9
- Taloned Swoop 8-10
- Prairie Wolf Alpha 9-10
- Elder Plainstrider 8-9
- Kodo Matriarch 11-12
- Kodo Bull 10
- Bristleback Interloper 9-10

(19) Venture Co. Buildings

- Enforcer Emilgund 11
- Venture Co. Worker 8-9

(20) Thunder Bluff

(21) Spirit Rise

(22) Elder Rise

(23) Hunter Rise

Redridge Mountains

East of Stormwind and Elwynn Forest is the town of Lakeshire, placed in the middle of the Redridge Mountains. Under siege by eastern Orc clans and hassled by Gnolls, things aren't simple for the people of Lakeshire currently. A great bridge that spans Lake Everstill is under repairs, even as enemy catapults lie in ruins along the southern ridgeline. To the north are Orcish Champions, known for their power and bravery, while the eastern groups have even greater leadership. Stonewatch Keep, on the far side of Lake Everstill sits as a constant reminder that peace has collapsed into a drawn-out war in Redridge.

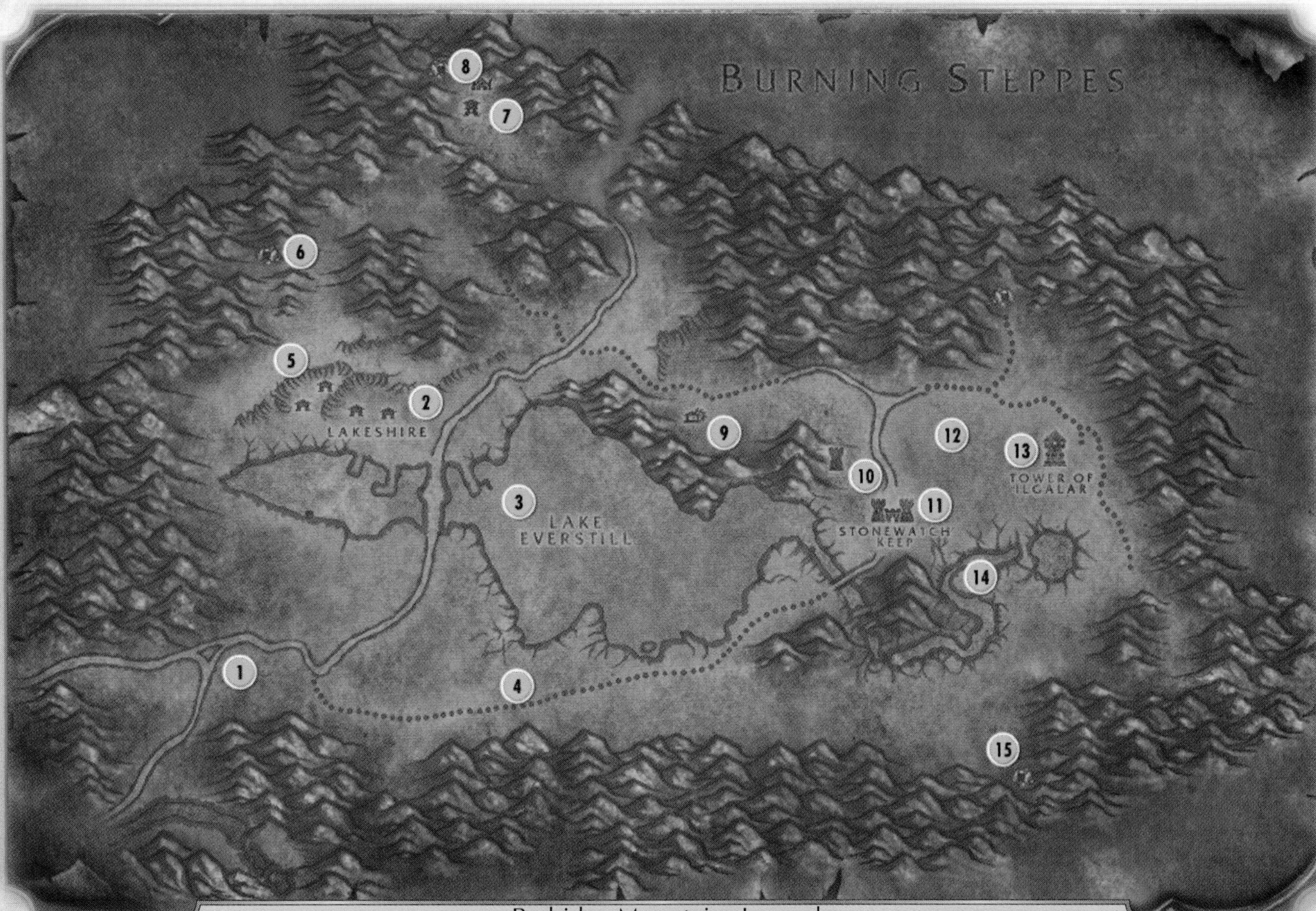

Redridge Mountains Legend

1 Three Corners
- Guard Parker 30 Quest
- Black Dragon Whelp 17-18
- Great Goretusk 16-17
- Redridge Mongrel 15-16
- Redridge Thrasher 14-15
- Tarantula 15-16

2 Lakeshire
- Alma Jainrose 20 Herbalism Trainer
- Ariena Stormfeather 55 Gryphon Master
- Chef Breanna 19 Quest
- Crystal Boughman 22 Cooking Trainer
- Darcy 15 Quest
- Deputy Feldon 33 Quest
- Foreman Oslow 20 Quest
- Innkeeper Brianna 30 Innkeeper
- Magistrate Solomon 36 Quest
- Marshal Marris 35 Quest
- Martie Jainrose 20 Quest
- Verner Osgood 25 Quest
- Bellygrub 24
- Blackrock Outrunner 20-21
- Great Goretusk 16-17

3 Lake Everstill
- Great Goretusk 16-17
- Murloc Flesheater 18-19
- Murloc Minor Tidecaller 17-18
- Murloc Scout 18-19
- Murloc Shorestriker 16-17
- Murloc Tidecaller 19-20

4 Lakeridge Highway
- Black Dragon Whelp 17-18
- Dire Condor 18-19
- Great Goretusk 16-17
- Murloc Minor Tidecaller 17-18
- Murloc Shorestriker 16-17
- Redridge Mongrel 16-17
- Redridge Poacher 16-17

5 Redridge Canyons
- Great Goretusk 16-17
- Redridge Alpha 21-22
- Redridge Basher 19-20
- Redridge Brute 17-18
- Redridge Mystic 18-19
- Yowler 25 Quest Target

6 Rethban Caverns
- Redridge Basher 19-20
- Redridge Drudger 20-21

7 Render's Camp
- Corporal Keeshan 25 Elite
- Blackrock Champion 24-25
- Blackrock Outrunner 20-21
- Blackrock Renegade 21-22
- Blackrock Summoner 22-23
- Blackrock Tracker 23-24

8 Render's Rock
- Blackrock Champion 24-25
- Blackrock Summoner 22-23
- Blackrock Tracker 23-24

9 Alther's Mill
- Black Dragon Whelp 17-18
- Dire Condor 18-19
- Great Goretusk 16-17
- Greater Tarantula 19-20

10 Stonewatch Tower
- Blackrock Grunt 19-20
- Blackrock Outrunner 19-20
- Blackrock Scout 20 Elite
- Blackrock Sentry 21-22 Elite
- Blackrock Shadowcaster 22-23 Elite

11 Stonewatch Keep
- Blackrock Gladiator 25 Elite
- Blackrock Hunter 24 Elite
- Blackrock Shadowcaster 22-23 Elite
- Gath'Ilzogg 26 Elite Quest Target
- Tharil'zun 24 Elite Quest Target

12 Galardell Valley
- Rabid Shadowhide Gnoll 21-22
- Shadowhide Brute 23-23
- Shadowhide Darkweaver 25-26
- Shadowhide Gnoll 22-23
- Shadowhide Slayer 25-26
- Shadowhide Warrior 24-25

13 Tower of Ilgalar
- Shadowhide Darkweaver 25-26
- Shadowhide Slayer 25-26
- Shadowhide Warrior 24-25
- Morganth

14 Stonewatch Falls
- Murloc Nightcrawler 21
- Murloc Tidecaller 19-20
- Shadowhide Darkweaver 25-26
- Shadowhide Slayer 25-26
- Shadowhide Warrior 24-25

15 Render's Valley
- Blackrock Outrunner 21
- Blackrock Renegade 21-22

Searing Gorge

West from the Badlands is the Searing Gorge, fed by lava flows. There are Dark Iron Dwarves and Elementals building up their forces to move on Nefarian and the Alliance. The Twilight Hammer lives in the northwest, holding true to ceremonies and beliefs of the old gods, and these people are not interested in making friends with any who draw near. Those who seek fame, fortune, mithril, and thorium are drawn here as moths to the flame.

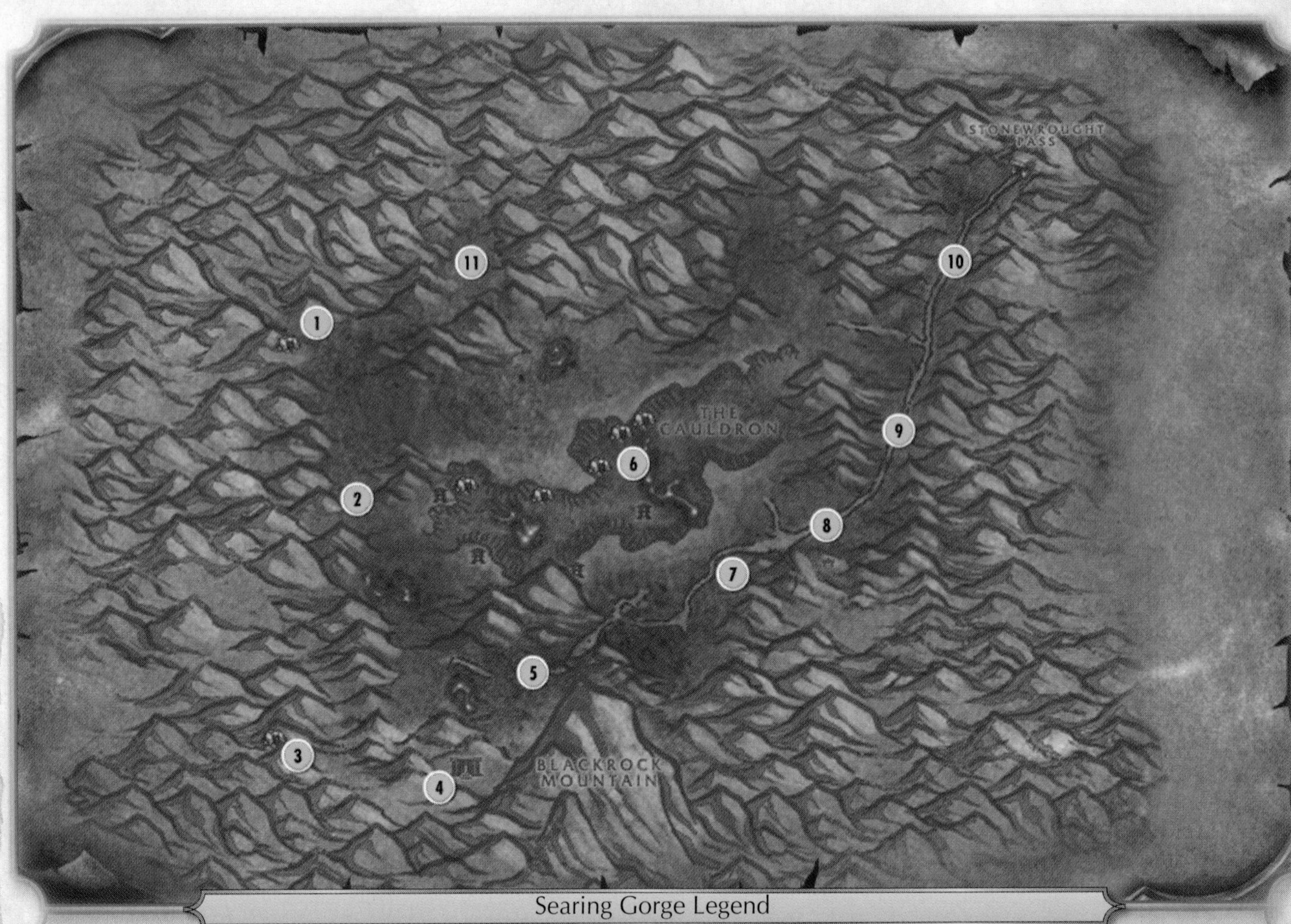

Searing Gorge Legend

1 Firewatch Ridge
- Twilight Dark Shaman 47-48 Elite
- Twilight Fire Guard 48-49 Elite
- Twilight Geomancer 50 Elite
- Twilight Idolater 50 Elite

2 Western Searing Gorge
- Greater Lava Spider 47-48
- Inferno Elemental 49
- Magma Elemental 46-47

3 Blackchar Cave
- Greater Lava Spider 48-49

4 Blackrock Mountain
- Entrance to Blackrock World Dungeon

5 SW Sear Gorge
- Graw Cornerstone 58 Vendor
- Graw Cornerstone's Guardian 48
- Greater Lava Spider 47-48
- Magma Elemental 46-48
- Searing Elemental 49

6 The Cauldron
- Blazing Elemental 45-47
- Dark Iron Slaver 45-46
- Dark Iron Taskmaster 47
- Heavy War Golem 48-49
- Magma Elemental 47-48
- Shadowsilk Poachers 47-48
- Slaved Worker 45-47

7 The Sea of Cinders
- Magma Elemental 47-48
- Searing Lava Spider 45-47

8 Tanner Camp
- Sarah Tanner 50 Master Elemental Leatherworker
- Glassweb Spider 43-45

9 Grimsilt Dig Site
- Dark Iron Geologist 43
- Dark Iron Watchman 44
- Glassweb Spider 43-35
- Tempered War Golem 45-46

10 Dustfire Valley
- Locked Door to Loch Modan
- Dark Iron Geologist 43
- Dark Iron Watchman 44
- Glassweb Spider 43-35
- Tempered War Golem 45-46

11 Thorium Point

Silithus

Climbing west, out of the steam of Un'Goro Crater, lies Silithus. This desert land is in a state of flux. The Cenarion Circle has bravely taken up arms to defend Azeroth from the inhabitants of Ahn'Qiraj, and the host of insect-monsters that call the various Hives home. Among the larger more visible dangers a thread of discord is sewn from the followers of the Twilight Hammer. Many dangers lurk in this mysterious land, but there is much to gain.

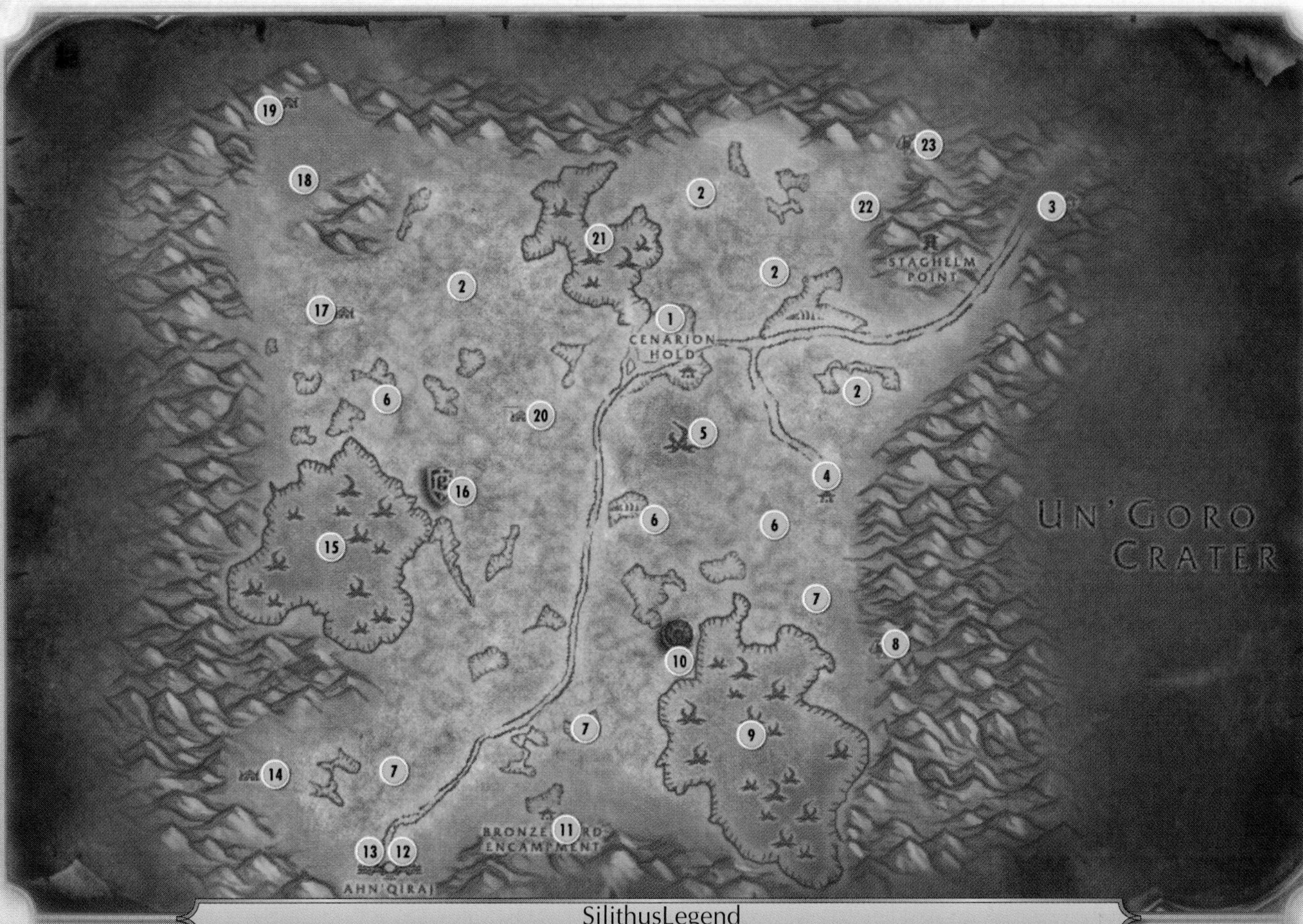

SilithusLegend

1 Cenarion Hold
- Runk Windtamer 55 Wind Rider Master
- Scout Bloodfist 55 Quest
- Squire Leoren Mal'derath 60 Stable Master
- Baristolth of the Shifting Sands 60 Quest
- Commander Mar'alith 62 Quest
- Mishta 58 General Trade Goods Vendor
- Windcaller Kaldon 60 Quest
- Cloud Skydancer 55 Hippogryph Master
- Rifleman Torrig 55 Quest
- Vish Kozus 61 Quest
- Garon Hutchins 60 Quest
- Windcaller Yessendra 55 Quest
- Aurel Goldleaf 60 Quest
- Dirk Thunderwood 60 Quest
- Calandrath 54 Innkeeper
- Keyl Swiftclaw 60 Quest
- Beetix Ficklespragg 57 Quest
- Noggle Ficklespragg 55 Quest
- Kania 54 Enchanting Supplier
- Vargus 57 Quest/Blacksmith
- Warden Haro 58 Quest
- Geologist Larksbane 60 Quest
- Bor Wildmane 57 Quest
- Huum Wildmane 60 Quest
- Khur Hornstriker 57 Reagent Vendor

2 Northern Desert
- Stonelash Scorpid 54-55
- Sand Skitterer 55-56
- Dredge Striker 55-56
- Dust Stormer 55-56

3 Valor's Rest
- Zannok Hidepiercer 59 Leatherworking Supplies
- Jarund Stoutstrider 55 Quest
- Layo Starstrike 55 Quest

4 Southwind Village
- Tortured Druid 55-56
- Tortured Sentinel 57
- Aendel Windspear 60 Recipe Vendor
- Hive'Ashi Drone 57-58

5 The Swarming Pillar
- Hive'Ashi Swarmer 57-58 Elite

6 Central Desert
- Stonelash Pincer 56
- Dredge Crusher 57-58
- Desert Rumbler 58
- Twilight Marauder 58
- Twilight Marauder Morna 58 Elite Boss

7 Southern Desert
- Stonelash Flayer 57-58
- Rock Stalker 57-58
- Cyclone Warrior 57-58
- Twilight Marauder 58
- Twilight Marauder Morna 58 Elite Boss

8 Ortell's Hideout
- Hermit Ortell 58 Quest

9 Hive'Regal
- Hive'Regal Spitfire 59-60 Elite
- Hive'Regal Hive Lord 59-62 Elite
- Hive'Regal Ambusher 59-60 Elite
- Hive'Regal Burrower 59-60 Elite
- Hive'Regal Slavemaker 59-60 Elite
- Mistress Natalia Mar'alith 62 Elite Boss
- Cenarion Scout Landion 60 Quest

10 Horde Encampment
- Krug Skullsplit 60 Quest
- Merok Longstride 60 Quest
- Shadow Priestess Shal 60 Quest
- Apothecary Quinard 55 Quest
- General Kirika 60 Quest

11 Bronzebeard Encampment
- Rutgar Glyphshaper 60 Quest
- Frankal Stonebridge 60 Quest
- Deathclasp 59 Elite Boss

12 The Scarab Wall

13 The Scarab Dias
- Jonathan the Revelator 61 Quest

14 Southern Twilight Camp
- Twilight Geolord 59-60
- Twilight Avenger 58-59
- Twilight Master 60
- Twilight Stonecaller 59-60
- Twilight Keeper Exeter 60
- Nelson the Nice 60 Elite

15 Hive'Zora
- Hive'Zora Reaver 59-60 Elite
- Hive'Zora Waywatcher 59 Elite
- Hive'Zora Wasp 58-59
- Hive'Zora Hive Sister 59-60 Elite
- Hive'Zora Tunneler 58 Elite
- Cenarion Scout Azenel 60 Quest

16 Alliance Encampment
- Janela Stouthammer 60 Quest
- Marshal Bluewall 60 Quest
- Captain Blackanvil 60 Quest
- Arcanist Nozzlespring 60 Quest
- Sergeant Carnes 60 Quest

17 Eastern Twilight Camp
- Twilight Geolord 59-60
- Twilight Avenger 58-59
- Twilight Stonecaller 59-60
- Twilight Keeper Mayna 60
- Twilight Prophet 60 Elite

18 The Crystal Vale
- Dust Stormer 55-57
- Desert Rumbler 57-58

19 Ravaged Twilight Camp
- Desert Rumbler 57-58
- Highlord Demitrian 62 Quest

20 Central Twilight Camp
- Twilight Geolord 59-60
- Twilight Avenger 58-59
- Twilight Stonecaller 59-60
- Twilight Keeper Havunth 60
- Twilight Prophet 60 Elite

21 Hive'Ashi
- Hive'Ashi Worker 57-58 Elite
- Hive'Ashi Swarmer 57-58 Elite
- Hive'Ashi Defender 58-59 Elite
- Hive'Ashi Sandstalker 58-59 Elite
- Hive'Ashi Stinger 57 Elite
- Cenarion Scout Jalia 60 Quest

22 Staghelm Point
- Twilight Overlord 60-61
- Twilight Avenger 59
- Dust Stormer 55
- Ralo'shan the Eternal Watcher 60 Quest

23 Twilight's Run
- Twilight Flamereaver 60
- Twilight Overlord 60-61
- Vyral the Vile 61

Silverpine Forest

The gloom of Silverpine is now a calming force for many of the area's residents. The Scourge control this area with a loose and rotting hand, and there are only a couple of areas that are hotly contested. Over on the east, in the middle of Lordamere Lake is a fortress where many Gnolls resist the attacks of the Forsaken. On the southern front, there are a number of mages of Dalaran who maintain a keep from which to launch strikes against their eternal foes. Apart from these enemies, the various elements of Worgen and disloyal Undead are dangerous forces for unwary travelers. Heroes from both the Horde and Alliance sometimes come here to battle Arugal, the lord and master of Shadowfang Keep.

Silverpine Forest Legend

1 North Tide's Hollow
- Moonrage Darksoul 13-14
- Moonrage Glutton 12-13

2 North Tide's Run
- Moonrage Darksoul 13-14
- Moonrage Glutton 12-13

3 The Skittering Dark
- Giant Grizzled Bear 12-13
- Moss Stalker 12-13

4 Skittering Dark Cave
- Mist Creeper 13-14
- Moss Stalker 12-13

5 The Dead Field
- Ferocious Grizzled Bear 11-12
- Giant Grizzled Bear 12-13
- Moonrage Glutton 12-13
- Mottled Worg 11-12
- Nightlash 14 Quest Target
- Rothide Gladerunner 11-12
- Rothide Mystic 12-13

6 The Ivar Patch
- Quinn Yorick 14 Quest
- Rane Yorick 15 Quest
- Mottled Worg 11-12
- Ravenclaw Slave 11-12

7 Maiden's Orchard
- Deathstalker Erland 11 Quest
- Mottled Worg 11-12
- Worg 10-11

8 The Shining Strand
- Vile Fin Shredder 12-13
- Vile Fin Tidehunter 13-14

9 Lordamere Lake
- Vile Fin Lakestalker 18-19
- Vile Fin Oracle 19-20

10 Fenris Isle
- Elder Lake Skulker 16-17
- Lake Skulker 15-16
- Rot Hide Brute 16-17
- Rot Hide Plague Weaver 17
- Rot Hide Savage 18-19
- Vile Fin Lakestalker 18-19
- Vile Fin Oracle 19-20

11 Fenris Keep
- Raging Rot Hide 18-19
- Rot Hide Savage 18-19

12 The Dawning Isles
- Elder Lake Creeper 18-19
- Elder Lake Skulker 16-17
- Lake Creeper 17-18
- Lake Skulker 15-16
- Vile Fin Shorecreeper 16-17
- Vile Fin Tidecaller 17-18

13 The Decrepit Ferry
- Fenwick Thatros 16
- Hand of Ravenclaw 15-16
- Ravenclaw Champion 14-15
- Ravenclaw Servant 13-14

14 The Sepulcher
- Apothecary Renferrel 14 Quest
- Dalar Dawnweaver 21 Quest
- Guillaume Sorouy 28 Journeyman Blacksmith
- High Executor Hadrec 30 Quest
- Innkeeper Bates 30 Innkeeper
- Johan Focht 19 Miner Trainer
- Karos Razok 55 Bat Handler
- Sarah Goode 30 Stable Master
- Shadow Priest Allistar 20 Quest
- Yuriv's Tombstone Quest Target
- Ferocious Grizzled Bear 11-12
- Moonrage Whitescalp 10-11

15 Deep Elm Mine
- Ferocious Grizzled Bear 11-12
- Grimson the Pale 15 Quest Target
- Moonrage Darksoul 13-14
- Moonrage Glutton 12-13

16 Deep Elm Canyons
- Dalaran Wizard 19-20
- Moonrage Bloodhowler 15-16
- Moonrage Darksoul 13-14
- Vile Fin Lakestalker 18-19
- Vile Fin Oracle 19-20

17 Olsen's Farthing
- Ravenclaw Raider 12-13
- Ravenclaw Slave 11-12

18 Shadowfang Keep
- Entrance to Shadowfang Keep World Dungeon

19 Pyrewood Village
- Dalaran Apprentice 13-14
- Giant Grizzled Bear 12-13
- Pyrewood Elder 14-15 Elite
- Pyrewood Sentry 15 Elite
- Pyrewood Watcher 14 Elite

20 Greymane Wall
- Bloodsnout Worg 16-17
- Haggard Refugee 18-19
- Moonrage Bloodhowler 15-16
- Sickly Refugee 19-29
- Valdred Moray 21 Quest Target

21 Ambermill
- Archmage Arateic 18 Quest Target
- Dalaran Conjurer 17-18
- Dalaran Protector 14-15
- Dalaran Warder 16-17
- Dalaran Watcher 18-19
- Dalaran Wizard 19-20

22 Beren's Peril
- Dalaran Watcher 18-19
- Dalaran Wizard 18-19
- Ravenclaw Drudger 19-20
- Ravenclaw Guardian 20-21

Stonetalon Mountains

Stonetalon Mountains can be found in the mountains between the Barrens and Desolace. The Tauren outpost of Sun Rock Retreat lies off the beaten path near the middle of the mountain and provides the Horde with the only local inn. The Peak itself houses an Alliance flight path and an Alliance vendor. Though home to many beasts, the wilderness is constantly being cut back by expanding goblin deforesters. In addition to the Barrens and Desolace, explorers can travel to and from Ashenvale forest via a secret tunnel that burrows through the foothills.

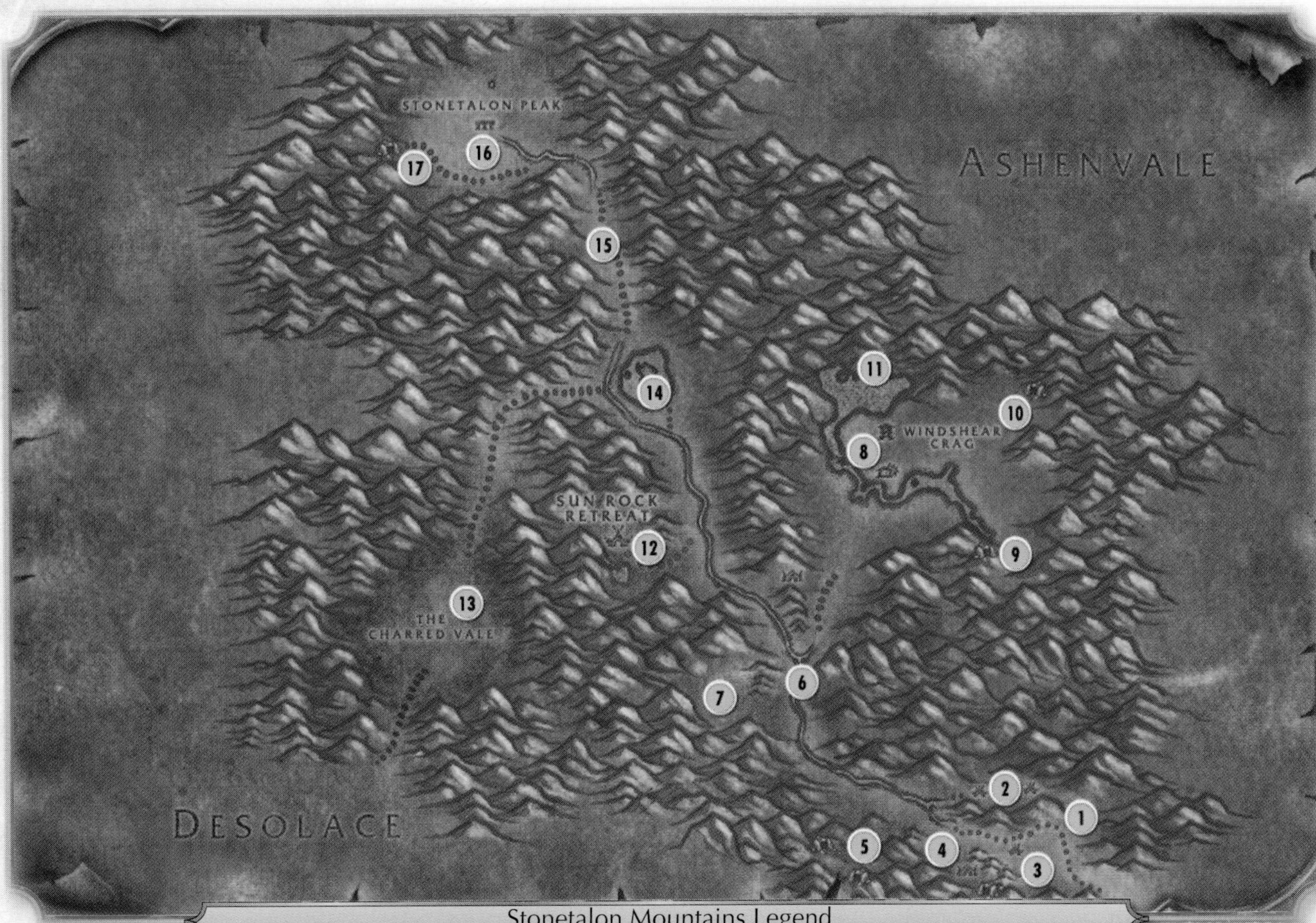

Stonetalon Mountains Legend

1 Camp Aparaje
- Grimtotem Mercenary 15
- Grimtotem Ruffian 15

2 Grimtotem Post
- Cliff Stormer 17
- Gorehoof the Black 17
- Grimtotem Brute 15-16
- Grimtotem Sorcerer 15-16
- Kaya Flathoof 15

3 Greatwood Vale
- Grimtotem Mercenary 15
- Grimtotem Ruffian 15

4 Malaka'jin
- Witch Doctor Jin'Zil 25 Quest
- Ken'Zigla 20 Quest
- Borand 30 Bowyer

5 Boulderslide Ravine

6 Web Winder Path
- Gaxim Rustfizzle 30 Quest
- Kaela Shadowspear 23 Quest
- Deepmoss Creeper 17-18
- Deepmoss Venomspitter 18-19

7 Sishir Canyon

8 Windshear Crag
- Ziz Fizziks 20 Quest
- Cliff Stormer 18-19
- Raging Cliff Stormer 19-20
- Deepmoss Venomspitter 18-19
- Deepmoss Webspinner 20-21
- Young Pridewing 19
- Venture Company Logger 19-20
- Venture Company Deforester 20
- Venture Company Operator 20,21
- XT:4 23
- XT:9 23

9 Windshear Mine
- Piznik 20 Quest
- Windshear Digger 21-22
- Windshear Geomancer 21-22
- Windshear Overlord 22-23
- Windshear Tunnelrat 21

10 Talondeep Path
- Braug Dimspirit 35 Quest

11 Cragpool Lake
- Nizzik 24 Vendor
- Venture Company Builder 22
- Venture Company Engineer 21-22
- Venture Company Machine Smith 22-23
- Gerenzo Wrenchwhistle 27
- Compact Harvest Reaper 22

12 Sun Rock Retreat
- Innkeeper Jayka 30 Innkeeper
- Tharm 55 Wind Ride Master
- Gereck Stable Master
- Jeeda 24 Vendor
- Krond 27 Butcher
- Grawnal 32 General Goods
- Stonetalon Grunt

13 The Charred Vale
- Blackened Basilisk 24
- Scorched Basilisk 28
- Singed Basilisk 25
- Rogue Flame Spirit 24
- Burning Ravager 24-25
- Burning Destroyer 25-26
- Charred Ancient 25
- Blackened Ancient 28
- Furious Stone Spirit 24-27
- Young Chimaera 24
- Fledgling Chimaera 25-27
- Chimaera Matriarch 28
- Bloodfury Harpy 23-24
- Bloodfury Ambusher 23-24
- Bloodfury Slayer 25-26
- Bloodfury Rogue Feather 25-26
- Bloodfury Windcaller 24
- Bloodfury Storm Witch 26-27

14 Mirkfallon Lake
- Pridewing Wyvern 21-22
- Pridewing Consort 22-23
- Pridewing Skyhunter 23-24
- Deepmoss Venomspitter 18-19
- Raging Cliff Stormer 19-20
- Antlered Courser 22
- Blackened Basilisk 24
- Rogue Flame Spirit 23

15 Stonetalon Mountain
- Braelyn Firehand 30 Quest
- Antlered Courser 22-23

16 Stonetalon Peak
- Teloren Hippogryph Master
- Chylina 24 Vendor
- Keeper Albagorm 30 Quest
- Sap Beast 22-23
- Corrosive Sap Beast 25
- Antlered Courser 22-23
- Great Courser 25
- Fey Dragon 24
- Wily Fey Dragon 26
- Twilight Hunter 23-24
- Son of Cenarius 25
- Daughter of Cenarius 23-25
- Cenarion Botanist 23-24
- Treant Ally 23

17 The Talon Den
- Cenarion Druid 26-27 Elite
- Cenarion Caretaker 25-26 Elite
- Mirkfallon Dryad 25 Elite
- Gatekeeper Kordurus 25 Elite

Stranglethorn Vale

At the southern end of the Eastern Kingdoms is an area of rivers, jungle, and coastline known as Stranglethorn Vale. This gigantic section of the continent is home to many beasts, and it is also a place where Goblins have and pirates are found in great numbers. The Horde settlement of Grom'Gol is here, along the western coast (accessed via Blimps from Orgrimmar and Undercity). To the south is Booty Bay, a neutral town that is truly a place where anything goes. Some of the finest hunters of big game in all of Azeroth come to Stranglethorn in hope of fighting the rarest of felines, apes, and raptors.

Stranglethorn Vale Legend

1 Rebel Camp
- Brother Nimetz 40 Quest
- Corporal Bluth 40 Vendor
- Corporal Kaleb 40 Quest
- Lieutenant Doren 40 Quest

2 Kurzen's Compound
- Kurzen Commando 34
- Kurzen Jungle Fighter 32-33
- Kurzen Medicine Man 32-33
- Kurzen War Panther 32-33
- Kurzen War Tiger 32
- Kurzen Wrangler 34

3 The Stockpile
- Colonel Kurzen 40 Elite Quest Target
- Kurzen Commando 34-35
- Kurzen Elite 36-37
- Kurzen Headshrinker 34-35
- Kurzen Shadow Hunter 38
- Kurzen Subchief 38
- Kurzen Witch Doctor 36

4 Northern Stranglethorn Vale
- Galvan the Ancient 60 Quest
- Bhag'thera 40 Quest Target
- Bloodscalp Beastmaster 34
- Bloodscalp Hunter 35
- Bloodscalp Scavenger 33
- Elder Stranglethorn Tiger 34-35
- Lastail Raptor 35
- Mistvale Gorilla 32-33
- Panther 32-33
- River Crocolisk 31
- Shadowmaw Panther 38
- Sharptooth Frenzy 31
- Stone Maw Basilisk 32
- Stranglethorn Tiger 33
- Stranglethorn Tigress 37-38
- Venture Company Mechanic 34
- Venture Company Miner 34-35
- Young Panther 30-31
- Young Stranglethorn Tiger 30-31

5 Nesingwary's Expedition
- Ajeck Rouack 40 Quest
- Barnil Stonepot 40 Quest
- Hemet Nesingwary 40 Quest
- Jaquilina Dramet 39 Axe Vendor
- Sir S. J. Erigadin 40 Quest
- River Crocolisk 30-31
- Young Stranglethorn Tiger 30-31

6 Ruins of Zul'Kunda
- Bloodscalp Beastmaster 34-35
- Bloodscalp Berserker 36-37
- Bloodscalp Headhunter 36-37
- Bloodscalp Hunter 34-35
- Bloodscalp Mystic 35
- Bloodscalp Scout 34-35
- Bloodscalp Tiger 35
- Bloodscalp Witch Doctor 37
- Nezzliok the Dire 40 Quest Target

7 Zuuldaia Ruins
- Bloodscalp Berserker 36-37
- Bloodscalp Headhunter 36-37
- Bloodscalp Witch Doctor 37

8 The Savage Coast
- Bloodscalp Axethrower 33
- Bloodscalp Shaman 34
- Crystal Spine Basilisk 34
- Elder Saltwater Crocolisk 38
- Lashtail Raptor 35
- Saltwater Crocolisk 35-36

9 Bal'lal Ruins
- Bloodscalp Axe Thrower 33
- Bloodscalp Shaman 33-34
- Bloodscalp Warrior 33-34

10 Tkashi Ruins
- Bloodscalp Axe Thrower 34
- Bloodscalp Shaman 33-34
- Bloodscalp Warrior 33-34

11 Lake Nazferiti
- Snapjaw Crocolisk 35-36
- Sharptooth Frenzy 31-32

12 Venture Company Operations Center
- Foreman Cozzle 38 Quest Target
- Venture Company Geologist 35-36
- Venture Company Mechanic 35

13 Venture Company Base Camp
- Venture Company Geologist 35-36
- Venture Company Mechanic 34
- Venture Company Shredder 37

14 Mosh'Ogg Ogre Mound
- Mosh'Ogg Lord 45 Elite
- Mosh'Ogg Mauler 43 Elite
- Mosh'Ogg Shaman 43 Elite
- Mosh'Ogg Spellcrafter 43-44 Elite
- Mosh'Ogg Warmonger 41-42 Elite

15 Mizjah Ruins
- Mosh'Ogg Brute 36-37
- Mosh'Ogg Witchdoctor 37

16 Southern Stranglethorn
- Se'Jib 50 Tribal Leatherworker
- Cold Eye Basilisk 39
- Jungle Thunderer 37-38
- Shadowmaw Panther 37
- Sharptooth Frenzy 32
- Stranglethorn Tigress 37-38

17 Balia'mah Ruins
- Skullsplitter Mystic 39
- Skullsplitter Axe Thrower 39-40
- Skullsplitter Warrior 39-40

18 Ruins of Zul'Mamwe
- Ana'thek the Cruel 45
- Kurzen Mindslave 44
- Mogh the Undying 44 Elite
- Skullsplitter Axe Thrower 39-40
- Skullsplitter Beastmaster 42
- Skullsplitter Berserker 43-44
- Skullsplitter Headhunter 43-44
- Skullsplitter Hunter 41-42
- Skullsplitter Mystic 39-40
- Skullsplitter Panther 41-42
- Skullsplitter Scout 41-42
- Skullsplitter Spiritchaster 44
- Skullsplitter Warrior 39-40
- Skullsplitter Witch Doctor 41-42

19 Venture Company Mine
- Venture Company Foreman 42
- Venture Company Strip Miner 40-41
- Venture Company Tinkerer 41

20 The Cape of Stranglethorn
- Jungle Stalker 40-41
- Shadowmaw Panther 37
- Thrashtail Basilisk 41-42

21 Southern Savage Coast
- Bloodsail Mage 40-41
- Bloodsail Raider 40-41
- Cold Eye Basilisk 39-40
- Jungle Stalker 40-41
- Naga Explorer 43-44

22 Gurubashi Arena
- Jungle Stalker 40-41

23 Bloodsail Compound
- Bloodsail Swashbuckler 42
- Bloodsail Warlock 42-43
- Jungle Stalker 40-41

24 Ruins of Jubuwal
- Jon-Jon the Crow 44
- Zanzil Hunter 44
- Zanzil Zombie 44

25 Crystalvein Mine
- Ironjaw Basilisk 43-44

26 Ruins of Aboraz
- Yenniku 41 Quest
- Chucky "Ten Thumbs" 43
- Zanzil Hunter 44
- Zanzil Naga 44
- Zanzil Witch Doctor 44
- Zanzil Zombie 43

27 The Crystal Shore
- Silverback Patriarch 43

28 Mistvale Valley
- Witch Doctor Unbagwa 50 Quest
- Elder Mistvale Gorilla 40-41
- Gorlash 47 Elite Quest Target

29 Nek'mani Wellspring
- Naga Explorer 43-44

30 Booty Bay
- "Sea Wolf" MacKinley 44 Quest
- "Shaky" Phillips 44 Quest
- Baron Revilgaz 60 Quest
- Brikk Keencraft 54 Blacksmith
- Captain Hecklebury Smotts 37 Quest
- Crank Fizzlebub 34 Quest
- Drizzlik 45 Quest
- First Mate Crazz 44 Quest
- Flora Silverwind 44 Herbalist
- Gramik Goodstitch 34 Tailor
- Gringer 55 Wind Rider Master
- Gyll 55 Gryphon Master
- Innkeeper Skindle 46 Innkeeper
- Kebok 35 Quest
- Krazek 35 Quest
- Narkk 42 Pet Vendor
- Oglethorpe Obnoticus 50 Gnome Engineer/Quest
- Rikqiz 43 Leatherworker
- Xizk Goodstitch 43 Tailor

31 Wild Shore
- Bloodsail Deckhand 43-44
- Bloodsail Elder Magus 44
- Bloodsail Mage 40-41
- Bloodsail Seadog 44-45
- Bloodsail Swabby 44
- Bloodsail Swashbuckler 42-43
- Bloodsail Warlock 42-43
- Brutus 43
- Captain Keelhaul 47
- Fleet Master Firallon 48
- Garr Salthoof 43
- Ironpatch 43
- Southern Sand Crawler 40-41

32 Jaguero Isle
- Princess Poobah 50 Quest
- Jaguero Stalker 50
- King Mukla 55 Quest Target
- Skymane Gorilla 50

33 Janeiro's Point
- Mok'rash 50 Elite Quest Target

34 Kal'al Ruins
- Murkgill Forager 35
- Murkgill Hunter 35-36
- Murkgill Lord 37
- Murkgill Warrior 35-36

35 Grom'gol Base Camp
- Angrun 40 Herbalist
- Brawn 35 Leatherworker
- Commander Aggro'gosh 55 Quest
- Far Seer Mok'thardin 45 Quest
- Kin'weelay 39 Quest
- Mudduk 40 Cook
- Nimboya 41 Quest
- Thysta 55 Wind Rider Master
- Zeppelin Master Nez'raz 60 Zeppelin Master

The World
Maps
Cities
Factions
Races
Classes

Swamp of Sorrows

Through Deadwind Pass, east from Duskwood, is the Swamp of Sorrows. Dragonkin dominate the eastern swamps, destroying any interlopers, while Murlocs, Spiders, and Horde patrols hold the south. Fortified and reinforced frequently is a Horde outpost in the south, in a spot where the Alliance simply has no control or ability to oust their troops. To the north many lost ones are found, though some are mad and aggressive to all, a few have wisdom to share.

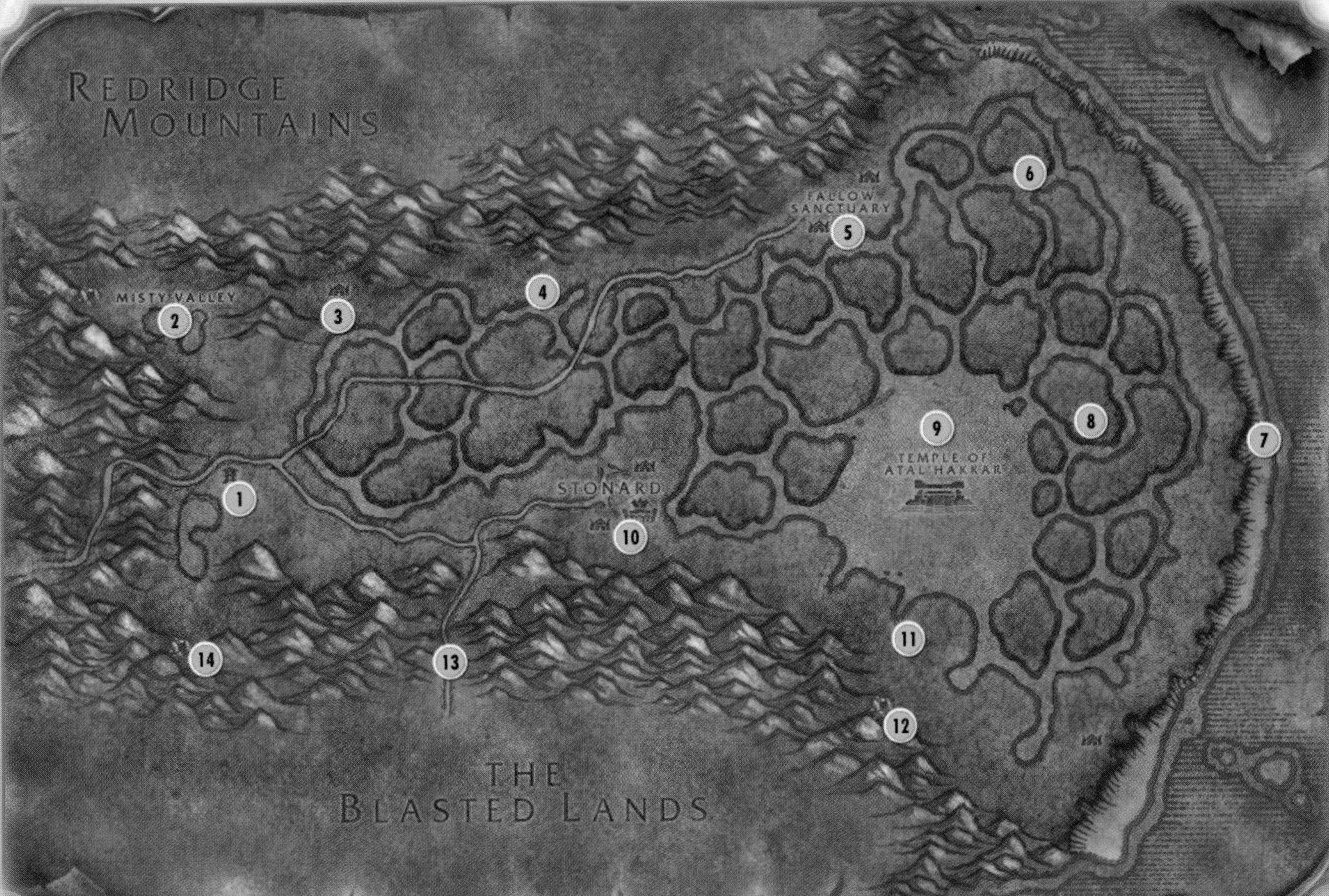

Swamp of Sorrows Legend

1. **Splinterspear Junction**
   - Sorrow Spinner 36
   - Stonard Scout 37
   - Swamp Jaguar 36
2. **Misty Valley**
   - Mire Lord 42
   - Swampwalker Elder 39-40
   - Swampwalker 38-39
   - Tangled Horror 40-41
3. **The Harborage**
   - Magtoor 42 Quest
   - Masat T'andr 44 Vendor
   - Draenel Exile 42
   - Swamp Jaguar 37
   - Young Sawtooth Crocolisk 35-36
4. **The Shifting Mire**
   - Lost One Fisherman 36
   - Lost One Muckdweller 36-37
   - Lost One Mudlurker 34
   - Noboru the Cudgel 39 Quest Target
   - Sawtooth Crocolisk 38
   - Sorrow Spinner 36-37
   - Swamp Jaguar 36-37
   - Swampwalker 39
   - Tangled Horror 40
5. **Fallow Sanctuary**
   - Galen Goodward 37 Quest
   - Lost One Chieftain 39
   - Lost One Cook 37
   - Lost One Fisherman 36
   - Lost One Hunter 36-37
   - Lost One Muckdweller 36-37
   - Lost One Riftseeker 37-38
   - Lost One Seer 38
   - Stonard Explorer 37-38
6. **Northern Swamp of Sorrows**
   - Sawtooth Crocolisk 38-39
   - Shadow Panther 39-40
   - Tangled Horror 40
7. **Misty Reed Strand**
   - Marsh Flesheater 43-44
   - Marsh Inkspewer 42-43
   - Marsh Murloc 41
   - Monstrous Crawler 43
   - Sawtooth Snapper 42
   - Silt Crawler 40-41
   - Stonard Explorer 38
8. **Sorrowmurk**
   - Elder Dragonkin 45 Elite
   - Sawtooth Snapper 41-42
   - Scalebane Captain 43-44 Elite
9. **Pool of Tears**
   - Green Scalebane 42 Elite
   - Green Wyrmkin 42 Elite
   - Scalebane Captain 43-44 Elite
10. **Stonard**
    - Breyk 55 Wind Rider Master
    - Dispatch Commander Ruag 60 Quest
    - Fel'zerul 60 Quest
    - Grunt Tharlak 55 Quest
    - Grunt Zuul 55 Quest
    - Helgrum the Swift 60 Quest
    - Rogvar 53 Alchemist
    - Stonard Cartographer 52
    - Stonard Grunt 55
    - Stonard Orc 50
    - Stonard Wayfinder 50-51
    - Zun'dartha 60 Quest
11. **Stagalbog**
    - Deathstrike Tarantula 40-41
    - Marsh Flesheater 43
    - Marsh Inkspewer 42-43
12. **Stagalbog Cave**
    - Marsh Flesheater 43
    - Marsh Inkspewer 42-43
    - Marsh Oracle 45
13. **Pass to Blasted Lands**
    - Fallen Hero of the Horde 60 Quest
14. **Itharius' Cave**
    - Itharius 45 Quest

Tanaris

Gadgetzan is one big desert with all the desert creatures you have come to expect by now. It has lizards, buzzards, elementals and more. There are also Dragons, Ogres and humans along with an instanced dungeon to test the mighty. If that's not enough, head north and check out the pirates, they always put on a good show. It's a good place to solo - especially to farm things you need like leather or cloth. Some great rare items drop here (Julie's Dagger). Beyond that, the zone is huge and easily shareable with others. There's a place right by the crater where the mobs drop herbs, so you can kill for the herbs instead of looking for them.

Tanaris Legend

1 Gadgetzan
- Senior Surveyor Fizzledowser 50 Quest
- Tran'rek 45 Quest
- Nixx Sprocketspring 55 Goblin Engineer
- Buzzek Bracketswing 55 Master Engineer
- Spigot Operator Luglunket 40 Quest
- Trenton Lighthammer 55 Quest
- Pikkle 45 Mining Trainer

2 Noonshade Ruins
- Wastewander Bandit 41-42
- Wastewander Thief 40-41

3 Steamwheedle Port
- Yeh'ikinya 40 Quest
- Prospector Ironboot 45 Quest
- Stoley 30 Quest
- Torta 45 Quest

4 Waterspring Field
- Wastewander Bandit 41-43
- Caliph Scorpidsting 46
- Wastewander Thief 40-42
- Wastewander Shadow Mage 40-43
- Wastewander Rogue 42-44
- Wastewander Assassin 43-46
- Scorpid Tail Lasher 44-45 Fire Roc 43-44
- Blisterpaw Hyena 43-45
- Glasshide Gazer 44-46

5 Zalashji's Den
- Zalashji 45

6 Wavestrider Beach

7 Caverns of Time
- Anachronos
- Chronalis
- Occulus 50 Elite
- Tick

8 Lost Rigger Cove
- Southsea Pirate 44-46
- Southsea Freebooter 43-45
- Andre Firebeard 45
- Southsea Dock Worker 44-46
- Southsea Swashbuckler 44-45

9 South Break Shore
- Coast Strider 48 Elite Giant
- Surf Glider 48-50

10 Lands End Beach
- Giant Surf Glider 48-50 Elite

11 The Gaping Chasm
- Glasshide Glazer 45
- Hazzali Sandreaver 49-51
- Hazzali Stinger 49
- Hazzali Stormer 49-50
- Hazzali Tunneler 48-49
- Hazzali Wasp 48
- Hazzali Worker 47-49

12 Broken Pillar
- Marvon Rivetseeker Quest NPC
- Blisterpaw Hyena 43-46
- Fire Roc 44-45
- Glasshide Gazer 43-45
- Scorpid Tail Lasher 43-46
- Scorpid Dunestalker 45-47
- Gusting Vortex 44-46

13 East Moon Ruins
- Rabid Blisterpaw 45-48
- Dunemaul Ogre 45-47
- Dunemaul Brute 45-48
- Dunemaul Enforcer 45-47
- Dunemaul Ogre Mage 45-48
- Dunemaul Warlock 45-48
- Glasshide Gazer 44-47
- Glasshide Petrifier 48-49

14 South Moon Ruins
- Dunemaul Enforcer 45-47
- Dunemaul Ogre Mage 45-48
- Dunemaul Warlock 45-48
- Dune Smasher 48-49
- Glasshide Petrifier 47-49
- Searing Roc 47-48
- Scorpid Dunestalker 46-47

15 Valley of the Watchers
- Prospector Gunstan 45 Explorers' League Quest
- Dune Smasher 48-49 Elite Giant
- Raging Dune Smasher 50 Elite
- Blisterpaw Hyena 43-46
- Glasshides Petrifier 47-49

16 Thistleshrub Valley
- Glasshide Petrifier 47-49
- Scorpid Dunestalker 46-47
- Thistleshrub Rootshaper 49-50
- Thistleshrub Dew Collector 48-49
- Gnarled Thistleshrub 48-50

17 Dunemaul Compound
- Rabid Blisterpaw 45-48
- Dunemaul Ogre 45-47
- Dunemaul Brute 45-48
- Dunemaul Enforcer 45-47
- Dunemaul Ogre Mage 45-48
- Dunemaul Warlock 45-48
- Glasshide Gazer 44-47

18 The Noxious Lair
- Centipaar Stinger 48-50
- Centipaar Swarmer 49-50
- Centipaar Wasp 47-49

19 Abyssal Sands
- Blisterpaw Hyena 44-46
- Scorpid Tail Lasher 43-44
- Fire Roc 43-45
- Glasshide Basilisk 43-
- Scorpid Dunecrawler 46-47
- Glasshide Gazer 45-46
- Land Rager 45-46

20 Sandsorrow Watch
- Ground Pounder 41-42
- Glasshide Basilisk 42-43
- Starving Blisterpaw 41-42
- Sandfury Hideskinner 42-43 Elite
- Sandfury Axe Thrower 42-44 Elite
- Sandfury Firecaller 43-44 Elite
- Sandfury Shadowcaster 43-44 Elite

21 Entrance to Zul'Farrak World Dungeon

Teldrassil

Teldrassil is the new home of the Night Elves. This distant homeland is far away from the safety of the Alliance lands, yet they are free from the focus of many enemies. Undead are not tolerated in this forest of life and beauty, and the Night Elves have many protectors that guard the land from any demonic taint. Beware though; the Firbolg and Timberlings who once existed in perfect balance with this land, have grown aggressive of late. The Druids of Teldrassil seek answers before the beasts and people of the land suffer their own madness.

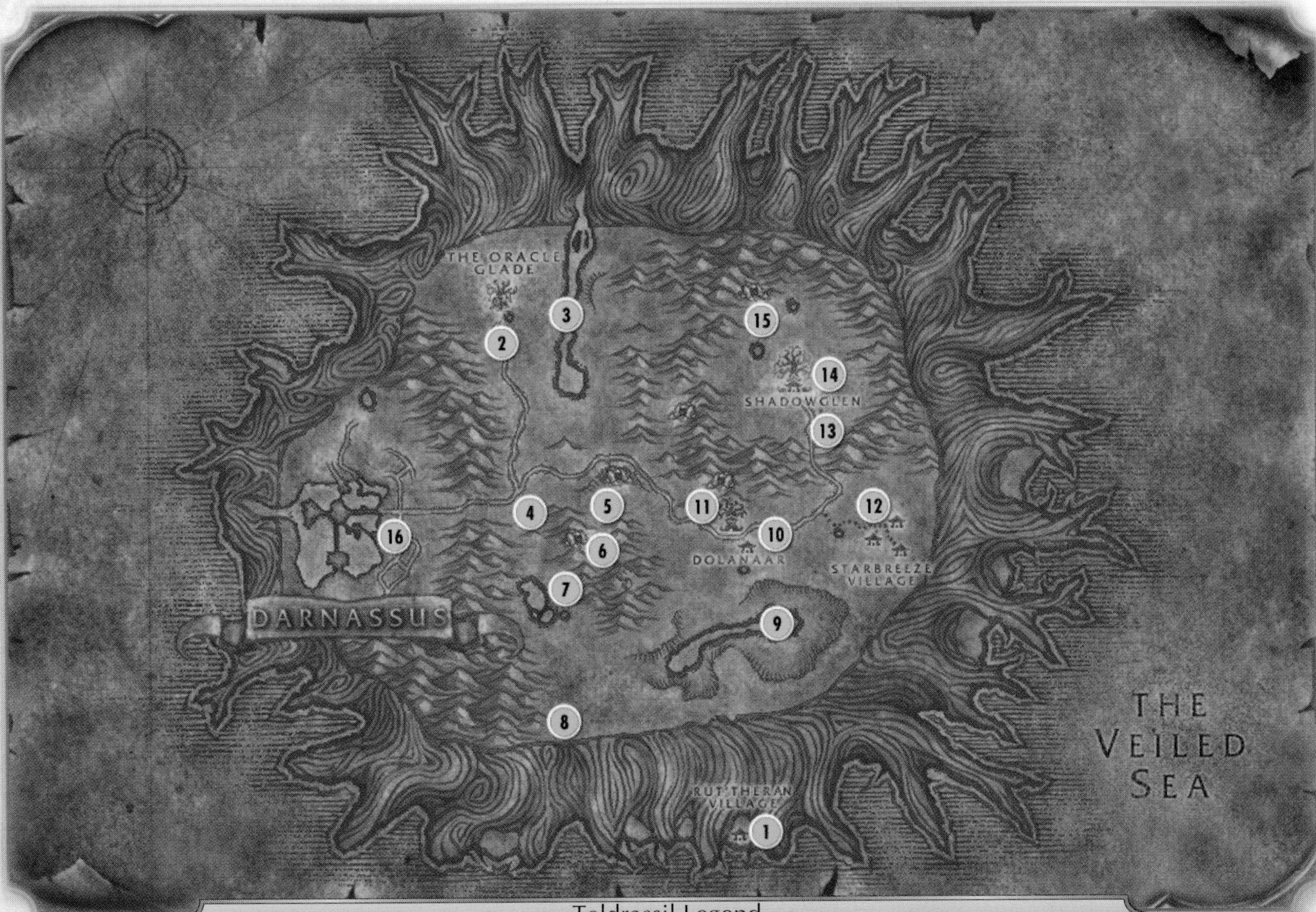

Teldrassil Legend

1 Rut'theran Village
- Boat to Auberdine
- Daryn Lightwind 30 Quest
- Erelas Ambersky 30 Quest
- Vesprystus 55 Hippogryph Master

2 The Oracle Glade
- Alanna Raveneye 29 Enchanter
- Mist 10 Quest
- Sentinel Arynia Cloudsbreak 10 Quest
- Strange-Leafed Plant
- Bloodfeather Fury 9-10
- Bloodfeather Harpy 8-9
- Bloodfeather Matriarch 11
- Bloodfeather Rogue 9
- Bloodfeather Sorceress 9
- Elder Nightsaber 8-9
- Feral Nightsaber 11
- Lady Sarthrah 12
- Minion of Sethir 10
- Sethir the Ancient 13 Quest Target
- Strigid Hunter 8-9
- Strigid Screecher 7-8
- Webwood Silkspinner 9

3 Wellspring River
- Blackmoss the Fetid 13 Quest Target
- Elder Timberling 11
- Timberling Mire Beast 9

4 Road to Darnassus
- Nadyia Maneweaver 30 Leatherworker
- Radnaal Maneweaver 19 Skinner
- Nightsaber Stalker 7-8
- Strigid Screecher 7-8
- Webwood Venomfang 7-8

5 Ban'ethil Hollow
- Agal 8 Quest Target
- Gnarlpine Ambusher 6-7
- Gnarlpine Defender 7
- Gnarlpine Shaman 8
- Webwood Venomfang 7-8

6 Ban'ethil Barrow Den
- Oben Rageclaw 40 Quest
- Gnarlpine Augur 9
- Gnarlpine Defender 7
- Gnarlpine Shaman 8
- Rageclaw 10 Quest Target

7 Pools of Arlithrien
- Nightsaber Stalker 7-8
- Strigid Screecher 7-8
- Webwood Venomfang 7-8

8 Gnarlpine Hold
- Strange-Fruited Plant
- Gnarlpine Avenger 10
- Gnarlpine Pathfinder 9-10
- Ursal the Mauler 12 Quest Target

9 Lake Al'Ameth
- Denalan 11 Quest
- Fel Cone (Ground Spawns)
- Timberling Seed (Ground Spawns)
- Oakenscowl 9+ Quest Target
- Timberling Bark Ripper 7-8
- Timberling Tramplers 8-9
- Timberling 5-6

10 Dolanaar
- Arthridas Bearmantle 11 Quest
- Byancie 22 First Aid
- Corithras Moonrage 10 Quest
- Cyndra Kindwhisper 28 Alchemist
- Innkeeper Keldamyr 30 Innkeeper
- Malorne Bladeleaf 17 Herbalist
- Sentinel Kyra Starsong 12 Quest
- Syral Bladeleaf 12 Quest
- Tallonkai Swiftroot 11 Quest
- Zarrin 13 Cook

11 Fel Rock
- Dark Sprite 6-7
- Lord Melenas 8 Quest Target
- Rascal Sprite 5-6
- Shadow Sprite 5-6
- Vicious Grell 7

12 Starbreeze Village
- Gaerolas Talvethren 7 Quest
- Zenn Foulhoof 7 Quest
- Ferocitas Dream Eater 8 Quest Target
- Gnarlpine Gardener 5
- Gnarlpine Mystic 6-7
- Gnarlpine Ursa 5-6
- Gnarlpine Warrior 6-7

13 Shadowglen
- Iverron 5 Quest
- Tarindrella 7 Quest
- Grell 2-3
- Grellkin 3-4
- Mangy Nightsaber 2-3
- Thistle Boar 2-3
- Webwood Spider 3-4
- Young Nightsaber 1-2
- Young Thistleboar 1-2

14 Aldrassil
- Conservator Ilthalaine 4 Quest
- Dirania Silvershine 8 Quest
- Gilshalan Windwalker 9 Quest
- Tenaron Stormgrip 10 Quest

15 Shadowthread Cave
- Webwood Egg (Ground Spawn)
- Githyliss the Vile 5 Quest Target
- Webwood Spider 3-4

16 Darnassus

Tirisfal Glades

Tirisfal Glades has seen the ravages of plague and the Scourge. The once vibrant villages and grand city of Lordaeron lay in ruins. Remnants of the Scourge still roam the land and the Forsaken who have awakened of their own free will are hunted by the Scarlet Crusade. Murlocs infect the northern shore and Rothide Gnolls have been seen taking over a farmstead just south of it. It is a land in constant turmoil.

Legend Tirisfal Glades

1 Deathknell
- Undertaker Mordo 5 Quest
- Executor Arren 5 Quest
- Deathguard Saltain 75 Quest
- Duskbat 1-2
- Young Scavenger 1-2
- Wretched Zombie 1-2
- Mindless Zombie 1-2
- Rattlecage Skeleton 2-3
- Mangy Duskbat 3-4
- Ragged Scavenger 2-3
- Scarlet Convert 3
- Mevin Korgal 5
- Calvin Montague 5 Quest

2 Night Web's Hollow
- Young Night Web Spider 2-3
- Night Web Spider 3-4

3 Solliden Farmstead
- Deathguard Simmer 23 Quest
- Greater Duskbat 6-7
- Decrepit Darkhound 5-6
- Tirisfal Farmhand 5-6
- Tirisfal Farmer 7
- Scarlet Warrior 6-7

4 Nightmare Vale
- Decrepit Hound 5-6
- Greater Duskbat 6-7
- Cursed Darkhound 7-8
- Scarlet Zealot 8-9
- Scarlet Missionary 7-8
- Captain Perrine 9

5 Stillwater Pond
- Decrepit Darkhound 5-6
- Cursed Darkhound 7-8
- Greater Duskbat 6-7
- Rotting Dead 5- 6
- Ravaged Corpse 6-7

6 Agamand Mills
- Cursed Darkhound 7-8
- Rattlecage Soldier 6-7
- Lost Soul 6
- Devlin Agamand 9
- Darkbone Caster 7-8
- Cracked Skull Soldier 8-9
- Nissa Agamand 10
- Thurman Agamand 10
- Gregor Agamand 10
- Rotting Ancestor 10-11
- Wailing Ancestor 9-11

7 Cold Hearth Manor
- Bowen Brisboi 24 Journeyman Tailor
- Ravaged Corpse 6-7
- Rotting Dead 5-6
- Vampiric Duskbat 8-9
- Cursed Darkhound 7-8
- Greater Duskbat 6-7

8 Brill
- Deathguard Dillinger 22 Quest
- Junior Apothecary Holland 20 Quest
- Faruza 5 Apprentice Herbalist
- Morganus 30 Stable Master
- Zachariah Post 30 Undead Horse Merchant
- Velma Warnam 30 Undead Horse Riding Instructor
- Executor Zygand 14 Quest
- Eliza Callen 12 Leather Armor Merchant
- Abigail Shiel 9 Trade Supplies
- Mrs. Winters 10 General Supplies
- Selina Weston 12 Alchemy & Herbalism Supplies

9 Garren's Haunt
- Rot Hide Gnoll 6-7
- Rot Hide Graverobber 6-7
- Rot Hide Mongrel 7-8
- Maggot Eye 10

10 Ruins of Lordaeron

11 Undercity

12 Brightwater Lake
- Clyde Kellen 16 Fisherman
- Cursed Darkhound 7-8
- Vampiric Duskbat 8-9

13 Balnir Farmstead
- Cursed Darkhound 7-8
- Vampiric Bat 8-9
- Bleeding Horror 9-11
- Wandering Spirit 10-11

14 The Bulwark
- Argent Quartermaster Hasana 58 Quest
- Argent Officer Garush 60 Quest
- High Executor Derrington 61 Quest
- Apothecary Dithers 58 Quest
- Shadow Priestess Vandis 60 Quest
- Alexi Barov 60 Quest

15 Crusader Outpost
- Scarlet Zealot 8-9
- Scarlet Friar 9-10
- Captain Vachon 11

16 Venomweb Vale
- Vampiric Duskbat 8-9
- Ravenous Darkhound 9-10
- Vicious Nightweb Spider 9-10

17 Faol's Rest
- Ravenous Darkhound 9-10

18 Whispering Gardens
- Entrance to Scarlet Monastery World Dungeon
- Scarlet Scout 29-30+
- Scarlet Magician 29-30+
- Scarlet Preserver 29-30+

19 Scarlet Watch Post
- Scarlet Friar 9-10
- Scarlet Vanguard 10-11
- Scarlet Bodyguard 10-11
- Scarlet Neophyte 10-11
- Captain Melrache 12

20 Zepplin to Orgrimmar and Grom'Gol-Outpost
- Deathguard Linnea 22 Quest
- Shelene Rhobart 25 Jouneyman Leatherworker
- Rand Rhobart 13 Skinner
- Martine Tramblay 15 Fishing Supplies

21 North Coast
- Vile Fin Minor Oracle 9-9
- Vile Fin Puddlejumper 7-8
- Vile Fin Muckdweller 9-10

22 Gunther's Retreat
- Gunther Arcanus 53 Quest
- Shambling Horror 7-8
- Hungering Dead 7-8
- Gunther's Minion 7-8

Un'Goro Crater

Un'Goro Crater is the blast from the past. The land is loaded with dinosaurs, walking plants, big bugs and elementals. As often happens in lands with such menacing flora and fauna, adventurers that have managed to get stuck there wish for your help and frequently offer quests. Targets are abundant and that helps with the kill quests. There is some collecting to be done, and there are some incredible quests that balance the whole mix out. It's not the biggest zone which is another plus. There's not an overwhelming amount of running for the quests, and that always helps.

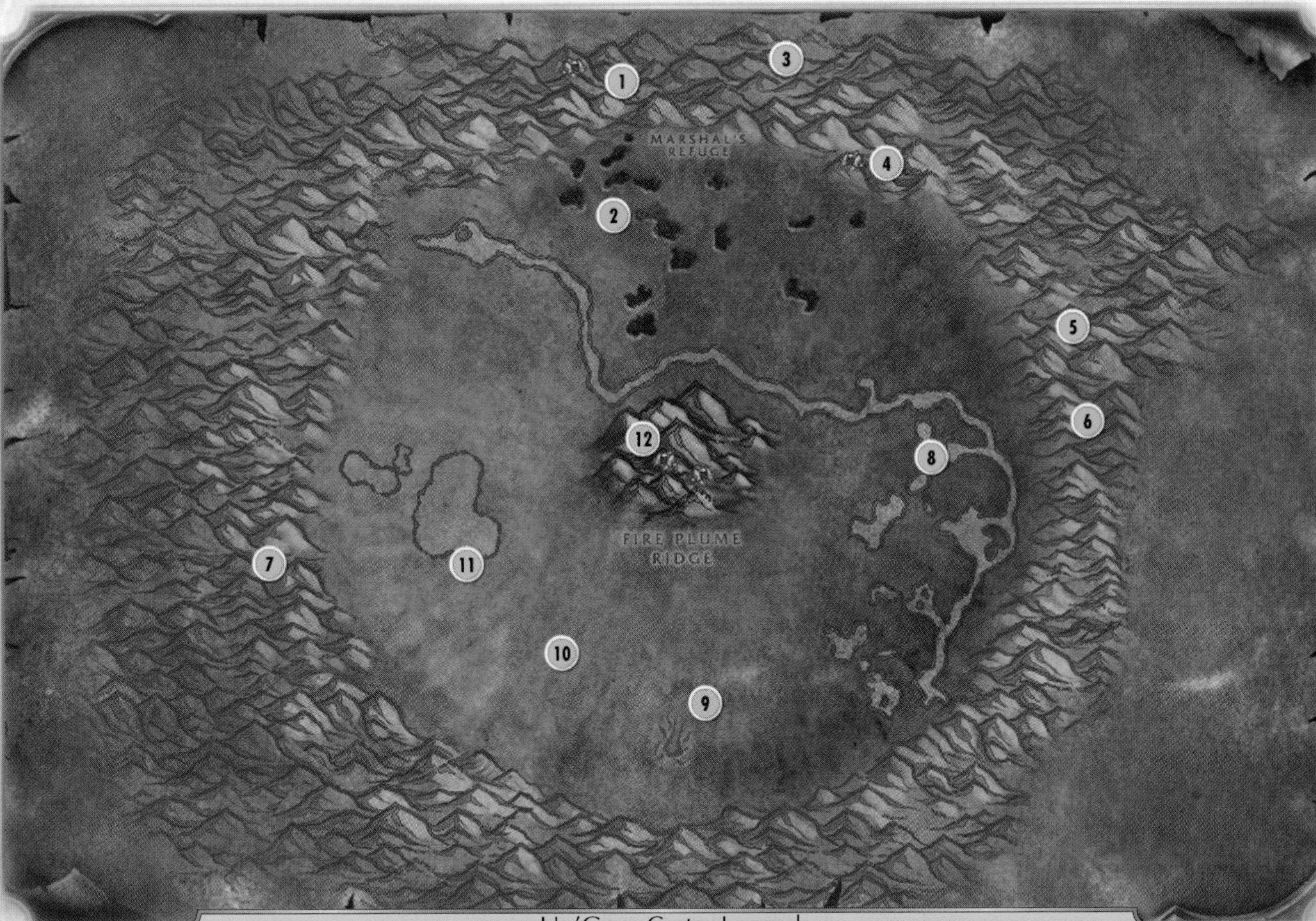

Un'Goro Crater Legend

1 Marshal's Refuge
Shizzle 40 Quest
Quixxil 40 Quest
Muigin 51 Quest
Petra Grossen 46 Quest
Dadanga 45 Quest
Hol'Anyee Marshal 45 Quest
Williden Marshal 48 Quest
Linken 40 Quest
Bloodpetal Pests 30-35

2 Lakkari Tar Pits
Karna Remtravel 45 Quest
Mor'Vek 60 "Ravasaur Trainer"
Tar Lurker 53-54
Tar Lord 53-54
Tar Beast 51-52
Tar Creeper 51-52
Primal ooze 50-51
Bloodpetal Flayer 51-52
Piemetradon 51-52
Stone Guardian 59-50 Elite
Young Diemetradon 50-51

3 Northern Crystal Pylon
Pterrordax 50-51

4 Fungal Rock
A-Me 01 48 Quest
Un'Goro Gorilla 50-51
Un'Goro Stomper 51-52
Un'Goro Thunderer 52-53
U'Cha 55

5 Ironstone Plateau
Fledgling Pterrordax 50

6 Eastern Stone Pylon
Fledgling Pterrordax 50
Pterrordax 50-52
Pterrordax 50-52

7 Western Crystal Pylon
Frenzied Pterrordax 52-53
Frenzied Pterrordax 52-53
Frenzied Pterrordax 52-53

8 The Marshlands
Ravasaur 48-49
Ravasaur Runner 49-50
Venomhide Ravasaur 50-51
Tyannodon 55Elite
Bloodpetal Lasher 49-50

9 The Slithering Scar
Gorishi Wasp 51-52
Gorishi Worker 51-52
Gorishi Reaver 52-53
Gorishi Stinger 52-53
Gorishi Tunneler 52-53

10 Terror Run
Glutinous Ooze 53-54
Bloodpetal Trapper 53-54
Elder Diemetradon 54-55
Spike Stegodon 53 Elite
Thunderstomp Stegodon 55 Elite
Plated Stegodon 53 Elite

11 Golakka Hot Springs
Elder Diemetradon 54-55
Bloodpetal Trapper 53-54
Glutinous Ooze 52-54
Krakle 60 Quest
Spiked Stegodon 52-54 Elite
Stegodon 53 Elite

12 Fire Plume Ridge
Scorching Elemental 53-54
Living Blaze 54-55
Blazerunner 56 Elite
Ironhide DevilSaur 55 Elite

The Western Plaguelands

Above the Alterac Mountains is the entrance to the Western Plaguelands. Tainted beasts, vicious Humans from the Scarlet Crusade, and a number of Scourge Undead live there. Cauldrons of bubbling liquids are guarded by the mindless dead. The Horde and the Alliance, so seldom to agree on matters, are both at war with the dangers posed by the Scourge, and this is the frontline of that battle. To the east is Darrowmere Lake, where Scholomance sits quietly in a deserted town. Walk here not, lest your group face trials of epic and deadly proportions.

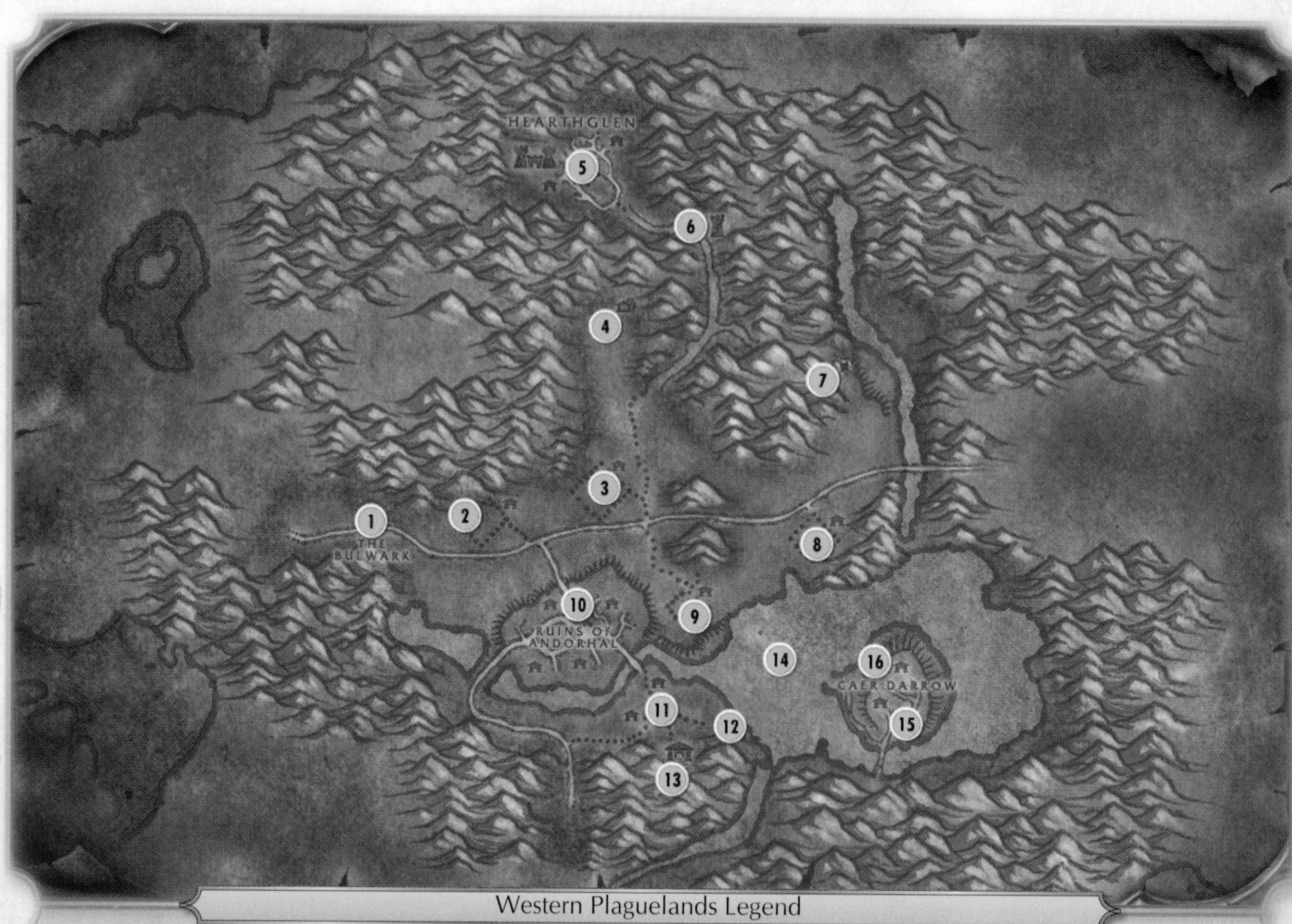

Western Plaguelands Legend

1 The Bulwark
- Carrion Vultures 52-53
- Diseased Black Bears 51-52
- Venom Mist Lurkers 51-52

2 Felstone Fields
- Scarlet Hound 52-54
- Scarlet Hunter 52-54
- Scarlet Ivoker 52-54
- Scarlet Medic 52-54
- Skelatal Flayer 50-52
- Skeletal Sorcerer 50-52
- Slavering Ghoul 50-52

3 Dalson's Tears
- Blighted Zombie 52-54
- Carrion Lurker 53-54
- Diseased Wolf 53-54
- Rotting Cadaver 52-54
- Skeletal Terror 52-54

4 Northridge Lumber
- Carrion Lurker 56-57
- Scarlet Knight 54-56
- Scarlet Lumberjack 54-56

5 Hearthglen
- Foremen Jerris 62 Elite
- High Protector Lorik 61 Elite
- Scarlet Paladin 55-56 Elite
- Scarlet Priest 56-57 Elite
- Scarlet Sentinel 55-56 Elite
- Scarlet Worker 55-57 Elite

6 Scarlet Tower
- High Clerist 63 Elite
- Scarlet Avenger 56-57
- Scarlet Knight 54-55
- Scarlet Mage 55-56
- Scarlet Spellbinder 57-58

7 The Weeping Cave
- Decaying Horror 55-56
- Devouring Ooze 55-56
- Plague Lurker 54-55
- Rotting Behemoth 55-56
- Vile Slime 54-55

8 Gahrron's Withering
- Hungering Wraith 56-58
- Plague Lurkers 54-55
- Taunting Vision 56-58
- Waling Death 56-58

9 The Writhing Haunt
- Fetid Zombie 55-56
- Freezing Ghoul 55-56
- Plague Lurker 54-55
- Rotting Ghoul 55-56

10 Ruins of Anderhol
- Cold Wraith 54-56 Elite
- Decrepit Guardian 56-57 Elite
- Flesh Golem 56-57 Elite
- Screaming Haunt 54-56 Elite
- Searing Ghoul 54-56 Elite
- Skeletal Acolyte 54-56 Elite
- Skeletal Executioner 55-56 Elite
- Skeletal Warlord 55-56 Elite
- Soulless Ghoul 54-56 Elite

11 Sorrow Hill
- Skeletal Flayers 50-51
- Slavering Ghouls 50-51

12 Uther's Tomb
- High Priest Thel'Danis 65

13 Sorrow Hill (Crypt)
- Lord Maldazzar
- Skeletal Flayers 50-51
- Skeletal Sorcerer 51-52
- Slavering Ghouls 50-51

14 Darrowmere Lake

15 Caer Darrow
- Artist Renfray 12
- Baker Masterson 37
- Caer Darrow Cannoneer
- Caer Darrow Citizen
- Caer Darrow Guardsman 54
- Caer Darrow Horseman 52-56
- Eva Sarkhoff 54
- Joseph Dirte 31
- Lucien Sarkhoff 55
- Magistrate Marduke 57
- Magnus Frostwake 50
- Melia 1
- Rory 35
- Sammy 1

16 Entrance to Scholomance World Dungeon

Westfall

Westfall is the bread basket of the southern lands. Once home to hundreds of the best farmers, the area is now sparsely populated; attacks from a huge band of Gnolls and increased activity by the Defias have almost driven everyone out of Westfall. Moonbrook is now a ghost town, save for the wandering of foul bandits, and none of the mines in the area are in the hands of good or honest folk. A militia of the people has formed and rallied around Sentinel Hill, one of the remaining bastions of resistance by the locals. Calling for help from Stormwind, they hold out and work to protect the remaining farms of Westfall.

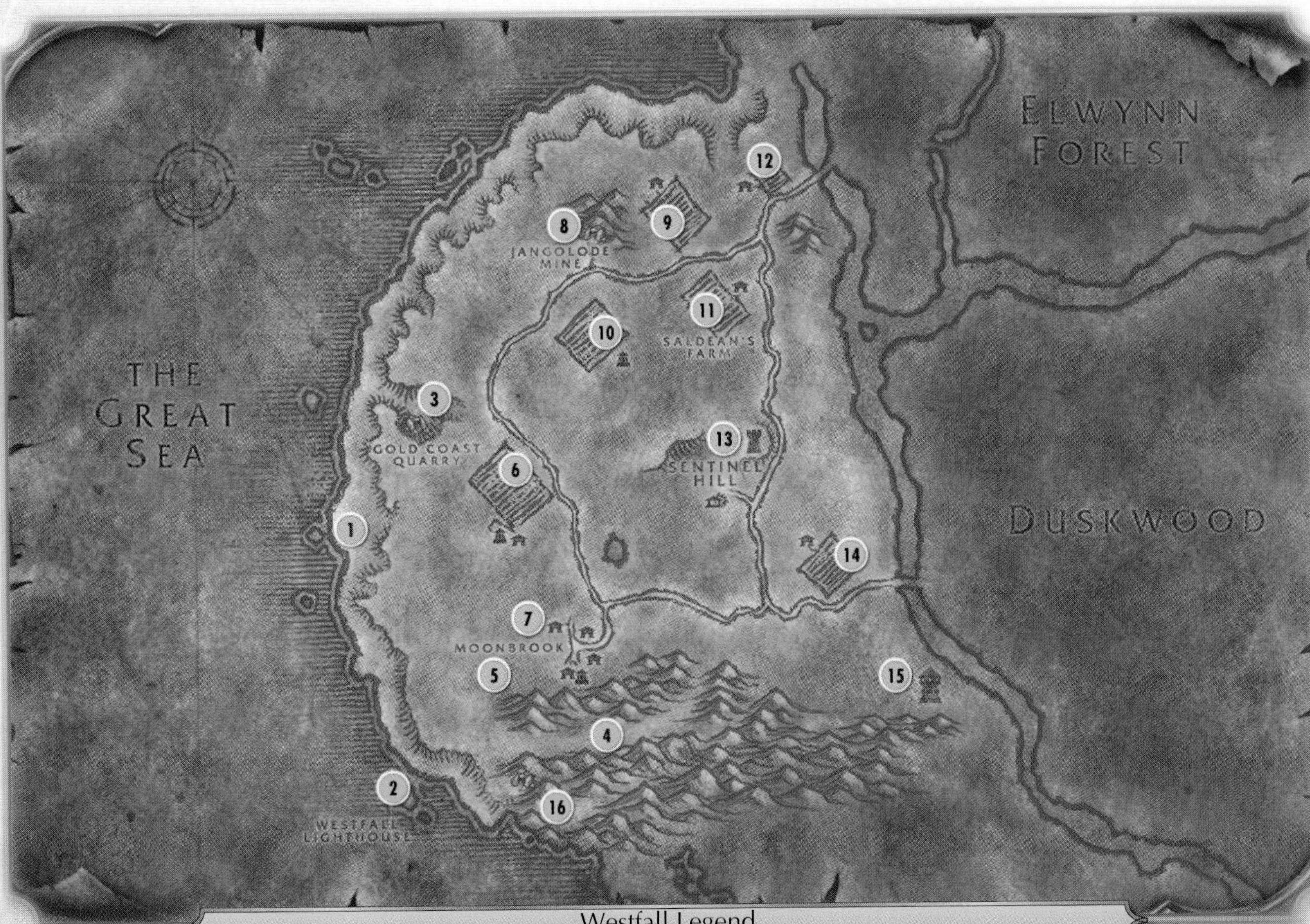

Westfall Legend

1 Longshore

Crawler 11-12
Greater Fleshripper 16-17
Murloc Coastrunner 12-13
Murloc Hunter 16-17
Murloc Minor Oracle 13-14
Murloc Netter 14-15
Murloc Oracle 17-18
Murloc Raider 11-12
Murloc Tidehunter 17-19
Murloc Warrior 15-16
Old Murk-Eye 20 Elite Quest Target
Riverpaw Herbalist 14-15
Riverpaw Mongrel 13-14
Sand Crawler 13-14
Sea Crawler 15-16
Shore Crawler 17-18

2 Westfall Lighthouse

Captain Grayson 30 Quest

3 Gold Coast Quarry

Coyote Packleader 12-13
Coyote 10-11
Defias Looter 13-14
Defias Looter 13-14
Defias Pillager 14-15
Defias Trapper 12-13
Fleshripper 13
Goretusk 14-15
Harvest Golem 11-12
Riverpaw Miner 14-15
Young Goretusk 12-13

4 The Dagger Hills

Grimbooze Thunderbrew 20 Quest
Defias Highwayman 17-18
Defias Knuckleduster 16-17
Defias Pathstalker 15-16

5 Demont's Place

Defias Knuckleduster 16-17
Defias Pathstalker 15-16
Defias Pillager 14-15
Fleshripper 13-14
Goretusk 14-15
Riverpaw Brute 15-16
Riverpaw Herbalist 14-15

6 Alexston Farmstead

Defias Looter 13-14
Defias Pillager 14-15
Defias Smuggler 11-12
Defias Trapper 13
Dust Devil 18-19
Foe Reaper 4000 20
Harvest Golem 11-12
Harvest Watcher 14-15

7 Moonbrook

Entrance to Deadmines Instance
Defias Looter 13-14
Defias Pillager 14-15
Fleshripper 13-14
Harvest Golem 11-12

8 Jangolode Mine

Coyote Packleader 12
Coyote 10-11
Defias Smuggler 11-12
Defias Trapper 12-13
Kobold Digger 12-13
Young Fleshripper 10-11

9 Furlbrow's Pumpkin Farm

Benny Blaanco 15
Coyote 10-11
Defias Looter 13-14
Defias Pillager 14-15
Defias Smuggler 11-12
Defias Trapper 12-13
Fleshripper 13-14
Harvest Watcher 14-15
Young Fleshripper 10-11
Young Goretusk 12-13

10 The Molsen Farm

Coyote 10-11
Harvest Golem 11-12
Harvest Watcher 14-15
Young Fleshripper 10-11

11 Saldean's Farm

Farmer Saldean 20 Quest
Salma Saldean 20 Quest
Coyote 10-11
Harvest Golem 11-12
Harvest Watcher 14-15
Young Fleshripper 10-11
Young Goretusk 12-13

12 The Jansen Stead

Farmer Furlbrow 20 Quest
Verna Furlbrow 20 Quest
Coyote 10-11
Defias Footpad 10-11
Riverpaw Gnoll 11-12
Rusty Harvest Golem 9-10
Young Fleshripper 11-12
Young Goretusk 12-13

13 Sentinel Hill

Captain Danuvin 33 Quest
Defias Traitor 15 Quest
Gryan Stoutmantle 35 Quest
Innkeeper Heather 30 Innkeeper
Kirk Maxwell 30 Stable Master
Protector Bialon 30 Quest
Scout Galiaan 30 Quest
Thor 55 Griffon Master
Defias Looter 13-14
Defias Pillager 14-15
Fleshripper 13-14
Goretusk 14-15
Great Goretusk 16-17
Greater Fleshripper 16-17
Young Fleshripper 10-11
Young Goretusk 12-13

14 The Dead Acre

Defias Knuckleduster 16-17
Great Goretusk 16-17
Greater Fleshripper 16-17
Harvest Reaper 17-18

15 The Dust Plains

Defias Tower Patroller 24
Defias Tower Sentry 24-25
Dust Devil 18-19
Great Goretusk 16-17
Klaven Mortwake 26 Elite Quest target
Riverpaw Bandit 16-17
Riverpaw Mystic 18-19
Riverpaw Taskmaster 17-18
Venture Co. Drone 22

16 Stilwell Farm

Daphne Stilwell 20

Wetlands

Sodden with moisure pouring off of the mountains and drifting in from sea, the Wetlands region is swamped with Slimes, Fen Dwellers, and a number of dangerous Humanoids. Gnolls, Orcs, and Dark Iron Dwarves hold various points in the south, east, and northern sections of the area. Out Menethil Harbor and most of the roads are safe from these troubles. For people interested in archeology, a large excavation site is located in the mountains just a tad east from Menethil. At the town itself, ships head out to Auberbine (in Darkshore), and Theramore (in the Dustwallow Marsh).

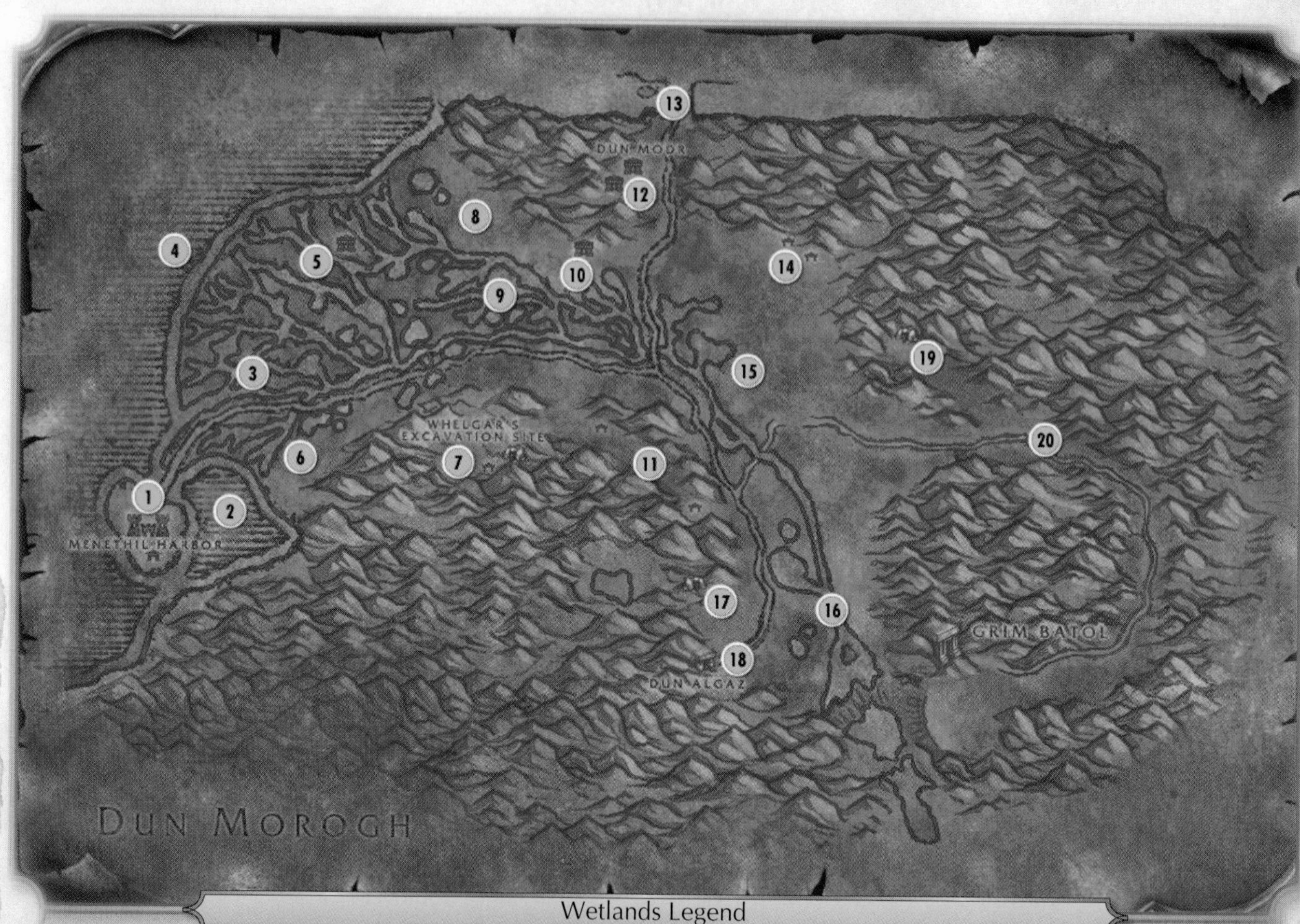

Wetlands Legend

1 Menethil

Archaeologist Flagongut 44 Quest
Bethaine Flinthammer 30 Stable Master
Captain Stoutfist 35 Quest
First Mate Fitzsimmons 30 Quest
Fremal Doohickey 30 First Aid
Glorin Steelbrow 25 Quest
Harlo Barnaby 25 Quest
Harold Riggs 25 Fishing
James Halloran 25 Quest
Junder Brokk 20 Quest
Mikhail 30 Quest
Red Jack Flint 22 Quest
Shellei Brondir 55 Gryphon Master
Sida 20 Quest
Tapoke "Slim" Jahn 34 Quest
Telurinon Moonshadow 25 Herbalism
Unger Statforth 25 Horse Vendor
Vincent Hyal 30 Quest

2 Menethil Bay

Bluegill Raider 28-29
Fen Dweller 20
Giant Wetlands Crocolisk 25-26
Wetlands Crocolisk 23-24
Young Wetlands Crocolisk 21-22

3 Bluegill Marsh

Bluegill Forager 22
Bluegill Muckdweller 23-24
Bluegill Murloc 20-21
Bluegill Oracle 26
Bluegill Puddlejumper 21-22
Bluegill Warrior 24-25
Fen Creeper 24-25
Fen Dweller 20-21
Giant Welands Crocolisk 25-26
Gobbler 22 Quest Target

4 The Lost Fleet

Captain Halyndor 30 Quest Target
Cursed Marine 27-28
Cursed Sailor 26-27
First Mate Snellig 29 Quest Target

5 Sundown Marsh

Fradd Swiftgear 24 Engineer Vendor
Wenna Silkbeard 29 Recipe Vendor
Fen Creeper 24-25
Giant Wetlands Crocolisk 25-26
Mosshide Alpha 27
Mosshide Brute 24-25
Mosshide Fenrunner 22
Mosshide Mystic 25-26
Mosshide Trapper 23-24
Wetlands Crocolisk 23-24
Young Wetlands Crocoolisk 21-22

6 Black Channel Marsh

Black Ooze 23
Mottled Raptor 22-23
Mottled Screecher 24-25

7 Whelgar's Excavation Site

Merrin Rockweaver 30 Quest
Ormer Ironbraid 25 Quest
Prospector Whelgar 30 Quest
Mottled Razormaw 25-26
Mottled Scytheclaw 25-26
Sarltooth 29 Quest Target

8 Saltspray Glen

Elder Razormaw 29
Fen Creeper 24
Fen Dweller 21
Fen Lord 26
Giant Wetlands Crocolisk 25-26
Highland Lashtail 24-25
Highland Raptor 23-24
Highland Razormaw 27-28
Highland Scytheclaw 25-26
Wetlands Crocolisk 23-24

9 Central Wetlands

Kixxie 25 Vendor
Black Slime 20
Fen Creeper 24
Fen Dweller 21
Fen Lord 26
Giant Wetlands Crocolisk 25-26
Mosshide Alpha 27
Mosshide Brute 24-25
Mosshide Fenrunner 22
Mosshide Mystic 25-26
Mosshide Trapper 23-24
Wetlands Crocolisk 23-24
Young Wetlands Crocoolisk 21-22

10 Ironbeard's Tomb

Black Ooze 23-24
Crimson Ooze 24-25

11 Angerfang Encampment

Chieftain Nek'rosh 32 Elite
Dragonmaw Battlemaster 30
Dragonmaw Bonewarder 27-28
Dragonmaw Centurion 29
Dragonmaw Raider 26-27
Dragonmaw Shadowwarder 29
Dragonmaw Swamprunner 28

12 Dun Modr

Dark Iron Entrepreneur 30 Vendor
Longbraid the Grim 35 Quest
Rhag Garmason 25 Quest
Dark Iron Demolitionist 30-31 Elite
Dark Iron Dwarf 27-28 Elite
Dark Iron Rifleman 27-28 Elite
Dark Iron Saboteur 28-29 Elite
Dark Iron Tunneler 29-30 Elite

13 Thandol Span

Comar Villard 22 Quest

14 Direforge Hill

Balgaras the Foul 34 Elite Quest Target
Black Ooze 24
Dark Iron Demolitionist 31 Elite
Dark Iron Dwarf 27-28 Elite
Dark Iron Saboteur 28-29 Elite
Dark Iron Tunneler 29-30 Elite
Highland Lashtail 25
Highland Raptor 24
Highland Scytheclaw 26

15 The Green Belt

Rethiel the Greenwarden 30 Quest
Black Ooze 24
Crimson Whelp 25-26
Highland Raptor 23-24
Lost Whelp 24-25
Red Whelp 24

16 Mosshide Fen

Black Ooze 23
Black Slime 21
Dark Iron Insurgent 18-19
Fen Dweller 20
Mosshide Fenrunner 22-23
Mosshide Gnoll 20-21
Mosshide Mistweaver 22
Mosshide Mongrel 22
Young Wetlands Crocolisk 21-22

17 Thelgen Rock

Cave Stalker 21-22
Leech Stalker 21

18 Dun Algaz

Dragonmaw Scout 19-20
Dragonmaw Grunt 20-21
Ma'ruk Wyrmscale 23

19 Raptor Ridge

Elder Razormaw 29
Highland Razormaw 27-28

20 Dragonmaw Gates

Red Dragonspawn 47-48
Red Scalebane 49
Red Wyrmkin 48-49
Scalebane Lieutenant 51-52
Scalebane Royal Guard 53-54
Wyrmkin Firebrand 52

Winterspring

The northern land of Winterspring is reached through a dangerous tunnel out of Felwood. The Furbolg who live there are hard to befriend. On the other side of the tunnel is Winterspring itself, where snow falls, geysers blast into the sky, and some of the greatest Yetis in all of Azeroth dwell. To escape from the cold and the monsters of Winterspring, look toward the center of the valley and speak with the Goblins who hold a neutral town there.

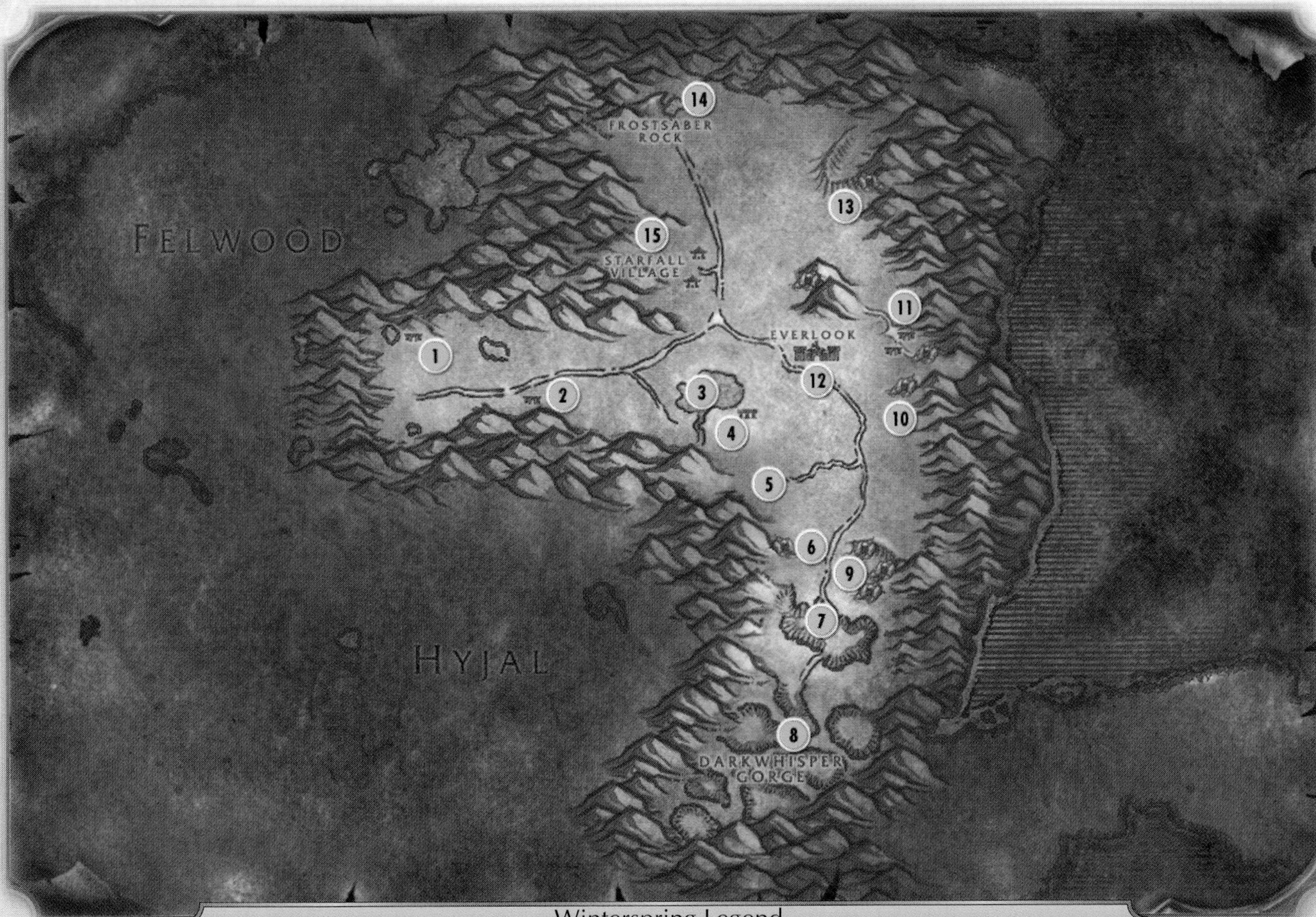

Winterspring Legend

1 Frostfire Hot Springs
- Fledgling Chillwind 54-55
- Ragged Owlbeast 53-55
- Rogue Ice Thistle 53-54
- Shardtooth Bear 53-54
- Winterfall Totemic 54-55
- Winterfall Pathfinder 53-54
- Winterfall Den Watcher 55-56

2 Timbermaw Post
- Winterfall Totemic 54-55
- Winterfall Pathfinder 53-54
- Winterfall Den Watcher 55-56

3 The ruins of Kel'Theril
- Anguished Highborn 55-56
- Suffering Highborn 54-55

4 Lake Kel'Theril
- Anguished Highborn 55-56
- Suffering Highborn 54-55

5 Mazthoril
- Brumeran 58 Elite
- Chillwind Chimera 55
- Cobalt Broodlings 55-56
- Cobalt Scalebane 56-57 Elite
- Cobalt Mageweaver 57-58 Elite
- Cobalt Welps 54
- Cobalt Wyrmkin 55-56 Elite
- Shardtooth Mauler 55
- Spell Eater 55-56
- Spellmaw 56 Elite
- Manaclaw 58 Elite
- Scryer 59 Elite
- Winterspring Owl 54-56

6 Dun Mandarr
- Berserker Owlbeast 57-58
- Crazed Owlbeast 58
- Elder Shardtooth 57-58
- Moontouched Owlbeast 58
- Winterspring Screecher 57-58

7 Frostwhisper Gorge
- Frostmaul Preserver 59-60 Elite
- Frostmaul Giant 59-60 Elite

8 Darkwhisper Gorge
- Hederine Initiate 59-60
- Hederine Manstalker 59-60 Elite
- Hedereine Slayer 59-60 Elite
- Vi'el 60

9 Owlwing Thicket
- Ranshalla 58
- Berserk Owl Beast 58-59
- Chillwind Ravager 59
- Crazed Owl Beast 56-57
- Moontouched Owl Beast 57-58

10 Ice Thistle Hills
- Chillwing Chimaera 55-57
- Ice Thistle Yeti 55-56
- Ice Thistle Patriarch 57-58
- Ice Thistle Matriarch 56-57
- Shardtooth Mauler 55-56
- Winterspring Owl 55-56

11 Winterfall Village
- Shardtooth 54-55
- Winterspring Owl 54-55
- Winterfall Ursa 57-58
- Winterfall Shaman 56-57
- Winterfall Den Watcher 55-56

12 Everlook
- Everlook Bruiser 65
- Maethrya 55 Elite Alliance Flight Master
- Yaugrek 55 Elite Horde Flight Master
- Meggi Peppinrocker 60
- Malyfous Darkhammer 55 The Thorium Brotherhood Quest
- Evie Whirlbrew 58 Alchemy Supplies Rare recipes
- Umi Rumplesnicker 57 Quest
- Azzleby 30 Stable Master
- Seril Scourbane 57
- Lilith the Lithe 55
- Qia Trade good supplies Rare Patterns
- Kilram 58
- Blixxrak 55 Light Armor Merchant
- Nixxrak 54 Heavy Armor Merchant
- Wixxrap 55 Weaponsmith And Gunsmith
- Jack Sterling 50
- Umaron Stragarelm 42
- Lunnix Sprocketslip 54 Mining supplier
- Felnok Steelspring 54
- Legacki 57
- Himmik 60 Food and Drink
- Jessica Redpath 50
- Gregor Greystone 55 Argent Dawn
- Innkeeper Vizzie 30
- Gogo 58
- Harco Wigglesworth 54
- Xizzer Fizzbolt 55 Engineer Supplier
- Chillwind Chimaera 57
- Shardtooth Mauler 56

13 The Hidden Grove
- Berserk Owl Beast 58-59
- Crazed Owl beast 56-57
- Moontouch Owl Beast 57-58

14 Frostsaber Rock
- Frostsaber Stalker 59-60
- Frostsaber Huntress 58-59
- Frostsaber Pride Watcher 60
- Frostsaber Cub 55-56
- Frostsaber 55-56

15 Starfall Village
- Syvrana 55 Trade Goods
- Lyranne Feathersong 56 Food and Drink
- Wynd Nightchaser 62
- Jaron Stoneshapper 55 Explorers' Club
- Natheril Raincaller 57 General Goods

The Cities of Azeroth

A HISTORY

The wars and plagues have claimed many cities throughout the history of Azeroth. While sand and vines bury and break the cities of the past, the people constantly rebuild new ones. These stand as beacons of light and civilization in times of trial.

Darnassus

At first glance Darnassus seems a tranquil refuge for the night elves and fitting replacement for their lost home in Ashenvale. However, Darnassus was created without nature's blessing and the creatures around this fair city suffer greatly for it. The great tree was planted for the most selfish of reasons, to regain their lost immortality by creating a tree that would bind their souls to the eternal world.

"Opulent" is the first word that may spring to mind when gazing around this grand city. It's a city alive and breathing with brightly colored foliage and softly glowing lights. Wisps float serenely along the pathways and large Ancient Protectors cast their gaze about them looking for any sign of danger.

The Tradesman's Terrace is in the south-western section of the city. Buildings of pagoda inspired architecture line the pathways with their signs prominently announcing the weapons and armor they are selling. One the west side of the city, the Temple of the Moon sits with a large welcoming walkway leading into the moonlit and mystical alcove within. A large alabaster statue stands proudly in the center of a pool of water. Trainers surround the lower ring around the pool and, at the top of the ramps, the Lady Tyrande Whisperwind herself stands.

To the east of the Temple, and in the center of the city surrounded by water, stands a large tree in the shape of a bear. Inside lies no heart, but the treasures of its citizens are kept here in the bank. Just slightly northwest of the bank sites the rune surrounded portal to Rut'theran Village on the sea. In the northern region of the city, small Protectors make their rounds, their woody creaking blends in with the sounds of the smaller creatures as they patrol through the Cenarion Enclave.

The eastern portion of the city contains the Craftsman's Terrace. Herein the various craftsmen sell their wares and train the next to carry on their traditions. So traveling crafters need not walk far, an Inn and Mailbox are also found here. It is a visually beautiful city and one worth making the trip to if you don't happen to be on the wrong side of the way.

Ironforge

The first dwarves came up from the depths of the earth and founded Khaz Modan, naming the mountain range after the Titan Khaz'goroth. Constructing an altar for their Titan father, the dwarves crafted a mighty forge within the heart of the mountain. Thus city that grew around the forge would be called "Ironforge" ever after.

With the loss of their beloved Gnomeregan to invaders, what was left of the gnomish people took residence within the safe halls of their friends and neighbors. The entrance to Ironforge can be imposing to any newcomer. It's large, stony façade and heavy metal portcullis look ready to shut out even the most powerful of the Titans.

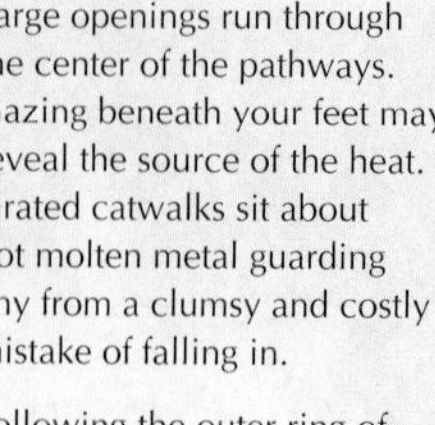

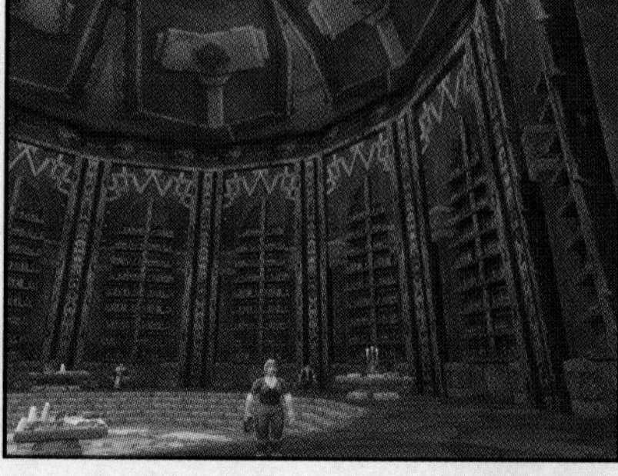

Within the city, the sounds of hammers falling rings out through the hustle and bustle. Large openings run through the center of the pathways. Gazing beneath your feet may reveal the source of the heat. Grated catwalks sit about hot molten metal guarding any from a clumsy and costly mistake of falling in.

Following the outer ring of the great city leads past the Military Quarter and toward Tinkertown. This is the gnomish region of the city made quite evident by the technological marvels even intertwined within their architecture. Overlarge gears rotate around walkways as you pass underneath. The King of gnomes, High Tinker Mekkatorque, stands watch over his people and watches as everyone comes and goes from the latest of innovations, the tram to and from Stormwind.

The library of Ironforge sits in the outer ring in the northeastern section of the city. The Explorer's League keeps watch over the many volumes of research and history they have managed to gather. Even with their love of the forge, dwarves have switched their focus to searching for their very own origins and embracing archaeology.

Perhaps the darkest of the areas are the Forlorn Caverns. Strangely enough, there seems to be some decent fishing for those looking for a break from the usual monotony of work. The northwestern area of the city houses the Mystic Ward. The vibrancy of the architecture is a striking contrast after emerging from the Forlorn Caverns. Within the very heart of the city is the Great Forge itself. Oversized anvils are worked on diligently by craftsmen that barely break a sweat although the heat is nearly unbearable. It is worth taking the time to walk through and get to know. There are always new surprises around every corner and it is a fitting home.

Stormwind

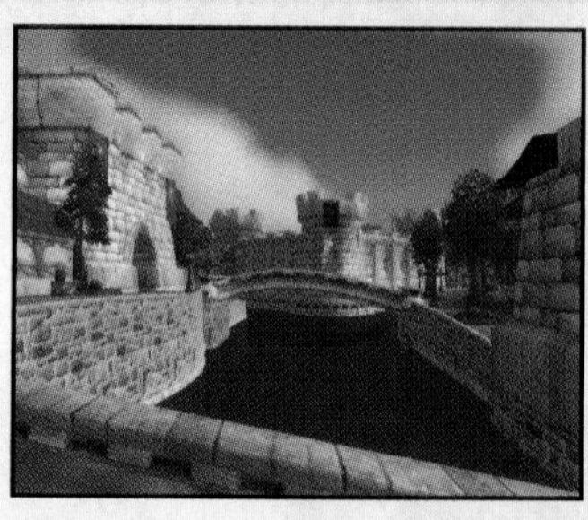

Stormwind is the last of the great human cities. With Lordaeron in the hands of the Forsaken and many of the cities that once housed the great kingdoms of humanity in ruins, Stormwind remains the center of commerce and safety.

The entrance to Stormwind itself is a testament to the legacy of heroes lost in time to the horrors of war. Each one bears a plague with the name of the honoree. It is rightly called the Valley of Heroes and all that enter it can't help but feel their chest swell in pride at the legacy of the Alliance.

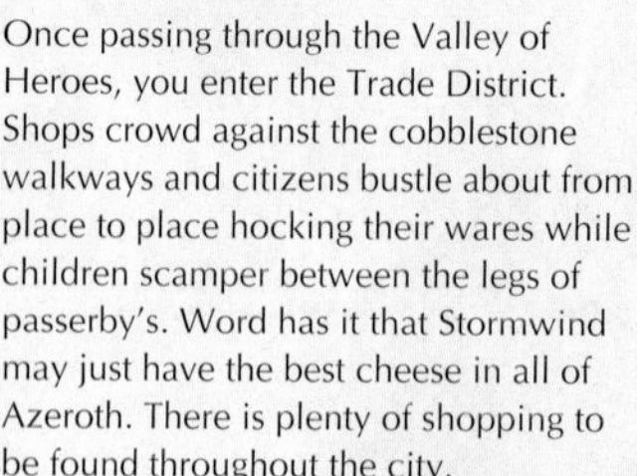

Once passing through the Valley of Heroes, you enter the Trade District. Shops crowd against the cobblestone walkways and citizens bustle about from place to place hocking their wares while children scamper between the legs of passerby's. Word has it that Stormwind may just have the best cheese in all of Azeroth. There is plenty of shopping to be found throughout the city.

To the right of the Trade District is Old Town. As you move in that direction, you'll notice the large canals that run through the city and more small shops line the waterways. Old Town is a smaller, more compact version of the Trade District. It has a cozy charm to it. North of Old Town lays the Dwarven District. It's a haze-covered area of the city as the pollution of the many fires settles over it. Large beast-like machines sit around the region of the city as if waiting to snatch up some imaginary creature for a snack.

Stormwind Keep lies between Old Town and the Dwarven District. The boy king, Anduin Wrynn, stands at court with his advisors, Lady Katrana Prestor and Lord Bolvar Fordragon, at his side. Few stop by to pay their respects. At the northernmost area of the city lies Cathedral Square. The tall spires of the Citadel of Light itself loom protectively over this portion of the city. Its beauty is unmatched and even children are brought by to tour and view where the great Paladins and Priests train.

The west is the Park where Druids go to find their center and train. The night elves have managed to bring a piece of Darnassus here by placing their own small torches on this green oasis among the clean white stones of Stormwind. Soldiers are lined up on the outer edges of receiving medical care from the wounds they received from riots that broke out among the Defias prisoners.

Within the Mage Quarter, a tall tower stands with a spiraling ramp twisting about it. It is truly one of the grandest wizard towers any could possibly hope to see. At the top lies a strange portal that swirls in luminescent green as if to peer out into the cosmos itself. Passing through leads deeper into the Wizard's Sanctum. There is plenty to explore throughout this great city and should you gain a thirst for doing so, stop by the Blue Recluse. They advertise a free drink and you can send out a postcard at the mailbox as well.

Orgrimmar

Named in honor of the legendary Orgrim Doomhammer, Orgrimmar was founded to be the capital of the orcs' new homeland. Built within a large, winding canyon in the harsh land of Durotar, Orgrimmar stands as one of the mightiest cities in the world.

After freeing his people from captivity among the humans, Thrall set out to brave the sea and bring his people to a new land to start a new society for the orcs. They named the land itself "Durotar" after his deceased father, the former chieftain of the Frostwolves. It is in Orgrimmar that the new seat of power resides for all of the orcs that survive to this day. No longer are the clans fractured and now they stand united as one nation.

The entrance to Orgrimmar yawns widely as the orc guards stand by. To the east of it stands the zeppelin Tower. The architecture is crude and yet speaks volumes of the craftsmen that built this city. Although different from conventionally accepted cities, none can say that there isn't a complex and harsh beauty invoked by the sight of Orgrimmar. Bonfires burn high atop the rocks and throughout the city, leaving a faint smoky haze.

The distinctive tile roofs of the city intermingle with the red rock of the terrain; wooden carvings shaped like horns, give off a menacing air as tanned hides are stretched over rooftops and across the rocks to filter out the relentless desert sun. After entering the city, the first region is the Valley of Strength. It serves as the central hub for banking and the buying and selling of all sorts of goods and services.

Just up the tower and across the rope bridge to the west lie the Valley of Spirits and the passageway to the western exit of the city. It is here fewer orcs are seen and more Trolls are apparent. In the Valley of Spirits the Trolls, who have also made a home in Durotar, teach some of the more mystic practices. North of the Valley of Strength is the shadier end of town: the Cleft of Shadow. From the area emanates a purple glow and within are the Warlocks and Rogues among some few vendors that serve their purpose.

Wrapping around the Cleft of Shadow is the Drag; it's filled with shops and trainers. This area is well-shaded from the ravages of the desert sun and a good place to cool off. The desert breeze can be heard blowing through the rocks. To the northeast, through the Drag, is the Valley of Honor where the orcs work their ways with metal and train their Warriors. There is even a small pond for a little fishing after a hard workout.

Out through the Drag once more, and following the curve of the path to the north, you'll find the Valley of Wisdom and the seat of power for Warchief Thrall. Even more impressive than the Grommash Hold, are the monolithic demon plates out front. It is the demon armor of Mannoroth himself set there to remind the orcs of the grand sacrifice made to defeat the beast and begin the path of reclaiming their honor. Even as crude as the city seems, it is a marvel of orc ingenuity and determination to live off a harsh land and thrive despite all odds.

Thunder Bluff

The great city of Thunder Bluff lies atop a series of mesas that overlook the verdant grasslands of Mulgore. The once nomadic Tauren recently established the city as a center for trade caravans, traveling craftsmen, and artisans of every kind. The proud city also stands as a refuge for the brave adventurers who stalk their dangerous prey through the plains of Mulgore and its surrounding areas. Long bridges of rope and wood span the chasms between the mesas, topped with tents, longhouses, colorfully painted totems, and spirit lodges. The mighty chief, Cairne Bloodhoof, watches over the bustling city, ensuring that the united Tauren tribes live in peace and security. Thunder Bluff sits high above the plains of Mulgore. The only means of arrival are by using the lifts from the plains below or flying in on one of the Wyverns that serve the area.

Brightly painted totems and tents made with stretched animal skins and wood struts lasted together sit atop the mesa giving the true feeling of being a part of a tribal community. The strong Tauren do much of their trade and banking on the main mesa. The winds are strong high atop the mesas and the Tauren capture this energy with brightly colored windmills atop the buildings. A series of rope bridges and towers interlink the varying levels and mesas into one continuous city.

Cairne Bloodhoof, leader of the Tauren, sits at the top level. All Tauren seeking his favor and the way of the hunter that is so precious to their very culture carry out his will.

To the southeast of the central bluff, connected by rope bridges, is the Hunter's Rise. Aspiring Hunters and Warriors train in the Hunter's Hall. Standing on the edge of the mesa here will give way to an amazing vista to the southeast. Watch your step however. There are no guardrails to keep you from falling to your death. The Tauren are more surefooted than that to care for such things. On the northern most mesa, the Elder Rise can be found where the wisest of Tauren reside. Druids can seek their council and learn more of their path in the Hall of Elders. The Spirit Rise lies to the west. The large head of a Kodo is fastened to the side of the building housing the Shaman trainers as if in silent watch and granting its power to those who train here.

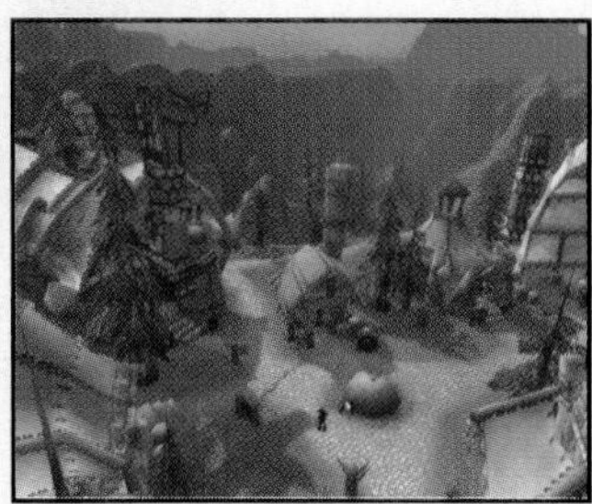

Along the side of the mesa is a path leading down into a cavern that resounds of dripping pools of water and quietly spoken conversation. Large yellow mushrooms surround the edges of the pools. The Priest and Mage trainers sit and patiently give their knowledge to those seeking their counsel. The mists of the pools rise ever so silently giving the already eerily glowing cavern a more surreal appearance.

Despite the simple nature of their city, the Tauren have all that is necessary for their people. They put their efforts into their accomplishments and leave their city simple and functional.

Undercity

Far beneath the ruined capital city of Lordaeron, the royal crypts have been turned into a bastion of power and undeath. Originally intended by Prince Arthas to be the Scourge's seat of power, the budding "Undercity" was abandoned when Arthas was recalled to aid the Lich King in distant Northrend. In Arthas' absence, the Dark Lady, Sylvannas Windrunner, led the rebel Forsaken to the Undercity, and claimed it as their own. Since taking up residence, the Forsaken have worked to complete the Undercity's construction by dredging the twisted maze of catacombs, tombs, and dungeons that Arthas began.

Once the seat of power for the humans, Lordaeron fell to the plague released by the Cult of the Damned. The new Lich King Arthas sought to make it his new home but found his conquest had been taken over by Lady Sylvannas. She has finished carving out what Arthas began building and claimed it for the Forsaken. While much of humanity has given up ever reclaiming Tirisfal Glades from the Scourge and Forsaken, a small band of Scarlet Crusaders still attempt to wrest back the cursed land from them. To the naked eye, the Ruins of Lordaeron look empty and uninhabitable. A Warlock will tell you otherwise. With a quick cast they can aid you in seeing the ghostly inhabitants that wander what appears to be an empty ruin.

Deeper in, the throne room sits bare and empty. The throne of a king destroyed by his own son is but a hollow shell of the greatness it once possessed. Swift moving elevators take you below the ruins. Undercity Guardians stand just outside the elevators; their large hulking forms past decay and oozing the remnants of the plague. The Trade Quarter is the heart of this city. Shops surround it on all levels and the bank sits prominently in the center. The grim décor of skulls and horns reflects the tastes of the denizens, all backlit by a constant green glowing pool of slime.

Taking the stairs down past the bank leads past auctioneers to an outer circle of merchants and canals. Each section of this part of the city is divided into quarters with and inner and outer ring and bridges spanning the river of ooze to connect them. Colorful banners of decaying fabric are draped around the entrances in a mockery of festivity while skulls on signs point the way to the different areas. The inner circle of this region houses merchants and profession trainers among more curious shops. The Undead have though of everything possible to help them in their pursuits.

The northeastern quarter of the city houses the Magic Quarter where Warlocks and Mages can train in their arts. A 'demonstration' of a Warlock pet is ongoing next to the building and can be quite informative. In the inner circle of this quarter robes and implements befitting a mage can be purchased. Moving clockwise takes you to the Rogue Quarter. Trainers wait here to improve the stealthy lives of all Rogues that come to them with greed and murder in their hearts. Within the inner circle, poisons and daggers can be purchased.

In the southwestern region of the city, the Apothecarium and the Royal Quarter are found. The Royal Apothecary Society does many of their experiments with the plague in this area. Their laboratory is something in and of itself to see with bits and pieces of various creatures strewn about and experiments being carried on in an adjoining room on some unlucky humans. The crackling static of their experiments and the occasional scream will set any visitor's hair on end.

Deep within the Royal Quarter the demon Varimathras stands at the side of the Dark Lady herself. His imposing figure is enough to make any be respectful of her every wish. To the northwest is the War Quarter. Warriors train and strain against target dummies while Priests stand along the building and gaze down at the occurrences. Nearby, the sewers lead out into the grounds of Tirisfal Glades near the Scarlet Crusades southern tower. The bats of Undercity use this as a means to gain access in and out of the city. If there was a pulse among the Forsaken, Undercity would resonate with it. Instead its cold and clammy countenance casts pallor among its visitors in what many would find unwelcoming. The Forsaken that reside here however, seem quite at ease at what their Dark Lady has carved out for them even with the remnants of the Scourge and overzealous Scarlet Crusade breathing down their necks.

World Factions and Reputation

Within the world of Azeroth there are many different groups whose view of you affects how they react to you. This may seem obvious, but many of the groups can come to respect or dislike you through your own actions.

The Horde and Alliance comprise factional teams. All opposing races start at "War" status. Your reputation with factions opposed to you cannot be changed.

Most allied races start with a "Friendly" reputation with other races in the core two groups (Alliance and Horde). The exception is the Forsaken. They start with lower reputation with Trolls, Tauren, and orcs just as Trolls, Tauren, and orcs start with lower reputation with the Forsaken.

While you cannot declare war on your own faction, your lack of actions prompt a lack of esteem from your superiors. Consider your actions and their repercussions carefully.

Reputation Levels	
Exalted:	The highest level of reputation a player can achieve with a faction
Revered:	Special reputation level reserved for special heroes
Honored:	10% discount on bought items from vendors
Friendly:	Standard reputation level for factions on the player's team
Neutral:	Starting reputation level for factions not on a player's team that are not KOS (Kill on Sight)
Unfriendly:	Cannot buy, sell, or interact
Hostile:	KOS
Hated:	KOS; all opposing team factions are set permanently to the lowest level here

WORLD FACTIONS

There are many groups in the world for your character to interact with. Only the Horde and Alliance factions are shown originally, but new groups appear as your character meets them for the first time. Included is a list of many of the factions, but many more are discovered during your travels in Azeroth

MONITORING YOUR REPUTATION

Players can check their current reputation with any faction they've had contact with by opening the Reputation tab on their character sheet in game. Using the hotkey, defaulted to "U", can be a faster way of accessing the tab.

Mousing over a faction shows how much reputation you have with them and how much you need to progress to the next level. Accomplishing tasks in game gives you a displayed amount of reputation, so it's fairly easy to calculate how much you need to accomplish to gain the next level.

CHANGING YOUR REPUTATION

There are three basic ways to raise your reputation with a faction. Each is explained below.

Quests

Accomplishing quests given by members of the faction is quick and doesn't take you out of your way. These quests often lead to Repeatable Quests or involve Killing. As such, quests are good first steps to raising your reputation.

Repeatable Quests

Blue question marks show NPCs with repeatable quests. These can be done an infinite number of times, which makes them part of the bread and butter of reputation grinding. Many repeatable quests involve killing so you get a double bang for your buck (you get the money and experience from the monsters while turning in the quest gives you the reputation increase).

KILLING

Everyone has enemies. Killing NPCs who are opposed to a faction can raise you reputation with that faction. The gain is often very little, but you also gain money and experience from the kill. Watch your combat log to see reputation changes as you kill new enemies.

As you gain in standing, the reputation you gain from killing enemies may diminish. The greatest hero of all time killing a lowly skeleton isn't very noteworthy after all.

Faction	How to Raise Reputation
Alliance	
Darnassus	Quests, Repeatable Quests
Gnomeregan Exiles	Quests, Repeatable Quests
Ironforge	Quests, Repeatable Quests
Stormwind	Quests, Repeatable Quests
Horde	
Darkspear Trolls	Quests, Repeatable Quests
Orgrimmar	Quests, Repeatable Quests
Thunder Bluff	Quests, Repeatable Quests
Undercity	Quests, Repeatable Quests
PvP Factions (Alliance/Horde)	
Stormpike Guard/Frostwolf Clan	Killing opposing players, Quests, Repeatable Quests, Capturing Objectives
League of Arathor/The Defilers	Gathering 200 Resources, Quests, Repeatable Quests, Capturing Objectives
Silverwing Sentinels/Warsong Outriders	Capturing an enemy flag, Quests, Repeatable Quests, Capturing Objectives
Steamwheedle Cartel	
Booty Bay	Quests, Repeatable Quests, Killing Bloodsail Buccaneers
Everlook	Quests, Repeatable Quests
Gadgetzan	Quests, Repeatable Quests
Ratchet	Quests, Repeatable Quests
Other	
Argent Dawn	Quests, Repeatable Quests, Killing Scourge
Bloodsail Buccaneers	Killing Booty Bay Guards
Cenarion Hold	Quests, Repeatable Quests
Darkmoon Faire	Quests, Repeatable Quests
Gelkis Clan Centaurs	Killing Magram Clan Centaurs
Hydraxian Waterlords	Quests, Killing specific mobs
Magram Clan Centaurs	Killing Gelkis Clan Centaurs
Ravenholdt	Killing Syndicate
Thorium Brotherhood	Quests, Repeatable Quests
Timbermaw Hold	Repeatable Quests, Killing Deadwood/Winterfall Furbolg
Wintersabre Trainers	Quests, Repeatable Quests

THE REWARDS

Raising your reputation can be a long and arduous process. You won't become the symbol of justice in a day, but the rewards make it worthwhile.

CORE FACTIONS

Raising your faction with Alliance, Horde, and Steamwheedle organizations gives the following bonuses:

Exalted:	Ability to learn how to ride another race's mount.
Honored:	10% Discount at all vendors allied with the faction.

PvP FACTIONS

Increasing your reputation with the PvP factions opens goods and services at the vendors near the entrance portals. Many of these items, weapons, and armor are superior to those of equal level found in your travels.

STORMPIKE GUARD

Item	Requirements	Set Name	Cost
Friendly			
Superior Healing Draught (Use: Restores 560 to 720 health)	Level 35, Usable only in Alterac Valley	N/A	5
Superior Mana Draught (Use: Restores 560 to 720 mana)	Level 35, Usable only in Alterac Valley	N/A	5
Stormpike Battle Tabard	N/A	N/A	1
(5)Alterac Heavy Runecloth Bandage (Use: Heals 2000 damage over 8 seconds)	First Aid 225	N/A	80
(5)Bottle Alterac Spring Water (Use: Restores 4410 mana over 30 seconds, Increases Spirit by 10 for 10 minutes)	Level 55, Must remain seated while drinking	N/A	50

Item	Requirements	Set Name	Cost
Honored			
Major Healing Draught (Use: Restores 980 to 1260 health)	Level 45, Usable only in Alterac Valley	N/A	9
Major Mana Draught (Use: Restores 980 to 1260 mana)	Level 45, Usable only in Alterac Valley	N/A	9
Stormpike Soldier's Cloak (Back, 43 Armor, +11 STA, +5 Frost Res., Equip: +24 Attack Power)	Level 55	N/A	6 79 50
Stormpike Sage's Cloak (Back, 43 Armor, +11 STA, +5 Frost Res., Equip: Increases damage and healing done by magical spells and effects by up to 14)	Level 55	N/A	6 84 40
Stormpike Soldier's Pendant (Neck, +15 STA, Equip: +18 Attack Power)	Level 55	N/A	6 44 83
Stormpike Sage's Pendant (Neck, +10 STA, +10 INT, Equip: Restores 4 mana per 5 seconds)	Level 55	N/A	6 44 83
Stormpike Plate Girdle (Plate Waist, 353 Armor, +18 STR, +7 AGI, +8 STA, +5 Frost Res.)	Level 55	N/A	4 26 99
Stormpike Mail Girdle (Mail Waist, 199 Armor, +12 AGI, +12 STA, +12 INT, +5 Frost Res.)	Level 55	N/A	6 40 48
Stormpike Leather Girdle (Leather Waist, 95 Armor, +11 STR, +10 AGI, +15 STA, +5 Frost Res.)	Level 55	N/A	5 33 74
Stormpike Cloth Girdle (Cloth Waist, 48 Armor, +11 STA, +10 INT, +5 Frost Res., Equip: Increases damage and healing done by magical spells and effects by up to 18)	Level 55	N/A	4 26 99
(5)Alterac mana Biscuit (Use: Restores 4410 health and 4410 mana over 30 seconds)	Level 51, Must remain seated while eating	N/A	63
(200) Ice Threaded Arrow (Adds 16.5 dps)	Level 51	N/A	54
(200) Ice Threaded Bullet (Adds 16.5 dps)	Level 51	N/A	54

Item	Requirements	Set Name	Cost
Revered			
Stormpike Battle Standard (Use: Place a Battle Standard with 1500 health that increases the damage of all party members that stay within 45 yards of the Battle Standard by 10%)	Lasts 2 minutes. Usable only in Alterac Valley	N/A	4 50
Electrified Dagger (One-Hand Dagger, 42.5 dps, +10 AGI, Chance on Hit: Blasts a target for 45 Nature damage)	Level 60	N/A	28 48 53
Crackling Staff (Staff, 55.6 dps, +25 STA, +16 INT, Equip: Increases damage and healing done by magical spells and effects by up to 15)	Level 60	N/A	35 86 72
Stormstrike Hammer (One-Hand Mace, 42.6 dps, +15 STR)	Level 60	N/A	28 90 23
Gnoll Skin Bandolier (16 Slot Ammo Pouch, Equip: Increases ranged attack speed by 15%)	Level 55	N/A	31 50
Harpy Hide Quiver (16 Slot Quiver, Equip: Increases ranged attack speed by 15%)	Level 55	N/A	31 50

Exalted			
Item	**Requirements**	**Set Name**	**Cost**
Stormpike Battle Charger (Use: Summons and dismisses a rideable Stormpike Battle Charger. This is a very fast mount)	Level 60	N/A	720
Lei of the Lifegiver (Off-Hand, Equip: Increases healing done by spells and effects by up to 53, Restores 3 mana per 5 seconds)	Level 60	N/A	45
Therazane's Touch (Off-Hand, Equip: Increases damage and healing done by magical spells and effects by up to 33)	Level 60	N/A	45
Tome of Arcane Domination (Off-Hand, Equip: Increases damage done by Arcane spells and effects by up to 34, Restores 3 mana every 5 seconds)	Level 60	N/A	45
Tome of Fiery Arcana (Off-Hand, Equip: Increases damage done by Fire spells and effects by up to 40)	Level 60	N/A	45
Tome of Shadow Force (Off-Hand, +8 STA, Equip: Increases damage done by Shadow spells and effects by up to 34)	Level 60	N/A	45
Tome of the Ice Lord (Off-Hand, +9 INT, Equip: Increases damage done by Frost spells and effects by up to 34)	Level 60	N/A	45
The Unstoppable Force (Two-Hand Mace, 61.4 dps, +19 STR, +15 STA, Equip: Improves your chance to get a critical strike by 2%, Chance on hit: Stuns target for 1 second)	Level 60	N/A	140 84 10
The Immovable Object (Shield, 2468 Armor, 44 Block, +15 STA, Equip: Increases the block value of your shield by 27)	Level 60	N/A	71 57 67
Don Julio's Band (Ring, +11 STA, Equip: Improves your chance to get a critical strike by 1%, Improves your chance to hit by 1%, +16 Attack Power)	Level 60	N/A	68
The Lobotomizer (One-Hand Dagger, 47.2 dps, Chance on hit: Wounds the target for 200 to 300 damage and lowers INT of target by 25 for 30 seconds)	Level 60	N/A	113 9 56
Don Rodrigo's Band (Ring, +7 STA, Equip: Improves your chance to get a critical strike with spells by 1%, Decreases the magical resistances of your spell targets by 20)	Level 60, Classes: Priest, Mage, Warlock	N/A	68

FROSTWOLF CLAN

Friendly			
Item	**Requirements**	**Set Name**	**Cost**
Superior Healing Draught (Use: Restores 560 to 720 health)	Level 35, Usable only in Alterac Valley	N/A	5
Superior Mana Draught (Use: Restores 560 to 720 mana)	Level 35, Usable only in Alterac Valley	N/A	5
Frostwolf Battle Tabard	N/A	N/A	1
(5)Alterac Heavy Runecloth Bandage (Use: Heals 2000 damage over 8 seconds)	First Aid 225	N/A	80
(5)Bottle Alterac Spring Water (Use: Restores 4410 mana over 30 seconds, Increases Spirit by 10 for 10 minutes)	Level 55, Must remain seated while drinking	N/A	50

Honored			
Item	**Requirements**	**Set Name**	**Cost**
Major Healing Draught (Use: Restores 980 to 1260 health)	Level 45, Usable only in Alterac Valley	N/A	9
Major Mana Draught (Use: Restores 980 to 1260 mana)	Level 45, Usable only in Alterac Valley	N/A	9
Frostwolf Legionnarie's Cloak (Back, 43 Armor, +11 STA, +5 Frost Res., Equip: +24 Attack Power)	Level 55	N/A	6 79 50
Frostwolf Advisor's Cloak (Back, 43 Armor, +11 STA, +5 Frost Res., Equip: Increases damage and healing done by magical spells and effects by up to 14)	Level 55	N/A	6 84 40
Frostwolf Legionnaire's Pendant (Neck, +15 STA, Equip: +18 Attack Power)	Level 55	N/A	6 44 83
Frostwolf Advisor's Pendant (Neck, +10 STA, +10 INT, Equip: Restores 4 mana per 5 seconds)	Level 55	N/A	6 44 83
Frostwolf Plate Belt (Plate Waist, 353 Armor, +18 STR, +7 AGI, +8 STA, +5 Frost Res.)	Level 55	N/A	4 26 99
Frostwolf Belt Girdle (Mail Waist, 199 Armor, +12 AGI, +12 STA, +12 INT, +5 Frost Res.)	Level 55	N/A	6 40 48
Frostwolf Leather Belt (Leather Waist, 95 Armor, +11 STR, +10 AGI, +15 STA, +5 Frost Res.)	Level 55	N/A	5 33 74
Frostwolf Cloth Belt (Cloth Waist, 48 Armor, +11 STA, +10 INT, +5 Frost Res., Equip: Increases damage and healing done by magical spells and effects by up to 18)	Level 55	N/A	4 26 99
(5)Alterac mana Biscuit (Use: Restores 4410 health and 4410 mana over 30 seconds)	Level 51, Must remain seated while eating	N/A	63
(200) Ice Threaded Arrow (Adds 16.5 dps)	Level 51	N/A	54
(200) Ice Threaded Bullet (Adds 16.5 dps)	Level 51	N/A	54

Revered			
Item	**Requirements**	**Set Name**	**Cost**
Frostwolf Battle Standard (Use: Place a Battle Standard with 1500 health that increases the damage of all party members that stay within 45 yards of the Battle Standard by 10%)	Lasts 2 minutes. Usable only in Alterac Valley	N/A	4 50
Glacial Blade (One-Hand Dagger, 42.5 dps, +10 AGI, Chance on Hit: Blasts a target for 45 Nature damage)	Level 60	N/A	28 48 53
Whiteout Staff (Staff, 55.6 dps, +25 STA, +16 INT, Equip: Increases damage and healing done by magical spells and effects by up to 15)	Level 60	N/A	35 86 72
Frostbite (One-Hand Mace, 42.6 dps, +15 STR)	Level 60	N/A	28 90 23
Gnoll Skin Bandolier (16 Slot Ammo Pouch, Equip: Increases ranged attack speed by 15%)	Level 55	N/A	31 50
Harpy Hide Quiver (16 Slot Quiver, Equip: Increases ranged attack speed by 15%)	Level 55	N/A	31 50

Exalted			
Item	**Requirements**	**Set Name**	**Cost**
Horn of the Frostwolf Howler (Use: Summons and dismisses a rideable Frostwolf Howler. This is a very fast mount)	Level 60	N/A	720
Lei of the Lifegiver (Off-Hand, Equip: Increases healing done by spells and effects by up to 53, Restores 3 mana per 5 seconds)	Level 60	N/A	45
Therazane's Touch (Off-Hand, Equip: Increases damage and healing done by magical spells and effects by up to 33)	Level 60	N/A	45
Tome of Arcane Domination (Off-Hand, Equip: Increases damage done by Arcane spells and effects by up to 34, Restores 3 mana every 5 seconds)	Level 60	N/A	45
Tome of Fiery Arcana (Off-Hand, Equip: Increases damage done by Fire spells and effects by up to 40)	Level 60	N/A	45
Tome of Shadow Force (Off-Hand, +8 STA, Equip: Increases damage done by Shadow spells and effects by up to 34)	Level 60	N/A	45

Exalted

Item	Requirements	Set Name	Cost
Tome of the Ice Lord (Off-Hand, +9 INT, Equip: Increases damage done by Frost spells and effects by up to 34)	Level 60	N/A	45
The Unstoppable Force (Two-Hand Mace, 61.4 dps, +19 STR, +15 STA, Equip: Improves your chance to get a critical strike by 2%, Chance on hit: Stuns target for 1 second)	Level 60	N/A	140 84 10
The Immovable Object (Shield, 2468 Armor, 44 Block, +15 STA, Equip: Increases the block value of your shield by 27)	Level 60	N/A	71 57 67
Don Julio's Band (Ring, +11 STA, Equip: Improves your chance to get a critical strike by 1%, Improves your chance to hit by 1%, +16 Attack Power)	Level 60	N/A	68
The Lobotomizer (One-Hand Dagger, 47.2 dps, Chance on hit: Wounds the target for 200 to 300 damage and lowers INT of target by 25 for 30 seconds)	Level 60	N/A	113 9 56
Don Rodrigo's Band (Ring, +7 STA, Equip: Improves your chance to get a critical strike with spells by 1%, Decreases the magical resistances of your spell targets by 20)	Level 60, Classes: Priest, Mage, Warlock	N/A	68

LEAGUE OF ARATHOR

Friendly

Item	Requirements	Set Name	Cost
Superior Healing Draught (Use: Restores 560 to 720 health)	Level 35, Usable only in Arathi Basin	N/A	5
Superior Mana Draught (Use: Restores 560 to 720 mana)	Level 35, Usable only in Arathi Basin	N/A	5
(5)Highlander's Field Ration (Use: Restores 1074 health and 2202 mana over 30 seconds)	Level 25, Must remain seated while eating. Usable only in Arathi Basin	N/A	10
(5)Highlander's Iron Ration (Use: Restores 1608 health and 3306 mana over 30 seconds)	Level 35, Must remain seated while eating. Usable only in Arathi Basin	N/A	15
(5)Highlander's Enriched Ration (Use: Restores 2148 health and 4410 mana over 30 seconds)	Level 45, Must remain seated while eating. Usable only in Arathi Basin	N/A	20
(5)Highlander's Silk Bandage (Use: Heals 640 damage over 8 seconds)	Level 25, First Aid (125), Usable only in Arathi Basin	N/A	10
(5)Highlander's Mageweave Bandage (Use: Heals 1104 damage over 8 seconds)	Level 35, First Aid (175), Usable only in Arathi Basin	N/A	15
(5)Highlander's Runecloth Bandage (Use: Heals 2000 damage over 8 seconds)	Level 45, First Aid (225), Usable only in Arathi Basin	N/A	20
Talisman of Arathor (Use: Absorbs 248 to 302 physical damage)	Level 28, Lasts 15 seconds	N/A	72 30
Talisman of Arathor (Use: Absorbs 310 to 378 physical damage)	Level 38, Lasts 15 seconds	N/A	1 52 30
Talisman of Arathor (Use: Absorbs 392 to 478 physical damage)	Level 48, Lasts 15 seconds	N/A	2 82 30
Talisman of Arathor (Use: Absorbs 495 to 605 physical damage)	Level 58, Lasts 15 seconds	N/A	4 12 30

Honored

Item	Requirements	Set Name	Cost
Highlander's Chain Girdle (Leather Waist, 61 Armor, +5 STA, Passive: +24 Attack Power)	Level 28, Classes: Hunter	N/A	93 73
Highlander's Chain Girdle (Mail Waist, 149 Armor, +6 STA, Passive: Improves your chance to get a critical strike by 1%, +8 Attack Power)	Level 40, Classes: Hunter	N/A	2 60 40
Highlander's Chain Girdle (Mail Waist, 178 Armor, +8 STA, Passive: Improves your chance to get a critical strike by 1%, +20 Attack Power)	Level 48, Classes: Hunter	N/A	4 93 73
Highlander's Chain Girdle (Mail Waist, 208 Armor, +10 STA, Passive: Improves your chance to get a critical strike by 1%, +34 Attack Power)	Level 58, Classes: Hunter	The Highlander's Determination	7 92 59
Highlander's Cloth Girdle (Cloth Waist, 88 Armor, +4 STA, +3 INT, Passive: Increases damage and healing done by magical spells and effects by up to 11)	Level 28, Classes: Warlock, Mage, Priest	N/A	72 7

Honored

Item	Requirements	Set Name	Cost
Highlander's Cloth Girdle (Cloth Waist, 105 Armor, +4 STA, +4 INT, Passive: Increases damage and healing done by magical spells and effects by up to 14)	Level 38, Classes: Warlock, Mage, Priest	N/A	1 66 84
Highlander's Cloth Girdle (Cloth Waist, 113 Armor, +6 STA, +5 INT, Passive: Improves your chance to get a critical strike with spells by 1%, Increases damage and healing done by magical spells and effects by up to 9)	Level 48, Classes: Warlock, Mage, Priest	N/A	3 36 19
Highlander's Cloth Girdle (Cloth Waist, 150 Armor, +7 STA, +6 INT, Passive: Improves your chance to get a critical strike with spells by 1%, Increases damage and healing done by magical spells and effects by up to 14)	Level 58, Classes: Warlock, Mage, Priest	The Highlander's Intent	5 36 1
Highlander's Lizardhide Girdle (Leather Waist, 91 Armor, +4 STA, +12 INT)	Level 28, Classes: Rogue, Druid	N/A	92 7
Highlander's Lizardhide Girdle (Leather Waist, 113 Armor, +4 STA, +15 INT)	Level 38, Classes: Rogue, Druid	N/A	2 13 14
Highlander's Lizardhide Girdle (Leather Waist, 136 Armor, +6 STA, +10 INT, Equip: Improves your chance to get a critical strike with spells by 1%)	Level 48, Classes: Rogue, Druid	N/A	4 29 52
Highlander's Lizardhide Girdle (Leather Waist, 159 Armor, +7 STA, +17 INT, Equip: Improves your chance to get a critical strike with spells by 1%)	Level 58, Classes: Rogue, Druid	The Highlander's Will	6 67 62
Highlander's Leather Girdle (Leather Waist, 91 Armor, +4 STA, +24 Attack Power)	Level 28, Classes: Rogue, Druid	N/A	89 41
Highlander's Leather Girdle (Leather Waist, 113 Armor, +4 STA, +30 Attack Power)	Level 38, Classes: Rogue, Druid	N/A	2 6 99
Highlander's Leather Girdle (Leather Waist, 136 Armor, +6 STA, Equip: Improves your chance to get a critical strike by 1%, +20 Attack Power)	Level 48, Classes: Rogue, Druid	N/A	4 17 8
Highlander's Leather Girdle (Leather Waist, 159 Armor, +7 STA, Equip: Improves your chance to get a critical strike by 1%, +34 Attack Power)	Level 58, Classes: Rogue, Druid	The Highlander's Purpose	6 65 29
Highlander's Lamellar Girdle (Mail Waist, 128 Armor, +11 STR, +4 STA, +5 INT)	Level 28, Classes: Paladin	N/A	1 3 75
Highlander's Lamellar Girdle (Plate Waist, 236 Armor, +12 STR, +6 STA, +6 INT)	Level 40, Classes: Paladin	N/A	1 60 8
Highlander's Lamellar Girdle (Plate Waist, 313 Armor, +11 STR, +4 STA, +8 INT, Equip: Improves your chance to get a critical strike by 1%)	Level 48, Classes: Paladin	N/A	3 47 32
Highlander's Lamellar Girdle (Plate Waist, 369 Armor, +15 STR, +6 STA, +10 INT, Equip: Improves your chance to get a critical strike by 1%)	Level 58, Classes: Paladin	The Highlander's Resolve	5 12 75
Highlander's Plate Girdle (Mail Waist, 128 Armor, +12 STR, +5 STA)	Level 28, Classes: Warrior, Paladin	N/A	1 2 94
Highlander's Plate Girdle (Plate Waist, 236 Armor, +15 STR, +6 STA,)	Level 40, Classes: Warrior, Paladin	N/A	1 58 83
Highlander's Plate Girdle (Plate Waist, 313 Armor, +10 STR, +8 STA)	Level 48, Classes: Warrior, Paladin	N/A	3 53 76
Highlander's Plate Girdle (Plate Waist, 369 Armor, +17 STR, +10 STA, Equip: Improves your chance to get a critical strike by 1%)	Level 58, Classes: Warrior, Paladin	The Highlander's Resolution	5 10 88

Revered

Item	Requirements	Set Name	Cost
Highlander's Chain Greaves (Leather Feet, 74 Armor, +8 AGI, +8 STA, Equip: Run speed increased slightly)	Level 28, Classes: Hunter	N/A	1 32 17
Highlander's Chain Greaves (Mail Feet, 183 Armor, +10 AGI, +10 STA, +3 INT, Equip: Run speed increased slightly)	Level 40, Classes: Hunter	N/A	3 68 75
Highlander's Chain Greaves (Mail Feet, 218 Armor, +12 AGI, +13 STA, +6 INT, Equip: Run speed increased slightly)	Level 48, Classes: Hunter	N/A	7 42 97
Highlander's Chain Greaves (Mail Feet, 255 Armor, +15 AGI, +16 STA, +8 INT, Equip: Run speed increased slightly)	Level 58, Classes: Hunter	The Highlander's Determination	12 24 28

Revered			
Item	Requirements	Set Name	Cost
Highlander's Cloth Boots (Cloth Feet, 84 Armor, +8 STA, Equip: Run speed increased slightly, Increases damage and healing done by magical spells and effects by up to 7)	Level 28, Classes: Priest, Mage, Warlock	N/A	1 6 92
Highlander's Cloth Boots (Cloth Feet, 103 Armor, +10 STA, +3 INT, Equip: Run speed increased slightly, Increases damage and healing done by magical spells and effects by up to 8)	Level 38, Classes: Priest, Mage, Warlock	N/A	2 47 49
Highlander's Cloth Boots (Cloth Feet, 132 Armor, +13 STA, +6 INT, Equip: Run speed increased slightly, Increases damage and healing done by magical spells and effects by up to 9)	Level 48, Classes: Priest, Mage, Warlock	N/A	4 98 73
Highlander's Cloth Boots (Cloth Feet, 161 Armor, +16 STA, +8 INT, Equip: Run speed increased slightly, Increases damage and healing done by magical spells and effects by up to 12)	Level 58, Classes: Priest, Mage, Warlock	The Highlander's Intent	7 46 19
Highlander's Lizardhide Boots (Leather Feet, 104 Armor, +5 AGI, +8 STA, +4 INT, Equip: Run speed increased slightly)	Level 28, Classes: Rogue, Druid	N/A	1 36 61
Highlander's Lizardhide Boots (Leather Feet, 129 Armor, +6 AGI, +10 STA, +5 INT, Equip: Run speed increased slightly, +6 Attack Power)	Level 38, Classes: Rogue, Druid	N/A	3 16 28
Highlander's Lizardhide Boots (Leather Feet, 145 Armor, +8 AGI, +13 STA, +7 INT, Equip: Run speed increased slightly, +12 Attack Power)	Level 48, Classes: Rogue, Druid	N/A	6 37 32
Highlander's Lizardhide Boots (Leather Feet, 181 Armor, +8 AGI, +16 STA, +8 INT, Equip: Run speed increased slightly, +16 Attack Power)	Level 58, Classes: Rogue, Druid	The Highlander's Will	9 29 14
Highlander's Leather Boots (Leather Feet, 104 Armor, +7 AGI, +8 STA, Equip: Run speed increased slighty)	Level 28, Classes: Rogue, Druid	N/A	1 32 64
Highlander's Leather Boots (Leather Feet, 129 Armor, +8 AGI, +10 STA, Equip: Run speed increased slighty, +6 Attack Power)	Level 38, Classes: Rogue, Druid	N/A	3 7 5
Highlander's Leather Boots (Leather Feet, 145 Armor, +11 AGI, +13 STA, Equip: Run speed increased slighty, +12 Attack Power)	Level 48, Classes: Rogue, Druid	N/A	6 18 68
Highlander's Leather Boots (Leather Feet, 181 Armor, +12 AGI, +16 STA, Equip: Run speed increased slighty, +16 Attack Power)	Level 58, Classes: Rogue, Druid	The Highlander's Purpose	9 25 64
Highlander's Lamellar Greaves (Mail Feet, 157 Armor, +6 STR, +6 AGI, +4 STA, +4 INT, Equip: Run speed increased slightly)	Level 28, Classes: Paladin	N/A	1 58 10
Highlander's Lamellar Greaves (Plate Feet, 289 Armor, +8 STR, +8 AGI, +6 STA, +6 INT, Equip: Run speed increased slightly)	Level 40, Classes: Paladin	N/A	2 42 87
Highlander's Lamellar Greaves (Plate Feet, 383 Armor, +11 STR, +10 AGI, +7 STA, +6 INT, Equip: Run speed increased slightly)	Level 48, Classes: Paladin	N/A	4 89 38
Highlander's Lamellar Greaves (Plate Feet, 452 Armor, +14 STR, +12 AGI, +8 STA, +8 INT, Equip: Run speed increased slightly)	Level 58, Classes: Paladin	The Highlander's Resolve	8 9 78
Highlander's Plate Greaves (Mail Feet, 157 Armor, +6 STR, +6 AGI, +6 STA, Equip: Run speed increased slightly)	Level 28, Classes: Warrior, Paladin	N/A	1 56 88
Highlander's Plate Greaves (Plate Feet, 289 Armor, +8 STR, +8 AGI, +8 STA, Equip: Run speed increased slightly)	Level 40, Classes: Warrior, Paladin	N/A	2 41 2
Highlander's Plate Greaves (Plate Feet, 383 Armor, +11 STR, +10 AGI, +10 STA, Equip: Run speed increased slightly)	Level 48, Classes: Warrior, Paladin	N/A	4 85 58
Highlander's Plate Greaves (Plate Feet, 452 Armor, +14 STR, +12 AGI, +12 STA, Equip: Run speed increased slightly)	Level 58, Classes: Warrior, Paladin	The Highlander's Resolution	8 6 90

Exalted			
Item	Requirements	Set Name	Cost
Highlander's Chain Pauldrons (Mail Shoulder, 312 Armor, +20 AGI, +18 STA, +17 INT)	Level 58, Classes: Hunter	The Highlander's Determination	16 59 3
Highlander's Epaulets (Cloth Shoulder, 185 Armor, +18 STA, +17 INT, Equip: Increases damage and healing done by magical spells and effects by up to 12, Restores 4 mana per 5 seconds)	Level 60, Classes: Priest, Mage, Warlock	The Highlander's Intent	11 56 54
Highlander's Lizardhide Shoulders (Leather Shoulder, 258 Armor, +12 AGI, +17 STA, +12 INT, Equip: +30 Attack Power)	Level 60, Classes: Rogue, Druid	The Highlander's Will	14 40 55
Highlander's Leather Spaulders (Leather Shoulder, 258 Armor, +18 AGI, +17 STA, Equip: +30 Attack Power)	Level 60, Classes: Rogue, Druid	The Highlander's Purpose	14 35 26
Highlander's Lamellar Spaulders (Plate Shoulder, 553 Armor, +18 STR, +17 AGI, +15 STA, +10 INT)	Level 60, Classes: Paladin	The Highlander's Resolve	11 13 70
Highlander's Plate Spaulders (Plate Shoulder, 553 Armor, +18 STR, +17 AGI, +20 STA)	Level 60, Classes: Warrior, Paladin	The Highlander's Resolution	11 9 46
Cloak of the Honor Guard (Back, 50 Armor, +5 AGI, +11 STA, Equip: +34 Attack Power)	Level 60	N/A	10 92 56
Ironbark Staff (Staff, 55.8 dps, 100 Armor, +19 STA, +10 INT, Equip: Improves your chance to get a critical strike with spells by 2%, Increases damage and healing done by magical spells and effects by up to 41)	Level 60	N/A	49 58 96
Sageclaw (One-Hand Dagger, 41.7 dps, +8 STA, Equip: Increases damage and healing done by magical spells and effects by up to 30, Improves your chance to get a critical strike with spells by 1%)	Level 60	N/A	39 81 26

THE DEFILERS

Friendly			
Item	Requirements	Set Name	Cost
Superior Healing Draught (Use: Restores 560 to 720 health)	Level 35, Usable only in Arathi Basin	N/A	5
Superior Mana Draught (Use: Restores 560 to 720 mana)	Level 35, Usable only in Arathi Basin	N/A	5
(5)Defiler's Field Ration (Use: Restores 1074 health and 2202 mana over 30 seconds)	Level 25, Must remain seated while eating. Usable only in Arathi Basin	N/A	10
(5)Defiler's Iron Ration (Use: Restores 1608 health and 3306 mana over 30 seconds)	Level 35, Must remain seated while eating. Usable only in Arathi Basin	N/A	15
(5)Defiler's Enriched Ration (Use: Restores 2148 health and 4410 mana over 30 seconds)	Level 45, Must remain seated while eating. Usable only in Arathi Basin	N/A	20
(5)Defiler's Silk Bandage (Use: Heals 640 damage over 8 seconds)	Level 25, First Aid (125), Usable only in Arathi Basin	N/A	10
(5)Defiler's Mageweave Bandage (Use: Heals 1104 damage over 8 seconds)	Level 35, First Aid (175), Usable only in Arathi Basin	N/A	15
(5)Defiler's Runecloth Bandage (Use: Heals 2000 damage over 8 seconds)	Level 45, First Aid (225), Usable only in Arathi Basin	N/A	20
Defiler's Talisman (Use: Absorbs 248 to 302 physical damage)	Level 28, Lasts 15 seconds	N/A	72 30
Defiler's Talisman (Use: Absorbs 310 to 378 physical damage)	Level 38, Lasts 15 seconds	N/A	1 52 30
Defiler's Talisman (Use: Absorbs 392 to 478 physical damage)	Level 48, Lasts 15 seconds	N/A	2 82 30
Defiler's Talisman (Use: Absorbs 495 to 605 physical damage)	Level 58, Lasts 15 seconds	N/A	4 12 30

Honored

Item	Requirements	Set Name	Cost
Defiler's Chain Girdle (Leather Waist, 61 Armor, +5 STA, Passive: +24 Attack Power)	Level 28, Classes: Hunter, Shaman	N/A	93 73
Defiler's Chain Girdle (Mail Waist, 149 Armor, +6 STA, Passive: Improves your chance to get a critical strike by 1%, +8 Attack Power)	Level 40, Classes: Hunter, Shaman	N/A	2 60 40
Defiler's Chain Girdle (Mail Waist, 178 Armor, +8 STA, Passive: Improves your chance to get a critical strike by 1%, +20 Attack Power)	Level 48, Classes: Hunter, Shaman	N/A	4 93 73
Defiler's Chain Girdle (Mail Waist, 208 Armor, +10 STA, Passive: Improves your chance to get a critical strike by 1%, +34 Attack Power)	Level 58, Classes: Hunter, Shaman	The Defiler's Determination	7 92 59
Defiler's Cloth Girdle (Cloth Waist, 88 Armor, +4 STA, +3 INT, Passive: Increases damage and healing done by magical spells and effects by up to 11)	Level 28, Classes: Warlock, Mage, Priest	N/A	72 7
Defiler's Cloth Girdle (Cloth Waist, 105 Armor, +4 STA, +4 INT, Passive: Increases damage and healing done by magical spells and effects by up to 14)	Level 38, Classes: Warlock, Mage, Priest	N/A	1 66 84
Defiler's Cloth Girdle (Cloth Waist, 113 Armor, +6 STA, +5 INT, Passive: Improves your chance to get a critical strike with spells by 1%, Increases damage and healing done by magical spells and effects by up to 9)	Level 48, Classes: Warlock, Mage, Priest	N/A	3 36 19
Defiler's Cloth Girdle (Cloth Waist, 150 Armor, +7 STA, +6 INT, Passive: Improves your chance to get a critical strike with spells by 1%, Increases damage and healing done by magical spells and effects by up to 14)	Level 58, Classes: Warlock, Mage, Priest	The Defiler's Intent	5 36 1
Defiler's Lizardhide Girdle (Leather Waist, 91 Armor, +4 STA, +12 INT)	Level 28, Classes: Rogue, Druid	N/A	92 7
Defiler's Lizardhide Girdle (Leather Waist, 113 Armor, +4 STA, +15 INT)	Level 38, Classes: Rogue, Druid	N/A	2 13 14
Defiler's Lizardhide Girdle (Leather Waist, 136 Armor, +6 STA, +10 INT, Equip: Improves your chance to get a critical strike with spells by 1%)	Level 48, Classes: Rogue, Druid	N/A	4 29 52
Defiler's Lizardhide Girdle (Leather Waist, 159 Armor, +7 STA, +17 INT, Equip: Improves your chance to get a critical strike with spells by 1%)	Level 58, Classes: Rogue, Druid	The Defiler's Will	6 67 62
Defiler's Leather Girdle (Leather Waist, 91 Armor, +4 STA, +24 Attack Power)	Level 28, Classes: Rogue, Druid	N/A	89 41
Defiler's Leather Girdle (Leather Waist, 113 Armor, +4 STA, +30 Attack Power)	Level 38, Classes: Rogue, Druid	N/A	2 6 99
Defiler's Leather Girdle (Leather Waist, 136 Armor, +6 STA, Equip: Improves your chance to get a critical strike by 1%, +20 Attack Power)	Level 48, Classes: Rogue, Druid	N/A	4 17 8
Defiler's Leather Girdle (Leather Waist, 159 Armor, +7 STA, Equip: Improves your chance to get a critical strike by 1%, +34 Attack Power)	Level 58, Classes: Rogue, Druid	The Defiler's Purpose	6 65 29
Defiler's Mail Girdle (Leather Waist, 61 Armor, +5 STA, +12 INT)	Level 28, Classes: Hunter, Shaman	N/A	91 74
Defiler's Mail Girdle (Mail Waist, 149 Armor, +6 STA, +15 INT)	Level 40, Classes: Hunter, Shaman	N/A	2 56 72
Defiler's Mail Girdle (Mail Waist, 178 Armor, +8 STA, +10 INT, Equip: Improves your chance to get a critical strike with spells by 1%)	Level 48, Classes: Hunter, Shaman	N/A	5 15 47
Defiler's Mail Girdle (Mail Waist, 208 Armor, +10 STA, +17 INT, Equip: Improves your chance to get a critical strike with spells by 1%)	Level 58, Classes: Hunter, Shaman	The Defiler's Fortitude	8 77 29
Defiler's Plate Girdle (Mail Waist, 128 Armor, +12 STR, +5 STA)	Level 28, Classes: Warrior	N/A	1 2 94
Defiler's Plate Girdle (Plate Waist, 236 Armor, +15 STR, +6 STA,)	Level 40, Classes: Warrior	N/A	1 58 83
Defiler's Plate Girdle (Plate Waist, 313 Armor, +10 STR, +8 STA)	Level 48, Classes: Warrior	N/A	3 53 76
Defiler's Plate Girdle (Plate Waist, 369 Armor, +17 STR, +10 STA, Equip: Improves your chance to get a critical strike by 1%)	Level 58, Classes: Warrior	The Defiler's Resolution	5 10 88

Revered

Item	Requirements	Set Name	Cost
Defiler's Chain Greaves (Leather Feet, 74 Armor, +8 AGI, +8 STA, Equip: Run speed increased slightly)	Level 28, Classes: Hunter	N/A	1 32 17
Defiler's Chain Greaves (Mail Feet, 183 Armor, +10 AGI, +10 STA, +3 INT, Equip: Run speed increased slightly)	Level 40, Classes: Hunter	N/A	3 68 75
Defiler's Chain Greaves (Mail Feet, 218 Armor, +12 AGI, +13 STA, +6 INT, Equip: Run speed increased slightly)	Level 48, Classes: Hunter	N/A	7 42 97
Defiler's Chain Greaves (Mail Feet, 255 Armor, +15 AGI, +16 STA, +8 INT, Equip: Run speed increased slightly)	Level 58, Classes: Hunter	The Defiler's Determination	12 24 28
Defiler's Cloth Boots (Cloth Feet, 84 Armor, +8 STA, Equip: Run speed increased slightly, Increases damage and healing done by magical spells and effects by up to 7)	Level 28, Classes: Priest, Mage, Warlock	N/A	1 6 92
Defiler's Cloth Boots (Cloth Feet, 103 Armor, +10 STA, +3 INT, Equip: Run speed increased slightly, Increases damage and healing done by magical spells and effects by up to 8)	Level 38, Classes: Priest, Mage, Warlock	N/A	2 47 49
Defiler's Cloth Boots (Cloth Feet, 132 Armor, +13 STA, +6 INT, Equip: Run speed increased slightly, Increases damage and healing done by magical spells and effects by up to 9)	Level 48, Classes: Priest, Mage, Warlock	N/A	4 98 73
Defiler's Cloth Boots (Cloth Feet, 161 Armor, +16 STA, +8 INT, Equip: Run speed increased slightly, Increases damage and healing done by magical spells and effects by up to 12)	Level 58, Classes: Priest, Mage, Warlock	The Defiler's Intent	7 46 19
Defiler's Lizardhide Boots (Leather Feet, 104 Armor, +5 AGI, +8 STA, +4 INT, Equip: Run speed increased slightly)	Level 28, Classes: Rogue, Druid	N/A	1 36 61
Defiler's Lizardhide Boots (Leather Feet, 129 Armor, +6 AGI, +10 STA, +5 INT, Equip: Run speed increased slightly, +6 Attack Power)	Level 38, Classes: Rogue, Druid	N/A	3 16 28
Defiler's Lizardhide Boots (Leather Feet, 145 Armor, +8 AGI, +13 STA, +7 INT, Equip: Run speed increased slightly, +12 Attack Power)	Level 48, Classes: Rogue, Druid	N/A	6 37 32
Defiler's Lizardhide Boots (Leather Feet, 181 Armor, +8 AGI, +16 STA, +8 INT, Equip: Run speed increased slightly, +16 Attack Power)	Level 58, Classes: Rogue, Druid	The Defiler's Will	9 29 14
Defiler's Leather Boots (Leather Feet, 104 Armor, +7 AGI, +8 STA, Equip: Run speed increased slighty)	Level 28, Classes: Rogue, Druid	N/A	1 32 64
Defiler's Leather Boots (Leather Feet, 129 Armor, +8 AGI, +10 STA, Equip: Run speed increased slighty, +6 Attack Power)	Level 38, Classes: Rogue, Druid	N/A	3 7 5
Defiler's Leather Boots (Leather Feet, 145 Armor, +11 AGI, +13 STA, Equip: Run speed increased slighty, +12 Attack Power)	Level 48, Classes: Rogue, Druid	N/A	6 18 68
Defiler's Leather Boots (Leather Feet, 181 Armor, +12 AGI, +16 STA, Equip: Run speed increased slighty, +16 Attack Power)	Level 58, Classes: Rogue, Druid	The Defiler's Purpose	9 25 64
Defiler's Mail Greaves (Leather Feet, 74 Armor, +8 AGI, +8 STA, Equip: Run speed increased slightly)	Level 28, Classes: Hunter, Shaman	N/A	1 39 60
Defiler's Mail Greaves (Mail Feet, 183 Armor, +10 AGI, +10 STA, +3 INT, Equip: Run speed increased slightly)	Level 40, Classes: Hunter, Shaman	N/A	3 89 54
Defiler's Mail Greaves (Mail Feet, 218 Armor, +12 AGI, +13 STA, +6 INT, Equip: Run speed increased slightly)	Level 48, Classes: Hunter, Shaman	N/A	7 93 48
Defiler's Mail Greaves (Mail Feet, 255 Armor, +15 AGI, +16 STA, +8 INT, Equip: Run speed increased slightly)	Level 58, Classes: Hunter, Shaman	The Defiler's Determination	11 54 59
Defiler's Plate Greaves (Mail Feet, 157 Armor, +6 STR, +6 AGI, +6 STA, Equip: Run speed increased slightly)	Level 28, Classes: Warrior	N/A	1 56 88
Defiler's Plate Greaves (Plate Feet, 289 Armor, +8 STR, +8 AGI, +8 STA, Equip: Run speed increased slightly)	Level 40, Classes: Warrior	N/A	2 41 2
Defiler's Plate Greaves (Plate Feet, 383 Armor, +11 STR, +10 AGI, +10 STA, Equip: Run speed increased slightly)	Level 48, Classes: Warrior	N/A	4 85 58
Defiler's Plate Greaves (Plate Feet, 452 Armor, +14 STR, +12 AGI, +12 STA, Equip: Run speed increased slightly)	Level 58, Classes: Warrior	The Defiler's Resolution	8 6 90

Exalted

Item	Requirements	Set Name	Cost
Defiler's Chain Pauldrons (Mail Shoulder, 312 Armor, +20 AGI, +18 STA, +17 INT)	Level 58, Classes: Hunter	The Defiler's Determination	16 59 3
Defiler's Epaulets (Cloth Shoulder, 185 Armor, +18 STA, +17 INT, Equip: Increases damage and healing done by magical spells and effects by up to 12, Restores 4 mana per 5 seconds)	Level 60, Classes: Priest, Mage, Warlock	The Defiler's Intent	11 56 54
Defiler's Lizardhide Shoulders (Leather Shoulder, 258 Armor, +12 AGI, +17 STA, +12 INT, Equip: +30 Attack Power)	Level 60, Classes: Rogue, Druid	The Defiler's Will	14 40 55
Defiler's Leather Spaulders (Leather Shoulder, 258 Armor, +18 AGI, +17 STA, Equip: +30 Attack Power)	Level 60, Classes: Rogue, Druid	The Defiler's Purpose	14 35 26
Defiler's Mail Pauldrons (Mail Shoulder, 312 Armor, +11 STR, +10 AGI, +18 STA, +17 INT, Equip: Restores 4 mana per 5 seconds)	Level 60, Classes: Hunter, Shaman	The Defiler's Fortitude	17 99 35
Defiler's Plate Spaulders (Plate Shoulder, 553 Armor, +18 STR, +17 AGI, +20 STA)	Level 60, Classes: Warrior, Paladin	The Defiler's Resolution	11 9 46
Deathguard's Cloak (Back, 50 Armor, +5 AGI, +11 STA, Equip: +34 Attack Power)	Level 60	N/A	10 92 56
Ironbark Staff (Staff, 55.8 dps, 100 Armor, +19 STA, +10 INT, Equip: Improves your chance to get a critical strike with spells by 2%, Increases damage and healing done by magical spells and effects by up to 41)	Level 60	N/A	49 58 96
Mindfang (One-Hand Dagger, 41.7 dps, 40 Armor, +8 STA, Equip: Increases damage and healing done by magical spells and effects by up to 30, Improves your chance to get a critical strike with spells by 1%)	Level 60	N/A	39 81 26

SILVERWING SENTINELS

Friendly

Item	Requirements	Set Name	Cost
Rune of Perfection (Trinket, +4 STA, Equip: Decreases the magical resistances of your spell targets by 10)	Level 20, Classes: Priest, Shaman, Mage, Warlock, Druid	N/A	2
Rune of Perfection (Trinket, +7 STA, Equip: Decreases the magical resistances of your spell targets by 20)	Level 40, Classes: Priest, Shaman, Mage, Warlock, Druid	N/A	4
Rune of Duty (Trinket, +4 STA, Equip: Restores 3 health every 5 seconds)	Level 20, Classes: Warrior, Paladin, Hunter, Rogue	N/A	4
Rune of Duty (Trinket, +7 STA, Equip: Restores 4 health every 5 seconds)	Level 40, Classes: Warrior, Paladin, Hunter, Rogue	N/A	4
Superior Healing Draught (Use: Restores 560 to 720 health)	Level 35, Usable only in Warsong Gulch	N/A	5
Superior Mana Draught (Use: Restores 560 to 720 mana)	Level 35, Usable only in Warsong Gulch	N/A	5
(5)Warsong Gulch Field Ration (Use: Restores 1074 health and 2202 mana over 30 seconds)	Level 25, Must remain seated while eating. Usable only in Warsong Gulch	N/A	10
(5)Warsong Gulch Iron Ration (Use: Restores 1608 health and 3306 mana over 30 seconds)	Level 35, Must remain seated while eating. Usable only in Warsong Gulch	N/A	15
(5)Warsong Gulch Enriched Ration (Use: Restores 2148 health and 4410 mana over 30 seconds)	Level 45, Must remain seated while eating. Usable only in Warsong Gulch	N/A	20
(5)Warsong Gulch Silk Bandage (Use: Heals 640 damage over 8 seconds)	Level 25, First Aid (125), Usable only in Warsong Gulch	N/A	10
(5)Warsong Gulch Mageweave Bandage (Use: Heals 1104 damage over 8 seconds)	Level 35, First Aid (175), Usable only in Warsong Gulch	N/A	15
(5)Warsong Gulch Runecloth Bandage (Use: Heals 2000 damage over 8 seconds)	Level 45, First Aid (225), Usable only in Warsong Gulch	N/A	20

Honored

Item	Requirements	Set Name	Cost
Caretaker's Cape (Back, 20 Armor, +4 STA, +2 SPI, Equip: Increases healing done by spells and effects by up to 9)	Level 18	N/A	36 50
Caretaker's Cape (Back, 25 Armor, +6 STA, +4 SPI, Equip: Increases healing done by spells and effects by up to 13)	Level 28	N/A	1 7 72
Caretaker's Cape (Back, 31 Armor, +8 STA, +5 SPI, Equip: Increases healing done by spells and effects by up to 18)	Level 38	N/A	2 49 34
Caretaker's Cape (Back, 38 Armor, +9 STA, +6 SPI, Equip: Increases healing done by spells and effects by up to 22)	Level 48	N/A	5 2 42
Caretaker's Cape (Back, 45 Armor, +11 STA, +8 SPI, Equip: Increases healing done by spells and effects by up to 26)	Level 58	N/A	7 69 43
Lorekeeper's Ring (Ring, +2 STA, Equip: Increases damage and healing done by magical spells and effects by up to 5, Restores 2 mana per 5 seconds)	Level 18	N/A	2
Lorekeeper's Ring (Ring, +4 STA, Equip: Increases damage and healing done by magical spells and effects by up to 7, Restores 2 mana per 5 seconds)	Level 28	N/A	2 75
Lorekeeper's Ring (Ring, +5 STA, Equip: Increases damage and healing done by magical spells and effects by up to 9, Restores 3 mana per 5 seconds)	Level 38	N/A	4 50
Lorekeeper's Ring (Ring, +6 STA, Equip: Increases damage and healing done by magical spells and effects by up to 12, Restores 4 mana per 5 seconds)	Level 48	N/A	6
Lorekeeper's Ring (Ring, +8 STA, Equip: Increases damage and healing done by magical spells and effects by up to 14, Restores 4 mana per 5 seconds)	Level 58	N/A	6 75
Sentinel's Medallion (Neck, +6 AGI, +2 STA)	Level 18	N/A	2
Sentinel's Medallion (Neck, +8 AGI, +5 STA)	Level 28	N/A	2 75
Sentinel's Medallion (Neck, +11 AGI, +7 STA)	Level 38	N/A	4 50
Sentinel's Medallion (Neck, +12 AGI, +8 STA)	Level 48	N/A	6
Sentinel's Medallion (Neck, +15 AGI, +10 STA)	Level 58	N/A	6 75
Protector's Band (Ring, +4 STR, +4 AGI, +2 STA)	Level 18	N/A	2
Protector's Band (Ring, +6 STR, +6 AGI, +4 STA)	Level 28	N/A	2 75
Protector's Band (Ring, +18 STR, +8 AGI, +5 STA)	Level 38	N/A	4 50
Protector's Band (Ring, +10 STR, +9 AGI, +6 STA)	Level 48	N/A	6
Protector's Band (Ring, +12 STR, +11 AGI, +8 STA)	Level 58	N/A	6 75
Major Healing Draught (Use: Restores 980 to 1260 health)	Level 45, Only usable in Warsong Gulch	N/A	9
Major Mana Draught (Use: Restores 980 to 1260 mana)	Level 45, Only usable in Warsong Gulch	N/A	9

Revered

Item	Requirements	Set Name	Cost
Lorekeeper's Staff (Staff, 19.7 dps, +8 STA, +4 INT, Equip: Restores 3 mana every 5 seconds)	Level 18	N/A	1 52 11
Lorekeeper's Staff (Staff, 27.8 dps, +11 STA, +7 INT, Equip: Restores 4 mana every 5 seconds)	Level 28	N/A	4 27 71
Lorekeeper's Staff (Staff, 38.1 dps, +14 STA, +9 INT, Equip: Restores 6 mana every 5 seconds)	Level 38	N/A	9 93 73
Lorekeeper's Staff (Staff, 45.9 dps, +18 STA, +11 INT, Equip: Restores 7 mana every 5 seconds)	Level 48	N/A	20 9 79
Lorekeeper's Staff (Staff, 54 dps, +21 STA, +13 INT, Equip: Restores 8 mana every 5 seconds)	Level 58	N/A	32 5 33
Outrunner's Bow (Bow, 11.7 dps)	Level 18	N/A	91 26
Outrunner's Bow (Bow, 16.7)	Level 28	N/A	2 56 63
Outrunner's Bow (Bow,22.7 dps, +3 AGI, +6 STA)	Level 38	N/A	5 96 24

Revered			
Item	**Requirements**	**Set Name**	**Cost**
Outrunner's Bow (Bow, 27.5 dps, +3 AGI, +8 STA)	Level 48	N/A	12 5 87
Outrunner's Bow (Bow, 32.3 dps, +4 AGI, +10 STA)	Level 58	N/A	18 53 62
Protector's Sword (One-Hand Sword, 15 dps, +4 STR, +2 STA)	Level 18	N/A	1 21 69
Protector's Sword (One-Hand Sword, 21.3 dps, +7 STR, +3 STA)	Level 28	N/A	3 42 17
Protector's Sword (One-Hand Sword, 29.3 dps, +8 STR, +3 STA)	Level 38	N/A	7 94 98
Protector's Sword (One-Hand Sword, 35.2 dps, +11 STR, +5 STA)	Level 48	N/A	16 7 83
Protector's Sword (One-Hand Sword, 41.5 dps, +13 STR, +5 STA)	Level 58	N/A	24 71 50
Sentinel's Blade (One-Hand Dagger, 15.3 dps, +4 AGI, +2 STA)	Level 18	N/A	1 21 69
Sentinel's Blade (One-Hand Dagger, 21.2 dps, +7 AGI, +3 STA)	Level 28	N/A	3 48 45
Sentinel's Blade (One-Hand Dagger, 29.1 dps, +8 AGI, +3 STA)	Level 38	N/A	8 67 91
Sentinel's Blade (One-Hand Dagger, 35 dps, +11 AGI, +5 STA)	Level 48	N/A	17 49 10
Sentinel's Blade (One-Hand Dagger, 41.5 dps, +13 AGI, +5 STA)	Level 58	N/A	25 26 44

Exalted			
Item	**Requirements**	**Set Name**	**Cost**
Silverwing Battle Tabard	N/A	N/A	4 50
Berserker Bracers (Plate Wrist, 229 Armor, +14 STR, +6 AGI, +8 STA)	Level 40	N/A	2 47 27
Berserker Bracers (Plate Wrist, 275 Armor, +17 STR, +7 AGI, +9 STA)	Level 50	N/A	4 81 75
Berserker Bracers (Plate Wrist, 323 Armor, +19 STR, +8 AGI, +11 STA)	Level 60	N/A	7 96 47
Dryad's Wrist Bindings (Cloth Wrist, 31 Armor, +6 STA, +6 INT, +5 SPI, Equip: Increases damage and healing done by magical spells and effects by up to 16)	Level 40	N/A	2 70 6
Dryad's Wrist Bindings (Cloth Wrist, 37 Armor, +7 STA, +6 INT, +6 SPI, Equip: Increases damage and healing done by magical spells and effects by up to 20)	Level 50	N/A	5 24 27
Dryad's Wrist Bindings (Cloth Wrist, 44 Armor, +8 STA, +8 INT, +7 SPI, Equip: Increases damage and healing done by magical spells and effects by up to 22)	Level 60	N/A	7 87 94
Forest Stalker's Bracers (Leather Wrist, 64 Armor, +8 STR, +14 AGI, +6 STA)	Level 40	N/A	3 9 9
Forest Stalker's Bracers (Leather Wrist, 75 Armor, +9 STR, +17 AGI, +7 STA)	Level 50	N/A	6 2 18
Forest Stalker's Bracers (Leather Wrist, 86 Armor, +11 STR, +19 AGI, +8 STA)	Level 60	N/A	9 8 27
Windtalker's Wristguards (Mail Wrist, 130 Armor, +6 STA, +6 INT, +5 SPI, Equip: +28 Attack Power)	Level 40	N/A	3 70 90
Windtalker's Wristguards (Mail Wrist, 156 Armor, +7 STA, +6 INT, +6 SPI, Equip: +34 Attack Power)	Level 50	N/A	7 22 62
Windtalker's Wristguards (Mail Wrist, 182 Armor, +8 STA, +8 INT, +7 SPI, Equip: +38 Attack Power)	Level 60	N/A	10 89 93
Sentinel's Silk Leggings (Cloth Leggings, 188 Armor, +23 STA, +19 INT, +10 SPI, Equip: Increases damage and healing done by magical spells and effects by up to 28)	Level 60	N/A	15 36 73
Sentinel's Lizardhide Pants (Leather Leggings, 263 Armor, +22 STR, +10 AGI, +22 STA, +22 INT, +9 SPI, Equip: Increases damage and healing done by magical spell and effects by up to 11)	Level 60	N/A	19 6 82
Sentinel's Leather Pants (Leather Leggings, 233 Armor, +28 AGI, +27 STA, Equip: Improves your chance to get a critical strike by 1%)	Level 60	N/A	18 99 77
Sentinel's Chain Leggings (Mail Leggings, 364 Armor, +35 AGI, +15 STA, Equip: Improves you chance to get a critical strike by 1% and improves you chance to hit by 1%)	Levl 60	N/A	21 79 86

Exalted			
Item	**Requirements**	**Set Name**	**Cost**
Sentinel's Lamellar Legguards (Plate Leggings, 646 Armor, +21 STR, +21 STA, Equip: Improves you chance to get a critical strike by 1% and improves you chance to hit by 1% and increases damage and healing done by magical spells and effects by up to 25)	Level 60	N/A	15 42 22
Sentinel's Plate Legguards (Plate Leggings, 646 Armor, +28 STR, +27 STA, Equip: Improves you chance to get a critical strike by 1% and improves you chance to hit by 1%)	Level 60	N/A	14 53 24

WARSONG OUTRIDERS

Friendly			
Item	**Requirements**	**Set Name**	**Cost**
Rune of Perfection (Trinket, +4 STA, Equip: Decreases the magical resistances of your spell targets by 10)	Level 20, Classes: Priest, Shaman, Mage, Warlock, Druid	N/A	2
Rune of Perfection (Trinket, +7 STA, Equip: Decreases the magical resistances of your spell targets by 20)	Level 40, Classes: Priest, Shaman, Mage, Warlock, Druid	N/A	4
Rune of Duty (Trinket, +4 STA, Equip: Restores 3 health every 5 seconds)	Level 20, Classes: Warrior, Paladin, Hunter, Rogue	N/A	4
Rune of Duty (Trinket, +7 STA, Equip: Restores 4 health every 5 seconds)	Level 40, Classes: Warrior, Paladin, Hunter, Rogue	N/A	4
Superior Healing Draught (Use: Restores 560 to 720 health)	Level 35, Usable only in Warsong Gulch	N/A	5
Superior Mana Draught (Use: Restores 560 to 720 mana)	Level 35, Usable only in Warsong Gulch	N/A	5
(5)Warsong Gulch Field Ration (Use: Restores 1074 health and 2202 mana over 30 seconds)	Level 25, Must remain seated while eating. Usable only in Warsong Gulch	N/A	10
(5)Warsong Gulch Iron Ration (Use: Restores 1608 health and 3306 mana over 30 seconds)	Level 35, Must remain seated while eating. Usable only in Warsong Gulch	N/A	15
(5)Warsong Gulch Enriched Ration (Use: Restores 2148 health and 4410 mana over 30 seconds)	Level 45, Must remain seated while eating. Usable only in Warsong Gulch	N/A	20
(5)Warsong Gulch Silk Bandage (Use: Heals 640 damage over 8 seconds)	Level 25, First Aid (125), Usable only in Warsong Gulch	N/A	10
(5)Warsong Gulch Mageweave Bandage (Use: Heals 1104 damage over 8 seconds)	Level 35, First Aid (175), Usable only in Warsong Gulch	N/A	15
(5)Warsong Gulch Runecloth Bandage (Use: Heals 2000 damage over 8 seconds)	Level 45, First Aid (225), Usable only in Warsong Gulch	N/A	20

Honored			
Item	**Requirements**	**Set Name**	**Cost**
Battle Healer's Cloak (Back, 20 Armor, +4 STA, +2 SPI, Equip: Increases healing done by spells and effects by up to 9)	Level 18	N/A	36 50
Battle Healer's Cloak (Back, 25 Armor, +6 STA, +4 SPI, Equip: Increases healing done by spells and effects by up to 13)	Level 28	N/A	1 7 72
Battle Healer's Cloak (Back, 31 Armor, +8 STA, +5 SPI, Equip: Increases healing done by spells and effects by up to 18)	Level 38	N/A	2 49 34
Battle Healer's Cloak (Back, 38 Armor, +9 STA, +6 SPI, Equip: Increases healing done by spells and effects by up to 22)	Level 48	N/A	5 2 42
Battle Healer's Cloak (Back, 45 Armor, +11 STA, +8 SPI, Equip: Increases healing done by spells and effects by up to 26)	Level 58	N/A	7 69 43
Advisor's Ring (Ring, +2 STA, Equip: Increases damage and healing done by magical spells and effects by up to 5, Restores 2 mana per 5 seconds)	Level 18	N/A	2

Honored

Item	Requirements	Set Name	Cost
Advisor's Ring (Ring, +4 STA, Equip: Increases damage and healing done by magical spells and effects by up to 7, Restores 2 mana per 5 seconds)	Level 28	N/A	2 75
Advisor's Ring (Ring, +5 STA, Equip: Increases damage and healing done by magical spells and effects by up to 9, Restores 3 mana per 5 seconds)	Level 38	N/A	4 50
Advisor's Ring (Ring, +6 STA, Equip: Increases damage and healing done by magical spells and effects by up to 12, Restores 4 mana per 5 seconds)	Level 48	N/A	6
Advisor's Ring (Ring, +8 STA, Equip: Increases damage and healing done by magical spells and effects by up to 14, Restores 4 mana per 5 seconds)	Level 58	N/A	6 75
Scout's Medallion (Neck, +6 AGI, +2 STA)	Level 18	N/A	2
Scout's Medallion (Neck, +8 AGI, +5 STA)	Level 28	N/A	2 75
Scout's Medallion (Neck, +11 AGI, +7 STA)	Level 38	N/A	4 50
Scout's Medallion (Neck, +12 AGI, +8 STA)	Level 48	N/A	6
Scout's Medallion (Neck, +15 AGI, +10 STA)	Level 58	N/A	6 75
Legionnaire's Band (Ring, +4 STR, +4 AGI, +2 STA)	Level 18	N/A	2
Legionnaire's Band (Ring, +6 STR, +6 AGI, +4 STA)	Level 28	N/A	2 75
Legionnaire's Band (Ring, +18 STR, +8 AGI, +5 STA)	Level 38	N/A	4 50
Legionnaire's Band (Ring, +10 STR, +9 AGI, +6 STA)	Level 48	N/A	6
Legionnaire's Band (Ring, +12 STR, +11 AGI, +8 STA)	Level 58	N/A	6 75
Major Healing Draught (Use: Restores 980 to 1260 health)	Level 45, Only usable in Warsong Gulch	N/A	9
Major Mana Draught (Use: Restores 980 to 1260 mana)	Level 45, Only usable in Warsong Gulch	N/A	9

Revered

Item	Requirements	Set Name	Cost
Advisor's Gnarled Staff (Staff, 19.7 dps, +8 STA, +4 INT, Equip: Restores 3 mana every 5 seconds)	Level 18	N/A	1 52 11
Advisor's Gnarled Staff (Staff, 27.8 dps, +11 STA, +7 INT, Equip: Restores 4 mana every 5 seconds)	Level 28	N/A	4 27 71
Advisor's Gnarled Staff (Staff, 38.1 dps, +14 STA, +9 INT, Equip: Restores 6 mana every 5 seconds)	Level 38	N/A	9 93 73
Advisor's Gnarled Staff (Staff, 45.9 dps, +18 STA, +11 INT, Equip: Restores 7 mana every 5 seconds)	Level 48	N/A	20 9 79
Advisor's Gnarled Staff (Staff, 54 dps, +21 STA, +13 INT, Equip: Restores 8 mana every 5 seconds)	Level 58	N/A	32 5 33
Outrider's Bow (Bow, 11.7 dps)	Level 18	N/A	91 26
Outrider's Bow (Bow, 16.7)	Level 28	N/A	2 56 63
Outrider's Bow (Bow,22.7 dps, +3 AGI, +6 STA)	Level 38	N/A	5 96 24
Outrider's Bow (Bow, 27.5 dps, +3 AGI, +8 STA)	Level 48	N/A	12 5 87
Outrider's Bow (Bow, 32.3 dps, +4 AGI, +10 STA)	Level 58	N/A	18 53 62
Legionnaire's Sword (One-Hand Sword, 15 dps, +4 STR, +2 STA)	Level 18	N/A	1 21 69
Legionnaire's Sword (One-Hand Sword, 21.3 dps, +7 STR, +3 STA)	Level 28	N/A	3 42 17
Legionnaire's Sword (One-Hand Sword, 29.3 dps, +8 STR, +3 STA)	Level 38	N/A	7 94 98
Legionnaire's Sword (One-Hand Sword, 35.2 dps, +11 STR, +5 STA)	Level 48	N/A	16 7 83
Legionnaire's Sword (One-Hand Sword, 41.5 dps, +13 STR, +5 STA)	Level 58	N/A	24 71 50
Scout's Blade (One-Hand Dagger, 15.3 dps, +4 AGI, +2 STA)	Level 18	N/A	1 21 69

Revered

Item	Requirements	Set Name	Cost
Scout's Blade (One-Hand Dagger, 21.2 dps, +7 AGI, +3 STA)	Level 28	N/A	3 48 45
Scout's Blade (One-Hand Dagger, 29.1 dps, +8 AGI, +3 STA)	Level 38	N/A	8 67 91
Scout's Blade (One-Hand Dagger, 35 dps, +11 AGI, +5 STA)	Level 48	N/A	17 49 10
Scout's Blade (One-Hand Dagger, 41.5 dps, +13 AGI, +5 STA)	Level 58	N/A	25 26 44

Exalted

Item	Requirements	Set Name	Cost
Warsong Battle Tabard	N/A	N/A	4 50
Berserker Bracers (Plate Wrist, 229 Armor, +14 STR, +6 AGI, +8 STA)	Level 40	N/A	2 47 27
Berserker Bracers (Plate Wrist, 275 Armor, +17 STR, +7 AGI, +9 STA)	Level 50	N/A	4 81 75
Berserker Bracers (Plate Wrist, 323 Armor, +19 STR, +8 AGI, +11 STA)	Level 60	N/A	7 96 47
Dryad's Wrist Bindings (Cloth Wrist, 31 Armor, +6 STA, +6 INT, +5 SPI, Equip: Increases damage and healing done by magical spells and effects by up to 16)	Level 40	N/A	2 70 6
Dryad's Wrist Bindings (Cloth Wrist, 37 Armor, +7 STA, +6 INT, +6 SPI, Equip: Increases damage and healing done by magical spells and effects by up to 20)	Level 50	N/A	5 24 27
Dryad's Wrist Bindings (Cloth Wrist, 44 Armor, +8 STA, +8 INT, +7 SPI, Equip: Increases damage and healing done by magical spells and effects by up to 22)	Level 60	N/A	7 87 94
Forest Stalker's Bracers (Leather Wrist, 64 Armor, +8 STR, +14 AGI, +6 STA)	Level 40	N/A	3 9 9
Forest Stalker's Bracers (Leather Wrist, 75 Armor, +9 STR, +17 AGI, +7 STA)	Level 50	N/A	6 2 18
Forest Stalker's Bracers (Leather Wrist, 86 Armor, +11 STR, +19 AGI, +8 STA)	Level 60	N/A	9 8 27
Windtalker's Wristguards (Mail Wrist, 130 Armor, +6 STA, +6 INT, +5 SPI, Equip: +28 Attack Power)	Level 40	N/A	3 70 90
Windtalker's Wristguards (Mail Wrist, 156 Armor, +7 STA, +6 INT, +6 SPI, Equip: +34 Attack Power)	Level 50	N/A	7 22 62
Windtalker's Wristguards (Mail Wrist, 182 Armor, +8 STA, +8 INT, +7 SPI, Equip: +38 Attack Power)	Level 60	N/A	10 89 93
Outrider's Silk Leggings (Cloth Leggings, 188 Armor, +23 STA, +19 INT, +10 SPI, Equip: Increases damage and healing done by magical spells and effects by up to 28)	Level 60	N/A	15 8 70
Outrider's Lizardhide Pants (Leather Leggings, 263 Armor, +22 STR, +10 AGI, +22 STA, +22 INT, +9 SPI, Equip: Increases damage and healing done by magical spell and effects by up to 11)	Level 60	N/A	19 84 15
Outrider's Leather Pants (Leather Leggings, 233 Armor, +28 AGI, +27 STA, Equip: Improves your chance to get a critical strike by 1%)	Level 60	N/A	19 77 10
Outrider's Chain Leggings (Mail Leggings, 364 Armor, +35 AGI, +15 STA, Equip: Improves you chance to get a critical strike by 1% and improves you chance to hit by 1%)	Levl 60	N/A	22 54 14
Outrider's Mail Leggings (Mail Leggings, 364 Armor, +14 STR, +22 STA, +22 INT, Equip: Improves you chance to get a critical strike by 1% and improves you chance to get a critical strike with spells by 1% and restores 6 mana per 5 sec)	Level 60	N/A	22 79 28
Outrider's Plate Legguards (Plate Leggings, 646 Armor, +28 STR, +27 STA, Equip: Improves you chance to get a critical strike by 1% and improves you chance to hit by 1%)	Level 60	N/A	14 91 63

Other Factions

ARGENT DAWN

Friendly

Item	Requirements	Set Name	Cost
(5)Enriched Mana Biscuit (Use: Restores 2148 health and 4410 mana over 30 seconds)	Level 45, Must remain seated while eating	N/A	60

Honored

Item	Requirements	Set Name	Cost
Recipe: Transmute Air to Fire (Use: Teaches you how to transmute Essence of Air into Essence of Fire)	Alchemy (275)	N/A	1 50
Plans: Girdle of the Dawn (Plate Waist, 341 Armor, +21 STR, +9 STA)	Blacksmithing (290)	N/A	2 20
Pattern: Dawn Treaders (Leather Feet, 114 Armor, +18 STA, Equip: Increases your chance to dodge an attack by 1%)	Leatherworking (290)	N/A	2 20
Pattern: Argent Boots (Cloth Feet, 57 Armor, +21 STA, +7 SPI, +4 Shadow Res.)	Tailoring (290)	N/A	2 20
Formula: Powerful Anti-Venom (Use: Target is cured of poisons up to level 60)	First Aid (300)	N/A	10
Formula: Enchant Bracer - mana (Use: Teaches you to permanently enchant a bracer to restore 4 mana every 5 seconds)	Enchanting (290)	N/A	3

Revered

Item	Requirements	Set Name	Cost
Plans: Gloves of the Dawn (Plate Hands, 417 Armor, +23 STR, +10 STA)	Blacksmithing (300)	N/A	4
Pattern: Golden Mantle of the Dawn (Leather Shoulder, 134 Armor, +22 STA, Equip: Increases your chance to dodge an attack by 1%)	Leatherworking (300), Dragonscale Leatherworking	N/A	4
Pattern: Argent Shoulders (Cloth Shoulder, 68 Armor, +23 STA, +8 SPI, +5 Shadow Res.)	Tailoring (300)	N/A	4
(5)Blessed Sunfruit (Use: Restores 1933 health over 27 seconds. Increases STR by 10 for 10 minutes)	Level 45, Must remain seated while eating	N/A	60
(5)Blessed Sunfruit Juice (Use: Restores 4410 mana over 30 seconds. Increases your SPI by 10 for 10 minutes)	Level 45, Must remain seated while drinking	N/A	60
Formula: Enchant Bracer - Healing (Use: Teaches you how to permanently enchant a bracer to increase the effects of healing spells by 24)	Enchanting (300)	N/A	6
Arcane Mantle of the Dawn (Use: Permanently adds 5 arcane resistance to a shoulder slot item)	N/A	N/A	9
Flame Mantle of the Dawn (Use: Permanently adds 5 fire resistance to a shoulder slot item)	N/A	N/A	9
Frost Mantle of the Dawn (Use: Permanently adds 5 frost resistance to a shoulder slot item)	N/A	N/A	9
Nature Mantle of the Dawn (Use: Permanently adds 5 nature resistance to a shoulder slot item)	N/A	N/A	9
Shadow Mantle of the Dawn (Use: Permanently adds 5 shadow resistance to a shoulder slot item)	N/A	N/A	9

Exalted

Item	Requirements	Set Name	Cost
Chromatic Mantle of the Dawn (Use: Permanently adds 5 resistance to all magic schools to a shoulder slot item)	N/A	N/A	36

CENARION CIRCLE

Friendly

Item	Requirements	Set Name	Cost
Pattern: Spitfire Bracers (Mail Wrist, 160 Armor, +9 AGI, +9 INT, Equip: Restores 4 mana every 5 seconds, Increases damage and healing done by magical spells and effects by up to 8)	Leatherworking (300)	N/A	4
Pattern: Sandstalker Bracers (Mail Wrist, 220 Armor, +7 STA, +15 Nature Res.)	Leatherworking (300)	N/A	4
Plans: Heavy Obsidian Belt (Plate Waist, 397 Armor, +25 STR, Equip: +5 all resistances)	Blacksmithing (300)	N/A	5
Plans: Ironvine Belt (Plate Waist, 408 Armor, +12 STA, +15 Nature Res., Equip: Increased Defense +3)	Blacksmithing (300)	N/A	5
Pattern: Sylvan Shoulders (Cloth Shoulder, 74 Armor, +18 STA, +20 Nature Res., Equip: Increases damage and healing done by magical spells and effects by up to 7)	Tailoring (300)	N/A	5
Pattern: Cenarion Herb Bag (20 Slot Herb Bag)	Tailoring (300)	N/A	2
Formula: Enchant Cloak - Greater Fire Resistance (Use: Teaches you how to permanently enchant a cloak to increase Fire Resistance by 15)	Enchanting (300)	N/A	10

Honored

Item	Requirements	Set Name	Cost
Pattern: Spitfire Gauntlets (Mail Hands, 228 Armor, +12 AGI, +12 INT, Equip: Restores 5 mana every 5 seconds, Increases damage and healing done by magical spells and effects by up to 11)	Leatherworking (300)	N/A	4
Pattern: Sandstalker Gauntlets (Mail Hands, 308 Armor, +9 STA, +20 Nature Res.)	Leatherworking (300)	N/A	4
Plans: Light Obsidian Belt (Mail Waist, 224 Armor, Equip: +24 Attack Power, Improves your chance to get a critical strike by 1%, +5 all resistances)	Blacksmithing (300)	N/A	5
Plans: Ironvine Gloves (Plate Hands, 454 Armor, +10 STA, +20 Nature Res., Equip: Increased Defense +10)	Blacksmithing (300)	N/A	5
Pattern: Sylvan Crown (Cloth Head, 80 Armor, +10 STA, +30 Nature Res., Equip: Increases damage and healing done by magical spells and effects by up to 18)	Tailoring (300)	N/A	5
Formula: Enchant Cloak - Greater Fire Resistance (Use: Teaches you how to permanently enchant a cloak to increase Fire Resistance by 15)	Enchanting (300)	N/A	10

Revered

Item	Requirements	Set Name	Cost
Pattern: Spitfire Breastplate (Mail Chest, 365 Armor, +16 AGI, +16 INT, Equip: Restores 6 mana per 5 seconds, Increases damage and healing done by magical spells and effects by up to 15)	Leatherworking (300)	N/A	4
Pattern: Sandstalker Breastplate (Mail Chest, 485 Armor, +13 STA, +25 Nature Res.)	Leatherworking (300)	N/A	4
Plans: Ironvine Breastplate (Plate Chest, 726 Armor, +15 STA, +30 Nature Res., Equip: Increased Defense +7)	Blacksmithing (300)	N/A	5
Pattern: Sylvan Vest (Cloth Chest, 98 Armor, +15 STA, +30 Nature Res., Equip: Increases damage and healing done by magical spells and effects by up to 12)	Tailoring (300)	N/A	5
Pattern: Gaea's Embrace (Back, 49 Armor, +6 STA, +20 Nature Res.)	Tailoring (300)	N/A	9
Pattern: Satchel of Cenarius (24 Slot Herb Bag)	Tailoring (300)	N/A	5

Exalted

Item	Requirements	Set Name	Cost
Pattern: Dreamscale Breastplate (Mail Chest, 434 Armor, +15 AGI, +15 STA, +14 INT, +30 Nature Resis., Equip: Restores 4 mana per 5 seconds)	Leatherworking (300), Dragonscale Leatherworking	N/A	6

THORIUM BROTHERHOOD

Friendly

Item	Requirements	Set Name	Cost
Formula: Enchant Weapon - Strength (Use: Teaches you how to permanently enchant a weapon to increase your strength by 15)	Enchanting (290)	N/A	3

Friendly			
Item	**Requirements**	**Set Name**	**Cost**
Plans: Dark Iron Bracers (Plate Wrist, 394 Armor, +7 STA, +18 Fire Res.)	Blacksmithing (295), Armorsmith	N/A	7
Pattern: Corehound Boots (Leather Feet, 126 Armor, +13 AGI, +10 STA, +24 Fire Res.)	Leatherworking (295), Tribal Leatherworking	N/A	15
Pattern: Molten Helm (Leather Head, 150 Armor, +16 STA, +29 Fire Res., Equip: Increases your chance to dodge an attack by 1%)	Leatherworking (300), Elemental Leatherworking	N/A	16
Pattern: Flarecore Gloves (Cloth Hands, 60 Armor, +10 STA, +14 INT, +25 Fire Res.)	Tailoring (300)	N/A	8
Recipe: Transmute Elemental Fire (Use: Teaches you how to transmute a Heart of Fire into three Elemental Fires)	Alchemy (300)	N/A	12

Honored			
Item	**Requirements**	**Set Name**	**Cost**
Pattern: Flarecore Mantle (Cloth Shoulder, 71 Armor, +9 STA, +10 INT, +10 SPI, +24 Fire Res.)	Tailoring (300)	N/A	18
Pattern: Flarecore Robe (Cloth Chest, 102 Armor, +35 STA, +15 Fire Res., Equip: Increases damage and healing done by magical spells and effects by up to 23)	Tailoring (300)	N/A	6
Pattern: Black Dragonscale Boots (Mail Feet, 270 Armor, +10 STA, +24 Fire Resl, Equip: +24 Attack Power)	Leatherworking (300), Dragonscale Leatherworking	Black DragonMail	16
Pattern: Lava Belt (Leather Waist, 223 Armor, +15 STA, +26 Fire Res.)	Leatherworking (300)	N/A	6
Plans: Fiery Chain Girdle (Mail Waist, 214 Armor, +10 STA, +9 INT, +8 SPI, +24 Fire Res.)	Blacksmithing (295), Armorsmith	N/A	9
Plans: Dark Iron Helm (Plate Head, 758 Armor, +20 STA, + 35 Fire Res.)	Blacksmithing (300), Armorsmith	N/A	6
Plans: Dark Iron Reaver (Main-Hand Sword, 42.7 dps, +10 STA, +6 Fire Res.)	Blacksmithing (300), Master Swordsmith	N/A	21
Plans: Dark Iron Destroyer (Main-Hand Axe, 42.7 dps, +10 STR, +6 Fire Res.)	Blacksmithing (300), Master Axesmith	N/A	21
Formula: Enchant Weapon - Mighty Spirit (Use: Teaches you how to permanently enchant a weapon to increase your spirit by 20)	Enchanting (300)	N/A	8

Revered			
Item	**Requirements**	**Set Name**	**Cost**
Pattern: Flarecore Leggings (Cloth Legs, 94 Armor, +21 STA, +16 Fire Res., Equip: Increases damage and healing done by magical spells and effects by up to 43)	Tailoring (300)	N/A	9
Pattern: Molten Belt (Leather Waist, 118 Armor, +28 AGI, +16 STA, +12 Fire Res.)	Leatherworking (300), Elemental Leatherworking	N/A	9
Pattern: Corehound Belt (Leather Waist, 118 Armor, +16 INT, +12 Fire Res., Equip: Increases healing done by spells and effects by up to 62)	Leatherworking (300), Tribal Leatherworking	N/A	9
Pattern: Chromatic Gauntlets (Mail Hands, 279 Armor, +5 Fire, Nature, Frost, Shadow Res., Equip: +44 Attack Power, Improves your chance to get a critical strike by 1%, Improves your chance to get a critical strike with spells by 1%)	Leatherworking (300), Dragonscale Leatherworking	N/A	9
Plans: Fiery Chain Shoulders (Mail Shoulder, 299 Armor, +10 STA, +14 INT, +25 Fire Res.)	Blacksmithing (300), Armorsmith	N/A	20
Plans: Dark Iron Leggings (Plate Legs, 778 Armor, +14 STA, +30 Fire Res.)	Blacksmithing (300), Armorsmith	N/A	18
Plans: Dark Iron Gauntlets (Plate Hands, 495 Armor, +12 AGI, +16 STA, +28 Fire Res.)	Blacksmithing (300), Armorsmith	N/A	8
Plans: Amnesty (One-Hand Dagger, 47.8 dps, Chance on Hit: Reduce your threat to the current target making them less likely to attack you)	Blacksmithing (300), Master Weaponsmith	N/A	7
Plans: Blackfury (Polearm, 62.6 dps, +35 STR, +15 STA, +10 Fire Res., Equip: Improves your chance to get a critical strike by 1%)	Blacksmithing (300), Weaponsmith	N/A	7
Formula: Enchant Weapon - Mighty Intellect (Use: Teaches you how to permanently enchant a weapon to increase your intellect by 22)	Enchanting (300)	N/A	10

Exalted			
Item	**Requirements**	**Set Name**	**Cost**
Plans: Blackguard (One-Hand Sword, 51.7 dps, +9 STA, Equip: Increases your chance to parry an attack by 1%)	Blacksmithing (300), Master Swordsmith	N/A	12
Plans: Nightfall (Two-Hand Axe, 67.0 dps, Chance of Hit: Reduces enemy's spell resistances by 60 for 5 seconds)	Blacksmithing (300), Master Axesmith	N/A	12
Plans: Ebon Hand (One-Hand Mace, 51.5 dps, +9 STA, +7 Fire Res., Chance on Hit: Sends a shadowy bolt at the enemy causing 125 to 275 Shadow damage)	Blacksmithing (300), Master Hammersmith	N/A	12
Plans: Dark Iron Boots (Plate Feet, 664 Armor, +28 Fire Res.)	Blacksmithing (300), Armorsmith	N/A	8

TIMBERMAW HOLD

Friendly			
Item	**Requirements**	**Set Name**	**Cost**
Pattern: Warbear Harness (Leather Chest, 158 Armor, +11 STR, +27 STA)	Leatherworking (275), Tribal Leatherworking	N/A	1 44
Pattern: Warbear Woolies (Leather Legs, 142 Armor, +28 STR, +12 STA)	Leatherworking (285), Tribal Leatherworking	N/A	1 98
Recipe: Transmute Earth to Water (Use: Teaches you how to transmute Essence of Earth into Essence of Water)	Alchemy (275)	N/A	1 35

Honored			
Item	**Requirements**	**Set Name**	**Cost**
Furbolg Medicine Pouch (Off-Hand, +10 STA, Use: Restores 100 health every 1 second for 10 seconds, 20 minute cooldown)	N/A	N/A	13 50
Furbolg Medicine Totem (Main-Hand Mace, 31 dps, +6 STA, +6 SPI)	N/A	N/A	11 98
Plans: Heavy Timbermaw Belt (Mail Waist, 193 Armor, +9 STA, Equip: +42 Attack Power)	Blacksmithing (290)	N/A	1 80
Plans: Might of the Timbermaw (Leather Waist, 93 Armor, +21 STR, +9 STA)	Leatherworking (290)	N/A	1 98
Pattern: Wisdom of the Timbermaw (Cloth Waist, 46 Armor, +21 INT, Equip: Restores 4 mana every 5 seconds)	Tailoring (290)	N/A	1 98
Formula: Enchant Weapon - Agility (Use: Teaches you how to permanently enchant a weapon to increase your agility by 15)	Enchanting (290)	N/A	2 70

Revered			
Item	**Requirements**	**Set Name**	**Cost**
Plans: Heavy Timbermaw Boots (Mail Feet, +23 STA, Equip: +20 Attack Power)	Blacksmithing (300)	N/A	3 60
Pattern: Timbermaw Brawlers (Leather Hands, 112 Armor, +23 STR, +10 STA)	Leatherworking (300)	N/A	3 60
Pattern: Mantle of the Timbermaw (Cloth Shoulder, 68 Armor, +21 INT, Equip: Restores 6 mana every 5 seconds)	Tailoring (300)	N/A	3 60

Exalted			
Item	**Requirements**	**Set Name**	**Cost**
Defender of the Timbermaw (Use: Call forth a Timbermaw Ancestor to fight at your side and heal you, 10 minute cooldown)	Quest	N/A	

ZANDALAR TRIBE

Friendly			
Item	**Requirements**	**Set Name**	**Cost**
Pattern: Bloodvine Boots (Cloth Feet, 63 Armor, +16 INT, Equip: Improves your chance to hit with spells by 1%, Increases damage and healing done by magical spells and effects by up to 19)	Tailoring (300)	Bloodvine Garb	5

Friendly

Item	Requirements	Set Name	Cost
Pattern: Primal Batskin Bracers (Leather Wrist, 79 Armor, +14 AGI, +7 STA, Equip: Improves your chance to hit by 1%)	Leatherworking (300)	Primal Batskin	5
Plans: Bloodsoul Gauntlets (Mail Hands, 238 Armor, +10 AGI, +17 STA, Equip: Improves your chance to get a critical strike by 1%)	Blacksmithing (300)	Bloodsoul Embrace	5
Plans: Darksoul Shoulders (Plate Shoulders, 507 Armor, +24 STA, Equip: Improves your chance to hit by 1%)	Blacksmithing (300)	The Darksoul	5
Schematic: Bloodvine Lens (Leather Head, 147 Armor, +12 STA, Equip: Improves your chance to get a critical strike by 2%, Slightly increases your stealth detection)	Engineering (300)	N/A	5
Recipe: Greater Dreamless Sleep (Use: Puts the imbiber in a dreamless sleep for 12 seconds. During that time the imbiber heals 2100 health and 2100 mana)	Alchemy (275)	N/A	5
Formula: Brilliant mana Oil (Use:While applied to a target weapon, it restores 12 mana to the caster every 5 seconds and increases the effect of healing spells by up to 25. Lasts 30 minutes)	Enchanting (300)	N/A	4

Honored

Item	Requirements	Set Name	Cost
Pattern: Bloodvine Leggings (Cloth Legs, 80 Armor, +6 INT, Equip: Improves your chance to hit with spells by 1%, Increases damage and healing done by magical spells and effects by up to 37)	Tailoring (300)	Bloodvine Garb	5
Pattern: Primal Batskin Gloves (Leather Hands, 113 Armor, +10 AGI, +9 STA, Equip: Improves your chance to hit by 2%)	Leatherworking (300)	Primal Batskin	5
Pattern: Blood Tiger Shoulders (Leather Shoulders, 136 Armor, +13 STR, +13 STA, +12 INT, +10 SPI)	Leatherworking (300)	Blood Tiger Harness	5
Plans: Bloodsoul Shoulders (Mail Shoulders, 286 Armor, +24 AGI, +10 STA)	Blacksmithing (300)	Bloodsoul Embrace	5
Plans: Darksoul Leggings (Plate Legs, 722 Armor, +22 STA, Equip: Improves your chance to hit by 2%)	Blacksmithing (300)	The Darksoul	5
Schematic: Bloodvine Goggles (Cloth Head, 75 Armor, Equip: Improves your chance to hit with spells by 2%, Improves your chance to get a critical strike with spells by 1%, Restores 9 mana every 5 seconds)	Engineering (300)	N/A	5
Recipe: Major Troll's Blood Potion (Use: Regenerate 20 health every 5 seconds for 1 hour)	Alchemy (290)	N/A	5
Formula: Brilliant Wizard Oil (Use: While applied to target weapon, it increases spell damage by up to 36 and increases Spell Critical chance by 1%. Lasts 30 minutes)	Enchanting (300)	N/A	4
(10)Essence Mango (Use: Restores 2550 health and 4410 mana over 30 seconds)	1 Zandalar Honor Token, Must remain seated while eating	N/A	

Revered

Item	Requirements	Set Name	Cost
Pattern: Bloodvine Vest (Cloth Chest, 92 Armor, +13 INT, Equip: Improves your chance to hit with spells by 2%)	Tailoring (300)	Bloodvine Garb	5
Pattern: Primal Batskin Jerkin (Leather Chest, 181 Armor, +32 AGI, +6 STA, Equip: Improves your chance to hit by 1%)	Leatherworking (300)	Primal Batskin	5
Plans: Bloodsoul Breastplate (Mail Chest, 381 Armor, +9 AGI, +13 STA, Equip: Improves your chance to get a critical strike by 2%)	Blacksmithing (300)	Bloodsoul Embrace	5
Plans: Darksoul Breastplate (Plate Chest, 736 Armor, +32 STA, Equip: Improves your chance to hit by 1%)	Blacksmithing (300)	The Darksoul	5
Pattern: Blood Tiger Breastplate (Leather Chest, 181 Armor, +17 STR, +17 STA, +16 INT, +13 SPI)	Leatherworking (300)	Blood Tiger Harness	5
Recipe: Mageblood Potion (Use: Regenerate 12 mana every 5 seconds for 1 hour)	Alchemy (275)	N/A	5

Revered

Item	Requirements	Set Name	Cost
Sheen of Zanza (Use: Increases the chance that the player will reflect hostile spells cast on them by 3% and grants a 100% chance to reflect the first spell cast on the user)	1 Zandalar Honor Tokens. Lasts 2 hours. Only one type of Zanza potion may be active at any given time.	N/A	
Spirit of Zanza (Use: Increases the players SPI by 50 and STA by 50)	3 Zandalar Honor Tokens. Lasts 2 hours. Only one type of Zanza potion may be active at any given time.	N/A	
Swiftness of Zanza (Use: Increases the player's run speed by 20%)	3 Zandalar Honor Tokens. Lasts 2 hours. Only one type of Zanza potion may be active at any given time.	N/A	

Exalted

Item	Requirements	Set Name	Cost
Recipe: Living Action Potion (Use: Makes you immune to stun and movement impairing effects for the next 5 seconds. Also removes existing stun and movement impairing effects)	Alchemy (285)	N/A	5
Zandalar Signet of Might (Use: Permanently adds 30 attack power to a shoulder slot item)	15 Zandalar Honor Tokens	N/A	
Zandalar Signet of Mojo (Use: Permanenty adds to a shoulder slot item increased damage and healing done by magical spells and effects by up to 18)	15 Zandalar Honor Tokens	N/A	
Zandalar Signet of Serenity (Use: Permanently adds to a shoulder slot item increases healing done by spells and effects up to 33)	15 Zandalar Honor Tokens	N/A	

The Races of Azeroth

World of Warcraft is a world built on war and conflict. The races of Azeroth have found themselves choosing sides and allying in order to stay safe from their many enemies and the creatures that roam it. Two factions have come of this; the Horde and the Alliance. Choosing a faction means choosing a side in a war, so consider carefully.

Alliance

Horde

Dwarf Gnome

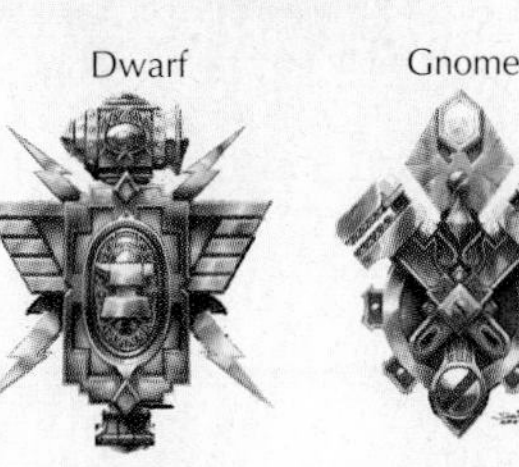

Orc Tauren

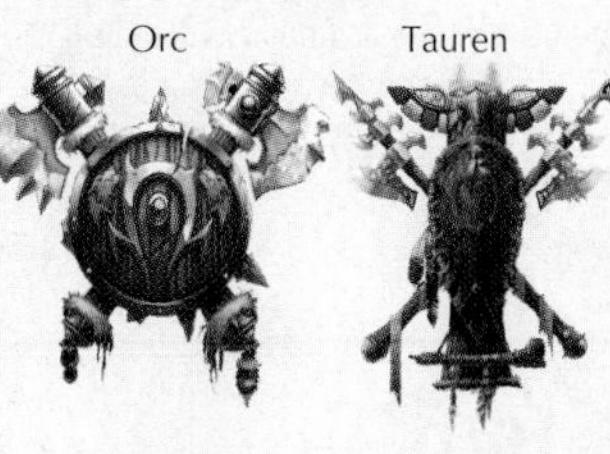

Human Night Elf

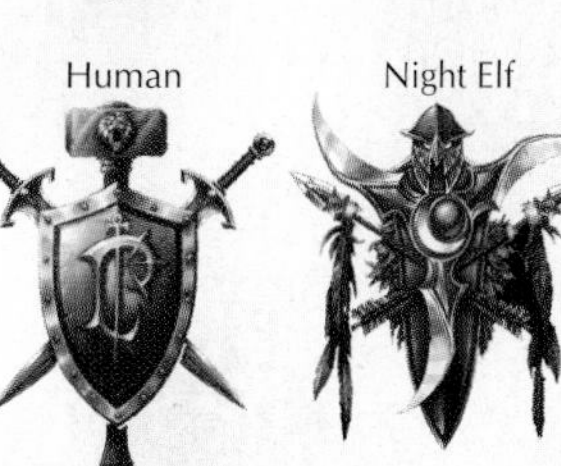

Troll Forsaken

DWARVES

Starting Statistics

Class	Strength	Agility	Stamina	Intellect	Spirit
Warrior	25	16	25	19	19
Paladin	24	16	25	19	20
Hunter	22	19	24	19	20
Rogue	23	19	24	19	19
Priest	22	16	23	21	22

Much like the stone and metal the dwarves shape so adeptly, the dwarves themselves are sturdy and durable. This gives them more physical staying power than some of the other races. While neither stupid nor clumsy, the dwarves are often the last to leave a battlefield.

Racial Traits

STONEFORM

Dwarves can gain certain aspects of stone for short periods of time. Activating Stoneform gives you immunity to poisons, disease, and bleed effects as well as increasing your Armor by 10% for 8 seconds. This ability has a 3 minute cooldown.

This is most useful when under heavy attack. The ability to purge existing poison, disease, and bleed effects can keep your health from dropping as quickly. Combined with the added Armor and you're more likely to survive long enough to finish the enemy or get healing.

TREASURE FINDING

The dwarves have been searching for treasures hidden in the very rock for longer than anyone can remember. It hasn't been until recently that the dwarves realized that concentrating allows them to find treasures above the ground as well. Activating this ability shows treasure chests on the mini map as yellow dots. This ability lasts until cancelled.

Using Treasure Finding can help you decide whether to venture down a side passage in a tunnel or check up a set of stairs. As a number of useful items are contained in chests, this has both survival and monetary uses. As only one type of tracking can be active at a time, characters with other tracking skills (Hunters, Herbalists, Miners) will get used to which tracking to have on at a given time.

FROST RESISTANCE

Life on the wintry peaks of Dun Morogh has left the dwarves resistance to icy wind. All dwarves have +10 to Cold Resistance. This is a passive ability and does not need to be activated in any way.

The upside of increased Cold Resistance, aside from lower heating bills, is lower damage from Cold-based attacks. As resistance increases both your chance to resist part of an attack's damage and your chance to fully resist the damage, Frost Resistance is quite useful. A full resist also keeps you from being affected by Cold-based Root and Snare effects.

GUN SPECIALIZATION

Friendly shooting competitions are commonplace at many dwarven holidays. As such, dwarves are more proficient with firearms and receive +5 to their maximum Gun Skill. As a passive trait Gun Specialization need not be activated.

The increased maximum Gun Skill offers several advantages if you're willing to put in the training time. As your Gun skill will be higher than normal for your level, you'll have a higher chance to hit your target and a higher chance for a critical strike when using your gun. Take the time to train your Gun skill to maximum.

LANGUAGES

While Dwarvish is still taught to all dwarven children, it isn't used as often as Common. Common is the native tongue of the humans and because they were many of the first tradesman to make connections outside their own race, Common became the tongue of tradesman. As people visited more of the foreign markets, Common spread more until it became the universal language that all Alliance races can speak. This has made a number of cooperative projects, both military and civilian, easier.

Brief History

The stoic dwarves of Ironforge spent countless generations mining treasures from deep within the earth. There, the dwarves unearthed a series of ruins that held secrets to their ancient heritage. Driven to discover the truth about his people's fabled origins, the great King Magni Bronzebeard ordered that the dwarves shift their industry from mining to archaeology. As part of the Grand Alliance, the stalwart dwarven armies have been called away to battle the merciless Horde in far away lands. In these perilous times, the defense of the mountain kingdom falls to brave dwarves like you. The spirits of the ancient kings watch over you and the very mountains are your strength. The future of your people is in your hands.

Some speculate that the dwarves are descended from the mysterious race known as the "Earthen". As the children of the Titans, they were to shape and guard the earth from deep within. With the implosion of the Well of Eternity, the Earthen sealed themselves away until some unknown event mysteriously woke them from their slumber. In time, they made their way to the surface and found homes within the mountains, founding their home of Ironforge.

Three clans rose among them, and they lived in relative peace among one another until High King Anvilmar passed away, leaving no heir. War broke out among the three factions until Madoran Bronzebeard at last managed to gain leverage and cast out the other clans. The Bronzebeards rule the Ironforge dwarves to this day.

Roleplaying Tips

Playing a dwarf can be quite enjoyable. They are a very passionate people. They work hard and they play hard. Dwarves will rarely stop before a task is complete. Whether this be to take an enemy keep, fully excavate a set of ruins, forge a unique sword, or relax after a day of work, dwarves give their full attention to whatever they are doing at the time. Each task has its own time and you should concentrate on the task at hand.

FORSAKEN

Starting Statistics

Class	Strength	Agility	Stamina	Intellect	Spirit
Warrior	22	18	23	18	25
Rogue	20	21	22	18	25
Priest	19	18	21	20	28
Mage	19	18	21	21	27
Warlock	19	18	22	20	27

The Forsaken have been freed from the chains of mortal bodies. They only continue to exist because of their dominant Spirit. While a higher Spirit benefits all classes with increased health and mana regeneration, the mystic classes make more use of it

Racial Traits

WILL OF THE FORSAKEN

The Forsaken have not been defeated by either death or the Lich King. When activated, the Will of the Forsaken makes them immune to Fear, Sleep, and Charm effects for five seconds. This can also be used to break free from already existing Fear, Sleep, and Charm effects and has a two minute cooldown.

With the most common forms of combat control being Fear, Sleep, and Charm, the benefit of being able to break these without outside assistance is amazing. In both PvP and PvE, you will be much more difficult to nullify quickly. All classes benefit from this trait.

CANNIBALIZE

Transcending death has given the Forsaken more than just the ability to move around as rotting flesh. They can repair their rotting flesh by consuming the flesh of the recently deceased. When activated, Cannibalize restores 7% of your total health every two seconds for a maximum of ten seconds. Only humanoid or undead corpses near the Forsaken can be used and any movement or damage taken will interrupt Cannibalize. It has a two minute cooldown.

While useful to all classes, this is most useful to melee classes as they have only their health to restore after combat. This can be used in both PvE and PvP to regenerate health quickly between battles.

UNDERWATER BREATHING

While the Forsaken have no need for breathing, extended time underwater causes their body to deteriorate and fall apart. This is not pleasant to see or experience. All Forsaken have a passive ability to remain underwater 300% more than living races.

While this trait doesn't seem like much at first, it's very useful to explorers and those who think out of the box. While others fear fighting or searching beneath the water, you can do so with little worry. In PvP, running into the water will force your enemy to engage you on your terms or allow you to escape.

SHADOW RESISTANCE

Undeath holds very few secrets for the Forsaken. Possibly powered by Shadow magic itself, they gain +10 to their Shadow Resistance. This trait is passive and does not need to be activated.

The upside of increased Shadow resistance is lower damage from Shadow-based attacks. Shadow resistance increases your chance to resist partial damage from a Shadow attack or effect as well as your chance to fully resist the effects. These effects include combat control abilities. Higher resistances are always useful.

LANGUAGES

The Forsaken are allied with the orcs but only use orcish when communicating with the other races of the Horde. They intentionally use Gutterspeak when conversing with each other as only Forsaken are taught it. The Forsaken have decided to keep their language from the other races so they can converse and plan without being overheard.

Brief History

Bound to the iron will of the tyrant Lich King, the vast Undead armies of the Scourge seek to eradicate all life on Azeroth. However, a group of renegades, led by the Banshee Sylvanus Windrunner, has broken away from the Scourge and freed themselves of the Lich King's domination. Known as the Forsaken, this group fights a constant battle not only to retain its freedom from the Scourge but also to slaughter those who would hunt them as monsters. With Sylvanus as their Banshee Queen, the Forsaken have built a dark stronghold beneath the ruins of Lordaeron's former capital. This hidden Undercity forms a sprawling labyrinth that sprawls beneath the haunted woods of Tirisfal Glades. Though the very land is cursed, the Scarlet Crusade still cling to their scattered holdings and obsess with the destruction of all undead. Convinced that the primitive races of the Horde can help them achieve victory over their enemies, the Forsaken have entered into an alliance of convienence. Harboring no true loyalty for their new allies, they go to any lengths to ensure their dark plans come to fruition. As one of the Forsaken, you must massacre any who pose a threat to the new order; human, Undead, or otherwise.

With Undeath comes new capabilities and immunities no other race is afforded. Just as the Forsaken do not need to draw breath, they have no mortal desires apart from survival. They are free to devote themselves to an unlife of working for their own revenge and power. Their dark lands are plagued by the remnants of the Scourge and the vile Scarlet Crusade, but they remain vigilant in their pursuit to rid themselves of both menaces and establish themselves as a dominant force on Azeroth.

Roleplaying Tips

The Forsaken are as varied as the humans they once were. Most died in very horrible and painful ways and feel nothing but hatred and the need for revenge. There are others who are able to see further and make much more long reaching plans...such as to kill all living things.

GNOMES

Starting Statistics

Class	Strength	Agility	Stamina	Intellect	Spirit
Warrior	18	23	21	24	20
Rogue	16	26	20	24	20
Mage	15	23	19	27	22
Warlock	15	23	20	26	22

At first look, gnomes appear much like children. Don't underestimate them, though. Those large eyes staring serenely at you hide a very active and articulate mind. They also keep your attention from the gnome's hands as he ties your bootlaces together.

Racial Traits

ESCAPE ARTIST

Very few races are as small as gnomes and most nets weren't made for them. Activating Escape Artist breaks all existing root and snare effects on you. It requires one and a half seconds to cast and one minute to cool down.

If a gnome puts their mind and fingers to it, nothing can hold them for long. Enemies that root or snare you to provide themselves with an escape route or to stop your escape are in for a rude surprise. The casting time can be slowed by taking damage, but the ability to escape some of the more common types of combat control is wonderful.

EXPANSIVE MIND

While very small, gnomes have curiosity and imagination that surpasses most people twice their height. All gnomes gain a 5% increase in their Intellect beyond other races. This is a passive trait and is always active.

The increased Intellect does a number of things. Higher Intellect makes weapon training faster as well as giving you more Mana to cast spells with. It also affects your chance to get a critical strike with spells. While faster weapon training helps the more physical classes in a modest way, the bonuses for casters are immense.

ARCANE RESISTANCE

The curiosity of gnomes knows no bounds. They have dabbled with so many things, both arcane and mundane, and had them blow up in their face, that they've become slightly resistant. +10 Arcane Resistance is a passive trait and does not need to be activated.

The upside of increased Arcane Resistance is lower damage from Arcane-based attacks. Arcane Resistance increases your chance to resist partial damage from an Arcane attack as well as your chance to fully resist the effects. These effects include combat control abilities. Higher resistances are always useful.

TECHNOLOGIST

Not everything gnomes do explodes. Many of their inventions work quite well, and they have pushed Engineering past the barriers of all other races except for the Goblins. All gnomes have +15 to their maximum Engineering Skill.

This allows them to learn more for each level of crafting. While a slim lead, it gives them the ability to understand certain schematics that Engineers of the same level would be unable to comprehend.

LANGUAGES

Listening to an excited gnome talk in your own language can sometimes be trying. Hearing them talk in their native gnomish will help you realize why no one takes the time to learn it aside from gnomes. As such, gnomes now teach Common to their children to make communication with other races more productive.

Brief History

The eccentric, often-brilliant gnomes are held as one of the most peculiar races of the world. With their obsession for developing radical new technologies and constructing marvels of mind-bending engineering, it's a wonder that any gnomes have survived to proliferate. Over the years, gnomes have contributed ingenious weapons to aid the Grand Alliance in its fierce battles against the Horde. Thriving within the wondrous city of Gnomeregan, the gnomes shared the resources of the forest of Dun Morogh peaks with their dwarven cousins. Yet recently, a barbaric menace rose up from the bowels of the earth and invaded Gnomeregan. The gnomes fought a valiant battle to save their beloved city. Nevertheless, Gnomeregan was irrevocably lost. The surviving gnomes fled to the safety of the dwarven stronghold of Ironforge. There they remain, devising strategies to retake their city. As a gnome of proud standing, it falls to you to answer the challenge and lead your curious people to a brighter future.

The gnomes work hard to this day within the well fortified halls of Ironforge to create bigger and better inventions. No problem is safe from gnomes. They will prevail and answers to every problem will be found.

It is their passion, and it can be seen in their choice of environs when visiting their small section of the city. With the energy they exhibit and their affinity for inventions, you begin to wonder if you should see a wind-up key in their backs.

Roleplaying Tips

Gnomes are insatiably curious and active. Very little slows them down and they are seldom idle for long. For this reason, few gnomes are curious about mundane things for terribly long. Most of them spend their days, and nights, trying to understand the two most powerful forces in the world: technology and magic.

HUMANS

Starting Statistics

Class	Strength	Agility	Stamina	Intellect	Spirit
Warrior	23	20	22	20	21
Paladin	22	20	22	20	22
Rogue	21	23	21	20	21
Priest	20	20	20	22	24
Mage	20	20	20	23	23
Warlock	20	20	21	22	23

Humans are very flexible. While most people think of humans as masters of no specific field, they can compete on every field. Their flexibility has allowed them to settle even the most inhospitable lands.

Racial Traits

PERCEPTION

Having enemies around them for so long, humans have become very good at peering into the shadows around them to see what lies hidden. Activating Perception increases your stealth detection radius by 10 yards. This lasts for 20 seconds and has a three minute cooldown.

This is useful whether your enemies are NPCs or PCs. Activating this before you enter an area where you suspect people hiding can reveal an ambush before you're surrounded. With 3 minute cooldown, organizing other humans grouped with you to stagger the ability makes it very powerful.

HUMAN SPIRIT

Partly romantic nonsense and partly truth, the unbreakable human spirit helps them to recover from many attacks more quickly. All humans get a 5% bonus to their Spirit.

An increased Spirit increases your natural health and mana regeneration rates. When out of combat and not casting, a higher Spirit helps you recover more quickly. This is an asset to every human regardless of class.

DIPLOMACY

While not the first race to interact with others, humans have a gift for establishing long friendships and trade agreements. Faction reputation gain is increased by 10% for humans.

This ability is extremely powerful for those that make use of it. A faster reputation gain enables you to attain reputation levels much more quickly and access crafting recipes and items with less work than people from other races. Crafters will find this ability immensely useful as will characters who participate in PvP (many PvP rewards are based on reputation).

SWORD AND MACE SPECIALIZATION

With so many devoted to martial pursuits, humans hold many competitions where combatants can test their skill without risking their life. The result is that all humans gain +5 to their maximum skill for Swords, Two-Handed Swords, Maces, and Two-Handed Maces.

The increased maximum for combat skills offers several advantages if you're willing to put in the training time. As your melee skill will be higher than standardly appropriate for your level, you'll have a higher chance to hit your target and a higher chance for a critical strike when using your sword or mace. Keep your combat skills at their maximum to take full advantage of this.

LANGUAGES

Humans have touched so many others they have created a legacy of cooperation and communication for the coming generations to enjoy. As one of the first races to work toward bring other races together in harmony, the native language of humans, Common, has been adopted as a global language for communication between races. While children of other races spend the time to master a second language, human children spend time learning about gnomish engineering, dwarven crafting, and night elf magic.

Brief History

The noble humans of Stormwind are a proud, tenacious race. Though the recent invasion of the Undead Scourge and demonic Burning Legion decimated their sister kingdom of Lordaeron, the defenders of Stormwind have stood vigilant against any who would threaten the sanctity of their lands. Nestled in the foothills of Elwynn Forest, Stormwind city is one of the last bastions of human power in the world. Ruled by the child-king Anduin Wrynn, the people of Stormwind remain steadfast in their commitment to the Grand Alliance. Backed by their stalwart allies, the armies of Stormwind have been called away to fight the savage Horde on distant battlefields. With the armies gone, the defense of Stormwind now falls to its proud citizens. You must defend the kingdom against the foul mongrels that encroach upon it and hunt down the subversive traitors who seek to destroy it from within. Now is the time for heroes; now Humanity's greatest chapter can be written.

Humans once lived a nomadic life in tribes wandering from place to place as the seasons changed or the hunting became lean. It wasn't until the rise of the Arathi that they began to form within one nation. They founded the fortified city of Strom and, as they grew, so did they gain the attention of the High Elves who, like them, were suffering brutal attacks from the Trolls. As allies, they beat back the Trolls, and the High Elves began to teach their newfound friends the ways of magic. With time, the humans also came into contact with the dwarves, and, while the dwarves were initially unsure of these strange new people, they developed a strong bond of friendship.

Over the years, the region of Lordaeron grew so large that it fractured into smaller kingdoms, each with its own beliefs, government, and lifestyle. The humans began to outstrip their teachers in the use of magic, which alarmed their High elf friends. The same corruption that had filled the world before was becoming evident. To combat this problem, the Council of Silvermoon joined with the Magocrat Lords of Arathor in a pact. They formed a secret order called the Guardians of Tirisfal. The Guardians sought to protect the world from the onslaught of the demons of the Burning Legion should they return. This legacy came to its end when the Guardian made a terrible misjudgement in her power and slew an avatar of the Demon Lord Sargeras a bit too easily. She then took his body and secreted it away where none could find it. However, Sargeras was too clever and instead hid his spirit inside her, later implanting his essence into her unborn child who would one day be the inheritor of her powers.

Roleplaying Tips

Partly because of their ability to live anywhere, humans are as varied as the world itself. While many are loyal citizens and defenders of Stormwind, there are those who care only for themselves. If there is one thing that links humans together, it would be their goal to be something better.

NIGHT ELVES

Starting Statistics

Class	Strength	Agility	Stamina	Intellect	Spirit
Warrior	20	25	21	20	20
Hunter	17	28	20	20	21
Rogue	18	28	20	20	20
Priest	17	25	19	22	23
Druid	18	25	19	22	22

Night elves are as agile as they are long lived. While casters find the extra chance to dodge appealing, melee classes love the added chance for a critical strike provided by the increased Agility.

Racial Traits

SHADOWMELD

Spending much of their time beneath the canopy of the forest, night elves have become adept at vanishing into the shadows. When out of combat and immobile, night elves can enter stealth mode by activating Shadowmeld. It lasts until canceled and has a ten second cooldown. Any action taken is considered movement and will cancel Shadowmeld.

The ability to hide from your enemies is of tremendous power. Hiding from NPCs can give you the time you need to recover from the last fight while hiding from other players also guarantees you get to start the fight on your terms.

QUICKNESS

Night elves are beyond agile. They move with the grace of a reed in the wind...always moving. Night elves gain a passive bonus of 1% to dodge.

Any time you are the focus of a melee attack, this trait might save you. For either casters trying to survive long enough for friends to come to their aid or melee attackers trying to survive long enough to kill their enemy, the added dodge can come in handy several times in every fight.

WISP SPIRIT

While most people must travel the world as ghosts after their death, the strong attunement to the world allows night elves to travel as wisps. This gives a 50% speed bonus, whereas others gain only a 25% speed bonus as ghosts.

In group settings this ability isn't as powerful unless your entire party is comprised of night elves. As a solo hero, this allows you to return to your body faster and thus continue your fight against evil more quickly.

NATURE RESISTANCE

You don't tend every beast of the woods without becoming more resistant to their poisons and fangs. Thus, night elves have a passive +10 Nature Resistance.

The upside of increased Nature Resistance is lower damage from Nature-based attacks. Nature Resistance increases your chance to resist partial damage from a Nature attack or effect as well as your chance to fully resist the effects. These effects include combat control abilities. Higher resistances are always useful.

LANGUAGES

Early in the friendship between the night elves and humans, it became apparent that much of the human population had neither the time nor patience to learn full Darnassian.

As communication is a cornerstone of friendship, the night elves decided to teach their population Common in addition to their own language. After several years every night elf was trained and can now communicate effortlessly in Common.

Brief History

For 10,000 years, the immortal night elves cultivated a druidic society within the shadowed recesses of Ashenvale forest. Yet recently, the catastrophic invasion of the Burning Legion shattered the tranquility of their ancient civilization. Led by the Arch Druid Malfurion Stormrage and the High Priestess Tyrande Whisperwind, the mightly night elves rose to challenge the demonic onslaught. Though victorious, the night elves were forced to sacrifice their cherished immortality and watch their beloved forests burn. Seeking to regain their immortality, a number of wayward Druids conspired to plant a special tree that would link their spirits to the eternal world. Despite Malfurion's warnings that nature would never bless such a selfish act, the Druids planted the great tree Teldrassil off the stormy coasts of northern Kalimdor. Within the twilight boughs of the colossal tree, the wondrous city of Darnassus took root. However, the great tree was not consecrated with nature's blessing and soon fell prey to the corruption of the Burning Legion. Now the wildlife and even the limbs of the great tree itself are tainted by a growing darkness. As one of the few night elves left in the world, it is your sworn duty to defend Darnassus and the wild children of nature against the Legion's encroaching corruption.

Night elves were once known as the Kaldorei and have lived on Kalimdor for thousands upon thousands of years. It was their delving into the magic of the Well of Eternity that caught the attention of Sargeras and the Burning Legion, and it was because of the night elves' misuse and addiction to magical power that caused the Great Maelstrom and creation of the evil Naga. Even Malfurion Stormrage's own brother Illidan played a major role in the destruction that followed. And yet, night elves have also brought beauty and triumphs to the world. Without their aid and sacrifices, the other races would have certainly been doomed. Their devotion to nature and healing the land is also well known. Even the betrayer Illidan contributed through the creation of the Moonwells. Thus many of the major events that have shaped Azeroth, both positively and negatively, can be traced back to the night elves. Perhaps it is a sense of responsibility that drives the night elves to this day to continue their vigil to safeguard and restore the natural world to what it once was.

Roleplaying Tips

As one of the longest living races in Azeroth, night elves tend to be slow to change. Slow to anger and slow to cool off, the night elves experience emotions as deeply, or perhaps more so, then the younger races. While generally slow to respond emotionally, their minds have seen much and tend to have a honed wit and sense of humor.

ORCS

Starting Statistics

Class	Strength	Agility	Stamina	Intellect	Spirit
Warrior	26	17	24	17	23
Hunter	23	20	23	17	24
Rogue	24	20	23	17	23
Shaman	24	17	23	18	25
Warlock	23	17	23	19	25

Centuries of demonic influence and war have honed orcs to be strong and lasting. With higher Strength and Stamina, orcs are adept at melee combat and a high Spirit gives them an edge as casters.

Racial Traits

BLOOD FURY

Screaming through the veins of orcs runs a fury that is monstrous when called upon and dangerous to be on the wrong side of. Activating Blood Fury increases your base melee Attack Power by 25% while decreasing all healing spells and effects on you by 50%. This state lasts for 15 seconds and has a two minute cooldown.

When the battle is desperate and your healer is out of mana, Blood Fury can pull you to victory. The primary downside to Blood Fury is the reduced effect of healing. If you are alone or your healer is out of mana, this isn't an issue since you won't be getting healing anyway. This ability is far better for melee classes as an increase to melee Attack Power doesn't really do anything if you're a caster staying at range.

HARDINESS

Surviving the wars against the human kingdoms and the land of Durotar have left the orcs more resistant to certain attacks. Thus orcs have a passive 25% chance to resist stun effects.

There are no downsides to having a resistance to stun effects. Melee classes are able to keep moving and attacking, and, while casters will have their casting delayed by the attacks, they won't be interrupted by the stun. This ability is equally useful in PvP and PvE.

COMMAND

Having been at the command of others before, orcs have firsthand knowledge of what works and what doesn't. Pets of orc Warlocks and Hunters deal 5% more damage. This ability is passive and does not need to be activated.

While this ability doesn't do much for Warriors, Rogues, or Shamans, it's a blessing to Warlocks and Hunters. Having a pet that deals more damage without having to pay for the increase means faster kills and better aggro management.

AXE SPECIALIZATION

The tree cutting hasn't been for naught. Orcs have become very adept in the use of axes and gain +5 to their maximum skill with both Axes and Two-Hand Axes. As a passive trait, Axe Specialization has no activation or cooldown.

The increased maximum for combat skills offers several advantages if you're willing to put in the training time. As your melee skill will be higher than standardly appropriate for your level, you'll have a higher chance to hit your target and a higher chance for a critical strike when using your axe. Keep your combat skills at their maximum to take full advantage of this.

LANGUAGES

From a young age, orcs are trained to keep themselves and those they care about safe. Many learn to walk the same time they hold their first weapon. With such a martial upbringing and so little time between wars, orcs have had little time to learn any languages beyond their own. It is fortunate that the rest of the Horde are so accommodating that orcish has become the common language between the races of the Horde.

Brief History

Long ago, the orcish Horde was corrupted by the Burning Legion and lured to the world of Azeroth. For 10 years, the orcs made war upon the human kingdoms of Stormwind and Lordaeron. Though the Horde was ultimately defeated and subjugated by the humans, a visionary young war chief named Thrall rose to lead his people in their darkest hour. Under Thrall's rule, the orcs freed themselves from the chains of demonic corruption and embrace their Shamanistic heritage. After breaking free of the human slave camps and wandering for years, the orcs have finally founded their own kingdom in the harsh wastelands of Durotar. Based in the warrior city of Orgrimmar, they stand ready to destroy all who would challenge their supremacy. As a proud defender of Durotar, it is your duty to crush your enemies both seen and unseen, for the nefarious agents of the Burning Legion still wander the land.

It was Sargeras' second-in-command, Kil'jaeden, who discovered Draenor and the races that lived there. Finding the orcs to be a race worth molding into a driving force of bloodlust, he began to corrupt them, turning them from their Shamanistic ways toward the powers of the Warlocks. The powerful Shaman Ner'zhul was seduced by the power of Kil'jaeden and all the demon offered, and it was not long before he led his people against the peaceful Draenei destroying many of them.

Despite the power Kil'jaeden had over Ner'zhul, he couldn't quite convince him to give the orcs completely over to the power of the Burning Legion. He instead recruited a new, more corruptible, young orc named Gul'dan. Gul'dan became an avid student and a powerful Warlock among his people.

In time, Gul'dan, under the manipulation of Kil'jaeden, maneuvered all of the orc clans into partaking in a ritual that would make them indebted slaves to the Burning Legion and give them a blood lust they could not quench. He then opened a portal into Azeroth, where the will of the Burning Legion was once more loosed upon the denizens of the land.

Roleplaying Tips

The orcs of Durotar have been through quite a lot. They have been corrupted by demons and forced into war after war.

Now free, orcs are quick to join in combat since that is what they know best. Some are loyal followers of Thrall and his ideals and wish to see their people free from the taint of the Burning Legion. There are others who still feel the fire burning inside of them and follow their Warchief Thrall into glorious battles.

TAUREN

Starting Statistics

Class	Strength	Agility	Stamina	Intellect	Spirit
Warrior	28	15	24	15	22
Hunter	25	18	23	15	23
Druid	26	15	22	17	24
Shaman	26	15	23	16	24

The Tauren are massive. Their Strength surpasses even that of the orcs and dwarves. Combine this with their high Stamina and Spirit, and the Tauren are practically made to fit melee classes; in fact, the more Intellectual caster classes aren't even available to them.

Racial Traits

WAR STOMP

No one can argue with a Tauren for long. When he or she puts her hoof down, everyone knows. War Stomp stuns up to five opponents within eight yards for two seconds when activated. It has a two minute cooldown and a one second casting time.

The ability to stop an enemy in their tracks is tremendous. Using War Stomp can stop a caster from finishing his spell, slow the escape of an enemy, or give you the moment you need to escape. While War Stomp won't win fights for you, its many uses and short cooldown ensure that it will be useful whenever you need it.

ENDURANCE

Tauren have been hunters and gatherers for generations. Whether in times of war or times of peace, they are constantly pushing and testing themselves. This never-ending training affords them a 5% increase in maximum health.

You can't go wrong with more hit points. While the classes that tend to be in the face of the enemy, such as Warriors benefit the most from this, the additional health can keep the softer classes alive long enough to finish the fight or for the Warrior to pull the enemies back. In a PvP setting, where longevity is never a guarantee, the addition health will help you contribute longer.

CULTIVATION

Understanding the delicate balance between the land and the Tauren has let them live more effectively with nature. They have learned how to gather in such a way as to avoid unnecessary damage to the plant and encourage its regrowth. All Tauren gain a passive +15 to their maximum Herbalism.

With an increase in your maximum Herbalism, you are able to harvest plants normally beyond your level. Keep this skill trained to maximum and the bonus will also reduce your failure rate.

NATURE RESISTANCE

You don't tend every beast of the woods without becoming more resistant to their poisons and fangs. Thus Tauren have a passive +10 Nature Resistance.

The upside of increased Nature Resistance is lower damage from Nature-based attacks. Nature Resistance increases your chance to resist partial damage from a Nature attack or effect as well as your chance to fully resist the effects. These effects include combat control abilities. Higher resistances are always useful.

LANGUAGES

The Tauren have adopted orcish as a trade language. While keeping their language, customs, and beliefs intact, the Tauren have found the value of conversing with the other races.

Brief History

Once a nomadic people, the Tauren roamed the endless plains of the Barrens hunting the mighty Kodo. Scattered across the land, the wandering tribes were only united by their common hatred for the marauding Centaur. Seeking aid against the Centaur, the chieftain Cairne Bloodhoof befriended the orcs, who had recently journeyed to Kalimdor. With the orcs' assistance, Cairne and his tribe were able to drive back the Centaur and claim the grasslands of Mulgore for their own. Upon the windswept mesa of Thunder Bluff, Bloodhoof built a refuge for his people. Over time, the scattered tribes united under a single banner. Though the noble Tauren are peaceful in nature, the rights of the great hunt are venerated as the heart of their spiritual culture. As a tribesman of Mulgore, you must test your skills in the wild and prove yourself in the great hunt.

The Tauren found mutual benefits in befriending the orcs and Trolls. While the orcs and Trolls helped the Tauren to drive back the Centaur and keep their lands safe, the Tauren have aided (and continue to aid) them on the spiritual path as a Shamanistic society.

Roleplaying Tips

While some view the Tauren as nothing more than brutes and hunters, they are much more. They have found a way to live with the land rather than off it. Though their size is immense, the Tauren are a patient and peaceful people on the whole.

TROLLS

Starting Statistics

Class	Strength	Agility	Stamina	Intellect	Spirit
Warrior	24	22	23	16	21
Hunter	21	25	22	16	22
Rogue	22	25	22	16	21
Priest	21	22	21	18	24
Shaman	22	22	22	17	23
Mage	21	22	21	19	23

Only one thing is similar among all Trolls. They are very adaptable to their profession. Trolls of any class can compete with those of other races. While their lower Intellect can be seen as a weakness, it isn't a great one and negligible at later levels.

Racial Traits

BERSERKING

Their adaptability manifests itself most when a Troll is backed into a corner. They can increase their body's functions to such a level that they enter a Berserk state. When activated, Berserking increases casting and attack speed by a base of 10%, increasing as the Troll's health lowers, and a maximum of 30%. The effects only last 10 seconds with a 3 minute cooldown.

The ability to increase your casting and attack speed, and thus your damage output, as you become weaker is incredible. Its cooldown is short enough that unless you are reckless, it will always be there when you need it.

REGENERATION

Everyone knows the stories of Trolls regrowing limbs in minutes. While these are exaggerations, Trolls have a 10% increased heath regeneration rate. Even more potent is that 10% of their total health regeneration remains active during combat. This is a passive ability and is always active.

While the increased health regeneration is great for recovering between battles, the real gem is the health regeneration during combat. Other races may have more hit points than you, but you recover yours during combat without the use of spells or potions. This can be of great value to any class.

BEAST SLAYING

When it comes to killing, the Trolls have been doing it for a long time. They've studied killing long enough that they receive a 5% damage bonus when attacking Beasts. This affects all Beasts, and only Beasts, and does not need to be activated.

This trait is valuable for any class as the target determines the bonus. Quests and dungeons with Beasts in them will be faster for you than other races as you can kill them more quickly. Choosing your targets with this in mind will help you take full advantage of this trait.

BOW AND THROWING WEAPON SPECIALIZATION

The Trolls are not strangers to ranged combat. They have been honing their skills for long enough to give them a +5 to their maximum Bow Skill and Throwing Weapon Skill. This is always active and has no cooldown.

The increased maximum skill offers several advantages if you're willing to put in the training time. As your Bow or Throwing Weapon skill will be higher than standardly appropriate for your level, you'll have a higher chance to hit your target and a higher chance for a critical strike when using these weapons. Take the time to train your Bow or Throwing Weapon skill to maximum.

LANGUAGES

The Darkspear tribe has allied itself closely with the orcs of Durotar, but they have not forgotten their own ways. Troll is still taught to the young, with orcish being taught in addition. Few dare to learn Troll as the Darkspear tribe tend to be very aggressive when asked about it.

Brief History

The vicious Trolls that populate the numerous jungle islands of the South Seas are renowned for the cruelty and dark mysticism. Barbarous and superstitious, they carry a seething hatred for all other races. Long since exiled from its ancestral homeland in Stranglethorn Vale, the Darkspear Tribe was nearly destroyed by rampaging Murlocs. Rescued by the young Warchief Thrall and his orcish warriors, the Darkspear tribe swore allegiance to the Horde. Led by the cunning Shadow Hunter, Vol'jin, the Darkspears now make their home in Durotar along with their orcish allies. As one of the only surviving Darkspears, it falls to you to regain the glory of your tribe.

The Trolls have a long history of war with the humans. Even before the Burning Legion came into the land, they had waged war against the humans and Elves with hit-and-run raiding parties. They hate the humans above all other races. After nearly being completely wiped from the face of Azeroth, however, they now relish in protecting their new home in Durotar and look for any reason to convince the remaining Horde of the complete treachery of humans. It was Grand Admiral Proudmoore's attack on the Horde that enraged them even more, and now the fires of hate burn even hotter within the breasts of the Trolls. For now, they cooperate with the remaining members of the Horde to maintain their homes and retain the alliances that let their people continue to rebuild.

Roleplaying Tips

The Trolls have learned to harness the power of hate. After using it for generations, they have become adept at its cultivation. Their hatred for the humans is well known, and few Trolls are without the burning need for spilt human blood.

Classes of Azeroth

This section offers a glimpse of the role that each class plays in Azeroth. All of the classes have played a part in the history of the world, and this shapes how they are viewed today. Choosing a class is an opportunity to immerse yourself in the past events and make a place for yourself in the future of the land.

DRUID

The keepers of nature, the Druids care for the natural world, its creatures, and the balance of existence. Many of them have watched over the world through the Emerald Dream, and ethereal realm that exists separate from Azeroth but intimately interwoven with it. This spirit world allows the regulation of the ebb and flow of nature and the evolutionary path of the world itself. It is the realm of one of the great Dragon Aspects; Ysera the Dreamer.

To help guide the course of the natural world, the Druids entered into the Emerald Dream, agreeing to exist apart from their friends and loved ones in an extended state of hibernation. However, because of the threat posed by Archimonde and the Burning Legion, the Druids awoke and used their power to fight to protect the world. Currently, some of the Druids have reentered the Emerald Dream, while others have stayed in Azeroth, working to repair the great damage that has been done to the natural order.

The Druids exist apart from the political boundaries empires and clans. What does it matter if one is Horde or Alliance in the great expanse of nature? The night elves and Tauren, united in their love of the land, have set aside their differences to work together, safeguarding Azeroth and helping to mend areas contaminated by pain and war. Therefore, the Druids offer hope of what all Azeroth could accomplish if all the races worked for the betterment of the world together.

HUNTER

The lands of Azeroth are home to a great many beasts, everything from wolves and cats to bears and large birds, to name but a few. These species care nothing for the war between Horde and Alliance; their lives are filled with their own struggle to find food and live from day to day. By the same token, there have always been those individuals who exist outside the boundaries of civilized society. These free spirits have found a connection to nature and a way of living with it. These wilderness people have taken the chance to explore the various lands of Azeroth and formed bonds linking themselves with the beasts of the world.

A Hunter is never without their weapon and their partner, the beast that they have formed a relationship with. The two of the work together and learn from each other. This allows the Hunter to embrace the natural world and their pets to be free from some of the more pressing aspects of their existence, such as finding prey and having a safe place to rest.

Some of the races have taken easily to this way of life. The Tauren and night elves have a great respect for nature as a whole, and working as partners with it is an extension of that. The Trolls, as well, have never moved far away from the rhythms of the natural world. For these people, becoming a Hunter allows them the chance to bond with nature and the beasts within it.

For others, it appeals to their independent spirit. The dwarves and orcs are strong individuals, and some of them have grown tired of the political bickering of the cities and accepted the wilderness as their homes. These are Hunters who seek to find their own ways in the world.

MAGE

The call of magic is a powerful one. Some have decided to dedicate their lives to it, studying it, practicing it, and spreading it throughout the world. In the history of Azeroth, no other kingdom fully embraced the force of magic as strongly as that of Dalaran, where the entire culture was guided by mages. As a political entity, Dalaran was a source of great knowledge not jaded by certain moral concerns, seeking only to understand the nature of magical power.

The kingdom of Dalaran is being rebuilt. Destroyed by the Burning Legion, its remnants have fled throughout the lands of Azeroth, and the practitioners of magic have taken new apprentices and students. This has led to knowledge of magic being spread throughout all of Azeroth.

In the Alliance lands, it is the humans and gnomes who look into the mystery of magic. The Trolls of Durotar have always been accused, rightly so, for dark mysticism while many of the Forsaken are from Dalaran itself and continue the pursuit of power.

PALADIN

The Paladins are the champions of Light and the defenders of the Alliance. Dedicated fighters, Paladins safeguard the populace and act as a symbol all can look up to. These men and women uphold honor and bravery, protect the people, honor the will of the nation, and bring light against the darkness.

Lordaeron was once the center for Paladins, a bright shining city that was a bastion of civilization. The defending Paladins were a great force of order and respect for their nation. However, there were dark forces at work, and a great sickness took hold of the land, spreading the curse of the undead throughout the country. Lordaeron was destroyed and some of its Paladins fell to corruption leaving the rest of the knightly order to fight against the undead and their former comrades.

The loyalty and brotherhood of the dwarves and humans make up the ranks of Paladins. These people are stout defenders and work within the boundaries of their political organizations. Beyond all else though, the Paladins are dedicated to ideals of honor and bravery. Light guides them.

PRIEST

Holy and Shadow are forces, separate from those of the world itself. There are those individuals that seek to use them within the world, dedicating themselves to these unseen forces. For these people, the use of these powers, requiring great study and great reverence.

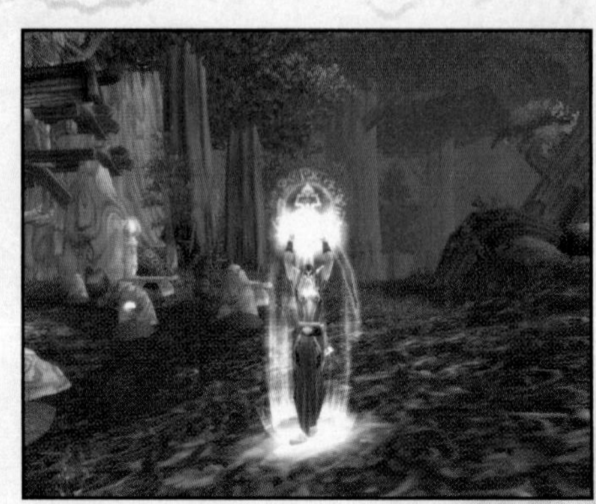

The pursuit of Holy magic is the love of life and healing, replenishing and protecting the caster and those for whom they care. Shadow is the opposite, a force of raw destructive power that damages the target and wounds the spirit. Both forces are powerful and require skill to use.

Those dedicated to healing of the mind and soul often become Priests, because of the appeal of Holy magic to salve the wounded. However, because of the strength that Shadow promises, darker individuals move to the profession as well. Of the races on Azeroth only humans, dwarves, night elves, Forsaken, and Trolls have all the pieces of the puzzle to unlock its teachings.

ROGUE

There have always been, and always will be, Rogues. These individuals use stealth and cunning to accomplish what a broadsword and shield can't. While the darker folk following this path are dangerous assassins, thieves, and brigands, there are those who train for the betterment of their own people. Spies put themselves at great risk and are perhaps the greatest rogues as they hide in front of an enemy instead of behind.

As times grew more dangerous, Rogues have learned to defend themselves. They have learned fighting styles that allow someone with the thinnest armor and two small blades to stand up to someone in chain wielding a hammer and shield. With the prominence of magic-wielders on battlefields and their ability to destroy standard troops, Rogues have been given an important duty. They must safeguard their friends by eliminating the enemy casters first.

Of all the races of Azeroth, only one will not accept training as a Rogue. The Tauren are not suited for the concept either physically or mentally. They believe the deception dishonorable. The ends justify the means for the other races.

SHAMAN

The Shaman are the spiritual leaders of their clans and tribes, guiding the peoples of the Horde to their destinies. Gifted with great insight, the Shaman seek to provide the best lives for their people within Azeroth. This common structure has formed a network among several disparate races.

The races of the Horde have always had strong beliefs and a willingness to defend them. In addition, most have a clan or tribal political structure with loyalty to their tribe being strongly valued. The Shaman help to meld these tribal forces together, so that all the various tribes and peoples can accomplish a unified goal that benefits all of them.

It was the Shaman of the orcs that lead them into Kalimdor and the Shaman of the Tauren and Trolls who helped them relearn their Shamanistic heritage. Of the Horde, only the Forsaken are without Shaman. This is a source of disquiet among the races as the Tauren, orcs, and Trolls have a common set of goals and the Forsaken may not share these.

WARLOCK

For some mages, the lure of dark power and knowledge proved too great for mere study. They found a new wellspring of chaotic magic, allowing them to reach into the strength of the demons. Gifted with the ability to manipulate these demonic forces, the Warlocks are powerful sorcerers, and the pacts that they form with demons are a sight of their devotion to the dark arts.

Demons are never far from a Warlock's call and the Warlock is a master at controlling them. These sinister creatures follow the Warlock's orders, attacking enemies and protecting their master. A Warlock's servant fights for them, and often the Warlock thinks nothing of sacrificing their demonic pet if the situation calls for it; a new summoning spell is all that it takes to drag the demon back to the world of Azeroth.

Because of their devotion to dark arts, Warlocks are feared and distrusted by most of the races. Within the lands of the Alliance, Warlocks are shunned and their places of teaching are outside major cities. Only humans and gnomes are curious enough to dabble with these forces. The orcs also have a great deal of suspicion toward Warlocks; most want nothing to do with demons every again, and orc history is replete with pain and anguish caused by demonic involvement. Only the Forsaken fully accept Warlocks as part of their civilization, giving them freedom and respect. However, despite the mistrust engendered by these practices, there will always be people who pursue dark and powerful knowledge.

WARRIOR

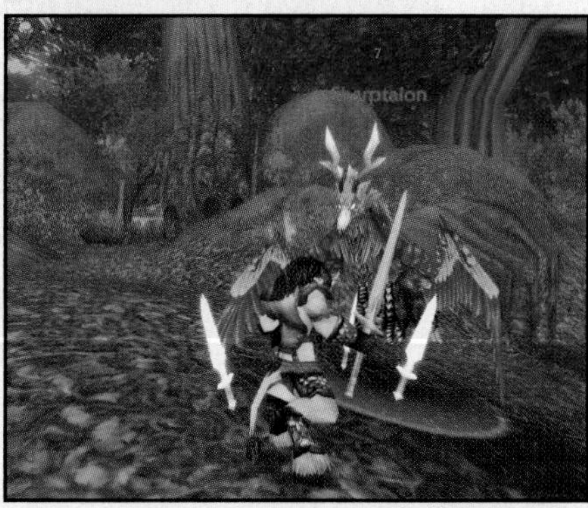

There have always been the Warriors who both defend their families and attack their enemies. While some spend their time training in hallowed halls to become powerful mystics, not everyone has that chance. The people living out on the frontier, away from large cities and the training there, have nothing to defend themselves with but a sword. They spend their days becoming stronger and faster. More than just their lives depend on their abilities…their family and friends live or die on their abilities.

Not everyone takes up arms to help others. There will always be those who are excited by the adrenaline rush of heated combat or simply enjoy watching life drain from an opponent's eyes. Whatever their reason for fighting, these men and women are the undisputed masters of melee combat. They train day and night mastering several stances of combat to be able to defeat any opponent that stands in front of them.

Any race that can forge weapons can train Warriors. humans, night elves, dwarves, and gnomes train Warriors and pit them against the mightiest of foes. Of the Horde, Tauren, Trolls, orcs, and Forsaken sharpen their blades and prepare for the coming war.

Beyond the Basics

Before getting involved with specific class abilities, data tables, templates, and so forth, it's important to evaluate play strategies that are used by all characters in World of Warcraft. This chapter explains various methods to improve your ability to gather money, rise in level, move around Azeroth, engage in combat, and find special areas.

Common Tactics

It takes considerable time to teach someone about World of Warcraft. This game has enough complexity to keep players on their tops for many days, even while learning the basics. This section is organized as well as possible to give you the tips and ideas to cut down on lost opportunities during that learning phase. There is always money and experience to be made, and there is no harm in starting from the beginning!

GAINING EXPERIENCE

Experience points get you closer to your next level. Characters progress from Levels 1 to 60 in WoW (and beyond toward level 70 later in 2006 when the expansion comes), and each advancement brings better attributes, higher health/mana, and the potential for greater deeds. Whether you focus on pulling in experience is one thing, but everyone gains levels if they enjoy the game and keep heading out into the wild.

Soloing Monsters

The most basic way to gain experience is to walk into an area with monsters and start fighting them. Every victory against a monster of equivalent level gets you experience. These points add up nicely if you try to kill monsters as quickly as possible. Trying to gain levels solely through monster killing is called "grinding" by many players. Some people find this method dull because it offers less variety of action compared to questing, going exploring, and so forth. Others feel relaxed by bringing down a stable flow of money, experience, and nasty monsters. There is nothing wrong with this method either way if it's what you like.

What Makes an Equivalent Mob

Monsters are worth experience if they are close to your character's level. There is allowed to be a 20% difference in levels between your character and the monster OR a difference of five levels (whichever is greater will be used).

Anything beneath this threshold gives zero experience when slain because the challenge is so trivial. However, such creatures still drop treasure.

Quick Equivalence Chart

Character Level	Allowed Levels of Difference
Until Level 25	5
30	6
40	8
50	10
60	12

Grinding itself can be a very fast method for leveling. Or, it can be slower than other available techniques; this entirely depends on the current level of your character, you equipment, local quest options, and more subtle aspects of play. Indeed, some grinders are able to gain levels with impressive speed by choosing a class build that is keen for soloing and finding areas where tandem fighting (going after one mob, then another right afterward, then another, etc.) is easy to do.

Checklist for a Good Grinding Area

- Many Monsters Available
- Enough Space Between Monsters That They Can be Fought Individually
- Creatures in Area Lack Powerful Special Abilities that Harm Your Class/Race (If you can't cure poison or disease, these are brutal on soloers, as are curses and many other debuffs)
- Monster Levels are Just Low Enough to Keep the Kills Fast and Downtime Short (a couple levels under your character for characters with modest gear, or monsters of equal level for those with better equipment)
- Few Players Compete for Kills in the Area
- A Vendor is Somewhat Accessible (for making repairs and dropping off loot items)
- Enemies Drop Cloth (if you bandage frequently)
- Preferably, a Graveyard is Close Enough to Shorten Downtime if an Accident Happens; This Isn't as Important as the Other Factors

INSTANCE GRINDING

Instance grinding is very different from grinding on monsters out in the field. Getting into a group of four or five characters and repeatedly taking on instances near your level is a wonderful way to get your character into better gear. It is not, however, a fast way to gain levels. Looking at pure experience per hour, instances are only better for the absolute worst grinding characters (e.g. people who specialize only on surviving, healing, and other non-damaging abilities).

This does not mean that you lose out in the long run by leveling in this way. Slow leveling often has a few perks. The longer you take at each level, the more money your character has throughout the game and the more your gear stays up-to-date.

Questing for Experience

During the lower levels (certainly through Levels 1 to 40), characters gain quite a bit of experience through questing. It isn't hard to gather multiple quests from towns in this period, and completing several at a time is both easy and exciting. The awards for turning in these quests catapult characters through their levels. And, when played correctly, the best elements of grinding and questing can be combined once players understand the locations they are visiting.

First off, it's useful to grind while approaching quest sites and while leaving them! If you have a quest in the northwest of The Barrens, asking you to kill Harpies, it is helpful to kill Centaur, Raptors, and other enemies on the way. Walking to the edge of a zone may take five or six minutes (more in a number of cases). That time is somewhat wasted if you simply travel because your characters are full on health and mana. Use those resources to blow through enemies quickly; be inefficient with mana, if you have it, because you are going to regenerate it as you go anyway.

Blast through the odd target here and there and you will find that experience gained per hour improves by a fair margin. This also makes traveling a lot more fun!

PICK AND CHOOSE

A subset of questing is to avoid getting all quests in a region while doing only those that fit your character's needs. This becomes quite common at the later levels, when people prefer to fight in certain regions, and dungeons.

To pick and choose with quests means to look through all available choices and decide which ones have rewards that you need OR which ones have targets that you want to kill anyway. This is a solid, mercenary approach. If your character likes to grind against Trolls in the Hinterlands, there is no reason on Azeroth not to help the local Dwarves (who have a few problems with said Trolls). Grinding is all well and good, but dropping off a quest each time you head back to sell loot nets practically free experience when you play in this manner.

Even at the lower levels, you may want to skip delivery quests or anything that you know takes a long time without keeping you hip-deep in slaughter. If experience is your goal, collecting ground spawns in areas without many enemies is a bad thing.

UNDERSTANDING ATTRIBUTES

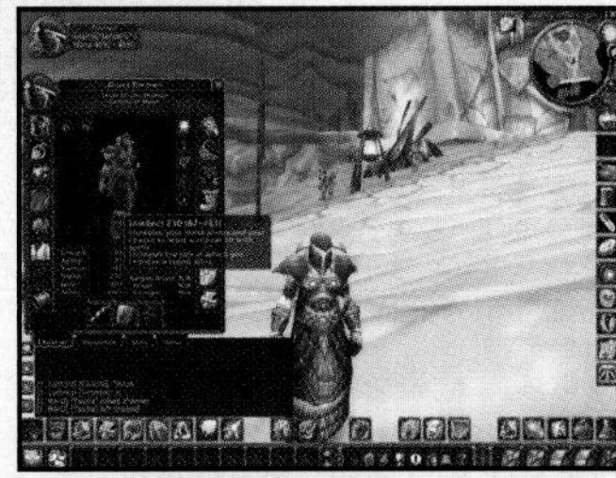

At the most basic level of play, higher attributes equal a better character. However, you are often forced to decide which attributes are the most important to your style of play. This means that it's crucial to understand what the attributes do, how they affects your class, and which systems can be influenced by your choices.

Attributes and What They Do

Attribute	Purpose
Strength	Improve Melee Damage (DPS), Raise Amount of Damage Absorbed by Shield Blocks
Agility	Higher % Chance to Dodge, Higher Critical Rate, Increases Damage for Some Characters (e.g. Hunters, Rogues)
Spirit	Improves Rate of Health/Mana Regeneration While Out of Combat
Stamina	Raises Health (One Points of Stamina Adds Ten Points of Health)
Intellect	Raises Mana (One Point of Intellect Adds Fifteen Points of Mana); Also Raises Critical Rates for Spellcasters

Strength improves your character's DPS and helps to block more damage from incoming attacks. Warriors always need a fair bit of strength, but all melee characters are interested in getting more when they can. Rogues need more Agility, but Strength isn't bad for them at all, and Hunters who do a bit more melee work (especially some Survival Hunters) take some Strength as well.

Agility affects Dodge and Critical percentages for all characters. This makes Agility a secondary damage attribute for tanks (Warriors, Paladins, etc.) and a primary damage attribute for Rogues and Hunters. The reason for this is that ranged damage is influenced by Agility. Also, Rogues receive half of their melee damage bonuses from Strength and half from Agility!

Spirit determines how much health/mana you regain with each tick of the game's clock. Health does not regenerate during normal combat, without items or abilities to grant such restoration. Mana regeneration, however, is only interrupted by casting spells (whether in battle or not). Your character's class makes a huge difference in what is regenerated. Warriors and Rogues, for instance, have no mana; their Spirit is used only for health regeneration. Hybrid classes (Druids, Hunters, Paladins, Shaman) are split between a moderate gain of health by their Spirit and a fair increase in mana as well. Then the heavier casters (Priests, Mages, and Warlocks) gain very little health from their Spirit but receive potentially large chunks of mana each tick. Spirit is one of the more complex attributes because it's either worthless, if you fight creatures out in the field or go against easier instances, or very important, if you are a caster taking on late-game raid monsters.

Stamina gives characters ten points of health for every point of Stamina they gain. This is a flat sum. Stamina can easily account for half (or more) of your character's health, even before the later stages of the game. Though having more health does nothing to increase a character's combat output, Stamina is still crucial. Classes that hold aggro to protect a group **need** to have high health. This gives healers a great deal more leeway in saving lives! Even hybrid classes and full casters need health though, especially if tougher dungeons are being run, if you solo, or if you plan to hit the Battlegrounds. In World of Warcraft, everyone gets beaten on, and even glass cannons want to survive a few hits before going down.

Intellect is similar to Stamina, though it gives mana to characters instead of health. Intellect also increases casters' rate for Critical spell effects; that is something that both healers and damage dealers are interested in getting. For non-casters, Intellect is almost a worthless Attribute. Rogues and Warriors are able to master Defense and Weapon Skills faster if they have a high Intellect, but this difference is not worth the loss of Stamina, Agility, etc. Also, getting an Arcane Intellect buff from Mages is more than enough to boost melee characters while learning new weaponry.

STAYING ON PAR

For each level of your character, there is a hidden par value for your attributes. This value is meant to reflect the improvements that are available to your character during advancement. If you stay at par, your percentages won't change in a major way; Critical rates, Dodging, and such are meant to be fluid yet stay within certain bounds.

If your character falls below par by having low-level equipment, not spending Talent points, or otherwise focusing on different elements, your percentage chance to achieve various effects may drop! Look at your character now and compare the numbers for Criticals and Dodge to what you had five levels ago; there is no guarantee of improvement in these things. You MUST increase your Agility to stay on par with melee/ranged Criticals and Dodge. You need to keep raising Intellect to maintain frequent spell Criticals.

By the same token, getting +20 to Stamina in your teen levels doesn't sound bad at all. A couple hundred more points of health. Great! But at level 58, you want to have at least a couple thousand more health for tanking enemies or PvPing.

How Do I Look at My Percentages?

To see your chance to Dodge and Critical opponents, open your Abilities Menu ("P" Key) and highlight these given aspects. They should be listed on the first page.

For even more interesting data, remove various pieces of equipment and notice the immediate and profound changes to said percentages. Equipment choices DO matter!

But How Do I Raise Attributes?

So if leveling raises your attributes and the par for said attributes, how do you actually keep up or even pull ahead with your true performance?

The key is to find equipment that focuses on the stats you need. As long as your character pushes to find Rare/Blue gear, starting around level 20, you can stay well ahead of par. Even if you stick to Uncommon/Green gear, you can stay close to or above par for your character.

Don't just take every weapon upgrade with higher DPS and every armor piece that raises your Damage Mitigation. This is **not** wise for the long run. Instead, look at the attributes given by each equipment piece you find. Choose two or three attributes that you are looking for, and make sure to get the most points possible for those.

First, avoid equipment pieces that only give one attribute bonus unless the piece is extremely good. You receive more total attribute points by choosing pieces with two or three attributes. When these are the two or three attributes you want already, this makes everything work out wonderfully.

Also, look for a consistent Enchanter in your guild or circle of friends. Have them help you increase your attributes. At all levels, Enchanters are able to add a fair number of points to your equipment pieces. Though pricey, this is a superb way to stay ahead of men and beasts that are competing against you.

Example: Warriors should avoid equipment that gives bonuses to Intellect and possibly Spirit as well, unless you greatly need the extra armor or your old equipment isn't giving you what you want either. Instead, search for appropriate Mail (or later Plate) that has Strength, Stamina, and Agility. If you tank a great deal, lean on Strength and Stamina. If you are more of a DPS Warrior, take all three and try to balance your needs.

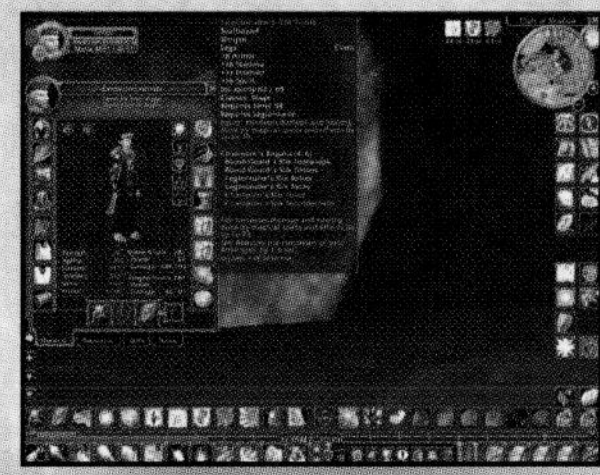

SPECIALIZING A CHARACTER

Nobody in WoW is meant to be exactly the same. There are many ways to configure your character for different forms of combat, and this goes well beyond a person's class. Use of Talents, style, equipment, and professions all make a difference in the end result.

The big question for each player is what do I want to accomplish in battle. Are you a healer, a damage dealer, or a support character? Do you want to be good for short bursts or for sustained effort? Is disruption of enemy forces more important to you than getting kills and glory?

Before jumping into the "how" end of things, we'll investigate the question of "why?"

Perks of Character Specialization

Customizing your character is an enjoyable experience because you are making an avatar into your own reflection of a class. You are leaving the simple distinction of Warrior/Rogue/Mage, etc. behind; what appears in its place is your representation of that class. Making a name for yourself, exploring new ideas and style choices, and seeking new modes of victory are all waiting down this path. The rewards are considerable.

If you stay along a general line, your character ends up with few weaknesses (only those given by your race/class). However, you are rarely able to play to your strengths unless you develop them. Specializing your character makes it much easier to win in battles where you are able to use your advantages.

Does this mean that you lose more often when you cannot play to your strengths if you heavily customize? Yes, it does. In a well-balanced game, there have to be penalties to your choices as well as perks, and WoW makes great efforts to balance your options.

The reason this isn't as much of a problem as it sounds is that a skilled player can often play to their strengths. Against many mobs and even some players, the ability to drive forward with your best abilities precludes the dangers of your weaknesses. That is why playing to your strengths and customizing is useful, doable, and a great deal of fun.

Using Your Talent Points

- Talents are gained from levels 10-60 (for 51 total Talent points)
- It is often powerful to specialize in two Talent trees, taking one until the mid 40s, then switching to a secondary Talent tree
- You can Respec Talents at your character's trainer for a scaling fee (this fee increases from one Gold, to five, and then to ten and beyond for additional Respecs)
- Talents greatly define what style of your class you wish to play

The most obvious form of customization is provided directly by the class system. At level ten, you start gaining Talents. The abilities gained from this system are very powerful, especially when people devote their characters into specific lines; the deeper stages of specific Talent lines are quite impressive and rewarding.

Before spending these points, take a *long* look at the lines available to your character. Because of the extended hours involved in reaching the higher levels, it's nice to know what you are getting into. Instead of taking any Talent that looks nice for now, try to come up with a path that nets as many permanent, useful Talents as possible.

On the whole, there are several varieties of Talent specializations. These are not identified directly, but an astute player can see where specific Talents are the most useful. Anything that reduces downtime and raises efficiency in battle is good for extended fighting against weaker targets; this is a style more for soloers than group members. On the other hand, abilities that are expensive but raise burst damage and effectiveness are critical in Instances and PvP fighting.

Decide what variety of character you are interested in playing. There is always the chance that your needs and interests will change, but many people know somewhat what they enjoy doing from the very beginning. Try to create a Talent path that advances the areas of the game you enjoy.

General Ability Tradeoffs		
Ability Type	Powerful For	Weakest In
Burst Damage/Healing	PvP	Group Settings
Efficient Damage/Healing	Soloing	PvP
Increased Potential Damage/Healing	Grouping/Instances	Soloing
Higher Damage Mitigation	Grouping/Tanks	Soloing
Disable Enemies	PvP	Efficient Experience Grinding

PvP builds are often about doing the greatest amount of activity in a short period. Instant abilities, helpful passive Talents, and other reactive perks are the focus here. Player vs. Player combat is often much shorter in duration than fighting against monsters in the field or in Instances. Thus, efficiency has less value compared to immediate power and survival. Specialize in burst healing or damage to be able to respond to the unpredictability of facing live, intelligent players in PvP combat.

Soloers need to be independent; they don't have backup healing, easy damage, or safety. This necessitates a build where the character is fully functional in multiple aspects of play. Efficiency is stressed because there are no allies to fall back on, and long downtime is a very bad thing if you don't have anyone to talk to or to keep the experience rolling. If you are a soloist, seek Talents that make your favorite actions more effective, then use those abilities to their fullest.

Group-friendly builds are some of the most specialized characters of all. These builds are intended to extend the weaker areas of many classes while honing specific strengths that are useful to allies. Seek increased potential in areas that are hailed by groups (better Damage Mitigation for a tank, more potent and dependable heals for a healer, and safe/constant damage from DPS classes). The group is present to negate the weaknesses of each member while extending the strengths of each member's build.

Remember that a soloist can group, a PvPer can and will farm Instances, and so forth. Everyone should be capable of filling a variety of roles, but it's going to be harder going against your element. Choose the line that makes your favorite role more enjoyable, because that is what you spend the most time doing.

This has given you an idea about how to think about Talents for your characters. This discussion has still occurred in a vacuum. Shortly, in the next chapter, you will learn about specific Talents choices and the tradeoffs involved with specializing each character class. These choices are too numerous and complex to evaluate here.

Honing Equipment

Talents are by no means the end of character customization. Equipment choices account for a great deal of a person's effectiveness. This doesn't boil down to a simple numbers game (i.e. Go for higher level gear all the time and don't stop). Rather, a focus on the type of equipment that completes your build is needed.

The most basic example is for casters who are rising in level. These characters need both Spirit and Intellect (Spirit for regaining mana and Intellect for having a large pool of Mana to draw from). A Soloist wants to have quite a high Spirit to maintain their mana and minimize downtime, since they are the ones casting in each battle. PvPers, at the other end, need to survive their current encounter no matter what the mana cost; they use Intellect for having the highest possible DPS for a given encounter. Even if recovery is slow as nails, they are free to drink water and cheer their victory.

Attribute Preference Examples		
Class/Style	Primary Attribute	Secondary Attribute
Defensive Tank	Agility and Stamina	Strength
Offensive Melee	Agility and Strength	Stamina
Rogue	Agility and Stamina	Strength
Melee Hybrid	Strength and Stamina	Intellect
Healing/Caster Hybrid	Stamina and Intellect	Spirit
PvP Caster	Stamina	Intellect
Group Caster	Intellect and Spirit	Stamina

These examples are neither exhaustive or absolute. There are major exceptions created when people see a niche that needs to be filled. Imagine a PvP Mage who enjoys going into large-scale battles that last for several minutes of direct fighting. Such a character might shun the pure Intellect model and grab more Spirit and +Damage gear for their favorite spell lines. The goal is not to memorize a specific table to select what you need. Instead, view the process that others use to create their customized equipment sets and see how it relates to your character.

WEAPON SPEED

Fast Weapons	*Slower Weapons*
Enhanced by Direct Plusses to Damage	Deal Damage in Bursts, Very Good for PvP
Better Against Casters	Do More Damage with "Instant Cast" Melee Attacks
Feel More Responsive	

Weapon speed has a number of complex aspects, and the system for it has changed several times during the evolution of WoW. Faster melee weapons were the ideal choices for Alpha and early Beta use, then things grew interesting. During early retail and for some time afterward, slow weapons grew to prominence because instant-use abilities would do so much damage with them. Rogues often tried to get the slowest available weaponry for their attacks, and Arms Warriors were no different.

In modern WoW, there have been changes to normalize the amount of damage instant melee and ranged weapon attacks deal. This makes a much wider variety of weaponry useful to characters, and in many ways is quite a positive change. All characters now have good reasons to go with each fast or slow weaponry. Faster ones are better for getting consistent DPS, poison use (for Rogues), or other +Damage On Hit abilities/items to work. General proc effects, however, are fine with any speed. And, if you want to have higher burst damage, the slower weapons are still superior for that.

Ask yourself where your character will do the most damage, in burst situations or extended fighting? For PvP, especially with physical classes, burst damage is very important. The moment you start dealing damage, someone is going to come after you. Crowd control abilities are soon to follow, and your DPS is going to shut down for a bit. That is why it's good to slap a character with a 3.8 second weapon shot! If they end up controlling or avoiding you for a few seconds afterward, you haven't lost much of anything. If you had been using a 1.2 second weapon, you would have missed at least a couple hits.

High-speed weapons are often better for PvE because of their consistency. You won't have sudden bursts that rip aggro off of things when you aren't ready for it, and neither will you have entire seconds of waiting for an attack when you just need to do a few points more.

Refining Your Playstyle

Once you have the Talents, equipment, and knowledge to support your interests, victory comes from refining the techniques you use in battle. Which attacks aren't as useful in light of your new Talents; which moves are now essential, and need to be used earlier in the fight? Try to work on pounding your techniques into a trim and effective weapon of their own. If you want to get really scientific about it, time your battles against monsters of the same type and level and see if you can reduce the period it takes to defeat them. The same method can be used to reduce damage taken (kill-time and limiting damage taken are often linked to some extent anyway).

Look at the abilities you use in battle. Which of these make the most difference over the course of the battle? If you have status buffs and debuffs, see if there are better times to cast them. Some of these can be done before battle is engaged, so work on mastering a lead in to fights that frees your character to use direct combat abilities as soon as possible.

Perhaps a change of quickbar is in order at this stage. One thing that slows players down a great deal is the inefficient use of the game's interface. Many players who take the time to reorganize their quickbars are impressed at the difference in their character's performance. Keep abilities that aren't used often on entirely different bars and streamline the buttons that are used in each and every combat. Try to use an ascending order that fits the progression of battle, such that your fingers know where to go without you losing time looking down at the keyboard.

Don't rely on the mouse to click abilities! Sure, you can put up extra quickbars from the Interface Menu and click on things that aren't needed in the heat of the moment (e.g. Hearthstones). For in-combat abilities, hotkeys are king!

Even these issues are part of customization. If something doesn't feel right, work hard to change it. Look through the key bindings and make sure everything is where you need it to be; Stance/Form shifting can be bound to keys as well. You may want to put those beneath your most active fingers to smooth the transitions. Warriors and Druids must be able to move from one stance/form to the next without any delay or problem; this is essential to their proper dominance in both PvE and PvP.

MAKING MONEY AND FINDING GEAR

Being an adept player is great, but money still makes the world go around. Buying from vendors and players is only one sink for money in WoW, and you are going to need plenty of cash just for those folks! Trainers take their fair share as well, and by the end of the day very few people have more gold than they need. So, how do you plan to stay in the black?

Understand Loot Tables

Being out in the wild is interesting when looking for treasure. Unlike the rewards for quests or defeating specific, named enemies, there are many random pieces of treasure that drop from normal creatures. This is entirely random within the bounds of loot tables.

Your characters receive the majority of simple Uncommon/Green items and trade items while out in the wild. While fighting easier creatures, you are likely to find high quantities of gear that is slightly beneath the monsters' level. Rare and Epic gear is extremely unlikely to drop from these easier fights, and when it does there is a fair chance that the item won't be one for you specifically.

Outdoor fighting is great for leveling, fine for getting trade materials, but is too unpredictable for gearing up characters beyond a certain point.

The drop-rate for Rare gear tremendously improves when you fight large groups of Elite monsters in dungeons. These Instanced areas also have set bosses with loot tables that are specific in what they drop (giving you the ability to know what is likely to fall each time they die, within a modest margin). Thus, gearing up is very much about hitting dungeons with your allies. Go into such fighting with a group of mixed character classes to reduce competition for high-end drops.

To find out what is available from a given encounter, look up a creature's loot table. This guide and a number of other Brady products, reveal where to get quite a few of the best items in the game. There are also online resources that allow you to search by monster name or item name/type to find out where equipment is gained. Asking other players where they found specific gear is yet another source of information.

Selling to Vendors

Just as the most simple way to gather experience comes from grinding against monsters, you can gather a great deal of money from selling loot to vendors. Almost all of the creatures in the wild have something worth selling (whether they are living, dead, beast, or construct). Fight against creatures at a fast rate and harvest their goodies for future sale to players and vendors.

Sell anything that cons grey to your character, then take a look into the uses for the various crafting items and other goodies that fall. If there is a market for the remainder of your inventory, hold onto that until you can make an Auction House run.

It's a very big mistake to be picky about the items you snag from monsters. Sure, some creatures are terrible about dropping good stuff (Slimes take forever before they started dropping fun stuff), but even these enemies occasionally have a rare gem or magical item. Beyond that, if you have tons of space in your bags, there is no reason not to grab everything in sight! It takes almost no time to sell items, and every single piece of gold adds up. Indeed, it sounds foolish not to loot a corpse with a mere silver piece on it. Why then, would anyone stop collecting vendor trash that could add up to many gold pieces in the long run?

For faster looting, hold down shift while right-clicking on bodies; this loots everything at once and is slightly faster for getting you on your way again. BoP items won't bind to you by doing this; a query bar rises instead, and you have the choice to take the item or leave it on the body.

A very wise investment early in your character's career is to buy bags from the Auction House. The vendor prices for bags are **never good for you**. Indeed, there are always crafters making bags for alts and newcomers, and you make a great deal of money in the long run by having larger packs to stash goodies. You never want to run out of space in a dungeon and have to pass up loot that could pay for one or two of your packs just by itself!

Oops, I Didn't Mean to Sell That

Vendors keep a list of the last ten items that you sold them. At any time, and without penalty to your finances, the vendors will allow you to buy back what you have sold them. This is such a nice function to prevent you from losing that Rare shield that you didn't mean to right-click while selling.

Gathering Materials

Profession	Means of Income
Skinning	Selling Leather on the Auction House (Much More Lucrative in the Later Levels)
Mining	Selling Metal and Stones on the Auction House (Iron is When This Becomes *Highly* Profitable)
Herbalism	Selling Herbs on the Auction House (Everything after the First Few Herbs are Worth Gold)
Enchanting	Break Uncommon and Rare Items And Auction The Materials

There are plenty of craftsfolk out there who need a constant supply of leather, cloth, metal, herbs, and magical powders. If you aren't interested in creating items, try out the gathering professions. In any event, selling the ingredients for crafted items to their creators is profitable throughout the levels. Use the Auction House to accomplish this unless you have friends or guild sources that need first crack at these items.

Knowing where to gather your items can make the difference between slim pickings and a lucrative trade. People don't usually go to Teldrassil for making it rich as a Miner, eh. Indeed, talk to other people and learn where some of the best spots are for getting the items you seek. Open fields have more beasts for leather, humanoid caves often have both metal deposits and cloth or leather to harvest, and herbs are specifically located because of their inability to grow in inhospitable regions.

Don't let your inventory control you either. You may harvest enough material to fill your bank vault and your packs, but understand what your merchandise is worth. Stay current on the going rates for your items and only slide a bit under that quantity when selling. A few silvers can attract a buyer almost as quickly as entire gold pieces worth of discounts. It's similar to running away from a bear when you have a gnome in your party; you don't have to outrun the bear (you just have to outrun the gnome). When competing against other sellers, there is no need to cut the market.

Farming for Loot

There may be specific places that bring in money at a fast pace for your character. Perhaps you have a group that brings down clusters of enemies quickly with AoEs. Or, you may have a favorite cave where there is metal, cloth, and vendor loot that sells half-decently. In any event, farming for money is a tradition with a long and glorious past.

Much like grinding for experience, you can grind with loot in mind. Find an area with as many of the target monsters as possible and hop to it. Though this is often a good solo practice, groups sometimes form with different needs. Perhaps you are trying to get an Uncommon or Rare Elemental drop (Breath of Wind or some equivalent item), and another character wishes to hunt for experience in the same area. Joining together can help both individuals; agree to divide loot in a way that lets you farm for your items while the grinder gets what they need as well.

Small teams with different Professions work nicely in this field as well. Having a person to skin, another to mine, a cloth gatherer, and so forth keeps the peace perfectly. Everyone can get what they want while journeying around the world without having to roll for items.

Hunting for Rares

Bind-on-Equip Rare items are extremely valuable. These blue pieces fetch a massive sum on the Auction House because people who are funding their alts are interested in getting the best gear without always putting in the work to hunt through dungeons or wait for drops that are never a given. Thus, you can strike it rich very easily by going through dungeons and waiting for the right pieces to drop.

A prime example of this comes from Shadowfang Keep. This Instance dungeon drops a Rare BoE piece every few runs (this is random, but making a few fast runs gives you a high chance of getting what you want). Because such pieces are going to be a few levels below the enemies that drop them, you can expect to find many items in the high teens from that dungeon. This makes Shadowfang Keep **ideal** for grabbing "twink" equipment to sell on the Auction House. Alts with a huge amount of money who want to camp at level 19 in the Battlegrounds sometimes pay 20-100 gold pieces for even these low-level items. One lucky drop that doesn't take more than a few hours of farming to find can fund your character for quite some time.

By the time you are in your 30s and 40s, your character can blow through Shadowfang Keep without any help, delays, or frustrations. Money, money, money.

Become One with the Auction House

- You Pay a Deposit Every Time You Post an Item on the Auction House (Based Off a Percentage of that Item's Value Multiplied by the Duration of the Auction)
- A Percentage of the Sell Price is Also Taken by the Auction House as a Fee (This Percentage is High for Neutral Auction Houses)
- You Won't See the Exact Duration of an Existing Auction; Instead, the System Lists a General Time (Short, Medium, Long, Very Long)
- The Upper Price for an Item is the Amount of the Current Bid on it; The Lower Value is the Amount Needed to Immediately Buy Out the Item
- Be Very Careful When Typing in Sale Values and Bid Quantities (A Slip Here can Cost You Dearly)
- Purchased Items and Money for Sales Appear in Characters' Mailboxes

The Auction House is a blessing in every way. Having a major center of trade opens the window for players to cooperate with everyone in their faction (and beyond, in the case of the neutral Auction Houses in the Goblin towns). Setting your Hearthstone to a capital city with an Auction House is rarely a bad choice, considering how often people return here to talk, trade, and find new items.

Sell useful items through the Auction House instead of vendoring them. Players who do this make far more money in the long run. There is a deposit every time you put items into the AH, and this increases proportionally as you set the timer for an auction for a longer duration. There is also a tax on final sales in the AH, and this is higher for the neutral Ahs.

The best bet for keeping your money flowing freely is to sell only your higher quality items (the ones that move quickly through the AH). People are rarely interested in equipment of low quality, so the profits for such items are higher through vendoring in a number of cases. Watch the AH by the searching for the very items you wish to sell and see what prices they are going for (and if people are really bidding on them). If the products aren't moving well, try a lower buyout than the other sellers.

If moving inventory is more important to you than the raw price, try very low starting bids. This really encourages impulse buying for anything useful; as long as the price is still low, players may push back and forth trying to keep their bid on the item. This sometimes leads to prices above what the players would have paid originally, but they become somewhat attached to the auction itself. You can't count on this, but it does happen.

Goods and Services

Profession/Ability	Service Provided
Alchemy	Selling Potions, Transmutes for Higher Metals and Elements (On Timers)
Blacksmith	Occasional Weapon or Mount Enhancements (Not Highly Valuable)
Enchanting	Wide Variety of Equipment Enhancements
Engineering	Make Scopes for Ranged Weapons, Make Ammo, Some Explosives Are Usable By Non-Engineers Also
Leatherworker	Cure Rugged Hides (On a Timer)
Tailor	Make Bags, Make Mooncloth (On a Timer)

- Orgrimmar and Undercity Are Major Trade Centers for the Horde
- Ironforge and Stormwind Are Major Trade Centers for the Alliance

Your characters can also make money by selling services to other players. Because everyone can master two professions (at most), it is common for players to need the services of other people from time to time. Blacksmiths attach Shield Spikes, Riding Spurs (for mounts), and other such goodies for weapons and armor. Enchanters prepare special concoctions to boost the power of items. Rogues can learn Lockpicking and open lockboxes for a tip or for goodwill.

When advertising your own skills, use the Trade Chat channel and prepare a text macro that quickly states your available skills and associated costs (if any). Try to keep this to one or two lines to prevent your message from filling up everyone's message windows. Use your macro periodically, but not more often than every few minutes. While doing this, participate in the channel and help others; it's useful to have a clientele that already knows who you are and respects your attitude.

To receive services, ask in Trade Chat if anyone has the skill level you seek in a profession. Be up front about what you want and they often are just as forthcoming about the price they require for their time. Don't by shy about saying "How much do you want?" if they don't list a specific sum. Under the friendly conditions, the other character may not answer firmly. Be sure to tip such people if you can afford to; it keeps the goodwill flowing and won't hurt you on any return visits.

Spending Your Wealth

There are more ways to spend money than to make it; that is the usual truth of things. Carefully choosing when and where to spend your hard-earned cash is very important, especially at low levels (where it's harder to make substantial amounts).

Learn Class Abilities First

Before looking for new items or having fun with your money, make sure that your character's abilities are current. Every even level, talk to your class trainers and see which new abilities are available. If you use said abilities or would like to, buy these before any purchases of equipment, services, or whatever else you enjoy. Having abilities trained to their fullest is extremely important, and the cost is minimal if you are willing to do some hunting on the side from time to time.

To avoid taking a more substantial hit to the wallet every two levels, it is possible to ignore some abilities (for some classes). If you are a Warrior who never uses Berserk Stance, don't train in Slam or Cleave. A sword-wielding Rogue could forego Backstab and Ambush for quite some time too. Almost all classes have abilities that they may not use, depending on playstyle. Save money in the short term by holding off on their purchase. It's always possible to return later and train these skills when the cost is lower (compared to your total earnings).

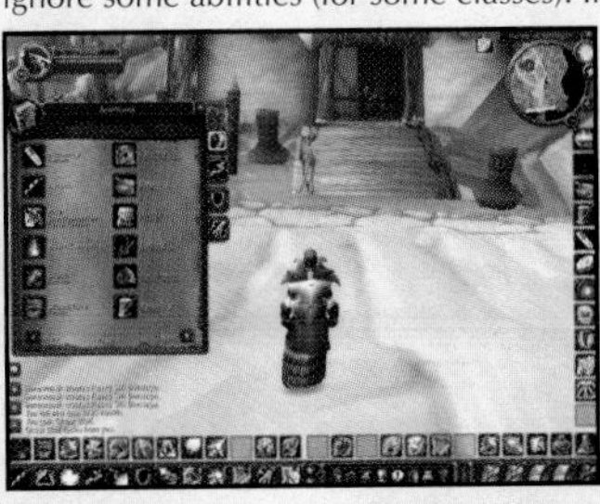

Restore Important Items

Whether you are finding, creating, or purchasing items that are used while adventuring, be certain to resupply from time to time. Bandages, food (for you or any pets), ammunition, repairs, potions, explosives, and other treats all cost time or money. If you enjoy using these goodies or at least fall in love with what they can do for you, put the money down and make sure your characters stays prepared.

Keep Equipment Up to Date

Many, many gold pieces go toward keeping your character's equipment up to date. At first, quests and general loot are able to keep characters up-to-speed. Decent items drop somewhat easily over the first 20 levels, and there are substantial numbers of quests with useful rewards.

In the mid-and-later levels, however, characters start to need better equipment. This necessitates going into dungeons more often and buying at least Uncommon items from the Auction House, with an occasional purchase of Rare gear. When doing this on a budget, look for the items you need over several days and only jump at bids that are priced below the norm. This saves you considerable money (at the cost of your time and patience). If you instead need an item as soon as possible, pay the premium and start buying out everything that looks nice; the sellers will love you.

Without a heavy investment in farming for money, you won't likely be able to purchase every Rare piece of equipment you like from the Auction House. The best middle road, for those of us who never have quite enough cash, is to plan your equipment ahead of time for every ten levels or so. Look at the Rare gear in each bracket and decide what your dream pieces are. Find out which of these can be sough directly and which are instead world drops (in other words, which ones are quite random).

Once you have done that, hunt for the pieces that drop in specific locations and only seek the Auction House for item slots that don't have any farmable choices for the next six to ten levels. By doing this, you only have to purchase a slot of gear from the Auction House every now and then.

The Bank

Using the bank saves characters from losing bag space. It's unfortunate to lose vendorable items because you have your bags loaded with ammunition, food, potions, skins, and whatever else has crept in there. Anything that isn't needed for a specific outing should be left in the bank vault and taken out at your convenience (especially trade goods).

For a one-time investment of cash, you can purchase extra bag slots in your bank vault. Notice how quickly the prices rise for additional slots; it is far more effective to use high-end bags than to purchase many bank slots. Each new tier of space costs more than the previous slot, so people need a heavy sum to unlock the later ones.

Though bags are a bit costly early on, crafters can save you tremendous time and frustration by creating some of the larger bags at a decent price. Ask your guild or friends if they know a good Tailor, then see if those folks are able to set you up with four larger bags at a fair cost. It's only worth buying bags from stores when you are entirely wealthy and only need a spare 6-Slot for an alt; otherwise, crafters are able to make bags at immensely lower prices.

Bags can drop from monsters as well. Though these aren't found with high frequency, you are going to find a few during your rise through the levels. These are best used to supplement your bank (rather than hoping to find four of the highest sized ones in any short period).

Bag Size by Loot Tables

Monster Level	Possible Bag Drop
1 to 10	6-Slot Bag (Linen Equivalent)
11-19	8-Slot Bag (Wool Equivalent)
20-29	10-Slot Bag (Silk Equivalent)
30-39	12-Slot Bag (Mageweave Equivalent)
40-49	Journeyman's Backpack (Runecloth Equivalent)
50-60	Traveler's Backpack (Mooncloth Equivalent)

Spend Wisely

The simple way to decide what to spend money on is to look at future earning potential. What items/skills are going to help you make money faster? Is it going to help you more to master a ranged weapon or get a new chest piece? Look at what your character does well and what they do poorly; spend money at both ends of that spectrum first, then deal with the in-between later. Mages deal tons of damage but die quickly (spend money on doing even more damage or on saving your rump). Don't fret over raising less important attributes, peripheral abilities, and other such concerns until you know that your best equipment is on par and your central abilities are fully trained.

Do a bit of research to avoid spending money at the wrong time. If there are important class quests coming up, you often have some nice items in your future; it's better to buy equipment for slots that aren't going to receive quest upgrades anytime soon. By the same token, don't waste serious gold enchanting an item that you are going to ditch in a level or two.

EXPLORING

Moving around the world and seeing the impressive variety of locations is a source of lasting joy. The zones in WoW are well differentiated, so it's a shame not to fully explore Kalimdor and the Eastern Kingdoms. This is a task that has subtle but worthwhile benefits for future play, as you also learn more about camp locations, monster variety, and other such matters while exploring.

Filling in Your Maps

Region maps start off without many locations uncovered. It is your responsibility to fill out the map over time by visiting the major points of interest. Each location you discover opens a new section of the map and awards you an exploration bonus (a slight gift of experience). Though this process isn't profitable by itself, given that hunting earns far more experience than wandering, it feels very good to have your maps uncovered for all major regions.

Instead of racing off to fully explore each map when you enter a new region, take the time to explore naturally, using the direction of quests and hunting to guide you. This way, you are never just exploring. You are finishing quests, making money, gaining experience from multiple sources, and having a good time too. If you choose to grind your way through an entire zone, fighting everything you see, the map uncovers just as nicely as if you spent all the time looking about and avoiding those fun skirmishes.

If you have trouble getting a specific section to come clear, try to walk closer to the major buildings, caves, and general landmarks inside that area. Just because a new text name appears in your map header doesn't mean that the area is uncovered (that doesn't happen until you receive the "You Have Discovered XXX" message and get the experience bonus. Walk deeper into each new area to find such bonuses.

Going into Smaller Dungeons

Dungeons are a useful point of interest because they often have heavy fighting, some metal or herb deposits, and quests to complete. Try to find where all of the dungeons are located when you are exploring even if you don't have quests for them at the time; it's common for quests to send people all around the world for various goals, and knowing where you are going can cut down on lost time.

Microdungeons are found in most regions. These areas are part of the normal terrain (in other words, you face no loading screen and can freely walk into the dungeons and back out without delay). There are often many monsters in microdungeons, but they won't usually be much tougher than the beasts and enemies walking out in the fields nearby. Unlike Instances, microdungeons aren't based on elite monsters, large pulls, and having a group to protect you.

Microdungeons are some of the best places to camp for metal in WoW. Though you can get more metal by running around entire areas, taking everything you see (once you know the spawn points for the deposits), there are several benefits to camping a cave. For one, the creatures there are worth plenty of experience if you are at the right level for fighting in the dungeon (which is often the case if you stay current on your Mining). Getting metal, experience, and loot at the same time is a major boon. Beyond that, the flow of metal out of a dungeon is reliable compared to searching external sources that people can mine casually.

For the best of both worlds, find all of the dungeons in a given region. Look on the maps once they are filled out to find caves and other places to explore, then go to each place at least one time. Record the items you need from each place (metal here, herbs there, cloth-dropping foes at this location, etc.), then create a loop. Visit one site, kill everything, take all of the items there, then move on to the second site. Moving around a zone in this fashion is amazing for raising gathering Professions, collecting materials to sell, and for gaining a moderate amount of experience.

Taking on World Dungeons

World dungeons are very different from microdungeons. As you might guess, these dungeons are much larger than their cousins. However, this is one of the superficial differences between the two. In fact, there are far more daunting challenges in world dungeons.

If you have missed the term Instance before, it means that an area is not part of the shared world. If twenty groups go there, twenty versions (e.g. Instances) of the dungeon are created. So, only your group is going to head into the fire; expect no surprise assistance or enemy intervention.

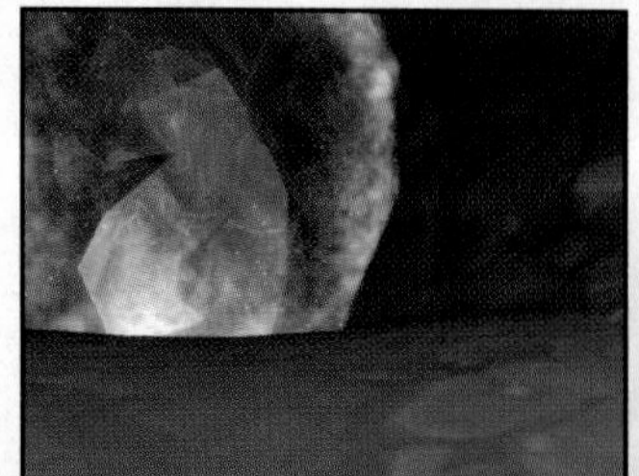

Traits of World Dungeons

- These Dungeons are Instanced (Every Group Goes into Their Own Version of the Dungeon)
- There is a Loading Screen to Mark the Separation Between the Shared Game World and the Instance
- Many Creatures in World Dungeons are Elite
- Battles Inside World Dungeons are Often Harder, Involve Scripted Bosses (in Some Cases), and Have Greater Rewards
- Horde and Alliance Members can do All World Dungeons (Even Those in Enemy Territory)

At the suggested levels, parties without five people and very impressive gear may have trouble. Unlike fighting out in the field, world dungeons are meant to challenge, frustrate, and even defeat parties that aren't experienced enough to survive the complex battles within. This is not a measure of a party's worth, as the vast majority of groups have to contend with full wipeouts and other such setbacks the first few times they try to overcome new world dungeons.

To make your attempts safer, be sure to mold the group before it heads into a world dungeon. Find people who you know and trust to play their characters with high skill. Beyond that, make sure everyone is willing to dedicate several hours to completing the task (most of the world dungeons are somewhat long, and having people leave in the middle can be disastrous for the group). Practice techniques against many of the creatures early in the dungeon and get a feel for the style of the place. In general, a group that has trouble early on needs a couple more levels or some better gear before they can complete that Instance.

Choose a very good leader for every Instance run. It is so important to have skilled and trusted leadership that a well-run group can function better than one with members of higher level, carrying better equipment. If you want to be a leader, run the Instance multiple times, look for key ways to avoid extra aggro, reduce fight times, and finish the boss battles without losing people left and right. Exchange strategies with other leaders and test out new methods frequently to keep your groups trim. With a good leader, Instances can be run sooner and without resorting to specific class combinations.

Always discuss loot rules and any pertinent etiquette **before** entering the actual Instance. In fact, get everything straightened out with other players before people head all the way out to the appropriate region for the dungeon crawl. If you think you need a dedicated healer, don't assume that a Shaman is specced for it. Ask them, "Are you comfortable being our primary healer?" If they say no, don't put them in your group to heal. If you only have that one slot left, apologize, then explain that you need to find a healer and thank them for their time.

What World Dungeons Should I Seek (And When)

Dungeon Name	Expected Levels	Region
Ragefire Chasm	13 to 18	Orgrimmar
Wailing Caverns	17 to 24	The Barrens
Deadmines	17 to 26	Westfall
Shadowfang Keep	22 to 30	Silverpine Forest
Blackfathom Deeps	24 to 32	Darkshore
The Stockades	24 to 32	Stormwind
Razorfen Kraul	25 to 35	The Barrens
Gnomeregan	29 to 38	Dun Morogh
Razorfen Downs	33 to 40	The Barrens
The Scarlet Monastery	34 to 45	Tirisfal Glades
Uldaman	35 to 47	The Badlands
Zul'Farrak	44 to 54	Tanaris Desert
Maraudon	46 to 55	Southwestern Desolace
The Sunken Temple	47 to 55	Swamp of Sorrows
Blackrock Depths	52+	Burning Steppes
Dire Maul	55+	Central Feralas
Scholomance	57+	Between Western and Eastern Plaguelands
Blackrock Spire	58+	Burning Steppes
Strathome	58+	Eastern Plaguelands

Common Tactics
Group Roles
Professions
Transportation
Mail System
Auction Houses
Guild Creation

Dungeon Etiquette

Be especially careful not to be impulsive or greedy during dungeon runs. It takes a great deal of time and work to get a good group together and push through a challenging dungeon for an hour (or two, or three). Because of that, it's even more important than ever to watch what you are doing.

Click Carefully: Many of the groups that don't run with a Master Looter are going to be using Group Loot or Need Before Greed. Either way, you are going to see many loot items appear. Listen carefully when group rules are explained, make any objections at that time, and do not break your contract with the group once everything is settled. Only roll the way you stated you would from the very beginning. There should be no changing the system, no calling dibs suddenly, and no sudden surprises.

Loot When You Are Safe: Do not run off to open chests, mine, harvest herbs, or do other activities during battle. By the same token, don't waste time looting corpses while a battle is still in progress. This is certain to get your group annoyed, and it risks people's safety.

Stay With the Group: Unless you are the one pulling monsters back to the group, stay with everyone else and don't wander. Failing to heed this is a sure way to pull an extra patroller back onto the group at just the wrong time.

Disagreements: Everyone thinks that they know how to do things the best way (well, it seems like everyone feels that way). It may be true that your ideas are better than the existing group leader. Regardless, do not call them out in the group chat at first. Message them privately with your clever ideas. They might very well use them! If the leader is outright rude, poor, or acts like a genuine nutter, consider telling the group your ideas then and see what they think. It's not likely to make things better, but it's a good second course to take.

If that fails, leave. Don't yell, don't whine, don't argue. Apologize and leave. This is the best way to keep your dignity without busting your head against the wall for hours on end.

Mind Those Pets: Note that pets can get entire groups into major trouble. If you send your pet into the wrong enemy group, everyone might die. If your pet paths oddly, everyone might die. If you leave your pet on aggressive, everyone in the group will strangle you (not quite, but don't do it). Use your pet carefully at all times. If you are about to drop to a lower area, put the pet away.

On the flipside, healers should look out for pets too. Hunters especially don't like losing their beloved allies, and it sure helps to have a free tank in the group. When you can spare the mana, keep those pets hale and hearty. Remember that you can target pets quickly using the same function key of that group member (e.g. if the third group member is a Hunter, hitting F3 would target the Hunter normally; tap the key a second time to target the pet instead)

Warlocks Are Not Your Toy: Warlocks can summon characters under certain circumstances. This requires the Warlock to use one of their items, get two other group members to help them, and takes their time and energy to put together. It is not their obligation to do this for you. If you are on the other side of the world as a group is forming, you should ask any Warlocks in the group if they are willing to summon you. Offer sincere thanks if they say yes. Offer a tip too (many of the Warlocks will say no). If the Warlock wants a tip, pay them a portion of what it would take you to get there anyway. Remember that you lose time and money to get places. If a Warlock wants 50 silver pieces for a summon, pay them and kill a few creatures while the group gets together. You can make the money in the time that Warlock just saved you!

Mage Food/Water: Mage Food and Water is a gift for dungeons. It saves people a massive amount of money. Again, offer to tip Mages when you ask for these favors, and certainly thank them for their time.

Warriors Pay the Price: Warriors don't have a major service to sell, and their repair bills are higher than anyone else's. It's sometimes tough to be a Warrior. For other classes, remember that. Help out your Warriors by giving them a bit of leeway on the items they roll Need for. Remember that most tanks need a two-handed weapon, a one-hander, a shield, perhaps a second one-hander, and a full list of tanking gear (perhaps a PvP set as well). Quite a few guilds help to gear up their Warriors for this reason. Love your Warrior. Support your Warrior. The good ones ensure that you don't eat dirt for a living.

"Heal Me Now:" Don't yell at your healers. Either they stink or they don't. If a healer is poor, they won't heal well no matter what you say. Don't invite those healers back into your groups, but don't ruin their night by calling them names either. You don't know if it's a nine-year-old behind that screen; they really might be doing their best already. You aren't obligated to play with people who are poor at their class (and you shouldn't), but don't get nasty just because you died. It happens. Healers get more blame than just about anyone. Think about that, empathize, and play a healer to level 60 yourself before getting too judgmental. Beyond that, you might have been doing something you shouldn't if you are getting a lot of aggro. If you aren't the main tank, maybe the healer shouldn't be healing you that much.

One Puller Only: Make sure one person is assigned for pulling monsters to a group. If that person messes up, let them die on their own and Resurrect them when the monsters are gone. If you aren't that person, don't start any fight unless you have no choice (e.g. a patroller is aggroing on the back of the group and is about to attack the Priest, so you attack it first).

Rely on the Main Assist: Make a macro to /assist "character who is main assist" and use that for your targeting. This is ideal for keeping the group's fire on one target.

Don't Run: Most of the time running gets you killed in Instances anyway. Unless your group leader orders everyone to ditch, hold your ground. If you are going to die, then die with honor.

Group Roles

Group Roles take the general knowledge and tactics of this chapter and expands on that to cover group functionality. Being able to control your character, rise in level and power, and find the right items is enough to bring you up in the ranks. However, a group with five soloers is not as effective as a group with five players who are skilled at grouping! There are tricks that work quite well when you have others on your side that would be worthless when tried solo. Learning these creates a synergy within well-played groups; that edge is what leads to victory in world dungeons, raids, and mass PvP combat.

ROLES: IN SHORT

Going past the terminology, players benefit from understanding what the true components of a group are capable of providing. Look at the following list and consider the way battles are won in a mathematical sense. By reducing incoming damage, shortening encounters, and extending survival time, characters of different roles are able to assist the greater needs of a group in separate ways. When facing various and unknown opponents, it is essential to have multiple answers to each problem.

Group Roles and Functions

Role	Importance in Battle
Mitigation/Tanking	Reduces Damage Directed at Group
Damage	Kills Enemies
Healer	Maintains Group

Various classes exist between these three niches, so the distinction we make here is one of action rather than an innate role. A Warrior, for example, can be both a damage dealer and a tank! Amusingly, Mages are quite the same; they deal damage to enemies while mitigating damage through crowd control.

The key to a successful group is to figure out what ratio of mitigation/damage/healing is needed for a given challenge, then to assemble a group that creates such a ratio.

Mitigation

Tanks and crowd controllers are intended to stop incoming damage in one way or another. Tanks gather enemies around themselves and force the aggro to stay put; this reduces incoming damage by keeping it centered on characters with high armor and survival rates. Crowd controls perform the same function by stopping enemy attacks, preventing their movement toward desirable targets, and so forth.

Warriors, Paladins, and Druids in Bear Form are able to survive hits far better than many of the other classes. These three tanks use abilities to get aggro then disable enemies as best as possible (e.g. Warriors use Demoralizing Shout and Thunder Clap to reduce incoming damage beyond what their plate armor already accomplishes).

Crowd controllers, like Mages, Warlocks, Rogues, and sometimes Priests try to take a specific enemy's damage entirely out of the battle for a time. Polymorph, Banish, Sap, Mind Control, and Shackle Undead are all abilities with the potential to stop enemies from being productive.

Obviously, characters can mitigate damage while still contributing to party health or DPS. A Warrior who is immensely survivable but can't hold aggro isn't of very much use. The key is to understand when to mitigate damage and when to switch toward other aspects of battle. See the following table for a better understanding of this.

Mitigation Abilities and When to Use Them

Class	Ability	When to Use
Druid	High Armor in Bear Form	During Battle: To Give Other Tanks Time to Regain Aggro or to Delay PvP Forces
Hunter	Traps	Before Combat: Traps Are Used to Slow Groups or Immobilize Individuals
Mage	Polymorph, Many Frost Spells	During Combat: Mages Take Enemies Out of Combat With Polymorph or Greatly Slow Groups With Ice Snare/Root Effects
Paladin	High Armor, Stuns	During Battle: Paladin Stuns Stop Enemies Fully for a Short Time, Paladin Armor Allows Them to Survive Aggro Gained from Healing
Priest	Shackle Undead, Psychic Scream, Mind Control	Various: Their Specific Uses Are Quite Powerful (Discussed in Character Chapter)
Rogue	Sap, Many Stuns, Blind	Before Combat: Rogue Saps Cause Very Long Incapacitation Time to Humanoids; In-Combat Stuns Are Also Useful Against PvP Enemies and Lesser Targets
Shaman	Frost Shock, Earthbind Totem	During Combat: Shamans Slow or Stop Enemy Forces Even on the Run
Warlock	Banish, Seduce, Fear	During Combat: Warlocks Are Able to Produce Very Long In-Combat Crowd Control
Warrior	High Armor, Immense Damage Mitigation, AOE Fear	During Combat: Warriors Get Aggro and Shut Down Incoming Enemy Damage

Whatever class you choose, understand the time and place for your mitigation. During light combat, mitigation is of less importance than healing or damage. When there are many incoming enemies (such as you see during many dungeons), mitigation becomes the most important aspect of group survivability. Without proper mitigation, healers won't be able to keep up.

Mitigation is also not a practice for any single member of the group. This is an ongoing and multi-faceted affair. The Warrior mitigates by engaging a full group of enemies, pulling them onto herself, and using abilities to reduce their damage. Then, a Mage in the same group uses Polymorph against a caster off in the distance to mitigate that enemy. The Shaman of the group drops totems to decrease the damage coming at the Warrior, and also uses Frost Shock to slow anything that breaks away from the Warrior and tries to get to her healers. Don't let enemies do what they want! Reduce their damage, reduce their movement, reduce their options. This is the key. The character chapter, Rising in the Ranks, goes into great length on this matter.

Damage Dealers

Almost every class can deal damage when configured properly. This person's duty is to knock down enemies quickly. Every foe that falls is unable to deal damage for the rest of the fight, meaning that DPS characters are able to protect the party by negating enemy activity in a permanent sense.

The most effective way for DPS characters to operate is to deal targeted damage to enemies who are most likely to die quickly (or to target the enemies who deal the most damage). To wound all enemies is not good enough for most situations; slaying targets is the true benefit of damage dealing! Thus, damage done by DPS characters needs to be concentrated so that each target dies as quickly as possible. A leader should be chosen among the damage dealers, and this person picks each target with a mind for kill rate vs. threat of target (this person is called the Main Assist). The faster the kill, the better the target. The more dangerous the target, the more important the kill. Quickly rate all of the enemies in a battle along these lines to decide what needs to be destroyed, then start opening the metaphoric can of beatdowns on your list.

The person chosen to be Main Assist should be a player who understands the given raid/dungeon area extremely well. For there, it helps if that person is a melee class (so that they are actually there in the action). Everyone else who is on damage duty needs to have an /assist macro for the Main Assist so that damage is properly focused.

Factors in Creating Your Own Hate List

To decide which targets come first, look at how past battles have gone. Which enemies deal the most damage to your party? Casters, creatures with major debuffs/combat control, and other such aggressive foes are usually high risk. Luckily, they are also softer kills. This ranks highly for both criteria you use.

Take down high damage or crowd control targets as soon as possible, then move on to foes with less opportunity. Often, the most enduring targets are the weakest, so they can be dispatched at the end of combat. Bosses are the big exception to this; removing any substantial allies a boss has may not be possible because of a boss' immense DPS (in other words, you may have to ignore fast kills to make a mad scramble against a superior target). Each boss fight has its own strategy and tactics, so that isn't something to worry about here.

Dealing Damage

Class	DPS Methods
Druid	Wield Weapons With High Stat Bonuses (Avoid Procs), Use Cat Form, Spec for Feral Combat
Hunter	Sustainable DPS is the Best in Game, Multishot + Pet + Rapid Fire + Stings Alone Add Up (Volley Against Large Groups)
Mage	Spec in Fire and Arcane, Use Many AoEs Against Groups of 3+ Enemies, Many Instants When Mana Efficiency Doesn't Matter
Paladin	Spec for Retribution, Rely on High-End Weaponry (Not Easy to Deal High DPS as a Paladin)
Priest	Not Often a DPS Class, Though Holy AoEs in Massed PvP, Shadow Spec for Ruining Single Targets
Rogue	High End Weapons, Backstab and Assassination for PvP Damage, Combat Spec for PvE
Shaman	Great Single-Target DPS Through Elemental or Enhancement Spec, Windfury Totem for Lucky Bursts; Poor for AoE DPS
Warlock	Spec with Affliction and Destruction, DOT Everyone, AoEs, Break Out the Dangerous Pets (e.g. Infernals)
Warrior	Spec for Arms or Fury (or Both), Heavy Gear Dependence, AoEs Assist Greatly (Sweeping Strikes/ Whirlwind), 2H Weapon or Dual Wield

Healer

Healers extend the length of time a group can survive in a battle; they also decrease downtime between battles to raise experience and money-gaining efficiency. This is done by using Mana to negate damage done against a group. With careful casting and high Spirit, these characters can dramatically lengthen the survival time of a group.

Also, there is a targeted advantage to the boost Healers provide. Though Tanks are able to reduce damage coming in against a party, they have only a few chances to turn the tide of battle if aggro is cemented and they fall close to death. If the Tank goes down because of this, all of the potential that protector brought to the group disappears in an instant. Healers smooth out damage so that individual members of the group do not die before their time. Proper healing ensures that Tanks last as long as possible, use all of their abilities and items, then only start to die off when the group has nothing left to give. Preventing premature deaths is as much a part of a Healer's service as ensuring total group survivability.

In tougher dungeons and end-game raids, healing is the only way to survive. Full DPS groups, even with crowd control, simply cannot make their way through the later portions of the game. In PvP, raiding, and even the harder five-man Instances, healers are a requirement. Priests are the acknowledged powerhouses of this, just as Warriors are the leaders of standard tanking. That said, Druids, Shamans, and Paladins that are willing to heal carefully are immensely powerful as well. Anyone who specializes in healing can fill the role nicely, and even characters without a Talent focus in healing can save lives!

These backup healers (such as Paladins or Druids/Shamans who haven't focused on healing) lack some of the healing efficiency and potential of a solid and true Healer. The best place for these backup healers is to be in a group with a full-time healer. Just as a backup tank is often ready to rip aggro off of group members when the main tank cannot, a backup healer exists to save the life of the primary healer or other characters when the worst luck happens.

During more frantic combat, it's hard to maintain composure. When multiple characters are taking damage and monsters are flying back and forth, it's essential that the healers focus on saving lives. Keep trickling the spells to the entire group while the Tanks hold all the aggro they can. Only unleash the massive, aggro-drawing flurry of heals when it's make or break time. Once that happens, hope that you can do enough to allow a secondary rezzer to survive and bring you back, because considerable aggro is coming your way.

Save the Tank!

There are times when healers have to make the hardest choice of all (to let some characters die while saving others). In dire fights, there won't always be mana to keep the entire group/raid alive. Even before end-game content, there are a number of encounters that greatly challenge any group that isn't higher in level or equipment. For these, a healer may have to acknowledge openly or in their own plans that some characters are expendable.

In general, the way to decide on healing priorities is to figure out what each person adds to the group. The main tank is the savior of a party because they control the aggro, protect the healers, and lower incoming damage in general. Keeping them alive is usually the top priority. After that, healers are the most important ones to save because they accomplish the same function (e.g. keep the group from wiping during an intense fight). Finally, the damage dealers are sorted. Within the damage dealers, the sorting is usually done by intelligence level of the player. Let players who foolishly deal too much damage and rip aggro off of the tanks often die. It's for the best; heals on those damage dealers risk the group!

An important exception to this list exists when a healer or damage dealer is out of mana. They are almost useless to the group then, and should only be saved if they are a rezzer.

Restoring Health

Class	Healing/Restoration
Druid	Heal Over Times, Direct Heals, Battle Rez
Hunter	Can Heal Their Pets
Mage	Offers Free Food/Water to Groups; Otherwise None
Paladin	Survivable Heals (They Want the Aggro), Powerful Lay on Hands (Once Per Hour), Rez
Priest	Best Heals in the Game, Efficient Healing, Increase Health Totals Through Buffs, Rez
Rogue	None
Shaman	Less Efficient Healing, Totems for Modest Healing Over Time, Totems for Mana Regeneration, Rez
Warlock	Can Heal Themselves, Soul Stone Rezzers to Rez Them in Case of Wipe
Warrior	Healers: These Guys/Girls Are Your Customers

Hybrid

As stated, most classes have elements in each of the three primary aspects. The devoted classes lean heavily toward one of the three roles (e.g. Priests are mostly healers), while the hybrid and support classes divide their skillsets somewhat evenly between the groups. Specialization within a class pushes characters closer toward one extreme or into a more versatile role.

Thus, no matter what character you choose to play, there are ways to become a bit of everything or ways to accentuate the strengths already found in the class. Characters that are specialized offer the greatest potential within their portion of the group roles, but end up requiring other characters to function normally. In other words, a Warrior who becomes a full tank loses so much DPS that they don't kill quickly on their own anymore. Priests with a full specialization on the Holy line are able to fight better than they used to, but still perform far better with a group there to help them survive.

For the players who want to fill the gaps in a group or be able to solo under a variety of conditions, the hybrid classes and specializations are preferable. Take a look at Druids (the epitome of a hybrid class). Druids can heal, deal ranged damage, fight in melee, stealth, and even get a combat rez. What can't Druids do? Nothing, quite honestly. Druids and other hybrid classes are never left without the ability to contribute; their only problem is in defining themselves while in the shadow of specialized classes/roles.

During the first fifty levels of the game, hybrids have a great deal of power. Druids can heal for a group of five and keep them going in an Instance, or they can switch to Bear Form and tank if there isn't a Warrior, or they can stay in Cat Form and deal damage. Restoration Shamans are easily heal for a group, just as Enhancement Shamans are fine tanks until the end-game challenges appear.

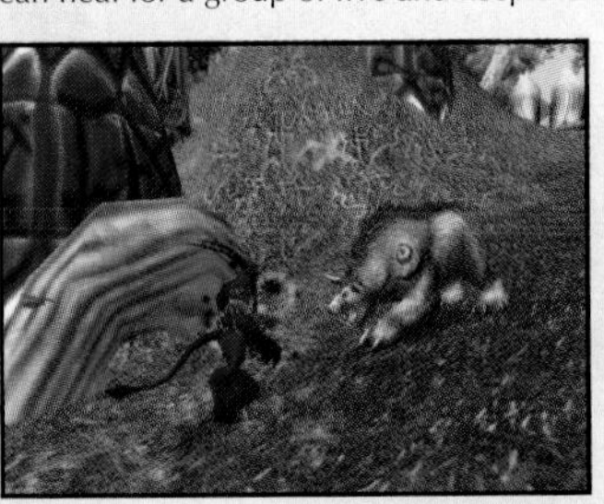

In late-game battles, the hybrid characters find their own niches. Backup healing, spare DPS, and other secondary roles never go out of fashion in raids. With a group of 40, there are many needs. When you play a hybrid class, be especially on the lookout in the long- and short-term for the needs of a guild, group, raid. If people need more healing, try to use more healing gear, respec your Talents if needed, and so forth. Become what is needed and there will always be a place for you.

Hybrid Class Potential

Class	Directions
Druid	Melee DPS/Tanking with Feral Combat (Cat and Bear Form), Ranged Damage with Balance (Caster Form), and Healing Through Restoration (Caster Form)
Paladin	Healing With Holy Talents, DPS With Retribution and 2H Weapons, Tanking With Protection (Though This is Difficult)
Shaman	Magical Damage With the Elemental Line, Tanking and Melee Damage with Enhancement, and Healing Through the Restoration Line

Professions

There is an entire section devoted to professions and other trades later in the guide, yet several aspects of the crafting system are worth developing here for incoming players. This section uncovers the basics of choosing your professions, the terminology of the system, and how to know what you are looking for in-game.

What Are Professions?

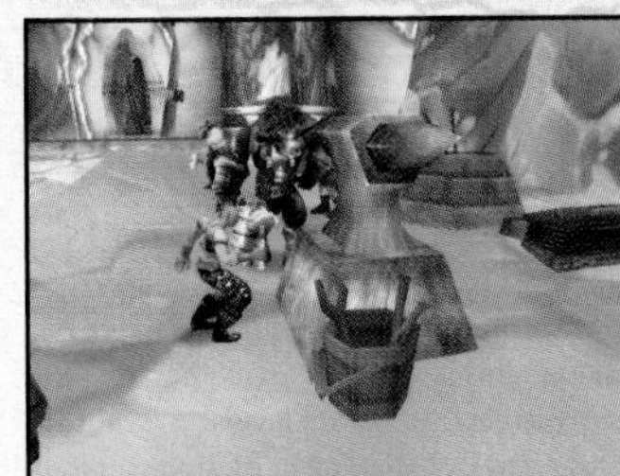

Professions cover the resource gathering and item creation systems in World of Warcraft. Each character is allowed to learn and maintain two professions, and doing so can be used for profit, improved equipment and usable items, or simply for the enjoyment of supporting friends/your guild.

List of Professions

Profession	Purpose	Benefits
Alchemy	Create Potions/Transmute Metals	Temporary Attribute Enhancement, Create High-End Metals, Elemental Transmutes
Blacksmithing	Forge Weapons, Chain/Plate Armor, and Peripheral Equipment	Increase Weapon Damage and Speed (for 2H), Improve Shields, Increase Mount Speed
Enchanting	Improve Equipment, Used to Create Goods used by Others	Sell Enchantments for Profit, Raise Attributes on Gear (Very Expensive Until High-Tier, Then Profits Are Immense)
Engineering	Construct Bombs, Rifles, and Accessories	Battle Pets, AoE Explosives, Ammunition, Scopes for Ranged Weapons
Herbalism	Gather Herbs	Ingredients for Alchemy, Sell for High Profit
Leatherworking	Make Leather Armor, Ammo Quivers/Pouches, and Armor Patches	Add Bonuses to Ranged Combat, Increase Armor Rating
Mining	Mine Metal	Ingredients for Blacksmithing and Engineering, Sell for High Profit
Skinning	Skin Beast Corpses for Leather	Ingredients for Leatherworking, Sell for Profit
Tailoring	Sew Cloth Armor and Items, Make Bags	Sell Bags to Other Characters

Professions have trainers (just like classes) that are found in small towns and large cities alike. There are higher concentrations of trainers in the capitals, and so much trade happens there that people often seek those specific trainers to do most of their work.

Trainers are needed to initially grab a profession, but they are also needed to gain new tiers of skill, and to pick up extra recipes for various items. All of these projects cost money, so it is often a question of much how time and money you wish to invest in a profession. In the later stages, some professions are worth sizable fortunes (especially the ones that gather resources for other professions). As long as you are willing to throw the extra energy into these skills, they are quite lucrative in the long run.

Learning how to create various items does not stop at the trainer. Hidden recipes can be found on monsters and special vendors around the world. Talk to other crafters to find out more about the locations of these items (and read the tables in our Crafting and Professions Chapter for more info as well).

WHAT ARE SECONDARY SKILLS?

List of Secondary Skills

Skill	Purpose	Benefits
Cooking	Create Food/Fires	Reduce Downtime w/ Food and Spirit Buffs
First Aid	Stitch Bandages	Allow for Fast Healing of Moderate Damage
Fishing	Collect Items from Water	Ingredients for Cooking, Spare Equipment, Find Recipes for Other Trades

Secondary Skills aren't limited by anything except time and money. Each character can take these skills whether they are interested in professions or not. In fact, many soloers take all three skills to reduce downtime and increase their self-sufficiency without losing constant money on store-bought food and such.

TRANSPORTATION

World of Warcraft takes place in Azeroth, a land that cannot be crossed quickly. There is much to see and do out there, and it sure helps to know how to get around! This section explains what the various means of transportation are, what their cost is, and what you can do to save the most time at the best prices.

POUNDING THE DIRT

Cost: None
Making it Cheaper: No Need
Making it Better: Boot Enchantment (Run Speed Increase)

The most basic form of transportation is to walk anywhere that you need to go. Though this is a very slow method, it certainly isn't costly. From level 1 forward, your character is going to do quite a bit of this. Even at the higher levels, when you have mounts at your disposal, walking is the primary means of travel within Instances and in areas where the monsters are plentiful (no need to waste time mounting when you can simple engage another target).

There are a few ways to enhance your basic walking speed. There are boot enchantments to add several percent to this (though modest, such enchantments certainly add up over longer distances or for PvP, when any bonus can be critical). Certain boots even come with a movement speed enchancement!

FLIGHT PATHS

Cost: Modest Copper or Silver
Making it Cheaper: Rep/PvP Rank Reduce Cost 10%
Making it Better: Not Possible

One of the most common forms of fast transport is to take the flight paths around Azeroth. Both factions have flight masters in just about every major city and town. The first time that you see a new flight master there is a green mark above their head to let you know that there is a new route to discover! Right click on the NPC to learn the route; after that point you can fly to and from that point without any problems (so long as you know at least one path that connects to the one in question).

Each character starts with the flight location from the nearby capital city. Most paths, however, you need to find by exploring the world. The first flight paths you are likely to actually discover are in The Barrens, Silverpine, Westfall, Loch Modan, or Darkshore.

After learning your flight paths, right click again on these NPCs to display a map of the continent you are currently on. From there, you get a view of all the points that connect to your current location. Highlight any of these to see the total cost for flying there, then left-click to select your target. These flights take several minutes, usually, but the trip is still a great deal faster than walking. Beyond that, you are free to go /afk and take care of looking up information, taking bio breaks, and so forth.

BOATS AND ZEPPELINS

Cost: None
Making it Cheaper: None
Making it Better: None

Boats and Zeppelins are provided as free forms of intercontinental travel. These are slower, in that you often have to wait for a modest period before the craft arrives, but characters without access to an appropriate Mage or Warlock have little choice in the matter.

Once a sea vessel or airship arrives, step onto the craft and wait for it to leave. There is a brief time for everyone to board, then the craft leaves the area. There is a loading period, and before long everyone should arrive safely at their destination. Note that jumping off of the zeppelins from very high altitudes can and will kill your character. Do not follow people off unless you are sure that you will be okay (this is most often an issue with the Tirisfal Glades tower, where people sometimes leap off early after Rogues or Mages who have means to reduce their falling damage).

In very odd cases where lag is high, a vessel might dump you. If that happens, try to reach land or safe water before your character dies from fatigue. In the case of falling off of a zeppelin from lag, simply retrieve your body and move on. When dumped too far out in the water, Rez at the Spirit Healer and move on. This happens so rarely that with a few thousand hours logged into WoW with the writing team, most have never seen this happen.

Zeppelins	
Location	Access To
East of Orgrimmar	Grom'gol (Stranglethorn Vale) and Undercity (Tirisfal Glades)
Grom'gol Basecamp	Orgrimmar (Durotar) and Undercity (Tirisfal Glades)
North of Undercity	Grom'gol (Stranglethorn Vale) and Orgrimmar (Durotar)

Boats	
Location	Access To
Auberdine	Rut'theran Village (Teldrassil), Menethil Harbor (Wetlands), Theramore (Dustwallow Marsh)
Booty Bay	Ratchet (The Barrens)
Menethil Harbor	Auberdine (Darkshore), Theramore (Dustwallow Marsh)
Ratchet	Booty Bay (Stranglethorn Vale)
Rut'theran Village	Auberdine (Darkshore)
Theramore	Auberdine (Darkshore), Menethil Harbor (Wetlands)
Western Feralas	Short Trip to Feathermoon

THE DEEPRUN TRAM

Cost: None
Making it Cheaper: None
Making it Better: None

The Deeprun Tram runs between Stormwind and Ironforge. Look in the northeast side of Stormwind, in the Dwarven Quarter, for one entrance to this free transport. Or, in Ironforge, seek Tinker Town.

Step onto the Tram when it arrives and wait for the journey to commence. This is a very short trip and even saves time over flying in a number of cases. You must stay alert on the Tram though, otherwise you miss your destination and end up on the return trip!

TRAVEL FORMS AND ABILITIES

Cost: Training Costs and Mana
Making it Cheaper: PvP Rank and Faction Rep Decreases Training Costs
Making it Better: Talents in Several Classes Exist to Improve Travel Forms

Hunters: Aspect of the Cheetah/Pack

Hunters learn Aspect of the Cheetah at level 20; this Aspect lets them move at 130% run speed, making it very useful to reach locations quickly. Switching between Aspects is instant, and this is another great boon. Hunters can immediately shift to a higher speed when there aren't any enemies nearby, then switch back as danger approaches.

At level 40, Aspect of the Pack is learned. This Aspect grants the same power of Aspect of the Cheetah to all group members within range. Getting through cleared areas of Instances has never been easier than with a Hunter using AotP!

The danger of these Aspects, and the reason they aren't used during battle, is that anyone under the influence of either Aspect is immediately dazed if they are damaged. Daze slows your character down greatly, and negates any of the benefits you were receiving from having the buff in the first place. Thus, take Aspect of the Cheetah off as soon as there is anything nasty approaching. In PvP especially, **beware Aspect of the Pack**. Everyone in your group getting dazed because of your mistake is going to cause a few sharp comments.

Shaman: Ghost Wolf

Shamans learn how to shift into their Ghost Wolf form at level 20. This form increases movement to 140% run speed. Only usable outdoors, this form is of great benefit for running around in the Battlegrounds, getting to quest locations, or for making herbing/mining runs. Through the use of Talents, Shamans can make their Ghost Wolf form faster to cast (in the heat of the Battlegrounds, this is a huge benefit). Certain class items and Talents together make Ghost Wolf even better by increasing run speed to a level that rivals that of a standard mount.

Shaman: Astral Recall

Astral Recall allows Shamans to essentially Hearth back to their bind point more often than normal characters. You can still use your Hearthstone normally, and when it is down, casting Astral Recall gets you home just as easily.

Druid: Travel Form

Though not learned until level 30, Druid Travel Form is very fast and useful. Moving at 140% of normal run speed, this form also adds the advantage of ditching movement debuffs during the Shapeshift and also protects the caster from Polymorph spells. Druids make wonderful runners in the Battlegrounds because of this, so long as their team is able to stop intercepting characters. In the 30-39 bracket, before mounts are introduced, Druids are the supreme flag runners of Warsong Gulch.

Rogue: Sprint

Rogue Sprint is a sudden burst of movement speed that lasts for 15 seconds (there is a five minute cooldown between uses). There are three ranks of Sprint, so the buff to movement increases as your character levels. This is a great ability for getting out of trouble, running flags in the Battlegrounds, moving at impressive speeds even while Stealthed, and so forth.

Warrior: Charge and Intercept

Warriors don't have a lot of abilities for getting around, but a clever Warrior learns to make their own path. While trying to run through groups of grey or green monsters in the levels before you own a mount, use Charge and later Intercept as well to leap forward. If you don't want to fight the monsters, Hamstring them and move on. Over time, this method truly does get you where you are going faster (and it's darn funny to watch).

MOUNTS

Cost: Up to 100 Gold at Level 40, Up to 900 Gold at Level 60
Making it Cheaper: Get Discounts for Honored Reputation w/ Pertinent Faction and for Rank 3 in PvP
Making it Better: Spurs Attach to Boots (Made by Blacksmiths, Increase Mount Run Speed), Zul'Farrak has a Carrot Trinket that Also Does This, Glove Enchantment

- Normal Mounts Cost 80 Gold Pieces; Move at 160% Running Speed
- Epic Mounts Cost 900 Gold Pieces; Move at 200% Running Speed
- It Costs 20 Gold Pieces to Master Riding; You Must Either Learn From Your Own Faction or Reach Exalted Status with Another Faction

The first tier of mounts are available after reaching character level 40. These cost 100 gold pieces before any discounts are given; a portion of the money goes toward learning how to actually ride such a creature, and the remaining money is for the purchase of the actual mount (20 gold pieces to learn riding, 80 gold pieces to get the mount itself).

Note that you can only learn how to ride a mount in your faction's capital from someone of the same race. Unless, that is, you reach Exalted reputation with other race (e.g. orcs can learn to ride Tauren Kodos **if** they reached Exalted status with Thunder Bluff).

Once you learn how to ride a mount, you can buy multiple mounts if you wish (though there is seldom a good reason to buy another mount until you reach level 60). At that time, epic mounts become available. Though extremely expensive, costing 1000 gold pieces before discounts, epic mounts travel faster than normal mounts and look better as well.

Once you own a mount, equip it to bind the mount to you, then place the icon on one of your quickbars for easy access. Mounting takes several seconds, so it is only useful for trips that take longer than six or so seconds. In other words, don't mount to move 50 yards and attack another creature. Dismounting is done by using the mount a second time ***or*** right-clicking on the buff icon that appears while you are riding.

There are several things that automatically dismount your character. Going indoors does this, as you cannot stay mounted in most indoor locations. Walking through water dismounts everyone too, so jump as far as you can when entering water. Certain types of crowd control also force a dismount (e.g. Polymorph).

Warlocks and Paladins Get Free Mounts

At level 40, Warlocks and Paladins receive quests to find their own mounts. These mounts have a specific appearance, cost nothing, and are fully functional in every way. This is quite a nice financial boon to these classes!

SUMMONING AND PORTALS

Cost: Reagents for Mages, Soul Shards for Warlocks
Making it Cheaper: Ask for Tips
Making it Better: None

As has been discussed in this guide, Mages and Warlocks have travel powers that help people to move immediately over immense distances. Mages past level 40 can portal entire teams from their current location to some of the major cities for their faction. Warlocks past level 20, on the other hand, use the souls of downed enemies to call group members to themselves.

Mage Teleports and Portals

- Mages Teleport Themselves to Cities Past Level 20, and Portal Groups of People When They Are Past Level 40
- Reagent Vendors Carry the Rune of Teleportation (Base 10 Silver Price), and the Rune of Portals (Base 20 Silver Price) that are Needed for These Spells

At levels 20 and 30, Mages master the ability to teleport themselves to the various capital cities of their faction. This requires a special reagent (Rune of Teleportation, found on Reagent Vendors). Because of this power, Mages should set their Hearthstones in the areas where they quest for experience and use teleportation to head back to capital cities. That way, the Mages almost never need to use slower forms of transportation except when moving into new areas entirely.

At levels 40 and 50, Mages can use these spells in a portal form, allowing other characters to instantly teleport as well. This requires a different reagent (a Rune of Portals). People who request such a service from Mages are likely to tip them for the immense time saved! These gateways last for a short period, and even people not in the Mage's group will be able to use the portals. Thus, folks who are on one continent are often able to save a huge amount of travel time by tipping a Mage 20 or more silver to open a portal to the other continent.

Warlock Summoning

- The Ritual of Summoning Requires a Level 20 or Higher Warlock, Two Group Members already with the Warlock, and the Desired Teleportee to be in Group as Well
- Warlocks Need to Use Soul Shards to Summon; This Also Takes Time, So Love/Tip Your Warlocks
- You Cannot Summon Someone Outside an Instance Into an Instance (They Must Zone Into the Instance Before Being Summoned)

After level 20, Warlocks can use their Ritual of Summoning to bring a person in their group to their current locations. The Warlock needs everyone involved to be in their group already. At least two people must already be with the Warlock to assist in creating the summoning portal, and the Warlock has to have Soul Shards on hand already. Soul Shards are gained by killing creatures while using Drain Soul on them. The Warlock casts the spell and remains in a channeling state while the two characters with the Warlock right click on the appearing portal.

To prevent a certain number of casual exploits with dungeon content, it was made impossible to summon characters outside of an Instance into that Instance. Thus, if a Warlock is already inside of a dungeon or similar place, the desired character must enter the Instance portal before summoning is usable on them, unless the Warlock and Assistants leave the instance.

The Mail System

The World of Warcraft mail system is extremely useful, easy to use, and costs very little. For just coppers a day, you can contact other members of your faction and send them letters, money, goods, or even sell items (through the Cash on Delivery system). This is a wonderful function of the game, and everyone should know about it.

WHAT CAN I DO?

- Mail Costs 30 Copper Pieces to Send
- Letters, Money, and Auction Items/Receipts Arrive Almost Instantly
- Items Take One Hour to Deliver
- You Can Send Your Alts Items/Money Directly Through the Mail (No Worrying About Middlemen!)

While standing near a mailbox, right click on the object. This brings up the mail screen. You are shown a list of pending messages, if there are any for your character. This Inbox screen is the default. Look at the tab on the bottom of the box and click on "Send Mail" to switch modes. From there, you can type in a character to send the mail to, a subject header, and any text for the body of your email.

The box in the lower-left is for any item that you wish to send. Though soulbound items cannot be sent through the mail, just about anything else can be. Also, type in any numbers for the gold, silver, and copper slots nearby to either send money to the person as well **or** to create a sell price for the item you are sending. The default is to send money, but the buttons in the lower right can be used to change this to COD if you like (Cash on Delivery). By doing so, the other person must pay the amount you type in to receive the item you are sending. COD can be held up to 30 days before purchase, so use wisely.

Scammers

You won't likely run into this during your World of Warcraft experience, but there are a few people who try to scam people out of money by sending items COD. If you get a gift-wrapped package of some sort from a person that you don't know, don't accept the charges. It's probably just a fish or something equally worthless.

WHERE CAN I DO IT?

- Mailboxes Look Slightly Different Between Regions, But Are Often Found by Inns or Banks (Highlight Them With Your Mouse to be Sure)

You can use these functions at any mailbox in either continent. The visual appearance of mailboxes is determined by region, but the general look of them remains similar. Also, you can find mailboxes in the same type of places throughout the world (near Inns and Banks most commonly). Mailboxes are placed in both major cities and minor towns, so it's very rare that you need to Hearth back just to take care of some mail.

HOW CAN I SEND GIFTS?

There are shops in the major cities where you can buy gift-wrapping paper. Right click on the paper, once purchased from a general vendor, then select the item you wish to wrap. Afterward, send the desired package in the mail to a friend!

Auction Houses: Gateway to Wealth

Auction Houses offer far more to the game than players might first suspect. These places are great meeting grounds for trade, and the wealth that pours from their vaults each day is legion. Use this section to learn about the tricks of the trade in WoW's Auction Houses.

THE BASICS

The first point of order is to learn how the Auction House is used. When you have items to sell or want to search for goodies to buy, travel to one of the capital cities in your faction (Orgrimmar, Thunder Bluff, or Undercity for Horde; Stormwind, Ironforge, or Darnassus for Alliance). Or, if you are reaching the higher levels, consider the neutral AHs (in Gadgetzan, Everlook, and Booty Bay). It is less expensive to use your faction's AHs, as the neutral ones charge a higher fee.

Once you find the NPCs who are listed as Auctioneers, right-click on them to open the Auction House. From here, you can browse for items to buy, check on current bids, and place your treasure up for auction.

Buying

From the initial screen you can browse and purchase items. At the top are systems to help you search for specific items. These filters allow you to search by:

Name	Type in a portion of an item's name or a type of stat modifier (such as Power, Falcon, etc.)
Level Range	Choose a minimum or maximum level for the item
Rarity	Choose the minimum quality level of the items (Rare would display blue items and onward)
Usable Items (Yes/No)	Will constrain results to items that you character can currently equip or use

Remember that equipment, usable items (potions, ammo, bandages, etc.), trade goods, and all manner of random drops can be found in the Auction House. Search through the entire AH at least once to get an idea for the scope of these auctions.

When you actually find an item you want, look at the display that appears on the main portion of the Auction House window; highlight the item you are interested in and read the information on that line. From left to right, there is the following type of data:

Icon	Picture of the item; Highlight this specifically to see the stats of the piece in question
Name of Item	Just the name
Minimum Level to Use/Equip Item	Useful for looking ahead and getting equipment to grow into
Time Left in Auction	Gives you an idea for the duration until the auction expires
Seller	Knowing the name might allow you to whisper and person and ask about where they found such a recipe, if they can make more of an item, etc.
Current Bid and Buyout Price	The top number on the right side is the current bid (you must bid a higher number to have a chance at the time); the lower number is the buyout price

Bidding on an item starts the war to see if you can wait out any other buyers. Auctions can be placed for as long as 24 hours, so only auctions listed at short (under 30 minutes), or medium (30 minutes to 2 hours) are going to close soon without a buyout. Once your bid is down, the game notifies you if another bidder comes forward on the item (and your existing bid money will return to your mailbox). If you really want a specific item but it has no buyout or one that you cannot afford, stay close to the Auction House when the Time Left reaches short and stay on top of the bidding.

A buyout immediately takes the full price for the listed item from you supplies, ends the auction, and mails the item to your mailbox. This is often rather costly for major pieces, but trade goods and lower-level items are usually bought out without the process being too painful.

Selling

Click on the third tab of the Auction House window (Auctions) to switch into selling mode. From here, drag and drop an item that you wish to post into the Auction Item box on the left. The default Starting Price that appears below is quite minimal, but it is enough to cover your costs. This default is useful for items of lower value that don't require a major investment of time to sell carefully.

Below that is the Auction Duration selection. Choose either a 2-hour run, an 8-hour auction (the default), or post the item for 24-hours. The deposit you pay to the Auction House will not be refunded if the item does not sell, and the price of said deposit increases proportionally with the duration of your auction. Still, many items are worth posting for 24-hours if you want to put them up at all. Give people the time to notice your goods, especially if you are posting items during off-hours.

If is entirely optional whether you want to post a buyout price for your items. Most of the time, it is very much in your interest to do this; many players aren't interested in start a buying war, especially for minor purchases. Trade goods, usable items, and even equipment are treats that people don't want to monitor, wait for, and potentially lose. Post a buyout price to allow the less patient buyers to grab what they want instantly. Your price can be a single copper higher than the starting price, or it can be immensely higher. There are reasons to go in either direction, and these are discussed shortly.

If you post an auction and suddenly find that you have changed your mind, select that item in the auctions tab and look at the bottom of your window. There is an option to close auctions; though you lose your deposit forever, this is **extremely** useful if you accidentally post something far below its value. Get it back soon! A few sharp buyers are watching the Auction Houses almost every hour of every day.

BEYOND THE BASICS

Most people learn quickly how to use the Auction House. It's so useful that you can hardly live without it sometimes. But there are many players who never actually stop and consider how much money there is to be made here. A level 15 character that has scrounged together a single gold piece can start an empire of wealth by wheeling and dealing on the AH.

Buy Low, Sell High

The old adage is both trite and truthful. The trick is to learn how low is for a given type of item and to figure out what high price the market will bear when selling. If you really want to master the Auction House on your server, keep a logbook for common item prices near your computer.

For items that are sold frequently (e.g. cloth, leather, potions), you can find the current prices quickly by searching as a buyer. See what other sellers are trying to get for their goods. You can post your auctions at a mere 5 silver discount and get some easy sales if everyone is clumping around the same price. As long as you aren't putting up much material, you aren't likely to start a seller's war.

One of the best ways to sell high is to sell when there aren't a lot of items being posted of the given type. If you check as a buyer and see a full page of Briarthorn, today might not be a good day to sell your stack (put it in the bank and wait). When you search late the next evening and see one or two other stacks, it is a very good time to sell. Even if sellers post low prices when there aren't many items for sale, try for a higher price anyway. Remember that those great deals are likely to buyout early. After that, your goods are the ones setting the price trend.

For goods that are always in demand for crafters and such, the middle of the week is a solid selling time; you won't have nearly as much competition. For equipment pieces, the weekends are better (because there are more buyers online, but sellers may not have the equipment pieces to compete with you). Trade goods are a more consistent market; the scarcity of good equipment pieces makes it possible to gouge people tremendously when there are more folks on.

High in a Bracket

Selling to PvPers in a great way to make money. Rare items that are levels x6-x9 in a given bracket are often worth a huge sum (e.g. level 16-19, 26-29). When selling these goods, be sure to start high. Losing a deposit, even a couple times, is not that big a deal compared to the long-term potential for a huge sale. Thus, don't undercut others who are selling similar items that don't drop as often. Wait, post your item a few times, and wait for that magical buyer to appear.

Rogue and Hunter twink gear is the best of all. There are always players creating PvP characters for the lower brackets. Thus, you can charge even more for powerful goods at the low levels when the items are for those classes. Level 16-19 Rogue gear can and does fetch hundreds of gold. Hunt through Shadowfang Keep looking for a lucky Bind-on-Equip drop, and you might just fund your character all the way into the 40s.

Don't feel guilty for gouging twink PvPers. The majority of those players have high-level characters already, more gold than they can handle, and are overgearing their characters in an attempt to dominate a given bracket. Almost nobody on the other side of the field is going to love the twinks, and even a number of people on their own side find this practice "weak" or "cheesy." So, gouge away! They can afford it.

Niche Markets

With work and some investment, you can corner a specific market, at least for a time. To do this, you must take the risk and buyout everything below a price threshold that you decide on. Afterward, you repost those items at your price and maintain an alert watch on the AH to keep the process going until other people naturally post their goods at the new price.

By maintaining a niche, you stand to make a fair sum, even while other sellers benefit from your work. If a specific group of sellers band together to undercut you and post at times when you aren't guarding the AH, the process must be started again.

Guild Creation and Upkeep

So you've decided that you want to start a guild. Guilds are an integral part of the game, allowing like-minded players to join together to achieve goals, not to mention getting to wear a really cool tabard. In explaining guilds, we'll cover the formation of a guild and its upkeep.

FORMING THE GUILD

A charter is the first item required on your path to having a guild. Charters may be purchased from Guild Masters located in each of the major cities. Local guards are quite eager to point the way, so it shouldn't be too hard to the necessary NPCs.

Alliance Charters	
City	NPC
Darnassus	Lysheana
Ironforge	Jondor Steelbrow
Stormwind City	Aldwin Laughlin

Horde Charters	
City	NPC
Orgrimmar	Urtrun Clanbringer
Thunder Bluff	Krumn
Undercity	Christopher Drakul

When you purchase your charter you are asked to supply a name for your guild. Be sure to choose an appropriate (non-offensive) name. Give the name some thought and allow it to express your guild and what it stands for. In the wee hours of the morning after you've been smashing Murlocs for hours on end, the name "Crazy Murloc Deathbringers" might sound completely appropriate. However, shorter names that roll off the tongue with ease are quite successful. Your guild tag will catch the attention of players, so be sure it's the kind of attention you're seeking.

Here's a suggestion that alleviates frustration when purchasing the charter; be sure to have two or three alternate versions of your guild name that you're comfortable with. Many times a name will be disallowed by Blizzard if it has been taken by another group.

Charters cost ten silver pieces and require 9 additional "signatures" for completion. This is easy if you have 9 friends running around waiting to come to your aid. However, many guilds are started by soliciting the aid of low-level characters in the starter zones. There is also a guild recruiting channel available in large cities where you can broadcast your new guild and need for signatures. Each signature must come from a separate account. In other words you can't have your buddy log onto his account and sign nine times with all of his characters. People who are already in guilds are also unable to sign your charter.

Once you have all of your signatures, return to the Guild Master and submit the charter.

Congratulations! Your guild has been formed. Each of the players who signed your charter receive a system message informing them that they are a founding member of your guild. These players automatically receive a default rank of "Member." The person who purchased the charter becomes the initial "Leader" of the guild.

GUILD COMMANDS

There are basic commands that guild leaders and officers use to perform certain actions while running a guild. The table below includes all of the current text commands for guild actions.

Crowning Another

There is a safeguard in place that prevents the guild from disbanding if a guild leader chooses to quit in the heat of the moment. A guild leader may not quit without designating another leader for the guild. This is not the case however if the guild leader chooses the /gdisband option.

Guild Commands

COMMAND	ACTION PERFORMED
/ginfo	Basic information about your guild
/g <message>	Sends chat text to all members of the guild
/o <message>	Sends chat text to all officers and leaders of the guild
/ginvite <player>	Invites player to join your guild
/gremove <player>	Removes player from guild
/gpromote <player>	Promotes player one rank
/gdemote <player>	Demotes player one rank
/gmotd <message>	Guild message seen by all members upon login to game
/gquit	Removes you from a guild
/groster	Provides a complete roster for guild (accessible to officers and leaders only)
/gleader <player>	Changes guild leader to chosen player. (guild leader command only)
/gdisband	Permanently disbands guild

You may also perform many guild commands through the guild screen. This screen can be opened by hitting the "O" key. Click on the "Guild" tab at the bottom of the screen to view information about your guild.

THE GUILD SCREEN

The guild screen shows members who are currently online. At the top of the screen you'll see "Show Offline Members." By clicking the box you'll be able to view a complete guild roster.

At the bottom of this list you'll see "Show Player Status." Click on the arrow icon to display additional guild status information.

You may sort each section by clicking on the title. For example if you click on "Level" the roster will be sorted by character level from lowest to highest or vice versa if you click one more time.

Name	The character's name
Zone	Location of the character
Level	That character's level
Class	The class of that guild member

By highlighting a member name and clicking on it you bring up an additional box that displays information for that particular player. Members who have been designated may demote, promote, or remove at this screen. Regular members may invite the selected character to a group by clicking "Group Invite" at the bottom right of the box.

Rank

The player's position in the guild as determined by the officers of the guild or by those members who are designated to alter ranks.

Note

This section is for public notes regarding the character. Only designated members may enter information here. It can be used to list Professions, let people know if this is an alt, or for inside jokes.

Last Online

Shows the last time the player was online. This is a useful tool for officers when tracking player activity.

GUILD FUNCTIONALITY

Guilds are created with 5 default ranks:

- Initiate
- Member
- Veteran
- Officer
- Leader

Only the guild leader may rename, add or remove ranks. A guild must have a minimum of five ranks and may create up to the maximum of ten ranks. When creating new ranks the system automatically makes the newest rank entered the entry level rank. Take care to enter your ranks from highest to lowest when creating new ones for your guild.

To add new ranks click on the "Guild Control" tab at the bottom right hand corner of the guild screen. Enter the rank name into the "Rank Label." Set the permissions for each rank by checking off the boxes that are appropriate.

Permissions

Command	Function
Speech	The member is allowed to enter text into the guild channel
Officerchat Listen	Allow designated members to read conversations in the officer chat channel
Officerchat Speak	Designated members can type messages in the officer chat channel
Promote	Members can promote other members of the guild
Demote	Members can demote other members of the guild
Invite Member	Members are permitted to invite players to the guild
Remove Player	Members can remove members from the guild
Set Motd	Member has the ability to set the guild message of the day
Edit Public Note	Member is able to edit public notes
View Officer Note	Member is able to view notes written by officers for players
Edit Officer Note	Member is able to change hidden officer notes for each player on the roster

RUNNING YOUR GUILD

Beyond the command, tabard, and charter, there is a great deal of social management that goes into a guild. A huge number of guilds run into problems with their player base at some time or another (bored, anxiety about end-game matters, ego conflicts, drama, and so forth). A skilled guild leader needs to be far more than a good player; these leaders need to be listeners, enforcers, and diplomats. It's not always easy, or sometimes even possible, to fill all of these roles at once! Sound a little intimidating? It should. Don't get involved with guild leadership unless you truly are ready and willing to devote some time and energy into herding cats!

Rules

COMMON GUILD ISSUES

- Loot Distribution
- Proper PvE and PvP Conduct
- Language Restrictions
- Required Play, Grouping, Etc.
- Roleplaying Matters

Creating a good foundation for a guild ensures a long, productive existence for it. This also promotes players who are happy to be members of that guild. If you haven't already done so, create a set of rules for guild members. Keep the rules simple. No one wants to read 43 pages of rules and regulations just to become a member of a guild. Games are meant to be fun and guilds are meant to enhance that experience. You can always adjust the rules as the need arises during the course of your adventures in Azeroth.

Most disputes within guilds arise from arguments over items. When creating your set of guild rules pay close attention to "Loot Rules." Once again, keep them simple. Members need to be aware of rules pertaining to item drops prior to venturing into Instances. Go over rules pertaining to item drops at the start of every group run. Yes, you've said them 100 times before, but stating the rules at the beginning of run through a dungeon alleviates arguments later (usually).

Make sure that members have easy access to these rules at all times.

LOOT DISTRIBUTION

Usually loot issues are easier to handle for the sub-60 levels. Many guilds are going to go with some form of Need Before Greed and stick to it. With the later levels, however, this is a big push to come up with a system for "fairly" distributing Epic loot (and beyond). DKPs, or Dragon Kill Points are used heavily by a number of WoW guilds to try and ensure that people who invest the most time in guild raids get the gear that they want. Other guilds may try to encourage Need Before Greed and rolling even in the raid instances, though this is not as common.

CONDUCT

Some guilds have standards of conduct even with people outside of the guild (or with the opposing faction). You may have things so that guild members must always accept duels, never run from PvP fights in the world, avoid Graveyard Camping for any reason, don't spit, or whatever else. These rules are highly subjective, based on the guild's interests, and should be adhered to by guild members. Anyone who signs on and understands the rules is free to walk away if they disagree.

If a guild member consistently breaks the rules of conduct, use a system of warnings and eventually remove the person from the guild if they are causing internal drama or strife. Be sure that the warning system is in writing, is fair, and is applied evenly whenever possible.

LANGUAGE RESTRICTIONS

If some words are taboo in your guild, be clear about it, correct people when they slip, and be very consistent. There isn't much to say about this matter, save that quite a few guild members have sore points about one word or another. Be sensible and treat guild chat as a large table in the middle of a restaurant; everyone can hear you, even strangers might catch an odd bit of conversation, and feelings can easily be hurt.

REQUIRED PLAY

Larger guilds may require a certain level of playtime per week/month for a person to stay in the guild. This may even be restricted to specific activities (members must participate in one MC/BWL Raid per week, members must put in ten hours of BG time per week). Be very clear with all new members about these requirements.

The trickiest time of all is when your guild considers placing new requirements on members. This is the type of scenario that splits guilds (sometimes taking even the members that wanted the change in the first place). Be very careful of placing demands on your player base.

ROLEPLAYING

Roleplaying guilds may have extra rules to demand that guild chat be IC (in character). For guilds of this sort, there is often a chat channel used on the side for speech outside of your character.

Forums

No one expects you to rush out and purchase a hosting plan or have someone design an elaborate Flash site for the guild. There are many free forum hosting sites available on the web.

On this site, place your guild rules in plain view for members and potential members.

Forums are great for posting information on dungeon crawls, roleplaying events, and guild communication. Be sure to setup a forum for Officers so that issues can be posted for all members in leadership positions.

Choosing Officers

A common drive when choosing officers is to hand out ranks to close friends, but this might not be the best choice for the guild. When you choose officers, be sure to select those players who have proven leadership skills and the ability to arbitrate disputes between members. Everyone handles things differently and it's a good idea to have a diversified group of people as officers.

Use promotions as rewards for dedication to the guild. Players want to upgrade their characters and there are many players who enjoy earning rank within the guild structure.

As a leader, remember to trust your officers and support their decisions. You've taken the time to select them and put them in charge; don't hover over them.

Recruiting

There are many ways to recruit members for your guild. There is no right or wrong way. Recruiting processes should be determined by your vision for the guild.

Do you want a guild with hundreds of members? Perhaps you want a small guild that will focus on exploring all of the content that the game provides. Guilds come in all sizes as well as types. Some guilds massively recruit members by issuing random invites in starter zones. A lot of role playing guilds use an interview process.

Do what's best for you and your guild.

The Tabard

Admit it. We all love those tabards. They show the community that we're all together in everything we do. Tabard selection can be a process that the guild leader handles or it can be a guild decision. Many guilds have members contribute what they can toward the purchase of the guild design. Tabard designs cost ten gold pieces. Individual tabards cost one gold piece (and are influenced by faction and PvP discounts).

THE TABARD VIEWER

Guild tabard designs are purchased from the Guild Master in major cities. Speak to the Guild Master and select "I'd like to create a Guild Crest." A guild tabard design may only be purchased by the guild leader but members may view the selections available.

Tabard Creation	
Icon	The image that appears on the front and back of the member tabard. Click the directional arrows to browse the available icons
Icon Color	Selects the icon color
Border	Selects the style of border for the tabard
Border Color	Select the border color
Background	Select the overall color for the tabard

Once you've made a choice for each selection click "Accept." The tabard design will appear on your equipped tabard. If members have trouble viewing the design on their tabards this is remedied with a quick logout and login.

Guild Events

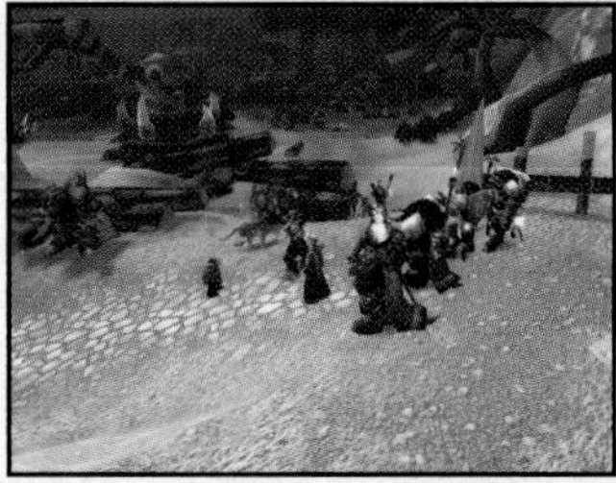

Even the most hardcore "lone wolf" player enjoys a planned guild event. Be sure to post the event several days in advance so that members can arrange to be present. The typical event is completing quests in an "Instance." These events bring experience and item upgrades for members.

Rewards and Discipline

Reward good behavior and punish bad behavior. No guild leader is perfect and sometimes members step over the line in regard to rules. Your members look to you and your officers to maintain the guild environment they expected when they joined. Offensive conversation in the guild channel, bad conduct on a guild raid, or constant belligerence can undermine a guild quickly if not dealt with just as quickly.

Reward members who show dedication to the guild. You don't have to empty your coin purse to do so. Acknowledging the generosity of a player's time, skills, and knowledge is just as good. You can create special ranks to show praise, have a forum for "Guild Mate of the Month," or an event to honor the player(s). A little praise goes a long way!

The secret to being a great guild leader or having a great guild is respect for the players who bear the tabard. The friendships that can develop from guild membership can be some of the most rewarding out there.

Druids are the keepers of nature and the world itself. Using their force of will and spirit, these protectors wander the Emerald Dream, focusing the power of the land. As a Druid, you have the power to become a defensive Bear, an aggressive Cat, an Aquatic creature, a Traveling feline, and use different spells to rejuvenate yourself and allies while dealing damage to enemies. Outside, where nature seems so close at hand, your control of roots are able to hold enemies in place, plaguing melee opponents and certain archers with frustration. Ultimately, Druids are jacks of all trades and masters of none; they can fill almost any role well, and round out groups splendidly.

Lore

We met above the Wailing Caverns and meditated for a short time to see if the stories were true. Indeed, I could feel that the place had become lost to our order, and that some of the finest Druids of the region were now against us. It was a sad thought, but we pushed it out of our minds and rose together. We were to go into the caves below in several groups, with my night elves going in second, after our Tauren friends cleared the way. Others were there, from both the so-called Alliance and Horde, preparing to compete over land, riches, and other banal things. Our order made great efforts to be past such concerns.

The Raptors below were different than the Sunscales outside; diseases of mind and body had affected them, turning them into something unnatural. Several of them had been hiding in peripheral caverns and came out when we passed deeper into the Wailing Caverns. I held a moment to bring my focus together, then raised my arms to call nature's strength into the room. My companions changed into their altered selves to defend us, as Calimos took the form of a great bear, and Mariyn became a cat to slip behind our attackers. Together, we lashed into the beasts until peace was granted them. Then we continued.

Our battles took us to the very end of Wailing Caverns, where the darkest monsters I have faced were waiting. The taint was in almost all things that lived in those hallowed chambers, but we returned it to a state of waiting. I don't think we could have succeeded without the Tauren's help, but isn't that the way of things? Together, we stood against this darkness, as we did against the Burning Legion. If we continue to cooperate, perhaps I will see the Emerald Dream again before I pass into the world.

Introduction to Playing the Class

If you like the idea of being able to play a different set of classes with the same character, Druids may be the perfect thing for you! These casters are able to heal, nuke, root, and engage in modest melee skirmishes, and they can use Shapeshifting to become powerful beasts. Through these forms, Druids can mimic Warriors and Rogues! This means that a Druid can act as a group's backup Tank, a melee DPS class, a ranged caster, or a spare Healer. It's hard to go wrong with options like that, and the Talent choices of a Druid make a huge difference in terms of customization.

Groups don't often grab a Druid as their first choice because of uncertainty over the Druid's specialization, but there are certainly ways to make a Druid appealing in solo play, group action, or PvP. With a focus on healing abilities, Druids are able to respond extremely well to backup and even some primary Healer duties. Specced for soloing, a Druid can rip through targets as a DPS attacker and switch from Cat Form to their Caster (natural) form to heal after battles; it's a low downtime, exciting way to work through the game's outside areas.

Also, people look to Druids for their stackable buffs; other classes are able to raise specific attributes (Intellect, Stamina, and sometimes Spirit from Mages and Priests). The Druid buffs add a damage shield, armor, and a bonus to all attributes and Resistances. At the end of the Feral Combat line, there is even an aura to buff Critical rates for everyone nearby while the Druid is in one of their animal forms. Druids are clearly one of the best classes in the game for pure buffs. Especially in the very late raid content of the game, nobody is going to turn away extra Resistance buffs!

Available Races	
Night Elf	Tauren

What do Attributes Mean to Me?	
Strength	Slightly Increased Damage
Stamina	Higher Health (Good for All Forms)
Agility	Raises Chance to Get a Critical Hit and Dodge, Raises Cat Form DPS (Best for Cat Form)
Intellect	Higher Mana Total, More Spell Criticals (Best for Caster Form)
Spirit	Improves Health/Mana Recovery in All Forms

ITEMS AND EQUIPMENT

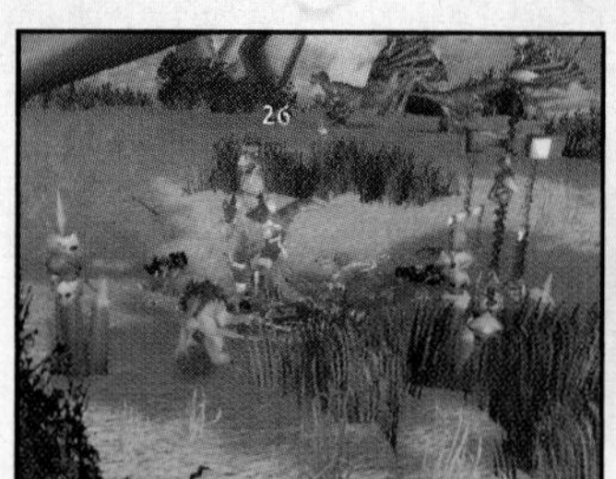

Druids start the game able to wear leather armor, and they never upgrade to anything heavier. These casters can initially wield staves without any problems. Beyond that, they are able to train in one- and two-handed maces, daggers, and fist weapons. Staves are desired for their bonuses to caster attributes, while weapons with Agility/Stamina bonuses are great for those interested in Cat Form damage. The best choice for your Druid is one that enhances your preferred style of fighting (Strength, Agility, Stamina if you prefer the melee aspects of Druids, or choose higher Intellect and Spirit to follow the caster line).

Procs In Animal Form

If you spend a great deal of time in Bear or Cat form, do not seek weaponry with Proc effects. These do not trigger while you are fighting as an animal, thus they are worthless to you. Instead, get items that increase your attributes!

Druids worry far more about armor than most of the other caster classes. The reason is that Druids end up tanking from time to time (while soloing, in PvP certainly, and even in certain groups). Bear Form adds some very nice bonuses to your armor, turning that feeble leather into something worthy of respect. Because Bear Form armor is calculated based on the armor a Druid has in their normal form, it is of great value to find Leather with nice stats. If powerful enchantments cannot be afforded, even simple armor patches are worth applying for this very reason.

Attributes are rough to deal with as a Druid (you need practically everything). Intellect is very nice to supplement the weaker mana pool of the Druid. Spirit helps all of the Forms to a decent extent. Beyond that, look for gear that improves your favorite form; Strength and Stamina for the mighty Bear, Agility and Stamina for the subtle Cat.

CHOOSING YOUR PROFESSION

Druids can benefit from a wide range of professions. Skinning and Leatherworking is an obvious combination for players who are new to the game; these players won't have access to as much higher-level equipment, the money for Rare gear, or the dungeon skills to comfortably delve for items early.

If you aren't worried about creating baseline equipment for your Druid, Herbalism and Alchemy are better choices. These carry far more potential for money by selling spare herbs. Moreover, potions are very nice for Druids because so many different attributes are useful to them. Thus, almost everything an Alchemist learns is put to use in one form or another.

As for secondary skills, Druids aren't driven to use them as often. Cooking and First Aid, while being staples for many melee classes, are are still of great use for Druids.

Class Abilities

Druid Abilities are divided by the form needed to cast them. For ranged magic, the Caster Form of the Druid is used. As a Bear, the Druid can take far more damage and use Warrior-type abilities. As a Cat, the Druid is stealthy and able to deal much higher damage.

Notice that the form of a Druid also dictates which secondary bar they have (mana for the Caster, Rage for the Bear, and Energy for the Cat).

Druid Forms

Form	Function	Survivability
Caster	Healing, Ranged Damage	Low
Bear	Tanking, Melee	High
Aquatic	Fast/Safe Water Travel	Low
Cat	Melee DPS, Stealth, Track Humanoids	Low
Travel	Super Fast Land Travel	Low
Dire Bear	Tanking, Melee	Immense
Moonkin	Buff to Group Spell Criticals, Balance Spell Use (Balance Talent)	High

Balance

Wrath

Wrath is a faster spell for direct damage (compared to the more powerful Starfire that you learn later). When there is a short interval for casting a ranged spell, use Wrath.

Rank	Level	Mana	Range	Casting Time	Cooldown	Cost to Train	Effects
1	1	20	30yd	1.5	—	—	Causes 12 to 14 Nature damage to the target
2	6	35	30yd	1.7	—	1	Causes 25 to 29 Nature damage to the target
3	14	55	30yd	2	—	9	Causes 44 to 52 Nature damage to the target
4	22	70	30yd	2	—	30	Causes 63 to 73 Nature damage to the target.
5	30	100	30yd	2	—	60	Causes 101 to 115 Nature damage to the target.
6	38	125	30yd	2	—	1 20	Causes 139 to 157 nature damage to the target.
7	46	155	30yd	2	—	2	Causes 188 to 210 Nature damage to the target.
8	54	180	30yd	2	—	2 80	Causes 236 to 264 Nature damage to the target.

Moonfire

Moonfire is a very powerful spell when used correctly. Spamable, because it is an instant, this spell is sometimes used as a way to dump mana into damage. However, this removes the power of the DOT that Moonfire places on a target, and ultimately destroys the mana efficiency of the spell.

Rank	Level	Mana	Range	Casting Time	Cooldown	Cost to Train	Effects
1	4	25	30yd	IC	—	1	Burns the enemy for 7 to 9 Arcane damage and then an additional 12 Arcane damage over 9 sec.
2	10	50	30yd	IC	—	3	Burns the enemy for 13 to 17 Arcane damage and then an additional 32 Arcane damage over 12 sec.
3	16	75	30yd	IC	—	18	Burns the enemy for 25 to 31 Arcane damage and then an additional 52 Arcane damage over 12 sec.
4	22	105	30yd	IC	—	30	Burns the enemy for 40 to 48 Arcane damage and then an additional 80 Arcane damage over 12 sec.
5	28	150	30yd	IC	—	50	Burns the enemy for 61 to 73 Arcane damage and then an additional 124 Arcane damage over 12 sec.
6	34	190	30yd	IC	—	1	Burns the enemy for 81 to 97 Arcane damage and then an additional 164 Arcane damage over 12 sec.
7	40	235	30yd	IC	—	1 90	Burns the enemy for 105 to 125 Arcane damage and then an additional 212 Arcane damage over 12 sec.
8	46	280	30yd	IC	—	2	Burns the enemy for 130 to 154 Arcane damage and then an additional 264 Arcane damage over 12 sec.
9	52	325	30yd	IC	—	2 60	Burns the enemy for 157 to 185 Arcane damage and then an additional 320 Arcane damage over 12 sec.
10	58	375	30yd	IC	—	3 20	Burns the enemy for 189 to 221 Arcane damage and then an additional 384 Arcane damage over 12 sec.

Thorns

Thorns is a ten minute buff that is castable on yourself or others. Ideal for anyone who is going to be tanking.

Rank	Level	Mana	Range	Casting Time	Cooldown	Cost to Train	Effects
1	6	35	30yd	IC	—	1	Thorns sprout from the friendly target causing 3 Nature damage to attackers when hit. Lasts 10 min.
2	14	60	30yd	IC	—	9	Thorns sprout from the friendly target causing 6 Nature damage to attackers when hit. Lasts 10 min.
3	24	105	30yd	IC	—	40	Thorns sprout from the friendly target causing 9 Nature damage to attackers when hit. Lasts 10 min.
4	34	170	30yd	IC	—	1	Thorns sprout from the friendly target causing 12 Nature damage to attackers when hit. Lasts 10 min.
5	44	240	30yd	IC	—	1 80	Thorns sprout from the friendly target causing 15 Nature damage to attackers when hit. Lasts 10 min.
6	54	320	30yd	IC	—	2 80	Thorns sprout from the friendly target causing 18 Nature damage to attackers when hit. Lasts 10 min.

Entangling Roots

Entangling Roots can only be cast outdoors. This spell has a long duration, only has a moderate chance to break on damage, and allows Druids to abuse melee targets.

Rank	Level	Mana	Range	Casting Time	Cooldown	Cost to Train	Effects
1	8	50	30yd	1.5	—	2	Roots the target in place and causes 20 nature damage over 12 sec. Only useable outdoors.
2	18	65	30yd	1.5	—	19	Roots the target in place and causes 50 nature damage over 15 sec. Only useable outdoors.
3	28	80	30yd	1.5	—	50	Roots the target in place and causes 90 nature damage over 18 sec. Only useable outdoors.
4	36	95	30yd	1.5	—	1 20	Roots the target in place and causes 140 nature damage over 21 sec. Only useable outdoors.
5	48	110	30yd	1.5	—	2 20	Roots the target in place and causes 200 nature damage over 24 sec. Only useable outdoors.
6	58	125	30yd	1.5	—	3 20	Roots the target in place and causes 270 nature damage over 27 sec. Only useable outdoors.

Nature's Grasp

Nature's Grasp is a Talent-learned ability that is used on your Druid. When active, the ability has a chance to proc when your Druid is attacked, casting a mana-free Entangling Roots on the aggressor. The Improved Nature's Grasp talent makes this "chance" 100%.

Rank	Level	Mana	Range	Casting Time	Cooldown	Cost to Train	Effects
1	10	50	—	IC	1 minute		While active, any time an enemy strikes the caster they have a 35% chance to become afflicted by Entangling Roots (Rank 1). Only useable outdoors. 1 charge. Lasts 45 sec.
2	18	65	—	IC	1 min	95	While active, any time an enemy strikes the caster they have a 35% chance to become afflicted by Entangling Roots (Rank 2). Only useable outdoors. 1 charge. Lasts 45 sec.
3	28	80	—	IC	1 min	2 50	While active, any time an enemy strikes the caster they have a 35% chance to become afflicted by Entangling Roots (Rank 3). Only useable outdoors. 1 charge. Lasts 45 sec.
4	38	95	—	IC	1 min	6	While active, any time an enemy strikes the caster they have a 35% chance to become afflicted by Entangling Roots (Rank 4). Only useable outdoors. 1 charge. Lasts 45 sec.
5	48	110	—	IC	1 min	11	While active, any time an enemy strikes the caster they have a 35% chance to become afflicted by Entangling Roots (Rank 5). Only useable outdoors. 1 charge. Lasts 45 sec.
6	58	125	—	IC	1 min	16	While active, any time an enemy strikes the caster they have a 35% chance to become afflicted by Entangling Roots (Rank 6). Only useable outdoors. 1 charge. Lasts 45 sec.

Faerie Fire

Faerie Fire debuffs the armor of an enemy and keeps them from being able to Stealth or use Invisibility.

Rank	Level	Mana	Range	Casting Time	Cooldown	Cost to Train	Effects
1	18	55	30yd	IC	—	19	Decrease the armor of the target by 175 for 40 sec. While affected, the target cannot stealth or turn invisible.
2	30	75	30yd	IC	—	60	Decrease the armor of the target by 285 for 40 sec. While affected, the target cannot stealth or turn invisible.
3	42	95	30yd	IC	—	1 60	Decrease the armor of the target by 395 for 40 sec. While affected, the target cannot stealth or turn invisible.
4	54	115	30yd	IC	—	2 80	Decrease the armor of the target by 505 for 40 sec. While affected, the target cannot stealth or turn invisible.

Hibernate

Hibernate casts a sleep spell on Beasts, Dragonkin, Ghost Wolf Shaman, Hunter pets, and Druid in Feral form.

Rank	Level	Mana	Range	Casting Time	Cooldown	Cost to Train	Effects
1	18	90	30yd	1.5sec	—	19	Forces the enemy target to sleep for up to 20 sec. Any damage will awaken the target. Only one target can be forced to hibernate at a time. Only works on Beasts and Dragonkin.
2	38	120	30yd	1.5sec	—	1 20	Forces the enemy target to sleep for up to 30 sec. Any damage will awaken the target. Only one target can be forced to hibernate at a time. Only works on Beasts and Dragonkin.
3	58	150	30yd	1.5sec	—	3 20	Forces the enemy target to sleep for up to 40 sec. Any damage will awaken the target. Only one target can be forced to hibernate at a time. Only works on Beasts and Dragonkin.

Omen of Clarity

Omen of Clarity is a Talent-learned ability that is cast on yourself. The buff allows Clearcasting a chance to proc after your melee attacks. The result is that the next spell or action requires no mana, Rage, or Energy!

Rank	Prerequisites	Effects
1	10 Points in Balance, 5 Points in Natural Weapons	Imbues the Druid with natural energy. Each of the druid's melee attacks has a chance of causing the caster to enter a Clearcasting state. The Clearcasting state reduces the Mana, Rage, or Energy cost of your next damage or healing spell or offensive ability by 100%. Lasts 5 minutes.

Starfire

Starfire is a great way to start fights when you are soloing. Though sporting a longer casting time, the damage and efficiency of this spell is noteworthy.

Rank	Level	Mana	Range	Casting Time	Cooldown	Cost to Train	Effects
1	20	95	30yd	3.5	—	20	Causes 89 to 109 Arcane damage to the target.
2	26	135	30yd	3.5	—	45	Causes 137 to 167 Arcane damage to the target
3	34	180	30yd	3.5	—	1	Causes 201 to 241 Arcane damage to the target.
4	42	230	30yd	3.5	—	1 60	Causes 280 to 334 Arcane damage to the target.
5	50	275	30yd	3.5	—	2 30	Causes 362 to 428 Arcane damage to the target.
6	58	315	30yd	3.5	—	3 20	Causes 445 to 525 Arcane damage to the target
7	60	340	30 yd	3.5 sec	—	—	Causes 496 to 584 Arcane damage to the target.

Soothe Animal

Soothe Animal reduces the aggro range of a Beast.

Rank	Level	Mana	Range	Casting Time	Cooldown	Cost to Train	Effects
1	22	50	40yd	1.5 sec	—	30	Soothes the target beast, reducing the range at which it will attack you by 10 yards. Only affects Beast targets level 40 or lower. Lasts 15 sec.
2	38	75	40yd	1.5 sec	—	1 20	Soothes the target beast, reducing the range at which it will attack you by 10 yards. Only affects Beast targets level 55 or lower. Lasts 15 sec.

Hurricane

Hurricane is a ranged channeled AoE that deals modest damage and reduces enemy attack speed.

Rank	Level	Mana	Range	Casting Time	Cooldown	Cost to Train	Effects
1	40	880	30 yd	IC	1 min	1 20	Creates a violent storm in the target area, causing 70 Nature damage to enemies every 1 sec, and reducing the attack speed of enemies by 20%. Lasts 10 sec. Druid must channel to maintain the spell.
2	50	1180	30 yd	IC	1 min	2 30	Creates a violent storm in the target area, causing 100 Nature damage to enemies every 1 sec, and reducing the attack speed of enemies by 20%. Lasts 10 sec. Druid must channel to maintain the spell.
3	60	1495	30 yd	IC	1 min	3 40	Creates a violent storm in the target area, causing 134 Nature damage to enemies every 1 sec, and reducing the attack speed of enemies by 20%. Lasts 10 sec. Druid must channel to maintain the spell.

Barkskin

Barkskin offers the ability to avoid spell interruptions from damage and reduces incoming physical damage by 20%. The cost is that your Druid's spells take a full second longer to cast, and melee speed is reduced by 20% for your character.

Rank	Level	Casting Time	Cooldown	Mana Cost	Cost to Train	Effects
1	44	IC	1 min	—	1 80	The druid's skin becomes as tough as bark. Physical Damage taken is reduced by 20%. While protected, damaging attacks will not cause spell-casting delays but non-instant spells take 1 sec longer to cast and melee combat is slowed by 25%. Lasts 15 sec.

Feral Combat

Demoralizing Roar

Demoralizing Roar acts like a Warrior's Demoralizing Shout. It causes an AoE debuff to enemy Attack Power.

Rank	Level	Rage	Range	Casting Time	Cooldown	Cost to Train	Effects
1	10	10	—	IC	—	3	The druid roars, decreasing nearby enemies' attack power by 30. Lasts 30 sec.
2	20	10	—	IC	—	20	The druid roars, decreasing nearby enemies' attack power by 50. Lasts 30 sec.
3	32	10	—	IC	—	80	The druid roars, decreasing nearby enemies' attack power by 65. Lasts 30 sec.
4	42	10	—	IC	—	1 60	The druid roars, decreasing nearby enemies' attack power by 100. Lasts 30 sec.
5	52	10	—	IC	—	2 60	The druid roars, decreasing nearby enemies' attack power by 130. Lasts 30 sec.

Enrage

Enrage generates 20 Free Rage, but reduces Bear Form armor by 16% and Dire Bear armor by 27%. Use this before a fight, wait for the ten seconds of debuff to expire, then engage a target.

Rank	Level	Rage	Range	Casting Time	Cooldown	Cost to Train	Effects

Bash

Bash is used to Stun a target for a short period. This only costs ten Rage, and is on a one-minute timer.

Rank	Level	Rage	Range	Casting Time	Cooldown	Cost to Train	Effects
1	14	10	9yd	IC	1 min	9	Stuns the target for 2 sec
2	30	10	9yd	IC	1 min	55	Stuns the target for 3 sec
3	46	10	9yd	IC	1 min	1 90	Stuns the target for 4 sec.

Swipe

Swipe deals light melee damage against up to three targets (while in Bear or Dire Bear Form). This is an instant attack.

Rank	Level	Rage	Range	Casting Time	Cooldown	Cost to Train	Effects
1	16	20	9yd	IC	4sec	18	Swipe 3 nearby enemies, inflicting 18 damage.
2	24	20	9yd	IC	4sec	40	Swipe 3 nearby enemies, inflicting 25 damage.
3	34	20	9yd	IC	4sec	1	Swipe 3 nearby enemies, inflicting 36 damage.
4	44	20	9yd	IC	4sec	1 80	Swipe 3 nearby enemies, inflicting 60 damage.
5	54	20	9yd	IC	4sec	2 80	Swipe 3 nearby enemies, inflicting 83 damage.

Maul

Maul is a Bear ability that is very similar to Heroic Strike. This uses a substantial amount of Rage. The bonus damage done and the increased Threat of the attack are both boons.

Rank	Level	Rage	Range	Casting Time	Cooldown	Cost to Train	Effects
1	10	15	—	Next Melee	—	10	Increases the druid's next attack by 18 damage.
2	18	15	—	Next Melee	—	19	Increases the druid's next attack by 27 damage.
3	26	15	—	Next Melee	—	45	Increases the druid's next attack by 37 damage.
4	34	15	—	Next Melee	—	1	Increases the druid's next attack by 49 damage.
5	42	15	—	Next Melee	—	1 60	Increases the druid's next attack by 71 damage.
6	50	15	—	Next Melee	—	2 30	Increases the druid's next attack by 101 damage.
7	58	15	—	Next Melee	—	3 20	Increases the druid's next attack by 128 damage.

Claw

Claw is a Cat Form ability that offers instant damage and a single Combo Point (much like a Rogue's Sinister Strike).

Rank	Level	Energy	Range	Casting Time	Cooldown	Cost to Train	Effects
1	20	45	9yd	IC	—	20	Claw the enemy, causing 27 additional damage. Awards 1 combo point.
2	28	45	9yd	IC	—	50	Claw the enemy, causing 39 additional damage. Awards 1 combo point.
3	38	45	9yd	IC	—	1 20	Claw the enemy, causing 57 additional damage. Awards 1 combo point.
4	48	45	9yd	IC	—	2 20	Claw the enemy, causing 88 additional damage. Awards 1 combo point.
5	58	45	9yd	IC	—	3 20	Claw the enemy, causing 115 additional damage. Awards 1 combo point.

Feral Charge

Feral Charge is a Bear Talent-learned ability that closes the distance with a target, interrupting any spells and immobilizing them for a short period.

Rank	Prerequisite	Effect
1	10 Points in Feral Combat	Requires Bear Form, Dire Bear Form. Causes you to charge an enemy, immobilizing and interrupting any spell being cast for 4 seconds. 8-25 yard range, costs 5+ Rage, 15 second cooldown.

Prowl

Prowl allows Druids in Cat Form to enter Stealth outside of combat.

Rank	Level	Energy	Range	Casting Time	Cooldown	Cost to Train	Effects
1	20	—	—	IC	10sec	20 ●	Allows the Druid to prowl around, but reduces your speed to 60% of normal. Lasts until cancelled.
2	40	—	—	IC	10sec	1 ● 40 ●	Allows the Druid to prowl around, but reduces your speed to 65% of normal. Lasts until cancelled.
3	60	—	—	IC	10sec	3 ● 40 ●	Allows the Druid to prowl around, but reduces your speed to 70% of normal. Lasts until cancelled.

Rip

Rip uses Cat Form Combo Points to deal a powerful DOT attack. Rip is a potent Finishing Move.

Rank	Level	Energy	Range	Casting Time	Cooldown	Cost to Train	Effects
1	20	30	9yd	IC	—	20 ●	Finishing move that causes damage over time. Damage increases per combo point: 1 point: 54 damage over 12 sec. 2 points: 90 damage over 12 sec. 3 points: 126 damage over 12 sec. 4 points: 162 damage over 12 sec. 5 points: 198 damage over 12 sec.
2	28	30	9yd	IC	—	50 ●	Finishing move that causes damage over time. Damage increases per combo point: 1 point: 78 damage over 12 sec. 2 points: 132 damage over 12 sec. 3 points: 186 damage over 12 sec. 4 points: 240 damage over 12 sec. 5 points: 294 damage over 12 sec.
3	36	30	9yd	IC	—	1 ● 10 ●	Finishing move that causes damage over time. Damage increases per combo point: 1 point : 108 damage over 12 sec. 2 points: 180 damage over 12 sec. 3 points: 252 damage over 12 sec. 4 points: 324 damage over 12 sec. 5 points: 396 damage over 12 sec.
4	44	30	9yd	IC	—	1 ● 80 ●	Finishing move that causes damage over time. Damage increases per combo point: 1 point : 156 damage over 12 sec. 2 points: 258 damage over 12 sec. 3 points: 360 damage over 12 sec. 4 points: 462 damage over 12 sec. 5 points: 564 damage over 12 sec.
5	52	30	9yd	IC	—	2 ● 60 ●	Finishing move that causes damage over time. Damage increases per combo point: 1 point: 216 damage over 12 sec. 2 points: 360 damage over 12 sec. 3 points:504 damage over 12 sec. 4 points: 648 damage over 12 sec. 5 points: 792 damage over 12 sec.
6	60	30	9yd	IC	—	3 ● 40 ●	Finishing move that causes damage over time. Damage increases per combo point: 1 point : 300 damage over 12 sec. 2 points: 498 damage over 12 sec. 3 points: 696 damage over 12 sec. 4 points: 894 damage over 12 sec. 5 points: 1092 damage over 12 sec.

Shred

Shred is a Cat Form's backstab. Use this from behind a target to deal very high damage in a single attack. Shred awards one Combo Point.

Rank	Level	Energy	Range	Casting Time	Cooldown	Cost to Train	Effects
1	22	60	9yd	IC	—	30 ●	Shred the target, causing 225% damage plus 54 to the target. Must be behind the target. Awards 1 combo point.
2	30	60	9yd	IC	—	60 ●	Shred the target, causing 225% damage plus 72 to the target. Must be behind the target. Awards 1 combo point.
3	38	60	9yd	IC	—	1 ● 20 ●	Shred the target, causing 225% damage plus 99 to the target. Must be behind the target. Awards 1 combo point.
4	46	60	9yd	IC	—	2 ●	Shred the target, causing 225% damage plus 144 to the target. Must be behind the target. Awards 1 combo point.
5	54	60	9yd	IC	—	2 ● 80 ●	Shred the target, causing 225% damage plus 180 to the target. Must be behind the target. Awards 1 combo point.

Rake

Rake is another Cat Form attack that is instant. This one deals some damage up front, but places a substantial DoT on the target. This awards a single Combo Point.

Rank	Level	Energy	Range	Casting Time	Cooldown	Cost to Train	Effects
1	24	40	9yd	IC	—	40 ●	Rake the target for 19 damage and an additional 39 damage over 9 sec. Awards one combo point.
2	34	40	9yd	IC	—	1 ●	Rake the target for 28 damage and an additional 57 damage over 9 sec. Awards one combo point.
3	44	40	9yd	IC	—	1 ● 80 ●	Rake the target for 43 damage and an additional 75 damage over 9 sec. Awards one combo point.
4	54	40	9yd	IC	—	2 ● 80 ●	Rake the target for 58 damage and an additional 96 damage over 9 sec. Awards one combo point.

Tiger's Fury

Tiger's Fury adds damage to every attack your Cat Form Druid makes for a short duration.

Rank	Level	Energy	Range	Casting Time	Cooldown	Cost to Train	Effects
1	24	30	—	IC	1 sec	40 ●	Increases damage done by 10 for 6 sec.
2	36	30	—	IC	1 sec	1 ● 10 ●	Increases damage done by 20 for 6 sec.
3	48	30	—	IC	1 sec	2 ● 20 ●	Increases damage done by 30 for 6 sec.
4	60	30	—	IC	1 sec	3 ● 40 ●	Increases damage done by 40 for 6 sec.

Dash

Dash is used in Cat Form and acts like a Sprint. Your character can even increase movement speed while Prowling.

Rank	Level	Energy	Casting Time	Cooldown	Cost to Train	Effects
1	26	—	IC	5 min	45 ●	Increases movement speed by 50% for 15 sec. Does not break Prowling.
2	46	—	IC	5 min	2 ●	Increases movement speed by 60 % for 15 sec. Does not break Prowling.

Challenging Roar

Challenging Roar forces all enemies to focus on your Bear for a short time. Because of the ten minute cooldown, this should only be used when aggro is going crazy and your group's healers are in danger.

Rank	Level	Rage	Range	Casting Time	Cooldown	Cost to Train	Effects
1	28	15	—	IC	10 min	50 ●	Forces all nearby enemies to focus on you for 6 seconds.

Cower

Cower is used in Cat Form to reduce aggro.

Rank	Level	Energy	Range	Casting Time	Cooldown	Cost to Train	Effects
1	28	20	9yd	IC	10 sec	50●	Cower, causing no damage but lowering your threat a small amount, making the enemy less likely to attack you.
2	40	20	9yd	IC	10 sec	1 ● 40 ●	Cower, causing no damage but lowering your threat a medium amount, making the enemy less likely to attack you.
3	52	20	9yd	IC	10 sec	2 ● 60 ●	Cower, causing no damage but lowering your threat a large amount, making the enemy less likely to attack you.

Faerie Fire (Feral)

Faerie Fire (Feral) is Talent-learned and functions just like normal Faerie Fire, but these versions can be used in Cat and Bear Forms.

Rank	Level	Rage	Range	Casting Time	Cooldown	Cost to Train	Effects
2	30	5	30yd	IC	—	10	Decrease the armor of the target by 285 for 40 sec. While affected, the target cannot stealth or turn invisible.
3	42	5	30yd	IC	—	1 50	Decrease the armor of the target by 395 for 40 sec. While affected, the target cannot stealth or turn invisible.
4	54	5	30yd	IC	—	2 70	Decrease the armor of the target by 505 for 40 sec. While affected, the target cannot stealth or turn invisible.

Ferocious Bite

Ferocious Bite is similar to a Rogue's Eviscerate. This ability works in Cat Form and converts Combo Points into instant damage.

Rank	Level	Casting Time	Cooldown	Energy Cost	Cost to Train	Effects
1	32	IC	—	35	80	Finishing movethat causes damage per combo point and converts each extra point of energy into 1.0 additional damage. Damage is increased by your Attack Power. 1 point : 50-66 damage, 2 points: 86-102 damage, 3 points: 122-138 damage, 4 points: 158-174 damage, 5 points: 194-210 damage
2	40	IC	—	35	1 26	Finishing move that causes damage per combo point and converts each extra point of energy into 1.5 additional damage. Damage is increased by your Attack Power. 1 point : 79-103 damage, 2 points: 138-162 damage, 3 points: 197-221 damage, 4 points: 256-280 damage, 5 points: 315-339 damage
3	48	IC	—	35	1 98	Finishing move that causes damage per combo point and converts each extra point of energy into 2.0 additional damage. Damage is increased by your Attack Power. 1 point : 122-162 damage, 2 points: 214-254 damage, 3 points: 306-346 damage, 4 points: 398-438 damage, 5 points: 490-530 damage
4	56	IC	—	35	2 70	Finishing move that causes damage per combo point and converts each extra point of energy into 2.5 additional damage. Damage is increased by your Attack Power. 1 point : 173-223 damage, 2 points: 301-351 damage, 3 points: 429-479 damage, 4 points: 557-607 damage, 5 points: 685-735 damage
5	60	IC	—	35	—	Finishing move that causes damage per combo point and converts each extra point of energy into 2.7 additional damage. Damage is increased by your Attack Power. 1 point : 199-259 damage, 2 points: 346-406 damage, 3 points: 493-553 damage, 4 points: 640-700 damage, 5 points: 787-847 damage

Ravage

Ravage is like the Rogue Ambush ability. Cat Form Druids use this from Prowl, and they must be behind the target. This also adds one Combo Point.

Rank	Level	Energy	Range	Casting Time	Cooldown	Cost to Train	Effects
1	32	60	9yd	IC	—	80	Ravage the target, causing 350% damage plus 147 to the target. Must be prowling and behind the target. Awards 1 combo point.
2	42	60	9yd	IC	—	1 60	Ravage the target, causing 350% damage plus 217 to the target. Must be prowling and behind the target. Awards 1 combo point.
3	50	60	9yd	IC	—	2 30	Ravage the target, causing 350% damage plus 273 to the target. Must be prowling and behind the target. Awards 1 combo point.
4	58	60	9yd	IC	—	3 20	Ravage the target, causing 350% damage plus 343 to the target. Must be prowling and behind the target. Awards 1 combo point.

Track Humanoid

Track Humanoids allows Druids in Cat Form to Track Humanoid targets on the mini-map.

Rank	Level	Mana	Range	Casting Time	Cooldown	Cost to Train	Effects
N/A	32	—	—	IC	—	80	Shows the location of all nearby humanoids on the minimap. Only one type of thing can be tracked at a time.

Leader of the Pack

Leader of the Pack is a Talent-learned ability that buffs the party's melee and ranged Critical rates!

Rank	Prerequisite	Effect
1	30 Points in Feral Combat	While in Cat, Bear, or Dire Bear Form, the Leader of the Pack increases ranged and melee critical chance of all party members within 45 yards by 3%. Passive ability.

Frenzied Regeneration

Frenzied Regeneration converts Bear Form Rage into health. If there are no enemies left nearby and you are about to switch to Caster or Cat Form, go ahead and dump your Rage for some extra health.

Rank	Level	Rage	Casting Time	Cooldown	Cost to Train	Effects
1	36	up to 10 per sec	IC	3 min		Converts up to 10 Rage per second into health for 10 sec. Each point of rage is converted into 15 health.
2	46	up to 10 per sec	IC	3 min	2	Converts up to 10 Rage per second into health for 10 sec. Each point of rage is converted into 15 health.
3	56	up to 10 per sec	IC	3 min	3	Converts up to 10 Rage per second into health for 10 sec. Each point of rage is converted into 20 health.

Restoration

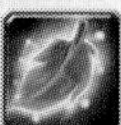

Healing Touch

Healing Touch is the slowest Druid heal spell. This is also the most powerful of the Druid heals, and is used when a large dose of health is needed without being needed as quickly.

Rank	Level	Mana	Range	Casting Time	Cooldown	Cost to Train	Effects
1	1	30	40yd	1.5sec	—	—	Heals a friendly target for 37 to 51
2	8	60	40yd	2sec	—	2	Heals a friendly target for 88 to 112.
3	14	120	40yd	2.5sec	—	9	Heals a friendly target for 195 to 243.
4	20	205	40yd	3	—	20	Heals a friendly target for 363 to 445.
5	26	300	40yd	3.5	—	45	Heals a friendly target for 572 to 694.
6	32	370	40yd	3.5	—	80	Heals a friendly target for 742 to 894.
7	38	445	40yd	3.5	—	1 20	Heals a friendly target for 936 to 1120.
8	44	545	40yd	3.5	—	1 80	Heals a friendly target for 1199 to 1427.
9	50	660	40yd	3.5	—	2 30	Heals a friendly target for 1516 to 1796.
10	56	790	40yd	3.5	—	3	Heals a friendly target for 1890 to 2230.
11	60	800	40 yd	3.5 sec	—	—	Heals a friendly target for 2267-2677.

Mark of the Wild

Mark of the Wild is a buff that covers more areas as it increases in rank. Eventually, Mark of the Wild adds to a friendly target's armor, attributes, and all Resistances.

Rank	Level	Mana	Range	Casting Time	Cooldown	Cost to Train	Effects
1	1	20	30yd	IC	—	10	Increases the friendly target's armor by 25 for 30 min.
2	10	50	30yd	IC	—	3	Increases the friendly target's armor by 65 and all attributes by 2 for 30 min.
3	20	100	30yd	IC	—	20	Increases the friendly target's armor by 105 and all attributes by 5 for 30 min.
4	30	160	30yd	IC	—	60	Increases the friendly target's armor by 150, all attributes by 6 and all resistances by 5 for 30 min.
5	40	240	30yd	IC	—	1 40	Increases the friendly target's armor by 195, all attributes by 8 and all resistances by 10 for 30 min.
6	50	340	30yd	IC	—	2 30	Increases the friendly target's armor by 240, all attributes by 10 and all resistances by 15 for 30 min.
7	60	445	30yd	IC	—	3 40	Increases the friendly target's armor by 285, all attributes by 12 and all resistances by 20 for 30 min.

Rejuvenation

Rejuvenation is an instant-cast heal over time.

Rank	Level	Mana	Range	Casting Time	Cooldown	Cost to Train	Effects
1	4	25	40yd	IC	—	1	Heals the target for 32 over 12 sec.
2	10	40	40yd	IC	—	3	Heals the target for 56 over 12 sec.
3	16	75	40yd	IC	—	18	Heals the target for 116 over 12 sec.
4	22	105	40yd	IC	—	30	Heals the target for 180 over 12 sec.
5	28	135	40yd	IC	—	50	Heals the target for 244 over 12 sec.
6	34	160	40yd	IC	—	1	Heals the target for 304 over 12 sec.
7	40	195	40yd	IC	—	1 40	Heals the target for 388 over 12 sec.
8	46	235	40yd	IC	—	2	Heals the target for 488 over 12 sec.
9	52	280	40yd	IC	—	2 60	Heals the target for 608 over 12 sec.
10	58	335	40yd	IC	—	3 20	Heals the target for 756 over 12 sec.
11	60	360	40 yd	IC	—	—	Heals the target for 888 over 12 sec.

Regrowth

Regrowth is a mixed instant heal and heal over time ability. With a shorter casting time than Healing Touch, Regrowth is best used to take care of the first dose of healing that a tank needs from a big fight.

Rank	Level	Mana	Range	Casting Time	Cooldown	Cost to Train	Effects
1	12	120	40yd	2sec	—	8	Heals a friendly target for 84 to 98 and another 98 over 21 sec.
2	18	205	40yd	2sec	—	19	Heals a friendly target for 164 to 188 and another 175 over 21 sec.
3	24	280	40yd	2sec	—	40	Heals a friendly target for 240 to 274 and another 259 over 21 sec.
4	30	350	40yd	2sec	—	60	Heals a friendly target for 318 to 360 and another 343 over 21 sec
5	36	420	40yd	2sec	—	1 10	Heals a friendly target for 405 to 457 and another 427 over 21 sec.
6	42	510	40yd	2sec	—	1 60	Heals a friendly target for 511 to 575 and another 546 over 21 sec.
7	48	615	40yd	2sec	—	2 20	Heals a friendly target for 646 to 724 and another 686 over 21 sec.
8	54	740	40yd	2sec	—	2 80	Heals a friendly target for 809 to 905 and another 861 over 21 sec.
9	60	880	40yd	2sec	—	3 40	Heals a friendly target for 1003 to 1119 and another 1064 over 21 sec.

Insect Swarm

Insect Swarm is a Talent-learned ability that delivers a light DoT and reduces the target's chance to hit by 2% for the duration of the effect.

Rank	Prerequisite	Effect
1	10 Points in Restoration	The enemy target is swarmed by insects, decreasing their chance to hit by 2% and causing 66 Nature damage over 12 seconds.

Rebirth

Rebirth uses a Seed reagent and a massive amount of a Druid's base mana, but the effects are dramatic. This is an in-combat Rez. Placed on a 30 minute timer, this is still a defining point for all Druids in group and raid situations.

Rank	Level	Mana	Reagent	Casting Time	Cooldown	Cost to Train	Effects
1	20	42	Maple Seed	2sec	30min	20	Returns the spirit to the body, restoring a dead target to life with 400 health and 700 mana.
2	30	42	Stranglethorn Seed	2sec	30min	60	Returns the spirit to the body, restoring a dead target to life with 750 health and 1200 mana.
3	40	42	Ashwood Seed	2sec	30min	1 40	Returns the spirit to the body, restoring a dead target to life with 1100 health and 1700 mana.
4	50	42	Hornbeam Seed	2sec	30min	2 30	Returns the spirit to the body, restoring a dead target to life with 1600 health and 2200 mana.
5	60	42	Ironwood Seed	2sec	30min	3 40	Returns the spirit to the body, restoring a dead target to life with 2200 health and 2800 mana.

Remove Curse

Remove Curse does exactly what you would expect; it removes curses. Only Mages and Druids can do this.

Rank	Level	Mana	Range	Casting Time	Cooldown	Cost to Train	Effects
N/A	24	5	30yd	IC	—	40	Dispels 1 curse from a friendly target.

Abolish Poison

Abolish Poison removes multiple poison effects over time.

Rank	Level	Mana	Range	Casting Time	Cooldown	Cost to Train	Effects
N/A	26	8	30 yd	IC	—	45	Attempts to cure 1 poison effect on the target, and one more poison effect every 2 seconds for 8 sec.

Nature's Swiftness

Nature's Swiftness is a Talent-learned ability on a three minute cooldown. After tapping this, your Druid's next Nature based spell is cast instantly.

Rank	Prerequisite	Effect
1	20 Points in Restoration, 5 Points in Improved Healing Touch	When activated, your next Nature spell becomes an instant cast spell.

Tranquility

Tranquility is a channeled ability that efficiency heals all group members over ten seconds. This produces very little aggro, and the amount healed is enough to make a substantial difference.

Rank	Level	Mana	Range	Casting Time	Cooldown	Cost to Train	Effects
1	30	375	—	IC	5 min	60	Regenerates all nearby group members for 94 every 2 seconds for 10 sec. Druids must channel to maintain the spell.
2	40	505	—	IC	5 min	1 40	Regenerates all nearby group members for 138 every 2 seconds for 10 sec. Druids must channel to maintain the spell.
3	50	695	—	IC	5 min	2 30	Regenerates all nearby group members for 205 every 2 seconds for 10 sec. Druids must channel to maintain the spell.
4	60	925	—	IC	5 min	3 40	Regenerates all nearby group members for 294 every 2 seconds for 10 sec. Druids must channel to maintain the spell.

Innervate

Innervate is a generic class ability. Innervate allows the target chosen to regenerate a massive amount of mana very quickly.

Rank	Minimum Level	Mana	Range	Casting Time	Cooldown	Cost to Train	Effects
1	40	62	30 yd	IC	6 minutes	1 40	Increases the target's Mana regeneration by 400% and allows 100% of the target's Mana regeneration to continue while casting. Lasts 20 sec.

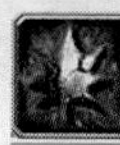

Swiftmend

Swiftmend is the final Talent-learned ability of the Restoration line. This spell consumes a heal over time effect in place of an instant heal.

Rank	Minimum Level	Mana	Range	Casting Time	Cooldown	Cost to Train	Effects
1	40	20% Base	40 yd	IC	15 seconds	—	Consumes a Rejuvenation or Regrowth effect on a friendly target to instantly heal them an amount equal to 12 sec. of Rejuvenation or 15 sec. of Regrowth.

Gift of the Wild

Gift of the Wild acts like Mark of the Wild but is cast on an entire group at once. Obtained from a dropped book.

Rank	Level	Mana	Range	Casting Time	Cooldown	Effects
1	50	900	40 yd	IC	—	Increases the armor of your party members by 240, all attributes by 10 and all resistances by 15 for one hour.
2	60	1200	40 yd	IC	—	Increases the armor of your party members by 285, all attributes by 12 and all resistances by 20 for one hour.

TALENTS

Druid Talents take the class far and wide, enabling the character to become a deft caster, a master of their Shifting forms, or a quality Healer (either in a primary role or as a backup to a Priest). The Balanced line offers many of the mystic improvements, raising the attack damage, efficiency, and critical potential of Druid combat spells. Feral Combat brings the Druid's Cat and Bear forms closer in-line with Rogues and Warriors, respectively, making the class far more effective at DPS work and Tanking. Finally, the Restoration line aids healing spells with decreased Threat, improved efficiency, and some interruption avoidance.

Balance

The Balance Talents are intended to make a Druid into a more capable caster. It becomes easier to root enemies (through Nature's Grasp and Improved Entangling Roots), while more damage/more efficient damage is dealt due to improvements to Wrath, Moonfire, and Starfire. The end point of the Balance Talents is the ability to Shapeshift into Moonkin Form. This allows casting Druids to use their Balance attack abilities from a form that is much more survivable (there is also an aura that adds 3% to the group's spell Critical rate).

Feral Combat

Feral Combat Talents allow your Bear Forms to survive longer, mitigate more damage, and disrupt enemies more easily. They also allow your Cat Form to deal more damage and act with greater stealth. The line culminates in an aura that raises physical Critical rates in your nearby group by 3%. This is the fastest Talent line for leveling your character because of the reduced downtime. Solo Druids benefit tremendously from the Feral Combat line.

Restoration

Though lowest on damage and survivability, the Restoration Druid line turns characters into healers. Greater mana efficiency, faster healing times, reduced interruption chances and threat from heals, and other such Talents are in this line. Druids that work with dungeon groups get the most use of the Restoration line, while solo Druids have perhaps the least to gain from it.

STRATEGIES

Playing a Druid varies greatly from area to area, group to group, and even from moment to moment. Because so much can be done to change the dynamic of a Druid in battle, it takes considerable practice to master all facets of this class. Once done, a Druid can seamlessly switch between the major roles of group members, taking over for anyone who falls short during a fight.

First off, be sure to have your keys bound so that Shapeshifting between forms is fast and easy. Using Control + the Function Keys is somewhat standard, but placing the keys beneath the quickbar numbers or anywhere close to your hand's natural placement is sensible too.

Combat in Caster Form

The enemy stands at maximum range when the Druid in Caster Form begins the attack. Starfire is used first, as its casting time is longer and the damage dealt is frontloaded. The enemy is struck and begins moving forward, so the Druid Moonfires instantly and casts Entangling Roots as soon as the global one-second timer completes. Still out of range for melee, the enemy is likely bound in place. The Starfires continue, and Wrath is used if time is running out and the Druid needs a final quick spell for some damage. If the slaughter lasts over 12 seconds, renew the Moonfire after the first one's DOT completes.

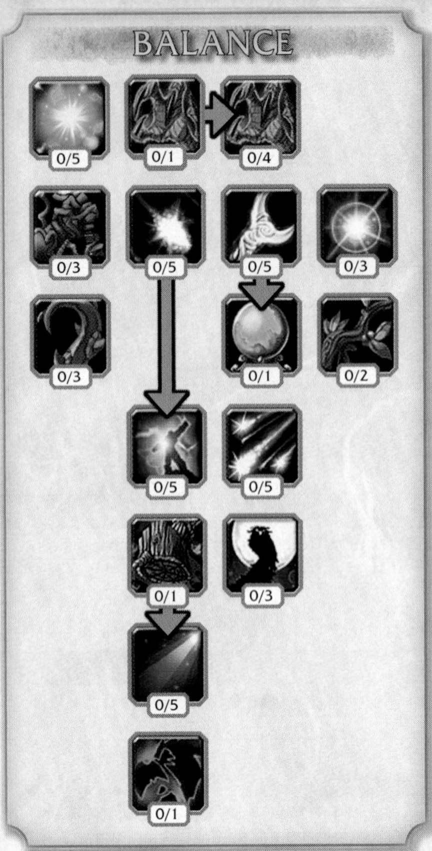

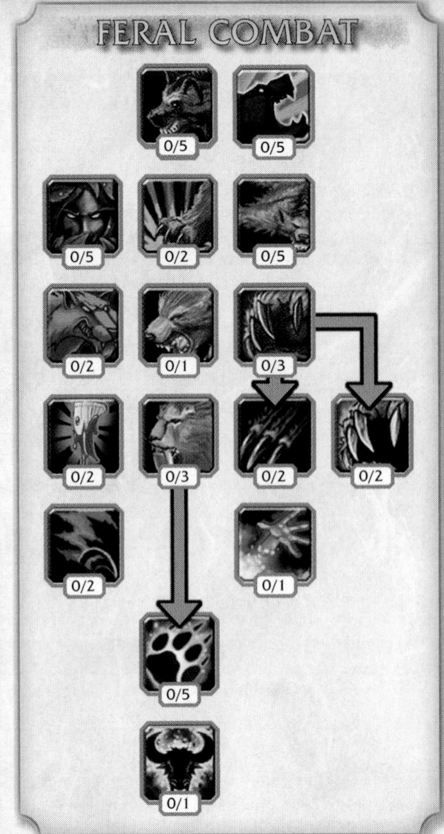

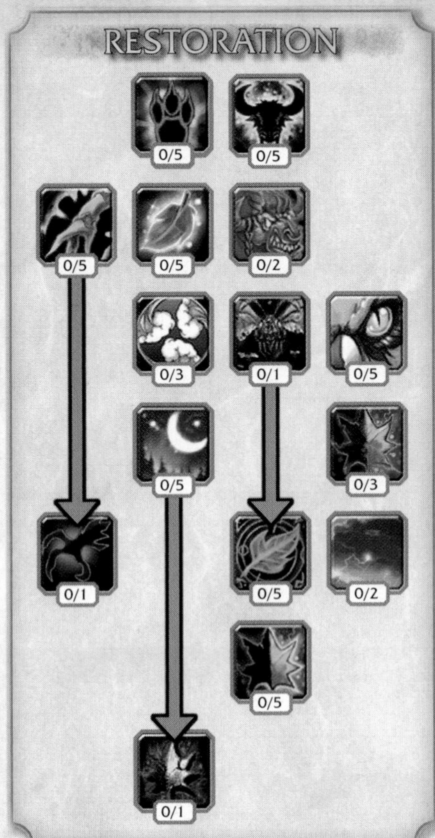

IMPROVED WRATH 5

Reduces the cast time of your Wrath spell by 0.1 seconds (Per Rank).

NATURE'S GRASP 1

While active, any time an enemy strikes the caster they have a 35% chance to become afflicted by Entangling Roots (Rank 1). Only useable outdoors. 1 charge. Lasts 45 seconds.

IMPROVED NATURE'S GRASP 4

Increases the chance for your Nature's Grasp to entangle an enemy by 15%. Progression 15%/30%/45%/65%.

IMPROVED ENTANGLING ROOTS 3

Gives you a 40% chance to avoid interruption caused by damage while casting Entangling Roots. Progression 40%/70%/100%.

IMPROVED MOONFIRE 5

Increases the damage and critical strike chance of your Moonfire spell by 2% (Per Rank).

NATURAL WEAPONS 5

Increases the damage you deal with physical attacks in all forms by 2% (Per Rank).

NATURAL SHAPESHIFTER 3

Reduces the mana cost of shapeshifting by 10% (Per Rank).

IMPROVED THORNS 3

Increases damage caused by your Thorns spell by 25% (Per Rank).

OMEN OF CLARITY 1

Imbues the Druid with natural energy. Each of the druid's melee attacks has a chance of causing the caster to enter a Clearcasting state. The Clearcasting state reduces the Mana, Rage, or Energy cost of your next damage or healing spell or offensive ability by 100%. Lasts 10 minutes.

NATURE'S REACH 2

Increases the range of your Wrath, Entangling Roots, Faerie Fire, Moonfire, Starfire, and Hurricane spells by 10% (Per Rank).

VENGEANCE 5

Increases the critical strike damage bonus of your Starfire, Moonfire, and Wrath spells by 20% (Per Rank).

IMPROVED STARFIRE 5

Reduces the cast time of Starfire by 0.1 seconds (Per Rank) and has 3% chance (Per Rank) to stun the target for 3 seconds.

NATURE'S GRACE 1

All spell criticals grace you with a blessing of nature, reducing the casting time of your next spell by 0.5 seconds.

MOONGLOW 3

Reduces the Mana cost of your Moonfire, Starfire, Wrath, Healing Touch, Regrowth, and Rejuvenation spells by 3% (Per Rank).

MOONFURY 5

Increases the damage done by your Starfire, Moonfire, and Wrath spells by 2% (Per Rank).

MOONKIN FORM 1

Transforms the druid into Moonkin Form. While in this form armor is increased by 360% and all party members within 30 yards have their spell critical chance increased by 3%. The Moonkin can only cast Balance spells while shapeshifted. The act of shapeshifting frees the caster of Polymorph and Movement Impairing effects.

FEROCITY 5

Reduces the cost of your Maul, Swipe, Claw, and Rake abilities by 1 Rage or Energy (Per Rank).

FERAL AGGRESSION 5

Increases the Attack Power reduction of your Demoralizing Roar by 8% (Per Rank) and the damage caused by your Ferocious Bite by 3% (Per Rank).

FERAL INSTINCT 5

Increases threat caused in Bear and Dire Bear Form by 3% (Per Rank) and reduces the chance enemies have to detect you while Prowling.

BRUTAL IMPACT 2

Increases the stun duration of your Bash and Pounce abilities by 0.5 seconds (Per Rank).

THICK HIDE 5

Increases your Armor contribution from items by 2% (Per Rank).

FELINE SWIFTNESS 2

Increases your movement speed by 15% (Per Rank) while outdoors in Cat Form and increases your chance to dodge while in Cat Form by 2% (Per Rank).

FERAL CHARGE 1

Requires Bear Form, Dire Bear Form. Causes you to charge an enemy, immobilizing and interrupting any spell being cast for 4 seconds.

SHARPENED CLAWS 3

Increases your critical strike chance while in Bear, Dire Bear, or Cat Form by 2% (Per Rank).

IMPROVED SHRED 3

Reduces the Energy cost of your Shred ability by 6 (Per Rank).

PREDATORY STRIKES 3

Increases your Attack Power in Cat, Bear, and Dire Bear Forms by 50% of your level (Per Rank).

BLOOD FRENZY 2

Your critical strikes from Cat Form abilities that add combo points have a 50% chance (Per Rank) to add an additional combo point.

PRIMAL FURY 2

Gives you a 50% chance (Per Rank) to gain an additional 5 Rage anytime you get a critical strike while in Bear and Dire Bear Form.

SAVAGE FURY 2

Increases the damage caused by your Claw, Rake, Maul and Swipe abilities by 10% (Per Rank).

FAERIE FIRE (FERAL) 1

Requires Cat Form, Bear Form, Dire Bear Form. Decreases the armor of the target by 175 for 40 seconds. While affected, the target cannot stealth or turn invisible.

HEART OF THE WILD 5

Increases your Intellect by 4% (Per Rank). In addition, while in Bear or Dire Bear Form your Stamina is increased by 4% (Per Rank) and while in Cat Form your Strength is increased by 4% (Per Rank).

LEADER OF THE PACK 1

While in Cat, Bear, or Dire Bear Form, the Leader of the Pack increases ranged and melee critical chance of all party members within 45 yards by 3%.

IMPROVED MARK OF THE WILD 5

Increases the effects of your Mark of the Wild and Gift of the Wild spells by 7% (Per Rank).

FUROR 5

Gives you a 20% chance (Per Rank) to gain 10 Rage when you shapeshift into Bear and Dire Bear form or 40 Energy when you shapeshift into Cat Form.

IMPROVED HEALING TOUCH 5

Reduces the cast time of your Healing Touch spell by 0.1 seconds (Per Rank).

NATURE'S FOCUS 5

Gives you a 14% chance (Per Rank)to avoid interruption caused by damage while casting the Healing Touch, Regrowth, and Tranquility spells.

IMPROVED ENRAGE 2

The Enrage ability now instantly generates 5 Rage (Per Rank).

REFLECTION 3

Allows 5% (Per Rank) of your Mana regeneration to continue while casting.

INSECT SWARM 1

The enemy target is swarmed by insects, decreasing their chance to hit by 2% and causing 66 Nature damage over 12 seconds.

SUBTLETY 5

Reduces the threat generated by your Healing spells by 4% (Per Rank).

TRANQUIL SPIRIT 5

Reduces the mana cost of your Healing Touch and Tranquility spells by 2% (Per Rank).

IMPROVED REJUVENATION 3

Increases the effect of your Rejuvenation spell by 5% (Per Rank).

NATURE'S SWIFTNESS 1

When activated, your next Nature spell becomes an instant cast spell.

GIFT OF NATURE 5

Increases the effect of all healing spells by 2% (Per Rank).

IMPROVED TRANQUILITY 2

Reduces threat caused by Tranquility by 40% (Per Rank).

IMPROVED REGROWTH 5

Increases the critical effect chance of your Regrowth Spell by 10% (Per Rank).

SWIFTMEND 1

Consumes a Rejuvenation or Regrowth effect on a friendly target to instantly heal them an amount equal to 12 sec. of Rejuvenation or 15 sec. of Regrowth.

Starfire is a very good spell for maintaining efficient damage, and its maximum damage dealt is quite good for a given level (compared to Wrath). What Wrath offers is the ability to dump a fair amount of Mana into a target over a short period, because of its brief casting time.

If you have Moonkin Form, from the Balanced Talents, stay in that shape unless you specifically need to heal. The increases survivability and spell Critical buff make the Moonkin Form very useful.

If Balance is your primary Talent line, having Hurricane can be a huge boon to Caster Form tactics. If multiple enemies are inbound against your group, it's powerful to be able to deal damage against them AND reduce their attack speed.

Moonfire Spam, Complaints, and Truth

Spamming Moonfire on the run is something that Druids can and will do from time to time. This is so painfully mana inefficient, that those who do it without a specific reason are being quite foolish. The base damage of Moonfire is not high at all for the mana invested, and the DOT overwrites itself constantly and resets the timer when the spam is being used, wasting hundreds of damage points.

When is it useful to waste your mana like this? When enemies are escaping and you are likely to either lose them or see them grab allies (a PvE situation). Or, in PvP when an enemy is on the run from you with the flag in Warsong Gulch. Perhaps your health is low, your chance for survival is poor even with healing, but you still have plenty of mana; this too would be a time for fast spamming of Moonfire just to dump some extra damage on a foe before your character falls.

Never Moonfire spam while grinding (it destroys your killrate in the long run). Neither should you do this in duels or other times when careful fighting and casting would net you greater results.

On the other side of this issue, players should not complain about getting killed by Moonfire spam. If you are on the run and getting hit from behind by a Druid, turn around and kill them! If you are running a flag or have to get away, understand that it's better for them to be Moonfiring you than using Entangling Roots, Wrath/Starfire, healing their incoming allies, etc. If you die to a simple Moonfire spam, it's likely that the Druid would have taken you out anyway (because of your character's low health, low levels, etc.). Moonfire is only deadly in spams when the Druid specializes both their Talents and gear for such casting; once again, this means that they are a soft target and you are always free to turn around and kill them!

Healing

As a backup healer, Druids are often called on to save other healers. When a Priest has gained too much aggro, shift to Caster Form and use spells to both save the healer in question and to get aggro onto yourself (it's better for the main tank to come and rip things off of you rather than worry about losing the primary healer). It's easy to switch into Bear Form once the aggro is on your Druid, and that prevents this action from being overly dangerous.

Remember when things are especially desperate to use the fastest order of healing spells. Regrowth for a good burst in only two seconds, then Rejuvenation for an Instant Heal Over Time, and finish with Healing Touch. Some people would try for the Instant HOT first, but the amount healed in the short term isn't enough; if your target is in danger of dying soon, it's better to cast Nature's Swiftness plus healing Touch or use Swiftmend. That buys enough time for Rejuvenation to work its wonders and for the Healing Touch to land.

Entangling Roots

When outdoors, it is possible to use Entangling Roots against enemies and move out of their attack range. While you begin regaining Mana, they continue to take light damage. This is a good way to handle adds; slap them with Entangling Roots and back away until they cannot contribute to the fight with any attacks. Handled correctly, this becomes a very substantial method of outdoor crowd control.

For PvP, Druids are able to Entangle Hunters and move to the sweet spot that is just outside of their melee range while being just inside their minimum missile range. Thus, only their pets can attack you. Hibernate the pet, Entangle the Hunter, and watch the poor sucker fume!

Before going into your alternate forms, use any spells or potions that are needed in future combat (these things aren't usable once in an Animal Form, but the effects transfers when you Shift). So, drink potions for Strength, Armor, etc. before going down on all fours.

Cat Form

Use Cat Form as a way to solo quickly or add DPS to a group. Druids deal very high damage in Cat Form, especially when specced in Feral Combat. The best trick with this is to lean on the DPS for several kills, until health begins to get low, then switch to your Caster Form for some healing magic. Restore any buffs, Shapeshift back into a Cat, and repeat the process.

In groups, the Cat offers high damage by harping on back attacks (Shred). When there is a high-level or generally skilled Tank holding aggro, this is a good choice for assisting the group's kill rate. It is easy to do more damage over time as a Cat than you can in Caster Form, and all of that mana you build up is perfect for going into a healing frenzy (between battles or when the group is in a pinch). It's hard not to fall in love with the Cat for this reason; Druids are constantly adding to the group without sacrificing healing potential or damage.

At Level 32, Druids in Cat Form can Track Humanoids. This is a rare ability that is gained only by Hunters. As such, Druids have a few perks in PvE and PvP combat. When trying to avoid or hunt down PvP opponents, this ability dramatically improves your group's chance to gaining initiative. Attacking when enemies are already engaged, distracted, or just looking the wrong way can be enough to overwhelm superior numbers and levels.

Speaking of Tracking

You may not have thought about it yet, but Druids aren't always counted as humanoids. In their Bear, Cat, Travel Form and Aquatic Forms, Druids are considered to be beasts! Because of that, Hunters who are relying on Track Humanoids won't be able to know that you are inbound.

Another issue to be aware of is that beast-specific abilities *will* work against Druids in their shapeshifted modes. You can be put to sleep by other Druids (using Hibernate). You can also be Feared by Hunters (using Scare Beast).

Bear Form

The Bear Form isn't as often needed as the Cat in group PvE because there are so many Warriors out in the world. Yet, the group you choose may have Fury Warriors or only Paladins for doing the Tank work, and they may need a bit of help. Bear Form is decent for Taunting, extremely solid for surviving damage, and can certainly make it worth a group's time to have a Druid. As with the Cat Form, save mana for important healing and switch back to Caster for bursts of activity.

If Bear Form is often needed in the groups you enjoy, invest in as high an Armor Rating as you can reach. Take Talents such as Thick Hide, use Defense Potions, and emulate as much of a Warrior's mentality as you can. Even using Armor Kits is sensible, considering that both Bear Forms multiply existing armor stats.

Read through the class description for Warriors to gain better ideas for Taunting, selecting the right targets to gather aggro, and so forth. Maul is tge most effective attack to generate threat. Swipe used at the same time as Maul is awesome for initial agro collection.

Travel Form in PvP

Travel Form makes Druids into the ultimate flag runners for the Warsong Gulch 30-39 bracket. Even afterward, Druids have a number of perks for running flags in this Battleground. Travel Form carries a 40% speed buff! Druids can use their Cat Form to Stealth around, grab the flag, then hurry outside to shift to Travel Form and move out. Unless snared or rooted, not much short of an epic mount can catch a Druid quickly. Beyond that, a Druid can shift to Caster and back to Travel Form to shake off a number of movement-debilitating effects!

On defense, Druids are just as potent in Warsong Gulch. These characters are able to root enemies for a very long period. Entangling Roots is a great spell for spotting long flag carriers while you wait for your buddies to show up. If a larger group of enemies is moving with the flag carrier, use Entangling Roots on their best healer instead; there is a very good chance that a foolish group will keep pressing forward toward their base, leaving the healer behind.

PvP Survivability

To defend areas, be ready to shift into Bear Form at the drop of a hat. Druids should rarely stay in their Caster Form or Cat Form if they are outnumbered. It's far wiser when the odds are against you, to stay in Bear and delay the enemies as long as possible. This is wonderfully effective in Arathi Basin, and also has its place in Alterac Valley and Warsong Gulch. Also, Kiting your foes in Travel Form while hitting flag cappers with Moonfire is an excellent stall tactic.

No matter what Talent line a Druid uses, they last only a few moments under direct assault while in Caster Form or Cat Form. Don't let people slaughter you like that. Wait for other members of your team to engage before moving into combat using these dangerous modes of healing or attack. Stay in Stealth from Cat Form until enemies are engaged so that you aren't targeted ahead of time by enemy damage dealers (and indeed, they *will* target you). Druids in PvP are seen foremost as healers, and for that they must be killed.

HUNTER

Hunters are primarily a ranged class that combines traps for damage or crowd control, pets for tanking, and brutal missile abilities with a modest array of melee survivability. Able to tame and train beasts in the wild, this class offers a tremendous amount of soloability, fast leveling, and excitement. Hunters have to invest in better bags, more food, and upkeep time while training any new pets. They also have the worst time in the initial levels (before they get their first pet).

Lore

There were too many in the camp for us to charge. The Scarlet Crusade wasn't stupid either; none would venture out of the camp alone. We decided to try and get a smaller group to come to us. Denegar, our Dwarven Warrior, volunteered to "ask if they had a cup of sugar and run back." Denegar had the heaviest armor of all of us, and we were still unsure if even he could survive the trip back with enemies at his back. I decided that I would do it. After all, we really needed that sugar.

I strung my bow and moved a bit closer. I took aim and waited until I had a good shot. I hit the fanatic in the shoulder. The man called to his friends before running toward me. I made a quick retreat back to the others. As the enemy made their charge, I shot my target in the leg. Now there were only two in the initial attack. Denegar made his intentions clear by swinging his two-handed axe above his head and bringing it down against the enemy's shield. It wasn't a hit, but the message was clear. Denegar was not to be ignored. As the Warriors closed in on Denegar, I pulled back and began peppering them with arrows. Their armor was as good as Denegar's. This wasn't to be a fast fight.

After several minutes, we had brought the first of the two enemies down. I was taking aim at the second when something moved on the edge of my vision. I dodged aside as a sword cut through the air I had occupied only a moment before. There was a Scarlet Warrior with two arrows in him and a very unhappy look on his face standing between me and the rest of the group. I had a bow in one hand, and an arrow in the other. A smile began to form as he advanced. That was long enough. Talon, my wolf companion and best friend, sank his teeth into the man's arm, dragging him to the ground. With his attention on Talon, I dropped my bow and arrow and unslung my two axes. With both of us attacking, the man couldn't fight effectively against either of us. After a few moments both Talon and I were sporting several wounds and our target was still standing. A look of horror crossed his face as a ball of fire slammed into his chest. This was followed by a scream of Dwarven rage and the arrival of the rest of the group. The Priest made quick work to restore the vigor Talon and I had lost through the fight. It had gone from two against one to six against one! The odds weren't in the Scarlet Crusader's favor.

Introduction to Playing the Class

Hunters have a certain mystique about them. The idea of fighting along side a life-long friend can be very appealing. The Hunter's strength is derived from combining the abilities of the Hunter with those of a pet. While this gives Hunters more choices than many classes, it takes practice and experimenting to find what works best in each situation.

At range, the Hunter is hard to beat. With high-damage attacks, movement-hindering abilities, and a pet to bite at the heels of attackers, fighting a Hunter at range is dangerous at best and foolhardy at worst. The movement-hindering abilities allow the Hunter to bring targets to a group in a more organized and less stressful fashion. For that reason, Hunters are prized by good groups as being one of the best pullers in Azeroth.

Starting with Leather armor and progressing to Mail at Level 40, Hunters aren't fragile. Combine this with dual-wield or a two-handed weapon and a pet, and they are almost as dangerous in melee if underestimated.

Hunters gain enough health to survive the attention of monsters for a short time. However, a long, drawn-out fight is something to be avoided as Hunters can't take nearly the hits Warriors, Paladins, or Druids can. Here is where the bond between Hunter and pet becomes so clear. Your companion is willing to do anything you ask. This includes keeping the attention of an enemy while you stay at long range and calmly fire away or sit on its hind-end waiting patiently for your commands.

Keeping you and your group safe is something your pet is happy to do. Keeping your pet safe is what Hunters do in return for that boundless loyalty.

Available Races	
Dwarf	Night Elf
Orc	Tauren
Troll	

What do Attributes Mean to Me?	
Strength	Increases Damage Done in Melee
Stamina	Higher Health
Agility	Raises Chance to Get a Critical Hit, Dodge, and Increases Damage Done at Range and in Melee
Intellect	More Mana, Better Chance for Critical Hits with Arcane Abilities (e.g. Volley, Arcane Missile), Faster Learning of Skills
Spirit	Improves Health and Mana Recovery

ITEMS AND EQUIPMENT

Properly equipped, a Hunter can function both in melee and at range. This flexibility gives you the choice of where to fight. Many Hunters choose to fight at range when possible as many of their abilities are dependant upon using Bows, Guns, or Crossbows.

Missile weapons offer your primary form of damage at range. As such, they must be kept up-to-date. This includes ammunition. Different types of arrows and shot provide different DPS bonuses. Always use the highest level ammunition available; becoming an Engineer and crafting your own ammunition helps with this for gun-users. Finding a weapon that does high DPS and has Agility bonuses is even better as Agility effects ranged damage. Scopes, made by Engineers, also contribute to range damage. Purchase these and seek Enchanters for +Agility enchantments for your melee weapons.

Food is fairly important to a Hunter...it's for your pet! Keeping pets fed and happy is as important as almost any equipment you could possibly buy. Hunters should restock their food supply before heading out of town. Be sure to know which foods your creature likes as well, because each species has different needs. Look at your pet's information page to learn about their food interests.

Quivers and ammo pouches give bonuses to firing speed. These containers only hold arrows or shot and take one of your bag slots. This means that where most classes have one backpack and four bags, Hunters end up with one backpack, three bags, and an ammunition container. Keep in mind that Hunters carry more food than many others (you're feeding two after all). So, Hunters have far less room than many characters.

Find equipment that raises your attributes and worry more about those bonuses than whether the piece has a particularly high Armor Rating. The foremost attribute for most Hunters is Agility. Agility heightens your Critical Hit chance, which is useful in both melee and ranged combat. Agility also increases damage in ranged combat and increases your Dodge rate and some damage in melee.

KEEPING A PET

Your pet is half of your character. Having a fully trained and leveled pet is very important. The first step is to find a pet you enjoy having that is the same level as you (or is at least close). After level 10, all Hunters undertake a quest given by their trainers. This quest explains how to tame pets. As your character progresses in level, this process becomes much easier. High-level Hunters are able to place a Freezing Trap, use Concussive Shot to start the action, then Tame. For low-level Hunters, it's a lonely and dangerous act. Use Concussive Shot from just beyond Tame's maximum range and start to Tame as soon as possible. Or, for beasts with a Stun or Knockdown, you should approach them and wait for them to use these powers before even trying to Tame (this way, they blow their chance to disrupt your Taming before you even bother to start).

Once the pet has agreed to become your friend, help the bond flourish by feeding it. Feeding raises a pet's Happiness. This level affects how much damage a pet does in combat, so it shouldn't be overlooked. Beyond that, you won't be able to train pets with their most important abilities unless those pets are loyal to you. Loyalty doesn't increase without a pet being Happy.

Pets Never Stop Eating

Your pet needs to be fed often. Watch its Happiness. Feed it whenever its Happiness Level falls. This ensures maximum damage and the best progression of Loyalty Level.

Your Pet's Happiness Can be Measured!

Happiness Level	Icon	Effect
Happy	Smiley Face	125% Damage; Gaining Loyalty
Content	Flat Expression	100% Damage; Gaining Loyalty
Unhappy	Frowning Face	75% Damage; Losing Loyalty

LOYALTY

As long as your current pet is Content or Happy, the creature's Loyalty rises. Each new pet can gain up to five levels of Loyalty; with each, there is an increase in the number of Training Points that can be spent teaching your buddy how to fight and survive. Before the first Loyalty level is reached, your pet is rebellious and won't be able to learn anything that costs points (though the pet will still use any innate powers that it has, and free abilities, such as Growl, can be taught).

Each Loyalty increase adds one Training Point per level of the creature. Thus, a level 55 Bear in Winterspring would gain 55 Training Points each time your Loyalty increased, for a total of 275 Training Points. Because innate abilities still cost Training Points, your first Loyalty improvement might not yield this full sum!

The best way to improve Loyalty is to keep your pet Happy at all times (a well fed pet is a Happy pet), and to take the creature into combat as often as possible. Loyalty increases at a **much** faster rate when your pets are involved in direct fighting. Thus, going /afk even with a Happy pet isn't a good technique for raising Loyalty.

LIONS, TIGERS, AND BEARS

There are many beasts in the world. Finding the one that is right for you might take a while and even change as your character develops. It takes quite some time for pets to really bond to their master, so avoid changing pets too often.

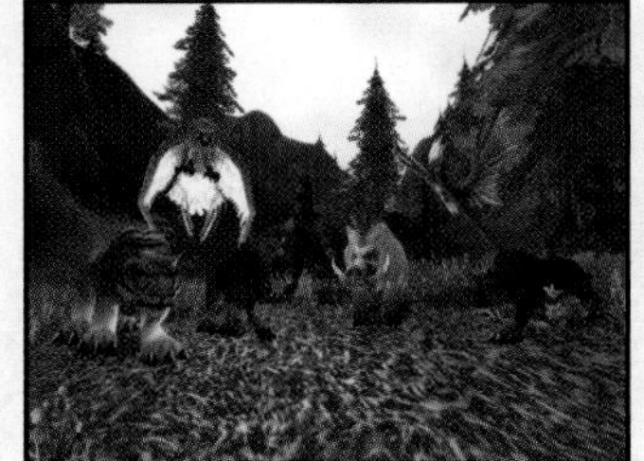

Not every beast can use all the abilities you teach. Some body-types are inadequate for performing certain attacks. Trying to teach a Raptor to Dive is amusing, but it is just impossible

Various beasts also have different diets. Bears and Nightsabres have no qualms about eating almost any meat you give them. Striders and Owls are a bit pickier about their food. Your pet's diet is listed in the Pet Details screen. One thing that is useful to know is that food must be of a certain level to impress your pet. Look at the Combat Log and see how much Happiness is gained by a specific food type. If the pet is only getting 8 or 16 Happiness per tick of eating, the food you are using is no longer entirely optimal. Just tossing any food you find down your pet's gullet might keep them Happy enough, but it's likely that you will need to feed them more often.

Another tip about feeding is that it takes some time. Have your Hunter solo a creature while your pet is eating (as long as the pet is on passive, this isn't a problem). Do this because telling your pet to attack stops the feeding and wastes the rest of the food. That can get pricey, and you need to feed pets more often. Watch the Combat Log to see when the message "Pet Happiness Effect Fades" comes up; that means that feeding time is over. Back to the fight, Kitty!

If you still don't have a Happy pet after a full feeding, go ahead and give your buddy some more food. There is no timer that alters how hungry your pet is, so you cannot gorge them.

EXCHANGING SKILLS WITH YOUR PET

Training has two facets. Hunters teach pets abilities and learn abilities from their pets. Many pets naturally have abilities. Learn these by watching your pet perform. This usually takes a short while before you gain the ability in the Beast Training menu. Once you know the ability, it's possible to teach the ability to any pet you gain that is physically capable of the act in question.

Because of this aspect, you need to Tame other beasts from time to time to learn their abilities. To do this, find the Stable Master in your current town and put your favorite pet in their keep. This way, you won't have to Abandon it to get a new creature. Head out into the wild, find the creature that has new abilities for you, and Tame it! Even if you don't want to keep the new pet, fight with it a few times, learn what you need to, then Abandon it (right-click on its portrait to do this). Once you have learned the ability you sought, return to the Stable Master and get your old pet back.

A number of Training Abilities are also learned from Pet Trainers in the major cities. Talk to these NPCs occasionally and see if they can give you anything. Growl, Resistances, Stamina, and Armor improvements are all gained in this way. Sprint, Attack Abilities, Stealth, and various innate actions are gained directly from pets.

This data was generously provided by Angela "Hyacinthe" Adams of the Good Intentions guild on Azjol-Nerub. A special thanks goes out to all the Hunters of Azeroth that constantly provide updates and other contributions to the table. <www.goodintentionsguild.info/hunters.html>

Trainer Abilities

Great Stamina

Rank	Required Level	Training Points	Cost	Effect
1	10	5	Passive	Adds 3 Stamina
2	12	10	Passive	Adds 5 Stamina
3	18	15	Passive	Adds 7 Stamina
4	24	25	Passive	Adds 10 Stamina
5	30	50	Passive	Adds 13 Stamina
6	36	75	Passive	Adds 17 Stamina
7	42	100	Passive	Adds 21 Stamina
8	48	125	Passive	Adds 26 Stamina
9	54	150	Passive	Adds 32 Stamina
10	60	185	Passive	Adds 40 Stamina

Natural Armor

Rank	Required Level	Training Points	Cost	Effect
1	10	1	Passive	Adds 50 Armor
2	12	5	Passive	Adds 100 Armor
3	18	10	Passive	Adds 160 Armor
4	24	15	Passive	Adds 240 Armor
5	30	25	Passive	Adds 330 Armor
6	36	50	Passive	Adds 430 Armor
7	42	75	Passive	Adds 550 Armor
8	48	100	Passive	Adds 675 Armor
9	54	125	Passive	Adds 810 Armor
10	60	150	Passive	Adds 1000 Armor

Resistances (Arcane, Fire, Frost, Nature, Shadow)

Rank	Required Level	Training Points	Cost	Effect
1	20	5 Each	Passive	Adds 30 Resistance of Selected Type (You Can Take All Five)
2	30	15 Each	Passive	Adds 60 Resistance of Selected Type (You Can Take All Five)
3	40	45 Each	Passive	Adds 90 Resistance of Selected Type (You Can Take All Five)
4	50	90 Each	Passive	Adds 120 Resistance of Selected Type (You Can Take All Five)

Growl

Rank	Required Level	Training Points	Cost	Effect
1	1	Free	15 Focus	Instant Taunt, 5 Second Cooldown, 5 Yard Range
2	10	Free	15 Focus	Instant Taunt, 5 Second Cooldown, 5 Yard Range
3	20	Free	15 Focus	Instant Taunt, 5 Second Cooldown, 5 Yard Range
4	30	Free	15 Focus	Instant Taunt, 5 Second Cooldown, 5 Yard Range
5	40	Free	15 Focus	Instant Taunt, 5 Second Cooldown, 5 Yard Range
6	50	Free	15 Focus	Instant Taunt, 5 Second Cooldown, 5 Yard Range
7	60	Free	15 Focus	Instant Taunt, 5 Second Cooldown, 5 Yard Range

Common Animal Abilities

Bite

Purpose: Focus-Efficient Damage

Not Usable By: Crabs, Scorpids, Owls

Rank	Required Level	Training Points	Cost	Effect
1	1	1	35 Focus	Instant Damage (7-9), 10 Second Cooldown, 5 Yard Range
2	8	4	35 Focus	Instant Damage (16-18), 10 Second Cooldown, 5 Yard Range
3	16	7	35 Focus	Instant Damage (24-28), 10 Second Cooldown, 5 Yard Range
4	24	10	35 Focus	Instant Damage (31-37), 10 Second Cooldown, 5 Yard Range
5	32	13	35 Focus	Instant Damage (40-48), 10 Second Cooldown, 5 Yard Range
6	40	17	35 Focus	Instant Damage (49-59), 10 Second Cooldown, 5 Yard Range
7	48	21	35 Focus	Instant Damage (66-80), 10 Second Cooldown, 5 Yard Range
8	56	25	35 Focus	Instant Damage (81-99), 10 Second Cooldown, 5 Yard Range

Where to Learn Bite (Rank 1)

- Dun Morogh: Snow Tracker Wolf (5-7), Winter Wolf (6-8)
- Durotar: Dreadmaw Crocolisk (9-11)
- Elwynn Forest: Gray Forest Wolf (7-8), Forest Spider (5-6)
- Mulgore: Prairie Stalker (7-8), Prairie Wolf (5-6), The Rake
- Teldrassil: Githyiss the Vile (5), Webwood Venomfang (7-8)
- Tirisfal Glades: Night Web Spider (3-4), Night Web Matriarch (5), Ragged Scavenger (2-3)

Where to Learn Bite (Rank 2)

- Barrens: Oasis Snapjaw (15-16)
- Dun Morogh: Starving Winter Wolf (8-9), Timber (10)
- Elwynn Forest: Mother Fang (10+), Prowler (9-10)
- Loch Modan: Forest Lurker (10-14), Loch Crocolisk (14-15)
- Mulgore: Prairie Wolf Alpha (9-10)
- Redridge Mountains: Tarantula (15-16)
- Teldrassil: Giant Webwood Spider (10-11), Lady Sathrah (12), Webwood Silkspinner (8-9)
- Tirisfal Glades: Vicious Nightweb Spider (9-10), Worg (10-11)
- Westfall: Coyote (10-11), Coyote Packleader (11-12)

Where to Learn Bite (Rank 3)

- Ashenvale: Ghostpaw Runner (19-20)
- Blackfathom Deeps: Aku'mai Fisher (23+), Ghamoo'Ra (25)
- Duskwood: Green Recluse (21-22), Lupos (23 elite)
- Hillsbrad Foothills: Forest Moss Creeper (20-21)
- Loch Modan: Wood Lurker (17-18)
- Redridge Mountains: Greater Tarantula (19-20)
- Silverpine Forest: Bloodsnout Worg (16-17)
- Stonetalon Peak: Besseleth (21+), Deepmoss Creeper (16-17), Deepmoss Webspinner (19-20)
- Wailing Caverns: Deviate Crocolisk (Elite)

Where to Learn Bite (Rank 4)

- Ashenvale: Ghostpaw Alpha (27-28), Wildthorn Lurker (27-29)
- Blackfathom Deeps: Aku'mai Snapjaw (26+-27+), Ghamoo-Ra (25+)
- Duskwood: Black Ravager (24-25), Black Ravager Mastiff (25-26), Naraxis
- Hillsbrad Foothills: Elder Moss Creeper (26-27), Giant Moss Creeper (24-25), Snapjaw (30-32)
- Wetlands: Giant Wetlands Crocolisk (25-26)

Where to Learn Bite (Rank 5)

- Arathi Highlands: Giant Plains Creeper (35-36), Plains Creeper (32-33)
- Badlands: Crag Coyote (35-36)
- Dustwallow Marsh: Darkfang Creeper (38-39), Darkfang Lurker (36-37), Darkfang Spider (35-36), Drywallow Crocolisk (35-36), Mottled Drywallow Crocolisk (38-39), Mudrock Tortoise (36-37)
- Thousand Needles: Sparkleshell Snapper(34-35)

Where to Learn Bite (Rank 6)

- Azshara: Timberweb Recluse (47-48), Badlands: Barnabus (38)
- Dustwallow Marsh: Deadmire (45), Drywallow Daggermaw (40+-41+), Mudrock Snapjaw (41-42)
- Felwood: Felpaw Wolf (47-48)
- Feralas: Longtooth Runner (40-41), Snarler (42), Undead Wolf (41, 47)
- Hinterlands: Old Cliff Jumper (42), Witherbark Broodguard (44-45)
- Searing Gorge: Rekk'tilac (48)
- Stormwind: Sewer Beast (Rare 50 Elite)
- Swamp of Sorrows: Deathstrike Tarantula (40-41), Sawtooth Snapper (41-42)

Where to Learn Bite (Rank 7)

- Felwood: Felpaw Ravager (51-52)
- Hinterlands: Ironback (51-52), Saltwater Snapjaw (49-50), Vilebranch Raiding Wolf (50-52 Elite)
- Searing Gorge: Rekk'tilac (48+)
- Tanaris: Giant Surf Gliders (48+-50+)
- Un'Goru Crater: Uhk'loc (52)
- Western Plagueland: Diseased Wolf (53-54), Plague Lurker (54-55)

Where to Learn Bite (Rank 8)

- Blackrock Spire: Bloodaxe Worg (55-57) In the patrols right before Halycon, and in the room right after Halycon

Claw

Purpose: Fast Damage

Not Usable By: Bats, Boars, Crocolisks, Gorillas, Hyenas, Spiders, Tall Striders, Turtles, Wind Serpents, Wolves

Rank	Required Level	Training Points	Cost	Effect
1	1	1	25 Focus	Instant Damage (4-6), No Cooldown, 5 Yard Range
2	8	4	25 Focus	Instant Damage (8-12), No Cooldown, 5 Yard Range
3	16	7	25 Focus	Instant Damage (12-16), No Cooldown, 5 Yard Range
4	24	10	25 Focus	Instant Damage (16-22), No Cooldown, 5 Yard Range
5	32	13	25 Focus	Instant Damage (21-29), No Cooldown, 5 Yard Range
6	40	17	25 Focus	Instant Damage (26-36), No Cooldown, 5 Yard Range
7	48	21	25 Focus	Instant Damage (35-49), No Cooldown, 5 Yard Range
8	56	25	25 Focus	Instant Damage (43-59), No Cooldown, 5 Yard Range

Where to Learn Claw (Rank 1)

- Dun Morogh: Ice Claw Bear (7-8)
- Durotar: Pygmy Surf Crawler (5-6), Sarkoth (4), Scorpid Workers (3)
- Teldrassil: Strigid Owl (5-6)

Where to Learn Claw (Rank 2)

- Darkshore: Thistle Bear (11-12), Tide Crawler (12-14)
- Dun Morogh: Bjarn (12+), Mangeclaw (11)
- Durotar: Deathflayer (11), Encrusted Surf Crawler (9-10), Venomtail Scorpid (9-10)
- Elwynn Forest: Young Forest Bear (8-9)
- Orgrimmar: Venom Scorpid (10-11)
- Silverpine: Bear
- Teldrassil: Strigid Hunter (8-9)

Where to Learn Claw (Rank 3)

- Ashenvale: Ashenvale Bear (20-24), Clattering Crawler (19-20)
- Blackfathom Deeps: Skittering Crustacean (22+-23+), Snapping Crustacean (23+-24+)
- Darkshore: Den Mother (18-19)
- Hillsbrad Foothills: Gray Bear (21-22)
- Loch Modan: Black Bear Patriarch (16-17), Ol' Sooty (20+)
- Westfall: Shore Crawler (17-18)

Where to Learn Claw (Rank 4)

- Ashenvale: Elder Ashenvale Bear (25-26), Mountain Lion (25)
- Blackfathom Deeps: Barbed Crustacean (25+-26+)
- Desolace: Scorpashi Snapper (30-31)
- Thousand Needles: Scorpid Reaver (30-31) in Shimmering Flats

Where to Learn Claw (Rank 5)

- Desolace: Scorpashi Lasher (34-35)
- Dustwallow Marsh: Drywallow Snapper (37-38)

Where to Learn Claw (Rank 6)

- Feralas: Ironfur Bear (41-42)
- Stranglethorn Vale: King Bangalash (43 Elite)
- Swamp of Sorrows: Monstrous Crawler (43-44), Silt Crawler (40-41)
- Tanaris: Scorpid Hunter (40-41)

Where to Learn Claw (Rank 7)

- Blasted Lands: Clack the Reaver (53+)
- Burning Steppes: Deathlash Scorpid (54-55)
- Felwood: Angerclaw Mauler (49-50), Ironbeak Hunter (50-52), Olm the Wise (52)
- Feralas: Ironfur Patriarch (48-49)
- Western Plaguelands: Diseased Grizzly (55-56)
- Winterspring: Shardtooth Bear (53-55), Winterspring Owl (54-56)

Where to Learn Claw (Rank 8)

- Winterspring: Elder Shardtooth (57-58), Winterspring Screecher (57-59)

Cower

Purpose: Reduce Pet Aggro

Not Usable By: N/A

Rank	Required Level	Training Points	Cost	Effect
1	5	8	15 Focus	Reduces Pet Aggro, 5 Second Cooldown
2	15	10	15 Focus	Reduces Pet Aggro, 5 Second Cooldown
3	25	12	15 Focus	Reduces Pet Aggro, 5 Second Cooldown
4	35	14	15 Focus	Reduces Pet Aggro, 5 Second Cooldown
5	45	16	15 Focus	Reduces Pet Aggro, 5 Second Cooldown
6	55	18	15 Focus	Reduces Pet Aggro, 5 Second Cooldown

Where to Learn Cower (Rank 1)

- Barrens: Elder Plainstrider (8-9), Fleeting Plainstrider (12-13)
- Darkshore: Foreststrider Fledging (11-13), Moonstalker Runt (10-11)
- Dun Morogh: Juvenile Snow Leopard (5-6)
- Durotar: Durotar Tiger (7-8)
- Mulgore: Elder Plainstrider (8-9), Flatland Cougar (7-8), Mazzranache (9)
- Teldrassil: Mangy Nightsaber (2), Nightsaber (5-6)
- Tirisfal Glades: Greater Duskbat (6-7)

Where to Learn Cower (Rank 2)

- Barrens: Ornery Plainstrider (16-17), Savannah Patriarch (15-16)
- Darkshore: Giant Foreststrider (17-19), Moonstalker Sire (17-18)
- Hillsbrad Foothills: Starving Mountain Lion (23-24)
- Stonetalon Mountains: Twilight Runner (23-24)

Where to Learn Cower (Rank 3)

- Hillsbrad Foothills: Feral Mountain Lion (27-28)
- Razorfen Kraul: Blind Hunter (32), Kraul Bat (31+)
- Stranglethorn Vale: Panther (32-33), Young Stranglethorn Panther (30-31), Young Stranglethorn Tiger (30-31)
- Thousand Needles: Crag Stalker (25-26)

Where to Learn Cower (Rank 4)

- Badlands: Ridge Huntress (38-39), Ridge Stalker (36-37)
- Uldaman: Shrike Bat (38-39)

Where to Learn Cower (Rank 5)

- Eastern Plaguelands: Noxious Plaguebat (54-56), Plaguebat (53-55)
- Stranglethorn Vale: Jaguero Stalker (50)

Where to Learn Cower (Rank 6)

- Eastern Plaguelands: Monstrous Plaguebat (56-58)
- Winterspring: Frostsaber Cub (55-56)

Dash

Purpose: Engages Target at High Speed

Not Usable By: Bears, Crabs, Crocolisks, Gorillas, Raptors, Scorpids, Spiders, Turtles, Flying Creatures

Rank	Required Level	Training Points	Cost	Effect
1	30	15	20 Focus	Increases Movement Speed by 40% for 15 Seconds, 30 Second Cooldown
2	40	20	20 Focus	Increases Movement Speed by 60% for 15 Seconds, 30 Second Cooldown
3	50	25	20 Focus	Increases Movement Speed by 80% for 15 Seconds, 30 Second Cooldown

Where to Learn Dash (Rank 1)

- Badlands: Broken Tooth (37), Crag Coyote (35-36), Elder Crag Coyote (39-40), Feral Crag Coyote (37-38)
- Desolace: Bonepaw Hyena (33-35), Magram Bonepaw (37-38)
- Scarlet Monastery: Scarlet Tracking Hound (33-34)
- Stranglethorn Vale: Kurzen War Tiger (32-33), Stranglethorn Tiger (32-33)
- Swamp of Sorrows: Swamp Jaguar (36-37)

Where to Learn Dash (Rank 2)

- Badlands: Ridge Stalker Patriarch (40-41)
- Blasted Lands: Ashmane Boar (48-49), Grunter (50)
- Feralas: Longtooth Runner (40-41)
- Hinterlands: Old Cliff Jumper (42), Silvermane Stalker (47-48)
- Stranglethorn Vale: Bhag'thera (40+), Elder Shadowmaw Panther (41-43), King Bangalash (43 Elite)
- Tanaris: Blisterpaw Hyena (44-45), Rabid Blisterpaw (47-48), Starving Blisterpaw (41-42)

Where to Learn Dash (Rank 3)

- Blackrock Spires: Blackrock Worg (54), Bloodaxe Worg (55-57)
- Blasted Lands: Hyena Ravage (Elite)
- Hinterlands: Vilebranch Raiding Wolf (50+-51+)
- Winterspring: Frostsaber Huntress (58-59), Frostsaber Stalker (59-60), Rak'shiri (rare blue frostsaber)

Dive

Purpose: Engages Target at High Speed

Not Usable By: Any Land Creature

Rank	Required Level	Training Points	Cost	Effect
1	30	15	20 Focus	Increases Movement Speed by 40% for 15 Seconds, 30 Second Cooldown
2	40	20	20 Focus	Increases Movement Speed by 60% for 15 Seconds, 30 Second Cooldown
3	50	25	20 Focus	Increases Movement Speed by 80% for 15 Seconds, 30 Second Cooldown

Where to Learn Dive (Rank 1)

- Arathi Highlands: Mesa Buzzard (34-35), Young Mesa Buzzard (31-32)
- Desolace: Dread Flyer (36-37)
- Razorfen Kraul: Razorfen Kraul Bat (30-31)
- Desolace: Dread Flyer (36-37)
- Uldaman: Shrike Bat (38-39)

Where to Learn Dive (Rank 2)

- Felwood: Ironbeak Owl (48-49)
- Feralas: Arash-ethis (49), Rogue Vale Screecher (45-46), Vale Screecher (41-42), Wind Serpent (44)
- Tanaris: Fire Roc (43-35), Roc (41-43)

Where to Learn Dive (Rank 3)

- Badlands: Zaricotl (55)
- Blasted Lands: Spiteflayer (52+)
- Eastern Plaguelands: Plaguebat (53-55)
- Felwood: Ironbeak Hunter (50-51), Ironbeak Screecher (52-53), Olm the Wise (52)
- Western Plaguelands: Carrion Vulture (51-52)
- Winterspring: Winterspring Owl (54-55), Winterspring Screecher (59)

Race-Specific Animal Abilities

Charge

Purpose: Charge Enemy, Stun Them, Increase Attack Power for Next Strike

Only Usable By: Boars

Rank	Required Level	Training Points	Cost	Effect
1	1	5	35 Focus	Charge, 1 Second Stun, +50 AP for Next Attack, 25 Second Cooldown
2	12	9	35 Focus	Charge, 1 Second Stun, +100 AP for Next Attack, 25 Second Cooldown
3	24	13	35 Focus	Charge, 1 Second Stun, +180 AP for Next Attack, 25 Second Cooldown
4	36	17	35 Focus	Charge, 1 Second Stun, +280 AP for Next Attack, 25 Second Cooldown
5	48	21	35 Focus	Charge, 1 Second Stun, +390 AP for Next Attack, 25 Second Cooldown
6	60	25	35 Focus	Charge, 1 Second Stun, +550 AP for Next Attack, 25 Second Cooldown

Where to Learn Charge (Rank 1)

- Durotar: Mottled Boar (1-2), Dire Mottled Boar (6-7), Elder Mottled Boar (8-9), Corrupted Mottled Boar (10-11)
- Dun Morogh: Small Crag Boar (3), Crag Boar (5-6), Large Crag Boar (6-7), Elder Crag Boar (7-8), Scarred Crag Boar (9-10)
- Elwynn Forest: Stonetusk Boar (5-6), Porcine Entourage (7), Rockhide Boar (7-8), Princess (9), Longsnout (10-11)
- Mulgore: Battleboar (3-4), Bristleback Battleboar (4-5)
- Teldrassil: Young Thistle Boar (1-2), Thistle Boar (2-3)

Where to Learn Charge (Rank 2)

- Loch Modan: Mangy Boar (15)
- Redridge Mountains: Great Goretusk (16-17)
- Westfall: Young Goretusk (12-13), Goretusk (14-15), Great Goretusk (16-17)

Where to Learn Charge (Rank 3)

- Razorfen Kraul: Agam'ar (24-25), Raging Agam'ar (25-26), Rotting Agam'ar (28)
- Redridge Mountains: Bellygrub (24)

Where to Learn Charge (Rank 5)

- Blasted Lands: Ashmane Boar (48-49)

Where to Learn Charge (Rank 6)

- Eastern Plaguelands: Plagued Swine (60)

Furious Howl

Purpose: Add Physical Damage to Next Attack for All Group Members

Only Usable By: Wolves

Rank	Required Level	Training Points	Cost	Effect
1	10	10	60 Focus	Adds 9-11 Damage on Next Physical Attack (All Group Members within 15 Yards), 10 Second Cooldown
2	24	15	60 Focus	Adds 18-22 Damage on Next Physical Attack (All Group Members within 15 Yards), 10 Second Cooldown
3	40	20	60 Focus	Adds 28-34 Damage on Next Physical Attack (All Group Members within 15 Yards), 10 Second Cooldown
4	58	25	60 Focus	Adds 45-57 Damage on Next Physical Attack (All Group Members within 15 Yards), 10 Second Cooldown

Where to Learn Furious Howl (Rank 1)

- Mulgore: Prairie Wolf Alpha (10)
- Silverpine Forest: Worg (10-12)
- Westfall: Coyote Packleader (11-12)

Where to Learn Furious Howl (Rank 2)

- Ashenvale: Ghostpaw Alpha (27-28)
- Badlands: Elder Crag Coyote (36-40)
- Duskwood: Black Ravager Mastiff (25-26)
- Feralas: Longtooth Howler (43-44)
- Hinterlands: Silvermane Howler (45-46)

Where to Learn Furious Howl (Rank 3)

- Felwood: Felpaw Wolf (47-48)
- Feralas: Longtooth Runner (40-41), Snarler (42)
- Hinterlands: Silvermane Wolf (43-44)

Where to Learn Furious Howl (Rank 4)

- Blackrock Spires: Bloodaxe Worg (55-57)

Lightning Breath

Purpose: Ranged, Nature-Damage Attack

Only Usable By: Winged Serpents

Rank	Required Level	Training Points	Cost	Effect
1	1	5	50 Focus	Deals 11-15 Nature Damage to One Target
2	12	10	50 Focus	Deals 21-25 Nature Damage to One Target
3	24	15	50 Focus	Deals 36-42 Nature Damage to One Target
4	36	15	50 Focus	Deals 51-61 Nature Damage to One Target
5	48	20	50 Focus	Deals 78-92 Nature Damage to One Target
6	60	25	50 Focus	Deals 99-113 Nature Damage to One Target

Where to Learn Lightning Breath (Rank 2)

- Barrens: Deviate Coiler (16 Elite), Deviate Dreadfang (21 Elite), Deviate Stinglash (16 Elite), Greater Thunderhawk (23), Thunderhawk Cloudscraper (20), Thunderhawk Hatchling (18, 20)

Where to Learn Lightning Breath (Rank 3)

- Barrens: Washte Pawne (25)
- Feralas: Rogue Vale Screecher (45-46), Vale Screecher (41-42)
- Thousand Needles: Cloud Serpent (25), Elder Cloud Serpent (27-28), Venemous Cloud Serpent (26)

Where to Learn Lightning Breath (Rank 4)

- Feralas: Rogue Vale Screecher (46), Vale Screecher (41)
- Sunken Temple (Swamp of Sorrows): Spawn of Hakkar (51 Elite)

Where to Learn Lightning Breath (Rank 5)

- Feralas: Arash-etish (49)
- Sunken Temple (Swamp of Sorrows): Hakkar'i Sappers (?), Hakkar'i Frostwings (?), Spawn of Hakkar (51 Elite)

Where to Learn Lightning Breath (Rank 6)

- Zul'Gurub: Son of Hakkar

Prowl

Purpose: Stealth, Strong Initial Attack

Only Usable By: Cats

Rank	Required Level	Training Points	Cost	Effect
1	30	15	40 Focus	Stealth w/ 50% Movement, 120% Initial Attack, 10 Second Cooldown
2	40	20	40 Focus	Stealth w/ 55% Movement, 135% Initial Attack, 10 Second Cooldown
3	50	25	40 Focus	Stealth w/ 60% Movement, 150% Initial Attack, 10 Second Cooldown

Where to Learn Prowl (Rank 1)

- Alterac: Mountain Lion (32-33)
- Badlands: Ridge Stalker (37)
- Stranglethorn Vale: Shadowmaw Panther (37-38)
- Swamp of Sorrows: Shadow Panther (39)

Where to Learn Prowl (Rank 2)

- Badlands: Ridge Stalker Patriarch (40-41)
- Stranglethorn Vale: Elder Shadowmaw Panther (42-43)

Where to Learn Prowl (Rank 3)

- Stranglethorn Vale: Jaguero Stalker (50)
- Winterspring: Frostsaber Stalker (59-60)

Scorpid Poison

Purpose: Poison DOT

Only Usable By: Scorpids

Rank	Required Level	Training Points	Cost	Effect
1	8	10	30 Focus	10 Nature Damage Over 8 Seconds, Stacks Up to 5 Times, 4 Second Cooldown
2	24	15	30 Focus	15 Nature Damage Over 8 Seconds, Stacks Up to 5 Times, 4 Second Cooldown
3	40	20	30 Focus	30 Nature Damage Over 8 Seconds, Stacks Up to 5 Times, 4 Second Cooldown
4	56	25	30 Focus	40 Nature Damage Over 8 Seconds, Stacks Up to 5 Times, 4 Second Cooldown

Where to Learn Scorpid Poison (Rank 1)

- Barrens: Silithid Creeper (20-21), Silithid Swarmer (21-22)
- Durotar: Corrupted Scorpid (10-11), Death Flayer (11), Venomtail Scorpid (9-10)

Where to Learn Scorpid Poison (Rank 2)

- Desolace: Scorpashi Snapper (30-31)
- Thousand Needles (Shimmering Flats): Scorpid Reaver (32), Scorpid Terror (33)

Where to Learn Scorpid Poison (Rank 3)

- Blasted Lands: Clack the Reaver (53), Scorpok Stinger (50-51)
- Burning Steppes: Deathlash Scorpid (54-55)
- Silithus: Stonelash Scorpid (53-55)
- Tanaris: Scorpid Dunestalker (47), Scorpid Hunter (40-41), Scorpid Tail Lasher (43-44)

Where to Learn Scorpid Poison (Rank 4)

- Burning Steppes: Fireclaw Scorpid (57), Firetail Scorpid (56-57)
- Silithus: Krellack (56), Stonelash Flayer (56-59), Stonelash Pincher (56-57)

Screech

Purpose: Light Damage, AoE Enemy Attack Power Reduction

Only Usable By: Bats, Carrion Birds, Owls

Rank	Required Level	Training Points	Cost	Effect
1	8	10	20 Focus	Single Target Takes 7-9 Damage, Nearby Enemies Lose 25 AP
2	24	15	20 Focus	Single Target Takes 12-16 Damage, Nearby Enemies Lose 50 AP
3	48	20	20 Focus	Single Target Takes 19-25 Damage, Nearby Enemies Lose 75 AP
4	56	25	20 Focus	Single Target Takes 26-46 Damage, Nearby Enemies Lose 100 AP

Where to Learn Screech (Rank 1)

- Westfall: Greater Fleshripper (16-17)

Where to Learn Screech (Rank 2)

- Desolace: Dread Ripper (39-40)
- Thousand Needles (Shimmering Flats): Salt Flats Vulture (34)
- Uldaman: Shrike Bat (38 Elite)

Where to Learn Screech (Rank 3)

- Felwood: Ironbeak Owl (48-49), Olm the Wise (52)
- Western Plaguelands: Carrion Vulture (50-52)

Where to Learn Screech (Rank 4)

- Eastern Plaguelands: Monstrous Plaguebat (56-58)
- Winterspring: Winterspring Screecher (57-59)

Shell Shield

Purpose: Immense Boost to Survivability

Only Usable By: Turtles

Rank	Required Level	Training Points	Cost	Effect
1	20	15	10 Focus	Halves Damage Taken, 43% Longer Between Attacks, 12 Second Duration, 3 Minute Cooldown

Where to Learn Shell Shield (Rank 1)

- Alterac Mountains: Turtle (?)
- Blackfathom Depths: Aku'mai Fisher (23+), Ghamoo'Ra (25+)
- Hillsbrad: Snapjaw (30-31)
- Tanaris: Giant Surf Glider (48-50 Elite)
- Wailing Caverns: Kresh (20 Elite)

Thunderstomp

Purpose: AoE Nature Damage

Only Usable By: Gorillas

Rank	Required Level	Training Points	Cost	Effect
1	30	15	60 Focus	Deals 67 to 77 Nature Damage to All Enemies Within 8 Yards, 1 Minute Cooldown
2	40	20	60 Focus	Deals 87 to 99 Nature Damage to All Enemies Within 8 Yards, 1 Minute Cooldown
3	50	25	60 Focus	Deals 115-133 Nature Damage to All Enemies Within 8 Yards, 1 Minute Cooldown

Where to Learn Thunderstomp (Rank 1)

- Stranglethorn Vale: Jungle Thunderer (37-38), Mistvale Gorilla (32-33)

Where to Learn Thunderstomp (Rank 2)

- Feralas: Groddoc Thunderer (49)
- Stranglethorn Vale: Elder Mistvale Gorilla (39-41)

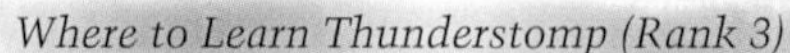

Where to Learn Thunderstomp (Rank 3)

- Un'Goro Crater: U'cha (55), Un'Goro Thunderer (52-53)

CHOOSING YOUR PROFESSION

For a first-time character, Skinning and Leatherworking offer a great deal to a Hunter (especially with Cooking and First Aid on the side). These give Hunters a great deal of independence. Cook your own food, and make plenty for any meat-eating creatures as well. Bandages for yourself or your pet, and craft armor from the creatures you kill.

A more damage-oriented option is to take Mining and Engineering as your professions. Combined, these allow Hunters to craft their own rifles and ammunition (a considerable boon indeed, given that store-bought ammo is lower DPS on the whole). Engineering also provides Scopes to increase ranged damage and explosives too!

Fishing is another secondary trade to consider. Some of the pets prefer fish instead of terrestrial meats, and it doesn't take too long to drop a line and pick up goodies for your pet in many locations. Though not a huge benefit, this is a slight money-saver for the cost-conscious players.

Class Abilities

Hunters, like casters, use Mana for their special attacks. These abilities either do extra Damage, hinder the enemy's abilities, protect the Hunter, or help the Hunter's Pet. Mana can be raised by items with +Intellect and it recovers fastest when you are not using abilities. A generic Hunter trick for saving Mana is to use abilities in a burst at the beginning or end of a fight, and to regenerate Mana for the rest of the fight while relying on your pet and autoshoot for DPS.

Be sure to optimize your Hunter's quickbars. This is a class with many abilities, and things can get very confusing if you toss everything together without rhyme or reason. Keep ranged abilities together, push melee abilities onto a secondary bar unless you are a Survival Hunter who does a great deal of melee fighting, and keep traps and tracking on entirely separate bars as well. This leads to clean ability use (relying on the keyboard for faster functionality instead of mouse-clicking, which is *way* too slow in most end game or PvP skirmishes).

Beast Mastery

Aspect of the Monkey

Aspect of the Monkey is used when your Hunter is in melee against a non-Warrior and wants to increase the chance for a Dodge to occur.

Rank	Level	Mana	Range	Casting Time	Cooldown	Cost to Train	Effect
N/A	4	20	—	IC	—	1	The hunter takes on the aspects of a monkey, increasing chance to dodge by 8%. Only one Aspect can be active at a time.

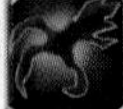

Aspect of the Hawk

Aspect of the Hawk increases the Ranged Attack Power of your Hunter (by a fair margin). This is often the default Aspect for Hunters as they rise through the levels.

Rank	Level	Mana	Range	Casting Time	Cooldown	Cost to Train	Effect
1	10	20	—	IC	—	4	The hunter takes on the aspects of the hawk, increasing Ranged Attack Power by 20. Only one Aspect can be active at a time.
2	18	35	—	IC	—	20	The hunter takes on the aspects of a hawk, increasing Ranged Attack Power by 35. Only one Aspect can be active at a time.
3	28	50	—	IC	—	80	The hunter takes on the aspects of the hawk, increasing Ranged Attack Power by 50. Only one Aspect can be active at a time.
4	38	70	—	IC	—	1 60	The hunter takes on the aspects of a hawk, increasing Ranged Attack Power by 70. Only one Aspect can be active at a time.
5	48	90	—	IC	—	3 20	The hunter takes on the aspects of a hawk, increasing Ranged Attack Power by 90. Only one aspect can be active at a time.
6	58	110	—	IC	—	4 80	The hunter takes on the aspects of a hawk, increasing Ranged Attack powers by 110. Only one Aspect can be active at a time.
7	60	120	—	IC	—	—	The Hunter takes on the Aspect of the Hawk, increasing Ranged Attack Power by 120. Only one Aspect can be active at a time.

Mend Pet

Mend Pet must be used within close proximity to your pet. This ability heals your beloved friend, generating a fair amount of Threat in the process. Be careful not to heal too often in battle!

Rank	Level	Mana	Range	Casting Time	Cooldown	Cost to Train	Effect
1	12	50	20 yd	Channeled	—	6	Heals your pet 20 health every second while you focus. Lasts 5 sec.
2	20	90	20 yd	Channeled	—	22	Heals your pet 38 health every second while you focus. Lasts 5 sec.
3	28	155	20 yd	Channeled	—	80	Heals your pet 68 health every second while you focus. Lasts 5 sec.
4	36	225	20 yd	Channeled	—	1 40	Heals your pet 103 health every second while you focus. Lasts 5 sec.
5	44	300	20 yd	Channeled	—	2 60	Heals your pet 142 health every second while you focus. Lasts 5 sec.
6	52	385	20 yd	Channeled	—	4	Heals your pet 189 health every second while you focus. Lasts 5 sec.
7	60	480	20 yd	Channeled	—	5	Heals your pet 245 health every second while you focus. Lasts 5 sec.

Eagle Eye

Eagle Eye allows Hunters to throw their view forward, scouting very distant positions

Rank	Level	Mana	Range	Casting Time	Cooldown	Cost to Train	Effect
N/A	14	25	50000 yd	Channeled	—	12	Zooms in the Hunter's vision. Only useable outdoors. Lasts 1 min.

Eyes of the Beast

Eyes of the Beast is an ability with great potential, and few Hunters use it as often as they should. Eyes of the Beast lets you take direct control of a pet! Use this to scout ahead even while indoors (which Eagle Eye can't do), to distract foes, lead enemies away from a desire camp or goal.

Rank	Level	Mana	Range	Casting Time	Cooldown	Cost to Train	Effect
N/A	14	20	50000 yd	2 sec	—	12	Take direct control of your pet and see through its eyes for 1 min.

Scare Beast

Scare Beast is a Fear ability that works against Beasts (even Druids in Feral form).

Rank	Level	Mana	Range	Casting Time	Cooldown	Cost to Train	Effect
1	14	35	10 yd	1.5 sec	30 sec	12	Scares a beast, causing it to run in fear for up to 10 sec. Damage caused may interrupt the effect. Only one beast can be feared at a time.
2	30	50	10 yd	1.5 sec	30 sec	80	Scares a beast, causing it to run in fear for up to 15 sec. Damage caused may interrupt the effect. Only one beast can be feared at a time.
3	46	75	10 yd	1.5 sec	30 sec	2 80	Scares a beast, causing it to run in fear for up to 20 sec. Damage caused may interrupt the effect. Only one beast can be feared at a time.

Aspect of the Cheetah

Aspect of the Cheetah is used as a modest travel ability. This Aspect raises a Hunter's movement rate by 30%! However, any damage dealt to your Hunter causes a Daze effect.

Rank	Level	Mana	Range	Casting Time	Cooldown	Cost to Train	Effect
N/A	20	40	—	IC	—	22	The hunter takes on the aspects of a cheetah, increasing movement speed by 30%. If the hunter takes damage she will be dazed for 4 sec. Only one Aspect can be active at a time.

Beast Lore

Beast Lore is a nifty ability that changes the details you receive about a given Beast. Instead of just knowing the creature's level and such, your Hunter can see their health, armor, Resistances, abilities known and diet.

Rank	Level	Mana	Range	Casting Time	Cooldown	Cost to Train	Effect
N/A	24	40	40 yd	IC	—	70	Gather information about the target beast. The tooltip will display damage, health, armor, any special resistances, and diet.

Intimidation

Intimidation is a Talent-learned ability that allows Beast Master Hunters to Stun targets with their pet.

Rank	Prerequisite	Effect
1	20 Points in Beast Mastery	Command your pet to intimidate the target on the next successful melee attack, causing a high amount of threat and stunning the target for 3 sec.

Aspect of the Beast

Aspect of the Beast is a PvP tool to be used against other Hunters, and Druids in Cat Form. When this Aspect is active, your Hunter will not show up on radar even when other classes are using Track Humanoids.

Rank	Level	Mana	Range	Casting Time	Cooldown	Cost to Train	Effect
N/A	30	50	IC	—	—	80	The hunter takes on the aspects of a beast, becoming untrackable.

Aspect of the Pack

Aspect of the Pack is a wonderful ability, but it can get you into real trouble. This Aspect grants Aspect of the Cheetah to your entire group (so long as they are within modest range). The Daze issue is now a threat to all of your allies.

Rank	Level	Mana	Range	Casting Time	Cooldown	Cost to Train	Effect
N/A	40	100	—	IC	—	1 80	The hunter and group members take on the aspects of a pack of cheetahs, increasing movement speed by 30%. If a pack member takes damage, they will be dazed for 4 sec. Only one Aspect can be active at a time.

Bestial Wrath

Bestial Wrath is a Talent-learned ability from the end of the Beast Mastery line. Beast Master Hunters can send their pets into a mighty rage, having them deal far more damage and be immune to almost all forms of crowd control.

Rank	Prerequisite	Effect
1	30 points in Beast Mastery, 1 Point in Intimidation	Send your pet into a rage causing 50% additional damage for 18 sec. While enraged, the beast cannot be stopped by any means.

Aspect of the Wild

Aspect of the Wild increases Nature Resistance for your group.

Rank	Level	Mana	Range	Casting Time	Cooldown	Cost to Train	Effect
1	46	90	—	IC	—	2 80	The hunter and group members within 30 yards take on the aspect of the wild, increasing Nature resistance by 45. Only one Aspect can be active at a time.
2	56	115	—	IC	—	4 60	The hunter and his group take on the aspect of the wild, increasing Nature resistance by 60. Only one Aspect can be active at a time.

Tranquilizing Shot

Tranquilizing Shot is an ability for Molten Core raiders. This is learned off of a book drop and is used to remove Frenzy effects from certain bosses (Magmadar of Molten Core is the prime example).

Rank	Level	Mana	Range	Casting Time	Cooldown	Effects
1	60	270	8-35 yd	IC	20 sec	Attempts to remove 1 Frenzy effect from an enemy creature.

Marksmanship

Serpent Sting

Serpent Sting is an instant, ranged DOT that deals a fair slice of damage.

Rank	Level	Mana	Range	Casting Time	Cooldown	Cost to Train	Effect
1	4	15	8-35 yd	IC	—	1	Stings the target, causing 20 Nature damage over 15 sec. Only one Sting per Hunter can be active on any one target.
2	10	30	8-35 yd	IC	—	4	Stings the target, causing 40 Nature damage over 15 sec. Only one Sting per Hunter can be active on any one target.
3	18	50	8-35 yd	IC	—	20	Stings the target, causing 80 Nature damage over 15 sec. Only one Sting per Hunter can be active on any one target.
4	26	80	8-35 yd	IC	—	70	Stings the target, causing 140 Nature damage over 15 sec. Only one Sting per Hunter can be active on any one target.
5	34	115	8-35 yd	IC	—	1 20	Stings the target, causing 210 Nature damage over 15 sec. Only one Sting per Hunter can be active on any one target.
6	42	150	8-35 yd	IC	—	2 40	Stings the target, causing 290 Nature damage over 15 sec. Only one Sting per Hunter can be active on any one target.
7	50	190	8-35 yd	IC	—	3 60	Stings the target, causing 385 Nature damage over 15 sec. Only one Sting per Hunter can be active on any one target.
8	58	230	8-35 yd	IC	—	4 80	Stings the target, causing 490 Nature damage over 15 sec. Only one Sting per Hunter can be active on any one target.
9	60	250	8-35 yd.	IC	—	—	Stings the target, causing 555 Nature damage over 15 sec. Only one Sting per Hunter can be active on any one target.

Arcane Shot

Arcane Shot is not very mana efficient on damage, but it is an instant attack that isn't mitigated by armor. In addition, anything that raises Arcane damage assists Arcane Shot (not that many Hunters are going to seek +Arcane gear except for specific circumstances).

Rank	Level	Mana	Range	Casting Time	Cooldown	Cost to Train	Effect
1	6	25	8-35 yd	IC	6 sec	1	An Instant shot that causes 13 Arcane Damage
2	12	35	8-35 yd	IC	6 sec	6	An Instant shot that causes 21 Arcane Damage
3	20	50	8-35 yd	IC	6 sec	22	An instant shot that causes 33 Arcane damage.
4	28	80	8-35 yd	IC	6 sec	80	An instant shot that causes 59 Arcane damage.
5	36	105	8-35 yd	IC	6 sec	1 40	An instant shot that causes 83 Arcane damage.
6	44	135	8-35 yd	IC	6 sec	2 60	An instant shot that causes 115 Arcane damage.
7	52	160	8-35 yd	IC	6 sec	4	An instant shot that causes 145 Arcane damage.
8	60	190	8-35 yd	IC	6 sec	5	An instant shot that causes 183 Arcane damage.

Hunter's Mark

Hunter's Mark places a debuff on a target that keeps them highlighted on your minimap (even if they Stealth in the future).

Rank	Level	Mana	Range	Casting Time	Cooldown	Cost to Train	Effect
1	6	15	100 yd	IC	—	1	Places the Hunter's Mark on the target, increasing the Ranged Attack Power of all attackers against that target by 20. In addition, the target of this ability can always be seen by the hunter whether it stealths or turns invisible. The target also appears on the mini-map. Lasts for 2 mins.
2	22	30	100 yd	IC	—	60	Places the Hunter's Mark on the target, increasing the Ranged Attack Power of all attackers against that target by 45. In addition, the target of this ability can always be seen by the hunter whether it stealths or turns invisible. The target also appears on the mini-map. Lasts for 2 mins.
3	40	45	100 yd	IC	—	1 80	Places the Hunter's Mark on the target, increasing the Ranged Attack Power of all attackers against that target by 75. In addition, the target of this ability can always be seen by the hunter whether it stealths or turns invisible. The target so appears on the mini-map. Lasts for 2 mins.
4	58	60	100 yd	IC	—	4 80	Places the Hunter's Mark on the target, increasing the Ranged Attack Power of all attackers against that target by 110. In addition, the target of this ability can always be seen by the hunter whether it stealths or turns invisible. The target also appears on the mini-map. Lasts for 2 mins.

Concussive Shot

Concussive Shot is an instant attack that is not used for damage. Instead, is slows targets (or outright Stuns them if you spec for it).

Rank	Level	Mana	Range	Casting Time	Cooldown	Cost to Train	Effect
N/A	8	5	8-35 yd	IC	12 sec	2	Dazes the target, slowing movement speed to 50% of normal for 4 sec.

Distracting Shot

Distracting Shot is an ability to add Threat to your Hunter.

Rank	Level	Mana	Range	Casting Time	Cooldown	Cost to Train	Effect
1	12	20	8-35 yd	IC	8 sec	6	Distract the target, causing threat.
2	20	30	8-35 yd	IC	8 sec	22	Distract the target, causing threat. More effective than Distracting Shot (Rank 1).
3	30	50	8-35 yd	IC	8 sec	80	Distract the target, causing threat. More effective than Distracting Shot (Rank 2).
4	40	70	8-35 yd	IC	8 sec	1 80	Distract the target, causing threat. More effective than Distracting Shot (Rank 3).
5	50	90	8-35 yd	IC	8 sec	3 60	Distract the target, causing threat. More effective than Distracting Shot (Rank 4).
6	60	110	8-35 yd	IC	8 sec	5	Distract the target, causing threat. More effective than Distracting Shot (Rank 5).

Multi-Shot

Multi-shot is a supreme damage dealer among the Hunter abilities. Strong and mana efficient even for single targets, this ability can damage up to three foes at once!

Rank	Level	Mana	Range	Casting Time	Cooldown	Cost to Train	Effect
1	18	100	8-35 yd	IC	10 sec	20	Fires several missiles, hitting 3 targets.
2	30	140	8-35 yd	IC	10 sec	80	Fires several missiles, hitting 3 targets for an additional 40 damage.
3	42	175	8-35 yd	IC	10 sec	2 40	Fires several missiles, hitting 3 targets for an additional 80 damage.
4	54	210	8-35 yd	IC	10 sec	4 20	Fires several missiles, hitting 3 targets for an additional 120 damage.
5	60	230	8-35 yd.	IC	10 sec	—	Fires several missiles, hitting 3 targets for an additional 150 damage.

Aimed Shot

Aimed Shot is a Talent-learned ability that takes a few seconds to cast but deals very high damage.

Rank	Minimum Level	Mana	Range	Casting Time	Cooldown	Cost to Train	Effect
1	20	68	8-35 yd	+3 sec	6 sec	—	Requires Ranged Weapon. An aimed shot that increases ranged damage by 70.
2	28	115	8-35 yd	+3 sec	6 sec	4	An aimed shot that increases ranged damage by 125.
3	36	160	8-35 yd	+3 sec	6 sec	7	An aimed shot that increases ranged damage by 200.
4	44	210	8-35 yd	+3 sec	6 sec	13	An aimed shot that increases ranged damage by 330.
5	52	260	8-35 yd	+3 sec	6 sec	20	An aimed shot that increases ranged damage by 460.
6	60	310	8-35 yd	+3 sec	6 sec	25	An aimed shot that increases ranged damage by 600.

Scorpid Sting

Scorpid Sting is a debuff Sting that reduces the Strength and Agility of the target.

Rank	Level	Mana	Range	Casting Time	Cooldown	Cost to Train	Effect
1	22	70	8-35 yd	IC	—	60	Stings the target, reducing Strength and Agility by 20 for 20 sec. Only one Sting per Hunter can be active on any one target.
2	32	90	8-35 yd	IC	—	1	Stings the target, reducing Strength and Agility by 29 for 20 sec. Only one Sting per Hunter can be active on any one target.
3	42	125	8-35 yd	IC	—	2 40	Stings the target, reducing Strength and Agility by 45 for 20 sec. Only one Sting per Hunter can be active on any one target.
4	52	165	8-35 yd	IC	—	4	Stings the target, reducing Strength and Agility by 68 for 20 sec. Only one Sting per Hunter can be active on any one target.

Rapid Fire

Rapid Fire increases ranged attack speed by 40% for 15 seconds, and it exists on a five minute timer. Use Rapid Fire for major engagements to increase your DPS substantially.

Rank	Level	Mana	Range	Casting Time	Cooldown	Cost to Train	Effect
N/A	26	100	—	IC	5 min.	70	Increases ranged attack speed by 40% for 15 seconds.

Scatter Shot

Scatter Shot is a Talent-learned ability that can be used even at fairly close range to Disorient a target.

Rank	Prerequisite	Effect
1	20 Points in Marksmanship	A short-range shot that deals 50% weapon damage and confuses the target for 4 sec. Any damage caused will remove the effect. 30 sec. Cooldown

Flare

Flare is the bane of Stealthers. Use this ability to light an area; any Stealther who moves within ten yards of that point over the next 30 seconds is revealed.

Rank	Level	Mana	Range	Casting Time	Cooldown	Cost to Train	Effect
N/A	32	50	30 yd	IC	15 sec	1	Exposes all hidden and invisible enemies within 10 yards of the targeted area for 30 sec.

Viper Sting

Viper Sting destroys the mana of casters. Place this Sting on mana-using targets as early as possible.

Rank	Level	Mana	Range	Casting Time	Cooldown	Cost to Train	Effect
1	36	135	8-35 yd	IC	—	1 40	Stings the target, draining 616 mana over 8 sec. Only one Sting per Hunter can be active on any one target.
2	46	175	8-35 yd	IC	—	2 80	Stings the target, draining 848 mana over 8 sec. Only one Sting per Hunter can be active on any one target.
3	56	215	8-35 yd	IC	—	4 60	Stings the target, draining 1108 mana over 8 sec. Only one Sting per Hunter can be active on any one target.

Trueshot Aura

Trueshot Aura is a Talent-learned ability at the end of the Marksmanship line. This Aura adds to Attack Power (both ranged and melee) for everyone in your group.

Rank	Minimum Level	Mana	Range	Casting Time	Cooldown	Cost to Train	Effect
1	40	325	—	IC	—	—	Increases the Ranged and Melee Attack Power of party members within 45 yards by 50. Lasts 30 min.
2	50	425	—	IC	—	18	Increases the Ranged and Melee Attack Power of party members within 45 yards by 75. Lasts 30 minutes.
3	60	525	—	IC	—	25	Increases the Ranged and Melee Attack Power of party members within 45 yards by 100. Lasts 30 minutes.

Volley

Volley is an AoE ability.

Rank	Level	Mana	Range	Casting Time	Cooldown	Cost to Train	Effect
1	40	350	8-35 yd	IC	1 min	1 80	Continuously fires a volley of ammo at the target area, causing 40 Arcane damage to enemy targets within 8 yards every second for 6 sec.
2	50	420	8-35 yd	IC	1 min	3 60	Continuously fires a volley of ammo at the target area, causing 50 Arcane damage to enemy targets within 8 yards every second for 6 sec.
3	58	490	8-35 yd	IC	1 min	4 80	Continuously fires a volley of ammo at the target area, causing 60 Arcane damage to enemy targets within 8 yards every second for 6 sec.

Raptor Strike

Raptor Strike increases the melee damage of your next attack by a moderate sum.

Rank	Level	Mana	Range	Casting Time	Cooldown	Cost to Train	Effect
1	1	15	—	Next Melee	6 sec	—	A strong attack that increases melee damage by 5.
2	8	25	—	Next Melee	6 sec	2	A strong attack that increases melee damage by 11.
3	16	35	—	Next Melee	6 sec	18	A strong attack that increases melee damage by 21.
4	24	45	—	Next Melee	6 sec	70	A strong attack that increases melee damage by 34.
5	32	55	—	Next Melee	6 sec	1	A strong attack that increases melee damage by 50.
6	40	70	—	Next Melee	6 sec	1 80	A strong attack that increases melee damage by 80.
7	48	85	—	Next Melee	6 sec	3 20	A strong attack that increases melee damage by 110.
8	56	100	—	Next Melee	6 sec	4 60	A strong attack that increases melee damage by 140.

Track Beasts

Tracking of various creature types is learned over the course of Hunter training (Beasts, Humanoids, Undead, Hidden, Elementals, Demons, Giants, Dragonkind).

Rank	Level	Mana	Range	Casting Time	Cooldown	Cost to Train	Effect
N/A	1	—	—	IC	—	10	Shows the location of all nearby Beasts on the minimap. Only one form of tracking can be active at a time.

Track Demons

Rank	Level	Mana	Range	Casting Time	Cooldown	Cost to Train	Effect
N/A	32	—	—	IC	—	1	Shows the location of all nearby demons on the minimap. Only one form of tracking can be active at a time.

Track Dragonkin

Rank	Level	Mana	Range	Casting Time	Cooldown	Cost to Train	Effect
N/A	50	—	—	IC	—	3 60	Shows the location of all nearby dragonkin on the minimap. Only one form of tracking can be active at a time.

Track Elementals

Rank	Level	Mana	Range	Casting Time	Cooldown	Cost to Train	Effect
N/A	26	—	—	—	—	70	Shows the location of all nearby elementals on the minimap. Only one form of tracking can be active at a time.

Track Giants

Rank	Level	Mana	Range	Casting Time	Cooldown	Cost to Train	Effect
N/A	40	—	—	—	—	1 80	Shows the location of all nearby giants on the minimap. Only one form of tracking can be active at a time.

Track Hidden

Rank	Level	Mana	Range	Casting Time	Cooldown	Cost to Train	Effect
N/A	24	—	—	IC	—	70	Increases stealth detection and shows hidden units within detection range on the minimap. Only one form of tracking can be active at a time.

Track Humanoids

Rank	Level	Mana	Range	Casting Time	Cooldown	Cost to Train	Effect
N/A	10	—	—	—	—	4	Shows the location of all nearby humanoids on the minimap. Only one form of tracking can be active at a time.

Track Undead

Rank	Level	Mana	Range	Casting Time	Cooldown	Cost to Train	Effect
N/A	18	—	—	IC	—	20	Shows the location of all nearby undead on the minimap. Only one form of tracking can be active at a time.

Wing Clip

Wing Clip is used by all Hunters. This melee ability Snares your target (and can even Immobilize them if you spec for it). There is no cooldown on Wing Clip either, meaning that a single Hunter can run through a group and Wing Clip everything in sight!

Rank	Level	Mana	Range	Casting Time	Cooldown	Cost to Train	Effect
1	12	40	5 yd	IC	—	6	Inflicts 5 damage and reduces the enemy target's movement speed to 50% of normal for 10 sec. Requires Melee Weapon.
2	38	60	5 yd	IC	—	1 60	Inflicts 25 damage and reduces the enemy target's movement speed to 45% of normal for 10 sec. Requires Melee Weapon.
3	60	80	5 yd	IC	—	5	Inflicts 50 damage and reduces the enemy target's movement speed to 40% of normal for 10 sec. Requires Melee Weapon.

Immolation Trap

Immolation Trap deals reasonably high damage to a single target when stepped on. Place these to help with fights where crowd control is not needed or wanted.

Rank	Level	Mana	Range	Casting Time	Cooldown	Cost to Train	Effect
1	16	50	—	IC	15 sec	18	Place a fire trap that will burn the first enemy to approach for 105 fire damage over 15 sec. Trap will exist for 1 min. Traps can only be placed when out of combat. Only one trap can be active at a time.
2	26	90	—	IC	15 sec	70	Place a fire trap that will burn the first enemy to approach for 215 fire damage over 15 sec. Trap will exist for 1 min. Traps can only be placed when out of combat. Only one trap can be active at a time.
3	36	135	—	IC	15 sec	1 40	Place a fire trap that will burn the first enemy to approach for 340 Fire damage over 15 sec. Trap will exist for 1 min. Traps can only be placed when out of combat. Only one trap can be active at a time.
4	46	190	—	IC	15 sec	2 80	Place a fire trap that will burn the first enemy to approach for 510 Fire damage over 15 sec. Trap will exist for 1 min. Traps can only be placed when out of combat. Only one trap can be active at a time.
5	56	245	—	IC	15 sec	4 60	Place a fire trap that will burn the first enemy to approach for 690 Fire damage over 15 sec. Trap will exist for 1 min. Traps can only be placed when out of combat. Only one trap can be active at a time.

Mongoose Bite

Mongoose Bite allows a moderate damage attack to be made instantly after your Hunter has dodged an enemy's strike.

Rank	Level	Mana	Range	Casting Time	Cooldown	Cost to Train	Effect
1	18	30	5 yd	IC	5 sec	18	Counterattack the enemy for 25 damage. Can only be performed after you dodge.
2	30	40	5 yd	IC	5 sec	80	Counterattack the enemy for 45 damage. Can only be performed after you dodge.
3	44	50	5 yd	IC	5 sec	2 60	Counterattack the enemy for 75 damage. Can only be performed after you dodge.
4	58	60	5 yd	IC	5 sec	4 80	Counterattack the enemy for 115 damage. Can only be performed after you dodge.

Deterrence

Deterrence is on a five minute cooldown. This is Talent-learned, and gives your Hunter ten seconds with a massive increased to Dodge and Parry.

Rank	Prerequisite	Effect
1	10 points in Survival	When activated, increases your Dodge and Parry chance by 25% for 10 sec.

Disengage

Disengage is a melee attack that can miss, but reduces Threat when it lands.

Rank	Level	Mana	Range	Casting Time	Cooldown	Cost to Train	Effect
1	20	50	5 yd	IC	—	22	Attempts to disengage from the target, reducing threat. Character exits combat mode.
2	34	100	5 yd	IC	—	1 20	Attempts to disengage from the target, reducing threat. Character exits combat mode. More effective than Disengage (Rank 1).
3	48	150	5 yd	IC	—	3 20	Attempts to disengage from the target, reducing threat. Character exits combat mode. More effective than Disengage (Rank 2).

Freezing Trap

Freezing Trap is used to disable a single target for a moderate period. Any damage dealt breaks this, and the duration isn't comparable to Polymorph, Shackle, and other high-end crowd control options.

Rank	Level	Mana	Range	Casting Time	Cooldown	Cost to Train	Effect
1	20	50	—	IC	15 sec	22	Place a frost trap that freezes the first enemy that approaches, preventing all action for up to 10 sec. Any damage caused will break the ice. Trap will exist for 1 min. Traps can only be placed when out of combat. Only one trap can be active at a time.
2	40	75	—	IC	15 sec	1 80	Place a frost trap that freezes the first enemy to approach, preventing all action for up to over 15 sec. Any damage caused will break the ice. Trap will exist for 1 min. Traps can only be placed when out of combat. Only one trap can be active at a time.
3	60	100	—	IC	15 sec	5	Place a frost trap that freezes the first enemy to approach, preventing all action for up to over 20 sec. Any damage caused will break the ice. Trap will exist for 1 min. Traps can only be placed when out of combat. Only one trap can be active at a time.

Frost Trap

Frost Trap is used more specifically than Freezing Trap. This AoE Snare slows enemies that pass through it.

Rank	Level	Mana	Range	Casting Time	Cooldown	Cost to Train	Effect
N/A	28	60	—	IC	15 sec	80	Place a frost trap that creates an ice slick around itself when the first enemy approaches it. All enemies within 10 yards will be slowed to 40% of their normal movement speed when in the area of effect. Trap will exist for 1 min. Traps can only be placed when out of combat. Only one trap can be active at a time.

Counterattack

Counterattack is a Talent-learned ability that lights up after your Hunter parries an attack. Modest damage is dealt, and an immediate five-second Immobilization is placed on the enemy target.

Rank	Minimum Level	Mana	Range	Casting Time	Cooldown	Cost to Train	Effect
1	30	45	5 yd	IC	—		A strike that becomes active after parrying an opponent's attack. This attack deals 40 damage and immobilizes the target for 5 sec. Counterattack cannot be blocked, dodged, or parried.
2	42	65	5 yd	IC	5 sec	12	A strike that becomes active after parrying an opponent's attack. This attack deals 70 damage and immobilizes the target for 5 sec. Counterattack cannot be blocked, dodged, or parried.
3	54	85	5 yd	IC	5 sec	21	A strike that becomes active after parrying an opponent's attack. This attack deals 110 damage and immobilizes the target for 5 sec. Counterattack cannot be blocked, dodged, or parried.

Feign Death

Feign Death is the bread and butter of Hunter deaggro toys. Feign Death after massive Criticals, after Multishots, or to get your Hunter out of combat so that traps can be placed.

Rank	Level	Mana	Casting Time	Cooldown	Cost to Train	Effect
N/A	30	80	IC	10 min	80	Feigns death which may trick enemies into ignoring you. Lasts up to 6 min. If the Hunter does not move before Feign Death expires, it will cause real death.

Explosive Trap

Explosive Trap is an AoE damage trap. Though dangerous because of the massive threat generated, this trap deals quite a heavy blow.

Rank	Level	Mana	Range	Casting Time	Cooldown	Cost to Train	Effect
1	34	275	—	IC	15 sec	1 20	Place a fire trap that explodes when an enemy approaches, causing 100 to 130 Fire damage and burning all enemies for 150 additional Fire damage over 20 sec to all within 10 yards. Trap will exist for 1 min. Traps can only be placed when out of combat. Only one trap can be active at a time.
2	44	395	—	IC	15 sec	2 60	Place a fire trap that explodes when an enemy approaches causing 139 to 187 Fire damage and burning all enemies for 240 additional Fire damage over 20 sec to all within 10 yards. Trap will exist for 1 min. Traps can only be placed when out of combat. Only one trap can be active at a time.
3	54	520	—	IC	15 sec	4 20	Place a fire trap that explodes when an enemy approaches causing 201 to 257 Fire damage and burning all enemies for 330 additional Fire damage over 20 sec to all within 10 yards. Trap will exist for 1 min. Traps can only be placed when out of combat. Only one trap can be active at a time.

Wyvern Sting

Wyvern Sting is a Talent-learned ability at the end of the Survival line. Adding yet another crowd control option to the Hunter's mix, Wyvern Sting puts a target to sleep for a fair duration.

Rank	Minimum Level	Mana	Range	Casting Time	Cooldown	Cost to Train	Effect
1	40	115	8 - 35 yds	IC	2 minutes	—	A stinging shot that puts the target to sleep for 12 sec. Any damage will cancel the effect. When the target wakes up, the Sting causes 300 Nature damage over 12 sec. Only useable out of combat. Only one Sting per Hunter can be active on the target at a time.
2	50	115	8 - 35 yds	IC	2 minutes	18	A stinging shot that puts the target to sleep for 12 sec. Any damage will cancel the effect. When the target wakes up, the Sting causes 420 Nature damage over 12 sec. Only useable out of combat. Only one Sting per Hunter can be active on the target at a time.
3	60	115	8 - 35 yds	IC	2 minutes	25	A stinging shot that puts the target to sleep for 12 sec. Any damage will cancel the effect. When the target wakes up, the Sting causes 600 Nature damage over 12 sec. Only useable out of combat. Only one Sting per Hunter can be active on the target at a time.

TALENTS

As with many classes, a Hunter's Talent choices are either defined by their playstyle or serve *to* define their playstyle. The PvE supremacy of Beast Mastery, the PvP artillery of a Marksmanship Hunter, and the complex interdiction of the Survival line all serve their masters well.

Beast Mastery

Beast Mastery is far and away one of the best Talent lines for leveling in World of Warcraft. Beast Master Hunters are able to solo very quickly, complete a wide range of quests, and experience death on such a seldom basis that Spirit Healers will not know you on a first-name basis. The reason for these things is that Beast Masters put so much into their pets! If anyone is going to die in a fight, it's likely to be your furry/scaly buddy (and your Hunter can scoot on out of there before the bitter end). Beyond that, the faster healing of pets and the reduced reliance on Hunter input into each fight allow Beast Masters to have effectively no downtime.

Look into this line for higher pet armor and health, improved outdoor pet speed (so nice), and damage improvements! These Hunter pets gain damage passively (higher standard damage and increased Critical rates) and actively (abilities like Bestial Wrath, which deals incredible damage and turns your pet into an unstoppable monster, for a time).

Marksmanship

Marksmanship Hunters are a frequent choice for those who want to deal damage directly. Though troubled at times by pets that are less survivable and a weak melee, Marksmanship Hunters provide burst and AoE damage that the other Hunters could only dream of reaching. With higher Critical chances at range, more damage done by Criticals, and improved base damage with such weapons, the passive DPS of Marksmanship Hunters is already high. Add to this several abilities that allow for even more options; Scatter Shot and Improved Concussive Shot allow you to keep enemies from closing the distance as easily, while Aimed Shot lets you deal cruel and unusual punishment to start ambushes or to slip in-between the cooldowns on your higher-damage Multishot!

A final perk of the Marksmanship line is that these Hunters gain an aura that helps the entire group (including your pet); Trueshot Aura raises Attack Power for everyone within range, and this effect stacks with Warriors' Battle Shout. Placed in a group with Hunters, Rogues, and Warriors, Trueshot Aura is divine!

Survival

With such valid Talent options in the first two lines, one might think that Survival is going to be the red-headed stepchild of the Hunter Talent choices. A number of younger Hunters might even believe this! Melee damage? Trap Improvements? Look deeper into this line; there are Talents in here that are so good that it hurts. The Talent options are more difficult and painful than it would first appear, eh?

Survival Hunters get a wonderful set of passive improvements (increased damage + Critical damage against specific targets, higher Parry, more health, better chance to hit, higher Agility, and more Criticals in melee and at range). Unbelievable. Though not the most frequent choice because the other two lines are so intuitive, an experience Hunter can do things of beauty as a Survivalist. Dealing more damage in melee and being more rugged allows these Hunters to eliminate the classes greatest weakness; PvP foes and enemies alike can close the distance and get a very nasty surprise. All of that is good already, then factor in the increased trap duration and difficult to resist such effects. Finally, Survivalists can combine a trap and their Wyvern Sting Talent to stop two different enemies from entering a fight. Few classes can match that!

Weaker for soloing than Beast Mastery and more difficult to play in PvP than Marksmanship, Survival is recommended for experienced Hunters who work well with their teams. In both PvP and PvE, Survivalists disrupt enemy forces with amazing skill

STRATEGIES

Hunter strategies often revolve around keep the enemies where *you* want them to be. This is true while soloing, in groups, and with several different specializations. What changes is the desired position of your enemy. Are you trying to work in maximal crowd control through traps and Wyvern Sting? What about keeping the enemy in melee with you while you Wing Clip everything (to help an ally)? Or, leave the enemy at long range, engaged by your pet. Read the following strategies to get an idea how Hunter's think and fight!

General Tips

Bringing the enemy down as quickly as possible is what the Hunter is made for. Cast Aspect of the Hawk and use Hunter's Mark on the target. This doesn't draw aggro, but increases all ranged damage dealt to your target. Send your pet in to attack since it takes a moment to get there. Begin the fight by using Serpent Sting so the DOT runs its full course. With your pet attacking and holding the enemy's attention (Growl is a good thing), keep shooting until the enemy is dead.

If the battle is to be a long one, use Serpent Sting early. It's an instant attack that causes damage over time. Have your pet using Growl whenever it has Health and you have aggro. This will help keep the enemy at range.

Change to Aspect of the Monkey when the enemy closes to melee. This will increase your Dodge rate and give you more opportunities to use Mongoose Bite. When the enemy runs, just wait for it to run a few steps and hit it with Arcane Shot.

Get comfortable moving from melee to range and back again. Knowing when to move into and out of melee combat helps you keep your health and mana high while still doing damage. If something breaks away from your pet, use a Wing Clip (followed with a Scattershot for Marksmanship Hunters), and get some distance before re-engaging. For fights where you know ahead of time that some aggro trading between you and your pet is needed, place a Frost or Freezing Trap ahead of time to give your enemies extra trouble when they come after you.

Mana only regenerates when you haven't cast for a short while. Keeping this in mind, cast your battle spells in bunches to allow regeneration between and during fights. Casting Arcane Shot every time it recharges increases your damage, but leaves you low on mana at the end of the fight. Only unload your mana supply if a fight is dangerous and threatening you (or your pet's) life.

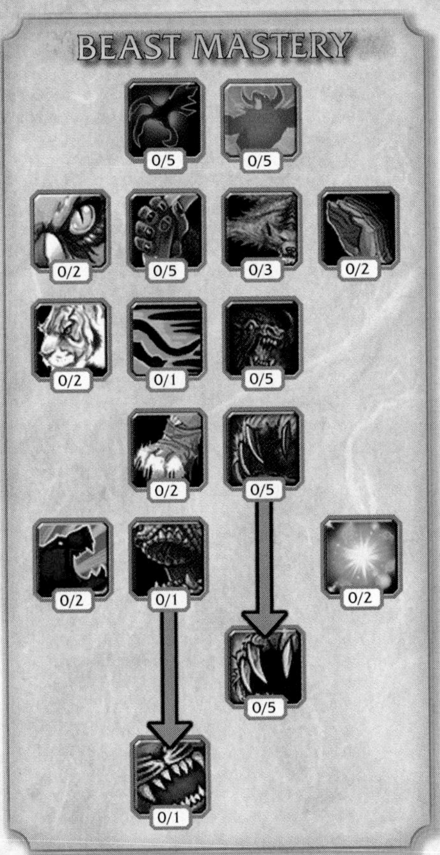

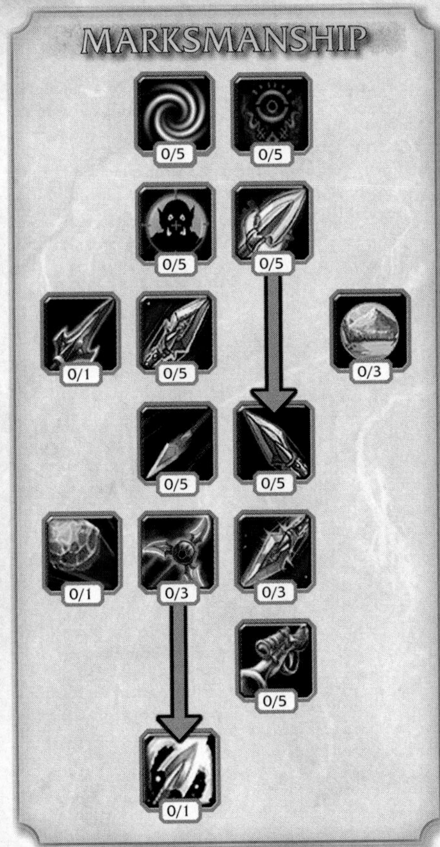

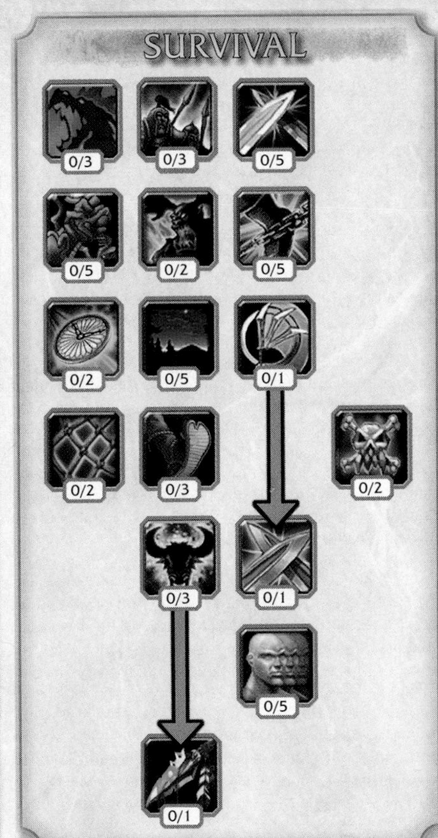

IMPROVED ASPECT OF THE HAWK 5

While Aspect of the Hawk is active, all normal ranged attacks have a 1% chance (Per Rank) of increasing ranged attack speed by 30% for 8 seconds.

ENDURANCE TRAINING 5

Increases the Health of your pets by 3% (Per Rank).

IMPROVED EYES OF THE BEAST 2

Increases the duration of your Eyes of the Beast by 30 seconds (Per Rank).

IMPROVED ASPECT OF THE MONKEY 5

Increases the Dodge bonus of your Aspect of the Monkey by 1% (Per Rank).

THICK HIDE 3

Increases the Armor rating of your pets by 10% (Per Rank).

IMPROVED REVIVE PET 2

Revive Pet's casting time is reduced by 3 seconds (Per Rank), mana cost is reduced by 20% (Per Rank), and increases the health your pet returns with by an additional 15% (Per Rank).

PATHFINDING 2

Increases the speed bonus of your Aspect of the Cheetah and Aspect of the Pack by 3% (Per Rank).

BESTIAL SWIFTNESS 1

Increases the outdoor movement speed of your pets by 30%.

UNLEASHED FURY 5

Increases the damage done by your pets by 4% (Per Rank).

IMPROVED MEND PET 2

Gives the Mend Pet Spell a 15% chance of cleansing 1 Curse, Disease, Magic or Poison effect from the pet each tick. Progression 15%/50%

FEROCITY 5

Increases the critical strike chance of your pets by 3% (Per Rank).

SPIRIT BOND 2

While your pet is active, you and your pet will regenerate 1% (Per Rank) of total health every 10 sec.

INTIMIDATION 1

Command your pet to intimidate the target on the next successful melee attack, causing a high amount of threat and stunning the target for 3 sec.

BESTIAL DISCIPLINE 2

Increases the Focus regeneration of your pets by 10% (Per Rank).

FRENZY 5

Gives your pet a 20% chance (Per Rank) to gain a 30% attack speed increase for 8 sec after dealing a critical strike.

BESTIAL WRATH 1

Send your pet into a rage causing 50% additional damage for 15 sec. While enraged, the beast cannot be stopped by any means.

IMPROVED CONCUSSIVE SHOT 5

Gives your Concussive Shot a 4% chance (Per Rank) to stun the target for 3 sec.

EFFICIENCY 5

Reduces the Mana cost of your Shots and Stings by 2% (Per Rank).

IMPROVED HUNTER'S MARK 5

Increases the Ranged Attack Power bonus of your Hunter's Mark spell by 3% (Per Rank).

LETHAL SHOTS 5

Increases your critical strike chance with ranged weapons by 1% (Per Rank).

AIMED SHOT 1

An aimed shot that increases ranged damage by 70.

IMPROVED ARCANE SHOT 5

Reduces the cooldown of your Arcane Shot by 0.2 sec (Per Rank).

HAWK EYE 3

Increases the range of your ranged weapons by 2 yards (Per Rank).

IMPROVED SERPENT STING 5

Increases the damage done by your Serpent Sting by 2% (Per Rank).

MORTAL SHOTS 5

Increases your ranged weapon critical strike damage bonus by 6% (Per Rank).

SCATTER SHOT 1

A short-range shot that deals 50% weapon damage and confuses the target for 4 sec. Any damage caused will remove the effect.

BARRAGE 3

Increases the damage done by your Multi-Shot and Volley spells by 5% (per rank).

IMPROVED SCORPID STING 3

Reduces the Stamina of targets affected by your Scorpid Sting by 10% (per rank) of the amount of the Strength reduced.

RANGED WEAPON SPECIALIZATION 5

Increases the damage you deal with ranged weapons by 1% (per rank).

TRUESHOT AURA 1

Increases the Ranged and Melee Attack Power of party members within 45 yards by 50. Lasts 30 min.

MONSTER SLAYING 3

Increases all damage caused against Beast, Giants and Dragonkin targets by 1% (Per Rank) and increases critical damage caused against Beasts, Giants, and Dragonkin targets by an additional 1% (Per Rank).

HUMANOID SLAYING 3

Increases all damage caused against Humanoid targets by 1% (Per Rank) and increases critical damage caused against Humanoid targets by an additional 1% (Per Rank).

DEFLECTION 5

Increases your Parry chance by 1% (Per Rank).

ENTRAPMENT 5

Gives your Immolation Trap, Frost Trap, and Explosive Trap a 5% chance (Per Rank) to entrap the target, preventing them from moving for 5 sec.

SAVAGE STRIKES 2

Increases the critical strike chance of Raptor Strike and Mongoose Bite by 10% (Per Rank).

IMPROVED WING CLIP 5

Gives your Wing Clip ability a 4% chance (Per Rank) to immobilize the target for 5 sec.

CLEVER TRAPS 2

Increases the duration of Freezing and Frost trap effects by 15% (Per Rank) and the damage of Immolation and Explosive trap effects by 15% (Per Rank).

SURVIVALIST 5

Increases total health by 2% (Per Rank).

DETERRENCE 1

When activated, increases your Dodge and Parry chance by 25% for 10 sec.

TRAP MASTERY 2

Decreases the chance enemies will resist trap effects by 5% (Per Rank).

SUREFOOTED 3

Increases hit chance by 1% (Per Rank) and increases the chance movement impairing effects will be resisted by 5% (Per Rank).

IMPROVED FEIGN DEATH 2

Reduces the chance your Feign Death ability will be resisted by 2% (Per Rank).

KILLER INSTINCT 3

Increases your critical strike chance with all attacks by 1% (Per Rank).

COUNTERATTACK 1

A strike that becomes active after parrying an opponent's attack. Deals 40 damage and immobilizes the target for 5 sec. Counterattack cannot be blocked, dodged, or parried.

LIGHTENING REFLEXES 5

Increases your Agility by 3% (Per Rank).

WYVERN STING 1

A stinging shot that puts the target to sleep for 12 sec. Any damage will cancel the effect. When the target wakes up, the Sting causes 300 Nature damage over 12 sec. Only useable out of combat. Only one Sting per Hunter can be active on the target at one time.

Pulling Like a Pro

The Hunter has many tools that aid in pulling. Using Hunter's Mark lets everyone know which enemy you intend to shoot. This helps a great deal when coordinating attacks with other party members.

Set a trap before you pull. Freeze Traps Root a single enemy giving you and your party more time to act against other foes. As an example, pretend that you are in Stratholme, looking at a group of undead. The Priest in your group plans to shackle one of the elite targets, and you are the Hunter. Place a Freeze Trap and shoot one of the deeper targets that isn't elite (for a fast kill). The first monster to add is going to come after you and run straight into that trap. Almost free crowd control! With this action, your group is focused on killing one target before it can do anything major, another is Shackled, and a third is frozen. Half of the enemies are out of the way already.

If only one enemy is coming, consider using the Immolation Trap. Once aggro is consolidated, just drag the enemy over the trap for added damage. Or, in major battles (PvP and such), use an Explosive Trap for AoE damage.

Bringing one enemy at a time to a group makes managing aggro easier and keeps everyone on the same target. This can turn even the most stressful areas into organized fighting. Even when larger groups are linked together (in many dungeons), a Hunter is able to ensure that only the intended group comes instead of a large group *and* patrollers *and* an extra group.

Part of pulling is avoiding unintended pulls. Many enemies run for help when they get low on Health. You or your group may not be prepared for a second wave if the first has not been dealt with. Have Wing Clip ready to slow fleeing enemies or Concuss them if they get too far away for Wing Clip.

One final piece of wisdom; when pulling, be ready to Feign Death if things go wrong. If two groups and a patroller all start to move in, Feign Death instantly, let your pet die, and tell your the group to stay back. The creatures won't aggro on your group unless they attack, heal, or otherwise interfere. The mobs will eat your buddy and head home. Get up, Rez your pet, and try again. This avoids group wipes for a great deal less suffering.

The First Shot

Remember a few things when making the first attack against an enemy. If you are pulling targets to you, note that instant attacks are best for timing purposes. Arcane Shot taps instantly and gets your target on the move. Using a Sting is just as fast, but these won't target you as quickly (and that is bad if you are competing for monsters with other people or groups).

When trying to get specific monsters in dungeons, line up your target carefully. After selecting and marking the foe, wait until the creature or group is away from patrollers (the Rogue's distract can help here) or any other non-linked entities that might add. If you pull a patroller while a group is near, you are going to get everyone! This is why Hunters are sent out to carefully pick patrollers from maximum range when they aren't near buddies.

Be cognizant of enemies' paths as they run after you. Do not pull targets through other groups when they are aggroing. This causes everything else to add to your existing pull (not a good situation).

Use Tracking to find out where the monsters are in an area. There might be things just around the corner (or a patrol on the way). Knowing that ahead of time avoids the problem of sticking your head out into an ambush.

Using Your Pet

Pets are the most important part of a Hunter's lineup. These allies deal damage for you, tank for you, and can survive far more abuse than one might imagine. With extra armor, health, and various Resistances, pets can almost survive like a well-geared Warrior.

First point of order is to bind Pet Attack to a key that is very easy to use. Make this a key that is by one of your hands, because you are going to use Pet Attack all the time.

Send pets to engage targets at range, and leave Growl on unless your pet is not meant to tank (e.g. Instance groups with a good Warrior). Use autoshoot and your desired Sting early in the fight, and hold briefly on harder-hitting abilities to ensure that Growl lands and that your pet is fully ticking-off the target. Then, use Multishot, Aimed Shot, and other high-damage attacks. After level 30, remember to Feign Death after large bursts of damage to keep the aggro firmly cemented on your pet.

Even in a group with a good tank, remember that your pet is a fast and sturdy offtank. When a single creature breaks away from the tank and goes after someone else (probably a healer), sick your pet on it to gain aggro, then tell your pet to attack the main creature being damaged by the group again. This causes the extra monster to run back to the main battle area on the heels of your pet; the main tank is going to have a much easier time holding aggro when all of the monsters are clustered in such a way.

If you can offtank with your pet, remember to keep traps in front of healers, and use your damage carefully, groups reinvite you *time and time again.*

Long-Term Damage

Autoshot, a good quiver/ammo pouch, high-end ammo, and a fine missile weapon are good for damage. But these aren't enough for brutal killing. Indeed, Hunters have abilities that push their damage potential into the highest strata, especially during longer fights. Learn what you are capable of dishing out!

All Hunters gain Multishot. This may sound like an AoE option for you, but it isn't. Multishot only hits three people; even Warriors are better suited for AoE than that paltry sum. Rather, Multishot is more like free damage! Even against a single target, Multishot is an ability that lets you take a free attack at relatively high-damage. After your normal shot flies, tap Multishot and watch the extra attack land. Very nice! If there are two or three targets, this ability goes from wonderful to amazingly wonderful. Use Multishot *all the time* once you master the art of losing aggro. It is very common for Hunters to toss a brutal Multishot into a cluster of enemies and Feign Death before a single target breaks rank.

Rapid Fire is on enough of a cooldown that you won't want to use it casually. Wait for the tougher fights (larger pulls, boss fights, and such). During those engagements, use Rapid Fire after your pet or prime tank has gathered aggro fully.

Volley is a Hunter's sincere AoE choice. Those somewhat low on damage dealt, this attack becomes valuable when there are four or more targets in a given location. While Mages, Warlocks, and even Priests are called on for an AoE fight, remember to stay at range and prepared Volley. Don't use this attack until after the primary AoE characters have started their actions; you don't want to get early aggro and pull the targets back to you. Wait until the casters have started blowing everything apart, then launch your Volley! Afterward, toss a Multishot, Feign Death, and do what you can to help finish any stragglers.

Hunters with Aimed Shot can slip it between normal shoots to deal the most damage. Enormous DPS is possible with a Hunter alternating between Aimed Shot and Multi-Shot.

Feign Death

Level 30 grants Feign Death. Love it and live by it. When soloing or grouping, use this to keep aggro fully off of your Hunter. Creatures that make it all the way over to you have a chance of resisting Feign Death, so use this ability before aggro is even coming your way. Aimed Shot just criticaled? Feign Death *now*! Multishot hit three targets and the tank only is focusing on one of them? You know what to do.

If a Feign Death isn't done early enough, you may not want to even try. If you are toward the back of the group, understand that a Feign Death might switch the aggro of the creature to the nearby casters. Nobody likes Hunters who do this! The tank is going to hate you. The healers are going to hate you. Even Rogues shake their heads and grit their teeth at that point. The reason is that the whole group must now work as quickly as possible to get aggro back where it should be, and that chaos is dangerous.

If aggro gets all the way to your doorstep, go into melee and bring the creature back to your tank. A good tank will easily pull the foe off of you and get back to work. Never run away from the group. Trust people to save you. And if they fail, remember that bad groups always end sooner rather than later.

A selfish time to use Feign Death is during a group wipe. If all of the healers have gone down and the battle is hopeless, retreat to an area that is away from patrollers and other enemies, then Feign Death. The group will wipe, but you can pop back up later. To make this survival a bit more group-friendly, if you took Engineering keep a set of Goblin Jumper Cables on your person. Use these to Resurrect one of the group's Rezzers, if you can. There, you have just become one more point of insurance against a total wipeout!

Mastering Your Radar

Tracking offers so much to a good Hunter. But you can't just sit back and expect the information to come to you! There are many different forms of Tracking, and only one can be active at a given time. Track Humanoids is the standard for PvP work, but remember that classes can switch to animal forms (Track Beasts).

In PvE situations, a dungeon might require a Hunter to shift between two or three forms of Tracking. While wandering through Maraudon, Giants, Elementals, and Beasts are all present. Once you know an Instance well, this becomes a matter of switching to the correct Tracking type ahead of time. When you don't know what types of enemies are ahead, try using a few forms of Tracking while the group is on the move. If anything pops up suddenly, stop and inform everyone.

When a more experienced person is in the group, be clear with them that you want as much information as possible. Say "I haven't been in here before. What type of Tracking should I use?" Hunters should ask a lot of questions, because in future runs people are going to look to you for information. They want to know when the patrollers are coming. They want to know if "that rare spawn is up." Mediocre Hunters are just plain DPS. Good Hunters are scouts, killers, and offtanks in a single package.

Mages are the ranged damage-dealers in World of Warcraft. These masters of elemental fire and cold have studied the arcane arts for years, dedicating themselves to the destruction of their enemies. Though fragile in melee combat, Mages are able to make themselves known on the field of battle. Strong enough on single-target DPS, the Mage offers even greater AoE options, the ability to slow/disrupt many targets, and the utility of in-battle crowd control as well. We didn't even mention that they can create free food and water (for health and mana), did we?

Lore

The cries of battle carried over the forest like a melody. I felt so many precious souls being brought again into the world: new, fresh, dedicated to a different cause. The right concoction of plague, violence, and temporary unpleasantness was always a good way to make people see things in a new light.

Waiting for our Warriors to bring the ranks of human invaders together, I poked my head up (ever so slightly) and saw that the time was approaching. The humans and several of their Alliance vermin were closing in for the kill; that is how they saw it at least. Visibly, our Warriors below were in a bad place. As they feigned disorder and feigned retreat, I readied the true attack. Looking over at Ishnaron, my Warlock ally, I nodded. He knew what to do.

Calmly we strode to the top of the hill. Ishnaron's Void Walker glided through the shadows and laid into the humans, distracting them. Our Warriors turned and began to fight with renewed vigor, and I summoned the power of frost to lock them in place before I began a mighty blizzard. The humans called out to one another, lost in the sudden storm.

With my storm of cold finished, I too turned to the strength of flame, and a wave of rippling fire tore through the tangle of living and dying men. They called to their healers for salvation, not realizing that those feeble creatures had died moments ago. The battle had been over before it ever began.

Introduction to Playing the Class

Mages love to bring damage to the table, whether to individual targets or entire groups. Using a massive amount of mana, this is a class with burst damage galore. Though Mages are sometimes glass cannons (all damage and no defense), the truth is that Mages can survive quite well as long as they temper their casting. Using spells at the right time can make all the difference between unsurvivable aggro and being in the clear.

The first defense of a Mage comes through range. Mage spells are cast at long range and are very deadly. Beyond the range itself, there is some use to the delay between a successful cast and the spell's impact. Most long-range Mage spells are bolts, so there is time to start casting a second spell before your first bolt impacts (against monsters, this is a great boon). Cast at maximum range for almost everything you do and allow as much reaction time as possible when seeing if there are adds.

Speaking of adds, Mages have an ability that they love while soloing and while playing in groups for crowd control-Polymorph. Turning enemies into sheep prevents them from doing any damage to you or your friends for a considerable duration. Unlike some forms of crowd control, Polymorph can be cast whether you or the creature are in battle, and even while you are being attacked directly. Though diminishing returns prevent Mages from hitting the same target with Polymorph too many times, it is quite possible to shift between Polymorph targets (getting close to the full duration for each).

Mages also get a powerful Intellect buff (for themselves and allies, meaning that all casters are quickly your best friends). Mages can also summon free food and drink so that everyone in the group recovers quickly during downtime. Later on, Mages summon Mana Gems for themselves (for fast Mana recovery during combat).

Using area-of-effect magic, Mages are able to do horrendous damage to large groups without delay. This gives a major place to Mages in large-scale PvP and when fighting in groups tailored for besting monsters with AoE tactics.

Available Races			
Gnome	Human	Troll	Undead

What do Attributes Mean to Me?	
Strength	No Mages Care
Stamina	Higher Health (Essential for PvP)
Agility	No Mages Care
Intellect	More Mana, Higher Spell Critical Changes
Spirit	Improved Regeneration of Health/Mana

Items and Equipment

Armor doesn't make the same difference for Mages that it does for Warriors; after all, you are wearing cloth garments, not mithril plates! The spells you use and the specialization you choose determine your effectiveness most of the time. That said, the attribute given by high-end gear help Mages to cast more spells, survive longer, and deal somewhat higher damage as well.

Instead of looking for DPS, weapon speed, improved Armor Rating, and similar values, Mages try to collect items that improve Intellect, + spell damage, Spirit, and sometimes Stamina as well. This is done to keep the casters casting as much as possible. Spirit equipment won't help your total casting or Critical hits, but it sure improves Mana regeneration. Intellect is a heavy attribute because Criticals and maximum mana come from that attribute.

Mixed equipment choices are very good. It's common to find good cloth items that add to both Intellect and Spirit. Solo Mages and those engaged in small group activities benefit more from Intellect than from Spirit. Yet, raid Mages and those with the right equipment/specialization are able to get a fair amount of mana restored even while casting. Under those circumstances, Spirit does make a huge difference in your total casting potential.

Items that add +Damage for Fire, Frost, or Arcane spells are certainly an option for Mages. If you are trying to raise your burst-damage potential, these are even better than some of their rivals.

Choosing Your Profession

Mages have a number of solid profession choices. Taking Tailoring is useful for creating modest gear earlier on in your career (to help with staying up-to-date before tackling tougher enemies). Because Tailoring doesn't have a Gathering profession, you are free to take Enchanting with it. Between the two, you are able to make and enchant your own items. Tailoring is a good sister-trade to Enchanting anyway, because Tailors are able to gather materials, make their own items, then break them for Enchanting reagents!

Herbalism and Alchemy allow Mages to create a number of potions to boost their spell damage and Resistance against enemy spells. Combined with Fishing (to gain certain rare ingredients), this is a solid combo.

Cooking isn't the most useful skill to grab on the side; Mages have such immediate access to food and drink that making additional sustenance isn't as impressive.

Class Abilities

The three types of magic available to this class are Arcane, Fire, and Frost. Arcane spells offer crowd control, short-range AoEs, food/water creation, and an Intellect buff (usable on self or allies).

Fire magic provides long range, wonderful damage efficiency, harder-hitting AoEs, and only a light amount of utility. This is where you find damage and more damage. If you want a Mage for the killing, this is where you will find many spells to fall in love with.

Frost magic is made for slowing and disrupting enemies while hurting them. These spells deal enough damage to get by while contributing Snare or Root effects. For PvP or group support, Frost is a very reliable choice.

Arcane Spells

Arcane Power

Rank	Prerequisites	Effect
1	3 Points in Arcane Instability, 30 Points in Arcane	When activated, your spells deal 35% more damage while costing 35% more mana to cast. This effect lasts 15 sec.

Arcane Intellect

Arcane Intellect is cast on yourself and just about any mana-using person you see. This spell greatly helps anyone with mana because it increases their total casting ability while additionally raising their chance for a Critical with magical spells/effects.

Rank	Level	Mana	Range	Casting Time	Cooldown	Cost to Train	Effect
1	1	60	30 yd	IC	—	10	Increase the target's Intellect by 2 for 30 min.
2	14	185	30 yd	IC	—	9	Increases the target's Intellect by 7 for 30 min.
3	28	520	30 yd	IC	—	70	Increases the target's Intellect by 15 for 30 min.
4	42	945	30 yd	IC	—	1 80	Increases the target's Intellect by 22 for 30 min.
5	56	1510	30 yd	IC	—	3 80	Increases the target's Intellect by 31 for 30 min.

Arcane Brilliance

Rank	Level	Mana	Reagent	Range	Casting Time	Effects
1	56	3400	Arcane Powder	40 yd	IC	Increases the Intellect of your party by 31 for one hour.

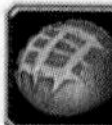

Conjure Food

Conjure Food and Water is a blessing, but everybody wants some of your free stuff.

Rank	Level	Mana	Range	Casting Time	Cooldown	Cost to Train	Effect
1	6	60	Inventory	3 sec	—	1	Conjures 2 muffins, providing the mage and his allies with something to eat. Conjured items disappear if logged out for more than 15 minutes.
2	12	105	Inventory	3 sec	—	6	Conjures 2 loaves of bread, providing the mage and his allies with something to eat. Conjured items disappear if logged out for more than 15 minutes.
3	22	180	Inventory	3 sec	—	30	Conjures 2 loaves of rye, providing the mage and his allies with something to eat. Conjured items disappear if logged out for more than 15 minutes.
4	32	285	Inventory	3 sec	—	1	Conjures 2 loaves of pumpernickel, providing the mage and his allies with something to eat. Conjured items disappear if logged out for more than 15 minutes.
5	42	420	Inventory	3 sec	—	1 80	Conjures 2 loaves of sourdough, providing the mage and his allies with something to eat. Conjured items disappear if logged out for more than 15 minutes.
6	52	585	Inventory	3 sec	—	3 50	Conjures 2 sweet rolls, providing the mage and his allies with something to eat. Conjured items disappear if logged out for more than 15 minutes.
7	60	705	Inventory	3 sec	—	3 50	Conjures 10 cinnamon rolls, providing the mage and his allies with something to eat. Conjured items disappear if logged out for more than 15 minutes.

Conjure Water

Rank	Level	Mana	Range	Casting Time	Cooldown	Cost to Train	Effect
1	4	60	Inventory	3 sec	—	1	Conjures 2 bottles of water, providing the mage and his allies with something to drink. Conjured items disappear if logged out for more than 15 minutes.
2	10	105	Inventory	3 sec	—	4	Conjures 2 bottles of fresh water, providing the mage and his allies with something to drink. Conjured items disappear if logged out for more than 15 minutes.
3	20	180	Inventory	3 sec	—	20	Conjures 2 bottles of purified water, providing the mage and his allies with something to drink. Conjured items disappear if logged out for more than 15 minutes.
4	30	285	Inventory	3 sec	—	80	Conjures 2 bottles of spring water, providing the mage and his allies with something to drink. Conjured items disappear if logged out for more than 15 minutes.
5	40	420	Inventory	3 sec	—	1 50	Conjures 2 bottles of mineral water, providing the mage and his allies with something to drink. Conjured items disappear if logged out for more than 15 minutes.
6	50	585	Inventory	3 sec	—	3 20	Conjures 2 bottles of sparkling water, providing the mage and his allies with something to drink. Conjured items disappear if logged out for more than 15 minutes.
7	60	780	Inventory	3 sec	—	—	Conjures 10 bottles of crystal water, providing the mage and his allies with something to drink. Conjured items disappear if logged out for more than 15 minutes.

Arcane Missiles

Arcane Missles when used with the appropriate talents, can be cast without any chance of being interrupted.

Rank	Level	Mana	Range	Casting Time	Cooldown	Cost to Train	Effect
1	8	85	30 yd	Channeled	—	2	Launches Arcane Missiles at the enemy, causing 24 Arcane damage each second for 3 seconds
2	16	140	30 yd	Channeled	—	15	Launches Arcane Missiles at the enemy, causing 36 Arcane damage each second for 4 sec.
3	24	235	30 yd	Channeled	—	40	Launches Arcane Missiles at the enemy, causing 56 Arcane damage each second for 5 sec.
4	32	320	30 yd	Channeled	—	1 10	Launches Arcane Missiles at the enemy, causing 83 Arcane damage each second for 5 sec.
5	40	410	30 yd	Channeled	—	1 50	Launches Arcane Missiles at the enemy, causing 115 Arcane damage each second for 5 sec.
6	48	500	30 yd	Channeled	—	2 50	Launches Arcane Missiles at the enemy, causing 159 Arcane damage each second for 5 sec.
7	56	595	30 yd	Channeled	—	3 80	Launches Arcane Missiles at the enemy, causing 202 Arcane damage each second for 5 sec.
8	56	655	30 yd	Channeled	Channeled	—	Launches Arcane Missiles at the enemy, causing 230 Arcane damage each second for 5 sec.

Polymorph

Polymorph is an in-battle crowd control spell that is amazingly powerful. Use this early on in battles to prevent a dangerous or long-lasting enemy from joining in a battle until your team is ready.

Rank	Level	Mana	Range	Casting Time	Cooldown	Cost to Train	Effect
1	8	60	30 yd	1.5 sec	—	2	Transforms the enemy into a sheep, forcing it to wander around for up to 20 sec. While wandering, the sheep cannot attack or cast spells but will regenerate very quickly. Any damage will transform the target back into its normal form. Only one target can be polymorphed at a time. Only works on Beasts, Humanoids and Critters
2	20	90	30 yd	1.5 sec	—	20	Transforms the enemy into a sheep, forcing it to wander around for up to 30 sec. While wandering, the sheep cannot attack or cast spells but will regenerate very quickly. Any damage will transform the target back into its normal form. Only one target can be polymorphed at a time. Only works on Beasts, Humanoids and Critters.
3	40	120	30 yd	1.5 sec	—	1 50	Transforms the enemy into a sheep, forcing it to wander around for up to 40 sec. While wandering, the sheep cannot attack or cast spells but will regenerate very quickly. Any damage will transform the target back into its normal form. Only one target can be polymorphed at a time. Only works on Beasts, Humanoids and Critters.
4	60	150	30 yd	1.5 sec	—	4 20	Transforms the enemy into a sheep, forcing it to wander around for up to 50 sec. While wandering, the sheep cannot attack or cast spells but will regenerate very quickly. Any damage will transform the target back into its normal form. Only one target can be polymorphed at a time. Only works on Beasts, Humanoids and Critters.

Polymorph: Pig

Rank	Level	Mana	Range	Casting Time	Cooldown	Cost to Train	Effect
1	60	150	30 yd	1.5 sec	—	—	Transforms the enemy into a pig, forcing it to wander around for up to 50 seconds. While wandering, the pig cannot attack or cast spells but will regenerate very quickly. Any damage will transform the target back into its normal form. Only one target can be polymorphed at a time. Only works on Beasts, Humanoids and Critters.

Dampen Magic

Dampen Magic is wonderful when you are facing casters and lack magical healing support from allies.

Rank	Level	Mana	Range	Casting Time	Cooldown	Cost to Train	Effect
1	12	100	30 yd	IC	—	6	Dampens magic used against the targeted party member, decreasing damage taken from spells by 10 and healing spells by 20. Lasts 10 min.
2	24	200	30 yd	IC	—	40	Dampens magic used against the targeted party member, decreasing damage taken from spells by up to 20 and healing spells by up to 40. Lasts 10 min.
3	36	300	30 yd	IC	—	1 30	Dampens magic used against the targeted party member, decreasing damage taken from spells by up to 30 and healing spells by up to 60. Lasts 10 min.
4	48	400	30 yd	IC	—	2 80	Dampens magic used against the targeted party member, decreasing damage taken from spells by up to 40 and healing spells by up to 80. Lasts 10 min.
5	60	500	30 yd	IC	—	4 20	Dampens magic used against the targeted party member, decreasing damage taken from spells by up to 50 and healing spells by up to 100. Lasts 10 min.

Amplify Magic

Amplify Magic allows the primary tank to receive greater healing for ten minutes with only a brief expense of mana but at acost of more magic damage!

Rank	Level	Mana	Range	Casting Time	Cooldown	Cost to Train	Effect
1	18	150	30 yd	IC	—	18	Amplifies magic used against the targeted party member, increasing damage taken from spells by 15 and healing spells by 30. Lasts 10 min.
2	30	250	30 yd	IC	—	80	Amplifies magic used against the targeted party member, increasing damage taken from spells by up to 25 and healing spells by up to 50. Lasts 10 min.
3	42	350	30 yd	IC	—	1 80	Amplifies magic used against the targeted party member, increasing damage taken from spells by up to 35 and healing spells by up to 70. Lasts 10 min.
4	54	450	30 yd	IC	—	3 60	Amplifies magic used against the targeted party member, increasing damage taken from spells by up to 45 and healing spells by up to 90. Lasts 10 min.

Slow Fall

Slow Fall is nice trick ability. Castable on yourself, it allows Mages to leap safely from high places.

Rank	Level	Mana	Range	Casting Time	Cooldown	Cost to Train	Effect
N/A	12	40	Self	IC	—	6	Slows falling speed for 30 sec.

Arcane Explosion

Arcane Explosion is a point blank AoE spell. Because it is used so quickly, this is an AoE of choice for fast bursts of damage against many light targets.

Rank	Level	Mana	Range	Casting Time	Cooldown	Cost to Train	Effect
1	14	75	—	—	—	9	Causes an explosion of arcane magic around the caster, causing 32 to 36 Arcane damage to all targets within 10 yards.
2	22	120	—	—	—	30	Causes an explosion of arcane magic around the caster, causing 57 to 63 Arcane damage to all targets within 10 yards.
3	30	185	—	—	—	80	Causes an explosion of arcane magic around the caster, causing 97 to 105 Arcane damage to all targets within 10 yards.
4	38	250	—	—	—	1 20	Causes an explosion of arcane magic around the caster, causing 139 to 151 Arcane damage to all targets within 10 yards.
5	46	315	—	—	—	2 60	Causes an explosion of arcane magic around the caster, causing 186 to 202 Arcane damage to all targets within 10 yards.
6	54	390	—	—	—	3 60	Causes an explosion of arcane magic around the caster, causing 243 to 263 Arcane damage to all targets within 10 yards.

Detect Magic

Detect Magic is another spell that is underused. Cast this to find out what positive effects are on an enemy target.

Rank	Level	Mana	Range	Casting Time	Cooldown	Cost to Train	Effect
N/A	16	35	40 yd	IC	—	15	Detects beneficial magic effects on the target for 2 min.

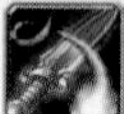

Remove Curse

Remove Curse spells are wonderful. Mages and Druids are able to take off these negative effects!

Rank	Level	Mana	Range	Casting Time	Cooldown	Cost to Train	Effect
1	18	22	30 yd	IC	—	18	Removes 1 Curse from a friendly target.

Blink

Blink is a protective ability that teleports a Mage forward a modest distance.

Rank	Level	Mana	Range	Casting Time	Cooldown	Cost to Train	Effect
1	20	77	Self	IC	15 seconds	20	Teleports the caster 20 yards forward, unless something is in the way. Also frees the caster from any bonds.

Evocation

Evocation is an ability for massive mana regeneration over a short period. Though the cooldown is substantial (ten minutes), Evocation should be used to get a free mana bar when it is needed the most.

Rank	Level	Mana	Range	Casting Time	Cooldown	Cost to Train	Effect
1	20	—	—	Channeled	8 minutes		While channeling this spell, your mana regeneration is active and increased by 1500%. Lasts 8 sec.

Presence of Mind

Rank	Prerequisites	Effect
1	20 Points in Arcane	When activated, your next Mage spell with a casting tim of less than 10 sec becomes an instant cast spell.

Mana Shield

Mana Shield allows Mages to protect themselves against damage at the expense of mana. Activate this before death AoE runs (when your mana total means very little compared to your survivability).

Rank	Level	Mana	Range	Casting Time	Cooldown	Cost to Train	Effect
1	20	40	Self	IC	—	20	Absorbs 120 physical damage, draining mana instead. Drains 2.0 mana per damage absorbed. Lasts 1 min.
2	28	60	Self	IC	—	70	Absorbs 210 physical damage, draining mana instead. Drains 2.0 mana per damage absorbed. Lasts 1 min.
3	36	80	Self	IC	—	1 30	Absorbs 300 physical damage, draining mana instead. Drains 2.0 mana per damage absorbed. Lasts 1 min.
4	44	100	Self	IC	—	2 30	Absorbs 390 physical damage, draining mana instead. Drains 2.0 mana per damage absorbed. Lasts 1 min.
5	52	120	Self	IC	—	3 50	Absorbs 480 physical damage, draining mana instead. Drains 2.0 mana per damage absorbed. Lasts 1 min.
6	60	140	Self	IC	—	4 20	Absorbs 570 physical damage, draining mana instead. Drains 2.0 mana per damage absorbed. Lasts 1 min.

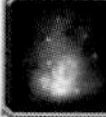

Counterspell

Counterspell is a life or death ability against enemy casters. Wait until they are casting a spell (whether it be healing or damage), then Counterspell to Silence the foe for several seconds and stop the specific school of magic they were using for even longer.

Rank	Level	Mana	Range	Casting Time	Cooldown	Cost to Train	Effect
1	24	100	30 yd	IC	30 seconds	40	Counters the enemy's spell, preventing him any spell in that school of magic being cast for 10 sec. Generates a high amount of threat.

Conjure Mana Agate

Conjure Mana Stones are used to give Mages a reserve for their mana.

Rank	Level	Mana	Range	Casting Time	Cooldown	Cost to Train	Effect
N/A	28	530	Inventory	3 sec	—	70	Conjures a Mana Agate that can be used to instantly restore 375 to 425 mana. Conjured items disappear if logged out for more than 15 minutes.

Conjure Mana Citrine

Rank	Level	Mana	Range	Casting Time	Cooldown	Cost to Train	Effect
N/A	48	1130	Inventory	3 sec	—	2 80	Conjures a Mana Citrine that can be used to instantly restore 775 to 925 mana. Conjured items disappear if logged out for more than 15 minutes.

Conjure Mana Jade

Rank	Level	Mana	Range	Casting Time	Cooldown	Cost to Train	Effect
N/A	38	800	Inventory	3 sec	—	1 40	Conjures a Mana Jade that can be used to instantly restore 550 to 650 mana. Conjured items disappear if logged out for more than 15 minutes.

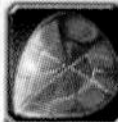

Conjure Mana Ruby

Rank	Level	Mana	Range	Casting Time	Cooldown	Cost to Train	Effect
N/A	58	1470	Inventory	3 sec	—	4	Conjures a Mana Ruby that can be used to instantly restore 1000 to 1200 mana. Conjured items disappear if logged out for more than 15 minutes.

Mage Armor

Mage Armor doesn't have the same survivability as the Ice Armor buff, and you can only use one at a time. However, against casters who stay at range, Mage Armor is better.

Rank	Level	Mana	Range	Casting Time	Cooldown	Cost to Train	Effect
1	34	270	Self	IC	—		Increases your resistance to all magic by 5 and allows 30% of your mana regeneration to continue while casting. Lasts 30 min.
2	46	380	Self	IC	—		Increases your resistance to all magic by 10 and allows 30% of your mana regeneration to continue while casting. Lasts 30 min.
3	58	490	Self	IC	—		Increases your resistance to all magic by 15 and allows 30% of your mana regeneration to continue while casting. Lasts 30 min.

Fire Spells

Combustion

Rank	Prerequisites	Effect
1	3 Points in Fire Power, 30 Points in Fire	When activated, this spell causes each Fire damage spell you cast to increase your critical strike chance with Fire damage spells by 10%. This effect lasts until you have caused 3 critical strikes with Fire spells.

Fireball

Fireball is the quintessential fire spell. This offers a long-range bolt with high damage and very high mana efficiency.

Rank	Level	Mana	Range	Casting Time	Cooldown	Cost to Train	Effect
1	1	30	30 yd	1.5 sec	—	—	Hurls a fiery ball that causes 14 to 22 fire damage and an additional 2 damage over 4 sec.
2	6	45	35 yd	2 sec	—	1	Hurls a fiery ball that causes 31 to 45 fire damage and an additional 3 damage over 4 sec.
3	12	65	35 yd	2 sec	—	6	Hurls a fiery ball that causes 55 to 75 fire damage and an additional 6 damage over 6 sec.
4	18	95	35 yd	2.5 sec	—	18	Hurls a fiery ball that causes 84 to 116 fire damage and an additional 12 damage over 8 sec.
5	24	140	35 yd	3.5 sec	—	40	Hurls a fiery ball that causes 139 to 187 fire damage and an additional 20 damage over 8 sec.
6	30	185	35 yd	3.5 sec	—	80	Hurls a fiery ball that causes 199 to 265 fire damage and an additional 28 damage over 8 sec.
7	36	220	35 yd	3.5 sec	—	1 30	Hurls a fiery ball that causes 255 to 335 fire damage and an additional 32 damage over 8 sec.
8	42	260	35 yd	3.5 sec	—	1 80	Hurls a fiery ball that causes 318 to 414 fire damage and an additional 40 damage over 8 sec.
9	48	305	35 yd	3.5 sec	—	2 80	Hurls a fiery ball that causes 392 to 506 fire damage and an additional 52 damage over 8 sec.
10	54	350	35 yd	3.5 sec	—	3 60	Hurls a fiery ball that causes 475 to 609 fire damage and an additional 60 damage over 8 sec.
11	60	395	35 yd	3.5 sec	—	4 20	Hurls a fiery ball that causes 561 to 715 fire damage and an additional 72 damage over 8 sec.
12	60	410	35 yd	3.5	—		Hurls a fiery ball that causes 596 to 760 fire damage and an additional 76 damage over 8 sec.

Fire Blast

Fire Blast is an instant spell that deals a fair amount of damage but loses some efficiency. Use this when enemies are almost dead and need to be finished off.

Rank	Level	Mana	Range	Casting Time	Cooldown	Cost to Train	Effect
1	6	40	20 yd	IC	8 seconds	1	Blasts the enemy with fire for 24 to 32 fire damage.
2	14	75	20 yd	IC	8 seconds	9	Blasts the enemy with fire for 57 to 71 fire damage.
3	22	115	20 yd	IC	8 seconds	30	Blasts the enemy with fire for 103 to 127 fire damage.
4	30	165	20 yd	IC	8 seconds	80	Blasts the enemy with fire for 168 to 202 fire damage.
5	38	220	20 yd	IC	8 seconds	1 40	Blasts the enemy with fire for 242 to 290 fire damage.
6	46	280	20 yd	IC	8 seconds	2 60	Blasts the enemy with fire for 332 to 394 fire damage.
7	54	340	20 yd	IC	8 seconds	3 60	Blasts the enemy with fire for 431 to 509 fire damage.

Flamestrike

Flamestrike is an AoE that doesn't have a cooldown but does have a casting time. This spell becomes mana efficient when there are three or more enemies clustered together.

Rank	Level	Mana	Range	Casting Time	Cooldown	Cost to Train	Effect
1	16	195	30 yd	3 sec	—	15	Calls down a pillar of fire, burning all enemies within the area for 52 to 68 fire damage and an additional 48 damage over 8 sec.
2	24	330	30 yd	3 sec	—	40	Calls down a pillar of fire, burning all enemies within the area for 96 to 123 fire damage and an additional 88 damage over 8 sec.
3	32	490	30 yd	3 sec	—	1	Calls down a pillar of fire, burning all enemies within the area for 154 to 192 fire damage and an additional 140 damage over 8 sec.
4	40	650	30 yd	3 sec	—	1 50	Calls down a pillar of fire, burning all enemies within the area for 220 to 272 fire damage and an additional 196 damage over 8 sec.
5	48	815	30 yd	3 sec	—	2 80	Calls down a pillar of fire, burning all enemies within the area for 291 to 359 fire damage and an additional 264 damage over 8 sec.
6	56	990	30 yd	3 sec	—	3 80	Calls down a pillar of fire, burning all enemies within the area for 375 to 459 fire damage and an additional 340 damage over 8 sec.

Fire Ward

Fire Ward is a useful spell in certain circumstance. Cast this ahead of time on yourself before fights with known fire enemies.

Rank	Level	Mana	Range	Casting Time	Cooldown	Cost to Train	Effect
1	20	85	Self	IC	30 seconds	20	Absorbs 105 fire damage. Lasts 30 sec.
2	30	135	Self	IC	30 seconds	80	Absorbs 185 fire damage. Lasts 30 sec.
3	40	195	Self	IC	30 seconds	1 50	Absorbs 300 fire damage. Lasts 30 sec.
4	50	255	Self	IC	30 seconds	3 20	Absorbs 430 fire damage. Lasts 30 sec.
5	60	320	Self	IC	30 seconds	4 20	Absorbs 585 fire damage. Lasts 30 sec.

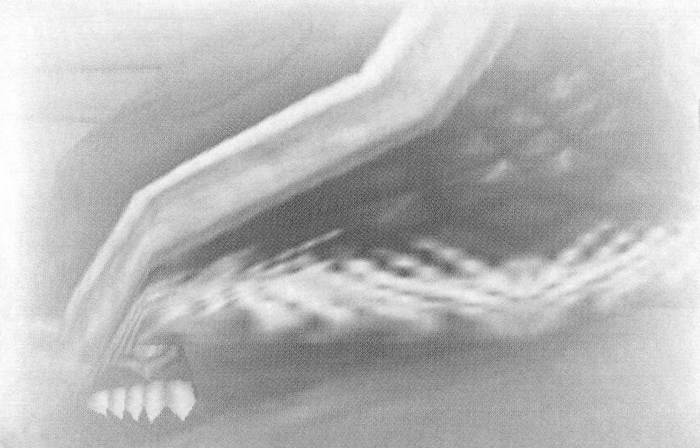

Pyroblast

Pyroblast is a Talent-learned ability that is very slow to cast. Outright damage and mana efficiency from Pyroblast are extremely high, and Mages can start fights with this to give themselves a major burst against a target that isn't coming toward them.

Rank	Minimum Level	Mana	Range	Casting Time	Cooldown	Cost to Train	Effect
1	20	125	35 yd	6 sec	—	—	Hurls an immense fiery boulder that causes 148 to 195 Fire damage and an additional 56 Fire damage over 12 sec.
2	24	150	35 yd	6 sec	—	10	Hurls an immense fiery boulder that causes 180 to 236 fire damage and an additional 72 damage over 12 sec.
3	30	195	35 yd	6 sec	—	20	Hurls an immense fiery boulder that causes 255 to 327 fire damage and an additional 96 damage over 12 sec.
4	36	240	35 yd	6 sec	—	32 50	Hurls an immense fiery boulder that causes 329 to 419 fire damage and an additional 124 damage over 12 sec.
5	42	285	35 yd	6 sec	—	45	Hurls an immense fiery boulder that causes 407 to 515 fire damage and an additional 156 damage over 12 sec.
6	48	335	35 yd	6 sec	—	70	Hurls an immense fiery boulder that causes 503 to 631 fire damage and an additional 188 damage over 12 sec.
7	54	385	35 yd	6 sec	—	90	Hurls an immense fiery boulder that causes 600 to 750 fire damage and an additional 228 damage over 12 sec.
8	60	440	35 yd	6 sec	—	1 50	Hurls an immense fiery boulder that causes 716 to 890 fire damage and an additional 268 damage over 12 sec.

Scorch

Scorch is another spell with massive damage efficiency. With a shorter casting time than Fireball, Scorch has more windows of opportunity, especially during intense fights/PvP situations.

Rank	Level	Mana	Range	Casting Time	Cooldown	Cost to Train	Effect
1	22	50	30 yd	1.5 sec	—	30	Scorch the enemy for 53 to 65 fire damage.
2	28	65	30 yd	1.5 sec	—	70	Scorch the enemy for 77 to 93 fire damage.
3	34	80	30 yd	1.5 sec	—	1 20	Scorch the enemy for 100 to 122 fire damage.
4	40	100	30 yd	1.5 sec	—	1 50	Scorch the enemy for 133 to 159 fire damage.
5	46	115	30 yd	1.5 sec	—	2 60	Scorch the enemy for 162 to 192 fire damage.
6	52	135	30 yd	1.5 sec	—	3 50	Scorch the enemy for 200 to 239 fire damage.
7	58	150	30 yd	1.5 sec	—	5	Scorch the enemy for 233 to 275 fire damage.

Blast Wave

Blast Wave is a Talent-learned ability that gives Fire Mages another AoE! This one is can be used instantly, is a point-blank AoE spell, and Dazes the enemies as well as dealing damage to them.

Rank	Minimum Level	Mana	Range	Casting Time	Cooldown	Cost to Train	Effect
1	30	215	—	IC	45 seconds	—	A wave of flame radiates outward from the caster, damaging all enemies caught within the blast for 160 to 192 fire damage, and dazing them for 6 sec.
2	36	270	—	IC	45 seconds	32 50	A wave of flame radiates outward from the caster, damaging all enemies caught within the blast for 201 to 241 fire damage, and dazing them for 6 sec.
3	44	355	—	IC	45 seconds	57 50	A wave of flame radiates outward from the caster, damaging all enemies caught within the blast for 277 to 329 fire damage, and dazing them for 6 sec.
4	52	450	—	IC	45 seconds	87 50	A wave of flame radiates outward from the caster, damaging all enemies caught within the blast for 365 to 433 fire damage, and dazing them for 6 sec.
5	60	460	—	IC	45 seconds	1 5	A wave of flame radiates outward from the caster, damaging all enemies caught within the blast for 462 to 544 fire damage, and dazing them for 6 sec.

Frost Spells

Ice Armor

Rank	Level	Mana	Range	Casting Time	Cooldown	Cost to Train	Effect
1	30	240	Self	IC	—	80	Increases armor by 290 and frost resistance by 6. If an enemy strikes the caster, they may have their movement slowed to 70% and attacks slowed by 20%. Lasts 30 min.
2	40	320	Self	IC	—	1 50	Increases armor by 380 and frost resistance by 9. If an enemy strikes the caster, they may have their movement slowed to 70% and attacks slowed by 20%. Lasts 30 min.
3	50	510	Self	IC	—	3 20	Increases armor by 470 and frost resistance by 12. If an enemy strikes the caster, they may have their movement slowed to 70% and attacks slowed by 20%. Lasts 30 min.
4	60	500	Self	IC	—	4 20	Increases armor by 560 and frost resistance by 15. If an enemy strikes the caster, they may have their movement slowed to 70% and attacks slowed by 20%. Lasts 30 min.

Cold Snap

Rank	Prerequisites	Effect
1	10 Points in Frost	When activated, this spell finishes the cooldown on all of your Frost spells

Frostbolt

Frostbolt is not made to delivering damage as well as Fireball, but it is a faster spell, still has high efficiency, and Snares targets.

Rank	Level	Mana	Range	Casting Time	Cooldown	Cost to Train	Effect
1	4	25	30 yd	1.5 sec	—	1	Launches a bolt of frost at the enemy, causing 18 to 20 frost damage and slowing movement speed to 60% of normal for 5 sec.
2	8	35	30 yd	1.8 sec	—	2	Launches a bolt of frost at the enemy, causing 31 to 35 frost damage and slowing movement speed to 60% of normal for 5 sec.
3	14	50	30 yd	2.2 sec	—	9	Launches a bolt of frost at the enemy, causing 51 to 57 frost damage and slowing movement speed to 60% of normal for 6 sec.
4	20	65	30 yd	2.6 sec	—	20	Launches a bolt of frost at the enemy, causing 74 to 82 frost damage and slowing movement speed to 60% of normal for 7 sec.
5	26	100	30 yd	3 sec	—	50	Launches a bolt of frost at the enemy, causing 126 to 138 frost damage and slowing movement speed to 60% of normal for 7 sec.
6	32	130	30 yd	3 sec	—	1	Launches a bolt of frost at the enemy, causing 174 to 190 frost damage and slowing movement speed to 60% of normal for 8 sec.
7	38	160	30 yd	3 sec	—	1 40	Launches a bolt of frost at the enemy, causing 227 to 247 frost damage and slowing movement speed to 60% of normal for 8 sec.
8	44	195	30 yd	3 sec	—	2 30	Launches a bolt of frost at the enemy, causing 292 to 316 frost damage and slowing movement speed to 60% of normal for 9 sec.
9	50	225	30 yd	3 sec	—	3 20	Launches a bolt of frost at the enemy, causing 353 to 383 frost damage and slowing movement speed to 60% of normal for 9 sec.
10	56	260	30 yd	3 sec	—	3 80	Launches a bolt of frost at the enemy, causing 429 to 463 frost damage and slowing movement speed to 60% of normal for 9 sec.
11	60	290	30 yd	3 sec	—	—	Launches a bolt of frost at the enemy, causing 515 to 550 Frost damage and slowing movement speed to 60 % of normal for 9 sec.

Frost Armor

Frost Armor adds major survivability against melee forces to your Mage. Enemies that strike you when this buff is active are usually Snared, giving you a much easier time getting away from them.

Rank	Level	Mana	Range	Casting Time	Cooldown	Cost to Train	Effect
1	1	60	Self	IC	—	—	Increase armor by 30. If an enemy strikes the caster, they may have their movement slowed by 70% and attacks slowed by 20% for 5 sec. Lasts 30 min.
2	10	110	Self	IC	—	4	Increases armor by 110. If an enemy strikes the caster, they may have their movement slowed to 70% and attacks slowed by 20% for 5 sec. Lasts 30 min.
3	20	170	Self	IC	—	20	Increases armor by 200. If an enemy strikes the caster, they may have their movement slowed to 70% and attacks slowed by 20% for 5 sec. Lasts 30 min.

Frost Nova

Frost Nova is an AoE to stop enemies immediately. A full Root is in effect for the duration of the spell.

Rank	Level	Mana	Range	Casting Time	Cooldown	Cost to Train	Effect
1	10	55	—	IC	25 sec	4	Blasts enemies near the caster for 19 to 22 Frost damage and freezes them in place for up to 8 sec. Damage caused may interrupt the effect.
2	26	85	—	IC	25 sec	50	Blasts enemies near the caster for 33 to 37 Frost damage and freezes them in place for up to 8 sec. Damage caused may interrupt the effect.
3	40	115	—	IC	25 sec	1 50	Blasts enemies near the caster for 52 to 58 Frost damage and freezes them in place for up to 8 sec. Damage caused may interrupt the effect.
4	54	145	—	IC	25 sec	3 60	Blasts enemies near the caster for 71 to 79 Frost damage and freezes them in place for up to 8 sec. Damage caused may interrupt the effect.

Blizzard

Blizzard is a channeled AoE that deals moderate damage over eight seconds. For Frost-specced Mages, this spell has the potential to slow enemies as well as injure them.

Rank	Level	Mana	Range	Casting Time	Cooldown	Cost to Train	Effect
1	20	320	30 yd	Channeled	—	20	Ice shards pelt the target area doing 200 damage over 8 sec.
2	28	520	30 yd	Channeled	—	70	Ice shards pelt the target area doing 352 damage over 8 sec.
3	36	720	30 yd	Channeled	—	1 30	Ice shards pelt the target area doing 520 damage over 8 sec.
4	44	935	30 yd	Channeled	—	2 30	Ice shards pelt the target area doing 720 damage over 8 sec.
5	52	1160	30 yd	Channeled	—	3 50	Ice shards pelt the target area doing 936 damage over 8 sec.
6	60	1400	30 yd	Channeled	—	4 20	Ice shards pelt the target area doing 1192 damage over 8 sec.

Frost Ward

Frost Ward acts like Fire Ward, but covers Frost Damage.

Rank	Level	Mana	Range	Casting Time	Cooldown	Cost to Train	Effect
1	22	85	Self	IC	30 sec	30	Absorbs 105 frost damage. Lasts 30 sec.
2	32	135	Self	IC	30 sec	1	Absorbs 185 frost damage. Lasts 30 sec.
3	42	195	Self	IC	30 sec	1 80	Absorbs 300 frost damage. Lasts 30 sec.
4	52	255	Self	IC	30 sec	3 50	Absorbs 430 frost damage. Lasts 30 sec.

Cone of Cold

Cone of Cold is an AoE that focuses on targets in front of the caster. Use this to deal damage to an incoming group and slow them for eight seconds.

Rank	Level	Mana	Range	Casting Time	Cooldown	Cost to Train	Effect
1	26	210	—	IC	10 sec	50	Targets in a cone in front of the caster take 98 to 108 frost damage and are slowed to 50% of normal speed for 8 sec.
2	34	290	—	IC	10 sec	1 20	Targets in a cone in front of the caster take 146 to 160 frost damage and are slowed to 50% of normal speed for 8 sec.
3	42	380	—	IC	10 sec	1 80	Targets in a cone in front of the caster take 213 to 234 frost damage and are slowed to 50% of normal speed for 8 sec.
4	50	465	—	IC	10 sec	3 20	Targets in a cone in front of the caster take 277 to 304 frost damage and are slowed to 50% of normal speed for 8 sec.
5	58	555	—	IC	10 sec	4	Targets in a cone in front of the caster take 335 to 365 frost damage and are slowed to 50% of normal speed for 8 sec.

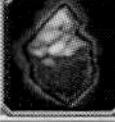

Ice Block

Ice Block comes from the Frost Talent line and is used to block enemy damage. At later levels, this allows a Frost Mage to block damage and avoid interruptions to casting as long as the Barrier lasts.

Rank	Minimum Level	Mana	Range	Casting Time	Cooldown	Cost to Train	Effect
1	30	15	Self	IC	5 minutes	—	You become encased in a block of ice, protecting you from all physical attacks and spells for 10 sesc, but during that time you cannot attack, move or cast spells.

Ice Barrier

Ice Barrier comes from the Frost Talent line and is used to block enemy damage.

Rank	Minimum Level	Mana	Range	Casting Time	Cooldown	Cost to Train	Effect
1	40	305	Self	IC	2 minutes	—	Instantly shields you, absorbing 455 damage. Lasts 1 min. While the shield holds, spells will not be interrupted.
2	46	360	Self	IC	2 minutes	65	Instantly shields you, absorbing 549 damage. Lasts 1 min. While the shield holds, spells will not be interrupted.
3	52	420	Self	IC	2 minutes	87 50	Instantly shields you, absorbing 678 damage. Lasts 1 min. While the shield holds, spells will not be interrupted.
4	58	480	Self	IC	2 minutes	1	Instantly shields you, absorbing 818 damage. Lasts 1 min. While the shield holds, spells will not be interrupted.

TALENTS

Mage Talents have changed a great deal over the retail period of World of Warcraft. Taking Arcane as a primary or secondary tree was almost a given in the old days. Elemental builds and even tri-Talent builds are becoming possible. Take a long look at your preferred playstyle before dedicating to any build, and don't be afraid to respec and try a few things out in the long run (it's worth the money).

Arcane Line

Arcane Talents are wonderful for raising Mana efficiency, Damage, and base functionality for the class. With an improved Intellect buff, Presence of Mind (for essentially a massive, Instant cast), and occasional free spells, this line has a bit of everything. If forced to declare a focus, however, Arcane Talents would likely be classified as burst damage. Arcane Power and Presence of Mind are both late Talents in the line that create solid burst potential.

Fire Line

Fire Talents make Mages into even more powerful casters at range (with longer-range bolts, a chance for Stuns, and major Fire Talents are extremely functional. Added abilities improve the Fire line's power to bring AoE's into a battle (Blast Wave) or deal huge damage from surprise attacks (Pyroblast). This is the most common choice for damage over time, and Fire's burst damage is pretty darn wonderful too.

Frost Line

Frost Talents are there to frustrate and halt enemy advances. Though lacking in the power to immediately bring down enemy troops in the same way, this specialization improves the Chill Effects of almost all Frost magic. Also, Root effects are added to additional spells, making it even harder for melee enemies to advance on groups that have Frost Mages at the ready. Mages who place utility above DPS gain the most from Frost Talents.

Portal Magic

A time-saving feature of the Mages is that they are able to Teleport themselves (and later their group as well) to major cities across Azeroth. This power is gained at Level 20, and it limited to the two central cities of your faction at that time. Later, at Level 30, the more distant capital is added. At level 40, the initial group portals are learned, then the distant targets are mastered at level 50.

It costs a light amount of money to use these. You buy the reagents for the spells from specialty vendors. Before discounts, Mages use 10 silver for a Teleport, and 20 silver for a Portal. Thus, a tip is absolutely essential if you want a Mage to Portal you somewhere and they aren't in your group.

STRATEGIES

Mages are all about keen strategy and tactics. This is one of those classes that dies easily if you aren't fast on your feet and good with your keys, because your Armor Rating isn't going to stay close to decent. In fact, Mages and damage mitigation only go together in the sentence, Mages have *no* damage mitigation. So, avoid the damage entirely and stay mobile.

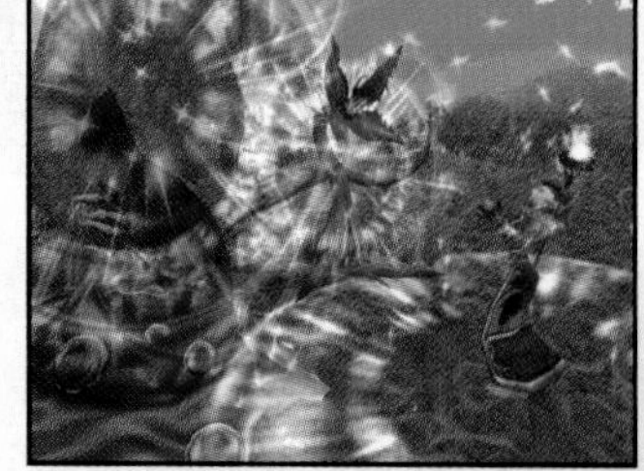

The key is to find ways to maximize the spell line(s) you enjoy the most. On the whole, Mages use a primary spell line with small pieces from the other two, and this is more than a Talent issue. Indeed, the spell lines have entirely different purposes, and your strategy should reflect the spells you prefer using (or vice versa).

Ewe Can't Live Without Polymorph

As early as level eight, you receive the Polymorph spell. To practice its use, save up your full supply of mana and intentionally take on two monsters at the same time. Normally, this is a very bad situation, because Mages cannot mitigate damage in any positive way. So, use your best Fireball on one target and "Sheep" the other opponent to prevent them from adding into combat immediately. Use kiting tricks to blow down the initial target then choose whether to proceed with the second foe (who will soon come out of Polymorph) or run away.

Master Polymorph and learn which targets are best to hit with it. Let your group's configuration determine a great deal in the higher instances. If your group is good at fast killing, Polymorph the most dangerous target. If your group can last a long time but kills slowly, Polymorph the less-damaging targets that take a longer time to destroy. This way, you are always taking a target out of the fight that would cause the most problems for your given group.

Fast Soloing

With Mages and Priests alike, soloing is a very important issue. These are classes that are soft and exposed when brought into direct combat unprepared, and their heavy use of mana means that downtime is high unless you know what you are doing!

For Mages, the key is to avoid the lure of free damage. In a life-or-death struggle, a Mage can pull out instant after instant. The issue here is that these instants have a high cost, and you won't be able to take down four or five enemies in a row without drinking while relying on instants. A mana-efficient style can do that (and more). Use spells like Fireball, Frostbolt, and Scorch to deal damage. Rely on the spell that is efficient and within your specialization. Fireball, Fireball, Frost Nova, back off from melee range, Fireball, Scorch. Without a single critical that would take down a modest target. With Mage Armor on, this would keep a soloer going for several targets in a row without any problems.

Use a strong wand to finish off enemies that are down to low health. Instead of wasting a boatload of mana, rely on the free attacks that wands provide. Whether the enemies are close by or running away, they are doomed!

Only use mana gems to save yourself during intense battles. Creating these isn't an efficient process. Consider them backups, not a standard part of your casting ritual.

Obviously, a mixture of very high Intellect and high + damage gear are essential for soloing as well. Stamina (while of great importance for PvP), is a tertiary stat while leveling. Your Mage won't need a lot of it, because enemies spend most of their time at range. Create a stack of food and use that to restore the dings that your Mage takes from time-to-time, and you won't have any problems. This is done while drinking anyway, so it doesn't even take extra time.

Ideal Use of Food and Water

Remember that your food and water are almost free (just a minor use of mana and brief casting periods). Don't ever resort to standing around. If you have free time and need health or mana, eat or drink. Five seconds free, and that is all because your group is about to pull? Drink anyway. *It is free*! Taking sips between pulls in a group is a wonderful way to keep your DPS high without constantly annoying the group by requesting med time.

You don't even have to engage in combat immediately when in a group. Tanks are not overly enthusiastic about the idea of you tossing a Crit Fireball half-a-second after they charge into combat. So, make sure you get that final tick of health or mana before standing up and joining in on the fun. Encourage others to do this as well!

Hand food and water out to groups like candy. If you arrive at a quest area, dungeon, or whatnot ahead of time, start making food and water. Toss two stacks of free water at every caster, and a stack of food at everyone. If you need to make more later, fine. It is amazing how much time is saved by free goodies. And, any time you are grouping, this is going to be a wasted minute here or there (waited for the zeppelin, boat, odd character, disconnected person, etc.).

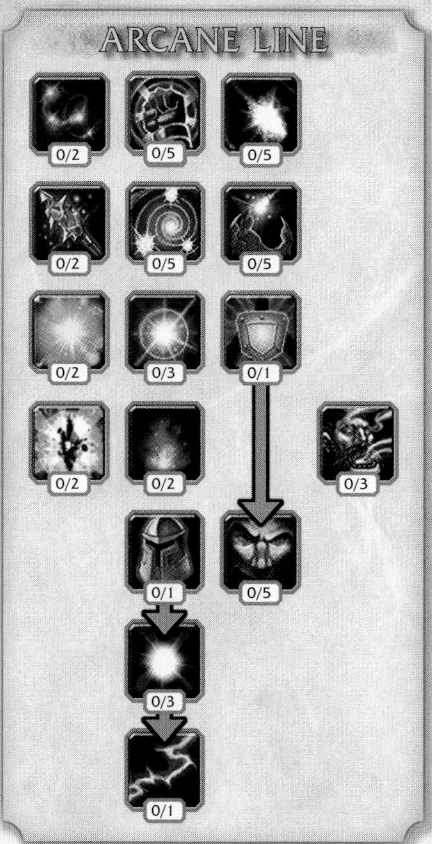

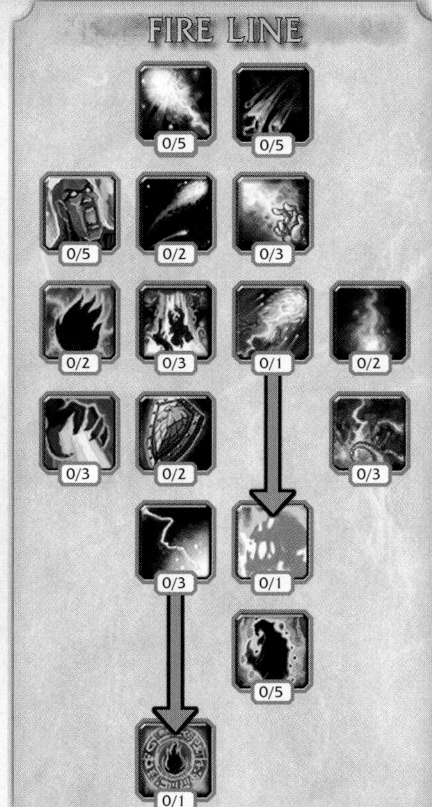

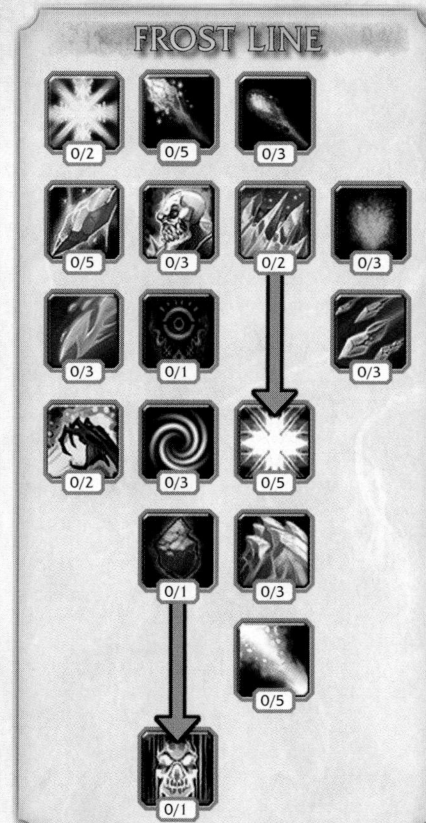

ARCANE SUBTLETY 2

Reduces your target's resistance to all your spells by 5 (Per Rank) and reduces threat of Arcane spells by 20% (Per Rank).

ARCANE FOCUS 5

Reduces the chance that the opponent can resist your arcane spells by 2% (Per Rank).

IMPROVED ARCANE MISSILES 5

Gives you a 20% chance (Per Rank) to avoid interruption caused by damage while channeling Arcane Missiles

WAND SPECIALIZATION 2

Increases your damage with Wands by 13%. Progression: 13%/25%.

MAGIC ABSORPTION 5

Increases all resistances by 2 (Per Rank) and causes all spells you resist to restore 1% (Per Rank) of your total mana.

ARCANE CONCENTRATION 5

Gives you a 2% (Per Rank) chance of entering a Clearcasting state after any damage spell hits a target. The Clearcasting state reduces the mana cost of your next damage spell by 100%.

MAGIC ATTUNEMENT 2

Increase the effect of your Amplify Magic and Dampen Magic spells by 25% (Per Rank).

IMPROVED ARCANE EXPLOSION 3

Increases the critical strike chance of your Arcane Explosion by an additional 2% (Per Rank).

ARCANE RESILIENCE 1

Increases your armor by an amount equal to 50% of your Intellect.

IMPROVED MANA SHIELD 2

Decreases the mana lost per point of damage taken when Mana Shield is active by 10% (Per Rank).

IMPROVED COUNTERSPELL 2

Gives your Counterspell a 50% chance (Per Rank) to silence the target for 4 sec.

ARCANE MEDITATION 3

Allows 5% (Per Rank) of your Mana regeneration to continue while casting

PRESENCE OF MIND 1

When activated, your next Mage spell with a casting time of less than 10 sec becomes an instant cast spell.

ARCANE MIND 5

Increases your maximum Mana by 2% (Per Rank).

ARCANE INSTABILITY 3

Increases your spell damage and critical strike chance by 1% (Per Rank).

ARCANE POWER 1

When activated, your spells deal 35% more damage while costing 35% more mana to cast. This effect lasts 15 sec.

IMPROVED FIREBALL 5

Reduces the casting time of your Fireball spell by 0.1 seconds (Per Rank).

IMPACT 5

Gives your Fire spells a 2% chance (Per Rank) to stun the target for 2 seconds.

IGNITE 5

Your critical strikes from Fire damage spells cause the target to burn for an additional 8% of your spell's damage (Per Rank) over 4 seconds

FLAME THROWING 2

Increases the range of your fire spells by 3 yards (Per Rank).

IMPROVED FIRE BLAST 3

Reduces the cooldown of your Fire Blast by 0.5 seconds - Progression: 0.5/1/1.5

INCINERATE 2

Increases the critical strike chance of your Fire Blast and Scorch spells by 2% (Per Rank).

IMPROVED FLAMESTRIKE 3

Increases the critical strike chance of your Flamestrike spell by 5% (Per Rank).

PYROBLAST 1

Hurls an immense fiery boulder that causes 148-195 fire damage and an additional 56 fire damage over 12 sec.

BURNING SOUL 2

Gives your fire spells a 35% (Per Rank) chance to not lose casting time when you take damage and reduces the threat caused by your Fire spells by 15% (Per Rank).

IMPROVED SCORCH 3

Your Scorch spells have a 33% (Progression: 33%/66%/100%) chance to cause your target to be vulnerable to Fire damage. This vulnerability increases the Fire damage dealt to your target by 3% and lasts 15 sec. Stacks up to 5 times.

IMPROVED FIRE WARD 2

Causes your Fire Ward to have a 10% (Per Rank) chance to reflect Fire spells while active.

MASTER OF ELEMENTS 3

Your Fire and Frost spell criticials will refund 10% (Per Rank) of the mana cost.

CRITICAL MASS 3

Increases the critical strike chance of your fire spells by 2% (Per Rank).

BLAST WAVE 1

A wave of flame radiates outward from the caster, damaging all enemies caught within the blast for 160 to 192 Fire damage, and dazing them for 6 sec.

FIRE POWER 5

Increases the damage done by your fire spells by 2% (Per Rank).

COMBUSTION 1

When activated, this spell causes each Fire damage spell you cast to increase your critical strike chance with Fire damage spells by 10%. This effect lasts until you have causes 3 critical strikes with Fire spells.

FROST WARDING 2

Increases the armor and resistances given by your Frost Armor and Ice Armor spells by 15% (Per Rank). In addition, gives your Frost Ward a 10% (Per Rank) chance to reflect Frost Spells and effects while active.

IMPROVED FROSTBOLT 5

Reduces the casting time of Frostbolt spell by 0.1 seconds (Per Rank).

ELEMENTAL PRECISION 3

Reduces the chance that the opponent can resist your Frost and Fire spells by 2% (Per Rank).

ICE SHARDS 5

Increases the critical strike damage bonus of your Frost spells by 20% (Per Rank).

FROSTBITE 3

Gives your Chill effects a 5% (Per Rank) chance to freeze the target for 5 sec.

IMPROVED FROST NOVA 2

Reduces the cooldown of your Frost Nova spell by 2 sec (Per Rank).

PERMAFROST 3

Increases the duration of your Chill effects by 1 sec (Per Rank) and reduces the targets speed by an additional 4% (Progression: 4%/7%/10%).

PIERCING ICE 3

Increases the damage done by your Frost spells by 2% (Per Rank).

COLD SNAP 1

When activated, this spell finishes the cooldown on all of your Frost spells.

IMPROVED BLIZZARD 3

Adds a chill effect to your Blizzard spell. This effect lowers the target's movement speed by 30% (Progression: 30%/50%/65%) Lasts 1.5 sec.

ARCTIC REACH 2

Increases the range of your Frostbolt and Blizzard spells and the radius of your Frost Nova and Cone of Cold spells by 10% (Per Rank).

FROST CHANNELING 3

Reduces the Mana cost of your Frost spells by 5% (Per Rank) and the threat caused by your Frost spells by 10% (Per Rank).

SHATTER 5

Increases the critical strike chance of your Frost spells against frozen targets by 10% (Per Rank).

ICE BLOCK 1

You become encased in a block of ice, protecting you from all physical attacks and spells for 10 sec, but during that time you cannot attack, move, or cast spells.

IMPROVED CONE OF COLD 3

Increases the damage dealt by your Cone of Cold spell by 15%. Progression: 15%/25%/35%

WINTER'S CHILL 3

Gives your Frost damage spells a 20% (Per Rank) chance to apply the Winter's Chill effect, which increases the chance a Frost spell will critically hit the target by 2% for 15 sec. Stacks up to 5 times.

ICE BARRIER 1

Instantly shields you, absorbing 438 damage. Lasts 1 min. While the shield holds, spells will not be interrupted.

Fun in PvP

You might be wondering if Mages are fun in PvP? The answer is a resounding, yes! You have to be a little crazy to bounce around with your fragile cloth being your only protection. However, fast-reacting Mages are still tough to kill.

In Warsong Gulch, Mages make strong defenders, good people for midfield, and useful assistants to a flag carrier. Only in rare cases should they carry a flag themselves, but a skilled Mage can even carry a flag successfully using a number of tricks.

For Arathi Basin, Mages can oddly serve a similar function to Rogues. They are very good at taking poorly-defended sites. If the enemies leave an area with only one defender, a Mage has *many* chances to win. First off, Polymorph the defender and take the flag. This prevents reinforcements from arriving with Rez cycles. After that, you only have one person to solo (and you can always call for assistance now that you have your foot in the door).

On defense, Mages Polymorph healers or other casters. If the other side has a clear leader (someone who kills well, acts intelligently, and so forth), keep them sheeped all the time. Chain Polymorph, even with the diminishing returns; this act takes the person out of the battle for quite some time, and it also upsets them. It's not fun to be controlled for that long. Your actions might throw off the enemy's calm and controlled state of mind.

Use higher ledges and recesses to give yourself as many chances for casting ambushes as possible. You aren't a tough character, no matter how much Stamina your Mage finds. Thus, start fights! Don't let other people see where you are until it's too late. Stay on the balcony above the flag room in Warsong Gulch if you hear that enemies are coming in by the tunnel. Move to the roof if you hear that they are using the ramp. Or, if they are coming in from all sides, hide in the cubby to the side of the flag and wait for your opportunity.

Use every tool you have to stay alive (don't laugh, many people forget how many toys they have). The first time you are engaged while running off or fighting, use Blink. If the enemies close the gap again, use Frost Nova. If they are coming in again, try Cone of Cold. Check your timers; Blink is almost up again!

In PvP, Ice Armor is a very wise choice. Mana efficiency isn't nearly as important in the Battlegrounds. Survival is! And Ice Armor is one of the better tools for keeping enemies from engaging multiple times in melee.

When large packs of enemies gather, sell your life dearly. Raise Mana Shield, drop every instant AoE you can, and keep up the pressure until your Mage drops. Against four or more packed enemies, this deals so much damage that the healers are in deep trouble. Any allies that come to help you are likely to have a much easier fight, even if you go down in the process.

Paladin

Paladins are the high-survivability melee fighters of the Eastern Kingdoms. With their heavy armor and robust physique, they have the ability to absorb an enemy's attacks, making them strong secondary tanks. It is in difficult situations that Paladins truly shine, and their use of Holy magic allows them some of a Healer's powers, including the ability to heal themselves, others, and to resurrect the fallen. Because of their mixture of healing and tanking, a Paladin makes a wonderfully self-sufficient soloer, as well as an asset in any good group.

Lore

Duskwood used to be a forest of brightly lit glades and shining leaves. Now, the sunlight doesn't reach the woodland floor, and everything is colored with a bluish haze. The townsfolk of Darkshire even whisper that their allies have forsaken them, as the Undead infest the graveyards and wander the land, attacking any unwary traveler. But the Light never leaves any place or anyone's heart fully, and I had come to give what aid I could in defense of the people.

That morning, death came to the streets of Darkshire as an abomination stalked through the town itself. I heard the calls of the town crier as the Night Watch, the citizen's militia, rallied. Other brave defenders of the Alliance came to the cry as well: a strong Warrior, a dedicated Priest, and a slim night elf Rogue. Standing beside them, basking in an Aura of Devotion, I knew that we could outlast whatever the darkness brought.

We smelled the creature before we saw it, but as it came out of the fog it was obvious that this was no natural beast. Cobbled together of sickly pale flesh and putrescent organs, it immediately set upon us. My first attempt to exorcize the creature met with little success, so I slammed my mace hard into its midsection, whispering a prayer under my breath as I did so.

We fought well and hard that day. Using the strength of the crusader, the Priest and I attacked with Holy magic and strikes. The Warrior and Rogue did their parts as well, and I healed them as the monster's blows pummeled down. But this creature was strong, very strong. At one point, I was forced to call upon the Light to protect me from the creature's attacks, and its fist rained down without effect upon a shield of Light itself. This gave the Priest the time needed to save our group, and as I watched, the Warrior finally gave the strikes needed to collapse the abomination.

Together, we had all stood against one of the worst horrors ever to walk Azeroth. One day, we will reclaim Duskwood, and all its citizens can roam in tranquil gardens and bright glades again. Until that day, may the Light protect and guide us, and give us all the strength to stand against the darkness!

Introduction to Playing the Class

Playing a Paladin requires getting into a different mindset from many of the other classes. Instead of getting joy from each kill, there is great enjoyment from keeping yourself and other group members alive despite all manner of problems. Settle in for slow fights (especially while soloing), and laugh at the feeble monsters that try to take your character down.

As with Warriors, it's very useful to have several equipment pieces for varying occasions. Use a two-handed weapon while soloing and rely on the best damage abilities at your disposal. Bandage after fights, don't use as much mana for healing, and try to keep wading through enemies as much as possible. Then, when a group needs you in an instance, break out the one-hander and shield for survivability. These choices can even be made during a single fight (use a two-hander when your Paladin doesn't have aggro to do more damage, then pull out the shield if too much starts coming your way).

Though unable to easily or predictably gather aggro through direct attack, Paladins can assist the main tank on a target and use their holy spells in conjunction with Judgement of Righteousness to regain aggro if the creature gets onto a softer person. If the Priest gets aggro, a Paladin can immediately start healing the Priest to both protect them and try to gather extra aggro.

Because Paladins are not major killers in PvP, some people are less interested in using them there. Yet, Paladins can accomplish certain tasks extremely well! In Warsong Gulch, Paladins escort flag runners incredible well. Blessing of Freedom, a healer in plate, and Cleanse are amazing together. In Arathi Basin, Paladins defend points forever (it takes so long to kill them, and they can always use Divine Shield or other such abilities to save themselves). As long as the Paladins fight a few feet away from the flag, it takes the enemies too long to capture the flag before you come out of your protected state and hit them. It's so nice.

In raids, Paladins use their Greater Blessings to provide the gathered classes with major benefits. Greater Blessing of Wisdom really helps to keep casters going in those longer fights. Blessing of Salvation is wonderful for keeping the aggro off of targets that are dealing high damage or doing the most healing (just don't cast it on the tanks please). Resistance Auras are also a powerful tool for the late game, where being able to add another 60 points of Resistance can make all the difference! Paladins are relegated to supporting roles for these end-game encounters, but they are truly wonderful at filling that slot.

Available Races	
Dwarf	Human

What do Attributes Mean to Me?	
Strength	Increases Melee Damage and Amount Absorbed by Shield Blocks
Stamina	Raises Health
Agility	High Dodge and Critical Rate
Intellect	Increases Mana, Spell Crit %
Spirit	Added Health/Mana Regeneration

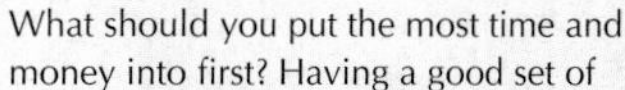

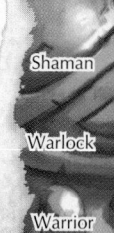

Items and Equipment

Paladins are equipment dependent. To do their best in the field and the dungeon, they need to have up-to-date armor and weapons, the best that they can afford or acquire. Also, to keep aggro and do damage, you want as powerful a weapon as you can get, and that means investing time and money into your equipment.

What should you put the most time and money into first? Having a good set of chest and leg armor is one of the best investments that you can make. This allows you to absorb the most amount of hits and keeps you in the fight the longest. Having that good set of armor allows you to conserve your mana to use for either healing or damage work (casting Seals, Judging enemies, Stuns, etc.).

If you really want to be the ultimate in survivability, use a shield, one-handed weapon, and spec for Protection. A shield can add large amounts to your Paladin's Armor Rating. Next, put a Shield Spike on it to add some offensive power. Keep your eyes open for quests that give shield rewards or look in the Auction House for one that suits you.

Try to keep that Armor Rating as high as you can. Don't be worried about being spendy with armor, because the survivability makes up for it a dozen times over. For an extra boost, try to get very good pieces enchanted with extra Stamina. At higher levels, adding Crusader to your weaponry is not only appropriate, but this adds to both DPS and survivability.

In terms of what attributes to look for, Stamina is always appreciated. There is never anything wrong with more health. If you find that you are soloing a lot, concentrate a bit more on Strength and Agility to raise your damage and shorten the length of fights. On the other hand, if you group more, lean a bit more on Intellect. This gives you the ability to do more healing work. Major Paladin healers need quite a slice of Intellect, both for the extra healing and for the increased chance to score Critical heals.

If you are playing more of a support Paladin, be careful to avoid weapons with proc abilities instead of attribute bonuses. Support Paladins need all of the Intellect and Stamina they can get, and weapons with proc abilities often have fewer points in attributes (or none at all). Mana regeneration gear and + to spell damage and healing are also very important for raiding Paladins.

CHOOSING YOUR PROFESSION

Knowing how to make your own equipment is a wonderful thing for Paladins. If you want to invest in crafted armor, move into Mining and Blacksmithing. Paladins are very good with the whole self-sufficiency thing, and making your own armor/weapons follows that perfectly. In addition, it's rather enjoyable to be out gathering usable materials while exploring the world at the same time.

For a PvP Paladin, or one interested in doing a great deal of soloing, Engineering is a wonderful thing to pick up. Paladins have fewer interrupts and possess almost no ranged abilities. This makes it amazingly powerful to rely on Engineering to deal AoE damage, light Stuns, and hit targets at range. Using Bombs to interrupt an enemy's spell can be very helpful, sometimes making all the difference in difficult fights where magic is being tossed at you.

A Paladin's biggest downtime problem is running out of mana. Alchemy and Herbalism can keep that in check by allowing a Paladin to make mana potions, which can help in a fix. As long as a Paladin has the mana, they are ready to fight, and more fighting means more experience. Beyond that, the bonuses gained from various potions help Paladins increase both their DPS and survivability. Spare herbs can be sold as well, adding to your funds for equipment upgrades.

First Aid, as for almost all melee or hybrid classes, comes in handy a great deal. Though you can always heal your character during or between fights, the use of bandages conserves mana! Especially when fighting humanoid mobs, that drop the cloth you need for First Aid, this cuts down on downtime tremendously. Cooking isn't as powerful for restoring health quickly, but its potential benefits for Stamina and Spirit are both noticed by soloing Paladins.

Class Abilities

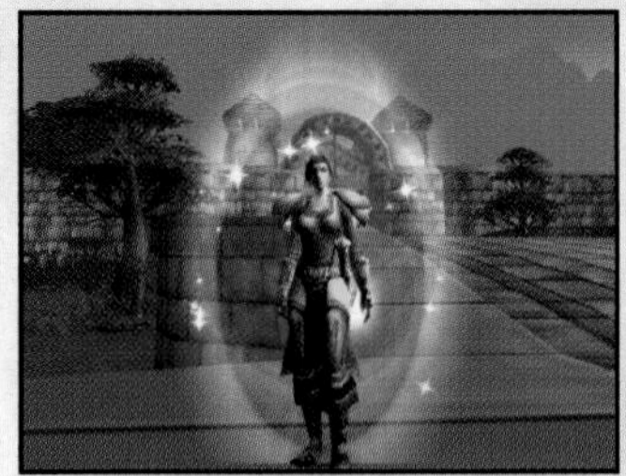

Paladins gain their anti-Undead abilities, healing, and Holy damage from the Holy skill line. Primarily, these abilities exist to keep your Paladin alive and to assist groups. When fighting Undead, the abilities become more combat oriented.

Protection abilities center around stopping enemies from killing or harming the Paladin and various allies. Stun enemy attackers, reduce Threat for soft allies in the group, and allow tanks to take those hits better.

Retribution neither heals nor protects; it is there to deal what damage a Paladin can master. Damaging Seals are found here, aggressive Auras, and the Judgement ability (to break Seals and cause potent effects on enemies).

Holy

Holy Light

Holy Light is one of the major healing abilities for Paladins. Though slower than Flash of Light and less efficient, this spell heals a great deal more per casting.

Rank	Level	Mana	Range	Casting Time	Cooldown	Cost to Train	Effect
1	1	35	40 yd	2.5 sec	—	N/A	Heals a friendly target for 39 to 47.
2	6	60	40 yd	2.5 sec	—	1	Heals a friendly target for 76 to 90.
3	14	110	40 yd	2.5 sec	—	20	Heals a friendly target for 159 to 187.
4	22	190	40 yd	2.5 sec	—	40	Heals a friendly target for 310 to 356.
5	30	275	40 yd	2.5 sec	—	1 10	Heals a friendly target for 491 to 553.
6	38	365	40 yd	2.5 sec	—	1 60	Heals a friendly target for 698 to 780.
7	46	465	40 yd	2.5 sec	—	2 40	Heals a friendly target for 945 to 1053.
8	54	580	40 yd	2.5 sec	—	4	Heals a friendly target for 1246 to 1388.
9	60	660	40 yd	2.5 sec	—	—	Heals a friendly target for 1590 to 1770.

Seal of Righteousness

Seal of Righteousness deals Holy damage to targets during a Paladin's melee attacks. When combine with Seal of the Crusader + Judgement, this can do a fair bit of damage (that doesn't get mitigated by Armor Rating or Resistances).

Rank	Level	Mana	Range	Casting Time	Cooldown	Cost to Train	Effect
1	1	20	Self	IC	—	—	Fills the Paladin with holy spirit for 30 sec, giving each melee attack an additional 1 to 4 Holy damage. Only one Seal can be active on the Paladin at any one time. Unleashing this Seal's energy will cause 12 Holy damage to an enemy.
2	10	40	Self	IC	—	3	Fills the Paladin with holy spirit for 30 sec, giving each melee attack an additional 2 to 8 Holy damage. Only one Seal can be active on the Paladin at any one time. Unleashing this Seal's energy will cause 25 to 27 Holy damage to an enemy.
3	18	60	Self	IC	—	35	Fills the Paladin with holy spirit for 30 sec, giving each melee attack an additional 4 to 14 Holy damage. Only one Seal can be active on the Paladin at any one time. Unleashing this Seal's energy will cause 39 to 43 Holy damage to an enemy.
4	26	90	Self	IC	—	60	Fills the Paladin with holy spirit for 30 sec, giving each melee attack an additional 6 to 21 Holy damage. Only one Seal can be active on the Paladin at any one time. Unleashing this Seal's energy will cause 57 to 63 Holy damage to an enemy.
5	34	120	Self	IC	—	1 30	Fills the Paladin with holy spirit for 30 sec, giving each melee attack an additional 4 to 31 Holy damage. Only one Seal can be active on the Paladin at any one time. Unleashing this Seal's energy will cause 78 to 86 Holy damage to an enemy.
6	42	140	Self	IC	—	2 10	Fills the Paladin with holy spirit for 30 sec, giving each melee attack an additional 12 to 43 Holy damage. Only one Seal can be active on the Paladin at any one time. Unleashing this Seal's energy will cause 102 to 112 Holy damage to an enemy.
7	50	170	Self	IC	—	2 80	Fills the Paladin with holy spirit for 30 sec, giving each melee attack an additional 16 to 56 Holy damage. Only one Seal can be active on the Paladin at any one time. Unleashing this Seal's energy will cause 131-143 Holy damage to an enemy.
8	58	200	Self	IC	—	4 40	Fills the Paladin with holy spirit for 30 sec, giving each melee attack an additional 20 to 71 Holy damage. Only one Seal can be active on the Paladin at any one time. Unleashing this Seal's energy will cause 162 to 178 Holy damage to an enemy.

Purify

Purify removes one poison and one disease effect from a target.

Rank	Level	Mana	Range	Casting Time	Cooldown	Cost to Train	Effect
N/A	8	4	30 yd	IC	—	1	Purifies the friendly target, removing 1 disease effect and 1 poison effect.

Lay on Hands

Lay on Hands is on a one-hour cooldown without Talents, but this ability has tremendous power. Your Paladin uses all of their remaining mana to instantly heal one target.

Rank	Level	Mana	Range	Casting Time	Cooldown	Cost to Train	Effect
1	10	100%	20 yd	IC	60 min	3 ●	Heals a friendly target for an amount equal to the Paladin's maximum health. Drains all of the Paladin's remaining mana when used.
2	30	100%	20 yd	IC	60 min	1 ● 10 ●	Heals a friendly target for an amount equal to the Paladin's maximum health and restores 250 of their mana. Drains all of the Paladin's remaining mana when used.
3	50	100%	20 yd	IC	60 min	2 ● 80 ●	Heals a friendly target for an amount equal to the Paladin's maximum health and restores 550 of their mana. Drains all of the Paladin's remaining mana when used.

Redemption

Redemption is a costly, out-of-combat Resurrection spell.

Rank	Level	Mana	Range	Casting Time	Cooldown	Cost to Train	Effect
1	12	60% of Base Mana	30 yd	10 sec	—	—	Brings a dead player back to life with 65 health and 120 mana. Cannot be cast when in combat.
2	24	60% of Base Mana	30 yd	10 sec	—	50 ●	Brings a dead player back to life with 150 health and 260 mana. Cannot be cast when in combat.
3	36	60% of Base Mana	30 yd	10 sec	—	1 ● 40 ●	Brings a dead player back to life with 250 health and 420 mana. Cannot be cast when in combat.
4	48	60% of Base Mana	30 yd	10 sec	—	2 ● 60 ●	Brings a dead player back to life with 400 health and 600 mana. Cannot be cast when in combat.
5	60	60% of Base Mana	30 yd	10 sec	—	4 ● 60 ●	Brings a dead player back to life with 600 health and 800 mana. Cannot be cast when in combat.

Blessing of Wisdom

Blessing of Wisdom restores mana every five seconds for the target.

Rank	Level	Mana	Range	Casting Time	Cooldown	Cost to Train	Effect
1	14	30	30 yd	IC	—	20 ●	Places a Blessing on the friendly target, restoring 10 mana every 5 seconds for 5 min. Players may only have one Blessing on them per Paladin at any one time.
2	24	45	30 yd	IC	—	50 ●	Places a Blessing on the friendly target, restoring 15 mana every 5 seconds for 5 min. Players may only have one Blessing on them per Paladin at any one time.
3	34	65	30 yd	IC	—	1 ● 30 ●	Places a Blessing on the friendly target, restoring 20 mana every 5 seconds for 5 min. Players may only have one Blessing on them per Paladin at any one time.
4	44	90	30 yd	IC	—	2 ● 20 ●	Places a Blessing on the friendly target, restoring 25 mana every 5 seconds for 5 min. Players may only have one Blessing on them per Paladin at any one time.
5	54	115	30 yd	IC	—	4 ●	Places a Blessing on the friendly target, restoring 30 mana every 5 seconds for 5 min. Players may only have one Blessing on them per Paladin at any one time.
6	60	125	30 yd	IC	—	—	Places a Blessing on the friendly target, restoring 33 Mana every 5 seconds for 5 min. Players may only have on Blessing on them per Paladin at any one time.

Greater Blessing of Wisdom

Rank	Level	Mana	Reagent	Range	Casting Time	Cooldown	Cost to Train	Effect
1	54	230	Symbol of Kings	30 yd	IC	—	4 ● 60 ●	Gives all members of the raid or group that share the same class as the target the Greater Blessing of Wisdom, restoring 30 mana every 5 sec for 15 min. Players can only have one Blessing on them per Paladin at any one time.
2	60	250	Symbol of Kings	30 yd	IC	—	4 ● 60 ●	Gives all members of the raid or group that share the same class as the target the Greater Blessing of Wisdom, restoring 33 mana every 5 sec for 15 min. Players can only have one Blessing on them per Paladin at any one time.

Consecration

Consecration is Talent-learned low-damage AoE ability. Paladins drop the AoE on the ground around themselves, instantly damaging nearby foes with Holy magic. This is extremely mana-inefficient unless there are many enemies nearby.

Rank	Minimum Level	Mana	Range	Casting Time	Cooldown		Cost to Train	Effect
1	20	135	—	IC	8 seconds	—		Consecrates the land beneath the Paladin, doing 64 Holy Damage over 8 sec to enemies who enter the area.
2	30	235	—	IC	8 seconds	—	2 ●	Consecrates the land beneath the Paladin, doing 120 Holy Damage over 8 sec to enemies who enter the area.
3	40	320	—	IC	8 seconds	—	10 ●	Consecrates the land beneath the Paladin, doing 192 Holy Damage over 8 sec to enemies who enter the area.
4	50	435	—	IC	8 seconds	—	14 ●	Consecrates the land beneath the Paladin, doing 280 Holy Damage over 8 sec to enemies who enter the area.
5	60	565	—	IC	8 seconds	—	23 ●	Consecrates the land beneath the Paladin, doing 384 Holy Damage over 8 sec to enemies who enter the area.

Exorcism

Exorcism deals instant, ranged damage to Undead or Demon targets (Forsaken players do not count, though Warlock pets do).

Rank	Level	Mana	Range	Casting Time	Cooldown	Cost to Train	Effect
1	20	85	30 yd	IC	15 sec	40 ●	Causes 84 to 96 holy damage to an Undead or Demon target.
2	28	135	30 yd	IC	15 sec	90 ●	Causes 152 to 172 holy damage to an undead target or demon.
3	36	180	30 yd	IC	15 sec	1 ● 40 ●	Causes 217 to 245 holy damage to an Undead or Demon target.
4	44	235	30 yd	IC	15 sec	2 ● 20 ●	Causes 304 to 342 holy damage to an Undead or Demon target.
5	52	285	30 yd	IC	15 sec	3 ● 40 ●	Causes 393 to 439 holy damage to an Undead or Demon target.
6	60	345	30 yd	IC	15 sec	4 ● 60 ●	Causes 505 to 563 holy damage to an Undead or Demon target.

Flash of Light

Flash of Light is an amazingly efficient healing spell (nothing in the game can really touch this, especially if your Paladin specs for Holy Talents). The problem is that the HPS output (health per second) is very low.

Rank	Level	Mana	Range	Casting Time	Cooldown	Cost to Train	Effect
1	20	35	40 yd	IC	—	40	Heals a friendly target for 62 to 72.
2	26	50	40 yd	1.5 sec	—	60	Heals a friendly target for 96 to 110.
3	34	70	40 yd	1.5 sec	—	1 30	Heals a friendly target for 145 to 163.
4	42	90	40 yd	1.5 sec	—	2 10	Heals a friendly target for 197 to 221.
5	50	115	40 yd	1.5 sec	—	2 80	Heals a friendly target for 267 to 299.
6	58	140	40 yd	1.5 sec	—	4 40	Heals a friendly target for 343 to 383.

Turn Undead

Turn Undead is a very inexpensive Fear spell that works against Undead (not Forsaken).

Rank	Level	Mana	Range	Casting Time	Cooldown	Cost to Train	Effect
1	24	35	20 yd	1.5 sec	—	50	The targeted undead enemy will be compelled to flee for up to 10 sec. Damage caused may interrupt the effect. Only one target can be turned at a time.
2	38	50	20 yd	1.5 sec	30 sec	1 80	The targeted undead enemy will be compelled to flee for up to 15 sec. Damage caused may interrupt the effect. Only one target can be turned at a time.
3	52	75	20 yd	1.5 sec	30 sec	3 20	The targeted undead enemy will be compelled to flee for up to 20 sec. Damage caused may interrupt the effect. Only one target can be turned at a time.

Sense Undead

Sense Undead allows Paladins to Track Undead, as per the Hunter ability(does not work on Forsaken).

Rank	Level	Mana	Range	Casting Time	Cooldown	Cost to Train	Effect
N/A	20	—	—	IC	—	—	Shows the location of all nearby undead on the minimap until cancelled. Only one type of tracking can be used at a time.

Divine Favor

Divine Favor is a Talent-learned ability on a two-minute cooldown. This guarantees that the next Flash of Light, Holy Light, or Holy Shock that is cast will be a Critical.

Rank	Minimum Level	Mana	Range	Casting Time	Cooldown	Cost to Train	Effect
1	30	60	—	IC	2 minutes	—	When activated, gives your next Flash of Light or Holy Light spell a 100% critical effect chance.

Seal of Light

Seal of Light adds a chance to gain health on melee attacks. When used with Judgement, this puts the effect on the enemy giving your teammates in melee a chance to gain health after a successful hit.

Rank	Level	Mana	Range	Casting Time	Cooldown	Cost to Train	Effect
1	30	110	—	IC	—	1 10	Fills the Paladin with divine light for 30 sec, giving each melee attack a chance to heal the Paladin for 39. Only one Seal can be active on the Paladin at any one time. Unleashing this Seal's energy will judge an enemy for 30 sec, granting melee attacks made against the judged enemy a chance of healing the attacker for 25. Only one Judgment per Paladin can be active at any one time. Your melee strikes will refresh the spell's duration.
2	40	140	—	IC	—	2	Fills the Paladin with divine light for 30 sec, giving each melee attack a chance to heal the Paladin for 53. Only one Seal can be active on the Paladin at any one time. Unleashing this Seal's energy will judge an enemy for 30 sec, granting melee attacks made against the judged enemy a chance of healing the attacker for 34. Only one Judgment per Paladin can be active at any one time. Your melee strikes will refresh the spell's duration.
3	50	180	—	IC	—	2 80	Fills the Paladin with divine light for 30 sec, giving each melee attack a chance to heal the Paladin for 76. Only one Seal can be active on the Paladin at any one time. Unleashing this Seal's energy will judge an enemy for 30 sec, granting melee attacks made against the judged enemy a chance of healing the attacker for 49. Only one Judgment per Paladin can be active at any one time. Your melee strikes will refresh the spell's duration.
4	60	210	—	IC	—	4 60	Fills the Paladin with divine light for 30 sec, giving each melee attack a chance to heal the Paladin for 94. Only one Seal can be active on the Paladin at any one time. Unleashing this Seal's energy will judge an enemy for 30 sec, granting melee attacks made against the judged enemy a chance of healing the attacker for 61. Only one Judgment per Paladin can be active at any one time. Your melee strikes will refresh the spell's duration.

Seal of Wisdom

Seal of Wisdom gives Paladins a chance to regain mana with each attack. When Judged, this effect works for all characters fighting.

Rank	Level	Mana	Range	Casting Time	Cooldown	Cost to Train	Effect
1	38	135	Self	IC	—	1 60	Fills the Paladin with divine wisdom for 30 sec, giving each melee attack a chance to restore 50 of the Paladin's mana. Only one Seal can be active on the Paladin at any one time. Unleashing this Seal's energy will judge an enemy for 10 sec, granting attacks and spells used against the judged enemy a chance to restore 33 mana to the attacker. Your melee attacks will refresh the spell's duration. Only one Judgment per Paladin can be active at any one time.
2	48	170	Self	IC	—	2 60	Fills the Paladin with divine wisdom for 30 sec, giving each melee attack a chance to restore 71 of the Paladin's mana. Only one Seal can be active on the Paladin at any one time. Unleashing this Seal's energy will judge an enemy for 10 sec, granting attacks and spells used against the judged enemy a chance to restore 46 mana to the attacker. Your melee attacks will refresh the spell's duration. Only one Judgment per Paladin can be active at any one time.
3	58	200	Self	IC	—	4 40	Fills the Paladin with divine wisdom for 30 sec, giving each melee attack a chance to restore 90 of the Paladin's mana. Only one Seal can be active on the Paladin at any one time. Unleashing this Seal's energy will judge an enemy for 10 sec, granting attacks and spells used against the judged enemy a chance to restore 59 mana to the attacker. Your melee attacks will refresh the spell's duration. Only one Judgment per Paladin can be active at any one time.

Blessing of Light

Blessing of Light increases the power of Holy Light and Flash of Light on the target. If there are multiple Paladins working with the same tank, this is an amazing ability.

Rank	Level	Mana	Range	Casting Time	Cooldown	Cost to Train	Effect
1	40	85	30 yd	IC	—	2	Places a Blessing on the friendly target, increasing the effects of Holy Light spells used on the target by up to 210 and the effect of Flash of Light spells used on the target by up to 60. Lasts 5 min. Players may only have one Blessing on them per Paladin at any one time.
2	50	110	30 yd	IC	—	2 80	Places a Blessing on the friendly target, increasing the effects of Holy Light spells used on the target by up to 300 and the effect of Flash of Light spells used on the target by up to 85. Lasts 5 min. Players may only have one Blessing on them per Paladin at any one time.
3	60	135	30 yd	IC	—	4 60	Places a Blessing on the friendly target, increasing the effects of Holy Light spells used on the target by up to 400 and the effect of Flash of Light spells used on the target by up to 115. Lasts 5 min. Players may only have one Blessing on them per Paladin at any one time.

Greater Blessing of Light

Rank	Level	Mana	Reagent	Range	Casting Time	Cooldown	Cost to Train	Effect
1	60	260	Symbol of Kings	30 yd	IC	—	4 60	Gives all members of the raid or group that share the same class with the target the Greater Blessing of Light, increasing the effects of Holy Light spells used on the target by up to 400 and Flash of Light spells used on the target by up to 115. Lasts 15 min. Players may only have one Blessing on them per Paladin at any one time.

Holy Shock

Holy Shock is a Talent-learned ability with a 30-second cooldown. Paladins can use this to either deal Holy damage or instantly heal a target (depending on whether the target is a friend or foe).

Rank	Minimum Level	Mana	Range	Casting Time	Cooldown	Cost to Train	Effect
1	40	255	20 yd	IC	30 seconds	—	Blasts the target with Holy energy, causing 204 to 220 Holy damage to an enemy, or 204 to 220 healing to an ally.
2	48	275	20 yd	IC	30 seconds	—	Blasts the target with Holy energy, causing 279 to 301 Holy damage to an enemy, or 279 to 301 healing to an ally.
1	40	255	20 yd	IC	30 seconds	—	Blasts the target with Holy energy, causing 365 to 395 Holy damage to an enemy, or 365 to 395 healing to an ally.

Cleanse

Rank	Level	Mana	Range	Casting Time	Cooldown	Cost to Train	Effect
N/A	42	4	30 yd	IC	—	2 10	Cleanses a friendly target, removing 1 poison effect, 1 disease effect, and 1 magic effect.

Hammer of Wrath

Hammer of Wrath deals Holy, ranged damage by throwing a hammer at the wounded target. This can only be used on foes that are at or below 20% health, and the damage is substantial for a short-casting time.

Rank	Level	Mana	Range	Casting Time	Cooldown	Cost to Train	Effect
1	44	295	30 yd	1 sec	6 sec	2 20	Hurls a hammer that strikes an enemy for 304 to 336 Holy Damage. Only useable on enemies that have 20% or less health.
2	52	360	30 yd	1 sec	6 sec	3 40	Hurls a hammer that strikes an enemy for 399 to 441 Holy Damage. Only useable on enemies that have 20% or less health.
3	60	425	30 yd	1 sec	6 sec	4 60	Hurls a hammer that strikes an enemy for 504 to 556 Holy Damage. Only useable on enemies that have 20% or less health.

Holy Wrath

Holy Wrath deals AoE damage to Undead and Demons (as usual, not to Forsaken). The one-minute cooldown timer keeps Paladins from being able to spam Holy Wrath.

Rank	Level	Mana	Range	Casting Time	Cooldown	Cost to Train	Effect
1	50	645	—	2 sec	1 min	2 80	Sends bolts of holy power in all directions, causing 362 to 428 Holy damage to all Undead and Demon targets within 20 yards.
2	60	805	—	2 sec	1 min	4 60	Sends bolts of holy power in all directions, causing 490 to 576 Holy damage to all Undead and Demon targets within 20 yards.

Protection

Devotion Aura

Devotion Aura provides an armor increase for everyone in the Paladin's group.

Rank	Level	Mana	Range	Casting Time	Cooldown	Cost to Train	Effect
1	1	N/A	30 yd	IC	—	10 [c]	Gives 55 additional armor to party members within 30 yards. Players may only have one Aura on them per Paladin at any one time.
2	10	N/A	30 yd	IC	—	3	Gives 160 additional armor to party members within 30 yards. Players may only have one Aura on them per Paladin at any one time.
3	20	N/A	30 yd	IC	—	40	Gives 275 additional armor to party members within 30 yards. Players may only have one Aura on them per Paladin at any one time.
4	30	N/A	30 yd	IC	—	1 10	Gives 390 additional armor to party members within 30 yards. Players may only have one Aura on them per Paladin at any one time.
5	40	N/A	30 yd	IC	—	2	Gives 505 additional armor to party members within 30 yards. Players may only have one Aura on them per Paladin at any one time.
6	50	N/A	30 yd	IC	—	2 80	Gives 620 additional armor to party members within 30 yards. Players may only have one Aura on them per Paladin at any one time.
7	60	N/A	30 yd	IC	—	4 60	Gives 735 additional armor to party members within 30 yards. Players may only have one Aura on them per Paladin at any one time.

Divine Protection

Divine Protection shields a Paladin from harm for a brief period. This is usable every five minutes and places a Forbearance debuff on the Paladin. This prevents them from being affected by Divine Shield or Blessing of Protection for 60 seconds.

Rank	Level	Mana	Range	Casting Time	Cooldown	Cost to Train	Effect
1	6	15	Self	IC	5 min	1	You are protected from all physical attacks and spells for 6 sec, but during that time you cannot attack or use physical abilities yourself. Once protected, the target cannot be made invulnerable by Divine Shield, Divine Protection, or Blessing of Protection again for 1 min.
2	18	35	Self	IC	5 min	35	You are protected from all physical attacks and spells for 8 sec, but during that time you cannot attack or use physical abilities yourself. Once protected, the target cannot be made invulnerable by Divine Shield, Divine Protection, or Blessing of Protection again for 1 min.

Hammer of Justice

Hammer of Justice offers a short-range, instant Stun to against a single target.

Rank	Level	Mana	Range	Casting Time	Cooldown	Cost to Train	Effect
1	8	30	10 yd	IC	1 min	2	Stuns the target for 3 sec.
2	24	50	10 yd	IC	1 min	50	Stuns the target for 4 sec.
3	40	75	10 yd	IC	1 min	2	Stuns the target for 5 sec.
4	54	100	10 yd	IC	1 min	5 80	Stuns the target for 6 sec.

Blessing of Protection

Blessing of Protection is used to provide Divine Protection for an ally. This shields them from all harm for a short period, allowing them to use non-physical actions without disruption.

Rank	Level	Mana	Range	Casting Time	Cooldown	Cost to Train	Effect
1	10	25	30 yd	IC	5 min	3	A targeted party member is protected from all physical attacks for 6 sec, but during that time they cannot attack or use physical abilities. Players may only have one Blessing on them per Paladin at any one time. Once protected, the target cannot be made invulnerable by Divine Shield, Divine Protection, or Blessing of Protection again for 1 min.
2	24	45	30 yd	IC	5 min	50	A targeted party member is protected from all physical attacks for 8 sec, but during that time they cannot attack or use physical abilities. Players may only have one Blessing on them per Paladin at any one time. Once protected, the target cannot be made invulnerable by Divine Shield, Divine Protection, or Blessing of Protection again for 1 min.
3	38	65	30 yd	IC	5 min	1 60	A targeted party member is protected from all physical attacks for 10 sec, but during that time they cannot attack or use physical abilities. Players may only have one Blessing on them per Paladin at any one time. Once protected, the target cannot be made invulnerable by Divine Shield, Divine Protection, or Blessing of Protection again for 1 min.

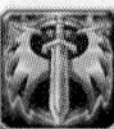

Righteous Fury

Righteous Fury increases the Threat generation of a Paladin's Holy attacks by 60% for 30 minutes.

Rank	Level	Mana	Range	Casting Time	Cooldown	Cost to Train	Effect
N/A	16	49	—	IC	—	30	Increases the threat generated by your Holy attacks by 60%. Lasts 30 min.

Blessing of Freedom

Blessing of Freedom adds immunity to movement-impairing effects for a short time. This is amazingly powerful for escaping from areas, for running the flag in Warsong Gulch, and for helping others to do the same.

Rank	Level	Mana	Range	Casting Time	Cooldown		Cost to Train	Effect
N/A	6	35	30 yd	IC	20 sec	—	35	Places a Blessing on the friendly target, granting immunity to movement impairing effects for 10 sec. Players may only have one Blessing on them per Paladin at any one time.

Blessing of Kings

Blessing of Kings is a Talent-learned ability that is mainly useful on hybrid classes. This Blessing increases all of the target's attributes by 10%.

Rank	Minimum Level	Mana	Range	Casting Time	Cooldown	Cost to Train	Effect
1	20	75	30 yd	IC	—	—	Places a Blessing on the friendly target, increasing total stats by 10% for 5 min. Players may have one Blessing on them per Paladin at any one time.

Greater Blessing of Kings

Rank	Level	Mana	Range	Casting Time	Cooldown	Cost to Train	Effect
1	60	150	30 yd	IC	—	23	Gives all members of the raid or group that share the same class with the target the Greater Blessing of Kings, increasing total stats by 10% for 15 min. Players may only have one Blessing per Paladin at any one time. Requires Symbol of Kings

Concentration Aura

Concentration Aura adds a 35% chance to avoid disruption from damage. Healers and AoE casters are going to be very happy with this Aura.

Rank	Level	Mana	Range	Casting Time	Cooldown	Cost to Train	Effect
N/A	22	N/A	Party	IC	—	40	Gives a 35% chance of ignoring spell interruption when damaged to all party members within 30 yards. Players may only have one Aura on them per Paladin at any one time.

Seal of Justice

Seal of Justice gives your Paladin's melee attacks a chance to Stun the target for two seconds. When Judged, this Seal prevents enemies from fleeing in PvE combat (and has no use in PvP).

Rank	Level	Mana	Range	Casting Time	Cooldown	Cost to Train	Effect
N/A	22	21	—	IC	—	40	Fills the Paladin with the spirit of justice for 30 sec, giving each melee attack a chance to stun for 2 sec. Only one Seal can be active one the Paladin at any one time. Unleashing this Seal's energy will judge an enemy for 10 sec, preventing them from fleeing. Only one Judgment per Paladin can be active at any one time.

Blessing of Salvation

Blessing of Salvation reduces Threat generation by 30% while active. This is an amazing Blessing for many classes, and it gets even better in the high-end game.

Rank	Level	Mana	Range	Casting Time	Cooldown	Cost to Train	Effect
N/A	26	13	30 yd	IC	—	60	Places a Blessing on the party member, reducing the amount of all threat generated by 30% for 5 min. Players may only have one Blessing on them per Paladin at any one time.

Shadow Resistance Aura

Resistance Auras (Shadow, Fire, Frost) are either worthless for a given fight or *essential.* Adding up to 60 to a specific Resistance without any upkeep is enough to add both damage mitigation and avoidance of dangerous effects during scary fights.

Rank	Level	Mana	Range	Casting Time	Cooldown	Cost to Train	Effect
1	28	N/A	Party	IC	—	90	Gives 30 additional Shadow resistance to all party members within 30 yards. Players may only have one Aura on them per Paladin at any one time.
2	40	N/A	Party	IC	—	2	Gives 45 additional Shadow resistance to all party members within 30 yards. Players may only have one Aura on them per Paladin at any one time.
3	52	N/A	Party	IC	—	3 40	Gives 60 additional Shadow resistance to all party members within 30 yards. Players may only have one Aura on them per Paladin at any one time.

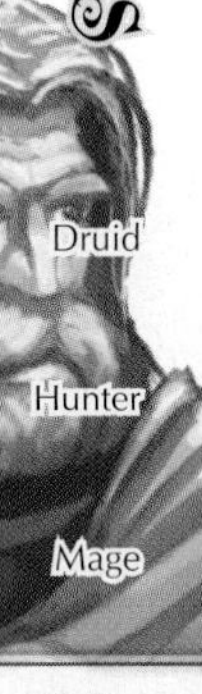

Fire Resistance Aura

Rank	Level	Mana	Range	Casting Time	Cooldown	Cost to Train	Effect
1	36	—	Party	IC	—	1 40	Gives 30 additional Fire resistance to all party members within 30 yards. Players may only have one Aura on them per Paladin at any one time.
2	48	—	Party	IC	—	2 60	Gives 45 additional Fire resistance to all party members within 30 yards. Players may only have one Aura on them per Paladin at any one time.
3	60	—	Party	IC	—	4 20	Gives 60 additional Fire resistance to all party members within 30 yards. Players may only have one Aura on them per Paladin at any one time.

Frost Resistance Aura

Rank	Level	Mana	Range	Casting Time	Cooldown	Cost to Train	Effect
1	32	—	Party	IC	—	1 20	Gives 30 additional Frost resistance to all party members within 30 yards. Players may only have one Aura on them per Paladin at any one time.
2	44	—	Party	IC	—	2 20	Gives 45 additional Frost resistance to all party members within 30 yards. Players may only have one Aura on them per Paladin at any one time.
3	56	—	Party	IC	—	4 20	Gives 60 additional Frost resistance to all party members within 30 yards. Players may only have one Aura on them per Paladin at any one time.

Blessing of Sanctuary

Blessing of Sanctuary is a Talent-learned ability used to increase the damage done during a block (through a Holy damage proc). This also reduces the damage done to the target! Main tanks benefit immensely from Sanctuary.

Rank	Minimum Level	Mana	Range	Casting Time	Cooldown	Cost to Train	Effect
1	30	60	30 yd	IC	—	—	Places a Blessing on the friendly target, reducing damage dealt from all sources by up to 7 for 5 min. In addition, when the target blocks a melee attack the attacker will take 14 Holy damage. Players may only have one Blessing on them per Paladin at any one time.
2	40	85	30 yd	IC	—	10	Places a Blessing on the friendly target, reducing damage dealt from all sources by up to 14 for 5 min. In addition, when the target blocks a melee attack, the attacker will take 21 Holy damage. Players may only have one Blessing on them per Paladin at any given time.
3	50	110	30 yd	IC	—	14	Places a Blessing on the friendly target, reducing damage dealt from all sources by up to 19 for 5 min. In addition, when the target blocks a melee attack, the attacker will take 28 Holy damage. Players may only have one Blessing on them per Paladin at any given time.
4	60	135	30 yd	IC	—	23	Places a Blessing on the friendly target, reducing damage dealt from all sources by up to 24 for 5 min. In addition, when the target blocks a melee attack, the attacker will take 35 Holy damage. Players may only have one Blessing on them per Paladin at any given time.

Greater Blessing of Sanctuary

Rank	Level	Mana	Range	Casting Time	Cooldown	Cost to Train	Effect
1	60	270	30 yd	IC	—	23	Gives all member of the raid or group that share the same class with the target the Greater Blessing of Sanctuary, reducing damage dealt from all sources by up to 24 for 15 min. In addition, when the target blocks a melee attack the attacker will take 35 Holy damage. Players may only have one Blessing per Paladin at any one time. Requires Symbol of Kings.

Divine Intervention

Divine Intervention is a wipe prevention ability on a one-hour cooldown. Use this to sacrifice your Paladin's life and remove a targeted ally from battle. This removes all aggro from the person and makes them invulnerable for three minutes, though they cannot act during this time.

Rank	Level	Mana	Reagent	Range	Casting Time	Cooldown	Cost to Train	Effect
N/A	30	—	Symbol of Divinity	20 yd	IC	60 min	1 10	The paladin sacrifices herself to remove the targeted party member from harm's way. Enemies will stop attacking the protected party member, who will be immune to all harmful attacks but cannot take any action for 3 min.

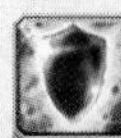

Divine Shield

Divine Shield is another bubble ability that shields a Paladin from all harm for a short period. Paladins under the effect of Divine Shield are still able to attack, though at 50% of their normal speed.

Rank	Level	Mana	Range	Casting Time	Cooldown	Cost to Train	Effect
1	34	75	Self	IC	—	1 30	Protects the Paladin from all damage and spells for 10 sec, but reduces attack speed by 50%. Once protected, the target cannot be made invulnerable by Divine Shield, Divine Protection, or Blessing of Protection again for 1 min.
2	50	110	Self	IC	—	2 80	Protects the Paladin from all damage and spells for 12 sec, but reduces attack speed by 50%. Once protected, the target cannot be made invulnerable by Divine Shield, Divine Protection, or Blessing of Protection again for 1 min.

Holy Shield

Holy Shield is a Talent-learned ability that increases the chance to block by 30% and deals Holy damage to the next four enemies that are blocked. This lasts for up to ten seconds (or the four charges), and has a ten-second cooldown.

Rank	Minimum Level	Mana	Range	Casting Time	Cooldown	Cost to Train	Effect
1	40	175	—	IC	10 seconds	—	Requires Shield. Increases chance to block by 30% for 10 sec and deals 50 Holy damage for each attack blocked while active. Each block expends a charge. 4 charges.
2	50	225	—	IC	10 sec	14	Increases chance to block by 30 % for 10 sec and deals 95 Holy Damage for each attack blocked while active. Damage caused by Holy Shield causes 20% additional threat. Each block expends a charge. 4 charges.
3	60	280	—	IC	10 sec	23	Increases chance to block by 30 % for 10 sec and deals 130 Holy Damage for each attack blocked while active. Damage caused by Holy Shield causes 20% additional threat. Each block expends a charge. 4 charges

Blessing of Sacrifice

Blessing of Sacrifice allow Paladins to spread out the damage done to their group. Use this on a main tank so that some of the damage done against them is transferred to your Paladin.

Rank	Level	Mana	Range	Casting Time	Cooldown	Cost to Train	Effect
1	46	80	30 yd	IC	—	2 40	Places a Blessing on the party member, transferring 45 damage taken per hit to the caster. Lasts 30 sec. Players may only have one Blessing on them per Paladin at any one time.
2	54	100	30 yd	IC	—	4	Places a Blessing on the party member, transferring 55 damage taken per hit to the caster. Lasts 30 sec. Players may only have one Blessing on them per Paladin at any one time.

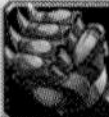

Blessing of Might

Blessing of Might adds to the Melee Attack Power of the target. Use this on Rogues and other physical DPS characters for the greatest effect.

Rank	Level	Mana	Range	Casting Time	Cooldown	Cost to Train	Effect
1	4	20	30 yd	IC	—	1	Places a Blessing on the friendly target, increasing attack power by 20 for 5 min. Players may only have one Blessing on them per Paladin at any one time.
2	12	30	30 yd	IC	—	10	Places a Blessing on the friendly target, increasing attack power by 35 for 5 min. Players may only have one Blessing on them per Paladin at any one time.
3	22	45	30 yd	IC	—	40	Places a Blessing on the friendly target, increasing attack power by 55 for 5 min. Players may only have one Blessing on them per Paladin at any one time.
4	32	60	30 yd	IC	—	1 20	Places a Blessing on the friendly target, increasing attack power by 85 for 5 min. Players may only have one Blessing on them per Paladin at any one time.
5	42	85	30 yd	IC	—	2 10	Places a Blessing on the friendly target, increasing attack power by 115 for 5 min. Players may only have one Blessing on them per Paladin at any one time.
6	52	110	30 yd	IC	—	3 40	Places a Blessing on the friendly target, increasing attack power by 155 for 5 min. Players may only have one Blessing on them per Paladin at any one time.
7	60	130	30 yd	IC	—	—	Places a Blessing on the friendly target, increasing attack power by 185 for 5 min. Players may only have one Blessing on them per Paladin at any one time.

Greater Blessing of Might

Rank	Level	Mana	Range	Casting Time	Cooldown	Cost to Train	Effect
1	52	220	30 yd	IC	—	4 60	Gives all members of the raid or group that share the same class with the target the Greater Blessing of Might, increasing attack power by 155 for 15 min. Players may only have one Blessing per Paladin at any one time.
2	60	260	30 yd	IC	—	4 60	Gives all members of the raid or group that share the same class with the target the Greater Blessing of Might, increasing attack power by 185 for 15 min. Players may only have one Blessing per Paladin at any one time.

Judgment

Judgement is a curious ability. After a Paladin casts a Seal, Judgement is used to break that Seal (ending its effect) and produce a different Judgement effect. Each Seal has a different power when Judged.

Rank	Level	Mana	Range	Casting Time	Cooldown	Cost to Train	Effect
1	4	9	10 yd	IC	15 sec	1	Unleashes the energy of a Seal spell upon the enemy. Refer to individual Seals for Judgment effect.

Seal of the Crusader

Seal of the Crusader increases the Attack Power and speed of Paladin attacks (though lowers their damage per hit to negate the DPS improvements of the speed itself).

Rank	Level	Mana	Range	Casting Time	Cooldown	Cost to Train	Effect
1	6	25	Self	IC	—	1	Fills the Paladin with the spirit of a crusader for 30 sec, granting 31 attack power. The Paladin also attacks 40% faster, but deals less damage with each attack. Only one Seal can be active on the Paladin at any one time. Unleashing this seal's energy will judge an enemy for 10 sec, increasing Holy damage taken by up to 20. Your melee strikes will refresh this spell's duration. Only one Judgment per Paladin can be active at any one time.
2	12	40	Self	IC	—	10	Fills the Paladin with the spirit of a crusader for 30 sec, granting 51 attack power. The Paladin also attacks 40% faster, but deals less damage with each attack. Only one Seal can be active on the Paladin at any one time. Unleashing this seal's energy will judge an enemy for 10 sec, increasing Holy damage taken by up to 30. Your melee strikes will refresh this spell's duration. Only one Judgment per Paladin can be active at any one time.
3	22	65	Self	IC	—	40	Fills the Paladin with the spirit of a crusader for 30 sec, granting 94 attack power. The Paladin also attacks 40% faster, but deals less damage with each attack. Only one Seal can be active on the Paladin at any one time. Unleashing this seal's energy will judge an enemy for 10 sec, increasing Holy damage taken by up to 50. Your melee strikes will refresh this spell's duration. Only one Judgment per Paladin can be active at any one time.
4	32	90	Self	IC	—	1 20	Fills the Paladin with the spirit of a crusader for 30 sec, granting 145 attack power. The Paladin also attacks 40% faster, but deals less damage with each attack. Only one Seal can be active on the Paladin at any one time. Unleashing this seal's energy will judge an enemy for 10 sec, increasing Holy damage taken by up to 80. Your melee strikes will refresh this spell's duration. Only one Judgment per Paladin can be active at any one time.
5	42	125	Self	IC	—	2 10	Fills the Paladin with the spirit of a crusader for 30 sec, granting 221 attack power. The Paladin also attacks 40% faster, but deals less damage with each attack. Only one Seal can be active on the Paladin at any one time. Unleashing this seal's energy will judge an enemy for 30 sec, increasing Holy damage taken by up to 110. Your melee strikes will refresh this spell's duration. Only one Judgment per Paladin can be active at any one time.
6	52	165	Self	IC	—	3 40	Fills the Paladin with the spirit of a crusader for 30 sec, granting 306 attack power. The Paladin also attacks 40% faster, but deals less damage with each attack. Only one Seal can be active on the Paladin at any one time. Unleashing this seal's energy will judge an enemy for 10 sec, increasing Holy damage taken by up to 140. Your melee strikes will refresh this spell's duration. Only one Judgment per Paladin can be active at any one time.

Retribution Aura

Retribution Aura deals Holy damage to any creature that strikes a group member. This Aura is most effective against large groups of fast-attacking monsters that are non-elites.

Rank	Level	Mana	Range	Casting Time	Cooldown	Cost to Train	Effect
1	16	N/A	Party	IC	—	30	Causes 5 holy damage to any creature that strikes a party member within 30 yards. Players may only have one Aura on them per Paladin at any one time.
2	26	N/A	Party	IC	—	60	Causes 8 holy damage to any creature that strikes a party member within 30 yards. Players may only have one Aura on them per Paladin at any one time.
3	36	N/A	Party	IC	—	1 40	Causes 12 holy damage to any creature that strikes a party member within 30 yards. Players may only have one Aura on them per Paladin at any one time.
4	46	N/A	Party	IC	—	2 40	Causes 16 holy damage to any creature that strikes a party member within 30 yards. Players may only have one Aura on them per Paladin at any one time.
5	56	N/A	Party	IC	—	4 20	Causes 20 holy damage to any creature that strikes a party member within 30 yards. Players may only have one Aura on them per Paladin at any one time.

Seal of Command

Seal of Command is a Talent-learned ability that procs additional Holy damage on some melee attacks. Judging Seal of Command deals instant Holy damage (and does even more than usual if the target is under a Stun effect).

Rank	Minimum Level	Mana	Range	Casting Time	Cooldown	Cost to Train	Effect
1	20	65	—	IC	—	—	Gives the Paladin a chance to deal additional Holy damage equal to 70% of the damage of the attack. Only one Seal can be active on the Paladin at any one time. Lasts 30 sec. Unleashing this Seal's energy will judge an enemy, instantly causing 68 to 74 damage, 137 to 147 if the target is stunned.
2	30	110	—	IC	—	5 ● 50 ●	Gives the Paladin a chance to deal additional Holy Damage equal to 70% of the damage of the attack. Only one Seal can be active on the Paladin at any one time. Lasts 30 sec. Unleashing the Seal's energy will judge an enemy, instantly causing 73 to 80 Holy Damage, 146 to 160 if the target is stunned or incapacitated.
3	40	140	—	IC	—	10 ●	Gives the Paladin a chance to deal additional Holy Damage equal to 70% of the damage of the attack. Only one Seal can be active on the Paladin at any one time. Lasts 30 sec. Unleashing the Seal's energy will judge an enemy, instantly causing 102 to 112 Holy Damage, 204 to 224 if the target is stunned or incapacitated.
4	50	180	—	IC	—	14 ●	Gives the Paladin a chance to deal additional Holy Damage equal to 70% of the damage of the attack. Only one Seal can be active on the Paladin at any one time. Lasts 30 sec. Unleashing the Seal's energy will judge an enemy, instantly causing 130 to 144 Holy Damage, 261 to 287 if the target is stunned or incapacitated.
5	60	210	—	IC	—	23 ●	Gives the Paladin a chance to deal additional Holy Damage equal to 70% of the damage of the attack. Only one Seal can be active on the Paladin at any one time. Lasts 30 sec. Unleashing the Seal's energy will judge an enemy, instantly causing 169 to 187 Holy Damage, 339 to 373 if the target is stunned or incapacitated.

Sanctity Aura

Sanctity Aura is a Talent-learned ability that increases group Holy damage.

Rank	Minimum Level	Mana	Range	Casting Time	Cooldown	Cost to Train	Effect
1	30	—	—	IC	—		Increases Holy damage done by party members within 30 yards by 10%. Players may only have one Aura on them per Paladin at any one time.

Repentance

Repentance is a Talent-learned ability that disables Humanoid targets for six seconds. Any damage taken by the target during that time ends the effect.

Rank	Minimum Level	Mana	Range	Casting Time	Cooldown	Cost to Train	Effect
1	40	60	20 yd	IC	1 minute		Puts the enemy target in a state of meditation for up to 6 sec. Any damage caused will awaken the target. Only works against Humanoids.

Talents

Paladin Talents fall mostly into a two-way split: support and damage. Holy and Protection Talents heavily supplement each other, and both serve to create a Paladin that supports groups and raids with incredible power. The DPS output of such Paladins is awful. However, their effectiveness is keeping members alive, throwing aggro where it belongs, and assisting with heals more than makes up for this. On the other side, Retribution is a tree for damage. With the correct gear, use of Retribution abilities, and a specialization in the Retribution Talents, a Paladin can become a DPS class. This comes at the sacrifice in group capabilities if taken very far. Decide which type of Paladin you want to play, and don't let others make that choice for you.

Holy

Divine Intellect, Spiritual Focus, Illumination, Divine Favor, and Holy Power define the healing potential of this line. Paladins with this lineup are able to heal efficiently and supplement primary healers at an amazing level. Though unable to get the heals of immense size that a Priest would look forward to, a Holy Paladin can cast for days on end, even when other classes have worriedly called "OOM!"

Protection

Protection is rarely taken for the sheer joy of its Talents, and for a soloing Paladin it is a lesser choice for fast XPing and questing. However, groups stand to gain immensely from the hidden beauty of Protection Talents. Improved Devotion Aura, Guardian's Favor, Blessing of Kings, Improved Hammer of Justice, Improved Concentration Aura (amazing in AoE groups), and Blessing of Sanctuary all have their place.

Retribution

Retribution is a fast and enjoyable soloer line, with the ability to turn Paladins into successful burst damage characters. Though less productive in large groups and raids, where many classes can become strong DPS dealers, none would argue that there is a lot of fun to be had here. Even for group-friendly Paladins, it's certainly not a bad idea to try leveling with Retribution and respect to another tree later on, if raiding catches your fancy. Benediction, Improved Seal of the Crusader, Conviction, Seal of Command (so good), Improved Two-Handed Weapons, Sanctity Aura, Vengeance, and Repentance all work exceedingly well together.

Strategies

Paladin gameplay is greatly defined by their choice of survivability. The difference between a fast Paladin fight and a drawn-out Paladin fight can be measured in minutes, not in seconds. Learning when to take risks leads to faster leveling and treasure gathering, while mastery of survivability is critical for PvP and dungeon delving.

General Tips

A Paladin should always keep as many toys and goodies around as possible. Though all classes benefit from potions, bandages, trinkets, and other goodies, for Paladins they are a must. Paladins often are forced into niches by their Talents and playstyle, and having items to round out their characters prevents trouble on the road ahead. For example, a Retribution Paladin is able to wade through monsters at a much greater rate than a Holy Paladin. But, they use their mana for damage and have more downtime to deal with after healing themselves. Food and bandages make up for that.

Keep one of your rear bags filled with various treats. Always have a full stack of bandages, food that gives bonuses, perhaps material for making fires, sharpening/weightstones, potions for Strength or Attack Power, spare Trinkets, and so forth. Use it all! Anything that increases a Paladin's kill rate or downtime is addressing the lone obstacle on the way to victory.

As mentioned earlier in the section, Engineering is a wonderful choice for Paladins. The lack of consistent, ranged firepower is curbed by the addition of bombs and other Engineering toys. Trinkets that deal ranged damage also aid Paladins greatly.

For Paladins with lower DPS, remember to quest heavily while leveling. All low DPS classes benefit immensely from quest experience.

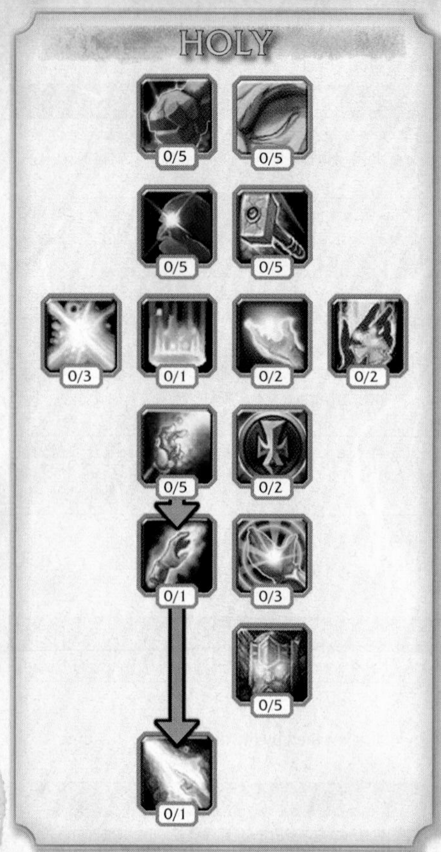

DIVINE STRENGTH 5

Increases your Strength by 2%.

DIVINE INTELLECT 5

Increases your total Intellect by 2%.

SPIRITUAL FOCUS 5

Gives you Flash of Light and Holy Light spells a 14% chance to not lose casting time when you take damage.

IMPROVED SEAL OF RIGHTEOUSNESS 5

Increases the damage done by your Seal of Righteousness and Judgement of Righteousness by 3%.

HEALING LIGHT 3

Increases the amount healed by your Holy Light and Flash of Light spells by 4%.

CONSECRATION 1

Consecrates the land beneath the Paladin, doing 64 Holy damage over 8 seconds to enemies who enter the area.

IMPROVED LAY ON HANDS 2

Gives the target of your Lay on Hands spell a 15% bonus to their armor value from items for 2 mins. In addition, the cooldown of your Lay on Hands is reduced by 10 mins.

UNYIELDING FAITH 2

Increases your chance to resist Fear and Disorient effects by an additional 5%.

ILLUMINATION 5

After getting a critical effect from your Flash of Light, Holy Shock, or Holy Light spell, gives you 20% chance to gain Mana equal to the base cost of your spell.

IMPROVED BLESSING OF WISDOM 2

Increases the effect of your Blessing of Wisdom spell by 10%.

DIVINE FAVO 1R

When activated, gives your next Flash of Light, Holy Light or Holy Shock spell a 100% critical effect chance.

LASTING JUDGMENT 3

Increases the duration of your Judgment of Light and Judgment of Wisdom by 10 secs.

HOLY POWER 5

Increases the critical effect chance of your Holy spells by 1%.

HOLY SHOCK 1

Blasts the target with Holy energy, causing 204 to 220 Holy damage to an enemy, or 204 to 220 healing to an ally.

IMPROVED DEVOTION AURA 5

Increases the armor bonus of your Devotion aura by 5%

REDOUBT 5

Increases your chance to block attacks with your shield by 6% after being the victim of a critical strike. Lasts 10 secs or 5 blocks.

PRECISION 3

Increases your chance to hit with melee weapons by 1%

GUARDIAN'S FAVOR 2

Reduces the cooldown of your Blessing of Protection by 60 secs and increases the duration of your Blessing of Freedom 3 secs.

TOUGHNESS 5

Increases your armor value from items by 2%.

BLESSING OF KINGS 1

Places a Blessing on the friendly target, increasing total stats by 10% for 5 mins. Players may only have one Blessing on them per Paladin at any one time.

IMPROVED RIGHTEOUS FURY 3

Increases the amount of threat generated by your Righteous Fury spell by 16%.

SHIELD SPECIALIZATION 3

Increases the amount of damage absorbed by your shield by 10%.

ANTICIPATION 5

Increases your Defense skill by 2.

IMPROVED HAMMER OF JUSTICE 3

Decreases the cooldown of your Hammer of Justice spell by 5 secs.

IMPROVED CONCENTRATION AURA 3

Increases the effect of you Concentration Aura by an additional 5% and gives all group members affected by the aura an additional 5% chance to resist Silence and Interrupt effects.

BLESSING OF SANCTUARY 1

Places a Blessing on the friendly target, reducing damage dealt from all sources by up to 7 for 5 mins. In addition, when the target blocks a melee attack the attacker will take 14 Holy damage. Players may only have one Blessing on them per Paladin at any one time.

RECKONING 5

Gives you a 20% chance to gain an extra attack after being the victim of a critical strike.

ONE-HANDED WEAPON SPECIALIZATION 5

Increases the damage you deal with one-handed melee weapons by 2%.

HOLY SHIELD 1

Increases chance to block by 30% for 10 secs and deals 50 Holy damage for each attack blocked while active. Each block expends a charge. 4 charges.

IMPROVED BLESSING OF MIGHT 5

Increases the Attack Power bonus of your Blessing of Might by 4%.

BENEDICTION 5

Reduces the Mana cost of your Judgment and Seal spells by 3%.

IMPROVED JUDGMENT 2

Decreases the cooldown of you Judgement spell by 1 sec.

IMPROVED SEAL OF THE CRUSADER 3

Increases the Attack Power bonus of you Seal of the Crusader and the Holy damage increase of your Judgment of the Crusader by 5%.

DEFLECTION 5

Increases you Parry chance by 1%.

VINDICATION 3

Gives the Paladin's damaging melee attacks a chance to reduce the target's Strength and Agility by 5% for 10 secs.

CONVICTION 5

Increases your chance to get a critical strike with melee weapons by 1%.

SEAL OF COMMAND 1

Gives the Paladin a chance to deal additional Holy damage equal to 70% of normal weapon damage. Only one Seal can be active on the Paladin at any one time. Lasts 30 secs.

PURSUIT OF JUSTICE 2

Increases movement and mounted movement speed by 4%. This does not stack with other movement speed increasing effects.

EYE FOR AN EYE 2

All spell criticals against you cause 15% of the damage taken to the caster as well. The damage caused by Eye for an Eye will not exceed 50% of the Paladin's total health.

IMPROVED RETRIBUTION AURA 2

Increases the damage done by your Retribution Aura by 25%.

TWO-HANDED WEAPON SPECIALIZATION 3

Increases the damage you deal with two-handed melee weapons by 2%.

SANCTITY AURA 1

Increases Holy damage done by party members within 30 yards by 10%. Players may only have one Aura on them per Paladin at any one time.

VENGEANCE 5

Gives you a 3% bonus to Physical and Holy damage you deal for 8 secs after dealing a critical strike from a swing, spell, or ability.

REPENTANCE 1

Puts the enemy target in a state of meditation for up to 6 secs. Any damage caused will awaken the target. Only works against Humanoids.

Using Auras

- Auras Last Until Changed
- One Aura Per Paladin Can Affect a Group at a Given Time
- Auras of Different Types Can be Used in Multiple Paladin Groups

Each Paladin can maintain a single Aura. These affect the entire group and don't need to be messed with unless your Paladin is shifting to a different Aura. Group members need to be within 30 yds. to the Paladin to gain the benefits from these.

When there are multiple Paladins in the group, use multiple Auras. All of them add their bonuses to group members!

Aura List

Aura Name	Effect	Best Used For
Concentration	Reduces Chance of Spell Interruption	Groups with Many Healers or AoE Casters
Devotion	Increased Armor Rating	Increased Mitigation Against Non-Magical Enemies
Resistance (Fire, Frost, Shadow)	Improves One Specific Resistance	Battles Against Elemental Enemies, Warlocks, Demons, etc. (Choose the Appropriate Resistance Type)
Retribution	Deals Holy Damage to All Attackers in Melee	Fighting Large Groups of Light Enemies
Sanctity	Improves Holy Damage	Soloing with Retribution Abilities; Groups of Priests and Paladins DPSing

Understanding Blessings

- Blessings Have a Relatively Short Duration, Compared to Other Buffs
- One Blessing per Paladin Can Be Active on a Given Character
- Only Different Blessings from Multiple Paladins Work Together (e.g. You Cannot Stack four Blessings of Might on One Rogue)

Normal Blessings are different from Auras; these are used on specific characters. Each Blessing is basically a short-term buff with a fairly substantial influence of character power. It takes quite a bit of doing to keep an entire group running with the proper Blessings, but it's worth the effort.

Choose from your available Blessings and tailor each one to the target's performance within the group. When Blessing everyone, pick the one for your character first. This way, you know when your Blessing falls and when the others will need their Blessings renewed.

At higher levels, Greater Blessings become available. These require inexpensive reagents, and the spells are used on entire class types in raids. Thus, a Greater Blessing of Sanctuary could be cast on a Warrior to give the benefit to *all* Warriors in the raid with your Paladin.

Blessing List

Blessing Name	Effect	Best Used For
Freedom	Immunity to Movement-Impairing Effects, Lasts Ten Seconds	Flag Carries in WSG, Fleeing Enemies, General PvP
Kings	Increases Target's Attributes by 10%	Classes That Use Four or Five Attributes
Light	Improves Flash of Light and Holy Light	Groups/Raids with Multiple Paladin Healers
Might	Adds Melee Attack Power to the Target	All Melee Characters in Easy Areas, Fury Warriors, Rogues, Hunter Pets
Protection	Shields Target From All Harm, Short Duration	Primary Healers, AoE Casters in Trouble
Sacrifice	Redirects Damage from the Target to the Paladin	Boss Fights
Salvation	Reduces Threat Generation by 30%	Super DPS Classes in Raid Situations, Healers
Sanctuary	Reduces Damage, Adds Holy Damage to Blocks	Main or Secondary Tanks
Wisdom	Restores Mana over Time	Helping Healers and Magical DPSers in Long Encounters

Seals Too?

- Seals Are Used to Buff the Casting Paladin
- Only One Seal Can Be Active At a Given Point
- Seals Can Be Judged to End the Effect Prematurely And Enact an Instant Effect

Seals are one of the more complex toys that Paladins gain as they level. These abilities have two forms. Each one is used initially as a buff for the Paladin; many of the Seals increase combat potential directly, with ways to restore health, mana, or deal damage.

Then, for a moderate mana cost, these Seals can be Judged! With this second skill, the Seal is converted to the Judgement form of the ability. The result is often either more damaging or enables an entire group to gain the benefits of the ability. The effect of a Seal is removed when Judgement is used, though the Seal can always be recast.

Many of the Seals are meant to work well together. We've already mentioned one of the classic Retribution combos: Seal of the Crusader, Judgement (to make them take more Holy damage), then Seal of Command (to add Holy damage to attacks). From there, Paladins that need even more stopping power can Stun the enemy with Hammer of Justice and use Judgement of Command to deal instant, heavy damage.

Seal List

Seal Name	Effect	Judgement	Best Used For
Command	Adds Holy Damage to Melee Attacks	Instant Holy Damage (Even More If Enemy is Stunned)	Paladin DPS Mode
Crusader	Raises Attack Power, Attack Speed	Increases Holy Damage Taken by Target	Dealing Damage, Setting up Seal of Command
Justice	Chance to Stun Target in Melee	Prevents Target from Fleeing	Add Minor Mitigation against Casters and Runners
Light	Chance to Heal Paladins during Melee Attacks	Chance to Heal Allies When They Strike Target Enemy	Groups With Many Melee Characters (Especially Rogues/ Feral Druids)
Righteousness	Adds Holy Damage to Each Melee Attack	Deals Instant Holy Damage	Moderate DPS for Non-Retribution Pallies
Wisdom	Chance to Restore Mana on Melee	Chance for All Allies to Restore Mana w/ Spells/Melee against Target	Assists Hybrid and Caster Parties, Good for Soloing

Priests are the ultimate Healers in World of Warcraft. Without the healing spells of a Priest, many a Warrior would not be able to survive grabbing five enemies, nor would a Mage live through their finest AoE casting. It is those healing spells that make a Priest extremely valuable to groups, and few parties turn down a skilled Healer. However, a Priest's usefulness is not limited to healing spells. These characters are also offensive casters, doing damage using both Holy and Shadow magic. Left to their own devices, Priests are no fading flowers resigned to depend on the good graces of others; instead, they are fully capable of defending themselves, performing damage-dealing spells, and avoiding some of the worst aspects of an enemy's attacks.

Lore

What started as a tiny battle was quickly becoming a widespread conflict. It seemed as though the entire area was embroiled with orcs. The din of battle washed away the peace of yesterday and the promises of tomorrow.

We had come to Stonewatch Keep, in the Redridge Mountains, to defend Lakeshire and its citizens. In particular, we were searching for Tharil'zun, an orc known for his cleverness and aggression. Lakeshire would never be safe as long as this creature held command, and we could not rest without hard proof of his demise. We would leave Stonewatch Keep only with Tharil'zun's head.

But an orc and his head are not easily parted, and Tharil'zun was far from alone. All it had taken was one of his retinue to scurry away like a coward and warn others. Suddenly, we found ourselves overwhelmed by orcs of enormous ferocity, strength, and the ability to use dark magic.

At first, I added what damage I could by using Holy Smite. But our group was quickly taking damage, and I rushed to their assistance with healing spells. The Warrior, Tielyn, nodded at me in response to the new energy that flooded into her and continued her grim task of slicing into the enemy. Suddenly, I heard Anat, a Mage, cry out. Standing over her, sword raised high, was a thick-bodied orc fighter. In mere seconds, that sword would swing down and cut the Mage's life and I would lose my dearest of friends; I shaped through great force and will the power of the Light into an unwavering Shield. The orc's sword crashed down upon the barrier, but Anat remained unharmed. The orc even looked surprised as Anat rallied, focusing her magic into a bolt she sent into the beast's face.

No longer secure enough to hang back, Tharil'zun himself entered the battle. Knowing that I would have to ensure that our little group survived his onslaught, I used only a small amount of offensive Shadow magic against him: enough to ensure a steady decrease of his power through a simple word: Pain. After that, my attention was completely enwrapped in healing our group, keeping Tielyn, Anat, and the others as safe and healthy as possible. Finally, with a last strangled gasp, Tharil'zun fell forward, dead.

We saved many good people of Lakeshire, I know. And, more importantly, none of my friends were lost in the battle. To help your friends and stop your enemies is the truest thing that anyone can accomplish, and we did a great deed today.

Introduction to Playing the Class

There are several classes with healing potential, but none of them outheals a Priest. This is a class with a wide range of different healing abilities, and Priests have the most powerful and efficient healing spells of any character in the game.

It is this healing ability that ensures that Priests always have a valuable place in any group. There are always spots available for someone who is willing to keep the rest of the group dealing damage and killing enemies.

However, Priests are not always relegated to only healing duties, and they are capable of doing damage against monsters on their own. The proper placement of an offensive spell can do as much to save a party member as a well-timed heal. In addition, this means that Priests are perfectly capable of dispatching their own enemies, and they do not need to be constantly shepherded by escorts.

Keep in mind, though, that being a Priest is a matter of temperament. If you find that you enjoy casting large amounts of offensive spells and hate healing, then a Mage may be more your cup of tea. Similarly, if you only want to heal occasionally and want to do more melee damage, Paladins and Shamans have some similar abilities to Priests and far more survivability.

What Priests' don't have is the heavy armor to withstand a determined assault. Faced with multiple opponents or high-damage enemies, a Priest's cloth armor is no barrier. The use of Power Word: Shield, a temporary spell that absorbs damage and keeps a character from being interrupted, can only go so far. It's best for a Priest to keep fights short, sweet, and at range as much as possible.

If you enjoy saving other people and want to throw in a bit of offensive damage on your own, being a Priest is a great choice. You can really have a wonderful time with some of the more social aspects of World of Warcraft as well as be a competent soloer if you find that is what you want.

Available Races	
Dwarf	Human
Night Elf	Troll
Undead	

What Do Attributes Mean to Me?	
Strength	Higher Melee Damage (Not So Important)
Stamina	Higher Health
Agility	Higher Chance to Dodge, More Melee Criticals (Only Useful to a Few Priests)
Intellect	Higher Mana Pool and Greater Chance for Critical Heals
Spirit	Greater Mana and Health Regeneration

ITEMS AND EQUIPMENT

What you are equipped with is not as important as what bonuses your character's equipment has. There are three major attributes that your character should concentrate on: Intellect, Spirit, and Stamina.

The choice between Intellect and Spirit is a most interesting one. Intellect increases the amount of mana that a Priest has available to them. More mana means that they can cast greater amounts of spells before resting (both more healing and damage spells). In addition, Priests with high Intellect have a higher chance of landing Critical heals and attacks with those spells.

On the other hand, both healing and damage spells are magic intensive. It is very easy for a Priest to cast away all of their mana, leaving them to rely on their melee damage or magical wands. This is not a good situation for a Priest to be in, and Priests with little mana are very vulnerable. If you have a high Spirit, you can cast your spells more freely, knowing that your character can regenerate mana while doing some fighting. This also decreases your downtime, and that's very useful for a Priest.

Choosing between Spirit and Intellect is a very personal decision, and there are benefits to each. Try and experiment so that you can find the set of armor that works best for what you want to do. If you find that you run out of mana frequently and cannot cast the number of spells that you want, concentrate more on Intellect. If your casting is high but you can't regenerate magic as well (say, in a group where the few heals that you have to make are very expensive), invest more in Spirit gear.

The only other attribute to look for in equipment is Stamina. Stamina is tied to how much health a Priest has. Because Priests don't have heavy armor (or even modest armor), even little improvements in Stamina are useful. If at all possible, increase your amount of health or armor by supplementing your equipment with enchantments.

Investing in a weapon is also a personal decision. Keep an eye out for ones that raise the attributes that you want. Maces, Daggers, and Staves are all valid choices, and some of them give very nice bonuses to Spirit and Intellect (Staves in particular). Staves are often focused more toward caster attributes, so they are a sound investment for many Priests.

Wands are important to purchase for doing damage when your mana is depleted. These ranged weapons cost nothing to activate (a huge plus), and allow your character to plug away at targets, not accruing very much aggro, while regeneration mana. It is very nice to have a melee weapon that gives you the bonuses you need while relying on wands for simple damage

CHOOSING YOUR PROFESSION

Enchanting is an interesting Profession to explore as a Priest. In this profession, you break apart equipment pieces into usable components. These components are your ingredients for enchanting armor and weapons. Enchanting gives bonuses to attributes or damage (and can even be used to add special effects and abilities to items). Because Intellect and Stamina are easily enhanced through Enchanting, this is a solid choice!

As a cloth wearer, Tailoring allows a Priest to create their own armor. The early Tailoring recipes create equipment that doesn't have any major bonuses to attributes, but later products are quite powerful. As a Tailor, Priests use the cloth materials that drop from humanoid mobs, so gathering the majority of the crafting ingredients is simply a matter of fighting enemies. In addition, Enchanting and Tailoring work well together (Tailoring can be used to create items that are broken down into Enchanting parts).

If those professions aren't to your liking, try Alchemy and Herbalism; these are certainly good for supporting yourself and group members. Or, take Mining and Engineering. Having items that stun enemies is very useful, and most people won't expect Priests to be breaking out explosives.

Class Abilities

There are three major lines of Class Abilities for Priests: Holy, Shadow, and Discipline. The use of these abilities always has an associated cost in mana. There are both defensive and offensive effects for Holy and Shadow, and the proper mixture of them is important for a Priest.

Below are the tables listing these Class Abilities with their associated information.

Discipline

Power Word: Fortitude

Power Word: Fortitude is a buff that is castable on your Priest and other characters as well. This lasts for 30 minutes and raises Stamina. At later levels, Priests search for books to learn Prayer of Fortitude, a spell that buffs the entire group with a one-hour version of this spell (this costs a reagent).

Rank	Level	Mana	Range	Casting Time	Cooldown	Cost to Train	Effect
1	1	60	30 yd	IC	—	10	Power infuses the target increasing their Stamina by 3 for 30 min.
2	12	155	30 yd	IC	—	8	Power infuses the target increasing their Stamina by 8 for 30 min.
3	24	400	30 yd	IC	—	50	Power infuses the target increasing their Stamina by 20 for 30 min.
4	36	745	30 yd	IC	—	1 40	Power infuses the target increasing their Stamina by 32 for 30 min.
5	48	1170	30 yd	IC	—	2 80	Power infuses the target increasing their Stamina by 43 for 30 min.
6	60	1695	30 yd	IC	—	4 60	Power infuses the target increasing their Stamina by 54 for 30 min.

Prayer of Fortitude (Party)

Rank	Level	Mana	Range	Casting Time	Reagent	Cost to Train	Effect
1	48	2600	40 yd	IC	Holy Candle	—	Power infuses the target's party, increasing their Stamina by 55 for 1 hour.
2	60	3400	40 yd	IC	Sacred Candle	—	Power infuses the target's party, increasing their Stamina by 70 for 1 hour.

Power Word: Shield

Power Word: Shield is a potent tool for pre-battle protection or for sudden changes in battle. This spell protects the target from a moderate amount of damage, and casting is not interrupted by damage while the Shield is in effect!

Rank	Level	Mana	Range	Casting Time	Cooldown	Cost to Train	Effect
1	6	45	40 yd	IC	4 sec	1	Draws on the soul of the party member to shield them, absorbing 44 damage. Lasts 30 sec. While the shield holds, spell casting will not be interrupted by damage. Once shielded, the target cannot be shielded again for 15 sec.
2	12	80	40 yd	IC	4 sec	8	Draws on the soul of the party member to shield them, absorbing 88 damage. Lasts 30 sec. While the shield holds, spell casting will not be interrupted by damage. Once shielded, the target cannot be shielded again for 15 sec.
3	18	130	40 yd	IC	4 sec	20	Draws on the soul of the party member to shield them, absorbing 158 damage. Lasts 30 sec. While the shield holds, spell casting will not be interrupted by damage. Once shielded, the target cannot be shielded again for 15 sec.
4	24	175	40 yd	IC	4 sec	50	Draws on the soul of the party member to shield them, absorbing 234 damage. Lasts 30 sec. While the shield holds, spell casting will not be interrupted by damage. Once shielded, the target cannot be shielded again for 15 sec.
5	30	210	40 yd	IC	4 sec	1	Draws on the soul of the party member to shield them, absorbing 301 damage. Lasts 30 sec. While the shield holds, spell casting will not be interrupted by damage. Once shielded, the target cannot be shielded again for 15 sec.
6	36	250	40 yd	IC	4 sec	1 40	Draws on the soul of the party member to shield them, absorbing 381 damage. Lasts 30 sec. While the shield holds, spell casting will not be interrupted by damage. Once shielded, the target cannot be shielded again for 15 sec.
7	42	300	40 yd	IC	4 sec	2 20	Draws on the soul of the party member to shield them, absorbing 484 damage. Lasts 30 sec. While the shield holds, spell casting will not be interrupted by damage. Once shielded, the target cannot be shielded again for 15 sec.
8	48	355	40 yd	IC	4 sec	2 80	Draws on the soul of the party member to shield them, absorbing 605 damage. Lasts 30 sec. While the shield holds, spell casting will not be interrupted by damage. Once shielded, the target cannot be shielded again for 15 sec.
9	54	425	40 yd	IC	4 sec	4	Draws on the soul of the party member to shield them, absorbing 44 763 damage. Lasts 30 sec. While the shield holds, spell casting will not be interrupted by damage. Once shielded, the target cannot be shielded again for 15 sec.
10	60	500	40 yd	IC	4 sec	4 60	Draws on the soul of the party member to shield them, absorbing 942 damage. Lasts 30 sec. While the shield holds, spell casting will not be interrupted by damage. Once shielded, the target cannot be shielded again for 15 sec.

Starshards (Night Elf only)

Starshards is a spell learned only by night elf Priests. This channeled spell deals Arcane damage to the target.

Rank	Level	Mana	Range	Casting Time	Cooldown	Cost to Train	Effect
1	10	50	30 yd	Channeled	—	—	Rains starshards down on the enemy target's head, causing 84 Arcane damage over 6 sec.
2	18	85	30 yd	Channeled	—	1	Rains starshards down on the enemy target's head, causing 162 Arcane damage over 6 sec.
3	26	140	30 yd	Channeled	—	3	Rains starshards down on the enemy target's head, causing 288 Arcane damage over 6 sec.
4	34	190	30 yd	Channeled	—	6	Rains starshards down on the enemy target's head, causing 414 Arcane damage over 6 sec.
5	42	245	30 yd	Channeled	—	11	Rains starshards down on the enemy target's head, causing 570 Arcane damage over 6 sec.
6	50	300	30 yd	Channeled	—	15	Rains starshards down on the enemy target's head, causing 756 Arcane damage over 6 sec.
7	58	350	30 yd	Channeled	—	22	Rains starshards down on the enemy target's head, causing 936 Arcane damage over 6 sec.

Inner Fire

Inner Fire increases the armor of a Priest for either ten minutes or until all of its charges are used (there are 20 charges, and each time the Priest is hit a charge is used).

Rank	Level	Mana	Range	Casting Time	Cooldown	Cost to Train	Effect
1	12	30	—	IC	—	8	A burst of Holy energy fills the caster, increasing armor by 315. Each melee or ranged damage hit against the priest will remove one charge. Lasts 10 min or until 20 charges are used.
2	20	65	—	IC	—	30	A burst of Holy energy fills the caster, increasing armor by 495. Each melee or ranged damage hit against the priest will remove one charge. Lasts 10 min or until 20 charges are used.
3	30	105	—	IC	—	1	A burst of Holy energy fills the caster, increasing armor by 720. Each melee or ranged damage hit against the priest will remove one charge. Lasts 10 min or until 20 charges are used.
4	40	165	—	IC	—	1 80	A burst of Holy energy fills the caster, increasing armor by 945. Each melee or ranged damage hit against the priest will remove one charge. Lasts 10 min or until 20 charges are used.
5	50	235	—	IC	—	3	A burst of Holy energy fills the caster, increasing armor by 1170. Each melee or ranged damage hit against the priest will remove one charge. Lasts 10 min or until 20 charges are used.
6	60	315	—	IC	—	4 60	A burst of Holy energy fills the caster, increasing armor by 1395. Each melee or ranged damage hit against the priest will remove one charge. Lasts 10 min or until 20 charges are used.

Dispel Magic

Dispel Magic may appear to be a humble spell, but there is a great deal of power hidden here. This spell either removes one negative effect from a friendly target, or removes one positive effect from an enemy.

Rank	Level	Mana	Range	Casting Time	Cooldown	Cost to Train	Effect
1	18	Variable	30 yd	IC	—	20	Dispels magic on the target, removing 1 harmful spell from a friend or 1 beneficial spell from an enemy.
2	36	Variable	30 yd	IC	—	1 40	Dispels magic on the target, removing 2 harmful spell from a friend or 2 beneficial spell from an enemy.

Elune's Grace (Night Elf only)

Elune's Grace is a night elf spell that is on a five-minute cooldown. Cast this for 15 seconds of decreased ranged damage taken and increased Dodge.

Rank	Level	Mana	Range	Casting Time	Cooldown	Cost to Train	Effect
1	20	60	—	IC	5 min	—	Reduces the ranged damage taken by 21 and increases chance to dodge by 10% for 15 sec.
2	30	105	—	IC	5 min	5	Reduces the ranged damage taken by 33 and increases chance to dodge by 10% for 15 sec.
3	40	145	—	IC	5 min	9	Reduces the ranged damage taken by 52 and increases chance to dodge by 10% for 15 sec.
4	50	195	—	IC	5 min	15	Reduces the ranged damage taken by 75 and increases chance to dodge by 10% for 15 sec.
5	60	240	—	IC	5 min	23	Reduces the ranged damage taken by 95 and increases chance to dodge by 10% for 15 sec

Feedback (Human only)

Feedback is a human Priest spell that puts a 15-second mana burn effect on you. When other casters hit your Priest with a spell, they lose a minor amount of mana and take an equivalent DOT.

Rank	Level	Mana	Range	Casting Time	Cooldown	Cost to Train	Effect
1	20	140	—	IC	3 min	—	The priest becomes surrounded with anti-magic energy. Any successful spell cast against the priest will burn 18 of the attacker's Mana, causing 1 Shadow damage for each point of Mana burned. Lasts 15 sec.
2	30	245	—	IC	3 min	5	The priest becomes surrounded with anti-magic energy. Any successful spell cast against the priest will burn 35 of the attacker's Mana, causing 1 Shadow damage for each point of Mana burned. Lasts 15 sec.
3	40	355	—	IC	3 min	9	The priest becomes surrounded with anti-magic energy. Any successful spell cast against the priest will burn 54 of the attacker's Mana, causing 1 Shadow damage for each point of Mana burned. Lasts 15 sec.
4	50	470	—	IC	3 min	15	The priest becomes surrounded with anti-magic energy. Any successful spell cast against the priest will burn 77 of the attacker's Mana, causing 1 Shadow damage for each point of Mana burned. Lasts 15 sec.
5	60	580	—	IC	3 min	23	The priest becomes surrounded with anti-magic energy. Any successful spell cast against the priest will burn 105 of the attacker's Mana, causing 1 Shadow damage for each point of Mana burned. Lasts 15 sec.

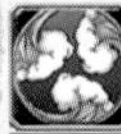

Inner Focus

Inner Focus is a Talent-learned ability on a three-minute cooldown. Using this raises the Critical chance of your next spell by 25% and eliminates its casting cost.

Rank	Minimum Level	Mana	Range	Casting Time	Cooldown	Cost to Train	Effect
1	20	—	—	IC	3 minutes	—	When activated, reduces the Mana cost of your next spell by 100% and increases its critical effect chance by 25% if it is capable of a critical effect.

Shackle Undead

Shackle Undead is one of the crowd control gems of the Priest class. This is used to take an Undead target out of the battle a variable period (any damage breaks this, so stay away from the gold-encircled target please).

Rank	Level	Mana	Range	Casting Time	Cooldown	Cost to Train	Effect
1	20	90	30 yd	1.5 sec	—	30	Shackles the target undead enemy for up to 30 sec. The shackled unit is unable to move, attack or cast spells. Any damage caused will release the target. Only one target can be shackled at a time.
2	40	120	30 yd	1.5 sec	—	1 80	Shackles the target undead enemy for up to 40 sec. The shackled unit is unable to move, attack or cast spells. Any damage caused will release the target. Only one target can be shackled at a time.
3	60	150	30 yd	1.5 sec	—	4 60	Shackles the target undead enemy for up to 50 sec. The shackled unit is unable to move, attack or cast spells. Any damage caused will release the target. Only one target can be shackled at a time.

Mana Burn

Mana Burn sucks the mana right out of a caster within range and deals half of the quantity taken as Shadow damage!

Rank	Level	Mana	Range	Casting Time	Cooldown	Cost to Train	Effect
1	24	95	30 yd	3 sec	—	50	Drains 191 to 203 mana from a target. For each mana drained in this way., the target takes 0.5 Shadow damage.
2	32	140	30 yd	3 sec	—	1 10	Drains 309 to 329 mana from a target. For each mana drained in this way, the target takes 0.5 Shadow damage.
3	40	185	30 yd	3 sec	—	1 80	Drains 442 to 468 mana from a target. For each mana drained in this way, the target takes 0.5 Shadow damage.
4	48	225	30 yd	3 sec	—	2 80	Drains 576 to 610 mana from a target. For each mana drained in this way., the target takes 0.5 Shadow damage.
5	56	270	30 yd	3 sec	—	4 20	Drains 738 to 780 mana from a target. For each mana drained in this way., the target takes 0.5 Shadow damage.

Divine Spirit

Divine Spirit is a Talent-learned buff. This provides a long-lasting improvement to Spirit for the target.

Rank	Minimum Level	Mana	Range	Casting Time	Cooldown	Cost to Train	Effect
1	30	285	30 yd	IC	—	—	Holy power infuses the target, increasing their Spirit by 17 for 30 min.
2	40	420	30 yd	IC	—	9	Holy power infuses the target, increasing their Spirit by 23 for 30 min.
3	50	785	30 yd	IC	—	15	Holy power infuses the target, increasing their Spirit by 33 for 30 min.
4	60	970	30 yd	IC	—	23	Holy power infuses the target, increasing their Spirit by 40 for 30 min.

Prayer of Spirit

Rank	Level	Mana	Range	Casting Time	Reagent	Cost to Train	Effect
1	60	1940	40 yd	IC	Sacred Candle	23	Power infuses the target's party, increasing their Spirit by 40 for 1 hour.

Levitate

Levitate requires a reagent but allows Priests to slowly float to the ground when leaping off of higher edges.

Rank	Level	Mana	Reagent	Casting Time	Cooldown	Cost to Train	Effect
N/A	34	100	Light Feather	IC	—	1 20	Allows the caster to levitate, floating a few feet above the ground. While levitating, you will fall at a reduced speed and travel over water-like surfaces. Any damage will cancel the effect. Lasts 2 min.

Power Infusion

Power Infusion is a Talent-learned ability that is on a three-minute timer. For 15 seconds, the target gets a 20% boost to healing and magical damage.

Rank	Minimum Level	Mana	Range	Casting Time	Cooldown	Cost to Train	Effect
1	40	182	30 yd	IC	3 minutes	—	Infuses the target with power, increasing their spell damage and healing by 20%. Lasts 15 sec.

Holy

Lesser Heal

Lesser Heal is a fast-casting healing spell for the low levels.

Rank	Level	Mana	Range	Casting Time	Cooldown	Cost to Train	Effect
1	1	30	40 yd	1.5 sec	—	—	Heal your target for 46 to 56.
2	4	45	40 yd	2 sec	—	1	Heal your target for 71 to 85.
3	10	75	40 yd	2.5 sec	—	3	Heal your target for 135 to 157.

Smite

Smite is a Holy spell for dealing damage. For Priests that are talented in Spiritual Guidance and have high Spirit, Smite can deal a surprising sum of damage.

Rank	Level	Mana	Range	Casting Time	Cooldown	Cost to Train	Effect
1	1	20	30 yd	1.5 sec	—	—	Smite an enemy for 13 to 17 Holy damage.
2	6	30	30 yd	2 sec	—	1	Smite an enemy for 25 to 31 Holy damage.
3	14	60	30 yd	2.5 sec	—	12	Smite an enemy for 54 to 62 Holy damage.
4	22	95	30 yd	2.5 sec	—	40	Smite an enemy for 91 to 105 Holy damage.
5	30	140	30 yd	2.5 sec	—	1	Smite an enemy for 150 to 170 Holy damage.
6	38	185	30 yd	2.5 sec	—	1 60	Smite an enemy for 212 to 240 Holy damage.
7	46	230	30 yd	2.5 sec	—	2 60	Smite an enemy for 287 to 323 Holy damage.
8	54	280	30 yd	2.5 sec	—	4	Smite an enemy for 371 to 415 Holy damage.

Renew

Renew is a modest heal over time spell. Though Priests are not the most effective class for such heals, Renew serves to supplement their healing repertoire.

Rank	Level	Mana	Range	Casting Time	Cooldown	Cost to Train	Effect
1	8	30	40 yd	IC	—	2	Heals the target of 45 damage over 15 sec.
2	14	65	40 yd	IC	—	12	Heals the target of 100 damage over 15 sec.
3	20	105	40 yd	IC	—	30	Heals the target of 175 damage over 15 sec.
4	26	140	40 yd	IC	—	60	Heals the target of 245 damage over 15 sec.
5	32	170	40 yd	IC	—	1 10	Heals the target of 315 damage over 15 sec.
6	38	205	40 yd	IC	—	1 60	Heals the target of 400 damage over 15 sec.
7	44	250	40 yd	IC	—	2 40	Heals the target of 510 damage over 15 sec.
8	50	305	40 yd	IC	—	3	Heals the target of 650 damage over 15 sec.
9	56	365	40 yd	IC	—	4 20	Heals the target of 810 damage over 15 sec.
10	60	410	40 yd	IC	—	—	Heals the target of 970 damage over 15 sec.

Desperate Prayer (Dwarf and Human only)

Desperate Prayer is a spell for human and Dwarven Priests. This is on a ten-minute cooldown and instantly heals the caster.

Rank	Level	Mana	Range	Casting Time	Cooldown	Cost to Train	Effect
1	10	—	—	IC	10 min	—	Instantly heals the caster for 134 to 170.
2	18	—	—	IC	10 min	1	Instantly heals the caster for 263 to 325.
3	26	—	—	IC	10 min	3	Instantly heals the caster for 447 to 543.
4	34	—	—	IC	10 min	6	Instantly heals the caster for 588 to 708.
5	42	—	—	IC	10 min	11	Instantly heals the caster for 834 to 994.
6	50	—	—	IC	10 min	15	Instantly heals the caster for 1101 to 1305.
7	58	—	—	IC	10 min	22	Instantly heals the caster for 1324 to 1562.

Resurrection

Resurrection is an out-of-combat spell to bring the dead back to life (in a good way). Cast this on fallen characters from your faction to bring them back.

Rank	Level	Mana	Range	Casting Time	Cooldown	Cost to Train	Effect
1	10	75%	30 yd	10 sec	—	3	Brings a dead player back to life with 70 health and 135 mana. Cannot be cast when in combat.
2	22	75%	30 yd	10 sec	—	40	Brings a dead player back to life with 160 health and 300 mana. Cannot be cast when in combat.
3	34	75%	30 yd	10 sec	—	1 20	Brings a dead player back to life with 300 health and 520 mana. Cannot be cast when in combat.
4	46	75%	30 yd	10 sec	—	2 60	Brings a dead player back to life with 500 health and 750 mana. Cannot be cast when in combat.
5	58	75%	30 yd	10 sec	—	4 40	Brings a dead player back to life with 750 health and 1000 mana. Cannot be cast when in combat.

Cure Disease

Cure Disease removes one disease effect from the target.

Rank	Level	Mana	Range	Casting Time	Cooldown	Cost to Train	Effect
N/A	14	Variable	30 yd	IC	—	12	Removes 1 disease from the friendly target.

Heal

Heal takes over for Lesser Heal. This spell is a medium-casting time heal, compared to what Priests get later on.

Rank	Level	Mana	Range	Casting Time	Cooldown	Cost to Train	Effect
1	16	155	40 yd	3 sec	—	16	Heal your target for 295 to 341.
2	22	205	40 yd	3 sec	—	40	Heal your target for 429 to 491.
3	28	255	40 yd	3 sec	—	80	Heal your target for 566 to 642.
4	34	305	40 yd	3 sec	—	1 20	Heal your target for 712 to 804.

Fear Ward (Dwarf only)

Fear Ward is a dwarven Priest spell, and it is clearly one of the finest PvP and PvE spells of this type. With only a 30-second cooldown, a Priest can cast this on a target and protect them from the next Fear effect that lands within ten minutes.

Rank	Level	Mana	Range	Casting Time	Cooldown	Cost to Train	Effect
1	20	100	30 yd	IC	30 sec	—	Wards the friendly target against Fear. The next Fear effect used against the target will fail, using up the ward. Lasts 10 min.

Flash Heal

Flash Heal is a fast-cast heal spell. Though lacking the heavy artillery of Greater Healing, Flash Heal is sometimes needed just to keep a target going (in a small group or PvP situation).

Rank	Level	Mana	Range	Casting Time	Cooldown	Cost to Train	Effect
1	20	125	40 yd	1.5 sec	—	30	Heals a friendly target for 193 to 237.
2	26	155	40 yd	1.5 sec	—	60	Heals a friendly target for 258 to 314.
3	32	185	40 yd	1.5 sec	—	1 10	Heals a friendly target for 327 to 393.
4	38	215	40 yd	1.5 sec	—	1 60	Heals a friendly target for 400 to 478.
5	44	265	40 yd	1.5 sec	—	2 40	Heals a friendly target for 518 to 616.
6	50	315	40 yd	1.5 sec	—	3	Heals a friendly target for 644 to 764.
7	56	380	40 yd	1.5 sec	—	4 20	Heals a friendly target for 812 to 958.

Holy Nova

Holy Nova is a Talent-learned AoE damage + healing spell that causes no Threat for the Priest. Though awfully inefficient, the Holy Nova heals all group members.

Rank	Minimum Level	Mana	Range	Casting Time	Cooldown	Cost to Train	Effect
1	20	185	10 yd	IC	—		Causes an explosion of holy light around the caster, causing 28 to 32 Holy damage to all enemy targets within 10 yards and healing all party members within 10 yards for 52 to 60. These effects cause no threat.
2	28	290	10 yd	IC	—	4	Causes an explosion of holy light around the caster, causing 50 to 58 Holy damage to all enemy targets within 10 yards and healing all party members within 10 yards for 86 to 98. These effects cause no threat.
3	36	400	10 yd	IC	—	7	Causes an explosion of holy light around the caster, causing 76 to 88 Holy damage to all enemy targets within 10 yards and healing all party members within 10 yards for 121 to 139. These effects cause no threat.
4	44	520	10 yd	IC	—	12	Causes an explosion of holy light around the caster, causing 106 to 122 Holy damage to all enemy targets within 10 yards and healing all party members within 10 yards for 161 to 187. These effects cause no threat.
5	52	635	10 yd	IC	—	19	Causes an explosion of holy light around the caster, causing 140 to 162 Holy damage to all enemy targets within 10 yards and healing all party members within 10 yards for 235 to 271. These effects cause no threat.
6	60	750	10 yd	IC	—	23	Causes an explosion of holy light around the caster, causing 181 to 209 Holy damage to all enemy targets within 10 yards and healing all party members within 10 yards for 302 to 350. These effects cause no threat.

Prayer of Healing

Prayer of Healing needs 3 or more group members to need 1000+ hps to become efficient. In raids, this spell can be extremely helpful.

Rank	Level	Mana	Range	Casting Time	Cooldown	Cost to Train	Effect
1	30	410	30 yd	3 sec	—	1	A powerful prayer heals party members within 30 yards for 301 to 321.
2	40	560	30 yd	3 sec	—	1 80	A powerful prayer heals party members within 30 yards for 444 to 472.
3	50	770	30 yd	3 sec	—	3	A powerful prayer heals party members within 30 yards for 657 to 695.
4	60	1030	30 yd	3 sec	—	4 60	A powerful prayer heals party members within 30 yards for 939 to 991.
5	60	1070	30 yd	3 sec	—	—	A powerful prayer heals party members within 30 yards for 1041 to 1099.

Spirit of Redemption

Spirit of Redemption is a Talent-learned ability that allows Holy Priests to last for ten seconds after their death, healing without cost as often as possible. No damage or ability can put a stop to this special period of assistance.

Rank	Prerequisite	Effect
1	20 points in Holy	Upon death, the priest becomes the Spirit of Redemption for 10 sec. The Spirit of Redemption cannot move, attack, be attacked or targeted by any spell or effects. While in this form, the priest can cast any healing spell free of cost. When the effect ends, the priest dies.

Abolish Disease

Abolish Disease removes one disease effect instantly, then cures another every five seconds (for a duration of 20 seconds).

Rank	Level	Mana	Range	Casting Time	Cooldown	Cost to Train	Effect
N/A	32	Variable	30 yd	IC	—	1 10	Attempts to cure 1 disease effect on the target and 1 more disease effect every 5 seconds for 20 sec.

Greater Heal

Greater Heal is the final step in the "Heal" progression. Greater Heal is a slow spell to cast, but it heals a tremendous quantity of damage. Greater Heal is more efficient than Flash Heal and Renew (by quite a margin).

Rank	Level	Mana	Range	Casting Time	Cooldown	Cost to Train	Effect
1	40	370	40 yd	3 sec	—	1 80	A slow casting spell that heals a single target for 899 to 1013.
2	46	455	40 yd	3 sec	—	2 60	A slow casting spell that heals a single target for 1149 to 1289.
3	52	545	40 yd	3 sec	—	3 80	A slow casting spell that heals a single target for 1437 to 1609.
4	58	655	40 yd	3 sec	—	4 40	A slow casting spell that heals a single target for 1798 to 2006.
5	60	710	40 yd	3 sec	—	—	A slow casting spell that heals a single target for 1966 to 2194.

Lightwell

Lightwell is an interesting Talent-learned ability for Holy Priests. This drops a well by the Priest that group members can use to add a heal over time effect to themselves. Any damage taken cancels this effect, so it isn't useful for main tanks during direct combat.

Rank	Minimum Level	Mana	Range	Casting Time	Cooldown	Cost to Train	Effect
1	40	225	—	3 sec	10 minutes	—	Creates a holy Lightwell near the priest. Friendly targets can click the Lightwell to restore 800 health over 10 sec. Being attacked cancels the effect. Lightwell lasts for 3 min or 5 charges.
2	50	295	—	3 sec	10 min	12	Creates a holy Lightwell near the priest. Friendly targets can click the Lightwell to restore 1165 health over 10 sec. Being attacked cancels the effect. Lightwell lasts for 3 min or 5 charges.
3	60	365	—	3 sec	10 min	15	Creates a holy Lightwell near the priest. Friendly targets can click the Lightwell to restore 1600 health over 10 sec. Being attacked cancels the effect. Lightwell lasts for 3 min or 5 charges.

Shadow

Shadow Word: Pain

Shadow Word: Pain is an instant ability that deals heavy damage over time.

Rank	Level	Mana	Range	Casting Time	Cooldown	Cost to Train	Effect
1	4	25	30 yd	IC	—	1	A word of darkness that causes 30 Shadow damage over 18 sec.
2	10	50	30 yd	IC	—	3	A word of darkness that causes 66 Shadow damage over 18 sec.
3	18	95	30 yd	IC	—	20	A word of darkness that causes 132 Shadow damage over 18 sec.
4	26	155	30 yd	IC	—	60	A word of darkness that causes 234 Shadow damage over 18 sec.
5	34	230	30 yd	IC	—	1 20	A word of darkness that causes 366 Shadow damage over 18 sec.
6	42	305	30 yd	IC	—	2 20	A word of darkness that causes 510 Shadow damage over 18 sec.
7	50	385	30 yd	IC	—	3	A word of darkness that causes 672 Shadow damage over 18 sec.
8	58	470	30 yd	IC	—	4 40	A word of darkness that causes 852 Shadow damage over 18 sec.

Fade

Fade discourages enemies from attacking your Priest. This instantly lowers the Threat against your Priest for ten seconds.

Rank	Level	Mana	Range	Casting Time	Cooldown	Cost to Train	Effect
1	8	40	—	IC	30 sec	2	Fade out, discouraging enemies from attacking you for 10 sec.
2	20	75	—	IC	30 sec	30	Fade out, discouraging enemies from attacking you for 10 sec. More effective than Fade (rank 1).
3	30	125	—	IC	30 sec	1	Fade out, discouraging enemies from attacking you for 10 sec. More effective than Fade (rank 2).
4	40	175	—	IC	30 sec	1 80	Fade out, discouraging enemies from attacking you for 10 sec. More effective than Fade (rank 3).
5	50	225	—	IC	30 sec	3	Fade out, discouraging enemies from attacking you for 10 sec. More effective than Fade (rank 4).
6	60	275	—	IC	30 sec	4 60	Fade out, discouraging enemies from attacking you for 10 sec. More effective than Fade (rank 5).

Hex of Weakness (Troll only)

Hex of Weakness is a Troll Priest spell that reduces damage caused by the target and debuffs healing spell effectiveness as well.

Rank	Level	Mana	Range	Casting Time	Cooldown	Cost to Train	Effect
1	10	35	30 yd	IC	—	—	Weakens the target enemy, reducing damage caused by 2 and reducing the effectiveness of any healing by 20%. Lasts 2 min.
2	20	55	30 yd	IC	—	1 50	Weakens the target enemy, reducing damage caused by 4 and reducing the effectiveness of any healing by 20%. Lasts 2 min.
3	30	90	30 yd	IC	—	5	Weakens the target enemy, reducing damage caused by 7 and reducing the effectiveness of any healing by 20%. Lasts 2 min.
4	40	130	30 yd	IC	—	9	Weakens the target enemy, reducing damage caused by 11 and reducing the effectiveness of any healing by 20%. Lasts 2 min.
5	50	180	30 yd	IC	—	15	Weakens the target enemy, reducing damage caused by 15 and reducing the effectiveness of any healing by 20%. Lasts 2 min.
6	60	240	30 yd	IC	—	—	Weakens the target enemy, reducing damage caused by 20 and reducing the effectiveness of any healing by 20%. Lasts 2 min.

Mind Blast

Mind Blast deals a high amount of Shadow damage to a target with only a short casting time. The downside of this wonderful spell is that there is high Threat generation above and beyond the damage dealt.

Rank	Level	Mana	Range	Casting Time	Cooldown	Cost to Train	Effect
1	10	50	30 yd	1.5 sec	8 sec	3	Blasts the target for 39 to 43 Shadow damage, but causes a high amount of threat.
2	16	80	30 yd	1.5 sec	8 sec	16	Blasts the target for 72 to 78 Shadow damage, but causes a high amount of threat.
3	22	110	30 yd	1.5 sec	8 sec	40	Blasts the target for 112 to 120 Shadow damage, but causes a high amount of threat.
4	28	150	30 yd	1.5 sec	8 sec	80	Blasts the target for 167 to 177 Shadow damage, but causes a high amount of threat.
5	34	185	30 yd	1.5 sec	8 sec	1 20	Blasts the target for 217 to 231 Shadow damage, but causes a high amount of threat.
6	40	225	30 yd	1.5 sec	8 sec	1 80	Blasts the target for 279 to 297 Shadow damage, but causes a high amount of threat.
7	46	265	30 yd	1.5 sec	8 sec	2 60	Blasts the target for 346 to 366 Shadow damage, but causes a high amount of threat.
8	52	310	30 yd	1.5 sec	8 sec	3 80	Blasts the target for 425 to 449 Shadow damage, but causes a high amount of threat.
9	58	350	30 yd	1.5 sec	8 sec	4 40	Blasts the target for 503 to 531 Shadow damage, but causes a high amount of threat.

Touch of Weakness (Undead only)

Touch of Weakness is a Forsaken Priest ability that is cast on oneself. The next enemy that hits such a Priest in melee takes minor Shadow damage and is debuffed to deal less damage for the next two minutes.

Rank	Level	Mana	Range	Casting Time	Cooldown	Cost to Train	Effect
1	10	25	—	IC	—	—	The next melee attack against the caster will cause 8 Shadow damage and reduce the damage caused by the attacker by 2 for 2 min.
2	20	45	—	IC	—	1 50	The next melee attack against the caster will cause 15 Shadow damage and reduce the damage caused by the attacker by 4 for 2 min.
3	30	75	—	IC	—	5	The next melee attack against the caster will cause 24 Shadow damage and reduce the damage caused by the attacker by 7 for 2 min.
4	40	105	—	IC	—	9	The next melee attack against the caster will cause 35 Shadow damage and reduce the damage caused by the attacker by 11 for 2 min.
5	50	145	—	IC	—	15	The next melee attack against the caster will cause 48 Shadow damage and reduce the damage caused by the attacker by 15 for 2 min.
6	60	195	—	IC	—	23	The next melee attack against the caster will cause 64 Shadow damage and reduce the damage caused by the attacker by 20 for 2 min.

Psychic Scream

Psychic Scream is an AoE Fear spell that is cast instantly (while on a 30-second cooldown). Useful for escapes, PvP disruption, and last ditch crowd control in careful PvE encounters, Psychic Scream is very powerful.

Rank	Level	Mana	Range	Casting Time	Cooldown	Cost to Train	Effect
1	14	100	8 yd	IC	30 sec	12	The caster lets out a psychic scream, causing 2 enemies within 8 yards to flee for 8 sec. Damage caused may interrupt the effect.
2	28	140	8 yd	IC	30 sec	80	The caster lets out a psychic scream, causing 3 enemies within 8 yards to flee for 8 sec. Damage caused may interrupt the effect.
3	42	180	8 yd	IC	30 sec	2 20	The caster lets out a psychic scream, causing 4 enemies within 8 yards to flee for 8 sec. Damage caused may interrupt the effect.
4	56	210	8 yd	IC	30 sec	4 20	The caster lets out a psychic scream, causing 5 enemies within 8 yards to flee for 8 sec. Damage caused may interrupt the effect.

Devouring Plague (Undead only)

Devouring Plague is a Forsaken Priest ability that costs a great deal of mana. However, this Shadow ability deals heavy damage over time and heals the Priest in the process.

Rank	Level	Mana	Range	Casting Time	Cooldown	Cost to Train	Effect
1	20	215	30 yd	IC	3 min	—	Afflicts the target with a disease that causes 152 Shadow damage over 24 sec. Damage caused by the Devouring Plague heals the caster.
2	28	350	30 yd	IC	3 min	4	Afflicts the target with a disease that causes 272 Shadow damage over 24 sec. Damage caused by the Devouring Plague heals the caster.
3	36	495	30 yd	IC	3 min	7	Afflicts the target with a disease that causes 400 Shadow damage over 24 sec. Damage caused by the Devouring Plague heals the caster.
4	44	645	30 yd	IC	3 min	12	Afflicts the target with a disease that causes 544 Shadow damage over 24 sec. Damage caused by the Devouring Plague heals the caster.
5	52	810	30 yd	IC	3 min	19	Afflicts the target with a disease that causes 712 Shadow damage over 24 sec. Damage caused by the Devouring Plague heals the caster.
6	60	985	30 yd	IC	3 min	23	Afflicts the target with a disease that causes 904 Shadow damage over 24 sec. Damage caused by the Devouring Plague heals the caster.

Mind Flay

Mind Flay is a Talent-learned ability that deals moderate damage over a short period. A Snare affects the target, reducing their speed to 50% of normal.

Rank	Minimum Level	Mana	Range	Casting Time	Cooldown	Cost to Train	Effect
1	20	45	20 yd	Channeled	—	—	Assault the target's mind with Shadow energy, causing 75 Shadow damage over 3 sec and slowing the target to 50% of their movement speed.
2	28	70	20 yd	Channeled	—	4	Assault the target's mind with Shadow energy, causing 126 Shadow damage over 3 sec and slowing the target to 50% of their movement speed.
3	36	100	20 yd	Channeled	—	7	Assault the target's mind with Shadow energy, causing 186 Shadow damage over 3 sec and slowing the target to 50% of their movement speed.
4	44	135	20 yd	Channeled	—	12	Assault the target's mind with Shadow energy, causing 261 Shadow damage over 3 sec and slowing the target to 50% of their movement speed.
5	52	165	20 yd	Channeled	—	19	Assault the target's mind with Shadow energy, causing 330 Shadow damage over 3 sec and slowing the target to 50% of their movement speed.
6	60	205	20 yd	Channeled	—	23	Assault the target's mind with Shadow energy, causing 426 Shadow damage over 3 sec and slowing the target to 50% of their movement speed.

Mind Soothe

Mind Soothe reduces the aggro range of Humanoid targets. If resisted, this spell will agro the target.

Rank	Level	Mana	Range	Casting Time	Cooldown	Cost to Train	Effect
1	20	50	40 yd	IC	—	30	Soothes the target, reducing the range at which it will attack you by 10 yards. Only affects Humanoid targets level 40 or lower. Lasts 15 sec.
2	36	70	40 yd	IC	—	1 40	Soothes the target, reducing the range at which it will attack you by 10 yards. Only affects Humanoid targets level 55 or lower. Lasts 15 sec.
3	52	90	40 yd	IC	—	3 80	Soothes the target, reducing the range at which it will attack you by 10 yards. Only affects Humanoid targets level 70 or lower. Lasts 15 sec.

Shadowguard (Troll only)

Shadowguard is a Troll Priest ability that puts a three charge damage shield around him/her. Enemies attacking the Priest take Shadow damage and use a charge each time (though only one charge can be used per target every few seconds).

Rank	Level	Mana	Range	Casting Time	Cooldown	Cost to Train	Effect
1	20	50	—	IC	—	—	The caster is surrounded by shadows. When the spell, melee or ranged attack hits the caster, the attacker will be struck for 20 Shadow damage. Attackers can only be damaged once every few seconds. This damage causes no threat. 3 charges. Lasts 10 min.
2	28	85	—	IC	—	4	The caster is surrounded by shadows. When the spell, melee or ranged attack hits the caster, the attacker will be struck for 35 Shadow damage. Attackers can only be damaged once every few seconds. This damage causes no threat. 3 charges. Lasts 10 min.
3	36	120	—	IC	—	7	The caster is surrounded by shadows. When the spell, melee or ranged attack hits the caster, the attacker will be struck for 51 Shadow damage. Attackers can only be damaged once every few seconds. This damage causes no threat. 3 charges. Lasts 10 min.
4	44	160	—	IC	—	12	The caster is surrounded by shadows. When the spell, melee or ranged attack hits the caster, the attacker will be struck for 70 Shadow damage. Attackers can only be damaged once every few seconds. This damage causes no threat. 3 charges. Lasts 10 min.
5	52	200	—	IC	—	19	The caster is surrounded by shadows. When the spell, melee or ranged attack hits the caster, the attacker will be struck for 90 Shadow damage. Attackers can only be damaged once every few seconds. This damage causes no threat. 3 charges. Lasts 10 min.
6	60	250	—	IC	—	23	The caster is surrounded by shadows. When the spell, melee or ranged attack hits the caster, the attacker will be struck for 116 Shadow damage. Attackers can only be damaged once every few seconds. This damage causes no threat. 3 charges. Lasts 10 min.

Mind Vision

Mind Vision puts your sight in the eyes of the targeted character. Use this in PvP to learn more about the location and distribution of enemy forces. In Warsong Gulch, create a macro to /target <Name of Flag Carrier> and spam that while searching for the foe.

Rank	Level	Mana	Range	Casting Time	Cooldown	Cost to Train	Effect
1	22	65	100 yd	Channeled	—	40	Allows the caster to see through the target's eyes for 1 min.
2	44	150	50000 yd	Channeled	—	2 40	Allows the caster to see through the target's eyes for 1 min. Will not work if the target is in another instance or on another continent.

Mind Control

Mind Control is a very risky spell, but it yields great rewards. In PvP and PvE, this takes control of a Humanoid target and allows you to use their basic melee attacks, at 80% normal speed.

Rank	Level	Mana	Range	Casting Time	Cooldown	Cost to Train	Effect
1	30	350	20 yd	3 sec	—	1	Controls a humanoid mind up to level 32, but slows its attack speed by 20%. Lasts up to 1 min.
2	44	550	20 yd	3 sec	—	2 40	Controls a humanoid mind up to level 47, but slows its attack speed by 20%. Lasts up to 1 min.
3	58	750	20 yd	3 sec	—	4 40	Controls a humanoid mind up to level 62, but slows its attack speed by 20%. Lasts up to 1 min.

Shadow Protection

Shadow Protection adds a substantial Shadow Resistance buff for the target.

Rank	Level	Mana	Range	Casting Time	Cooldown	Cost to Train	Effect
1	30	250	30 yd	IC	—	1	Increases the target's resistance to Shadow spells by 30 for 10 min.
2	42	450	30 yd	IC	—	2 20	Increases the target's resistance to Shadow spells by 45 for 10 min.
3	56	650	30 yd	IC	—	4 20	Increases the target's resistance to Shadow spells by 60 for 10 min.

Prayer of Shadow Protection

Rank	Level	Mana	Range	Casting Time	Reagent	Cost to Train	Effect
1	56	1300	40 yd	IC	Sacred Candle	—	Power infuses the target's party, increasing their Shadow resistance by 60 for 20 min.

Silence

Silence is a Talent-learned ability that prevents the target from casting any spells or using vocal abilities for five seconds.

Rank	Minimum Level	Mana	Range	Casting Time	Cooldown	Cost to Train	Effect
1	30	225	20 yd	IC	45 seconds	—	Silences the target, preventing them from casting spells for 5 sec.

Vampiric Embrace

Vampiric Embrace is a Talent-learned ability that allows Shadow Priests to heal their groups with the damage done to enemies.

Rank	Minimum Level	Mana	Range	Casting Time	Cooldown	Cost to Train	Effect
1	40	40	30 yd	IC	10 seconds	—	Afflicts your target with Shadow energy that causes all party members to be healed for 20% of any Shadow spell damage you deal for 1 min.

Shadowform

Shadowform is a Talent-learned ability that transforms the Priest into a creature of nightmares. Damage dealt by Shadow magic is increased by 15% in this form, and physical damage taken is reduced by the same amount. The only downside of Shadowform is that the Priest cannot use Holy spells while transformed.

Rank	Minimum Level	Mana	Range	Casting Time	Cooldown	Cost to Train	Effect
1	40	550 mana	—	IC	1.5 seconds		Assume a Shadowform, increasing your Shadow damage by 15% and reducing Physical damage done to you by 15%. However, you may not cast Holy spells while in this form.

Talents

Priest Talents are fiercely debated, and there are many builds for success. Damage, healing, survivability for groups, and additional buffs are hidden in there. Clearly, the Shadow line offers a great deal of hindrance and damage for PvP, and some great solo opportunities as well. Holy Talents make a Priest an even better healer and a more efficient healer; the effect on small groups is immense. Discipline allows Priests to cast both healing and damaging spells for longer periods and have harder-hitting results. In effect, all of these lines are viable so the choices are difficult.

Discipline

The Discipline Talents are very useful for raid situations, where not every Priest needs to be a Holy master. It is very useful to add Priests that can Spirit buff (Divine Spirit), Cast for long periods during raid encounters (Meditation, Inner Focus, Mental Strength), and deal more burst damage (Force of Will, Power Infusion).

Taking Discipline as a sub-line for Holy or Shadow does wonderful things for your mana efficiency. Taking Discipline as a primary line helps to balance your healing/damage dealing capabilities.

Holy

Holy Talents do not box a Priest into being a fulltime healer like they used to, but they certainly make Priests into the leaders of healing for a group or raid. Faster healing (Divine Fury) mixes with improvements to healing range and efficiency (Holy Specialization, Inspiration, Holy Reach, Improved Healing, Spiritual Guidance, Spiritual Healing). On top of that, Holy Priests have access to continued casting even after their deaths (Spirit of Redemption), and to healing over time that can be deployed even before battle (Lightwell).

If you want to see heals in the several-thousand point margin, this is the line for you. Every Warrior will love you if you are a Holy Priest. Beyond that, the combination of Holy Priests and a well-played main tank create the core of almost all raid groups.

Shadow

Shadow Priests level faster, solo quite well, deal a fair sum of damage (Improved Shadow Word: Pain, Improved Mind Blast, Shadow Weaving, Darkness, and Shadowform), and are far more than just group support on the fields of PvP (Blackout, Improved Psychic Scream, Mind Flay, and Silence). This Talent line brings somewhat less to a PvE group than the others, but that doesn't mean that Shadow Priests can't drop into their normal forms and do some fine healing when they are needed.

Priests that solo a great deal should seriously consider the damage and low downtime of Shadow sub Discipline. Together, these lines create a Priest that keeps going and going. Shadow sub Discipline or Discipline sub Shadow are both incredible for leveling, and many Priests take these for a fun way up to the higher levels.

STRATEGIES

The core Priest strategy involves the proper mixture of offensive and defensive spells that allows you to keep high amounts of mana. Much of this depends on whether or not you are in a group: that is, whether your primary role is healing or doing damage. No matter what your specialization, your Priest is able to deal damage and heal perfectly well. Remember that! If a group needs you to be acting as more of a healer, hold off on Mind Blast, Mind Flay, Smites, etc. Save that mana for the team. If there are a few healers, however, lend a bit more mana to DPS so that fights don't take an eternity (too much healing and not enough damage can get groups killed).

General Tips

Keep your Stamina buff up at all times. Having that extra health can make a big difference for anyone, and the first thing you should do before moving out into the world should be to buff yourself. By the same token, as you add members to your group, give them each a Stamina buff. This especially makes a difference for other casters, who need all the health they can get. And main tanks, as always, stack health on top of health, so they always want the best that you can give them.

Be efficient. Greater Healing and its earlier variants are more mana-efficient than Flash Heals and Renew. The only downside to using this power healing spell is that it takes slightly longer to cast and has the potential for overhealing. If your tank is only down by a thousand health, healing for two-thousand health is halving your efficiency. As long as a fight is under control, the best way to keep mana high while healing is to use bigger heal spells, less often. Try Flash Heal when the fighting is more desperate and you are working to get a target stabilized.

Power Word: Shield is a very nice ability, but it is very mana intensive. In a group, only use it in emergency situations or for shielding a main tank ahead of a fight. When you put a Shield on a main tank ahead of a battle, your Priest avoids the dangers of early aggro; the seconds this earns may be more than enough to allow your tank to steal aggro for the full fight. Then, only resort to Shield use if a character is either going to die or be severely interrupted in spellcasting by damage. Shields are instant and can give you time to cast authentic healing spells as needed, and the delay in casting interruption is especially good for other healers and AoE casters.

If you are soloing, then Power Word: Shield is good to use right before you start off the fight. This keeps you from being interrupted or having to cast healing spells instead of offensive spells. This works especially well if the enemies you fight are fast-attacking ones, like Wolves or Cats.

Remember that Shadow Word: Pain is a superb DOT. Even when you are a healer, it is very wise to keep this efficient spell ticking away on a target that your group is attempting to defeat. It's not going to take too much time or mana to get Pain going (being that it is an instant), so there is no reason not to keep Pain on primary targets.

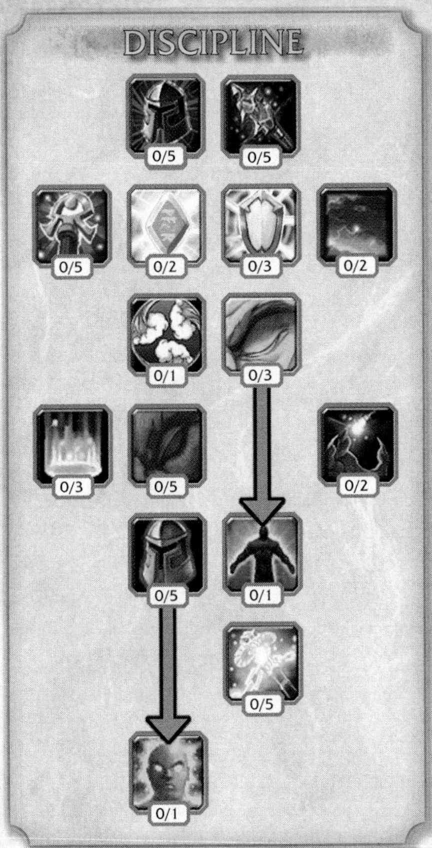

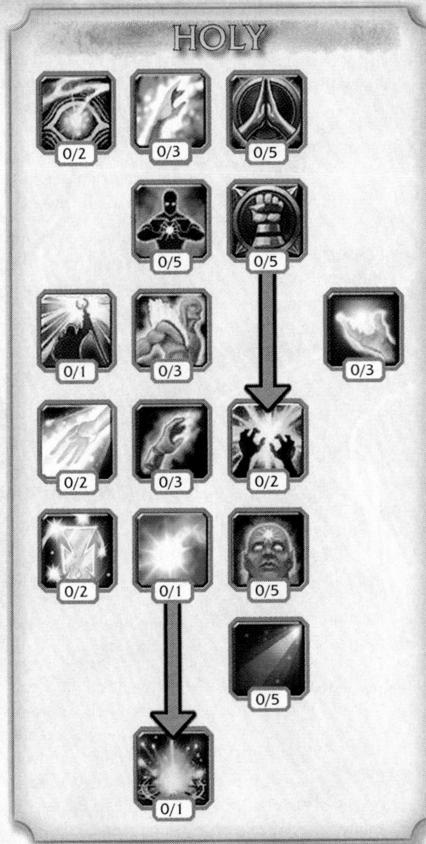

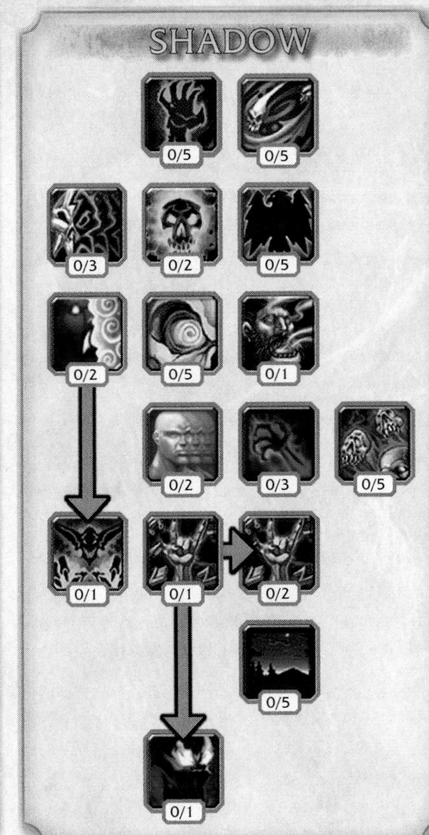

UNBREAKABLE WILL — 5

Increases your chance to Stun, Fear, and Silence by 3%.

WAND SPECIALIZATION — 5

Increases your damage with Wands by 5%.

SILENT RESOLVE — 5

Reduces the threat generated by your spells by 4%.

IMPROVED POWER WORD: FORTITUDE — 2

Increases the effect of your Power Word: Fortitude and Prayer of Fortitude by 15%.

IMPROVED POWER WORD: SHIELD — 3

Increases the damage absorbed by your Power Word: Shield by 5%.

MARTYRDOM — 2

Gives you a 50% chance to gain the Focused Casting effect that lasts for 6 secs after being the victim of a melee or ranged critical strike. The Focused Casting effect prevents you from losing casting time when taking damage and increases resistance to Interrupt effects by 10%.

INNER FOCUS — 1

When activated, reduces the Mana cost of your next spell by 100% and increases its critical effect chance by 25% if capable.

MEDITATION — 3

Allows 5% of you Mana regeneration to continue while casting.

IMPROVED INNER FIRE — 3

Increases the beneficial effects of you Inner Fire spell by 10%.

MENTAL AGILITY — 5

Reduces the Mana cost of your instant cast spells by 2%.

IMPROVED MANA BURN — 2

Reduces the casting time of you Mana Burn spell by 0.25 secs.

MENTAL STRENGTH — 5

Increases your maximum Mana by 2%.

DIVINE SPIRIT — 1

Holy Power infuses the target, increasing their Spirit by 17 for 30 mins.

FORCE OF WILL — 5

Increases your spell damage by 1% and the critical strike chance of your offensive spells by 1%.

POWER INFUSION — 1

Infuses the target with power, increasing their spell damage and healing by 20%. Lasts 15 secs.

HEALING FOCUS — 2

Gives you a 35% chance to avoid interruption caused by damage while casting a healing spell.

IMPROVED RENEW — 3

Increases the amount healed by your Renew spell by 5%.

HOLY SPECIALIZATION — 5

Increases the critical effect chance of you Holy spells by 1%.

SPELL WARDING — 5

Reduces all spell damage taken by 2%.

DIVINE FURY — 5

Reduces the casting time of your Smite, Holy Fire, Heal and Greater Heal spells by 0.1 sec.

HOLY NOVA — 1

Causes an explosion of holy light around the caster, causing 28 to 32 Holy damage to all enemies within 10 yards and healing all party members within 10 yards for 52 to 60. These effects cause no threat.

BLESSED RECOVERY — 3

After being struck by a melee or ranged critical hit, heal 8% of the damage taken over 6 secs.

INSPIRATION — 3

Increases your target's armor by 8% for 15 secs after getting a critical effect from you Flash Heal, Heal, Greater Heal, or Prayer of Healing spell.

HOLY REACH — 2

Increases the range of you Smite and Holy Fire spells and the radius of your Prayer of Healing and Holy Nova spells by 10%.

IMPROVED HEALING — 3

Reduces the Mana cost of you Lesser Heal, Heal, and Greater Heal spells by 5%.

SEARING LIGHT — 2

Increases the damage of you Smite and Holy Fire spells by 5%.

IMPROVED PRAYER OF HEALING — 2

Reduces the Mana cost of your Prayer of Healing spell by 10%.

SPIRIT OF REDEMPTION — 1

Upon death, the Priest become the Spirit of Redemption for 10 secs. The Spirit cannot move, attack, be attacked, or targeted by any spells or effects. While in this form, the Priest can cast any healing spell free of cost. When the effect ends the Priest dies.

SPIRITUAL GUIDANCE — 5

Increases spell damage and healing by up to 5% of you total Spirit.

SPIRITUAL HEALING — 5

Increases the amount healed by your healing spells by 2%.

LIGHTWELL — 1

Creates a holy Lightwell near the Priest. Friendly targets can click the Lightwell to restore 800 health over 10 secs. Being attacked cancels the effect. Lightwell lasts for 3 mins or 5 charges.

SPIRIT TAP — 5

Gives you a 20% chance to gain a 100% bonus to your Spirit after killing a target that yields experience. For the duration, your Mana will regenerate at a 50% rate while casting. Lasts 15 secs.

BLACKOUT — 5

Gives your Shadow damage spells a 2% chance to stun the target for 3 secs.

SHADOW AFFINITY — 3

Reduces the threat generated by your Shadow spells by 8%.

IMPROVED SHADOW WORD: PAIN — 2

Increases the duration of your Shadow Word: Pain spell by 3 secs.

SHADOW FOCUS — 5

Reduces your target's chance to resist your Shadow spells by 2%.

IMPROVED PSYCHIC SCREAM — 2

Reduces the cooldown of your Psychic Scream spell by 2 secs.

IMPROVED MIND BLAST — 5

Reduces the cooldown of you Mind Blast spell by 0.5 sec.

MIND FLAY — 1

Assault the target's mind with Shadow energy, causing 75 damage over 3 secs and slowing the target to 50% of their movement speed.

IMPROVED FADE — 2

Decreases the cooldown of you Fade ability by 3 secs.

SHADOW REACH — 3

Increases the range of your Shadow damage spells by 6%.

SHADOW WEAVING — 5

Your Shadow damage spells have a 20% chance to cause your target to be vulnerable to Shadow damage. This vulnerability increases the Shadow damage dealt to your target by 3% and lasts for 15 secs. Stacks up to 5 times.

SILENCE — 1

Silences the target, preventing them from casting spells for 5 secs.

VAMPIRIC EMBRACE — 1

Afflicts your target with Shadow energy that causes all party members to be healed for 20% of any Shadow damage you deal for 1 min.

IMPROVED VAMPIRIC EMBRACE — 2

Increases the percentage healed by Vampiric Embrace by an additional 5%.

DARKNESS — 5

Increases your Shadow spell damage by 2%.

SHADOWFORM — 1

Assume a Shadowform, increasing your Shadow damage by 15% and reducing Physical damage done to you by 15%. However, you may not cast Holy spells while in this form.

All by Your Lonesome?

In World of Warcraft, it is completely possible for every class to solo up to maximum level, and this includes cloth-wearing Healers. Instead of being dependent on a group, Priests on their own are very powerful, independent entities.

The primary goal as a solo Priest is to minimize the time that you spend regenerating mana. First off, if you are sitting you aren't getting experience. Second, drinks are monetarily expensive, and there are better ways to spend your money (e.g. training, getting better gear).

Strongly consider specializing in Shadow Magic while leveling, because that line dramatically improves a Priest's kill rate. Start fights with a Mind Blast and Shadow Word: Pain to get your timer started and some damage going. If you have Mind Flay, slow the enemy's approach with that while continuing to lay on the damage. At higher levels, this is combined with Vampiric Embrace to make up for damage taken during the fighting!

Only use mana on survivability when it is absolutely necessary. If your Priest goes into every fight with a Power Word: Shield, Inner Fire, and Renew, you are going to drink through a river of water. Even with a Mage buddy to give you freebies, this is not an ideal method of play. Taking a bit of damage isn't that bad a thing, considering that health comes back on its own between battles. A slap here or there means very little, and one Greater Heal after a few fights or the use of Vampiric Embrace negates these issues.

Instead, save Renew, Power Word: Shield, and such for battles where things are going wrong. If an enemy comes with a friend that you weren't expecting, use the Shield to continue casting without delays. Put the Shadow Word: Pain on both/all targets early on, and be sure to restore the DOT when it drops. If things are getting too desperate, use Psychic Scream and bugger out before the enemies have a chance to return with buddies.

Group Dynamics

Your primary role in a group is that of healer. Your job is to keep people alive and fighting. If the fight is well in hand, you can toss in a few offensive spells (just don't Mind Blast to start off the fight), but by and large you let other characters do damage while you allow them to keep taking the hits. It's a tradeoff: you don't get injured, the monster gets hurt, and people who ordinarily couldn't handle concentrated aggro get to do heavy damage.

Every time that you heal, you generate a certain amount of Threat. This really begins to come into play when your group is fighting multiple targets. If you heal too soon, you become the center of aggression, and that really puts a crimp in further healing (or living through the battle). So before you heal, keep an eye on who the enemies are fighting and how the fight is progressing. Try to give Tanks enough time to damage all of the enemies who are incoming before starting heavy spell work. Warriors/Paladins don't need to be at full health all the time anyway; it makes them angry not to be at least a little injured.

There is also a definite order as to who should be healed first. Casters are the most fragile and need healing quickly if they are struck; use Flash Heal to get them what they need. As long as the main tank is a good one, these lighter targets won't take hits for long anyway. A main tank should be able to Taunt the stray foes off of people, Sunder it, and still focus back to the primary foe.

If everyone is taking damage, worry only about healing the main tank and other healers. When people start to die in a very ugly pull, it's essential that you keep tanks/healers going until the end. Losing DPS is never a good thing, but Rogues, Hunter Pets, the Hunters themselves, and Mages are the characters that are most expendable. If you lose the main tank in most fights, things get very scary. If you lose the healers, it's over.

If everyone in your party is looking injured, don't hesitate to use Prayer of Healing. And while it is true that these spells do cause Threat, like any other heal spell, they do not automatically cause you to be the sole focus of monster aggression. Instead, they are a very good and useful way of keeping an entire group active and fighting in a nasty situation. Prayer of Healing is situational, and pristine fights often deal with healing only the main tank. However, the reality is that things can, will, and do go wrong, and AoE heals are a good backup. Holy Priests can also spam Holy Nova; though inefficient, the mix of healing allies and damaging enemies is good when people get totally mobbed.

There are also several things that a Priest can do to avoid enemy attention. Fade discourages enemies from attacking you; use this immediately if you are jumped by a monster during a group engagement.

Psychic Scream is godly in PvP and is a great survival tool while soloing, but be careful about using it in groups. A tough pull that is scaring you is going to go a lot worse if you Scream and end up getting an extra monster or two as a result. Scream if a group is trying to evacuate or if the area is extremely clear of additional foes (this won't happen often).

Mind Control

In terms of crowd control at higher levels, Priests do gain the ability to temporarily control enemies. This spell is called Mind Control and it only works on humanoid targets. The enemies get a chance to break free every five seconds, and a PvE target that breaks Mind Control rarely stops attacking the Priest. Thus, all characters need to focus fire on the failed target, Stunlock the darn thing if possible, and bring it down.

Mind Control is a great way to take down a single target in a group of elites before the party engages any monsters. Doing this allows the Priest to attack the enemy group with itself! The monsters are going to tear apart their traitorous member, and that is the end of things. You are even able, in some dungeons, to jump Mind Controlled targets off ledges and down to cleared areas. By doing so, you cause the entire group of aggroed enemies to chase their member down to the previous area. Your buddies can then pick one or two elites off of the pile and kill them while the rest kill their MCed victim. In one smooth action, your group has taken down three elites with almost no danger. When the rest of the group returns, kill them.

In PvP, Mind Control is less useful most of the time, but it has its place. When there are high bridges (northern Alterac Valley), or nasty cliffs (Lumber Mill, Arathi Basin), Mind Control is very efficient for taking a foe out of the fight. Cast the spell, jump the poor fool to their death, and go back to the fighting. Or, if you are really mean in the open field, Mind Control someone and send them into a large group of monsters. The monsters do the work for you this way. Remove the Mind Control at the last moment, and watch the person try to escape. This victim is doomed to take Durability loss on their death (because it's not a PvP death). Note that this is not nice and the agro will switch to you when the person dies. Reserve that type of treatment for people who have been camping graveyards, hassling lowbies, and so forth.

When approaching PvE enemies, use Mind Sooth to reduce their aggro range (Mind Control does not have a long range). Your Priest has to stay fairly close to the target as well; the farther away the creature gets, the greater a chance that the spell breaks and end early.

Additionally, some PvE targets are able to use their healing, buffs, and other abilities while Mind Controlled. Because of that, certain healers and casters are wonderful to Mind Control. Grab these and let them get the aggro for using their abilities instead of keeping it on yourself.

Just remember that Mind Control is often a major gamble. It can do tremendous things (for good or for ill). Let groups know when you know what you are doing with Mind Control and when you are experimenting with new ideas. If they are reticent, be willing to hold off and try your tricks some other time. If they say "Go for it!" you know that they are onboard and are willing to deal with any slipups without getting whiney.

Rogues are a very interesting and complex melee class in World of Warcraft. These Stealthers are able to stay out of sight (with a bit of luck and planning), and their surprise attacks are able to bring down soft targets at an alarming rate. Though challenged by and wary of enemies in heavy armor, Rogues grin and strike fear into the hearts of anyone who isn't hidden under a veil of steel. Rarely surpassed in PvP capabilities, Rogues are also fast levelers and devourers of PvE content. It is only in the very late game raids that Rogues face their greatest challenge (surviving mass aggro and AoEs in fights where dealing the most damage isn't always a good thing).

Lore

The night was dark and silent...I was glad for it. The wind swept over me and the barren flatland of my playground. The Quillboars walked around me ignorant to their danger, but they were foolish creatures, and I am Saslen; they would know me only when I allowed it...such short lived knowledge.

I turned back toward a far hill and used my dagger to reflect moonlight toward my companions. They could see it well enough to understand my message, "Four". Gothara, Wertala, and Sinsear were ready to go.

Gliding into position, I struck.

One of the Quillboars bent over, knocked unconscious. Its peers barely noticed, their attention drawn to a mighty Tauren charging their small camp. Moving with speed, Gothara looked like a small mountain. As the creatures turned to face the Tauren Warrior, she roared. The moment of truth had arrived and found the Quillboars lacking. Those who engaged her struck like children; there were many who did not strike at all.

I began moving toward the battle. Wertala's voice was steady as she chanted the seven Troll words for pain: one of the Quillboars convulsed, bubbly snorts of mucous and blood sounded from its short flat snout. Sinsear, with his Voidwalker in tow, summoned dark shadows—the Void. Yet, one of the Quillboars was undaunted.

Standing in the back, this creature started to bring the power of elemental flame out of the land. Already heavily engaged, the others wouldn't be able to bring their full force against this foe until it was too late. But I had my own plan.

I was behind the caster in an instant. It still knew nothing of my presence, consumed by incantations. The wind suddenly stopped, as if the whole of the Barrens held its breath, anticipating my strike...the wait was short. I stabbed deep into its back. The shriek of the caster-pig seemed to revive the wind, now howling over the battle, the wind and cries merging into a frenzied opus of darkness and death. The caster, who turned to look at me with fear-filled eyes, began to mumble. The Quillboar stumbled over the words, slurring them. The poison was already in full effect.

There were other enemies yet to fell, so I had no time to tarry. A final cut offered rest to the Quillboar. The creature's companions called for assistance, but only the night heard their miserable cries. Soon, they fell just like their friend. Only the initial Quillboar was alive, trying to rouse itself from my Sap. When it finally looked up, Gothara stomped the ground, paralyzing him with fright. I cut with impunity. So simple...

Introduction to Playing the Class

Rogues require an aggressive mindset. This needs to be tempered with a certain degree of patience as well; Rogues don't charge straight in to combat and take the hits. Indeed, the best way to succeed as a Rogue is to prepare the perfect attack, then go nuts once everything comes together.

First off, spec for really high damage. Almost all groups are going to expect DPS from your character. If you want to be even more than that for other players, spec in the Subtlety Talent line and train yourself for scouting, crowd control, and general group support.

Maximize +Critical, +Hit, and Agility gear to reach those high damage numbers, and think about how you want to deal said damage. For sustained damage, Rogues can use Combat Talents and abilities, larger weapons (swords most commonly), and rely on more direct tactics. Instead of backstabbing and using Stealth for Ambush, these Rogues go for more Stuns and Sinister Strikes. That is very effective in PvE.

To do the great bursts, look into the Assassination Talents, a wicked set of daggers, and use Stealth to start battles with painful attacks. With a high-damage weapon, Assassination Talents, and a good Ambush, Rogues start a fight with an enormous advantage.

In either event, skilled rogues devour low health opponents, in PvE and PvP. For grinding and farming items, this should be kept in mind. And in the Battlegrounds, know your place! Don't hop out and try to take down the biggest Warrior on the enemy team unless you have backup. Instead, Sap the brute and kill any healers or casters in the area! Take the quick, easy kills that can be done with burst damage or Stuns. Anything tougher can wait until there are more people to assist you.

And that is the biggest thing for most Rogues to understand; you are not a one-man wrecking crew. Rogues are more than that, and less. They are scouts for the attack force, can time attacks wonderfully, provide detailed information, annoy enemies beyond belief, Stun and CC opponents, and so forth. But you don't take groups on directly! That is what Warriors are for, bless their tanky little hearts.

An interesting facet of Rogue play is that these characters don't use mana. Instead, they have Energy. This starts at 100 (a full, yellow bar), and restores itself quickly. Unlike Warriors, it doesn't matter whether you are in-combat, getting hit, etc. Energy comes back all the time.

The next aspect of battle is that your standard moves (Sinister Strike, Backstab, Ambush, Hemorrhage, etc.) add Combo Points to your target. These points are saved up, from one to five, and are used to complete Finishing Moves only usable on the target that the Combo Points are saved on (although the Slice and Dice effect does carry over).. A Finishing Move removes all of the Combo Points from your target and enacts a powerful effect: instant damage, increased attack speed for your Rogue, DOTs, and so forth.

Available Races	
Dwarf	Gnome
Human	Night Elf
Orc	Troll
Undead	

What do Attributes Mean to Me?	
Strength	Slightly Increased Melee Damage
Stamina	More Health
Agility	Substantial Increase in Critical Hit Rate, Improved Melee Damage, Higher Chance to Dodge, Increases Armor
Intellect	Faster Rate for Gaining Weapon Skills (Trivial)
Spirit	Improves Hit Point Recovery (Almost Worthless)

Items and Equipment

Rogues love their weapons, as do any melee class. Whether a Rogue is going to go for daggers, swords, or maces depends heavily on build (Talents play the biggest part). There are a number of issues here, including the fact that some abilities are impossible with heavier weapons. Ambush and Backstab, two hard-hitting attacks in the Rogue's lineup, are only possible with daggers.

Slower weapons are used more often with Sinister Strike, dealing immediate damage without the worry of position or Stealth. If you prefer dealing damage over time, Combat Rogues do quite well. If Stealth and massive, sudden damage are your goals, a very slow dagger is absolutely divine. This is a very sound model for PvP, where burst damage is king.

As for armor, look for Agility and Stamina in high numbers. These attributes are needed for just about all Rogue builds. If soloing, keep as much Stamina as possible; it makes a huge difference in what you can survive.

At the higher levels, keep a good eye out for +Hit and +Critical equipment as well. These are the bread and butter of good Rogues in the late game. Rogues are always dual wielding (gaining this ability as early as level 10)! Thus, a high +Hit bonus is also of importance.

Ranged weapons are key for pulling if you don't want to rely on Sap. Get something you are comfortable using and rely on that for getting creatures out of thick spots. Because these aren't your primary sources of damage, it isn't as important to keep ranged weapons fully up-to-date. In fact, the attribute bonuses of a good ranged weapon are far more important than the damage dealt; Bows with Stamina and Agility are certainly out there, and if there isn't a Hunter who needs it instead, take them!

Poisons offer a massive boost to your DPS. Rogues are able to use these after reaching Level 20. Invest in quality poisons and use them frequently when fighting anything of importance. Instant Poison is good for short fights against low-level monsters. Deadly Poison stacks well and procs nicely, so it's pretty solid against Elites and other long-fight targets. Mind-Numbing Poison is a gem for disrupting the activity of casters. Crippling Poison keeps mobs from wandering to far away.

One nice perk of being a Rogue is that you can Pick Locks. This is a very useful skill for opening Lockboxes, Chests, and even gates in certain dungeons that otherwise require quest keys and a greater investment of time. After learning Lock Picking from your trainer and completing the class quest to gain the Thieves Tools, use the initial quest box to raise their skill for a fair time before leaving. Afterward, there are places in the world that are useful for raising your skill; you can also advertise in the General or Trade Channels to let people know that you are unlocking boxes (they get the loot, you get easy skillups).

Lockpicking Skillups

Skill	Location
1-100	Chests for the Lockpicking Quest
101-175	Poison Quest Chests and from chests in Durnholde Keep
176-225	Scarlet Monastery Doors
226-250	Sturdy Junkboxes and from chests off shore at Ethel Rethor in Desolace
251-280	Heavy Junkboxes and from chests in Lost Rigger Cove
281-300	High-End Instance Doors

CHOOSING YOUR PROFESSION

Rogues have a fair number of choices when it comes to their professions. Skinning and Leatherworking are perfectly fine for getting you into some adequate armor; being able to make pouches for ammo isn't a horrible thing either. At higher levels, your Skinning can also help to offset the cost of constant weapon searching and poison purchases.

For more damage, the combo of Mining and Engineering is suitable for all classes. Rogues benefit even more from having Bombs because they are in direct combat so often. Coupled with the innate power of this class to Stun enemies all the time, Bombs are even better!

Secondary skills are very important to Rogues. Without heavy armor or the ability to heal magically, Rogues usually fall in love with Cooking and First Aid. Rogues kill quickly but take a lot of damage as well, so reducing downtime greatly improves their experience efficiency.

Fishing is even useful for Rogues; there is a chance to improve your Lockpicking while using Fishing (you never know what is going to bob to the surface, eh).

Class Abilities

Assassination covers a number of Stealth attacks and finishing moves. These abilities often do very high damage and are critical for starting and ending fights (burst damage galore). The Combat line is what a Rogue brings to melee when they are engaged in melee without Stealth. Finally, the line of Subtlety controls Stealth itself, Vanishing from encounters and crowd control.

Finally, Rogues have a special set of abilities beyond the normal three-way-split. Poisons are learned at level 20, and these are applied to Rogue weapons at all times. Though somewhat costly, these add a major amount of damage or utility to a Rogue's attacks.

Assassination

Eviscerate

Eviscerate is a high-damage Finishing Move. This turns Combo Points directly into damage.

Rank	Level	Energy	Cost to Train	Effects
1	1	35	—	Finishing move that causes damage per combo point. 1 point: 7-11 damage, 2 points: 13-17 damage, 3 points: 19-23 damage, 4 points: 25-29 damage, 5 points: 31-35 damage.
2	8	35	2	Finishing move that causes damage per combo point. 1 point: 16-24 damage, 2 points: 29-37 damage, 3 points: 42-50 damage, 4 points: 55-63 damage, 5 points: 68-76 damage.
3	16	35	18	Finishing move that causes damage per combo point. 1 point: 29-43 damage, 2 points: 52-66 damage, 3 points: 75-89 damage, 4 points: 98-112 damage, 5 points: 121-135 damage.
4	24	35	50	Finishing move that causes damage per combo point. 1 point: 47-67 damage, 2 points: 84-104 damage, 3 points: 121-141 damage, 4 points: 158-178 damage, 5 points: 195-215 damage.
5	32	35	1 20	Finishing move that causes damage per combo point. 1 point: 69-99 damage, 2 points: 123-153 damage, 3 points: 177-207 damage, 4 points: 231-261 damage, 5 points: 285-315 damage.
6	40	35	2	Finishing move that causes damage per combo point. 1 point: 104-148 damage, 2 points: 186-230 damage, 3 points: 268-312 damage, 4 points: 350-394 damage, 5 points: 432-476 damage.
7	48	35	3 30	Finishing move that causes damage per combo point. 1 point: 158-226 damage, 2 points: 282-350 damage, 3 points: 406-474 damage, 4 points: 530-598 damage, 5 points: 654-722 damage.
8	56	35	5	Finishing move that causes damage per combo point. 1 point: 216-312 damage, 2 points: 384-480 damage, 3 points: 552-648 damage, 4 points: 720-816 damage, 5 points: 888-984 damage.

Slice and Dice

Slice and Dice improves base attack speed by at least 20%. This Finishing Move lasts for a longer period depending on the number of Combo Points held when it is used.

Rank	Level	Energy	Cost to Train	Effects
1	10	25	3	Finishing move that increases melee attack speed by 20%. Lasts longer per combo point. 1 point: 9 seconds, 2 points: 12 seconds, 3 points: 15 seconds, 4 points: 18 seconds, 5 points: 21 seconds.
2	42	25	2 70	Finishing move that increases melee attack speed by 30%. Lasts longer per combo point. 1 point: 9 seconds, 2 points: 12 seconds, 3 points: 15 seconds, 4 points: 18 seconds, 5 points: 21 seconds

Expose Armor

Expose Armor is a Finishing Move that is often used when soloing heavier opponents (bosses, high-armor monsters).

Rank	Level	Energy	Cost to Train	Effects
1	14	25	12	Finishing move that exposes the target for 30 seconds, reducing armor per combo point. 1 point: 80 armor, 2 points: 160 armor, 3 points: 240 armor, 4 points: 320 armor, 5 points: 400 armor.
2	26	25	60	Finishing move that exposes the target for 30 seconds, reducing armor per combo point. 1 point: 145 armor, 2 points: 290 armor, 3 points: 435 armor, 4 points: 580 armor, 5 points: 725 armor.
3	36	25	1 60	Finishing move that exposes the target for 30 seconds, reducing armor per combo point. 1 point: 210 armor, 2 points: 420 armor, 3 points: 630 armor, 4 points: 840 armor, 5 points: 1050 armor.
4	46	25	3 10	Finishing move that exposes the target for 30 seconds, reducing armor per combo point. 1 point: 275 armor, 2 points: 550 armor, 3 points: 825 armor, 4 points: 1100 armor, 5 points: 1375 armor.
5	56	25	5	Finishing move that exposes the target for 30 seconds, reducing armor per combo point. 1 point: 340 armor, 2 points: 680 armor, 3 points: 1020 armor, 4 points: 1360 armor, 5 points: 1700 armor.

Garrote

Garrote is a Combo Builder that starts from Stealth. Use this to land a DOT on the target.

Rank	Level	Energy	Cost to Train	Effects
1	14	50	12	Garrote the enemy, causing 108 damage over 18 seconds. Must be stealthed and behind the target. Awards 1 combo point.
2	22	50	40	Garrote the enemy, causing 162 damage over 18 seconds. Must be stealthed and behind the target. Awards 1 combo point.
3	30	50	1	Garrote the enemy, causing 222 damage over 18 seconds. Must be stealthed and behind the target. Awards 1 combo point.
4	38	50	1 80	Garrote the enemy, causing 282 damage over 18 seconds. Must be stealthed and behind the target. Awards 1 combo point.
5	46	50	3 10	Garrote the enemy, causing 348 damage over 18 seconds. Must be stealthed and behind the target. Awards 1 combo point.
6	54	50	4 80	Garrote the enemy, causing 438 damage over 18 seconds. Must be stealthed and behind the target. Awards 1 combo point.

Ambush

Ambush is a Combo Builder that starts from Stealth. You cannot use Ambush without having a dagger in your main hand

Rank	Level	Energy	Cost to Train	Effects
1	18	60	29	Ambush the target, causing 250% weapon damage plus 70 to the target. Must be stealthed and behind the target. Requires a dagger in the main hand. Awards 1 combo point.
2	26	60	60	Ambush the target, causing 250% weapon damage plus 100 to the target. Must be stealthed and behind the target. Requires a dagger in the main hand. Awards 1 combo point.
3	34	60	1 40	Ambush the target, causing 250% weapon damage plus 125 to the target. Must be stealthed and behind the target. Requires a dagger in the main hand. Awards 1 combo point.
4	42	60	2 70	Ambush the target, causing 250% weapon damage plus 185 to the target. Must be stealthed and behind the target. Requires a dagger in the main hand. Awards 1 combo point.
5	50	60	3 50	Ambush the target, causing 250% weapon damage plus 230 to the target. Must be stealthed and behind the target. Requires a dagger in the main hand. Awards 1 combo point.
6	58	60	5 20	Ambush the target, causing 250% weapon damage plus 290 to the target. Must be stealthed and behind the target. Requires a dagger in the main hand. Awards 1 combo point.

Rupture

Rupture is a Finishing Move that puts a DOT on the target.

Rank	Level	Energy	Cost to Train	Effects
1	20	25	30	Finishing move that causes damage over time. Lasts longer per combo point. 1 point: 45 damage over 6 seconds, 2 points: 75 damage over 10 seconds, 3 points: 105 damage over 14 seconds, 4 points: 135 damage over 18 seconds, 5 points: 165 damage over 22 seconds.
2	28	25	80	Finishing move that causes damage over time. Lasts longer per combo point. 1 point: 69 damage over 6 seconds, 2 points: 115 damage over 10 seconds, 3 points: 161 damage over 14 seconds, 4 points: 207 damage over 18 seconds, 5 points: 253 damage over 22 seconds
3	36	25	1 [60 sp]	Finishing move that causes damage over time. Lasts longer per combo point. 1 point: 96 damage over 6 seconds, 2 points: 160 damage over 10 seconds, 3 points: 224 damage over 14 seconds, 4 points: 288 damage over 18 seconds, 5 points: 352 damage over 22 seconds
4	44	25	2 90	Finishing move that causes damage over time. Lasts longer per combo point. 1 point: 135 damage over 6 seconds, 2 points: 225 damage over 10 seconds, 3 points: 315 damage over 14 seconds, 4 points: 405 damage over 18 seconds, 5 points: 495 damage over 22 seconds
5	52	25	4 60	Finishing move that causes damage over time. Lasts longer per combo point. 1 point: 186 damage over 6 seconds, 2 points: 310 damage over 10 seconds, 3 points: 434 damage over 14 seconds, 4 points: 558 damage over 18 seconds, 5 points: 682 damage over 22 seconds
6	60	25	5 40	Finishing move that causes damage over time. Lasts longer per combo point. 1 point: 255 damage over 6 seconds, 2 points: 425 damage over 10 seconds, 3 points: 595 damage over 14 seconds, 4 points: 765 damage over 18 seconds, 5 points: 935 damage over 22 seconds

Cheap Shot

Cheap Shot is an opening Stun from Stealth that adds two Combo Points, and possibly three is specced right.

Rank	Level	Energy	Cost to Train	Effects
N/A	26	60	60	Stuns the target for 4 seconds. Must be stealthed. Awards 2 combo points.

Cold Blood

Cold Blood is a Talent-learned ability on a three-minute timer. Using this guarantees that the next Sinister Strike, Backstab, Ambush, or Eviscerate will score a Critical as long as it hits. If you miss the attack, such is life. Ambush and Eviscerate are used most commonly with this because of their potential for catastrophic damage on Criticals.

Rank	Prerequisite	Effect
1	20 Points in Assassination	When activated, increases the critical strike chance of your next Sinister Strike, Backstab, Ambush, or Eviscerate by 100%.

Kidney Shot

Kidney Shot is a Finishing Move that Stuns the opponent longer per combo point. While stunned by a Kidney Shot the victim also takes increased damage from all types of attacks.

Rank	Level	Energy	Cost to Train	Effects
1	30	25	1	Finishing move that stuns the target. Lasts longer per combo point. 1 point: 1 second, 2 point: 2 seconds, 3 points: 3 seconds, 4 points: 4 seconds, 5 points: 5 seconds.
2	50	25	3 50	Finishing move that stuns the target. Lasts longer per combo point. 1 point: 2 second, 2 point: 3 seconds, 3 points: 4 seconds, 4 points: 5 seconds, 5 points: 6 seconds.

Combat

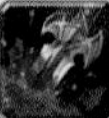

Backstab

Backstab is a Combo Builder that requires a dagger and for your Rogue to be standing behind the target. Because Stealth is not required, Rogues can do this in active combat.

Rank	Level	Energy	Cost to Train	Effects
1	4	60	1	Backstab the target, causing 150% weapon damage plus 15 to the target. Must be behind the target. Requires a dagger in the main hand. Awards 1 combo point.
2	12	60	8	Backstab the target, causing 150% weapon damage plus 30 to the target. Must be behind the target. Requires a dagger in the main hand. Awards 1 combo point.
3	20	60	30	Backstab the target, causing 150% weapon damage plus 48 to the target. Must be behind the target. Requires a dagger in the main hand. Awards 1 combo point.
4	28	60	80	Backstab the target, causing 150% weapon damage plus 69 to the target. Must be behind the target. Requires a dagger in the main hand. Awards 1 combo point.
5	36	60	1 60	Backstab the target, causing 150% weapon damage plus 90 to the target. Must be behind the target. Requires a dagger in the main hand. Awards 1 combo point.
6	44	60	2 90	Backstab the target, causing 150% weapon damage plus 135 to the target. Must be behind the target. Requires a dagger in the main hand. Awards 1 combo point.
7	52	60	4 60	Backstab the target, causing 150% weapon damage plus 165 to the target. Must be behind the target. Requires a dagger in the main hand. Awards 1 combo point.
8	60	60	5 40	Backstab the target, causing 150% weapon damage plus 210 to the target. Must be behind the target. Requires a dagger in the main hand. Awards 1 combo point.
9	60	60	—	Backstab the target, causing 150% weapon damage plus 225 to the target. Must be behind the target. Requires a dagger in the main hand. Awards 1 combo point.

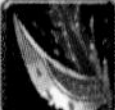

Gouge

Gouge is a Combo Builder that incapacitates opponents for four seconds. Your character sheaths their weapons after using Gouge because any damage inflicted on the target breaks this effect.

Rank	Level	Energy	Cost to Train	Effects
1	6	45	1	Causes 10 damage, incapacitating the opponent for 4 seconds and turns off your attack. Target must be facing you. Any damage caused will revive the target. Awards 1 combo point. 10 sec cooldown.
2	18	45	29	Causes 20 damage, incapacitating the opponent for 4 seconds and turns off your attack. Target must be facing you. Any damage caused will revive the target. Awards 1 combo point. 10 sec cooldown.
3	32	45	1 20	Causes 32 damage, incapacitating the opponent for 4 seconds and turns off your attack. Target must be facing you. Any damage caused will revive the target. Awards 1 combo point. 10 sec cooldown.
4	46	45	3 10	Causes 55 damage, incapacitating the opponent for 4 seconds and turns off your attack. Target must be facing you. Any damage caused will revive the target. Awards 1 combo point. 10 sec cooldown.
5	60	45	5 40	Causes 75 damage, incapacitating the opponent for 4 seconds and turns off your attack. Target must be facing you. Any damage caused will revive the target. Awards 1 combo point. 10 sec cooldown.

Sinister Strike

Sinister Strike is a damaging attack that adds one Combo Point.

Rank	Level	Energy	Cost to Train	Effects
1	1	40	—	An instant strike that causes 3 damage in addition to your normal weapon damage. Awards 1 combo point.
2	6	40	1	An instant strike that causes 6 damage in addition to your normal weapon damage. Awards 1 combo point.
3	14	40	12	An instant strike that causes 10 damage in addition to your normal weapon damage. Awards 1 combo point.
4	22	40	40	An instant strike that causes 15 damage in addition to your normal weapon damage. Awards 1 combo point.
5	30	40	1	An instant strike that causes 22 damage in addition to your normal weapon damage. Awards 1 combo point.
6	38	40	1 80	An instant strike that causes 33 damage in addition to your normal weapon damage. Awards 1 combo point.
7	46	40	3 10	An instant strike that causes 52 damage in addition to your normal weapon damage. Awards 1 combo point.
8	54	40	4 80	An instant strike that causes 68 damage in addition to your normal weapon damage. Awards 1 combo point.

Evasion

Evasion is an ability on a five-minute cooldown that dramatically raises your Rogue's Dodge rate. This lasts for 15 seconds, and it very effective against monsters, Rogues, melee Hunters, and pets.

Rank	Level	Energy	Cost to Train	Effects
N/A	8	N/A	2	The rogue's dodge chance will increase by 50% for 15 seconds. 5 min cooldown.

Sprint

Sprint raises a Rogue's movement speed for 15 seconds. If specced right this removes all movement impairing effects.

Rank	Level	Energy	Cost to Train	Effects
1	10	—	3	Increases the rogue's movement speed by 50% for 15 seconds. Does not break stealth. 5 minute cooldown.
2	34	—	1 40	Increases the rogue's movement speed by 60% for 15 seconds. Does not break stealth. 5 minute cooldown.
3	58	—	5 20	Increases the rogue's movement speed by 70% for 15 seconds. Does not break stealth. 5 minute cooldown.

Kick

Kick instantly interrupts casters and prevents them from using the same school of magic for several seconds.

Rank	Level	Energy	Cost to Train	Effects
1	12	25	8	A quick kick that injures a single foe for 15 damage. It also interrupts spellcasting and prevents any spell in that school from being cast for 5 seconds. 10 second cooldown.
2	26	25	60	A quick kick that injures a single foe for 30 damage. It also interrupts spellcasting and prevents any spell in that school from being cast for 5 seconds. 10 second cooldown.
3	42	25	2 70	A quick kick that injures a single foe for 45 damage. It also interrupts spellcasting and prevents any spell in that school from being cast for 5 seconds. 10 second cooldown.
4	58	25	5 20	A quick kick that injures a single foe for 80 damage. It also interrupts spellcasting and prevents any spell in that school from being cast for 5 seconds. 10 second cooldown.

Feint

Feint works to reduce Threat against your targeted enemy.

Rank	Level	Energy	Cost to Train	Effects
1	16	20	18	Performs a feint, causing no damage but lowering your threat by a large amount, making the enemy less likely to attack you. 10 second cooldown.
2	28	20	80	Performs a feint, causing no damage but lowering your threat by a large amount, making the enemy less likely to attack you. More effective than Feint (Rank 1). 10 second cooldown.
3	40	20	2	Performs a feint, causing no damage but lowering your threat by a large amount, making the enemy less likely to attack you. More effective than Feint (Rank 2). 10 second cooldown.
4	52	20	3 68	Performs a feint, causing no damage but lowering your threat by a large amount, making the enemy less likely to attack you. More effective than Feint (Rank 3). 10 second cooldown.
5	60	20	—	Performs a feint, causing no damage but lowering your threat by a large amount, making the enemy less likely to attack you. More effective than Feint (Rank 4). 10 second cooldown.

Riposte

Riposte is a Talent-learned ability that, after a successful Parry, causes weapon damage, bonus damage on top of that, and Disarms the opponent for six seconds.

Rank	Prerequisite	Effect
1	10 Points in Combat, 5 Points in Deflection	A strike that becomes active after parrying an opponent's attack. This attack deals 150% weapon damage and disarms the target for 6 seconds.

Blade Flurry

Blade Flurry is a Talent-learned ability on a two-minute cooldown. When used, this increases your Rogue's attack speed and allows a second target to be hit with each swing.

Rank	Prerequisite	Effect
1	20 Points in Combat	Increases your attack speed by 20%. In addition, attacks strike an additional nearby opponent. Lasts 15 seconds.

Adrenaline Rush

Adrenaline Rush is a Talent-learned ability that doubles Energy regeneration for 15 seconds (this is on a five-minute cooldown). Combine with Blade Flurry to steal a couple of enemies and obliterate them.

Rank	Prerequisite	Effect
1	30 Points in Combat	Increases your Energy regeneration rate by 100% for 15 seconds.

Subtlety

Stealth

Stealth is a key feature of Rogues. This ability allows your Rogue to enter a state that is much harder for both monsters and characters to detect. Stealth is used to engage targets when they are unaware. Several of the Rogue's best damage/Stun abilities rely on Stealth.

Rank	Level	Energy	Cost to Train	Effects
1	1	—	10	Allows the Rogue to sneak around but reduces your speed to 50% of normal. Lasts until cancelled.
2	20	—	30	Allows the Rogue to sneak around but reduces your speed to 60% of normal. Lasts until cancelled.
3	40	—	2	Allows the Rogue to sneak around but reduces your speed to 65% of normal. Lasts until cancelled.
4	60	—	5 40	Allows the Rogue to sneak around but reduces your speed to 70% of normal. Lasts until cancelled.

Pick Pocket

Pick Pocket does exactly as it appears. Humaniod NPCs can have their pockets picked in or outside of battle. Distract is a sister skill as using this skill from behind is safest.

Rank	Level	Energy	Cost to Train	Effects
N/A	4	—	1	Picks the target's pocket. Requires Stealth.

Sap

Sap is a crowd control ability that is used from Stealth. This takes a Humanoid target out for combat for a very long duration. Unless specialized with Improved Sap, you will exit your stealthed mode.

Rank	Level	Energy	Cost to Train	Effects
1	10	65	3	Incapacitates the target for up to 25 seconds. Must be stealthed. Only works on Humanoids that are not in combat. Any damage caused will revive the target. Only 1 target may be sapped at a time.
2	28	65	80	Incapacitates the target for up to 35 seconds. Must be stealthed. Only works on Humanoids that are not in combat. Any damage caused will revive the target. Only 1 target may be sapped at a time.
3	48	65	3 30	Incapacitates the target for up to 25 seconds. Must be stealthed. Only works on Humanoids that are not in combat. Any damage caused will revive the target. Only 1 target may be sapped at a time.

Ghostly Strike

Ghostly Strike is a Talent-learned ability that deals immediate weapon + bonus damage, adds a Combo Point, and increases the Rogue's chance to Dodge by 15% for seven seconds.

Rank	Prerequisite	Effect
1	10 Points in Subtlety	A strike that deals 125% weapon damage and increases your chance to dodge by 15% for 7 seconds. Awards 1 combo point.

Distract

Distract causes all foes in the area to look towards the center of your target wheel.

Rank	Level	Energy	Cost to Train	Effects
N/A	22	30	40	Throws a distraction, attracting the attention of all nearby monsters for 10 seconds. Does not break stealth.

Vanish

Vanish breaks effects that impair movement and puts your Rogue immediately into a state of enhanced Stealth. This also removes all aggro from your Rogue, making Vanish useful for soloing, PvP, and PvE groups/raids.

Rank	Level	Energy	Cost to Train	Effects
1	22	—	40	Allows the rogue to vanish from sight, entering an improved stealth mode for 10 seconds. Also breaks movement impairing effects. Requires Flash Powder. 5 min cooldown.
2	42	—	2 43	Allows the rogue to vanish from sight, entering an improved stealth mode for 10 seconds. Also breaks movement impairing effects. Requires Flash Powder. 5 minute cooldown. More Effective than Vanish (Rank 1).

Detect Traps

Detect Traps is a passive ability that lets you spot both Hunter traps and various dungeon hazards.

Rank	Level	Energy	Cost to Train	Effects
N/A	24	—	50	Hidden traps will become visible for 3 minutes.

Disarm Traps

Disarm Trap is not used very often, but it works to disable traps that your Rogue has detected.

Rank	Level	Energy	Cost to Train	Effects
N/A	30	—	1	Sneak up on the trap in order to disarm it. Don't get too close or the trap will go off. Requires Detect Traps and Thieves' Tools.

Preparation

Preparation is a Talent-learned ability on a ten-minute cooldown. This immediately finishes the cooldown on all of your Rogue's abilities!

Rank	Minimum Level	Energy	Range	Cost to Train	Effects
1	30	—	—	—	When activated, this ability immediately finishes the cooldown on your other Rogue abilities. 10 min cooldown.

Blind

Blind is an ability on a five-minute timer that Disorients your target for up to ten seconds. However, any damage breaks the Blind effect.

Rank	Level	Energy	Cost to Train	Effects
N/A	34	30	1 40	Blinds the target, causing it to wander at 40% of move speed disoriented for up to 10 seconds. Any damage caused will remove the effect. Requires Blinding Powder. 5 minute cooldown.

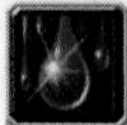

Hemorrhage

Hemorrhage is a Talent-learned ability, deep in the Subtlety line. This ability debuffs a target so that it takes more damage from melee strikes for the next 30 attacks from *all* melee characters attacking it.

Rank	Level	Energy	Cost to Train	Effects
2	46	35	77 50	An instant strike that damages the opponent and causes the target to hemorrhage, increasing any Physical damage dealt to the target by up to 5. Lasts 30 charges or 15 seconds. Awards 1 combo point.
3	58	35	1 30	An instant strike that damages the opponent and causes the target to hemorrhage, increasing any Physical damage dealt to the target by up to 7. Lasts 30 charges or 15 seconds. Awards 1 combo point.

Premeditation

Premeditation is a Talent-learned ability that adds two Combo Points to a target. The Combo Points must be used in the next 10 seconds or they are lost. This abilty is on a a two-minute cooldown.

Rank	Minimum Level	Energy	Range	Cost to Train	Effects
1	40	-10	15 yd	—	When used, adds 2 combo points to your target. The target must become engaged in combat within 10 sec or the combo points are lost. 2 min cooldown.

Safe Fall

Safe Fall passively reduces falling damage. This allows Rogues to jump from higher places without dying, though there is still an upper limit.

Rank	Level	Energy	Cost to Train	Effects
N/A	40	N/A	2	Reduces damage from falling.

Talents

Rogue Talents lines are all about damage and setting yourself up to do more damage. The pivotal points between these lines is to figure out when you *want* to deal said damage. Assassination brings better poison possibilities and hits VERY hard coming out of Stealth. Look here to have the best burst DPS early in a fight (including a move to start a fight with a critical Ambush at enhanced damage).

Combat Mastery puts its damage into a steady stream. Ignoring the short burst, the Combat line focuses on dealing its best damage over longer fights. Better weapon abilities, improvements to Dual-Wielding, and more efficient special attacks are here.

Subtlety is indeed a modest line for raw damage, but it reveals its strength through improvements to Stealth movement, anti-detection, reduced costs to several attacks, and better crowd control. This is not a soloers line; rather, Subtlety is for Rogues who want to engage in large amounts of scouting, PvP, and infiltration. Subtlety also brings the most utility for five-characters groups and raids.

Assassination

Assassination is filled with must-have treats for the damage dealers out there. Even specs that focus on groupability or damage over time are going to be happy taking a few of the early Assassination Talents. Malice is hard to live without for any Rogue build (free Crits left and right). Ruthlessness is a wonderful ability to maintaining momentum, in PvP and PvE; combine this with Relentless Strikes. Remorseless Attacks is fun while leveling, though certainly falls down in usefulness in the late-game. Murder and Improved Slice and Dice are excellent for Rogues of various specializations.

For Rogues who are in Assassination for the long haul, add Lethality for even higher burst damage, Cold Blood (an essential Talent for promising Crits on five-point Eviscerates or Ambush openers). Seal Fate and Vigor are icing on the cake, capping the Assassination line with even more frontloaded damage. You can't go wrong with these for PvP, and PvE DPS slots are still nicely filled with such Rogues.

Combat

Improved Sinister Strike starts off the Combat line, and things keep piling on the damage-over-time aspect from there. For sword users (and mace users as well), this is the tree for you. Always take Precision while leveling, as that extra 5% chance to hit is a massive boon; don't drop this Talent until your Rogue has high-end gear with 5-6% to Hit already.

Riposte offers both damage and mitigation in battle, especially for duels and soloing. Riposte has almost no Energy cost, deals high damage, and Disarms the opponent! Don't miss Dual Wield Specialization either, as this adds very consistent damage for low and high-end Rogues. Blade Flurry, like Riposte, is a must. Rogues are never going to be available for true AoE, but having a second target is a PvP boon, a soloing lifesaver, and can help a great deal in group PvE when your group is focused on blowing creatures down.

Sword Specialization is the most common selection for Rogues of this line. Using two swords means that a Rogue is going to proc very often (compared to dagger Rogues), and that the damage over time from this melee character is going to be immense. Sword Spec obviously enhances that! Grab Weapon Expertise to increase your weapon skills (and thus your chance to hit and make critical strikes). And if you are already in that deep, Aggression and Adrenaline Rush are must-haves as well. Adrenaline Rush alone allows a Combat Rogue to put 100% and more of their potential into a boss fight, and its timer is only a five-minute one; even in fast dungeon runs, this allows every boss fight to be a glorious moment.

Subtlety

Master of Deception is in the first tier of Subtlety, and it is immensely important in PvP and for group-friendly Rogues. Being able to wander around without nearly as wide a detection radius is essential for good Sap runs and for approaching flags on the Battlegrounds. When taken with Improved Sap, Subtlety Rogues become extremely useful for five-man dungeon runs in the mid and late game. These take the Rogue class from a moderate crowd control position and elevate them to a much higher tier.

Preparation is deep in the Subtlety line, but is allows for so many tricks. Better escapes, more damage, and many frustrated enemies are created with Prep. Doubled with Premeditation, at the end of the line, this allows Rogues to do some amazing bursts even without full Assassination Talents.

Opportunity and Improved Backstab help with raising the consistent damage level of this line, and Hemorrhage happily replaces Sinister Strike toward the later game. Serrated Blades increases your damage substantially against armored foes in both PvP and PvE and is much more useful than simply being the prerequisite for Hemorrhage.When there are substantial groups of melee attackers, this ability deals more than enough total damage to be worthwhile!

Ghostly Strike, while not being terribly efficient on its own, doubles well with Setup and heavier weaponry. It's always useful for Rogues to have sword and dagger weapon options, and Subtlety Rogues can happily enjoy the best of both worlds by Ambushing with their daggers then settling in for easy Combo Points with their swords.

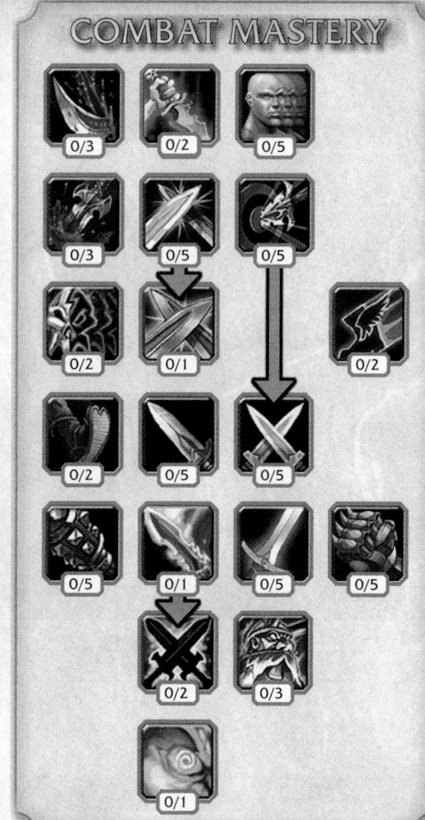

Druid
Hunter
Mage
Paladin
Priest
Rogue
Shaman
Warlock
Warrior

IMPROVED EVISCERATE 3

Increases the damage done by your Eviscerate ability by 5% (Per Rank)

REMORSELESS ATTACKS 2

Gives you a 20% damage bonus (Per Rank) on your next Sinister Strike, Backstab, Ambush, or Ghost Strike after killing an opponent

MALICE 5

Increases your critical strike chance by 1% (Per Rank)

RUTHLESSNESS 3

Gives your finishing moves a 20% chance (Per Rank) to add a combo point to your target

MURDER 2

Increases damage to Humanoid, Beasts, Giants, and Dragonkin by 2% (Per Rank)

IMPROVED SLICE AND DICE 3

Increases the duration of your Slice and Dice ability by 15% (Per Rank)

RELENTLESS STRIKES 1

Your finishing moves have a 20% chance per combo point to restore 25 energy

IMPROVED EXPOSE ARMOR 2

Increases the armor reduced by your Expose Armor ability by 15% (Per Rank)

LETHALITY 5

Increases the damage done by your critical strikes by 6% (Per Rank) when using the Sinister Strike, Gouge, Backstab, Ghost Strike and Hemorrhage ability.

VILE POISONS 5

Increases the damage dealt by your poisons by 4% and gives your poisons an 8% chance to resist dispel effects (Per Rank).

IMPROVED POISONS 5

Adds a 2% chance (Per Rank) to apply poisons to a target

IMPROVED KIDNEY SHOT 3

While affected by your Kidney Shot ability, the target receives an additional 3% damage (Per Rank) from all sources

COLD BLOOD 1

Instant cast—3 min cooldown—When activated, your next Sinister Strike, Backstab, Ambush or Eviscerate is guaranteed a critical strike.

SEAL FATE 5

You have a 20% chance (Per Rank) to add an extra combo point when you critical with abilities that add combo points

VIGOR 1

Increases your maximum Energy by 10

IMPROVED GOUGE 3

Increases the effect duration of your Gouge ability by 0.5 secs (Per Rank)

IMPROVED SINISTER STRIKE 2

Reduces the Energy cost of your Sinister Strike ability by 3 - Progression: 3/5

LIGHTNING REFLEXES 5

Increases your Dodge chance by 1% (Per Rank)

IMPROVED BACKSTAB 3

Increases the critical strike chance of your Backstab ability by 10% (Per Rank)

DEFLECTION 5

Increases your Parry chance by 1% (Per Rank)

PRECISION 5

Increases your chance to hit with melee weapons by 1% (Per Rank)

ENDURANCE 2

Reduces the cooldown of your Sprint and Evasion abilities by 45 seconds (Per Rank)

RIPOSTE 1

This Instant ability is usable after a Parry; it deals 150% weapon damage and disarms the enemy for six seconds

IMPROVED SPRINT 3

Gives you a 50% chance (Per Rank) to remove all movement impairing affects

IMPROVED KICK 2

Adds a 50% chance (Per Rank) that your target also becomes Silenced for 2 seconds after being kicked

DAGGER SPECIALIZATION 5

Increases your chance to get a critical strike with Daggers by 1% (Per Rank)

DUAL WIELD SPECIALIZATION 5

Increases the damage done by your offhand weapon by 10% (Per Rank)

MACE SPECIALIZATION 5

Improves your Mace skill by 1 (Per Rank) and adds a 1% (Per Rank) chance to stun on a strike.

BLADE FLURRY 1

25 Energy, Instant cast, 5 min Cooldown, Req melee weapon- Increases your attack speed by 20%. In addition your normal melee weapon swings strike an additional nearby opponent. Lasts 15 sec.

SWORD SPECIALIZATION 5

Increases your chance to get an extra swing with Swords by 1%—Progression: 1%/2%/3%/4%/6%

FIST WEAPON SPECIALIZATION 5

Increases your chance to get a critical strike with Fist Weapons by 1% (Per Rank)

WEAPON EXPERTISE 2

Increases your skill with Swords, Fists, and Daggers—Progression: 3%/5%

AGGRESSION 3

Increases damage done by Sinister Stike and Eviscerate by 2% (Per Rank)

ADRENALINE RUSH 1

Instant cast 6 min cooldown; doubles your Energy regeneration rate for 15 seconds

MASTER OF DECEPTION 5

Improves your ability to avoid detection with each Rank

OPPORTUNITY 5

Increases the damage dealt when striking from behind with your Backstab, Garrote or Ambush abilities by 4% (Per Rank)

SLEIGHT OF HAND 2

Reduces the chance of being critically struck by ranged and melee attacks by 1% (Per Rank) and increases the threat reduction of Feint by 10% (Per Rank)

ELUSIVENESS 2

Reduces the cooldown of your Vanish, and Blind abilities by 45 sec (Per Rank)

CAMOUFLAGE 5

Increases your speed while Stealthed by 3% (Per Rank) and your cooldown by 1 second (Per Rank)

INITIATIVE 3

Gives you a 25% chance (Per Rank) to add an additional combo point to your target when using your Ambush, Garrote or Cheap Shot ability.

GHOSTLY STRIKE 1

40 Energy Instant Cast 20 sec cooldown 7yd range—A strike that deals 125%weapon damage and increases your chance to dodge by 15% for 5 sec. Awards 1 combo point.

IMPROVED AMBUSH 3

Increases the critical strike chance of your Ambush ability by 15% - ProgressionL 15%/30%/40%

SETUP 3

Gives you a 15% chance (Per Rank) to add a Combo Point to your target after dodging their attack.

IMPROVED SAP 3

Gives you a 30% chance (Per Rank) to return to Stealth mode after using your Sap ability.

SERRATED BLADES 3

Ignore an amount of Armor/Level—Progression: 1.67/3.34/5.00—and increases the damage done by Rupture by 10% (Per Rank)

HEIGHTENED SENSES 2

Increases your Stealth detection and reduces the chance you are hit by spells and ranged attacks by 1% (Per Rank)

PREPARATION 1

Instant cast- 10 min cooldown When activated, this ability immediately finishes the cooldown on your other Rogue abilities.

DIRTY DEEDS 2

Reduces the cost of Cheap Shot and Garrote by 10 (Per Rank) (Per Rank)

HEMORRHAGE 1

Engages an Instant strike that that adds a combo point and a debuff that increases melee damage to that target by 3 for 30 hits or 15 seconds

DEADLINESS 5

Increases your Attack Power by 2% (Per Rank)

PREMEDITATION 1

10 Energy, 1 sec cast, 2 min cooldown, 7 yd range- When used, adds 2 combo points to your target.

STRATEGIES

Rogue strategies rely heavily on the Talent line that they favor, but there are some tricks that are universal to the class. Many of these can be mastered early in a Rogue's career, allowing them to break out from the central mold as they grow.

Poisons

Carry around several poisons to use for varying situations. Crippling Poison is only useful if you don't have a class nearby to help Snare enemies in PvE (though it is *always* a wise choice in PvP). Mind-Numbing Poison really helps against casters (and is only surpassed if you have a Warlock in your party to sit on them instead). Instant Poison knocks down targets in short fights. Deadly Poison is the king of longer fights with its higher chance to activate and stacking (very nice to keep on an offhand weapon).

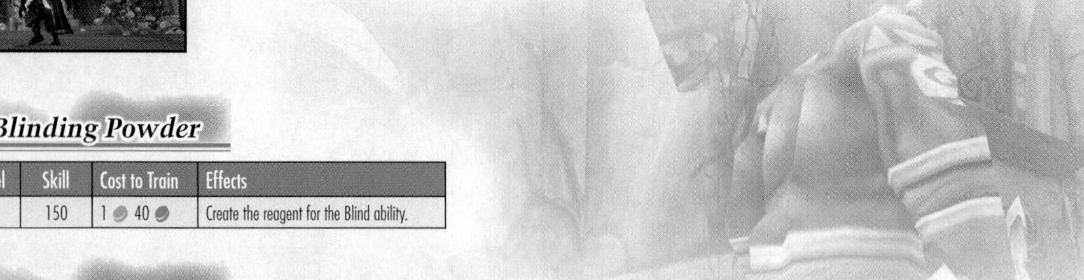

Blinding Powder

Rank	Level	Skill	Cost to Train	Effects
N/A	34	150	1 40	Create the reagent for the Blind ability.

Crippling Poison

Rank	Level	Skill	Cost to Train	Effects
1	20	1	30	Coats a weapon with poison that lasts for 30 minutes. Each strike as a 30% chance of poisoning the enemy, slowing their movement speed to 50% of normal for 12 seconds.
2	50	230	3 50	Coats a weapon with poison that lasts for 30 minutes. Each strike as a 30% chance of poisoning the enemy, slowing their movement speed to 30% of normal for 12 seconds.

Deadly Poison

Rank	Level	Skill	Cost to Train	Effects
1	30	130	1	Coats a weapon with a poison that lasts 30 minutes. Each strike has a 30% chance of poisoning the enemy for 40-44 Nature damage over 12 seconds. Stacks up to 5 times on a single target. 60 charges.
2	38	170	1 80	Coats a weapon with a poison that lasts 30 minutes. Each strike has a 30% chance of poisoning the enemy for 56-60 Nature damage over 12 seconds. Stacks up to 5 times on a single target. 75 charges.
3	46	210	3 10	Coats a weapon with a poison that lasts 30 minutes. Each strike has a 30% chance of poisoning the enemy for 92 Nature damage over 12 seconds. Stacks up to 5 times on a single target. 90 charges.
4	54	250	4 80	Coats a weapon with a poison that lasts 30 minutes. Each strike has a 30% chance of poisoning the enemy for 124-128 Nature damage over 12 seconds. Stacks up to 5 times on a single target. 105 charges.
5	60	275	—	Coats a weapon with poison that lasts for 30 minutes. Each strike has a 30% chance of poisoning the enemy for 136 Nature Damage over 12 sec. Stacks up to 5 times on a single target. 105 charges.

Instant Poison

Rank	Level	Skill	Cost to Train	Effects
1	20	1	—	Coats a weapon with poison that lasts 30 minutes. Each strike has a 20% chance of poisoning the enemy which instantly inflicts 21-29 Nature damage. 55 charges.
2	28	120	80	Coats a weapon with poison that lasts 30 minutes. Each strike has a 20% chance of poisoning the enemy which instantly inflicts 34-44 Nature damage. 55 charges.
3	36	160	1 60	Coats a weapon with poison that lasts 30 minutes. Each strike has a 20% chance of poisoning the enemy which instantly inflicts 50-65 Nature damage. 70 charges.
4	44	200	2 90	Coats a weapon with poison that lasts 30 minutes. Each strike has a 20% chance of poisoning the enemy which instantly inflicts 77-98 Nature damage. 85 charges.
5	52	240	4 60	Coats a weapon with poison that lasts 30 minutes. Each strike has a 20% chance of poisoning the enemy which instantly inflicts 105-136 Nature damage. 100 charges.
6	60	280	5 40	Coats a weapon with poison that lasts 30 minutes. Each strike has a 20% chance of poisoning the enemy which instantly inflicts 128-171 Nature damage. 115 charges.

Mind-Numbing Poison

Rank	Level	Skill	Cost to Train	Effects
1	24	100	50	Coats a weapon with a poison that lasts for 30 minutes. Each strike has a 20% chance of poisoning the enemy, increasing their casting time by 40% for 10 seconds. 50 charges.
2	38	170	1 80	Coats a weapon with a poison that lasts for 30 minutes. Each strike has a 20% chance of poisoning the enemy, increasing their casting time by 50% for 12 seconds. 75 charges.
3	52	240	4 60	Coats a weapon with a poison that lasts for 30 minutes. Each strike has a 20% chance of poisoning the enemy, increasing their casting time by 60% for 14 seconds. 100 charges.

Wound Poison

Rank	Level	Skill	Cost to Train	Effects
1	32	140	1 20	Coats a weapon with a poison that lasts for 30 minutes. Each strike has a 30% chance of poisoning the enemy, reducing all healing effects used on them by 55 for 15 seconds. Stacks up to 5 times on a single target. 60 charges.
2	40	180	2	Coats a weapon with a poison that lasts for 30 minutes. Each strike has a 30% chance of poisoning the enemy, reducing all healing effects used on them by 75 for 15 seconds. Stacks up to 5 times on a single target. 60 charges.
3	48	220	3 30	Coats a weapon with a poison that lasts for 30 minutes. Each strike has a 30% chance of poisoning the enemy, reducing all healing effects used on them by 105 for 15 seconds. Stacks up to 5 times on a single target. 60 charges.
4	56	260	5	Coats a weapon with a poison that lasts for 30 minutes. Each strike has a 30% chance of poisoning the enemy, reducing all healing effects used on them by 135 for 15 seconds. Stacks up to 5 times on a single target. 60 charges.

Money!

Rogues have to spend piles of money on weapons, slightly better armor, enchantments, poisons, and potions. Add to this food needs and the lost income of keeping cloth (for First Aid) instead of selling it, and Rogues seem very poor. Luckily, this doesn't end up being too bad if you know what you are doing. After all, Rogues kill at a wonderful rate, and that brings in the money even faster than it leaves.

Skinning, if taken, offers one route to greater cash. After even a short time, Skinning shines as a way to make considerable funds, especially when materials are sold through the Auction House instead of vendored. The other gathering crafts are not able to increase their rates very well (you can only find so many herbs in a region, and you can only mine so many veins before having to travel and wait). Skinning, however, benefits heavily from a high killrate.

Pick Pocketing Humanoid monsters is a good way to find extra items that vendor well. Beyond that, there are sometimes higher-quality items on these creatures, so this is a skill worthy of using often. Humanoid monsters are already a fairly good source of income, since they drop money and cloth in the first place; combining this with Pick Pocketing is a pleasant boost. If you are already planning on using Cheap Shot or Ambush to open, it doesn't even take much extra time to use Pick Pockets (though this does slow leveling slightly).

Rogues blow through lower-level dungeons without taking much time. This makes them a powerful class for finding bind-on-equip rare items to sell on the Auction House. Take Enchanting, break the bind-on-pickup items to sell on the Auction House for other Enchanters. Between these two actions, your Rogue is likely to be rolling in the money.

Slapping on Combo Points

Many Rogue builds, regardless of Talents, use combo points heavily. These are required for all finishing moves, whether you are trying to score damage, reduce enemy armor, or keep those fiends out of commission as long as possible.

Use moves like Sinister Strike and Hemorrhage for fast accrual of Combo Points. Sinister Strike can be used well with swords to deal high damage while working toward potent Eviscerates. To stay low in profile, Hemorrhage raises group damage against a foe, costs less, and still provides that needed Combo Point.

For fights where winning is more important than speed, remember to use Gouge and wait for its full timer before attacking again. This gives you a free Combo Point, and it frustrates the heck out of PvP enemies.

Stealth

Stealth is both offensive and defensive in nature, depending on who is creeping out in the bushes. Defensively, Stealth takes you away from harm by keeping your Rogue hidden from monsters and dangerous players. At longer range, things simply won't be able to see you; this exact distance of this varies tremendously, so it's wise to test often to get a feel for your "safe" range.

What Control Stealth Detection Ranges?	
[li]	Level Differences Between the Rogue and the Viewer
[li]	Line of Sight (Creatures Don't "See" Behind Themselves)
[li]	Monster/Character Type (Hunters and Certain Monsters Detect Stealthers at Longer Range)
[li]	Talents (i.e. Master of Deception)
[li]	Gear (i.e. Nightscape Boots)

Be wary of approaching targets that are higher-level than you without getting well behind them first. If you stand in a target's line-of-sight, it takes *much* higher Subtlety to stay hidden. Once revealed, you are a sitting duck (free to spells, abilities, ranged weapons, and general monster aggro). Use Distract to keep things from looking your way.

The Best Targets

The best targets are found in enemies who die quickly. This is true for almost everyone, but Rogues have the ability to take many foes down quickly if the enemy has light armor. Using high DPS to its fullest, the Rogue can do so much damage that few enemies can ramp up to their full capabilities. Some may even die before getting to attack (ouch)!

Part of this rests in going after lower-level targets when you are grinding for experience. Anything of higher level is going to keep you missing a moderate amount of the time, and this is a *very* bad thing for a Rogue (you can't afford to whiff on those early attacks). Stick to enemies a level or two beneath you and go through them at maximum speed.

Anything that isn't wearing heavy armor is a good target, but PvE casters are the best. Don't forget to save Energy for a Kick to disrupt casting. Add Gouge to that for a secondary interrupt, and things are sounding even better. Though Mind Numbing Poison looks great on paper for these fights, it's really unimportant for most PvP and PvE uses, considering that Rogues are already the interruption kings and queens.

Wait a moment before interrupting slow spells; get in an extra slice or two before using your abilities (this effectively "wastes" the caster's time with a spell that is going to fail anyway). This also ensures that you don't waste an interrupt on an ability that is instant but has a visual component.

Adds are very bad for Rogues because of the low damage tolerance this class displays. That is another reason that Rogues love to solo enemies slightly beneath their level. When enemies are paired or too close to avoid adds, use Stealth, Sap one target, then kill the other first. Sap provides a considerable window for bringing down foes in solo and group environments.

Vanish and Feint, You Crazy Fiend!

Many Rogues, especially those that PvP often, are used to doing as much damage as they can. In a group setting, that isn't always a good idea. Warriors can hold a *great deal* of aggro, but not in the first few moments of a battle. When dealing damage early in a boss fight or an otherwise major encounter, use Feint to keep the target's attention off of your Rogue. If you get way too much aggro (e.g. Sword Spec just procced six times, yikes!!!), Vanish immediately. This clears that dreaded aggro and lets your Warrior keep up the fun. Another good idea is to wait...yes, wait! A mob with three Sunders on it *rarely* leaves the warrior.

Do not go after secondary targets either. For some reason, quite a few Rogues see themselves as backup tanks. This is only true when all of your timers are being used. As a last-ditch effort, Evasion is a good way for Rogues to dodge-tank an add and keep a healer alive. Just wait and only do this when the group is in *real* trouble. If there is an offtank already, such as a Fury Warrior, let them pull adds off of healers. You kill; you don't tank. Leather doesn't rhyme with cloth, but in your case, maybe it should. Rogues die quickly, and poorly played Rogues die often.

For the longer explanation of why Rogues must not get aggro, think about the reason why you would pull a creature off of a healer; to save them from the aggro, right? But you won't. As you begin to tank the creature, the healer needs to start healing you. That puts the aggro right back on them, and thus the chain continues with the creature bouncing back and forth while you and the healer rise on its Threat list. Meanwhile, the Warrior cries.

What you can do, and this is fun stuff, is to Disorient, Stun, Blind, and otherwise mess with monsters that peel off of the tank. Blind or Gouge such a foe and leave it be. Vanish and Cheapshot. Don't DPS things that are uncontrolled, but trying to disable them until the Warrior has time to reestablish aggro is absolutely fine.

Shaman

Shaman invoke the powers of air, earth, fire, and water to increase their melee effectiveness, attack at range, aid themselves and teammates, hinder enemies, and heal. This plethora of abilities make them a very solid choice for the solo player while still being a respectable choice for the more social. The array of spells is confusing at first, but given practice, the Shaman can fulfill nearly any open spot in a group and be quite a devastating opponent.

Lore

I asked the Earthmother for strength as I looked over the bodies of the fallen Tauren, dwarves, and Goblins. A tremendous battle between the fair people of Bloodhoof Village and the defilers of Venture Company had taken place near some of the eastern mines. I was returning to Thunder Bluff at the time, but I heard of the battle from several young Warriors who were resting, hoping to make another run at the remaining Venture Company workers.

I had gone to the mines alone, seething with anger, and now the dead were my only companions. Begging the grace of the spirits of the world, I brought the Tauren back to themselves and bid them leave. "Return later and cleanse the place of any foulness that remains," I spoke. They must have seen something in my eyes, for it is rarely the place of our people to walk away when the land is ravaged, but they obeyed by order, still shaken from the return to their bodies.

I gripped by axe and shield tightly and ran into the mines. The workers of the Venture Company looked far less than beasts to me; given the gift of thought and will, yet choosing to twist it against the earth. At first I fought like a brave Warrior, blocking their attacks and hacking into flesh and bone with the strength of my arms. Yet more of the workers came, and their supervisors followed. Though tested by hundreds of battles, I was not immune to their push. I threw down a Totem of Stoneskin and felt my body harden against the enemy's blows.

Their push failed and I had a moment's respite. I used this time to heal my wounds and charge my weapon with the power of Rock! The next Goblin who came forward was bitten foully by my axe's swing and fell to the ground. Still more followed, and I felt that my anger had gotten me into a place from which I could no longer retreat. If this was my death, so be it, but the mine would be cleared of its darkness.

Then, as I saw at least six more enemies come out from the final room of the mines, I heard steps behind me and knew that I would be lost if they were Venture Company reinforcements. Yet, it was my people. They had ignored my words after all; bellowing like a storm, they crashed into the room and devoured the Goblins with fast and ferocious swings. When all was done, the mine was clear. The younger Tauren searched the bodies of the Goblins and found whatever they sought. They seemed happy to be alive, and honored to have saved a small corner of our land from harm.

I too was warmed by our victory. There is a greater joy in serving the world; it was too bad the people of Venture Company had turned their eyes from such beauty.

Introduction to Playing the Class

These spiritual leaders have a bond with the world. It's different from that of the Druid in that Shaman call power from the four elements. Air, earth, fire, and water answer the call of the Shaman through spells and totems.

Some of the Shaman's greatest power rests in their totems. While only being able to use one totem of each elemental type (these are gained through quests as you progress) at a time, the Shaman has many options for each totem. Knowing which totem to use takes practice and can make the life of yourself and your group easier.

As one of the few classes that can heal themselves and others, Shaman are often called upon to group with the more martial and mystic classes and keep them alive. This is something the Shaman does well, but it's not all they do.

Starting with Leather armor and progressing to Mail at Level 40, Shaman aren't fragile. They can carry shields as well and this makes them quite hearty. With an enchant on their weapon, enemies aren't going to find a soft and squishy healer if they engage a Shaman.

Many of the spells Shaman gain, allow them to live through quite a lot. Surviving the attention of a monster or two for a short time is very easy, while lasting through a long fight is more trying. They work well as tanks in the lower levels, but should avoid the role as the enemies become more difficult.

Shaman work best when helping others. They can heal melee classes and buff casters with totems. With their damage from melee or spells, they aid parties in defeating enemies. Knowing which task to take on when takes practice, but mastering it makes you a sought after addition to any party.

Available Races	
Orc	Tauren
Troll	

What do Attributes Mean to Me?	
Strength	Increases Damage Done in Melee and Damage Blocked by Shield
Stamina	Higher Health
Agility	Raises Chance to Get a Critical Hit and Dodge
Intellect	More Mana, Better Chance for Critical Hits with Spells Faster Learning of Skills
Spirit	Improves Health and Mana Recovery

Items and Equipment

Shaman have plenty of needs when it comes to equipment. Because Shaman are so versatile, they need gear that holds up to many tests. High armor, a good shield, substantial DPS from a relatively fast weapon, and multiple attribute bonuses are desirable. Simply put, keeping your equipment up-to-date is going to take most of your time and money.

For melee, a good shield and solid armor pieces make a huge difference. Because Shaman are limited to Leather armor during the lower levels, it's hard to survive major aggro (this improves later on by learning to wear Mail at level 40). The good news is that it isn't hard to find attributes you need; the bad news is that you need almost everything.

Strength and Agility are useful, but they are secondary to Intellect, Stamina, and Spirit. Work on getting the best bonuses in your three primary stats while leveling and try not to focus too much on which of the three you are getting from a given item (just look for the best total bonuses to the three and let that guide you in item selection). Later on, you have more leeway to decide which direction to focus on. Stamina is incredibly useful for melee-centered and soloing Shaman. Intellect saves groups on a daily basis, and Spirit builds are fun for grinding and evading downtime.

While Shaman can use Staves, this removes your ability to wield a shield. Take a careful look at the weapons. If you are going to have the monster's attention, shield and one-hand weapon are a more sensible combination. If you are grouped with someone who has the monster's attention choose the weapon that gives you the highest damage (if you want to attack the enemy directly) or better stats (if you want to stand back and heal the party). Weapons can be switched in battle and should be if an events change your role in a group.

A Large Wardrobe

As Shaman can fill so many different roles, they tend to develop at least two different suits of equipment.

For soloing or backup tanking, they often have a high Stamina and Armor suit while for healing they tend to have a high Intellect suit with bonuses to healing spells.

This may sound expensive at first (and it is), don't look to buy two sets of equipment. Instead watch for item upgrades that can be useful in either capacity and dedicate a bank bag to holding the suit you aren't wearing.

CHOOSING YOUR PROFESSION

Alchemy and Herbalism are very good professions for a Shaman. Having constant access to attribute buffs, extra defense, and a supply of Health/Mana potions can shore up any weak side to your character. As Shaman are dependant on all attributes, they also use a wider variety of potions and thus can get much more from them then most classes.

For a first-time character, Skinning and Leatherworking are also good choices. Being able to craft your own armor keeps you from falling behind and allows you to use more of your money to keep your weapon up-to-date. At higher levels, when you learn to wear Mail armor, choosing the Dragonscale Leatherworking specialty allows you to continue making useful armor for yourself.

If you already have friends who are heavily into Alchemy and you aren't worried about making your own armor, Enchanting is a great profession to master. Being able to customize your equipment without the massive expense of going to other players can help direct your finances toward higher-end gear and allow you to keep gear slightly longer as the bonuses your enchanting give make it take longer to become outdated.

At first, secondary skills don't seem to come into play as often with a Shaman as they do with non-magic classes. Having the ability to heal makes First Aid and Cooking a bit less impressive, but you will often find your mana doesn't stretch as far as you want. Cooking can increase both Stamina and Spirit which is advantageous. First Aid allows you to heal yourself between fights while allowing your mana to regenerate. These combined can drastically reduce your downtime and have you fighting much quicker.

Class Abilities

All of a Shaman's abilities are tied to their mana. Shaman live or die depending on whether or not they have mana. Because mana regenerates faster when you aren't casting, use your abilities in bursts and allow time to pass between these bursts to regain mana. This isn't always possible, but should be done whenever the opportunity arises.

With very different abilities to use based on whether you are alone or with a group, keeping your quickbars optimized makes you more effective and your gameplay more enjoyable. No one wants to be searching their quickbars for a spell while in combat. Keep your totems clumped together by type of fight and on a separate bar since you won't always use them. Keep your damage spells together, and your healing and dispelling spells together. This leads to clean ability use (rely on the keyboard for faster functionality instead of mouse-clicking).

Elemental Combat

Elemental Mastery

Rank	Prerequisites	Effect
1	1 Point in Elemental Fury, 30 Points in Elemental	When activated, this spell gives your next Fire, Frost, or Nature damage spell a 100% critical strike chance and reduces the mana cost by 100%.

Earth Shock

Earth Shock has two primary uses. It's fast Nature damage for a lot of mana and is useful in fights against enemies that hit very hard. Its second use is as a ranged interrupt.

Rank	Level	Mana	Range	Casting Time	Cooldown	Cost To Train	Effect
1	4	30	20 yd	IC	6 seconds	1	Instantly shocks the target with concussive force, causing 19 to 22 Nature damage. It also interrupts spellcasting and prevents any spell in that school from being cast for 2 sec. Causes a high amount of threat.
2	8	50	20 yd	IC	6 seconds	1	Instantly shocks the target with concussive force, causing 35 to 38 Nature damage. It also interrupts spellcasting and prevents any spell in that school from being cast for 2 sec. Causes a high amount of threat.
3	14	85	20 yd	IC	6 seconds	9	Instantly shocks the target with concussive force, causing 60 to 65 Nature damage. It also interrupts spellcasting and prevents any spell in that school from being cast for 2 sec. Causes a high amount of threat.
4	24	145	20 yd	IC	6 seconds	35	Instantly shocks the target with concussive force, causing 126 to 134 Nature damage. It also interrupts spellcasting and prevents any spell in that school from being cast for 2 sec. Causes a high amount of threat.
5	36	240	20 yd	IC	6 seconds	1	Instantly shocks the target with concussive force, causing 235 to 249 Nature damage. It also interrupts spellcasting and prevents any spell in that school from being cast for 2 sec. Causes a high amount of threat.
6	48	345	20 yd	IC	6 seconds	2 20	Instantly shocks the target with concussive force, causing 372 to 394 Nature damage. It also interrupts spellcasting and prevents any spell in that school from being cast for 2 sec. Causes a high amount of threat.
7	60	405	20 yd	IC	6 seconds	3 40	Instantly shocks the target with concussive force, causing 517 to 545 Nature damage. It also interrupts spellcasting and prevents any spell in that school from being cast for 2 sec. Causes a high amount of threat.

Earthbind Totem

Earthbind Totem snares multiple enemies if they are near the totem.

Rank	Level	Mana	Range	Casting Time	Cooldown	Cost To Train	Effect
1	12	84	—	IC	15 seconds	1	Summons an Earthbind Totem with 5 health at the feet of the caster for 45 sec that slows the movement speed of enemies with 10 yards.

Lighting Bolt

Lightning Bolt is a single target, ranged, Nature spell.

Rank	Level	Mana	Range	Casting Time	Cooldown	Cost To Train	Effect
1	1	15	30 yd	1.5 sec	—	—	Casts a bolt of lightning at the target for 15 to 17 Nature damage.
2	8	30	30 yd	2 sec	—	1	Casts a bolt of lightning at the target for 28 to 33 Nature damage.
3	14	45	30 yd	2.5 sec	—	9	Casts a bolt of lightning at the target for 48 to 57 Nature damage.
4	20	75	30 yd	3 sec	—	22	Casts a bolt of lightning at the target for 88 to 100 Nature damage.
5	26	105	30 yd	3 sec	—	40	Casts a bolt of lightning at the target for 131 to 149 Nature damage.
6	32	135	30 yd	3 sec	—	80	Casts a bolt of lightning at the target for 172 to 194 damage.
7	38	165	30 yd	3 sec	—	1 10	Casts a bolt of lightning at the target for 235 to 264 Nature damage.
8	44	195	30 yd	3 sec	—	1 80	Casts a bolt of lightning at the target for 291 to 326 Nature damage.
9	50	230	30 yd	3 sec	—	2 40	Casts a bolt of lightning at the target for 357 to 400 damage.
10	56	265	30 yd	3 sec	—	3	Casts a bolt of lightning at the target for 419 to 467 Nature damage.

Stoneclaw Totem

Stoneclaw Totem is very useful when too many enemies are attacking you. It's an area of effect taunting totem.

Rank	Level	Mana	Range	Casting Time	Cooldown	Cost To Train	Effect
1	8	15	—	IC	30 seconds	1 ●	Summons a Stoneclaw Totem with 65 health at the feet of the caster for 15 sec that taunts creatures within 8 yards to attack it.
2	18	30	—	IC	30 seconds	20 ●	Summons a Stoneclaw Totem with 150 health at the feet of the caster for 15 sec that taunts creatures within 8 yards to attack it.
3	28	55	—	IC	30 seconds	60 ●	Summons a Stoneclaw Totem with 220 health at the feet of the caster for 15 sec that taunts creatures within 8 yards to attack it.
4	38	75	—	IC	30 seconds	1 ● 10 ●	Summons a Stoneclaw Totem with 280 health at the feet of the caster for 15 sec that taunts creatures within 8 yards to attack it.
5	48	105	—	IC	30 seconds	2 ● 20 ●	Summons a Stoneclaw Totem with 390 health at the feet of the caster for 15 sec that taunts creatures within 8 yards to attack it.
6	58	140	—	IC	30 seconds	3 ● 20 ●	Summons a Stoneclaw Totem with 480 health at the feet of the caster for 15 sec that taunts creatures within 8 yards to attack it.

Flame Shock

Flame Shock, like Earth Shock, has two primary abilities. It's instant Fire damage and causes Fire damage over time.

Rank	Level	Mana	Range	Casting Time	Cooldown	Cost To Train	Effect
1	10	55	20 yd	IC	6 seconds	4 ●	Instantly sears the target with fire, causing 25 Fire damage immediately and 28 Fire damage over 12 sec.
2	18	95	20 yd	IC	6 seconds	20 ●	Instantly sears the target with fire, causing 51 Fire damage immediately and 48 Fire damage over 12 sec.
3	28	160	20 yd	IC	6 seconds	60 ●	Instantly sears the target with fire, causing 94 to 95 Fire damage immediately and 96 Fire damage over 12 sec.
4	40	250	20 yd	IC	6 seconds	1 ● 20 ●	Instantly sears the target with fire, causing 163 to 164 Fire damage immediately and 168 Fire damage over 12 sec.
5	52	345	20 yd	IC	6 seconds	2 ● 70 ●	Instantly sears the target with fire, causing 241 to 242 Fire damage immediately and 256 Fire damage over 12 sec.

Fire Nova Totem

Fire Nova Totem doesn't do anything when you first put it down, but somehow it annoys everything in the area. Have solid aggro before using this totem and hold the enemies for the four seconds it takes to blast all enemies close by with Fire damage or it just isn't worth it.

Rank	Level	Mana	Range	Casting Time	Cooldown	Cost To Train	Effect
1	12	95	—	IC	15 seconds	8 ●	Summons a Fire Nova Totem that has 5 health and lasts 5 sec. Unless it is destroyed within 4 sec., the totem inflicts 53 to 62 fire damage to enemies within 10 yd.
2	22	151	—	IC	15 seconds	30[sp]	Summons a Fire Nova Totem that has 5 health and lasts 5 sec. Unless it is destroyed within 4 sec., the totem inflicts 110 to 124 fire damage to enemies within 10 yd.
3	32	266	—	IC	15 seconds	80 ●	Summons a Fire Nova Totem that has 5 health and lasts 5 sec. Unless it is destroyed within 4 sec., the totem inflicts 195 to 219 fire damage to enemies within 10 yd.
4	42	375	—	IC	15 seconds	1 ● 60 ●	Summons a Fire Nova Totem that has 5 health and lasts 5 sec. Unless it is destroyed within 4 sec., the totem inflicts 295 to 331 fire damage to enemies within 10 yd.
5	52	520	—	IC	15 seconds	2 ● 70 ●	Summons a Fire Nova Totem that has 5 health and lasts 5 sec. Unless it is destroyed within 4 sec., the totem inflicts 409 to 456 fire damage to enemies within 10 yd.

Purge

Purge removes beneficial magic effects from an enemy. It's instant and can be used while moving.

Rank	Level	Mana	Range	Casting Time	Cooldown	Cost To Train	Effect
1	12	10% of base	30 yd	IC	—	8 ●	Purges the enemy target, removing 1 magic effect.
2	32	10% of base	30 yd	IC	—	80 ●	Purges the enemy target, removing 2 magic effects.

Searing Totem

Searing Totem is the only single target damage totem you have. It tends to pick its target fairly randomly.

Rank	Level	Mana	Range	Casting Time	Cooldown	Cost To Train	Effect
1	10	25	—	IC	—	—	Summons a Searing Totem with 5 health at your feet for 30 sec that repeatedly attacks an enemy within 20 yds for 9 to 11 Fire damage.
2	20	45	—	IC	—	22 ●	Summons a Searing Totem with 5 health at your feet for 35 sec that attacks an enemy within 20 yards for 13 to 17 Fire damage.
3	30	75	—	IC	—	70 ●	Summons a Searing Totem with 5 health at your feet for 40 sec that attacks an enemy within 20 yards for 19 to 25 Fire damage.
4	40	110	—	IC	—	1 ● 20 ●	Summons a Searing Totem with 5 health at your feet for 45 sec that attacks an enemy within 20 yards for 26 to 34 Fire damage.
5	50	145	—	IC	—	2 ● 40 ●	Summons a Searing Totem with 5 health at your feet for 50 sec that attacks an enemy within 20 yards for 33 to 45 Fire damage.
6	60	170	—	IC	—	3 ● 40 ●	Summons a Searing Totem with 5 health at your feet for 55 sec that attacks an enemy within 20 yards for 40 to 54 Fire damage.

Frost Shock

Frost Shock, like the other shock spells, has two components. The first is instant damage. The second component reduces the target's movement rate for eight seconds.

Rank	Level	Mana	Range	Casting Time	Cooldown	Cost To Train	Effect
1	20	115	20 yd	IC	6 seconds	22 ●	Instantly shocks the target with frost, causing 95 to 101 Frost damage and slowing movement speed to 50% of normal. Lasts 8 sec.
2	34	225	20 yd	IC	6 seconds	90 ●	Instantly shocks the target with frost, causing 215 to 230 Frost damage and slowing movement speed to 50% of normal. Lasts 8 sec.
3	46	325	20 yd	IC	6 seconds	2 ●	Instantly shocks the target with frost, causing 345 to 366 Frost damage and slowing movement speed to 50% of normal. Lasts 8 sec.
4	58	430	20 yd	IC	6 seconds	3 ● 20 ●	Instantly shocks the target with frost, causing 486 to 514 Frost damage and slowing movement speed to 50% of normal. Lasts 8 sec.

Magma Totem

Magma Totem is a fairly reliable AoE Fire damage totem. It tends to live longer than Fire Nova Totem since enemies don't target it as quickly.

Rank	Level	Mana	Range	Casting Time	Cooldown	Cost To Train	Effect
1	26	230	—	IC	—	40 ●	Summons a Magma Totem with 5 health at the feet of the caster for 20 sec that causes 22 Fire damage to creatures within 8 yards every 2 seconds.
2	36	360	—	IC	—	1 ●	Summons a Magma Totem with 5 health at the feet of the caster for 20 sec that causes 37 Fire damage to creatures within 8 yards every 2 seconds.
3	46	500	—	IC	—	2 ●	Summons a Magma Totem with 5 health at the feet of the caster for 20 sec that causes 54 Fire damage to creatures within 8 yards every 2 seconds.
4	56	650	—	IC	—	3 ●	Summons a Magma Totem with 5 health at the feet of the caster for 20 sec that causes 75 Fire damage to creatures within 8 yards every 2 seconds.

Chain Lightning

Chain Lightning has a short cast time then Lightning Bolt, but costs more and has a cooldown.

Rank	Level	Mana	Range	Casting Time	Cooldown	Cost To Train	Effect
1	32	280	30 yd	2.5 sec	6 seconds	80	Hurls a lightning bolt at the enemy, dealing 220 to 227 nature damage and then jumping to additional nearby enemies. Each jump reduces the damage by 30%. Affects 3 total targets.
2	40	380	30 yd	2.5 sec	6 seconds	1 20	Hurls a lightning bolt at the enemy, dealing 288 to 323 nature damage and then jumping to additional nearby enemies. Each jump reduces the damage by 30%. Affects 3 total targets.
3	48	490	30 yd	2.5 sec	6 seconds	2 20	Hurls a lightning bolt at the enemy, dealing 391 to 438 nature damage and then jumping to additional nearby enemies. Each jump reduces the damage by 30%. Affects 3 total targets.
4	56	605	30 yd	2.5 sec	6 seconds	3	Hurls a lightning bolt at the enemy, dealing 493 to 551 nature damage and then jumping to additional nearby enemies. Each jump reduces the damage by 30%. Affects 3 total targets.

Enhancement

Stormstrike

Rank	Prerequisite	Effect
1	30 Points in Enhancement	Gives you an extra attack. In addition, the next 2 sources of Nature damage dealt to the target are increased by 20%. Lasts 12 secs.

Flametongue Totem

Rank	Level	Mana	Range	Casting Time	Cooldown	Cost To Train	Effect
1	28	90	—	IC	—	60	Summons a Flametongue Totem with 5 health at the feet of the caster. The totem enchants all party members' main-hand weapons with fire if they are within 20 yards. Each hit causes 6.4 to 19.6 additional Fire damage, based on the speed of the weapon. Slower weapons cause more fire damage per swing. Lasts 2 min.
2	38	140	—	IC	—	1 10	Summons a Flametongue Totem with 5 health at the feet of the caster. The totem enchants all party members' main-hand weapons with fire if they are within 20 yards. Each hit causes 9 to 27.9 additional Fire damage, based on the speed of the weapon. Slower weapons cause more fire damage per swing. Lasts 2 min.
3	48	200	—	IC	—	2 20	Summons a Flametongue Totem with 5 health at the feet of the caster. The totem enchants all party members' main-hand weapons with fire if they are within 20 yards. Each hit causes 12.3 to 37.9 additional Fire damage, based on the speed of the weapon. Slower weapons cause more fire damage per swing. Lasts 2 min.
4	58	275	—	IC	—	3 20	Summons a Flametongue Totem with 5 health at the feet of the caster. The totem enchants all party members' main-hand weapons with fire if they are within 20 yards. Each hit causes 15.8 to 48.7 additional Fire damage, based on the speed of the weapon. Slower weapons cause more fire damage per swing. Lasts 2 min.

Rockbiter Weapon

Rockbiter Weapon is your first weapon enhancement, but it never loses its purpose. It directly increases your attack power and thus your damage. It also increases the threat generated by each swing.

Rank	Level	Mana	Range	Casting Time	Cooldown	Cost To Train	Effect
1	1	15	—	IC	—	10	Imbue the Shaman's weapon, increasing attack power by 29 and allowing melee attacks to cause additional threat when using that weapon. Lasts for 5 minutes.
2	8	25	—	IC	—	1	Imbue the Shaman's weapon, increasing attack power by 58 and allowing melee attacks to cause additional threat when using that weapon. Lasts for 5 minutes.
3	16	50	—	IC	—	18	Imbue the Shaman's weapon, increasing attack power by 88 and allowing melee attacks to cause additional threat when using that weapon. Lasts for 5 minutes.
4	24	75	—	IC	—	35	Imbue the Shaman's weapon, increasing attack power by 129 and allowing melee attacks to cause additional threat when using that weapon. Lasts for 5 minutes.
5	34	100	—	IC	—	90	Imbue the Shaman's weapon, increasing attack power by 211 and allowing melee attacks to cause additional threat when using that weapon. Lasts for 5 minutes.
6	44	125	—	IC	—	1 80	Imbue the Shaman's weapon, increasing attack power by 393 and allowing melee attacks to cause additional threat when using that weapon. Lasts for 5 minutes.
7	54	150	—	IC	—	2 90	Imbue the Shaman's weapon, increasing attack power by 554 and allowing melee attacks to cause additional threat when using that weapon. Lasts for 5 minutes.

Lighting Shield

Lightning Shield increases the damage you deal if enemies are attacking you. It's a reactive shield that has three charges.

Rank	Level	Mana	Range	Casting Time	Cooldown	Cost To Train	Effect
1	8	45	—	IC	—	1	The caster is surrounded by 3 balls of lightning. When a spell, melee or ranged attack hits the caster, the attacker will be struck for 13 Nature damage. This expends one lightning ball. Only one ball will fire every few seconds. Lasts 10 min.
2	16	80	—	IC	—	18	The caster is surrounded by 3 balls of lightning. When a spell, melee or ranged attack hits the caster, the attacker will be struck for 29 Nature damage. This expends one lightning ball. Only one ball will fire every few seconds. Lasts 10 min.
3	24	125	—	IC	—	35	The caster is surrounded by 3 balls of lightning. When a spell, melee or ranged attack hits the caster, the attacker will be struck for 51 Nature damage. This expends one lightning ball. Only one ball will fire every few seconds. Lasts 10 min.
4	32	180	—	IC	—	80	The caster is surrounded by 3 balls of lightning. When a spell, melee or ranged attack hits the caster, the attacker will be struck for 80 Nature damage. This expends one lightning ball. Only one ball will fire every few seconds. Lasts 10 min.
5	40	240	—	IC	—	1 20	The caster is surrounded by 3 balls of lightning. When a spell, melee or ranged attack hits the caster, the attacker will be struck for 114 Nature damage. This expends one lightning ball. Only one ball will fire every few seconds. Lasts 10 min.
6	48	305	—	IC	—	2 20	The caster is surrounded by 3 balls of lightning. When a spell, melee or ranged attack hits the caster, the attacker will be struck for 154 Nature damage. This expends one lightning ball. Only one ball will fire every few seconds. Lasts 10 min.
7	56	370	—	IC	—	3	The caster is surrounded by 3 balls of lightning. When a spell, melee or ranged attack hits the caster, the attacker will be struck for 198 Nature damage. This expends one lightning ball. Only one ball will fire every few seconds. Lasts 10 min.

Flametongue Weapon

Flametongue Weapon complements your weapon enhancement list. It adds Fire damage to each swing of your weapon.

Rank	Level	Mana	Range	Casting Time	Cooldown	Cost To Train	Effect
1	10	30	—	IC	—	4	Imbue the Shaman's weapon with fire. Each hit causes 4.2 to 13 additional Fire damage, based on the speed of the weapon. Slower weapons cause more fire damage per swing. Lasts for 5 minutes.
2	18	55	—	IC	—	22	Imbue the Shaman's weapon with fire. Each hit causes 6.2 to 19.2 additional Fire damage, based on the speed of the weapon. Slower weapons cause more fire damage per swing. Lasts for 5 minutes.
3	26	80	—	IC	—	40	Imbue the Shaman's weapon with fire. Each hit causes 9.3 to 28.6 additional Fire damage, based on the speed of the weapon. Slower weapons cause more fire damage per swing. Lasts for 5 minutes.
4	36	105	—	IC	—	1	Imbue the Shaman's weapon with fire. Each hit causes 14.9 to 45.8 additional Fire damage, based on the speed of the weapon. Slower weapons cause more fire damage per swing. Lasts for 5 minutes.
5	46	130	—	IC	—	2	Imbue the Shaman's weapon with fire. Each hit causes 24.4 to 75 additional Fire damage, based on the speed of the weapon. Slower weapons cause more fire damage per swing. Lasts for 5 minutes.
6	56	155	—	IC	—	3	Imbue the Shaman's weapon with fire. Each hit causes 32.4 to 99.9 additional Fire damage, based on the speed of the weapon. Slower weapons cause more fire damage per swing. Lasts for 5 minutes.

Strength of Earth Totem

Strength of Earth Totem increases the strength of any party members in range.

Rank	Level	Mana	Range	Casting Time	Cooldown	Cost To Train	Effect
1	10	25	—	IC	—	4	Summons a Strength of Earth Totem with 5 health at the feet of the caster. The totem increases the strength of party members within 20 yards by 10. Lasts 2 min.
2	24	65	—	IC	—	35	Summons a Strength of Earth Totem with 5 health at the feet of the caster. The totem increases the strength of party members within 20 yards by 20. Lasts 2 min.
3	38	155	—	IC	—	1 10	Summons a Strength of Earth Totem with 5 health at the feet of the caster. The totem increases the strength of party members within 20 yards by 36. Lasts 2 min.
4	52	275	—	IC	—	2 70	Summons a Strength of Earth Totem with 5 health at the feet of the caster. The totem increases the strength of party members within 20 yards by 61. Lasts 2 min.
5	60	340	—	IC	—	—	Summons a Strength of Earth Totem with 5 health at the feet of the caster. The totem increases the strength of party members within 20 yards by 77. Lasts 2 min.

Stoneskin Totem

Stoneskin Totem is a mainstay of many Shaman. It reduces the damage of all melee attacks against you or other party members in range.

Rank	Level	Mana	Range	Casting Time	Cooldown	Cost To Train	Effect
1	4	30	—	IC	—	—	Summons a Stoneskin Totem with 5 health at the feet of the caster. The totem protects party members within 20 yards, reducing melee damage taken by 4. Lasts 45 sec.
2	14	60	—	IC	—	9	Summons a Stoneskin Totem with 5 health at the feet of the caster. The totem protects party members within 20 yards, reducing melee damage taken by 7. Lasts 1 min.
3	24	90	—	IC	—	35	Summons a Stoneskin Totem with 5 health at the feet of the caster. The totem protects party members within 20 yards, reducing melee damage taken by 11. Lasts 1 min.
4	34	115	—	IC	—	90	Summons a Stoneskin Totem with 5 health at the feet of the caster. The totem protects party members within 20 yards, reducing melee damage taken by 16. Lasts 1 min.
5	44	160	—	IC	—	1 80	Summons a Stoneskin Totem with 5 health at the feet of the caster. The totem protects party members within 20 yards, reducing melee damage taken by 22. Lasts 1 min.
6	54	210	—	IC	—	2 90	Summons a Stoneskin Totem with 5 health at the feet of the caster. The totem protects party members within 20 yards, reducing melee damage taken by 30. Lasts 1 min.

Frostbrand Weapon

Frostbrand Weapon is another good choice when you don't want aggro. It deals Cold damage and slows the movement speed of enemies on each hit.

Rank	Level	Mana	Range	Casting Time	Cooldown	Cost To Train	Effect
1	20	60	—	IC	—	22	Imbue the Shaman's weapon with frost. Each hit has a chance of causing 35 additional Frost damage and slowing the target's movement speed by 25% for 8 sec. Lasts for 5 minutes.
2	28	85	—	IC	—	60	Imbue the Shaman's weapon with frost. Each hit has a chance of causing 53 additional Frost damage and slowing the target's movement speed by 25% for 8 sec. Lasts for 5 minutes.
3	38	110	—	IC	—	1 10	Imbue the Shaman's weapon with frost. Each hit has a chance of causing 84 additional Frost damage and slowing the target's movement speed by 25% for 8 sec. Lasts for 5 minutes.
4	48	135	—	IC	—	2 20	Imbue the Shaman's weapon with frost. Each hit has a chance of causing 134 additional Frost damage and slowing the target's movement speed by 25% for 8 sec. Lasts for 5 minutes.
5	58	160	—	IC	—	3 20	Imbue the Shaman's weapon with frost. Each hit has a chance of causing 175 additional Frost damage and slowing the target's movement speed by 25% for 8 sec. Lasts for 5 minutes.

Ghost Wolf

Ghost Wolf is the Shaman's travel form. It increases the Shaman's speed significantly and with the appropriate talent choice, its casting time is trivial.

Rank	Level	Mana	Range	Casting Time	Cooldown	Cost To Train	Effect
N/A	20	100	—	3 sec	—	22	Turns the shaman into a Ghost Wolf, increasing speed by 40%. Only useable outdoors.

Water Breathing

Water Breathing can be cast with only the cost of a Shiny Fish Scale. It allows the target to travel beneath the water without worrying about drowning.

Rank	Level	Mana	Reagent	Range	Casting Time	Cooldown	Cost To Train	Effect
N/A	22	50	Shiny Fish Scales	30	IC	—	30	Allows the target to breath underwater for 10 min.

Frost Resistance Totem

Frost Resistance Totem, like all resistance totems, is best used in a group.

Rank	Level	Mana	Range	Casting Time	Cooldown	Cost To Train	Effect
1	24	75	—	IC	—	35	Summons a Frost Resistance Totem with 5 health at the feet of the caster for 1 min. The totem increases party members' frost resistance by 30, if within 20 yards.
2	38	150	—	IC	—	1 10	Summons a Frost Resistance Totem with 5 health at the feet of the caster for 1 min. The totem increases party members' frost resistance by 45, if within 20 yards.
3	54	180	—	IC	—	2 90	Summons a Frost Resistance Totem with 5 health at the feet of the caster for 1 min. The totem increases party members' frost resistance by 60, if within 20 yards.

Far Sight

Far Sight can only be used outdoors. It moves the Shaman's consciousness to another location that is within line of sight of the Shaman's body.

Rank	Level	Mana	Range	Casting Time	Cooldown	Cost To Train	Effect
N/A	26	80	50000	2 sec	—	40	Changes the caster's viewpoint to the targeted location. Lasts 60 seconds. Only useable outdoors.

Fire Resistance Totem

Fire Resistance Totem is best used in a group. Unlike many of the other resistance totems however, Fire Resistance Totem is used fairly often as many of the high-end dungeons and raids have enemies that use Fire based attacks.

Rank	Level	Mana	Range	Casting Time	Cooldown	Cost To Train	Effect
1	28	75	—	IC	—	60	Summons a Fire Resistance Totem with 5 health at the feet of the caster for 1 min that increases the fire resistance of party members within 20 yards by 30.
2	42	120	—	IC	—	1 60	Summons a Fire Resistance Totem with 5 health at the feet of the caster for 1 min that increases the fire resistance of party members within 20 yards by 45.
3	58	180	—	IC	—	3 20	Summons a Fire Resistance Totem with 5 health at the feet of the caster for 1 min that increases the fire resistance of party members within 20 yards by 60.

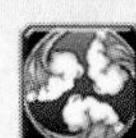

Water Walking

Water Walking is both fun and useful. Beyond running around your friends while they swim across a river or lake, you can cast this spell on other people to increase the entire group's travel speed. Any damage taken dispels this effect and it requires one Fish Oil.

Rank	Level	Mana	Reagent	Range	Casting Time	Cooldown	Cost To Train	Effect
N/A	28	95	Fish Oil	30	IC	—	60	Allows the friendly target to walk across water for 10 min. Any damage caused will cancel the effect.

Astral Recall

Astral Recall transports the Shaman back to his or her bind point. Since it only has a fifteen minute cooldown, it's better than a Hearthstone, and you can still use your Hearthstone

Rank	Level	Mana	Range	Casting Time	Cooldown	Cost To Train	Effect
N/A	30	150	—	10 sec	15 minutes	70	Yanks the caster through the twisting nether back to his home location.

Grounding Totem

Grounding Totem can protect you and your teammates from harmful spells.

Rank	Level	Mana	Range	Casting Time	Cooldown	Cost To Train	Effect
N/A	30	6% of base	—	IC	15 seconds	70	Summons a Grounding Totem with 5 health at the feet of the caster that will redirect one harmful spell cast on a nearby party member to itself every 10 seconds. Will not redirect area of effect spells. Lasts 45 secs.

Nature Resistance Totem

Nature Resistance Totem increases all party members Nature Resistance as long as they are within range.

Rank	Level	Mana	Range	Casting Time	Cooldown	Cost To Train	Effect
1	30	75	—	IC	—	70	Summons a Nature Resistance Totem with 5 health at the feet of the caster for 1 min that increases the nature resistance of party members within 20 yards by 30.
2	44	120	—	IC	—	1 80	Summons a Nature Resistance Totem with 5 health at the feet of the caster for 1 min that increases the nature resistance of party members within 20 yards by 45.
3	60	180	—	IC	—	3 40	Summons a Nature Resistance Totem with 5 health at the feet of the caster for 1 min that increases the nature resistance of party members within 20 yards by 60.

Windfury Weapon

Windfury Weapon is useful to all Shaman, but very useful to Shaman using two-handed weapons or very slow one-handed weapons. This gives you weapon a chance to take two addition swings immediately with an attack power bonus.

Rank	Level	Mana	Range	Casting Time	Cooldown	Cost To Train	Effect
1	30	90	—	IC	—	70	Imbue the Shaman's weapon with wind. Each hit has a 20% chance of granting you 2 extra attacks with 46 extra attack power. Lasts for 5 minutes.
2	40	115	—	IC	—	1 20	Imbue the Shaman's weapon with wind. Each hit has a 20% chance of granting you 2 extra attacks with 119 extra attack power. Lasts for 5 minutes.
3	50	140	—	IC	—	2 40	Imbue the Shaman's weapon with wind. Each hit has a 20% chance of granting you 2 extra attacks with 249 extra attack power. Lasts for 5 minutes.
4	60	165	—	IC	—	3 40	Imbue the Shaman's weapon with wind. Each hit has a 20% chance of granting you 2 extra attacks with 333 extra attack power. Lasts for 5 minutes.

Windfury Totem

Windfury Totem works very similarly to Windfury Weapon. This gives all party members a chance to take an addition swing with an attack power bonus.

Rank	Level	Mana	Range	Casting Time	Cooldown	Cost To Train	Effect
1	32	115	—	IC	—	80	Summons a Windfury Totem with 5 health at the feet of the caster. The totem enchants all party members main-hand weapons with wind, if they are within 20 yards. Each hit has a 20% chance of granting the attacker 1 extra attack with 122 extra attack power. Lasts 2 min.
2	42	175	—	IC	—	1 60	Summons a Windfury Totem with 5 health at the feet of the caster. The totem enchants all party members main-hand weapons with wind, if they are within 20 yards. Each hit has a 20% chance of granting the attacker 1 extra attack with 229 extra attack power. Lasts 2 min.
3	52	250	—	IC	—	2 70	Summons a Windfury Totem with 5 health at the feet of the caster. The totem enchants all party members main-hand weapons with wind, if they are within 20 yards. Each hit has a 20% chance of granting the attacker 1 extra attack with 315 extra attack power. Lasts 2 min.

Sentry Totem

Sentry Totem immediately shifts the Shaman's view to the totem. To switch back and forth, click on the icon at the top of the screen.

Rank	Level	Mana	Range	Casting Time	Cooldown	Cost To Train	Effect
N/A	34	65	—	IC	—	90	Summons an immobile Sentry Totem with 100 health at your feet for 5 min that allows vision of nearby area and warns of enemies that attack it. Right-click on buff to switch back and forth between totem sight and Shaman sight.

Windwall Totem

Windwall Totem is very similar to the Stoneskin Totem. It reduces the damage from ranged attacks.

Rank	Level	Mana	Range	Casting Time	Cooldown	Cost To Train	Effect
1	36	115	—	IC	—	1	Summons a Windwall Totem with 5 health at the feet of the caster. The totem protects party members within 20 yards, reducing ranged damage taken by 32. Lasts 2 mins.
2	46	170	—	IC	—	2	Summons a Windwall Totem with 5 health at the feet of the caster. The totem protects party members within 20 yards, reducing ranged damage taken by 50. Lasts 2 mins.
3	56	225	—	IC	—	3	Summons a Windwall Totem with 5 health at the feet of the caster. The totem protects party members within 20 yards, reducing ranged damage taken by 64. Lasts 2 mins.

Grace of Air Totem

Grace of Air Totem is most effective in parties with Hunters and Rogues. It increases the agility of party members nearby.

Rank	Level	Mana	Range	Casting Time	Cooldown	Cost To Train	Effect
1	42	155	—	IC	—	1 60	Summons a Grace of Air Totem with 5 health at the feet of the caster. The totem increases the agility of party members within 20 yards by 43. Lasts 1.25 min.
2	56	250	—	IC	—	3	Summons a Grace of Air Totem with 5 health at the feet of the caster. The totem increases the agility of party members within 20 yards by 67. Lasts 1.50 min.
3	60	310	—	IC	—	—	Summons a Grace of Air Totem with 5 health at the feet of the caster. The totem increases the agility of party members within 20 yds by 77. Lasts 2 min.

Restoration

Tranquil Air Totem

Rank	Minimum Level	Mana	Range	Casting Time	Cooldown	Cost To Train	Effect
1	50	8% of base	—	IC	—	2 40	Summons a Tranquil Air Totem with 5 health at the feet of the caster. The totem reduces the threat caused by all party members within 20 yards by 20%. Lasts 2 mins.

Healing Wave

Healing Wave is your basic and largest heal. It's casting time increases with each rank and can only be slightly reduced by talent choices.

Rank	Level	Mana	Range	Casting Time	Cooldown	Cost To Train	Effect
1	1	25	40 yd	1.5 sec	—	—	Heals a friendly target for 34 to 44.
2	6	45	40 yd	2 sec	—	1	Heals a friendly target for 64 to 78.
3	12	80	40 yd	2.5 sec	—	8	Heals a friendly target for 129 to 155.
4	18	155	40 yd	3 sec	—	20	Heals a friendly target for 268 to 316.
5	24	200	40 yd	3 sec	—	35	Heals a friendly target for 376 to 440.
6	32	265	40 yd	3 sec	—	80	Heals a friendly target for 536 to 622.
7	40	340	40 yd	3 sec	—	1 20	Heals a friendly target for 740 to 854.
8	48	440	40 yd	3 sec	—	2 20	Heals a friendly target for 1017 to 1167.
9	56	560	40 yd	3 sec	—	3	Heals a friendly target for 1367 to 1561.
10	60	620	40 yd	3 sec	—	—	Heals a friendly target for 1620 to 1850.

Ancestral Spirit

Ancestral Spirit allows the Shaman to resurrect others. This can be used on people in your party or not, but cannot be used to resurrect enemy forces.

Rank	Level	Mana	Range	Casting Time	Cooldown	Cost To Train	Effect
1	12	90% of base	30 yd	10 sec	—	8	Returns the spirit to the body, restoring a dead target to life with 65 health and 120 mana. Cannot be cast when in combat.
2	24	90% of base	30 yd	10 sec	—	35	Returns the spirit to the body, restoring a dead target to life with 150 health and 260 mana. Cannot be cast when in combat.
3	36	90% of base	30 yd	10 sec	—	1	Returns the spirit to the body, restoring a dead target to life with 250 health and 420 mana. Cannot be cast when in combat.
4	48	90% of base	30 yd	10 sec	—	2 20	Returns the spirit to the body, restoring a dead target to life with 400 health and 600 mana. Cannot be cast when in combat.
5	60	90% of base	30 yd	10 sec	—	3 40	Returns the spirit to the body, restoring a dead target to life with 600 health and 800 mana. Cannot be cast when in combat.

Cure Poison

Cure Poison is an instant spell, use it if a single party member is poisoned in a fight or if your Poison Cleansing Totem isn't acting quickly enough to keep the party clean.

Rank	Level	Mana	Range	Casting Time	Cooldown	Cost To Train	Effect
1	16	9% of base	30 yd	IC	—	18	Cures 1 poison effect on the target.

Tremor Totem

Tremor Totem can save a party. This totem shakes the ground around it and can dispel sleep, fear, and charm effects.

Rank	Level	Mana	Range	Casting Time	Cooldown	Cost To Train	Effect
N/A	18	75	—	IC	—	20	Summons a Tremor Totem with 5 health at the feet of the caster that shakes the ground around it, removing Fear, Charm, and Sleep effects from party members within 20 yards. Lasts 1.5 min.

Lesser Healing Wave

Lesser Healing Wave is your fastest heal without use of talents. This heal is most useful when softer party members are under attack as it's more important to keep what little health they have restored than to conserve mana.

Rank	Level	Mana	Range	Casting Time	Cooldown	Cost To Train	Effect
1	20	105	40 yd	1.5 sec	—	22	Heals a friendly target for 162 to 186.
2	28	145	40 yd	1.5 sec	—	60	Heals a friendly target for 247 to 281.
3	36	185	40 yd	1.5 sec	—	1	Heals a friendly target for 337 to 381.
4	44	235	40 yd	1.5 sec	—	1 80	Heals a friendly target for 458 to 514.
5	52	305	40 yd	1.5 sec	—	2 70	Heals a friendly target for 631 to 705.
6	60	380	40 yd	1.5 sec	—	3 40	Heals a friendly target for 832 to 928.

Cure Disease

Cure Disease is instant and should be used immediately when a party member is infected as some diseases can quickly spread to the entire party.

Rank	Level	Mana	Range	Casting Time	Cooldown	Cost To Train	Effect
1	22	9% of base	30 yd	IC	—	30	Cures 1 disease on the target.

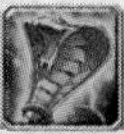

Poison Cleansing Totem

Poison Cleansing Totem is a water totem, but is far more mana efficient if you're fighting an enemy that will poison multiple party members or poison several times.

Rank	Level	Mana	Range	Casting Time	Cooldown	Cost To Train	Effect
N/A	22	10% of base	—	IC	—	30	Summons a Poison Cleansing Totem with 5 Health at the feet of the caster that attempts to remove 1 poison effect from party members within 20 yards every 5 seconds. Lasts 2 mins.

Healing Stream Totem

Healing Stream Totem slowly restores your party's health. It shouldn't be used as the sole healing a party receives, but it can certainly supplement healing.

Rank	Level	Mana	Range	Casting Time	Cooldown	Cost To Train	Effect
1	20	40	—	IC	—	—	Summons a Healing Stream Totem with 5 health at the feet of the caster for 1 min that heals group members within 20 yards for 6 every 2 sec.
2	30	50	—	IC	—	70	Summons a Healing Stream Totem with 5 health at the feet of the caster for 1 min that heals group members within 20 yards for 8 every 2 seconds.
3	40	60	—	IC	—	1 20	Summons a Healing Stream Totem with 5 health at the feet of the caster for 1 min that heals group members within 20 yards for 10 every 2 seconds.
4	50	70	—	IC	—	2 40	Summons a Healing Stream Totem with 5 health at the feet of the caster for 1 min that heals group members within 20 yards for 12 every 2 seconds.
5	60	80	—	IC	—	3 40	Summons a Healing Stream Totem with 5 health at the feet of the caster for 1 min that heals group members within 20 yards for 14 every 2 seconds.

Mana Spring Totem

Mana Spring Totem, similar to Healing Stream Totem, slowly restores the mana of party members. It's useful if you have multiple mana users in your party.

Rank	Level	Mana	Range	Casting Time	Cooldown	Cost To Train	Effect
1	26	40	—	IC	—	40	Summons a Mana Spring Totem with 5 health at the feet of the caster for 1 min that restores 4 mana every 2 seconds to group members within 20 yards.
2	36	60	—	IC	—	1	Summons a Mana Spring Totem with 5 health at the feet of the caster for 1 min that restores 6 mana every 2 seconds to group members within 20 yards.
3	46	80	—	IC	—	2	Summons a Mana Spring Totem with 5 health at the feet of the caster for 1 min that restores 8 mana every 2 seconds to group members within 20 yards.
4	56	100	—	IC	—	3	Summons a Mana Spring Totem with 5 health at the feet of the caster for 1 min that restores 10 mana every 2 seconds to group members within 20 yards.

Reincarnation

Reincarnation allows a Shaman to resurrect themselves. This has a long cooldown (one hour without talents) and requires the Shaman to have an Ankh in her inventory (which is consumed on resurrection).

Rank	Level	Reagent	Range	Casting Time	Cooldown	Cost To Train	Effect
N/A	30	Ankh	Self	IC	1 hour	70	Allows you to resurrect yourself upon death with 20% health and mana. Useable once per hour.

Disease Cleansing Totem

Disease Cleasing Totem periodically clears one disease effect from all party members in range. Against multiple enemies that use disease effects, this totem is very mana efficient.

Rank	Level	Mana	Range	Casting Time	Cooldown	Cost To Train	Effect
N/A	38	10% of base	—	IC	—	1 10	Summons a Disease Cleansing Totem with 5 health at the feet of the caster that attempts to remove 1 disease effect from party members within 20 yards every 5 seconds. Lasts 2 mins.

Chain Heal

Chain Heal is a slower cast heal that heals up to three targets if they are close enough together. It isn't as powerful as either of the healing waves, but allows you to heal multiple people at once.

Rank	Level	Mana	Range	Casting Time	Cooldown	Cost To Train	Effect
1	40	260	40 yd	2.5 sec	—	1 20	Heals the friendly target for 320 to 368, then jumps to heal additional nearby targets. If cast on a party member, the heal will only jump to other party members. Each jump reduces the effectiveness of the heal by 50%. Heals 3 ranged targets.
2	46	315	40 yd	2.5 sec	—	2	Heals the friendly target for 405 to 465, then jumps to heal additional nearby targets. If cast on a party member, the heal will only jump to other party members. Each jump reduces the effectiveness of the heal by 50%. Heals 3 ranged targets.
3	54	405	40 yd	2.5 sec	—	2 90	Heals the friendly target for 551 to 629, then jumps to heal additional nearby targets. If cast on a party member, the heal will only jump to other party members. Each jump reduces the effectiveness of the heal by 50%. Heals 3 ranged targets.

Mana Tide Totem

Mana Tide Totem is learned through talents, but can be extremely useful in long fights. It restores a reasonable amount of mana to all party members in range quickly.

Rank	Minimum Level	Mana	Range	Casting Time	Cooldown	Cost To Train	Effect
1	40	20	—	IC	5 minutes	—	Summons a Mana Tide Totem with 5 health at the feet of the caster for 12 sec that restores 170 mana every 3 seconds to group members within 20 yards.
2	48	40	—	IC	5 minutes	55	Summons a Mana Tide Totem with 5 health at the feet of the caster for 12 sec that restores 230 mana every 3 seconds to group members within 20 yards.
3	58	60	—	IC	5 minutes	80	Summons a Mana Tide Totem with 5 health at the feet of the caster for 12 sec that restores 290 mana every 3 seconds to group members within 20 yards.

Nature's Swiftness

Rank	Prerequisites	Effect
1	5 Points in Tidal Mastery, 20 Points in Restoration	When activated your next Nature spell with a casting time less than 10 sec becomes an instant cast spell.

TALENTS

The Shaman class can fulfill a variety of roles. The talents you choose determine which roles you can fill well and which you are mediocre at. The raw damage of the Elemental tree, the melee capabilities of the Enhancement tree, or the sustaining power of the Restoration tree are all viable options. Read each carefully and choose the one that fits your view of the Shaman.

ELEMENTAL

The Elemental tree gives a number of abilities that increase the damage, add effects to, or increase the duration of your spells. Its ability to cause large bursts of damage and to hinder enemies make it an intuitive choice for the PvP Shaman. Shaman tend to have smaller mana pools than other casters, but with this line, you can do comparable damage until your mana depletes.

This line is best for reducing the cooldown, while increasing damage and critical chance, of your shock spells. It also increases the hindering ability of your Earthbind Totem, the damage of your fire totems, and improves your lightning spells significantly. Elemental Shaman are fairly feared in PvP as they can deal a lot of damage very quickly. In PvE, this tree can get you in trouble if not moderated. You deal a lot of damage very quickly, but have no tools to reduce your threat. Cast in moderation or end up tanking the enemy.

ENHANCEMENT

Enhancement Shaman can stand shoulder to shoulder with Warriors and Rogues. They concentrate on developing their melee damage and mitigation while increasing the power of their group-effecting totems. Learning to wield two-handed maces and axes is a sign of what Enhancement Shaman are all about; increasing melee damage by ignoring the more traditional healing and casting roles.

Many Shaman take some of the Enhancement tree for at least the increase in mana. PvP oriented Shaman love the decrease in Ghostwolf casting time as it makes them very mobile on the field. The heavy Enhancement Shaman enjoy a higher block chance (if they are using a shield), a higher parry chance, higher critical strike chance with weapons, and increased weapon damage over all. At lower levels, these Shaman can even perform the role of tank in dungeon groups. This shouldn't be attempted in later dungeons as the difference in mitigation between plate and mail armor becomes more pronounced as enemies deal more damage.

RESTORATION

While any Shaman can heal when needed, the Restoration Shaman excels at it. They give up the increased damage of the Elemental line, and the improved melee of the Enhancement line, to significantly increase their ability to heal. While the healing power of a Restoration Shaman cannot rival that of a Rejuvenation Druid or Holy Priest, it can make for a wonderful backup healer or even a primary healer.

Restoration Shaman have no ability to remove aggro once it's on them, but they can reduce the threat generated by their healing spells and can reduce the interruption caused by damage. This allows you to continue healing yourself or others when enemies have turned their focus to you. With the increased survivability granted by your mail armor and shield, you can survive long enough for your party to pull the enemies off you. Increasing the critical chance of healing spells and giving you an instant spell every few minutes makes you adept at keeping party members alive, while adding a number of effects to the targets of your heals (increased armor and increased healing efficiency) makes your main tank even more powerful.

Restoration Shaman aren't as devastating in PvP as Elemental Shaman and slower at soloing than Enhancement Shaman. The real bread and butter of the Restoration line comes from what they can bring to a party.

STRATEGIES

The primary factor in determining Shaman strategy rests on the duration of an upcoming fight. In longer fights, Shaman bring more and more interesting things to a group (and even to some extent gain this complexity while soloing). Shaman are most efficient and exciting when pressured into using many of their special AoE totems, which are pivotal in distinguishing this class from its rivals.

SURVIVAL

When you and your group are threatened, the class has many tricks to come out on top. In battles where there is risk to the party and a powerful monster (or a number of lesser foes), it's amazing to see what the totems can accomplish over time. Drop your Stoneskin Totem and reduce incoming damage right off the bat!

Reducing each enemy attacks by six points (for example), adds up to hundreds of saved mana in healing when a group goes through 15-20 rounds of attacks against multiple foes. Considering this totem lasts for an entire minute, those numbers are entirely legitimate.

The same math applies to Healing Stream Totems. Though each tick seems like a trivial sum of health to restore, these powerhouses of Heal Over Time efficiency cost very little to drop, take no time to prepare, and account for about an entire Lesser Healing Wave worth of health to *each* member of the party who is damaged during the next minute. You just can't beat efficiency like that, even if only one or two party members are taking damage.

BACKUP HEALING

Shaman have the ability to fight up close and do magical damage, so there are times when it doesn't seem like it is a Shaman's "duty" to heal. This is a complex issue, and, in the end, it is a personal decision, but there are a few points to make.

Shaman have the ability to save lives, as do all healing classes. Dealing damage saves lives when the damage brings down a target that is threatening the group. Healing saves a life when it restores a person who would have fallen before the attacking enemies were slain. If you are in a group that is about to lose a member due to an attack, it is your responsibility to drop into healing duties for a time. Even in a selfish sense, everyone benefits from keeping each member alive during a fight because losing a person leads to major downtime (for a corpse run or for resurrection).

And, from a mana perspective, it costs much more to bring someone back from the dead than it does to give them a bit of healing.

Looked at from a different angle, there is a great deal of good to be done by a secondary healer. Shaman have much better armor than Priests, especially in the later game. Healing a wounded character saves the primary healer from getting aggro; this is doubly important when the person being healed is the primary healer.

Shaman specced in the Restoration tree actually become quite skilled in healing. Combining this and an Intellect equipment build, a person can support entire groups as if playing a traditional Priest

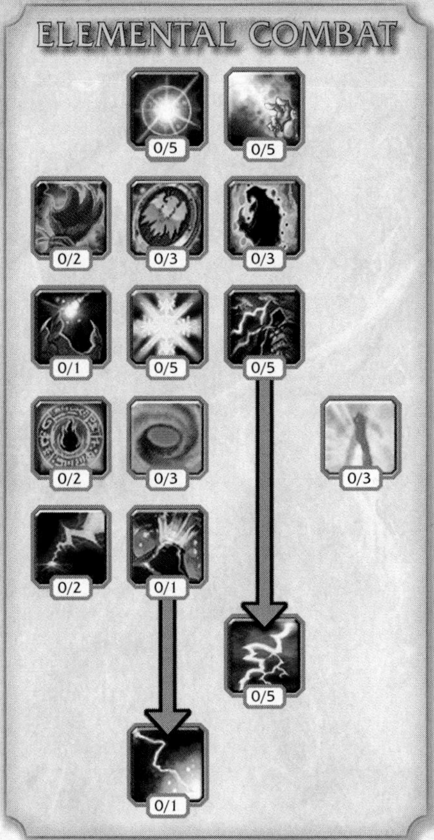

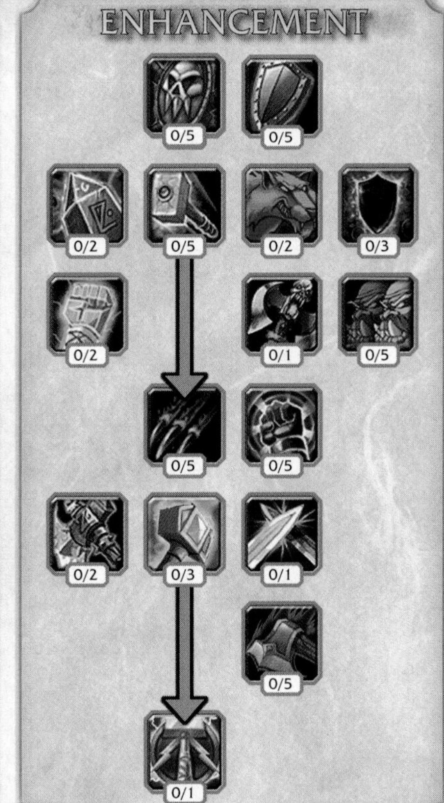

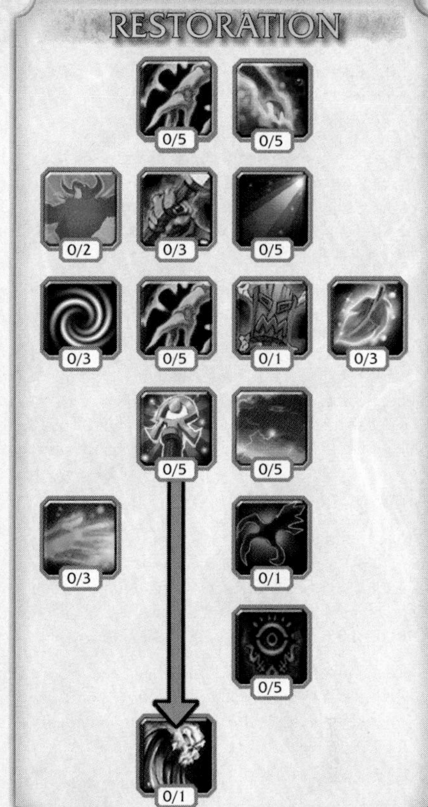

CONVECTION 5

Reduces the Mana cost of your Shock, Lightning Bolt and Chain Lightning spells by 2% (Per Rank).

CONCUSSION 5

Increases the damage done by your Lightning Bolt, Chain Lightning and Shock spells by 1% (Per Rank).

EARTH'S GRASP 2

Increases the Health of your Stoneclaw Totem by 25% (Per Rank) and your Earthbind Totem by 10% (Per Rank).

ELEMENTAL WARDING 3

Reduces damage taken from Fire, Frost and Nature effects by 4%. Progression 4/7/10.

CALL OF FLAME 3

Increases the damage done by your Fire Totems by 5% (Per Rank).

ELEMENTAL FOCUS 1

Gives you a 10% chance to enter a Clearcasting state after casting any Fire, Frost, or Nature damage spell. The Clearcasting state reduces the mana cost of your next damage spell by 100%.

REVERBERATION 5

Reduces the cooldown of your Shock spells by 0.2 sec (Per Rank).

CALL OF THUNDER 5

Increases the critical strike chance of your Lightning Bolt and Chain Lightning spells by 1%. Progression 1/2/3/4/6

IMPROVED FIRE NOVA TOTEM 2

Reduces the delay before your Fire Nova Totem activates by 1 sec. (Per Rank) and decreases the threat generated by your Magma Totem by 25% (Per Rank).

EYE OF THE STORM 3

Gives you a 33% chance to gain the Focused Casting effect that lasts for 6 sec after being the victim of a melee or ranged critical strike. The Focused Casting effect prevents you from losing casting time when taking damage. Progression 33/66/100.

ELEMENTAL DEVASTATION 3

Your offensive spell crits will increase your chance to get a critical strike with melee attacks by 3% (Per Rank) for 10 sec.

STORM REACH 2

Increases the range of your Lightning Bolt and Chain Lightning spells by 3 yards (Per Rank).

ELEMENTAL FURY 1

Increases the critical strike damage bonus of your Searing, Magma, and Fire Nova Totems and your Fire, Frost, and Nature spells by 100%.

LIGHTNING MASTERY 5

Reduces the cast time of your Lightning Bolt and Chain Lightning spells by 0.2 sec (Per Rank).

ELEMENTAL MASTERY 1

When activated, this spell gives your next Fire, Frost, or Nature damage spell a 100% critical strike chance and reduces the mana cost by 100%.

ANCESTRAL KNOWLEDGE 5

Increases your maximum Mana by 1% (Per Rank).

SHIELD SPECIALIZATION 5

Increases your chance to block attacks with a shield by 1% (Per Rank) and increases the amount blocked by 5% (Per Rank).

GUARDIAN TOTEMS 2

Increases the amount of damage reduced by your Stoneskin Totem and Windwall Totem by 10% (Per Rank) and the cooldown of your Grounding Totem by 1 sec. (Per Rank).

THUNDERING STRIKES 5

Improves your chance to get a critical strike with your weapon attacks by 1% (Per Rank).

IMPROVED GHOST WOLF 2

Reduces the cast time of your Ghost Wolf spell by 1 sec (Per Rank).

IMPROVED LIGHTNING SHIELD 3

Increases the damage done by your Lightning Shield orbs by 5% (Per Rank).

ENHANCING TOTEMS 2

Increases the effect of your Strength of Earth and Grace of Air Totems by 8%. Progression 8/15.

TWO-HANDED AXES AND MACES 1

Allows you to use Two-Handed Axes and Two-Handed Maces.

ANTICIPATION 5

Increases your chance to dodge by an additional 1% (Per Rank).

FLURRY 5

Increases your attack speed by 10% for your next 3 swings after dealing a critical strike. Progression: 10%/15%/20%/25%/30%

TOUGHNESS 5

Increases your armor value from items by 2% (Per Rank).

IMPROVED WEAPON TOTEMS 2

Increases the melee attack power bonus of your Windfury Totem by 15% (Per Rank) and increases the damage caused by your Flametongue Totem by 6% (Per Rank).

ELEMENTAL WEAPONS 3

Increases the melee attack power bonus of your Rockbiter Weapon by 7% (Progression 7/14/20), your Windfury Weapon effect by 13% (Progression 13/27/40) and increases the damage caused by your Flametongue Weapon and Frostbrand Weapon by 5% (Per Rank).

PARRY 1

Gives a chance to parry enemy melee attacks.

WEAPON MASTERY 5

Increases the damage you deal with all weapons by 2%.

STORMSTRIKE 1

Gives you an extra attack. In addition, the next 2 sources of Nature damage dealt to the target are increased by 20%. Lasts 12 secs.

IMPROVED HEALING WAVE 5

Reduces the casting time of your Healing Wave spell by 0.1 sec (Per Rank).

TIDAL FOCUS 5

Reduces the Mana cost of your healing spells by 1% (Per Rank).

IMPROVED REINCARNATION 2

Reduces the cooldown of your Reincarnation spell by 10 min (Per Rank) and increases the amount of health and mana you reincarnate with by an additional 10% (Per Rank).

ANCESTRAL HEALING 3

Increases your target's armor value from items by 8% (Progression 8/16/25) for 15 sec after getting a critical effect from one of your healing spells.

TOTEMIC FOCUS 5

Reduces the Mana cost of your totems by 5% (Per Rank).

NATURE'S GUIDANCE 3

Increases your chance to hit with melee attacks and spells by 1% (Per Rank).

HEALING FOCUS 5

Gives you a 14% chance (Per Rank) to avoid interruption caused by damage while casting any healing spell.

TOTEMIC MASTERY 1

Restoration The radius of your totems that affect friendly targets is increased to 30 yd.

HEALING GRACE 3

Reduces the threat generated by your healing spells by 5% (Per Rank).

RESTORATIVE TOTEMS 5

Increases the effect of your Mana Spring and Healing Stream Totems by 5% (Per Rank).

TIDAL MASTERY 5

Increases the critical effect chance of your healing and lightning spells by 1% (Per Rank).

HEALING WAY 3

Your Healing Wave spells have a 33% (Progression 33/66/100) chance to increase the subsequent Healing Wave spells on that target by 6% for 15 sec. This effect will stack up to 3 times.

NATURE'S SWIFTNESS 1

When activated your next Nature spell with a casting time less than 10 sec becomes an instant cast spell.

PURIFICATION 5

Increases the effectiveness of your healing spells by 2% (Per Rank).

MANA TIDE TOTEM 1

Summons a Mana Tide Totem with 5 health at the feet of the caster for 12 sec that restores 170 mana every 3 seconds to group members within 20 yards.

Backup Tanking

Though not as armored as Warriors and not as evasive as Rogues, Shaman can perform quite adequately as backup tanks if the party is fighting too many for the tank to hold. Earthshock to gain the target's interest, and switch back to the party's primary target.

Keeping the target where the main tank can see it keeps him from running around looking for the ping-ponged mob and gives him a chance to pull it off you if your health gets too low. Healing yourself keeps you alive and further angers the enemy. Should the enemy peel off of you, hit it with another Earthshock to remind it that you aren't to be trifled with.

This has a few dangers as Shaman have no way to reduce threat once they have generated it. Once an enemy is on you, it often takes someone taunting it off or simply killing it.

Remember that you are sturdier than many of the other classes out there. If you see an enemy break off the tank and make a run at a softer party member, pull it off and drag it back to the main tank. With all enemies kept near the tank, it makes his job much easier and thus makes the party's chances of survival much higher.

Working With Other Shaman

Shaman can only drop one totem from a given element at a time. Having multiple Shaman in a party allows for many more totems to be dropped. While the totems do not stack (two Stoneskin Totems don't double the amount absorbed for example), having other Shaman around allows you to divvy totem duties and stack many more effects on the party.

Determine in advance who drops what. Having one drop Windfury Totem and Stoneskin Totem while another drops Grace of Air Totem and Strength of Earth Totem greatly increases the damage your party deals while still reducing the damage taken by enemies.

The only totems that stack are damage totems. Two Magma Totems inflict double the damage to all enemies in the area. Multiple Shaman can be quite damaging without ever engaging the enemy.

As for additional duties, they can be divided as well. If healing is in good shape with just one of the Shaman staying on backup duty, the other can switch to a more aggressive posture and help knock the enemies down faster. In the event that your casting draws brief aggro, use Lightning Shield and deal even more damage, efficiently.

Which Weapon Buff?

Shaman have a number of choices when it comes to enchanting their weapons. The first thing to keep in mind is that weapon buffs do not stack with weapon totems. This means that using Rockbiter Weapon and Windfury Totem do not grant you both bonuses.

The most difficult decisions are in a party. As a solo adventurer, Shaman use whichever weapon buff they personally enjoy or is more effective against the current enemy (Flametongue Weapon doesn't do much against a fire elemental for instance).

In groups, Shaman should use a weapon buff that is consistent with the role they are performing. If the only healer in a group, avoid using Rockbiter Weapon as the additional threat generated isn't worth the damage increase. Instead use Frostbrand or Flametongue Weapon to increase your damage slightly without generating unnecessary threat.

Controlling Aggro

While Shaman have no way to reduce threat already generated, they still have a number of tools to control aggro in group settings. The primary use of their tools is to collect aggro. When using them to keep softer party members from harm, there are few downsides to this. If the main tank is controlling aggro without help, there is no need to use these, but if the main tank is having trouble, a little work on your part can salvage a poor fight.

Using Rockbiter Weapon keeps a target on you even with other party members blasting away (provided they don't overdo it). It generates more damage than your attacks normally would and is great for holding an enemy while others finish it.

Earthshock generates a lot of threat quickly. It deals modest damage instantly and really pisses the enemy off. Use this to pull undamaged enemies off softer party members. One Earthshock holds an enemy's interest for quite some time, but it won't be enough to give your tank trouble when she tries to pull the enemy off you.

Healing is another way to draw aggro from undamaged enemies. Healing the most damage person in the party (while a good idea as it helps them survive) also builds a reasonable bit of threat. Healing yourself keeps you alive and continues to add threat to the enemies. Do this when your tank is having a really tough time and your party isn't focusing fire well.

Kiting and Hindering

An unhindered Shaman can kite one or more enemies quite well. If you're kiting a single enemy, hit them with Frostshock as fast as it recycles and keep moving. This forces the enemy to move at a much slower speed while still generating threat so the enemy will continue following you.

In PvP, this is a ruthless and vile tactic that nearly ensures victory against an unskilled opponent. It's far more difficult to kite skilled PvP players. Another option in PvP is to drop an Earthbind Totem to slow a larger force of enemies. Dropping it near doorways and in bushes makes it more difficult to see and thus more difficult to destroy before the enemy runs through it.

In PvE, kiting multiple opponents can be quite useful if your party wouldn't survive a direct attack against them. Hit the enemy with Chain Lightning to generate early threat and drop an Earthbind Totem before running off. Heal yourself and others to keep the enemies following you and not focusing on your totems. You party can pull the enemies off one at a time and kill them while you kite the others. This takes a lot of mana and the party should be ready to jump in if you get dazed.

Know Where to Be

Shaman have a lot they can do. Keep an eye on where the enemy is and how much health and mana each party member has at all times. Be ready to jump in if things start going poorly. If the Druid has too much aggro from healing, the Warrior and Rogue can pull the monster off, but they have no ability to heal the Druid.

On the other side of the coin, if a Warrior has fallen and enemies are running at the Priest, the Rogue can hold one enemy, but she won't be able to hold them all. With some fast work, you can collect aggro and save the rest of the party.

As one of the only classes that can heal, cast, and deal damage at the same time, you have a great deal of power…and just as much responsibility.

Warlocks are draped in shadow and intrigue. While others shun the power of demon summoning and control, a rare few understand that power is merely a tool to be used as one sees fit. Without taking advantage of power, we are sure to be the victims of it.

These casters are different than Mages, though damage can still be a focus for them. Warlocks use a mix of direct, magical assault and demonic pets to accomplish various tasks. Synergistically, these forces allow Warlocks to kill very efficiently over time. One great joy is that these summoners are able to choose from different types of pets as they level (starting with a Mage-like Imp, but leading toward pets that can tank, deal moderate damage and offering some crowd control, detect Stealth and Dispel effects, and deal massive damage).

Warlocks start with the mystic staples: bolts from range for direct damage. From there, however, the variety expands immensely, and even over the first few training sessions the true beauty of the class begins to appear. Warlocks master multiple forms of damage over time and debuffs to weaken their opponent. To top off the pile of tricks, these casters can create items to instantly heal themselves (or allies if given away) and ones that bring back the dead! Warlocks can even summon grouped allies from other parts of the world, instantly joining them with the bulk of the party before heading into danger. These abilities turn Warlocks into a utility class as well as a DPS class. Did we forget to mention the horrifying AoEs?

Warlocks may sound challenging, or even a little daunting; they are! And, it's worth your time and practice to learn about these clever casters. If you want power at range and thrive on complex tricks and techniques, don't listen to those Mages who pretend to understand true power. Keep reading to learn the truth.

Lore

The door swung shut, but a cold wind had blown into the tavern. Several of the locals looked up at me, but they didn't stare for long. Mages came through Goldshire all the time, and to them I seemed about as common as any caster with a mind for flame and glory. I purchased some basic supplies and made myself a fixture of the room for a time, waiting until nobody knew or cared what I was doing, then I slipped into the back room and down the staircase.

Though I had never been to this place before, I had heard from others where to seek my trainer. There, in the dark storage room under the tavern, I found barrels of aging whisky and ale. The place smelled dry and a bit stale, but there was something else hovering in the air; an almost imperceptible hint of intensity.

"Who are you?" a voice queried from the darkness.

I concentrated for a few moments instead of responding, bringing a powerful energy to bear in the room and a light shone where before there was nothing. Out of that stepped my Imp, snarling for a moment in its petulant manner.

"I come as a man who wishes to learn," I said to the shadowy figure near the wall. "I have already begun my journey, but there is much still that I do not understand. Others have said that you are a person who can help me."

"We must all help ourselves," the other said while stepping slightly forward. "Yet," he added, "I can guide you toward greater things."

The stairs above us creaked for a moment, sounding as if someone was about to descend. Both of our hands reached into the folds of our robes, bringing out wands that cracked with a dark aura. Nothing approached; it was merely some buffoon upstairs who had wandered too heavily on the floor.

I smiled as I put my wand away. "I am ready."

Introduction to Playing the Class

Warlocks are a class with a great deal of finesse. Certainly, there are easier classes to try when you first enter the World of Warcraft, but these casters have so much potential for utility, damage, and excitement, that they are a must-try class somewhere along your journey.

The simple philosophy of Warlocks is one of attrition; the enemies can't kill you before your damage over time kills them. And indeed, attrition is easy for Warlocks to rely on. With multiple, stacking DOTs, Warlocks can place a massive amount of damage on a target with almost no casting time (these are on short casting timers or are instants). DOT, DOT, DOT, Fear, rinse, and repeat. There are other ways of cracking mobs, but this is extremely reliable and can be relatively fast while maintaining full mana for the next engagement. Thus, the Warlock has almost no downtime between fights.

Another facet of this is that Warlocks have a very thin line between their health and mana. Health is *easily* converted into mana through Life Tap. And to some extent, mana can be converted into health through Life Drain. Because Warlocks also have Healthstones to act as free health in a pinch, this means that there is almost always something in reserve for those tougher fights.

Pet choices define a Hunter because pets do so much damage and are essential tanking buddies. That isn't always the case for Warlock pets; the Warlock is easily more of a damage dealer, and not all of a Warlock's pets can take a hand at tanking. That said, the abilities these creatures bring to the class offer immense variety of play.

When the monsters aren't a threat (e.g. a good group or soft monsters), the Imp is relied on for easy damage at range, more health, and a damage shield for melee. The Voidwalker can tank like a fiend, survive almost anything, and hold that aggro; sadly, he hits like a weary kitten. The Succubus does more melee damage, can seduce Humanoids for crowd control, and likes whips. Finally, there is a Felhunter that warns of stealthers, can eat magic to Dispel effects, they can Silence casters, and even reduce melee Attack Power of enemies.

In the later game, Warlocks have quests for their mount and epic mount (major cost savers), and they also learn how to summon and "control" pets with immense power. Infernals and Doomguards are scary, difficult to control, and fun as heck to throw against your enemies.

Due to spells like Hellfire, Warlocks have AoE potential that surpasses almost all other classes. The life expectancy of a Warlock who does this work is low without proper healing, but the results are amazing to watch. Think about dealing a couple-hundred DPS with a channeled spell for *every* target! It's as fun as it sounds.

Available Races	
Gnome	Human
Orc	Undead

What do Attributes Mean to Me?	
Strength	Improved Melee for Sword Attacks (Not So Great)
Stamina	Higher Health (Extremely Important)
Agility	Improved Dodge Rate
Intellect	Higher Mana Total, More Criticals from Spells
Spirit	Improved Health and Mana Recovery

Items and Equipment

Warlocks aren't as dependent on equipment as a number of their rivals. Indeed, having a good wand and high bonuses to Stamina and Intellect are enough by themselves to place Warlocks in a fairly good spot. These casters have many facets of play that revolve around the timing of their ability use, so stats are reduced slightly in importance (not to the point of being on the sidelines, of course).

The primary focus for a Warlock is to collect a heavy supply of Intellect and Stamina gear. With proper pet use, Warlocks can have some very effective and long fights against difficult opponents. The Intellect is always there for having a good mana pool. Stamina, on the other hand, is for both survival and for having a backup mana pool. This might not make sense yet, but it will in time. The short version is that Warlocks can easily turn health into mana! Thus, more health either means that you live longer or can cast harder.

Wands have already been mentioned; these ranged weapons are perfect for adding to solo or group damage when your mana is depleted (or when you wish to start regenerating mana as a monster dies of your DOTs). Stay current with these weapons as often as possible and practice their use and timing to make sure you get the maximum amount of damage.

Stamina enchantments are easy to obtain, and the lower-tier ones are often relatively cheap even if you purchase them from non-guildies. Get as much +Stamina enchanting done as possible when you can afford it; at early, mid, and later levels, this really adds to a Warlocks capabilities.

One odd point of note; a number of other casters would far rather have mana potions instead of health potions. After all, most of them can convert mana into health very efficiently. And even if they can't do that (e.g. Mages), there is far more importance in having mana to destroy enemies and survive. Casters cannot live on health alone! But with Warlocks, that is the converse. There are many situations when a Warlock needs health, and these casters can lay on plenty of damage without a huge mana pool.

CHOOSING YOUR PROFESSION

Warlocks can be happy with several choices in tradeskills. Tailoring and Enchanting both have allure because of their wide use in creating and improving moderate-to-high quality items for casters. This is a very good route for the solo Warlock.

Warlocks in large guilds may prefer Herbalism and Alchemy, for the potion potential. Yet, Warlocks don't use potions quite as often as some of the other casters because of their ability to shift mana into health and health into mana (though different abilities).

Because Warlocks get dinged up from time to time and like to use their health for various projects, it's very nice to have Cooking and First Aid to improve the efficiency of these powers. Quickly increasing your mana supply on the move and using First Aid to shore up any health problems can keep a Warlock at top form. Forsaken Warlocks especially are able to have fun with their health (cast a lot, use Life Tap, bandage here and there, eat some corpses, etc.).

Class Abilities

Warlock abilities are able to cause massive trouble to enemies through DOTs, debuffs, and some direct damage. In addition, a Warlock's choice of pet modifies which buffs are cast on allies and how militant the Warlock is against enemies (Imps for some damage at range and buff utility, Succubus for melee damage and crowd control, Voidwalker for tanking/defense, etc.).

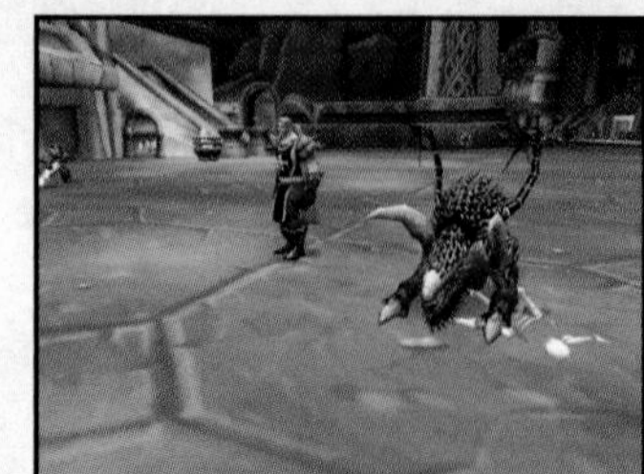

Affliction

Corruption

Corruption is the first Affliction DOT. Through Talents, this can become an instant DOT, just like Curse of Agony. Because Corruption only lasts for 12 seconds, it needs to be renewed on powerful enemies.

Rank	Level	Mana	Range	Casting Time	Cooldown	Cost to Train	Effect
1	4	35	30 yd	2.0 sec	—	1	Corrupts the target, causing 42 damage over 12 sec.
2	14	55	30 yd	2.0 sec	—	9	Corrupts the target, causing 91 damage over 15 sec.
3	24	100	30 yd	2.0 sec	—	30	Corrupts the target, causing 184 damage over 18 sec.
4	34	160	30 yd	2.0 sec	—	80	Corrupts the target, causing 324 damage over 18 sec.
5	44	225	30 yd	2.0 sec	—	1 20	Corrupts the target, causing 486 damage over 18 sec.
6	54	290	30 yd	2.0 sec	—	2	Corrupts the target, causing 666 damage over 18 sec.

Curse of Weakness

Curse of Weakness reduces damage caused by the target for up to two minutes. This isn't used terribly often, as only one Curse (per Warlock) can be active on a target.

Rank	Level	Mana	Range	Casting Time	Cooldown	Cost to Train	Effect
1	4	20	30 yd	IC	—	1	Damage caused by the target is reduced by 3 for 2 min. Only one Curse per Warlock can be active on any one target.
2	12	30	30 yd	IC	—	6	Damage caused by the target is reduced by 6 for 2 min. Only one Curse per Warlock can be active on any one target.
3	22	70	30 yd	IC	—	25	Damage caused by the target is reduced by 10 for 2 min. Only one Curse per Warlock can be active on any one target.
4	32	95	30 yd	IC	—	70	Damage caused by the target is reduced by 15 for 2 min. Only one Curse per Warlock can be active on any one target.
5	42	130	30 yd	IC	—	1 10	Damage caused by the target is reduced by 22 for 2 min. Only one Curse per Warlock can be active on any one target.

Life Tap

Life Tap converts health into mana without delay.

Rank	Level	HP	Range	Casting Time	Cooldown	Cost to Train	Effect
1	6	25	—	IC	—	1	Converts 25 health into 25 mana.
2	16	60	—	IC	—	12	Converts 60 health into 65 mana.
3	26	115	—	IC	—	40	Converts 115 health into 130 mana.
4	36	185	—	IC	—	90	Converts 185 health into 210 mana.
5	46	265	—	IC	—	1 30	Converts 265 health into 300 mana.

Curse of Agony

Curse of Agony is an instant long-term mana efficient DOT. For standard targets, this is the default Curse for bringing the foe down and collecting experience.

Rank	Level	Mana	Range	Casting Time	Cooldown	Cost to Train	Effect
1	8	25	30 yd	IC	—	2	Curses the target with agony, causing 84 Shadow damage over 24 sec. This damage is dealt slowly at first, and builds up as the Curse reaches its full duration. Only one Curse per Warlock can be active on any one target.
2	18	50	30 yd	IC	—	15	Curses the target with agony, causing 180 Shadow damage over 24 sec. This damage is dealt slowly at first, and builds up as the Curse reaches its full duration. Only one Curse per Warlock can be active on any one target.
3	28	90	30 yd	IC	—	50	Curses the target with agony, causing 324 Shadow damage over 24 sec. This damage is dealt slowly at first, and builds up as the Curse reaches its full duration. Only one Curse per Warlock can be active on any one target.
4	38	130	30 yd	IC	—	1	Curses the target with agony, causing 504 Shadow damage over 24 sec. This damage is dealt slowly at first, and builds up as the Curse reaches its full duration. Only one Curse per Warlock can be active on any one target.
5	48	170	30 yd	IC	—	1 40	Curses the target with agony, causing 780 Shadow damage over 24 sec. This damage is dealt slowly at first, and builds up as the Curse reaches its full duration. Only one Curse per Warlock can be active on any one target.
6	58	215	30 yd	IC	—	2 40	Curses the target with agony, causing 1044 Shadow damage over 24 sec. This damage is dealt slowly at first, and builds up as the Curse reaches its full duration. Only one Curse per Warlock can be active on any one target.

Fear

Fear is the bread and butter of Warlock crowd control. Damage may interrupt Fear, but it still takes time from the target to refocus and return to the Warlock.

Rank	Level	Mana	Range	Casting Time	Cooldown	Cost to Train	Effect
1	8	30	20 yd	1.5 sec	—	2	Strikes fear in the enemy, causing it to run in fear for up to 10 sec. Damage caused may interrupt the effect. Only 1 target can be feared at a time.
2	32	30	20 yd	1.5 sec	—	70	Strikes fear in the enemy, causing it to run in fear for up to 15 sec. Damage caused may interrupt the effect. Only 1 target can be feared at a time.
3	56	30	20 yd	1.5 sec	—	2 20	Strikes fear in the enemy, causing it to run in fear for up to 20 sec. Damage caused may interrupt the effect. Only 1 target can be feared at a time.

Drain Soul

Drain Soul is the first method Warlocks gain to find Soul Shards (these are needed for almost all Summons, and for a few normal spells as well). This channeled spell does a modest amount of damage; your Warlock receives a Soul Shard from the target if it dies while the Drain Soul is still in effect.

Rank	Level	Mana	Range	Casting Time	Cooldown	Cost to Train	Effect
1	10	55	30 yd	IC	—	3	Drains the soul of the target, causing 55 Shadow damage over 15 sec. If the target dies while being drained, and yields experience or honor, the caster gains a Soul Shard. Soul Shards are required for other spells.
2	24	125	30 yd	IC	—	30	Drains the soul of the target, causing 155 Shadow damage over 15 sec. If the target dies while being drained, and yields experience or honor, the caster gains a Soul Shard. Soul Shards are required for other spells.
3	38	210	30 yd	IC	—	1	Drains the soul of the target, causing 295 Shadow damage over 15 sec. If the target dies while being drained, and yields experience or honor, the caster gains a Soul Shard. Soul Shards are required for other spells.
4	52	290	30 yd	IC	—	1 80	Drains the soul of the target, causing 455 Shadow damage over 15 sec. If the target dies while being drained, and yields experience or honor, the caster gains a Soul Shard. Soul Shards are required for other spells.

Curse of Recklessness

Curse of Recklessness is a complex spell, and it doesn't come into play often. This Curse prevents a target from fleeing, makes it immune to Fear effects, reduces armor, and increases melee Attack Power.

Rank	Level	Mana	Range	Casting Time	Cooldown	Cost to Train	Effect
1	14	35	30 yd	IC	—	9	Curses the target with recklessness, increasing attack power by 20 but reducing armor by 140 for 2 min. Cursed enemies will not flee and will ignore fear effects. Only one Curse per Warlock can be active on any one target.
2	28	60	30 yd	IC	—	50	Curses the target with recklessness, increasing attack power by 45 but reducing armor by 290 for 2 min. Cursed enemies will not flee and will ignore fear effects. Only one Curse per Warlock can be active on any one target.
3	42	90	30 yd	IC	—	1 20	Curses the target with recklessness, increasing attack power by 65 but reducing armor by 465 for 2 min. Cursed enemies will not flee and will ignore fear effects. Only one Curse per Warlock can be active on any one target.
4	56	115	30 yd	IC	—	2 20	Curses the target with recklessness, increasing attack power by 90 but reducing armor by 640 for 2 min. Cursed enemies will not flee and will ignore fear effects. Only one Curse per Warlock can be active on any one target.

Drain Life

Drain Life is a critical ability for certain Warlock builds. If you plan on draintanking, stack on the DOTs, keep your pet on full damage, and uses Drain Life to negate as much incoming damage as possible.

Rank	Level	Mana	Range	Casting Time	Cooldown	Cost to Train	Effect
1	14	55	20 yd	IC	—	9	Transfers 10 health every second from the target to the caster. Lasts 5 sec.
2	22	85	20 yd	IC	—	25	Transfers 17 health every second from the target to the caster. Lasts 5 sec.
3	30	135	20 yd	IC	—	60	Transfers 29 health every second from the target to the caster. Lasts 5 sec.
4	38	185	20 yd	IC	—	1	Transfers 41 health every second from the target to the caster. Lasts 5 sec
5	46	240	20 yd	IC	—	1 30	Transfers 55 health every second from the target to the caster. Lasts 5 sec.
6	54	300	20 yd	IC	—	2	Transfers 71 health every second from the target to the caster. Lasts 5 sec.

Amplify Curse

Amplify Curse is a Talent-learned ability that is usable every three minutes. This increases the effectiveness of Curse of Agony, Curse of Weakness, or Curse of Exhaustion.

Rank	Minimum Level	Mana	Range	Casting Time	Cooldown	Cost to Train	Effect
1	20	—	—	IC	3 minutes	—	Increases the effect of your next Curse of Weakness or Curse of Agony by 50% or your next Curse of Exhaustion by 20%.

Drain Mana

Drain Mana takes mana from your foe, giving it to you and leaving them without the tools to keep themselves alive while dealing damage against you.

Rank	Level	Mana	Range	Casting Time	Cooldown	Cost to Train	Effect
1	24	95	20 yd	IC	—	30	Transfers 42 mana every 1 sec from the target to the caster. Lasts 5 sec.
2	34	155	20 yd	IC	—	80	Transfers 68 mana every 1 sec from the target to the caster. Lasts 5 sec.
3	44	225	20 yd	IC	—	1 20	Transfers 99 mana every 1 sec from the target to the caster. Lasts 5 sec.
4	54	310	20 yd	IC	—	2	Transfers 136 mana every 1 sec from the target to the caster. Lasts 5 sec.

Curse of Tongues

Curse of Tongues is an anti-caster ability that adds considerably to casting times.

Rank	Level	Mana	Range	Casting Time	Cooldown	Cost to Train	Effect
1	26	80	30 yd	IC	—	40	Forces the target to speak in Demonic, slowing the casting time of all spells by 50%. Only one Curse per Warlock can be active on any one target. Lasts 30 sec.
2	50	110	30 yd	IC	—	1 50	Forces the target to speak in Demonic, slowing the casting time of all spells by 60%. Only one Curse per Warlock can be active on any one target. Lasts 30 sec.

Banish

Banish is a crowd control spell that works against Demons and Elementals. During this time, the enemy can't be damaged by anyone.

Rank	Level	Mana	Range	Casting Time	Cooldown	Cost to Train	Effect
N/A	28	100	30 yd	1 sec	20 min	50	Banished the enemy target, preventing all action but making it invulnerable for up to 30 sec. Only one target can be banished at a time.

Curse of Exhaustion

Curse of Exhaustion is a Talent-learned ability that Snares targets. With additional Talents, this becomes enough of a Snare to modestly impair melee enemies.

Rank	Minimum Level	Mana	Range	Casting Time	Cooldown	Cost to Train	Effect
1	30	108	30 yd	IC	—	—	Reduces the target's speed to 90% of normal for 12 sec. Only one Curse per Warlock can be active on any one target.

Siphon Life

Siphon Life is a Talent-learned ability that restores a modest amount of life while draining it away from the target. Because this is an instant-cast spell, it leaves the Warlock free to deal DPS.

Rank	Minimum Level	Mana	Range	Casting Time	Cooldown	Cost to Train	Effect
1	30	150	30 yd	IC	—	—	Transfers 15 health from the target to the caster every 3 sec. Lasts 30 sec.
2	38	205	30 yd	IC	—	5	Transfers 22 health from the target to the caster every 3 sec. Lasts 30 sec.
3	48	285	30 yd	IC	—	7	Transfers 33 health from the target to the caster every 3 sec. Lasts 30 sec.
4	58	365	30 yd	IC	—	12	Transfers 45 health from the target to the caster every 3 sec. Lasts 30 sec.

Curse of the Elements

Curse of Elements screams raid-friendly in a loud voice. A single use of Curse of Elements is enough to place a five-minute debuff on a target that reduces Fire and Frost Resistance.

Rank	Level	Mana	Range	Casting Time	Cooldown	Cost to Train	Effect
1	32	100	30 yd	IC	—	70	Curses the target, reducing Fire and Frost resistances by 45 and increasing Fire and Frost damage by 6% for 5 min. Only one Curse per Warlock can be active on any one target.
2	46	150	30 yd	IC	—	1 30	Curses the target, reducing Fire and Frost resistances by 60 and increasing Fire and Frost damage by 8% for 5 min. for 5 min. Only one Curse per Warlock can be active on any one target.
3	60	200	30 yd	IC	—	2 60	Curses the target, reducing Fire and Frost resistances by 75 and increasing Fire and Frost damage by 10% for 5 min. for 5 min. Only one Curse per Warlock can be active on any one target.

Dark Pact

Dark Pack is a Talent-learned ability that completes the Affliction line. This ability steals mana from your "beloved" pet and converts it into your own.

Rank	Minimum Level	Mana	Range	Casting Time	Cooldown	Cost to Train	Effect
1	40	—	20 yd	IC	—	—	Drains 150 of your pet's Mana, returning 100% to you.
2	50	—	20 yd	IC	—	7 50	Drains 200 of your pet's Mana, returning 100% to you.
3	60	—	20 yd	IC	—	13	Drains 250 of your pet's Mana, returning 100% to you.

Howl of Terror

Howl of Terror causes up to five nearby enemies to flee in Terror. Though damage to the targets may cause the effect to end early, this is a great spell for getting out of major trouble.

Rank	Level	Mana	Range	Casting Time	Cooldown	Cost to Train	Effect
1	40	150	—	2 sec	40 sec	1 10	Howl, causing all enemies within 10 yds to flee in terror for 10 sec. Damage caused may interrupt the effect.
2	54	200	—	2 sec	40 sec	2	Howl, causing all enemies within 10 yds to flee in terror for 15 sec. Damage caused may interrupt the effect.

Death Coil

Death Coil is an instant spell that deals damage (restoring damage dealt to your Warlock's total), and placing a short-term Horror effect on the target for the duration. Though this has a two-minute cooldown timer, it should be used as often as possible in PvP.

Rank	Level	Mana	Range	Casting Time	Cooldown	Cost to Train	Effect
1	42	430	30 yd	IC	2 min	1 10	Causes the enemy target to run in horror for 3 sec and causes 287 Shadow damage. The caster gains 100% of the damage caused in health.
2	50	495	30 yd	IC	2 min	1 50	Causes the enemy target to run in horror for 3 sec and causes 375 Shadow damage. The caster gains 100% of the damage caused in health.
3	58	565	30 yd	IC	2 min	2 40	Causes the enemy target to run in horror for 3 sec and causes 470 Shadow damage. The caster gains 100% of the damage caused in health.

Curse of Shadow

Curse of Shadow is like Curse of Elements, but Arcane and Shadow Resistances are lowered instead.

Rank	Level	Mana	Range	Casting Time	Cooldown	Cost to Train	Effect
1	44	150	30 yd	IC	—	1 20	Curses the target for 5 min, reducing Shadow and Arcane resistances by 60 and increasing Shadow and Arcane damage taken by 8%. Only one Curse per Warlock can be active on any one target.
2	56	200	30 yd	IC	—	2 20	Curses the target for 5 min, reducing Shadow and Arcane resistances by 75 and increasing Shadow and Arcane damage taken by 10%. Only one Curse per Warlock can be active on any one target.

Curse of Doom

Curse of Doom places a Curse on a target that deals several thousand damage over one minute. If this kills the target, there is a small chance that a Doom Guard is summoned next to your Warlock! Have Banish ready, cast Curse of Shadow, then try to Enslave the Doom Guard.

Rank	Level	Mana	Range	Casting Time	Cooldown	Cost to Train	Effect
N/A	60	300	30 yd	IC	1 min	2 60	Curses the target with impending Doom, causing 3200 Shadow Damage after 1 min. If the target dies from this damage, there is a chance that a Doomguard will be summoned. Cannot be cast on players.

Demonology

Health Funnel

Health Funnel channels health from you into your pet.

Rank	Level	HP	Range	Casting Time	Cooldown	Cost to Train	Effect
1	12	11 + 5/ sec	20 yd	Channeled	—	6	Gives 12 health to the caster's pet every second for 10 sec as long as the caster channels.
2	20	15 + 10/ sec	20 yd	Channeled	—	20	Gives 24 health to the caster's pet every second for 10 sec as long as the caster channels.
3	28	24 + 17/ sec	20 yd	Channeled	—	50	Gives 43 health to the caster's pet every second for 10 sec as long as the caster channels.
4	36	39 + 24/ sec	20 yd	Channeled	—	90	Gives 64 health to the caster's pet every second for 10 sec as long as the caster channels.
5	44	45 + 33/ sec	20 yd	Channeled	—	1 20	Gives 89 health to the caster's pet every second for 10 sec as long as the caster channels.
6	52	62 + 42/ sec	20 yd	Channeled	—	1 80	Gives 119 health to the caster's pet every second for 10 sec as long as the caster channels.
7	60	79 + 52/ sec	20 yd	Channeled	—	2 60	Gives 153 health to the caster's pet every second for 10 sec as long as the caster channels.

Create Healthstone

Create Healthstone require one Soul Shard to create. These are used to restore health instantly (think of it as a free potion).

Ability	Level	Mana	Casting Time	Cooldown	Cost to Train	Effect
Create Healthstone (Minor)	10	95	3 sec	—	3	Creates a Minor Healthstone that can be used to instantly restore 100 health. Conjured Items disappear if logged out for more than 15 min. Requires Soul Shard.
Create Healthstone (Lesser)	22	240	3 sec	—	25	Creates a Lesser Healthstone that can be used to instantly restore 250 health. Conjured Items disappear if logged out for more than 15 min. Requires Soul Shard.
Create Healthstone	34	475	3 sec	—	80	Creates a Healthstone that can be used to instantly restore 500 health. Conjured Items disappear if logged out for more than 15 min. Requires Soul Shard.
Create Healthstone (Greater)	46	750	3 sec	—	1 30	Creates a Greater Healthstone that can be used to instantly restore 800 health. Conjured Items disappear if logged out for more than 15 min. Requires Soul Shard.
Create Healthstone (Major)	58	1120	3 sec	—	2 40	Creates a Major Healthstone that can be used to instantly restore 1200 health. Conjured Items disappear if logged out for more than 15 min. Requires Soul Shard.

Demon Skin

Demon Skin/Demon Armor are spells that buff Warlocks for 30 minutes. Eventually, these help with armor, Shadow Resistance, and health regeneration as well.

Rank	Level	Mana	Range	Casting Time	Cooldown	Cost to Train	Effect
2	10	120	—	IC	—	3	Protects the caster, increasing armor by 120 and restores 5 health per 5 sec for 30 min.

Demon Armor

Rank	Level	Mana	Range	Casting Time	Cooldown	Cost to Train	Effect
1	20	275	—	IC	—	20	Protects the caster, increasing armor by 210, Shadow resistance by 3 and restores 7 health every 5 sec. for 30 min.
2	30	520	—	IC	—	60	Protects the caster, increasing armor by 300, Shadow resistance by 6 and restores 9 health every 5 sec. for 30 min.
3	40	800	—	IC	—	1 10	Protects the caster, increasing armor by 390, Shadow resistance by 9 and restores 11 health every 5 sec. for 30 min.
4	50	1150	—	IC	—	1 50	Protects the caster, increasing armor by 480, Shadow resistance by 12 and restores 13 health every 5 sec. for 30 min.
5	60	1580	—	IC	—	2 60	Protects the caster, increasing armor by 570, Shadow resistance by 15 and restores 15 health every 5 sec. for 30 min.

Unending Breath

Unending Breath allows the target of the spell to breathe underwater for ten minutes.

Rank	Level	Mana	Range	Casting Time	Cooldown	Cost to Train	Effect
N/A	16	50	30 yd	IC	—	12	Allows the target to breath underwater for 10 min.

Create Soulstone

Create Soulstone requires a Soul Shard. This creates an item that gives the holder a chance to Resurrect in the event of their death.

Ability	Level	Mana	Casting Time	Cooldown	Cost to Train	Effect
Create Soulstone (Minor)	18	170	3 sec	—	15	Creates a Minor Soulstone. The Soulstone can be used to store one target's soul. If the target dies while his soul is stored, he will be able to resurrect with 400 health and 700 mana. Conjured items disappear if logged out for more than 15 min.
Create Soulstone (Lesser)	30	170	3 sec	—	60	Creates a Soulstone. The Soulstone can be used to store one target's soul. If the target dies while his soul is stored, he will be able to resurrect with 750 health and 1200 mana. Conjured items disappear if logged out for more than 15 min.
Create Soulstone	40	170	3 sec	—	1 10	Creates a Soulstone. The Soulstone can be used to store one target's soul. If the target dies while his soul is stored, he will be able to resurrect with 1100 health and 1700 mana. Conjured items disappear if logged out for more than 15 min.
Create Soulstone (Greater)	50	170	3 sec	—	1 50	Creates a Soulstone. The Soulstone can be used to store one target's soul. If the target dies while his soul is stored, he will be able to resurrect with 2200 health and 2800 mana. Conjured items disappear if logged out for more than 15 min.

Fel Domination

Fel Domination is a Talent-learned ability that is on a 15-minute cooldown. Not only does this greatly reduce the summoning time of your next pet; it halves the mana cost of the summoning as well.

Rank	Minimum Level	Mana	Range	Casting Time	Cooldown	Cost to Train	Effect
1	20	—	—	IC	15 minutes	—	Your next Imp, Voidwalker, Succubus, or Felhunter Summon spell has its casting time reduced by 5 sec and its Mana cost reduced by 50%.

Ritual of Summoning

Ritual of Summoning requires a Soul Shard, two group members at your current location, and a target in your group. Cast the spell on the target; this creates a portal. Then, have the two group members right-click on the portal to assist in the summoning. This instantly ports the target to you.

Rank	Level	Mana	Range	Casting Time	Cooldown	Cost to Train	Effect
N/A	20	300	30 yd	5 sec	—	20	Begins a ritual that summons the targeted group member. Requires the caster and 2 additional people to complete the ritual. In order to participate, all players must be out of combat and right-click the portal and not move until the ritual is complete. Requires a Soul Shard.

Eye of Kilrogg

Eye of Kilrogg summons a stealthy eye that your Warlock can control. This is used to scout distant areas.

Rank	Level	Mana	Range	Casting Time	Cooldown	Cost to Train	Effect
N/A	22	100	50000 yd	5 sec	—	25	Summons an Eye of Kilrogg and binds your vision to it. The eye us stealthy and quick, but very fragile.

Sense Demons

Sense Demons allows for Demon Tracking on your mini-map.

Rank	Level	Mana	Range	Casting Time	Cooldown	Cost to Train	Effect
1	24	—	—	[IC]	—	30	Shows the location of all nearby demons on the mini-map until cancelled. Only one type of tracking can be used at a time.

Detect Invisibility

Detect Invisibility is used to detect creatures that are using Invisibility effects (Stealth does not fall into this category).

Ability	Level	Mana	Range	Casting Time	Cooldown	Cost to Train	Effect
Detect Lesser Invisibility	26	50	30 yd	IC	—	40	Allows the friendly target to detect lesser invisibility for 10 min.
Detect Invisibility	38	90	30 yd	IC	—	1	Allows the friendly target to detect invisibility for 10 min.
Detect Greater Invisibility	50	140	30 yd	IC	—	1 50	Allows the friendly target to detect greater invisibility for 10 min.

Create Firestone

Create Firestone requires a Soul Shard, and is used for increasing melee and fire-based spell damage. Firestones are held in the offhand, and can only be used by Warlocks.

Ability	Level	Mana	Casting Time	Cooldown	Cost to Train	Effect
Create Firestone (Lesser)	28	500	3 sec	—	50	Creates a Lesser Firestone which can be equipped in the off hand. When equipped, enchants the main hand weapon with fire, granting each attack a chance to deal 25 to 35 additional Fire damage. In addition, equipping the Lesser Firestone increases damage done by Fire spells by 10. Conjured Items disappear if logged out for more than 15 min. Requires Soul Shard.
Create Firestone	36	700	3 sec	—	90	Creates a Firestone which can be equipped in the off hand. When equipped, enchants the main hand weapon with fire, granting each attack a chance to deal 40 to 60 additional Fire damage. In addition, equipping the Lesser Firestone increases damage done by Fire spells by 14. Conjured Items disappear if logged out for more than 15 min. Requires Soul Shard.
Create Firestone (Greater)	46	900	3 sec	—	1 30	Creates a Greater Firestone which can be equipped in the off hand. When equipped, enchants the main hand weapon with fire, granting each attack a chance to deal 60 to 90 additional Fire damage. In addition, equipping the Lesser Firestone increases damage done by Fire spells by 17. Conjured Items disappear if logged out for more than 15 min. Requires Soul Shard.
Create Firestone (Major)	56	1100	3 sec	—	2 20	When equipped, enchants the main hand weapon with fire, granting each attack a chance to deal 80 to 120 additional Fire damage. In addition, equipping the Lesser Firestone increases damage done by Fire spells by 21. Conjured Items disappear if logged out for more than 15 min. Requires Soul Shard.

Demonic Sacrifice

Demonic Sacrifice is a Talent-learned ability that gives Warlocks up to a 30 minute buff for getting rid of their pet.

Rank	Minimum Level	Mana	Range	Casting Time	Cooldown	Cost to Train	Effect
1	30	—	—	IC	15 minutes	—	When activated sacrifices your summoned demon to grant you an effect which lasts 30 min. The effect is cancedlled if any demon is summoned. Progression: Imp (Increases Fire Damage by 15%), Voidwalker (Restores 3% of total health every 4 sec), Succubus (Increases your Shadow Damage by 15%), Felhunter (Restores 2% of total Mana every 4 sec).

Enslave Demon

Enslave Demon is used to take control of a Demon; you cannot do this and keep your existing pet going (one Demon at a time). Enslave Demon won't last forever, and it can break early. Cast Curse of Shadow on the targets before Enslaving them to push the odds for a full timer in your favor.

Rank	Level	Mana	Range	Casting Time	Cooldown	Cost to Train	Effect
1	30	300	30 yd	3 sec	—	60	Enslaves the target demon, up to level 32, forcing it to do your bidding. While enslaved, the demon's attack speed is slowed by 30% and its casting speed is slowed by 30%. Lasts up to 5 min. If you repeatedly enslave the same demon, it will become more difficult to control with each attempt. Requires a Souls Shard.
2	44	500	30 yd	3 sec	—	1 20	Enslaves the target demon, up to level 47, forcing it to do your bidding. While enslaved, the demon's attack speed is slowed by 30% and its casting speed is slowed by 30 Lasts up to 5 min. If you repeatedly enslave the same demon, it will become more difficult to control with each attempt. Requires a Souls Shard.
3	58	700	30 yd	3 sec	—	2 40	Enslaves the target demon, up to level 62, forcing it to do your bidding. While enslaved, the demon's attack speed is slowed by 30% and its casting speed is slowed by 30%. Lasts up to 5 min. If you repeatedly enslave the same demon, it will become more difficult to control with each attempt. Requires a Souls Shard.

Shadow Ward

Shadow Ward is only on a 30-second cooldown, but its duration is only 30 seconds as well. Use this to buff a target against Shadow damage.

Rank	Level	Mana	Range	Casting Time	Cooldown	Cost to Train	Effect
1	32	135	—	IC	30 sec	70	Absorbs 185 shadow damage. Lasts 30 sec.
2	42	195	—	IC	30 sec	1 10	Absorbs 300 shadow damage. Lasts 30 sec.
3	52	255	—	IC	30 sec	1 80	Absorbs 430 shadow damage. Lasts 30 sec

Create Spellstone

Create Spellstone requires a Soul Shard. When equipped, they raise the Critical rate for a Warlock's spells by 1%. When used, the Spellstone creates an anti-magic shield for a decent sum of health.

Ability	Level	Mana	Casting Time	Cooldown	Cost to Train	Effect
Create Spellstone	36	500	5 sec	—	90	Creates a Spellstone for the caster. When equipped and used, the Spellstone removes all magic effects from the caster and will absorb 400 magic damage for 1 min. Conjured Items disappear if logged out for more than 15 min. Requires Soul Shard.
Create Spellstone (Greater)	48	750	5 sec	—	1 40	Creates a Greater Spellstone for the caster. When equipped and used, the Greater Spellstone removes all magic effects from the caster and will absorb 650 magic damage for 1 min. Conjured Items disappear if logged out for more than 15 min. Requires Soul Shard.
Create Spellstone (Major)	60	1000	5 sec	—	2 60	Creates a Major Spellstone for the caster. When equipped and used, the Major Spellstone removes all magic effects from the caster and will absorb 900 magic damage for 1 min. Conjured Items disappear if logged out for more than 15 min. Requires Soul Shard.

Soul Link

Soul Link is a Talent-learned ability that transfers 30% of the damage taken by the Warlock to their pet. There is also a buff to the damage rate of both the Warlock and the pet while this is active.

Rank	Minimum Level	Mana	Range	Casting Time	Cooldown	Cost to Train	Effect
1	40	270	100 yd	IC	—		When active, 30% of all damage taken by the caster is taken by your summoned demon instead. In addition, both the demon and the master will inflict 3% more damage. Lasts as long as the demon is active.

Inferno

Inferno is a summon that requires an Infernal Stone and can only be used once an hour. This calls an Infernal down from the sky, delivering an AoE Stun for two seconds. Your Warlock gets five minutes of free control over this "pet" before Enslave Demon needs to be used.

Rank	Level	Mana	Range	Casting Time	Cooldown	Reagent	Effect
1	50	100% of Base Mana	30 yd	2 sec	60 min	Infernal Stone	Summons a meteor from the Twisting Nether, causing 200 Fire damage and stunning all enemy targets in the area for 2 sec. An Infernal rises from the crater, under the command of the caster for 5 min. Once control is lost, the Infernal must be Enslaved to maintain control. Can only be used outdoors.

Ritual of Doom

Ritual of Doom requires a Demonic Figuring reagent (costing a full gold piece), all of the Warlocks mana, and can only be used once an hour. This offers another way to summon a Doomguard. Warlocks need to have a group with four other people to begin the ritual and at the completion of casting Ritual of Doom, one of your "buddies" is killed off to create the Doomguard. Cast Curse of Shadow and Enslave Demon to grab the Doomguard and bend it to your will. Note that the Doomguard from this Ritual is *more* powerful than the Doomguard from Curse of Doom.

Rank	Level	Mana	Range	Casting Time	Cooldown	Reagent	Effect
1	60	100% of Base Mana	30 yd	10 sec	60 min	Demonic Figurine	Begins a ritual that sacrifices a random participant to summon a doomguard. The doomguard must be immediately enslaved of it will attack the ritual participants. Requires the caster and 4 additional party members to complete the ritual. In order to participate, all players must right-click the portal and not move until the ritual is complete.

Destruction

Shadow Bolt

Shadow Bolt deals ranged, Shadow damage to a target. This is not the mana efficient attack for a Warlock, but it does offer a fair amount of damage especially when added to a pile of existing DOTs.

Rank	Level	Mana	Range	Casting Time	Cooldown	Cost to Train	Effect
2	6	40	30 yd	2.2 sec	—	1	Sends a shadowy bolt at the enemy, causing 23 to 29 shadow damage.
3	12	70	30 yd	2.8 sec	—	6	Sends a shadowy bolt at the enemy, causing 48 to 56 shadow damage.
4	20	110	30 yd	3 sec	—	20	Sends a shadowy bolt at the enemy, causing 86 to 98 shadow damage.
5	28	160	30 yd	3 sec	—	50	Sends a shadowy bolt at the enemy, causing 142 to 162 shadow damage.
6	36	210	30 yd	3 sec	—	90	Sends a shadowy bolt at the enemy, causing 204 to 230 shadow damage.
7	44	260	35 yd	2.8 sec	—	1 20	Sends a shadowy bolt at the enemy, causing 281 to 315 shadow damage.
8	52	309	35 yd	2.8 sec	—	1 80	Sends a shadowy bolt at the enemy, causing 360 to 402 shadow damage.
9	60	363	35 yd	2.8 sec	—	2 60	Sends a shadowy bolt at the enemy, causing 455 to 507 shadow damage.
10	60	380	30 yd	3 sec	—	—	Sends a shadowy bolt at the enemy, causing 482 to 538 Shadow damage.

Immolate

Immolate is a short-casting Fire spell that deals some of its damage up front, but the bulk of the pain as a DOT.

Rank	Level	Mana	Range	Casting Time	Cooldown	Cost to Train	Effect
1	1	25	30 yd	2 sec	—	10	Burns the enemy for 8 Fire damage and then an additional 20 Fire damage over 15 sec.
2	10	45	30 yd	2 sec	—	3	Burns the enemy for 19 Fire damage and then an additional 40 Fire damage over 15 sec.
3	20	90	30 yd	2 sec	—	20	Burns the enemy for 45 Fire damage and then an additional 90 Fire damage over 15 sec.
4	30	155	30 yd	2 sec	—	60	Burns the enemy for 90 Fire damage and then an additional 165 Fire damage over15 sec.
5	40	216	30 yd	1.8 sec	—	1 10	Burns the enemy for 173 Fire damage and then an additional 330 Fire damage over 15 sec.
6	50	295	30 yd	1.5 sec	—	1 50	Burns the enemy for 255 Fire damage and then an additional 485 Fire damage over 15 sec.
7	60	370	30 yd	1.5 sec	—	2 60	Burns the enemy for 343 Fire damage and then an additional 645 Fire damage over 15 sec.
8	60	380	30 yd	2 sec	—	—	Burns the enemy for 279 Fire Damage and then an additional 510 Fire damage over 15 sec.

Searing Pain

Searing Pain deals its full sum of Fire damage up front (a rarity for Warlocks). This causes much higher Threat than spamming Shadow Bolt.

Rank	Level	Mana	Range	Casting Time	Cooldown	Cost to Train	Effect
1	18	50	30 yd	1.5 sec	—	15	Inflict searing pain on the enemy target, causing 34 to 42 Fire damage. Causes a high amount of threat.
2	26	75	30 yd	1.5 sec	—	40	Inflict searing pain on the enemy target, causing 59 to 71 Fire damage. Causes a high amount of threat.
3	34	100	30 yd	1.5 sec	—	80	Inflict searing pain on the enemy target, causing 86 to 104 Fire damage. Causes a high amount of threat.
4	42	127	30 yd	1.5 sec	—	1 10	Inflict searing pain on the enemy target, causing 122 to 146 Fire damage. Causes a high amount of threat.
5	50	152	30 yd	1.5 sec	—	1 50	Inflict searing pain on the enemy target, causing 158 to 188 Fire damage. Causes a high amount of threat.
6	58	185	30 yd	1.5 sec	—	2 40	Inflict searing pain on the enemy target, causing 204 to 240 Fire damage. Causes a high amount of threat.

Rain of Fire

Rain of Fire is a channeled AoE that deals substantial damage to your enemies. This is cast at range, and does not benefit heavily from bonus to damage from gear.

Rank	Level	Mana	Range	Casting Time	Cooldown	Cost to Train	Effect
1	20	295	30 yd	IC	—	20	Calls down a fiery rain to burn enemies in the area of effect for 168 Fire damage over 8 sec.
2	34	605	30 yd	IC	—	80	Calls down a fiery rain to burn enemies in the area of effect for 384 Fire damage over 8 sec.
3	46	885	30 yd	IC	—	1 30	Calls down a fiery rain to burn enemies in the area of effect for 620 damage over 8 sec.
4	58	1185	30 yd	IC	—	2 40	Calls down a fiery rain to burn enemies in the area of effect for 904 Fire damage over 8 sec.

Shadowburn

Shadowburn is a Talent-learned ability on a 15-second cooldown. Warlocks cast this as an instant spell to deal Shadow damage that is fairly heavy. Shadowburn requires a Soul Shard, it gives your Warlock a free Soul Shard if the target dies within several seconds of the attack.

Rank	Minimum Level	Mana	Reagent	Range	Casting Time	Cooldown	Cost to Train	Effect
1	20	105	Soul Shard	20 yd	IC	15 seconds	—	Instantly blasts the target for 91 to 104 Shadow damage. If the target dies from Shadowburn, and yields experience or honor, the caster gains a Soul Shard.
2	24	130	Soul Shard	20 yd	IC	15 sec	1 50	Instantly blasts the target for 115 to 131 damage. If the target dies within 5 sec from Shadowburn and yields experience of honor, the caster gains a Soul Shard.
3	32	190	Soul Shard	20 yd	IC	15 sec	3 50	Instantly blasts the target for 186 to 210 damage. If the target dies within 5 sec from Shadowburn and yields experience of honor, the caster gains a Soul Shard.
4	40	245	Soul Shard	20 yd	IC	15 sec	5 50	Instantly blasts the target for 261 to 293 damage. If the target dies within 5 sec from Shadowburn and yields experience of honor, the caster gains a Soul Shard.
5	48	305	Soul Shard	20 yd	IC	15 sec	7	Instantly blasts the target for 350 to 392 damage. If the target dies within 5 sec from Shadowburn and yields experience of honor, the caster gains a Soul Shard.
6	56	365	Soul Shard	20 yd	IC	15 sec	11	Instantly blasts the target for 450 to 502 damage. If the target dies within 5 sec from Shadowburn and yields experience of honor, the caster gains a Soul Shard.

Hellfire

Hellfire is the type of spell that makes other characters roll Warlock alts. This point blank AoE deals unrepentant damage, rarely rivaled by AoEs. Your Warlock is going to get massive aggro, take damage from Hellfire itself (unavoidably), and require major attention from your group.

Rank	Level	Mana	Range	Casting Time	Cooldown	Cost to Train	Effect
1	30	645	—	IC	—	60	Ignites the area surrounding the caster, causing 83 Fire damage to himself and 83 fire damage to all nearby enemies every 1 sec. Lasts 15 sec.
2	42	975	—	IC	—	1 10	Ignites the area surrounding the caster, causing 139 Fire damage to himself and 145 fire damage to all nearby enemies every 1 sec. Lasts 15 sec.
3	54	1300	—	IC	—	2	Ignites the area surrounding the caster, causing 208 Fire damage to himself and 216 fire damage to all nearby enemies every 1 sec. Lasts 15 sec.

Conflagrate

Conflagrate is a Talent-learned ability that consumes an existing Immolate effect on a target and deals a major dose of instant damage.

Rank	Minimum Level	Mana	Range	Casting Time	Cooldown	Cost to Train	Effect
1	40	165	36 yd	IC	10 seconds	—	Ignites a target that is already afflicted by Immolate, dealing 249 to 316 Fire damage and consuming the Immolate spell.
2	48	200	30 yd	IC	10 sec	7	Ignites a target that is already affected by Immolate, dealing 316 to 396 Fire Damage and consuming the Immolate spell.
3	54	230	30 yd	IC	10 sec	10	Ignites a target that is already affected by Immolate, dealing 383 to 479 Fire Damage and consuming the Immolate spell.
4	60	255	30 yd	IC	10 sec	13	Ignites a target that is already affected by Immolate, dealing 447-557 Fire Damage and consuming the Immolate spell.

Soul Fire

Soul Fire is a slow spell to cast, has a one-minute cooldown, and it consumes a Soul Shard when used. However, the Fire damage dealt by this spell is lewd and unfair (for the target).

Rank	Level	Mana	Range	Casting Time	Cooldown	Cost to Train	Effect
1	48	305	30 yd	6 sec	1 min	1 40	Burn the enemy's soul, causing 623-783 Fire damage.
2	56	335	30 yd	6 sec	1 min	2 20	Burns the enemy's soul, causing 703-881 Fire damage.

Imp Abilities

Fireball deals ranged Fire damage to targets. This is not a massive quantity, but it supplements exiting Warlock attacks well, especially in cases where a melee pet would be troublesome due to enemy AoEs.

Blood Pact increases the Stamina of group members in range. This stacks with Priest and Druid buffs, allowing for all characters to reach very high sums of health! This is quite a bonus for a group with a solid main tank.

Phase Shift turns your Imp invisible when it is not attacking. This is quite useful in dungeon situations, where pets can path oddly and cause huge problems when they aren't dismissed. When the Imp is out and Phase Shifted, he'll path right through enemies with causing wipes, though players who aren't used to it might lose a bit of sphincter control while seeing it.

Fire Shield is another tank-friendly spell. This buffs the target with a damage shield, helping to cement damage on the main tank, especially when fast attackers are involved.

Voidwalker Abilities

Torment is a powerful Taunt that Voidwalkers use to keep their primary target engaged. This has no value in PvP, but does wonderful things in solo PvE for holding aggro even when the Warlock is using higher-Threat attacks.

Sacrifice destroys the Voidwalker but gives the Warlock a shield for the next 30 seconds. This is wonderful for PvE and PvP escapes, and it really one of the only PvP functions of the Voidwalker (for Warlocks who are making death runs at the enemy and want to survive that much longer).

Consume Shadows is used outside of combat to restore Voidwalker health. This takes them ten seconds to channel. Considering how often Voidwalkers are beaten upon, this is a necessary ability that is used all the time.

Suffering is an AoE Taunt that costs a great deal of mana from the Voidwalker. This gives the Warlock enough Threat leeway to throw DOTs onto secondary and tertiary targets while letting the first enemy die. Then, the Warlock helps to finish off whatever health is left on the initial foe, then start blasting away at the next foe.

Succubus Abilities

Lash of Pain deals instant Shadow damage when the Succubus uses it. She can score Criticals off of LoP, bringing Succubus DPS up to a fairly high level for a Warlock pet.

Soothing Kiss is an ability to reduce Threat on the Succubus, much like the ability for Hunter's pets to Cower. Usually, the Succubus doesn't get a lot of aggro, so this isn't an ability that she needs to have on autocast.

Seduction is the most prominent ability of a Succubus. This is used as crowd control against Humanoids, especially in PvP situations. When there are many casters present, Warlocks go with Felhunters in PvP. When there are more physical classes, the Succubus becomes dominant. This ability offers crowd control over a modest period, and gives the Warlock time to prepare the distance and casting for very nice spell chains.

Lesser Invisibility makes it look like your Warlock doesn't have any pets with them. At range, younger PvPers might even mistake your Warlock for another type of caster if they don't specifically highlight you for your level/class information. In any event, this protects your Succubus from a fast attack that would quickly kill her. Left on Passive, she is then reserved for Seduction! Even experienced players won't often have the time or ability to detect her and take her down, as they have other things to worry about.

Felhunter Abilities

Devour Magic takes a positive effect away from an enemy or removes a negative effect from an ally. This process heals the Felhunter as well! This function is incredible for group support in PvP and PvE situations, where many negative effects are devastating. Because this only has an eight-second cooldown, Felhunters really help Paladins and Priests to keep groups clear from harm.

Tainted Blood reduces the Attack Power of enemies that strike the Felhunter in melee (and this stacks up to five times). It's better not to keep this on autocast at all in PvP, where very few people are going to go after your pet.

Spell Lock is an instant ability to Silence an enemy for three seconds; if that target was already casting, they cannot use a spell from the same school of magic for an even longer period. An amazingly useful against PvE and PvP casters.

Paranoia detects stealthers very well. Rogues and Druids in Cat Form are not going to be able to sneak up on a Warlock with a Felhunter out. This makes Warlocks wonderful for defending flag rooms, choke points, and so forth in PvP.

Talents

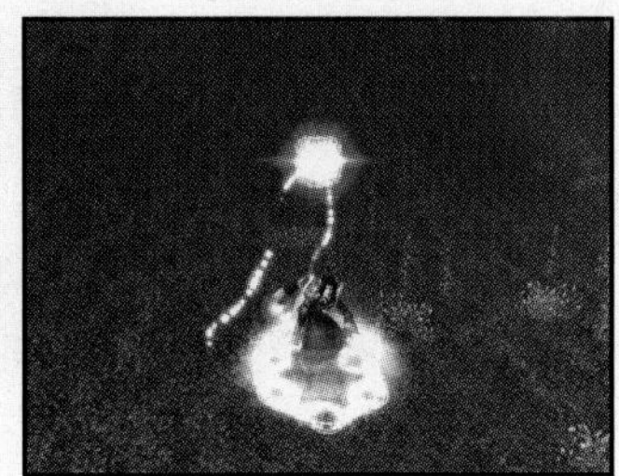

Warlock Talents are able to hone this class toward one of several ends. The Affliction line makes Warlocks even more effective with long-term satisfaction (better damage over time, higher efficiency with debuffs and DOTs, chances for instant casting from time-to-time, etc.).

Demonology allows Warlocks to survive well beyond their normal means. This Talent tree develops pet abilities and gives PvP and PvE Warlocks immense survivability.

Destruction goes toward the direct end of Warlock attacks, greatly improving the output of a Warlock's fire and bolt spells. Later in the line, there are Talents to improve the chance and power of critical spells.

Affliction

Affliction is a zero-downtime tree of Talents that allows for very fast leveling. The combination of Talents to improve your already mana-efficient abilities is quite impressive.

Take Improved Corruption (always), because this saves amazing levels of casting time during the early fights. Warlocks can rattle off Curse of Agony and Corruption on multiple targets, even in large-scale PvP, without wasting time or much mana. This really puts pressure on healers for enemy PvPers, and it works just as well in PvE.

Improved Drain Soul helps with leveling speed, but also look into Improved Life Drain. For specific Warlock builds, this can be a valuable addition (if you plan on tanking for your pet instead of relying on the Voidwalker). Fel Concentration is a *must have* Talent for that style of play, because it prevents your Warlock from being disrupted heavily when Draining in close combat.

Nightfall and Grim Reach are both too much fun to miss. Grim Reach gives you the extra range to help with giving more lead time against targets in PvP and PvE. Nightfall allows for instant Shadowbolts from time to time and it procs most often from Corruption (something that Affliction Warlocks use on every target, all the time).

For PvP, go ahead and take Curse of Exhaustion and its Improved Talents. For PvE though, this doesn't end up being nearly as useful. Instead, grab Siphon Life, then return to earlier tiers for a few points to take Talents that you kind of wanted (Improved Life Tap, Suppression, etc.).

Shadow Mastery and Dark Pact complete the tree, and anyone putting more than 20 points into Affliction is going to want to finish the line and enjoy these major perks.

Your Warlock is never going to run out of mana with this build, the Threat they accumulate is low, but the damage over time is still very high. Wonderful for skilled soloers, superb in PvE groups, and capable in PvP.

Demonology

Demonology is an odd line, and the things your Warlock gets from it are varied. Improved Imp is quite good in the earlier levels, though Demonic Embrace is a Talent that becomes indispensable later on because of its huge improvement to sustained Warlock combat.

Fel Intellect is a champion of the next tier, with its improvement to mana for all standard pets. This makes quite a difference in damage output or survivability, depending on the pet you are using. If combined with an Affliction build, Fel Intellect is doubly rewarding.

Improved Succubus is a keen choice for PvP Warlocks, primarily because of its improvements to Seduction duration and Lash of Pain damage. Soloers who rely on the Voidwalker are going to be lured in by Fel Stamina instead, with its noteworthy boost to pet health.

Take Unholy Power for its damage improvements; though this won't redefine your character, it certainly helps the nag-ability of your pets to wear away at their targets.

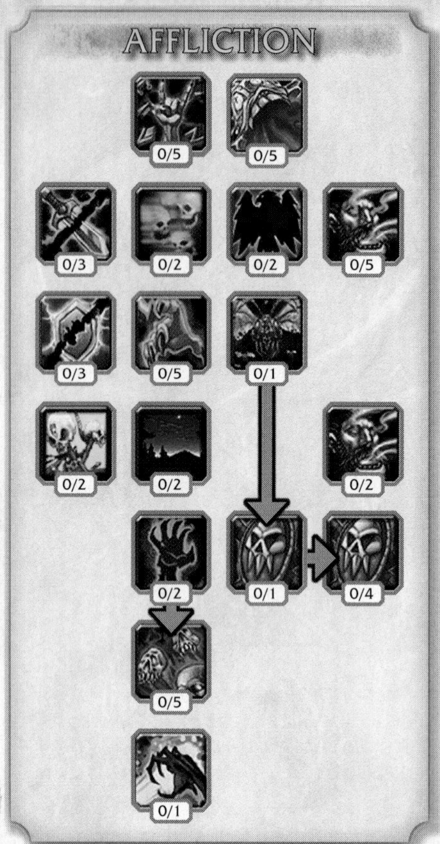

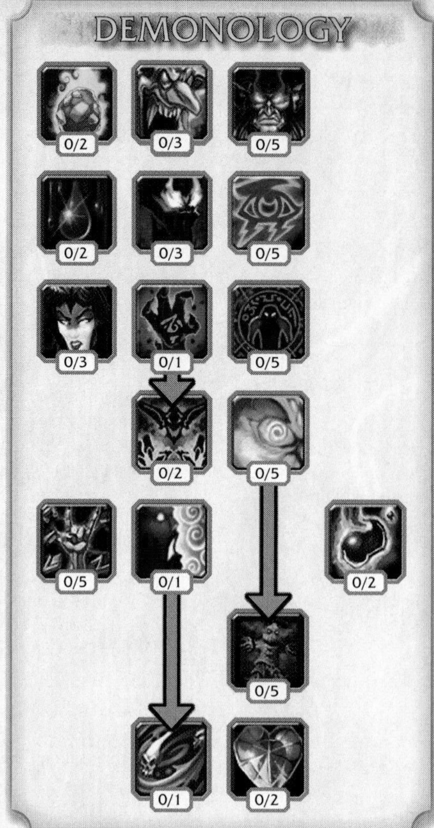

SUPPRESSION 5

Reduces the chance for enemies to resist your Affliction spells by 2% (Per Rank)

IMPROVED CORRUPTION 5

Reduces the casting time of your Corruption spell by 0.4 sec (Per Rank)

IMPROVED CURSE OF WEAKNESS 3

Increases the effect of your Curse of Weakness by 6%. - Progression: 6%/13%/20%

IMPROVED DRAIN SOUL 2

Gives you a 50% chance (Per Rank) to increase mana regen by 100% if your target dies while you are casting Drain Soul

IMPROVED LIFE TAP 2

Increases the amount of Mana awarded by your Life Tap spell by 10% (Per Rank)

IMPROVED DRAIN LIFE 5

Increases the Health drained by your Drain Life spell by 2% (Per Rank)

IMPROVED CURSE OF AGONY 3

Increases the damage done by Curse of Agony by 2% (Per Rank)

FEL CONCENTRATION 5

Gives you a 14% chance (Per Rank) to avoid interruption caused by damage while channeling the Drain Life, Drain Mana, or Drain Soul spell.

AMPLIFY CURSE 1

Instant Cast 5 min cooldown Increases the effect of your next Curse of Weakness, Curse of Agony, or Curse of Exhaustion by 50%.

GRIM REACH 2

Increases the range of your Affliction spells by 10% (Per Rank)

NIGHTFALL 2

Gives your Corruption and Drain Life spells a 2% chance to cause you to enter a Shadow Trance state after damaging the opponent. The Shadow Trance state reduces the casting time of your next Shadow Bolt spell by 100%. - Progression 2%/3%

IMPROVED DRAIN MANA 2

Causes 15% of mana drained by this spell (Per Rank) to damage your target

SIPHON LIFE 1

150 Mana 1.5 sec cast 30yd range Transfers 15 health from the target to thecaster every 3 sec. Lasts 30sec.

CURSE OF EXHAUSTION 1

17 Mana Instant Cast 30 yd range Reduces the target's speed to 90% of normal for 15 sec. Only one Curse per Warlock can be active on any one target.

IMPROVED CURSE OF EXHAUSTION 4

Increases the speed reduction of your Curse of Exhaustion by 5% (Per Rank)

SHADOW MASTERY 5

Increases the damage dealt by your Shadow spells by 2% (Per Rank)

DARK PACT 1

Instant Cast 20 yrd range Drains 250 of your pet's Mana returning 100% to you.

IMPROVED HEALTHSTONE 2

Increases the amount of health returned by a Healthstone by 10% (Per Rank)

IMPROVED IMP 3

Increases the effect of an Imp's Firebolt, Fire Shield, and Bloodpact by 10% (Per Rank)

DEMONIC EMBRACE 5

Increases your total Stamina by 3% (Per Rank) at a loss of 1% of your Stamina (Also Per Rank)

IMPROVED HEALTH FUNNEL 2

Increases the amount of health returned by Health Funnel by 10% (Per Rank)

IMPROVED VOIDWALKER 3

Increases the effects of your Voidwalker's Torment, Consume Shadows, and Suffering by 8% - Progression: 8%/16%/25%

FEL INTELLECT 5

Increases the maximum mana of your pets by 3% (Per Rank)

IMPROVED SUCCUBUS 3

Increases the effect of your Succubus' Lash of Pain, Soothing Kiss, and Lesser Invisibility by 8% - Progression: 8%/16%/25%

FEL DOMINATION 1

Adds an Instant ability that reduces pet summoning time by 5.5 seconds, and lowers mana cost by 50%

FEL STAMINA 5

Increases the maximum health of your pets by 2% (Per Rank)

MASTER SUMMONER 2

Reduces the summoning time of your pets by 2 seconds (Per Rank)

UNHOLY POWER 5

Increases melee damage done by your pets by 3% (Per Rank)

IMPROVED ENSLAVE DEMON 5

Reduces the attack speed/casting speed penalty of your controlled demons by 2% (Per Rank)

DEMONIC SACRIFICE 1

Sacrifices your pet for a 30 minute buff - Progression: Imp (Increases Fire Damage by 15%), Voidwalker (Increases health by 15%), Succubus (Increases Shadow Damage by 15%), Felhunter (Increases mana by 20%)

IMPROVED FIRESTONE 2

Increases the damage done by your Firestones by 15% (Per Rank)

MASTER DEMONOLOGIST 2

Reduces the mana cost and casting time of all stone-creation spells by 20% (Per Rank)

SOUL LINK 1

Adds an Instant ability that splits damage taken between you and your pet for 30 seconds

IMPROVED SPELLSTONE 2

Increases the amount of damage absorbed by your Spellstones by 15% (Per Rank)

IMPROVED SHADOW BOLT 5

Your Shadow Bolt critical strikes increase the next 4 sources of Shadow damage dealt to the target by 4% (Per Rank)

CATACLYSM 5

Reduces the Mana cost of your Destruction spells by 1% (Per Rank)

BANE 5

Reduces the casting time of your Shadow Bolt and Immolate spells by 0.1 sec (Per Rank)

AFTERMATH 5

Gives your Destruction spells a 2% chance (Per Rank) to daze the target for 5 sec.

IMPROVED FIREBOLT 2

Reduces the casting time of your Imp's Firebolt spell by 0.5 sec (Per Rank)

IMPROVED LASH OF PAIN 2

Reduces the cooldown of your Succubus' Lash of Pain spell by 3 sec (Per Rank)

DEVASTATION 5

Increases the critical strike chance of your Destruction spells by 1% (Per Rank)

SHADOWBURN 1

130 mana, Instant cast 15 sec cooldown 20yd range Reagents: Soul Shard- Instantly blasts the target with 125 to 150 Shadow damage. This spell generates less threat than would normally be caused. Requires 1 Soul Shard. Awards 1 Soul Shard if the target dies from Shadowburn.

INTENSITY 2

Gives you a 35% chance (Per Rank) to resist interruption caused by damage while channeling the Rain of Fire or Hellfire spell.

DESTRUCTIVE REACH 2

Increases the range of your Destruction spells by 10% (Per Rank)

IMPROVED SEARING PAIN 5

Increases the critical strike chance of your Searing Pain spell by 2% (Per Rank)

PYROCLASM 2

Gives your Rain of Fire and Hellfire spells a 12% chance to stun the target for 3 sec. - Progression: 12%/25%

IMPROVED IMMOLATE 5

Increases the initial damage of your immolate spell by 5% (Per Rank)

RUIN 1

Increases the damage done by your critical strikes by 100%.

EMBERSTORM 5

Increases the damage done by your Fire spells by 2% (Per Rank)

CONFLAGRATE 1

220 Mana 1.5 sec cast 10 sec cooldown 20yd range Ignites a target that is already afflicted by Immolate, dealing 214 to 256 damage and consuming the Immolate spell.

Demonic Sacrifice must be taken; it is one of the most incredible Talents in the Demonology line. With this, a Warlock can Sacrifice any of their pets for fairly major buffs, and the Voidwalker specifically turns the Warlock into an unstoppable machine of AoE destruction. If these AoE death rushes excite you, take Improved Firestone as well; this doesn't add a major damage boost, but it's bigger than it first appears.

Master Demonologist is a passive effect that improves all of your standard pets; take all five ranks of this.

Half of the entire point in taking Demonology past the first couple of tiers is to get Soul Link. For PvP and solo PvE functionality, Soul Link causes Warlocks to survive as it they were real tanks.

Demonology, taken heavily, is very good as a first-time choice for characters who are learning the game (that isn't to say that experienced players won't fall in love with it too). Instead, the idea is that Warlocks with these Talents are extremely hard to bring down. They can solo, using their Voidwalker, and beat down almost anything in their way. The process is slower than Affliction or Destruction Talents, but you always have your finger on a series of "I win" buttons to either win the fight outright or at least survive to resummon your pet and try again.

Destruction

Improved Shadow Bolt is decent for a solo player and only gets better when you have more buddies around. Warlocks and Shadow Priests working together get are very mean with these tricks.

Bane and Aftermath are both great in the second tier. In the long-run, you might grab both of them. In the short-term, use Bane for its consistent improvements to Warlock casting speeds, or take Aftermath if you want sporadic effects (for most, Aftermath becomes much better in later levels).

Steal Shadowburn as soon as possible, as it is a perfect spell for burst damage, finishing targets, and so forth (and being another Shadow spell, it fills out the Destruction line anyway). Then, take Devastation; this cannot be left behind.

The choices are difficult again in the next line. If you solo or PvP a lot, take Improved Searing Pain now. If you join small groups for PvE more often or deal with large-scale PvP, Take Intensity and Destructive Reach first (you are going to get all of these eventually anyway).

Immediately grab Ruin in the next tier; it is so powerful that anyone who doesn't take it while making a Destruction build is either a fool or a genius beyond their time. Take all five points of Improved Immolate, then get four points of Emberstorm.

The damage in this line is now crippling for burst use in soloing and PvP. Complete the process with Conflagrate, then return and fill out the spec with the final point of Emberstorm, Pyroclasm (if AoEs are very important to your character), and Aftermath/Bane, from earlier levels.

This takes a massive investment in a single Talent line, but the results are quite worthwhile. Though inefficient, compared to Affliction Warlocks, Destruction casters are able to burst in PvP and take down almost anything on the field. They are feared and respected wherever they go, and there are only a few character types that are eager to face this build.

In PvE, Destruction Warlocks have more downtime, require a bit of extra cash (for greater supplies of water and potions), and must be careful about their Threat generation in groups without a masterful main tank. That said, they add a great deal to the overall damage output.

STRATEGIES

Okay, it's time to head out into the field and bring down enemies. There are great ways to do this as a Warlock, especially if you are patient. After level ten, when you have the choice of Imp or Voidwalker as pets, the game gets quite interesting. From there, Warlocks level and receive more and more choices, eventually becoming one of the most complex classes in the game.

Some General Tips

Your Curses make a huge difference in the outcome of a battle, whether you are alone or in a group. Curse of Tongues is the best way to say hello to casters, Curse of Elements/Shadow is vicious in groups with multiple casters or for times when you plan on unleashing many Fire or Shadow spells. If there are other Warlocks in the group, work out which Curses are going to be used. This keeps you from stepping on each other's toes.

Remember to avoid heavy Threat abilities early in a fight when you are grouped. Shadowbolt is only a little naughty, Searing Pain is extremely naughty, and AoEs or Soul Fire are right out. Wait for tanks to have serious aggro before playing around with high damage/high Threat abilities.

When working with an AoE group, keep Healthstones available (and on your quick-bar) at all times. Keep the Voidwalker out for immediate Sacrifice, and get used to dying. AoE groups are for high-risk/high-reward playing.

Soul Shards

Always keep a heavy supply of Soul Shards around. These items are needed for so much of a Warlock's utility that it's very dangerous to run out of them. Summoning allies, grabbing more important pets, and even some of the special class spells later down the road cost shards. Don't be shy about having an entire bag dedicated to keeping extra shards, and replace these as soon as possible when the supply starts to drop. Also look into the special bags for Soul Shards that are made by Tailors; these give you even more space for large group of Shards (e.g. Core Felcloth Bag, Soul Pouch).

Remember that only enemies that are worth experience/honor to your Warlock can drop Soul Shards. Killing rabbits and cows is not going to get you what you need.

Give various stones to your allies in a group as soon as possible, as they can be useful at any point. Be sure to give a Soul Stone to group Rezzer first, and a Healthstone to the main tank first; they are the ones that are most important to protect from a wipeout.

When grouping or raiding, fill extra bag space with Soul Shards before you enter a dungeon. The greatest and most difficult press for Shards is during the first few minutes, when a group is getting ready. Your Warlock is needed for Healthstones aplenty, Summoning your pet, Summoning straggling group/raid members, Soulstones, and so forth. And, you don't want to tap out! Even if it fills two bags or more with Shards, go into groups prepared. After all, those Shards will be long gone from at least one bag by the time you get enough loot to worry about the space, so it's not like your Warlock is going to miss out on treasure.

If you need more Shards before a run, let people know. For smaller groups that aren't facing raid-level challenges, there are usually offers for a few folks to head outside of the dungeon and help you kill a few targets while waiting for the group/raid to get together. For friendly runs, this is no big deal at all (just don't rely on this for scheduled raids and such, where people want to start at a specific time).

Standing Alone

As stated, the Voidwalker is critical to safe soloing. This tank of a pet is able to keep enemies' attention fairly well. For you to do your part, stick with DOTs and wand activity and watch the creatures fall into death without realizing that you are the one to blame. Slap Corruption, Curse of Agony, and a nice Immolate on targets once the Voidwalker has them in melee and switch to your wand for the conclusion.

For adds that your Voidwalker can handle, slap DOTs on them as well, after the Voidwalker has gotten their attention. A more dangerous add can be Feared to give yourself time to bring down the first target. If it looks like Fear is going to backfire (by drawing more monsters), slam the initial target with all DOTs, then a Searing Pain to get it off of your pet and divide the damage between yourself and the Voidwalker; this isn't optimal, but it's a last-ditch method that works in a pinch. Kill the first creature and turn on the second once your Voidwalker is ready for it.

If things get worse, Sacrifice your Voidwalker for extra time and run like Fel!

Another type of solo work altogether (and not for the faint of heart or light of skill) is to tank consistently for your pets. Ditch the Voidwalker and use your Imp or Succubus for this, for their high damage potential. This is often an Affliction Warlock's specialty; Draintank the enemy by using DOTs, Drain Life to keep yourself afloat, and switch to the wand for the kill if mana conservation is ever needed. With the right spec, this brings in experience at an immense rate.

Pet Choices in a Group

Bring out the beloved Succubus or Imp in a group and watch the DPS of your extended character improve. Though the Imp is a dangerous creature if it stays in active mode, you can keep from pulling many accidental enemies by setting the monster to Passive and controlling him carefully. With the Imp's Fire Bolts and damage shield, he adds quite a percentage to a group's overall performance.

The Succubus is at her best when a skilled Tank is at the lead of a group. Work with the Tank so that they know to keep the Succubus at the enemy's back (to avoid Cleaves and other front-targeted AoEs). The Succubus is obviously a great choice for added crowd control against Humanoids as well, in PvE and PvP. Seduce Humanoid adds while the group maintains focus on their primary target.

The Felhunter isn't a choice for damage, but the creature's utility is quite welcome. If your group is facing casters, the Felhunter has no peer. Even groups that have a Paladin or Priest benefit from the Felhunter's Devour Magic ability.

WARRIOR

Warriors are the protectors in World of Warcraft. These brave souls fight for both the Horde and Alliance, and neither side would survive for long without their perseverance. Fighting primarily in melee, Warriors use their heavy armor and damage mitigation to endure the attention of monsters; their role in a group is to gather as much of that aggression as possible. By doing this, weaker classes are left free to use their healing, higher DPS, and other such abilities without fear of reprisal and death. Both in the field and in dungeons, Warriors always have a place in a skilled group. When soloing or assisting other Warriors, these fighters reveal that underneath the armor there is a savage killer than is able to sacrifice mitigation for destructive power.

Lore

We approached the ancient homeland of the spiteful gnomes, and putrescence filled the air we breathed. The smell was one of the worst things I could have imagined. It poured like steam out of the tunnels around us, but it came from the very gnomes lived in the ruined city. They were fouled with disease, a fate worse than many would have wished even for the wasteful beasts.

I heard Illiathu, our Shaman, cry out. Three of the demonic things had charged her, and I knew her strength would fail before long against such an onslaught. Crying with all the strength the Earthmother allows me, I ran over and leapt onto the first. It stood still for a moment, paralyzed with fear even as my axe struck home. The others would have continued their attacks on Illiathu, intent on her falling Totems, but I was on them as well.

Swinging left and right, mocking their horrid faces and torturous heritage, I got their attention every way I knew how. They turned to me and struck helplessly against the finest steel our crafters can forge. The earth's bounty protected me. Illiathu used her time well, and the few wounds that had blossomed under my armor tightened and ceased to bleed. I felt no pain.

The two Forsaken with us were doing all of the killing; no great surprise there. With small blades and burning fire, they were the ones destroying the gnomes, but I wounded all of the foes during the fray, tearing the armor from their bilious forms and knocking aside their steel before it landed home. When we left later that day, our mission successful, not a single ally was left behind in the darkness.

Nothing will defeat the Horde as long as there are people ready to stand in the way of evil. We Tauren believe in the power of the Earthmother, and the Scourge, Burning Legion, gnomes, dwarves, and humans will not stop us from protecting our people.

Introduction to Playing the Class

Warriors are very easy to pick up, but it takes an immense amount of time to master them. Some people perceive the class as being forced into one role by their specializations, but no Talent configuration truly pigeonholes a Warrior with skill. Bring along a wide range of weapons, and watch how easy it is for a Warrior to be a DPS class or a tank, at any time.

The key is to master stance switching and weapon selection. Within the same fight, a Warrior can start as a DPS class (using dual wield or a two-handed weapon), bring down some light targets, then switch to tank mode (with a one-handed weapon and shield) to deal with adds or a specifically powerful creature. Battle Stance offers consistent damage and control, while fast use of Berserker Stance is nice for Whirlwind AoEs and Berserk Rage. Then, when you need to generate more Threat against single targets and survive longer, drop into Defensive Stance.

Warriors can change their Threat generation and survivability at the drop of a hat. The difference between Berserker Stance and Defensive Stance alone is 20% in terms of incoming damage. Add a shield to that, and a Defensive Stance Warrior is taking well over 30% less damage. Demoralizing Shout, switch quickly to Battle Stance for a Thunder Clap, and now the enemies are really hitting like kittens. Not enough? Use Shield Block and Disarm (if possible).

Even Arms and Fury Warriors are extremely hard to kill when they use their stances correctly and keep a full range of equipment ready to go. All Warriors, of all types, should have a shield, one or two single-handed weapons, and a two-handed weapon. These should be in your bags, all the time, fully repaired before dungeon runs. There is a time and place for everything!

Bind stance-switching to keys that are easily accessible. Master them, be able to switch without losing time to think, and keep an organized quickbar that is as intuitive as possible for you. Keep shout abilities in the same location for all of your stances, and leave interrupts on similar keys as well.

One interested thing about Warriors is that they lack mana. Instead, they gain the power to use their abilities from Rage. This builds when a Warrior takes or deals damage (there are a few class abilities to generate Rage as well). The more damage you deal or take at a given time, the more Rage you will get. This makes it essential to keep your weapons upgraded as often as possible. Rage deteriorates between fights, when a Warrior is out of battle, so it helps greatly to have as little downtime as possible.

Available Races	
Dwarf	Gnome
Human	Night Elf
Orc	Tauren
Troll	Undead

What do Attributes Mean to Me?	
Strength	Increases Melee Damage Greatly, Improves Amount of Damage Absorbed During a Block
Stamina	Higher Health
Agility	Raises Chance to Get a Critical Hit, Dodge
Intellect	Faster Rate for Gaining Weapon Skills (Worthless)
Spirit	Improves Health Recovery (Worthless)

ITEMS AND EQUIPMENT

Warriors are more dependent on equipment than any other class; their weapons need to be as deadly as possible when it comes to DPS (for the damage itself, for increased Threat generation, and for getting more Rage). They also need armor that is extremely up-to-date, and peripheral items that raise Stamina and Strength are at a premium for dungeon runs. Add bandages, food, and even some explosives to the mix, and Warriors are often laden with goodies. Most of the time, they are pretty darn poor as well!

Okay, so what are your priorities? As a Warrior, whether you solo or join a group, a massive investment in armor is required. Unless you are going with a two-handed weapon, a shield is one of your best items. Keep searching for quests with shield rewards and look for dungeons where high-quality shields drop.

Try to keep your Armor Rating as high as possible while being somewhat picky about which pieces you grab. When available, armor pieces with similar stats should be distinguished by the attributes they raise. A Warrior who goes for survivability wants to have as much Stamina as possible on their equipment. Enchant your items and always be on the lookout to replace gear that isn't quite right for your stats with better pieces. Stamina is almost always the first pick for a Warrior, with Strength and Agility following behind. Spirit and Intellect are just about worthless, and should practically be avoided in favor of getting other attributes.

Weapons with procs instead of attributes must be chosen carefully; your Warrior needs those combat attributes to function well, so it's always a tough tradeoff. Don't go for a proc unless the effect on hit is extremely good. For defensive one-handed weapons, only look for procs that raise Armor Rating, Defense, add healing, or other survival-based elements. For dual-wield or two-handed choices, go for procs that are aggressive and deal enough damage to be worth giving up the stats.

In regard to attributes themselves, Stamina is needed in PvP and PvE. Only Fury offtanks are likely to look for less of this attribute than other Warriors, but even they aren't going to ignore it. The more complex choice is the decision between Strength and Agility. For burst damage (e.g. PvP Arms Warriors), Agility should be taken pretty heavily. A high Critical rate is essential for burst damage. However, for steady Threat to keep monsters on your Warrior, a high Strength is far more useful. Strength adds to base damage, so it won't matter if you are getting the Criticals or not; high damage at a smooth rate is extremely important for a good tank.

At the higher levels, when you start to see +Hit and +Critical items, remember that a Warrior wants to have about +5% to Hit (maybe +6% in a pinch, but that is a stretch). There is no ceiling for how much +Critical gear you want, but generally figure that a point in +Critical is worth almost 20 Agility for you.

Items that raise Defense are also part of the mix. Higher-tier items usually add to several attributes, then have a bonus to +Hit/+Crit/+Defense. This means that even with your best gear, there is going to be a rough choice. Hit and Crit more, or take that lovely Defense? Defense allows for higher burst defense, if that makes any sense to you. Warriors with a high Defense receive fewer Critical hits from enemies. Don't give up Stamina for Defense, and only give up your damage-dealing statistics if your Warrior is holding aggro without any problems in all of your groups. Defense means nothing if you aren't dealing enough damage and using your abilities well enough to maintain aggro at all times!

CHOOSING YOUR PROFESSION

Many first-time Warriors go for Blacksmithing and Mining; they are an intuitive combination. They also let a lot of Warrior down, sadly. There aren't many Blacksmithing items before the very late-game that are good enough to keep a Warrior protected well (and the early to mid weapons are horrible). Warriors need/want the best-of-the-best gear possible, and almost all of that is going to come from dungeon delving. Only take Blacksmithing if you are serious about getting it up to its maximum value and working hard to find rare or epic recipes; those are the only Blacksmithing items that really draw people in.

Not as many early Warriors take Herbalism/Alchemy, but this is actually a very wise choice. Warriors drink more potions, on the whole, than a lot of classes. Being able to make your own is very important unless you have a guild or friend that is willing to do the work for you. Warriors gain so much from the extra Strength, Agility, Critical rate, and such that potions provide.

For a PvP Warrior, Engineering is a solid choice (also paired with Mining). Having bombs and some of the gadgets that Engineering provides is effective for turning the tide of nasty battles, especially if you are a very active fighter. Charge ahead of your group, use bombs to disrupt the incoming enemy lines, then continue forward for the softer targets. A short Stun and some extra damage is more than enough to push initiative in your group's favor, and a frontline character has a greater chance to make these things happen.

Even more useful to a Warrior in action, however, are the secondary trades. Cooking and First Aid are very powerful for reducing downtime and limiting your need to buy expensive food from local vendors. Keep both of these trades at a fair level and use them heavily to improve your kill rate. Even in groups this does very good things (reducing the burden on your healers can greatly shorten quest and dungeon times).

Class Abilities

Rage is on a scale from 0 to 100, and unlike other classes, it stays at zero when you aren't engaged in combat. When a Warrior strikes enemies or is hit by them, the Rage Meter goes up. Using points from this bar engages various abilities to defend the Warrior, do extra Damage, help the group, or otherwise aid in combat.

Below are the tables for these abilities, broken down by their limitations.

Arms

Heroic Strike

Heroic Strike is an ability that generates **massive** Threat! It is a Rage sink, but has its purposes.

Rank	Level	Stance	Rage	Cost to Train	Effects
1	1	All	-15	—	A strong attack that increases melee damage by 11 and causes a high amount of threat.
2	8	All	-15	2	A strong attack that increases melee damage by 21 and causes a high amount of threat.
3	16	All	-15	20	A strong attack that increases melee damage by 32 and causes a high amount of threat.
4	24	All	-15	80	A strong attack that increases melee damage by 44 and causes a high amount of threat.
5	32	All	-15	1 40	A strong attack that increases melee damage by 58 and causes a high amount of threat.
6	40	All	-15	2 20	A strong attack that increases melee damage by 80 and causes a high amount of threat.
7	48	All	-15	4	A strong attack that increases melee damage by 111 and causes a high amount of threat.
8	56	All	-15	9 80	A strong attack that increases melee damage by 138 and causes a high amount of threat.
9	60	All	-15	—	A strong attack that increases melee damage by 157 and causes a high amount of threat.

Charge

Charge is a blessing from the heavens. This allows your Warrior to enter melee from range. It also generates bonus Rage and causes a trivial Stun effect to interrupt casters.

Rank	Level	Stance	Rage	Cost to Train	Effects
1	4	Battle	9	1	Charge an enemy, generate 9 Rage, and stun it for 1 sec. Cannot be used in combat. 15 second cooldown.
2	26	Battle	12	1	Charge an enemy, generate 12 Rage, and stun it for 1 sec. Cannot be used in combat. 15 second cooldown.
3	46	Battle	15	3 60	Charge an enemy, generate 15 Rage, and stun it for 1 sec. Cannot be used in combat. 15 second cooldown.

Rend

Rend produces a laughable DOT on a target. This occurs instantly and doesn't require much Rage. Don't use Rend for the damage done, use it for its DOT effect.

Rank	Level	Stance	Rage	Cost to Train	Effects
1	4	Battle, Defensive	-10	1	Wounds the target, causing them to bleed for 15 damage over 9 seconds.
2	10	Battle, Defensive	-10	6	Wounds the target, causing them to bleed for 28 damage over 12 seconds.
3	20	Battle, Defensive	-10	40	Wounds the target, causing them to bleed for 45 damage over 15 seconds.
4	30	Battle, Defensive	-10	1 20	Wounds the target, causing them to bleed for 66 damage over 18 seconds.
5	40	Battle, Defensive	-10	2 20	Wounds the target, causing them to bleed for 98 damage over 21 seconds.
6	50	Battle, Defensive	-10	4 20	Wounds the target, causing them to bleed for 126 damage over 21 seconds.
7	60	Battle, Defensive	-10	6 20	Wounds the target, causing them to bleed for 147 damage over 21 seconds.

Thunder Clap

Thunder Clap deals Nature damage for up to four enemies and reduces their attack speed for a modest time. This offers more damage mitigation than it appears, and even in fights against single enemies, Thunder Clap is worthwhile.

Rank	Level	Stance	Rage	Cost to Train	Effects
1	6	Battle	-20	1	Blasts nearby enemies with thunder, slowing their attack speed by 10% for 10 seconds and doing 10 damage to them. Will affect up to 4 targets. 4 second cooldown.
2	18	Battle	-20	30	Blasts nearby enemies with thunder, slowing their attack speed by 10% for 14 seconds and doing 23 damage to them. Will affect up to 4 targets. 4 second cooldown.
3	28	Battle	-20	1 10	Blasts nearby enemies with thunder, slowing their attack speed by 10% for 18 seconds and doing 37 damage to them. Will affect up to 4 targets. 4 second cooldown.
4	38	Battle	-20	2	Blasts nearby enemies with thunder, slowing their attack speed by 10% for 22 seconds and doing 55 damage to them. Will affect up to 4 targets. 4 second cooldown.
5	48	Battle	-20	4	Blasts nearby enemies with thunder, slowing their attack speed by 10% for 26 seconds and doing 82 damage to them. Will affect up to 4 targets. 4 second cooldown.
6	58	Battle	-20	6	Blasts nearby enemies with thunder, slowing their attack speed by 10% for 30 seconds and doing 103 damage to them. Will affect up to 4 targets. 4 second cooldown.

Hamstring

Hamstring deals trivial damage but produces a Snare effect on your target.

Rank	Level	Stance	Rage	Cost to Train	Effects
1	8	Battle, Berserk	-10	2	Maims the enemy, causing 5 damage and slowing the enemy's movement to 60% of normal for 15 seconds.
2	32	Battle, Berserk	-10	1 40	Maims the enemy, causing 18 damage and slowing the enemy's movement to 55% of normal for 15 seconds.
3	54	Battle, Berserk	-10	5 60	Maims the enemy, causing 45 damage and slowing the enemy's movement to 50% of normal for 15 seconds.

Overpower

Overpower is the Rogue destroyer. This ability uses almost no Rage and deals a full weapon attack with bonus damage to anyone who dares to Dodge your Warrior's hits (even special attack Dodges trigger this). With a slight investment in the Arms Talent line, this also gains a +50% chance to Critical.

Rank	Level	Stance	Rage	Cost to Train	Effects
1	12	Battle	-5	10	Instantly overpowers the enemy, causing weapon damage plus 5. Only usable after the target dodges. The Overpower cannot be blocked, dodged, or parried. 5 second cooldown.
2	28	Battle	-5	1 10	Instantly overpowers the enemy, causing weapon damage plus 15. Only usable after the target dodges. The Overpower cannot be blocked, dodged, or parried. 5 second cooldown.
3	44	Battle	-5	3 40	Instantly overpowers the enemy, causing weapon damage plus 25. Only usable after the target dodges. The Overpower cannot be blocked, dodged, or parried. 5 second cooldown.
4	60	Battle	-5	6 20	Instantly overpowers the enemy, causing weapon damage plus 35. Only usable after the target dodges. The Overpower cannot be blocked, dodged, or parried. 5 second cooldown.

Mocking Blow

Mocking Blow is on a two-minute cooldown. This instant strike deals a light amount of damage, causes increased Threat, and forces the PvE enemy to attack your Warrior for a short time.

Rank	Level	Stance	Rage	Cost to Train	Effects
1	16	Battle	-10	20	A mocking attack that causes 22 damage, a moderate amount of threat, and forces the target to focus its attacks on you for 6 seconds. 2 min cooldown.
2	26	Battle	-10	1	A mocking attack that causes 31 damage a moderate amount of threat, and forces the target to focus its attacks on you for 6 seconds. 2 min cooldown.
3	36	Battle	-10	1 80	A mocking attack that causes 46 damage a moderate amount of threat, and forces the target to focus its attacks on you for 6 seconds. 2 min cooldown.
4	46	Battle	-10	3 60	A mocking attack that causes 71 damage a moderate amount of threat, and forces the target to focus its attacks on you for 6 seconds. 2 min cooldown.
5	56	Battle	-10	5 80	A mocking attack that causes 93 damage a moderate amount of threat, and forces the target to focus its attacks on you for 6 seconds. 2 min cooldown.

Anger Management

Anger Management is a Talent-learned ability that changes the rate of Rage decay you receive outside of battle.

Rank	Prerequisite	Effect
1	10 Point in Arms, 5 Points in Tactical Mastery	Reduces the time required for your Rage to decay while out of combat by 30% (Per Rank).

Retaliation

Retaliation is on a 30-minute cooldown, linked with Shield Wall and Recklessness (thus, only one of these abilities can be used every half-an-hour). Retaliation itself allows a Warrior to counterattack, at full damage, every time they are struck from the front.

Rank	Level	Stance	Rage	Cost to Train	Effects
N/A	20	Battle	—	40	Instantly counterattack any enemy that strikes you in melee for 15 sec. Melee attacks from behind cannot be counterattacked. A maximum of 30 attacks will cause retaliation. 30 minute cooldown.

Sweeping Strikes

Sweeping Strikes is a Talent-learned ability that gives your Warrior's next five melee swings the ability to hit an additional target.

Rank	Prerequisite	Effect
1	20 Points in Arms, Battle Stance, Your next 5 melee weapon swings strike an additional enemy.	Mortal Strike is a Talent-learned ability that deals an instant attack with moderate bonus damage and adds a debuff on the target that halves healing effectiveness.

Mortal Strike

Mortal Strike is a Talent-learned ability that deals an instant attack with moderate bonus damage and adds a debuff on the target that halves healing effectiveness.

Rank	Minimum Level	Stance	Rage	Range	Cost to Train	Effects
1	40	All	-30	5 yd	—	A vicious strike that deals weapon damage plus 85 and wounds the target, reducing the effectiveness of any healing by 50% for 10 sec. Requires Melee Weapon. 6 sec cooldown.
2	48	All	-30	5 yd	—	A vicious strike that deals weapon damage plus 110 and wounds the target, reducing the effectiveness of any healing by 50% for 10 sec. Requires Melee Weapon. 6 sec cooldown.
3	54	All	-30	5 yd	—	A vicious strike that deals weapon damage plus 135 and wounds the target, reducing the effectiveness of any healing by 50% for 10 sec. Requires Melee Weapon. 6 sec cooldown.
4	60	All	-30	5 yd	—	A vicious strike that deals weapon damage plus 160 and wounds the target, reducing the effectiveness of any healing by 50% for 10 sec. Requires Melee Weapon. 6 sec cooldown.

Battle Shout

Battle Shout unleashes an AoE buff to Melee Attack Power.

Rank	Level	Stance	Rage	Cost to Train	Effects
1	1	All	-10	10	The warrior shouts, increasing the attack power of all party members within 20 yards by 15. Lasts 2 min.
2	12	All	-10	10	The warrior shouts, increasing the attack power of all party members within 20 yards by 35. Lasts 2 min.
3	22	All	-10	60	The warrior shouts, increasing the attack power of all party members within 20 yards by 55. Lasts 2 min.
4	32	All	-10	1 40	The warrior shouts, increasing the attack power of all party members within 20 yards by 85. Lasts 2 min.
5	42	All	-10	3 20	The warrior shouts, increasing the attack power of all party members within 20 yards by 130. Lasts 2 min.
6	52	All	-10	5 40	The warrior shouts, increasing the attack power of all party members within 20 yards by 185. Lasts 2 min.
7	60	All	-10	—	The warrior shouts, increasing the attack power of all party members within 20 yards by 232. Lasts 2 min.

Demoralizing Shout

Demoralizing Shout is another AoE shout. This time, the effect is on your enemies. They receive a debuff to their Attack Power.

Rank	Level	Stance	Rage	Cost to Train	Effects
1	14	All	-10	15	Reduces the attack power of all enemies within 10 yds by 35 for 30 seconds.
2	24	All	-10	80	Reduces the attack power of all enemies within 10 yds by 55 for 30 seconds.
3	34	All	-10	1 60	Reduces the attack power of all enemies within 10 yds by 70 for 30 seconds.
4	44	All	-10	3 40	Reduces the attack power of all enemies within 10 yds by 105 for 30 seconds.
5	54	All	-10	5 60	Reduces the attack power of all enemies within 10 yds by 140 for 30 seconds.

Cleave

Cleave costs a fair sum of Rage (20 Rage plus your next melee swing), but it hits your target and an additional foe.

Rank	Level	Stance	Rage	Cost to Train	Effects
1	20	All	-20	40	A sweeping attack that does your weapon damage plus 5 to your target and his nearest ally.
2	30	All	-20	1 20	A sweeping attack that does your weapon damage plus 10 to your target and his nearest ally.
3	40	All	-20	2 20	A sweeping attack that does your weapon damage plus 18 to your target and his nearest ally.
4	50	All	-20	4 20	A sweeping attack that does your weapon damage plus 32 to your target and his nearest ally.
5	60	All	-20	6 20	A sweeping attack that does your weapon damage plus 50 to your target and his nearest ally.

Piercing Howl

Piercing Howl is an AoE that reduces movement speed.

Rank	Prerequisite	Effect
1	10 Points on Fury	Causes all enemies near the warrior to be dazed for 6 seconds.

Intimidating Shout

Intimidating Shout instantly causes up to five enemies to be struck with Fear. Note that many of them will run around willy-nilly, and could cause PvE adds to an existing fight.

Rank	Level	Stance	Rage	Cost to Train	Effects
N/A	22	All	-25	60	The warrior shouts, causing the targeted enemy to cower in fear. Up to 5 total nearby enemies will flee in fear. Lasts 8 sec. 3 minute cooldown.

Execute

Execute becomes available when an enemy drops below 20% of their full health. This strike eats up all of the Rage your Warrior has, but the damage output is fairly substantial.

Rank	Level	Stance	Rage	Cost to Train	Effects
1	24	Battle, Berserker	-15	80	Attempt to finish off a wounded foe, causing 125 damage and converting each extra point of rage into 3 additional damage. Only useable on targets with 20% or less health.
2	32	Battle, Berserker	-15	1 40	Attempt to finish off a wounded foe, causing 200 damage and converting each extra point of rage into 6 additional damage Only useable on targets with 20% or less health.
3	40	Battle, Berserker	-15	2 20	Attempt to finish off a wounded foe, causing 325 damage and converting each extra point of rage into 9 additional damage Only useable on targets with 20% or less health.
4	48	Battle, Berserker	-15	4	Attempt to finish off a wounded foe, causing 450 damage and converting each extra point of rage into 12 additional damage Can only be used on targets with 20% or less health.
5	56	Battle, Berserker	-15	5 80	Attempt to finish off a wounded foe, causing 600 damage and converting each extra point of rage into 15 additional damage Only useable on targets with 20% or less health.

Challenging Shout

Challenging Shout is an emergency aggro ability on a ten-minute cooldown. This causes an AoE shout that pulls all aggro onto your Warrior.

Rank	Level	Stance	Rage	Cost to Train	Effects
N/A	26	All	-5	1 90	Forces all nearby enemies to focus attacks on you for 6 seconds. 10 minute cooldown.

Death Wish

Death Wish is a Talent-learned ability on a three-minute cooldown. Though this increases your Warrior's physical damage by 20% and makes the character immune to Fear, it also lowers Armor Rating and Resistances.

Rank	Prerequisite	Effect
1	20 Points in Fury	When activated. increases your physical damage by 20% and makes you immune to Fear effects but lowers your armor and all resistances by 20%. Lasts 30 sec.

Intercept

Intercept is used in Berserker Stance to close the distance between your Warrior and an enemy. This does more damage than Charge, has a longer Stun, and can be used during combat.

Rank	Level	Stance	Rage	Cost to Train	Effects
1	30	Berserker	-15	—	Charge an enemy, causing 40 damage and stunning it for 3 seconds. 30 second cooldown.
2	42	Berserker	-15	4 40	Charge an enemy, causing 45 damage and stunning it for 3 seconds. 30 second cooldown.
3	52	Berserker	-15	5 30	Charge an enemy, causing 65 damage and stunning it for 3 seconds. 30 second cooldown.

Slam

Slam is a situational ability. Wait until just after a normal attack, then Slam to deal a full-damage hit after a short casting time. Slam can be interrupted, Slam can fail if the enemy moves away, and Slam isn't useful if your weapon has a low min and max damage.

Rank	Level	Stance	Rage	Cost to Train	Effects
1	30	All	-15	1 20	Slams the opponent, causing weapon damage plus 32. 1.5 second cast time.
2	38	All	-15	2	Slams the opponent, causing weapon damage plus 43.
3	46	All	-15	3 60	Slams the opponent, causing weapon damage plus 68. 1.5 second cast time.
4	54	All	-15	5 60	Slams the opponent, causing weapon damage plus 87. 1.5 second cast time.

Berserker Rage

Berserk Rage is a wonderful ability. Even without the Fury Talents to generate free Rage when using this, the ability provides both immunity to Fear for ten seconds, and extra Rage generation when taking damage.

Rank	Level	Stance	Rage	Cost to Train	Effects
N/A	32	Berserker	—	1 40	The warrior enters a berserker rage, becoming immune to Fear and Incapacitate effects and generating extra rage when taking damage. Lasts 10 seconds. 30 second cooldown.

Whirlwind

Whirlwind delivers an AoE attack that hits up to four targets instantly. This is amazingly Rage-efficient.

Rank	Level	Stance	Rage	Cost to Train	Effects
N/A	36	Berserker	-25	1 80	In a whirlwind of steel you attack up to 4 enemies within 8 yards, causing weapon damage to each enemy.

Pummel

Pummel allows Warriors to interrupt casters without having a shield equipped (normally, a Shield Bash is used if you aren't carrying a two-handed weapon).

Rank	Level	Stance	Rage	Cost to Train	Effects
1	38	Berserker	-10	2	Pummel the target for 20 damage. It also interrupts spellcasting and prevents any spell in that school from being cast for 4 seconds. 10 second cooldown.
2	58	Berserker	-10	4 80	Pummel the target for 50 damage. It also interrupts spellcasting and prevents any spell in that school from being cast for 4 seconds. 10 second cooldown.

Bloodthirst

Bloodthirst is a Talent-learned ability that deals damage instantly based off of Attack Power and restores health to your Warrior for up to the next five swings.

Rank	Minimum Level	Stance	Rage	Range	Cost to Train	Effects
1	40	All	-30	5 yd	—	Instantly attack the target, causing damage equal to 45% of your attack power. In addition, the next 5 successful melee attacks will restore 10 health. This effect lasts 8 sec. 6 sec cooldown.
2	48	All	-30	5 yd	—	Instantly attack the target, causing damage equal to 45% of your attack power. In addition, the next 5 successful melee attacks will restore 13 health. This effect lasts 8 sec. 6 sec cooldown.
1	54	All	-30	5 yd	—	Instantly attack the target, causing damage equal to 45% of your attack power. In addition, the next 5 successful melee attacks will restore 17 health. This effect lasts 8 sec. 6 sec cooldown.
1	60	All	-30	5 yd	—	Instantly attack the target, causing damage equal to 45% of your attack power. In addition, the next 5 successful melee attacks will restore 20 health. This effect lasts 8 sec. 6 sec cooldown.

Recklessness

Recklessness is on the 30-minute cooldown with Retaliation and Shield Wall. This one should not be used while tanking, because it increases incoming damage by 20%. However, most strikes delivered are going to be Criticals for 15 seconds.

Rank	Level	Stance	Rage	Cost to Train	Effects
N/A	50	Berserker	—	4 20	The warrior will cause critical hits with most attacks, and will be immune to Fear effects for the next 15 seconds, but all damage taken is increased by 20%. 30 minute cooldown.

Protection

Blood Rage

Bloodrage costs a fair slice of health to use, but it can be done in battle or outside of combat to gain an instant ten Rage and another ten Rage over a short period.

Rank	Level	Stance	Rage	Cost to Train	Effects
N/A	10	All	20	6	Generates 10 Rage at the cost of Health and then generates an additional 10 Rage over 10 seconds. The warrior is considered in combat for the duration. 1 minute cooldown.

Taunt

Taunt is exactly what is appears. Nothing hidden here.

Rank	Level	Stance	Rage	Cost to Train	Effects
N/A	10	Defensive	—	—	Taunts the target to attack you, but has no effect if the target is already attacking you. 10 second cooldown.

Sunder Armor

Sunder Armor is meant to be used all the time. This reduces the target's damage mitigation, and the effect can be stacked up to five times. This generates good aggro.

Rank	Level	Stance	Rage	Cost to Train	Effects
1	10	All	-15	—	Sunders the target's armor, reducing it by 90 per Sunder Armor and causes a high amount of threat. Can be applied up to 5 times. Lasts 30 seconds.
2	22	All	-15	60	Sunders the target's armor, reducing it by 180 per Sunder Armor and causes a high amount of threat. Can be applied up to 5 times. Lasts 30 seconds.
3	34	All	-15	1 60	Sunders the target's armor, reducing it by 270 per Sunder Armor and causes a high amount of threat. Can be applied up to 5 times. Lasts 30 seconds.
4	46	All	-15	3 60	Sunders the target's armor, reducing it by 360 per Sunder Armor and causes a high amount of threat. Can be applied up to 5 times. Lasts 30 seconds.
5	58	All	-15	6	Sunders the target's armor, reducing it by 450 per Sunder Armor and causes a high amount of threat. Can be applied up to 5 times. Lasts 30 seconds.

Shield Bash

Shield Bash is used to interrupt casters. Wait until they are a second or two into their casting, then *bonk* them out of their ability.

Rank	Level	Stance	Rage	Cost to Train	Effects
1	12	Battle, Defensive	-10	10	Bashes the target with your shield for 6 damage. It also interrupts spellcasting and prevents any spell in that school from being cast for 6 seconds. Must have a shield equipped. 12 second cooldown.
2	32	Battle, Defensive	-10	1 40	Bashes the target with your shield for 18 damage. It also interrupts spellcasting and prevents any spell in that school from being cast for 6 seconds. Must have a shield equipped. 12 second cooldown.
3	52	Battle, Defensive	-10	5 40	Bashes the target with your shield for 45 damage. It also interrupts spellcasting and prevents any spell in that school from being cast for 6 seconds. Must have a shield equipped. 12 second cooldown.

Revenge

Revenge shares a cooldown with Overpower and is only usable in Defensive Stance. This is triggered after your character Blocks, Dodges, or Parries. The counterattack made is not high on damage, but it costs very little Rage and carries a high bonus Threat.

Rank	Level	Stance	Rage	Cost to Train	Effects
1	14	Defensive	-5	15	Instantly counterattack an enemy for 12 to 14 damage and a high amount of threat. Revenge must follow a block, dodge, or parry. 5 second cooldown.
2	24	Defensive	-5	80	Instantly counterattack an enemy for 18 to 22 damage and a high amount of threat. Revenge must follow a block, dodge, or parry. 5 second cooldown.
3	34	Defensive	-5	1 60	Instantly counterattack an enemy for 25 to 31 damage and a high amount of threat. Revenge must follow a block, dodge, or parry. 5 second cooldown.
4	44	Defensive	-5	3 40	Instantly counterattack an enemy for 43 to 53 damage and a high amount of threat. Revenge must follow a block, dodge, or parry. 5 second cooldown.
5	54	Defensive	-5	5 60	Instantly counterattack an enemy for 64 to 78 damage and a high amount of threat. Revenge must follow a block, dodge, or parry. 5 second cooldown.
6	60	Defensive	5	—	Instantly counterattack an enemy for 81 to 99 damage and a high amount of threat. Revenge must follow a block, dodge, or parry. 5 second cooldown.

Shield Block

Shield Block almost certifies that your Warrior will block the next incoming attack (it adds 75% to your chance), and the effect lasts until you make a Block or until five seconds has elapsed.

Rank	Level	Stance	Rage	Cost to Train	Effects
N/A	16	Defensive	-10	20	Increases chance to block by 75% for 5 seconds, but will only block 1 attack.

Disarm

Disarm rips the weapon out of an enemy's hands for ten seconds.

Rank	Level	Stance	Rage	Cost to Train	Effects
N/A	18	Defensive	-20	30	Disarm the enemy's weapon for 10 seconds. 1 minute cooldown.

Last Stand

Last Stand is a Talent-learned ability on a ten-minute cooldown. This gives your Warrior a 30% health bonus for 20 seconds. Use this when your health is low during a major encounter to give healers time to save your tanky life.

Rank	Prerequisite	Effect
1	10 Points in Protection, 2 Points in Improved Bloodrage	When activated, this ability temporarily grants you 30% of your maximum Hit Points for 20 seconds. After the effect expires, the hit points are lost.

Shield Wall

Shield Wall shares the notorious 30-minute Warrior cooldown. This adds ten seconds of reduced damage from almost all sources (-75% damage).

Rank	Level	Stance	Rage	Cost to Train	Effects
N/A	28	Defensive	—	1 10	Reduces the damage taken from melee attacks, ranged attacks and spells by 75% for 10 seconds. 30 minute cooldown.

Concussion Blow

Concussion Blow is a Talent-learned ability that instantly Stuns an opponent for five seconds.

Rank	Prerequisites	Effect
1	20 Points in Protection	Stuns the opponent for 5 seconds.

Shield Slam

Shield Slam is another Talent-learned ability. This one crowns the Protection tree, and allows Warriors with shields to deal moderate damage, gain extra Threat, and possibly Dispel an effect on the target as well.

Rank	Minimum Level	Stance	Rage	Range	Cost to Train	Effects
1	40	Defensive	-30	5 yd	—	Slam the target with your shield, causing 288 to 352 damage and has a 50% chance of dispelling 1 magic effect on the target. Also causes a high amount of threat. 6 sec cooldown.
2	48	Defensive	-30	5 yd	—	Slam the target with your shield, causing 342 to 418 damage and has a 50% chance of dispelling 1 magic effect on the target. Also causes a high amount of threat. 6 sec cooldown.
3	54	Defensive	-30	5 yd	—	Slam the target with your shield, causing 396 to 484 damage and has a 50% chance of dispelling 1 magic effect on the target. Also causes a high amount of threat. 6 sec cooldown.

Talents

Warriors Talents really help to push your characters toward either the defensive or aggressive ends of the spectrum. It's hard to walk the middle ground with a Warrior, and weapon choice plays into this quite distinctly. Arms is seen as major PvP line or a secondary selection for other Warriors, and it focuses on flexibility and burst damage. Fury is all about higher damage over time and a number of survival tools that might surprise you. The Protection line encourages one-handed weapons, a shield, and mitigation through survival and Stuns.

Arms

The Arms line is often heralded as the best for PvP (though all three lines are capable and have their place on the field, this carries some truth). Arms is certainly the best Talent line for burst damage!

Deflection is almost a must have for just about any Warrior; five percent to Parry is a very big deal no matter how you look at it. From there, Improved Charge and Tactical Mastery both should be taken. Tactical Mastery is not fun in the least, and it costs a full five Talent Points. It's also mandatory. No Warrior can function very well without it. This Talent alone allows your Warrior to switch between Stances and retain up to 25 Rage. Switch to Berserk for an instant Whirlwind (doable), switch to Defensive Stance, Taunt, Sunder Armor, back to Battle Stance (doable without losing momentum). You need Tactical Mastery.

Improved Overpower is also kind of a must, even for Protection Warriors. This is just too fun to pass up. But that ends the forced Arms Talents. After that, it gets more interesting.

Arms/PvP types should avoid Improved Heroic Strike, and Improved Thunder Clap. Instead, get your Two-Handed Weapon Spec, Sweeping Strikes, choose a weapon spec (Sword or Axe, most likely), then take Improved Hamstring, and Mortal Strike.

Improved Hamstring is great in the Battlegrounds for Rooting target over a short period. Your Warrior can even spam Hamstring until this effect lands! Sweeping Strikes gives you much more AoE potential to support an AoE group, and Mortal Strike speaks for itself. No Arms Warrior goes that deep and ditches Mortal Strike.

Then, with those in place, take Improved Rend (yuk), Deep Wounds (nice), and Impale (brutal). This lineup gives your Warrior a major increase to their Critical damage output. With the proper Agility and +Crit gear, this gives you burst damage all over the place. Charge, normal hit, Mortal Strike, hit them so hard that Execute just lit. You know what to do from there.

This places a fairly high burden on your Arms line, but the results are very nice. You can try to ditch some of Deflection, Improved Charge, and another point from the grouping to try and score 20 points into Fury (for Enrage). This is all a matter of playstyle preferences.

Fury

Fury is a more gentle mistress than the Arms line. You won't need to put 31 or more points in here to maximize the tree. Instead, take Cruelty (no matter what kind of Warrior you are).

Unbridled Wrath is horrid except for those who dual wield constantly, and it's barely good enough for them. Improved Demoralizing Shout is far more useful to the majority of Warrior builds. Take Piercing Howl in the third tier if you PvP a great deal, but possibly skip it if you only do PvE (it's quite situational there). Improved Battle Shout is always going to be a solid choice, as it's almost free Attack Power.

In the next line, take Enrage fully. If you are this far into the tree, you can't help but use this Talent. While soloing, it's incredible. While tanking, it's stunning. Only Warriors that offtank all the time, never act as main tank, and never solo should avoid Enrage.

Death Wish is a must grab, even though it too is situational. Then, choose whether to take Improved Intercept (for PvP types especially), Improved Slam (for heavy offtanks), or go back up for Blood Craze and one point of Improved Execute (for main tanks who still love the Fury line).

Take Flurry to full. Every Fury Warrior who gets this far needs to have it, and it's useful to almost any weapon build or situation. Improved Berserk Rage should also be taken, as it comes in handy often.

Bloodthirst completes the table. Dealing damage based off of Attack Power allows Bloodthirst to scale very well with certain gear types, and the extra damage is quite fun for soloing. Even as an offtank in the raid game, it's always good to steal life in any way possible, because the healers are always focused on keeping main tanks alive.

This Fury combination gives Warriors major damage output over time. When scoring Critical or being struck by Criticals, these Warriors go crazy. They can more Rage than any other build, and they are able to hold aggro quite well. Though surpassed as tanks by Protection Warriors, these folks can still do a very good job as either offtanks or main tanks. The only thing you really give up is the promised burst damage from heavy Arms Talents.

Protection

The Protection line always seems to be changing. You can always rely on it to be somewhat tepid at soloing, slow for leveling, but amazing for raiders and for tanks who want to hold the most aggro and survive the longest. Without argument, it's much easier to be the main tank for a group when you are a Protection Warrior. Other builds can get the job done, but there are safety nets here and allow your group to survive even when things start going wrong.

Shield Specialization starts off the tree well, with a bit of extra Rage generation and slightly higher mitigation of damage, due to increased Blocks. In the next line, always take Improved Bloodrage and Toughness, though you might have to come back later to polish off the last two points of Toughness. Iron Will is PvP ability most often, and can be ditched most of the time by PvE folks.

Land Stand is your first major wipe prevention Talent. This Talent is good at almost any level, and really helps with raid-level content. Its cooldown is short enough that Last Stand can be used in just about every boss fight your Warrior gets into. Use it, love it.

The other third-tier Talents are also wonderful, and they present some mean choices. Improved Shield Block is impossible to leave behind (it just offers too much extra mitigation, so take at least one point in it for the added Block). Then, put three points into Improved Revenge if you are trying to level as a Protection Warrior or Defiance if you are reaching the endgame. Defiance, with its higher Threat generation, is amazing in the later game. Improved Revenge only offers Stuns, and those become less and less useful in the endgame.

Improved Sunder Armor and Improved Taunt are the immediate selections for the next tier. Improved Disarm only has value in PvP, quite honestly.

Fill out the rest of the Protection line if you are going this far. The extra damage from one-handed Specialization makes a huge difference in holding aggro while tanking. Getting more time from Shield Wall is another raid-saver. And Shield Slam is fun for PvP damage while being a Protection Warrior and a major boost in PvE for holding aggro in Defensive Stance.

Protection Warriors are usually seen as the least fun. This build is powerful, have no doubt, but you won't be able to keep up with Fury and Arms warriors for extended damage or burst damage. What you can do is promise a 40-man raid that you can last through major damage and extended damage that would destroy a main tank of another build. How many gold pieces of repairs is that going to save your guild when you face new dungeons? How much sooner are your buddies going to complete that next boss fight? Protection Warriors are the safest choices for main tank, and it's hard to put a value on that, even if you lose a great deal of your damage output.

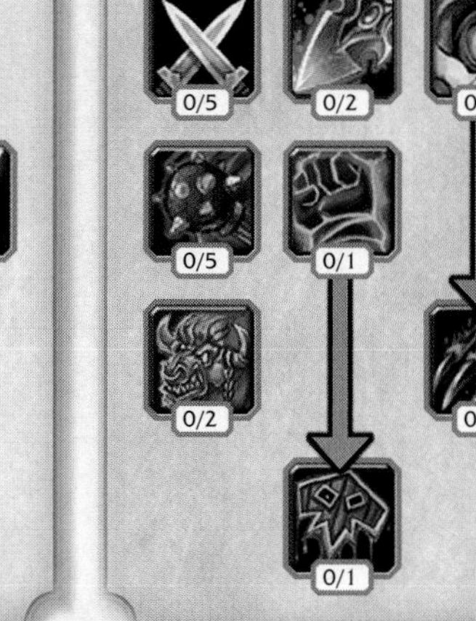

IMPROVED HEROIC STRIKE	3

Reduces the cost of your Heroic Strike ability by 1 Rage point (Per Rank).

DEFLECTION 5

Increases your Parry by 1% (Per Rank).

IMPROVED REND 3

Increases the bleed damage done by your Rend ability by 15%. Progression 15%/25%/35%.

IMPROVED CHARGE 2

Increases the amount of Rage generated by your Charge ability by 3 (Per Rank).

TACTICAL MASTERY 5

You retain up to 5 of your rage points (per Rank) when you change stances.

IMPROVED THUNDER CLAP 3

Reduces the cost of your Thunder Clap ability by 1 rage point. Progression 1/2/4.

IMPROVED OVERPOWER 2

Increases the critical strike chance of your Overpower ability by 25% (Per Rank).

ANGER MANAGEMENT 1

Reduces the time required for your Rage to decay while out of combat by 30% (Per Rank).

DEEP WOUNDS 3

Your critical strikes causes the opponent to bleed, dealing 20% (Per Rank) of your melee weapon's damage over 12 seconds.

TWO-HANDED WEAPON SPECIALIZATION 5

Increases the damage you deal with two-handed melee weapons by 1% (Per Rank).

IMPALE 2

Increases the critical strike damage bonus of your abilities in Battle Defensive, and Berserker stance by 10% (Per Rank).

AXE SPECIALIZATION 5

Increases your chance to get a critical strike with Axes by 1% (Per Rank).

SWEEPING STRIKES 1

Your next 5 melee weapon swings strike an additional enemy.

MACE SPECIALIZATION 5

Gives you a 1% chance to stun your target for 3 sec with a Mace. Progression 1%/2%/3%/4%/6%

SWORD SPECIALIZATION 5

Gives you a 1% chance (Per Rank) to get an extra attack on the same target after dealing damage with your Sword.

POLEARM SPECIALIZATION 5

Increases your chance to get a critical strike with Polearms by 1% (Per Rank).

IMPROVED HAMSTRING 3

Gives your Hamstring ability a 5% chance (Per Rank) to immobilize a target for 5 sec.

MORTAL STRIKE 1

A vicious strike that deals weapon damage plus 85 and wounds the target, reducing the effectiveness of any healing by 50% for 10 seconds.

BOOMING VOICE 5

Increases the area effect and duration of your Battle Shout and Demoralizing Shout by 10% (Per Rank).

CRUELTY 5

Increases your chance to get a critical strike with melee weapons by 1% (Per Rank).

IMPROVED DEMORALIZING SHOUT 5

Increases the Attack Power reduction of your Demoralizing Shout by 8% (Per Rank).

UNBRIDLED WRATH 5

Gives you a 8% chance (Per Rank) to generate an additional Rage point when you deal melee damage with a weapon.

IMPROVED CLEAVE 3

Increases the bonus damage of your Cleave ability by 40% (Per Rank).

PIERCING HOWL 1

Causes all enemies near the warrior to be dazed for 6 seconds.

BLOOD CRAZE 3

Regenerates 1% (Per Rank) of your total health after being the victim of a critical strike.

IMPROVED BATTLE SHOUT 5

Increases the Attack Power bonus of your Battle Shout by 5% (Per Rank).

DUAL WIELD SPECIALIZATION 5

Increases the damage done by your offhand weapon by 5% (Per Rank).

IMPROVED EXECUTE 2

Reduces the Rage cost of your Execute ability. Progression 2/5.

ENRAGE 5

Gives you a 5% melee damage bonus (Per Rank) for 12 seconds up to a maximum of 12 swings after being the victim of a critical strike.

IMPROVED SLAM 5

Decreases the casting time of your Slam ability by 0.1 seconds (Per Rank).

DEATH WISH 1

When activated, increases your physical damage by 20% and makes you immune to Fear effects but lowers your armor and all resistances by 20%. Lasts 30 sec.

IMPROVED INTERCEPT 2

Reduces the cooldown of your Intercept ability by 5 seconds (Per Rank).

IMPROVED BERSERKER RAGE 2

The Berserker Rage ability will generate 5 rage (Per Rank) when used.

FLURRY 5

Increases your attack speed by 10% for your next 3 swings after dealing a critical strike. Progression 10%/15%/20%/25%/30%.

BLOODTHIRST 1

Instantly attack the target, causing damage equal to 40% of your attack power. In addition, the next 5 successful melee attacks will restore 10 health. This effect lasts 8 sec.

SHIELD SPECIALIZATION 5

Increases your chance to block attacks with a shield by 1% (Per Rank) and has a 20% chance (Per Rank) to generate 1 Rage when a block occurs.

ANTICIPATION 5

Increases your Defense skill by 2 (Per Rank).

IMPROVED BLOODRAGE 2

Reduces the Health cost of your Bloodrage ability by 25% (Per Rank).

TOUGHNESS 5

Increases your armor value from items by 2% (Per Rank).

IRON WILL 5

Increases your chance to resist stun and charm effects by 3% (Per Rank).

LAST STAND 1

When activated, this ability temporarily grants you 30% of your maximum Hit Points for 20 seconds. After the effect expires, the hit points are lost.

IMPROVED SHIELD BLOCK 3

Allows your Shield Block ability to block an additional attack, and increases the duration by 0.5 seconds (Per Rank).

IMPROVED REVENGE 3

Gives your Revenge ability a 20% chance to stun the target for 3 seconds. Progression 20%/30%/40%.

DEFIANCE 5

Increases the threat generated by your attacks by 3% (Per Rank) while in Defensive Stance.

IMPROVED SUNDER ARMOR 3

Reduces the cost of your Sunder Armor ability by 1 rage point (Per Rank).

IMPROVED DISARM 3

Increases the duration of your Disarm ability by 1 sec (Per Rank).

IMPROVED TAUNT 2

Reduces the cooldown of your Taunt ability by 1 sec (Per Rank).

IMPROVED SHIELD WALL 2

Increases the effect duration of your Shield Wall ability by 3 sec. Progression 3/5.

CONCUSSION BLOW 1

Stuns the opponent for 5 seconds.

IMPROVED SHIELD BASH 2

Gives your Shield Bash ability a 50% chance (Per Rank) to silence the target for 3 seconds.

ONE HANDED WEAPON SPECIALIZATION 5

Increases the damage you deal with a One-Handed melee weapon by 2% (Per Rank).

SHIELD SLAM 1

Slam the target with your shield, causing 288 to 352 damage and has a 50% chance of dispelling 1 magic effect on the target. Also causes a high amount of threat.

STRATEGIES

It takes months to master the full breadth of Warrior abilities and functionality, but a couple pages of tips can get you odd to a good start. This biggest point of all is to be flexible. Warriors aren't a one-trick pony; not by a long shot. This is a class with damage and mitigation galore, and most games aren't like that with their tanks. Blizzard was very good to us; usually, tanks absorb damage and have no fun at anything else. If you play Warriors long enough, you'll start to expect more out of MOG life, and that is a beautiful thing.

GENERAL TIPS

Always have food, bandages, healing potions, and something to buff Strength or Stamina on hand. Your bags should also have a shield and a full assortment of weapons. Be prepared. Use this toys all of the time for faster leveling and a greater joy of killing. Even if you aren't a Blacksmith, also keep Sharpening Stones on-hand for increased weapon damage.

Become close friends with an Enchanter, or become one. Warriors love the +Stamina enchantments, and the weapon enchantments are even better. Crusader is your best friend: anything that lets you heal yourself in battle while getting a Strength buff is almost too good to be true. Don't be afraid to put down the money for these on your high-end weapons.

Run dungeons as often as possible. Not only are Warriors needed in these, but most of the best gear while leveling is found on bosses in dungeons. This is true for all classes, but Warriors stand to gain so much more. What we mean is that a Mage in cruddy gear is outperformed moderately by a Mage in good gear. Skill means almost everything to those caster folks. For a Warrior, skill and gear work hand-in-hand. If you get your Warrior decked out in the best goodies, you become a god of battle: dealing damage, mitigating a ton of incoming problems, and winning friends wherever you go. Get your gear! Though working to do this slows down leveling dramatically, because dungeons aren't good places to get experience, the process of leveling is tremendously more fun when you have the right gear.

And after all, aren't you playing your Warrior to have fun?

BEING FAIR ABOUT AGGRO

Some demands are fair from groups. They want you to hold aggro, within reason. They want you to have a shield for big battles, boss fights, or higher-level monsters. They need you to know when to Taunt and use Defensive Stance, even when Battle Stance is more to your liking. These are fair things to expect.

Don't, on the other hand, let people force you to stay in Defensive Stance, with a sword and shield, all the time. If you are holding aggro and the healers aren't tapping out of mana every fight, feel free to put a bit more DPS on the pile. You don't have to be a Protection Warrior to tank, and you don't have to sit in Defensive Stance all day to hold aggro. Let the situation dictate how you play. If you have the aggro under control, tell people that you know what you are doing and don't let them backseat tank.

If you are losing aggro, stay in Defensive Stance more and remember to use Sunder Armor, Heroic Strike, Revenge, and other abilities that give you a lot of Threat. If that still isn't enough, remember that your group mates have a responsibility to deal with aggro as well. Is there one specific person ripping aggro off you? If it's a healer, you are probably doing something wrong, or your group just isn't up to the dungeon quite yet. However, if it's a DPS class, *they should look at themselves first.* Other classes using abilities with extra Threat may be causing trouble (Mind Blast, Searing Pain, Mages spamming their instants or AoEing, Rogues that aren't using Feint, Hunters that Multishot without Feign Death, etc.). Let these DPSers know to cool off slightly, and give you more time to cement aggro.

ARE STANCES JUST ABOUT ABILITIES?

Some abilities are reserved for specific stances, but that isn't all that stances do. Look at the following table.

Stance	Performance
Battle Stance	Full Damage, Decreased Threat
Defensive Stance	-10% Damage Dealt, -10% Damage Receive, Greatly Increase Threat
Berserker Stance	+3% Critical Rate, +10% Damage Received, Decreased Threat

As you can see, Berserker Stance is not a wise stance to stay in when you have a great deal of aggro. Having +3% to your Critical rate isn't worth it. That said, you can switch into a stance, use an ability, and quickly pop back out of it (this is why Tactical Mastery is a required Talent). Use Berserker Stance for Berserk Rage, Whirlwind, or Pummel.

By the same token, if you don't want/need Threat, don't stick around in Defensive Stance. Use it for Taunting a single mob as a backup tank, or to Disarm, but don't reduce your damage by 10% if you aren't trying to either grab aggro or mitigate damage!

Damage-point per damage-point, Defensive Stance is the ideal way to keep firm aggro. Though the numbers look nice in Battle Stance and Berserker Stance, the change in Threat from these stances make it impossible to hold aggro nearly as well as someone in Defense Stance, even when they are dealing a fraction of your damage.

NOBODY FIGHTS FAIR

PvP is great for Warriors that have mastered the class. With the proper gear, there are probably one of the top two or three classes in the game. Without high-end gear and a lot of skill, things aren't so easy. The problem is that everyone knows what you want to do (get in close and hammer on people). Because of that, each class does everything in their power to keep you at range. Druids use Entangling Roots, Mages Frost Nova/Blink and Keep you at range, Priests and Warlocks Fear you away and lay down the damage.

The key is to know how to close distances quickly. Charge the moment you get a chance in PvP. Don't hesitate, don't think, don't even select targets if a few enemies come around a corner. Charge first, target second. Even if you have to charge a Hunter pet that is ahead of a group, go ahead (at least you get the free Rage and cover most of the gap).

Next, master the switch to Berserker Stance and use Intercept. This is the PvP gift to Warriors. Intercept lets you catch up with fleeing people and Stun them long enough to get your Hamstring off. Then, even if you are Snared, they are in the same boat. No fast running away for those cowards. Destroy them!

Buy the PvP Trinket (the Insignia) as soon as you can. Even a few Battleground matches are enough to start gaining ranks, and this opens the first reward. The PvP Trinket gets Warriors out of Snare/Root problems. Use this Trinket heavily in PvP, keep it on your quickbar, and surprise those people who think they just locked you in place. Free Action Potions aren't a bad investment either.

Keep your two-handed weapon out in PvP. Enemies don't stick around for dual wielders to get many shots off. For that reason, you end up losing some of their DPS efficiency. Two-handed weapons only need one opportunity for a hit every few seconds. That means that it's easier to keep your attacks going even when folks are running behind you, trying to Stun your character, and so forth.

Since your weapon is your only source of damage invest in a weapon chain. There are also several pieces of equipment that grant your immunity to disarm.

I WANT MORE AGGRO

Charge a group, use Demoralizing Shout to get group aggro, Thunder Clap to cement it. Switch to Berserker Stance, hit Berserk Rage if you are Fury specced, Whirlwind, use Mortal Strike/Blood Thirst/Shield Slam to burn any spare Rage, then drop to Defensive Stance and start to focus on a single target.

Sunder Armor early on, use Revenge any time it appears, and tap Heroic Strike with spare Rage for a ton of extra Threat. If a second target runs off and you don't have an offtank to deal with it, switch targets, Taunt, Sunder Armor, then go back to your main foe.

If you are having particular problems with one monster, go to Battle Stance and use Mocking Blow. If you lose the whole group, try Challenging Shout.

Use items that keep you afloat earlier in a fight, when you have less aggro. This keeps your healers from stealing peripheral monsters. Any trinkets that absorb damage, for instance, are good to use at the start of a fight with many enemies.

If you can't get a target to aggro on you, Stun them with whatever you have: Bombs, the Tauren's Warstomp, Concussive Blow, Improved Revenge. This way, at least the foe isn't killing your buddies.

DUNGEONS AND RAIDS

What is the Difference Between a Dungeon and a Raid?

At the core, there is only one difference between a dungeon group and a raid. Dungeon groups have a maximum of 5 characters while Raids have anywhere from 6 to 40. This very simple distinction makes the two very different however. As the size of a group increases, specialization in each character is fundamentally necessary.

Dungeons

Instance Dungeons in World of Warcraft should be done in groups of five. Instances often allow as many as ten, but quests are not able to be completed.

ROLES IN A DUNGEON

Role Table

Role	Responsibility	Classes
Tank	Gather, Maintain, and Survive Aggro	Warrior, Druid, Paladin, Shaman
Secondary Tank (Off-tank)	Pull Aggro from non-tank members	Warrior, Druid, Paladin, Shaman, Warlock, Hunter
Healer	Keep Party Members Alive	Priest, Druid, Shaman, Paladin
Crowd Control (CC)	Neutralize Enemies	Mage, Rogue, Hunter, Priest, Warlock
Damage (DPS)	Kill Enemies	Rogue, Mage, Warlock, Hunter, Druid
Area of Effect Damage (AoE)	Damage multiple enemies at once	Mage, Warlock, Hunter, Warrior, Druid, Priest
Resurrection (Rez)	Revive Fallen Members	Priest, Shaman, Paladin, Druid
Wipe Recovery	Resurrect or Survive a Total Party Wipe	Paladin, Warlock, Shaman, Engineer

That's More Than Five Roles!

While you are limited to five members in your party, there are many jobs to do. Many characters can fill multiple roles. A Priest can be Healer, Crowd Control, and Resurrection while a Hunter can be Secondary Tank, Damage, and Crowd Control.

Some roles take more attention than others. No one should ever be both Tank and Healer. It's too much responsibility and doesn't work.

Tank

As one of the most important roles, a good tank can make a party while a bad tank can break one. The party tank should start the fights to get early aggro, and use abilities to maintain the aggro. Often this is done after all forms of CC are in effect.

WARRIOR

Warriors make the best tanks. They have the heaviest armor (mail until level 40 when they learn to wear plate), can use a shield, have abilities to hold single enemies, and abilities to hold multiple enemies. Taunt and Mocking Blow are useful to pull an enemy's attention off another party member while Sunder Armor and Heroic Strike cause higher threat and are useful for keeping an enemy on you. When all goes wrong, Challenging Shout pulls all enemies in range onto you. Combine these abilities with Defensive Stance, Demoralizing Shout, Shield Block, and Shield Wall and you've seen the very basic abilities a Warrior can bring to the table as a tank.

DRUID

At first, Druids seem like a poor choice as a tank. Their leather armor doesn't stand up to much. Only Druids using Bear Form or Dire Bear Form should be considered for the role of tank. Speccing in the Feral talent tree makes you even more effective. As a bear (or dire bear), the Druid's armor is increased greatly and they gain access to a number of abilities that help them substitute nicely. Feral Charge and Maul work well to keep a single target's attention, while Swipe and Demoralizing Roar affect multiple enemies. With a Druid as your tank, your group needs to be careful about focusing fire as the Druid doesn't have as many ways to quickly peel aggro off other members.

PALADIN

Like Warriors, Paladins have access to the heaviest armor in the game (mail until level 40 when they learn to wear plate) and can equip a shield. This combined with their ability to heal themselves, can make the Paladin extremely durable as a tank. They aren't quite as effective with holding aggro as a Warrior, but they have a number of abilities to aid them. Blessing of Salvation keeps other party members from drawing as much threat. Blessing of Sanctuary reduces all damage, while Seal of Justice and Hammer of Justice can stun an enemy to further reduce the damage they deal. Righteous Fury multiplies the threat generated by the Paladin's holy spells. Used in conjunction with Holy Shield and Consecrate, this creates a decent amount of threat. Paladins are very good at reducing the damage enemies can deal to a party, but not as talented at maintaining the attention of several enemies. Keep your parties fire focused when using a Paladin as tank.

SHAMAN

Of all the classes that can perform the role of tank, Shaman are the most dangerous. They have several tools to hold aggro, but they can only wear leather (and mail after level 40). While a Shaman can be a passable tank for instance groups until level 50 or so, the instances after that are much more difficult for the Shaman to survive in. While Stoneskin Totem reduces melee damage dealt to the party and Shaman can equip shields, it's their ability to hold aggro that qualifies them to fill the role of tank. Rockbiter Weapon and Earth Shock generate great amounts of threat, while Windfury Weapon can dramatically increase the Shaman's damage output for a short time. Shaman make better secondary tanks, but can be used as tanks if absolutely needed.

Secondary Tank

If party members aren't focusing fire well enough or an enemy resists CC or you just plain get unlucky, enemies jump from the tank to your healers or dps. Rather than having the tank run around trying to regain aggro, it's better to have an off-tank grab the aggro and pull it back to the main tank before returning to the primary target or simply tie it up.

WARRIOR

As having all the tools to be primary tank, Warriors are fully qualified as secondary tanks. Using Taunt or Mocking Blow (to pull aggro off another party member) in conjunction with Sunder Armor or Heroic Strike (to build aggro quickly) allows the Warrior to perform this role with flying colors. Warriors acting as secondary tanks should consider switching to a two-handed weapon or using Berserk Stance to increase their damage to the primary tank's target when they aren't acting as off-tank.

DRUID

As secondary tanks aren't always needed, the Druid is free to use whatever form he or she chooses when not performing this role. When a party member pulls aggro off the main tank, a Druid can shift to Bear or Dire Bear Form and keep the enemy tied up until the main tank can pull it off. Another option is to tear aggro off the other party member and move to the front lines so the main tank can pull it off you. Once the job of secondary tank is accomplished, the Druid is free to return to the role they were fulfilling prior.

PALADIN

Paladins have a few more tools as secondary tank than they do as primary tank. Without many opponents to interfere with their casting, Paladins can use heals as well as their damage to pull aggro off party members. Holy Shock can be used as instant damage against the enemy or to instantly heal a friend and give you enough time to pull the enemy off. Stun the target with Hammer of Justice, then use Judgement of Command because the threat is multiplied by Righteous Fury. As with Warriors, Paladins fulfilling this role should consider using a two-handed weapon to increase their damage as their heavy armor is enough to keep them alive against a single enemy.

SHAMAN

The aggro grabbing tools of the Shaman make them a great choice for this role. A quick Earthshock combine with a Lesser Healing Wave can quickly pull aggro off a party member. As you'll likely only have a single enemy on you, the survivability problems of the Shaman aren't an issue. Your armor is enough to keep you alive until the party is ready to deal with your target. Using a two-handed weapon increases a Shaman's damage output, but have a shield bridges the gap between their armor and the heavier types. Consider using a one-handed weapon and a shield until your enemy is dead or looking at the main tank before pulling out your two-handed weapon.

WARLOCK

Clad in cloth, the Warlock doesn't seem a wise choice for a secondary tank. Indeed, they are very poor choices for this role. However, their pets are great choices for it. A Voidwalker has an impressive amount of health and is fairly durable. The best part about it is the Warlock's ability to simply summon another one outside of combat, if their pet dies. This allows you to sic your Voidwalker on an enemy, have it use Torment to grab and maintain aggro, and forget about it as you go back to the primary target. If a Warlock is to fulfill this role, let them know ahead of time as it takes a good while to summon a Voidwalker and their other pets are generally poor choices for secondary tanks.

HUNTER

Both a Hunter and their pet can fulfill this role. Putting a pet on an enemy and Growling keeps that enemy tied up until the pet is dead or Cowers it off. Hunters speccing in the Beast Mastery talent tree have pets that can nearly rival Warriors for their durability and ability to maintain the attention of an enemy.

The Hunter can also fulfill this role. Distracting Shot followed by Arcane Shot is often enough to pull an enemy off a softer party member. With leather armor (mail after level 40), the Hunter isn't nearly as killable as other party members. Once the tank is ready to pull aggro off the Hunter, using Disengage or Feign Death makes this much easier. The ability to quickly pull and drop aggro combined with a pet, make Hunters an almost optimal choice for this role.

HEALER

This role is fairly self explanatory, but there are a few subtleties to it. Healing someone is pretty straight forward. Using the right heal at the right time is a bit more difficult. A Healer's first priority is to keep the tank alive. The second priority being to keep themselves alive (who will heal after you are dead?) and healing others comes third. A Healer's mana should be watched by the entire party as once it runs out, things get more serious.

PRIEST

The Priest is the first obvious choice as healer. With heals of several sizes, the Priest can avoid overhealing and drawing aggro. The other assets of the Priest are their buffs. Power Word: Fortitude is a long duration buff that increases the party member's Stamina, and thus their health. Power Word: Shield is a very short term buff that absorbs damage. This draws more aggro, but can give the party the time it needs to pull an enemy off before a member dies. Shielding the tank before battle begins avoids the aggro issue and gives the tank several moments to generate threat before taking damage. Drawing aggro isn't the worst problem of the Priest, as using Fade reduces your threat level considerably.

DRUID

While in caster form, the Druid has a great many tools for the role of healer. They have the standard heals of varying size to keep from overhealing and drawing aggro, but their true strength lies elsewhere. Mark of the Wild is a long term buff that increases all stats and armor of a party member. This increases health while decreasing incoming damage. Regrowth and Rejuvenation are both heal over time spells. This allows the Druid to heal while spreading out the threat they draw. Using these before a battle begins ensures that damage is being healed without the attention of the Druid or drawing aggro.

SHAMAN

Shaman have a number of tools to buff and heal party members. In addition to the standard heals of differing size to keep from overhealing and drawing aggro, their totems can heal and buff party members. Healing Stream Totem and Mana Spring Totem restore health and mana to all party members in range. While not having any way to reduce the amount of threat they are drawing, Shaman wear heavier armor and can survive unwanted aggro longer.

PALADIN

Paladins have fewer tools for this role, but can be used as a backup or when none of the other classes are available. Blessing of Protection can keep a party member safe from physical attacks for a short duration. This gives the Paladin enough time to heal the party member or the party to kill the enemy. The greatest tools the Paladin has for this role are the wide array of blessings. Blessing of Light coupled with Flash of Light (rank 3) can be cast repeatedly with very high mana efficiency. As blessings have short durations, the Paladin will be very busying keeping them active. A Paladin's Lay on Hands can turn a disastrous situation into a livable one. As it uses all the Paladin's mana, it's a last ditch effort to safe a party and once it's used, the party is without further healing.

CROWD CONTROL

It's always easier to survive three enemies attacking you than four. CC keeps enemies tied up for lengthy periods without lowering your damage or increasing your risk. CC is often broken any time the affected enemy takes damage. There are two distinct types of CC; in-combat and out-of-combat.

Out-of-Combat CC tends to last longer, but can only be used when you or the enemy is out of combat. Groups using any of these abilities should use them before the fight begins.

MAGE

Mages are useful crowd control in a variety of circumstances. Should there be a single enemy the party can't deal with at the time, a Polymorph neutralizes them for a good long time; as long as the enemy is a humanoid, beast, or critter. When the Polymorph breaks, it can be recast with only a duration penalty. Frost Bolt and Cone of Cold can snare single enemies, while Mages have other tools to hamper the movement of enemy groups. Frost Nova roots for several seconds, while Fire and Ice specced Mages can make use of Blast Wave and Improved Blizzard. Counterspell is also a powerful means of controlling a caster

ROGUE

Both in-combat and out-of-combat, CC is what the Rogue brings to a group. Sap can only be used on humanoids and before combat begins. It can only be used on one enemy and the Rogue is detected immediately by other enemies unless he or she has the Improved Sap talent. Blind lasts for several seconds and takes a reagent. Gouge is a nearly free CC, but doesn't last long and can only be used if the enemy is facing the Rogue. Only lasting a few seconds, Gouge can barely be called CC, but it can be useful in emergency situations. Kidney Shot also works if things start ot get chaotic.

HUNTER

Most Hunter abilities are out-of-combat crowd control. Traps can only be used if the Hunter is out of combat. This can be accomplished before the battle begins or by using Feign Death (provided your pet isn't engaged). Freezing Trap creates an area that slows all enemies who enter, while Frost Trap can encase a single enemy in a block of ice for an extended period of time. If the Hunter is specced in the Survival talent tree, Wyvern Sting can also be used to put an enemy to sleep before combat begins. Marksmanship Hunters have a short in-combat CC in Scatter Shot. This is only useful in emergencies when a few seconds makes the difference.

PRIEST

Priests have three forms of CC. Psychic Scream sends nearby enemies running in fear for several seconds. This gets them off your party, but may send them into more enemies and make the situation much worse. Use this ability with extreme caution in the confined spaces of instances. Shackle Undead can only affect undead enemies, but very few classes have any ability to CC undead, so it's still fairly powerful. It neutralizes the enemy for several seconds and can be recast if broken with only a duration penalty. The third is Mind Control. It is dangerous to use in pick-up groups, but for a seasoned group this is a powerful way to start a fight.

WARLOCK

Enemies can be CCed several ways by a Warlock. Demons and elementals can be Banished for a long time. Banish can be recast and cannot be broken until the duration passes. During the time it is banished, the demon or elemental is immune to damage. Fear causes a single enemy to flee, while Howl of Terror causes several enemies to flee. This gets them off the party, but can make the situation worse if the fleeing enemies find friends to bring back. Deathcoil is a short duration fear, but is really only useful in emergencies. The final form of CC the Warlock possesses, is actually a pet ability. The Succubus can use Seduction to CC a humanoid target for extended durations.

Damage

Doing damage is easy. Doing a lot of damage is a little harder. Doing a lot of damage and living to tell about it is even more difficult. Focusing all the damage so things die quickly and aggro is maintained...that is the penultimate.

Start slow with the damage and increase it as the enemy's health drops. This helps your tank maintain aggro until you're ready to finish it.

ROGUE

With so many tools to deal damage and avoid aggro, the Rogue is a great selection for this role. Deadly Poison and Instant Poison can proc extra damage on every swing the Rogue makes. Using damage over time abilities (Garrote, Deadly Poison, and Rupture) against harder targets keep the Rogue from getting aggro as quickly while using fast damage abilities (Ambush, Backstab, Sinister Strike, Instant Poison, and Eviscerate) can kill weaker targets very quickly. Slice and Dice is a good finisher for those pesky bosses. Feint can keep a Rogue from generating too much threat and Vanish can be used in emergencies to dump threat quickly.

MAGE

Mages are all about damage. Once aggro is established, Mages should feel free to blast away, but don't start with Pyroblast or any other large spells. Keep these for your second or third volley against a target. Instead start with Arcane Missles, Fireball, or Frost Bolt. These don't do quite as much damage, but Mages should start small and finish big. As the fight progresses and the enemy's health drops, start throwing everything you have at it. Pyroblast, if you're specced in the Fire talent tree, Scorch, and Fire Blast throws a good bit of damage in a short period of time. Being able to create their own water, Mages shouldn't be worried about mana efficiency against weaker enemies as they can recover between fights.

WARLOCK

Many of the Warlock's spells don't do much up front damage. Against weaker opponents, the Warlock isn't ideal. Against very tough enemies, however, the Warlock's DoTs really start to shine. Any of the pets the Warlock can choose from aid in doing damage with the Succubus being most damaging. Throwing Corruption, Curse of Agony, and Immolate on an enemy doesn't do much damage at first, but as the seconds pass, the enemy's health continuously drops. Being able to Drain Mana or Drain Health, also make the Warlock great for longer fights as they can maintain consistent damage. If you are Destruction specialized, Shadowbolts with an occasional Conflagrate deals awesome damage.

HUNTER

Constantly firing arrows or bullets at an enemy makes the Hunter a valid choice for a damage slot. To increase the damage they are putting out, Hunters can use Serpent Sting, Aimed Shot (if they are specced in the Marksmanship talent tree), and Arcane Shot. If the party is fighting a single enemy, using Multi-Shot adds further damage. In fights where fast damage is important, Rapid Fire and Beastial Wrath (if you are specced in the Beast Mastery talent tree) increases the damage of the Hunter and the pet for a short duration and have a fairly short cooldown.

DRUID

When in Cat Form, Druids function a great deal like Rogues. The reduced survivability of this form is offset by the increased damage potential. As such, a Cat Form Druid makes a perfectly acceptable damage slot occupant. For quick fights against weaker enemies, starting with Ravage, using Shred or Claw to build combo points, and finishing with Ferocious Bite does a great deal of damage in a very short time. Using the DoT abilities of Cat Form is more ideal for longer fights against tougher opponents. Begin with Pounce, use Rake and Shred to build combo points, and finish with Rip. While this does just as much damage, it spreads it out over time and makes it easier for the tank to maintain aggro.

Area of Effect Damage

There are times in dungeons where it takes far too long to kill the enemies one at a time and trying to do so can result in the entire group dying. For these fights, (often against a dozen or more non-elite enemies) being able to damage many at once is the wisest course of action. This must be done quickly as only very skilled tanks can hold aggro against multiple enemies in these situations.

MAGE

One of the kings of AoE damage is the Mage. Arcane Explosion allows the Mage to continue doing AoE damage even while being attacked because of its instant cast time and limited targeting time (it is cast with you as the center of the effect). Blizzard and Flame Strike can be cast at range, but have differing effects. Flame Strike does damage immediately and continues damaging any enemies in the area over time. Blizzard is a channeled spell and does damage over the duration of the cast, but can slow the enemy's approach if you have the Improved Blizzard talent. Often a good line up is to start with Blizzard or Flame Strike and switch to Arcane Explosion as the enemy advances on you.

HUNTER

Hunters are a good second place when it comes to the AoE slot. They can do almost as much damage to almost as many targets as a Mage. Setting an Explosive Trap before the fight and using Multi-Shot then Volley throws a lot of damage out very quickly and generates a great deal of threat. Feign Death to allow the tank to grab aggro, before putting another Explosive Trap and backing off to Multi-Shot and Volley again. Keeping you pet on Passive and not attacking allows you to set another trap.

WARLOCK

Warlocks have a number of tools that qualify them for an AoE slot. Warlocks have a ranged AoE (Rain of Fire) and a point blank AoE (Hellfire). If the Warlock is the only AoE party member, they should start the fight with their Voidwalker. Cast Rain of Fire until the enemies closes with you and begins attacking. Sacrifice your Voidwalker to protect you from casting interruptions and use Hellfire to finish the enemies. While not having as many tools as the Mage, the Warlock is still quite impressive in this position.

WARRIOR

Few people think of a Warrior in the damage slot, let alone the AoE damage slot. Warriors have a few abilities that can be used in each fight, and a few tricks that can be used in very difficult fights. Switching to a two-hand weapon and using Whirlwind and Cleave allows the Warrior to hit multiple enemies for reasonable damage. Warriors speccing in the Arms talent tree can use Sweeping Strikes to hit extra targets for a short duration and a moderate cooldown (30 seconds). In very tough fights, Warriors can use Challenging Shout (10 minute cooldown) to force all enemies to attack them, then use Retaliation (30 minute cooldown) to counter-attack each enemy. This tactic results in devastating damage, but can only be used every 30 minutes and is often saved for particularly dangerous fights.

DRUID

Druids only have one spell to add to an AoE engagement. They don't have the versatility to be a primary or only AoE party member, but they can support another. Hurricane is a channeled spell and should be done very early in the fight. This draws aggro onto the Druid. Shift into Bear Form or Dire Bear Form to survive the enemy damage, while the primary AoE member (free from interruption for the next few seconds) finishes the enemies.

PRIEST

A Priest's contribution, like the Druid's isn't as impressive, but can certainly supplement. Holy Nova doesn't do as much damage, but doesn't draw any aggro. While only available to Priests that spec in the Holy talent tree, Holy Nova can add enough damage to finish enemies before they finish your primary AoE member.

Resurrection

No matter how careful you are, there is always the chance that something will go wrong and someone in the party dies. Having someone who can resurrect a fallen member (rezzer) can save the time of running back to your body, or save the entire run if enemies have respawned behind you.

PRIEST

Resurrection can be cast any time outside of combat and doesn't have a cooldown. The fallen party member must be within line of sight. If the party member has already released their spirit, cast the spell, then click on the body to target the person's corpse.

SHAMAN

Shaman have very similar restrictions as Priests. Ancestral Spirit cannot be used during combat and has no cooldown. Line of sight and range are still concerns and players who have released can be rezzed in a similar fashion by casting the spell before clicking on their corpse.

PALADIN

Paladins can ask Redemption for dead party members. Constricted by line of sight, range, and combat just as Priests are, Paladins are not often the primary rezzers, but they are just as qualified for the position.

DRUID

The Druid has the most restrictions on their ability to rez others, but make up for it by having one of the common restrictions removed. Rebirth is the only rez spell that can be cast during combat. It costs a reagent each time it is used (the reagent varies depending on level) and has a 30 minute cooldown. Line of sight and range are still issues, but Druids are generally secondary or emergency rezzers.

Wipe Recovery

Total party wipes happen sooner or later and can be a crushing blow to morale, but having a fast way to recover from them can save time and your entire run as enemies may have respawned between the instance entrance and where your party died.

WARLOCK

By far, the Warlock is the easiest and most versatile class to use as wipe recovery. For the cost of a Soul Shard, the Warlock can use Create Soul Stone for a party member. This allows the 'stoned' person to instantly resurrect himself instead of releasing their spirit. The soul stone buff lasts one hour, has a 30 minute cooldown, and needs to be renewed. Instanly rezzing yourself uses the stone, so choose when to resurrect yourself carefully. Classes that can resurrect others are almost always the ones chosen to have their soul stored.

PALADIN

Paladin wipe recovery is a little trickier to use and is more like wipe prevention. By using a Symbol of Divinity and sacrificing themselves, Paladins can call upon Divine Intervention and remove a party member from combat and all danger for 3 minutes. At the end of the duration, the party member can be attacked as normal, so it should be cast on someone who can resurrect others and is outside of the enemy's aggro detection. Couple this with the restriction of having to cast Divine Intervention before the person dies makes proper use of this spell nearly an art form.

SHAMAN

Shaman are the only class that can resurrect themselves (and only themselves) without any form of setup (aside from buying the Ankhs before they came). Reincarnation has a one hour cooldown (unless you have taken the Improved Reincarnation talent), and consumes an Ankh each time it is used. Also possessing the ability to resurrect others, Reincarnation makes Shaman quite ideal at recovering from wipes. As Shaman can resurrect themselves, they are often a poor choice for Soul Stones, unless they have used their Ankh recently.

ENGINEERS

Hunters or Rogues with Engineer skill can remove themselves from combat (FD or Vanish), then use Goblin Jumper Cables to restore a priest. Remember, Goblin Jumper Cables are unreliable.

Dungeon Listing

Dungeon Quick Table

Level Range	Dungeon	Zone
13-18	Ragefire Chasm	Orgrimmar
17-24	Wailing Caverns	Barrens
17-24	Deadmines	Westfall
22-26	Shadowfang Keep	Silverpine Forest
24-28	Blackfathom Deeps	Ashenvale
24-28	The Stockades	Stormwind
25-30	Razorfen Kraul	Barrens
29-38	Gnomeregan	Dun Morogh
33-40	Razorfen Downs	Barrens
34-45	The Scarlet Monastery	Tirisfal Glades
35-47	Uldaman	Badlands
44-50	Zul'Farrak	Tanaris
47-55	The Sunken Temple	Swamp of Sorrows
45-50	Maraudon	Desolace
52+	Blackrock Depths	Searing Gorge/Burning Steppes
55+	Dire Maul	Feralas
58+	Stratholme	Eastern Plaguelands
57+	Scholomance	Western Plaguelands
58+	Blackrock Spire	Searing Gorge/Burning Steppes

Ragefire Chasm

Zone:	Orgrimmar
Level Range:	13-18
Primary Enemies:	Humanoid
Special Items:	None
Entrance Requirements:	None

Ragefire Chasm is only accessible to Horde parties as it lies deep within the heart of orc and Troll territory. It's a good training ground for groups as many of the things you will encounter in later instances are present here.

It's fairly important to have a good variety in classes as there is little overlap with abilities at this level. Having a tank is always important. A Warrior is the best choice, but a Shaman or Druid in bear form can be used also. Druids, Priests, and Shaman all have the ability to act as a healer, but don't ask a Druid or Shaman to be both healer and tank. Mages are very useful for their Polymorph spell's ability to control combat.

After the more difficult jobs are filled, it's time to add some damage to your group. Every class can add damage. Extra Warriors can serve as backup for the main tank while they cut through the enemies. Additional Priests can serve as backup healers while they blast the enemies with the power of shadows.

What makes this particular Instance troublesome is that most classes have yet to acquire many of their class-defining skills so CC can be a major issue.

Wailing Caverns

Zone:	Barrens
Level Range:	17-24
Primary Enemies:	Humanoid, Beast
Special Items:	Embrace of the Viper armor set
Entrance Requirements:	None

The primary enemies are humanoids and beasts. This means both Rogues and Druids can be used to control pulls in addition to Mages. A number of the enemies cast their own crowd control spells and having someone to wake sleeping members or interrupt enemy attacks is vital. Warriors, Rogues, and Shaman all have interrupts and should watch for casters. Green glowing effects usually warn of healing spells, while white glowing effects warn of sleeping spells. Priests can Dispel Magic and Shaman can use Tremor Totems to wake party members.

The last few enemies really puts your tank and healer to the test. Having a highly skilled tank and healer make these fights seem easy while having less skilled members will make these fights nightmares.

For the collectors in us all, the Embrace of the Viper leather armor set drops from enemies in Wailing Caverns. While ideally for a Druid, the pieces of this set are quite good for their level and can be used by a number of classes.

Deadmines

Zone:	Westfall
Level Range:	17-24
Primary Enemies:	Humanoid
Special Items:	Defias Leather armor set
Entrance Requirements:	None

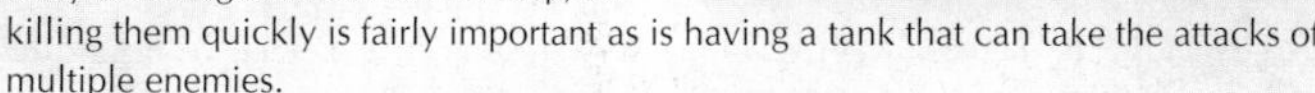

With almost an entire instance of humanoids, Mages and Rogues are primary choices for crowd control. Enemies are fairly close together but run for help, so killing them quickly is fairly important as is having a tank that can take the attacks of multiple enemies.

In the Deadmines, but not quite in the instance you will find undead. While the undead portion is fairly small, Priests can take up the CC duties while you're there. Deeper in the dungeon are casters. Once you begin meeting the casters, have an interrupt order ready as their spells (primarily fire based) can be quite damaging and are cast at range. Consider Polymorphing casters if running to them to interrupt casting risks pulling more enemies.

The Defias Leather armor set is quite nice. Rogues, Hunters, and Shaman are certain to enjoy the armor, while Warriors and Paladins may even find the bonuses to their liking.

Shadowfang Keep

Zone:	Silverpine Forest
Level Range:	22-26
Primary Enemies:	Undead
Special Items:	None
Entrance Requirements:	None

Shadowfang Keep has few humanoid targets but an abundance of undead. Many of the enemies are immune to shadow magic, so Warlocks should switch to their fire spells while Priests should make use of their holy spells. Have a Priest to CC the undead while a Mage can CC the few living enemies, makes pulls more manageable.

The enemies also use a variety of abilities to debuff your party. Magic, Disease, and Curse debuffs will surely be cast on your party, and having someone who can remove them makes your run much faster and safer. Priests can Dispel Magic debuffs. Shaman and Priests can remove disease effects. Mages and Druids can remove curses. These abilities take little mana or attention so can be done in addition to the member's standard role.

Blackfathom Deeps

Zone:	Ashenvale
Level Range:	24-28
Primary Enemies:	Humanoid
Special Items:	None
Entrance Requirements:	None

Be certain to have a group with crowd control, many interrupts, and some good armor. There are some very large fights in the Deeps, and you often are faced with multiple casters.

While the instance has a number of enemy types, the larger fights are against humanoid targets or against too many targets to effectively CC. Mages and Rogues make good choices for controlling pulls. Bring someone in for some AoE work as there are a couple fights at the end that can be very dangerous and confusing.

The Stockade

Zone:	Stormwind
Level Range:	24-28
Primary Enemies:	Humanoid
Special Items:	None
Entrance Requirements:	None

Just as Ragefire Chasm is only accessible to Horde parties, The Stockade is only accessible to Alliance groups. Standing in the very center of Stormwind (the very heart of the Alliance), only fools would attempt to enter the Stockade as Horde parties.

The Stockade is a short dungeon populated nearly exclusively by humanoids. Having a Mage or Rogue to help control the pulls and an off-tank to keep the enemies from jumping on casters is ideal, but not fully required. Though the pulls are larger than much you have dealt with so far, do not attempt to use AoEs to kill the targets more quickly as they are all elites and can kill your AoE members very quickly.

Razorfen Kraul

Zone:	Barrens
Level Range:	25-30
Primary Enemies:	Humanoid, Beast
Special Items:	None
Entrance Requirements:	None

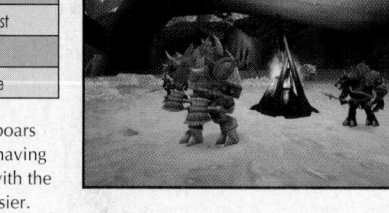

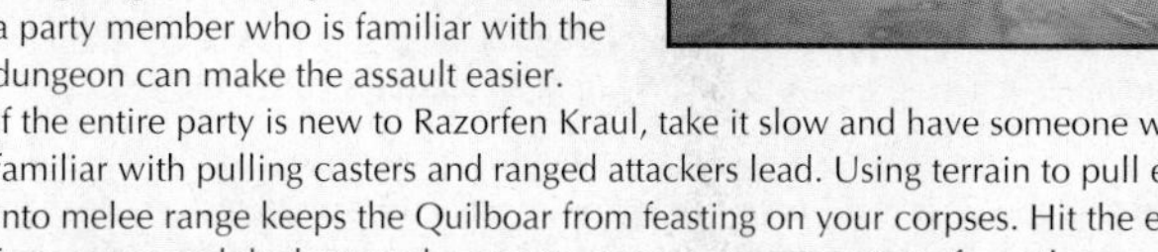

Because of the multitude of Quilboars using magic and ranged attacks, having a party member who is familiar with the dungeon can make the assault easier.
If the entire party is new to Razorfen Kraul, take it slow and have someone who is familiar with pulling casters and ranged attackers lead. Using terrain to pull enemies into melee range keeps the Quilboar from feasting on your corpses. Hit the enemies from range and duck around a corner or run past your party to force the enemy to come closer.

Characters with ranged interrupts make this easier. Mages with Counterspell and Shaman with Earth Shock can force enemy casters to come to you. Several of the fights within are against enemies that do tremendous damage. Using anything but a Warrior or Paladin for your tank is doable but risky.

Gnomeregan

Zone:	Dun Morogh
Level Range:	29-38
Primary Enemies:	Humanoid
Special Items:	None
Entrance Requirements:	Horde parties need to complete Chief Engineer Scooty to use the teleporter in Booty Bay

Many of the fights within Gnomeregan are against enemies that are highly resistant or immune to most forms of CC. Having an off-tank watching for enemies that escape the attention of the tank is important. As enemy groups are close together, having a character with a ranged attack pull the enemies back to the party is preferable.

There are many things that can go wrong in Gnomeregan. Druids have a hard time keeping up as rezzers, so a Priest, Paladin, or Shaman is preferable. Warlocks, Shaman, and Paladins gain their wipe recovery abilities at level 30 and you should have one in the party as one unlucky pull can doom your group.

Razorfen Downs

Zone:	Barrens
Level Range:	33-40
Primary Enemies:	Undead, Humanoid
Special Items:	None
Entrance Requirements:	None

While forming your party, consider bringing someone who can cure diseases. The Quilboar have forged an alliance with the Scourge. You'll be afflicted with many diseases as you travel through Razorfen Downs and having the ability to cure them makes this assault easier, even possible to some groups.

A number of fights have several enemies. Having strong AoE potential in the party can make these fights much easier. Mages and Warlocks are ideal for this with Hunters being a reasonable backup.

With so many undead in the area, most forms of CC are useless. Having a Priest to shackle can make quite a difference.

The Scarlet Monastery

Zone:	Tirisfal Glades
Level Range:	34-45
Primary Enemies:	Humanoid
Special Items:	Chain of the Scarlet Crusade armor set
Entrance Requirements:	The Scarlet Key is required to enter the Cathedral or Armory.

This dungeon is split into four parts with four separate portals. The Library and Graveyard can be accessed at any time, but the Armor and Cathedral are behind closed doors (the key can be obtained in either of the unlocked portions). Rogues who are highly skilled at picking locks can open the doors (this is also a wonderful place to train lockpicking). For this reason many parties only do one portion of the instance at a time.

The Scarlet Crusade allows very little deviation in their order. This instance is almost entirely humanoid (making Mages, Warlocks, and Rogues very useful for controlling pulls), but undead run rampant in the graveyard portion (making Priests the only viable CC).

There are very few non-elite enemies in the dungeon, but having at least one person with an AoE ability makes the final fight in the Armory much more fun. The humans are very social and run for help. Kill them quickly and have someone ready to snare enemies to prevent late additions to a fight (crippling poison is your friend).

Those visiting the Scarlet Monastery for loot should keep an eye out for the Chain of the Scarlet Crusade. This mail armor set has some wonderful stats but is very near an armor change level. Warriors and Paladins switch to plate armor soon after level 40, and Hunters and Shaman can't use any of the pieces until level 40.

Uldaman

Zone:	Badlands
Level Range:	35-47
Primary Enemies:	Humanoid, Golem
Special Items:	None
Entrance Requirements:	None

The dwarves and Troggs early in the dungeon can be CCed like any other humanoids, but as you progress deeper the enemies become more difficult to CC. Take an off-tank to keep extra enemies from getting to your softer members.

Having a party member with high armor and high HP is crucial for surviving this dungeon. Chain-wearing classes can handle the Shadowforge dwarves and the Troggs, but when you reach the Golems, you need someone in plate. The Golems hit extremely hard and have very high health. Another necessity for Uldaman is including classes that have snare or root abilities. Many enemies flee when at low health and there are always more enemies close by.

Zul'Farrak

Zone:	Tanaris
Level Range:	44-50
Primary Enemies:	Humanoid, Beast
Special Items:	None
Entrance Requirements:	The Mallet of Zul'Farrak is required to spawn Gaz'rilla.

Most of the fights in the troll city involve several humanoid enemies. Rogues, Warlocks, and Mages make your fights more manageable. The hardest fights are against swarms of enemies, so having a strong AoE member (Mage or Warlock) and a support AoE member (Druid, Warrior, Hunter, or Priest) is important.

Focus fire well and your enemies drop quickly. Fracturing damage will be the end of your party as many of the enemies possess high health and run when wounded. One party member is unlikely to be able to kill a runner before it finds friends so stay on the same target and be ready to root or snare fleeing enemies.

The Sunken Temple

Zone:	Swamp of Sorrows
Level Range:	47-55
Primary Enemies:	Humanoid, Undead, Wyrmkin
Special Items:	None
Entrance Requirements:	The Ancient Egg is required to spawn the Avatar of Hakkar.

The population of enemies is as varied as this dungeon is complex. Though only one portal allows access to the temple, there is a major split between the upper and lower floors of the dungeon. Check with your party to make sure everyone has the same goal before entering as there are quests for both levels.

Your party will be bloated if you try to bring someone for each type of CC in the dungeon. Instead, use whatever CC you have when you can and make the best with the other fights. Priests can shackle the undead trolls while Rogues, Warlocks, and Mages can CC the living trolls and only Druids can sleep the Wyrmkin.

The final fight of the instance is against the Shade of Eranikus which can cast sleep on party members. Have an off-tank ready to pickup the duties if the tank is put to sleep as it cannot be dispelled.

Maraudon

Zone:	Desolace
Level Range:	45-50
Primary Enemies:	Demon, Elemental, Beast
Special Items:	The Sceptre of Celebras allows teleporting to the center of the instance.
Entrance Requirements:	None

There is very little that can be CCed in Maraudon. The satyrs and elementals can be banished by Warlocks, but that's about it. Instead stack your group with damage so enemies can be killed quickly and healing to keep your tank alive.

Having an off-tank proves invaluable when you fight small groups of tough opponents (Warlock and Hunter pets work best) and having multiple ranged damage classes make some of the earlier fights against the slimes easier (the slimes do AoE damage).

Running the purple side and orange side of Maraudon completely gives you the opportunity to create the Sceptre of Celebras. This allows you to portal past much of the instance and straight to the final portion. Groups often do 'Princess runs', meaning they intend to port in. Specify early which entrance you are taking.

Blackrock Depths

Zone: Searing Gorge/Burning Steppes
Level Range: 52+
Primary Enemies: Humanoid, Elemental, Beast
Special Items: None
Entrance Requirements: The Shadowforge Key unlocks the deeper portion of the instances

Having a party with combat control is essential as many fights involve a large number of enemies. Sap, Polymorph, Mind Control, and Banish are all extremely useful in the chambers under the mountain.

The largest fights are against humanoids, but the most difficult fights will be against elementals. As Warlocks can CC both types (Seduce and Banish), they are extremely useful.

Large enemy groups often include healers. These should be interrupted until they can be killed. Having several members with spell interrupts is very important.

Dire Maul

Zone: Feralas
Level Range: 55+
Primary Enemies: Elemental, Humanoid, Demon
Special Items: Ogre Tannin (required to make the Ogre Suit) is acquired in the northern wing.
Entrance Requirements: The Crescent Key is required to enter the northern or western wings.

Dire Maul is another dungeon with several wings. The eastern wing is the only unlocked wing and is where you acquire the key for the other two wings (north and west). Very few groups do all of Dire Maul in a single sitting (it's just too long), so specify which side you intend to do when recruiting party members. Rogues who are highly skilled at picking locks can open all the doors.

The enemies and fights vary greatly among the wings. With the proliferation of satyrs in the east wing, Warlocks make a good choice for CC. The ghosts and elementals in the west wing make Priests and Warlocks good choices. The north wing is mostly ogres. This makes Rogues, Mages, Warlocks, and Priests all valid choices for CC.

There are fights in all the wings where several weaker enemies attack you. One AoE member makes these fights faster, but is not a requirement to defeat them.

Stratholme

Zone: Eastern Plaguelands
Level Range: 58+
Primary Enemies: Undead
Special Items: The Key to the City allows entrance through the back door. Parts of the Beaststalker, Devout, Dreadmist, Elements, Lightforge, Magister, Shadowcraft, Valor, Wildheart armor sets drop.
Entrance Requirements: None

The ruins of Stratholme are home to both the living and unliving survivors of the plague. Most groups only do one wing of the dungeon at a time, but some do both. Knowing your goals ahead of time makes your choices easier.

West side (also known as live side or scarlet side) has many undead in the beginning, but the harder fights are against fewer and tougher humanoid targets so Rogues, Warlocks, and Mages are useful for CC purposes.

East side (also known as undead side or Baron side) is populated by the undead. Many of the fights are against large groups of elite and non-elite undead. Priests can CC an elite each fight while the party kills the non-elites first. This can be done with AoEs, but is dangerous and should be discussed first. Without at least one strong AoE class, however, some of the later fights are very difficult.

Stratholme is the first of the three dungeons that contribute to your first dungeon armor set. While several enemies can drop various pieces of different sets, Baron Rivendare is the only enemy in the game who drops the leggings for all the sets.

Scholomance

Zone: Western Plaguelands
Level Range: 57+
Primary Enemies: Undead, Humanoid
Special Items: The Blood of Innocents is required to spawn Kirtonos the Herald. Parts of the Beaststalker, Devout, Dreadmist, Elements, Lightforge, Magister, Shadowcraft, Valor, Wildheart armor sets drop. The Cadaver, Bloodmail, Necropile, and Deathbone armor sets can be found.
Entrance Requirements: The Skeleton Key is required to enter Scholomance.

Scholomance is locked. The key can only be obtained by completing a quest chain that begins at Chillwind Point and the Bulwark for Alliance and Horde individuals. A Rogue with a high lockpicking skill can open the door as well.

The dungeon is almost entirely populated with undead and some humanoids. Priests, Mages, and Warlocks are prime choices for CC. Rogues with Improved Sap can also fill the slot, but Rogues without it shouldn't attempt to Sap (they can still fill a damage slot).

Several of the fights are against multiple enemies. Some are against very tough opponents making an off-tank very useful, while others are against many weaker enemies making AoE members useful.

Scholomance also has parts of the first dungeon armor set. Many of the enemies within drop various parts of the sets, but Darkmaster Gandling is the only enemy in the game who possess the head piece for the sets.

Lower Blackrock Spire

Zone: Searing Gorge/Burning Steppes
Level Range: 58+
Primary Enemies: Humanoid
Special Items: Parts of the Beaststalker, Devout, Dreadmist, Elements, Lightforge, Magister, Shadowcraft, Valor, Wildheart armor sets drop. The Spider's Kiss weapon set drops.
Entrance Requirements: None

Blackrock Spire is a single instance, but is separated between a non-raid portion (lower) and a raid portion (upper). The door to upper can only be opened by obtaining the key through a quest chain that begins inside lower Blackrock Spire. Rogues cannot pick this door as it is magically shut and only the key can open it.

The enemies in the spire are predominantly humanoid. This makes Improved Sap Rogues, Warlocks, and Mages very good choices for their ability to control the pulls. Hunters make an excellent addition with their traps as the enemies hit very hard but don't often attack in large groups.

CC is good, but a well equipped and skilled tank is better. As most of the fights aren't as large as in Scholomance or Stratholme, Paladins and Druids can make successful tanks.

Many of the enemies in lower Blackrock Spire drop parts of the dungeon armor sets. General Drakkisath drops the chest piece for all the dungeon sets.

Raids

There are many tasks that are simply too large for a single group of five to handle. Some of these only require a second group while others require nearly an entire army.

HOW TO FORM A RAID

Forming a raid is slightly different to forming a group. Invite people into your group as normal. When you have the first five people, open your social window (defaulted to 'o') and select the Raid tab. Push Convert to Raid and continue inviting.

There are two things that make the inviting process easier and faster.

Promoting others: With the raid window open, right click on a members name and promote them. This makes them an assistant and allows them to aid with inviting others.
Long names: Some people have very long or difficult to type names. If the person has spoken recently, right click on their name in the chat box and invite them.

ROLES IN A RAID

Role Table		
Role	Responsibility	Classes
Main Tank	Gather, Maintain, and Survive Aggro	Warrior, Druid
Backup Tank	Gather, Maintain, and Survive Aggro on Boss adds	Warrior, Druid,, Paladin
Secondary Tank (Off-tank)	Pull Aggro from non-tank members	Warrior, Druid, Paladin
Healer	Keep Party Members Alive	Priest, Druid, Shaman, Paladin
Debuff Removal	Remove Damaging and Debilitating Debuffs	Priest, Paladin, Druid, Shaman, Mage
Crowd Control (CC)	Neutralize Enemies	Mage, Rogue, Hunter, Priest, Warlock
Mitigation	Reduces Damage Dealt by Enemies	Rogue, Warlock, Priest, Shaman, Druid, Hunter, Warrior, Paladin
Burst Damage (DPS)	Kill Enemies Quickly	Mage, Rogue, Druid
Sustained Damage (DPS)	Maintain High Damage Level Over Time	Hunter, Rogue, Warlock, Warriors
Area of Effect Damage (AoE)	Damage multiple enemies at once	Mage, Warlock, Hunter, Warrior, Druid, Priest
Resurrection (Rez)	Revive Fallen Members	Priest, Shaman, Paladin, Druid
Wipe Recovery	Ressurect or Survive a Total Party Wipe	Paladin, Warlock, Shaman, Engineer

That's A Lot!

Depending on which raid you are attending, not all of these roles need to be filled. Crowd Control is very important in Upper Blackrock Spire, while Decursers and Dispellers are necessary to take on Lord Kazzak.

MAIN TANK

As one of the most important roles, a good tank can make a party while a bad tank can break one. The main tank should start the fights to get early aggro, and use abilities to maintain the aggro. Against the most vicious of the raid enemies, main tanks often need very high resists in addition to high armor, defense, and health. Some fights involve several enemies that are immune to CC, so there may be several main tanks in your raid.

WARRIOR

Warriors make the best tanks. They have the heaviest armor (plate), can use a shield, have abilities to hold single enemies, and abilities to hold multiple enemies.

DRUID

Only Druids using Dire Bear Form and specced in the Feral talent tree should be considered for this role. As a dire bear, the Druid's armor is increased greatly and they gain access to a number of abilities that help them fill this role.

BACKUP TANK

This person is generally bored until boss fights. This role becomes the raid's only hope when there are adds in boss encounters.

WARRIOR

As with main tanks, Warriors make the greatest backup tanks. They have the armor and shield to survive against a tough opponent and have several abilities to turn the fight around at a moments notice. Charge brings you into battle with rage to burn. If you were already engaged and have little rage, use Blood Rage. Taunt, Mocking Blow, and Challenging Shout will pull the enemy's attention very quickly. Follow with a few Sunder Armors to lock aggro onto you.

DRUID

Only Druids using Dire Bear Form and specced in the Feral talent tree should be considered for this role. The Druid only has a few abilities to pick up aggro quickly. Cooperation from the rest of the raid is essential for a Druid to fill this role. Challenging Roar is your only tool to gathering aggro quickly. With its ten minute cooldown, it's only useful in emergency situations, but that's what this is. Frenzied Regeneration can keep you alive longer without taxing your healers as much, but drains your rage, so be careful about using it.

PALADIN

Like Warriors, Paladins have access to the heaviest armor in the game (plate) and can equip a shield. This combined with their ability to heal themselves, can make the Paladin extremely durable as a tank.

SECONDARY TANK

If party members aren't focusing fire well enough or an enemy resists CC or you just plain get unlucky, enemies will jump from the tank to your healers or dps. Rather than having the tank run around trying to regain aggro, it's better to have an off-tank grab the aggro and pull it back to the main tank before returning to the primary target or simply tie it up.

WARRIOR

As having all the tools to be primary tank, Warriors are fully qualified as secondary tanks.

DRUID

As secondary tanks aren't always needed, the Druid is free to use whatever form he or she chooses when not performing this role. When a party member pulls aggro off the main tank, a Druid can shift to Bear or Dire Bear Form and keep the enemy tied up until the main tank can pull it off. Once the job of secondary tank is accomplished, the Druid is free to return to the role they were fulfilling prior.

PALADIN

Paladins have a few more tools as secondary tank than they do as primary tank. Without many opponents to interfere with their casting, Paladins can use their heals as well as their damage to pull aggro off party members.

HEALER

In raids, there are often multiple healers. This is necessary as the enemies are either more numerous (meaning more tanks to heal) or more devastating. Determining who heals who and when is important and avoids wasting mana. There are several ways to divvy the duties of healing:

One Healer Per Group: Putting one healer in each group and making each only responsible for their group spreads the healing out a good bit, but some healers will be lax while others (the healer with the main tank) over-taxed.
One Healer at a Time: Having a single healer casting all the heals until they are out of mana can allow your raid to last longer against certain opponents as the healers not actively healing are regenerating mana. The major downside is when damage comes it too quickly for a single healer to deal with and people start dying or the healer pulls aggro.
Only Use Small Heals: Using smaller heals splits aggro more effectively, but depletes your healer's mana more quickly (as smaller heals are less mana efficient). It gives all the healers a chance to interrupt their casting if their target gains health from another caster.

PRIEST

The Priest is the first obvious choice as healer. With heals of several sizes, the Priest can avoid overhealing and drawing aggro.

DRUID

While in caster form, the Druid has a great many tools for the role of healer. Regrowth and Rejuvenation are both heal over time spells. This allows the Druid to heal while spreading out the threat they draw. Using these before a battle begins ensures that damage is being healed without the attention of the Druid or drawing aggro.

SHAMAN

Shaman have a number of tools to buff and heal party members. In addition to the standard heals of differing size to keep from overhealing and drawing aggro, their totems can heal and buff party members.

PALADIN

Paladins have fewer tools for this role, but can be used as a backup.

DEBUFF REMOVAL

Debuffs can be crippling to a raid. Many of these abilities hamper you, while some do damage, and some even force you character to fight for the wrong side. Recognizing and dispelling these effects make fights much less difficult.

Most fights, the character will have another role and remove debuffs as needed. There are four types of removable debuffs; magic, poison, curse, and disease. Only a couple classes can remove each type.

Debuff Removal

Debuff	Class (Ability)
Magic	Priest (Dispel Magic), Paladin (Cleanse)
Poison	Druid (Abolish Poison), Shaman (Cure Poison, Poison Cleansing Totem), Paladin (Cleanse)
Curse	Druid (Remove Curse), Mage (Remove Lesser Curse)
Disease	Shaman (Cure Disease, Disease Cleasing Totem), Paladin (Cleanse), Priest (Cure Disease, Abolish Disease)

CROWD CONTROL

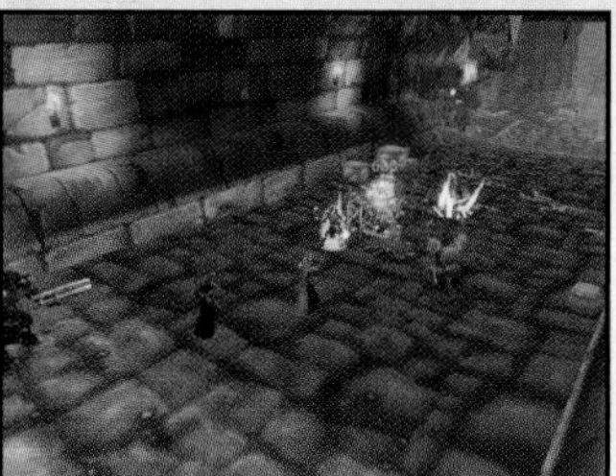

CC keeps enemies tied up for lengthy periods without lowering your damage or increasing your risk. Many forms of CC are broken any time the affected enemy takes damage. There are two distinct types of CC; in-combat and out-of-combat.

Out-of-Combat CC tends to last longer, but can only be used when you or the enemy is out of combat. Groups using any of these abilities should use them before the fight begins.

MAGE

Mages are useful crowd control in a variety of circumstances. Should there be a single enemy the party can't deal with at the time, a Polymorph neutralizes them for a good long time; as long as the enemy is a humanoid, beast, or critter. When the Polymorph breaks, it can be recast with only a duration penalty.

ROGUE

Both in-combat and out-of-combat CC is what the Rogue brings to a group. Sap can only be used on humanoids and before combat begins. Blind lasts for several seconds and takes a reagent.

HUNTER

Most Hunter abilities are out-of-combat crowd control. Traps can only be used if the Hunter is out of combat. This can be accomplished before the battle begins or by using Feign Death (provided your pet isn't engaged). Freezing Trap creates an area that slows all enemies who enter, while Frost Trap can encase a single enemy in a block of ice for an extended period of time.

PRIEST

Priests have two forms of CC. Psychic Scream sends nearby enemies running in fear for several seconds (rarely is this used in Raids). Shackle Undead can only affect undead enemies, but very few classes have any ability to CC undead, so it's still fairly powerful.

WARLOCK

Enemies can be CCed several ways by a Warlock. Demons and elementals can be Banished for a long time. Banish can be recast and cannot be broken until the duration passes. The Warlock's Succubus can use Seduction to CC a humanoid target for extended durations.

MITIGATION

Many of the enemies you may fight deal to much damage to survive alone. Even with a healer helping, your tank will likely die if some of the damage is not mitigated. Nearly every class has the ability to reduce the damage dealt to your main tank. With people working on concert, even the most damaging enemies become manageable. Note, most bosses are immune to stuns, disarms, etc.

ROGUE

Against any opponent not immune to stun, Rogues are one of the greatest mitigation classes. Opening a fight with Cheap Shot leaves the enemy stunned for several seconds. Use Sinister Strike or Backstab to build combo points before finishing with Kidney Shot to leave the enemy stunned once again. Multiple Rogues staggering their stuns can keep an enemy stunned from the start of the fight until the end. Against stun immune targets, a well-timed Kick still interrupts casting.

WARLOCK

Just as enemy curses make your party weaker, Warlock curses make enemies weaker. Curse of Tongues increases the casting time on enemy spells and is quite useful against casters. Lengthening the cast time gives the rest of the raid more time to interrupt the spell. Against melee enemies, Curse of Weakness can drastically reduce the amount of damage they are dealing. By debuffing the enemy, Warlocks are able to mitigate a reasonable amount of damage.

PRIEST

Priests have a number of abilities that can be used to reduce the damage a raid takes. Mana Burn can destroy an enemy caster's mana pool and render them unable to cast spells, while Shadow Protection raises the resistance of members to shadow damage. Power Word: Shield surrounds a raid member, protecting them from damage, until the shield is destroyed. As an instant spell, it's very useful for emergency mitigation, but used before a fight begins reduces the amount of damage your tank takes from an enemy groups first volley.

SHAMAN

Shaman are able to reduce magical and physical damage taken by party members. Stoneskin Totem reduces damage on all melee attacks to party members while Windwall Totem reduces all physical ranged attacks. Grounding Totem can absorb non-AoE spells cast at the party. Well-timed Earthshocks interrupt enemy casting and the Nature, Fire, and Frost Resistance Totems reduce the damage from the appropriate types of spells to party members.

Why Isn't Everyone Getting the Totem Buffs?

Totems only affect raid members who are in the same party as the Shaman who dropped them. For this reason, it's not a great idea to have all the Shaman in the same party.

DRUID

Druids have a couple abilities that can mitigate damage. Mark of the Wild increases the armor of raid members (in addition to increases their stats). If the Druid is using bear or dire bear form, they also have Demoralizing Roar (which decreases enemy attack power) and Bash (which stuns for a short while). Druids aren't terribly adept at damage mitigation, but they can do it if needed.

HUNTER

Like Druids, Hunters only have a couple abilities that mitigate damage raid members take. Aspect of the Wild increases the nature resistance of all party members and, by doing so, reduces the damage from nature effects. Scorpid Sting reduces the enemy's strength and agility. While not terribly useful against caster enemies, it can have a noticeable effect against melee targets. Marksmanship Hunters have a change to stun an enemy when using Concussive Shot.

WARRIOR

Warriors not fulfilling a tanking role can assist the tank greatly with a number of abilities. Disarm can reduce the damage a humanoid melee enemy can deal by quite a bit, while Protection Warriors can even stun the enemy for several seconds with Concussion Blow. Thunderclap and Demoralizing Shout reduce enemy attack speed and attack power, rendering their physical attacks much less damaging. If the enemy is a caster, Pummel and Shield Bash can interrupt a spell when timed well.

PALADIN

Much like a Rogue, a Paladin's primary ability to mitigate damage to others is through stuns. Hammer of Justice and Seal of Justice can keep an enemy from doing much at all. When timed with a Rogue or another Paladin, enemies can be stunned for quite some time. Paladins have other tricks however. Paladins can surround themselves and their party members in Shadow, Fire, or Frost Resistance Auras. This reduces the damage of shadow, fire, or frost effects by increasing resistances. Greater Blessing of Sanctuary reduces all incoming damage to raid members and Devotion Aura can raise group members' armor. As one of the best ways for a Paladin to mitigate damage, Blessing of Sacrifice transfers some of the damage taken by a target to the Paladin.

Burst Damage

Burst damage is useful when getting to a boss. The weaker enemies around the boss or in the dungeon can often be killed before they can significantly damage your party. Burst damage characters often have lower survivability, but if the fight is finished quickly it doesn't matter. Even with downtime afterward, it's often a better plan to use burst DPS on weaker enemies.

ROGUE

Many Rogues can dish out a great deal of damage very quickly. Without worrying about avoiding aggro, they can push their damage even higher. Ambush is a good way to start a fight. Garrote and Cheap Shot are options for non-dagger Rogues. Use Backstab or Sinister Strike to build combo points quickly. If the enemy isn't going down fast enough, consider using Thistle Tea to restore your energy when it depletes. Finish the fight with a several combo-point Eviscerate. Having Instant Poison on your weapons further adds quick damage.

MAGE

Mages are wonderful with burst damage. They have several tools that can quickly turn their sizable mana pool into damage. Start the fight with Combustion and Pyroblast if you're specced in the Fire talent tree or Arcane Power if you chose the Arcane tree. If you're clearing several groups, use your abilities with cooldowns more sparingly, but remember that you'll be drinking between battles anyway. Follow up with Cone of Cold and Fireblast. Both of these are instants. Cast Arcane Missles while you wait for Cone of Cold and Fireblast to cool down. Continue throwing your mana at the enemy until they are dead.

DRUID

When in Cat Form, Druids function a great deal like Rogues. The reduced survivability of this form is offset by the increased damage potential. As such, a Cat Form Druid makes a perfectly acceptable burst damage slot occupant. Start with Ravage, using Shred or Claw to build combo points, and finishing with Ferocious Bite. This does a good bit of damage in a very short time and is exactly why you're here.

Sustained Damage

Many enemies are too tough to blown down with burst DPS. In these cases, it's more important to be able to sustain a high level of damage for a prolonged time. The damage is often lower than burst DPS, but spreading the damage out (making it easier for the tank to hold aggro) is very important.

ROGUE

Rogues have a number of tools that make them a good choice for this role. Starting a fight with Garrote guarantees you'll do nearly as much damage as an Ambush (if you're specced for it)...just over several seconds. Use Backstab or Sinister Strike to build combo points. Mix a Feint in to keep your threat level low. When you've built up combo points, use Slice and Dice for sustained DPS. Coating your weapons with Deadly Poison adds more damage but spreads it out just like the abilities mentioned. Keep the DPS moving and have Vanish ready if the enemy turns to you.

WARLOCK

Many of the Warlock's spells don't do much up front damage which makes them ideal for longer fights. Any of the pets Warlocks can choose from aid in doing damage with the Succubus causing the most damage herself, but the Imp allows the Warlock to caster longer. Throwing Corruption, Curse of Agony, and Immolate on an enemy doesn't do much damage at first, but as the seconds pass, the enemy's health continues to drop. Being able to Drain Mana or Drain Health as needed keeps the Warlock doing damage consistently. Should you run out of mana, use Dark Pact (if you're an Affliction Warlock) to steal some from your pet. Another option when you run out of mana is to use Life Tap to trade your health for mana.

HUNTER

Constantly firing arrows or bullets at an enemy makes the Hunter a valid choice for this role. Auto Fire keeps the Hunter doing damage, provided you are able to stay at range, while the pet can chew on the enemy. To increase the damage they are putting out, Hunters can use Serpent Sting (though it takes up a debuff slot), Aimed Shot (if they are specced in the Marksmanship talent tree), and Arcane Shot. Use your special abilities until you are low on mana then stop casting. Auto Fire keeps the damage going while allowing you to regenerate mana. In the larger fights, use Feign Death often to keep your threat level low.

Area of Effect Damage

There are times in dungeons where it takes far too long to kill the enemies one at a time and trying to do so can result in the entire group dying. For these fights, often against a dozen or more non-elite enemies, being able to damage many at once is the wisest course of action.

MAGE

Arcane Explosion allows the Mage to continue doing AoE damage even while being attacked because of its instant cast time and limited targeting time (it is cast with you as the center of the effect). Blizzard and Flame Strike can be cast at range, but have differing effects. Often a good line up is to start with Blizzard or Flame Strike and switch to Arcane Explosion as the enemy advances on you.

HUNTER

Hunters are a good second place when it comes to the AoE slot. Setting an Explosive Trap before the fight and using Multi-Shot then Volley throws a lot of damage out very quickly and generates a great deal of threat. Feign Death to allow the tank to grab aggro. Keep your pet on Passive.

WARLOCK

Warlocks have a number of tools that qualify them for an AoE slot. Warlocks have a ranged AoE (Rain of Fire) and a point blank AoE (Hellfire).

Resurrection

Having someone who can resurrect a fallen member can save the time of running back to your body, or save the entire run if enemies have respawned behind you.

PRIEST

Resurrection can be cast any time outside of combat and doesn't have a cooldown.

SHAMAN

Ancestral Spirit cannot be used during combat and has no cooldown.

PALADIN

Paladins can ask Redemption for dead party members.

DRUID

Rebirth is the only rez spell that can be cast during combat. It costs a reagent each time it is used (the reagent varies depending on level) and has a 30 minute cooldown.

Wipe Recovery

Total party wipes happen, especially in Raids. Having good wipe recovery is the only thing that keeps the Raid going.

WARLOCK

For the cost of a Soul Shard, the Warlock can use Create Soul Stone for a party member. This allows the 'stoned' person to instantly resurrect himself instead of releasing their spirit. The soul stone buff lasts one hour, has a one hour cooldown, and needs to be renewed. Classes that can resurrect should be given stones.

PALADIN

By using a Symbol of Divinity and sacrificing themselves, Paladins can call upon Divine Intervention and remove a party member from combat and all danger for 3 minutes. At the end of the duration, the party member can be attacked as normal, so it should be cast on someone who can resurrect others and is outside of the enemy's aggro detection.

SHAMAN

Reincarnation has a one hour cooldown (unless you have taken the Improved Reincarnation talent), and consumes an Ankh each time it is used.

ORGANIZING A RAID

Once you have everyone in a raid, it's important to move people into group configurations that are beneficial to your goal. In the raid window, the raid leader can simply click and drag people from one group to another.

The most obvious way to organize people is as several small groups; each with their own healer, tank, dps, etc. This is a very balanced way to do it and is often a good start. As you become more comfortable with organizing raids and knowing the abilities of all the classes, forming specialized groups becomes quite powerful.

The following are merely examples of specialized groups. Knowing your raid-mates, their abilities, and their play style will be the ultimate factors in group placement.

Main tank

Class	Role
Warrior	Main Tank
Paladin/Shaman	Healer/Mitigation
Warlock w/Imp	Damage
Priest	Healer/Mitigation
Druid	Healer

This group would be quite durable. It would have all the healing the Main Tank would need and have the Backup Tank ready to take over should something go wrong. With the mitigation and healing provided by the Paladin or Shaman, the Warrior would become even more durable

Ranged Damage

Class	Role
Shaman	Heal/Buff
Hunter w/Wolf	Damage/Buff
Hunter w/Wolf	Damage/Buff
Hunter w/Wolf	Damage/Buff
Hunter w/Wolf	Damage/Buff

This group is a bit stale, but it's still effective. The Shaman using Grace of Air Totem increases the agility of all the Hunters in the group. The Hunters should keep their wolves near (rather than sending them to attack) and use their Furious Howl manually. If the Hunters time it well, always have the Furious Howl buff and each attack has its damage raised significantly. The Shaman is fairly superfluous and can be replaced by a Feral Druid or a Paladin using Blessing of Might.

AoE Damage

Class	Role
Ice Mage	AoE Damage
Fire Mage	AoE Damage
Warlock	AoE Damage
Warrior	Tank/AoE Damage
Priest	Healer/Mitigation/AoE Damage

Starting the fight with dual Blizzards and a Rain of Fire might scare most people, but there is a method to this madness. When the enemies approach the casters, the Priest uses Power Word: Shield and the Warrior Charges and uses Challenging Shout. Once all aggro is on the Warrior, pull back so all enemies are in front of you and use Retaliation (30 minute cooldown and not fully necessary if you're saving the ability for Shield Wall). The enemies won't be pulling off the Warrior for some time so use Arcane Explosion, Holy Nova (if you're Holy specced), Hellfire, and Whirlwind to finish the enemies quickly.

Melee DPS

Class	Role
Fury Warrior	Damage/Buff
Rogue	Damage
Shaman	Damage/Buff
Feral Druid	Damage/Buff
Hunter w/Wolf	Damage/Buff

Any of these classes can deal damage on their own, but together they can buff each other and further raise their damage. The Warrior raises everyone's attack power with Battle Shout. The Shaman raises everyone's strength with Strength of Earth Totem and increases melee attacks with Windfury Totem or raises agility with Grace of Air Totem. The Feral Druid increases everyone's critical chance with Leader of the Pack. The Hunter has their pet use focus only on Furious Growl which raises the damage of each person's next attack. Combine all of these together and this group puts out the damage.

Sustained Magic Damage

Class	Role
Warlock	Sustained Damage
Warlock	Sustained Damage
Warlock	Sustained Damage
Shadow Priest	Damage
Paladin	Healer

One Warlock uses Curse of Shadows while another uses Curse of Elements to keep the targets shadow and fire resistance low while the other uses Curse of Agony. After that, everyone starts throwing shadow damage and DoTs. Corruption, Immolate, and Shadow Word: Pain all stack and will keep doing damage as you switch to Firebolt, Shadowbolt, Mind Flay, and Mind Blast. The Priest should use Fade often to keep his or her threat lower. The Paladin brings a good bit to the party with emergency healing and his Blessing of Wisdom which regenerates mana for each party member. A Shaman using Mana Spring Totem can be substituted or a Balance Druid in Moonkin form to increase spell critical chance. This is a highly specialized group, it is almost always better to assign a Warlock to a tank.

WHAT IS THE DIFFERENCE BETWEEN A RAID INSTANCE AND AN OUTDOOR RAID?

Raid Instances take place inside an instanced dungeon. This means you cannot have any outside assistance, but it also means you won't have any outside interference (especially on PvP servers). Raid Instances are often long dungeons with many smaller enemies leading to the larger threat.

Outdoor Raids occur in the world. People from outside your raid can help or hinder your attempt at these targets. You may also be competing with others as these enemies often take several days to respawn. Outdoor Raids are often in areas where your raid will have to fight past small groups of enemies to get to the boss, but not nearly as many as a dungeon raid.

Raid Listing

Raid Quick Table

Name	Zone	Player Limit
Upper Blackrock Spire	Searing Gorge/Burning Steppes	10
Ruins of Ahn'Qiraj	Silithus	20
Zul'Gurub	Stranglethorn Vale	20
Blackwing Lair	Blackrock Spire	40
Molten Core	Blackrock Depths	40
Naxxramas	Western Plaguelands	40
Onyxia's Lair	Dustwallow Marsh	40
Temple of Ahn'Qiraj	Silithus	40

Upper Blackrock Spire

Zone: Searing Gorge/Burning Steppes	
Level Range: 58-60	
Player Limit: 10	
Primary Enemies: Humanoid, Wyrmkin	
Special Items: Parts of the Beaststalker, Devout, Dreadmist, Elements, Lightforge, Magister, Shadowcraft, Valor, Wildheart armor sets drop. Dal'Rend's Sacred Charge weapon set drops.	
Entrance Requirements: A completed Seal of Ascension is required to enter the upper floors of Blackrock Spire	

…ake a left in the first room to the sealed …ns. The path is filled with the humanoids and Wyrmkin loyal to the Black Dragonflight.

Having Mages and Druids for CC is quite important as is having a heavily armored tank and watchful healer. The enemies at the end of the instance hit very hard. Have your wipe recovery stay well back from a fight so that if a wipe occurs they can rez safely without re-aggroing the enemies.

Zul'Gurub

Zone: Stranglethorn Vale	
Level Range: 60+	
Player Limit: 20	
Primary Enemies: Humanoid	
Special Items: Many armor and weapon pieces including class specific armor sets.	
Entrance Requirements: None	

While the outcasts of the ancient Gurubashi Empire fled to the Swamp of Sorrows to continue their worship of the blood god Hakkar, they soon found that only in the capital of the shattered empire could Hakkar be fully summoned. The capital has been taken by the Atal'ai and the preparations to summon Hakkar have been completed.

The other troll tribes have sent their greatest High Priests, but to no avail. Rather than defeating Hakkar and his followers, these mighty spiritual warriors have been taken by Hakkar and are now counted among his allies.

The quests for Zul'Gurub are obtained on a small island off the northwest coast of Stranglethorn Vale. The entrance to Zul'Gurub, in northeastern Stranglethorn Vale, is guarded by a few trolls but you can easily run past them and zone into the area.

Molten Core

Zone: Blackrock Depths	
Level Range: 60+	
Player Limit: 40	
Primary Enemies: Elemental, Demon	
Special Items: Class-specific epic armor sets as well as many epic weapons. The starter for the Priest and Hunter epic quests drops here.	
Entrance Requirements: Attunement to the Core	

While there is no key to Molten Core, you can't take all 40 people through Blackrock Depths each time. There is a Blood Elf who offers a quest that allows you to be 'attuned' to Molten Core. Once the quest is complete, you can enter Molten Core from the Blood Elf rather than going all the way through Blackrock Depths.

Molten Core is a cave of molten rock and creatures that flourish in the impressive heat. With many targets being opposed to the Hydraxian Waterlords, this is a good place to increase your reputation as you will need it to summon some of the more powerful monsters in Molten Core.

Bring your fire resistance gear and couple good secondary tanks. Many of the enemies throw off any CC you put on them and have to be tanked individually. Focus your fire and kill the enemies one at a time.

Onyxia's Lair

Zone: Dustwallow Marsh	
Level Range: 60+	
Player Limit: 40	
Primary Enemies: Wyrmkin	
Special Items: A plethora of rare and epic items can be found in the horde of the dragon.	
Entrance Requirements: Completing the Marshal Windsor or Warlord's Command quest chain is required for Alliance and Horde raids to enter Onyxia's Lair. Blackhand's Command	

While a very short instance, it is very challen… a great deal of trouble and Onyxia herself is no pushover. Be ready with your fire resistance gear.

Blackwing Lair

Zone: Upper Blackrock Spire	
Level Range: 60+	
Player Limit: 40	
Primary Enemies: Humanoid, Wyrmkin	
Special Items: Many armor and weapon pieces including class specific armor sets.	
Entrance Requirements: None	

Lord Nefarion commands his agents from high atop Blackrock Spire. Like Molten Core, the entrance to Blackwing Lair is within another instance (Upper Blackrock Spire). To become attuned, kill the Quartermaster outside Blackrock Spire and read his orders. Once the quest is begun, proceed into Upper Blackrock Spire and kill Drakkisath. With him dead, use the orb behind him to complete your attunement. In the future, you are able to enter Blackwing Lair by using the orb where you found the Quartermaster.

The fights within Blackwing Lair are quite varied and exciting. Each fight is extremely different from the previous and it will take several attempts before your raid will progress through this raid instance. Be prepared for the wipes and be ready to think about new strategies that will lead you to victory.

Ruins of Ahn'Qiraj

Zone: Silithus
Level Range: 60+
Player Limit: 20
Primary Enemies: Constructs, Silithid
Special Items: Many armor and weapon pieces including class specific armor sets.
Entrance Requirements: The Gates of Ahn'Qiraj world event must be completed before the Ruins of Ahn'Qiraj can be entered.

Following the War of the Shifting Sands, the Qiraji were left in a devastated city cut off from the world. Though not defeated, they were sealed within. Many generations have passed, but the Qiraji have not been idle. The Ruins of Ahn'Qiraj are teeming with an army anxious to strike against Azeroth.

As the primary enemies are constructs and silithids, there are few ways to CC them. Instead concentrate on using tanks to hold them while your raid blows them down.

Temple of Ahn'Qiraj

Zone: Silithus
Level Range: 60+
Player Limit: 40
Primary Enemies: Silithid
Special Items: Many armor and weapon pieces including class specific armor sets.
Entrance Requirements: The Gates of Ahn'Qiraj world event must be completed before the Temple of Ahn'Qiraj can be entered.

The War of the Shifting Sands never reached the center of the city. Even as the outskirts were laid to waste, the Temple of Ahn'Qiraj was never taken. The breeding grounds were never destroyed and the leadership was never attacked.

After so many generations have passed, the armies are ready. The monument to unspeakable gods is not one to be taken lightly. Many of the enemies will have unique abilities and will take several attempts before they can be defeated. Repair your armor before you enter as you'll need all the durability you have and be prepared for many deaths.

Naxxramas

Zone: Eastern Plaguelands
Level Range: 60+
Player Limit: 40
Primary Enemies: Undead, Beasts
Special Items: Many armor and weapon pieces including class specific armor sets.
Entrance Requirements: Gaining reputation with Argent Dawn at Light's hope Chapel allows you to enter Naxxramas cheaper.

Honored	Revered	Exalted
5x Arcane Crystal	2x Arcane Crystal	Free
2x Nexus Crystal	1x Nexus Crystal	
60	30	
1x Righteous Orb		

Floating above the greenish haze of Eastern Plaguelands, Naxxramas is the ultimate destination for those helping the Argent Dawn.

Both the living and unliving servants of the Lich King aid Kel'Thuzad in Naxxramas. The Necropolis has everything that is needed to wage war against Azeroth. Defeating this unbelievable evil will mean far more than victory…it will mean survival.

Druids, Priests, and Mages make excellent choices for CC classes, but be ready to encounter enemies that are immune to CC entirely. Have several off-tanks and healers ready for fights against large groups of enemies.

Shaped like a giant wheel, there are four wings in the Necropolis, determine which wing you intend to enter before the raid forms. This will save hurt feelings and time.

EXISTING OUTDOOR RAIDS

Outdoor Table

Name	Zone
Ysondre	Ashenvale, Feralas, Duskwood, The Hinterlands
Taerar	Ashenvale, Feralas, Duskwood, The Hinterlands
Lethon	Ashenvale, Feralas, Duskwood, The Hinterlands
Emeriss	Ashenvale, Feralas, Duskwood, The Hinterlands
Azurgos	Azshara
Lord Kazzak	The Blasted Lands

Dragons of Nightmare

Something has happened within the Emerald Dream. Ysera's four most trusted lieutenants have emerged from the dream, but they are tainted. They attack anyone who comes near and some of them have visible signs of the taint.

There are several things that all four dragons have in common.

1. Generate floating green clouds that cause Sleep.
2. Green Dragon Breath which slows ability cooldowns.
3. Attack members behind with Tail Swipe.
4. Use specific abilities at 75%, 50%, and 25% health.
5. Are guarded by groups of green dragonkin and drakes.

YSONDRE

Zone: Ashenvale, Feralas, Duskwood, The Hinterlands
Level Range: 60+
Primary Damage Type: Nature
Special Items: Many items of epic and rare quality.

As one of the Dragons of Nightmare, Ysondre shares the sleep, breath, and tail swipe abilities of her brethren. Have your raid prepared to avoid the green clouds and your main tank ready to keep Ysondre facing away from the largest portion of the raid.

As her health drops, Ysondre summons several druids who attack members of your raid. Ysondre also has a Lightning Wave attack that she uses against the main tank. This does considerable nature damage and can leap from one person to the next. Avoid keeping people too close to the main tank to reduce the overall damage done by this ability. The more people you bring to this fight, the more damage you do, but the more chaotic things become.

TAERAR

Taerar also shares the tail swipe, green dragon breath, and sleep attacks. Have your raid prepared to avoid the green clouds and stay away from the front of Taerar.

As his health drops, Taerar will become a full shadow and summon three Shades of Taerar. These look identical to Taerar and have many of his abilities. They have fewer hitpoints and must be killed before Taerar engages your raid again. Only the true Taerar has the ability to fear large portions of your raid. Fear immunity and dispelling effects greatly aids your success. The more people you bring to this fight, the more damage you do, but the more chaotic things become.

Zone: Ashenvale, Feralas, Duskwood, The Hinterlands
Level Range: 60+
Primary Damage Type: Nature
Special Items: Many items of epic and rare quality.

LETHON

Tail swipe, green dragon breath, and sleep are all abilities Lethon shares with the other Dragons of Nightmare. Keep your raid away from the floating green clouds and to the sides of Lethon to reduce the effectiveness of his attacks.

As the battle with Lethon continues, he often casts Shadowbolt Whirl that hits everyone in the raid. This makes life on healers more difficult so be ready. With his health falling, Lethon stuns your entire raid for a few seconds and summon wraiths from your bodies. These travel toward Lethon slowly and heal him when contact is made. Be ready to AoE these to death or face a reinvigorated dragon. The more people you bring to this fight, the more damage you do, but the more chaotic things become and the more people possibly healing him.

Zone:	Ashenvale, Feralas, Duskwood, The Hinterlands
Level Range:	60+
Primary Damage Type:	Nature, Shadow
Special Items:	Many items of epic and rare quality.

EMERISS

As one of the Dragons of Nightmare, Emeriss also possesses the sleep, breath, and tail swipe abilities. Avoid standing in front of her (unless you're the main tank), behind her, or in the floating green clouds.

Throughout the fight, Emeriss casts infections on your raid members. These cause the targeted member to inflict massive damage to all nearby members over several seconds. Should you get hit with this, run away from others until it can be dispelled. Emeriss, when her health drops, will release a DoT that deals 100% of your health over 10 seconds. A single heal keeps you from dying, but won't leave you with much health. Be ready to dispel and heal quickly after she does this.

Zone:	Ashenvale, Feralas, Duskwood, The Hinterlands
Level Range:	60+
Primary Damage Type:	Nature
Special Items:	Many items of epic and rare quality.

AZUREGOS

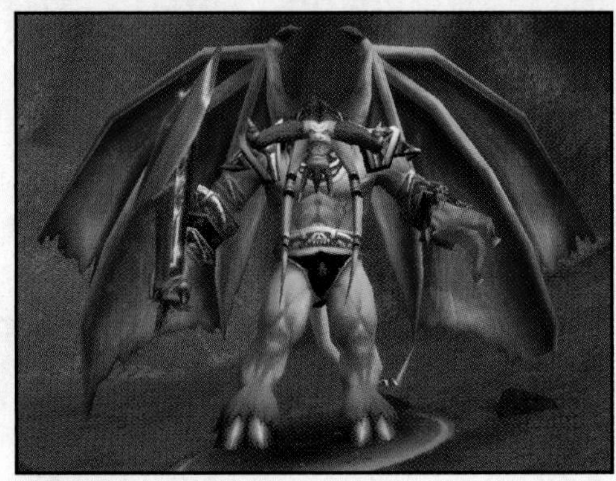

Azuregos guards the magical secrets of Azshara. He does not attack you until provoked. This makes assembling a raid easier as he patrols around. Clear any of the mobs in the area before engaging Azuregos.

The ancient blue dragon has many tricks to use against your raid. Keep everyone close enough to get teleported with him, but far enough away to avoid his AoEs. Don't attempt to resurrect after he's killed you as he will freeze you every time he uses a cold attack until the fifteen minute debuff wears off.

Zone:	Azshara
Level Range:	60+
Primary Damage Type:	Cold
Special Items:	Many items of epic and rare quality.

LORD KAZZAK

Safe within the Tainted Scar, Lord Kazzak prepares for his attack on the world. Move your raid into position as one group as the patrolling demons in the scar are very dangerous and will kill any small groups wandering through.

Lord Kazzak has several shadow attacks and curses that make him rather difficult to defeat. Keep all curses and magic debuffs dispelled and be ready for a quick fight. Should the fight take too long and Kazzak become bored, he begins casting shadowbolt volleys every couple seconds until your raid is dead. Do not bring more than 40 people against Kazzak. Any larger force (pets included) cause Kazzak to cast shadowbolt volleys every couple seconds until your raid is dead.

Zone:	The Blasted Lands
Level Range:	60+
Primary Damage Type:	Shadow
Special Items:	Many items of epic and rare quality.

When World of Warcraft released, there wasn't nearly as much to say about player versus player combat. Everything was handled in duels, or out in the open fields, and these contests were for personal distinction alone. With the introduction of the Battlegrounds, the Honor System, and some substantial balances for the character classes, things have changes immensely. This chapter does all that it can to explain the rules, concepts, and purpose of PvP combat in World of Warcraft. It also goes into specifics about the various locations for such conflict, and how to come out on top in your many engagements.

PvP 101

Though there are many specifics in PvP combat, there are also a number of universal traits. The Honor System, gaining Ranks, rules of conduct, and many strategies are shared between the various Battlegrounds and in the open field. Before trying to master Warsong Gulch, Arathi Basin, or the legendary Alterac Valley, a person must try to understand how PvP works, at its core.

HONOR AND REPUTATION

One of the first questions that new players wonder is what you can get through PvP. You don't get experience from killing other characters, and even victory in the Battlegrounds awards such a modest level of experience that it won't be a major focus for anyone there. Instead, PvP offers Honor, Reputation (Battlegrounds Only), fun, and a number of equipment rewards.

There are two major paths of equipment upgrades that are earned from the Battlegrounds. Honor is gained from just about any PvP action (winning a Battleground, sometimes losing a Battleground, slaying a target that is not grey to your character, taking part in a raid against an enemy faction's leader, etc.). This Honor is gathered for a full week, then is calculated during server maintenance to see how your character has performed compared to other characters of the same faction. You are then given a Standing (from first, which would be the most honor gained on the server for your faction, to all of the Standing values for those who PvPed at all). The higher your Standing, the more your character's Rank will progress. There are 14 PvP Ranks, though characters start without any Rank at all. After each maintenance, your character has the chance to gain or lose Rank; this is a dynamic system that pushes characters to PvP constantly if they want to achieve or even maintain the higher Ranks in the game.

The Long and Short of Honor System Terms

- Honor: Gained for Kills and Battleground Activity; Used at the End of the Week, then Are Reset
- Standing: Calculated After Server Maintenance for Each Week, Used to Determine Whether Your Character Gains or Loses Rating Points
- Rank: Your Current PvP Title; This Determines What Rewards You Can Access from Your Faction; Rank/Title is Based Off of Your Character's Current Rating Points
- Rating: The Actual Measure of Your Character's Honor System Progress; This is More Accurate Than Rank, But Cannot Be Seen In-Game

At first this might seem complex, and some aspects of it genuinely are. Many people participate in the Honor System without fully understanding how it works. That is fine; they only need to get out there and fight if they want a few Ranks. But to conquer the system and get the most out of it, people need to sit down and really see what is going on behind the scenes.

UNDERSTANDING HONOR, STANDING, RATINGS, AND RANK

A Quick Look at the Ranks

Rank	Rating Points	Required Level	Alliance Title	Horde Title	Reward
1	Score 25 Kills in a Week	N/A	Private	Scout	Tabard
2	2,000	N/A	Corporal	Grunt	Trinket (Removes Certain Status Effects)
3	5,000	N/A	Sergeant	Sergeant	Rare Cloak; 10% Discount on Items/Requires From Faction Merchants
4	10,000	33	Master Sergeant	Senior Sergeant	Rare Necklace
5	15,000	38	Sergeant Major	First Sergeant	Rare Bracers
6	20,000	41	Knight	Stone Guard	Entry to Officer's Brackets in Racial Capital, Officer's Tabard, Inexpensive Potions
7	25,000	44	Knight-Lieutenant	Blood Guard	Rare Boots and Gloves (PvP Set)
8	30,000	46	Knight-Captain	Legionnaire	Rare Chest and Leggings (PvP Set)
9	35,000	48	Knight-Champion	Centurion	Battle Standard (Enhances Health to Allies, Reusable)
10	40,000	51	Lieutenant Commander	Champion	Rare Helm and Shoulders (PvP Set Complete)
11	45,000	53	Commander	Lieutenant General	Inexpensive Epic Mount (Unique Appearance), Ability to Chat in Defense Channels
12	50,000	55	Marshal	General	Epic Gloves, Leggings, and Boots (Upgraded PvP Set)
13	55,000	57	Field Marshal	Warlord	Epic Helm, Shoulders, and Chest (Upgraded PvP Set Complete)
14	60,000	60	Grand Marshal	High Warlord	Epic Weapons/Shield

Rules of Rank Advancement

- Rating Advances By Having a High Standing (End the Week With More Honor Than Others)
- Rating Decays Every Week; You Are In a Fight to Earn More Than You Lose
- Because Lower Level Battlegrounds and Characters Are Worth Fewer Honor Points, Competition for High Standing Isn't Possible Before the Higher Brackets
- Rating/Rank is Capped at Various Levels; Only a Character at Level 60 Can Reach Rank 14 (All Brackets Have a Cap of Some Sort Before Then)
- Dishonorable Kills (Taking Out Civilians) Immediately Reduces Your Rating, Effectively Lowering Your Rank Progress

If Standing gets you the Rating/Ranks you need, and a high Standing is based on getting more Honor than other characters in your faction, the obvious question is how to get the most Honor.

Duels get you nothing of any sort. Open field PvP is almost worthless, contributing only a small amount of Honor over time. In reality, the higher Ranks are not accessible without entering the Battlegrounds. In these battles, your character gains a high sum of Honor for victories while still getting supplemental Honor for the kills that naturally take place during the contest. Because Battlegrounds have Reputations (and rewards) of their own, the vast majority of focused PvP takes place within them.

Knowing that the Battlegrounds are the place to go for Honor, your next step is to find a solid team to play with. Sure, PUGing the BGs (going into the Battlegrounds by queueing on your own) is okay here and there. But to get a ton of Honor, start forming groups ahead of time. Join a good PvP guild, or just find a number of friends who are skilled in PvP and enjoy playing with you. This helps teamwork immensely, and leads to victory after victory in many engagements.

If Honor and victories are even more important, make sure that your guild has a voice chat server of some sort so that they can always be on a voice chat program while in the Battlegrounds. It's much faster to hit a key and say "Incoming Ramp" than to type it. In fact, speaking even allows you to quickly convey "Three incoming ramp, a Paladin, a Druid, and a Priest." Get as many people as possible on voice chat and get the folks to speak out about important actions in the Battlegrounds.

With these systems in place, practice and play often. Investing more hours into the PvP system is always a way to increase the Honor you are getting each week. A couple of hours here and there are easily enough to pull your character up through the first few Ranks. As the climb continues, you need to put in more time. Competition starts at Rank 4, but it is trivial. You only need to be placing somewhere in the top few hundred to make consistent progress. It isn't until Rank 8 or 9 that casual players in the PvP system start to really push themselves for progress.

By Rank 11, even those people in a good guild that PvPs often start to see real challenges. To advance at that stage, your character has to be placing in the very high Standings every week. And to reach Rank 14, you need to be able to steal that top slot on your faction for a couple of weeks in a row. It's possible to hit Rank 14 by getting in the top three Standing Slots, but you can't afford to see far below the leader in Honor, whatever the case.

Moving through the PvP Ranks takes a few months, even if you devote all of your WoW time to PvPing. And, depending on the level of PvP on your server, hitting Ranks 12 and beyond may demand ten or more hours of PvP per day. Anyone can get through the lower Ranks (and enjoy their rewards). Anyone can eventually get enough Reputation to enjoy the Battleground-specific rewards! And most players can even hit the middle-Officer Ranks without too much trouble. Just be aware that going to Rank 11 and beyond requires major work and dedication to PvP and the game itself. Skill can only take you so far; time, time, and more time are needed in the end.

For the highest Ranks in the system, many players start to organize themselves even between the guilds. Quite a few servers have formed a queue for advancing to the highest Ranks. This way, the high-end players enter into an agreement to allow specific people to get the highest totals. By avoiding competition between each other in this fashion, they dramatically reduce the level of tension in the process and allow themselves more free time to do other WoW activities or even logoff (it does happen). Use the PvP Rankings from the worldofwarcraft.com site to find out who you are competing with at the highest tiers. Talk to them and see what can be worked out; it's always worth a try!

Can I Make Rank 14?

The answer is probably no, even if you are incredibly good. Rank 14 is never about skill (some players make Rank 14 and stink at PvP, while others are just as good as you might expect from someone who PvPs constantly).

The highest PvP levels are entirely about having the right group to play with all the time, investing a massive amount of gameplay into PvP every week for a few months or more, and in winning constantly. If you PUG, you won't make it. If you can't roll a bunch of enemy PUGs, you won't make it. If you have a job or social life that takes you away from the game during prime PvP hours, it's going to be brutally hard.

Try out the system and see what types of Standing you can make. If your level of time investment can get you into the higher Standings in the 50s bracket, there is a real chance for you. If not, shoot for a Rank that is realistic and don't stress yourself out about the process. The game is supposed to be fun for you, and PvP certainly can be. Don't worry about things that you can't change; do your best and grab the rewards available to you.

After all, the Reputation rewards are rather good by themselves, and combined with a decent Rank they equip a character quite nicely throughout the levels.

Diminishing Returns and Wasted Effort

- A person's honor decreases by 10% each time you kill them in a Battlground
- Honor From Kills Does Not Mean Very Much in the Long Run
- Your Sum Total of Honorable Kills Does Nothing, Means Nothing, is Worth Nothing

Further information about Honor is useful for your progress. Many players who are new to the system don't believe that the Bonus Honor from the Battlegrounds is the key to success in achieving a higher Rating. Instead, these players try to farm Honor from repeatedly killing their enemies. Not only does this make for a less interesting and longer match, but it doesn't pay off! Observe the following table.

Diminishing Returns for Repeatedly Killing the Same Person

Times Killed	Percentage of Full Honor Value
1	100%
2	90%
3	80%
4	70%
5+	60%, 50%, 40%, etc.

This table shows what happens when you and your groups kill the same person repeatedly. The first time a specific enemy character is slain, they yield their full Honor value to you (up to several hundred points). The second kill is reduced to 75% of the total value, and so on from there.

Honor gained from kills is purely supplemental for this reason. You can't farm targets; you can't gain major Rating from mass slaughter, and so forth. This is even more reason not to camp graveyards, not to farm kills in the Battlegrounds, and to push for your objectives!

Every 24 hours, the diminishing returns system resets, and those who you killed yesterday go back to being worth a full value (until you trash them again). This system is the main reason why places like Alterac Valley and open field PvP sites are not ultimate honorfests.

Rating Decay

- Your Character Loses 20% of Their Accrued Rating Every Week
- In the Higher Ranks, 20% of Your Rating Leads to Slower and Slower Progress Because This Value Becomes Greatly Higher
- There is a Safety Net That Prevents You From Losing More than 2,500 Rating Per Week if You Go Into the Negatives (This is usually Half a Rank)

Every week, after maintenance, your character has their Rating for the completed week compared to their old Rating. If you didn't PvP much at all, it is likely to you will lose points from your overall Rating. This can cause you to fall up to half a Rank per week.

If you look at the required Rating values for the Ranks, you can see why the 20% Rating penalty per week becomes so fierce. At the lowest part of Rank 13, this means that your character needs to get at least 11,000 Rating Points per week just to break even. That means getting a substantial percentage of the number one character's Honor total. The person with the highest Standing only gets 13,000, so we're not talking about a very high margin for slipups.

There isn't a set total for Rating Given to anyone below first Standing. While the number one person gets that lovely 13,000, everyone else receives an amount weighted by their percentage of the leader's Honor. So, if you got the number two slots and only missed by a hair, don't fret! Your character is still going to get a sum in the high 12,000s (12,920 for example).

There Can Be Only One

Despite all of the rules for progression that we just mentioned, there are some exceptions. The system is set up to prevent too many characters from being in the higher Ranks at the same time. When passing into the really high Ranks (11 and up), this number dwindles to a paltry sum.

This is yet another reason why many players work together and form queues for getting into the higher Ranks. Once a person has gotten to their desired goal, it is important for them to fall back and make room for other players in their faction. Someone who was crazy enough to camp Rank 14 would be keeping the rest of their faction from reaching it. Though rare, more than one Rank 14 player can exist at one time on a server.

Thus, get your gear and get out! You can certainly still BG and will be happily welcomed into your old groups. But try not to BG so much that you threaten to get into the top 20 Standing positions. That way, the people who need the high Ranks can push you out of the way.

A Few More Tips

If you are trying for those highest Ranks, remember these final words of advice. First, learn to love Warsong. Stomping PUGs in Warsong Gulch offers the best Honor/hour in the game. Arathi Basin matches **can** be even better if you are able to seize a 5-0 victory in five or six minutes, but there are some problems with that. It's not easy against any team worth a darn. It's also extremely unlikely that such teams will queue constantly and let your guild/PvP group obliterate them.

Thus, Warsong is the most consistent source for defeatable PUGs. Be nice and respectful to the enemies (to keep them queueing and to be a good person). Beyond that, remember to bring your appropriate PvP gear and trinkets, keep the Stamina high, buy Healing Potions and possibly Free Action Potions as well if you like to run the flag.

If Ranks are that important, choose Talents specifically for the Battleground that you plan to camp. Don't worry about PvE Talents and survivability if all that you do and plan on doing for several months will involve Battleground work. Keep an eye out for anything that will improve your burst damage or limit enemy capabilities. Stuns are great, instant attacks are wonderful too. Mana efficiency is less important, considering that you won't often live for too long once you start casting heavily.

Rules, Even in War

Another general theme of PvP is the sense of proper conduct that runs through its most respected players. There are many people who are going to break into an "us vs. them" mentality, and those are the types that often a lot more difficult to work with. If you want to play on consistent, mature, and skilled teams, it usually means learning the rules of conduct and sticking to them at all times.

You might wonder what is fair and what is unfair on the field of war. By the terms of the game, almost everything is kosher in the Battlegrounds; using /spit and /rude, slaughtering people two seconds after they Rez, and being a general jerk to friend and enemy alike is not going to get you kicked off the server (unless you use language that violates the ToS, obviously).

What those actions may do, however, is get you blacklisted from the best PvP groups available. That is a very bad thing, because the rate of Honor for PUGs isn't even close to what a skilled group can rake in. And for the higher Ranks, even a single group hitting more Honor than you is going to prevent you from moving forward well.

Thus, whether you believe in being nasty to the enemies or not, it's very much to your advantage to learn how to behave in the way that your server deems appropriate. The specifics of that may vary a fair bit, but we'll still discuss some of the usual problems that come up here; that way, you at least know the sides before you have to choose which one to take.

Graveyard Camping

Graveyard Camp is considered a normal tactic on PvP servers. Though frowned upon, don't be surprised to see it more since the cross-server Battleground merger of 1.12

In Arathi Basin, never approach the file graveyard for the other side; these are located at the northwestern hill for the Alliance and the southeastern hill for the Horde. Don't climb the hill, don't let enemies kite you up there, and just stay away. If the other side is outnumbered and being 5-0ed there, just let them stay back if they don't want to fight. Keep it painless, take your free victory, and be happy it isn't happening to you. Never rub it in.

In Warsong Gulch, there on time when you want to attack the graveyard. Yup, you guessed it; when their flag runner stands in the middle of the graveyard. This is done by turtling teams to give them the best chance to keep constant healing on their carrier. With enough healers, it can be very hard to defeat without a good group of crowd controllers (and you just might not have said crowd controllers in your raid). When that is the case, hop on every healer that Rezzes and kill em outright until the flag runner is dead and the flag is returned. That is the **only** exception to the rule when in Warsong.

In Alterac Valley, graveyard camping is built into the system somewhat. Because the teams are forced to capture graveyards, there are times you simply have to clear out recent rezzers to ensure that it is safe to capture and hold the area. Don't laugh, spit, or be a jerk about it. Just kill the targets, get it done, and move on. As long as your side isn't mean about the process, the enemies are likely to understand that it's just something that had to happen.

Spitting and Other Emotes

This problem comes up all the time. Some people really like to /spit on their foes. You will see it, and you might see it a lot (depending on your server). Even on some RP servers, there is a sense that /spit is an insult to the player and not the character. That isn't universal, but it is a commonly-held view. Unless you truly wish to insult an enemy and are willing to risk offending even your own team, avoid using the Spit Emote.

For roleplaying or just having fun, try /shake, /grin, and /roar instead. There are many cool emotes out there that don't have the same weight as /spit. Also, remember that /say and non-standard emotes /em "Other Test" are not viewable by the other side. Don't use these to try and convey a message, because they won't get across.

Laughing at other players is another emote that might be taken personally. This won't evoke the same response at spitting, and sometimes it just makes sense (e.g. That Paladin just bubbled with the flag, omg /lol). If you do this a lot though, and do care about being nice to the other side, try a /hug or a /comfort to go along with it. Let people know that you aren't ripping into them, but laughing at the situation.

Because the system Blizzard uses to garble text between the factions is consistent, people have figured out how to state something that is gibberish to their own team and understandable by the other side. Please don't use this to insult the other team; it's not funny or amusing to many people, and it gets old pretty quickly.

Text Spamming

Spamming /say or /yell in the BGs can also get to be a major pain. Don't create macros to tap and fill people's textbars. This annoys folks on both sides of the fight, and it isn't going to win you terribly many friends. If you have specific messages for your team, keep it in /raid or /party chat.

If you are roleplaying and have a battlecry or something similar, use it sparingly. There is nothing wrong with doing this; try to keep the message short, and only use it from time to time. There is a big difference between spamming something to be a pain and doing some roleplaying (most characters on both sides will recognize this).

Item Use

This is an issue that is brought up from time-to-time; people complain about the use or over-use of items in the Battlegrounds. People with more money are going to drink a great number of potions, including Healing/Mana Potions, attribute-enhancing ones, and even Flasks in truly extreme cases. Free Action and Swiftness Potions are used commonly, and quite a few Engineering pieces too.

There is nothing wrong with this; the rules of the game and even the rules of decency say nothing about avoiding money use for the BGs. You can choose not to use these items, and that is fine too, but there is no way that both sides are going to enter into an agreement to abstain from all of their toys. Indeed, some players get the most joy out of using Mind Control Caps, Rocket Boots, and a way array of Trinkets.

Get used to Purging/Dispelling when you see heavy item users on the field; for a slight use of mana, you get to rip effects right off of these characters, wasting money and cooldowns in the process!

Bracket Camping/Twinking

Each bracket starts at x0 and goes up to x9 (except for the capped bracket, for players of the highest level). Thus, the first bracket is 10-19, then 20-29, and so forth. For brackets like the 10-19 and 50-59, it is extremely common to find bracket campers; those who are staying at the highest level of the BGs and avoiding experience. These are folks who are trying to get either more honor in a somewhat easier bracket, or they are specifically Twinking to get an edge over others in PvP (this is most often the case with level 19 characters).

The issue itself becomes rather complex. There is nothing in the game rules that says a person has to level up, and twinking is not an avoidable thing either. Blizzard is likely to limit some of the potential for twinkers in the future; it has been stated that high-tier Enchantments are going to be limited to higher-level characters at some point in the future. This will relieve some of the pressure on the earlier brackets.

Okay, so what does twinking look like? Expect a certain type of level 19 player to have almost all Rare equipment (AH purchased), be wielding high DPS weaponry, and be using Enchantments that are very expensive. Life Stealing is one of the most brutal Enchantments for this tier of Battlegrounds. Rogues are one of the most common twink classes because their DPS is already quite capable in the high teens, while Warriors don't have enough of their abilities, and casters can only do so much to twink their characters.

Twinking does have a vague wrongness. There isn't anything against the rules here, but non-twinks in the lower brackets have no chance against you. A level 10-15 character can be one-shotted by a twink. Even level 19 characters are doomed against a dual-Lifesteal Rogue. Play how you want, and have a good time, but realize that people don't like to be splattered without even a fighting chance. Not everyone has a level 60 character already for easy funds, and not everyone is willing to play the Auction House for hours trying to make smooth deals. Thus, not everyone can twink their characters. It's not a fair fight.

A bracket camper, on the other hand, has no specific gear. They may be wonderfully equipped or poorly equipped. These characters are simply put in the Battlegrounds to reach a certain objective before moving on. Some bracket campers are really cool folks who just have PvP goals to reach. Others are trying to keep an edge in PvP as long as possible. On some servers there is antagonism between capped players and those one level below them. You can reach Rank 13 at level 59, meaning that most of the PvP journey can be spent without leveling to 60. It's easier to find and roll PUGs in the 50s (where equipment is lower, the levels are obviously varied, and more fresh blood moves through).

There is no clear cut right and wrong here. The best way to avoid drama and difficulty is to keep a good attitude, play with friends, and avoid the folks on both sides of the issue if they start to get nasty. Whether you bracket camp or not, keep a clean smile, fight a fair fight, and most PvPers will like you. Those who don't can take a kind leap off the side of the Lumber Mill.

Strategy and Tactics

Time to get new players started with a few general tips. We'll get into BG-specific tips farther down, but the ideas here are useful almost anywhere.

Communication is Essential

This can't be stressed enough. The only way to way consistently against good teams is to have effective communication with the rest of your allies. The Battlegrounds aren't about killing; they are focused on goals: running a flag, capturing resource locations, and pushing up the field toward the enemy's base. These are not done well without a plan.

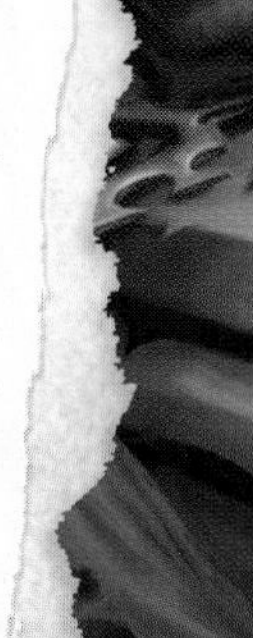

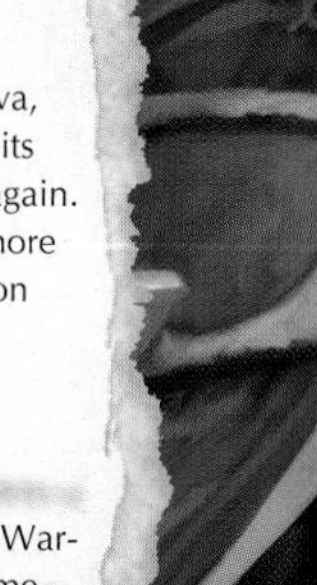

Whether you are using text or voice chat, effective communication takes a fair bit of practice. Don't give people more or less information than they need. Warn defenders about incoming targets and their numbers. Call for attackers to form at a specific site, and let them know when to hit.

If you aren't the leader of a raid, listen closely to what is being said, then contribute information that would be valuable to the leader. State when you see defenders moving about, notify is sites are light on defense or heavy, and so forth.

Learn to get this information across efficiently. Instead of saying/typing "There are five people coming toward out ramp," try "inc ramp 5." Lingo is used heavily in all of the BGs. Expect everything possible to be abbreviated when text is used, and even over voice some of this sticks.

Examples of Communication

Poor Form	Good Form	Meaning
ZERG!!!!111	6+ Inc Farm	Six or more people are rushing toward the Farm
Flag Lost	Ramp	The flag was taken, and the runner is going out to our ramp
Healers NOW	Kill Kith, Then Chay	Take down Kith the Priest, as she is healing their people; Take Out Chay After Kith is dead
Get their flag	Push Ramp now	Push forward into the enemy base using their ramp
Hold midfield	Rez, form on me, and stay with me	After your characters Rez, group together on my location

The more specific your information, the more powerful it becomes. Do everything possible to learn the lingo of your server and master it. Then, practice conveying information during downtime or even minor breaks within combat. If you get Stunned for four seconds, then type "FC Balcony" (enemy flag carrier is on the balcony). If you get Sapped by a defensive point, type "LM!" hit enter, then "Sapped, flag in trouble!" (the first line means Lumber Mill, then they get the next line, I'm crowd controlled and the flag is being captured).

Don't leave Caps Lock on, don't curse, and never yell at your teammates. This is asking for a loss. The last thing that you want to do is sow discord within the ranks of your buddies. If a game is already going poorly, any drama is going to make things a lot worse. Winning teams are much better able to roll with the punches than those teams that have already gotten beaten up a few times. Try to keep an upbeat attitude about it all, and spread that to others when you can. Ignore the naysayers and fools who are fast to decry every player and pitfall that appears.

Not a Soloers Paradise

Solo players are the bane of the Battlegrounds, even when they are effective killers. Cooperation allows for a synergistic increase to a raid's firepower. Thus, soloers are taking away from the group's potential even if they play their classes well.

Picture a scenario where one team has six people crossing the field in Warsong Gulch; they are grouped tightly together, their healers are ready to heal, their DPSers are set to target with a main assist on their leader, and so forth. The other side is crossing the field with seven characters, but they are strung out across the landscape. The first group hits them in pockets, facing two or three each time. When that happens, their crowd controllers keep all but the prime target Stunned or otherwise out of commission and the rest of the group obliterates the primary foe. This takes almost no time or mana, and the healers quickly restore the health of anyone who gets hurt.

The first group is very likely to reach the other side of the field without a single casualty, even though they were outnumbered at the beginning of the run. This is because the other group didn't focus fire, didn't stay together, didn't have a chance to heal, and so forth.

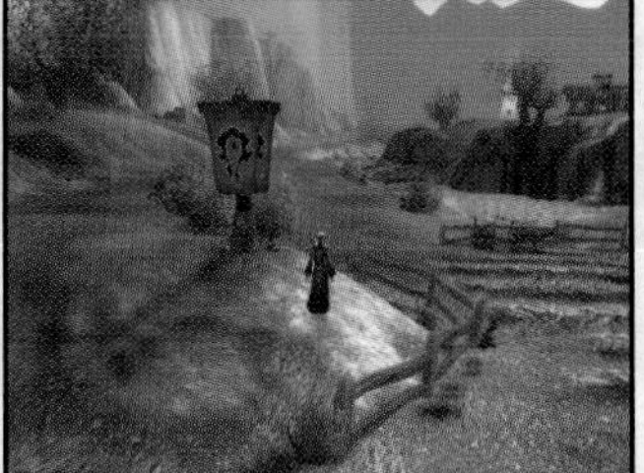

This event isn't theoretical. It happens, and it happens a lot. Stay grouped, stay together on offense and defense, and support your buddies. Attack the targets that they are already attacking, and do all that you can to heal and protect those allies who are being beaten upon. Attacking everything at once doesn't work in PvE, so why should it fare any better here?

Don't make solo runs for flags/goals unless you see a massive lapse in the enemy's defense. Even then, let people know what you are doing and why you are doing it. "They just ditched the Stables entirely, I'm NJing it."

Use your minimap to coordinate groupwork. Hit Shift + M to bring up the extra map and move toward your buddies if you are separated from them. There is no excuse for not knowing where people are!

Defense, Defense, Defense!

Too many players underestimate the value of light but solid defense. Having too many players near a flag is a waste of resources that can spell for a long game or even a loss. Indeed, you need to have a trim but effective defense at all times.

Arathi Basin is the best example of a Battleground where this is true at all times; there are five points to defend (if you are lucky), and only up to 15 players on each side. There **must** be a single person at all owned sites at all times. Even if you think that a site is completely safe, it's amazingly important to have a set of eye there, watching for stealthers and people who might be hidden in the terrain. Enemies are always hoping to find an undefended site; never give it to them!

During fierce contests you are going to need more than a single defender. A lone person won't slow anyone down. If they are immediately CCed through Sap or Polymorph there is plenty of time to capture the flag. If the enemies are being smart, a pair of defenders is well more than twice as powerful. It's much harder for the enemies to crowd control two people at once without making an obvious move toward the site. Beyond that, a direct attack requires that both characters die before the flag is captured. This leaves a window for the first character to Rez and return to the fight! If you are really lucky, the second person will die and do the same, allowing a duo to sometimes face four or five people and win in the long run.

All of that said, avoid the turtle in most circumstances. If you place six or seven people at a single point, there enemies are going to figure out a way to beat you. Turtling on defense slows games, hurts everyone's Honor, and leads to way too many defeats. Turtling is only useful for buying time (so it's a nice way to stall after a few people /afk or leave the BG because another one popped). Turtle to wait for reinforcements, then start the offense again.

To defeat a turtle, use crowd control. Psychic Scream, Howl of Terror, Frost Nova, Frost Traps, and other such abilities make it very hard for a larger force to bring its DPS to bear. This makes it quite possible to jump in, steal a flag, and head out again. This is most prominent in Warsong Gulch. For the other BGs, where there are more targets, the enemies are likely to just avoid your turtle and take everything else on the field.

Burst Damage

PvP kills are most easily gained by burst damage. Take a look at Fury and Arms Warriors to see a great example of this; the Fury Warriors deal more damage over time, so they should be awesome at PvP, right? It's true that they are still good, but Arms Warriors are able to frontload a ton of their damage. Charge, hit, Hamstring, hit, Mortal Strike, and watch the opponent's squirm as they try to respond. They just took a boatload of damage; even if they get some distance, they have a lot of health to make up, and that Arms Warrior is happily enjoying his cooldowns for another big swing. Fury Warriors, who often use faster attacks, are forced to stick to enemies to maximize their DPS, and that just isn't possible in PvP.

The reason bursts are easier to maintain is that PvP combat is filled with Stuns, Snares, Roots, fast movement by opponents, some lag, and many other problems to get in the way of fast attacks. This encourages big hits rather than many hits.

Even better is that big hits scare people. When they lose a third of their health in a moment or two, it's harder for the victim to concentrate on doing damage in return. It's also harder for their healers to respond; laying heavy damage on one target makes it possible to kill the person even when they have a whole team ready to try and save them. Two or three burst damage types working in concert can kill a flag carrier before a single heal lands!

Good burst abilities/equipment includes Mortal Strike, Aimed Shot, two-handed weapons, Pyroblast, Soul Fire, and Ambush. Anything with high cost or high charge times is likely to be fun in PvP. These lend themselves toward sudden strikes from behind, Stealth, out of sight, and so forth. Even classes without any ability to hide can surprise foes in PvP. A Warrior hiding inside of a bush might not be seen as an enemy rushes toward the Farm in Arathi Basin. This allows the Warrior to start with a Charge, from behind, getting them quite a bit of Rage and some damage before the victim even responds.

Using and Knowing the Terrain

The map is not the terrain! Get your character into a wide range of PvP activities, and you will soon start to see opportunities that were not initially available. There are many ways to get into various locations, and finding places to hide for surprise attacks is amazingly easy. Though some classes can Track and figure out where you are, only Hunters are especially good at doing this under a variety of circumstances. For almost every other target, the terrain is your friend!

Look for bushes, small buildings, tiny corners to hide in, and balconies to jump down from. These positions are all over the place, in world PvP and in the Battlegrounds. Don't fight foolishly when you have a choice; start from range, observe your enemies, stay hidden and wait for your team to arrive, and only get close to foes when you are a melee class.

A few classes have ways to observe the battlefield even while tucked away in safe locations (e.g. Warlocks, Hunters, Priests, Shaman). Use your class' abilities to look around an area when you are out of sight. If enemies come close, surprise them after informing your team where they are and how many there are. If you can scout at really long range, report on enemy force activity when there isn't direct fighting in your area; this allows defenders to accomplish several goals at the same time!

Healers

Healers are the blessing and bane of PvP, depending on whether they are on your side or the enemy's. Be prepared for healing classes to save important targets time and time again. This is why your team has to murder healers first, always.

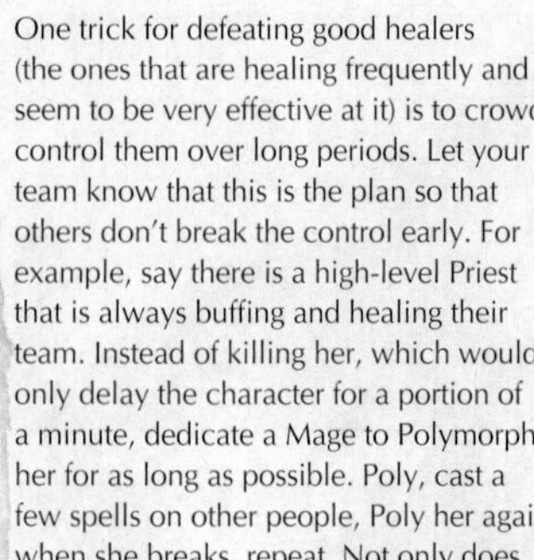

It's not nice, but slaughtering healers is a face of PvP. Druids and Priests are first on the chopping block; they are squishy and concerted assault. Allow the ones that are in animal or Shadow Form to live while other healers die, but switch back as soon as they revert to Caster Form or non-Shadow Form. Then, take down the Shamans/Paladins on the other team. These targets take longer, but they can't heal as well either, especially once the aggro turns their way.

One trick for defeating good healers (the ones that are healing frequently and seem to be very effective at it) is to crowd control them over long periods. Let your team know that this is the plan so that others don't break the control early. For example, say there is a high-level Priest that is always buffing and healing their team. Instead of killing her, which would only delay the character for a portion of a minute, dedicate a Mage to Polymorph her for as long as possible. Poly, cast a few spells on other people, Poly her again when she breaks, repeat. Not only does this keep the person out of combat for as long as possible, it frustrates them to no end. It's not fun to be chain crowd controlled. And though it's mean to say this, you don't want the best healers on the other team to have too much fun.

If you are one of the aforementioned healers, remember to stay out of sight as often as possible. Use terrain, obstacles that don't break line of sight for your spells, buildings, and other characters to hide yourself. Don't charge in with the main group; let other players engage and get the attention of foes before you enter casting range.
If the other team isn't highly skilled, they aren't as likely to look past the Warriors, Hunters, and other obvious attackers that are jumping onto them. If they do not notice you, use disruptive abilities to delay the enemies while your DPSers beat on them (Psychic Scream, Earthbind Totem, Entangling Roots, and such).

Crowd Control and Disruption

Crowd control is about as important as healing for the Battlegrounds (and sometimes it's even more valuable to a team). Use your class' crowd control abilities as often as possible. Your goal out in the field isn't to kill as many foes as possible, except in very odd cases. Indeed, you are there to capture a flag, hold terrain, etc. Killing isn't needed for that, but disruption is.

Crowd Control and Disruption Abilities

Class	Abilities to Use Heavily
Druid	Entangling Roots (godly against melee targets and flag carriers), Hibernate (Hunter Pets, Feral Druids, Ghost Wolf Shamans)
Hunter	Freezing and Frost Traps (on choke points), Wing Clip and Concussive Shot (flag carriers, melee targets), Wyvern Sting (anyone), Scare Beast (Pets, Feral Druids, Ghost Wolf Shamans)
Mage	Polymorph (anyone), Frost Nova/Cone of Cold/Blizzard (groups of foes supporting their team)
Paladin	Hammer of Justice (best against casters), Repentance
Priest	Psychic Scream (packets of enemies), Mind Control (especially when cliffs are nearby), Mind Flay
Rogue	Sap (healers, as usual), Many Stuns, Crippling Poison
Shaman	Earthbind Totem (slows group or singles wonderfully), Frost Shock
Warlock	All Fear Abilities (these destroy team coordination), Seduce (with Succubus), Curse of Exhaustion
Warrior	Hamstring (use this on everyone), Piercing Howl (wonderful to keep reinforcements from getting to their flag carriers), Intimidating Shout (breaking turtle defenses), Protection Warrior Stuns

Power-Ups in the Battlegrounds

Be on the lookout for areas where special power-ups spawn in the Battlegrounds. These items are fairly useful, and their proper use certainly helps to win games for the side that dominates them.

In Arathi Basin, all of these power-ups spawn near the resource nodes. Look in the mine cart about the Gold Mines, inside the house at the farm, in the center of the mill at the Lumber Mill, and just inside the Stables. These power-ups rotate between all three types of effects. The respawn rate for the Gold Mine power-ups seems to be faster than the others.

In Warsong Gulch there are also several power-up locations. Inside the main tunnel for each base is a cubby area where a Speed power-up spawns. Use this for getting out of the base when capturing a flag; if you are a defender of the base, make sure to get this whenever possible to prevent attackers from snagging it.

There are also outdoor buildings in Warsong Gulch, in the southwestern part of the field and in the northeast there are Berserking power-ups; these are especially useful for taking out the early rush of people who are crossing the field toward your base. Then, smaller buildings on the southeast and northwest have Restoration power-ups.

Battleground Power-Ups

Name	Effect	Duration	Found in
Berserking	30% Increased Damage, 10% More Damage Taken	One Minute	Arathi Basin (Near Resource Points), Warsong Gulch (Outdoor Buildings)
Restoration	Restores 10% Health/Mana/Pet Happiness per Second	Ten Seconds	Arathi Basin (Near Resource Points), Warsong Gulch (Outdoor Buildings)
Speed	Doubles Movement Speed	Ten Seconds	Arathi Basin (Near Resource Points), Warsong Gulch (Base Tunnels)

The Stealther Conundrum

It's never easy to stay on defense when you know that stealthers could be lining up their best attacks against you. There are quite a few abilities that deal with this problem, and many people don't know about at first. The Hunter ability, Flare, is obviously intended to reveal Stealthers. But, anything that deals damage in an area-of-effect is useful as well. When stealther activity is suspected, use the abilities to keep Stealthers at bay or to actively break them out of Stealth Mode.

Detecting or Breaking Stealth

Class	Abilities to Use Heavily
Druid	Switch to Cat Form and Stealth Yourself
Hunter	Flare, All Traps, Leave Pets on Aggressive (If They Spot the Stealthers, They'll Attack Very Quickly)
Mage	Arcane Explosion
Paladin	Consecration (If Learned)
Priest	Shield If You Expect Stealthers Inc
Rogue	Stealth Yourself
Shaman	Magma Totem, Drop to Ghost Wolf for Sap Immunity
Warlock	Use Felhunter to Detect Stealthers; Warlocks Destroy Stealthers
Warrior	Use Bloodrage and Get Battleshout up (Bloodrage Puts Warriors In Combat, Making Them Immune to Sap for a Time)

I Thought That Ability Was Useless

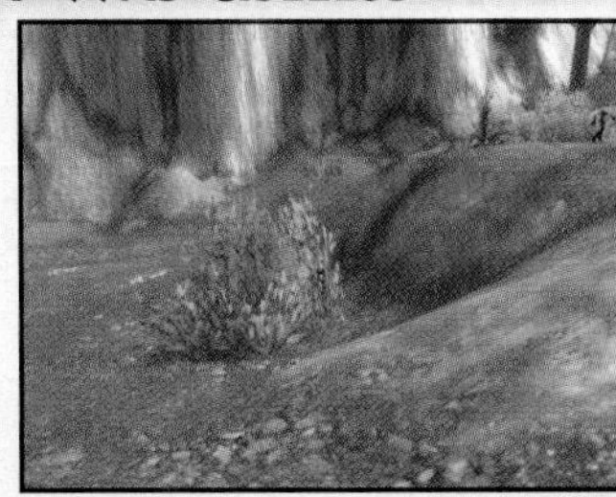

Abilities function so different in PvP than they do in PvE. Some of the things that are very useful normally become worthless (e.g. anything relating to Threat). On the flipside, a number of abilities that are rarely bothered with become quite potent, such as the scouting abilities like Eagle Eye.

Play around with all of your class' abilities in PvP to see how they function. You might be surprised what combinations become available.

Locations for PvP

There are different locations for PvP, with varying rewards and strategies. Though it would take a full book of its own to go into the massive level of detail for higher-level Warcraft PvP, this offers a brief overview of what can be done.

DUELING

- Standard Rewards: Nothing Tangible
- Honor: None
- Goal: Practice PvP Techniques
- Requirements: None

Dueling can be engaged with members of either faction, though it will flag your character for combat if you duel a person of the opposing faction when they are flagged (or if they flag during the fight).

This form of battle does not cause the death of either character, no Honor is awarded, but otherwise this fight occurs like a normal 1-on-1. Nobody can interfere with the encounter, and if either side runs too far from the duel flag that appears the battle will end (resulting in a loss for the fleeing person).

Losses and victories are not recorded in any way, so these have no effect on your character at all. Duels are done to pass the time, have fun, and test out techniques. Note that these have very little bearing on true PvP because the Battlegrounds are for group-on-group fighting. The best duelist in the world still needs solid communication skills to accomplish anything worthwhile in BG PvP.

Remember to establish "rules" before going into a duel. If you get deeply upset when other people blow timers, use potions, etc., then let that be known well before the fight starts. Otherwise, everything goes.

To maximize your successes in duels, come up with a plan ahead of time. Use burst damage, kiting, or outright attrition, and stick with your theme. If you are going for burst damage, don't waste anything on drawing the fight out. If you are kiting, learn how far you can run, keep your enemy Snared/Rooted, and so forth. For attrition combat, slap down the DOTs and keep your foe controlled or at range as much as possible.

WORLD PVP

- Standard Rewards: Just Honor
- Honor: Very Low
- Goal: Kill Enemy Faction Leaders, Sow Anarchy, Just Fight
- Requirements: None

World PvP consists mostly of rolling PvP encounters (small fights on PvP servers) and raids on towns or cities. The smaller encounters behave somewhat like duels, but often start with one side at a great disadvantage. Instead of having people face off against each other, one side is usually taken by surprise due to Stealth, terrain, already being engaged, etc.

To reduce the problem of being rolled in world PvP, watch your back while fighting various monsters, stay in a group for questing, and don't let your health stay low for very long, even if it means using bandages more often. Treat every minute as if it could be your last, and assume that there is always a Stealther nearby. Even when there isn't, it's always possible that a few people could come over the hill at any moment.

Going after towns and cities is more direct, and it requires quite a few more people. Get a group, or preferably a raid, together. If you only have five to ten people, head to a smaller place, like Astranaar or Hammerfall. The distant locales of these places prevent massive numbers of people from arriving quickly to counter you; instead, a moderate assortment of levels and classes should be there or soon arrive. This makes for a somewhat fair fight.

If your raid has 30 or more people, try for a major location, and keep trying to rally more and more people from your side to join in. Take on one of the major cities from the other faction, and keep the pressure going. During primetime hours, it's nearly impossible to kill an enemy faction's leaders (the leader of each city). But during off-hours, it is possible to kill these tough targets if your raid uses skill and speed to clear their way through the city.

When defending against these attacks, remember that time is on your side. It is easier to get reinforcements for your forces than it is for their group, and Rezzing is also easier for the defenders, who often have many places and people to hide and protect them. Because of this, it is easier to make the enemy forces pay dearly for every inch, even if it means that your character is doomed. Use AoE death runs to soften large groups of attackers. Be sure to spam Snare abilities when enemies try to rush through an area; don't let them bypass guards, NPCs, and other hindrances! Snare, Fear, Daze, and do whatever you can to keep the NPCs beating on your targets for as long as possible.

Because of diminishing returns, you can't get a lot of Honor from world PvP even if you kill a fair number of people per day. This is a very fun form of combat, and it is purely based on the fighting (instead of on capturing terrain or flags). But, you won't reach the higher PvP ranks by doing things this way.

WARSONG GULCH

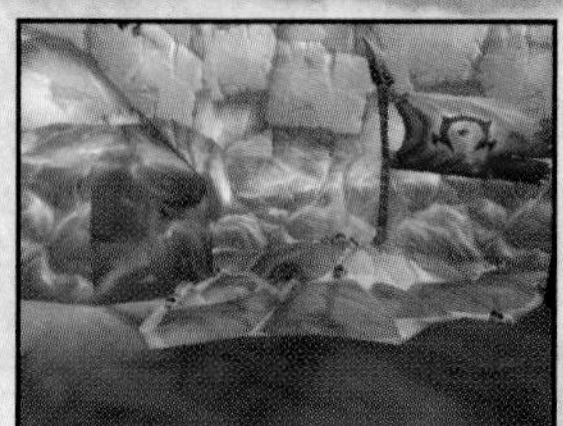

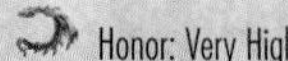

- Standard Rewards: A Trinket, Rare Equipment (Rings, Bow, Staff, Sword, Dagger, Necklace), Epic Bracer, Epic Leggings
- Honor: Very High
- Goal: Capture the Enemy's Flag Three Times
- Requirements: Five People per Team Minimum

Warsong Gulch is the first Battleground that most young PvPers will encounter. From level ten forward, this BG is available, and it only takes five people queued from each side to open the Gulch.

There are two bases, the Alliance one in the north, and a Horde one in the south. Between them is an open field that is wide enough to allow for groups to pass each other without spotting the movement of their foes.

The goal is to reach the enemy base, right click on their flag to capture it, then return and place their flag on top of yours (by walking over it). If the enemies take your flag in the meanwhile, you won't be able to score. Flag carriers drop the flags if they are made immune to damage, mount, or right click on the flag icon, on the upper-right side of their screen.

The key is to figure out exactly how many people you need on defense, how many should stay in midfield to thwart enemy actions, and how many should go after the flag. Normally, you want your smallest group to be on pure defense. Then, use most of the raid for attack if the enemy is turtling or split your forces between flag running and midfield if the enemy is being more aggressive.

The only graveyards in Warsong Gulch are just to the right as a defender walks out of their base. These are up on hills to prevent enemies from easily getting to them for ganking, but foes can come into the bases by the main tunnels and leave up top to enter the graveyards (or they can take the ramps on the left side of the base and move over to the graveyards from there).

Flag carriers receive massive attention and often need at least one dedicated healer; sometimes three won't be enough. Keep shields and healing spells coming while other characters slow the attackers to keep them away from the carrier. It is essential that one escorting person stays near the carrier at all times, to pick up the flag if the carrier is slain. Doing this, your side can pass off the enemy's flag multiple times on the way home, with Rezzers returning to help with the run as quickly as possible.

For defenders, the goal is to right click on a flag when it drops. Once you see that a carrier is going to collapse, position the cursor above their heads and start to right-click rapidly. This raises the chance that your character will return the flag if it falls.

Remember that everyone except the flag carrier can still use mounts in the 40+ brackets. Thus, people on both sides can move rapidly into position. For these more intense brackets, tougher carriers are sometimes required. During earlier brackets, when speed is a greater factor, softer classes have an edge (Mages can Blink, Druids with Travel Form destroy the 30s bracket, Shamans with Ghost Wolf are always nice, etc.).

Don't try to defend from the flag room most of the time. Though it's nice to have one person who stays very close to the flag (primarily to call out the direction of enemy flag runners as they flee), it's best to hit enemy forces **before** they reach the flag room. Think about this; hitting an enemy force ahead of time means that some of your slain defenders get to respawn and hit the force again before they reach the flag. Attackers have to travel across the entire field, to this attrition favors the defending team! If you hole up in the flag room, the other team has a chance of being all the way outside the base by the time your fallen members respawn. There is no advantage to that!

When attacking, stay as tightly grouped as possible. New players have a strong tendency to fragment and string their way into the enemy base. Defenders aren't going to be like that (most of the time); they are going to be sticking together. That gives them the opportunity to bum rush your lone attackers, eat them alive, and be at full health for the new loner. Don't let three, grouped defenders beat six, soloing attackers by falling for this.

Silverwing Hold

Warsong Lumber Mill

Warsong Gulch Legend

1. Horde Base
2. Flag Rooms
3. Tunnels
4. Ramps
5. Graveyards
6. Powerup Buildings
7. Battleground Exit Portals
8. Midfield
9. Alliance Base

Mastering the Gulch

For a confident team, a very aggressive front is quite lucrative for fast matches and high honor. Nobody is going to get the most out of these events by having both sides turtles, so it is important to get a strong offense going. To do that, form the groups so that only one or two people are planning to stay behind in the base. As a risky gambit, you can even have these people come out to midfield to assist in the fighting.

Remember that defending your flag **is not** about keeping the enemies from touching it; it is about preventing enemies from getting back to their base with your flag. Thus, it's very useful to dominate midfield and destroy enemy flag carriers as they come out of the base. Non-stealthers have a hard time making it in at all when people do this, and stealthers are not at their best when carrying flags across a heavy midfield.

Be ready to stop carriers who are using maximum speed! That is the best counter to this heavy offense/midfield technique. A single Rogue or Druid can easily get your flag, and they might have the ability to go across the field at very high speed. This demands a midfield team that cooperates well, communicates immediately, and knows have to stop/slow flag runners.

Also expect to deal with Sprint Potions, Free Action Potions, and other toys. Dedicated runners blow these all the time, especially on older servers. For those targets, be certain to come at them with many types of delaying techniques. If the roots/snares won't work, try to polymorph and wait out the potion/buff that is helping the runner. This also gives you midfield team more time to get other there (you always want to have a few people beating on runners).

An entirely different technique is to wear enemies down emotionally with a heavy turtle. This is not the way to win outright! Rather, it is a method that diminishes a powerful enemy team's ability to work together. It is often considered dishonorable, but is very effective and needs to be discussed.

You realize that you are facing an enemy team that is extremely good. They might be as good as your people; they might even be a good better. However, you still have folks who are willing to work together. So, to buy time and frustrate your foes, you order everyone except a lone stealther onto defense. You them proceed to trash wave after wave of foes until the enemies lose their cohesion. At that time you shift your force into a more aggressive stance and push to the other side of the field.

During this, your stealther keeps the other team honest. If they try to rush with all or almost all of their people, the stealther should grab the enemy flag and try to carefully move home. Avoid the center of midfield in this case, and choose a side to stay along. Scoring under these circumstances can happen! The best timing is to start a flag run just as a big fight is approaching at the home base. That way, your stealther can get the flag and be on the way home before a number of the enemies respawn.

Turtling should not be a choice that people take under normal circumstances. It's slower than a more aggressive stance, and that means fewer points of honor. This is a last resort, and should be reserved for tougher fights.

ARATHI BASIN

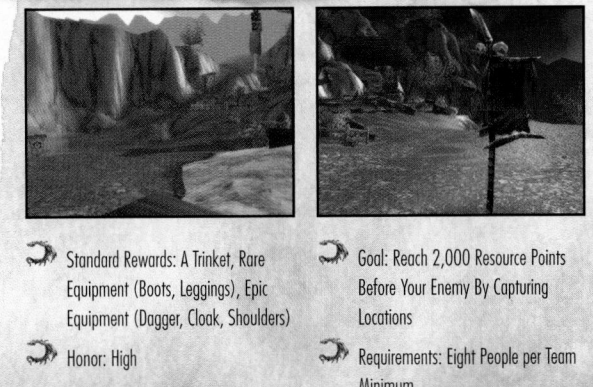

- Standard Rewards: A Trinket, Rare Equipment (Boots, Leggings), Epic Equipment (Dagger, Cloak, Shoulders)
- Honor: High
- Goal: Reach 2,000 Resource Points Before Your Enemy By Capturing Locations
- Requirements: Eight People per Team Minimum

Arathi Basin is really in a class of its own; this Battleground is a race with a dynamic timelimit. Unlike the other Battlegrounds, both sides are in a rush to reach a goal that will occur sooner or later. You will never see a one-hour Arathi Basin, because somebody is going to hit 2000 point sooner or later; these matches last from 8 to 40 minutes, and are most often around 25 for a complete match.

Trollbane Hall

Defiler's Den

Arathi Basin Legend

1. Horde Base
2. Farm Flag
3. Farm Graveyard
4. Lumber Mill Flag
5. Lumber Mill Graveyard
6. Blacksmith Flag
7. Blacksmith Graveyard
8. Gold Mine Flag
9. Gold Mine Graveyard
10. Stables Flag
11. Stables Graveyard
12. Alliance Base
13. Powerup Location (Random Powerup)

There are five resource nodes (Farm, Gold Mine, Blacksmith, Lumber Mill, and Stables). Each generates resources for the team that controls them. If one team holds three and the other holds two, the leading team will gain 50% more points over time. With a 4-to-1 lead, the winning team gets points at quadruple the speed. And with a 5-0 occurring, points come in at an amazing rate, finishing the match at a very early point.

So, your team wants to get as many sites as they can comfortably hold. It's no good to rush for all five sites and lose your battles at four of them, so there is a great deal of strategy and tactical work in figuring out what to hit. Initially, the Alliance gets the Stables while the Horde gets the Farm. The bulk of the forces for both sides rush on to contest the three other sites while a minimal defense guards the "safe" areas while they convert.

After right-clicking on a flag, it takes one minute for the site to become yours. While contested, it only takes the other team a few seconds to right click and defend the flag (or, in the case that nobody hold the site beforehand, the site becomes contested in their favor). If the other team previously possessed the site, they can score a Defense; this instantly puts the site back in their possession.

Once a site is under control, resources begin to flow from it. In addition, the Spirit Healer at that location becomes active for the controlling side. This makes it easier to defend the area. Contested sites have no active Spirit Healer for either side; this is why it is very important for attackers to hit the flag early. You don't want a stream of reinforcements to appear every 30 seconds!

Use shorthand to let people know about the sites (Farm for the Farm, Mine for the Gold Mine, LM for the Lumber Mill, Stab for Stables, and BS for the Blacksmith). Keep everyone abreast of enemy movements; from good vantage points like the Lumber Mill, your people can see a huge portion of the map.

Because it takes several seconds to use the flags, it is quite possible to interrupt attackers. Use instant abilities to deal damage and knock them off of the flag. If they don't turn to fight you, continue to deal damage to thwart their efforts. If several people pile onto a flag, drop totems, use any AoEs you have, try group Fear abilities, and so forth.

Defenders should try to fight near the flags whenever possible. Even if drawn off, by a Hunter, you must keep your eyes on the flag at all times. When someone jumps onto it, be ready to hurry back and shoot them, hit them, or do whatever you can. As an attacker, it's wise to draw people off as often as you can. If there are too many defenders to defeat, send one person ahead of the group to annoy and flee from the defenders; if they are stupid enough to chase the lone attacker, move in with others and take the site. This works more often than you might think.

Try not to let your sites get divided. Holding the Stables, Blacksmith, and Farm puts you in the lead. But, it also presents a daunting fight, because your forces are strung out across the map. When you can, try to hold territory that supports other nodes. Keeping the LM and Farm in the south, and taking the BS means that you have a triangle of defense that is extremely hard to break. From the BS, your people can see attack forces coming to either side, so your defenders always know what is being hit and can quickly rush to intercept a large group.

Low DPS classes have much more value in Arathi Basin than they do in many other PvP situations. As a defender in the Basin, your job is **not** to kill enemies. It's true! Your job is to slow enemies down for long enough that reinforcements respawn or arrive from other points. Thus, you don't need to kill to be a great defender.

Paladins, Druids in Bear Form, Priests, Protection Warriors, and other survivors have a great place in the Basin. Use their abilities to heal, slow, disrupt, and antagonize enemies. Paladins are so good at this that they have quite a reputation for annoyance; take damage while defending the flag, bubble, heal, drop bubble and attack anyone who got on the flag. For Druids, stay away from the flag, use Moonfire at range to disrupt capturing attackers, then switch to Travel Form and flee if too many people come after you. Even if the enemies are much higher in level, repeating this is wonderfully successful.

The best attackers are classes that have long-duration crowd control or high burst damage. Rogues and Mages have an especially good time Sap/Polymorphing targets and capturing the flags when there are solo defenders. For groups of attackers, lay on the DPS while focusing on enemy healers first. Once your group outnumbers the defenders, have one person try to ninja the flag (by grabbing it during the fighting). If the defenders don't see this, you win. If you do, it disrupts their current battleplan because someone needs to break off and stop the capture.

Overseeing the Basin

There are two major schools of thought on the leadership of Arathi Basin forces. For dealing with groups of people who are not as experienced in the game, one technique is to assign groups very clearly and encourage people to stick with their group the entire battle. A group is assigned for full attack work, another two groups for defense, then you have a floater group that defends sites if a third or fourth site is gained or joins the attackers if the team is behind.

The upside of a rigid team structure is that it gives inexperienced players the ability to follow veterans more closely and learn from them. Most of the strategy is clean, and obvious, and that helps to avoid confusion.

The downside of this pattern is that it lacks the strength and flexibility displayed by a team of full floaters! Such a team follows the other school of thought, that each force of 15 can be used fluidly. Those attackers require immense communication because they choose the ideal number of defenders for each site, at a given moment. As more people are needed for attack or specific defense, individual players call out that they will shift into that task.

For example, a fluid team leaves a single person at the farm early in the match while a heavy force hits the mill, BS, and mine. All three are taken, but the enemies swing around and are about to hit the farm with a few troops. The lone farm defender calls for help "Inc Farm 3," and two characters respond that they are going to the farm to assist.

Though this model has immense potential, it requires wonderful players who are used to working together. Quite PvPers make it difficult to determine where the force is needed, and a lack of discipline undermines the benefits that flexibility provides.

ALTERAC VALLEY

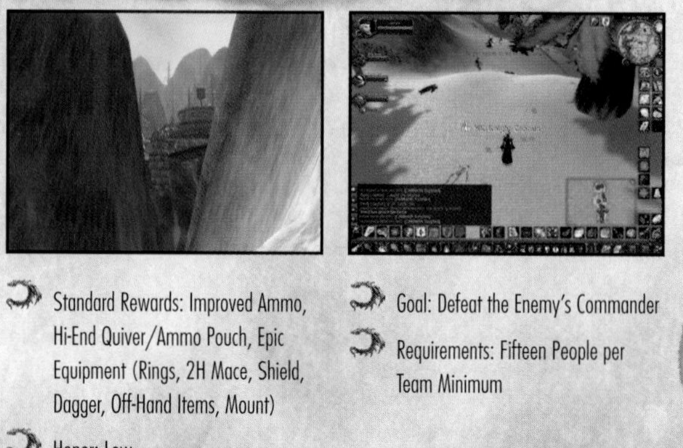

- Standard Rewards: Improved Ammo, Hi-End Quiver/Ammo Pouch, Epic Equipment (Rings, 2H Mace, Shield, Dagger, Off-Hand Items, Mount)
- Honor: Low
- Goal: Defeat the Enemy's Commander
- Requirements: Fifteen People per Team Minimum

Alterac Valley isn't available until the higher levels are reached. From level 50 onward, this is the Battleground that tests and defies many players. Up to 40 characters can enter Alterac Valley at the same time (per team), meaning that leadership is extremely difficult here. It's unusual to have everyone know each other and accept commands perfectly.

The goal is to push to the other team's base. The Alliance holds the northern keep, and the Horde leader is in the south. Killing the commander for the other team instantly ends the battle, but there is a lot to do along the way. There are resources to gather (mines are taken from NPC enemies to harvest for ground troops, Wolves and Rams are used to create cavalry, and Wing Commanders are rescued to summon aerial forces). Beyond that, Armor Scraps are taken from bodies and given to the Blacksmiths at your team's base to upgrade NPC armor. Blood is taken from bodies as well, and this is given to the summoner NPC at your team's base for calling a massive, elite creature later in the battle.

Thus, everything has a use in Alterac Valley. The rank and file characters are going to fight over graveyards, which are taken to keep the focus of the battle in different areas. Defenders work to hamper enemy forces, and can accomplish a great deal with AoE death runs, especially in the base defense (where elite NPCs are there to assist).

Along the way north/south, your team tries to take out enemy sub-bosses and locations. This not only reduces the attack force of your enemy (by removing their buffs); it also increases Honor of your side and adds additional Elite NPCs to guard your own leader.

There are quests for Alterac Valley that are given by the NPCs at the formal entrance to the zone (in the Alterac Mountains), and there are additional quests given by NPC inside the Battleground. Try to complete these as you go, and don't worry about finishing each on your first run through the Battleground. Try to get one or two done each time; the first one that is really important is the quest to clear the caves by your main base. This is a quest for either side, and the result is that you get an item to port back to your main base (very useful in Alterac Valley).

Try to have just a few, assigned people loot the bodies. This helps to keep the teams from having everyone run back every 30-40 minutes. Beyond that, the rewards are shared evenly, so there is no reason to have everyone waste their time looting.

AoEs are the king of Alterac Valley, on offense and defense. Mages and Warlocks especially are able to blast through massive groups of people who are trying to hold an area. Use these death rushes initially to soften a force, then hit them with standard DPS to finish the task. When taking flags or holding flags, keep the AoEs pounding on everyone to prevent them from having the opportunity to stay out of combat, touch flags, and so forth. The side that has fewer AoE characters is forced to be extremely aggressive when taking areas (if they can't take something quickly, the superior AoE forces of their enemy are likely to settle in and defend for a **long** time).

Beating the Valley

Even with the reduction in NPCs on the field (done in previous patches), defenders are still able to hold areas quite brutally if one side abandons there attempt to take enemy territory. These turtles heavily favor the faction with a higher player population. The players that drop out of the long matches eventually aren't replaced for the side with fewer members, leading to an imbalance in sides.

Luckily, the revamp to the battleground system makes it so that populations are smoother than they once were. Server clusters are better balanced and have the potential for both sides to receive reinforcements even late in the evening. Because of this, turtling doesn't have quite the finality that it once did.

There are still extensive arguments over the need to take and hold as many sights as possible in Alterac Valley. If you lets your enemies take many of your sites, this increases the number of defenders at the enemy commander's location (not a good thing). However, devoting people to slow or stop your enemy's advance keeps your main force from going forward as quickly too.

There isn't a clear or simple answer to this. Each commander has to decide how to distribute their forces. A heavy assault early on leads to a strong push, but it allows your enemies to do the same. Ultimately, both groups end up facing a powerful wall at the end of the match where turtling is quite successful.

One alternative that is very potent (if you have the right team for it), is to have a capable defense that holds the enemy in a stalemate while one or two stealth groups hit the targets on the opponent's end of the map. Taking four Rogues and a Druid in each of these groups makes it possible to stay in full stealth, have healing, and be strong enough to free Wing Commanders, kill enemy targets, and seize lightly-defended Graveyards. Of course, you need ten stealthers with skill to be able to try this.

Alterac Valley Legend

1. Frostwolf Keep (Commander: Drek'Thar)
2. Wildpaw Cavern (Trinket Quest Target)
3. Frostwolf Graveyard
4. Coldtooth Mine (Horde Mine)
5. Horde Starting Point
6. Iceblood Garrison (Horde Captain: Galvangar)
7. Iceblood Graveyard
8. Field of Strife
9. Snowfall Graveyard
10. Stonehearth Outpost (Alliance Captain: Balinda Stonehearth)
11. Stonehearth Graveyard
12. Icewing Cavern (Trinket Quest Target)
13. Stormpike Graveyard
14. Alliance Starting Point
15. Irondeep Mine (Alliance Mine)
16. Dun Baldar (Commander: Vanndar Stormpike)
17. Tower Point
18. Iceblood Tower
19. Stonehearth Bunker
20. Icewing Bunker
21. Lumber Mill Area
22. Ram Territory (Cavalry Targets)
23. Wolf Territory (Cavalry Targets)

Crafting & Professions

Choosing a Path

Azeroth is full of many exciting discoveries and, for some, it comes in the form of its robust crafting system. Players can create various items and equipment as long as they have the right materials, tools, and know-how.

Players are restricted to two primary professions per character. Those choices are: Alchemy, Blacksmithing, Enchanting, Engineering, Herbalism, Leatherworking, Mining, Skinning, and Tailoring. To complement these profession options, there are secondary skills available to all characters. Secondary professions are not limited in the amount you can learn so every character can learn all three: Cooking, First Aid, and Fishing.

Professions are a way to improve your character by offering more adventuring options beyond questing and grinding. The available products are wondrous: weapons and armor, potions and oils, bombs and shrinking devices. True, you can't do all of them at once, so one of your first decisions is which professions and secondary skills you'd like to explore.

Consider the Options

Each class may, at first glance, look to be geared toward a certain profession. Decide what's important to you. Do you wish to have a profession that can supplement your character class or one focused solely on extra cash flow? Are you interested in more effective combat (PvE and PvP) with gadgets and bombs or does having the ability to enchant your equipment sound more interesting? You're not restricted to a specific profession based on your class. Mages can be Blacksmiths if they wish and Paladins can work with cloth; it's up to you.

Primary

There are two primary types of professions; gathering and manufacturing.

Gathering professions are used to harvest materials from the world and prepare them to be used by a manufacturing profession. Gathering professions aren't reliant on other professions, but in such cases the gains are purely monetary.

Manufacturing professions use materials obtained from several sources to create new products or services. These rely heavily on gathering professions (the two exceptions are Enchanting and Tailoring).

Profession Quick List

Profession	Typical Partner Skill	Profession Type	Description
Alchemist	Herbalism	Manufacturer	Makes potions and elixirs with various attributes. Transmutation of metals and elements is also available to those that reach higher levels of Alchemy.
Blacksmith	Mining	Manufacturer	Makes mail and plate armor, as well as metal weapons of all types. At higher levels of skill Blacksmiths can choose to specialize in either Weaponsmithing or Armorsmithing. Weaponsmiths are able to further specialize in Axesmithing, Hammersmithing, or Swordsmithing.
Enchanter	Any	Gatherer/ Manufacturer	Disenchants uncommon or rarer items to attain resources. Enchants weapons and armor with permanent spell effects.
Engineer	Mining	Manufacturer	Engineers create gadgets, guns, bombs, etc. Many of the gadgets are usable only by other Engineers. The also create mechanical pets and trinkets. At later levels, Engineers can choose to specialize in Goblin or Gnomish Engineering.
Herbalist	Alchemy	Gatherer	Trackingdown herbs to be used by other professions. Alchemists, Enchanters, and Leatherworkers are just a few of the professions that use herbs on occasion (with Alchemists being dependant on them).
Leatherworker	Skinning	Manufacturer	Creates leather armor at lower levels and branches into both leather and mail armor at higher levels. Leatherworkers can also produce armor kits that can increase the armor on certain equipment. Proficient Leatherworkers can specialize in either Tribal Leatherworking, Elemental Leatherworking, or Dragonscale Leatherworking.
Miner	Blacksmithing or Engineering	Gatherer	Discovering the mining deposits of ore is restricted to Miners. In addition to the raw ore, rare gems can be found within the earth. Miners also smelt the ore into bars that other professions can make use of.
Skinner	Leatherworking	Gatherer	Harvests the leather and hides from beasts slain in combat. Skinners supplement many of the professions to a small extent with Leatherworkers being fully reliant on them.
Tailor	Any	Manufacturer	Creates cloth armor and bolts from the cloth pieces found on the bodies of enemies. Tailors can also create bags to increase characters' inventory space (these are generally quite sought after). As the primary sources of cloth are dead enemies, Tailors are only slightly dependant on Miners, Skinners, and Herbalists for some of the more rare materials.

Secondary Skill Quick List

Trade Skill	Description
Cook	Gather meats and parts of slain beasts and turn it into useful foods that replenish health. At higher levels certain foods also give statistic bonuses for a limited time.
First Aid	Uses cloth from fallen enemies to create bandages. These can be used to quickly heal yourself or others between fights.
Fisher	Gathers fish and treasure from the bodies of water spread across Azeroth. Alchemists make use of some fish while Tailors, Leatherworkers, Blacksmiths and Enchanters use various pearls.

All items necessary to excel in your chosen line of work can be purchased from others in the game if necessary. It's very possible to be an Engineer if you have the gold to buy the ore and stone you need. Guilds and friends are often key (exploited) in providing materials for such pursuits. Teamwork can be a huge advantage. One person producing ore to barter for armor and weapons is the foundation of a budding economy.

Of course, there's no rule saying that you must "make" something. Some players focus on gather resources in exchange for gold or lower costing equipment. There's plenty of room for players who wish nothing else than to sell the bounty of the land. The truth is, those with an abundance of gold are often willing to pay a premium in lieu of gathering the materials themselves. Gathering raw resources is almost free (the only expense is the price of a pick or skinning knife, and training), so anything you make is profit.

The obvious goal is to become the best crafter possible, regardless of which profession you choose. Maximizing your gold to do so in the cheapest and most efficient way possible is key. Everything available to crafters has a color. For example, Tailoring patterns and ore deposits each have a specific color depending on your level in the appropriate profession.

Difficulty vs. Reward

Color	Difficulty	Reward
Gray	None	These tasks are effortless and cannot fail unless interrupted. No skill gains are possible.
Green	Trivial	Very easy tasks that rarely fail. Skill gains are rare, but possible.
Yellow	Average	With a modest chance of failure, the chance for skill gain is significant.
Orange	Challenge	Failures are common (you won't lose any materials…only time) and skill gains are guaranteed on success.
Red	Impossible	Your skill is too low currently to even attempt these tasks.

It doesn't matter if you're Mining, Tailoring, Smithing, etc. These colors are uniform across the crafts. If you're trying to level up, focus on tasks that give a solid return while using as little of your resource pool as necessary. A good example of a trade off is when a yellow recipe uses two items and an orange uses six. Sure, you get a point for the orange one, but by making the yellow you have the potential for gaining three points with the same materials. However, there's also a slim risk that you'll make no progress.

Always watch for the change in color as you level. If you're just creating the same item over and over, it could very well change to a green status and have little value beyond the item itself. It doesn't always happen on a set number so pay attention (but it does tend to happen at five and ten number breaks). For this one reason, it's not always smart to hit the "create all" button. Follow this rule: if you're interested in skilling up, pay attention. If you want the items, create as many as you like.

All professions have specific trainers that teach their craft. The six capital cities typically house them all, but there are trainers hidden in the wild, in smaller towns, and even in dungeons/instances that offer more specialized training. It's important to visit the main trainers once ever 5-10 ranks while starting out. After you begin attaining higher levels, pay attention to your rank and only visit when you must. As you learn new skills, they're automatically added to your menu. You need to advance in a profession to learn better skills.

Ranks

Rank	Maximum Skill Level
Apprentice	75
Journeyman	150
Expert	225
Artisan	300

Not all trainers can teach you something new. As you level up, it's inevitable that you begin to surpass the knowledge of some trainers. When you've learned all a trainer can teach you, they often point you in the direction of the next trainer for you to contact.

Plans, recipes, and schematics can be purchased at your trainer. However, there are some that are dropped, received as quest rewards, or purchased from merchants throughout Azeroth. Some drops are extremely rare. Getting your hands on a rare set of plans and being the first to make that item for the market can make you quite rich quite quickly. Dropped plans generally make more powerful items. Rare plans, recipes, etc. are often some of the items that create the most voracious bidding. If you find a recipe or schematic as a drop, make sure to consult with someone before tossing it on the Auction House for a few silver.

ENVIRONMENT

Some items require you to travel to them. An anvil isn't something that you can put in your backpack and carry around. When something like this is required, it is noted in the recipe/pattern. You don't need to click the item, just stand near it, to make use of it.

Equipment and Tools

Some professions require equipment, but not all of them. Blacksmiths need a hammer (Blacksmith's Hammer), but Herbalists need only their hands. There are three types of equipment geared toward the professions in the game.

STORE-BOUGHT

Items and components like Blacksmith's Hammers, Mining Picks, Skinning Knives, vials, thread, etc. are all purchasable from vendors. You can generally get most items at the general vendors and you only need to buy these once. In the case of equipment, they simply need to be in your packs (not your bank) and you use the item once you initiate the action, whether it's mining ore or skinning a boar. However, for vials, thread, flux, etc. you need the item on you.

PLAYER-MADE

Some skills, as you level, require the trader to use different, player-made items. This can be a potion for a Tailoring pattern or an Arclight Spanner for an Engineer. Keep the items in your packs when you wish to use them.

Gathering Professions

The skills of Mining, Skinning, and Herbalism are gathering skills. You won't be making anything, or need to make anything to gather. These vocations supply other professions with resources.

HERBALISM

Your first skill is Find Herbs. Drag this icon from your ability book (defaulted to "p") onto a hotbar. Push the corresponding number or click it to activate. Once you activate it you'll only need to refresh it on death or after logging in.

While out adventuring, yellow dots appear on your mini-map. These denote an herbs location. If you mouse over the dot, you can discover which type of herb is shown.

When you're next to the plant, mouse over it to check the skill level required to harvest it. If you are able to harvest it, right-click on the plant to gather the herbs. It takes a few seconds and, if you're successful, a loot window opens with the herbs you found. To speed this you can hold shift and right-click the plant. The time to harvest will be the same, but it puts the fruit of your labor directly into your pack instead of bringing up a loot window.

It's possible to get as many as three herbs from each harvest as well as a bonus herb (Swiftthistle can be found in Mageroyal, Bruiseweed, Briarthorn, etc.).

Herb Name	Herbalism Skill Requirement	Alterac Mountains	Arathi Highlands	Ashenvale	Azshara	Badlands	Barrens	Blasted Lands	Burning Steppes	Darkshore	Deadwind Pass	Desolace	Dun Morogh	Durotar	Duskwood	Dustwallow Marsh	Eastern Plaguelands	Elwynn Forest	Felwood	Feralas	Hillsbrad	Hinterlands	Loch Modan	Moonglade	Mulgore	Redridge Mountains	Searing Gorge	Silithus	Silverpine Forest	Stonetalon Mountains	Stranglethorn Vale	Swamp of Sorrows	Tanaris	Teldrassil	Thousand Needles	Tirisfal Glades	Un'Goro Crater	Western Plaguelands	Westfall	Wetlands	Winterspring
Arthas' Tears	220																●		●																		●			
Black Lotus	300								●								●																								●
Blindweed	235																															●					●				
Briarthorn	70			●			●			●					●						●		●			●			●	●									●	●	
Bruiseweed	100	●	●	●			●			●		●			●						●		●			●			●	●					●				●	●	
Dreamfoil	270				●				●								●		●																		●	●			
Earthroot	15						●			●			●	●				●					●		●				●					●		●			●		
Fadeleaf	160	●	●			●										●						●									●	●									
Firebloom	205					●		●																			●						●								
Ghost Mushroom	245											●										●																			
Golden Sansam	260				●				●								●		●	●		●															●				
Goldthorn	170	●	●		●	●										●				●		●									●	●									
Grave Moss	120	●	●				●					●			●																									●	
Gromsblood	250							●				●							●																						
Icecap	290																																								●
Khadgar's Whisker	185	●	●		●	●										●				●	●	●									●	●									
Kingsblood	125	●	●	●		●	●					●			●	●					●									●	●	●			●					●	
Liferoot	150	●	●	●								●				●				●	●	●									●	●								●	
Mageroyal	50			●			●			●					●						●		●			●			●	●				●					●	●	
Mountain Silversage	280				●				●								●		●																		●	●			●
Peacebloom	1						●			●			●	●				●					●		●				●					●		●			●		
Plaguebloom	285																●		●																			●			
Purple Lotus	210			●	●	●														●		●									●		●								
Silverleaf	1						●			●			●	●				●					●		●				●					●		●			●		
Stranglekelp	85	●	●	●	●					●						●					●								●		●	●							●	●	
Sungrass	230				●			●	●								●		●	●		●															●	●			
Swiftthistle*																																									
Wild Steelbloom	115	●	●	●		●	●					●			●						●									●	●				●					●	
Wildvine**																																									
Wintersbite	195	●																																							

* Found with Mageroyal or Briarthorn

** Found with Purple Lotus and off Trolls in Hinterlands and Stranglethorn Vale

MINING

Mining ore is crucial to the economy and may be used by your other profession. Copper, tin, and others are available at the swing of a pick, but jewels await the lucky. Find Minerals is the first skill granted to miners. Buy a Mining Pick, and head out to find your copper. Drag this icon from your ability book (defaulted to "p") onto a hotbar. Push the corresponding number or click it to activate. It remains active until you log, die, or change tracking types. A yellow dot appears on your mini-map when ore is nearby.

Mouse over the yellow dot to discover what kind of mineral awaits. Once you reach the vein, mouse over it to check the required skill level.

Right-click the node to begin mining. After a few swings, your character kneels down to check what you've found and a loot window opens. If you fail, simply try again. To speed the process, you can hold shift and right-click the vein to immediately deposit the spoils in your back after a success.

Unlike herbs, mines have to be used several times before they are depleted. If you fail to mine anything on your first try, you still have the chance to skill up until you mine ore for the first time on that vein. Failing to mine does not count against getting a skill-up.

Once you gather a load of ore, return to a forge and smelt it into bars. Again, pull the Smelting icon from your ability book (defaulted to "p") and drag it onto you hotbar. Activate the skill to bring up the smelting menu. Click "create all" or "create" to smelt the ore into useable bars.

Ore Name	Mining Skill Requirement	Alterac Mountains	Arathi Highlands	Ashenvale	Azshara	Badlands	Barrens	Blasted Lands	Burning Steppes	Darkshore	Deadwind Pass	Desolace	Dun Morogh	Durotar	Duskwood	Dustwallow Marsh	Eastern Plaguelands	Elwynn Forest	Felwood	Feralas	Hillsbrad
Copper	1	●		●			●			●		●	●	●	●			●			●
Dark Iron	230								●												
Gold	155	●	●	●	●	●		●	●			●			●	●	●		●	●	●
Incendicite	65																				
Indurium	150					●															
Iron	125	●	●	●		●		●	●			●			●	●				●	●
Lesser Bloodstone	75		●																		
Mithril	175	●	●		●	●		●	●			●				●	●		●	●	●
Rich Thorium	270				●				●								●				
Silver	75	●	●	●		●	●			●		●			●	●				●	●
Small Thorium	250							●	●								●		●	●	
Tin	65	●	●	●			●			●		●			●						●
Truesilver	230	●	●		●	●		●	●			●				●	●		●	●	●

Ore Name	Hinterlands	Loch Modan	Moonglade	Mulgore	Redridge Mountains	Searing Gorge	Silithus	Silverpine Forest	Stonetalon Mountains	Stranglethorn Vale	Swamp of Sorrows	Tanaris	Teldrassil	Thousand Needles	Tirisfal Glades	Un'Goro Crater	Western Plaguelands	Westfall	Wetlands	Winterspring
Copper		●		●	●			●	●					●	●			●	●	
Dark Iron						●														
Gold	●					●	●		●	●	●	●		●			●		●	●
Incendicite																			●	
Indurium																				
Iron						●			●	●	●	●		●			●		●	●
Lesser Bloodstone																				
Mithril	●					●	●		●	●	●	●		●			●			●
Rich Thorium							●									●	●			●
Silver	●	●			●	●		●	●	●	●	●		●			●		●	●
Small Thorium	●					●	●					●				●	●			●
Tin		●			●			●	●	●				●				●	●	
Truesilver	●					●	●		●	●	●	●		●			●			●

SKINNING

When beasts are killed in the wild, Skinners swoop in to take the hides and any leather from their corpses. You need a Skinning Knife in your pack to strip the hide from the corpse (only after the corpse is fully looted can be skinned). Right-click on the body and wait for the skinning to be finished. A loot window appears. You can bypass the loot window if you hold shift when you right-click.

The types of leather and hide depend on the level of the animal you're skinning and a bit of randomness. Animals bordering on the next tier may have several of the lower tier instead of one of the higher tier. As the enemy's level increases, the level of leather received increases as well.

What's This?

Not all enemies are skinned for leather alone. Dragonkin, scorpids, turtles, and many others can be skinned for scales, as well as leather.

One thing you notice while hunting is that groups without a Skinner tend to leave corpses strewn about. It's quite a find and Skinners often follow such parties and clean up after them for some time.

Manufacturing Professions

Making items can be very rewarding. The ability to take raw resources and use what knowledge you've gained to create useful armor, weapons, potions, or enchants is worth pursuing. It's not a bad way to increase the size of your purse either.

All the skills ramp up quickly at first but, as you gain higher levels, your progress slows to a more steady pace. As long as you continue to make items of appropriate levels you continue to skill up. Having a guild to supply you with gold or resources is a great way to whip through the early levels, but it can be done without any aid as well. Even on your own you'll be able to become an artisan in your chosen field with the proper application of time.

Along with the decrease in skill gain, notice the additional components many of the higher level items require. A high end item may require you to adventure for a week to accumulate enough rare materials to create it. It's common to see such a rare item sell for great money if it's used in a recipe or pattern. Pearls and gems are common examples of additional components.

It's fair to say that if you bought all the resources to create a high level item that someone, in return, is going to have to pay a pretty penny to have you create it for them. However, some items require you to pay more for the resources than buyers are willing to pay for the completed item. Be careful when choosing what to make and what to buy.

There are times when money is no object. If you can make a robe that doubles a caster's current bonuses, they will likely pay a good deal for it.

ALCHEMY

Taking herbs, mixing them in a vial, and creating a potion that makes you several feet taller sounds exciting, no? The low level potions are typically the least interesting, but that makes them no less useful. Low level adventurers would be glad to pay for Lesser, and even Minor, Healing and Mana Potions. However, it's the high end potions and elixirs that really get people to dig into their pockets.

Invisibility Potions, Strength Potions, Defense Potions, Agility Potions—all of these are within reach of the alchemist. The list is huge and everyone has their favorites. There are no tools required for this profession, but you have to purchase vials constantly.

To create a potion, open your ability menu (defaulted to "p") and drag the Alchemy icon onto a hotbar. Activating the icon opens the Alchemy menu and immediately displays what potions you know how to create.

Click on the name of the potion to discover which reagents you need. It shows how many of each item as well. Make sure you have all the appropriate ingredients (including the vials) in your bags before trying to create potions. The menu indicates which potions you can make and how many of each (depending on your resources) can be made also. Mouse over the icon to see what the effects of the potion are.

As soon as you create a potion, it appears in your packs. To use it, either right-click it or drag it onto your hotbar for quick access.

Alchemists can also transmute semi-rare ore and elements into rarer types. You can, given the appropriate skill and a Philosopher's Stone, transmute iron to gold, mithril to truesilver, and more. Transmutes have a cooldown of one to two days, but are well worth the wait.

It's not hard to level up this skill if you have Herbalism. The herbs you find are free and, as long as you remember to have your Find Herbs skill active, you don't have to go out of your way. Groupmates, guildmates, and strangers in the field appreciate useful potions, and you're likely to develop quite a fan-base. They also sell very well in the auction houses.

No Room

If you're trying to create potions when your bags are full, you won't be able to add the potion to your inventory. This may become a problem at the lower levels when inventory space is limited. Making use of the bank to store your herbs when you aren't making potions is a good idea and will save you a headache.

Alchemy

TITLE/DESCRIPTION	REGION	GRID LOC	NAME
Artisan Alchemist	Darnassus (26)	G-2	Ainethil
Artisan Alchemist	Undercity (88)	F-7	Doctor Herbert Halsey
Expert Alchemist	Ashenvale (12)	G-6	Kylanna
Expert Alchemist	Darnassus (26)	G-2	Sylvanna Forestmoon
Expert Alchemist	Dustwallow Marsh (38)	H-5	Alchemist Narett
Expert Alchemist	Hillsbrad Foothills (48)	G-2	Serge Hinott
Expert Alchemist	Ironforge (52)	I-5	Tally Berryfizz
Expert Alchemist	Orgrimmar (60)	G-3	Yelmak
Expert Alchemist	Stormwind (72)	G-8	Lilyssia Nightbreeze
Expert Alchemist	Stranglethorn Vale (74)	B-8	Jaxin Chong
Expert Alchemist	Thunder Bluff (84)	E-3	Bena Winterhoof
Expert Alchemist	Undercity (88)	G-7	Doctor Marsh
Journeyman Alchemist	Darnassus (26)	G-2	Milla Fairancora
Journeyman Alchemist	Durotar (34)	H-7	Miao'zan
Journeyman Alchemist	Elwynn Forest (42)	E-5	Alchemist Mallory
Journeyman Alchemist	Ironforge (52)	I-5	Vosur Brakthel
Journeyman Alchemist	Loch Modan (54)	E-5	Ghak Healtouch
Journeyman Alchemist	Orgrimmar (60)	G-3	Whuut
Journeyman Alchemist	Stormwind (72)	G-8	Tel'Athir
Journeyman Alchemist	Teldrassil (80)	G-6	Cyndra Kindwhisper
Journeyman Alchemist	Thunder Bluff (84)	E-3	Kray
Journeyman Alchemist	Tirisfal Glades (86)	H-5	Carolai Anise
Journeyman Alchemist	Undercity (88)	F-7	Doctor Martin Felben
Master Alchemist	Feralas (46)	C-4	Kylanna Windwhisper
Master Alchemist	Swamp of Sorrows (76)	F-5	Rogvar

BLACKSMITHING

Smiths are some of the most popular crafters. Not only do you create mail and plate armor, but weapons too! True, only four of the nine classes ever require a Blacksmith for armoring needs, but each class could benefit from a new weapon now and then. Even Priests choose to learn how to use daggers when they need. However, the best creations require leather, cloth, jewels, and more.

A Blacksmith's Hammer must be in your pack. Though that may sound obvious, it's often forgotten in the bank or ditched in the field for more bag space. You'll also need an anvil upon which to bang that hammer. Pull the Blacksmithing icon from your ability book (defaulted to "p") onto a hotbar and activate it. Your Blacksmithing menu pops up and shows all plans currently available.

Click on the name of the plan to see what components it requires. It shows you how many of each component you have in your bags and how many items of that plan you can make. It also gives you the option to make one or many in a row. Mouse over the icon of the item to see its stats.

Once you've made an item, it drops into your packs automatically. By level 250, it's difficult to find a trainer in a main city that can teach you anything new. However, by finding dropped patterns and hidden trainers, you can continue to progress in your craft. Some quests offer rewards for you also. These require you to craft certain items and, in return, they teach you new patterns. One of the quest lines leads you to the Mithril Order. It's not an easy quest chain, but the reward is the ability to craft a full suit of mithril plate armor!

Once you've attained a high enough skill level, you must choose a new path. Decide whether you wish to focus on weapons and carry the title Weaponsmith or become an Armorsmith. Both paths require quests and both are mutually exclusive. If you choose one path, the other is forever closed to this character. If become a Weaponsmith interests you, you may be interested to discover that an even more specialized choices await. The mutally exclusive Hammersmith, Swordsmith, and Axesmith titles are often required for the highest level weapon patterns.

Blacksmithing is not a very fast skill to increase. You're often sharing ore available to Engineers and they're not scarce. Other Blacksmiths also compete for available ore and gems in the auction houses. It's expensive to buy since the demand is so high. In the early stages, it doesn't seem that bad, but it gets worse.

It's not a get rich quick profession, but some of the high end items are truly impressive. Of course, it's because they are so difficult to make. Casual players can expect to either drop a good chunk of money on the resources or spend several weeks gather all the materials required. Take it slow and don't rush.

The good news is you can make some money. Every class needs something at a certain level. The market demands for Blacksmiths fill these gaps and this gives you that extra surge of cash you need. You won't sell most of what you make early on, but certain pieces sell like clean air in Gnomeregan.

Blacksmithing

TITLE/DESCRIPTION	REGION	GRID LOC	NAME
Armorsmith	Orgrimmar (60)	J-2	Okothos Ironrager
Armorsmith	Ironforge	F-4	Grumnus Steelshaper
Artisan Blacksmith	Ironforge (52)	G-4	Bengus Deepforge
Artisan Blacksmith	Orgrimmar (60)	J-2, K-2	Saru Steelfury
Artisan Blacksmith of the Mithril Order	Stranglethorn Vale (74)	F-2	Galvan the Ancient
Expert Blacksmith	Barrens (18)	F-3	Traugh
Expert Blacksmith	Duskwood (36)	J-5	Clarise Gnarltree
Expert Blacksmith	Ironforge (52)	G-4	Rotgath Stonebeard
Expert Blacksmith	Orgrimmar (60)	J-2	Snarl
Expert Blacksmith	Stormwind (72)	H-2	Therum Deepforge
Expert Blacksmith	Thunder Bluff (84)	D-6	Karn Stonehoof
Expert Blacksmith	Undercity (88)	I-3	James Van Brunt
Journeyman Blacksmith	Darkshore (24)	F-4	Delfrum Flintbeard
Journeyman Blacksmith	Dun Morogh (32)	F-5	Tognus Flintfire
Journeyman Blacksmith	Durotar (34)	H-4	Dwukk
Journeyman Blacksmith	Elwynn Forest (42)	E-6	Smith Argus
Journeyman Blacksmith	Ironforge (52)	G-4	Groum Stonebeard
Journeyman Blacksmith	Orgrimmar (60)	J-2	Ug'thok
Journeyman Blacksmith	Silverpine Forest (68)	F-4	Guillaume Sorouy
Journeyman Blacksmith	Stormwind (72)	I-2, J-2	Dane Lindgren
Journeyman Blacksmith	Thunder Bluff (84)	D-6	Thrag Stonehoof
Journeyman Blacksmith	Undercity (88)	H-3	Basil Frye
Master Blacksmith	Stranglethorn Vale (74)	C-8	Brikk Keencraft
Weaponsmith	Orgrimmar (60)	J-2	Borgosh Corebender
Weaponsmith	Ironforge	F-4	Ironus Coldsteel

ENCHANTING

This is probably the simplest profession and also the most expensive to master. Components are not gathered from the field or from the corpses of beasts; instead, you must disenchant items of worth. This, of course, implies that you must find or purchase the items to be disenchanted. Disenchanting destroys the original item and leaves you with components to be used plying your trade. Items of higher level or rarer quality disenchant into better materials.

Only the Good Stuff

Only items of Uncommon quality or higher (Rare, Epic, Legendary, etc.) can be disenchanted for resources. You're not going to be able to get anything from common items.

Nearly every magical item can be disenchanted. The difficult part about this method of resource gathering is that you really need to think twice about destroying some item. If an item was given to you from a quest and its soulbound, but you can't use it, the choice is still difficult. These items sell for a good bit. In the long run, enchanting can make up for the long and expensive trek to artisan.

If you are with a party while hunting that doesn't need a certain item, ask for it; you may find that your party is willing to let you have a great deal of items. It's a standard to see a guild Enchanter snagging anything that someone doesn't immediately need. The Enchanter needs to keep everyone's weapons glowing, but that's a fair trade for resources that are typically hard to come by.

To disenchant an item, open your ability book (defaulted to "p") and drag the Disenchant skill onto a hotbar. Activate the ability and then click on the item you wish to disenchant. Grab the items from the loot menu and continue.

Once you've obtained a reasonable supply of dust and shards, move the Enchanting icon onto your hotbar in a similar fashion. Activating the Enchanting skill brings up a window that shows all enchants you are currently proficient with.

Click any recipe to see the components required. To enchant an item, open your inventory (or have someone put an item in the "Will Not Be Traded" slot of the trade window). Activate the appropriate enchant and click on the item. Enchantments are permanent until replaced. If you wish to replace an enchantment, it erases the previous one in favor of the new one.

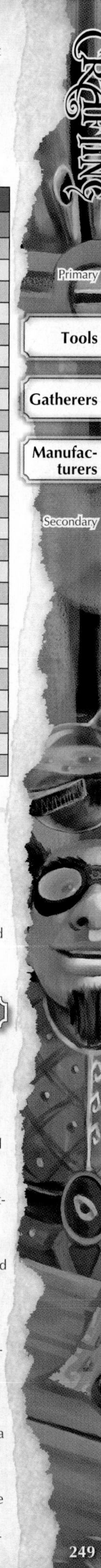

The quickest way to master this profession is to have friends willing to offer items that they don't need. Whether this is through a guild or just a group of players you've begun to hang out with, it's nice to be up front and explain to them that you've chosen the path of the Enchanter. Be generous with your services and you're certain to receive goodwill in kind.

Low-level Enchanters underbid one another to level up quickly. However, by the time they reach a level with solid enchantments that people crave, the prices skyrocket. The resources aren't cheap and the enchantments are permanent. Imagine two Warriors. Each has attained level 50 and they're wearing the same equipment, they've chosen the same talents and use their abilities in the same fashion. However, one has every possible item enchanted and the other is in unenchanted equipment. Who's going to win?

People are constantly trying to get the edge over the competition and enchantments are sure ways to do that. If you're planning on holding onto an item for a while, get it enchanted early on and really take advantage of it.

Enchanting

TITLE/DESCRIPTION	REGION	GRID LOC	NAME
Artisan Enchanter	Elwynn Forest (42)	I-7	Kitta Firewind
Artisan Enchanter	Stonetalon Mountains (70)	F-6	Hgarth
Expert Enchanter	Darnassus (26)	H-1	Taladan
Expert Enchanter	Feralas (46)	C-4	Xylinnia Starshine
Expert Enchanter	Ironforge (52)	H-4	Gimble Thistlefuzz
Expert Enchanter	Orgrimmar (60)	F-4	Godan
Expert Enchanter	Stormwind (72)	F-6	Lucan Cordell
Expert Enchanter	Thunder Bluff (84)	E-4	Teg Dawnstrider
Expert Enchanter	Undercity (88)	I-6	Lavinia Crowe
Journeyman Enchanter	Darnassus (26)	H-1	Lalina Summermoon
Journeyman Enchanter	Ironforge (52)	H-4	Thonys Pillarstone
Journeyman Enchanter	Orgrimmar (60)	F-4	Jhag
Journeyman Enchanter	Stormwind (72)	F-6	Betty Quin
Journeyman Enchanter	Teldrassil (80)	D-3	Alanna Raveneye
Journeyman Enchanter	Thunder Bluff (84)	E-4	Mot Dawnstrider
Journeyman Enchanter	Tirisfal Glades (86)	H-5	Vance Undergloom
Journeyman Enchanter	Undercity (88)	I-6	Malcomb Wynn
Master Enchanter	Badlands (16)	G-1	Annora

Items

Item	Skill Level	Source	Reagent(s)
Lesser Magic Wand	15	Trained	1 Simple Wood, 1 Lesser Magic Essence
Minor Wizard Oil	45	Found	1 Maple Seed, 1 Empty Via, l2 Strange Dust
Greater Magic Wand	70	Trained	1 Simple Wood, 1 Greater Magic Essence
Runed Silver Rod	100	Trained	1 Silver Rod, 6 Strange Dust, 3 Greater Magic Essence, 1 Shadowgem
Runed Golden Rod	150	Trained	1 Golden Rod, 1 Iridescent Pearl, 2 Greater Astral Essence, 2 Soul Dust
Lesser Mystic Wand	150	Trained	1 Star Wood, 1 Lesser Mystic Essence, 1 Soul Dust
Minor Mana Oil	150	Found	2 Maple Seed, 1 Leaded Vial, 3 Soul Dust
Greater Mystic Wand	175	Trained	1 Star Wood, 1 Greater Mystic Essence, 1 Vision Dust
Runed Truesilver Rod	200	Trained	1 Truesilver Rod, 1 Black Pearl, 2 Greater Mystic Essence, 2 Vision Dust
Lesser Wizard Oil	200	Found	2 Stranglethorn Seed, 1 Leaded Vial, 3 Vision Dust
Lesser Mana Oil	250	Found	2 Purple Lotus, 3 Dream Dust, 1 Crystal Vial
Smoking Heart of the Mountain	265	Found	1 Blood of the Mountain, 1 Essence of Fire, 3 Small Brilliant Shard
Wizard Oil	275	Found	2 Firebloom, 1 Crystal Vial, 3 Illusion Dust
Runed Arcanite Rod	290	Found	1 Arcanite Rod, 1 Golden Pearl, 2 Large Brilliant Shard, 4 Small Brilliant Shard, 4 Greater Eternal Essence, 10 Illusion Dust
Brilliant Wizard Oil	300	Found	3 Firebloom, 1 Imbued Vial, 2 Large Brilliant Shard
Brilliant Mana Oil	300	Found	3 Purple Lotus, 1 Imbued Vial, 2 Large Brilliant Shard

Enchantments

Enchantment	Skill Level	Source	Reagent(s)
Enchant Bracer - Minor Health	1	Trained	1 Strange Dust
Enchant Chest - Minor Health	1	Trained	1 Strange Dust
Enchant Bracer - Minor Deflect	10	Trained	1 Lesser Magic Essence, 1 Strange Dust
Enchant Chest - Minor Mana	20	Found	1 Lesser Magic Essence
Enchant Chest - Minor Absorption	40	Trained	1 Lesser Magic Essence, 2 Strange Dust
Enchant Cloak - Minor Resistance	45	Trained	2 Lesser Magic Essence, 1 Strange Dust
Journeyman Enchanting	50	Trained	
Enchant Bracer - Minor Stamina	50	Trained	2 Lesser Magic Essence, 3 Strange Dust
Enchant Chest - Lesser Health	60	Trained	2 Lesser Magic Essence, 2 Strange Dust
Enchant Bracer - Minor Spirit	60	Found	2 Lesser Magic Essence
Enchant Cloak - Minor Protection	70	Found	1 Greater Magic Essence, 3 Strange Dust
Enchant Bracer - Minor Strength	80	Trained	5 Strange Dust
Enchant Bracer - Minor Agility	80	Trained	1 Greater Magic Essence, 2 Strange Dust

Enchantments

Enchantment	Skill Level	Source	Reagent(s)
Enchant Chest - Lesser Mana	80	Found	1 Greater Magic Essence, 1 Lesser Magic Essence
Enchant Weapon - Minor Beast Slayer	90	Found	2 Greater Magic Essence, 4 Strange Dust
Enchant Weapon - Minor Striking	90	Trained	1 Small Glimmering Shard, 1 Greater Magic Essence, 2 Strange Dust
Enchant 2H Weapon - Lesser Intellect	100	Found	3 Greater Magic Essence
Enchant 2H Weapon - Minor Impact	100	Trained	1 Small Glimmering Shard, 4 Strange Dust
Enchant Shield - Minor Stamina	100	Trained	1 Lesser Astral Essence, 2 Strange Dust
Enchant 2H Weapon - Lesser Spirit	110	Found	1 Lesser Astral Essence, 6 Strange Dust
Enchant Cloak - Minor Agility	110	Found	1 Lesser Astral Essence
Enchant Cloak - Lesser Protection	115	Trained	1 Small Glimmering Shard, 6 Strange Dust
Enchant Shield - Lesser Protection	115	Found	1 Small Glimmering Shard, 1 Lesser Astral Essence, 1 Strange Dust
Enchant Bracer - Lesser Spirit	120	Found	2 Lesser Astral Essence
Enchant Chest - Health	120	Trained	1 Lesser Astral Essence, 4 Strange Dust
Expert Enchanting	125	Trained	
Enchant Boots - Minor Agility	125	Found	2 Lesser Astral Essence, 6 Strange Dust
Enchant Boots - Minor Stamina	125	Found	8 Strange Dust
Enchant Cloak - Lesser Fire Resistance	125	Trained	1 Fire Oil, 1 Lesser Astral Essence
Enchant Shield - Lesser Spirit	130	Trained	2 Lesser Astral Essence, 4 Strange Dust
Enchant Bracer - Lesser Stamina	130	Trained	2 Soul Dust
Enchant Cloak - Lesser Shadow Resist	135	Found	1 Shadow Protection Potion, 1 Greater Astral Essence
Enchant Weapon - Lesser Striking	140	Trained	1 Large Glimmering Shard, 2 Soul Dust
Enchant Bracer - Lesser Strength	140	Found	2 Soul Dust
Enchant Chest - Lesser Absorption	140	Trained	1 Large Glimmering Shard, 1 Greater Astral Essence, 2 Strange Dust
Enchant Gloves - Herbalism	145	Found	3 Kingsblood, 1 Sould Dust
Enchant Gloves - Fishing	145	Found	3 Blackmouth Oil, 1 Soul Dust
Enchant Gloves - Mining	145	Found	3 Iron Ore, 1 Soul Dust
Enchant 2H Weapon - Lesser Impact	145	Trained	1 Large Glimmering Shard, 3 Soul Dust
Enchant Chest - Mana	145	Trained	1 Greater Astral Essence, 2 Lesser Astral Essence
Enchant Bracer - Lesser Intellect	145	Trained	2 Greater Astral Essence
Enchant Chest - Minor Stats	150	Trained	1 Greater Astral Essence, 1 Large Glimmering Shard, 1 Soul Dust
Enchant Shield - Lesser Stamina	155	Trained	1 Lesser Mystic Essence, 1 Soul Dust
Enchant Cloak - Defense	155	Trained	1 Small Glowing Shard, 3 Soul Dust
Enchant Boots - Lesser Agility	160	Trained	1 Lesser Mystic Essence, 1 Soul Dust
Enchant Chest - Greater Health	160	Trained	3 Soul Dust
Enchant Bracer - Spirit	165	Trained	1 Lesser Mystic Essence
Enchant Boots - Lesser Stamina	170	Trained	4 Soul Dust
Enchant Bracer - Lesser Deflection	170	Found	1 Mystic Essence, 2 Soul Dust
Enchant Bracer - Stamina	170	Trained	6 Soul Dust
Enchant Weapon - Lesser Elemental Slayer	175	Found	1 Elemental Earth, 1 Small Glowing Shard, 1 Lesser Mystic Essence
Enchant Weapon - Lesser Beastslayer	175	Found	2 Large Fang, 1 Small Glowing Shard, 1 Lesser Mystic Essence
Enchant Cloak - Fire Resistance	175	Trained	1 Elemental Fire, 1 Lesser Mystic Essence
Enchant Shield - Spirit	180	Trained	1 Greater Mystic Essence, 1 Vision Dust
Enchant Bracer - Strength	180	Trained	1 Vision Dust
Enchant Chest - Greater Mana	185	Trained	1 Greater Mystic Essence
Enchant Boots - Lesser Spirit	190	Found	1 Greater Mystic Essence, 2 Lesser Mystic Essence
Enchant Weapon - Winter's Might	190	Found	2 Wintersbite, 1 Large Glowing Shard, 3 Greater Mystic Essence, 3 Vision Dust
Enchant Shield - Lesser Block	195	Found	1 Large Glowing Shard, 2 Greater Mystic Essence, 2 Vision Dust
Enchant Weapon - Striking	195	Trained	1 Large Glowing Shard, 2 Greater Mystic Essence
Artisan Enchanting	200	Trained	
Enchant 2H Weapon - Impact	200	Trained	1 Large Glowing Shard, 4 Vision Dust
Enchant Gloves - Skinning	200	Found	3 Green Whelp Scale, 1 Vision Dust
Enchant Chest - Lesser Stats	200	Trained	1 Large Glowing Shard, 2 Greater Mystic Essence, 2 Vision Dust
Enchant Cloak - Greater Defense	205	Trained	3 Vision Dust
Enchant Cloak - Resistance	205	Trained	1 Lesser Nether Essence
Enchant Shield - Stamina	210	Found	5 Vision Dust
Enchant Bracer - Intellect	210	Trained	2 Lesser Nether Essence
Enchant Gloves - Agility	210	Trained	1 Lesser Nether Essence, 1 Vision Dust
Enchant Gloves - Advanced Mining	215	Found	3 Truesilver Bar, 3 Vision Dust
Enchant Boots - Stamina	215	Trained	5 Vision Dust
Enchant Bracer - Greater Spirit	220	Found	3 Lesser Nether Essence, 1 Vision Dust
Enchant Chest - Superior Health	220	Trained	6 Vision Dust
Enchant Cloak - Lesser Agility	225	Found	2 Lesser Nether EssenceEnchantment
Enchant Gloves - Advanced Herbalism	225	Found	3 Sungrass, 3 Vision Dust
Enchant Gloves - Strength	225	Trained	2 Lesser Nether Essence, 3 Vision Dust
Enchant Boots - Minor Speed	225	Trained	1 Aquamarine, 1 Small Radiant Shard, 1 Lesser Nether Essence
Enchant Shield - Greater Spirit	230	Trained	1 Greater Nether Essence, 2 Dream Dust
Enchant Weapon - Demonslaying	230	Found	1 Elixir of Demonslaying, 1 Small Radiant Shard, 2 Dream Dust
Enchant Chest - Superior Mana	230	Trained	1 Greater Nether Essence, 2 Lesser Nether Essence
Enchant Boots - Agility	235	Trained	2 Greater Nether Essence
Enchant Shield - Frost Resistance	235	Found	1 Frost Oil, 1 Large Radiant Shard
Enchant Bracer - Deflection	235	Found	1 Greater Nether Essence, 2 Dream Dust
Enchant Bracer - Greater Strength	240	Trained	1 Greater Nether Essence, 2 Dream Dust
Enchant 2H Weapon - Greater Impact	240	Trained	2 Large Radiant Shard, 2 Dream Dust

Enchantments			
Enchantment	**Skill Level**	**Source**	**Reagent(s)**
Enchant Bracer - Greater Stamina	245	Found	3 Dream Dust
Enchant Chest - Stats	245	Trained	1 Large Radiant Shard, 1 Greater Nether Essence, 1 Dream Dust
Enchant Weapon - Greater Striking	245	Trained	2 Large Radiant Shard, 2 Greater Nether Essence
Enchanted Thorium	250	Trained	1 Thorium Bar, 3 Dream Dust
Enchanted Leather	250	Trained	1 Rugged Leather, 1 Lesser Nether Essence
Enchant Gloves - Minor Haste	250	Trained	2 Large Radiant Shard, 2 Wildvine
Enchant Gloves - Riding Skill	250	Found	2 Large Radiant Shard, 3 Dream Dust
Enchant Bracer - Greater Intellect	255	Found	3 Lesser Eternal Essence
Enchant Boots - Greater Stamina	260	Found	10 Dream Dust
Enchant Weapon - Fiery Weapon	265	Found	4 Large Radiant Shard, 1 Essence of Fire
Enchant Cloak - Greater Resistance	265	Found	1 Globe of Water, 1 Breath of Wind, 1 Ichor of Undeath, 1 Core of Earth, 1 Heart of Fire, 2 Lesser Eternal Essence
Enchant Shield - Greater Stamina	265	Found	10 Dream Dust
Enchant Bracer - Superior Spirit	270	Found	3 Lesser Eternal Essence, 10 Illusion Dust
Enchant Gloves - Greater Agility	270	Found	3 Lesser Eternal Essence, 3 Illusion Dust
Enchant Boots - Spirit	275	Found	2 Greater Eternal Essence, 1 Lesser Eternal Essence
Enchant Chest - Major Health	275	Found	1 Small Brilliant Shard, 6 Illusion Dust
Enchant Shield - Superior Spirit	280	Found	2 Greater Eternal Essence, 4 Illusion Dust
Enchant Weapon - Icy Chill	285	Found	1 Essence of Water, 1 Essence of Air, 1 Icecap, 4 Small Brilliant Shard
Enchant Cloak - Superior Defense	285	Found	8 Illusion Dust
Enchant Chest - Major Mana	290	Found	1 Small Brilliant Shard, 3 Greater Eternal Essence
Enchant Weapon - Strength	290	Found	2 Essence of Earth, 6 Large Brilliant Shard, 6 Greater Eternal Essence, 4 Illusion Dust
Enchant Weapon - Agility	290	Found	2 Essence of Air, 6 Large Brilliant Shard, 6 Greater Eternal Essence, 4 Illusion Dust
Enchant Bracer - Mana Regeration	290	Found	2 Essence of Water, 4 Greater Eternal Essence, 16 Illusion Dust
Enchant 2H Weapon - Agility	290	Found	4 Essence of Air, 10 Large Brilliant Shard, 6 Greater Eternal Essence, 14 Illusion Dust
Enchant Gloves - Greater Strength	295	Found	4 Greater Eternal Essence, 4 Illusion Dust
Enchant Boots - Greater Agility	295	Found	8 Greater Eternal Essence
Enchant Bracer - Superior Strength	295	Found	6 Greater Eternal Essence, 6 Illusion Dust
Enchant 2H Weapon - Superior Impact	295	Found	4 Large Brilliant Shard, 10 Illusion Dust
Enchant Weapon - Unholy Weapon	295	Found	4 Essence of Undeath, 4 Large Brilliant Shard
Enchant 2H Weapon - Major Intellect	300	Found	2 Large Brilliant Shard, 12 Greater Eternal Essence
Enchant Weapon - Superior Striking	300	Found	2 Large Brilliant Shard, 10 Greater Eternal Essence
Enchant Bracer - Superior Stamina	300	Found	15 Illusion Dust
Enchant Weapon - Crusader	300	Found	2 Righteous Orb, 4 Large Brilliant Shard
Enchant Chest - Greater Stats	300	Found	4 Large Brilliant Shard, 10 Greater Eternal Essence, 15 Illusion Dust
Enchant Weapon - Lifestealing	300	Found	6 Essence of Undeath, 6 Living Essence, 6 Large Brilliant Shard
Enchant 2H Weapon - Major Spirit	300	Found	2 Large Brilliant Shard, 12 Greater Eternal Essence
Enchant Weapon - Spell Power	300	Found	4 Essence of Fire, 4 Essence of Water, 4 Essence of Air, 2 Golden Pearl, 4 Large Brilliant Shard, 12 Greater Eternal Essence
Enchant Weapon - Healing Power	300	Found	6 Living Essence, 6 Essence of Water, 1 Righteous Orb, 4 Large Brilliant Shard, 8 Greater Eternal Essence
Enchant Bracer - Healing Power	300	Found	6 Living Essence, 2 Large Brilliant Shard, 4 Greater Eternal Essence, 20 Illusion Dust
Enchant Weapon - Mighty Spirit	300	Found	10 Large Brilliant Shard, 8 Greater Eternal Essence, 15 Illusion Dust
Enchant Weapon - Mighty Intellect	300	Found	15 Large Brilliant Shard, 12 Greater Eternal Essence, 20 Illusion Dust
Enchant Gloves - Threat	300	Found	8 Larvic Acid, 4 Nexus Crystal, 6 Large Brilliant Shard
Enchant Gloves - Shadow Power	300	Found	6 Essence of Undeath, 3 Nexus Crystal, 10 Large Brilliant Shard
Enchant Gloves - Frost Power	300	Found	4 Essence of Water, 3 Nexus Crystal, 10 Large Brilliant Shard
Enchant Gloves - Fire Power	300	Found	4 Essence of Fire, 2 Nexus Crystal, 10 Large Brilliant Shard
Enchant Gloves - Healing Power	300	Found	1 Righteous Orb, 3 Nexus Crystal, 8 Large Brilliant Shard
Enchant Gloves - Superior Agility	300	Found	4 Essence of Air, 3 Nexus Crystal, 8 Large Brilliant Shard
Enchant Cloak - Greater Fire Resistance	300	Found	4 Essence of Fire, 3 Nexus Crystal, 8 Large Brilliant Shard
Enchant Cloak - Greater Nature Resistance	300	Found	4 Living Essence, 2 Nexus Crystal, 8 Large Brilliant Shard
Enchant Cloak - Stealth	300	Found	2 Black Lotus, 3 Nexus Crystal, 8 Large Brilliant Shard
Enchant Cloak - Subtlety	300	Found	2 Black Diamond, 4 Nexus Crystal, 6 Large Brilliant Shard
Enchant Cloak - Dodge	300	Found	8 Guardian Stone, 3 Nexus Crystal, 8 Large Brilliant Shard

ENGINEERING

If you like toys, gadgets and things that go *boom,* become an Engineer. It's a great match if you've already chosen to be a Miner since you use a lot of stone and ore. Gems are also used in Engineering and miners have the greatest access to them. Engineers can create bombs, guns, pets that are cute, pets that attack, and pets that explode. It's definitely not a boring profession.

Snag the Engineering icon from your ability book (defaulted to "p") and place it on a hotbar. Activate it to bring up your Engineering window.

Click on the name of a schematic to see what components are needed, what tools are required, and how much you have in your inventory. You can also mouse over the item to see what it does before making it.

Click the "create" or "create all" button to make the item. It's put directly into your pack on creation.

Bombs and Dynamite: Right-click the icon if it's in your pack or use your hotbar for faster access. A green circle appears once you've activated it. Choose the area of effect and left-click to toss your creation into the world. **Pets:** Pets work from your pack or hotbar keys as well. Battle Chickens and Mithril Dragonlings fight alongside you for some time while Explosive Sheep run at the enemy and...explode.

Trinkets: Many items constructed at higher levels are trinkets. There are two trinket slots on your character screen (defaulted to "c"). Trinkets must be equipped to be used and can't be swapped during combat. Activate a trinket by clicking on it from your character screen or using a hotbar key. Trinkets have cooldowns varying from five minutes to an hour. If you have a lot of trinkets, it's best to switch them out as you use them. The time works whether it's equipped or in your bag. However, if you carry five of the same item, Battle Chickens for example, they have a shared cooldown. So, using one activates the timer on all of them. There's no need to have more that one of any trinket equipped at the same time.

At skill level 150, you must pick Goblin Engineering or Gnome Engineering. Goblins are more of the blow'em up type and gnomes love to make gadgets and trinkets. Either takes a quest to get and once you learn one, this character is forever locked out of the other.

Engineering is the anti-wealth skill. Just about everything you make can only be used by other Engineers and there's a good chance that they can make their own. Rare schematics are the only things that give you a bit of an edge over the competition. Hold onto those and try to get as much as you can from this career. This path is all about improving your character. You make bombs, pets, goggles, parachutes, lasers, and all kinds of things that blow up and burn. It's what the killers and PvPers like to use. You'll be broke, but you'll be a walking time bomb with a bag full of tricks to pull out for a multitude of reasons.

Engineering			
TITLE/DESCRIPTION	**REGION**	**GRID LOC**	**NAME**
Artisan Engineer	Ironforge (52)	I-4	Springspindle Fizzlegear
Artisan Engineer	Orgrimmar (60)	I-3, J-3	Roxxik
Expert Engineer	Duskwood (36)	K-5	Finbus Geargrind
Expert Engineer	Ironforge (52)	I-4	Trixie Quikswitch
Expert Engineer	Orgrimmar (60)	I-3, J-3	Nogg
Expert Engineer	Stormwind (72)	H-1	Lilliam Sparkspindle
Expert Engineer	Undercity (88)	K-7	Franklin Lloyd
Journeyman Engineer	Barrens (18)	H-4	Tinkerwiz
Journeyman Engineer	Darkshore (24)	F-4	Jenna Lemkenilli
Journeyman Engineer	Dun Morogh (32)	G-5	Bronk Guzzlegear
Journeyman Engineer	Durotar (34)	H-4	Mukdrak
Journeyman Engineer	Ironforge (52)	I-4	Jemma Quikswitch
Journeyman Engineer	Loch Modan (54)	F-1	Deek Fizzlebizz
Journeyman Engineer	Mulgore (58)	H-3	Twizwick Sprocketgrind
Journeyman Engineer	Orgrimmar (60)	I-3, J-3	Thund
Journeyman Engineer	Stormwind (72)	H-1	Sprite Jumpsprocket
Journeyman Engineer	Undercity (88)	K-7	Graham Van Talen
Master Engineer	Tanaris (78)	H-3	Buzzek Bracketswing
Master Gnome Engineer	Ironforge (52)	J-5	Tinkmaster Overspark
Master Gnome Engineer	Stranglethorn Vale (74)	B-8	Oglethorpe Obnoticus
Master Goblin Engineer	Barrens (18)	H-4	Vazario Linkgrease
Master Goblin Engineer	Tanaris (78)	H-3	Nixx Sprocketspring

LEATHERWORKING

Leather armor is something that many classes need desperately, especially early. Leatherworkers can gain access to mail armor at higher levels. Skinning, obviously, is a fantastic partner profession to have. Controlling your own resources is a great way to gain an edge over those wishing to buy from other players.

Open you ability book (defaulted to "p") and drag the Leatherworking icon onto a hotbar. Activating the ability brings up your Leatherworking screen. At first, you don't know much but that changes quickly. Click the name of a pattern to see how many of what components are required. Mousing over the item reveals the stats of the item.

Once you begin to make even the simplest of armor pieces, you'll need to visit your trainer often to learn new recipes. As your skill increases, the breadth of what you can craft increases and your ability to skill up slows.

You can create items one at a time or several one after another. Created items are automatically dropped into your packs.

At rank 225, you have three specialties to choose from; Tribal, Elemental, and Dragonscale. Each one requires a quest to learn and they are mutually exclusive. Once your character chooses one, they can never choose another. Tribal Leatherworking uses the special leathers taken from unusually creatures in the land. As the items are all leather, it's suited for Druids and Rogues most. Elemental Leatherworking harnesses the powers of the elementals running around the world. Also leather armor, Elemental Leatherworkers often sell their wares to Druids and Rogues. Dragonscale Leatherworking creates mail armor from the scaled beasts of the land and is generally sold to Shamans and Hunters, who at higher levels wear mail instead of leather armor.

Leatherworking combined with Skinning is a very intuitive and lucrative trade. You supply your trade by killing things you're already killing. There is no need to go out of your way for stray herbs or ore. While Leatherworkers are confined to armor, they can also make armor kits. These can be applied to any type of armor for the head, hands, chest, or legs slot and increase the armor of the item.

There another bonus to being a less-flashy profession. Chances are that when you're in a group, you'll be the only person collecting skins. Wearing the armor you make keeps you up to date and generally ahead of the curve until the late game. End game gear is hard to make and requires components that are difficult to find in large quantities.

Leatherworking

TITLE/DESCRIPTION	REGION	GRID LOC	NAME
Artisan Leatherworker	Darnassus (26)	I-2	Telonis
Artisan Leatherworker	Thunder Bluff (84)	D-4	Una
Expert Leathercrafter	Desolace (30)	G-6	Narv Hidecrafter
Expert Leatherworker	Ashenvale (12)	E-5	Aayndia Floralwind
Expert Leatherworker	Barrens (18)	F-6	Krulmoo Fullmoon
Expert Leatherworker	Darnassus (26)	I-2	Faldron
Expert Leatherworker	Ironforge (52)	E-3	Fimble Finespindle
Expert Leatherworker	Orgrimmar (60)	H-4	Karolek
Expert Leatherworker	Stormwind (72)	J-5	Simon Tanner
Expert Leatherworker	Stranglethorn Vale (74)	C-3	Brown
Expert Leatherworker	Thunder Bluff (84)	E-4	Tarn
Expert Leatherworker	Undercity (88)	I-6	Arthur Moore
Journeyman Leatherworker	Barrens (18)	E-4	Waldor
Journeyman Leatherworker	Barrens (18)	E-4	Waldor
Journeyman Leatherworker	Darnassus (26)	I-2	Darianna
Journeyman Leatherworker	Elwynn Forest (42)	F-6	Adele Fielder
Journeyman Leatherworker	Ironforge (52)	E-3	Gretta Finespindle
Journeyman Leatherworker	Mulgore (58)	E-6	Chaw Stronghide
Journeyman Leatherworker	Orgrimmar (60)	H-4	Kamari
Journeyman Leatherworker	Stormwind (72)	J-5	Randal Worth
Journeyman Leatherworker	Teldrassil (80)	E-5	Nadyia Maneweaver
Journeyman Leatherworker	Thunder Bluff (84)	D-4	Mak
Journeyman Leatherworker	Tirisfal Glades (86)	I-6	Shelene Rhobart
Journeyman Leatherworker	Undercity (88)	J-6	Dan Golthas
Master Dragonscale Leatherworker	Azshara (14)	D-6	Peter Galen
Master Dragonscale Leatherworker	Badlands (16)	I-6	Thorkaf Dragoneye
Master Elemental Leatherworker	Searing Gorge (64)	H-7	Sarah Tanner
Master Leatherworker	Feralas (46)	I-4	Hahrona Ironhide
Master Leatherworking Trainer	The Hinterlands (50)	B-4	Drakk Stonehand
Master Tribal Leatherworker	Stranglethorn Vale (74)	D-4	Se'Jib
Tribal Leatherworking Trainer	Feralas (46)	K-5	Caryssia Moonhunter

TAILORING

When people think of Tailors they immediately think of cloth armor. However, when a non-caster thinks of Tailors, they think of bags! Sure, Tailors make cloth armor and caster chase after them in droves trying to pick up some of the nicer equipment, but bags and cloaks are used by everyone.

Open your ability book (defaulted to "p") and drag the Tailoring icon onto a hotbar. Click or push the appropriate hotkey to activate the icon and open you Tailoring window.

Click on the name of a pattern to see what components are needed to create the item. It shows you how many of each component you have in your bags and how many items of the pattern you can create. It gives you the option to make one or many in a row. To see what the pattern makes, mouse over the icon and the item's statistics are shown. Once an item is made, it is automatically put into your packs.

There isn't a partner profession needed for Tailoring. The main supplies for this skill are cloth which is dropped by humanoid enemies. By killing humanoid mobs, which is inevitable, you build a supply of cloth. Tailors also buy a lot of thread and dye from the vendors however. These items cannot by found in the field, so be ready to put down some money whenever you want to make an item. Since Tailoring doesn't need a partner profession to gather materials, you can choose one of the other gathering professions and sell the harvest to make up the money you spend making items.

In addition to the obvious, Tailors learn several patterns that have little combat value and are strickly for role players. Tuxedos, dresses, shirts, and the like are all within the realm of learning for a Tailor.

Tailoring

TITLE/DESCRIPTION	REGION	GRID LOC	NAME
Artisan Tailor	Stormwind (72)	G-7	Georgio Bolero
Artisan Tailor	Undercity (88)	J-3	Josef Gregorian
Expert Tailor	Barrens (18)	F-6	Mahani
Expert Tailor	Darnassus (26)	H-2	Me'lynn
Expert Tailor	Ironforge (52)	F-3	Jormund Stonebrow
Expert Tailor	Orgrimmar (60)	H-5	Magar
Expert Tailor	Stormwind (72)	F-8	Sellandus
Expert Tailor	Stranglethorn Vale (74)	B-8	Grarnik Goodstitch
Expert Tailor	Thunder Bluff (84)	E-4	Tepa
Expert Tailor	Undercity (88)	J-3	Rhiannon Davis
Journeyman Tailor	Barrens (18)	F-3	Kil'hala
Journeyman Tailor	Darkshore (24)	F-4	Grondal Moonbreeze
Journeyman Tailor	Darnassus (26)	I-2	Trianna
Journeyman Tailor	Elwynn Forest (42)	K-7	Eldrin
Journeyman Tailor	Ironforge (52)	F-3	Uthrar Threx
Journeyman Tailor	Orgrimmar (60)	H-5	Snang
Journeyman Tailor	Stormwind (72)	G-7	Lawrence Schneider
Journeyman Tailor	Thunder Bluff (84)	E-4	Vhan
Journeyman Tailor	Tirisfal Glades (86)	G-5	Bowen Brisboise
Journeyman Tailor	Undercity (88)	J-3	Victor Ward
Master Shadoweave Tailor	Stormwind (72)	D-8	Jalane Ayrole
Master Shadoweave Tailor	Undercity (88)	L-2	Josephine Lister
Master Tailor	Dustwallow Marsh (38)	I-5	Timothy Worthington
Master Tailor	Hillsbrad Foothills (48)	H-2	Daryl Stack

SECONDARY SKILLS

Secondary skills have no restrictions on how many a player can learn. Anyone can learn them and they don't count against your maximum of two professions. So, if you wish to take all three, go nuts! These skills general reduce your downtime and/or help your cash flow.

COOKING

Raw meat is often found on the beasts of Azeroth. However, turning piles of flesh, legs, ribs, eggs, etc. into delicacies is the cook's advantage. The food that cooks create often heals at a better rate than store-bought food. In addition, it often gives a short statistic bonus if you eat enough. Animals drop all sorts of ingredients for the avid cook.

To use your Cooking skill, open you ability book (defaulted to "p") and drag the icon onto a hotbar. Open the Cooking menu by clicking on the icon or pushing the appropriate hotkey and see what recipes you've mastered.

Click on the name of a recipe to see what ingredients you need. It shows how many of each ingredient you currently possess in addition to how many of the item you can currently cook.

Finished food is placed in your packs automatically, but a fire is needed to make anything. Using fires you find in the world is convenient unless you happen to be in the middle of nowhere. Merchants sell Simple Wood and Flint and Tinder. You only need one Flint and Tinder, but you need one Simple Wood for each fire you create. This allows you to cook almost anywhere!

Cooking

TITLE/DESCRIPTION	NAME	REGION	GRID LOC
Butcher	Sherman Femmel	Redridge Mountains (62)	C-4
Butcher	Dirge Quikcleave	Tanaris (78)	H-3
Cook	Duhng	Barrens (18)	G-3
Cook	Tomas	Elwynn Forest (42)	F-7

Cooking			
TITLE/DESCRIPTION	NAME	REGION	GRID LOC
Cook	Pyall Silentstride	Mulgore (58)	E-6
Cook	Zarrin	Teldrassil (80)	G-6
Cooking Trainer	Alegorn	Darnassus (26)	F-2
Cooking Trainer	Cook Ghilm	Dun Morogh (32)	I-5
Cooking Trainer	Gremlock Pilsnor	Dun Morogh (32)	F-5
Cooking Trainer	Daryl Riknussun	Ironforge (52)	H-4
Cooking Trainer	Zamja	Orgrimmar (60)	G-5
Cooking Trainer	Crystal Boughman	Redridge Mountains (62)	B-4
Cooking Trainer	Stephen Ryback	Stormwind (72)	K-4
Cooking Trainer	Aska Mistrunner	Thunder Bluff (84)	F-5
Cooking Trainer	Eunice Burch	Undercity (88)	H-4, I-4
Recipe Trainer	Henry Stern	Barrens (18)	F-9
Superior Butcher	Slagg	Arathi Highlands (10)	J-3

FIRST AID

First Aid offers non-healers the opportunity to heal themselves and others. No, it's not as amazing as the magical healing abilities of the Priest, Druid, Shaman, or Paladin, but it's something! It's great for those non-healers while they're soloing or for a quick fix when your main healer goes down. Bandages of all types can heal wounds and lessen downtime. Also, Anti-Venom can cure poison and halt the steady assault on your health.

When you apply a bandage, it activates instantly, healing over time, wither 6 or 8 seconds. A character must wait 60 seconds after a bandage is applied before another can be used. First Aid is a stop gap or emergency measure and isn't intended to be the focus of a characters combat time. If you're hit at any time during the bandaging, the healing is stopped and you are left with the debuff. Bandaging the main tank usually doesn't do much because of this, but it can be the difference in a close fight.

Pull the First Aid icon from your ability book (defaulted to "p") onto a hotbar and activate it to open your First Aid window. Click on the item to see how much cloth is required to create the bandage and how many you can create presently. Bandages are automatically placed in your packs upon creation.

You never have enough cloth. There are times when you sell excess cloth only to run out of bandages the next day. Many players keep large quantities in their bank and several stacks on them at all times. Bandages are best used after a fight and perfect for soloing. Applying one right after a fight can keep you going endlessly with little downtime. Remember, if you get hit while applying a bandage, you lose the healing and retain the 60 second cooldown timer. Once you learn the next level of bandage and are pulling in enough of the required cloth, sell the old bandages.

To apply a bandage simply select the target you wish to heal (using F1 for you and F2-F5 for other party members is fast and easy) and push the hotkey you have the bandages set to. If you don't want to lose your current target and it's an enemy, you can activate the bandage then select your target.

First Aid			
TITLE/DESCRIPTION	NAME	REGION	GRID LOC
First Aid Trainer	Dannelor	Darnassus (26)	G-1
First Aid Trainer	Rawrk	Durotar (34)	H-4
First Aid Trainer	Nissa Firestone	Ironforge (52)	G-6
First Aid Trainer	Vira Younghoof	Mulgore (58)	E-6
First Aid Trainer	Arnok	Orgrimmar (60)	C-8
First Aid Trainer	Shaina Fuller	Stormwind (72)	F-3
First Aid Trainer	Byancie	Teldrassil (80)	G-6
First Aid Trainer	Pand Stonebinder	Thunder Bluff (84)	C-2
First Aid Trainer	Nurse Neela	Tirisfal Glades (86)	H-5
First Aid Trainer	Mary Edras	Undercity (88)	J-5
First Aid Trainer	Fremal Doohickey	Wetlands (96)	A-6
Physician	Thamner Pol	Dun Morogh (32)	F-5
Physician	Michelle Belle	Elwynn Forest (42)	F-7
Trauma Surgeon (First Aid)	Doctor Gregory Victor	Arathi Highlands (10)	J-4
Trauma Surgeon (First Aid)	Doctor Gustaf VonHowzen	Dustwallow Marsh (38)	I-5

FISHING

Fishing has two nice perks to it. The general ability is to catch fish. Fish can be cooked into some useful foods. It's great for Hunters with pets that eat fish. Some skills, like Alchemy, use certain types of fish in their recipes.

The second ability is the possibility of hauling up clams, boxes, chests, and mollusks. These can have items of worth or gems within and are quite a find!

Open your ability book (defaulted to "p") and drag the Fishing icon onto a hotbar. Equip your fishing pole (these can be bought at many vendors and stronger poles can be found or given as quest rewards). Move to a body of water and use the Fishing ability.

Fishing			
TITLE/DESCRIPTION	NAME	REGION	GRID LOC
Artisan Fisherman	Nat Pagle	Dustwallow Marsh (38)	H-6
Butcher	Sherman Femmel	Redridge Mountains (62)	C-4
Fisherman	Kil'Hiwana	Ashenvale (12)	B-4
Fisherman	Kilxx	Barrens (18)	H-4
Fisherman	Zizzek	Barrens (18)	H-4
Fisherman	Heldan Galesong	Darkshore (24)	E-6
Fisherman	Lui'Mala	Desolace (30)	B-7
Fisherman	Paxton Ganter	Dun Morogh (32)	E-4
Fisherman	Lau'Tiki	Durotar (34)	H-8
Fisherman	Lee Brown	Elwynn Forest (42)	F-6
Fisherman	Brannock	Feralas (46)	C-4
Fisherman	Donald Rabonne	Hillsbrad Foothills (48)	F-6
Fisherman	Warg Deepwater	Loch Modan (54)	E-4
Fisherman	Uthan Stillwater	Mulgore (58)	E-6
Fisherman	Androl Oakhand	Teldrassil (80)	G-9
Fisherman	Clyde Kellen	Tirisfal Glades (86)	I-5
Fishing Trainer	Astaia	Darnassus (26)	F-5
Fishing Trainer	Grimnur Stonebrand	Ironforge (52)	F-1
Fishing Trainer	Lumak	Orgrimmar (60)	I-3
Fishing Trainer	Matthew Hooper	Redridge Mountains (62)	C-5
Fishing Trainer	Arnold Leland	Stormwind (72)	G-6
Fishing Trainer	Kah Mistrunner	Thunder Bluff (84)	F-5
Fishing Trainer	Armand Cromwell	Undercity (88)	K-3
Fishing Trainer	Harold Riggs	Wetlands (96)	A-6
Superior Fisherman	Myizz Luckycatch	Stranglethorn Vale (74)	B-8

Fishing Poles			
M Lev	Weapon Name	Vendor Value	Notes
1	Fishing Pole	4	
1	Blump Family Fishing Pole	1 87	Fishing Skill +3
5	Strong Fishing Pole	1 80	Fishing Skill +5
15	Darkwood Fishing Pole	10 66	Fishing Skill +15
25	Big Iron Fishing Pole	33 78	Fishing Skill +20

You cast line and bobber into the water and wait. Keep your mouse hovering over the bobber and wait for a fish to bite (this is shown by the bobber...bobbing). Click on the bobber to reel in your catch. If you were successful, your bounty shows in a loot window.

Fishing Poles Don't Make Good Weapons

Be sure to equip your weapons before going into combat. This can happen if an enemy comes upon you while fishing or if you simply move onto other activities. Hitting someone with a Fishing Pole, while funny, isn't effective.

Fresh and ocean waters have different types of fish as do some of the rare ponds and lakes in Azeroth. The best way to skill up is to fish in areas where your character can defeat the enemies. This keeps you fishing in areas where you can succeed and allows you to defend yourself if a monster wanders too close. Purchasing and using lures can temporary increase you fishing skill to make transitioning into a new area easier.

Lures					
Skill Required	Name	Fishing Bonus	Obtained	Cost	
0	Shiny Bauble	25	Vendor		50
50	Nightcrawlers	50	Vendor	1	
100	Bright Baubles	75	Vendor	2	50
100	Aquadynamic Fish Attractor	100	Engineering	N/A	

To use a lure, open your inventory. Right click on the lure and then left click on your fishing pole. Lures only last a certain length of time, but your skill can be greatly increased by these.

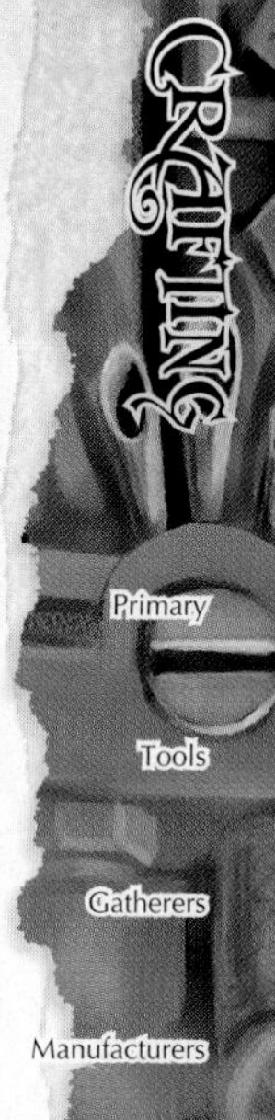

QUEST

Alterac Mountains

Title	Location	Faction	Min Level	Con Level	Starter Location	Finisher	Prerequisite	Max XP	Cash Reward
Taretha's Gift	Alterac Mountains	Horde	29	40	Elysa—Loch Modan	Krusk	Lord Aliden Perenolde	3900	
CHOICE OF: 1 Mantis Boots or 1 Brigand's Pauldrons									
Valik	Alterac Mountains	Horde	29	34	Henchman Valik—Alterac Mountains Sofera's Naze	Henchman Valik		270	
REWARD: 1 Syndicate Missive									
The Ensorcelled Parchment	Alterac Mountains	Alliance	30	40	Ensorcelled Parchment	Loremaster Dibbs		775	
Frostmaw	Alterac Mountains	Horde	26	37	Melor Stonehoof—Thunder Bluff	Melor Stonehoof	Steelsnap	4250	
REWARD: 1 Spirit Hunter Headdress									
You're a Mean One...	Alterac Mountains	Horde	30	60	Strange Snowman—Alterac Mountains	Kaymard Copperpinch	Stolen Winter Veil Treats	3300	
You're a Mean One...	Alterac Mountains	Alliance	30	60	Strange Snowman—Alterac Mountains	Wulmort Jinglepocket	Stolen Winter Veil Treats	3300	

Alterac Valley - BG

Title	Location	Faction	Min Level	Con Level	Starter Location	Finisher	Prerequisite	Max XP	Cash Reward
Irondeep Supplies	Alterac Valley - Alliance	Alliance	51	55	Stormpike Quartermaster—Alterac Valley	Stormpike Quartermaster			40●
Coldtooth Supplies	Alterac Valley - Horde	Alliance	51	55	Stormpike Quartermaster—Alterac Valley	Stormpike Quartermaster			40●
More Armor Scraps	Alterac Valley - Alliance	Alliance	51	60		Murgot Deepforge	Armor Scraps		
Begin the Attack!	Alterac Valley - Alliance	Alliance	1	60		Field Marshal Teravaine			
Ivus the Forest Lord	Alterac Valley - Alliance	Alliance	51	60		Arch Druid Renferal			
Call of Air - Vipore's Fleet	Alterac Valley - Alliance	Alliance	51	60		Wing Commander Vipore			
Call of Air - Slidore's Fleet	Alterac Valley - Alliance	Alliance	51	60		Wing Commander Slidore			
Call of Air - Ichman's Fleet	Alterac Valley - Alliance	Alliance	51	60		Wing Commander Ichman			
Ram Riding Harnesses	Alterac Valley - Alliance	Alliance	51	60		Stormpike Ram Rider Commander			
Empty Stables	Alterac Valley - Alliance	Alliance	51	60	Stormpike Stable Master—Alterac Valley	Stormpike Stable Master			
Alterac Valley Graveyards	Alterac Valley - Alliance	Alliance	51	60	Sergeant Durgen Stormpike—Alterac Valley	Sergeant Durgen Stormpike		6600	90●
Towers and Bunkers	Alterac Valley - Alliance	Alliance	51	60	Sergeant Durgen Stormpike—Alterac Valley	Sergeant Durgen Stormpike		6600	90●
The Quartermaster	Alterac Valley - Alliance	Alliance	51	60	Mountaineer Boombellow—Alterac Valley	Stormpike Quartermaster		650	
Capture a Mine	Alterac Valley - Alliance	Alliance	51	60	Sergeant Durgen Stormpike—Alterac Valley	Sergeant Durgen Stormpike		6600	90●
The Battle of Alterac	Alterac Valley - Alliance	Alliance	51	60	Prospector Stonehewer—Alterac Valley	Prospector Stonehewer		9950	2●70●
Proving Grounds	Alterac Valley - Alliance	Alliance	51	60	Lieutenant Haggerdin—Alterac Valley	Lieutenant Haggerdin		6600	
REWARD: 1 Stormpike Insignia Rank 1, 1The Frostwolf Artichoke									
Rise and Be Recognized	Alterac Valley - Alliance	Alliance	51	60		Lieutenant Haggerdin	Proving Grounds	6600	
REWARD: 1 Stormpike Insignia Rank 2									
Honored Amongst the Guard	Alterac Valley - Alliance	Alliance	51	60		Lieutenant Haggerdin	Rise and Be Recognized	6600	
REWARD: 1 Stormpike Insignia Rank 3									
Earned Reverence	Alterac Valley - Alliance	Alliance	51	60		Lieutenant Haggerdin	Honored Amongst the Guard	8300	
REWARD: 1 Stormpike Insignia Rank 4									
Legendary Heroes	Alterac Valley - Alliance	Alliance	51	60		Lieutenant Haggerdin	Earned Reverence	9950	
REWARD: 1 Stormpike Insignia Rank 5									
The Eye of Command	Alterac Valley - Alliance	Alliance	51	60		Lieutenant Haggerdin	Legendary Heroes	9950	
REWARD: 1 Stormpike Insignia Rank 6									
Armor Scraps	Alterac Valley - Alliance	Alliance	51	60	Murgot Deepforge—Alterac Valley	Murgot Deepforge		6600	
The Sovereign Imperative	Alterac Valley - Alliance	Alliance	51	60	Lieutenant Rotimer—Ironforge	Lieutenant Haggerdin		6600	
Brotherly Love	Alterac Valley - Alliance	Alliance	51	60	Commander Karl Philips—Alterac Valley	Commander Karl Philips		6600	
Fallen Sky Lords	Alterac Valley - Alliance	Alliance	51	60	Commander Duffy—Alterac Valley	Commander Duffy		6600	
Crystal Cluster	Alterac Valley - Alliance	Alliance	51	60		Arch Druid Renferal			
Hero of the Stormpike	Alterac Valley - Alliance	Alliance	51	60		Prospector Stonehewer	The Battle of Alterac	650	
CHOICE OF: 1 Bloodseeker or 1 Ice Barbed Spear or 1 Wand of Biting Cold or 1 Cold Forged Hammer									
More Booty!	Alterac Valley - Horde	Horde	51	60		Smith Regzar	Enemy Booty		
Lokholar the Ice Lord	Alterac Valley - Horde	Horde	51	60		Primalist Thurloga			
Call of Air - Guse's Fleet	Alterac Valley - Horde	Horde	51	60		Wing Commander Guse			
Call of Air - Jeztor's Fleet	Alterac Valley - Horde	Horde	51	60		Wing Commander Jeztor			
Call of Air - Mulverick's Fleet	Alterac Valley - Horde	Horde	51	60		Wing Commander Mulverick			
Launch the Attack!	Alterac Valley - Horde	Horde	1	60		Warmaster Garrick			
Coldtooth Supplies	Alterac Valley - Alliance	Horde	51	55	Frostwolf Quartermaster—Alterac Valley	Frostwolf Quartermaster			85●
Irondeep Supplies	Alterac Valley - Horde	Horde	51	55	Frostwolf Quartermaster—Alterac Valley	Frostwolf Quartermaster			85●
Empty Stables	Alterac Valley - Horde	Horde	51	60	Frostwolf Stable Master—Alterac Valley	Frostwolf Stable Master			
Ram Hide Harnesses	Alterac Valley - Horde	Horde	51	60		Frostwolf Wolf Rider Commander			
The Graveyards of Alterac	Alterac Valley - Horde	Horde	51	60	Corporal Teeka Bloodsnarl—Alterac Valley	Corporal Teeka Bloodsnarl		6600	90●
Towers and Bunkers	Alterac Valley - Horde	Horde	51	60	Corporal Teeka Bloodsnarl—Alterac Valley	Corporal Teeka Bloodsnarl		6600	90●
Speak with our Quartermaster	Alterac Valley - Horde	Horde	51	60	Jotek—Alterac Valley	Frostwolf Quartermaster		650	85●
Capture a Mine	Alterac Valley - Horde	Horde	51	60	Frostwolf Quartermaster—Alterac Valley	Corporal Teeka Bloodsnarl		6600	1●80●
The Battle for Alterac	Alterac Valley - Horde	Horde	51	60	Voggah Deathgrip—Alterac Valley	Voggah Deathgrip		9950	2●70●
Proving Grounds	Alterac Valley - Horde	Horde	51	60	Warmaster Laggrond—Alterac Valley	Warmaster Laggrond		6600	
REWARD: 1 Frostwolf Insignia Rank 1, 1Peeling the Onion									
Rise and Be Recognized	Alterac Valley - Horde	Horde	51	60		Warmaster Laggrond	Proving Grounds	6600	
REWARD: 1 Frostwolf Insignia Rank 2									
Honored Amongst the Clan	Alterac Valley - Horde	Horde	51	60		Warmaster Laggrond	Rise and Be Recognized	6600	
REWARD: 1 Frostwolf Insignia Rank 3									
Earned Reverence	Alterac Valley - Horde	Horde	51	60		Warmaster Laggrond	Honored Amongst the Clan	8300	
REWARD: 1 Frostwolf Insignia Rank 4									
Legendary Heroes	Alterac Valley - Horde	Horde	51	60		Warmaster Laggrond	Earned Reverence	9950	
REWARD: 1 Frostwolf Insignia Rank 5									
The Eye of Command	Alterac Valley - Horde	Horde	51	60		Warmaster Laggrond	Legendary Heroes	9950	
REWARD: 1 Frostwolf Insignia Rank 6									
Enemy Booty	Alterac Valley - Horde	Horde	51	60	Smith Regzar—Alterac Valley	Smith Regzar		6600	
In Defense of Frostwolf	Alterac Valley - Horde	Horde	51	60	Frostwolf Ambassador Rokhstrom—Orgrimmar	Warmaster Laggrond		6600	
Brotherly Love	Alterac Valley - Horde	Horde	51	60	Commander Louis Philips—Alterac Valley	Commander Louis Philips		6600	
Fallen Sky Lords	Alterac Valley - Horde	Horde	51	60	Commander Mulfort—Alterac Valley	Commander Mulfort		6600	
A Gallon of Blood	Alterac Valley - Horde	Horde	51	60		Primalist Thurloga			
Hero of the Frostwolf	Alterac Valley - Horde	Horde	51	60		Voggah Deathgrip	The Battle for Alterac	650	
CHOICE OF: 1 Bloodseeker or 1 Ice Barbed Spear or 1 Wand of Biting Cold or 1 Cold Forged Hammer									

Arathi Basin - BG

Title	Location	Faction	Min Level	Con Level	Starter Location	Finisher	Prerequisite	Max XP	Cash Reward
The Battle for Arathi Basin!	Arathi Basin	Alliance	50	55	Field Marshal Oslight—Arathi Highlands Refuge Pointe Humanoid	Field Marshal Oslight		5650	1●65●
Control Four Bases	Arathi Basin	Alliance	60	60	Field Marshal Oslight—Arathi Highlands Refuge Pointe Humanoid	Field Marshal Oslight	The Battle for Arathi Basin!	9950	2●70●
Control Five Bases	Arathi Basin	Alliance	60	60	Field Marshal Oslight—Arathi Highlands Refuge Pointe Humanoid	Field Marshal Oslight	Control Four Bases	9950	2●70●
REWARD: 1 Arathor Battle Tabard									
The Battle for Arathi Basin!	Arathi Basin	Horde	50	55	Deathmaster Dwire—Arathi Highlands	Deathmaster Dwire		5650	1●65●
Take Four Bases	Arathi Basin	Horde	60	60	Deathmaster Dwire—Arathi Highlands	Deathmaster Dwire	The Battle for Arathi Basin!	9950	2●70●
Take Five Bases	Arathi Basin	Horde	60	60	Deathmaster Dwire—Arathi Highlands	Deathmaster Dwire	Take Four Bases	9950	2●70●
REWARD: 1 Battle Tabard of the Defilers									
The Battle for Arathi Basin!	Arathi Basin	Alliance	40	45	Field Marshal Oslight—Arathi Highlands Refuge Pointe Humanoid	Field Marshal Oslight		3900	1●30●
The Battle for Arathi Basin!	Arathi Basin	Alliance	30	35	Field Marshal Oslight—Arathi Highlands Refuge Pointe Humanoid	Field Marshal Oslight		2750	75●
The Battle for Arathi Basin!	Arathi Basin	Alliance	20	25	Field Marshal Oslight—Arathi Highlands Refuge Pointe Humanoid	Field Marshal Oslight		2000	35●
The Battle for Arathi Basin!	Arathi Basin	Horde	40	45	Deathmaster Dwire—Arathi Highlands	Deathmaster Dwire		3900	1●30●

Title	Location	Faction	Min Level	Con Level	Starter Location	Finisher	Prerequisite	Max XP	Cash Reward
The Battle for Arathi Basin!	Arathi Basin	Horde	30	35	Deathmaster Dwire—Arathi Highlands	Deathmaster Dwire		2750	75
The Battle for Arathi Basin!	Arathi Basin	Horde	20	25	Deathmaster Dwire—Arathi Highlands	Deathmaster Dwire		2000	35
Sigil of Strom	Arathi Highlands	Horde	32	37	Zengu—Arathi Highlands Hammerfall	Zengu		2850	40
The Broken Sigil	Arathi Highlands	Horde	32	40	Zengu—Arathi Highlands Hammerfall	Tor'gan	Sigil of Strom	3150	50
Sigil of Thoradin	Arathi Highlands	Horde	32	40	Tor'gan—Arathi Highlands Hammerfall	Zengu	The Broken Sigil	320	
The Princess Trapped	Arathi Highlands	Both	30	37	Shards of Myzrael— Arathi	Iridescent Shards		2850	
Sigil of Arathor	Arathi Highlands	Horde	32	41	Zengu—Arathi Highlands Hammerfall	Zengu	Sigil of Thoradin	3300	55
Sigil of Trollbane	Arathi Highlands	Horde	32	42	Zengu—Arathi Highlands Hammerfall	Zengu	Sigil of Arathor	3450	55
Trol'kalar	Arathi Highlands	Horde	32	42	Zengu—Arathi Highlands Hammerfall	Trollbane's Tomb	Sigil of Trollbane	850	
Trol'kalar	Arathi Highlands	Horde	32	42	Trollbane's Tomb— Arathi	Zengu	Trol'kalar	4300	
CHOICE OF: 1 Blood-tinged Armor or 1 Pit Fighter's Shield									
Stones of Binding	Arathi Highlands	Both	30	38	Shards of Myzrael— Arathi	Stone of Inner Binding	The Princess Trapped	2850	
Breaking the Keystone	Arathi Highlands	Both	30	42	Iridescent Shards— Arathi	Keystone	Stones of Binding	3450	
Myzrael's Allies	Arathi Highlands	Alliance	30	40	Shards of Myzrael— Arathi	Gerrig Bonegrip	Breaking the Keystone	2350	
Hammerfall	Arathi Highlands	Horde	29	34	Gor'mul—Arathi Highlands Hammerfall	Tor'gan		270	
Summoning the Princess	Arathi Highlands	Both	30	50	Theldurin the Lost—Badlands	Shards of Myzrael	The Lost Fragments	7100	
REWARD: 1 Pulsating Crystalline Shard									
Hints of a New Plague?	Arathi Highlands	Alliance	30	36	Quae—Arathi Highlands Go'Shek Farm	Kinelory	Hints of a New Plague?		
Hints of a New Plague?	Arathi Highlands	Alliance	30	36	Quae—Arathi Highlands Go'Shek Farm	Quae	Hints of a New Plague?	2800	
Hints of a New Plague?	Arathi Highlands	Alliance	30	33	Phin Odelic—Hillsbrad Southshore	Quae		1300	
Hints of a New Plague?	Arathi Highlands	Alliance	30	37	Kinelory—Arathi Highlands Go'Shek Farm	Quae	Hints of a New Plague?	2850	
Hints of a New Plague?	Arathi Highlands	Alliance	30	37	Quae—Arathi Highlands Go'Shek Farm	Phin Odelic	Hints of a New Plague?	3350	
CHOICE OF: 1 Dustfall Robes or 1 Lightstep Leggings									
Deep Sea Salvage	Arathi Highlands	Both	35	40	First Mate Nilzlix—Arathi Highlands Faldir's Cove	First Mate Nilzlix	Land Ho!	3150	
REWARD: 1 Black Water Hammer									
Land Ho!	Arathi Highlands	Both	35	35	Lolo the Lookout—Arathi Highlands Faldir's Cove	Shakes O'Breen		700	
Drowned Sorrows	Arathi Highlands	Both	35	40	Captain Steelgut—Arathi Highlands Faldir's Cove	Captain Steelgut	Land Ho!	3150	
REWARD: 1 Seawolf Gloves									
Sunken Treasure	Arathi Highlands	Both	35	40	Professor Phizzlethorpe—Arathi Highlands Faldir's Cove	Doctor Draxlegauge	Land Ho!	3150	
Sunken Treasure	Arathi Highlands	Both	35	40	Doctor Draxlegauge—Arathi Highlands Faldir's Cove	Doctor Draxlegauge	Sunken Treasure	3900	
CHOICE OF: 1 Gnomish Zapper or 1 Servomechanic Sledgehammer									
Death From Below	Arathi Highlands	Both	35	44	Shakes O'Breen—Arathi Highland Faldir's Cove Monster Human	Shakes O'Breen	Sunken Treasure	4650	
CHOICE OF: 1 Coldwater Ring or 1 Seafire Band									
Sunken Treasure	Arathi Highlands	Both	35	40	Doctor Draxlegauge—Arathi Highlands Faldir's Cove	Shakes O'Breen	Sunken Treasure	1550	
Sunken Treasure	Arathi Highlands	Both	35	40	Shakes O'Breen—Arathi Highland Faldir's Cove Monster Human	Fleet Master Seahorn	Sunken Treasure	3150	
Sunken Treasure	Arathi Highlands	Both	35	40	Fleet Master Seahorn—Stranglethorn Booty Bay	Shakes O'Breen	Sunken Treasure	3150	
Foul Magics	Arathi Highlands	Horde	30	33	Tor'gan—Arathi Highlands Hammerfall	Tor'gan		2650	
Raising Spirits	Arathi Highlands	Horde	29	34	Tor'gan—Arathi Highlands Hammerfall	Tor'gan	Hammerfall	2700	
Foul Magics	Arathi Highlands	Horde	35	40	Tor'gan—Arathi Highlands Hammerfall	Tor'gan	Foul Magics	3150	
CHOICE OF: 1 White Drakeskin Cap or 1 Radiant Silver Bracers									
Raising Spirits	Arathi Highlands	Horde	29	34	Tor'gan—Arathi Highlands Hammerfall	Gor'mul	Raising Spirits	270	
Raising Spirits	Arathi Highlands	Horde	29	34	Gor'mul—Arathi Highlands Hammerfall	Tor'gan	Raising Spirits	270	
Call to Arms	Arathi Highlands	Horde	30	32	Drum Fel—Arathi Highlands Hammerfall	Drum Fel		2550	
Call to Arms	Arathi Highlands	Horde	30	38	Drum Fel—Arathi Highlands Hammerfall	Drum Fel	Call to Arms	2850	
Call to Arms	Arathi Highlands	Horde	30	40	Drum Fel—Arathi Highlands Hammerfall	Drum Fel	Call to Arms	3150	50
CHOICE OF: 1 Silent Hunter or 1 Skullsplitter									
The Real Threat	Arathi Highlands	Horde	30	40	Korin Fel—Arathi Highlands Hammerfall	Korin Fel	Call to Arms	3900	
CHOICE OF: 1 Mistspray Kilt or 1 Sword of Hammerfall									
Northfold Manor	Arathi Highlands	Alliance	30	31	Captain Nials—Arathi Highlands Refuge Pointe	Captain Nials		2500	
Stromgarde Badges	Arathi Highlands	Alliance	30	37	Captain Nials—Arathi Highlands Refuge Pointe	Captain Nials	Northfold Manor	3550	
REWARD: 1 Stromgarde Cavalry Leggings									
Wanted! Marez Cowl	Arathi Highlands	Alliance	30	39	Wanted Board— Arathi Highlands Refuge Pointe	Captain Nials		3750	
REWARD: 1 Arcane Runed Bracers									
Wanted! Otto and Falconcrest	Arathi Highlands	Alliance	30	40	Wanted Board— Arathi Highlands Refuge Pointe	Captain Nials		3900	
CHOICE OF: 1 Rod of Sorrow or 1 War Rider Bracers									
Myzrael's Allies	Arathi Highlands	Horde	30	40	Stone Circle, Key—Arathi	Zaruk	Breaking the Keystone	2350	
Malin's Request	Arathi Highlands	Alliance	30	32	Archmage Malin—Stormwind	Skuerto	Worth Its Weight in Gold	1950	
Worth Its Weight in Gold	Arathi Highlands	Alliance	30	36	Apprentice Kryten—Arathi Highlands Refuge Pointe	Apprentice Kryten		3500	75
The Lost Fragments	Arathi Highlands	Both	30	41	Theldurin the Lost—Badlands	Theldurin the Lost	Theldurin the Lost	3300	
Wand over Fist	Arathi Highlands	Alliance	30	39	Skuerto—Arathi Highlands Refuge Pointe	Skuerto	Worth Its Weight in Gold	3000	
Trelane's Defenses	Arathi Highlands	Alliance	30	39	Skuerto—Arathi Highlands Refuge Pointe	Apprentice Kryten	Wand over Fist	3000	
An Apprentice's Enchantment	Arathi Highlands	Alliance	30	39	Apprentice Kryten—Arathi Highlands Refuge Pointe	Skuerto	Trelane's Defenses	300	
Attack on the Tower	Arathi Highlands	Alliance	30	39	Skuerto—Arathi Highlands Refuge Pointe	Skuerto	An Apprentice's Enchantment	3000	
Malin's Request	Arathi Highlands	Alliance	30	39	Skuerto—Arathi Highlands Refuge Pointe	Archmage Malin	Attack on the Tower	3750	90
CHOICE OF: 1 Vigilant Buckler or 1 Wingborne Boots									
Guile of the Raptor	Arathi Highlands	Horde	29	37	Tor'gan—Arathi Highlands Hammerfall	Tor'gan	Raising Spirits	2850	
Guile of the Raptor	Arathi Highlands	Horde	29	37	Tor'gan—Arathi Highlands Hammerfall	Gor'mul	Guile of the Raptor	290	
Guile of the Raptor	Arathi Highlands	Horde	29	37	Gor'mul—Arathi Highlands Hammerfall	Tor'gan	Guile of the Raptor	2850	
REWARD: 1 Call of the Raptor									
Elemental Leatherworking	Arathi Highlands	Horde	40	55	Brumn Winterhoof—Arathi Highlands	Brumn Winterhoof	Dragonscale Leatherworking	4200	
Triage	Arathi Highlands	Horde	35	45	Doctor Gregory Victor—Arathi	Doctor Gregory Victor		3900	
Arathor Basic Care Package	Arathi Highlands	Alliance	25	34		Samuel Hawke		270	
REWARD: 1 Arathor Basic Care Package									
Arathor Standard Care Package	Arathi Highlands	Alliance	35	44		Samuel Hawke		380	
REWARD: 1 Arathor Standard Care Package									
Arathor Advanced Care Package	Arathi Highlands	Alliance	45	60		Samuel Hawke		650	
REWARD: 1 Arathor Advanced Care Package									
Defiler's Basic Care Package	Arathi Highlands	Horde	25	34		Rutherford Twing		270	
REWARD: 1 Defiler's Basic Care Package									
Defiler's Standard Care Package	Arathi Highlands	Horde	35	44		Rutherford Twing		380	
REWARD: 1 Defiler's Standard Care Package									
Defiler's Advanced Care Package	Arathi Highlands	Horde	45	60		Rutherford Twing		650	
REWARD: 1 Defiler's Advanced Care Package									
Sharptalon's Claw	Ashenvale	Horde	20	30	Sharptalon's Claw	Senani Thunderheart	The Ashenvale Hunt	2450	
Ursangous's Paw	Ashenvale	Horde	20	24	Ursangous's Paw	Senani Thunderheart	The Ashenvale Hunt	1950	
Shadumbra's Head	Ashenvale	Horde	20	27	Shadumbra's Head	Senani Thunderheart	The Ashenvale Hunt	2200	
Stonetalon Standstill	Ashenvale	Horde	23	25	Mastok Wrilehiss—Ashenvale	Mastok Wrilehiss		2000	18
Between a Rock and a Thistlefur	Ashenvale	Horde	21	24	Karang Amakkar—Ashenvale	Karang Amakkar		1950	17
The Hunt Completed	Ashenvale	Horde	20	30		Senani Thunderheart	Ursangous's Paw	3050	
REWARD: 1 Wildhunter Cloak									
Je'neu of the Earthen Ring	Ashenvale	Horde	23	27	Mastok Wrilehiss—Ashenvale	Je'neu Sancrea	The Befouled Element	2200	
CHOICE OF: 1 Deftkin Belt or 1 Driftmire Shield or 1 Soft Willow Cape									
The Tower of Althalaxx	Ashenvale	Alliance	13	21	Delgren the Purifier—Ashenvale	Delgren the Purifier	The Tower of Althalaxx	1650	
The Tower of Althalaxx	Ashenvale	Alliance	13	24	Delgren the Purifier—Ashenvale	Delgren the Purifier	The Tower of Althalaxx	1950	
CHOICE OF: 1 Clergy Ring or 1 Staff of the Purifier									
Supplies to Auberdine	Ashenvale	Alliance	19	24	Feero Ironhand—Ashenvale	Delgren the Purifier	The Tower of Althalaxx	2900	50
CHOICE OF: 1 Everglow Lantern or 1 Chestplate of Kor									
Trek to Ashenvale	Ashenvale	Alliance	15	19	Sentinel Selarin—Darkshore Auberdine	Raene Wolfrunner		370	

Ashenvale cont'd

Title	Location	Faction	Min Level	Con Level	Starter Location	Finisher	Prerequisite	Max XP	Cash Reward
Raene's Cleansing	Ashenvale	Alliance	18	19	Raene Wolfrunner—Ashenvale Astranaar	Teronis' Corpse		1450	
The Ancient Statuette	Ashenvale	Alliance	19	20	Talen—Ashenvale	Talen		1150	9
The Zoram Strand	Ashenvale	Alliance	14	19	Shindrell Swiftfire—Ashenvale Astranaar	Shindrell Swiftfire		1450	11
Ruuzel	Ashenvale	Alliance	20	25	Talen—Ashenvale	Talen	The Ancient Statuette	2250	
REWARD: 1 Robes of Antiquity									
Bathran's Hair	Ashenvale	Alliance	20	20	Orendil Broadleaf—Ashenvale	Orendil Broadleaf		775	
Forsaken Diseases	Ashenvale	Alliance	24	29	Kayneth Stillwind—Ashenvale	Kayneth Stillwind		2350	
Insane Druids	Ashenvale	Alliance	24	32	Kayneth Stillwind—Ashenvale	Kayneth Stillwind	Forsaken Diseases	3200	
REWARD: 1 Emil's Brand									
Elemental Bracers	Ashenvale	Alliance	20	24	Sentinel Velene Starstrike—Ashenvale	Sentinel Velene Starstrike		1950	
Mage Summoner	Ashenvale	Alliance	20	25	Sentinel Velene Starstrike—Ashenvale	Sentinel Velene Starstrike	Elemental Bracers	2550	
REWARD: 1 Light of Elune									
Orendil's Cure	Ashenvale	Alliance	20	20	Orendil Broadleaf—Ashenvale	Pelturas Whitemoon	Bathran's Hair	1950	25
Vile Satyr! Dryads in Danger!	Ashenvale	Alliance	26	32	Illiyana—Ashenvale	Anilia		2550	
The Howling Vale	Ashenvale	Alliance	25	30	Sentinel Melyria Frostshadow—Ashenvale Astranaar	Sentinel Melyria Frostshadow		2450	25
Raene's Cleansing	Ashenvale	Alliance	18	21	Teronis' Corpse—Ashenvale	Raene Wolfrunner	Raene's Cleansing	1250	
Raene's Cleansing	Ashenvale	Alliance	18	21	Raene Wolfrunner—Ashenvale Astranaar	Shael'dryn	Raene's Cleansing	825	
An Aggressive Defense	Ashenvale	Alliance	18	24	Raene Wolfrunner—Ashenvale Astranaar	Raene Wolfrunner	Raene's Cleansing	1950	17
REWARD: 10 Moist Cornbread, 10Melon Juice									
Raene's Cleansing	Ashenvale	Alliance	18	27	Shael'dryn—Ashenvale	Shael'dryn	Raene's Cleansing	2200	
Raene's Cleansing	Ashenvale	Alliance	18	28	Shael'dryn—Ashenvale	Shael'dryn	Raene's Cleansing	2300	
Raene's Cleansing	Ashenvale	Alliance	18	28	Shael'dryn—Ashenvale	Hidden Shrine	Raene's Cleansing	1700	
REWARD: 1 Dartol's Rod of Transformation									
Raene's Cleansing	Ashenvale	Alliance	18	28	Shael'dryn—Ashenvale	Raene Wolfrunner	Raene's Cleansing	230	
Raene's Cleansing	Ashenvale	Alliance	18	28	Raene Wolfrunner—Ashenvale Astranaar	Krolg	Raene's Cleansing	1700	
The Branch of Cenarius	Ashenvale	Alliance	26	32	Anilia—Ashenvale	Illiyana	Vile Satyr! Dryads in Danger!	2550	
CHOICE OF: 1 Faerie Mantle or 1 Brightscale Girdle									
Satyr Slaying!	Ashenvale	Alliance	26	32	Illiyana—Ashenvale	Illiyana	The Branch of Cenarius	2550	30
Elune's Tear	Ashenvale	Alliance	20	22	Pelturas Whitemoon—Ashenvale Astranaar	Pelturas Whitemoon	Orendil's Cure	1750	14
The Ruins of Stardust	Ashenvale	Alliance	20	23	Pelturas Whitemoon—Ashenvale Astranaar	Pelturas Whitemoon	Elune's Tear	1850	15
Fallen Sky Lake	Ashenvale	Alliance	20	30	Pelturas Whitemoon—Ashenvale Astranaar	Pelturas Whitemoon	The Ruins of Stardust	3050	
CHOICE OF: 1 Snapbrook Armor or 1 Beastial Manacles or 1 Luminescent Amice									
Velinde Starsong	Ashenvale	Alliance	25	30	Sentinel Melyria Frostshadow—Ashenvale Astranaar	Thyn'tel Bladeweaver	The Howling Vale	600	
Raene's Cleansing	Ashenvale	Alliance	18	30	Krolg—Ashenvale	Krolg	Raene's Cleansing	2450	
Raene's Cleansing	Ashenvale	Alliance	18	30	Krolg—Ashenvale	Raene Wolfrunner	Raene's Cleansing	3050	
CHOICE OF: 1 Glacial Stone or 1 Gutterblade REWARD: 1 Ring of Pure Silver									
Culling the Threat	Ashenvale	Alliance	18	25	Raene Wolfrunner—Ashenvale Astranaar	Raene Wolfrunner		2000	18
REWARD: 2 Restoring Balm									
Raene's Cleansing	Ashenvale	Alliance	18	28	Hidden Shrine—Ashenvale	Shael'dryn	Raene's Cleansing	230	
Journey to Stonetalon Peak	Ashenvale	Alliance	18	18	Faldreas Goeth'Shael—Ashenvale Astranaar	Keeper Albagorm	Reclaiming the Charred Vale	675	
The Tower of Althalaxx	Ashenvale	Alliance	13	28	Delgren the Purifier—Ashenvale	Delgren the Purifier	The Tower of Althalaxx	2300	
The Tower of Althalaxx	Ashenvale	Alliance	13	28	Delgren the Purifier—Ashenvale	Balthule Shadowstrike	The Tower of Althalaxx	575	
The Befouled Element	Ashenvale	Horde	23	27	Befouled Water Globe	Mastok Wrilehiss		550	
Kayneth Stillwind	Ashenvale	Alliance	24	29	Shindrell Swiftfire—Ashenvale Astranaar	Kayneth Stillwind		600	
The Ashenvale Hunt	Ashenvale	Horde	20	20		Senani Thunderheart			
Satyr Horns	Ashenvale	Horde	21	26	Pixel—Ashenvale	Pixel		2100	20
Naga at the Zoram Strand	Ashenvale	Horde	14	19	Marukai—Ashenvale	Marukai		1450	
Troll Charm	Ashenvale	Horde	19	24	Mitsuwa—Ashenvale	Mitsuwa		1950	17
Freedom to Ruul	Ashenvale	Horde	19	24	Ruul Snowhoof—Ashenvale Unique Tauren	Yama Snowhoof		2400	
Ashenvale Outrunners	Ashenvale	Horde	19	24	Kuray'bin—Ashenvale	Kuray'bin		1950	
The Lost Pages	Ashenvale	Horde	23	30	Gurda Ragescar—Ashenvale	Gurda Ragescar		3650	
CHOICE OF: 1 Shredder Operating Gloves or 1 Oilrag Handwraps									
Report to Kadrak	Ashenvale	Horde	17	19	Thork—Barrens Crossroads	Kadrak		150	
Report to Kadrak	Ashenvale	Horde	17	19	Darn Talongrip—Orgrimmar	Kadrak		150	
The Warsong Reports	Ashenvale	Horde	17	19	Kadrak—Barrens	Kadrak		1800	20
Torek's Assault	Ashenvale	Horde	20	24	Torek—Ashenvale	Ertog Ragetusk		2400	17
CHOICE OF: 1 Polished Walking Staff or 1 Slatemetal Cutlass									
Warsong Runner Update	Ashenvale	Horde	17	19		Warsong Runner			
REWARD: 1 Warsong Runner Update									
Warsong Outrider Update	Ashenvale	Horde	17	25		Warsong Outrider			
REWARD: 1 Warsong Outrider Update									
Warsong Scout Update	Ashenvale	Horde	17	21		Warsong Scout			
REWARD: 1 Warsong Scout Update									
Trouble in the Deeps	Ashenvale	Horde	17	22	Tsunaman—Stonetalon Mountain	Je'neu Sancrea		440	
The Essence of Aku'Mai	Ashenvale	Horde	17	22	Je'neu Sancrea—Ashenvale	Je'neu Sancrea		1750	14
Allegiance to the Old Gods	Ashenvale	Horde	17	22	Damp Note	Je'neu Sancrea		1750	11
Allegiance to the Old Gods	Ashenvale	Horde	17	26	Je'neu Sancrea—Ashenvale	Je'neu Sancrea	Allegiance to the Old Gods	2650	40
CHOICE OF: 1 Band of the Fist or 1 Chestnut Mantle									
Warsong Supplies	Ashenvale	Horde	22	27	Locke Okarr—Ashenvale Warsong	Locke Okarr		2750	
CHOICE OF: 1 Warsong Sash or 1 Warsong Boots or 1 Warsong Gauntlets									
Warsong Saw Blades	Ashenvale	Horde	22	27		Pixel			
REWARD: 1 Warsong Saw Blades									
King of the Foulweald	Ashenvale	Horde	21	26	Karang Amakkar—Ashenvale	Karang Amakkar	Between a Rock and a Thistlefur	2650	20
CHOICE OF: 1 Boorguard Tunic or 1 Cobalt Legguards									
Vorsha the Lasher	Ashenvale	Horde	20	23	Muglash—Ashenvale	Warsong Runner		2300	
REWARD: 1 Horn Ring									
Amongst the Ruins	Ashenvale	Horde	21	27	Je'neu Sancrea—Ashenvale	Je'neu Sancrea		2750	45
Baron Aquanis	Ashenvale	Horde	21	30	Strange Water Globe	Je'neu Sancrea		3050	
CHOICE OF: 1 Outlaw Sabre or 1 Witch's Finger									
Sentinel Basic Care Package	Ashenvale	Alliance	25	34		Illiyana Moonblaze		270	
REWARD: 1 Sentinel Basic Care Package									
Sentinel Standard Care Package	Ashenvale	Alliance	35	44		Illiyana Moonblaze		380	
REWARD: 1 Sentinel Standard Care Package									
Sentinel Advanced Care Package	Ashenvale	Alliance	45	60		Illiyana Moonblaze		650	
REWARD: 1 Sentinel Advanced Care Package									
Outrider Basic Care Package	Ashenvale	Horde	25	34		Kelm Hargunth		270	
REWARD: 1 Outrider Basic Care Package									
Outrider Standard Care Package	Ashenvale	Horde	35	44		Kelm Hargunth		380	
REWARD: 1 Outrider Standard Care Package									
Outrider Advanced Care Package	Ashenvale	Horde	45	60		Kelm Hargunth		650	
REWARD: 1 Outrider Advanced Care Package									

Azshara

Title	Location	Faction	Min Level	Con Level	Starter Location	Finisher	Prerequisite	Max XP	Cash Reward
A Crew Under Fire	Azshara	Both	48	57	Captain Vanessa Beltis—Azshara	Captain Vanessa Beltis		600	
Return Trip	Azshara	Both	45	55		Nyrill			
Meeting with the Master	Azshara	Both	45	55		Sanath Lim-yo			
Stealing Knowledge	Azshara	Horde	45	52	Jediga—Azshara	Jediga		5100	
Delivery to Magatha	Azshara	Horde	45	52	Jediga—Azshara	Magatha Grimtotem	Stealing Knowledge	2550	
Delivery to Jes'rimon	Azshara	Horde	45	52	Jediga—Azshara	Jes'rimon	Stealing Knowledge	2550	40
Delivery to Andron Gant	Azshara	Horde	45	52	Jediga—Azshara	Andron Gant	Stealing Knowledge	2550	60

Ashenvale
Badlands

AZSHARA

Title	Location	Faction	Min Level	Con Level	Starter Location	Finisher	Prerequisite	Max XP	Cash Reward
Delivery to Archmage Xylem	Azshara	Horde	45	52	Jediga—Azshara	Archmage Xylem	Stealing Knowledge	2550	40s
Magatha's Payment to Jediga	Azshara	Horde	45	52	Magatha Grimtotem—Thunder Bluff	Jediga	Delivery to Magatha	3800	60s
Jes'rimon's Payment to Jediga	Azshara	Horde	45	52	Jes'rimon—Orgrimmar	Jediga	Delivery to Jes'rimon	3800	60s
Andron's Payment to Jediga	Azshara	Horde	45	52	Andron Gant—Undercity	Jediga	Delivery to Andron Gant	3800	75s
Xylem's Payment to Jediga	Azshara	Horde	45	52	Archmage Xylem—Azshara	Jediga	Delivery to Archmage Xylem	3800	60s
Kim'jael Indeed!	Azshara	Both	47	53	Kim'jael—Azshara	Kim'jael		6550	8s
REWARD: 3 M73 Frag Grenade									
Dragonscale Leatherworking	Azshara	Alliance	40	55	Peter Galen—Azshara	Peter Galen	Tribal Leatherworking	4200	
Kim'jael's "Missing" Equipment	Azshara	Both	47	53	Kim'jael—Azshara	Kim'jael	Kim'jael Indeed!	6550	1g 60s
Spiritual Unrest	Azshara	Both	45	47	Loh'atu—Azshara	Loh'atu		4200	50s
A Land Filled with Hatred	Azshara	Both	45	47	Loh'atu—Azshara	Loh'atu		4200	70s
Courser Antlers	Azshara	Both	50	52	Ogtinc—Azshara	Ogtinc		5100	
Wavethrashing	Azshara	Both	50	52	Ogtinc—Azshara	Ogtinc	Courser Antlers	5100	
The Green Drake	Azshara	Both	50	52	Ogtinc—Azshara	Ogtinc	Wavethrashing	6350	
CHOICE OF: 1 Hunting Spear or 1 Devilsaur Eye or 1 Devilsaur Tooth									
Sealed Azure Bag	Azshara	Both	50	52	Lord Jorach Ravenholdt—Hillsbrad Chateau Ravenholdt	Archmage Xylem		5100	60s
Encoded Fragments	Azshara	Both	50	52	Archmage Xylem—Azshara	Archmage Xylem	Sealed Azure Bag	5100	
The Azure Key	Azshara	Both	50	52	Archmage Xylem—Azshara	Lord Jorach Ravenholdt	Encoded Fragments	6350	75s
CHOICE OF: 1 Ebon Mask or 1 Whisperwalk Boots or 1 Duskbat Drape									
Magic Dust	Azshara	Both	50	52	Archmage Xylem—Azshara	Archmage Xylem		5100	
The Siren's Coral	Azshara	Both	50	52	Archmage Xylem—Azshara	Archmage Xylem	Magic Dust	5100	75s
Destroy Morphaz	Azshara	Both	50	52	Archmage Xylem—Azshara	Archmage Xylem	The Siren's Coral	6350	1g 55s
CHOICE OF: 1 Glacial Spike or 1 Arcane Crystal Pendant or 1 Fire Ruby									
Of Coursers We Know	Azshara	Both	50	52	Ogtinc—Azshara	Ogtinc		5100	
The Ichor of Undeath	Azshara	Both	50	52	Ogtinc—Azshara	Ogtinc	Of Coursers We Know	5100	
Blood of Morphaz	Azshara	Both	50	52	Ogtinc—Azshara	Greta Mosshoof	The Ichor of Undeath	6350	1g 55s
CHOICE OF: 1 Blessed Prayer Beads or 1 Woestave or 1 Circle of Hope									

BADLANDS

Title	Location	Faction	Min Level	Con Level	Starter Location	Finisher	Prerequisite	Max XP	Cash Reward
Barbecued Buzzard Wings	Badlands	Both	33	40	Rigglefuzz—Badlands Valley of Fangs	Rigglefuzz		2350	
REWARD: 2 Barbecued Buzzard Wing, 14609									
Agmond's Fate	Badlands	Alliance	30	38	Prospector Ironband—Loch Modan	Prospector Ironband	Murdaloc	2850	
REWARD: 1 Prospector Gloves									
Pearl Diving	Badlands	Alliance	30	37	Rigglefuzz—Badlands Valley of Fangs	Rigglefuzz		3550	
CHOICE OF: 1 Flash Rifle or 1 Flash Wand REWARD: 1 Flash Bomb									
Fiery Blaze Enchantments	Badlands	Alliance	40	45	Sigrun Ironhew—Badlands	Sigrun Ironhew		3900	
REWARD: 1 Fiery Blaze Enchantment									
The Black Box	Badlands	Alliance	30	40	Corroded Black Box	Pilot Longbeard		2350	50s
Solution to Doom	Badlands	Both	30	40	Theldurin the Lost—Badlands	Theldurin the Lost		3150	
REWARD: 1 Doomsayer's Robe									
Study of the Elements: Rock	Badlands	Both	35	37	Lotwil Veriatus—Badlands	Lotwil Veriatus		2850	
Study of the Elements: Rock	Badlands	Both	35	39	Lotwil Veriatus—Badlands	Lotwil Veriatus	Study of the Elements: Rock	3000	
Study of the Elements: Rock	Badlands	Both	35	42	Lotwil Veriatus—Badlands	Lotwil Veriatus	Study of the Elements: Rock	3450	
Coolant Heads Prevail	Badlands	Both	35	37	Lotwil Veriatus—Badlands	Lotwil Veriatus		2850	
Gyro... What?	Badlands	Both	35	37	Lotwil Veriatus—Badlands	Lotwil Veriatus	Coolant Heads Prevail	2850	
Liquid Stone	Badlands	Both	35	37	Lucien Tosselwrench—Badlands	Lucien Tosselwrench	Gyro... What?	2100	
REWARD: 1 Recipe: Lesser Stoneshield Potion, 2Lesser Stoneshield Potion									
Stone Is Better than Cloth	Badlands	Both	35	42	Lucien Tosselwrench—Badlands	Lucien Tosselwrench	Study of the Elements: Rock	2550	
REWARD: 1 Enchanted Stonecloth Bracers									
Tremors of the Earth	Badlands	Alliance	40	50	Garek—Badlands	Garek	Tremors of the Earth	5900	
CHOICE OF: 1 Blazewind Breastplate or 1 Prismscale Hauberk or 1 Warforged Chestplate or 1 Mindburst Medallion									
Mirages	Badlands	Alliance	35	38	Sigrun Ironhew—Badlands	Sigrun Ironhew		2150	
A Dwarf and His Tools	Badlands	Alliance	35	35	Prospector Ryedol—Badlands	Prospector Ryedol		2750	
REWARD: 1 Ryedol's Hammer									
A Sign of Hope	Badlands	Alliance	35	35	Crumpled Map—Badlands	Prospector Ryedol		1350	
A Sign of Hope	Badlands	Alliance	35	35	Prospector Ryedol—Badlands	Hammertoe Grez	A Sign of Hope	2750	
Amulet of Secrets	Badlands	Alliance	35	40	Hammertoe Grez—Uldaman	Hammertoe Grez	A Sign of Hope	3150	
Prospect of Faith	Badlands	Alliance	35	40	Hammertoe Grez—Uldaman	Prospector Ryedol	Amulet of Secrets	2350	
Prospect of Faith	Badlands	Alliance	35	40	Prospector Ryedol—Badlands	Historian Karnik	Prospect of Faith	3150	
Passing Word of a Threat	Badlands	Alliance	35	40	Historian Karnik—Ironforge	Advisor Belgrum	Prospect of Faith	1550	
Passing Word of a Threat	Badlands	Alliance	35	40	Advisor Belgrum—Ironforge	Historian Karnik	Passing Word of a Threat	2350	
To Ironforge for Yagyin's Digest	Badlands	Alliance	30	40	Theldurin the Lost—Badlands	Gerrig Bonegrip	Solution to Doom	775	
To the Undercity for Yagyin's Digest	Badlands	Horde	30	40	Theldurin the Lost—Badlands	Keeper Bel'dugur	Solution to Doom	775	
Tremors of the Earth	Badlands	Alliance	40	43	Garek—Badlands	Garek	Mirages	3600	
Scrounging	Badlands	Alliance	35	40	Sigrun Ironhew—Badlands	Sigrun Ironhew	Mirages	3150	
CHOICE OF: 1 Salbac Shield or 1 Ironheel Boots									
This Is Going to Be Hard	Badlands	Both	35	42	Lotwil Veriatus—Badlands	Lucien Tosselwrench	Study of the Elements: Rock		
Forbidden Knowledge	Badlands	Horde	30	40	Keeper Bel'dugur—Undercity	Theldurin the Lost	The Star, the Hand and the Heart	2350	
REWARD: 1 Skull of Impending Doom									
Find Agmond	Badlands	Alliance	30	38	Prospector Ironband—Loch Modan	Battered Dwarven Skeleton		1450	4s
REWARD: 1 Ripped Prospector Belt, 1Jade, 22776									
Murdaloc	Badlands	Alliance	30	42	Agmond's Corpse—Badlands	Prospector Ironband	Find Agmond	3450	
REWARD: 1 Rock Pulverizer									
An Ambassador of Evil	Badlands	Alliance	35	44	Historian Karnik—Ironforge	Advisor Belgrum	Passing Word of a Threat	4650	1g 25s
REWARD: 1 Dwarf Captain's Sword									
This Is Going to Be Hard	Badlands	Both	35	42	Lucien Tosselwrench—Badlands	Lotwil Veriatus	This Is Going to Be Hard		
This Is Going to Be Hard	Badlands	Both	35	45	Lotwil Veriatus—Badlands	Lotwil Veriatus	This Is Going to Be Hard	4850	
REWARD: 1 Nifty Stopwatch									
Seal of the Earth	Badlands	Alliance	40	50		Seal of the Earth			
Broken Alliances	Badlands	Horde	40	43	Gorn—Badlands	Gorn		3600	
Broken Alliances	Badlands	Horde	40	50	Gorn—Badlands	Gorn	Broken Alliances	5900	
CHOICE OF: 1 Blazewind Breastplate or 1 Prismscale Hauberk or 1 Warforged Chestplate or 1 Mindburst Medallion									
Seal of the Earth	Badlands	Horde	40	50		Seal of the Earth			
The Lost Tablets of Will	Badlands	Alliance	35	45	Advisor Belgrum—Ironforge	Advisor Belgrum	An Ambassador of Evil	5850	1g 30s
REWARD: 1 Medal of Courage									
Flash Bomb Recipe	Badlands	Alliance	30	37		Rigglefuzz	Pearl Diving		
REWARD: 1 Schematic: Flash Bomb									
Uldaman Reagent Run	Badlands	Horde	36	42	Jarkal Mossmeld—Badlands	Jarkal Mossmeld	Badlands Reagent Run	3450	55s
REWARD: 5 Restorative Potion									
Badlands Reagent Run II	Badlands	Horde	40	44	Jarkal Mossmeld—Badlands	Jarkal Mossmeld	Uldaman Reagent Run	3750	
Badlands Reagent Run	Badlands	Horde	36	39	Jarkal Mossmeld—Badlands	Jarkal Mossmeld		3000	45s
Translating the Journal	Badlands	Horde	37	42	Jarkal Mossmeld—Badlands	Jarkal Mossmeld	Translating the Journal	350	
Find the Gems and Power Source	Badlands	Horde	37	44	Jarkal Mossmeld—Badlands	Jarkal Mossmeld	Translating the Journal	3750	
Deliver the Gems	Badlands	Horde	37	44	Jarkal Mossmeld—Badlands	Dran Droffers	Find the Gems and Power Source	1850	1g 25s
Power Stones	Badlands	Both	30	36	Rigglefuzz—Badlands Valley of Fangs	Rigglefuzz		3500	
CHOICE OF: 1 Energized Stone Circle or 1 Duracin Bracers or 1 Everlast Boots									
Dreadmaul Rock	Badlands	Horde	48	52	Thal'trak Proudtusk—Badlands	Sha'ni Proudtusk		5100	
Disharmony of Flame	Badlands	Horde	48	52	Thunderheart—Badlands	Thunderheart		5100	1g 55s
Disharmony of Fire	Badlands	Horde	48	56	Thunderheart—Badlands	Thunderheart	Disharmony of Flame	7300	2g 55s
CHOICE OF: 1 Sunborne Cape or 1 Nightfall Gloves or 1 Crypt Demon Bracers or 1 Stalwart Clutch									

Badlands cont'd

Title	Location	Faction	Min Level	Con Level	Starter Location	Finisher	Prerequisite	Max XP	Cash Reward
Commander Gor'shak	Badlands	Horde	48	52	Galamav the Marksman—Badlands	Commander Gor'shak	Disharmony of Flame	5100	
The Rise of the Machines	Badlands	Horde	52	54	Hierophant Theodora Mulvadania—Badlands	Hierophant Theodora Mulvadania		5450	1 65
The Rise of the Machines	Badlands	Horde	52	54	Hierophant Theodora Mulvadania—Badlands	Lotwil Veriatus	The Rise of the Machines	1350	
The Rise of the Machines	Badlands	Horde	52	58	Lotwil Veriatus—Badlands	Lotwil Veriatus	The Rise of the Machines	6200	2 65
CHOICE OF: 1 Azure Moon Amice or 1 Raincaster Drape or 1 Basaltscale Armor or 1 Lavaplate Gauntlets									
KILL ON SIGHT: Dark Iron Dwarves	Badlands	Horde	48	52	Wanted Poster—Badlands	Warlord Goretooth		5100	1 55
KILL ON SIGHT: High Ranking Dark Iron Officials	Badlands	Horde	50	54	Wanted Poster—Badlands	Warlord Goretooth	KILL ON SIGHT: Dark Iron Dwarves	5450	1 65
Grark Lorkrub	Badlands	Horde	52	58	Lexlort—Badlands	Grark Lorkrub	KILL ON SIGHT: High Ranking Dark Iron Officials	6200	
Operation: Death to Angerforge	Badlands	Horde	52	58	Warlord Goretooth—Badlands	Warlord Goretooth	KILL ON SIGHT: Dark Iron Dwarves	7750	2 65
REWARD: 1 Conqueror's Medallion									
The Pack Mistress	Badlands	Horde	55	59	Galamav the Marksman—Badlands	Galamav the Marksman		6400	1 80
CHOICE OF: 1 Astoria Robes or 1 Traphook Jerkin or 1 Jadescale Breastplate									
Warlord's Command	Badlands	Horde	55	60	Warlord Goretooth's Command	Warlord Goretooth		8550	1 85
CHOICE OF: 1 Wyrmthalak's Shackles or 1 Omokk's Girth Restrainer or 1 Halycon's Muzzle or 1 Vosh'gajin's Strand or 1 Voone's Vice Grips									
Eitrigg's Wisdom	Badlands	Horde	55	60	Warlord Goretooth—Badlands	Thrall	Warlord's Command	6600	
Operative Bijou	Badlands	Horde	55	59	Lexlort—Badlands	Bijou		6400	
Dragonscale Leatherworking	Badlands	Horde	40	55	Thorkaf Dragoneye—Badlands	Thorkaf Dragoneye	Elemental Leatherworking	4200	
The Last Element	Badlands	Horde	48	54	Shadowmage Vivian Lagrave—Badlands	Shadowmage Vivian Lagrave	Disharmony of Flame	5450	2 45
REWARD: 1 Lagrave's Seal									

Barrens

Title	Location	Faction	Min Level	Con Level	Starter Location	Finisher	Prerequisite	Max XP	Cash Reward
Call of Water	Barrens	Horde	20	23	Islen Waterseer—Barrens	Brazier of Everfount	Call of Water	1400	
Call of Water	Barrens	Horde	20	23	Minor Manifestation of Water—Silverpine	Islen Waterseer	Call of Water	2750	
REWARD: 1 Water Totem									
Call of Water	Barrens	Horde	20	23	Brazier of Everfount—Silverpine	Minor Manifestation of Water	Call of Water	1250	
Call of Water	Barrens	Horde	20	23	Brine—Barrens	Islen Waterseer	Call of Water	460	
REWARD: 1 Water Sapta									
Chen's Empty Keg	Barrens	Horde	11	15	Chen's Empty Keg—Barrens	Brewmaster Drohn		1050	
Chen's Empty Keg	Barrens	Horde	11	15	Brewmaster Drohn—Barrens Ratchet	Brewmaster Drohn	Chen's Empty Keg	1350	
REWARD: 5 Stormstout									
Chen's Empty Keg	Barrens	Horde	11	24	Brewmaster Drohn—Barrens Ratchet	Brewmaster Drohn	Chen's Empty Keg	975	
REWARD: 5 Trogg Ale									
Gann's Reclamation	Barrens	Horde	17	23	Gann Stonespire—Barrens Southern Barrens	Gann Stonespire		1850	12 50
Plainstrider Menace	Barrens	Horde	10	12	Sergra Darkthorn—Barrens Crossroads	Sergra Darkthorn		900	5
The Zhevra	Barrens	Horde	10	13	Sergra Darkthorn—Barrens Crossroads	Sergra Darkthorn	Plainstrider Menace	900	6
Revenge of Gann	Barrens	Horde	17	26	Gann Stonespire—Barrens Southern Barrens	Gann Stonespire	Gann's Reclamation	2100	20
Fungal Spores	Barrens	Horde	10	15	Apothecary Helbrim—Barrens Crossroads	Apothecary Helbrim		1050	7
Revenge of Gann	Barrens	Horde	17	26	Gann Stonespire—Barrens Southern Barrens	Gann Stonespire	Revenge of Gann	2100	20
REWARD: 1 Totemic Clan Ring									
Kolkar Leaders	Barrens	Horde	11	16	Regthar Deathgate—The Barrens	Regthar Deathgate		875	8
Verog the Dervish	Barrens	Horde	11	18	Regthar Deathgate—The Barrens	Regthar Deathgate	Kolkar Leaders	1000	10
Hezrul Bloodmark	Barrens	Horde	11	19	Regthar Deathgate—The Barrens	Regthar Deathgate	Verog the Dervish	1100	8
REWARD: 1 Bounty Hunter's Ring									
Apothecary Zamah	Barrens	Horde	10	15	Apothecary Helbrim—Barrens Crossroads	Apothecary Zamah	Fungal Spores	800	
CHOICE OF: 4 Elixir of Minor Fortitude or 4 Elixir of Minor Agility or 3 Minor Rejuvenation Potion 2 Swiftness Potion REWARD: 1 Cauldron Stirrer									
Centaur Bracers	Barrens	Horde	9	14	Regthar Deathgate—The Barrens	Regthar Deathgate		1250	
CHOICE OF: 1 Orcish Battle Bow or 1 Pointed Axe or 1 Stonewood Hammer									
The Tear of the Moons	Barrens	Horde	22	30	Feegly the Exiled—Barrens Bael Modan	Feegly the Exiled		2450	25
Ignition	Barrens	Both	13	18	Wizzlecrank's Shredder—Barrens	Wizzlecrank's Shredder		1350	
Dig Rat Stew	Barrens	Horde	15	23	Grub—Barrens	Grub		1850	
REWARD: 1 Recipe: Dig Rat Stew, 5Dig Rat Stew, 1Apothecary Gloves									
The Escape	Barrens	Both	13	18	Wizzlecrank's Shredder—Barrens	Sputtervalve	Ignition	1700	3 50
CHOICE OF: 1 Flaring Baton or 1 Greasy Tinker's Pants									
Raptor Horns	Barrens	Both	13	18	Mebok Mizzyrix—Barrens Ratchet Goblin	Mebok Mizzyrix		1350	
REWARD: 5 Raptor Punch, 1Barkeeper's Cloak									
Root Samples	Barrens	Both	9	16	Mebok Mizzyrix—Barrens Ratchet Goblin	Mebok Mizzyrix		1150	8
REWARD: 1 Spore-covered Tunic									
Harpy Raiders	Barrens	Horde	12	15	Darsok Swiftdagger—Barrens Crossroads	Darsok Swiftdagger		1050	7
Egg Hunt	Barrens	Horde	17	22	Korran—Barrens Crossroads	Korran		1750	
CHOICE OF: 1 Harlequin Robes or 1 Violet Scale Armor									
Raptor Thieves	Barrens	Horde	9	13	Gazrog—Barrens Crossroads	Gazrog		900	6
The Forgotten Pools	Barrens	Horde	10	13	Tonga Runetotem—Barrens Crossroads	Tonga Runetotem		675	
Disrupt the Attacks	Barrens	Horde	9	12	Thork—Barrens Crossroads	Thork		900	
The Disruption Ends	Barrens	Horde	9	15	Thork—Barrens Crossroads	Thork	Disrupt the Attacks	1050	
CHOICE OF: 1 Binding Girdle or 1 Cinched Belt									
Isha Awak	Barrens	Horde	10	27	Mahren Skyseer—Barrens	Mahren Skyseer	Mahren Skyseer	2750	
CHOICE OF: 1 Branding Rod or 1 Ward of the Vale REWARD: 1 Beastmaster's Girdle									
Mahren Skyseer	Barrens	Horde	9	27	Jorn Skyseer—Barrens Camp Taurajo	Mahren Skyseer	Cry of the Thunderhawk	550	
Harpy Lieutenants	Barrens	Horde	12	16	Darsok Swiftdagger—Barrens Crossroads	Darsok Swiftdagger	Harpy Raiders	1150	8
Serena Bloodfeather	Barrens	Horde	12	20	Darsok Swiftdagger—Barrens Crossroads	Darsok Swiftdagger	Harpy Lieutenants	1950	
CHOICE OF: 1 Elegant Shortsword or 1 Harpy Skinner or 1 Zhovur Axe									
The Stagnant Oasis	Barrens	Horde	10	16	Tonga Runetotem—Barrens Crossroads	Tonga Runetotem	The Forgotten Pools	1150	
Tribes at War	Barrens	Horde	14	21	Mangletooth—Barrens	Mangletooth		1650	
Betrayal from Within	Barrens	Horde	17	25	Mangletooth—Barrens	Mangletooth	Blood Shards of Agamaggan	1500	
Altered Beings	Barrens	Horde	10	16	Tonga Runetotem—Barrens Crossroads	Tonga Runetotem	The Stagnant Oasis	1150	8
Echeyakee	Barrens	Horde	10	16	Sergra Darkthorn—Barrens Crossroads	Sergra Darkthorn	Prowlers of the Barrens	1450	
Ishamuhale	Barrens	Horde	10	19	Jorn Skyseer—Barrens Camp Taurajo	Jorn Skyseer	Jorn Skyseer	1800	
Lakota'mani	Barrens	Horde	10	22	Hoof of Lakota'mani	Jorn Skyseer		1300	
Owatanka	Barrens	Horde	10	24	Owatanka's Tailspike	Jorn Skyseer		1450	
Washte Pawne	Barrens	Horde	10	25	Washte Pawne's Feather	Jorn Skyseer		1500	
Southsea Freebooters	Barrens	Both	9	14	Gazlowe—Barrens Ratchet	Gazlowe		750	5
Stolen Booty	Barrens	Both	9	16	Gazlowe—Barrens Ratchet	Gazlowe	The Missing Shipment	1150	8
CHOICE OF: 1 Wayfaring Gloves or 1 Padded Lamellar Boots									
Spirit of the Wind	Barrens	Horde	14	20		Mangletooth	Blood Shards of Agamaggan		
The Missing Shipment	Barrens	Both	9	14	Gazlowe—Barrens Ratchet	Wharfmaster Dizzywig	Southsea Freebooters	100	
The Guns of Northwatch	Barrens	Horde	13	20	Captain Thalo'thas Brightsun—Barrens Ratchet	Captain Thalo'thas Brightsun		1550	
CHOICE OF: 1 Privateer Musket or 1 Sea Dog Britches									
The Missing Shipment	Barrens	Both	9	14	Wharfmaster Dizzywig—Barrens Ratchet	Gazlowe	The Missing Shipment	100	
Weapons of CHOICE	Barrens	Horde	17	24	Tatternack Steelforge—Barrens Camp Taurajo	Tatternack Steelforge		1950	
CHOICE OF: 1 Demolition Hammer or 1 Everglow Lantern									
Samophlange	Barrens	Both	10	14	Sputtervalve—Barrens Ratchet	Control Console		750	
WANTED: Baron Longshore	Barrens	Both	11	16	Wanted Poster—Barrens	Gazlowe		1150	6 80
Miner's Fortune	Barrens	Both	13	18	Wharfmaster Dizzywig—Barrens Ratchet	Wharfmaster Dizzywig		1700	
REWARD: 1 A Sack of Coins									
The Harvester	Barrens	Horde	10	24	Harvester's Head	Jorn Skyseer		2400	
Free From the Hold	Barrens	Horde	13	20	Gilthares Firebough—Barrens	Captain Thalo'thas Brightsun		1950	25
CHOICE OF: 1 Buckled Boots or 1 Riveted Gauntlets									

Title	Location	Faction	Min Level	Con Level	Starter Location	Finisher	Prerequisite	Max XP	Cash Reward
Consumed by Hatred	Barrens	Horde	14	20	Mankrik—Barrens Crossroad	Mankrik		1950	
CHOICE OF: 1 Boar Hunter's Cape or 1 Grassland Sash									
Samophlange	Barrens	Both	10	14	Control Console—Barrens	Control Console	Samophlange	490	
Samophlange	Barrens	Both	10	14	Control Console—Barrens	Control Console	Samophlange	750	
Samophlange	Barrens	Both	10	16	Control Console—Barrens	Sputtervalve	Samophlange	1150	
CHOICE OF: 1 Engineer's Hammer or 1 Welding Shield									
Prowlers of the Barrens	Barrens	Horde	10	15	Sergra Darkthorn—Barrens Crossroads	Sergra Darkthorn	The Zhevra	1050	7
The Angry Scytheclaws	Barrens	Horde	10	17	Sergra Darkthorn—Barrens Crossroads	Sergra Darkthorn	Echeyakee	1250	9
Betrayal from Within	Barrens	Horde	17	25	Mangletooth—Barrens	Thork	Betrayal from Within	3050	
CHOICE OF: 1 Barkshell Tunic or 1 Dry Moss Tunic									
Enraged Thunder Lizards	Barrens	Horde	10	18	Jorn Skyseer—Barrens Camp Taurajo	Jorn Skyseer	Ishamuhale	1700	
Cry of the Thunderhawk	Barrens	Horde	10	20	Jorn Skyseer—Barrens Camp Taurajo	Jorn Skyseer	Enraged Thunder Lizards	1950	
CHOICE OF: 1 Cobalt Buckler or 1 Wind Rider Staff REWARD: 1 Gloves of the Moon									
The Demon Seed	Barrens	Horde	9	14	Ak'Zeloth—Barrens	Ak'Zeloth	Ak'Zeloth	1250	
REWARD: 1 Banshee Armor									
Flawed Power Stone	Barrens	Horde	1	14		Flawed Power Stone			
REWARD: 1 Flawed Power Stone									
Trouble at the Docks	Barrens	Both	14	18	Crane Operator Bigglefuzz—Barrens Ratchet	Crane Operator Bigglefuzz		1350	10
Water Sapta	Barrens	Horde	20	20		Islen Waterseer	Call of Water		
REWARD: 1 Water Sapta									
Passage to Booty Bay	Barrens	Alliance	25	30	Wharfmaster Dizzywig—Barrens Ratchet	Caravaneer Ruzzgot	The Barrens Port	600	
Letter to Jin'Zil	Barrens	Horde	15	20	Darsok Swiftdagger—Barrens Crossroads	Witch Doctor Jin'Zil	Serena Bloodfeather	1550	
Deepmoss Spider Eggs	Barrens	Both	15	20	Mebok Mizzyrix—Barrens Ratchet Goblin	Mebok Mizzyrix		1950	13
Further Instructions	Barrens	Both	16	27	Sputtervalve—Barrens Ratchet	Ziz Fizziks	Further Instructions	1100	
Call of Water	Barrens	Horde	20	23	Tiev Mordune—Silverpine North Tide's Run	Tiev Mordune	Call of Water		
Goblin Sponsorship	Barrens	Both	29	37	Gazlowe—Barrens Ratchet	Wharfmaster Lozgil	Goblin Sponsorship	700	
Ziz Fizziks	Barrens	Both	16	21	Sputtervalve—Barrens Ratchet	Ziz Fizziks	Super Reaper 6000	420	
Smart Drinks	Barrens	Both	13	18	Mebok Mizzyrix—Barrens Ratchet Goblin	Mebok Mizzyrix	Raptor Horns	1350	8
Wharfmaster Dizzywig	Barrens	Horde	9	11	Apothecary Helbrim—Barrens Crossroads	Wharfmaster Dizzywig		440	
Call of Water	Barrens	Horde	20	20	Searn Fi				
REWARDDer—Orgrimmar	Islen Waterseer		775						
Call of Water	Barrens	Horde	20	20	Xanis Flameweaver—Thunder Bluff	Islen Waterseer		775	
Call of Water	Barrens	Horde	20	22	Islen Waterseer—Barrens	Brine		440	
Call of Water	Barrens	Horde	20	23	Brine—Barrens	Brine	Call of Water	1400	
Call of Water	Barrens	Horde	20	22	Brine—Barrens	Brine	Call of Water	875	
Call of Water	Barrens	Horde	20	22	Brine—Barrens	Brine	Call of Water	1300	
The Orb of Soran'ruk	Barrens	Both	20	25	Doan Karhan—Barrens Southern Barrens	Doan Karhan		2550	
CHOICE OF: 1 Orb of Soran'ruk or 1 Staff of Soran'ruk									
Tome of the Cabal	Barrens	Alliance	30	30	Strahad Farsan—Barrens	Krom Stoutarm		600	
The Binding	Barrens	Both	30	30	Strahad Farsan—Barrens	Strahad Farsan	Tome of the Cabal	2450	
REWARD: 1 Box of Souls									
Components for the Enchanted Gold Bloodrobe	Barrens	Both	31	31	Menara Voidrender—Barrens	Menara Voidrender		2500	
Fragments of the Orb of Orahil	Barrens	Both	35	40	Menara Voidrender—Barrens	Tabetha	Knowledge of the Orb of Orahil	3150	
Tome of the Cabal	Barrens	Horde	30	30	Strahad Farsan—Barrens	Jorah Annison		600	
Plundering the Plunderers	Barrens	Horde	16	18	Wrenix the Wretched—Barrens Ratchet	Wrenix the Wretched	Wrenix of Ratchet	1350	
REWARD: 10 Thistle Tea									
Mission: Possible But Not Probable	Barrens	Horde	20	24		Shenthul	Deep Cover	1950	
REWARD: 1 Recipe: Thistle Tea									
Call of Water	Barrens	Horde	20	20	Swart—Durotar Razor Hill	Islen Waterseer		775	
Call of Water	Barrens	Horde	20	20	Narm Skychaser—Mulgore Bloodhoof Village	Islen Waterseer		775	
Jorn Skyseer	Barrens	Horde	10	18	Sergra Darkthorn—Barrens Crossroads	Jorn Skyseer	The Angry Scytheclaws	140	
Stolen Silver	Barrens	Horde	9	18	Gazrog—Barrens Crossroads	Gazrog	Raptor Thieves	1350	10
CHOICE OF: 1 Rambling Boots or 1 Settler's Leggings									
Mura Runetotem	Barrens	Horde	10	15	Tonga Runetotem—Barrens Crossroads	Mura Runetotem	Altered Beings	1050	
CHOICE OF: 1 Jackseed Belt or 1 Sower's Cloak									
The Runed Scroll	Barrens	Horde	15	25	Runed Scroll	Kadrak		2550	
Horde Presence	Barrens	Horde	15	29	Kadrak—Barrens	Kadrak	The Runed Scroll	2950	
CHOICE OF: 1 Trailblazer Boots or 1 Jutebraid Gloves									
Goblin Engineering	Barrens	Both	30	47	Tinkerwiz—Barrens Ratchet	Nixx Sprocketspring	The Pledge of Secrecy	420	
Gnome Engineering	Barrens	Alliance	30	47	Tinkerwiz—Barrens Ratchet	Tinkmaster Overspark	The Pledge of Secrecy	420	
Gnome Engineering	Barrens	Horde	30	47	Tinkerwiz—Barrens Ratchet	Oglethorpe Obnoticus	The Pledge of Secrecy	420	
Membership Card Renewal	Barrens	Both	30	47		Vazario Linkgrease	Show Your Work		
REWARD: 1 Goblin Engineer Membership Card									
Wenikee Boltbucket	Barrens	Horde	10	14	Sputtervalve—Barrens Ratchet	Wenikee Boltbucket	Samophlange	490	
Nugget Slugs	Barrens	Horde	10	15	Wenikee Boltbucket—Barrens	Wenikee Boltbucket	Wenikee Boltbucket	1050	
Rilli Greasygob	Barrens	Horde	10	18	Wenikee Boltbucket—Barrens	Rilli Greasygob	Nugget Slugs	340	
Samophlange Manual	Barrens	Horde	10	19	Rilli Greasygob—Orgrimmar	Rilli Greasygob	Rilli Greasygob	1800	
CHOICE OF: 1 Tork Wrench or 1 Samophlange Screwdriver									
Counterattack!	Barrens	Horde	11	20	Regthar Deathgate—The Barrens	Regthar Deathgate	Hezrul Bloodmark	1950	25
In Search of Menara Voidrender	Barrens	Alliance	31	31	Briarthorn—Ironforge	Menara Voidrender		625	
In Search of Menara Voidrender	Barrens	Horde	31	31	Zevrost—Orgrimmar	Menara Voidrender		625	
In Search of Menara Voidrender	Barrens	Alliance	31	31	Demisette Cloyce—Stormwind	Menara Voidrender		625	
In Search of Menara Voidrender	Barrens	Horde	31	31	Kaal Soulreaper—Undercity	Menara Voidrender		625	
Components for the Enchanted Gold Bloodrobe	Barrens	Both	31	34	Menara Voidrender—Barrens	Xizk Goodstitch	Components for the Enchanted Gold Bloodrobe	2000	
Components for the Enchanted Gold Bloodrobe	Barrens	Both	31	34	Xizk Goodstitch—Stranglethorn Booty Bay	Menara Voidrender	Components for the Enchanted Gold Bloodrobe	1350	
Components for the Enchanted Gold Bloodrobe	Barrens	Both	31	37	Menara Voidrender—Barrens	Menara Voidrender	Components for the Enchanted Gold Bloodrobe	2850	
Components for the Enchanted Gold Bloodrobe	Barrens	Both	31	37	Menara Voidrender—Barrens	Menara Voidrender	Components for the Enchanted Gold Bloodrobe	2100	
Fine Gold Thread	Barrens	Both	31	37		Xizk Goodstitch	Components for the Enchanted Gold Bloodrobe		
REWARD: 1 Fine Gold Thread									
The Completed Robe	Barrens	Both	31	38	Menara Voidrender—Barrens	Menara Voidrender	Components for the Enchanted Gold Bloodrobe	3550	
REWARD: 1 Enchanted Gold Bloodrobe									
Lost in Battle	Barrens	Horde	14	20	Mankrik—Barrens Crossroad	Mankrik		1150	9
Cleansing of the Orb of Orahil	Barrens	Both	35	40	Tabetha—Dustwallow Marsh The Quagmire	Tabetha	Fragments of the Orb of Orahil	2350	
REWARD: 1 Cleansed Infernal Orb									
Shard of a Felhound	Barrens	Both	35	40	Acolyte Wytula—Barrens	Menara Voidrender	Knowledge of the Orb of Orahil	2350	
Shard of an Infernal	Barrens	Both	35	40	Acolyte Magaz—Barrens	Menara Voidrender	Knowledge of the Orb of Orahil	2350	
The Completed Orb of Dar'Orahil	Barrens	Both	35	40	Menara Voidrender—Barrens	Menara Voidrender	Returning the Cleansed Orb	3900	
CHOICE OF: 1 Orb of Dar'Orahil or 1 Staff of Dar'Orahil									
Knowledge of the Orb of Orahil	Barrens	Alliance	35	35	Briarthorn—Ironforge	Menara Voidrender		1350	
Knowledge of the Orb of Orahil	Barrens	Horde	35	35	Zevrost—Orgrimmar	Menara Voidrender		1350	
Knowledge of the Orb of Orahil	Barrens	Alliance	35	35	Demisette Cloyce—Stormwind	Menara Voidrender		1350	
Knowledge of the Orb of Orahil	Barrens	Horde	35	35	Kaal Soulreaper—Undercity	Menara Voidrender		1350	

Barrens cont'd

Title	Location	Faction	Min Level	Con Level	Starter Location	Finisher	Prerequisite	Max XP	Cash Reward
The Completed Orb of Noh'Orahil	Barrens	Both	35	40	Menara Voidrender—Barrens	Menara Voidrender	Returning the Cleansed Orb	3900	
CHOICE OF: 1 Orb of Noh'Orahil or 1 Staff of Noh'Orahil									
Returning the Cleansed Orb	Barrens	Both	35	40	Tabetha—Dustwallow Marsh The Quagmire	Menara Voidrender	Cleansing of the Orb of Orahil	1550	
Supplies for the Crossroads	Barrens	Horde	9	14	Thork—Barrens Crossroads	Thork		975	6●
Agamaggan's Strength	Barrens	Horde	14	20		Mangletooth	Blood Shards of Agamaggan		
Agamaggan's Agility	Barrens	Horde	14	20		Mangletooth	Blood Shards of Agamaggan		
Wisdom of Agamaggan	Barrens	Horde	14	20		Mangletooth	Blood Shards of Agamaggan		
Rising Spirit	Barrens	Horde	14	20		Mangletooth	Blood Shards of Agamaggan		
Razorhide	Barrens	Horde	14	20		Mangletooth	Blood Shards of Agamaggan		
Blood Shards of Agamaggan	Barrens	Horde	14	21	Mangletooth—Barrens	Mangletooth	Tribes at War	1250	
Gathering the Cure	Barrens	Horde	14	14	Tonga Runetotem—Barrens Crossroads	Tonga Runetotem	The Principal Source	750	
Curing the Sick	Barrens	Horde	14	14	Tonga Runetotem—Barrens Crossroads	Dendrite Starblaze	Gathering the Cure	750	
REWARD: 1 Veildust Medicine Bag									
A Bundle of Hides	Barrens	Horde	10	10	Jahan Hawkwing—Barrens Crossroads	Devrak		210	
Ride to Thunder Bluff	Barrens	Horde	10	10	Devrak—Barrens Crossroads	Ahanu	A Bundle of Hides	420	1●75●
Tal the Wind Rider Master	Barrens	Horde	10	10	Ahanu—Thunder Bluff	Tal	Ride to Thunder Bluff	210	
Return to Jahan	Barrens	Horde	10	10	Tal—Thunder Bluff	Jahan Hawkwing	Tal the Wind Rider Master	1050	3●50●
Meats to Orgrimmar	Barrens	Horde	10	10	Zargh—Barrens Crossroads	Devrak		210	
The Ashenvale Hunt	Barrens	Horde	20	20	Jorn Skyseer—Barrens Camp Taurajo	Senani Thunderheart	Ishamuhale	390	
Ride to Orgrimmar	Barrens	Horde	10	10	Devrak—Barrens Crossroads	Innkeeper Gryshka	Meats to Orgrimmar	420	1●75●
Doras the Wind Rider Master	Barrens	Horde	10	10	Innkeeper Gryshka—Orgrimmar	Doras	Ride to Orgrimmar	210	
Return to the Crossroads.	Barrens	Horde	10	10	Doras—Orgrimmar	Zargh	Doras the Wind Rider Master	1050	3●50●
Mending Old Wounds	Barrens	Both	15	60		Mupsi Shacklefridd			

Blasted Lands

Title	Location	Faction	Min Level	Con Level	Starter Location	Finisher	Prerequisite	Max XP	Cash Reward
Supplies for Nethergarde	Blasted Lands	Alliance	40	45	Watchmaster Sorigal—Duskwood Darkshire	Quartermaster Lungertz		2900	50●
Vital Supplies	Blasted Lands	Alliance	40	45	High Sorcerer Andromath—Stormwind	Watchmaster Sorigal	Supplies for Nethergarde	975	
To Serve Kum'isha	Blasted Lands	Both	45	55	Kum'isha the Collector—Blasted Lands	Kum'isha the Collector		8450	
REWARD: 1 Emerald Encrusted Chest									
Kum'isha's Endeavors	Blasted Lands	Both	45	55	Kum'isha the Collector—Blasted Lands	Kum'isha the Collector	To Serve Kum'isha	5650	
REWARD: 1 Emerald Encrusted Chest									
Snickerfang Jowls	Blasted Lands	Both	45	50	Bloodmage Drazial—Blasted Lands	Bloodmage Drazial		4700	
REWARD: 1 R.O.I.D.S.									
Rage of Ages	Blasted Lands	Both	45	50	Bloodmage Drazial—Blasted Lands	Bloodmage Drazial	Snickerfang Jowls		
REWARD: 1 R.O.I.D.S.									
A Boar's Vitality	Blasted Lands	Both	45	50	Bloodmage Drazial—Blasted Lands	Bloodmage Drazial		4700	
REWARD: 1 Lung Juice Cocktail									
Spirit of the Boar	Blasted Lands	Both	45	50	Bloodmage Drazial—Blasted Lands	Bloodmage Drazial	A Boar's Vitality		
REWARD: 1 Lung Juice Cocktail									
The Decisive Striker	Blasted Lands	Both	45	50	Bloodmage Drazial—Blasted Lands	Bloodmage Drazial		4700	
REWARD: 1 Ground Scorpok Assay									
Salt of the Scorpok	Blasted Lands	Both	45	50	Bloodmage Drazial—Blasted Lands	Bloodmage Drazial	The Decisive Striker		
REWARD: 1 Ground Scorpok Assay									
The Basilisk's Bite	Blasted Lands	Both	45	50	Bloodmage Lynnore—Blasted Lands	Bloodmage Lynnore		4700	
REWARD: 1 Cerebral Cortex Compound									
Infallible Mind	Blasted Lands	Both	45	50	Bloodmage Lynnore—Blasted Lands	Bloodmage Lynnore	The Basilisk's Bite		
REWARD: 1 Cerebral Cortex Compound									
Vulture's Vigor	Blasted Lands	Both	45	50	Bloodmage Lynnore—Blasted Lands	Bloodmage Lynnore		4700	
REWARD: 1 Gizzard Gum									
Spiritual Domination	Blasted Lands	Both	45	50	Bloodmage Lynnore—Blasted Lands	Bloodmage Lynnore	Vulture's Vigor		
REWARD: 1 Gizzard Gum									
The Disgraced One	Blasted Lands	Horde	45	50	Fallen Hero of the Horde—Blasted Lands	Dispatch Commander Ruag	Fall From Grace	1200	
The Missing Orders	Blasted Lands	Horde	45	50	Dispatch Commander Ruag—Swamp of Sorrows Stonard	Bengor	The Disgraced One	1200	
The Swamp Talker	Blasted Lands	Horde	45	55	Bengor—Swamp of Sorrows Stonard	Fallen Hero of the Horde	The Missing Orders	5650	
The Stones That Bind Us	Blasted Lands	Both	45	57	Fallen Hero of the Horde—Blasted Lands	Fallen Hero of the Horde	A Tale of Sorrow	7550	
Heroes of Old	Blasted Lands	Both	45	57	Corporal Thund Splithoof—Blasted Lands	Spectral Lockbox	Heroes of Old	6000	
REWARD: 1 Shard of Afrasa									
Heroes of Old	Blasted Lands	Both	45	57	Fallen Hero of the Horde—Blasted Lands	Corporal Thund Splithoof	The Stones That Bind Us	3000	
Kirith	Blasted Lands	Both	45	58	Fallen Hero of the Horde—Blasted Lands	Spirit of Kirith	Heroes of Old	6200	
The Cover of Darkness	Blasted Lands	Both	45	60	Spirit of Kirith—Blasted Lands	Fallen Hero of the Horde	Kirith	3300	
The Demon Hunter	Blasted Lands	Both	45	60	Fallen Hero of the Horde—Blasted Lands	Loramus Thalipedes	The Cover of Darkness	6600	
Petty Squabbles	Blasted Lands	Alliance	50	57	Ambassador Ardalan—Blasted Lands	Fallen Hero of the Horde		4500	
Fall From Grace	Blasted Lands	Horde	45	50	Fallen Hero of the Horde—Blasted Lands	Fallen Hero of the Horde		470	
A Tale of Sorrow	Blasted Lands	Both	45	57	Fallen Hero of the Horde—Blasted Lands	Fallen Hero of the Horde	Petty Squabbles	600	
Loramus	Blasted Lands	Both	45	57	Loramus Thalipedes—Azshara	Loramus Thalipedes	The Demon Hunter	600	
Everything Counts In Large Amounts	Blasted Lands	Both	45	55	Kum'isha the Collector—Blasted Lands	Kum'isha the Collector		5650	
REWARD: 1 Kum'isha's Junk									
One Draenei's Junk...	Blasted Lands	Both	45	55	Kum'isha the Collector—Blasted Lands	Kum'isha the Collector	Everything Counts In Large Amounts		
REWARD: 1 Kum'isha's Junk									
Breaking the Ward	Blasted Lands	Both	45	58	Loramus Thalipedes—Azshara	Loramus Thalipedes	Loramus	3100	
The Name of the Beast	Blasted Lands	Both	45	58	Loramus Thalipedes—Azshara	Lord Arkkoroc	Breaking the Ward	6200	
The Name of the Beast	Blasted Lands	Both	45	58	Lord Arkkoroc—Azshara	Lord Arkkoroc	The Name of the Beast	6200	2●65●
The Name of the Beast	Blasted Lands	Both	45	58	Lord Arkkoroc—Azshara	Loramus Thalipedes	The Name of the Beast	3100	
Azsharite	Blasted Lands	Both	45	58	Loramus Thalipedes—Azshara	Loramus Thalipedes	The Name of the Beast	7750	2●65●
The Formation of Felbane	Blasted Lands	Both	45	58	Loramus Thalipedes—Azshara	Galvan the Ancient	Azsharite	4650	
Enchanted Azsharite Fel Weaponry	Blasted Lands	Both	45	58	Galvan the Ancient—Stranglethorn	Galvan the Ancient	The Formation of Felbane	625	
CHOICE OF: 1 Enchanted Azsharite Felbane Dagger or 1 Enchanted Azsharite Felbane Staff or 1 Enchanted Azsharite Felbane Sword									
Return to the Blasted Lands	Blasted Lands	Both	45	58	Galvan the Ancient—Stranglethorn	Fallen Hero of the Horde	Enchanted Azsharite Fel Weaponry	1550	
Uniting the Shattered Amulet	Blasted Lands	Both	45	60	Fallen Hero of the Horde—Blasted Lands	Fallen Hero of the Horde	Return to the Blasted Lands	8300	
You Are Rakh'likh, Demon	Blasted Lands	Both	45	60	Fallen Hero of the Horde—Blasted Lands	Fallen Hero of the Horde	Uniting the Shattered Amulet	9950	2●70●
REWARD: 1 Necklace of Sanctuary, 1Demon's Blood, 1Demon Hide Sack									
Warrior Kinship	Blasted Lands	Both	50	52	Fallen Hero of the Horde—Blasted Lands	Fallen Hero of the Horde		5100	
War on the Shadowsworn	Blasted Lands	Both	50	53	Fallen Hero of the Horde—Blasted Lands	Fallen Hero of the Horde	Warrior Kinship	5100	
Voodoo Feathers	Blasted Lands	Both	50	52	Fallen Hero of the Horde—Blasted Lands	Fallen Hero of the Horde	War on the Shadowsworn	6350	
CHOICE OF: 1 Fury Visor or 1 Diamond Flask or 1 Razorsteel Shoulders									

Burning Steppes

Title	Location	Faction	Min Level	Con Level	Starter Location	Finisher	Prerequisite	Max XP	Cash Reward
Dark Iron Legacy	Burning Steppes	Both	48	52	Franclorn Forgewright—Burning Steppes	Franclorn Forgewright		500	
Dark Iron Legacy	Burning Steppes	Both	48	52	Franclorn Forgewright—Burning Steppes	Monument of Franclorn Forgewright	Dark Iron Legacy	5100	2●30●
REWARD: 1 Shadowforge Key									
Krom'Grul	Burning Steppes	Horde	48	53	Sha'ni Proudtusk—Burning Steppes	Thal'trak Proudtusk	Dreadmaul Rock	5250	
REWARD: 1 Sha'ni's Ring									
Extinguish the Firegut	Burning Steppes	Alliance	48	52	Oralius—Burning Steppes	Oralius		5100	
Gor'tesh the Brute Lord	Burning Steppes	Alliance	48	53	Oralius—Burning Steppes	Oralius	Extinguish the Firegut	5250	
Ogre Head On A Stick = Party	Burning Steppes	Alliance	48	53	Oralius—Burning Steppes	Oralius	Gor'tesh the Brute Lord	5250	2●40●
CHOICE OF: 1 Maddening Gauntlets or 1 Choking Band									
A Taste of Flame	Burning Steppes	Both	52	54	Cyrus Therepentous—Burning Steppes	Cyrus Therepentous	Trinkets...	5450	
A Taste of Flame	Burning Steppes	Both	52	54	Cyrus Therepentous—Burning Steppes	Cyrus Therepentous	Trinkets...	5450	
A Taste of Flame	Burning Steppes	Both	52	58	Cyrus Therepentous—Burning Steppes	Cyrus Therepentous	A Taste of Flame	6200	2●65●
CHOICE OF: 1 Shaleskin Cape or 1 Wyrmhide Spaulders or 1 Valconian Sash									
Precarious Predicament	Burning Steppes	Horde	52	58	Grark Lorkrub—Burning Steppes	Lexlort	Grark Lorkrub	7750	2●65●
Dragonkin Menace	Burning Steppes	Alliance	48	54	Helendis Riverhorn—Burning Steppes	Helendis Riverhorn		5450	1●65●

Title	Location	Faction	Min Level	Con Level	Starter Location	Finisher	Prerequisite	Max XP	Cash Reward
The True Masters	Burning Steppes	Alliance	48	54	Helendis Riverhorn—Burning Steppes	Magistrate Solomon	Dragonkin Menace	4100	
The True Masters	Burning Steppes	Alliance	48	54	Marshal Maxwell—Burning Steppes	Marshal Maxwell	The True Masters	550	
Marshal Windsor	Burning Steppes	Alliance	48	54	Marshal Maxwell—Burning Steppes	Marshal Windsor	The True Masters	5450	
Overmaster Pyron	Burning Steppes	Alliance	48	52	Jalinda Sprig—Burning Steppes	Jalinda Sprig		5100	1●55●
Incendius!	Burning Steppes	Alliance	48	56	Jalinda Sprig—Burning Steppes	Jalinda Sprig	Overmaster Pyron	5800	85●
CHOICE OF: 1 Sunborne Cape or 1 Nightfall Gloves or 1 Crypt Demon Bracers or 1 Stalwart Clutch									
FIFTY! YEP!	Burning Steppes	Alliance	50	56	Oralius—Burning Steppes	Oralius		5800	85●
The Good Stuff	Burning Steppes	Alliance	50	56	Oralius—Burning Steppes	Oralius		5800	85●
REWARD: 1 A Dingy Fanny Pack									
Tablet of the Seven	Burning Steppes	Both	50	50	Maxwort Uberglint—Burning Steppes	Maxwort Uberglint		2350	75●
Libram of Rumination	Burning Steppes	Both	50	55		Mathredis Firestar			
REWARD: 1 Lesser Arcanum of Rumination									
Libram of Constitution	Burning Steppes	Both	50	55		Mathredis Firestar			
REWARD: 1 Lesser Arcanum of Constitution									
Libram of Tenacity	Burning Steppes	Both	50	55		Mathredis Firestar			
REWARD: 1 Lesser Arcanum of Tenacity									
Libram of Resilience	Burning Steppes	Both	50	55		Mathredis Firestar			
REWARD: 1 Lesser Arcanum of Resilience									
Libram of Voracity	Burning Steppes	Both	50	55		Mathredis Firestar			
CHOICE OF: 1 Lesser Arcanum of Voracity or 1 Lesser Arcanum of Voracity or 1 Lesser Arcanum of Voracity or 1 Lesser Arcanum of Voracity or 1 Lesser Arcanum of Voracity									
Put Her Down	Burning Steppes	Alliance	55	59	Helendis Riverhorn—Burning Steppes	Helendis Riverhorn		6400	1●80●
CHOICE OF: 1 Astoria Robes or 1 Traphook Jerkin or 1 Jadescale Breastplate									
Broodling Essence	Burning Steppes	Both	50	52	Tinkee Steamboil—Burning Steppes	Tinkee Steamboil		5100	75●
Kibler's Exotic Pets	Burning Steppes	Both	55	59	Kibler—Burning Steppes	Kibler		6400	90●
REWARD: 1 Worg Carrier									
Egg Freezing	Burning Steppes	Both	57	60	Tinkee Steamboil—Burning Steppes	Tinkee Steamboil	Return to Tinkee	8300	1●80●
REWARD: 1 Eggscilloscope									
Egg Collection	Burning Steppes	Both	57	60	Tinkee Steamboil—Burning Steppes	Tinkee Steamboil	Egg Freezing	9950	2●70●
Doomrigger's Clasp	Burning Steppes	Alliance	57	60	Mayara Brightwing—Burning Steppes	Mayara Brightwing		1650	
Delivery to Ridgewell	Burning Steppes	Alliance	57	60	Mayara Brightwing—Burning Steppes	Count Remington Ridgewell	Doomrigger's Clasp	6600	2●70●
CHOICE OF: 1 Swiftfoot Treads or 1 Blinkstrike Armguards									
Mayara Brightwing	Burning Steppes	Alliance	57	60	Count Remington Ridgewell—Stormwind	Mayara Brightwing		650	
Felnok Steelspring	Burning Steppes	Both	50	54	Tinkee Steamboil—Burning Steppes	Felnok Steelspring	Broodling Essence	2700	
Chillwind Horns	Burning Steppes	Both	50	54	Felnok Steelspring—Winterspring Everlook	Felnok Steelspring	Felnok Steelspring	5450	
Return to Tinkee	Burning Steppes	Both	50	54	Felnok Steelspring—Winterspring Everlook	Tinkee Steamboil	Chillwind Horns	2700	
CHOICE OF: 1 Blitzcleaver or 1 Grave Scepter									
En-Ay-Es-Tee-Why	Burning Steppes	Both	55	59	Kibler—Burning Steppes	Kibler		6400	90●
REWARD: 1 Smolderweb Carrier									
Mother's Milk	Burning Steppes	Both	55	60	Ragged John—Burning Steppes	Ragged John		9950	1●80●
REWARD: 1 Ragged John's Neverending Cup									
Tinkee Steamboil	Burning Steppes	Both	57	60	Felnok Steelspring—Winterspring Everlook	Tinkee Steamboil	Return to Tinkee	650	
Maxwell's Mission	Burning Steppes	Alliance	55	60	Marshal Maxwell—Burning Steppes	Marshal Maxwell	Message to Maxwell	8550	1●80●
CHOICE OF: 1 Wyrmthalak's Shackles or 1 Omokk's Girth Restrainer or 1 Halycon's Muzzle or 1 Vosh'gajin's Strand or 1 Voone's Vice Grips									
General Drakkisath's Demise	Burning Steppes	Alliance	55	60	Marshal Maxwell—Burning Steppes	Marshal Maxwell	General Drakkisath's Command	9950	2●70●
CHOICE OF: 1 Mark of Tyranny or 1 Eye of the Beast or 1 Blackhand's Breadth									
Stormwind Rendezvous	Burning Steppes	Alliance	50	60	Marshal Maxwell—Burning Steppes	Reginald Windsor	Jail Break!	650	
Mor'zul Bloodbringer	Burning Steppes	Horde	60	58	Kurgul—Orgrimmar	Mor'zul Bloodbringer		625	
Rage of Blood	Burning Steppes	Both	60	58	Mor'zul Bloodbringer—Burning Steppes	Mor'zul Bloodbringer		7750	
Wildeyes	Burning Steppes	Both	60	58	Mor'zul Bloodbringer—Burning Steppes	Gorzeeki Wildeyes	Rage of Blood	3100	
Lord Banehollow	Burning Steppes	Both	60	58	Gorzeeki Wildeyes—Burning Steppes	Lord Banehollow		6200	
Ulathek the Traitor	Burning Steppes	Both	60	58	Lord Banehollow—Felwood Monster Dreadlord Unique Elite	Lord Banehollow	Lord Banehollow	6200	
Xorothian Stardust	Burning Steppes	Both	60	60	Lord Banehollow—Felwood Monster Dreadlord Unique Elite	Gorzeeki Wildeyes	Ulathek the Traitor	6600	
Bell of Dethmoora	Burning Steppes	Both	60	60	Mor'zul Bloodbringer—Burning Steppes	Gorzeeki Wildeyes	Wildeyes	6600	
Wheel of the Black March	Burning Steppes	Both	60	60	Mor'zul Bloodbringer—Burning Steppes	Gorzeeki Wildeyes	Wildeyes	6600	
Doomsday Candle	Burning Steppes	Both	60	60	Mor'zul Bloodbringer—Burning Steppes	Gorzeeki Wildeyes	Wildeyes	6600	
Imp Delivery	Burning Steppes	Both	60	60	Gorzeeki Wildeyes—Burning Steppes	Gorzeeki Wildeyes	Xorothian Stardust	6600	
Arcanite	Burning Steppes	Both	60	60	Gorzeeki Wildeyes—Burning Steppes	Gorzeeki Wildeyes	Bell of Dethmoora	6600	
Dreadsteed of Xoroth	Burning Steppes	Both	60	60	Mor'zul Bloodbringer—Burning Steppes	Dreadsteed Spirit	Arcanite	7050	
A New Threat	Coldridge Valley	Alliance	1	2	Balir Frosthammer—Dun Morogh Anvilmar	Balir Frosthammer	Dwarven Outfitters	170	
CHOICE OF: 1 Bear Shawl or 1 Rustic Belt or 1 Snow Boots									
Dwarven Outfitters	Coldridge Valley	Alliance	1	1	Sten Stoutarm—Dun Morogh Anvilmar	Sten Stoutarm		80	
CHOICE OF: 1 Rabbit Handler Gloves or 1 Wolf Handler Gloves or 1 Boar Handler Gloves									
The Troll Cave	Coldridge Valley	Alliance	1	4	Grelin Whitebeard—Dun Morogh Anvilmar	Grelin Whitebeard		360	
CHOICE OF: 1 Anvilmar Hand Axe or 1 Anvilmar Hammer or 1 Anvilmar Knife or 1 Anvilmar Sledge REWARD: 3 Healing Herb									
The Boar Hunter	Coldridge Valley	Alliance	1	3	Talin Keeneye—Dun Morogh Anvilmar	Talin Keeneye		250	
CHOICE OF: 1 Dwarven Cloth Britches or 1 Dwarven Leather Pants									
The Stolen Journal	Coldridge Valley	Alliance	1	5	Grelin Whitebeard—Dun Morogh Anvilmar	Grelin Whitebeard	The Troll Cave	550	
CHOICE OF: 1 Dwarven Kite Shield or 1 Smooth Walking Staff									
Coldridge Valley Mail Delivery	Coldridge Valley	Alliance	1	3	Sten Stoutarm—Dun Morogh Anvilmar	Talin Keeneye	Dwarven Outfitters	190	
Coldridge Valley Mail Delivery	Coldridge Valley	Alliance	1	4	Talin Keeneye—Dun Morogh Anvilmar	Grelin Whitebeard	Coldridge Valley Mail Delivery	270	7●
Senir's Observations	Coldridge Valley	Alliance	1	5	Grelin Whitebeard—Dun Morogh Anvilmar	Mountaineer Thalos	The Stolen Journal	340	
Senir's Observations	Coldridge Valley	Alliance	1	5	Mountaineer Thalos—Dun Morogh Anvilmar	Senir Whitebeard	Senir's Observations	340	
Beginnings	Coldridge Valley	Alliance	1	4	Alamar Grimm—Dun Morogh Anvilmar	Alamar Grimm		360	
Supplies to Tannok	Coldridge Valley	Alliance	1	5	Hands Springsprocket—Dun Morogh Anvilmar	Tannok Frosthammer		110	
CHOICE OF: 5 Tough Jerky or 5 Refreshing Spring Water									
Simple Rune	Coldridge Valley	Alliance	1	1	Sten Stoutarm—Dun Morogh Anvilmar	Thran Khorman	Dwarven Outfitters	40	
Consecrated Rune	Coldridge Valley	Alliance	1	1	Sten Stoutarm—Dun Morogh Anvilmar	Bromos Grummner	Dwarven Outfitters	40	
Etched Rune	Coldridge Valley	Alliance	1	1	Sten Stoutarm—Dun Morogh Anvilmar	Thorgas Grimson	Dwarven Outfitters	40	
Encrypted Rune	Coldridge Valley	Alliance	1	1	Sten Stoutarm—Dun Morogh Anvilmar	Solm Hargrin	Dwarven Outfitters	40	
Hallowed Rune	Coldridge Valley	Alliance	1	1	Sten Stoutarm—Dun Morogh Anvilmar	Branstock Khalder	Dwarven Outfitters	40	
Simple Memorandum	Coldridge Valley	Alliance	1	1	Sten Stoutarm—Dun Morogh Anvilmar	Thran Khorman	Dwarven Outfitters	40	
Encrypted Memorandum	Coldridge Valley	Alliance	1	1	Sten Stoutarm—Dun Morogh Anvilmar	Solm Hargrin	Dwarven Outfitters	40	
Glyphic Memorandum	Coldridge Valley	Alliance	1	1	Sten Stoutarm—Dun Morogh Anvilmar	Marryk Nurribit	Dwarven Outfitters	40	
Tainted Memorandum	Coldridge Valley	Alliance	1	1	Sten Stoutarm—Dun Morogh Anvilmar	Alamar Grimm	Dwarven Outfitters	40	
A Refugee's Quandary	Coldridge Valley	Alliance	3	3	Felix Whindlebolt—Dun Morogh Anvilmar	Felix Whindlebolt		250	50●
Scalding Mornbrew Delivery	Coldridge Valley	Alliance	4	5	Nori Pridedrift—Dun Morogh Anvilmar	Durnan Furcutter		230	
Bring Back the Mug	Coldridge Valley	Alliance	4	5	Durnan Furcutter—Dun Morogh Anvilmar	Nori Pridedrift	Scalding Mornbrew Delivery	450	50●
Welcome!	Coldridge Valley	Alliance	1	1	Coldridge Valley Gift Voucher	Yori Crackhelm			
CHOICE OF: 1 Diablo Stone or 1 Panda Collar or 1 Zergling Leash									
Carnival Boots	Darkmoon Faire	Both	1	60		Chronos			
REWARD: 1 Darkmoon Faire Prize Ticket									
Carnival Jerkins	Darkmoon Faire	Both	10	60		Chronos			
REWARD: 4 Darkmoon Faire Prize Ticket									
The World's Largest Gnome!	Darkmoon Faire	Both	20	60		Chronos			
REWARD: 8 Darkmoon Faire Prize Ticket									
Crocolisk Boy and the Bearded Murloc	Darkmoon Faire	Both	30	60		Chronos			
REWARD: 12 Darkmoon Faire Prize Ticket									

Darkmoon Faire cont'd

Title	Location	Faction	Min Level	Con Level	Starter Location	Finisher	Prerequisite	Max XP	Cash Reward
Armor Kits	Darkmoon Faire	Both	40	60		Chronos			
REWARD: 20 Darkmoon Faire Prize Ticket									
Coarse Weightstone	Darkmoon Faire	Both	1	60		Kerri Hicks			
REWARD: 1 Darkmoon Faire Prize Ticket									
Heavy Grinding Stone	Darkmoon Faire	Both	10	60		Kerri Hicks			
REWARD: 4 Darkmoon Faire Prize Ticket									
Green Iron Bracers	Darkmoon Faire	Both	20	60		Kerri Hicks			
REWARD: 8 Darkmoon Faire Prize Ticket									
Big Black Mace	Darkmoon Faire	Both	30	60		Kerri Hicks			
REWARD: 12 Darkmoon Faire Prize Ticket									
Rituals of Strength	Darkmoon Faire	Both	40	60		Kerri Hicks			
REWARD: 20 Darkmoon Faire Prize Ticket									
Copper Modulator	Darkmoon Faire	Both	1	60		Rinling			
REWARD: 1 Darkmoon Faire Prize Ticket									
Whirring Bronze Gizmo	Darkmoon Faire	Both	10	60		Rinling			
REWARD: 4 Darkmoon Faire Prize Ticket									
Green Fireworks	Darkmoon Faire	Both	20	60		Rinling			
REWARD: 8 Darkmoon Faire Prize Ticket									
Mechanical Repair Kits	Darkmoon Faire	Both	30	60		Rinling			
REWARD: 12 Darkmoon Faire Prize Ticket									
Thorium Widget	Darkmoon Faire	Both	40	60		Rinling			
REWARD: 20 Darkmoon Faire Prize Ticket									
Small Furry Paws	Darkmoon Faire	Both	1	60		Yebb Neblegear			
REWARD: 1 Darkmoon Faire Prize Ticket									
Torn Bear Pelts	Darkmoon Faire	Both	10	60		Yebb Neblegear			
REWARD: 4 Darkmoon Faire Prize Ticket									
Soft Bushy Tails	Darkmoon Faire	Both	20	60		Yebb Neblegear			
REWARD: 8 Darkmoon Faire Prize Ticket									
Vibrant Plumes	Darkmoon Faire	Both	30	60		Yebb Neblegear			
REWARD: 12 Darkmoon Faire Prize Ticket									
Evil Bat Eyes	Darkmoon Faire	Both	40	60		Yebb Neblegear			
REWARD: 20 Darkmoon Faire Prize Ticket									
Darkmoon Beast Deck	Darkmoon Faire	Alliance	1	55	Beasts Deck	Professor Thaddeus Paleo		550	
REWARD: 1 Darkmoon Card: Blue Dragon									
Darkmoon Portals Deck	Darkmoon Faire	Alliance	1	55	Portals Deck	Professor Thaddeus Paleo		550	
REWARD: 1 Darkmoon Card: Twisting Nether									
Darkmoon Warlords Deck	Darkmoon Faire	Alliance	1	55	Warlords Deck	Professor Thaddeus Paleo		550	
REWARD: 1 Darkmoon Card: Heroism									
Darkmoon Elementals Deck	Darkmoon Faire	Alliance	1	55	Elementals Deck	Professor Thaddeus Paleo		550	
REWARD: 1 Darkmoon Card: Maelstrom									
5 Tickets - Darkmoon Flower	Darkmoon Faire	Both	6	60		Gelvas Grimegate			
REWARD: 1 Darkmoon Flower									
5 Tickets - Minor Darkmoon Prize	Darkmoon Faire	Both	15	60		Gelvas Grimegate			
REWARD: 1 Minor Darkmoon Prize									
12 Tickets - Lesser Darkmoon Prize	Darkmoon Faire	Both	30	60		Gelvas Grimegate			
REWARD: 1 Lesser Darkmoon Prize									
40 Tickets - Greater Darkmoon Prize	Darkmoon Faire	Both	45	60		Gelvas Grimegate			
REWARD: 1 Greater Darkmoon Prize									
50 Tickets - Darkmoon Storage Box	Darkmoon Faire	Both	6	60		Gelvas Grimegate			
REWARD: 1 Darkmoon Storage Box									
10 Tickets - Last Month's Mutton	Darkmoon Faire	Both	25	60		Gelvas Grimegate			
REWARD: 1 Last Month's Mutton									
50 Tickets - Last Year's Mutton	Darkmoon Faire	Both	45	60		Gelvas Grimegate			
REWARD: 1 Last Year's Mutton									
Your Fortune Awaits You...	Darkmoon Faire	Both	10	60	Sayge's Fortune #23	Mysterious Eastvale Haystack		650	
REWARD: 1 Mysterious Lockbox									
Your Fortune Awaits You...	Darkmoon Faire	Both	10	60	Sayge's Fortune #24	Mysterious Deadmines Chest		650	
REWARD: 1 Mysterious Lockbox									
More Dense Grinding Stones	Darkmoon Faire	Both	40	60		Kerri Hicks			
REWARD: 20 Darkmoon Faire Prize Ticket									
1200 Tickets - Orb of the Darkmoon	Darkmoon Faire	Both	55	60		Gelvas Grimegate			
REWARD: 1 Orb of the Darkmoon									
More Armor Kits	Darkmoon Faire	Both	40	60		Chronos			
REWARD: 20 Darkmoon Faire Prize Ticket									
More Thorium Widgets	Darkmoon Faire	Both	40	60		Rinling			
REWARD: 20 Darkmoon Faire Prize Ticket									
More Bat Eyes	Darkmoon Faire	Both	40	60		Yebb Neblegear			
REWARD: 20 Darkmoon Faire Prize Ticket									
Your Fortune Awaits You...	Darkmoon Faire	Both	10	60	Sayge's Fortune #25	Mysterious Wailing Caverns Chest		650	
REWARD: 1 Mysterious Lockbox									
Your Fortune Awaits You...	Darkmoon Faire	Both	10	60	Sayge's Fortune #27	Mysterious Tree Stump		650	
REWARD: 1 Mysterious Lockbox									
Spawn of Jubjub	Darkmoon Faire	Both	1	1		Morja			
REWARD: 1 Unhatched Jubling Egg									
1200 Tickets - Amulet of the Darkmoon	Darkmoon Faire	Both	55	60		Gelvas Grimegate			
REWARD: 1 Amulet of the Darkmoon									
Glowing Scorpid Blood	Darkmoon Faire	Both	40	60		Yebb Neblegear			
REWARD: 20 Darkmoon Faire Prize Ticket									
More Glowing Scorpid Blood	Darkmoon Faire	Both	40	60		Yebb Neblegear			
REWARD: 20 Darkmoon Faire Prize Ticket									
40 Tickets - Schematic: Steam Tonk Controller	Darkmoon Faire	Both	45	60		Gelvas Grimegate			
REWARD: 1 Schematic: Steam Tonk Controller									

Darkshore

Title	Location	Faction	Min Level	Con Level	Starter Location	Finisher	Prerequisite	Max XP	Cash Reward
The Absent Minded Prospector	Darkshore	Alliance	15	20	Archaeologist Hollee—Darkshore Auberdine	Prospector Remtravel		1150	
The Absent Minded Prospector	Darkshore	Alliance	15	20	Prospector Remtravel—Darkshore	Archaeologist Hollee	The Absent Minded Prospector	1950	
The Absent Minded Prospector	Darkshore	Alliance	15	20	Archaeologist Hollee—Darkshore Auberdine	Chief Archaeologist Greywhisker	The Absent Minded Prospector	1150	
CHOICE OF: 1 Hammerfist Gloves or 1 Windfelt Gloves or 1 Relic Hunter Belt									
The Absent Minded Prospector	Darkshore	Alliance	15	20	Chief Archaeologist Greywhisker—Darnassus	Archaeologist Flagongut	The Absent Minded Prospector	1550	
The Absent Minded Prospector	Darkshore	Alliance	15	24	Archaeologist Flagongut—Darnassus	Archaeologist Flagongut	The Absent Minded Prospector	2400	
CHOICE OF: 1 Relic Blade or 1 Skullchipper									
The Master's Glaive	Darkshore	Alliance	12	17	Onu—Darkshore	Scrying Bowl	Onu	625	
Therylune's Escape	Darkshore	Alliance	10	18	Therylune—Darkshore Dryad Unique	Therysil		1350	10
Cave Mushrooms	Darkshore	Alliance	12	17	Barithras Moonshade—Darkshore Auberdine	Barithras Moonshade		1250	9
REWARD: 1 Gustweald Cloak, 10Red-speckled Mushroom									
Onu	Darkshore	Alliance	12	17	Barithras Moonshade—Darkshore Auberdine	Onu	Cave Mushrooms	625	
The Twilight Camp	Darkshore	Alliance	12	17	Scrying Bowl—Darkshore	Twilight Tome	The Master's Glaive	1250	9
Return to Onu	Darkshore	Alliance	12	17	Twilight Tome	Onu	The Twilight Camp	950	7
Mathystra Relics	Darkshore	Alliance	12	20	Onu—Darkshore	Onu	Return to Onu	1950	
CHOICE OF: 1 Hardwood Cudgel or 1 Woodsman Sword									

Title	Location	Faction	Min Level	Con Level	Starter Location	Finisher	Prerequisite	Max XP	Cash Reward
The Fall of Ameth'Aran	Darkshore	Alliance	9	12	Sentinel Tysha Moonblade—Darkshore	Sentinel Tysha Moonblade		900	5●
Bashal'Aran	Darkshore	Alliance	7	12	Thundris Windweaver—Darkshore Auberdine	Asterion		675	
Bashal'Aran	Darkshore	Alliance	7	12	Asterion—Darkshore	Asterion	Bashal'Aran	900	
Bashal'Aran	Darkshore	Alliance	7	13	Asterion—Darkshore	Asterion	Bashal'Aran	900	
Bashal'Aran	Darkshore	Alliance	7	13	Asterion—Darkshore	Asterion	Bashal'Aran	675	
CHOICE OF: 1 Explorer's Vest or 1 Vagabond Leggings or 1 Elven Wand									
Tools of the Highborne	Darkshore	Alliance	9	12	Thundris Windweaver—Darkshore Auberdine	Thundris Windweaver		900	5●
REWARD: 1 Ivy Cuffs									
Onu is meditating	Darkshore	Alliance	1	1		Onu	The Master's Glaive		
REWARD: 1 Phial of Scrying									
Onu is meditating	Darkshore	Alliance	1	1		Onu	The Twilight Camp		
REWARD: 1 Phial of Scrying									
For Love Eternal	Darkshore	Alliance	11	16	Cerellean Whiteclaw—Darkshore Auberdine	Cerellean Whiteclaw		875	
REWARD: 1 Tear of Grief									
The Tower of Althalaxx	Darkshore	Alliance	13	18	Sentinel Elissa Starbreeze—Darkshore Auberdine	Balthule Shadowstrike		675	
The Tower of Althalaxx	Darkshore	Alliance	13	18	Balthule Shadowstrike—Darkshore	Balthule Shadowstrike	The Tower of Althalaxx	1350	10●
The Tower of Althalaxx	Darkshore	Alliance	13	18	Balthule Shadowstrike—Darkshore	Delgren the Purifier	The Tower of Althalaxx	1000	
The Powers Below	Darkshore	Alliance	10	20	Book: The Powers Below	Gerrig Bonegrip		1950	
The Tower of Althalaxx	Darkshore	Alliance	13	31	Balthule Shadowstrike—Darkshore	Delgren the Purifier	The Tower of Althalaxx	2500	
CHOICE OF: 1 Pious Legwraps or 1 Seraph's Strike									
Deep Ocean, Vast Sea	Darkshore	Alliance	13	17	Gorbold Steelhand—Dwarf	Gorbold Steelhand		1250	
CHOICE OF: 1 Welldrip Gloves or 1 Noosegrip Gauntlets									
Buzzbox 827	Darkshore	Alliance	7	10	Wizbang Cranktoggle—Darkshore Auberdine	Buzzbox 827		850	3● 50●
How Big a Threat?	Darkshore	Alliance	10	14	Terenthis—Darkshore Auberdine	Terenthis		750	
How Big a Threat?	Darkshore	Alliance	10	14	Terenthis—Darkshore Auberdine	Terenthis	How Big a Threat?	975	
A Lost Master	Darkshore	Alliance	10	20	Terenthis—Darkshore Auberdine	Terenthis	How Big a Threat?	1550	
A Lost Master	Darkshore	Alliance	10	20	Terenthis—Darkshore Auberdine	Volcor	A Lost Master	775	
Escape Through Force	Darkshore	Alliance	10	22	Volcor—Darkshore	Terenthis	A Lost Master	1750	17●
REWARD: 1 Steadfast Cinch									
Escape Through Stealth	Darkshore	Alliance	10	20	Volcor—Darkshore	Terenthis	A Lost Master	775	6●
REWARD: 1 Scarab Trousers									
Buzzbox 411	Darkshore	Alliance	7	12	Buzzbox 827—Darkshore	Buzzbox 411	Buzzbox 827	1150	10●
Buzzbox 323	Darkshore	Alliance	7	14	Buzzbox 411—Darkshore	Buzzbox 323	Buzzbox 411	975	6●
Buzzbox 525	Darkshore	Alliance	7	16	Buzzbox 323—Darkshore	Buzzbox 525	Buzzbox 323	1150	8●
REWARD: 1 Wizbang's Gunnysack, 5Wizbang's Special Brew									
Fruit of the Sea	Darkshore	Alliance	15	17	Gubber Blump—Darkshore Auberdine	Gubber Blump		1250	
CHOICE OF: 1 Shucking Gloves or 1 Crustacean Boots									
The Family and the Fishing Pole	Darkshore	Alliance	10	14	Gubber Blump—Darkshore Auberdine	Gubber Blump		975	
REWARD: 1 Blump Family Fishing Pole									
The Tower of Althalaxx	Darkshore	Alliance	13	31	Balthule Shadowstrike—Darkshore	Balthule Shadowstrike	The Tower of Althalaxx	2500	
Researching the Corruption	Darkshore	Alliance	18	24	Gershala Nightwhisper—Darkshore Auberdine	Gershala Nightwhisper		2400	35●
CHOICE OF: 1 Beetle Clasps or 1 Prelacy Cape									
Gaffer Jacks	Darkshore	Alliance	10	12	Wizbang Cranktoggle—Darkshore Auberdine	Wizbang Cranktoggle		460	2● 50●
Electropellers	Darkshore	Alliance	10	12	Wizbang Cranktoggle—Darkshore Auberdine	Wizbang Cranktoggle	Gaffer Jacks	900	5●
REWARD: 20 Aquadynamic Fish Lens									
Gyromast's Revenge	Darkshore	Alliance	14	20	Gelkak Gyromast—Darkshore	Gelkak Gyromast	Gyromast's Retrieval	1150	9●
REWARD: 5 Elixir of Water Breathing									
Gyromast's Retrieval	Darkshore	Alliance	14	20	Gelkak Gyromast—Darkshore	Gelkak Gyromast		1550	12●
Plagued Lands	Darkshore	Alliance	10	14	Tharnariun Treetender—Darkshore	Tharnariun Treetender		975	6●
Cleansing of the Infected	Darkshore	Alliance	10	16	Tharnariun Treetender—Darkshore	Tharnariun Treetender	Plagued Lands	1150	
Tharnariun's Hope	Darkshore	Alliance	10	18	Tharnariun Treetender—Darkshore	Tharnariun Treetender	Cleansing of the Infected	1350	
CHOICE OF: 1 Evergreen Gloves or 1 Timberland Cape									
Easy Strider Living	Darkshore	Alliance	9	12	Alanndarian Nightsong—Darkshore	Alanndarian Nightsong		900	
REWARD: 1 Recipe: Strider Stew, 5Strider Stew									
Washed Ashore	Darkshore	Alliance	11	13	Gwennyth Bly'Leggonde—Darkshore Auberdine	Gwennyth Bly'Leggonde		675	10●
Washed Ashore	Darkshore	Alliance	11	14	Gwennyth Bly'Leggonde—Darkshore Auberdine	Gwennyth Bly'Leggonde	Washed Ashore	975	
CHOICE OF: 1 Sandcomber Boots or 1 Dryweed Belt or 1 Clamshell Bracers									
Beached Sea Turtle	Darkshore	Alliance	11	13	Beached Sea Turtle—Darkshore	Gwennyth Bly'Leggonde	Washed Ashore	460	3●
Beached Sea Creature	Darkshore	Alliance	11	13	Beached Sea Creature—Darkshore	Gwennyth Bly'Leggonde	Washed Ashore	460	3●
Beached Sea Turtle	Darkshore	Alliance	12	15	Beached Sea Turtle—Darkshore	Gwennyth Bly'Leggonde	Washed Ashore	550	3● 50●
Beached Sea Turtle	Darkshore	Alliance	12	15	Beached Sea Turtle—Darkshore	Gwennyth Bly'Leggonde	Washed Ashore	550	3● 50●
Beached Sea Creature	Darkshore	Alliance	12	14	Beached Sea Creature—Darkshore	Gwennyth Bly'Leggonde	Washed Ashore	490	3●
Beached Sea Creature	Darkshore	Alliance	12	16	Beached Sea Creature—Darkshore	Gwennyth Bly'Leggonde	Washed Ashore	575	4●
Beached Sea Turtle	Darkshore	Alliance	13	19	Beached Sea Turtle—Darkshore	Gwennyth Bly'Leggonde	Washed Ashore	750	5●
Beached Sea Turtle	Darkshore	Alliance	13	19	Beached Sea Turtle—Darkshore	Gwennyth Bly'Leggonde	Washed Ashore	725	5●
Beached Sea Creature	Darkshore	Alliance	13	19	Beached Sea Creature—Darkshore	Gwennyth Bly'Leggonde	Washed Ashore	725	5●
WANTED: Murkdeep!	Darkshore	Alliance	15	18	Wanted Poster—Darkshore	Sentinel Glynda Nal'Shea		1700	
CHOICE OF: 1 Timberland Armguards or 1 Ridgeback Bracers or 1 Breakwater Girdle									
Thundris Windweaver	Darkshore	Alliance	11	15	Terenthis—Darkshore Auberdine	Thundris Windweaver	How Big a Threat?	110	
The Cliffspring River	Darkshore	Alliance	11	15	Thundris Windweaver—Darkshore Auberdine	Thundris Windweaver	Thundris Windweaver	800	
The Blackwood Corrupted	Darkshore	Alliance	15	18	Thundris Windweaver—Darkshore Auberdine	Thundris Windweaver	The Cliffspring River	1700	20●
CHOICE OF: 1 Moonstone Wand or 1 Wildkeeper Leggings or 1 Guststorm Legguards									
The Red Crystal	Darkshore	Alliance	12	14	Sentinel Glynda Nal'Shea—Darkshore Auberdine	Sentinel Glynda Nal'Shea		490	6●
As Water Cascades	Darkshore	Alliance	12	14	Sentinel Glynda Nal'Shea—Darkshore Auberdine	Mysterious Red Crystal	The Red Crystal	490	
The Fragments Within	Darkshore	Alliance	12	14	Mysterious Red Crystal—Darkshore	Sentinel Glynda Nal'Shea	As Water Cascades	975	
CHOICE OF: 1 Briarsteel Shortsword or 1 Curvewood Dagger or 1 Oakthrush Staff									
The Sleeper Has Awakened	Darkshore	Alliance	17	20	Kerlonian Evershade—Darkshore	Liladris Moonriver		1550	
CHOICE OF: 1 Owlsight Rifle or 1 Jadefinger Baton or 1 Steelcap Shield									
One Shot. One Kill.	Darkshore	Alliance	10	15	Sentinel Aynasha—Darkshore	Sentinel Onaeya		1050	14●
Gathering the Cure	Darkshore	Alliance	14	14	Alanndarian Nightsong—Darkshore	Alanndarian Nightsong	The Principal Source	750	
Curing the Sick	Darkshore	Alliance	14	14	Alanndarian Nightsong—Darkshore	Dendrite Starblaze	Gathering the Cure	750	
REWARD: 1 Veildust Medicine Bag									
The Bounty of Teldrassil	Darkshore	Alliance	10	10	Nessa Shadowsong—Teldrassil Rut'theran Village	Vesprystus		210	
Flight to Auberdine	Darkshore	Alliance	10	10	Vesprystus—Teldrassil Rut'theran Village Night Elf Taxi Elite	Laird	The Bounty of Teldrassil	420	
Return to Nessa	Darkshore	Alliance	10	10	Laird—Darkshore Auberdine	Nessa Shadowsong	Flight to Auberdine	1050	2● 50●
Nessa Shadowsong	Darkshore	Alliance	10	10	Mydrannul—Night Elf	Nessa Shadowsong		210	
A Lesson to Learn	Darnassus	Alliance	16	16	Mathrengyl Bearwalker—Night Elf	Dendrite Starblaze		120	
Trouble In Darkshore?	Darnassus	Alliance	14	14	Chief Archaeologist Greywhisker—Darnassus	Archaeologist Hollee	The Absent Minded Prospector	490	
Tumors	Darnassus	Alliance	4	9	Rellian Greenspyre—Darnassus	Rellian Greenspyre	Rellian Greenspyre	975	6●
REWARD: 1 Pruning Knife									
Velinde's Effects	Darnassus	Alliance	25	30	Thyn'tel Bladeweaver—Darnassus	Thyn'tel Bladeweaver	Velinde Starsong	600	
The Barrens Port	Darnassus	Alliance	25	30	Thyn'tel Bladeweaver—Darnassus	Wharfmaster Dizzywig	Velinde's Effects	1200	
The New Frontier	Darnassus	Alliance	54	55	Herald Moonstalker—Darnassus	Arch Druid Fandral Staghelm		550	
In Search of Thaelrid	Darnassus	Alliance	18	24	Dawnwatcher Shaedlass—Darnassus	Argent Guard Thaelrid	Blackfathom Villainy	2400	
Twilight Falls	Darnassus	Alliance	20	25	Argent Guard Manados—Darnassus	Argent Guard Manados		2550	
REWARD: 1 Nimbus Boots, 1Heartwood Girdle									
Moonglow Vest	Darnassus	Alliance	8	18	Lotherias—Darnassus Unique Night Elf	Lotherias		1350	
REWARD: 1 Pattern: Moonglow Vest									

Darnassus cont'd

Title	Location	Faction	Min Level	Con Level	Starter Location	Finisher	Prerequisite	Max XP	Cash Reward
Erion's Behest	Darnassus	Alliance	16	16	Erion Shadewhisper—Night Elf	Renzik "The Shiv"	Redridge Rendezvous	575	
Assisting Arch Druid Staghelm	Darnassus	Alliance	47	50	Innkeeper Saelienne—Darnassus	Arch Druid Fandral Staghelm		470	
Un'Goro Soil	Darnassus	Alliance	47	50	Arch Druid Fandral Staghelm—Darnassus	Jenal		4700	1● 45●
Morrowgrain Research	Darnassus	Alliance	47	50	Arch Druid Fandral Staghelm—Darnassus	Mathrengyl Bearwalker	Un'Goro Soil	470	
REWARD: 20 Packet of Tharlendris Seeds									
Morrowgrain Research	Darnassus	Alliance	47	50	Mathrengyl Bearwalker—Night Elf	Mathrengyl Bearwalker	Morrowgrain Research	4700	
REWARD: 1 Cenarion Circle Cache									
Morrowgrain to Darnassus	Darnassus	Alliance	47	55		Mathrengyl Bearwalker	Morrowgrain Research	4700	
REWARD: 1 Cenarion Circle Cache									
March of the Silithid	Darnassus	Alliance	50	53	Gracina Spiritmight—Darnassus	Alchemist Pestlezugg	Rise of the Silithid	525	
Calm Before the Storm	Darnassus	Alliance	50	54	Gracina Spiritmight—Darnassus	Idriana	Calm Before the Storm	8150	
CHOICE OF: 1 Oblivion Orb or 1 Snarkshaw Spaulders or 1 Eschewal Greaves									
A Call to Arms: The Plaguelands!	Darnassus	Alliance	50	50	Herald Moonstalker—Darnassus	Commander Ashlam Valorfist		470	
Stars of Elune	Darnassus	Alliance	10	10		Priestess Alathea			
Returning Home	Darnassus	Alliance	10	10	Priestess Josetta—Elwynn Goldshire	Priestess Alathea		210	
Returning Home	Darnassus	Alliance	10	10	Laurna Morninglight—Teldrassil Dolanaar	Priestess Alathea		210	
Returning Home	Darnassus	Alliance	10	10	Maxan Anvol—Dun Morogh Kharanos	Priestess Alathea		210	
Returning Home	Darnassus	Alliance	10	10	High Priestess Laurena—Stormwind	Priestess Alathea		210	
Returning Home	Darnassus	Alliance	10	10	Nara Meideros—Stormwind	Priestess Alathea		210	
Returning Home	Darnassus	Alliance	10	10	High Priest Rohan—Ironforge	Priestess Alathea		210	
Elune's Grace	Darnassus	Alliance	20	20		Priestess Alathea			
Elune's Grace	Darnassus	Alliance	20	20	High Priestess Laurena—Stormwind	Priestess Alathea		390	
Elune's Grace	Darnassus	Alliance	20	20	Nara Meideros—Stormwind	Priestess Alathea		390	
Elune's Grace	Darnassus	Alliance	20	20	High Priest Rohan—Ironforge	Priestess Alathea		390	
Moonglade	Darnassus	Alliance	10	10	Mathrengyl Bearwalker—Night Elf	Dendrite Starblaze		210	
Heeding the Call	Darnassus	Alliance	10	10	Denatharion—Night Elf	Mathrengyl Bearwalker		85	
Body and Heart	Darnassus	Alliance	10	10	Mathrengyl Bearwalker—Night Elf	Mathrengyl Bearwalker	Back to Darnassus	850	
Lessons Anew	Darnassus	Alliance	14	14	Mathrengyl Bearwalker—Night Elf	Dendrite Starblaze		100	
The New Frontier	Darnassus	Alliance	54	55	Arch Druid Fandral Staghelm—Darnassus	Mathrengyl Bearwalker	The New Frontier	550	
Rabine Saturna	Darnassus	Alliance	54	55	Mathrengyl Bearwalker—Night Elf	Rabine Saturna	The New Frontier	1400	
Frostsaber Replacement	Darnassus	Horde	60	1		Lelanai			
CHOICE OF: 1 Reins of the Swift Stormsaber or 1 Reins of the Swift Frostsaber or 1 Reins of the Swift Mistsaber									
Nightsaber Replacement	Darnassus	Horde	60	1		Lelanai			
CHOICE OF: 1 Reins of the Swift Stormsaber or 1 Reins of the Swift Frostsaber or 1 Reins of the Swift Mistsaber									
A Donation of Wool	Darnassus	Alliance	12	60		Raedon Duskstriker		650	
A Donation of Silk	Darnassus	Alliance	26	60		Raedon Duskstriker		1650	
A Donation of Mageweave	Darnassus	Alliance	40	60		Raedon Duskstriker		3300	
A Donation of Runecloth	Darnassus	Alliance	50	60		Raedon Duskstriker	A Donation of Wool	6600	
Additional Runecloth	Darnassus	Alliance	50	60		Raedon Duskstriker	A Donation of Runecloth		
Dancing for Marzipan	Darnassus	Alliance	10	60	Innkeeper Saelienne—Darnassus	Innkeeper Saelienne			
REWARD: 1 Darnassus Marzipan									
The Lunar Festival	Darnassus	Alliance	1	60		Lunar Festival Harbinger			

Deathknell

Title	Location	Faction	Min Level	Con Level	Starter Location	Finisher	Prerequisite	Max XP	Cash Reward
A Rogue's Deal	Deathknell	Horde	1	5		Innkeeper Renee		110	
CHOICE OF: 5 Forest Mushroom Cap or 5 Refreshing Spring Water									
Rude Awakening	Deathknell	Horde	1	1	Undertaker Mordo—Tirisfal Glades Deathknell	Shadow Priest Sarvis		40	
The Mindless Ones	Deathknell	Horde	1	2	Shadow Priest Sarvis—Tirisfal Glades Deathknell	Shadow Priest Sarvis		170	
CHOICE OF: 1 Flax Gloves or 1 Battered Cloak									
The Damned	Deathknell	Horde	2	2	Novice Elreth—Tirisfal Glades Deathknell	Novice Elreth		170	
CHOICE OF: 1 Flax Bracers or 1 Old Leather Belt									
Night Web's Hollow	Deathknell	Horde	2	4	Executor Arren—Tirisfal Glades Deathknell	Executor Arren	The Damned	360	
CHOICE OF: 1 Flax Vest or 1 Rugged Mail Vest or 1 Zombie Skin Leggings									
The Scarlet Crusade	Deathknell	Horde	2	4	Executor Arren—Tirisfal Glades Deathknell	Executor Arren	Night Web's Hollow	360	
CHOICE OF: 1 Forsaken Dagger or 1 Forsaken Maul or 1 Forsaken Shortsword or 1 Forsaken Bastard Sword REWARD: 5 Refreshing Spring Water									
The Red Messenger	Deathknell	Horde	2	5	Executor Arren—Tirisfal Glades Deathknell	Executor Arren	The Scarlet Crusade	675	
CHOICE OF: 1 Executor Staff or 1 Deathguard Buckler									
Vital Intelligence	Deathknell	Horde	2	5	Executor Arren—Tirisfal Glades Deathknell	Executor Zygand	The Red Messenger	340	75●
A Rogue's Deal	Deathknell	Horde	1	5	Calvin Montague—Tirisfal Glades Deathknell	Calvin Montague	A Rogue's Deal	110	
Piercing the Veil	Deathknell	Horde	1	3	Venya Marthand—Tirisfal Glades Deathknell	Venya Marthand		190	
Simple Scroll	Deathknell	Horde	1	1	Shadow Priest Sarvis—Tirisfal Glades Deathknell	Dannal Stern	The Mindless Ones	40	
Encrypted Scroll	Deathknell	Horde	1	1	Shadow Priest Sarvis—Tirisfal Glades Deathknell	David Trias	The Mindless Ones	40	
Hallowed Scroll	Deathknell	Horde	1	1	Shadow Priest Sarvis—Tirisfal Glades Deathknell	Dark Cleric Duesten	The Mindless Ones	40	
Glyphic Scroll	Deathknell	Horde	1	1	Shadow Priest Sarvis—Tirisfal Glades Deathknell	Isabella	The Mindless Ones	40	
Tainted Scroll	Deathknell	Horde	1	1	Shadow Priest Sarvis—Tirisfal Glades Deathknell	Maximillion	The Mindless Ones	40	
Rattling the Rattlecages	Deathknell	Horde	1	3	Shadow Priest Sarvis—Tirisfal Glades Deathknell	Shadow Priest Sarvis	The Mindless Ones	250	
CHOICE OF: 1 Flax Boots or 1 Scavenger Tunic or 1 Roamer's Leggings									
Scavenging Deathknell	Deathknell	Horde	2	3	Deathguard Saltain—Tirisfal Glades Deathknell	Deathguard Saltain	The Damned	320	
CHOICE OF: 1 Flax Belt or 1 Rustmetal Bracers or 1 Short Duskbat Cape									
Welcome!	Deathknell	Horde	1	1	Deathknell Gift Voucher	Claire Willower			
CHOICE OF: 1 Diablo Stone or 1 Panda Collar or 1 Zergling Leash									
Marla's Last Wish	Deathknell	Horde	3	5	Novice Elreth—Tirisfal Glades Deathknell	Novice Elreth	The Damned	450	

DR Tram

Title	Location	Faction	Min Level	Con Level	Starter Location	Finisher	Prerequisite	Max XP	Cash Reward
Deeprun Rat Roundup	Deeprun Tram	Alliance	10	12	Monty—Squirrel TokenDeeprun Tram	Monty		900	
Me Brother, Nipsy	Deeprun Tram	Alliance	10	12	Monty—Squirrel TokenDeeprun Tram	Nipsy	Deeprun Rat Roundup	90	5●
REWARD: 10 Deeprun Rat Kabob									

Desolace

Title	Location	Faction	Min Level	Con Level	Starter Location	Finisher	Prerequisite	Max XP	Cash Reward
Get Me Out of Here!	Desolace	Both	34	39	Melizza Brimbuzzle—Desolace	Hornizz Brimbuzzle		2250	45●
Ghost-o-plasm Round Up	Desolace	Both	34	39	Hornizz Brimbuzzle—Desolace Kodo Graveyard	Hornizz Brimbuzzle		2250	45●
CHOICE OF: 1 Condor Bracers or 1 Anchorhold Buckler									
Down the Scarlet Path	Desolace	Alliance	34	39	Brother Anton—Desolace Nijel's Point	Brother Anton		3000	45●
Regthar Deathgate	Desolace	Horde	30	32	Nazgrel—Orgrimmar	Regthar Deathgate	The Kolkar of Desolace	650	
The Kolkar of Desolace	Desolace	Horde	30	32	Regthar Deathgate—The Barrens	Felgur Twocuts		650	
Khan Dez'hepah	Desolace	Horde	30	35	Felgur Twocuts—Desolace Ghost Walker Post	Felgur Twocuts		3450	
Centaur Bounty	Desolace	Horde	30	31	Felgur Twocuts—Desolace Ghost Walker Post	Felgur Twocuts	Khan Dez'hepah	3750	
CHOICE OF: 1 Lilac Sash or 1 Braced Handguards									
Magram Alliance	Desolace	Horde	30	33	Gurda Wildmane—Desolace Ghost Walker Post	Warug		650	
Gelkis Alliance	Desolace	Horde	30	33	Gurda Wildmane—Desolace Ghost Walker Post	Uthek the Wise		650	
Broken Tears	Desolace	Both	30	33	Warug—Desolace	Warug	Assault on the Kolkar	2650	
Stealing Supplies	Desolace	Both	30	35	Uthek the Wise—Desolace	Uthek the Wise	Raid on the Kolkar	1350	
CHOICE OF: 200 Silver Star 200 Feathered Arrow 200 Exploding Shot									
Gizmo for Warug	Desolace	Both	30	35	Warug—Desolace	Warug	Broken Tears	2050	
Ongeku	Desolace	Both	30	37	Uthek the Wise—Desolace	Uthek the Wise	Stealing Supplies	2850	
Khan Jehn	Desolace	Both	30	37	Uthek the Wise—Desolace	Uthek the Wise	Ongeku	2850	
Khan Shaka	Desolace	Both	30	37	Warug—Desolace	Warug	Gizmo for Warug	2850	
Khan Hratha	Desolace	Both	30	42	Uthek the Wise—Desolace	Uthek the Wise	Khan Jehn	4300	
CHOICE OF: 1 Gelkis Marauder Chain or 1 Uthek's Finger									
Khan Hratha	Desolace	Both	30	42	Warug—Desolace	Warug	Khan Shaka	4300	
CHOICE OF: 1 Magram Hunter's Belt or 1 Ceremonial Centaur Blanket									
Strange Alliance	Desolace	Alliance	30	35	Captain Pentigast—Desolace Nijel's Point	Uthek the Wise		2050	
Raid on the Kolkar	Desolace	Alliance	30	32	Uthek the Wise—Desolace	Uthek the Wise	Strange Alliance	2550	
Brutal Politics	Desolace	Alliance	30	35	Captain Pentigast—Desolace Nijel's Point	Warug		2050	

Title	Location	Faction	Min Level	Con Level	Starter Location	Finisher	Prerequisite	Max XP	Cash Reward
Assault on the Kolkar	Desolace	Alliance	30	32	Warug—Desolace	Warug	Brutal Politics	2550	
Centaur Bounty	Desolace	Alliance	30	31	Corporal Melkins—Desolace Nijel's Point	Corporal Melkins		3750	
REWARD: 1 Ring of Calm									
Vahlarriel's Search	Desolace	Alliance	30	33	Vahlarriel Demonslayer—Desolace Nijel's Point	Malem Chest		1950	
Vahlarriel's Search	Desolace	Alliance	30	33	Vahlarriel Demonslayer—Desolace Nijel's Point	Dalinda Malem	Vahlarriel's Search	2650	
Search for Tyranis	Desolace	Alliance	30	33	Dalinda Malem—Desolace Thunder Axe Fortress	Dalinda Malem	Vahlarriel's Search	2650	
Return to Vahlarriel	Desolace	Alliance	30	33	Dalinda Malem—Desolace Thunder Axe Fortress	Vahlarriel Demonslayer	Search for Tyranis	3300	
CHOICE OF: 1 Grappler's Belt or 1 Gloves of Insight or 1 Garrison Cloak or 1 Moonlit Amice									
The Karnitol Shipwreck	Desolace	Alliance	30	39	Kreldig Ungor—Desolace Nijel's Point	Karnitol's Chest	Reclaimers' Business in Desolace	3000	
The Karnitol Shipwreck	Desolace	Alliance	30	39	Karnitol's Chest—Desolace	Kreldig Ungor	The Karnitol Shipwreck	1500	
The Karnitol Shipwreck	Desolace	Alliance	30	39	Kreldig Ungor—Desolace Nijel's Point	Kreldig Ungor	The Karnitol Shipwreck	3000	
The Karnitol Shipwreck	Desolace	Alliance	30	39	Kreldig Ungor—Desolace Nijel's Point	Roetten Stonehammer	The Karnitol Shipwreck	1500	
CHOICE OF: 1 Hellion Boots or 1 Sanguine Pauldrons									
Reagents for Reclaimers Inc.	Desolace	Alliance	30	33	Kreldig Ungor—Desolace Nijel's Point	Kreldig Ungor	Reclaimers' Business in Desolace	2650	35●
Reagents for Reclaimers Inc.	Desolace	Alliance	30	35	Kreldig Ungor—Desolace Nijel's Point	Kreldig Ungor	Reagents for Reclaimers Inc.	2750	25●
Vahlarriel's Search	Desolace	Alliance	30	33	Malem Chest—Desolace	Vahlarriel Demonslayer	Vahlarriel's Search	1950	
Reagents for Reclaimers Inc.	Desolace	Alliance	30	40	Kreldig Ungor—Desolace Nijel's Point	Kreldig Ungor	Reagents for Reclaimers Inc.	3150	35●
Reagents for Reclaimers Inc.	Desolace	Alliance	30	40	Kreldig Ungor—Desolace Nijel's Point	Roetten Stonehammer	Reagents for Reclaimers Inc.	3150	35●
CHOICE OF: 1 Auric Bracers or 1 Stormfire Gauntlets									
Hand of Iruxos	Desolace	Horde	32	38	Taiga Wisemane—Desolace	Taiga Wisemane		2850	45●
Catch of the Day	Desolace	Horde	32	37	Nataka Longhorn—Desolace Ghost Walker Post	Nataka Longhorn		2100	
CHOICE OF: 3 Mithril Ore or 5 Thick Leather or 5 Mageweave Cloth									
Fish in a Bucket	Desolace	Horde	25	1		Jinar'Zillen			50●
REWARD: 1 Bloodbelly Fish									
Bone Collector	Desolace	Both	33	39	Bibbly F'utzbuckle—Desolace Kormek's Hut	Bibbly F'utzbuckle		2250	
REWARD: 1 Kodobone Necklace									
Kodo Roundup	Desolace	Both	30	34	Smeed Scrabblescrew—Desolace	Smeed Scrabblescrew		2000	
CHOICE OF: 1 Kodo Rustler Boots or 1 Wrangling Spaulders									
Portals of the Legion	Desolace	Horde	32	38	Taiga Wisemane—Desolace	Taiga Wisemane	Hand of Iruxos	3550	
CHOICE OF: 1 Gripsteel Wristguards or 1 Braidfur Gloves									
Sceptre of Light	Desolace	Both	30	33	Azore Aldamort—Desolace	Azore Aldamort		2650	35●
Hunting in Stranglethorn	Desolace	Horde	28	31	Roon Wildmane—Desolace Shadowprey Tauren	Hemet Nesingwary		1250	
Bodyguard for Hire	Desolace	Both	30	35	Cork Gizelton—Desolace	Smeed Scrabblescrew		2750	40●40●
REWARD: 1 Trader's Ring									
Gizelton Caravan	Desolace	Both	32	38	Rigger Gizelton—Desolace	Smeed Scrabblescrew		2850	65●38●
CHOICE OF: 1 Sidegunner Shottie or 1 Kodo Brander or 1 Studded Ring Shield									
Book of the Ancients	Desolace	Both	30	38	Azore Aldamort—Desolace	Azore Aldamort	Sceptre of Light	3550	45●
CHOICE OF: 1 Silkstream Cuffs or 1 Arcmetal Shoulders									
Brother Anton	Desolace	Alliance	34	39	Brother Crowley—Stormwind	Brother Anton		300	
Clam Bait	Desolace	Horde	31	35	Mai'Lahii—Desolace Shadowprey Village	Mai'Lahii		2750	
CHOICE OF: 1 Pardoc Grips or 1 Ringtail Girdle or 1 Bracesteel Belt									
Other Fish to Fry	Desolace	Horde	32	36	Drulzegar Skraghook—Desolace	Drulzegar Skraghook		2800	40●
Claim Rackmore's Treasure!	Desolace	Both	30	36	Rackmore's Log—Desolace	Rackmore's Chest		2800	
REWARD: 1 Captain Rackmore's Wheel, 1Captain Rackmore's Tiller									
The Testament of Rexxar	Desolace	Horde	55	60	Rexxar—Desolace	Myranda the Hag	The Champion of the Horde	4950	
Blood of the Black Dragon Champion	Desolace	Horde	55	60	Rexxar—Desolace	Rexxar	Ascension...	9950	
REWARD: 1 Drakefire Amulet									
Frostmane Hold	Dun Morogh	Alliance	7	9	Senir Whitebeard—Dun Morogh Kharanos	Senir Whitebeard		600	
CHOICE OF: 1 Warm Winter Robe or 1 Stone Buckler									
The Reports	Dun Morogh	Alliance	1	10	Senir Whitebeard—Dun Morogh Kharanos	Senator Barin Redstone	Frostmane Hold	420	1●75●
Distracting Jarven	Dun Morogh	Alliance	1	7		Jarven Thunderbrew			
Bitter Rivals	Dun Morogh	Alliance	2	6	Marleth Barleybrew—Dun Morogh Brewnall	Unguarded Thunder Ale Barrel		140	
Return to Marleth	Dun Morogh	Alliance	2	7	Guarded Thunder Ale Barrel—Dun Morogh	Marleth Barleybrew	Bitter Rivals	625	1●75●
Tundra MacGrann's Stolen Stash	Dun Morogh	Alliance	7	12	Tundra MacGrann—Dun Morogh	Tundra MacGrann		900	
CHOICE OF: 1 Ironwrought Bracers or 1 Wooly Mittens									
The Grizzled Den	Dun Morogh	Alliance	4	7	Pilot Stonegear—Dun Morogh Kharanos	Pilot Stonegear		625	1●75●
Protecting the Herd	Dun Morogh	Alliance	6	12	Rudra Amberstill—Dun Morogh	Rudra Amberstill		900	
CHOICE OF: 1 Rancher's Trousers or 1 Soft Leather Tunic or 1 Coldridge Hammer									
The Perfect Stout	Dun Morogh	Alliance	5	9	Rejold Barleybrew—Dun Morogh Brewnall	Rejold Barleybrew		775	
CHOICE OF: 1 Goat Fur Cloak or 1 Ivy-weave Bracers									
Stocking Jetsteam	Dun Morogh	Alliance	2	6	Pilot Bellowfiz—Dun Morogh Kharanos	Pilot Bellowfiz		675	2●50●
Evershine	Dun Morogh	Alliance	2	7	Pilot Bellowfiz—Dun Morogh Kharanos	Rejold Barleybrew	Stocking Jetsteam	160	
A Favor for Evershine	Dun Morogh	Alliance	2	8	Rejold Barleybrew—Dun Morogh Brewnall	Rejold Barleybrew	Evershine	525	
Return to Bellowfiz	Dun Morogh	Alliance	2	8	Rejold Barleybrew—Dun Morogh Brewnall	Pilot Bellowfiz	A Favor for Evershine	875	
CHOICE OF: 1 Sharp Axe or 1 Gnarled Short Staff or 1 Camping Knife									
Beer Basted Boar Ribs	Dun Morogh	Alliance	5	7	Ragnar Thunderbrew—Dun Morogh Kharanos	Ragnar Thunderbrew		625	1●75●
REWARD: 5 Beer Basted Boar Ribs, 1Recipe: Beer Basted Boar Ribs									
Tools for Steelgrill	Dun Morogh	Alliance	2	5	Tharek Blackstone—Dun Morogh Kharanos	Beldin Steelgrill		100	25●
Guarded Thunderbrew Barrel	Dun Morogh	Alliance	1	1		Guarded Thunder Ale Barrel			
Operation Recombobulation	Dun Morogh	Alliance	7	10	Razzle Sprysprocket—Dun Morogh Kharanos	Razzle Sprysprocket		850	
CHOICE OF: 1 Driving Gloves or 1 Oil-stained Cloak									
Shimmer Stout	Dun Morogh	Alliance	8	10	Rejold Barleybrew—Dun Morogh Brewnall	Mountaineer Barleybrew	The Perfect Stout	420	
Stout to Kadrell	Dun Morogh	Alliance	8	10	Mountaineer Barleybrew—Dun Morogh South Gate Outpost	Mountaineer Kadrell	Shimmer Stout	625	
Rejold's New Brew	Dun Morogh	Alliance	8	10	Tharek Blackstone—Dun Morogh Kharanos	Rejold Barleybrew	The Perfect Stout	85	
REWARD: 1 Mug of Shimmer Stout									
A Pilot's Revenge	Dun Morogh	Alliance	8	11	A Dwarven Corpse—Dun Morogh	Pilot Hammerfoot	The Lost Pilot	650	
CHOICE OF: 1 Craftsman's Dagger or 1 Compact Hammer									
The Lost Pilot	Dun Morogh	Alliance	8	10	Pilot Hammerfoot—Dun Morogh North Gate Outpost	A Dwarven Corpse		420	
REWARD: 1 Siege Brigade Vest									
Those Blasted Troggs!	Dun Morogh	Alliance	5	9	Foreman Stonebrow—Dun Morogh Gol'Bolar Quarry	Foreman Stonebrow		600	2●
The Public Servant	Dun Morogh	Alliance	6	11	Senator Mehr Stonehallow—Dun Morogh Gol'Bolar Quarry	Senator Mehr Stonehallow		650	3●
The Tome of Divinity	Dun Morogh	Alliance	12	12		Tiza Battleforge	The Tome of Divinity	460	
REWARD: 1 Tome of Divinity									
The Tome of Divinity	Dun Morogh	Alliance	12	12	Tome of Divinity	Tiza Battleforge			
The Tome of Divinity	Dun Morogh	Alliance	12	12	Tiza Battleforge—Ironforge	John Turner	The Tome of Divinity	460	
The Tome of Divinity	Dun Morogh	Alliance	12	13	John Turner—Ironforge	John Turner	The Tome of Divinity	900	
The Tome of Divinity	Dun Morogh	Alliance	12	13	John Turner—Ironforge	Tiza Battleforge	The Tome of Divinity	230	
The Tome of Divinity	Dun Morogh	Alliance	12	13	Tiza Battleforge—Ironforge	Muiredon Battleforge	The Tome of Divinity		
The Tome of Divinity	Dun Morogh	Alliance	12	13	Muiredon Battleforge—Ironforge	Narm Faulk	The Tome of Divinity	675	
The Tome of Divinity	Dun Morogh	Alliance	12	13		Muiredon Battleforge	The Tome of Divinity	675	
The Tome of Divinity	Dun Morogh	Alliance	12	13	Muiredon Battleforge—Ironforge	Tiza Battleforge	The Tome of Divinity	1150	
The Symbol of Life	Dun Morogh	Alliance	12	12		Tiza Battleforge	The Tome of Divinity		
REWARD: 1 Symbol of Life									
Road to Salvation	Dun Morogh	Alliance	10	10	Hogral Bakkan—Dun Morogh Kharanos	Hulfdan Blackbeard		420	
Onin's Report	Dun Morogh	Alliance	10	10	Onin MacHammar—Dun Morogh Dwarf	Hulfdan Blackbeard	Simple Subterfugin'	850	
REWARD: 1 Blade of Cunning									
Kingly Shakedown	Dun Morogh	Alliance	16	16	Hulfdan Blackbeard—Ironforge	Renzik "The Shiv"	Redridge Rendezvous	120	
To Hulfdan!	Dun Morogh	Alliance	16	16	Hogral Bakkan—Dun Morogh Kharanos	Hulfdan Blackbeard	Redridge Rendezvous	120	

Dun Morogh cont'd

Title	Location	Faction	Min Level	Con Level	Starter Location	Finisher	Prerequisite	Max XP	Cash Reward
The Only Cure is More Green Glow	Dun Morogh	Alliance	20	30	Irradiated Ozzie—Dun Morogh	Ozzie Togglevolt	Gnogaine	2450	25●
Tome of Divinity	Dun Morogh	Alliance	12	12	Azar Stronghammer—Dun Morogh Kharanos	Tiza Battleforge		90	
Tome of Divinity	Dun Morogh	Alliance	12	12	Brandur Ironhammer—Ironforge	Tiza Battleforge		90	
Tome of Divinity	Dun Morogh	Alliance	12	12	Lord Grayson Shadowbreaker—Stormwind	Tiza Battleforge		230	
Ammo for Rumbleshot	Dun Morogh	Alliance	5	6	Loslor Rudge—Dun Morogh Kharanos	Hegnar Rumbleshot		550	1●25●
Garments of the Light	Dun Morogh	Alliance	5	4	Maxan Anvol—Dun Morogh Kharanos	Maxan Anvol		270	
REWARD: 1 Friar's Robes of the Light									
In Favor of the Light	Dun Morogh	Alliance	5	4	Branstock Khalder—Dun Morogh Anvilmar	Maxan Anvol		90	
Frost Ram Exchange	Dun Morogh	Horde	60	1		Veron Amberstill			
CHOICE OF: 1 Swift Brown Ram or 1 Swift Gray Ram or 1 Swift White Ram									
Black Ram Exchange	Dun Morogh	Horde	60	1		Veron Amberstill			
CHOICE OF: 1 Swift Brown Ram or 1 Swift Gray Ram or 1 Swift White Ram									
Icy Blue Mechanostrider Replacement	Dun Morogh	Horde	60	1		Milli Featherwhistle			
CHOICE OF: 1 Swift Green Mechanostrider or 1 Swift White Mechanostrider or 1 Swift Yellow Mechanostrider									
White Mechanostrider Replacement	Dun Morogh	Horde	60	1		Milli Featherwhistle			
CHOICE OF: 1 Swift Green Mechanostrider or 1 Swift White Mechanostrider or 1 Swift Yellow Mechanostrider									

Dungeon Set

Title	Location	Faction	Min Level	Con Level	Starter Location	Finisher	Prerequisite	Max XP	Cash Reward
An Earnest Proposition	Dungeon Set 2.0	Alliance	58	60	Deliana—Ironforge The High Seat	Deliana		6600	
REWARD: 1 Darkmantle Bracers									
A Supernatural Device	Dungeon Set 2.0	Alliance	58	60	Deliana—Ironforge The High Seat	Mux Manascrambler	An Earnest Proposition	6600	
The Ectoplasmic Distiller	Dungeon Set 2.0	Both	58	60	Mux Manascrambler—Stranglethorn Vale Booty Bay	Mux Manascrambler	A Supernatural Device	6600	
REWARD: 1 Mux's Quality Goods									
An Earnest Proposition	Dungeon Set 2.0	Horde	58	60	Mokvar—Orgrimmar Valley of Wisdom	Mokvar		6600	
REWARD: 1 Deathmist Bracers									
Hunting for Ectoplasm	Dungeon Set 2.0	Both	58	60	Mux Manascrambler—Stranglethorn Vale Booty Bay	Mux Manascrambler	The Ectoplasmic Distiller	6600	90●
A Portable Power Source	Dungeon Set 2.0	Both	58	60	Mux Manascrambler—Stranglethorn Vale Booty Bay	Mux Manascrambler	Hunting for Ectoplasm	6600	90●
A Shifty Merchant	Dungeon Set 2.0	Both	58	60	Mux Manascrambler—Stranglethorn Vale Booty Bay	Mux Manascrambler	A Portable Power Source	3300	
A Supernatural Device	Dungeon Set 2.0	Horde	58	60	Mokvar—Orgrimmar Valley of Wisdom	Mux Manascrambler	An Earnest Proposition	6600	
Return to Deliana	Dungeon Set 2.0	Alliance	58	60	Mux Manascrambler—Stranglethorn Vale Booty Bay	Deliana	A Shifty Merchant	6600	
Just Compensation	Dungeon Set 2.0	Alliance	58	60	Deliana—Ironforge The High Seat	Deliana	Return to Deliana	9950	
REWARD: 1 Darkmantle Belt, 1Darkmantle Gloves									
In Search of Anthion	Dungeon Set 2.0	Alliance	58	60	Deliana—Ironforge The High Seat	Anthion Harmon	Just Compensation	6600	
Anthion's Strange Request	Dungeon Set 2.0	Both	58	60	Anthion Harmon—Eastern Plaguelands Stratholme	Anthion Harmon	Proof of Life	6600	
Anthion's Old Friend	Dungeon Set 2.0	Both	58	60	Anthion Harmon—Eastern Plaguelands Stratholme	Falrin Treeshaper	Anthion's Strange Request	6600	
Falrin's Vendetta	Dungeon Set 2.0	Both	58	60	Falrin Treeshaper—Dire Maul	Falrin Treeshaper	Anthion's Old Friend	6600	
CHOICE OF: 1 Beads of Ogre Might or 1 Beads of Ogre Mojo									
Return to Mokvar	Dungeon Set 2.0	Horde	58	60	Mux Manascrambler—Stranglethorn Vale Booty Bay	Mokvar	A Shifty Merchant	6600	
Just Compensation	Dungeon Set 2.0	Horde	58	60	Mokvar—Orgrimmar Valley of Wisdom	Mokvar	Return to Mokvar	9950	
REWARD: 1 Deathmist Belt, 1Deathmist Wraps									
Dead Man's Plea	Dungeon Set 2.0	Both	58	60	Anthion Harmon—Eastern Plaguelands Stratholme	Ysida Harmon	In Search of Anthion	8300	
REWARD: 1 Ysida's Satchel									
Proof of Life	Dungeon Set 2.0	Both	58	60		Anthion Harmon	Dead Man's Plea	6600	
The Instigator's Enchantment	Dungeon Set 2.0	Both	58	60	Falrin Treeshaper—Dire Maul	Falrin Treeshaper	Falrin's Vendetta	6600	
The Challenge	Dungeon Set 2.0	Both	58	60	Falrin Treeshaper—Dire Maul	Anthion Harmon	The Instigator's Enchantment	6600	
Anthion's Parting Words	Dungeon Set 2.0	Alliance	58	60	Anthion Harmon—Eastern Plaguelands Stratholme	Deliana	The Challenge	9950	
REWARD: 1 Darkmantle Boots, 1Darkmantle Pants, 1Darkmantle Spaulders									
Bodley's Unfortunate Fate	Dungeon Set 2.0	Alliance	58	60	Anthion Harmon—Eastern Plaguelands Stratholme	Bodley	Anthion's Parting Words	1650	
Three Kings of Flame	Dungeon Set 2.0	Both	58	60	Bodley—Blackrock Mountain	Bodley	Bodley's Unfortunate Fate	6600	
An Earnest Proposition	Dungeon Set 2.0	Alliance	58	60	Deliana—Ironforge The High Seat	Deliana		6600	
REWARD: 1 Soulforge Bracers									
An Earnest Proposition	Dungeon Set 2.0	Alliance	58	60	Deliana—Ironforge The High Seat	Deliana		6600	
REWARD: 1 Feralheart Bracers									
An Earnest Proposition	Dungeon Set 2.0	Alliance	58	60	Deliana—Ironforge The High Seat	Deliana		6600	
REWARD: 1 Virtuous Bracers									
An Earnest Proposition	Dungeon Set 2.0	Horde	58	60	Mokvar—Orgrimmar Valley of Wisdom	Mokvar		6600	
REWARD: 1 Sorcerer's Bindings									
An Earnest Proposition	Dungeon Set 2.0	Alliance	58	60	Deliana—Ironforge The High Seat	Deliana		6600	
REWARD: 1 Sorcerer's Bindings									
An Earnest Proposition	Dungeon Set 2.0	Alliance	58	60	Deliana—Ironforge The High Seat	Deliana		6600	
REWARD: 1 Deathmist Bracers									
An Earnest Proposition	Dungeon Set 2.0	Alliance	58	60	Deliana—Ironforge The High Seat	Deliana		6600	
REWARD: 1 Beastmaster's Bindings									
An Earnest Proposition	Dungeon Set 2.0	Horde	58	60	Mokvar—Orgrimmar Valley of Wisdom	Mokvar		6600	
REWARD: 1 Bracers of Heroism									
An Earnest Proposition	Dungeon Set 2.0	Alliance	58	60	Deliana—Ironforge The High Seat	Deliana		6600	
REWARD: 1 Bracers of Heroism									
An Earnest Proposition	Dungeon Set 2.0	Horde	58	60	Mokvar—Orgrimmar Valley of Wisdom	Mokvar		6600	
REWARD: 1 Beastmaster's Bindings									
Just Compensation	Dungeon Set 2.0	Alliance	58	60	Deliana—Ironforge The High Seat	Deliana	Return to Deliana	9950	
REWARD: 1 Feralheart Belt, 1Feralheart Gloves									
An Earnest Proposition	Dungeon Set 2.0	Horde	58	60	Mokvar—Orgrimmar Valley of Wisdom	Mokvar		6600	
REWARD: 1 Virtuous Bracers									
Just Compensation	Dungeon Set 2.0	Alliance	58	60	Deliana—Ironforge The High Seat	Deliana	Return to Deliana	9950	
REWARD: 1 Virtuous Belt, 1Virtuous Gloves									
Just Compensation	Dungeon Set 2.0	Alliance	58	60	Deliana—Ironforge The High Seat	Deliana	Return to Deliana	9950	
REWARD: 1 Sorcerer's Belt, 1Sorcerer's Gloves									
Just Compensation	Dungeon Set 2.0	Alliance	58	60	Deliana—Ironforge The High Seat	Deliana	Return to Deliana	9950	
REWARD: 1 Soulforge Belt, 1Soulforge Gauntlets									
Just Compensation	Dungeon Set 2.0	Alliance	58	60	Deliana—Ironforge The High Seat	Deliana	Return to Deliana	9950	
REWARD: 1 Deathmist Belt, 1Deathmist Wraps									
An Earnest Proposition	Dungeon Set 2.0	Horde	58	60	Mokvar—Orgrimmar Valley of Wisdom	Mokvar		6600	
REWARD: 1 Feralheart Bracers									
Just Compensation	Dungeon Set 2.0	Alliance	58	60	Deliana—Ironforge The High Seat	Deliana	Return to Deliana	9950	
REWARD: 1 Beastmaster's Belt, 1Beastmaster's Gloves									
Just Compensation	Dungeon Set 2.0	Alliance	58	60	Deliana—Ironforge The High Seat	Deliana	Return to Deliana	9950	
REWARD: 1 Belt of Heroism, 1Gauntlets of Heroism									
An Earnest Proposition	Dungeon Set 2.0	Horde	58	60	Mokvar—Orgrimmar Valley of Wisdom	Mokvar		6600	
REWARD: 1 Bindings of The Five Thunders									
An Earnest Proposition	Dungeon Set 2.0	Horde	58	60	Mokvar—Orgrimmar Valley of Wisdom	Mokvar		6600	
REWARD: 1 Darkmantle Bracers									
Anthion's Parting Words	Dungeon Set 2.0	Alliance	58	60	Anthion Harmon—Eastern Plaguelands Stratholme	Deliana	The Challenge	9950	
REWARD: 1 Feralheart Boots, 1Feralheart Kilt, 1Feralheart Spaulders									
Anthion's Parting Words	Dungeon Set 2.0	Alliance	58	60	Anthion Harmon—Eastern Plaguelands Stratholme	Deliana	The Challenge	9950	
REWARD: 1 Virtuous Sandals, 1Virtuous Skirt, 1Virtuous Mantle									
Anthion's Parting Words	Dungeon Set 2.0	Alliance	58	60	Anthion Harmon—Eastern Plaguelands Stratholme	Deliana	The Challenge	9950	
REWARD: 1 Sorcerer's Boots, 1Sorcerer's Leggings, 1Sorcerer's Mantle									
Anthion's Parting Words	Dungeon Set 2.0	Alliance	58	60	Anthion Harmon—Eastern Plaguelands Stratholme	Deliana	The Challenge	9950	
REWARD: 1 Soulforge Boots, 1Soulforge Legplates, 1Soulforge Spaulders									

Title	Location	Faction	Min Level	Con Level	Starter Location	Finisher	Prerequisite	Max XP	Cash Reward
Anthion's Parting Words	Dungeon Set 2.0	Alliance	58	60	Anthion Harmon—Eastern Plaguelands Stratholme	Deliana	The Challenge	9950	
REWARD: 1 Deathmist Sandals, 1Deathmist Leggings, 1Deathmist Mantle									
Anthion's Parting Words	Dungeon Set 2.0	Alliance	58	60	Anthion Harmon—Eastern Plaguelands Stratholme	Deliana	The Challenge	9950	
REWARD: 1 Beastmaster's Boots, 1Beastmaster's Pants, 1Beastmaster's Mantle									
Anthion's Parting Words	Dungeon Set 2.0	Alliance	58	60	Anthion Harmon—Eastern Plaguelands Stratholme	Deliana	The Challenge	9950	
REWARD: 1 Boots of Heroism, 1Legplates of Heroism, 1Spaulders of Heroism									
Just Compensation	Dungeon Set 2.0	Horde	58	60	Mokvar—Orgrimmar Valley of Wisdom	Mokvar	Return to Mokvar	9950	
REWARD: 1 Beastmaster's Belt, 1Beastmaster's Gloves									
Just Compensation	Dungeon Set 2.0	Horde	58	60	Mokvar—Orgrimmar Valley of Wisdom	Mokvar	Return to Mokvar	9950	
REWARD: 1 Belt of Heroism, 1Gauntlets of Heroism									
Just Compensation	Dungeon Set 2.0	Horde	58	60	Mokvar—Orgrimmar Valley of Wisdom	Mokvar	Return to Mokvar		
REWARD: 1 Virtuous Belt, 1Virtuous Gloves									
Just Compensation	Dungeon Set 2.0	Horde	58	60	Mokvar—Orgrimmar Valley of Wisdom	Mokvar	Return to Mokvar	9950	
REWARD: 1 Cord of The Five Thunders, 1Gauntlets of The Five Thunders									
In Search of Anthion	Dungeon Set 2.0	Horde	58	60	Mokvar—Orgrimmar Valley of Wisdom	Anthion Harmon	Just Compensation	6600	
Just Compensation	Dungeon Set 2.0	Horde	58	60	Mokvar—Orgrimmar Valley of Wisdom	Mokvar	Return to Mokvar	9950	
REWARD: 1 Sorcerer's Belt, 1Sorcerer's Gloves									
Components of Importance	Dungeon Set 2.0	Both	58	60	Bodley—Blackrock Mountain	Bodley	Three Kings of Flame	6600	
Just Compensation	Dungeon Set 2.0	Horde	58	60	Mokvar—Orgrimmar Valley of Wisdom	Mokvar	Return to Mokvar	9950	
REWARD: 1 Feralheart Belt, 1Feralheart Gloves									
Components of Importance	Dungeon Set 2.0	Both	58	60	Bodley—Blackrock Mountain	Bodley	Three Kings of Flame	6600	
Just Compensation	Dungeon Set 2.0	Horde	58	60	Mokvar—Orgrimmar Valley of Wisdom	Mokvar	Return to Mokvar	9950	
REWARD: 1 Darkmantle Gloves, 1Darkmantle Belt									
Components of Importance	Dungeon Set 2.0	Both	58	60	Bodley—Blackrock Mountain	Bodley	Three Kings of Flame	6600	
Components of Importance	Dungeon Set 2.0	Both	58	60	Bodley—Blackrock Mountain	Bodley	Three Kings of Flame	6600	
More Components of Importance	Dungeon Set 2.0	Both	58	60	Bodley—Blackrock Mountain	Bodley	I See Alcaz Island In Your Future...	6600	
CHOICE OF: 3 Bloodkelp Elixir of Dodging or 3 Bloodkelp Elixir of Resistance									
More Components of Importance	Dungeon Set 2.0	Both	58	60	Bodley—Blackrock Mountain	Bodley	I See Alcaz Island In Your Future...	6600	
CHOICE OF: 3 Bloodkelp Elixir of Dodging or 3 Bloodkelp Elixir of Resistance									
More Components of Importance	Dungeon Set 2.0	Both	58	60	Bodley—Blackrock Mountain	Bodley	I See Alcaz Island In Your Future...	6600	
CHOICE OF: 3 Bloodkelp Elixir of Dodging or 3 Bloodkelp Elixir of Resistance									
More Components of Importance	Dungeon Set 2.0	Both	58	60	Bodley—Blackrock Mountain	Bodley	I See Alcaz Island In Your Future...	6600	
CHOICE OF: 3 Bloodkelp Elixir of Dodging or 3 Bloodkelp Elixir of Resistance									
Anthion's Parting Words	Dungeon Set 2.0	Horde	58	60	Anthion Harmon—Eastern Plaguelands Stratholme	Mokvar	The Challenge	9950	
REWARD: 1 Feralheart Boots, 1Feralheart Kilt, 1Feralheart Spaulders									
Anthion's Parting Words	Dungeon Set 2.0	Horde	58	60	Anthion Harmon—Eastern Plaguelands Stratholme	Mokvar	The Challenge	9950	
REWARD: 1 Darkmantle Boots, 1Darkmantle Pants, 1Darkmantle Spaulders									
The Left Piece of Lord Valthalak's Amulet	Dungeon Set 2.0	Both	58	60	Bodley—Blackrock Mountain	Bodley	Components of Importance	8300	
Anthion's Parting Words	Dungeon Set 2.0	Horde	58	60	Anthion Harmon—Eastern Plaguelands Stratholme	Mokvar	The Challenge	9950	
REWARD: 1 Deathmist Sandals, 1Deathmist Leggings, 1Deathmist Mantle									
The Left Piece of Lord Valthalak's Amulet	Dungeon Set 2.0	Both	58	60	Bodley—Blackrock Mountain	Bodley	Components of Importance	8300	
Anthion's Parting Words	Dungeon Set 2.0	Horde	58	60	Anthion Harmon—Eastern Plaguelands Stratholme	Mokvar	The Challenge	9950	
REWARD: 1 Virtuous Sandals, 1Virtuous Skirt, 1Virtuous Mantle									
The Left Piece of Lord Valthalak's Amulet	Dungeon Set 2.0	Both	58	60	Bodley—Blackrock Mountain	Bodley	Components of Importance	8300	
The Left Piece of Lord Valthalak's Amulet	Dungeon Set 2.0	Both	58	60	Bodley—Blackrock Mountain	Bodley	Components of Importance	8300	
Anthion's Parting Words	Dungeon Set 2.0	Horde	58	60	Anthion Harmon—Eastern Plaguelands Stratholme	Mokvar	The Challenge	9950	
REWARD: 1 Sorcerer's Boots, 1Sorcerer's Leggings, 1Sorcerer's Mantle									
Anthion's Parting Words	Dungeon Set 2.0	Horde	58	60	Anthion Harmon—Eastern Plaguelands Stratholme	Mokvar	The Challenge	9950	
REWARD: 1 Beastmaster's Boots, 1Beastmaster's Pants, 1Beastmaster's Mantle									
I See Alcaz Island In Your Future...	Dungeon Set 2.0	Both	58	60	Bodley—Blackrock Mountain	Bodley	The Left Piece of Lord Valthalak's Amulet	6600	
The Right Piece of Lord Valthalak's Amulet	Dungeon Set 2.0	Both	58	60	Bodley—Blackrock Mountain	Bodley	More Components of Importance	8300	
The Right Piece of Lord Valthalak's Amulet	Dungeon Set 2.0	Both	58	60	Bodley—Blackrock Mountain	Bodley	More Components of Importance	8300	
The Right Piece of Lord Valthalak's Amulet	Dungeon Set 2.0	Both	58	60	Bodley—Blackrock Mountain	Bodley	More Components of Importance	8300	
The Right Piece of Lord Valthalak's Amulet	Dungeon Set 2.0	Both	58	60	Bodley—Blackrock Mountain	Bodley	More Components of Importance	8300	
Anthion's Parting Words	Dungeon Set 2.0	Horde	58	60	Anthion Harmon—Eastern Plaguelands Stratholme	Mokvar	The Challenge	9950	
REWARD: 1 Boots of The Five Thunders, 1Kilt of The Five Thunders, 1Pauldrons of The Five Thunders									
Anthion's Parting Words	Dungeon Set 2.0	Horde	58	60	Anthion Harmon—Eastern Plaguelands Stratholme	Mokvar	The Challenge	9950	
REWARD: 1 Boots of Heroism, 1Legplates of Heroism, 1Spaulders of Heroism									
Final Preparations	Dungeon Set 2.0	Both	58	60	Bodley—Blackrock Mountain	Bodley	The Right Piece of Lord Valthalak's Amulet	6600	
Back to the Beginning	Dungeon Set 2.0	Horde	58	60	Bodley—Blackrock Mountain	Mokvar	Return to Bodley	650	
Saving the Best for Last	Dungeon Set 2.0	Horde	58	60	Mokvar—Orgrimmar Valley of Wisdom	Mokvar	Back to the Beginning	1650	
REWARD: 1 Sorcerer's Crown, 1Sorcerer's Robes									
Mea Culpa, Lord Valthalak	Dungeon Set 2.0	Both	58	60	Bodley—Blackrock Mountain	Spirit of Lord Valthalak	Final Preparations	9950	
Return to Bodley	Dungeon Set 2.0	Both	58	60	Spirit of Lord Valthalak—Upper Blackrock Spire Monster Drakonid Elite	Bodley	Mea Culpa, Lord Valthalak	650	
REWARD: 1 Brazier of Invocation, 1Brazier of Invocation: User's Manual									
Saving the Best for Last	Dungeon Set 2.0	Horde	58	60	Mokvar—Orgrimmar Valley of Wisdom	Mokvar	Back to the Beginning	1650	
REWARD: 1 Coif of The Five Thunders, 1Vest of The Five Thunders									
Back to the Beginning	Dungeon Set 2.0	Alliance	58	60	Bodley—Blackrock Mountain	Deliana	Return to Bodley	650	
Saving the Best for Last	Dungeon Set 2.0	Horde	58	60	Mokvar—Orgrimmar Valley of Wisdom	Mokvar	Back to the Beginning	1650	
REWARD: 1 Deathmist Mask, 1Deathmist Robe									
Saving the Best for Last	Dungeon Set 2.0	Horde	58	60	Mokvar—Orgrimmar Valley of Wisdom	Mokvar	Back to the Beginning	1650	
REWARD: 1 Feralheart Cowl, 1Feralheart Vest									
Saving the Best for Last	Dungeon Set 2.0	Alliance	58	60	Deliana—Ironforge The High Seat	Deliana	Back to the Beginning	1650	
REWARD: 1 Feralheart Cowl, 1Feralheart Vest									
Saving the Best for Last	Dungeon Set 2.0	Horde	58	60	Mokvar—Orgrimmar Valley of Wisdom	Mokvar	Back to the Beginning	1650	
REWARD: 1 Beastmaster's Cap, 1Beastmaster's Tunic									
Saving the Best for Last	Dungeon Set 2.0	Alliance	58	60	Deliana—Ironforge The High Seat	Deliana	Back to the Beginning	1650	
REWARD: 1 Beastmaster's Cap, 1Beastmaster's Tunic									
Saving the Best for Last	Dungeon Set 2.0	Alliance	58	60	Deliana—Ironforge The High Seat	Deliana	Back to the Beginning	1650	
REWARD: 1 Virtuous Crown, 1Virtuous Robe									
Saving the Best for Last	Dungeon Set 2.0	Alliance	58	60	Deliana—Ironforge The High Seat	Deliana	Back to the Beginning	1650	
REWARD: 1 Helm of Heroism, 1Breastplate of Heroism									
Saving the Best for Last	Dungeon Set 2.0	Alliance	58	60	Deliana—Ironforge The High Seat	Deliana	Back to the Beginning	1650	
REWARD: 1 Soulforge Helm, 1Soulforge Breastplate									
Saving the Best for Last	Dungeon Set 2.0	Horde	58	60	Mokvar—Orgrimmar Valley of Wisdom	Mokvar	Back to the Beginning	1650	
REWARD: 1 Darkmantle Cap, 1Darkmantle Tunic									
Saving the Best for Last	Dungeon Set 2.0	Alliance	58	60	Deliana—Ironforge The High Seat	Deliana	Back to the Beginning	1650	
REWARD: 1 Darkmantle Cap, 1Darkmantle Tunic									
Saving the Best for Last	Dungeon Set 2.0	Alliance	58	60	Deliana—Ironforge The High Seat	Deliana	Back to the Beginning	1650	
REWARD: 1 Sorcerer's Crown, 1Sorcerer's Robes									
Saving the Best for Last	Dungeon Set 2.0	Alliance	58	60	Deliana—Ironforge The High Seat	Deliana	Back to the Beginning	1650	
REWARD: 1 Deathmist Mask, 1Deathmist Robe									
Saving the Best for Last	Dungeon Set 2.0	Horde	58	60	Mokvar—Orgrimmar Valley of Wisdom	Mokvar	Back to the Beginning	1650	
REWARD: 1 Virtuous Crown, 1Virtuous Robe									
Saving the Best for Last	Dungeon Set 2.0	Horde	58	60	Mokvar—Orgrimmar Valley of Wisdom	Mokvar	Back to the Beginning	1650	
REWARD: 1 Helm of Heroism, 1Breastplate of Heroism									

Durotar

Title	Location	Faction	Min Level	Con Level	Starter Location	Finisher	Prerequisite	Max XP	Cash Reward
Vanquish the Betrayers	Durotar	Horde	3	7	Gar'Thok—Durotar Razor Hill	Gar'Thok		625	1●75●
Thwarting Kolkar Aggression	Durotar	Horde	5	8	Lar Prowltusk—Durotar Sen'jin Village	Lar Prowltusk		700	
CHOICE OF: 1 Seasoned Fighter's Cloak or 1 Heavy Cord Bracers									
Carry Your Weight	Durotar	Horde	4	7	Furl Scornbrow—Durotar Razor Hill	Furl Scornbrow		625	
REWARD: 1 Handmade Leather Bag									
Dark Storms	Durotar	Horde	4	12	Orgnil Soulscar—Durotar Razor Hill	Orgnil Soulscar	Report to Orgnil	900	
REWARD: 1 Tiger Hide Boots									
Minshina's Skull	Durotar	Horde	4	9	Master Gadrin—Durotar Sen'jin Village	Master Gadrin		775	
REWARD: 1 Faintly Glowing Skull									
Ak'Zeloth	Durotar	Horde	4	13	Neeru Fireblade—Orgrimmar	Ak'Zeloth	Neeru Fireblade	460	
Need for a Cure	Durotar	Horde	7	9	Rhinag—Durotar	Rhinag		975	
CHOICE OF: 1 Charging Buckler or 1 Light Scorpid Armor									
Finding the Antidote	Durotar	Horde	7	9	Kor'ghan—Orgrimmar	Kor'ghan			
REWARD: 1 Venomtail Antidote									
Break a Few Eggs	Durotar	Horde	6	8	Cook Torka—Durotar	Cook Torka		700	2●25●
REWARD: 5 Tough Hunk of Bread, 5Tough Jerky									
Lost But Not Forgotten	Durotar	Horde	8	11	Misha Tor'kren—Durotar	Misha Tor'kren		875	
REWARD: 1 Handsewn Cloak									
Practical Prey	Durotar	Horde	5	8	Vel'rin Fang—Durotar Sen'jin Village	Vel'rin Fang		700	2●25●
A Solvent Spirit	Durotar	Horde	5	7	Master Vornal—Durotar Sen'jin Village	Master Vornal		625	1●75●
REWARD: 10 Really Sticky Glue									
Report to Orgnil	Durotar	Horde	4	7	Master Gadrin—Durotar Sen'jin Village	Orgnil Soulscar		320	
From The Wreckage....	Durotar	Horde	3	8	Gar'Thok—Durotar Razor Hill	Gar'Thok	Vanquish the Betrayers	700	
CHOICE OF: 1 Dirt-trodden Boots or 1 Sandrunner Wristguards or 1 Wide Metal Girdle									
Zalazane	Durotar	Horde	4	10	Master Gadrin—Durotar Sen'jin Village	Master Gadrin		850	
CHOICE OF: 1 Lightweight Boots or 1 Veiled Grips									
Skull Rock	Durotar	Horde	4	12	Margoz—Durotar Orc	Margoz	Margoz	900	
CHOICE OF: 1 Jagged Dagger or 1 Steady Bastard Sword or 1 Stinging Mace									
Margoz	Durotar	Horde	4	12	Orgnil Soulscar—Durotar Razor Hill	Margoz	Dark Storms	90	
Neeru Fireblade	Durotar	Horde	4	12	Margoz—Durotar Orc	Neeru Fireblade	Skull Rock	460	
The Admiral's Orders	Durotar	Horde	1	7	Aged Envelope	Gar'Thok		625	
The Admiral's Orders	Durotar	Horde	1	7	Gar'Thok—Durotar Razor Hill	Nazgrel	The Admiral's Orders	625	1●75●
Burning Shadows	Durotar	Horde	4	12	Eye of Burning Shadow	Neeru Fireblade		675	
Winds in the Desert	Durotar	Horde	7	9	Rezlok—Durotar	Rezlok		775	3●
Securing the Lines	Durotar	Horde	7	11	Rezlok—Durotar	Rezlok	Winds in the Desert	875	
CHOICE OF: 1 Harpy Wing Clipper or 1 Hickory Shortbow or 1 Blemished Wooden Staff									
Encroachment	Durotar	Horde	6	10	Gar'Thok—Durotar Razor Hill	Gar'Thok		625	2●50●
Conscript of the Horde	Durotar	Horde	10	12	Takrin Pathseeker—Durotar Razor Hill	Kargal Battlescar		460	
Crossroads Conscription	Durotar	Horde	10	12	Kargal Battlescar—Barrens	Sergra Darkthorn	Conscript of the Horde	900	
Fire Sapta	Durotar	Horde	10	13		Telf Joolam	Call of Fire		
REWARD: 1 Fire Sapta									
Gan'rul's Summons	Durotar	Horde	10	10	Ophek—Durotar Razor Hill	Gan'rul Bloodeye	Creature of the Void	210	
Call of Fire	Durotar	Horde	10	10	Searn Fi	REWARDer—Orgrimmar	Kranal Fiss	420	
Call of Fire	Durotar	Horde	10	10	Xanis Flameweaver—Thunder Bluff	Kranal Fiss		420	
Call of Fire	Durotar	Horde	10	11	Kranal Fiss—Barrens	Telf Joolam		650	
Call of Fire	Durotar	Horde	10	12	Telf Joolam—Durotar	Telf Joolam	Call of Fire	900	
REWARD: 1 Fire Sapta									
Call of Fire	Durotar	Horde	10	13	Telf Joolam—Durotar	Brazier of the Dormant Flame	Call of Fire	1150	
REWARD: 1 Torch of the Eternal Flame									
Call of Fire	Durotar	Horde	10	13	Brazier of the Dormant Flame—	Kranal Fiss	Call of Fire	1150	
REWARD: 1 Fire Totem									
Therzok	Durotar	Horde	10	10	Kaplak—Durotar Razor Hill	Therzok	The Shattered Hand	210	
A Peon's Burden	Durotar	Horde	1	5	Ukor—Durotar	Innkeeper Grosk		110	
CHOICE OF: 5 Tough Hunk of Bread or 5 Refreshing Spring Water									
To Orgrimmar!	Durotar	Horde	16	16	Kaplak—Durotar Razor Hill	Shenthul	Find the Shattered Hand	120	
Call of Fire	Durotar	Horde	10	10	Swart—Durotar Razor Hill	Kranal Fiss		420	
Call of Fire	Durotar	Horde	10	10	Narm Skychaser—Mulgore Bloodhoof Village	Kranal Fiss		420	
Your Place In The World	Durotar	Horde	1	1	Kaltunk—Durotar Valley of Trials	Gornek		40	
Garments of Spirituality	Durotar	Horde	5	4	Tai'jin—Durotar Razor Hill	Tai'jin		270	
REWARD: 1 Juju Hex Robes									
In Favor of Spirituality	Durotar	Horde	5	4	Ken'jai—Durotar Valley of Trials	Tai'jin		90	
Hex of Weakness	Durotar	Horde	10	10		Ur'kyo			
Hex of Weakness	Durotar	Horde	10	10	Tai'jin—Durotar Razor Hill	Ur'kyo		210	
Hex of Weakness	Durotar	Horde	10	10	Var'jun—Mulgore Bloodhoof Village	Ur'kyo		210	
Hex of Weakness	Durotar	Horde	10	10	Miles Welsh—Thunder Bluff	Ur'kyo		210	
Hex of Weakness	Durotar	Horde	10	10	Aelthalyste—Undercity	Ur'kyo		210	
Taming the Beast	Durotar	Horde	10	10	Thotar—Durotar Razor Hill	Thotar		850	
The Hunter's Path	Durotar	Horde	10	10	Sian'dur—Orgrimmar Valley of Honor	Thotar		85	
The Hunter's Path	Durotar	Horde	10	10	Una Ji'ro—Moonglade	Thotar		85	
The Hunter's Path	Durotar	Horde	10	10	Kary Thunderhorn—Thunder Bluff Hunter Rise	Thotar		85	
Training the Beast	Durotar	Horde	10	10	Thotar—Durotar Razor Hill	Ormak Grimshot	Taming the Beast	420	
Taming the Beast	Durotar	Horde	10	10	Thotar—Durotar Razor Hill	Thotar	Taming the Beast	850	
Taming the Beast	Durotar	Horde	10	10	Thotar—Durotar Razor Hill	Thotar	Taming the Beast	850	
Ivory Raptor Replacement	Durotar	Horde	60	1		Zjolnir			
CHOICE OF: 1 Swift Blue Raptor or 1 Swift Olive Raptor or 1 Swift Orange Raptor									
Red Raptor Replacement	Durotar	Horde	60	1		Zjolnir			
CHOICE OF: 1 Swift Blue Raptor or 1 Swift Olive Raptor or 1 Swift Orange Raptor									
Incoming Gumdrop	Durotar	Horde	10	60	Una Ji'ro—Moonglade	Kali Remik			
REWARD: 1 Darkspear Gumdrop									

Duskwood

Title	Location	Faction	Min Level	Con Level	Starter Location	Finisher	Prerequisite	Max XP	Cash Reward
Jitters' Growling Gut	Duskwood	Alliance	17	20	Jitters—Duskwood	Chef Grual		390	
Morbent Fel	Duskwood	Alliance	20	32	Sven Yorgen—Duskwood	Sven Yorgen	Armed and Ready	3850	
CHOICE OF: 1 Night Watch Pantaloons or 1 Watch Master's Cloak or 1 Sparkmetal Coif REWARD: 1 Torch of Holy Flame									
The Night Watch	Duskwood	Alliance	18	24	Commander Althea Ebonlocke—Duskwood Darkshire	Commander Althea Ebonlocke		1450	17●
The Night Watch	Duskwood	Alliance	18	26	Commander Althea Ebonlocke—Duskwood Darkshire	Commander Althea Ebonlocke	The Night Watch	2100	20●
The Night Watch	Duskwood	Alliance	18	30	Commander Althea Ebonlocke—Duskwood Darkshire	Commander Althea Ebonlocke	The Night Watch	2450	25●
CHOICE OF: 1 Bandolier of the Night Watch or 1 Quiver of the Night Watch or 1 Gunnysack of the Night Watch									
The Legend of Stalvan	Duskwood	Alliance	22	28	Madame Eva—Duskwood Darkshire	Clerk Daltry		230	
The Legend of Stalvan	Duskwood	Alliance	22	28	Clerk Daltry—Duskwood Darkshire	Old Footlocker	The Legend of Stalvan	1150	
The Legend of Stalvan	Duskwood	Alliance	22	28	Old Footlocker—	Clerk Daltry	The Legend of Stalvan	1700	
The Legend of Stalvan	Duskwood	Alliance	22	28	Clerk Daltry—Duskwood Darkshire	Innkeeper Farley	The Legend of Stalvan	575	
The Legend of Stalvan	Duskwood	Alliance	22	28	Innkeeper Farley—Elwynn Goldshire	Caretaker Folsom	The Legend of Stalvan	1700	
The Legend of Stalvan	Duskwood	Alliance	22	28	Caretaker Folsom—Stormwind	Sealed Crate	The Legend of Stalvan	230	
The Legend of Stalvan	Duskwood	Alliance	22	28	Sealed Crate—	Marshal Haggard	The Legend of Stalvan	1150	
The Legend of Stalvan	Duskwood	Alliance	22	28	Marshal Haggard—Elwynn	Marshal Haggard	The Legend of Stalvan	1150	
The Legend of Stalvan	Duskwood	Alliance	22	28	Marshal Haggard—Elwynn	Tavernkeep Smitts	The Legend of Stalvan	575	
The Legend of Stalvan	Duskwood	Alliance	22	28	Tavernkeep Smitts—Duskwood Darkshire	Commander Althea Ebonlocke	The Legend of Stalvan	230	
REWARD: 1 A Bloodstained Journal Page									
The Legend of Stalvan	Duskwood	Alliance	22	28	Commander Althea Ebonlocke—Duskwood Darkshire	Clerk Daltry	The Legend of Stalvan	230	

Title	Location	Faction	Min Level	Con Level	Starter Location	Finisher	Prerequisite	Max XP	Cash Reward
Seasoned Wolf Kabobs	Duskwood	Alliance	18	25	Chef Grual—Duskwood Darkshire	Chef Grual		2000	18●
REWARD: 4 Seasoned Wolf Kabob, 1Recipe: Seasoned Wolf Kabob									
Dusky Crab Cakes	Duskwood	Alliance	17	20	Chef Grual—Duskwood Darkshire	Chef Grual	Jitters' Growling Gut	775	
REWARD: 1 Recipe: Gooey Spider Cake									
Sven's Revenge	Duskwood	Alliance	20	25	Sven Yorgen—Duskwood	Mound of loose dirt		1000	
The Legend of Stalvan	Duskwood	Alliance	22	28	Clerk Daltry—Duskwood Darkshire	Commander Althea Ebonlocke	The Legend of Stalvan	230	
The Legend of Stalvan	Duskwood	Alliance	22	35	Commander Althea Ebonlocke—Duskwood Darkshire	Madame Eva	The Legend of Stalvan	4100	
CHOICE OF: 1 Crescent of Forlorn Spirits or 1 Ring of Forlorn Spirits									
The Totem of Infliction	Duskwood	Alliance	18	25	Madame Eva—Duskwood Darkshire	Madame Eva		2550	
REWARD: 1 Totem of Infliction									
Ghoulish Effigy	Duskwood	Alliance	20	27	Abercrombie—Duskwood	Abercrombie	Juice Delivery	1650	22●
Ogre Thieves	Duskwood	Alliance	20	30	Abercrombie—Duskwood	Abercrombie	Ghoulish Effigy	1200	14●
Supplies from Darkshire	Duskwood	Alliance	20	24	Abercrombie—Duskwood	Madame Eva		490	
Ghost Hair Thread	Duskwood	Alliance	20	24	Madame Eva—Duskwood Darkshire	Blind Mary	Supplies from Darkshire	490	
Return the Comb	Duskwood	Alliance	20	24	Blind Mary—Duskwood	Madame Eva	Ghost Hair Thread	200	1●75●
Gather Rot Blossoms	Duskwood	Alliance	20	24	Tavernkeep Smitts—Duskwood Darkshire	Tavernkeep Smitts	Zombie Juice	975	
Deliver the Thread	Duskwood	Alliance	20	24	Madame Eva—Duskwood Darkshire	Abercrombie	Return the Comb	1450	13●
Zombie Juice	Duskwood	Alliance	20	24	Abercrombie—Duskwood	Tavernkeep Smitts	Deliver the Thread	490	
Juice Delivery	Duskwood	Alliance	20	24	Tavernkeep Smitts—Duskwood Darkshire	Abercrombie	Gather Rot Blossoms	975	17●
Note to the Mayor	Duskwood	Alliance	20	30	Abercrombie—Duskwood	Lord Ello Ebonlocke	Ogre Thieves	600	
Raven Hill	Duskwood	Alliance	17	20	Elaine Carevin—Duskwood Darkshire	Jitters		390	
Deliveries to Sven	Duskwood	Alliance	17	23	Elaine Carevin—Duskwood Darkshire	Sven Yorgen		925	8●
The Hermit	Duskwood	Alliance	17	25	Elaine Carevin—Duskwood Darkshire	Abercrombie		1000	
Worgen in the Woods	Duskwood	Alliance	23	28	Calor—Duskwood Darkshire	Calor		1150	18●
Look To The Stars	Duskwood	Alliance	20	25	Viktori Prism'Antras—Duskwood Darkshire	Viktori Prism'Antras		2000	
Look To The Stars	Duskwood	Alliance	20	25	Viktori Prism'Antras—Duskwood Darkshire	Blind Mary	Look To The Stars	1000	
Look To The Stars	Duskwood	Alliance	20	25	Blind Mary—Duskwood	Viktori Prism'Antras	Look To The Stars	1500	
Look To The Stars	Duskwood	Alliance	20	30	Viktori Prism'Antras—Duskwood Darkshire	Viktori Prism'Antras	Look To The Stars	2450	
CHOICE OF: 1 Zodiac Gloves or 1 Belt of the Stars									
Worgen in the Woods	Duskwood	Alliance	23	29	Calor—Duskwood Darkshire	Calor	Worgen in the Woods	1750	19●
Worgen in the Woods	Duskwood	Alliance	23	31	Calor—Duskwood Darkshire	Calor	Worgen in the Woods	1900	22●
Worgen in the Woods	Duskwood	Alliance	23	31	Calor—Duskwood Darkshire	Jonathan Carevin	Worgen in the Woods	3150	
CHOICE OF: 1 Cloak of the Faith or 1 Shield of the Faith									
REWARD: 1 Consecrated Wand									
The Weathered Grave	Duskwood	Alliance	28	35	A Weathered Grave—Duskwood	Sirra Von'Indi		700	
Wolves at Our Heels	Duskwood	Alliance	19	21	Lars—Duskwood	Lars		1250	
REWARD: 5 Flash Bundle									
Morgan Ladimore	Duskwood	Alliance	28	35	Sirra Von'Indi—Duskwood Darkshire	Commander Althea Ebonlocke	The Weathered Grave	280	
REWARD: 1 The Story of Morgan Ladimore									
Mor'Ladim	Duskwood	Alliance	28	35	Commander Althea Ebonlocke—Duskwood Darkshire	Commander Althea Ebonlocke	Morgan Ladimore	2050	35●
The Daughter Who Lived	Duskwood	Alliance	28	35	Commander Althea Ebonlocke—Duskwood Darkshire	Watcher Ladimore	Mor'Ladim	280	
Sven's Camp	Duskwood	Alliance	20	25	Mound of Loose Dirt—Duskwood	Sven Yorgen	Sven's Revenge	1000	
A Daughter's Love	Duskwood	Alliance	28	35	Watcher Ladimore—Duskwood Darkshire	A Weathered Grave	The Daughter Who Lived	1350	
REWARD: 1 Archeus									
Return to Jitters	Duskwood	Alliance	17	20	Chef Grual—Duskwood Darkshire	Jitters	Dusky Crab Cakes	775	12●
Eight-Legged Menaces	Duskwood	Alliance	17	21	Watcher Dodds—Duskwood	Watcher Dodds		1250	
REWARD: 1 Night Watch Gauntlets									
Translate Abercrombie's Note	Duskwood	Alliance	20	30	Lord Ello Ebonlocke—Duskwood Darkshire	Sirra Von'Indi	Note to the Mayor	250	
Translation to Ello	Duskwood	Alliance	20	30	Sirra Von'Indi—Duskwood Darkshire	Lord Ello Ebonlocke	Wait for Sirra to Finish	250	
REWARD: 1 Translated Letter from The Embalmer									
Bride of the Embalmer	Duskwood	Alliance	20	30	Lord Ello Ebonlocke—Duskwood Darkshire	Lord Ello Ebonlocke	Translation to Ello	3650	
REWARD: 1 Mantle of Honor, 1Crest of Darkshire									
Digging Through the Dirt	Duskwood	Alliance	20	35		Eliza's Tombstone			
The Shadowy Figure	Duskwood	Alliance	20	25	Sven Yorgen—Duskwood	Madame Eva	Sven's Camp	500	
The Shadowy Search Continues	Duskwood	Alliance	20	25	Madame Eva—Duskwood Darkshire	Clerk Daltry	The Shadowy Figure	200	
Inquire at the Inn	Duskwood	Alliance	20	25	Clerk Daltry—Duskwood Darkshire	Tavernkeep Smitts	The Shadowy Search Continues	200	
Return to Sven	Duskwood	Alliance	20	25	Jitters—Duskwood	Sven Yorgen	Finding the Shadowy Figure	500	
Seeking Wisdom	Duskwood	Alliance	20	29	Sven Yorgen—Duskwood	Bishop Farthing	Proving Your Worth	600	
Proving Your Worth	Duskwood	Alliance	20	28	Sven Yorgen—Duskwood	Sven Yorgen	Return to Sven	2300	18●
An Old History Book	Duskwood	Alliance	20	25	An Old History Book	Milton Sheaf		1500	14●
Crime and Punishment	Duskwood	Alliance	22	26	Councilman Millstipe—Duskwood Darkshire	Councilman Millstipe		2100	
CHOICE OF: 1 Ambassador's Boots or 1 Darkshire Mail Leggings									
Wait for Sirra to Finish	Duskwood	Alliance	20	30	Sirra Von'Indi—Duskwood Darkshire	Sirra Von'Indi	Translate Abercrombie's Note	1850	
Finding the Shadowy Figure	Duskwood	Alliance	20	25	Tavernkeep Smitts—Duskwood Darkshire	Jitters	Inquire at the Inn	1000	
The Carevin Family	Duskwood	Alliance	25	30	Clerk Daltry—Duskwood Darkshire	Jonathan Carevin	The Caravan Road	250	25●
The Scythe of Elune	Duskwood	Alliance	25	30	Jonathan Carevin—Duskwood Darkshire	Jonathan Carevin	The Carevin Family	2450	25●
Answered Questions	Duskwood	Alliance	25	30	Jonathan Carevin—Duskwood Darkshire	Thyn'tel Bladeweaver	The Scythe of Elune	3050	
CHOICE OF: 1 Lunaris Bow or 1 Moonbeam Wand									
Nothing But The Truth	Duskwood	Horde	37	42	Deathstalker Zraedus—Duskwood	Apothecary Faustin		350	
Nothing But The Truth	Duskwood	Horde	37	42	Apothecary Faustin—Duskwood	Apothecary Faustin	Nothing But The Truth	4300	
CHOICE OF: 1 Cloak of Blight or 1 Cragwood Maul									
Nothing But The Truth	Duskwood	Horde	37	42	Apothecary Faustin—Duskwood	Deathstalker Zraedus	Nothing But The Truth	350	
Nothing But The Truth	Duskwood	Horde	37	42	Deathstalker Zraedus—Duskwood	Infiltrator Marksen	Nothing But The Truth	2550	
Overlord Mok'Morokk's Concern	Dustwallow	Horde	38	43	Overlord Mok'Morokk—Dustwallow Ogre	Overlord Mok'Morokk		4450	
REWARD: 1 Enormous Ogre Boots									
Army of the Black Dragon	Dustwallow	Horde	38	43	Tharg—Dustwallow Ogre	Tharg		4450	
CHOICE OF: 1 Tharg's Shoelace or 1 Tharg's Disk									
Identifying the Brood	Dustwallow	Horde	38	43	Draz'Zilb—Dustwallow Ogre	Draz'Zilb		5350	
CHOICE OF: 1 Scorched Cape or 1 Rustler Gloves									
The Brood of Onyxia	Dustwallow	Horde	38	43	Draz'Zilb—Dustwallow Ogre	Overlord Mok'Morokk	Identifying the Brood	360	
The Brood of Onyxia	Dustwallow	Horde	38	43	Overlord Mok'Morokk—Dustwallow Ogre	Draz'Zilb	The Brood of Onyxia	360	
The Brood of Onyxia	Dustwallow	Horde	38	45	Draz'Zilb—Dustwallow Ogre	Draz'Zilb	The Brood of Onyxia	4850	
CHOICE OF: 1 Encarmine Boots or 1 Boots of Zua'tec									
Challenge Overlord Mok'Morokk	Dustwallow	Horde	38	45	Overlord Mok'Morokk—Dustwallow Ogre	Draz'Zilb	The Brood of Onyxia	4850	
CHOICE OF: 1 Fiendish Skiv or 1 Chillnail Splinter									
Hungry!	Dustwallow	Both	32	36	Mudcrush Durtfeet—Dustwallow Ogre	Mudcrush Durtfeet		2800	
CHOICE OF: 1 Mud's Crushers or 1 Durtfeet Stompers									
Theramore Spies	Dustwallow	Horde	30	35	Nazeer Bloodpike—Dustwallow Marsh Brackenwall Village	Nazeer Bloodpike		2750	
The Theramore Docks	Dustwallow	Horde	30	35	Nazeer Bloodpike—Dustwallow Marsh Brackenwall Village	Nazeer Bloodpike	Theramore Spies	2750	
Jarl Needs a Blade	Dustwallow	Both	30	35	"Swamp Eye" Jarl—Dustwallow Marsh Swamplight Manor	"Swamp Eye" Jarl	Jarl Needs Eyes	3450	35●
REWARD: 1 Reedknot Ring, 1Artisan's Trousers									
Mudrock Soup and Bugs	Dustwallow	Alliance	33	38	Morgan Stern—Dustwallow Marsh Theramore Isle	Morgan Stern		2850	
Deadmire	Dustwallow	Horde	35	45	Melor Stonehoof—Thunder Bluff	Melor Stonehoof		3900	
Jarl Needs Eyes	Dustwallow	Both	30	35	"Swamp Eye" Jarl—Dustwallow Marsh Swamplight Manor	"Swamp Eye" Jarl	Soothing Spices	2750	
Soothing Spices	Dustwallow	Both	30	35	"Swamp Eye" Jarl—Dustwallow Marsh Swamplight Manor	"Swamp Eye" Jarl		1350	
REWARD: 20 Frog Leg Stew									
The Orc Report	Dustwallow	Alliance	30	35	Loose Dirt—	Theramore Lieutenant		700	
Captain Vimes	Dustwallow	Alliance	30	35	Theramore Lieutenant—Dustwallow Marsh Theramore Isle	Captain Garran Vimes	The Orc Report	2750	

Dustwallow Marsh cont'd

Title	Location	Faction	Min Level	Con Level	Starter Location	Finisher	Prerequisite	Max XP	Cash Reward
Stinky's Escape	Dustwallow	Alliance	30	37	"Stinky" Ignatz—Dustwallow Marsh	Morgan Stern		2850	40s
REWARD: 1 Elixir of Fortitude									
The Lost Report	Dustwallow	Horde	30	35	Loose Dirt—Dustwallo	Nazeer Bloodpike		2050	
The Severed Head	Dustwallow	Horde	30	35	Loose Dirt—Dustwallo	Nazeer Bloodpike	The Lost Report	2050	
The Troll Witchdoctor	Dustwallow	Horde	30	35	Nazeer Bloodpike—Dustwallow Marsh Brackenwall Village	Kin'weelay	The Severed Head	2750	
The Black Shield	Dustwallow	Horde	30	35	Black Shield—Dustwallo	Krog		700	
Lieutenant Paval Reethe	Dustwallow	Alliance	30	40	Theramore Guard Badge	Captain Garran Vimes	James Hyal	775	
The Black Shield	Dustwallow	Alliance	30	35	Black Shield—Dustwallo	Captain Garran Vimes	They Call Him Smiling Jim	700	
... and Bugs	Dustwallow	Alliance	33	40	Morgan Stern—Dustwallow Marsh Theramore Isle	Morgan Stern	Mudrock Soup and Bugs	3150	
REWARD: 1 Baroque Apron									
Lieutenant Paval Reethe	Dustwallow	Alliance	30	40	Captain Garran Vimes—Dustwallow Marsh Theramore Isle	Adjutant Tesoran	Lieutenant Paval Reethe	320	
Morgan Stern	Dustwallow	Alliance	33	38	Angus Stern—Stormwind	Morgan Stern	Mudrock Soup and Bugs	700	
Marg Speaks	Dustwallow	Horde	30	40	Bubbling Cauldron—Stranglethorn	Nazeer Bloodpike	The Troll Witchdoctor	3150	
Report to Zor	Dustwallow	Horde	30	40	Nazeer Bloodpike—Dustwallow Marsh Brackenwall Village	Zor Lonetree	Marg Speaks	3150	
Suspicious Hoofprints	Dustwallow	Horde	30	35	Hoofprints—Dustwallo	Krog		1350	
Lieutenant Paval Reethe	Dustwallow	Horde	30	37	Theramore Guard Badge	Krog		700	
Stinky's Escape	Dustwallow	Horde	30	37	"Stinky" Ignatz—Dustwallow Marsh	Mebok Mizzyrix		2850	
REWARD: 1 Elixir of Fortitude									
Feast at the Blue Recluse	Dustwallow	Alliance	30	37		Angus Stern	Stinky's Escape		
REWARD: 1 Moist Towelette									
Questioning Reethe	Dustwallow	Horde	30	37	Ogron—Dustwallow	Krog	Lieutenant Paval Reethe	3550	
CHOICE OF: 1 Eyepoker or 1 Blasting Hackbut									
The Black Shield	Dustwallow	Horde	30	37	Krog—Dustwallow Marsh Brackenwall Village	Mosarn	Questioning Reethe	1400	
They Call Him Smiling Jim	Dustwallow	Alliance	30	35	Guard Byron—Dustwallow Marsh Theramore	Captain Garran Vimes	James Hyal	280	
Suspicious Hoofprints	Dustwallow	Alliance	30	35	Hoofprints—Dustwallo	Captain Garran Vimes	James Hyal	1350	
Doelin's Men	Dustwallow	Alliance	30	38	Adjutant Tesoran—Dustwallow Marsh Theramore Isle	Captain Garran Vimes	Lieutenant Paval Reethe	290	
The Deserters	Dustwallow	Alliance	30	38	Captain Garran Vimes—Dustwallow Marsh Theramore Isle	Balos Jacken	Doelin's Men	2850	
The Deserters	Dustwallow	Alliance	30	38		Captain Garran Vimes	The Deserters	2850	
James Hyal	Dustwallow	Alliance	30	35	Connor Rivers—Stormwind	Vincent Hyal	They Call Him Smiling Jim	700	
James Hyal	Dustwallow	Alliance	30	35	Vincent Hyal—Wetlands Menethil	Clerk Lendry		700	
The Black Shield	Dustwallow	Alliance	30	35	Captain Garran Vimes—Dustwallow Marsh Theramore Isle	Caz Twosprocket	The Black Shield	280	
The Black Shield	Dustwallow	Alliance	30	35	Caz Twosprocket—Dustwallow Marsh Theramore Isle	Captain Garran Vimes	The Black Shield	1350	
The Black Shield	Dustwallow	Horde	30	35	Krog—Dustwallow Marsh Brackenwall Village	Do'gol	The Black Shield	280	
The Black Shield	Dustwallow	Horde	30	37	Do'gol—Dustwallow	Do'gol	The Black Shield	2850	
The Black Shield	Dustwallow	Horde	30	37	Do'gol—Dustwallow	Krog	The Black Shield	1400	
The Test of Skulls, Scryer	Dustwallow	Horde	55	60	Emberstrife—Dustwallow Marsh	Emberstrife	Emberstrife	6600	
The Test of Skulls, Somnus	Dustwallow	Horde	55	60	Emberstrife—Dustwallow Marsh	Emberstrife	Emberstrife	7250	
The Test of Skulls, Chronalis	Dustwallow	Horde	55	60	Emberstrife—Dustwallow Marsh	Emberstrife	Emberstrife	6600	
The Test of Skulls, Axtroz	Dustwallow	Horde	55	60	Emberstrife—Dustwallow Marsh	Emberstrife	The Test of Skulls, Scryer	6600	
Ascension...	Dustwallow	Horde	55	60	Emberstrife—Dustwallow Marsh	Rexxar	The Test of Skulls, Axtroz	5450	
Nat Pagle, Angler Extreme	Dustwallow	Both	35	45	Nat Pagle—Dustwallow Marsh	Nat Pagle		3900	
Service to the Horde	Dustwallow	Horde	30	40		Zor Lonetree	Report to Zor	1550	1g 50s
CHOICE OF: 1 Band of Allegiance or 1 Lonetree's Circle									

Eastern Plaguelands

Title	Location	Faction	Min Level	Con Level	Starter Location	Finisher	Prerequisite	Max XP	Cash Reward
Little Pamela	Eastern Plaguelands	Both	50	55	Marlene Redpath—Western Plaguelands	Pamela Redpath		2800	
Pamela's Doll	Eastern Plaguelands	Both	50	55	Pamela Redpath—Eastern Plaguelands	Pamela Redpath		2800	
Auntie Marlene	Eastern Plaguelands	Both	50	56	Pamela Redpath—Eastern Plaguelands	Marlene Redpath	Pamela's Doll	2900	
A Strange Historian	Eastern Plaguelands	Both	50	56	Marlene Redpath—Western Plaguelands	Chromie	Auntie Marlene	4350	
The Annals of Darrowshire	Eastern Plaguelands	Both	50	56	Chromie—Western Plaguelands Ruins of Anderhol	Chromie	A Strange Historian	5800	
Heroes of Darrowshire	Eastern Plaguelands	Both	50	56	Carlin Redpath—Eastern Plaguelands Light's Hope Chapel	Carlin Redpath	Brother Carlin	5800	
Villains of Darrowshire	Eastern Plaguelands	Both	50	57	Carlin Redpath—Eastern Plaguelands Light's Hope Chapel	Carlin Redpath	Brother Carlin	6000	
Marauders of Darrowshire	Eastern Plaguelands	Both	50	60	Carlin Redpath—Eastern Plaguelands Light's Hope Chapel	Carlin Redpath	Villains of Darrowshire	6600	
Brother Carlin	Eastern Plaguelands	Both	50	56	Chromie—Western Plaguelands Ruins of Anderhol	Carlin Redpath	The Annals of Darrowshire	2900	
Defenders of Darrowshire	Eastern Plaguelands	Both	50	55	Carlin Redpath—Eastern Plaguelands Light's Hope Chapel	Carlin Redpath		5650	
The Flesh Does Not Lie	Eastern Plaguelands	Both	55	60	Betina Bigglezink—Eastern Plaguelands Light's Hope Chapel	Betina Bigglezink		6600	1g 85s
The Active Agent	Eastern Plaguelands	Both	55	60	Betina Bigglezink—Eastern Plaguelands Light's Hope Chapel	Betina Bigglezink	The Flesh Does Not Lie	6850	
CHOICE OF: 1 Seal of the Dawn or 1 Rune of the Dawn									
The Great Fras Siabi	Eastern Plaguelands	Both	55	60	Smokey LaRue—Eastern Plaguelands Light's Hope Chapel	Smokey LaRue		8550	
REWARD: 1 Smokey's Lighter									
Uncle Carlin	Eastern Plaguelands	Both	50	56	Pamela Redpath—Eastern Plaguelands	Carlin Redpath	Pamela's Doll	2900	
Houses of the Holy	Eastern Plaguelands	Both	55	60	Leonid Barthalomew the Revered—Eastern Plaguelands Light's Hope Chapel	Leonid Barthalomew the Revered		6600	1g 80s
CHOICE OF: 1 Crown of the Penitent or 1 Band of the Penitent REWARD: 5 Superior Healing Potion, 5Greater Mana Potion									
The Archivist	Eastern Plaguelands	Both	55	60	Duke Nicholas Zverenhoff—Eastern Plaguelands Light's Hope Chapel	Duke Nicholas Zverenhoff		8300	1g 85s
Above and Beyond	Eastern Plaguelands	Both	55	60	Duke Nicholas Zverenhoff—Eastern Plaguelands Light's Hope Chapel	Duke Nicholas Zverenhoff	The Archivist	8300	
Lord Maxwell Tyrosus	Eastern Plaguelands	Both	55	60	Duke Nicholas Zverenhoff—Eastern Plaguelands Light's Hope Chapel	Lord Maxwell Tyrosus	Above and Beyond	6600	
The Argent Hold	Eastern Plaguelands	Both	55	60	Lord Maxwell Tyrosus—Eastern Plaguelands Light's Hope Chapel	The Argent Hold	Lord Maxwell Tyrosus	9950	2g 70s
CHOICE OF: 1 Argent Avenger or 1 Argent Defender or 1 Argent Crusader									
The Restless Souls	Eastern Plaguelands	Both	55	60	Caretaker Alen—Eastern Plaguelands Light's Hope Chapel	Egan		6850	
The Restless Souls	Eastern Plaguelands	Both	55	60	Egan—Eastern Plaguelands Scourgehold	Egan	The Restless Souls	8850	1g 85s
REWARD: 1 Testament of Hope									
Menethil's Gift	Eastern Plaguelands	Both	57	60	Leonid Barthalomew the Revered—Eastern Plaguelands Light's Hope Chapel	Menethil's Gift	The Dying, Ras Frostwhisper	6600	
Menethil's Gift	Eastern Plaguelands	Both	57	60	Menethil's Gift—Stratholme	Leonid Barthalomew the Revered	Menethil's Gift	8800	
Soulbound Keepsake	Eastern Plaguelands	Both	57	60	Leonid Barthalomew the Revered—Eastern Plaguelands Light's Hope Chapel	Magistrate Marduke	Menethil's Gift	5300	
Argent Dawn Commission	Eastern Plaguelands	Both	50	55		Duke Nicholas Zverenhoff		550	
REWARD: 1 Argent Dawn Commission									
Corruptor's Scourgestones	Eastern Plaguelands	Both	50	55		Duke Nicholas Zverenhoff	Argent Dawn Commission	550	
REWARD: 1 Argent Dawn Valor Token									
Invader's Scourgestones	Eastern Plaguelands	Both	50	55		Duke Nicholas Zverenhoff	Argent Dawn Commission	550	
REWARD: 1 Argent Dawn Valor Token									
Minion's Scourgestones	Eastern Plaguelands	Both	50	55		Duke Nicholas Zverenhoff	Argent Dawn Commission	550	
REWARD: 1 Argent Dawn Valor Token									
Mantles of the Dawn	Eastern Plaguelands	Both	55	60	Quartermaster Miranda Breechlock—Eastern Plaguelands Light's Hope Chapel	Quartermaster Miranda Breechlock	Argent Dawn Commission	6600	
Chromatic Mantle of the Dawn	Eastern Plaguelands	Both	55	60	Quartermaster Miranda Breechlock—Eastern Plaguelands Light's Hope Chapel	Quartermaster Miranda Breechlock	Mantles of the Dawn	8300	
REWARD: 1 Chromatic Mantle of the Dawn									
Sister Pamela	Eastern Plaguelands	Both	50	55	Jessica Redpath—Winterspring Everlook	Pamela Redpath		550	
The Battle of Darrowshire	Eastern Plaguelands	Both	55	60	Chromie—Western Plaguelands Ruins of Anderhol	Pamela Redpath	Return to Chromie	8300	
REWARD: 1 Tea with Sugar									
A Plague Upon Thee	Eastern Plaguelands	Horde	48	55	Mickey Levine—Western Plaguelands	Mickey Levine		5650	85s
A Plague Upon Thee	Eastern Plaguelands	Horde	48	55	Mickey Levine—Western Plaguelands	Termite Barrel	A Plague Upon Thee	2800	
A Plague Upon Thee	Eastern Plaguelands	Alliance	48	55	Nathaniel Dumah—Western Plaguelands	Nathaniel Dumah		5650	85s
A Plague Upon Thee	Eastern Plaguelands	Alliance	48	55	Nathaniel Dumah—Western Plaguelands	Termite Barrel	A Plague Upon Thee	2800	
Return to Chromie	Eastern Plaguelands	Both	50	60	Carlin Redpath—Eastern Plaguelands Light's Hope Chapel	Chromie	Marauders of Darrowshire	3300	
Hidden Treasures	Eastern Plaguelands	Both	50	60	Pamela Redpath—Eastern Plaguelands	Joseph's Chest	The Battle of Darrowshire	9950	
REWARD: 1 Ring of Protection, 1Archlight Talisman, 1Magebane Scion									
Zoeldarr the Outcast	Eastern Plaguelands	Both	50	55	Caretaker Alen—Eastern Plaguelands Light's Hope Chapel	Caretaker Alen		4200	65s

Title	Location	Faction	Min Level	Con Level	Starter Location	Finisher	Prerequisite	Max XP	Cash Reward
To Kill With Purpose	Eastern Plaguelands	Horde	54	58	Nathanos Blightcaller—Eastern Plaguelands	Nathanos Blightcaller		6200	90s
Hameya's Plea	Eastern Plaguelands	Both	54	60	Torn Scroll—Eastern Plaguelands	Mound of Dirt		6600	90s
REWARD: 1 Hameya's Slayer, 1Hameya's Cloak									
That's Asking A Lot	Eastern Plaguelands	Both	54	58	Smokey LaRue—Eastern Plaguelands Light's Hope Chapel	Smokey LaRue		6200	1g 75s
When Smokey Sings, I Get Violent	Eastern Plaguelands	Both	54	58	Smokey LaRue—Eastern Plaguelands Light's Hope Chapel	Smokey LaRue	That's Asking A Lot	6200	2g 65s
CHOICE OF: 1 Smokey's Explosive Launcher or 1 Smokey's Fireshooter REWARD: 10 Moist Towelette, 1Smokey's Drape									
Un-Life's Little Annoyances	Eastern Plaguelands	Horde	54	58	Nathanos Blightcaller—Eastern Plaguelands	Nathanos Blightcaller		6200	90s
The Ranger Lord's Behest	Eastern Plaguelands	Horde	54	60	Nathanos Blightcaller—Eastern Plaguelands	Nathanos Blightcaller		6600	90s
Duskwing, Oh How I Hate Thee...	Eastern Plaguelands	Horde	56	60	Nathanos Blightcaller—Eastern Plaguelands	Nathanos Blightcaller	To Kill With Purpose	6600	90s
CHOICE OF: 1 Duskwing Gloves or 1 Duskwing Mantle									
The Corpulent One	Eastern Plaguelands	Horde	56	60	Nathanos Blightcaller—Eastern Plaguelands	Nathanos Blightcaller	To Kill With Purpose	6600	90s
CHOICE OF: 1 Ichor Spitter or 1 Skullstone Hammer or 1 Sarah's Guide									
The Call to Command	Eastern Plaguelands	Horde	56	60	Nathanos Blightcaller—Eastern Plaguelands	Varimathras	Duskwing, Oh How I Hate Thee...	675	
The Crimson Courier	Eastern Plaguelands	Horde	56	60	Varimathras—Undercity	Nathanos Blightcaller	The Call to Command	6600	
Nathanos' Ruse	Eastern Plaguelands	Horde	56	60	Nathanos Blightcaller—Eastern Plaguelands	Crusader Lord Valdelmar	The Crimson Courier	6850	
Return to Nathanos	Eastern Plaguelands	Horde	56	60	Crusader Lord Valdelmar—Eastern Plaguelands Monster Human	Nathanos Blightcaller	Nathanos' Ruse	3400	
The Scarlet Oracle, Demetria	Eastern Plaguelands	Horde	56	60	Nathanos Blightcaller—Eastern Plaguelands	Nathanos Blightcaller	Return to Nathanos	8300	1g 80s
CHOICE OF: 1 Gorewood Bow or 1 Stormrager or 1 Sacred Protector									
Ramstein	Eastern Plaguelands	Horde	56	60	Nathanos Blightcaller—Eastern Plaguelands	Nathanos Blightcaller	Duskwing, Oh How I Hate Thee...	6600	1g 80s
CHOICE OF: 1 Royal Seal of Alexis or 1 Elemental Circle									
Augustus' Receipt Book	Eastern Plaguelands	Both	50	55	Augustus the Touched—Eastern Plaguelands	Augustus the Touched		1400	
A Plague Upon Thee	Eastern Plaguelands	Alliance	48	55	Termite Barrel—Western Plaguelands	Nathaniel Dumah	A Plague Upon Thee	5650	85s
A Plague Upon Thee	Eastern Plaguelands	Horde	48	55	Termite Barrel—Western Plaguelands	Mickey Levine	A Plague Upon Thee	5650	
A Warning	Eastern Plaguelands	Both	60	60		Eris Havenfire			
The Balance of Light and Shadow	Eastern Plaguelands	Both	60	60	Eris Havenfire—Eastern Plaguelands	Eris Havenfire	A Warning	9950	
REWARD: 1 Splinter of Nordrassil									
The Shadow Guard	Eastern Plaguelands	Both	60	60	Mataus the Wrathcaster—Eastern Plaguelands	Mataus the Wrathcaster			
REWARD: 1 Shadow Guard									
The Ice Guard	Eastern Plaguelands	Both	60	60	Mataus the Wrathcaster—Eastern Plaguelands	Mataus the Wrathcaster			
REWARD: 1 Ice Guard									
Binding the Dreadnaught	Eastern Plaguelands	Both	55	60	Korfax, Champion of the Light—Eastern Plaguelands	Korfax, Champion of the Light		6600	
REWARD: 1 Insignia of the Dawn									
Dark Iron Scraps	Eastern Plaguelands	Both	55	60		Korfax, Champion of the Light	Binding the Dreadnaught		
REWARD: 1 Insignia of the Dawn									
The Elemental Equation	Eastern Plaguelands	Both	55	60	Archmage Angela Dosantos—Eastern Plaguelands	Archmage Angela Dosantos			
REWARD: 1 Insignia of the Dawn									
Core of Elements	Eastern Plaguelands	Both	55	60		Archmage Angela Dosantos	The Elemental Equation		
REWARD: 1 Insignia of the Dawn									
Bonescythe Digs	Eastern Plaguelands	Both	55	60	Rohan the Assassin—Eastern Plaguelands	Rohan the Assassin		6600	
REWARD: 1 Insignia of the Crusade									
Bone Fragments	Eastern Plaguelands	Both	55	60		Rohan the Assassin	Bonescythe Digs		
REWARD: 1 Insignia of the Crusade									
Savage Flora	Eastern Plaguelands	Both	55	60	Rayne—Eastern Plaguelands	Rayne		6600	
CHOICE OF: 1 Insignia of the Crusade or 1 Insignia of the Dawn									
Savage Fronds	Eastern Plaguelands	Both	55	60		Rayne	Savage Flora		
CHOICE OF: 1 Insignia of the Dawn or 1 Insignia of the Crusade									
Cryptstalker Armor Doesn't Make Itself...	Eastern Plaguelands	Both	55	60	Huntsman Leopold—Eastern Plaguelands	Huntsman Leopold		6600	
REWARD: 1 Insignia of the Crusade									
Crypt Fiend Parts	Eastern Plaguelands	Both	55	60		Huntsman Leopold	Cryptstalker Armor Doesn't Make Itself...		
REWARD: 1 Insignia of the Crusade									
They Call Me "The Rooster"	Eastern Plaguelands	Both	55	60	Dispatch Commander Metz—Eastern Plaguelands Light's Hope Chapel	Dispatch Commander Metz		3300	
REWARD: 1 Sealed Craftsman's Writ									
Epic Armaments of Battle - Friend of the Dawn	Eastern Plaguelands	Both	55	60	Quartermaster Miranda Breechlock—Eastern Plaguelands Light's Hope Chapel	Quartermaster Miranda Breechlock			
CHOICE OF: 1 Amulet of the Dawn or 1 Bracers of Hope or 1 Bracers of Subterfuge or 1 Medallion of the Dawn or 1 Talisman of Ascendance or 1 The Purifier									
Superior Armaments of Battle - Friend of the Dawn	Eastern Plaguelands	Both	55	60	Quartermaster Miranda Breechlock—Eastern Plaguelands Light's Hope Chapel	Quartermaster Miranda Breechlock			
CHOICE OF: 1 Band of Piety or 1 Band of Resolution or 1 Verimonde's Last Resort or 1 Supply Bag or 1 Leggings of the Plague Hunter or 1 Sanctified Leather Helm									
Superior Armaments of Battle - Honored Amongst the Dawn	Eastern Plaguelands	Both	55	60	Quartermaster Miranda Breechlock—Eastern Plaguelands Light's Hope Chapel	Quartermaster Miranda Breechlock			
CHOICE OF: 1 Band of Piety or 1 Band of Resolution or 1 Verimonde's Last Resort or 1 Supply Bag or 1 Leggings of the Plague Hunter or 1 Sanctified Leather Helm									
Epic Armaments of Battle - Honored Amongst the Dawn	Eastern Plaguelands	Both	55	60	Quartermaster Miranda Breechlock—Eastern Plaguelands Light's Hope Chapel	Quartermaster Miranda Breechlock			
CHOICE OF: 1 Amulet of the Dawn or 1 Bracers of Hope or 1 Bracers of Subterfuge or 1 Medallion of the Dawn or 1 Talisman of Ascendance or 1 The Purifier									
Epic Armaments of Battle - Revered Amongst the Dawn	Eastern Plaguelands	Both	55	60	Quartermaster Miranda Breechlock—Eastern Plaguelands Light's Hope Chapel	Quartermaster Miranda Breechlock			
CHOICE OF: 1 Amulet of the Dawn or 1 Bracers of Hope or 1 Bracers of Subterfuge or 1 Medallion of the Dawn or 1 Talisman of Ascendance or 1 The Purifier									
Superior Armaments of Battle - Revered Amongst the Dawn	Eastern Plaguelands	Both	55	60	Quartermaster Miranda Breechlock—Eastern Plaguelands Light's Hope Chapel	Quartermaster Miranda Breechlock			
CHOICE OF: 1 Band of Piety or 1 Band of Resolution or 1 Verimonde's Last Resort or 1 Supply Bag or 1 Leggings of the Plague Hunter or 1 Sanctified Leather Helm									
Superior Armaments of Battle - Exalted Amongst the Dawn	Eastern Plaguelands	Both	55	60	Quartermaster Miranda Breechlock—Eastern Plaguelands Light's Hope Chapel	Quartermaster Miranda Breechlock			
CHOICE OF: 1 Band of Piety or 1 Band of Resolution or 1 Verimonde's Last Resort or 1 Supply Bag or 1 Leggings of the Plague Hunter or 1 Sanctified Leather Helm									
Epic Armaments of Battle - Exalted Amongst the Dawn	Eastern Plaguelands	Both	55	60	Quartermaster Miranda Breechlock—Eastern Plaguelands Light's Hope Chapel	Quartermaster Miranda Breechlock			
CHOICE OF: 1 Amulet of the Dawn or 1 Bracers of Hope or 1 Bracers of Subterfuge or 1 Medallion of the Dawn or 1 Talisman of Ascendance or 1 The Purifier									
Craftsman's Writ	Eastern Plaguelands	Both	55	60		Dispatch Commander Metz	They Call Me "The Rooster"		
REWARD: 1 Sealed Craftsman's Writ									
Craftsman's Writ - Dense Weightstone	Eastern Plaguelands	Both	55	60	Craftsman's Writ - Dense Weightstone	Packmaster Stonebruiser			
CHOICE OF: 1 Insignia of the Crusade or 1 Insignia of the Dawn									
Craftsman's Writ - Imperial Plate Chest	Eastern Plaguelands	Both	55	60	Craftsman's Writ - Imperial Plate Chest	Packmaster Stonebruiser			
CHOICE OF: 1 Insignia of the Crusade or 1 Insignia of the Dawn									
Craftsman's Writ - Volcanic Hammer	Eastern Plaguelands	Both	55	60	Craftsman's Writ - Volcanic Hammer	Packmaster Stonebruiser			
CHOICE OF: 1 Insignia of the Crusade or 1 Insignia of the Dawn									
Craftsman's Writ - Huge Thorium Battleaxe	Eastern Plaguelands	Both	55	60	Craftsman's Writ - Huge Thorium Battleaxe	Packmaster Stonebruiser			
CHOICE OF: 1 Insignia of the Crusade or 1 Insignia of the Dawn									
Craftsman's Writ - Radiant Circlet	Eastern Plaguelands	Both	55	60	Craftsman's Writ - Radiant Circlet	Packmaster Stonebruiser			
CHOICE OF: 1 Insignia of the Crusade or 1 Insignia of the Dawn									
Craftsman's Writ - Wicked Leather Headband	Eastern Plaguelands	Both	55	60	Craftsman's Writ - Wicked Leather Headband	Packmaster Stonebruiser			
CHOICE OF: 1 Insignia of the Crusade or 1 Insignia of the Dawn									
Craftsman's Writ - Rugged Armor Kit	Eastern Plaguelands	Both	55	60	Craftsman's Writ - Rugged Armor Kit	Packmaster Stonebruiser			
CHOICE OF: 1 Insignia of the Crusade or 1 Insignia of the Dawn									
Craftsman's Writ - Wicked Leather Belt	Eastern Plaguelands	Both	55	60	Craftsman's Writ - Wicked Leather Belt	Packmaster Stonebruiser			
CHOICE OF: 1 Insignia of the Crusade or 1 Insignia of the Dawn									
Craftsman's Writ - Runic Leather Pants	Eastern Plaguelands	Both	55	60	Craftsman's Writ - Runic Leather Pants	Packmaster Stonebruiser			
CHOICE OF: 1 Insignia of the Crusade or 1 Insignia of the Dawn									
Craftsman's Writ - Brightcloth Pants	Eastern Plaguelands	Both	55	60	Craftsman's Writ - Brightcloth Pants	Packmaster Stonebruiser			
CHOICE OF: 1 Insignia of the Crusade or 1 Insignia of the Dawn									
Craftsman's Writ - Runecloth Boots	Eastern Plaguelands	Both	55	60	Craftsman's Writ - Runecloth Boots	Packmaster Stonebruiser			

Eastern Plaguelands cont'd

Title	Location	Faction	Min Level	Con Level	Starter Location	Finisher	Prerequisite	Max XP	Cash Reward
CHOICE OF: 1 Insignia of the Crusade or 1 Insignia of the Dawn									
Craftsman's Writ - Runecloth Bag	Eastern Plaguelands	Both	55	60	Craftsman's Writ - Runecloth Bag	Packmaster Stonebruiser			
CHOICE OF: 1 Insignia of the Crusade or 1 Insignia of the Dawn									
Craftsman's Writ - Goblin Sapper Charge	Eastern Plaguelands	Both	55	60	Craftsman's Writ - Goblin Sapper Charge	Packmaster Stonebruiser			
CHOICE OF: 1 Insignia of the Crusade or 1 Insignia of the Dawn									
Craftsman's Writ - Thorium Grenade	Eastern Plaguelands	Both	55	60	Craftsman's Writ - Thorium Grenade	Packmaster Stonebruiser			
CHOICE OF: 1 Insignia of the Crusade or 1 Insignia of the Dawn									
Craftsman's Writ - Gnomish Battle Chicken	Eastern Plaguelands	Both	55	60	Craftsman's Writ - Gnomish Battle Chicken	Packmaster Stonebruiser			
CHOICE OF: 1 Insignia of the Crusade or 1 Insignia of the Dawn									
Craftsman's Writ - Thorium Tube	Eastern Plaguelands	Both	55	60	Craftsman's Writ - Thorium Tube	Packmaster Stonebruiser			
CHOICE OF: 1 Insignia of the Crusade or 1 Insignia of the Dawn									
Craftsman's Writ - Major Mana Potion	Eastern Plaguelands	Both	55	60	Craftsman's Writ - Major Mana Potion	Packmaster Stonebruiser			
CHOICE OF: 1 Insignia of the Crusade or 1 Insignia of the Dawn									
Craftsman's Writ - Greater Arcane Protection Potion	Eastern Plaguelands	Both	55	60	Craftsman's Writ - Greater Arcane Protection Potion	Packmaster Stonebruiser			
CHOICE OF: 1 Insignia of the Crusade or 1 Insignia of the Dawn									
Craftsman's Writ - Major Healing Potion	Eastern Plaguelands	Both	55	60	Craftsman's Writ - Major Healing Potion	Packmaster Stonebruiser			
CHOICE OF: 1 Insignia of the Crusade or 1 Insignia of the Dawn									
Craftsman's Writ - Flask of Petrification	Eastern Plaguelands	Both	55	60	Craftsman's Writ - Flask of Petrification	Packmaster Stonebruiser			
CHOICE OF: 1 Insignia of the Crusade or 1 Insignia of the Dawn									
Craftsman's Writ - Stonescale Eel	Eastern Plaguelands	Both	55	60	Craftsman's Writ - Stonescale Eel	Packmaster Stonebruiser			
CHOICE OF: 1 Insignia of the Crusade or 1 Insignia of the Dawn									
Craftsman's Writ - Plated Armorfish	Eastern Plaguelands	Both	55	60	Craftsman's Writ - Plated Armorfish	Packmaster Stonebruiser			
CHOICE OF: 1 Insignia of the Crusade or 1 Insignia of the Dawn									
Craftsman's Writ - Lightning Eel	Eastern Plaguelands	Both	55	60	Craftsman's Writ - Lightning Eel	Packmaster Stonebruiser			
CHOICE OF: 1 Insignia of the Crusade or 1 Insignia of the Dawn									
The Only Song I Know...	Eastern Plaguelands	Both	60	60	Craftsman Wilhelm—Eastern Plaguelands	Craftsman Wilhelm	Echoes of War		
CHOICE OF: 1 Glacial Leggings or 1 Icebane Leggings or 1 Icy Scale Leggings or 1 Polar Leggings									
Omarion's Handbook	Eastern Plaguelands	Both	60	60	Omarion's Handbook	Craftsman Wilhelm			
Icebane Gauntlets	Eastern Plaguelands	Both	60	60	Craftsman Wilhelm—Eastern Plaguelands	Craftsman Wilhelm	Omarion's Handbook		
REWARD: 1 Icebane Gauntlets									
Icebane Bracers	Eastern Plaguelands	Both	60	60	Craftsman Wilhelm—Eastern Plaguelands	Craftsman Wilhelm	Omarion's Handbook		
REWARD: 1 Icebane Bracers									
Icebane Breastplate	Eastern Plaguelands	Both	60	60	Craftsman Wilhelm—Eastern Plaguelands	Craftsman Wilhelm	Omarion's Handbook		
REWARD: 1 Icebane Breastplate									
Glacial Cloak	Eastern Plaguelands	Both	60	60	Craftsman Wilhelm—Eastern Plaguelands	Craftsman Wilhelm	Omarion's Handbook		
REWARD: 1 Glacial Cloak									
Glacial Wrists	Eastern Plaguelands	Both	60	60	Craftsman Wilhelm—Eastern Plaguelands	Craftsman Wilhelm	Omarion's Handbook		
REWARD: 1 Glacial Wrists									
Glacial Gloves	Eastern Plaguelands	Both	60	60	Craftsman Wilhelm—Eastern Plaguelands	Craftsman Wilhelm	Omarion's Handbook		
REWARD: 1 Glacial Gloves									
Glacial Vest	Eastern Plaguelands	Both	60	60	Craftsman Wilhelm—Eastern Plaguelands	Craftsman Wilhelm	Omarion's Handbook		
REWARD: 1 Glacial Vest									
Polar Bracers	Eastern Plaguelands	Both	60	60	Craftsman Wilhelm—Eastern Plaguelands	Craftsman Wilhelm	Omarion's Handbook		
REWARD: 1 Polar Bracers									
Polar Gloves	Eastern Plaguelands	Both	60	60	Craftsman Wilhelm—Eastern Plaguelands	Craftsman Wilhelm	Omarion's Handbook		
REWARD: 1 Polar Gloves									
Polar Tunic	Eastern Plaguelands	Both	60	60	Craftsman Wilhelm—Eastern Plaguelands	Craftsman Wilhelm	Omarion's Handbook		
REWARD: 1 Polar Tunic									
Icy Scale Bracers	Eastern Plaguelands	Both	60	60	Craftsman Wilhelm—Eastern Plaguelands	Craftsman Wilhelm	Omarion's Handbook		
REWARD: 1 Icy Scale Bracers									
Icy Scale Gauntlets	Eastern Plaguelands	Both	60	60	Craftsman Wilhelm—Eastern Plaguelands	Craftsman Wilhelm	Omarion's Handbook		
REWARD: 1 Icy Scale Gauntlets									
Icy Scale Breastplate	Eastern Plaguelands	Both	60	60	Craftsman Wilhelm—Eastern Plaguelands	Craftsman Wilhelm	Omarion's Handbook		
REWARD: 1 Icy Scale Breastplate									
The Fate of Ramaladni	Eastern Plaguelands	Both	60	60	Korfax, Champion of the Light—Eastern Plaguelands	Korfax, Champion of the Light	Echoes of War		
Ramaladni's Icy Grasp	Eastern Plaguelands	Both	60	60	Korfax, Champion of the Light—Eastern Plaguelands	Korfax, Champion of the Light	The Fate of Ramaladni		
REWARD: 1 Ramaladni's Icy Grasp									
Writ of Safe Passage	Eastern Plaguelands	Both	55	60		Dispatch Commander Metz			
CHOICE OF: 1 Insignia of the Dawn or 1 Insignia of the Crusade									
Craftsman's Writ - Runecloth Robe	Eastern Plaguelands	Both	55	60	Craftsman's Writ - Runecloth Robe	Packmaster Stonebruiser			
CHOICE OF: 1 Insignia of the Crusade or 1 Insignia of the Dawn									

Elwynn Forest

Title	Location	Faction	Min Level	Con Level	Starter Location	Finisher	Prerequisite	Max XP	Cash Reward
Riverpaw Gnoll Bounty	Elwynn Forest	Alliance	6	10	Deputy Rainer—Elwynn	Deputy Rainer	The Jasperlode Mine	850	
CHOICE OF: 1 Militia Buckler or 1 Urchin's Pants									
Give Gerard a Drink	Elwynn Forest	Alliance	1	1		Gerard Tiller			
REWARD: 1 Shiny Red Apple									
Further Concerns	Elwynn Forest	Alliance	7	10	Marshal Dughan—Elwynn Goldshire	Guard Thomas	A Fishy Peril	420	
Find the Lost Guards	Elwynn Forest	Alliance	7	10	Guard Thomas—Elwynn	A half-eaten body	Further Concerns	210	
Deliver Thomas' Report	Elwynn Forest	Alliance	7	10	Guard Thomas—Elwynn	Marshal Dughan	Report to Thomas	1050	7●
A Fishy Peril	Elwynn Forest	Alliance	7	10	Remy "Two Times"—Elwynn Goldshire	Marshal Dughan		85	
Discover Rolf's Fate	Elwynn Forest	Alliance	7	10	Half-eaten body—Elwynn	Rolf's corpse	Find the Lost Guards	420	
Bounty on Murlocs	Elwynn Forest	Alliance	7	10	Guard Thomas—Elwynn	Guard Thomas	Deliver Thomas' Report	850	
CHOICE OF: 1 Long Bayonet or 1 Solid Metal Club or 1 Well-used Sword									
Gold Dust Exchange	Elwynn Forest	Alliance	4	7	Remy "Two Times"—Elwynn Goldshire	Remy "Two Times"		625	1● 75●
REWARD: 1 Bag of Marbles									
Protect the Frontier	Elwynn Forest	Alliance	7	10	Guard Thomas—Elwynn	Guard Thomas		625	
REWARD: 2 Lesser Healing Potion									
Cloth and Leather Armor	Elwynn Forest	Alliance	7	10	Marshal Dughan—Elwynn Goldshire	Sara Timberlain	Deliver Thomas' Report	210	
CHOICE OF: 1 Well-stitched Robe or 1 Patched Pants									
Kobold Candles	Elwynn Forest	Alliance	3	7	William Pestle—Elwynn Goldshire	William Pestle		480	1● 25●
REWARD: 5 Glowing Wax Stick									
Shipment to Stormwind	Elwynn Forest	Alliance	3	7	William Pestle—Elwynn Goldshire	Morgan Pestle	Kobold Candles	800	3● 50●
Reward: 15 Explosive Rocket or 5 Oil of Olaf 2 Elixir of Lion's Strength									
The Fargodeep Mine	Elwynn Forest	Alliance	4	7	Marshal Dughan—Elwynn Goldshire	Marshal Dughan		480	1● 25●
Report to Thomas	Elwynn Forest	Alliance	7	10	Rolf's corpse—Elwynn	Guard Thomas	Discover Rolf's Fate	210	
The Jasperlode Mine	Elwynn Forest	Alliance	4	10	Marshal Dughan—Elwynn Goldshire	Marshal Dughan	The Fargodeep Mine	850	3● 50●
Red Linen Goods	Elwynn Forest	Alliance	4	9	Sara Timberlain—Elwynn	Sara Timberlain		775	
REWARD: 1 Red Linen Shirt, 1Red Linen Sash									
Back to Billy	Elwynn Forest	Alliance	5	6	"Auntie" Bernice Stonefield—Elwynn	Billy Maclure	Pie for Billy	140	
Lost Necklace	Elwynn Forest	Alliance	5	6	"Auntie" Bernice Stonefield—Elwynn	Billy Maclure		140	
Pie for Billy	Elwynn Forest	Alliance	5	6	Billy Maclure—Elwynn	"Auntie" Bernice Stonefield	Lost Necklace	410	
Goldtooth	Elwynn Forest	Alliance	5	8	Billy Maclure—Elwynn	"Auntie" Bernice Stonefield	Back to Billy	875	
REWARD: 1 Lion-stamped Gloves									
Princess Must Die!	Elwynn Forest	Alliance	6	9	Ma Stonefield—Elwynn	Ma Stonefield		775	
CHOICE OF: 1 Weather-worn Boots or 1 Brass-studded Bracers or 1 Farmer's Boots									
A Watchful Eye	Elwynn Forest	Alliance	20	21	Theocritus—Elwynn	Old Lion Statue		1250	

Title	Location	Faction	Min Level	Con Level	Starter Location	Finisher	Prerequisite	Max XP	Cash Reward
Young Lovers	Elwynn Forest	Alliance	5	6	Maybell Maclure—Elwynn	Tommy Joe Stonefield		140	
Note to William	Elwynn Forest	Alliance	5	6	Gramma Stonefield—Elwynn	William Pestle	Speak with Gramma	140	
Report to Gryan Stoutmantle	Elwynn Forest	Alliance	9	10	Marshal Haggard—Elwynn	Gryan Stoutmantle		625	
Speak with Gramma	Elwynn Forest	Alliance	5	6	Tommy Joe Stonefield—Elwynn	Gramma Stonefield	Young Lovers	140	
Collecting Kelp	Elwynn Forest	Alliance	5	7	William Pestle—Elwynn Goldshire	William Pestle	Note to William	320	
The Escape	Elwynn Forest	Alliance	5	7	William Pestle—Elwynn Goldshire	Maybell Maclure	Collecting Kelp	800	
REWARD: 5 Minor Healing Potion									
The Collector	Elwynn Forest	Alliance	7	10	Gold Pickup Schedule	Marshal Dughan		210	85
Manhunt	Elwynn Forest	Alliance	7	10		Marshal Dughan	The Collector	850	
CHOICE OF: 1 Stormwind Chain Gloves or 1 Elastic Wristguards									
Wanted: "Hogger"	Elwynn Forest	Alliance	5	11	Wanted Poster—Elwynn Goldshire	Marshal Dughan		875	
CHOICE OF: 1 Footman Tunic or 1 Stormwind Guard Leggings or 1 Balanced Fighting Stick									
Furlbrow's Deed	Elwynn Forest	Alliance	8	9	Westfall Deed	Farmer Furlbrow		600	
REWARD: 5 Ripe Watermelon, 5 Small Pumpkin									
Westbrook Garrison Needs Help!	Elwynn Forest	Alliance	6	10	Marshal Dughan—Elwynn Goldshire	Deputy Rainer	The Jasperlode Mine	210	
The Tome of Divinity	Elwynn Forest	Alliance	12	12		Duthorian Rall	The Tome of Divinity		
REWARD: 1 Tome of Divinity									
The Tome of Divinity	Elwynn Forest	Alliance	12	12	Tome of Divinity	Duthorian Rall		90	
The Tome of Divinity	Elwynn Forest	Alliance	12	12	Duthorian Rall—Stormwind	Stephanie Turner	The Tome of Divinity	460	
The Tome of Divinity	Elwynn Forest	Alliance	12	13	Stephanie Turner—Stormwind	Stephanie Turner	The Tome of Divinity	900	
Gakin's Summons	Elwynn Forest	Alliance	10	10	Remen Marcot—Elwynn	Gakin the Darkbinder	Surena Caledon	420	
The Tome of Divinity	Elwynn Forest	Alliance	12	13	Stephanie Turner—Stormwind	Duthorian Rall	The Tome of Divinity	230	
The Tome of Divinity	Elwynn Forest	Alliance	12	13	Duthorian Rall—Stormwind	Gazin Tenorm	The Tome of Divinity		
The Tome of Divinity	Elwynn Forest	Alliance	12	13	Gazin Tenorm—Stormwind	Henze Faulk	The Tome of Divinity	675	
The Tome of Divinity	Elwynn Forest	Alliance	12	13		Gazin Tenorm	The Tome of Divinity	675	
The Tome of Divinity	Elwynn Forest	Alliance	12	13	Gazin Tenorm—Stormwind	Duthorian Rall	The Tome of Divinity	1150	
The Symbol of Life	Elwynn Forest	Alliance	12	12		Duthorian Rall	The Tome of Divinity		
REWARD: 1 Symbol of Life									
Rest and Relaxation	Elwynn Forest	Alliance	1	5	Falkhaan Isenstrider—Elwynn Forest Northshire Abbey	Innkeeper Farley		100	
CHOICE OF: 5 Small Pumpkin or 5 Refreshing Spring Water									
Seek out SI: 7	Elwynn Forest	Alliance	10	10	Keryn Sylvius—Elwynn Goldshire	Master Mathias Shaw		210	
Redridge Rendezvous	Elwynn Forest	Alliance	16	16	Renzik "The Shiv"—Stormwind	Lucius		120	
SI:7	Elwynn Forest	Alliance	16	16	Keryn Sylvius—Elwynn Goldshire	Renzik "The Shiv"	Redridge Rendezvous	120	
Tome of Divinity	Elwynn Forest	Alliance	12	12	Brother Wilhelm—Elwynn Goldshire	Duthorian Rall		230	
Tome of Divinity	Elwynn Forest	Alliance	12	12	Brandur Ironhammer—Ironforge	Duthorian Rall		230	
A Bundle of Trouble	Elwynn Forest	Alliance	5	9	Supervisor Raelen—Elwynn	Supervisor Raelen		775	3
In Favor of the Light	Elwynn Forest	Alliance	5	4	Priestess Anetta—Elwynn Forest Northshire	Priestess Josetta		90	
Garments of the Light	Elwynn Forest	Alliance	5	4	Priestess Josetta—Elwynn Goldshire	Priestess Josetta		270	
REWARD: 1 Friar's Robes of the Light									
White Stallion Exchange	Elwynn Forest	Horde	60	1		Katie Hunter			
CHOICE OF: 1 Swift Brown Steed or 1 Swift Palomino or 1 Swift White Steed									
Palomino Exchange	Elwynn Forest	Horde	60	1		Katie Hunter			
CHOICE OF: 1 Swift Brown Steed or 1 Swift Palomino or 1 Swift White Steed									
Flute of Xavaric	Felwood	Alliance	49	54	Flute of Xavaric	Eridan Bluewind		5450	
Corrupted Windblossom	Felwood	Both	48	55		Corrupted Windblossom		550	
Corrupted Windblossom	Felwood	Both	48	55		Corrupted Windblossom		550	
Corrupted Windblossom	Felwood	Both	48	55		Corrupted Windblossom		550	
Corrupted Songflower	Felwood	Both	48	55		Corrupted Songflower		550	
Corrupted Songflower	Felwood	Both	48	55		Corrupted Songflower		550	
Corrupted Songflower	Felwood	Both	48	55		Corrupted Songflower		550	
Cleansing Felwood	Felwood	Alliance	48	55	Arathandris Silversky—Felwood Morlos'Aran	Arathandris Silversky		5650	
Cleansing Felwood	Felwood	Horde	48	55	Maybess Riverbreeze—Felwood	Maybess Riverbreeze		5650	
Salve via Hunting	Felwood	Alliance	48	55		Arathandris Silversky	Salve via Hunting		
REWARD: 2 Cenarion Plant Salve									
Salve via Mining	Felwood	Alliance	48	55		Arathandris Silversky	Salve via Mining		
REWARD: 2 Cenarion Plant Salve									
Salve via Gathering	Felwood	Alliance	48	55		Arathandris Silversky	Salve via Gathering		
REWARD: 2 Cenarion Plant Salve									
Salve via Skinning	Felwood	Alliance	48	55		Arathandris Silversky	Salve via Skinning		
REWARD: 2 Cenarion Plant Salve									
Salve via Disenchanting	Felwood	Alliance	48	55		Arathandris Silversky	Salve via Disenchanting		
REWARD: 2 Cenarion Plant Salve									
Salve via Hunting	Felwood	Horde	48	55		Maybess Riverbreeze	Salve via Hunting		
REWARD: 2 Cenarion Plant Salve									
Salve via Mining	Felwood	Horde	48	55		Maybess Riverbreeze	Salve via Mining		
REWARD: 2 Cenarion Plant Salve									
Salve via Gathering	Felwood	Horde	48	55		Maybess Riverbreeze	Salve via Gathering		
REWARD: 2 Cenarion Plant Salve									
Salve via Skinning	Felwood	Horde	48	55		Maybess Riverbreeze	Salve via Skinning		
REWARD: 2 Cenarion Plant Salve									
Salve via Disenchanting	Felwood	Horde	48	55		Maybess Riverbreeze	Salve via Disenchanting		
REWARD: 2 Cenarion Plant Salve									
Corrupted Songflower	Felwood	Both	48	55		Corrupted Songflower		550	
Corrupted Songflower	Felwood	Both	48	55		Corrupted Songflower		550	
Corrupted Windblossom	Felwood	Both	48	55		Corrupted Windblossom		550	
Corrupted Songflower	Felwood	Both	48	55		Corrupted Songflower		550	
Corrupted Whipper Root	Felwood	Both	48	55		Corrupted Whipper Root		550	
Corrupted Songflower	Felwood	Both	48	55		Corrupted Songflower		550	
Corrupted Night Dragon	Felwood	Both	48	55		Corrupted Night Dragon		550	
Corrupted Windblossom	Felwood	Both	48	55		Corrupted Windblossom		550	
Corrupted Windblossom	Felwood	Both	48	55		Corrupted Windblossom		550	
Ancient Spirit	Felwood	Alliance	49	56	Arei—Felwood Monster Ancient Protector	Kayneth Stillwind		7300	
CHOICE OF: 1 Ethereal Mist Cape or 1 Clouddrift Mantle									
Corrupted Windblossom	Felwood	Both	48	55		Corrupted Windblossom		550	
Corrupted Songflower	Felwood	Both	48	55		Corrupted Songflower		550	
Corrupted Windblossom	Felwood	Both	48	55		Corrupted Windblossom		550	
The Corruption of the Jadefire	Felwood	Alliance	49	54	Eridan Bluewind—Felwood Emerald Sanctuary	Eridan Bluewind		5450	
Felbound Ancients	Felwood	Alliance	49	54	Eridan Bluewind—Felwood Emerald Sanctuary	Eridan Bluewind	Flute of Xavaric	5450	
Purified!	Felwood	Alliance	49	54	Eridan Bluewind—Felwood Emerald Sanctuary	Eridan Bluewind	Felbound Ancients	5450	
REWARD: 1 Flute of the Ancients									
Corrupted Whipper Root	Felwood	Both	48	55		Corrupted Whipper Root		550	
Corrupted Whipper Root	Felwood	Both	48	55		Corrupted Whipper Root		550	
Corrupted Whipper Root	Felwood	Both	48	55		Corrupted Whipper Root		550	
Corrupted Whipper Root	Felwood	Both	48	55		Corrupted Whipper Root		550	
Corrupted Night Dragon	Felwood	Both	48	55		Corrupted Night Dragon		550	
Corrupted Night Dragon	Felwood	Both	48	55		Corrupted Night Dragon		550	

Felwood cont'd

Title	Location	Faction	Min Level	Con Level	Starter Location	Finisher	Prerequisite	Max XP	Cash Reward
Corrupted Whipper Root	Felwood	Both	48	55		Corrupted Whipper Root		550	
Corrupted Night Dragon	Felwood	Both	48	55		Corrupted Night Dragon		550	
Corrupted Songflower	Felwood	Both	48	55		Corrupted Songflower		550	
Corrupted Songflower	Felwood	Both	48	55		Corrupted Songflower		550	
Corrupted Windblossom	Felwood	Both	48	55		Corrupted Windblossom		550	
Corrupted Windblossom	Felwood	Both	48	55		Corrupted Windblossom		550	
Well of Corruption	Felwood	Horde	49	54	Winna Hazzard—Felwood Bloodvenom Post	Winna Hazzard		5400	
Corrupted Sabers	Felwood	Horde	49	54	Winna Hazzard—Felwood Bloodvenom Post	Winna Hazzard	Well of Corruption	5450	60●
Further Corruption	Felwood	Alliance	49	54	Eridan Bluewind—Felwood Emerald Sanctuary	Eridan Bluewind	The Corruption of the Jadefire	5450	
REWARD: 1 Breezecloud Bracers									
Forces of Jaedenar	Felwood	Both	48	51	Greta Mosshoof—Felwood Emerald Sanctuary	Greta Mosshoof		4900	
Verifying the Corruption	Felwood	Both	48	54	Taronn Redfeather—Felwood Emerald Sanctuary	Taronn Redfeather		6800	1●65●
Collection of the Corrupt Water	Felwood	Both	48	52	Greta Mosshoof—Felwood Emerald Sanctuary	Greta Mosshoof	Forces of Jaedenar	3800	
Seeking Spiritual Aid	Felwood	Both	48	52	Greta Mosshoof—Felwood Emerald Sanctuary	Islen Waterseer	Collection of the Corrupt Water	2550	
Cleansed Water Returns to Felwood	Felwood	Both	48	54	Islen Waterseer—Barrens	Greta Mosshoof	Seeking Spiritual Aid	2700	
Dousing the Flames of Protection	Felwood	Both	48	55	Greta Mosshoof—Felwood Emerald Sanctuary	Greta Mosshoof	Cleansed Water Returns to Felwood	5650	
A Strange Red Key	Felwood	Both	49	55	Blood Red Key	Captured Arko'narin		5650	
Rescue From Jaedenar	Felwood	Both	49	55	Captured Arko'narin—Felwood Shadow Hold	Jessir Moonbow	A Strange Red Key	5650	
Retribution of the Light	Felwood	Both	49	57	Jessir Moonbow—Felwood Emerald Sanctuary	Remains of Trey Lightforge	Rescue From Jaedenar	4500	
REWARD: 1 Remains of Trey Lightforge									
A Final Blow	Felwood	Both	48	58	Greta Mosshoof—Felwood Emerald Sanctuary	Greta Mosshoof	Dousing the Flames of Protection	9300	
CHOICE OF: 1 Brantwood Sash or 1 Blight Leather Gloves or 1 Gearforge Girdle									
The Remains of Trey Lightforge	Felwood	Both	49	57	Remains of Trey Lightforge—Felwood	Jessir Moonbow	Retribution of the Light	7550	22●
CHOICE OF: 1 Hunt Tracker Blade or 1 Tidecrest Blade									
Salve via Hunting	Felwood	Alliance	48	55		Arathandris Silversky	Cleansing Felwood	4200	
REWARD: 2 Cenarion Plant Salve									
Salve via Mining	Felwood	Alliance	48	55		Arathandris Silversky	Cleansing Felwood	4200	
REWARD: 2 Cenarion Plant Salve									
Salve via Gathering	Felwood	Alliance	48	55		Arathandris Silversky	Cleansing Felwood	4200	
REWARD: 2 Cenarion Plant Salve									
Salve via Skinning	Felwood	Alliance	48	55		Arathandris Silversky	Cleansing Felwood	4200	
REWARD: 2 Cenarion Plant Salve									
Salve via Disenchanting	Felwood	Alliance	48	55		Arathandris Silversky	Cleansing Felwood	4200	
REWARD: 2 Cenarion Plant Salve									
Salve via Hunting	Felwood	Horde	48	55		Maybess Riverbreeze	Cleansing Felwood	4200	
REWARD: 2 Cenarion Plant Salve									
Salve via Mining	Felwood	Horde	48	55		Maybess Riverbreeze	Cleansing Felwood	4200	
REWARD: 2 Cenarion Plant Salve									
Salve via Gathering	Felwood	Horde	48	55		Maybess Riverbreeze	Cleansing Felwood	4200	
REWARD: 2 Cenarion Plant Salve									
Salve via Skinning	Felwood	Horde	48	55		Maybess Riverbreeze	Cleansing Felwood	4200	
REWARD: 2 Cenarion Plant Salve									
Salve via Disenchanting	Felwood	Horde	48	55		Maybess Riverbreeze	Cleansing Felwood	4200	
REWARD: 2 Cenarion Plant Salve									
A Husband's Last Battle	Felwood	Horde	46	51	Dreka'Sur—Felwood	Dreka'Sur		4900	75●
What Niby Commands	Felwood	Both	50	50	Niby the Almighty—Felwood	Impsy			
Flawless Fel Essence	Felwood	Both	50	55	Impsy—Felwood	Impsy	What Niby Commands	5650	
Kroshius' Infernal Core	Felwood	Both	50	55	Impsy—Felwood	Niby the Almighty	Flawless Fel Essence	7050	
REWARD: 1 Shard of the Green Flame									
The Ancient Leaf	Felwood	Both	60	60	Ancient Petrified Leaf	Vartrus the Ancient		9950	
An Introduction	Felwood	Both	60	60		Vartrus the Ancient	The Ancient Leaf		
Ancient Sinew Wrapped Lamina	Felwood	Both	60	60	Hastat the Ancient—Felwood	Hastat the Ancient	An Introduction	10900	
REWARD: 1 Ancient Sinew Wrapped Lamina									
A Proper String	Felwood	Both	60	60	Stoma the Ancient—Felwood	Stoma the Ancient	An Introduction	9950	
REWARD: 1 Enchanted Black Dragon Sinew									
Stave of the Ancients	Felwood	Both	60	60	Vartrus the Ancient—Felwood	Vartrus the Ancient	An Introduction	9950	
REWARD: 1 Ancient Rune Etched Stave									
Hot and Itchy	Felwood	Both	50	52	Impsy—Felwood	Impsy	An Imp's Request	3800	
The Wrong Stuff	Felwood	Both	50	52	Impsy—Felwood	Impsy	Hot and Itchy	5100	
Trolls of a Feather	Felwood	Both	50	52	Impsy—Felwood	Impsy	The Wrong Stuff	6350	1●55●
CHOICE OF: 1 Soul Harvester or 1 Abyss Shard or 1 Robes of Servitude									
Timbermaw Ally	Felwood	Both	45	48	Grazle—Felwood Timbermaw Monster Furbolg Common	Grazle		4400	
CHOICE OF: 1 Earth Warder's Vest or 1 Belt of the Den Watcher									
Deadwood of the North	Felwood	Both	45	55	Nafien—Felwood Timbermaw Monster Furbolg Common	Nafien		5650	
CHOICE OF: 1 Leggings of the Ursa or 1 Helm of the Pathfinder									
Speak to Nafien	Felwood	Both	45	55	Grazle—Felwood Timbermaw Monster Furbolg Common	Nafien	Timbermaw Ally	550	
Speak to Salfa	Felwood	Both	45	55	Nafien—Felwood Timbermaw Monster Furbolg Common	Salfa	Deadwood of the North	550	
Feathers for Grazle	Felwood	Both	45	55		Grazle	Timbermaw Ally	550	
Feathers for Nafien	Felwood	Both	45	55		Nafien	Deadwood of the North	550	
Deadwood Ritual Totem	Felwood	Both	45	55	Deadwood Ritual Totem	Kernda		5650	85●
REWARD: 2 Major Healing Potion, 2Major Mana Potion									

Feralas

Title	Location	Faction	Min Level	Con Level	Starter Location	Finisher	Prerequisite	Max XP	Cash Reward
Find OOX-22/FE!	Feralas	Both	40	45	OOX-22/FE Distress Beacon	Homing Robot OOX-22/FE		3900	
Rescue OOX-22/FE!	Feralas	Both	40	45	Homing Robot OOX-22/FE—Feralas	Oglethorpe Obnoticus	Find OOX-22/FE!	4850	
CHOICE OF: 1 Failed Flying Experiment or 1 Chainlink Towel									
The Mark of Quality	Feralas	Alliance	40	46	Pratt McGrubben—Feralas Feathermoon	Pratt McGrubben		4050	
CHOICE OF: 1 Pratt's Handcrafted Boots or 1 Pratt's Handcrafted Gloves									
The Mark of Quality	Feralas	Horde	40	46	Jangdor Swiftstrider—Camp Mojache, Feralas	Jangdor Swiftstrider		4050	
CHOICE OF: 1 Jangdor's Handcrafted Boots or 1 Jangdor's Handcrafted Gloves									
The Giant Guardian	Feralas	Alliance	44	49	Rockbiter—Feralas	Shay Leafrunner		3400	
Wandering Shay	Feralas	Alliance	44	49	Shay Leafrunner—Feralas	Rockbiter	The Giant Guardian	4550	
CHOICE OF: 1 Granite Grips or 1 Vinehedge Cinch									
Wild Leather Armor	Feralas	Alliance	30	45	Pratt McGrubben—Feralas Feathermoon	Pratt McGrubben		1950	
Wild Leather Shoulders	Feralas	Alliance	30	45	Pratt McGrubben—Feralas Feathermoon	Pratt McGrubben	Wild Leather Armor	2900	
REWARD: 1 Pattern: Wild Leather Shoulders									
Wild Leather Vest	Feralas	Alliance	30	45	Pratt McGrubben—Feralas Feathermoon	Pratt McGrubben	Wild Leather Armor	2900	
REWARD: 1 Pattern: Wild Leather Vest									
Wild Leather Helmet	Feralas	Alliance	30	45	Pratt McGrubben—Feralas Feathermoon	Pratt McGrubben	Wild Leather Armor	2900	
REWARD: 1 Pattern: Wild Leather Helmet									
Wild Leather Boots	Feralas	Alliance	30	45	Pratt McGrubben—Feralas Feathermoon	Pratt McGrubben	Wild Leather Shoulders	2900	
REWARD: 1 Pattern: Wild Leather Boots									
Wild Leather Leggings	Feralas	Alliance	30	45	Pratt McGrubben—Feralas Feathermoon	Pratt McGrubben	Wild Leather Shoulders	2900	
REWARD: 1 Pattern: Wild Leather Leggings									
Master of the Wild Leather	Feralas	Alliance	30	45	Pratt McGrubben—Feralas Feathermoon	Telonis	Wild Leather Boots	3900	
REWARD: 1 Pattern: Wild Leather Cloak									
Wild Leather Armor	Feralas	Horde	30	45	Jangdor Swiftstrider—Camp Mojache, Feralas	Jangdor Swiftstrider		1950	
Wild Leather Shoulders	Feralas	Horde	30	45	Jangdor Swiftstrider—Camp Mojache, Feralas	Jangdor Swiftstrider	Wild Leather Armor	2900	
REWARD: 1 Pattern: Wild Leather Shoulders									
Wild Leather Vest	Feralas	Horde	30	45	Jangdor Swiftstrider—Camp Mojache, Feralas	Jangdor Swiftstrider	Wild Leather Armor	2900	

Title	Location	Faction	Min Level	Con Level	Starter Location	Finisher	Prerequisite	Max XP	Cash Reward
REWARD: 1 Pattern: Wild Leather Vest									
Wild Leather Helmet	Feralas	Horde	30	45	Jangdor Swiftstrider—Camp Mojache, Feralas	Jangdor Swiftstrider	Wild Leather Armor	2900	
REWARD: 1 Pattern: Wild Leather Helmet									
Wild Leather Boots	Feralas	Horde	30	45	Jangdor Swiftstrider—Camp Mojache, Feralas	Jangdor Swiftstrider	Wild Leather Shoulders	2900	
REWARD: 1 Pattern: Wild Leather Boots									
Wild Leather Leggings	Feralas	Horde	30	45	Jangdor Swiftstrider—Camp Mojache, Feralas	Jangdor Swiftstrider	Wild Leather Shoulders	2900	
REWARD: 1 Pattern: Wild Leather Leggings									
Master of the Wild Leather	Feralas	Horde	30	45	Jangdor Swiftstrider—Camp Mojache, Feralas	Una	Wild Leather Boots	3900	
REWARD: 1 Pattern: Wild Leather Cloak									
War on the Woodpaw	Feralas	Horde	39	42	Hadoken Swiftstrider—Feralas	Hadoken Swiftstrider		2550	
Alpha Strike	Feralas	Horde	39	43	Hadoken Swiftstrider—Feralas	Hadoken Swiftstrider	War on the Woodpaw	2700	
The Ruins of Solarsal	Feralas	Alliance	40	43	Shandris Feathermoon—Feralas Feathermoon Stronghold	Solarsal Gazebo		2700	
Return to Feathermoon Stronghold	Feralas	Alliance	40	43	Solarsal Gazebo—Feralas	Shandris Feathermoon	The Ruins of Solarsal	1800	
Against the Hatecrest	Feralas	Alliance	40	43	Latronicus Moonspear—Feralas Feathermoon	Latronicus Moonspear	Against the Hatecrest	2700	45
Against Lord Shalzaru	Feralas	Alliance	40	45	Latronicus Moonspear—Feralas Feathermoon	Latronicus Moonspear	Against the Hatecrest	2900	50
Delivering the Relic	Feralas	Alliance	40	45	Latronicus Moonspear—Feralas Feathermoon	Vestia Moonspear	Against Lord Shalzaru	3900	
CHOICE OF: 1 Dawnrider's Chestpiece or 1 Sentinel's Guard									
The Stave of Equinex	Feralas	Alliance	42	50	Troyas Moonbreeze—Feralas	Equinex Monolith	Return to Troyas	4700	
REWARD: 1 A Sparkling Stone									
Woodpaw Investigation	Feralas	Horde	39	43	Hadoken Swiftstrider—Feralas	Woodpaw Battle Map	Alpha Strike	1800	
The Battle Plans	Feralas	Horde	39	43	Woodpaw Battle Map—Feralas	Hadoken Swiftstrider	Woodpaw Investigation	3600	
CHOICE OF: 1 Earthclasp Barrier or 1 Rushridge Boots									
In Search of Knowledge	Feralas	Alliance	42	47	Troyas Moonbreeze—Feralas	Daryn Lightwind		420	
Feralas: A History	Feralas	Alliance	42	47	Feralas: A History—Feralas Rut'theran	Daryn Lightwind	In Search of Knowledge	420	
The Borrower	Feralas	Alliance	42	48	Daryn Lightwind—Teldrassil Rut'theran Village	Curgle Cranklehop	Feralas: A History	1100	
The Morrow Stone	Feralas	Alliance	42	50	Equinex Monolith—Feralas	Troyas Moonbreeze	The Stave of Equinex	4700	
CHOICE OF: 1 Cairnstone Sliver or 1 Seedtime Hoop									
Return to Troyas	Feralas	Alliance	42	48	Daryn Lightwind—Teldrassil Rut'theran Village	Troyas Moonbreeze	The Super Snapper FX	3300	
The Super Snapper FX	Feralas	Alliance	42	48	Curgle Cranklehop—Tanaris Gadgetzan	Daryn Lightwind	The Borrower	4400	
Freedom for All Creatures	Feralas	Alliance	38	47	Kindal Moonweaver—Feralas	Kindal Moonweaver		3150	
Doling Justice	Feralas	Alliance	38	47	Jer'kai Moonweaver—Feralas	Jer'kai Moonweaver	Freedom for All Creatures	3150	
Doling Justice	Feralas	Alliance	38	47	Jer'kai Moonweaver—Feralas	Tyrande Whisperwind	Doling Justice	5250	
CHOICE OF: 1 Firwillow Wristbands or 1 Nightscale Girdle									
A New Cloak's Sheen	Feralas	Horde	38	45	Krueg Skullsplitter—Thousand Needles	Krueg Skullsplitter		3900	
A Grim Discovery	Feralas	Horde	38	45	Krueg Skullsplitter—Thousand Needles	Krueg Skullsplitter	A New Cloak's Sheen	3900	
The Ogres of Feralas	Feralas	Horde	38	43	Rok Orhan—Feralas	Rok Orhan		2700	45
A Grim Discovery	Feralas	Horde	37	45	Krueg Skullsplitter—Thousand Needles	Belgrom Rockmaul	A Grim Discovery	4850	
CHOICE OF: 1 Battlehard Cape or 1 Jademoon Orb									
The Gordunni Scroll	Feralas	Horde	38	43	Gordunni Scroll	Rok Orhan		1800	
Dark Ceremony	Feralas	Horde	38	46	Rok Orhan—Feralas	Rok Orhan	The Gordunni Scroll	4050	
The Ogres of Feralas	Feralas	Horde	38	44	Rok Orhan—Feralas	Rok Orhan	The Ogres of Feralas	3750	
A Threat in Feralas	Feralas	Horde	38	43	Belgrom Rockmaul—Orgrimmar	Rok Orhan	The Ogres of Feralas	900	
The High Wilderness	Feralas	Alliance	39	44	Angelas Moonbreeze—Feralas	Angelas Moonbreeze		3750	65
Gordunni Cobalt	Feralas	Horde	38	43	Orwin Gizzmick—Feralas	Orwin Gizzmick		3600	
CHOICE OF: 1 Boots of the Maharishi or 1 Stargazer Cloak									
The Gordunni Orb	Feralas	Horde	38	47	Rok Orhan—Feralas	Uthel'nay	Dark Ceremony	2100	
Dark Heart	Feralas	Horde	45	50	Talo Thornhoof—Feralas Camp Mojache	Talo Thornhoof		5900	
CHOICE OF: 1 Wingcrest Gloves or 1 Stronghorn Girdle									
Vengeance on the Northspring	Feralas	Horde	45	50	Talo Thornhoof—Feralas Camp Mojache	Talo Thornhoof		3550	55
A Strange Request	Feralas	Horde	40	45	Witch Doctor Uzer'i—Feralas	Neeru Fireblade		1950	
Return to Witch Doctor Uzer'i	Feralas	Horde	40	45	Neeru Fireblade—Orgrimmar	Witch Doctor Uzer'i	A Strange Request	975	
Testing the Vessel	Feralas	Horde	40	47	Witch Doctor Uzer'i—Feralas	Witch Doctor Uzer'i	Return to Witch Doctor Uzer'i	4200	
Hippogryph Muisek	Feralas	Horde	40	47	Witch Doctor Uzer'i—Feralas	Witch Doctor Uzer'i	Testing the Vessel	4200	
Faerie Dragon Muisek	Feralas	Horde	40	45	Witch Doctor Uzer'i—Feralas	Witch Doctor Uzer'i	Hippogryph Muisek	3900	
Treant Muisek	Feralas	Horde	40	50	Witch Doctor Uzer'i—Feralas	Witch Doctor Uzer'i	Faerie Dragon Muisek	4700	
Mountain Giant Muisek	Feralas	Horde	40	50	Witch Doctor Uzer'i—Feralas	Witch Doctor Uzer'i	Treant Muisek	4700	
Natural Materials	Feralas	Horde	40	50	Witch Doctor Uzer'i—Feralas	Witch Doctor Uzer'i	Return to Witch Doctor Uzer'i	4700	
Weapons of Spirit	Feralas	Horde	40	50	Witch Doctor Uzer'i—Feralas	Witch Doctor Uzer'i	Mountain Giant Muisek	4700	
CHOICE OF: 1 Force of the Hippogryph or 1 Spirit of the Faerie Dragon or 1 Strength of the Treant or 1 Will of the Mountain Giant									
Against the Hatecrest	Feralas	Alliance	40	43	Shandris Feathermoon—Feralas Feathermoon Stronghold	Latronicus Moonspear	Return to Feathermoon Stronghold	360	
To the Top	Feralas	Alliance	25	25		Marli Wishrunner			
Jonespyre's Request	Feralas	Alliance	47	50	Innkeeper Shyria—Feralas Feathermoon	Quintis Jonespyre	Morrowgrain Research	470	
The Mystery of Morrowgrain	Feralas	Alliance	47	50	Eranikus Transformed—Moonglade	Quintis Jonespyre	Morrowgrain Research	4700	
CHOICE OF: 1 Quintis' Research Gloves or 1 Bark Iron Pauldrons									
Morrowgrain to Feathermoon Stronghold	Feralas	Alliance	47	55		Quintis Jonespyre	The Mystery of Morrowgrain	550	
REWARD: 10 Packet of Tharlendris Seeds									
An Orphan Looking For a Home	Feralas	Alliance	38	47		Quentin	Doling Justice	1050	
A Short Incubation	Feralas	Alliance	38	47	Quentin—Thousand Needles Mirage Raceway	Quentin	An Orphan Looking For a Home	2100	
The Newest Member of the Family	Feralas	Alliance	38	47	Quentin—Thousand Needles Mirage Raceway	Agnar Beastamer	A Short Incubation	4200	
The Videre Elixir	Feralas	Both	47	52		Gregan Brewspewer	It's a Secret to Everybody		
REWARD: 3 Videre Elixir									
The Strength of Corruption	Feralas	Horde	47	52	Talo Thornhoof—Feralas Camp Mojache	Talo Thornhoof		5100	
The Missing Courier	Feralas	Alliance	40	43	Latronicus Moonspear—Feralas Feathermoon	Ginro Hearthkindle		360	
The Missing Courier	Feralas	Alliance	40	43	Ginro Hearthkindle—Feralas Feathermoon	Wrecked Row Boat	The Missing Courier	2700	
Boat Wreckage	Feralas	Alliance	40	44	Wrecked Row Boat—Feralas	Ginro Hearthkindle	The Missing Courier	380	
The Knife Revealed	Feralas	Alliance	40	44	Ginro Hearthkindle—Feralas Feathermoon	Quintis Jonespyre	Boat Wreckage	380	
Psychometric Reading	Feralas	Alliance	40	44	Eranikus Transformed—Moonglade	Ginro Hearthkindle	The Knife Revealed	380	
The Woodpaw Gnolls	Feralas	Alliance	40	44	Ginro Hearthkindle—Feralas Feathermoon	Large Leather Backpacks	Psychometric Reading	2800	
The Writhing Deep	Feralas	Alliance	40	46	Large Leather Backpacks	Zukk'ash Pod	The Woodpaw Gnolls	3050	
Freed from the Hive	Feralas	Alliance	40	46	Zukk'ash Pod—Feralas	Ginro Hearthkindle	The Writhing Deep	4050	
A Hero's Welcome	Feralas	Alliance	40	46	Ginro Hearthkindle—Feralas Feathermoon	Shandris Feathermoon	Freed from the Hive	6050	
CHOICE OF: 1 Ceremonial Elven Blade or 1 Sanctimonial Rod									
Rise of the Silithid	Feralas	Alliance	40	46	Shandris Feathermoon—Feralas Feathermoon Stronghold	Gracina Spiritmight	A Hero's Welcome	410	
Thalanaar Delivery	Feralas	Alliance	40	44	Undelivered Parcel	Falfindel Waywarder		2800	65
Food for Baby	Feralas	Alliance	38	47	Agnar Beastamer—Hinterlands	Agnar Beastamer	The Newest Member of the Family	4200	
Becoming a Parent	Feralas	Alliance	37	48	Agnar Beastamer—Hinterlands	Agnar Beastamer	Food for Baby	440	
REWARD: 1 Sprite Darter Egg									
Tribal Leatherworking	Feralas	Alliance	40	55	Caryssia Moonhunter—Feralas Thalanaar	Caryssia Moonhunter	Master of the Wild Leather	4200	
Zapped Giants	Feralas	Both	45	48	Zorbin Fandazzle—Feralas	Zorbin Fandazzle		4400	
REWARD: 1 Zorbin's Mega-Slicer									
Fuel for the Zapping	Feralas	Both	45	48	Zorbin Fandazzle—Feralas	Zorbin Fandazzle		4400	70
REWARD: 1 Zorbin's Water Resistant Hat									
Again With the Zapped Giants	Feralas	Both	45	55	Zorbin Fandazzle—Feralas	Zorbin Fandazzle	Zapped Giants	550	
Refuel for the Zapping	Feralas	Both	45	55	Zorbin Fandazzle—Feralas	Zorbin Fandazzle	Fuel for the Zapping	550	
Zukk'ash Infestation	Feralas	Horde	39	45	Hadoken Swiftstrider—Feralas	Hadoken Swiftstrider	The Battle Plans	3900	
Stinglasher	Feralas	Horde	39	47	Hadoken Swiftstrider—Feralas	Hadoken Swiftstrider	The Battle Plans	4200	1 35
Zukk'ash Report	Feralas	Horde	39	48	Hadoken Swiftstrider—Feralas	Zilzibin Drumlore	Zukk'ash Infestation	4400	

Title	Location	Faction	Min Level	Con Level	Starter Location	Finisher	Prerequisite	Max XP	Cash Reward
CHOICE OF: 1 Ring of Subtlety or 1 Emerald Peak Spaulders									
Improved Quality	Feralas	Alliance	40	48	Pratt McGrubben—Feralas Feathermoon	Pratt McGrubben	The Mark of Quality	4400	
REWARD: 1 Pratt's Handcrafted Tunic									
Improved Quality	Feralas	Horde	40	48	Jangdor Swiftstrider—Camp Mojache, Feralas	Jangdor Swiftstrider	The Mark of Quality	4400	70
REWARD: 1 Jangdor's Handcrafted Tunic									
Pristine Yeti Hide	Feralas	Alliance	40	48	Pristine Yeti Hide	Pratt McGrubben	The Mark of Quality	2200	70
Perfect Yeti Hide	Feralas	Horde	40	48	Perfect Yeti Hide	Jangdor Swiftstrider	The Mark of Quality	440	7
Soothing Turtle Bisque	Tarren Mill	Horde	28	31	Christoph Jeffcoat—Hillsbrad Tarren Mill	Christoph Jeffcoat		2500	30
REWARD: 1 Recipe: Soothing Turtle Bisque, 3Soothing Turtle Bisque									
Time To Strike	Hillsbrad Foothills	Horde	19	20	Deathstalker Lesh—Hillsbrad Southpoint Tower	High Executor Darthalia		625	6
Elixir of Suffering	Hillsbrad Foothills	Horde	19	22	Apothecary Lydon—Hillsbrad Tarren Mill	Apothecary Lydon		1750	
The Rescue	Hillsbrad Foothills	Horde	17	22	Krusk—Hillsbrad Tarren Mill	Krusk		2200	
CHOICE OF: 1 Grunt Vest or 1 Orcish War Chain REWARD: 1 Recipe: Big Bear Steak									
Elixir of Suffering	Hillsbrad Foothills	Horde	19	22	Apothecary Lydon—Hillsbrad Tarren Mill	Umpi	Elixir of Suffering	180	
Crushridge Bounty	Hillsbrad Foothills	Alliance	30	36	Marshal Redpath—Hillsbrad Southshore	Marshal Redpath		3500	18
Elixir of Pain	Hillsbrad Foothills	Horde	21	24	Apothecary Lydon—Hillsbrad Tarren Mill	Apothecary Lydon		1950	
CHOICE OF: 1 Gloves of Brawn or 1 Stomping Boots or 1 Firewalker Boots REWARD: 1 Recipe: Hot Lion Chops									
Elixir of Pain	Hillsbrad Foothills	Horde	21	24	Apothecary Lydon—Hillsbrad Tarren Mill	Stanley	Elixir of Pain	1450	
Gol'dir	Hillsbrad Foothills	Horde	29	36	Krusk—Hillsbrad Tarren Mill	Gol'dir	Infiltration	2800	
Crushridge Warmongers	Hillsbrad Foothills	Alliance	30	40	Marshal Redpath—Hillsbrad Southshore	Marshal Redpath	Crushridge Bounty	4700	
CHOICE OF: 1 Burning Sliver or 1 Lunar Buckler									
Syndicate Assassins	Hillsbrad Foothills	Alliance	26	33	Magistrate Henry Maleb—Hillsbrad Southshore	Magistrate Henry Maleb		1950	
CHOICE OF: 1 Crusader Belt or 1 Insulated Sage Gloves									
Blackmoore's Legacy	Hillsbrad Foothills	Horde	29	36	Gol'dir—Hillsbrad Strahbrad	Krusk	Gol'dir	2100	
Lord Aliden Perenolde	Hillsbrad Foothills	Horde	29	42	Krusk—Hillsbrad Tarren Mill	Elysa	Blackmoore's Legacy	4300	
Elixir of Agony	Hillsbrad Foothills	Horde	24	28	Apothecary Lydon—Hillsbrad Tarren Mill	Apothecary Lydon		2300	25
REWARD: 3 Swiftness Potion, 5Healing Potion									
Foreboding Plans	Hillsbrad Foothills	Alliance	26	34	Syndicate Documents	Magistrate Henry Maleb		1350	
Encrypted Letter	Hillsbrad Foothills	Alliance	30	34	Syndicate Documents	Loremaster Dibbs		1350	
Noble Deaths	Hillsbrad Foothills	Alliance	26	36	Magistrate Henry Maleb—Hillsbrad Southshore	Magistrate Henry Maleb	Foreboding Plans	2800	40
Elixir of Agony	Hillsbrad Foothills	Horde	24	28	Apothecary Lydon—Hillsbrad Tarren Mill	Master Apothecary Faranell	Elixir of Agony	1150	25
Letter to Stormpike	Hillsbrad Foothills	Alliance	30	34	Loremaster Dibbs—Hillsbrad Southshore	Prospector Stormpike	Encrypted Letter	1350	
Elixir of Agony	Hillsbrad Foothills	Horde	24	30	Master Apothecary Faranell—Undercity	Apothecary Lydon	Elixir of Agony	3050	
CHOICE OF: 1 High Apothecary Cloak or 1 Meditative Sash									
Elixir of Agony	Hillsbrad Foothills	Horde	24	30	Apothecary Lydon—Hillsbrad Tarren Mill	Apothecary Lydon	Elixir of Agony	1200	
The Crown of Will	Hillsbrad Foothills	Horde	34	39	Melisara—Hillsbrad Tarren Mill	Melisara		2250	
The Crown of Will	Hillsbrad Foothills	Horde	34	41	Melisara—Hillsbrad Tarren Mill	Melisara	The Crown of Will	3300	
The Crown of Will	Hillsbrad Foothills	Horde	34	43	Melisara—Hillsbrad Tarren Mill	Melisara	The Crown of Will	4450	
The Crown of Will	Hillsbrad Foothills	Horde	34	43	Melisara—Hillsbrad Tarren Mill	Sharlindra	The Crown of Will	3600	
REWARD: 1 Ethereal Talisman									
Assassin's Contract	Hillsbrad Foothills	Alliance	30	38	Assassin's Contract	Magistrate Henry Maleb		700	
Baron's Demise	Hillsbrad Foothills	Alliance	30	40	Magistrate Henry Maleb—Hillsbrad Southshore	Magistrate Henry Maleb	Assassin's Contract	3900	1
Elixir of Agony	Hillsbrad Foothills	Horde	24	30	Apothecary Lydon—Hillsbrad Tarren Mill	Dusty Rug	Elixir of Agony	3650	
Battle of Hillsbrad	Hillsbrad Foothills	Horde	19	24	High Executor Darthalia—Hillsbrad Tarren Mill	High Executor Darthalia		1950	17
Battle of Hillsbrad	Hillsbrad Foothills	Horde	19	25	High Executor Darthalia—Hillsbrad Tarren Mill	High Executor Darthalia	Battle of Hillsbrad	2000	18
Battle of Hillsbrad	Hillsbrad Foothills	Horde	19	26	High Executor Darthalia—Hillsbrad Tarren Mill	High Executor Darthalia	Battle of Hillsbrad	2100	20
Battle of Hillsbrad	Hillsbrad Foothills	Horde	19	26	High Executor Darthalia—Hillsbrad Tarren Mill	High Executor Darthalia	Battle of Hillsbrad	2100	20
Infiltration	Hillsbrad Foothills	Horde	29	34	Krusk—Hillsbrad Tarren Mill	Krusk	The Rescue	2700	35
Down the Coast	Hillsbrad Foothills	Alliance	25	30	Lieutenant Farren Orinelle—Hillsbrad Southshore	Lieutenant Farren Orinelle		1850	13
Dark Council	Hillsbrad Foothills	Alliance	30	40	Magistrate Henry Maleb—Hillsbrad Southshore	Magistrate Henry Maleb	Further Mysteries	3150	50
Battle of Hillsbrad	Hillsbrad Foothills	Horde	19	28	High Executor Darthalia—Hillsbrad Tarren Mill	High Executor Darthalia	Battle of Hillsbrad	2300	25
Preserving Knowledge	Hillsbrad Foothills	Alliance	20	38	Loremaster Dibbs—Hillsbrad Southshore	Loremaster Dibbs	Southshore	3550	
Battle of Hillsbrad	Hillsbrad Foothills	Horde	19	30	High Executor Darthalia—Hillsbrad Tarren Mill	High Executor Darthalia	Battle of Hillsbrad	2450	25
Return to Milton	Hillsbrad Foothills	Alliance	20	38	Loremaster Dibbs—Hillsbrad Southshore	Milton Sheaf	Preserving Knowledge	3550	85
Prison Break In	Hillsbrad Foothills	Horde	30	34	Magus Wordeen Voidglare—Hillsbrad Tarren Mill	Magus Wordeen Voidglare		3350	
Dalaran Patrols	Hillsbrad Foothills	Horde	30	35	Magus Wordeen Voidglare—Hillsbrad Tarren Mill	Magus Wordeen Voidglare	Prison Break In	2050	
Souvenirs of Death	Hillsbrad Foothills	Horde	20	25	Deathguard Samsa—Hillsbrad Tarren Mill	Deathguard Samsa	Battle of Hillsbrad	2550	
REWARD: 1 Skull Ring									
Humbert's Sword	Hillsbrad Foothills	Horde	26	30	Deathguard Humbert—Hillsbrad Tarren Mill	Deathguard Humbert		3050	
CHOICE OF: 1 Ribbed Breastplate or 1 Mercenary Leggings									
WANTED: Syndicate Personnel	Hillsbrad Foothills	Horde	17	22	Wanted Poster—Hillsbrad	High Executor Darthalia		1750	14
Battle of Hillsbrad	Hillsbrad Foothills	Horde	19	32	High Executor Darthalia—Hillsbrad Tarren Mill	Varimathras	Battle of Hillsbrad	2550	
CHOICE OF: 1 Sacred Burial Trousers or 1 Deadskull Shield or 1 Runic Darkblade REWARD: 1 Band of the Undercity									
Helcular's Revenge	Hillsbrad Foothills	Horde	29	33	Novice Thaivand—Hillsbrad Tarren Mill	Novice Thaivand		2650	
Helcular's Revenge	Hillsbrad Foothills	Horde	29	33	Novice Thaivand—Hillsbrad Tarren Mill	Helcular's Grave	Helcular's Revenge	3300	
Stormpike's Deciphering	Hillsbrad Foothills	Alliance	28	40	Loremaster Dibbs—Hillsbrad Southshore	Prospector Stormpike	The Ensorcelled Parchment	1550	50
Soothing Turtle Bisque	Hillsbrad Foothills	Alliance	28	31	Chef Jessen—Hillsbrad Southshore	Chef Jessen		2500	30
REWARD: 1 Recipe: Soothing Turtle Bisque, 3Soothing Turtle Bisque									
Stone Tokens	Hillsbrad Foothills	Horde	30	32	Keeper Bel'varil—Hillsbrad Tarren Mill	Keeper Bel'varil		2550	30
Bracers of Binding	Hillsbrad Foothills	Horde	30	34	Keeper Bel'varil—Hillsbrad Tarren Mill	Keeper Bel'varil	Stone Tokens	2700	
Farren's Proof	Hillsbrad Foothills	Alliance	25	32	Lieutenant Farren Orinelle—Hillsbrad Southshore	Lieutenant Farren Orinelle	Down the Coast	2250	30
Farren's Proof	Hillsbrad Foothills	Alliance	25	32	Lieutenant Farren Orinelle—Hillsbrad Southshore	Marshal Redpath	Farren's Proof	260	
Farren's Proof	Hillsbrad Foothills	Alliance	25	32	Marshal Redpath—Hillsbrad Southshore	Lieutenant Farren Orinelle	Farren's Proof	260	
Stormwind Ho!	Hillsbrad Foothills	Alliance	25	32	Lieutenant Farren Orinelle—Hillsbrad Southshore	Lieutenant Farren Orinelle	Farren's Proof	1950	
REWARD: 1 Fish Gutter									
Reassignment	Hillsbrad Foothills	Alliance	25	32	Lieutenant Farren Orinelle—Hillsbrad Southshore	Major Samuelson	Stormwind Ho!	3200	
Costly Menace	Hillsbrad Foothills	Alliance	30	34	Darren Malvew—Hillsbrad Southshore	Darren Malvew		2700	
CHOICE OF: 1 Shepherd's Girdle or 1 Shepherd's Gloves REWARD: 1 Recipe: Tasty Lion Steak, 5Tasty Lion Steak									
Bartolo's Yeti Fur Cloak	Hillsbrad Foothills	Alliance	29	34	Bartolo Ginsetti—Hillsbrad Southshore	Bartolo Ginsetti		2700	
REWARD: 1 Yeti Fur Cloak									
WANTED: Baron Vardus	Hillsbrad Foothills	Horde	35	40	Wanted Poster—Hillsbrad	High Executor Darthalia	WANTED: Syndicate Personnel	3500	
REWARD: 1 Inferno Robe									
Dangerous!	Hillsbrad Foothills	Horde	19	28	Wanted Poster—Hillsbrad Tarren Mill	High Executor Darthalia		2300	
CHOICE OF: 1 Bow of Plunder or 1 Sentry Buckler or 1 Charred Wand REWARD: 1 Hooded Cowl									
The Hammer May Fall	Hillsbrad Foothills	Horde	30	32	Tallow—Hillsbrad Tarren Mill	Drum Fel	Call to Arms	2550	30
Blood of Innocents	Hillsbrad Foothills	Horde	13	23	Apothecary Lydon—Hillsbrad Tarren Mill	Apothecary Lydon	Journey to Tarren Mill	1850	
Return to Thunder Bluff	Hillsbrad Foothills	Horde	13	23	Apothecary Lydon—Hillsbrad Tarren Mill	Apothecary Zamah	Blood of Innocents	1400	
The Flying Machine Airport	Hillsbrad Foothills	Horde	13	23	Apothecary Zamah—Thunder Bluff	Apothecary Zamah	Return to Thunder Bluff	2300	30
Crashing the Wickerman Festival	Hillsbrad Foothills	Alliance	25	60	Sergeant Hartman—Hillsbrad Foothills Southshore	Sergeant Hartman		6600	
REWARD: 15 Hallow's End Pumpkin Treat									
Hinott's Assistance	Hillsbrad Foothills	Horde	20	20	Serge Hinott—Hillsbrad Tarren Mill	Serge Hinott	Hinott's Assistance	160	
REWARD: 1 Hinott's Oil									
The Manor, Ravenholdt	Hillsbrad Foothills	Both	24	24	Elegant Letter	Fahrad		1950	
Syndicate Emblems	Hillsbrad Foothills	Both	24	60		Ravenholdt Guard	The Manor, Ravenholdt		
Manna-Enriched Horse Feed	Hillsbrad Foothills	Alliance	60	60	Merideth Carlson—Hillsbrad Southshore	Merideth Carlson		650	
REWARD: 1 Manna-Enriched Horse Feed									
Junkboxes Needed	Hillsbrad Foothills	Both	50	60		Fahrad			

Title	Location	Faction	Min Level	Con Level	Starter Location	Finisher	Prerequisite	Max XP	Cash Reward
REWARD: 200 Dusksteel Throwing Knife									
The Power of Pine	Hillsbrad Foothills	Alliance	25	60	Sergeant Hartman—Hillsbrad Foothills Southshore	Sergeant Hartman		1650	
REWARD: 15 Hallow's End Pumpkin Treat									
Mastering the Elements	Hillsbrad Foothills	Horde	50	50	Bath'rah the Windwatcher—Alterac Mountains Chillwind Point	Bath'rah the Windwatcher	Elemental Mastery	3800	
Spirit Totem	Hillsbrad Foothills	Horde	50	52	Bath'rah the Windwatcher—Alterac Mountains Chillwind Point	Bath'rah the Windwatcher	Elemental Mastery	5100	
Da Voodoo	Hillsbrad Foothills	Horde	50	52	Bath'rah the Windwatcher—Alterac Mountains Chillwind Point	Bath'rah the Windwatcher	Spirit Totem	6350	1● 55●
CHOICE OF: 1 Azurite Fists or 1 Enamored Water Spirit or 1 Wildstaff									
A Sticky Situation	Hinterlands	Horde	42	48	Gilveradin Sunchaser—Hinterlands High Elf	Gilveradin Sunchaser	Ripple Recovery	4400	
Find OOX-09/HL!	Hinterlands	Both	43	48	OOX-09/HL Distress Beacon	Homing Robot OOX-09/HL		4400	
Rescue OOX-09/HL!	Hinterlands	Both	43	48	Homing Robot OOX-09/HL—Hinterlands	Oglethorpe Obnoticus	Find OOX-09/HL!	5450	
CHOICE OF: 1 Gnomish Inventor Boots or 1 Gnomish Water Sinking Device									
Jammal'an the Prophet	Hinterlands	Alliance	38	53	Atal'ai Exile—Hinterlands	Atal'ai Exile		6650	
CHOICE OF: 1 Rainstrider Leggings or 1 Helm of Exile									
Rin'ji is Trapped!	Hinterlands	Horde	42	47	Rin'ji—Hinterlands	Rin'ji's Secret		4200	
Rin'ji's Secret	Hinterlands	Horde	42	47	Rin'ji's Secret—Hinterlands	Oran Snakewrithe	Rin'ji is Trapped!	2100	
Skulk Rock Clean-up	Hinterlands	Alliance	40	48	Fraggar Thundermantle—Hinterlands Aerie Peak	Fraggar Thundermantle		4400	50●
Troll Necklace Bounty	Hinterlands	Alliance	40	45	Fraggar Thundermantle—Hinterlands Aerie Peak	Fraggar Thundermantle		3900	65●
Troll Necklace Bounty	Hinterlands	Alliance	40	45		Fraggar Thundermantle	Troll Necklace Bounty	390	
Grim Message	Hinterlands	Horde	35	42	Nimboya—Stranglethorn Grom'gol	Nimboya		3450	55●
Venom Bottles	Hinterlands	Horde	40	43	Venom Bottle—Hinterlands	Apothecary Lydon		3600	
Undamaged Venom Sac	Hinterlands	Horde	40	45	Apothecary Lydon—Hillsbrad Tarren Mill	Apothecary Lydon	Venom Bottles	3900	
Consult Master Gadrin	Hinterlands	Horde	40	45	Apothecary Lydon—Hillsbrad Tarren Mill	Master Gadrin	Undamaged Venom Sac	2900	
The Spider God	Hinterlands	Horde	40	45	Master Gadrin—Durotar Sen'jin Village	Master Gadrin	Consult Master Gadrin	4850	
Summoning Shadra	Hinterlands	Horde	40	55	Master Gadrin—Durotar Sen'jin Village	Apothecary Lydon	The Spider God	8450	
Venom to the Undercity	Hinterlands	Horde	40	55	Apothecary Lydon—Hillsbrad Tarren Mill	Master Apothecary Faranell	Summoning Shadra	8450	2● 50●
CHOICE OF: 1 Royal Highmark Vestments or 1 Honorguard Chestpiece or 1 Aegis of Battle									
Witherbark Cages	Hinterlands	Alliance	40	45	Gryphon Master Talonaxe—Hinterlands	Gryphon Master Talonaxe		3900	
The Altar of Zul	Hinterlands	Alliance	40	48	Gryphon Master Talonaxe—Hinterlands	Gryphon Master Talonaxe	Witherbark Cages	4400	
Thadius Grimshade	Hinterlands	Alliance	40	47	Gryphon Master Talonaxe—Hinterlands	Thadius Grimshade	The Altar of Zul	2100	
Nekrum's Medallion	Hinterlands	Alliance	40	47	Thadius Grimshade—Blasted Lands	Thadius Grimshade	Thadius Grimshade	5250	70●
The Divination	Hinterlands	Alliance	40	47	Thadius Grimshade—Blasted Lands	Thadius Grimshade	Nekrum's Medallion	1050	
Return to the Hinterlands	Hinterlands	Alliance	40	47	Thadius Grimshade—Blasted Lands	Gryphon Master Talonaxe	The Divination	2100	
Saving Sharpbeak	Hinterlands	Alliance	40	53	Gryphon Master Talonaxe—Hinterlands	Gryphon Master Talonaxe	Return to the Hinterlands	7900	2● 40●
CHOICE OF: 1 Gryphon Rider's Stormhammer or 1 Gryphon Rider's Leggings									
Favored of Elune?	Hinterlands	Alliance	42	47	Erelas Ambersky—Teldrassil Rut'theran Village	Erelas Ambersky		4200	1● 35●
Snapjaws, Mon!	Hinterlands	Horde	44	50	Katoom the Angler—Hinterlands Revantusk Village	Katoom the Angler		4700	75●
REWARD: 1 Nat Pagle's Extreme Angler FC-5000									
Gammerita, Mon!	Hinterlands	Horde	44	48	Katoom the Angler—Hinterlands Revantusk Village	Katoom the Angler		4400	1● 40●
Stalking the Stalkers	Hinterlands	Horde	44	48	Huntsman Markhor—Hinterlands Revantusk Village	Huntsman Markhor		4400	1● 40●
Hunt the Savages	Hinterlands	Horde	44	48	Huntsman Markhor—Hinterlands Revantusk Village	Huntsman Markhor		4400	1● 40●
Avenging the Fallen	Hinterlands	Horde	44	48	Huntsman Markhor—Hinterlands Revantusk Village	Huntsman Markhor		4400	1● 40●
Vilebranch Hooligans	Hinterlands	Horde	44	48	Smith Slagtree—Hinterlands Revantusk Village	Smith Slagtree		4400	1● 40●
Lord Lost His Lunch	Hinterlands	Horde	44	49	Lard—Hinterlands Revantusk Village	Lard		4550	1● 40●
REWARD: 1 Lard's Special Picnic Basket									
Message to the Wildhammer	Hinterlands	Horde	44	48	Otho Moji'ko—Hinterlands Revantusk Village	Otho Moji'ko		4400	
Another Message to the Wildhammer	Hinterlands	Horde	44	48	Otho Moji'ko—Hinterlands Revantusk Village	Otho Moji'ko	Message to the Wildhammer	5450	
The Final Message to the Wildhammer	Hinterlands	Horde	44	50	Otho Moji'ko—Hinterlands Revantusk Village	Otho Moji'ko	Another Message to the Wildhammer	5900	2● 20●
REWARD: 1 Owlbeast Hide Gloves									
Cannibalistic Cousins	Hinterlands	Horde	44	48	Mystic Yayo'jin—Hinterlands Revantusk Village	Mystic Yayo'jin		4400	1● 40●
Kidnapped Elder Torntusk!	Hinterlands	Horde	46	51	Primal Torntusk—Hinterlands Revantusk Village	Elder Torntusk		4900	
Recover the Key!	Hinterlands	Horde	46	51	Elder Torntusk—Hinterlands Revantusk Village	Elder Torntusk	Kidnapped Elder Torntusk!	6100	
Return to Primal Torntusk	Hinterlands	Horde	46	51	Elder Torntusk—Hinterlands Revantusk Village	Primal Torntusk	Recover the Key!	4900	2● 25●
CHOICE OF: 1 Highland Bow or 1 Flask of Forest Mojo									
Separation Anxiety	Hinterlands	Horde	46	50	Huntsman Markhor—Hinterlands Revantusk Village	Huntsman Markhor		5900	1● 45●
CHOICE OF: 1 Laquered Wooden Plate Legplates or 1 Greenleaf Handwraps									
Dark Vessels	Hinterlands	Horde	46	50	Primal Torntusk—Hinterlands Revantusk Village	Primal Torntusk		5900	
REWARD: 1 Nature's Breath									
Wanted: Vile Priestess Hexx and Her Minions	Hinterlands	Horde	46	51	Wanted Poster—Hinterlands	Primal Torntusk		6100	2● 25●
CHOICE OF: 1 Woven Ivy Necklace or 1 Deep Woodlands Cloak									
Job Opening: Guard Captain of Revantusk Village	Hinterlands	Horde	46	51	Wanted Poster—Hinterlands	Primal Torntusk		6100	2● 25●
REWARD: 1 Rune of the Guard Captain									
Stonegear's Search	Ironforge	Alliance	20	23	Pilot Longbeard—Ironforge	Pilot Stonegear	Search for Incendicite	460	
Further Mysteries	Ironforge	Alliance	30	34	Prospector Stormpike—Ironforge	Magistrate Henry Maleb	Letter to Stormpike	1350	
Sara Balloo's Plea	Ironforge	Alliance	25	30	Sara Balloo—Ironforge	King Magni Bronzebeard	Sully Balloo's Letter	1200	
A King's Tribute	Ironforge	Alliance	25	30	King Magni Bronzebeard—Ironforge	Grand Mason Marblesten	Sara Balloo's Plea	1200	
A King's Tribute	Ironforge	Alliance	25	31	Grand Mason Marblesten—Ironforge	Grand Mason Marblesten	A King's Tribute	2500	
A King's Tribute	Ironforge	Alliance	25	31	Grand Mason Marblesten—Ironforge	King Magni Bronzebeard	A King's Tribute	2500	
REWARD: 1 Ironforge Memorial Ring									
Ironband Wants You!	Ironforge	Alliance	30	37	Prospector Stormpike—Ironforge	Prospector Ironband	Find Agmond	700	
The Star, the Hand and the Heart	Ironforge	Alliance	30	44	Gerrig Bonegrip—Ironforge	Gerrig Bonegrip	To Ironforge for Yagyin's Digest	5600	
Knowledge in the Deeps	Ironforge	Alliance	10	23	Gerrig Bonegrip—Ironforge	Gerrig Bonegrip		2750	
REWARD: 1 Sustaining Ring									
The New Frontier	Ironforge	Alliance	54	55	Courier Hammerfall—Ironforge	Arch Druid Fandral Staghelm		550	
Mythology of the Titans	Ironforge	Alliance	28	38	Librarian Mae Paledust—Ironforge	Librarian Mae Paledust		3550	
REWARD: 1 Explorers' League Commendation									
Reclaimed Treasures	Ironforge	Alliance	33	43	Krom Stoutarm—Ironforge	Krom Stoutarm		3600	60●
Seeking the Kor Gem	Ironforge	Alliance	20	22	Thundris Windweaver—Darkshore Auberdine	Thundris Windweaver		440	
REWARD: 1 Purified Kor Gem									
Reclaimers' Business in Desolace	Ironforge	Alliance	30	33	Roetten Stonehammer—Ironforge	Kreldig Ungor		1300	
Supplying the Front	Ironforge	Alliance	1	12	Tormus Deepforge—Ironforge	Thorvald Deepforge		900	
REWARD: 1 Plans: Copper Chain Vest									
Gearing Redridge	Ironforge	Alliance	1	16	Tormus Deepforge—Ironforge	Verner Osgood		1150	
REWARD: 1 Plans: Ironforge Breastplate									
The Test of Righteousness	Ironforge	Alliance	20	21	Duthorian Rall—Stormwind	Jordan Stilwell	The Tome of Valor	825	
The Test of Righteousness	Ironforge	Alliance	20	22	Jordan Stilwell—Ironforge	Jordan Stilwell	The Test of Righteousness	2200	
Bailor's Ore Shipment	Ironforge	Alliance	20	22	Bailor Stonehand—Loch Modan Thelsamar	Bailor Stonehand		440	
REWARD: 1 Jordan's Refined Ore Shipment									
The Slaughtered Lamb	Ironforge	Alliance	10	10	Lago Blackwrench—Ironforge	Gakin the Darkbinder	Surena Caledon	420	
Gakin's Summons	Ironforge	Alliance	20	20	Lago Blackwrench—Ironforge	Gakin the Darkbinder	Devourer of Souls	390	
The Tome of Valor	Ironforge	Alliance	20	20		Tiza Battleforge	The Tome of Valor		
REWARD: 1 Tome of Valor									
Tome of the Cabal	Ironforge	Alliance	30	30	Krom Stoutarm—Ironforge	Krom Stoutarm	Tome of the Cabal	2450	
Tome of the Cabal	Ironforge	Alliance	30	30	Krom Stoutarm—Ironforge	Strahad Farsan	Tome of the Cabal	2450	
The Test of Righteousness	Ironforge	Alliance	20	22	Jordan Stilwell—Ironforge	Jordan Stilwell	The Test of Righteousness	2200	
REWARD: 1 Verigan's Fist									
Find Bingles	Ironforge	Alliance	12	15	Gnoarn—Ironforge	Bingles Blastenheimer		270	

Ironforge cont'd

Title	Location	Faction	Min Level	Con Level	Starter Location	Finisher	Prerequisite	Max XP	Cash Reward
Speak with Shoni	Ironforge	Alliance	15	15	Gnoarn—Ironforge	Shoni the Shilent		270	
Lore for a Price	Ironforge	Alliance	37	41	Talvash del Kissel—Ironforge	Talvash del Kissel	The Shattered Necklace	2450	
Back to Uldaman	Ironforge	Alliance	37	42	Talvash del Kissel—Ironforge	Remains of a Paladin	Lore for a Price	2550	
Simple Subterfugin'	Ironforge	Alliance	10	10	Hulfdan Blackbeard—Ironforge	Onin MacHammar	Road to Salvation	850	
Restoring the Necklace	Ironforge	Alliance	37	44		Talvash del Kissel	Restoring the Necklace	5600	
REWARD: 1 Talvash's Enhancing Necklace									
The Platinum Discs	Ironforge	Alliance	40	47	High Explorer Magellas—Ironforge	Dinita Stonemantle	The Platinum Discs	420	
CHOICE OF: 5 Superior Healing Potion or 5 Greater Mana Potion REWARD: 1 Thawpelt Sack									
The Brassbolts Brothers	Ironforge	Alliance	40	46	Klockmort Spannerspan—Ironforge	Wizzle Brassbolts	Gahz'rilla	410	
The Day After	Ironforge	Alliance	20	27	Gnoarn—Ironforge	Ozzie Togglevolt		220	
The Grand Betrayal	Ironforge	Alliance	25	35	High Tinker Mekkatorque—Ironforge	High Tinker Mekkatorque		2750	35
CHOICE OF: 1 Civinad Robes or 1 Triprunner Dungarees or 1 Dual Reinforced Leggings									
Data Rescue	Ironforge	Alliance	25	30	Master Mechanic Castpipe—Ironforge	Master Mechanic Castpipe		3650	25
REWARD: 1 Repairman's Cape, 1Mechanic's Pipehammer									
Castpipe's Task	Ironforge	Alliance	25	28	Gaxim Rustfizzle—Stonetalon Webwinder Path	Master Mechanic Castpipe	Data Rescue	230	
Seeing What Happens	Ironforge	Alliance	45	50	Historian Karnik—Ironforge	Uldum Pedestal	Portents of Uldum	4700	
Gnome Improvement	Ironforge	Alliance	28	35	Talvash del Kissel—Ironforge	Talvash del Kissel	Return of the Ring	2750	
REWARD: 1 Talvash's Gold Ring									
Portents of Uldum	Ironforge	Alliance	45	50	High Explorer Magellas—Ironforge	Historian Karnik	The Platinum Discs	470	
Replacement Phial	Ironforge	Alliance	37	42	Talvash del Kissel—Ironforge	Talvash del Kissel	Back to Uldaman		
REWARD: 1 Talvash's Phial of Scrying									
Passing the Burden	Ironforge	Alliance	45	52	Historian Karnik—Ironforge	Tymor		500	
Arcane Runes	Ironforge	Alliance	45	52	Tymor—Ironforge	Pilot Xiggs Fuselighter	Passing the Burden	2550	
An Easy Pickup	Ironforge	Alliance	45	52	Tymor—Ironforge	Xiggs Fuselighter			
Signal for Pickup	Ironforge	Alliance	45	52	Xiggs Fuselighter—Ironforge	Xiggs Fuselighter	An Easy Pickup		
REWARD: 1 Standard Issue Flare Gun									
Return to Tymor	Ironforge	Alliance	45	52	Pilot Xiggs Fuselighter—Azshara	Tymor	Arcane Runes	7600	
CHOICE OF: 1 Steelsmith Greaves or 1 Skullspell Orb									
Signal for Pickup	Ironforge	Alliance	45	52		Xiggs Fuselighter	Signal for Pickup		
REWARD: 1 Standard Issue Flare Gun									
Gnome Engineering	Ironforge	Alliance	30	47	Springspindle Fizzlegear—Ironforge	Tinkmaster Overspark	The Pledge of Secrecy	420	
The Pledge of Secrecy	Ironforge	Alliance	30	47	Tinkmaster Overspark—Ironforge	Tinkmaster Overspark	Gnome Engineering	420	
Show Your Work	Ironforge	Alliance	30	47	Tinkmaster Overspark—Ironforge	Tinkmaster Overspark	The Pledge of Secrecy	3150	
REWARD: 1 Gnome Engineer Membership Card									
Membership Card Renewal	Ironforge	Alliance	30	47		Tinkmaster Overspark	Show Your Work		
REWARD: 1 Gnome Engineer Membership Card									
The Smoldering Ruins of Thaurissan	Ironforge	Alliance	50	54	Royal Historian Archesonus—Ironforge	Royal Historian Archesonus	The Smoldering Ruins of Thaurissan	5450	1 65
REWARD: 1 Ring of the Aristocrat									
The Smoldering Ruins of Thaurissan	Ironforge	Alliance	50	54	Royal Historian Archesonus—Ironforge	Royal Historian Archesonus		550	
Assisting Arch Druid Staghelm	Ironforge	Alliance	47	50	Innkeeper Firebrew—Dwarf Ironforge	Arch Druid Fandral Staghelm		470	
Goblin Engineering	Ironforge	Alliance	30	47	Springspindle Fizzlegear—Ironforge	Nixx Sprocketspring	The Pledge of Secrecy	420	
Kharan Mighthammer	Ironforge	Alliance	50	59	King Magni Bronzebeard—Ironforge	Kharan Mighthammer	The Smoldering Ruins of Thaurissan	6400	
The Fate of the Kingdom	Ironforge	Alliance	50	59	King Magni Bronzebeard—Ironforge	Princess Moira Bronzebeard	The Bearer of Bad News	8050	
A Little Slime Goes a Long Way	Ironforge	Alliance	48	52	Laris Geardawdle—Ironforge	Laris Geardawdle		6350	
A Little Slime Goes a Long Way	Ironforge	Alliance	48	54	Laris Geardawdle—Ironforge	Laris Geardawdle	A Little Slime Goes a Long Way	6800	40
CHOICE OF: 1 Hazecover Boots or 1 Brazen Gauntlets									
A Call to Arms: The Plaguelands!	Ironforge	Alliance	50	50	Courier Hammerfall—Ironforge	Commander Ashlam Valorfist		470	
The Art of the Armorsmith	Ironforge	Alliance	40	40	Grumnus Steelshaper—Ironforge	Grumnus Steelshaper	The Way of the Weaponsmith		
The Way of the Weaponsmith	Ironforge	Alliance	40	40	Ironus Coldsteel—Ironforge	Ironus Coldsteel	The Art of the Armorsmith	3150	
A Lack of Fear	Ironforge	Alliance	20	20		High Priest Rohan			
A Lack of Fear	Ironforge	Alliance	20	20	High Priestess Laurena—Stormwind	High Priest Rohan		390	
A Lack of Fear	Ironforge	Alliance	20	20	Priestess Alathea—Darnassus	High Priest Rohan		390	
I Got Nothin' Left!	Ironforge	Alliance	35	45	Grimnur Stonebrand—Ironforge	Nat Pagle		975	
I Know A Guy...	Ironforge	Alliance	35	45	Daryl Riknussun—Ironforge	Dirge Quikcleave		975	
Alliance Trauma	Ironforge	Alliance	35	45	Nissa Firestone—Ironforge	Doctor Gustaf VanHowzen		975	
Greatfather Winter is Here!	Ironforge	Alliance	10	60	Wulmort Jinglepocket—Ironforge	Greatfather Winter		650	
Treats for Greatfather Winter	Ironforge	Alliance	10	60	Greatfather Winter—Ironforge	Greatfather Winter		1650	
REWARD: 1 Smokywood Pastures Gift Pack									
Stolen Winter Veil Treats	Ironforge	Alliance	30	60	Wulmort Jinglepocket—Ironforge	Strange Snowman		1650	
A Smokywood Pastures' Thank You!	Ironforge	Alliance	30	60	Wulmort Jinglepocket—Ironforge	Greatfather Winter	You're a Mean One...	4950	
REWARD: 1 Smokywood Pastures Special Gift									
The Reason for the Season	Ironforge	Alliance	10	60	Goli Krumn—Ironforge	Historian Karnik		650	
The Feast of Winter Veil	Ironforge	Alliance	10	60	Historian Karnik—Ironforge	King Magni Bronzebeard	The Reason for the Season	650	
Arrows Are For Sissies	Ironforge	Alliance	52	60		Artilleryman Sheldonore			
REWARD: 200 Thorium Headed Arrow									
To Show Due Judgment	Ironforge	Alliance	60	60	High Priest Rohan—Ironforge	Lord Grayson Shadowbreaker	Emphasis on Sacrifice	650	
Lord Grayson Shadowbreaker	Ironforge	Alliance	60	60	Brandur Ironhammer—Ironforge	Lord Grayson Shadowbreaker		650	
A Donation of Wool	Ironforge	Alliance	12	60		Mistina Steelshield		650	
A Donation of Silk	Ironforge	Alliance	26	60		Mistina Steelshield		1650	
A Donation of Mageweave	Ironforge	Alliance	40	60		Mistina Steelshield		3300	
A Donation of Runecloth	Ironforge	Alliance	50	60		Mistina Steelshield	A Donation of Wool	6600	
Additional Runecloth	Ironforge	Alliance	50	60		Mistina Steelshield	A Donation of Runecloth		
A Donation of Wool	Ironforge	Alliance	12	60		Bubulo Acerbus		650	
A Donation of Silk	Ironforge	Alliance	26	60		Bubulo Acerbus		1650	
A Donation of Mageweave	Ironforge	Alliance	40	60		Bubulo Acerbus		3300	
A Donation of Runecloth	Ironforge	Alliance	50	60		Bubulo Acerbus	A Donation of Wool	6600	
Additional Runecloth	Ironforge	Alliance	50	60		Bubulo Acerbus	A Donation of Runecloth		
The Darkmoon Faire	Ironforge	Alliance	6	60	Melnan Darkstone—Ironforge	Gelvas Grimegate		650	
REWARD: 5 Darkmoon Faire Prize Ticket									
Chicken Clucking for a Mint	Ironforge	Alliance	10	60	Innkeeper Firebrew—Ironforge	Innkeeper Firebrew			
REWARD: 1 Ironforge Mint									
Incoming Gumdrop	Ironforge	Alliance	10	60	Talvash del Kissel—Ironforge	Talvash del Kissel			
REWARD: 1 Gnomeregan Gumdrop									
Metzen the Reindeer	Ironforge	Alliance	40	60	Wulmort Jinglepocket—Ironforge	Wulmort Jinglepocket		4950	
REWARD: 5 Preserved Holly									
The Hero of the Day	Ironforge	Alliance	40	60	Wulmort Jinglepocket—Ironforge	Holly Preserver	Metzen the Reindeer		
REWARD: 5 Preserved Holly									
The Lunar Festival	Ironforge	Alliance	1	60		Lunar Festival Harbinger			

Kharanos

Title	Location	Faction	Min Level	Con Level	Starter Location	Finisher	Prerequisite	Max XP	Cash Reward
Taming the Beast	Kharanos	Alliance	10	10	Grif Wildheart—Dun Morogh Kharanos	Grif Wildheart		850	
The Hunter's Path	Kharanos	Alliance	10	10	Olmin Burningbeard—Ironforge Hall of Arms	Grif Wildheart		85	
The Hunter's Path	Kharanos	Alliance	10	10	Tristane Shadowstone—Dun Morogh Brewnall	Grif Wildheart		85	
The Hunter's Path	Kharanos	Alliance	10	10	Einris Brightspear—Stormwind Dwarven District	Grif Wildheart		85	
Taming the Beast	Kharanos	Alliance	10	10	Grif Wildheart—Dun Morogh Kharanos	Grif Wildheart	Taming the Beast	850	
Taming the Beast	Kharanos	Alliance	10	10	Grif Wildheart—Dun Morogh Kharanos	Grif Wildheart	Taming the Beast	850	
Training the Beast	Kharanos	Alliance	10	10	Grif Wildheart—Dun Morogh Kharanos	Belia Thundergranite	Taming the Beast	420	

LM

Title	Location	Faction	Min Level	Con Level	Starter Location	Finisher	Prerequisite	Max XP	Cash Reward
Uldaman Reagent Run	Loch Modan	Alliance	38	42	Ghak Healtouch—Loch Modan Thelsamar	Ghak Healtouch	Badlands Reagent Run	3450	55
REWARD: 5 Restorative Potion									
A Dark Threat Looms	Loch Modan	Alliance	16	18	Chief Engineer Hinderweir VII—Loch Modan	Ashlan Stonesmirk	A Dark Threat Looms	1350	

Loch Modan

Title	Location	Faction	Min Level	Con Level	Starter Location	Finisher	Prerequisite	Max XP	Cash Reward
A Dark Threat Looms	Loch Modan	Alliance	16	18	Suspicious Barrel—Loch Modan	Chief Engineer Hinderweir VII	A Dark Threat Looms	1350	
In Defense of the King's Lands	Loch Modan	Alliance	10	17	Captain Rugelfuss—Loch Modan	Captain Rugelfuss	In Defense of the King's Lands	1600	
CHOICE OF: 1 Frontier Britches or 1 Dwarven Defender or 1 Lucky Trousers									
In Defense of the King's Lands	Loch Modan	Alliance	10	12	Mountaineer Cobbleflint—Loch Modan	Mountaineer Cobbleflint		900	5
REWARD: 5 Dalaran Sharp									
In Defense of the King's Lands	Loch Modan	Alliance	10	15	Mountaineer Gravelgaw—Loch Modan	Mountaineer Gravelgaw	In Defense of the King's Lands	1050	7
REWARD: 3 Lesser Healing Potion									
A Dark Threat Looms	Loch Modan	Alliance	16	18	Chief Engineer Hinderweir VII—Loch Modan	Suspicious Barrel		675	
Mercenaries	Loch Modan	Alliance	15	19	Magistrate Bluntnose—Loch Modan	Magistrate Bluntnose		1800	20
WANTED: Chok'sul	Loch Modan	Both	17	22	Wanted Poster—Loch Modan	Magistrate Bluntnose		1750	
CHOICE OF: 1 Durable Chain Shoulders or 1 Kimbra Boots REWARD: 1 Minor Channeling Ring									
A Hunter's Boast	Loch Modan	Alliance	11	16	Daryl the Youngling—Loch Modan	Daryl the Youngling		875	
CHOICE OF: 1 Daryl's Hunting Bow or 1 Daryl's Hunting Rifle									
A Hunter's Challenge	Loch Modan	Alliance	11	17	Daryl the Youngling—Loch Modan	Daryl the Youngling	A Hunter's Boast	950	
REWARD: 1 Fine Cloth Shirt, 1Daryl's Shortsword									
In Defense of the King's Lands	Loch Modan	Alliance	10	15	Mountaineer Wallbang—Loch Modan	Mountaineer Wallbang	In Defense of the King's Lands	1050	7
REWARD: 3 Coarse Sharpening Stone									
The Trogg Threat	Loch Modan	Alliance	10	12	Captain Rugelfuss—Loch Modan	Captain Rugelfuss		900	5
Vyrin's Revenge	Loch Modan	Alliance	15	20	Vyrin Swiftwind—Loch Modan	Daryl the Youngling	A Hunter's Challenge	775	
Resupplying the Excavation	Loch Modan	Alliance	10	15	Jern Hornhelm—Loch Modan Thelsamar	Huldar	Powder to Ironband	270	
A Dark Threat Looms	Loch Modan	Alliance	16	18	Ashlan Stonesmirk—Wetlands	Chief Engineer Hinderweir VII	A Dark Threat Looms	340	
A Dark Threat Looms	Loch Modan	Alliance	16	18	Chief Engineer Hinderweir VII—Loch Modan	Chief Engineer Hinderweir VII	A Dark Threat Looms	1350	
A Dark Threat Looms	Loch Modan	Alliance	16	18	Chief Engineer Hinderweir VII—Loch Modan	Explosive Charge	A Dark Threat Looms	675	
A Dark Threat Looms	Loch Modan	Alliance	16	20	Explosive Charge—Loch Modan	Chief Engineer Hinderweir VII	A Dark Threat Looms	1950	
CHOICE OF: 1 Dwarven Tree Chopper or 1 Thornblade									
Gathering Idols	Loch Modan	Alliance	13	18	Magmar Fellhew—Loch Modan	Magmar Fellhew		1350	
CHOICE OF: 1 Dwarven Flamestick or 1 Trogg Slicer or 1 Thelsamar Axe									
Excavation Progress Report	Loch Modan	Alliance	10	15	Prospector Ironband—Loch Modan	Jern Hornhelm		270	
Report to Ironforge	Loch Modan	Alliance	10	15	Jern Hornhelm—Loch Modan Thelsamar	Prospector Stormpike	Excavation Progress Report	550	1 75
Powder to Ironband	Loch Modan	Alliance	10	15	Prospector Stormpike—Ironforge	Jern Hornhelm	Report to Ironforge	270	
Filthy Paws	Loch Modan	Alliance	9	15	Mountaineer Stormpike—Loch Modan	Mountaineer Stormpike		1350	
CHOICE OF: 1 Ironheart Chain or 1 Robe of the Keeper or 1 Ironplate Buckler									
Protecting the Shipment	Loch Modan	Alliance	10	15	Miran—Loch Modan	Prospector Ironband	After the Ambush	1050	
CHOICE OF: 1 Foreman Belt or 1 Mud Stompers									
Crocolisk Hunting	Loch Modan	Alliance	10	15	Marek Ironheart—Loch Modan	Marek Ironheart		1050	
REWARD: 1 Recipe: Crocolisk Steak, 1Rugged Cape									
Rat Catching	Loch Modan	Alliance	10	11	Mountaineer Kadrell—Loch Modan Thelsamar	Mountaineer Kadrell		875	4
CHOICE OF: 1 Burnt Hide Bracers or 1 Cavalier's Boots									
Thelsamar Blood Sausages	Loch Modan	Alliance	7	11	Vidra Hearthstove—Loch Modan	Vidra Hearthstove		875	4
REWARD: 5 Blood Sausage, 1Recipe: Blood Sausage									
Ironband's Excavation	Loch Modan	Alliance	13	18	Jern Hornhelm—Loch Modan Thelsamar	Magmar Fellhew	Gathering Idols	340	
After the Ambush	Loch Modan	Alliance	10	15	Huldar—Loch Modan	Miran	Resupplying the Excavation	110	
Vyrin's Revenge	Loch Modan	Alliance	15	20	Daryl the Youngling—Loch Modan	Vyrin Swiftwind	Vyrin's Revenge	1550	
CHOICE OF: 1 Hunting Ammo Sack or 1 Hunting Quiver									
Stormpike's Order	Loch Modan	Alliance	9	14	Mountaineer Stormpike—Loch Modan	Furen Longbeard		975	6
Mountaineer Stormpike's Task	Loch Modan	Alliance	9	15	Mountaineer Kadrell—Loch Modan Thelsamar	Mountaineer Stormpike	Stormpike's Order	550	
Bingles' Missing Supplies	Loch Modan	Alliance	12	15	Bingles Blastenheimer—Loch Modan	Bingles Blastenheimer		1050	7
REWARD: 1 Bingles' Flying Gloves									
Badlands Reagent Run	Loch Modan	Alliance	36	39	Ghak Healtouch—Loch Modan Thelsamar	Ghak Healtouch		3000	45
Badlands Reagent Run II	Loch Modan	Alliance	40	44	Ghak Healtouch—Loch Modan Thelsamar	Ghak Healtouch	Uldaman Reagent Run	3750	
Honor Students	Loch Modan	Alliance	10	10	Brock Stoneseeker—Loch Modan Thelsamar Mining Trainer	Thorgrum Borrelson		210	
Gryth Thurden	Loch Modan	Alliance	10	10	Golnir Bouldertoe—Ironforge	Gryth Thurden	Ride to Ironforge	210	
Ride to Ironforge	Loch Modan	Alliance	10	10	Thorgrum Borrelson—Loch Modan	Golnir Bouldertoe	Honor Students	420	1 75
Return to Brock	Loch Modan	Alliance	10	10	Gryth Thurden—Ironforge	Brock Stoneseeker	Gryth Thurden	1050	3 50
Trial of the Lake	Moonglade	Horde	16	16	Dendrite Starblaze—Moonglade	Tajarri	A Lesson to Learn	875	
Trial of the Lake	Moonglade	Alliance	16	16	Dendrite Starblaze—Moonglade	Tajarri	A Lesson to Learn	875	
Trial of the Sea Lion	Moonglade	Horde	16	16	Tajarri—Moonglade	Dendrite Starblaze	Trial of the Lake	875	
Aquatic Form	Moonglade	Horde	16	16	Dendrite Starblaze—Moonglade	Turak Runetotem	Trial of the Sea Lion	1150	
REWARD: 1 Aquarius Belt									
Trial of the Sea Lion	Moonglade	Alliance	16	16	Tajarri—Moonglade	Dendrite Starblaze	Trial of the Lake	875	
Wasteland	Moonglade	Both	54	55	Rabine Saturna—Moonglade	Loyo Starstrike	Rabine Saturna	2800	
Under the Chitin Was...	Moonglade	Both	54	57		Umber	Uncovering Past Secrets	3000	
Aquatic Form	Moonglade	Alliance	16	16	Dendrite Starblaze—Moonglade	Mathrengyl Bearwalker	Trial of the Sea Lion	1150	
REWARD: 1 Aquarius Belt									
Shards of the Felvine	Moonglade	Both	56	60	Rabine Saturna—Moonglade	Rabine Saturna	A Reliquary of Purity	8300	
CHOICE OF: 1 Milli's Shield or 1 Milli's Lexicon									
A Reliquary of Purity	Moonglade	Both	56	60		Rabine Saturna		6600	
Great Bear Spirit	Moonglade	Alliance	10	10	Dendrite Starblaze—Moonglade	Dendrite Starblaze	Moonglade	420	
Great Bear Spirit	Moonglade	Horde	10	10	Dendrite Starblaze—Moonglade	Dendrite Starblaze	Moonglade	420	
Back to Darnassus	Moonglade	Alliance	10	10	Dendrite Starblaze—Moonglade	Mathrengyl Bearwalker	Great Bear Spirit	85	
Back to Thunder Bluff	Moonglade	Horde	10	10	Dendrite Starblaze—Moonglade	Turak Runetotem	Great Bear Spirit	85	
The Principal Source	Moonglade	Alliance	14	14	Dendrite Starblaze—Moonglade	Alanndarian Nightsong	Lessons Anew	750	
Power over Poison	Moonglade	Alliance	14	14	Dendrite Starblaze—Moonglade	Mathrengyl Bearwalker	Curing the Sick	975	
The Principal Source	Moonglade	Horde	14	14	Dendrite Starblaze—Moonglade	Tonga Runetotem	Lessons Anew	750	
Power over Poison	Moonglade	Horde	14	14	Dendrite Starblaze—Moonglade	Turak Runetotem	Curing the Sick	975	
Uncovering Past Secrets	Moonglade	Both	54	57	Umber—Moonglade	Rabine Saturna	Umber, Archivist	7550	1 70
CHOICE OF: 1 Ring of Living Stone or 1 Glowing Crystal Ring									
Elune's Candle	Moonglade	Both	10	60		Valadar Starsong			
REWARD: 1 Elune's Candle, 1Lunar Festival Fireworks Pack									
Festival Dumplings	Moonglade	Both	1	60		Valadar Starsong			
REWARD: 8 Festival Dumplings									
Festive Lunar Dresses	Moonglade	Both	1	60		Valadar Starsong			
CHOICE OF: 1 Festive Green Dress or 1 Festive Pink Dress or 1 Festive Purple Dress REWARD: 1 Lunar Festival Fireworks Pack									
Festive Lunar Pant Suits	Moonglade	Both	1	60		Valadar Starsong			
CHOICE OF: 1 Festive Black Pant Suit or 1 Festive Blue Pant Suit or 1 Festive Teal Pant Suit REWARD: 1 Lunar Festival Fireworks Pack									
Elune's Blessing	Moonglade	Both	40	60	Valadar Starsong—Moonglade	Valadar Starsong		6600	90
REWARD: 1 Elune's Lantern, 1Lunar Festival Fireworks Pack, 37912									
Small Rockets	Moonglade	Both	25	60		Fariel Starsong			
REWARD: 1 Small Rocket Recipes, 1Lunar Festival Fireworks Pack									
Firework Launcher	Moonglade	Both	45	60		Fariel Starsong			
REWARD: 1 Schematic: Firework Launcher, 1Lunar Festival Fireworks Pack									
Festive Recipes	Moonglade	Both	50	60		Fariel Starsong			
CHOICE OF: 1 Pattern: Festival Dress or 1 Pattern: Festival Suit REWARD: 1 Lunar Festival Fireworks Pack									
Large Rockets	Moonglade	Both	35	60		Fariel Starsong			
REWARD: 1 Large Rocket Recipes, 1Lunar Festival Fireworks Pack									
Cluster Rockets	Moonglade	Both	45	60		Fariel Starsong			
REWARD: 1 Cluster Rocket Recipes, 1Lunar Festival Fireworks Pack									
Large Cluster Rockets	Moonglade	Both	55	60		Fariel Starsong			

Moonglade

Moonglade cont'd

Title	Location	Faction	Min Level	Con Level	Starter Location	Finisher	Prerequisite	Max XP	Cash Reward
REWARD: 1 Large Cluster Rocket Recipes, 1Lunar Festival Fireworks Pack									
Cluster Launcher	Moonglade	Both	55	60		Fariel Starsong			
REWARD: 1 Schematic: Cluster Launcher, 1Lunar Festival Fireworks Pack									

Mulgore

Title	Location	Faction	Min Level	Con Level	Starter Location	Finisher	Prerequisite	Max XP	Cash Reward
Dangers of the Windfury	Mulgore	Horde	5	8	Ruul Eagletalon—Mulgore Bloodhoof	Ruul Eagletalon		700	2●25●
Sharing the Land	Mulgore	Horde	1	6	Baine Bloodhoof—Mulgore Bloodhoof	Baine Bloodhoof		550	1●25●
REWARD: 25 Flash Pellet									
Dwarven Digging	Mulgore	Horde	6	8	Baine Bloodhoof—Mulgore Bloodhoof	Baine Bloodhoof		700	
CHOICE OF: 1 Fortified Bindings or 1 Rough-hewn Kodo Leggings									
Poison Water	Mulgore	Horde	4	5	Mull Thunderhorn—Mulgore Bloodhoof	Mull Thunderhorn		450	
The Ravaged Caravan	Mulgore	Horde	5	8	Morin Cloudstalker—Mulgore	Sealed Supply Crate		525	
The Ravaged Caravan	Mulgore	Horde	5	8	Venture Co. Crate—Mulgore	Morin Cloudstalker	The Ravaged Caravan	525	
Winterhoof Cleansing	Mulgore	Horde	4	6	Mull Thunderhorn—Mulgore Bloodhoof	Mull Thunderhorn	Poison Water	550	
Thunderhorn Totem	Mulgore	Horde	4	7	Mull Thunderhorn—Mulgore Bloodhoof	Mull Thunderhorn	Winterhoof Cleansing	625	
Thunderhorn Cleansing	Mulgore	Horde	4	8	Mull Thunderhorn—Mulgore Bloodhoof	Mull Thunderhorn	Thunderhorn Totem	700	
REWARD: 1 Thunderhorn Cloak									
Wildmane Totem	Mulgore	Horde	4	10	Mull Thunderhorn—Mulgore Bloodhoof	Mull Thunderhorn	Thunderhorn Cleansing	850	
Wildmane Cleansing	Mulgore	Horde	4	10	Mull Thunderhorn—Mulgore Bloodhoof	Mull Thunderhorn	Wildmane Totem	1050	
CHOICE OF: 1 Ceremonial Tomahawk or 1 Dreamwatcher Staff									
Swoop Hunting	Mulgore	Horde	4	6	Harken Windtotem—Mulgore Bloodhoof	Harken Windtotem		675	2●50●
The Venture Co.	Mulgore	Horde	5	10	Morin Cloudstalker—Mulgore	Morin Cloudstalker	The Ravaged Caravan	625	2●50●
Supervisor Fizsprocket	Mulgore	Horde	5	12	Morin Cloudstalker—Mulgore	Morin Cloudstalker	The Ravaged Caravan	900	4●45●
CHOICE OF: 1 Compact Fighting Knife or 1 Goblin Smasher									
Mazzranache	Mulgore	Horde	5	8	Maur Raincaller—Mulgore Bloodhoof	Maur Raincaller		700	49●
CHOICE OF: 1 Cliff Runner Boots or 1 Plains Hunter Wristguards									
Rite of Vision	Mulgore	Horde	3	6	Baine Bloodhoof—Mulgore Bloodhoof	Zarlman Two-Moons		55	
The Demon Scarred Cloak	Mulgore	Horde	6	12	Demon Scarred Cloak	Skorn Whitecloud		900	3●40●
CHOICE OF: 1 Skorn's Hammer or 1 Skorn's Rifle									
Rite of Vision	Mulgore	Horde	3	7	Zarlman Two-Moons—Mulgore Bloodhoof	Zarlman Two-Moons	Rite of Vision	625	
Rite of Vision	Mulgore	Horde	3	7	Zarlman Two-Moons—Mulgore Bloodhoof	Seer Wiserunner	Rite of Vision	480	
CHOICE OF: 1 Rainwalker Boots or 1 Sun-beaten Cloak									
Rite of Wisdom	Mulgore	Horde	3	10	Seer Wiserunner—Mulgore	Ancestral Spirit	Rite of Vision	850	
Journey into Thunder Bluff	Mulgore	Horde	3	10	Ancestral Spirit—Mulgore	Cairne Bloodhoof	Rite of Wisdom	420	
Rites of the Earthmother	Mulgore	Horde	3	14	Cairne Bloodhoof—Thunder Bluff High Rise	Cairne Bloodhoof	Journey into Thunder Bluff	1250	
REWARD: 1 Kodo Hunter's Leggings									
A Sacred Burial	Mulgore	Horde	7	10	Lorekeeper Raintotem—Mulgore Tauren	Lorekeeper Raintotem		625	2●50●
Journey to the Crossroads	Mulgore	Horde	9	12	Kirge Sternhorn—Barrens Camp Taurajo	Thork	Plainstrider Menace	230	
The Hunter's Way	Mulgore	Horde	10	10	Skorn Whitecloud—Mulgore Bloodhoof	Melor Stonehoof	Plainstrider Menace	850	
Heeding the Call	Mulgore	Horde	10	10	Gennia Runetotem—Mulgore Bloodhoof Village	Turak Runetotem		85	
Taming the Beast	Mulgore	Horde	10	10	Yaw Sharpmane—Mulgore Bloodhoof Village	Yaw Sharpmane		850	
The Hunter's Path	Mulgore	Horde	10	10	Kary Thunderhorn—Thunder Bluff Hunter Rise	Yaw Sharpmane		85	
The Hunter's Path	Mulgore	Horde	10	10	Sian'dur—Orgrimmar Valley of Honor	Yaw Sharpmane		85	
The Hunter's Path	Mulgore	Horde	10	10	Thotar—Durotar Razor Hill	Yaw Sharpmane		85	
Taming the Beast	Mulgore	Horde	10	10	Yaw Sharpmane—Mulgore Bloodhoof Village	Yaw Sharpmane	Taming the Beast	850	
Taming the Beast	Mulgore	Horde	10	10	Yaw Sharpmane—Mulgore Bloodhoof Village	Yaw Sharpmane	Taming the Beast	850	
Training the Beast	Mulgore	Horde	10	10	Yaw Sharpmane—Mulgore Bloodhoof Village	Holt Thunderhorn	Taming the Beast	420	
New Kodo - Teal	Mulgore	Horde	60	1		Harb Clawhoof			
CHOICE OF: 1 Great Brown Kodo or 1 Great Gray Kodo or 1 Great White Kodo									
New Kodo - Green	Mulgore	Horde	60	1		Harb Clawhoof			
CHOICE OF: 1 Great Brown Kodo or 1 Great Gray Kodo or 1 Great White Kodo									

Northshire

Title	Location	Faction	Min Level	Con Level	Starter Location	Finisher	Prerequisite	Max XP	Cash Reward
Bounty on Garrick Padfoot	Northshire	Alliance	2	5	Deputy Willem—Elwynn Forest Northshire	Deputy Willem	Brotherhood of Thieves	340	
CHOICE OF: 1 Tapered Pants or 1 Layered Tunic or 1 Ensign Cloak									
Kobold Camp Cleanup	Northshire	Alliance	1	2	Marshal McBride—Elwynn Forest Northshire	Marshal McBride	A Threat Within	170	25●
Investigate Echo Ridge	Northshire	Alliance	1	3	Marshal McBride—Elwynn Forest Northshire	Marshal McBride	Kobold Camp Cleanup	250	40●
Brotherhood of Thieves	Northshire	Alliance	2	4	Deputy Willem—Elwynn Forest Northshire	Deputy Willem	A Threat Within	360	
CHOICE OF: 1 Militia Dagger or 1 Militia Hammer or 1 Militia Shortsword or 1 Militia Warhammer or 1 Militia Quarterstaff									
Skirmish at Echo Ridge	Northshire	Alliance	1	5	Marshal McBride—Elwynn Forest Northshire	Marshal McBride	Investigate Echo Ridge	450	
CHOICE OF: 1 Outfitter Belt or 1 Outfitter Boots or 1 Outfitter Gloves									
Wolves Across the Border	Northshire	Alliance	1	2	Eagan Peltskinner—Elwynn Forest Northshire	Eagan Peltskinner		170	
CHOICE OF: 1 Soft Fur-lined Shoes or 1 Wolfskin Bracers									
Report to Goldshire	Northshire	Alliance	1	5	Marshal McBride—Elwynn Forest Northshire	Marshal Dughan	Skirmish at Echo Ridge	230	
REWARD: 1 Pikeman Shield									
A Threat Within	Northshire	Alliance	1	1	Deputy Willem—Elwynn Forest Northshire	Marshal McBride		40	
The Stolen Tome	Northshire	Alliance	1	4	Drusilla La Salle—Elwynn Forest Northshire	Drusilla La Salle	Beginnings	360	
Simple Letter	Northshire	Alliance	1	1	Marshal McBride—Elwynn Forest Northshire	Llane Beshere	Kobold Camp Cleanup	40	
Consecrated Letter	Northshire	Alliance	1	1	Marshal McBride—Elwynn Forest Northshire	Brother Sammuel	Kobold Camp Cleanup	40	
Encrypted Letter	Northshire	Alliance	1	1	Marshal McBride—Elwynn Forest Northshire	Jorik Kerridan	Kobold Camp Cleanup	40	
Hallowed Letter	Northshire	Alliance	1	1	Marshal McBride—Elwynn Forest Northshire	Priestess Anetta	Kobold Camp Cleanup	40	
Glyphic Letter	Northshire	Alliance	1	1	Marshal McBride—Elwynn Forest Northshire	Khelden Bremen	Kobold Camp Cleanup	40	
Tainted Letter	Northshire	Alliance	1	1	Marshal McBride—Elwynn Forest Northshire	Drusilla La Salle	Kobold Camp Cleanup	40	
Milly Osworth	Northshire	Alliance	2	4	Deputy Willem—Elwynn Forest Northshire	Milly Osworth	Brotherhood of Thieves	35	
Milly's Harvest	Northshire	Alliance	2	4	Milly Osworth—Elwynn Forest Northshire	Milly Osworth	Brotherhood of Thieves	180	
Grape Manifest	Northshire	Alliance	2	4	Milly Osworth—Elwynn Forest Northshire	Brother Neals	Milly's Harvest	360	
CHOICE OF: 1 Wine-stained Cloak or 1 Latched Belt									
Eagan Peltskinner	Northshire	Alliance	1	2	Deputy Willem—Elwynn Forest Northshire	Eagan Peltskinner	A Threat Within	85	
Welcome!	Northshire	Alliance	1	1	Northshire Gift Voucher	Merissa Stilwell			
CHOICE OF: 1 Diablo Stone or 1 Panda Collar or 1 Zergling Leash									

Orgrimmar

Title	Location	Faction	Min Level	Con Level	Starter Location	Finisher	Prerequisite	Max XP	Cash Reward
Ripple Delivery	Orgrimmar	Horde	42	48	Gilveradin Sunchaser—Hinterlands High Elf	Dran Droffers	A Sticky Situation	4400	1●40●
Children's Week	Orgrimmar	Horde	10	60		Orcish Orphan			
The Ashenvale Hunt	Orgrimmar	Horde	20	20	Warcaller Gorlach—Orgrimmar	Senani Thunderheart		160	
Ripple Recovery	Orgrimmar	Horde	42	48	Dran Droffers—Orgrimmar	Malton Droffers		440	
Ripple Recovery	Orgrimmar	Horde	42	48	Malton Droffers—Orgrimmar	Gilveradin Sunchaser	Ripple Recovery	4400	
Assisting Arch Druid Runetotem	Orgrimmar	Horde	47	50	Innkeeper Gryshka—Orgrimmar	Arch Druid Hamuul Runetotem		470	
The New Frontier	Orgrimmar	Horde	54	55	Warcaller Gorlach—Orgrimmar	Arch Druid Hamuul Runetotem		550	
The Spirits of Stonetalon	Orgrimmar	Horde	13	17	Zor Lonetree—Orgrimmar	Seereth Stonebreak	Goblin Invaders	320	
Alliance Relations	Orgrimmar	Horde	30	30	Craven Drok—Orgrimmar	Keldran		600	
Alliance Relations	Orgrimmar	Horde	30	30	Keldran—Orgrimmar	Takata Steelblade	Alliance Relations	1200	
Alliance Relations	Orgrimmar	Horde	30	33	Takata Steelblade—Desolace Ghost Walker Post	Maurin Bonesplitter	Alliance Relations	270	
Befouled by Satyr	Orgrimmar	Horde	25	33	Takata Steelblade—Desolace Ghost Walker Post	Takata Steelblade	Alliance Relations	2650	
The Burning of Spirits	Orgrimmar	Horde	25	33	Maurin Bonesplitter—Desolace Ghost Walker Post	Maurin Bonesplitter	Alliance Relations	2650	
Alliance Relations	Orgrimmar	Horde	30	33	Takata Steelblade—Desolace Ghost Walker Post	Keldran	Befouled by Satyr	2650	
CHOICE OF: 1 Gloves of Kapelan or 1 Swiftrunner Cape									
The Corrupter	Orgrimmar	Horde	25	33	Flayed Demon Skin	Maurin Bonesplitter		1300	
The Corrupter	Orgrimmar	Horde	25	33	Maurin Bonesplitter—Desolace Ghost Walker Post	Maurin Bonesplitter	The Corrupter	2650	
The Corrupter	Orgrimmar	Horde	25	35	Maurin Bonesplitter—Desolace Ghost Walker Post	Maurin Bonesplitter	The Corrupter	2750	
The Corrupter	Orgrimmar	Horde	25	33	Maurin Bonesplitter—Desolace Ghost Walker Post	Takata Steelblade	The Corrupter	270	
The Corrupter	Orgrimmar	Horde	25	40	Takata Steelblade—Desolace Ghost Walker Post	Takata Steelblade	The Corrupter	3900	
CHOICE OF: 1 Basalt Buckler or 1 Enforcer Pauldrons									
Creature of the Void	Orgrimmar	Horde	10	11	Gan'rul Bloodeye—Orgrimmar	Gan'rul Bloodeye	Creature of the Void	875	

Title	Location	Faction	Min Level	Con Level	Starter Location	Finisher	Prerequisite	Max XP	Cash Reward
The Binding	Orgrimmar	Horde	10	11	Gan'rul Bloodeye—Orgrimmar	Gan'rul Bloodeye	Creature of the Void	650	
Devourer of Souls	Orgrimmar	Horde	20	20	Gan'rul Bloodeye—Orgrimmar	Cazul	Devourer of Souls	160	
Blind Cazul	Orgrimmar	Horde	20	20	Cazul—Orgrimmar	Zankaja	Devourer of Souls	390	
News of Dogran	Orgrimmar	Horde	20	20	Zankaja—Orgrimmar	Gazrog	Blind Cazul	390	
News of Dogran	Orgrimmar	Horde	20	20	Gazrog—Barrens Crossroads	Ken'zigla	News of Dogran	775	
Ken'zigla's Draught	Orgrimmar	Horde	20	20	Ken'zigla—Stonetalon Malaka'jin	Grunt Logmar	News of Dogran	1550	
Love's Gift	Orgrimmar	Horde	20	20	Grunt Dogran—Barrens	Gan'rul Bloodeye	Dogran's Captivity	390	
The Binding	Orgrimmar	Horde	20	20	Gan'rul Bloodeye—Orgrimmar	Gan'rul Bloodeye	Love's Gift	1150	
REWARD: 1 Small Soul Pouch									
Dogran's Captivity	Orgrimmar	Horde	20	20	Grunt Logmar—Barrens	Grunt Dogran	Ken'zigla's Draught	1150	
The Shattered Hand	Orgrimmar	Horde	10	13	Therzok—Orgrimmar	Therzok	The Shattered Hand	460	
REWARD: 1 Blade of Cunning									
The Shattered Hand	Orgrimmar	Horde	10	13	Therzok—Orgrimmar	Therzok		675	
Necklace Recovery	Orgrimmar	Horde	37	41	Dran Droffers—Orgrimmar	Dran Droffers		2450	
Necklace Recovery, Take 2	Orgrimmar	Horde	37	41	Dran Droffers—Orgrimmar	Remains of a Paladin	Necklace Recovery	2450	
Necklace Recovery, Take 3	Orgrimmar	Horde	37	44	Dran Droffers—Orgrimmar	Jarkal Mossmeld	Deliver the Gems	5600	
REWARD: 1 Jarkal's Enhancing Necklace									
Zando'zan	Orgrimmar	Horde	16	16	Shenthul—Orgrimmar	Zando'zan			
Wrenix of Ratchet	Orgrimmar	Horde	16	16	Zando'zan—Orgrimmar	Wrenix the Wretched	Zando'zan	120	
Deep Cover	Orgrimmar	Horde	20	20	Shenthul—Orgrimmar	Taskmaster Fizzule	The Shattered Salute	1150	
REWARD: 1 Fizzule's Whistle									
The Shattered Salute	Orgrimmar	Horde	20	20	Shenthul—Orgrimmar	Shenthul		160	
Hinott's Assistance	Orgrimmar	Horde	20	26	Shenthul—Orgrimmar	Serge Hinott	Mission: Possible But Not Probable	1050	
Barbaric Battlements	Orgrimmar	Horde	32	32	Orokk Omosh—Orgrimmar	Orokk Omosh		2550	
REWARD: 1 Plans: Barbaric Iron Breastplate									
On Iron Pauldrons	Orgrimmar	Horde	32	32	Orokk Omosh—Orgrimmar	Orokk Omosh	Barbaric Battlements	2550	
REWARD: 1 Plans: Barbaric Iron Shoulders									
Trampled Under Foot	Orgrimmar	Horde	32	36	Orokk Omosh—Orgrimmar	Orokk Omosh	On Iron Pauldrons	2800	
REWARD: 1 Plans: Barbaric Iron Boots									
Horns of Frenzy	Orgrimmar	Horde	32	36	Orokk Omosh—Orgrimmar	Orokk Omosh	Trampled Under Foot	2800	
REWARD: 1 Plans: Barbaric Iron Helm									
Joys of Omosh	Orgrimmar	Horde	32	36	Orokk Omosh—Orgrimmar	Orokk Omosh	On Iron Pauldrons	280	
REWARD: 1 Plans: Barbaric Iron Gloves									
The Old Ways	Orgrimmar	Horde	40	40	Aturk the Anvil—Orgrimmar	Aturk the Anvil		3150	
Booty Bay or Bust!	Orgrimmar	Horde	40	40	Ox—Orgrimmar	McGavan	The Old Ways	1550	
Rig Wars	Orgrimmar	Horde	25	35	Nogg—Orgrimmar	Nogg		2750	
CHOICE OF: 1 Civinad Robes or 1 Triprunner Dungarees or 1 Dual Reinforced Leggings									
Chief Engineer Scooty	Orgrimmar	Horde	20	35	Sovik—Orgrimmar	Scooty		280	
Nogg's Ring Redo	Orgrimmar	Horde	28	35	Nogg—Orgrimmar	Nogg	Return of the Ring	2750	
REWARD: 1 Nogg's Gold Ring									
Seeking Strahad	Orgrimmar	Horde	30	30	Gan'rul Bloodeye—Orgrimmar	Strahad Farsan		600	
Betrayed	Orgrimmar	Horde	44	53	Belgrom Rockmaul—Orgrimmar	Ag'tor Bloodfist		2650	
Betrayed	Orgrimmar	Horde	44	53	Ag'tor Bloodfist—Azshara	Kaldorei Tome of Summoning	Betrayed	3950	
Betrayed	Orgrimmar	Horde	44	56	Kaldorei Tome of Summoning—Azshara	Ag'tor Bloodfist	Betrayed	4350	
Betrayed	Orgrimmar	Horde	44	56	Ag'tor Bloodfist—Azshara	Belgrom Rockmaul	Betrayed	7300	
CHOICE OF: 1 Pyrestone Orb or 1 Belgrom's Hammer									
The Eastern Kingdoms	Orgrimmar	Horde	48	54	Thrall—Orgrimmar Grommash Hold	Thrall	What Is Going On?		
The Royal Rescue	Orgrimmar	Horde	48	59	Thrall—Orgrimmar Grommash Hold	Princess Moira Bronzebeard	The Eastern Kingdoms	8050	
Bone-Bladed Weapons	Orgrimmar	Horde	48	52	Jes'rimon—Orgrimmar	Jes'rimon		5100	40●
CHOICE OF: 1 White Bone Band or 1 White Bone Shredder or 1 White Bone Spear									
March of the Silithid	Orgrimmar	Horde	50	53	Zilzibin Drumlore—Orgrimmar	Alchemist Pestlezugg	Rise of the Silithid	525	
Calm Before the Storm	Orgrimmar	Horde	50	54	Zilzibin Drumlore—Orgrimmar	Karus	Calm Before the Storm	8150	
CHOICE OF: 1 Oblivion Orb or 1 Snarkshaw Spaulders or 1 Eschewal Greaves									
For The Horde!	Orgrimmar	Horde	55	60	Thrall—Orgrimmar Grommash Hold	Thrall	Eitrigg's Wisdom	10900	2● 85●
CHOICE OF: 1 Mark of Tyranny or 1 Eye of the Beast or 1 Blackhand's Breadth									
A Call to Arms: The Plaguelands!	Orgrimmar	Horde	50	50	Warcaller Gorlach—Orgrimmar	High Executor Derrington		470	
The Art of the Armorsmith	Orgrimmar	Horde	40	50	Okothos Ironrager—Orgrimmar	Okothos Ironrager	The Way of the Weaponsmith	3150	
The Way of the Weaponsmith	Orgrimmar	Horde	40	40	Borgosh Corebender—Orgrimmar	Borgosh Corebender	The Art of the Armorsmith	3150	
Shadowguard	Orgrimmar	Horde	20	20	Miles Welsh—Thunder Bluff	Ur'kyo		390	
Shadowguard	Orgrimmar	Horde	20	20	Aelthalyste—Undercity	Ur'kyo		390	
Shadowguard	Orgrimmar	Horde	20	20		Ur'kyo			
Hidden Enemies	Orgrimmar	Horde	9	12	Thrall—Orgrimmar Grommash Hold	Thrall		900	2● 50●
Hidden Enemies	Orgrimmar	Horde	9	12	Thrall—Orgrimmar Grommash Hold	Thrall	Hidden Enemies	460	
Hidden Enemies	Orgrimmar	Horde	9	16	Thrall—Orgrimmar Grommash Hold	Thrall	Hidden Enemies	1150	8●
Hidden Enemies	Orgrimmar	Horde	9	15	Thrall—Orgrimmar Grommash Hold	Neeru Fireblade	Hidden Enemies	110	
Hidden Enemies	Orgrimmar	Horde	9	16	Neeru Fireblade—Orgrimmar	Thrall	Hidden Enemies	1450	
CHOICE OF: 1 Kris of Orgrimmar or 1 Hammer of Orgrimmar or 1 Axe of Orgrimmar or 1 Staff of Orgrimmar									
Slaying the Beast	Orgrimmar	Horde	9	16	Neeru Fireblade—Orgrimmar	Neeru Fireblade		1150	
Heeding the Call	Orgrimmar	Horde	10	10	Innkeeper Gryshka—Orgrimmar	Turak Runetotem		85	
What the Wind Carries	Orgrimmar	Horde	55	60	Thrall—Orgrimmar Grommash Hold	Thrall	For The Horde!	650	
The Champion of the Horde	Orgrimmar	Horde	55	60	Thrall—Orgrimmar Grommash Hold	Rexxar	What the Wind Carries	3650	
You Too Good.	Orgrimmar	Horde	35	45	Lumak—Orgrimmar	Nat Pagle		975	
To Gadgetzan You Go!	Orgrimmar	Horde	35	45	Zamja—Orgrimmar	Dirge Quikcleave		975	
Horde Trauma	Orgrimmar	Horde	35	45	Arnok—Orgrimmar	Doctor Gregory Victor		975	
Great-father Winter is Here!	Orgrimmar	Horde	10	60	Kaymard Copperpinch—Orgrimmar Valley of Strength	Great-father Winter		650	
Treats for Great-father Winter	Orgrimmar	Horde	10	60	Great-father Winter—Orgrimmar Valley of Strength	Great-father Winter		1650	
REWARD: 1 Smokywood Pastures Gift Pack									
Stolen Winter Veil Treats	Orgrimmar	Horde	30	60	Kaymard Copperpinch—Orgrimmar Valley of Strength	Strange Snowman		1650	
The Reason for the Season	Orgrimmar	Horde	10	60	Furmund—Orgrimmar Valley of Strength	Sagorne Creststrider		650	
A Smokywood Pastures' Thank You!	Orgrimmar	Horde	30	60	Kaymard Copperpinch—Orgrimmar Valley of Strength	Great-father Winter	You're a Mean One...	4950	
REWARD: 1 Smokywood Pastures Special Gift									
The Feast of Winter Veil	Orgrimmar	Horde	10	60	Sagorne Creststrider—Orgrimmar	Cairne Bloodhoof	The Reason for the Season	650	
A Fair Trade	Orgrimmar	Horde	52	60		Bounty Hunter Kolark			
REWARD: 200 Thorium Headed Arrow									
Victory for the Horde	Orgrimmar	Horde	60	60	Head of Onyxia	Thrall		13250	
For All To See	Orgrimmar	Horde	60	60	Thrall—Orgrimmar Grommash Hold	Overlord Runthak	Victory for the Horde	9950	
CHOICE OF: 1 Onyxia Blood Talisman or 1 Dragonslayer's Signet or 1 Onyxia Tooth Pendant									
The Journey Has Just Begun	Orgrimmar	Horde	60	60		Overlord Runthak	For All To See		
Wolf Swapping - Arctic Wolf	Orgrimmar	Horde	60	1		Ogunaro Wolfrunner			
CHOICE OF: 1 Horn of the Swift Brown Wolf or 1 Horn of the Swift Gray Wolf or 1 Horn of the Swift Timber Wolf									
Wolf Swapping - Red Wolf	Orgrimmar	Horde	60	1		Ogunaro Wolfrunner			
CHOICE OF: 1 Horn of the Swift Brown Wolf or 1 Horn of the Swift Gray Wolf or 1 Horn of the Swift Timber Wolf									
Material Assistance	Orgrimmar	Horde	58	60	Sagorne Creststrider—Orgrimmar	Sagorne Creststrider		4950	
Again Into the Great Ossuary	Orgrimmar	Horde	58	60		Sagorne Creststrider	The Darkreaver Menace		
REWARD: 1 Divination Scryer									
The Lord of Blackrock	Orgrimmar	Horde	60	60	Head of Nefarian	Thrall		9950	
The Lord of Blackrock	Orgrimmar	Horde	60	60	Thrall—Orgrimmar Grommash Hold	High Overlord Saurfang	The Lord of Blackrock	9950	
CHOICE OF: 1 Master Dragonslayer's Medallion or 1 Master Dragonslayer's Orb or 1 Master Dragonslayer's Ring									

Orgrimmar cont'd

Title	Location	Faction	Min Level	Con Level	Starter Location	Finisher	Prerequisite	Max XP	Cash Reward
A Donation of Runecloth	Orgrimmar	Horde	50	60		Rashona Straglash	A Donation of Wool	6600	
A Donation of Wool	Orgrimmar	Horde	12	60		Rashona Straglash		650	
A Donation of Silk	Orgrimmar	Horde	26	60		Rashona Straglash		1650	
A Donation of Mageweave	Orgrimmar	Horde	40	60		Rashona Straglash		3300	
Additional Runecloth	Orgrimmar	Horde	50	60		Rashona Straglash	A Donation of Runecloth		
A Donation of Wool	Orgrimmar	Horde	12	60		Vehena		650	
A Donation of Silk	Orgrimmar	Horde	26	60		Vehena		1650	
A Donation of Mageweave	Orgrimmar	Horde	40	60		Vehena		3300	
A Donation of Runecloth	Orgrimmar	Horde	50	60		Vehena	A Donation of Wool	6600	
Additional Runecloth	Orgrimmar	Horde	50	60		Vehena	A Donation of Runecloth		
The Darkmoon Faire	Orgrimmar	Horde	6	60	Kruban Darkblade—Orgrimmar	Gelvas Grimegate		650	
REWARD: 5 Darkmoon Faire Prize Ticket									
The Darkreaver Menace	Orgrimmar	Horde	58	60	Sagorne Creststrider—Orgrimmar	Sagorne Creststrider	Material Assistance	9950	
REWARD: 1 Skyfury Helm									
Hallow's End Treats for Spoops!	Orgrimmar	Horde	10	60	Spoops—Orgrimmar	Spoops		1650	
REWARD: 30 Hallow's End Pumpkin Treat									
Flexing for Nougat	Orgrimmar	Horde	10	60	Innkeeper Gryshka—Orgrimmar	Innkeeper Gryshka			
REWARD: 1 Orgrimmar Nougat									
Metzen the Reindeer	Orgrimmar	Horde	40	60	Kaymard Copperpinch—Orgrimmar Valley of Strength	Kaymard Copperpinch		4950	
REWARD: 5 Preserved Holly									
The Hero of the Day	Orgrimmar	Horde	40	60	Kaymard Copperpinch—Orgrimmar Valley of Strength	Holly Preserver	Metzen the Reindeer		
REWARD: 5 Preserved Holly									
The Lunar Festival	Orgrimmar	Horde	1	60		Lunar Festival Harbinger			

Ratchet

Title	Location	Faction	Min Level	Con Level	Starter Location	Finisher	Prerequisite	Max XP	Cash Reward
Summon Felsteed	Ratchet	Horde	40	40	Zevrost—Orgrimmar	Strahad Farsan		320	
Summon Felsteed	Ratchet	Alliance	40	40	Briarthorn—Ironforge	Strahad Farsan		320	
Summon Felsteed	Ratchet	Alliance	40	40	Demisette Cloyce—Stormwind	Strahad Farsan		320	
Summon Felsteed	Ratchet	Horde	40	40	Kaal Soulreaper—Undercity	Strahad Farsan		320	
Summon Felsteed	Ratchet	Both	40	40	Strahad Farsan—Barrens	Strahad Farsan		320	
Volcanic Activity	Ratchet	Both	49	55	Liv Rizzlefix—Barrens Ratchet	Liv Rizzlefix		5650	85●

Red Cloud Mesa

Title	Location	Faction	Min Level	Con Level	Starter Location	Finisher	Prerequisite	Max XP	Cash Reward
The Hunt Begins	Red Cloud Mesa	Horde	1	2	Grull Hawkwind—Mulgore Camp Narache	Grull Hawkwind		170	
CHOICE OF: 1 Nomadic Belt or 1 Painted Chain Gloves									
The Hunt Continues	Red Cloud Mesa	Horde	1	3	Grull Hawkwind—Mulgore Camp Narache	Grull Hawkwind	The Hunt Begins	250	
CHOICE OF: 1 Nomadic Bracers or 1 Painted Chain Belt									
A Humble Task	Red Cloud Mesa	Horde	1	2	Chief Hawkwind—Mulgore Camp Narache	Greatmother Hawkwind	A Humble Task	85	17●
A Humble Task	Red Cloud Mesa	Horde	1	3	Greatmother Hawkwind—Mulgore Red Cloud Mesa	Chief Hawkwind		250	40●
Rites of the Earthmother	Red Cloud Mesa	Horde	1	3	Chief Hawkwind—Mulgore Camp Narache	Seer Graytongue	A Humble Task	250	
Rite of Strength	Red Cloud Mesa	Horde	1	4	Seer Graytongue—Mulgore Red Cloud Mesa	Chief Hawkwind	Rites of the Earthmother	450	
CHOICE OF: 1 Rock Mace or 1 Stone Tomahawk or 1 Whittling Knife or 1 Elder's Cane or 1 Brave's Axe									
Rites of the Earthmother	Red Cloud Mesa	Horde	1	5	Chief Hawkwind—Mulgore Camp Narache	Baine Bloodhoof	Rite of Strength	340	
The Battleboars	Red Cloud Mesa	Horde	1	4	Grull Hawkwind—Mulgore Camp Narache	Grull Hawkwind	The Hunt Continues	450	
REWARD: 1 Nomadic Vest, 10Tough Hunk of Bread									
Attack on Camp Narache	Red Cloud Mesa	Horde	1	4	Dirt-stained Map	Chief Hawkwind		360	
REWARD: 1 Thick Bark Buckler									
Earth Sapta	Red Cloud Mesa	Horde	4	4		Seer Ravenfeather	Call of Earth		
REWARD: 1 Earth Sapta									
Call of Earth	Red Cloud Mesa	Horde	4	4	Seer Ravenfeather—Mulgore Camp Narache	Seer Ravenfeather	Call of Earth	270	
Call of Earth	Red Cloud Mesa	Horde	4	4	Seer Ravenfeather—Mulgore Camp Narache	Minor Manifestation of Earth	Call of Earth	180	
Call of Earth	Red Cloud Mesa	Horde	4	4	Minor Manifestation of Earth—Mulgore	Seer Ravenfeather	Call of Earth	450	
REWARD: 1 Earth Totem									
A Task Unfinished	Red Cloud Mesa	Horde	1	5	Antur Fallow—Mulgore Red Cloud Mesa	Innkeeper Kauth		110	
CHOICE OF: 5 Tough Hunk of Bread or 5 Refreshing Spring Water									
Simple Note	Red Cloud Mesa	Horde	1	1	Grull Hawkwind—Mulgore Camp Narache	Harutt Thunderhorn	The Hunt Begins	40	
Etched Note	Red Cloud Mesa	Horde	1	1	Grull Hawkwind—Mulgore Camp Narache	Lanka Farshot	The Hunt Begins	40	
Rune-Inscribed Note	Red Cloud Mesa	Horde	1	1	Grull Hawkwind—Mulgore Camp Narache	Meela Dawnstrider	The Hunt Begins	40	
Verdant Note	Red Cloud Mesa	Horde	1	1	Grull Hawkwind—Mulgore Camp Narache	Gart Mistrunner	The Hunt Begins	40	
Break Sharptusk!	Red Cloud Mesa	Horde	3	5	Brave Windfeather—Mulgore Camp Narache	Brave Windfeather		675	
CHOICE OF: 1 Painted Chain Leggings or 1 Nomadic Gloves									
Welcome!	Red Cloud Mesa	Horde	1	1	Camp Narache Gift Voucher	Vorn Skyseer			
CHOICE OF: 1 Diablo Stone or 1 Panda Collar or 1 Zergling Leash									

Redridge Mountains

Title	Location	Faction	Min Level	Con Level	Starter Location	Finisher	Prerequisite	Max XP	Cash Reward
Tharil'zun	Redridge Mountains	Alliance	18	25	Marshal Marris—Redridge Lakeshire	Marshal Marris	Blackrock Menace	2550	
CHOICE OF: 1 Fire Hardened Buckler or 1 Orc Crusher									
Blackrock Menace	Redridge Mountains	Alliance	18	21	Marshal Marris—Redridge Lakeshire	Marshal Marris		1650	13●
An Unwelcome Guest	Redridge Mountains	Alliance	18	24	Martie Jainrose—Redridge Lakeshire	Martie Jainrose		1950	17●
REWARD: 1 Bouquet of Scarlet Begonias									
The Everstill Bridge	Redridge Mountains	Alliance	15	20	Foreman Oslow—Redridge Lakeshire	Foreman Oslow	The Lost Tools	1550	
CHOICE OF: 1 Smith's Trousers or 1 Bridgeworker's Gloves or 1 Riding Gloves									
Solomon's Law	Redridge Mountains	Alliance	17	23	Bailiff Conacher—Redridge Lakeshire	Bailiff Conacher		1850	15●
Redridge Goulash	Redridge Mountains	Alliance	15	18	Chef Breanna—Redridge Lakeshire	Chef Breanna		1350	10●
REWARD: 5 Redridge Goulash, 1Recipe: Redridge Goulash									
Shadow Magic	Redridge Mountains	Alliance	18	23	Marshal Marris—Redridge Lakeshire	Marshal Marris	Blackrock Menace	2300	30●
Dry Times	Redridge Mountains	Alliance	12	15	Barkeep Daniels—Redridge Lakeshire	Barkeep Daniels		1050	
REWARD: 1 Finely Woven Cloak, 1A Bulging Coin Purse									
The Price of Shoes	Redridge Mountains	Alliance	14	18	Verner Osgood—Redridge Lakeshire	Smith Argus		340	
Return to Verner	Redridge Mountains	Alliance	13	18	Smith Argus—Elwynn Goldshire	Verner Osgood	The Price of Shoes	675	5●
Messenger to Stormwind	Redridge Mountains	Alliance	14	14	Magistrate Solomon—Redridge Lakeshire	General Marcus Jonathan		490	
Messenger to Stormwind	Redridge Mountains	Alliance	14	14	General Marcus Jonathan—Stormwind	Magistrate Solomon	Messenger to Stormwind	250	1●50●
Underbelly Scales	Redridge Mountains	Alliance	14	18	Verner Osgood—Redridge Lakeshire	Verner Osgood	Return to Verner	1700	
CHOICE OF: 1 Black Whelp Boots or 1 Black Whelp Gloves									
A Baying of Gnolls	Redridge Mountains	Alliance	15	20		Verner Osgood	Return to Verner	1150	9●
The Lost Tools	Redridge Mountains	Alliance	15	16	Foreman Oslow—Redridge Lakeshire	Foreman Oslow		875	
REWARD: 2 Medium Armor Kit									
Howling in the Hills	Redridge Mountains	Alliance	15	25		Verner Osgood	A Baying of Gnolls	2000	
CHOICE OF: 1 Ring of Iron Will or 1 Gold Militia Boots									
Selling Fish	Redridge Mountains	Alliance	16	21	Dockmaster Baren—Redridge Lakeshire	Dockmaster Baren		1250	10●
REWARD: 1 Murloc Fin Soup, 1Recipe: Murloc Fin Soup, 5Fishliver Oil									
Blackrock Bounty	Redridge Mountains	Alliance	20	25	Guard Howe—Redridge Lakeshire	Guard Howe		2000	18●
A Free Lunch	Redridge Mountains	Alliance	12	15	Darcy—Redridge Lakeshire	Guard Parker		550	
Visit the Herbalist	Redridge Mountains	Alliance	12	15	Guard Parker—Redridge	Martie Jainrose	A Free Lunch	270	
Delivering Daffodils	Redridge Mountains	Alliance	12	15	Martie Jainrose—Redridge Lakeshire	Darcy	Visit the Herbalist	270	
REWARD: 10 Sauteed Sunfish									
Messenger to Westfall	Redridge Mountains	Alliance	14	14	Magistrate Solomon—Redridge Lakeshire	Gryan Stoutmantle	Messenger to Stormwind	490	
Messenger to Westfall	Redridge Mountains	Alliance	14	14	Gryan Stoutmantle—Westfall	Magistrate Solomon	Messenger to Westfall	250	1●50●
Messenger to Darkshire	Redridge Mountains	Alliance	18	18	Magistrate Solomon—Redridge Lakeshire	Lord Ello Ebonlocke	Messenger to Westfall	1000	
Messenger to Darkshire	Redridge Mountains	Alliance	18	18	Lord Ello Ebonlocke—Duskwood Darkshire	Magistrate Solomon	Messenger to Darkshire	340	2●50●
Murloc Poachers	Redridge Mountains	Alliance	20	20	Dockmaster Baren—Redridge Lakeshire	Dockmaster Baren		1550	
REWARD: 1 Dwarven Fishing Pole									
Wanted: Gath'Ilzogg	Redridge Mountains	Alliance	15	26	Wanted Poster—Redridge Lakeshire	Magistrate Solomon		2650	40●

Title	Location	Faction	Min Level	Con Level	Starter Location	Finisher	Prerequisite	Max XP	Cash Reward
Theocritus' Retrieval	Redridge Mountains	Alliance	15	23	Glowing Shadowhide Pendant	Theocritus		1400	12●
REWARD: 3 Restoring Balm									
Wanted: Lieutenant Fangore	Redridge Mountains	Alliance	15	26	Wanted Poster—Redridge Lakeshire	Magistrate Solomon		2650	40●
Missing In Action	Redridge Mountains	Alliance	19	25	Corporal Keeshan—Redridge	Marshal Marris		2550	
CHOICE OF: 1 Robe of Solomon or 1 Deputy Chain Coat or 1 Bone-studded Leather									
Encroaching Gnolls	Redridge Mountains	Alliance	11	16	Guard Parker—Redridge	Deputy Feldon		290	2●
Assessing the Threat	Redridge Mountains	Alliance	11	17	Deputy Feldon—Redridge Lakeshire	Deputy Feldon	Encroaching Gnolls	950	7●
Looking Further	Redridge Mountains	Alliance	20	22	Old Lion Statue—Redridge	An Empty Jar	A Watchful Eye	1300	
Morganth	Redridge Mountains	Alliance	20	27	Theocritus—Elwynn	Theocritus	Looking Further	2750	
REWARD: 1 Rose Mantle									
What Comes Around...	Redridge Mountains	Alliance	22	25	Guard Berton—Redridge Lakeshire	Guard Berton		2000	
CHOICE OF: 1 Lucine Longsword or 1 Hardened Root Staff									
Alther's Mill	Redridge Mountains	Alliance	16	20	Lucius—Redridge Lakeshire	Lucius	Redridge Rendezvous	1550	
REWARD: 1 Certificate of Thievery									
Hilary's Necklace	Redridge Mountains	Alliance	12	15	Shawn—Redridge Lakeshire	Hilary		1350	
The True Masters	Redridge Mountains	Alliance	48	54	Magistrate Solomon—Redridge Lakeshire	Highlord Bolvar Fordragon	The True Masters	4100	
The True Masters	Redridge Mountains	Alliance	48	54	Magistrate Solomon—Redridge Lakeshire	Marshal Maxwell	The True Masters	550	
The Horn of the Beast	Searing Gorge	Alliance	40	48	Margol's Horn	Mountaineer Pebblebitty		5450	
Proof of Deed	Searing Gorge	Alliance	40	48	Mountaineer Pebblebitty—Loch Modan	Curator Thorius	The Horn of the Beast	4400	1●40●
At Last!	Searing Gorge	Alliance	40	48	Curator Thorius—Ironforge	Mountaineer Pebblebitty	Proof of Deed	4400	
REWARD: 1 Key to Searing Gorge									
Suntara Stones	Searing Gorge	Alliance	40	48	Dorius Stonetender—Searing Gorge	Singed Letter		4400	
Suntara Stones	Searing Gorge	Alliance	40	48	Singed Letter	Curator Thorius	Suntara Stones	4400	1●40●
Dwarven Justice	Searing Gorge	Alliance	40	55	Curator Thorius—Ironforge	Dying Archaeologist	Suntara Stones	5650	
Release Them	Searing Gorge	Alliance	40	52	Dying Archaeologist—Searing Gorge	Altar of Suntara	Dwarven Justice	5100	
Prayer to Elune	Searing Gorge	Alliance	40	50	Zamael Lunthistle—Searing Gorge	Zamael Lunthistle		470	
Prayer to Elune	Searing Gorge	Alliance	40	50	Zamael Lunthistle—Searing Gorge	Astarii Starseeker	Prayer to Elune	5900	1●45●
CHOICE OF: 1 Kaylari Shoulders or 1 Runesteel Vambraces									
Shadoweaver	Searing Gorge	Both	40	50	Nilith Lokrav—Searing Gorge	Nilith Lokrav		4700	1●45●
REWARD: 1 Shadowy Bracers									
The Undermarket	Searing Gorge	Both	40	50	Nilith Lokrav—Searing Gorge	Nilith Lokrav	Shadoweaver	4700	
REWARD: 1 Shadowy Belt, 1Kovic's Trading Satchel									
The Undermarket	Searing Gorge	Both	40	50	Nilith Lokrav—Searing Gorge	Vizzklick	The Undermarket	4700	75●
REWARD: 1 Pattern: Shadoweave Mask									
Divine Retribution	Searing Gorge	Both	40	48	Kalaran Windblade—Searing Gorge	Kalaran Windblade		440	
The Flawless Flame	Searing Gorge	Both	40	48	Kalaran Windblade—Searing Gorge	Kalaran Windblade	Divine Retribution	4400	1●40●
Forging the Shaft	Searing Gorge	Both	40	48	Kalaran Windblade—Searing Gorge	Kalaran Windblade	The Flawless Flame	4400	1●40●
The Flame's Casing	Searing Gorge	Both	40	50	Kalaran Windblade—Searing Gorge	Kalaran Windblade	Forging the Shaft	4700	75●
The Torch of Retribution	Searing Gorge	Both	40	50	Kalaran Windblade—Searing Gorge	Kalaran Windblade	The Flame's Casing	470	
The Torch of Retribution	Searing Gorge	Both	40	50	Kalaran Windblade—Searing Gorge	Torch of Retribution	The Torch of Retribution	4700	
REWARD: 1 Torch of Retribution									
Squire Maltrake	Searing Gorge	Both	40	50	Kalaran Windblade—Searing Gorge	Squire Maltrake	The Torch of Retribution	470	
Set Them Ablaze!	Searing Gorge	Both	40	52	Squire Maltrake—Searing Gorge	Squire Maltrake	Squire Maltrake	7600	2●30●
CHOICE OF: 1 Dragonflight Leggings or 1 Drakefire Headguard or 1 Axe of the Ebon Drake									
Trinkets...	Searing Gorge	Both	40	50	Hoard of the Black Dragonflight—Searing Gorge	Hoard of the Black Dragonflight	Set Them Ablaze!	470	
REWARD: 1 Hoard of the Black Dragonflight									
Rise, Obsidion!	Searing Gorge	Alliance	40	52	Dying Archaeologist—Searing Gorge	Curator Thorius	Release Them	7600	
CHOICE OF: 1 Centurion Legplates or 1 Lordrec Helmet or 1 Ring of Fortitude									
Caught!	Searing Gorge	Both	43	45	Wooden Outhouse—Searing Gorge	Wooden Outhouse		3900	
Ledger from Tanaris	Searing Gorge	Both	43	46	Wooden Outhouse—Searing Gorge	Krinkle Goodsteel	Caught!	5050	
CHOICE OF: 1 Charged Lightning Rod or 1 Girdle of Reprisal									
The Key to Freedom	Searing Gorge	Both	43	47	Grimesilt Outhouse Key	Wooden Outhouse		5250	
Elemental Leatherworking	Searing Gorge	Alliance	40	55	Sarah Tanner—Searing Gorge	Sarah Tanner	Dragonscale Leatherworking	4200	
WANTED: Overseer Maltorius	Searing Gorge	Both	45	50	Wanted Poster—Searing Gorge	Lookout Captain Lolo Longstriker		4700	
CHOICE OF: 1 Seared Mail Vest or 1 Charred Leather Tunic									
Look at the Size of It!	Searing Gorge	Both	45	50	Chambermaid Pillaclencher's Pillow	Evonice Sootsmoker		4700	
REWARD: 1 Evonice's Landin' Pilla									
What the Flux?	Searing Gorge	Both	45	50	Master Smith Burninate—Searing Gorge	Master Smith Burninate		4700	75●
Curse These Fat Fingers	Searing Gorge	Both	45	49	Hansel Heavyhands—Searing Gorge	Hansel Heavyhands		4550	70●
REWARD: 1 Slagplate Gauntlets									
Fiery Menace!	Searing Gorge	Both	45	49	Hansel Heavyhands—Searing Gorge	Hansel Heavyhands		4550	70●
REWARD: 1 Seared Mail Girdle									
Incendosaurs? Whateverosaur is More Like It	Searing Gorge	Both	45	49	Hansel Heavyhands—Searing Gorge	Hansel Heavyhands		4550	70●
REWARD: 1 Luffa									
STOLEN: Smithing Tuyere and Lookout's Spyglass	Searing Gorge	Both	45	48	Wanted Poster—Searing Gorge	Taskmaster Scrange		4400	1●40●
CHOICE OF: 1 Slagplate Leggings or 1 Everwarm Handwraps									
JOB OPPORTUNITY: Culling the Competition	Searing Gorge	Both	45	48	Wanted Poster—Searing Gorge	Taskmaster Scrange		4400	2●10●
Restoring Fiery Flux Supplies via Kingsblood	Searing Gorge	Both	45	60		Master Smith Burninate	What the Flux?		
Gaining Acceptance	Searing Gorge	Both	45	60		Master Smith Burninate	What the Flux?		
Restoring Fiery Flux Supplies via Iron	Searing Gorge	Both	45	60		Master Smith Burninate	What the Flux?		
Restoring Fiery Flux Supplies via Heavy Leather	Searing Gorge	Both	45	60		Master Smith Burninate	What the Flux?		
The Balance of Nature	Shadowglen	Alliance	1	2	Conservator Ilthalaine—Teldrassil Shadowglen	Conservator Ilthalaine		170	35●
CHOICE OF: 1 Archery Training Gloves or 1 Stemleaf Bracers									
The Balance of Nature	Shadowglen	Alliance	1	3	Conservator Ilthalaine—Teldrassil Shadowglen	Conservator Ilthalaine	The Balance of Nature	250	50●
CHOICE OF: 1 Draped Cloak or 1 Blackened Leather Belt									
The Woodland Protector	Shadowglen	Alliance	1	1	Melithar Staghelm—Teldrassil Shadowglen	Tarindrella		40	
The Woodland Protector	Shadowglen	Alliance	1	3	Tarindrella—Teldrassil Shadowglen	Tarindrella	The Woodland Protector	250	
CHOICE OF: 1 Canopy Leggings or 1 Tracking Boots or 1 Viny Gloves REWARD: 3 Healing Herb									
Webwood Venom	Shadowglen	Alliance	3	4	Gilshalan Windwalker—Teldrassil Shadowglen	Gilshalan Windwalker		360	
CHOICE OF: 1 Thistlewood Maul or 1 Thistlewood Dagger or 1 Thistlewood Staff or 1 Thistlewood Blade									
Webwood Egg	Shadowglen	Alliance	1	5	Gilshalan Windwalker—Teldrassil Shadowglen	Gilshalan Windwalker	Webwood Venom	550	
CHOICE OF: 1 Woodland Shield or 1 Woodland Tunic or 1 Woodland Robes									
Tenaron's Summons	Shadowglen	Alliance	1	5	Melithar Staghelm—Teldrassil Shadowglen	Tenaron Stormgrip	Webwood Egg	45	
Crown of the Earth	Shadowglen	Alliance	1	5	Tenaron Stormgrip—Teldrassil Shadowglen	Tenaron Stormgrip	Tenaron's Summons	340	
Crown of the Earth	Shadowglen	Alliance	1	5	Tenaron Stormgrip—Teldrassil Shadowglen	Corithras Moonrage	Crown of the Earth	230	
Simple Sigil	Shadowglen	Alliance	1	1	Conservator Ilthalaine—Teldrassil Shadowglen	Alyissia	The Balance of Nature	40	
Etched Sigil	Shadowglen	Alliance	1	1	Conservator Ilthalaine—Teldrassil Shadowglen	Ayanna Everstride	The Balance of Nature	40	
Encrypted Sigil	Shadowglen	Alliance	1	1	Conservator Ilthalaine—Teldrassil Shadowglen	Frahun Shadewhisper	The Balance of Nature	40	
Hallowed Sigil	Shadowglen	Alliance	1	1	Conservator Ilthalaine—Teldrassil Shadowglen	Shanda	The Balance of Nature	40	
Verdant Sigil	Shadowglen	Alliance	1	1	Conservator Ilthalaine—Teldrassil Shadowglen	Mardant Strongoak	The Balance of Nature	40	
A Good Friend	Shadowglen	Alliance	2	4	Dirania Silvershine—Teldrassil Shadowglen	Iverron		270	
Welcome!	Shadowglen	Alliance	1	1	Shadowglen Gift Voucher	Orenthil Whisperwind			
CHOICE OF: 1 Diablo Stone or 1 Panda Collar or 1 Zergling Leash									
The Spirits of Southwind	Silithus	Both	54	55	Layo Starstrike—Silithus	Layo Starstrike	Wasteland	5650	
Hive in the Tower	Silithus	Both	54	57	Layo Starstrike—Silithus	Layo Starstrike	The Spirits of Southwind	6000	
Umber, Archivist	Silithus	Both	54	57	Layo Starstrike—Silithus	Umber	Hive in the Tower	3000	

Title	Location	Faction	Min Level	Con Level	Starter Location	Finisher	Prerequisite	Max XP	Cash Reward
Examine the Vessel	Silithus	Both	60	60	Vessel of Rebirth	Highlord Demitrian			
Thunderaan the Windseeker	Silithus	Both	60	60	Highlord Demitrian—Silithus	Highlord Demitrian	Examine the Vessel	10900	
Rise, Thunderfury!	Silithus	Both	60	60	Dormant Wind Kissed Blade	Highlord Demitrian	Thunderaan the Windseeker	10900	
REWARD: 1 Thunderfury, Blessed Blade of the Windseeker									
Taking Back Silithus	Silithus	Alliance	54	55	Cenarion Emissary Jademoon—Ironforge	Windcaller Proudhorn		2800	
Taking Back Silithus	Silithus	Horde	54	55	Cenarion Emissary Blackhoof—Orgrimmar	Windcaller Proudhorn		2800	
Deadly Desert Venom	Silithus	Both	54	55	Beetix Ficklespragg—Silithus	Beetix Ficklespragg		5650	85●
Noggle's Last Hope	Silithus	Both	54	57	Beetix Ficklespragg—Silithus	Beetix Ficklespragg	Deadly Desert Venom	6000	65●
CHOICE OF: 2 Major Healing Potion or 1 Major Mana Potion									
The Twilight Lexicon	Silithus	Both	54	60	Hermit Ortell—Silithus	Hermit Ortell	The Deserter	8300	90●
Securing the Supply Lines	Silithus	Both	54	55	Windcaller Proudhorn—Silithus	Windcaller Proudhorn		5650	85●
Stepping Up Security	Silithus	Both	54	57	Windcaller Proudhorn—Silithus	Windcaller Proudhorn	Securing the Supply Lines	6000	1● 70●
Noggle's Lost Satchel	Silithus	Both	54	58	Noggle Ficklespragg—Silithus	Noggle Ficklespragg	Noggle's Last Hope	6200	
CHOICE OF: 2 Elixir of the Mongoose 2 Elixir of the Sages									
Wanted - Deathclasp, Terror of the Sands	Silithus	Both	54	59	Wanted Poster—Silithus	Vish Kozus		8050	1● 80●
CHOICE OF: 1 Sandstrider's Mark or 1 Black Crystal Dagger									
The Twilight Mystery	Silithus	Both	54	58	Geologist Larksbane—Silithus	Geologist Larksbane		6200	90●
The Deserter	Silithus	Both	54	59	Geologist Larksbane—Silithus	Hermit Ortell	The Twilight Mystery	4800	90●
What Tomorrow Brings	Silithus	Both	60	60	Baristolth of the Shifting Sands—Silithus	Baristolth of the Shifting Sands		6600	
A Terrible Purpose	Silithus	Both	54	60	Hermit Ortell—Silithus	Commander Mar'alith	The Twilight Lexicon	6600	1● 80●
Only One May Rise	Silithus	Both	60	60	Baristolth of the Shifting Sands—Silithus	Baristolth of the Shifting Sands	What Tomorrow Brings	6600	
The Path of the Righteous	Silithus	Both	60	60	Baristolth of the Shifting Sands—Silithus	Baristolth of the Shifting Sands	Only One May Rise	6600	
REWARD: 1 Proxy of Nozdormu									
The Hand of the Righteous	Silithus	Both	60	60	Baristolth of the Shifting Sands—Silithus	Baristolth of the Shifting Sands	The Path of the Righteous	650	
REWARD: 1 Proxy of Nozdormu									
Anachronos	Silithus	Both	60	60	Baristolth of the Shifting Sands—Silithus	Anachronos	The Path of the Righteous		
Dearest Natalia	Silithus	Both	58	60	Commander Mar'alith—Silithus	Commander Mar'alith		6600	
Long Forgotten Memories	Silithus	Both	60	60	Anachronos—Tanaris	Crystalline Tear	Anachronos	6600	
Into The Maw of Madness	Silithus	Both	58	60	Commander Mar'alith—Silithus	Commander Mar'alith	Dearest Natalia	9950	2● 80●
REWARD: 1 Corrupted Blackwood Staff									
Desert Recipe	Silithus	Both	54	57	Calandrath—Silithus	Sandy Cookbook		3000	
Brann Bronzebeard's Lost Letter	Silithus	Both	58	60	Brann Bronzebeard's Lost Letter	Rutgar Glyphshaper		8300	
REWARD: 1 Brann's Trusty Pick									
Glyph Chasing	Silithus	Both	58	60	Rutgar Glyphshaper—Silithus	Rutgar Glyphshaper	Dearest Natalia	8800	2● 80●
Breaking the Code	Silithus	Both	58	60	Frankal Stonebridge—Silithus	Frankal Stonebridge	Dearest Natalia	8300	2● 70●
Sharing the Knowledge	Silithus	Both	54	57	Sandy Cookbook—Silithus	Calandrath	Desert Recipe	6000	85●
Unraveling the Mystery	Silithus	Both	58	60	Rutgar Glyphshaper—Silithus	Geologist Larksbane	Glyph Chasing	5300	
The Calling	Silithus	Both	58	60	Geologist Larksbane—Silithus	Geologist Larksbane	Unraveling the Mystery	9950	
Armaments of War	Silithus	Both	58	60		Geologist Larksbane	The Calling	7250	
REWARD: 1 Cenarion Reservist's Legplates, 1Crystal Encrusted Greaves									
Kitchen Assistance	Silithus	Both	54	57	Calandrath—Silithus	Calandrath	Sharing the Knowledge	3000	1● 70●
Secret Communication	Silithus	Both	57	60	Bor Wildmane—Silithus	Bor Wildmane		6600	1● 80●
Encrypted Twilight Texts	Silithus	Both	57	60		Bor Wildmane	Secret Communication		
Twilight Geolords	Silithus	Both	60	60	Huum Wildmane—Silithus Cenarion Hold Tauren	Huum Wildmane		6600	
Vyral the Vile	Silithus	Both	60	60	Huum Wildmane—Silithus Cenarion Hold Tauren	Huum Wildmane	Twilight Geolords	6600	90●
CHOICE OF: 1 Desert Wind Gauntlets or 1 Sunprism Pendant									
True Believers	Silithus	Both	54	59	Hermit Ortell—Silithus	Hermit Ortell	The Twilight Lexicon	6400	90●
Still Believing	Silithus	Both	54	59		Hermit Ortell	True Believers		45●
Aurel Goldleaf	Silithus	Both	60	60	Huum Wildmane—Silithus Cenarion Hold Tauren	Aurel Goldleaf		650	
Dukes of the Council	Silithus	Both	60	60	Aurel Goldleaf—Silithus Cenarion Hold	Aurel Goldleaf		6600	
REWARD: 1 Twilight Cultist Medallion of Station									
Medallion of Station	Silithus	Both	60	60		Aurel Goldleaf	Dukes of the Council	6600	
REWARD: 1 Twilight Cultist Medallion of Station									
Lords of the Council	Silithus	Both	60	60	Aurel Goldleaf—Silithus Cenarion Hold	Aurel Goldleaf		6600	
REWARD: 1 Twilight Cultist Ring of Lordship									
Twilight Ring of Lordship	Silithus	Both	60	60		Aurel Goldleaf	Lords of the Council		
REWARD: 1 Twilight Cultist Ring of Lordship									
Goldleaf's Discovery	Silithus	Both	60	60	Huum Wildmane—Silithus Cenarion Hold Tauren	Aurel Goldleaf		650	
Signet of the Dukes	Silithus	Both	60	60	Bor Wildmane—Silithus	Bor Wildmane	Dukes of the Council	8800	1● 85●
REWARD: 1 Sack of Spoils									
Bor Wildmane	Silithus	Both	60	60	Aurel Goldleaf—Silithus Cenarion Hold	Bor Wildmane	Dukes of the Council	650	
Bor Wishes to Speak	Silithus	Both	60	60	Aurel Goldleaf—Silithus Cenarion Hold	Bor Wildmane	Lords of the Council	650	
Scepter of the Council	Silithus	Both	60	60	Bor Wildmane—Silithus	Bor Wildmane	Lords of the Council	10550	1● 85●
REWARD: 1 Chest of Spoils									
Abyssal Contacts	Silithus	Both	60	60	Bor Wildmane—Silithus	Bor Wildmane		6600	90●
REWARD: 1 Bag of Spoils									
Abyssal Crests	Silithus	Both	60	60		Bor Wildmane	Abyssal Contacts		
REWARD: 1 Bag of Spoils									
Abyssal Signets	Silithus	Both	60	60		Bor Wildmane	Signet of the Dukes		
REWARD: 1 Sack of Spoils									
Abyssal Scepters	Silithus	Both	60	60		Bor Wildmane	Scepter of the Council	3500	
REWARD: 1 Chest of Spoils									
Armaments of War	Silithus	Both	58	60		Geologist Larksbane	The Calling	6600	
REWARD: 1 Cenarion Reservist's Legplates, 1Crystal Lined Greaves									
Armaments of War	Silithus	Both	58	60		Geologist Larksbane	The Calling	6600	
REWARD: 1 Cenarion Reservist's Legguards, 1Desertstalkers's Gauntlets									
Armaments of War	Silithus	Both	58	60		Geologist Larksbane	The Calling	6600	
REWARD: 1 Cenarion Reservist's Leggings, 1Dunestalker's Boots									
Armaments of War	Silithus	Both	58	60		Geologist Larksbane	The Calling	6600	
REWARD: 1 Cenarion Reservist's Pants, 1Desert Bloom Gloves									
Armaments of War	Silithus	Both	58	60		Geologist Larksbane	The Calling	6600	
REWARD: 1 Cenarion Reservist's Legguards, 1Wastewalker's Gauntlets									
Armaments of War	Silithus	Both	58	60		Geologist Larksbane	The Calling	6600	
REWARD: 1 Cenarion Reservist's Pants, 1Sandworm Skin Gloves									
Armaments of War	Silithus	Both	58	60		Geologist Larksbane	The Calling	6600	
REWARD: 1 Cenarion Reservist's Leggings, 1Sandstorm Boots									
Bandages for the Field	Silithus	Alliance	60	60	Logistics Task Briefing X	Windcaller Proudhorn		650	
REWARD: 1 Cenarion Logistics Badge, 1Followup Logistics Assignment									
Desert Survival Kits	Silithus	Alliance	60	60	Logistics Task Briefing I	Calandrath		650	
REWARD: 1 Cenarion Logistics Badge, 1Logistics Assignment									
Twilight Battle Orders	Silithus	Both	60	60	Tactical Task Briefing X	Commander Mar'alith		650	
REWARD: 1 Cenarion Tactical Badge, 1Tactical Assignment									
Target: Hive'Ashi Stingers	Silithus	Both	60	60	Combat Task Briefing XII	Commander Mar'alith		650	
REWARD: 1 Cenarion Combat Badge									
Target: Hive'Ashi Workers	Silithus	Both	60	60	Combat Task Briefing III	Commander Mar'alith		650	
REWARD: 1 Cenarion Combat Badge									
Field Duty	Silithus	Alliance	60	60	Windcaller Kaldon—Silithus	Windcaller Kaldon			

Title	Location	Faction	Min Level	Con Level	Starter Location	Finisher	Prerequisite	Max XP	Cash Reward
CHOICE OF: 1 Combat Assignment or 1 Logistics Assignment or 1 Tactical Assignment									
Field Duty Papers	Silithus	Alliance	60	60		Captain Blackanvil			
REWARD: 1 Signed Field Duty Papers									
A Pawn on the Eternal Board	Silithus	Both	60	60	Crystalline Tear—Silithus	Anachronos	Long Forgotten Memories	6600	
Hive'Zora Scout Report	Silithus	Both	60	60	Tactical Task Briefing VI	Windcaller Proudhorn		650	
REWARD: 1 Cenarion Tactical Badge, 1Followup Tactical Assignment									
Hoary Templar	Silithus	Both	60	60	Tactical Task Briefing IV	Bor Wildmane		650	
REWARD: 1 Cenarion Tactical Badge, 1Tactical Assignment									
Earthen Templar	Silithus	Both	60	60	Tactical Task Briefing III	Bor Wildmane		650	
REWARD: 1 Cenarion Tactical Badge, 1Followup Tactical Assignment									
Crimson Templar	Silithus	Both	60	60	Tactical Task Briefing II	Bor Wildmane		650	
REWARD: 1 Cenarion Tactical Badge, 1Tactical Assignment									
The Four Dukes	Silithus	Both	60	60	Tactical Task Briefing V	Commander Mar'alith		650	
REWARD: 1 Mark of Cenarius									
Target: Hive'Zora Hive Sisters	Silithus	Both	60	60	Combat Task Briefing V	Commander Mar'alith		650	
REWARD: 1 Cenarion Combat Badge									
Boots for the Guard	Silithus	Alliance	60	60	Logistics Task Briefing II	Vish Kozus		650	
REWARD: 1 Cenarion Logistics Badge, 1Logistics Assignment									
Grinding Stones for the Guard	Silithus	Alliance	60	60	Logistics Task Briefing III	Vish Kozus		650	
REWARD: 1 Cenarion Logistics Badge, 1Logistics Assignment									
Volunteer's Battlegear	Silithus	Both	60	60	Vargus—Silithus	Vargus	Cenarion Battlegear	3300	
CHOICE OF: 1 Gloves of Earthen Power or 1 Band of Earthen Wrath or 1 Earthweave Cloak									
The Charge of the Dragonflights	Silithus	Both	60	60		Anachronos	A Pawn on the Eternal Board	650	
Veteran's Battlegear	Silithus	Both	60	60	Vargus—Silithus	Vargus	Cenarion Battlegear	3300	
CHOICE OF: 1 Grace of Earth or 1 Band of Earthen Might or 1 Earthpower Vest									
Champion's Battlegear	Silithus	Both	60	60	Vargus—Silithus	Vargus	Cenarion Battlegear		
CHOICE OF: 1 Fist of Cenarius or 1 Wrath of Cenarius or 1 Earthstrike									
Stalwart's Battlegear	Silithus	Both	60	60	Vargus—Silithus	Vargus	Cenarion Battlegear	3300	
CHOICE OF: 1 Deeprock Bracers or 1 Earthcalm Orb or 1 Rockfury Bracers or 1 Might of Cenarius									
Target: Hive'Zora Tunnelers	Silithus	Both	60	60	Combat Task Briefing VII	Commander Mar'alith		650	
REWARD: 1 Cenarion Combat Badge									
Field Duty	Silithus	Horde	60	60	Windcaller Kaldon—Silithus	Windcaller Kaldon			
CHOICE OF: 1 Combat Assignment or 1 Logistics Assignment or 1 Tactical Assignment									
Field Duty Papers	Silithus	Horde	60	60		Krug Skullsplit			
REWARD: 1 Signed Field Duty Papers									
Azure Templar	Silithus	Both	60	60	Tactical Task Briefing I	Bor Wildmane		650	
REWARD: 1 Cenarion Tactical Badge, 1Followup Tactical Assignment									
Hive'Regal Scout Report	Silithus	Both	60	60	Tactical Task Briefing VII	Windcaller Proudhorn		650	
REWARD: 1 Cenarion Tactical Badge, 1Followup Tactical Assignment									
Hive'Ashi Scout Report	Silithus	Both	60	60	Tactical Task Briefing VIII	Windcaller Proudhorn		650	
REWARD: 1 Cenarion Tactical Badge, 1Tactical Assignment									
Twilight Marauders	Silithus	Both	60	60	Tactical Task Briefing IX	Windcaller Proudhorn		650	
REWARD: 1 Cenarion Tactical Badge, 1Followup Tactical Assignment									
Target: Hive'Ashi Defenders	Silithus	Both	60	60	Combat Task Briefing I	Commander Mar'alith		650	
REWARD: 1 Cenarion Combat Badge									
Target: Hive'Ashi Sandstalkers	Silithus	Both	60	60	Combat Task Briefing II	Commander Mar'alith		650	
REWARD: 1 Cenarion Combat Badge									
Target: Hive'Zora Waywatchers	Silithus	Both	60	60	Combat Task Briefing VI	Commander Mar'alith		650	
REWARD: 1 Cenarion Combat Badge									
Target: Hive'Zora Reavers	Silithus	Both	60	60	Combat Task Briefing IV	Commander Mar'alith		650	
REWARD: 1 Cenarion Combat Badge									
Target: Hive'Regal Ambushers	Silithus	Both	60	60	Combat Task Briefing VIII	Commander Mar'alith		650	
REWARD: 1 Cenarion Combat Badge									
Target: Hive'Regal Spitfires	Silithus	Both	60	60	Combat Task Briefing IX	Commander Mar'alith		650	
REWARD: 1 Cenarion Combat Badge									
Target: Hive'Regal Slavemakers	Silithus	Both	60	60	Combat Task Briefing X	Commander Mar'alith		650	
REWARD: 1 Cenarion Combat Badge									
Target: Hive'Regal Burrowers	Silithus	Both	60	60	Combat Task Briefing XI	Commander Mar'alith		650	
REWARD: 1 Cenarion Combat Badge									
The Ironforge Brigade Needs Explosives!	Silithus	Alliance	60	60	Logistics Task Briefing IV	Arcanist Nozzlespring		650	
REWARD: 1 Cenarion Logistics Badge, 1Followup Logistics Assignment									
Scrying Materials	Silithus	Alliance	60	60	Logistics Task Briefing V	Geologist Larksbane		650	
REWARD: 1 Cenarion Logistics Badge, 1Followup Logistics Assignment									
Armor Kits for the Field	Silithus	Alliance	60	60	Logistics Task Briefing VII	Janela Stouthammer		650	
REWARD: 1 Cenarion Logistics Badge, 1Followup Logistics Assignment									
Arms for the Field	Silithus	Alliance	60	60	Logistics Task Briefing VI	Janela Stouthammer		650	
REWARD: 1 Cenarion Logistics Badge, 1Followup Logistics Assignment									
Uniform Supplies	Silithus	Alliance	60	60	Logistics Task Briefing VIII	Windcaller Proudhorn		650	
REWARD: 1 Cenarion Logistics Badge, 1Logistics Assignment									
Extraordinary Materials	Silithus	Alliance	60	60	Logistics Task Briefing IX	Vargus		650	
REWARD: 1 Cenarion Logistics Badge, 1Logistics Assignment									
The Orgrimmar Legion Needs Mojo!	Silithus	Horde	60	60	Logistics Task Briefing IV	Shadow Priestess Shai		650	
REWARD: 1 Cenarion Logistics Badge, 1Followup Logistics Assignment									
Arms for the Field	Silithus	Horde	60	60	Logistics Task Briefing VI	Merok Longstride		650	
REWARD: 1 Cenarion Logistics Badge, 1Followup Logistics Assignment									
Armor Kits for the Field	Silithus	Horde	60	60	Logistics Task Briefing VII	Merok Longstride		650	
REWARD: 1 Cenarion Logistics Badge, 1Followup Logistics Assignment									
Cenarion Battlegear	Silithus	Both	60	60	Windcaller Kaldon—Silithus	Vargus			
Desert Survival Kits	Silithus	Horde	60	60	Logistics Task Briefing I	Calandrath		650	
REWARD: 1 Cenarion Logistics Badge, 1Logistics Assignment									
Boots for the Guard	Silithus	Horde	60	60	Logistics Task Briefing II	Vish Kozus		650	
REWARD: 1 Cenarion Logistics Badge, 1Logistics Assignment									
Grinding Stones for the Guard	Silithus	Horde	60	60	Logistics Task Briefing III	Vish Kozus		650	
REWARD: 1 Cenarion Logistics Badge, 1Logistics Assignment									
Scrying Materials	Silithus	Horde	60	60	Logistics Task Briefing V	Geologist Larksbane		650	
REWARD: 1 Cenarion Logistics Badge, 1Followup Logistics Assignment									
Uniform Supplies	Silithus	Horde	60	60	Logistics Task Briefing VIII	Windcaller Proudhorn		650	
REWARD: 1 Cenarion Logistics Badge, 1Logistics Assignment									
Extraordinary Materials	Silithus	Horde	60	60	Logistics Task Briefing IX	Vargus		650	
REWARD: 1 Cenarion Logistics Badge, 1Logistics Assignment									
Bandages for the Field	Silithus	Horde	60	60	Logistics Task Briefing X	Windcaller Proudhorn		650	
REWARD: 1 Cenarion Logistics Badge, 1Followup Logistics Assignment									
The Ultimate Deception	Silithus	Both	60	60	Logistics Task Briefing XI	Aurel Goldleaf		650	
REWARD: 1 Mark of Remulos									
Secrets of the Colossus - Ashi	Silithus	Both	51	60		Oglethorpe Obnoticus		9950	2 70
REWARD: 1 Colossal Bag of Loot									
Secrets of the Colossus - Regal	Silithus	Both	51	60		Overseer Oilfist		9950	2 70

Silithus cont'd

Title	Location	Faction	Min Level	Con Level	Starter Location	Finisher	Prerequisite	Max XP	Cash Reward
REWARD: 1 Colossal Bag of Loot									
Secrets of the Colossus - Zora	Silithus	Both	51	60		Lord Maxwell Tyrosus		9950	2●70●
REWARD: 1 Colossal Bag of Loot									
The Perfect Poison	Silithus	Both	60	60	Dirk Thunderwood—Silithus Ravenholdt	Dirk Thunderwood		6600	
CHOICE OF: 1 Ravenholdt Slicer or 1 Shivsprocket's Shiv or 1 The Thunderwood Poker or 1 Doomulus Prime or 1 Fahrad's Reloading Repeater or 1 Simone's Cultivating Hammer									
A Humble Offering	Silithus	Both	58	60	Aurel Goldleaf—Silithus Cenarion Hold	Aurel Goldleaf			
REWARD: 1 Band of Cenarius									
Allegiance to Cenarion Circle	Silithus	Both	60	60		Windcaller Kaldon			

Silverpine

Title	Location	Faction	Min Level	Con Level	Starter Location	Finisher	Prerequisite	Max XP	Cash Reward
Arugal's Folly	Silverpine	Horde	9	15	Dalar Dawnweaver—Silverpine The Sepulcher	Dalar Dawnweaver	Arugal's Folly	1350	
CHOICE OF: 1 Logsplitter or 1 Bonegrinding Pestle or 1 Cinder Wand									
Prove Your Worth	Silverpine	Horde	9	10	Dalar Dawnweaver—Silverpine The Sepulcher	Dalar Dawnweaver		850	3●50●
Arugal's Folly	Silverpine	Horde	9	11	Dalar Dawnweaver—Silverpine The Sepulcher	Dalar Dawnweaver	Prove Your Worth	875	
Arugal's Folly	Silverpine	Horde	9	14	Dalar Dawnweaver—Silverpine The Sepulcher	Dalar Dawnweaver	Arugal's Folly	975	6●
Arugal's Folly	Silverpine	Horde	9	15	Dalar Dawnweaver—Silverpine The Sepulcher	Dalar Dawnweaver	Arugal's Folly	1050	7●
Ivar the Foul	Silverpine	Horde	10	12	Rane Yorick—Silverpine	Rane Yorick	Return to Quinn	675	3●50●
CHOICE OF: 1 Quilted Bracers or 1 Weathered Belt									
Lost Deathstalkers	Silverpine	Horde	10	12	High Executor Hadrec—Silverpine The Sepulcher	Rane Yorick	Wild Hearts		
Wild Hearts	Silverpine	Horde	10	11	Rane Yorick—Silverpine	Apothecary Renferrel		440	
REWARD: 1 Recipe: Discolored Healing Potion, 1Discolored Healing Potion									
Return to Quinn	Silverpine	Horde	10	11	Apothecary Renferrel—Silverpine The Sepulcher	Quinn Yorick	Wild Hearts	650	
Escorting Erland	Silverpine	Horde	10	11	Deathstalker Erland—Silverpine	Rane Yorick		875	
REWARD: 1 Deathstalker Shortsword									
The Dead Fields	Silverpine	Horde	10	14	High Executor Hadrec—Silverpine The Sepulcher	High Executor Hadrec		975	6●
REWARD: 1 Reconnaissance Boots									
The Decrepit Ferry	Silverpine	Horde	10	16	High Executor Hadrec—Silverpine The Sepulcher	Corpse Laden Boat	The Dead Fields	875	
Rot Hide Clues	Silverpine	Horde	10	16	Corpse Laden Boat—Silverpine The Sepulcher	High Executor Hadrec	The Decrepit Ferry	290	
The Engraved Ring	Silverpine	Horde	10	16	High Executor Hadrec—Silverpine The Sepulcher	Magistrate Sevren	Rot Hide Clues	575	
Raleigh and the Undercity	Silverpine	Horde	10	16	Magistrate Sevren—Tirisfal Glades Brill	Raleigh Andrean	The Engraved Ring	575	
Assault on Fenris Isle	Silverpine	Horde	10	24	High Executor Hadrec—Silverpine The Sepulcher	High Executor Hadrec	Report to Hadrec	1950	
CHOICE OF: 1 High Robe of the Adjudicator or 1 Talonstrike									
Rot Hide Ichor	Silverpine	Horde	10	17	High Executor Hadrec—Silverpine The Sepulcher	Apothecary Renferrel	Rot Hide Clues	1250	9●
Rot Hide Origins	Silverpine	Horde	10	17	Apothecary Renferrel—Silverpine The Sepulcher	Bethor Iceshard	Rot Hide Ichor	320	
Thule Ravenclaw	Silverpine	Horde	10	16	Bethor Iceshard—Undercity	Apothecary Renferrel	Rot Hide Origins	290	
REWARD: 1 Bethor's Potion									
A Recipe For Death	Silverpine	Horde	9	12	Apothecary Renferrel—Silverpine The Sepulcher	Master Apothecary Faranell		900	5●
REWARD: 20 Senggin Root									
Report to Hadrec	Silverpine	Horde	10	16	Apothecary Renferrel—Silverpine The Sepulcher	High Executor Hadrec	Thule Ravenclaw	575	
CHOICE OF: 5 Coarse Weightstone or 5 Coarse Sharpening Stone REWARD: 1 Medium Armor Kit									
The Deathstalkers' Report	Silverpine	Horde	10	11	Rane Yorick—Silverpine	High Executor Hadrec	Escorting Erland	440	2●
A Recipe For Death	Silverpine	Horde	9	15	Master Apothecary Faranell—Undercity	Apothecary Renferrel	A Recipe For Death	1350	14●
A Recipe For Death	Silverpine	Horde	9	18	Apothecary Renferrel—Silverpine The Sepulcher	Master Apothecary Faranell	A Recipe For Death	2050	
CHOICE OF: 1 Nightglow Concoction or 1 Acidproof Cloak REWARD: 1 Elixir of Minor Fortitude, 1Swiftness Potion									
Pyrewood Ambush	Silverpine	Horde	12	15	Deathstalker Faerleia—Silverpine	Deathstalker Faerleia		1350	14●
CHOICE OF: 1 Faerleia's Shield or 1 Stretched Leather Trousers or 1 Mystic Shawl									
Resting in Pieces	Silverpine	Horde	12	17	A Talking Head	Shallow Grave		625	
The Hidden Niche	Silverpine	Horde	12	18	Shallow Grave—Silverpine The Sepulcher	Dusty Shelf	Resting in Pieces	675	5●
Border Crossings	Silverpine	Horde	10	14	Shadow Priest Allister—Silverpine The Sepulcher	Dalaran Crate		975	
Maps and Runes	Silverpine	Both	10	14	Dalaran Crate—Silverpine The Sepulcher	Shadow Priest Allister	Border Crossings	750	5●
Ambermill Investigations	Silverpine	Horde	10	16	Shadow Priest Allister—Silverpine The Sepulcher	Shadow Priest Allister	Dalaran's Intentions	1150	8●
The Weaver	Silverpine	Horde	10	22	Shadow Priest Allister—Silverpine The Sepulcher	Shadow Priest Allister	Ambermill Investigations	1750	
CHOICE OF: 1 Ceranium Rod or 1 Camouflaged Tunic									
Dalar's Analysis	Silverpine	Horde	10	14	Shadow Priest Allister—Silverpine The Sepulcher	Dalar Dawnweaver	Maps and Runes	100	
Dalaran's Intentions	Silverpine	Horde	10	14	Dalar Dawnweaver—Silverpine The Sepulcher	Shadow Priest Allister	Dalar's Analysis	100	
Wand to Bethor	Silverpine	Horde	12	18	Dusty Shelf—Silverpine	Bethor Iceshard	The Hidden Niche	1700	
CHOICE OF: 1 Stamped Trousers or 1 Rugged Mail Gloves or 1 Serrated Knife									
Journey to Hillsbrad Foothills	Silverpine	Horde	19	20	Apothecary Renferrel—Silverpine The Sepulcher	Apothecary Lydon		1150	9●
Beren's Peril	Silverpine	Horde	16	21	Shadow Priest Allister—Silverpine The Sepulcher	Shadow Priest Allister		1250	
REWARD: 1 Wand of Decay									
Arugal Must Die	Silverpine	Horde	18	27	Dalar Dawnweaver—Silverpine The Sepulcher	Dalar Dawnweaver		3300	
REWARD: 1 Seal of Sylvanas									
Sample for Helbrim	Silverpine	Horde	10	15	Apothecary Zinge—Undercity	Apothecary Helbrim	Zinge's Delivery	1050	
CHOICE OF: 1 Brewer's Gloves or 1 Long Draping Cape									
Zinge's Delivery	Silverpine	Horde	10	15	Apothecary Renferrel—Silverpine The Sepulcher	Apothecary Zinge	Speak with Renferrel	110	
Speak with Renferrel	Silverpine	Horde	10	12	High Executor Hadrec—Silverpine The Sepulcher	Apothecary Renferrel	The Deathstalkers' Report	90	
Supplying the Sepulcher	Silverpine	Horde	10	10	Deathguard Podrig—Silverpine The Sepulcher	Karos Razok		210	
Michael Garrett	Silverpine	Horde	10	10	Gordon Wendham—Undercity	Michael Garrett	Ride to the Undercity	210	
Ride to the Undercity	Silverpine	Horde	10	10	Karos Razok—Silverpine The Sepulcher	Gordon Wendham	Supplying the Sepulcher	420	
Return to Podrig	Silverpine	Horde	10	10	Michael Garrett—Undercity	Deathguard Podrig	Michael Garrett	1050	3●50●

Stonetalon Mountains

Title	Location	Faction	Min Level	Con Level	Starter Location	Finisher	Prerequisite	Max XP	Cash Reward
Reclaiming the Charred Vale	Stonetalon Mountains	Alliance	20	27	Keeper Albagorm—Stonetalon	Keeper Albagorm		2200	
Jin'Zil's Forest Magic	Stonetalon Mountains	Horde	20	26	Witch Doctor Jin'Zil—Stonetalon Malaka'jin	Witch Doctor Jin'Zil		2100	
CHOICE OF: 1 Voodoo Mantle or 1 Hexed Bracers									
Reclaiming the Charred Vale	Stonetalon Mountains	Alliance	20	27	Keeper Albagorm—Stonetalon	Falfindel Waywarder	Reclaiming the Charred Vale	2200	
CHOICE OF: 1 Tempered Bracers or 1 Constable Buckler									
Goblin Invaders	Stonetalon Mountains	Horde	13	19	Seereth Stonebreak—The Barrens	Seereth Stonebreak		1450	11●
The Elder Crone	Stonetalon Mountains	Horde	13	18	Seereth Stonebreak—The Barrens	Magatha Grimtotem	Goblin Invaders	675	
Shredding Machines	Stonetalon Mountains	Horde	13	23	Seereth Stonebreak—The Barrens	Seereth Stonebreak	Goblin Invaders	1850	12●50●
On Guard in Stonetalon	Stonetalon Mountains	Alliance	17	21	Sentinel Thenysil—Ashenvale	Kaela Shadowspear		825	
A Gnome's Respite	Stonetalon Mountains	Alliance	17	21	Gaxim Rustfizzle—Stonetalon Webwinder Path	Gaxim Rustfizzle	On Guard in Stonetalon	1650	
An Old Colleague	Stonetalon Mountains	Alliance	17	21	Gaxim Rustfizzle—Stonetalon Webwinder Path	Lomac Gearstrip	A Gnome's Respite	825	
Ineptitude + Chemicals = Fun	Stonetalon Mountains	Alliance	17	21	Lomac Gearstrip—Ironforge	Lomac Gearstrip	An Old Colleague	1650	
Ineptitude + Chemicals = Fun	Stonetalon Mountains	Alliance	17	21	Lomac Gearstrip—Ironforge	Gaxim Rustfizzle	Ineptitude + Chemicals = Fun	825	
A Scroll from Mauren	Stonetalon Mountains	Alliance	17	21	Gaxim Rustfizzle—Stonetalon Webwinder Path	Collin Mauren	A Gnome's Respite	825	
Devils in Westfall	Stonetalon Mountains	Alliance	17	21	Collin Mauren—Stormwind	Collin Mauren	A Scroll from Mauren	1650	
Special Delivery for Gaxim	Stonetalon Mountains	Alliance	17	21	Collin Mauren—Stormwind	Gaxim Rustfizzle	Devils in Westfall	850	
Retrieval for Mauren	Stonetalon Mountains	Alliance	17	26	Collin Mauren—Stormwind	Collin Mauren		2100	
REWARD: 1 Spellcrafter Wand									
Covert Ops - Alpha	Stonetalon Mountains	Alliance	17	22	Gaxim Rustfizzle—Stonetalon Webwinder Path	Gaxim Rustfizzle	Special Delivery for Gaxim	2200	
Covert Ops - Beta	Stonetalon Mountains	Alliance	17	22	Gaxim Rustfizzle—Stonetalon Webwinder Path	Gaxim Rustfizzle	Special Delivery for Gaxim	2200	
Reception from Tyrande	Stonetalon Mountains	Alliance	17	28	Sentinel Thenysil—Ashenvale	Tyrande Whisperwind	Update for Sentinel Thenysil	3400	
CHOICE OF: 1 Efflorescent Robe or 1 Grizzly Tunic or 1 Wildwood Chain REWARD: 1 Band of Elven Grace									
Update for Sentinel Thenysil	Stonetalon Mountains	Alliance	17	22	Kaela Shadowspear—Stonetalon Webwinder Path	Sentinel Thenysil	Enraged Spirits	875	
Enraged Spirits	Stonetalon Mountains	Alliance	20	26	Kaela Shadowspear—Stonetalon Webwinder Path	Kaela Shadowspear	Kaela's Update	2100	20●
Wounded Ancients	Stonetalon Mountains	Alliance	22	28	Kaela Shadowspear—Stonetalon Webwinder Path	Kaela Shadowspear	Kaela's Update	2300	25●
On Guard in Stonetalon	Stonetalon Mountains	Alliance	17	21	Kaela Shadowspear—Stonetalon Webwinder Path	Gaxim Rustfizzle	On Guard in Stonetalon	170	
Cenarius' Legacy	Stonetalon Mountains	Horde	20	25	Braelyn Firehand—Stonetalon Stonetalon Mountains	Braelyn Firehand		1500	
Ordanus	Stonetalon Mountains	Horde	20	29	Braelyn Firehand—Stonetalon Stonetalon Mountains	Braelyn Firehand	Cenarius' Legacy	2350	
The Den	Stonetalon Mountains	Horde	20	29	Braelyn Firehand—Stonetalon Stonetalon Mountains	Talon Den Hoard	Ordanus	2950	

Title	Location	Faction	Min Level	Con Level	Starter Location	Finisher	Prerequisite	Max XP	Cash Reward
REWARD: 1 Sacred Band, 1Panther Armor, 1Juggernaut Leggings									
Gerenzo's Orders	Stonetalon Mountains	Both	17	22	Piznik—Stonetalon Windshear Mine	Piznik		2200	
Kaela's Update	Stonetalon Mountains	Alliance	17	22	Gaxim Rustfizzle—Stonetalon Webwinder Path	Kaela Shadowspear	Covert Ops - Alpha	180	
Gerenzo's Orders	Stonetalon Mountains	Both	17	22	Piznik—Stonetalon Windshear Mine	Ziz Fizziks	Gerenzo's Orders	1300	
REWARD: 1 Dredge Boots									
Super Reaper 6000	Stonetalon Mountains	Both	16	21	Ziz Fizziks—Stonetalon Windshear Crag	Ziz Fizziks		1650	
Further Instructions	Stonetalon Mountains	Both	16	21	Ziz Fizziks—Stonetalon Windshear Crag	Sputtervalve	Super Reaper 6000	825	
Gerenzo Wrenchwhistle	Stonetalon Mountains	Both	16	27	Ziz Fizziks—Stonetalon Windshear Crag	Ziz Fizziks	Further Instructions	2200	10●
CHOICE OF: 1 Engineer's Cloak or 1 Draftsman Boots									
Pridewings of Stonetalon	Stonetalon Mountains	Alliance	18	21	Shindrell Swiftfire—Ashenvale Astranaar	Shindrell Swiftfire	The Zoram Strand	1650	13●
Calling in the Reserves	Stonetalon Mountains	Horde	23	28	Maggran Earthbinder—Stonetalon Mountain	Grish Longrunner		1150	12●
Harpies Threaten	Stonetalon Mountains	Horde	18	26	Maggran Earthbinder—Stonetalon Mountain	Maggran Earthbinder		2100	20●
Bloodfury Bloodline	Stonetalon Mountains	Horde	18	26	Maggran Earthbinder—Stonetalon Mountain	Maggran Earthbinder	Harpies Threaten	2100	
CHOICE OF: 1 Spritekin Cloak or 1 Screecher Belt									
Arachnophobia	Stonetalon Mountains	Horde	15	21	Wanted Poster—Besseleth	Maggran Earthbinder		1650	
CHOICE OF: 1 Claystone Shortsword or 1 Clear Crystal Rod									
Cycle of Rebirth	Stonetalon Mountains	Horde	17	23	Tammra Windfield—Stonetalon Mountain	Tammra Windfield		1400	
New Life	Stonetalon Mountains	Horde	17	25	Tammra Windfield—Stonetalon Mountain	Tammra Windfield	Cycle of Rebirth	2000	
CHOICE OF: 1 Windseeker Boots or 1 Sandspire Gloves									
Elemental War	Stonetalon Mountains	Horde	19	25	Tsunaman—Stonetalon Mountain	Tsunaman		2000	
Kaya's Alive	Stonetalon Mountains	Horde	12	18	Makaba Flathoof—Stonetalon	Tammra Windfield	Protect Kaya	1000	
Boulderslide Ravine	Stonetalon Mountains	Horde	14	18	Mor'rogal—Stonetalon Mountain	Mor'rogal		1350	
Blood Feeders	Stonetalon Mountains	Horde	13	19	Xen'Zilla—Stonetalon	Xen'Zilla		1450	11●
Earthen Arise	Stonetalon Mountains	Horde	14	20	Mor'rogal—Stonetalon Mountain	Mor'rogal	Boulderslide Ravine	1550	
CHOICE OF: 1 Owlbeard Bracers or 1 Wolfmane Wristguards									
Protect Kaya	Stonetalon Mountains	Horde	12	18	Kaya Flathoof—Stonetalon	Makaba Flathoof		1350	
Avenge My Village	Stonetalon Mountains	Horde	12	18	Makaba Flathoof—Stonetalon	Makaba Flathoof		1350	
Kill Grundig Darkcloud	Stonetalon Mountains	Horde	12	18	Makaba Flathoof—Stonetalon	Makaba Flathoof	Avenge My Village	1350	10●
Oh Brother. . .	Stormwind	Alliance	15	20	Wilder Thistlenettle—Stormwind	Wilder Thistlenettle		1550	
REWARD: 1 Miner's Revenge									
Collecting Memories	Stormwind	Alliance	14	18	Wilder Thistlenettle—Stormwind	Wilder Thistlenettle		1350	
CHOICE OF: 1 Tunneler's Boots or 1 Dusty Mining Gloves									
A Meal Served Cold	Stormwind	Alliance	35	40	Angus Stern—Stormwind	Angus Stern		4700	1● 50●
The Doomed Fleet	Stormwind	Alliance	20	29	Bishop Farthing—Stormwind	Glorin Steelbrow	Seeking Wisdom	1200	
Armed and Ready	Stormwind	Alliance	20	29	Grimand Elmore—Stormwind	Sven Yorgen	Blessed Arm	600	
Wine Shop Advert	Stormwind	Alliance	1	2	Renato Gallina—Stormwind	Suzetta Gallina		130	
REWARD: 1 Bottle of Pinot Noir									
Harlan Needs a Resupply	Stormwind	Alliance	1	2	Harlan Bagley—Stormwind	Rema Schneider		85	17●
Package for Thurman	Stormwind	Alliance	1	2	Rema Schneider—Stormwind	Thurman Schneider		130	
A Noble Brew	Stormwind	Alliance	25	30	Zardeth of the Black Claw—Stormwind	Zardeth of the Black Claw		2450	25●
A Noble Brew	Stormwind	Alliance	25	30	Zardeth of the Black Claw—Stormwind	Lord Baurles K. Wishock	A Noble Brew	2450	25●
Speaking of Fortitude	Stormwind	Alliance	20	24	Brother Kristoff—Stormwind	Milton Sheaf		200	
Brother Paxton	Stormwind	Alliance	20	24	Milton Sheaf—Stormwind	Brother Paxton	Speaking of Fortitude	490	
Ink Supplies	Stormwind	Alliance	20	24	Brother Paxton—Elwynn Forest Northshire	Foreman Oslow	Brother Paxton	490	
Return to Kristoff	Stormwind	Alliance	20	24	Brother Paxton—Elwynn Forest Northshire	Brother Kristoff	Rethban Ore	1950	
REWARD: 1 Wandering Boots									
Rethban Ore	Stormwind	Alliance	20	24	Foreman Oslow—Redridge Lakeshire	Brother Paxton	Ink Supplies	975	
Look to an Old Friend	Stormwind	Alliance	16	31	Master Mathias Shaw—Stormwind	Elling Trias	Shadow of the Past	250	
Stormpike's Delivery	Stormwind	Alliance	9	15	Grimand Elmore—Stormwind	Mountaineer Stormpike		1050	7●
The Unsent Letter	Stormwind	Alliance	16	22	An Unsent Letter	Baros Alexston		875	7●
Quell The Uprising	Stormwind	Alliance	22	26	Warden Thelwater—Stormwind	Warden Thelwater		2650	40●
The Color of Blood	Stormwind	Alliance	22	26	Nikova Raskol—Stormwind	Nikova Raskol		2650	40●
Bazil Thredd	Stormwind	Alliance	16	22	Baros Alexston—Stormwind	Warden Thelwater	The Unsent Letter	440	
The Stockade Riots	Stormwind	Alliance	16	29	Warden Thelwater—Stormwind	Warden Thelwater	Bazil Thredd	2350	25●
The Curious Visitor	Stormwind	Alliance	16	29	Warden Thelwater—Stormwind	Baros Alexston	The Stockade Riots	600	
Shadow of the Past	Stormwind	Alliance	16	29	Baros Alexston—Stormwind	Master Mathias Shaw	The Curious Visitor	600	
The Head of the Beast	Stormwind	Alliance	16	31	Elling Trias—Stormwind	Master Mathias Shaw	The Attack!	250	
Brotherhood's End	Stormwind	Alliance	16	31	Master Mathias Shaw—Stormwind	Baros Alexston	The Head of the Beast	325	
An Audience with the King	Stormwind	Alliance	16	31	Baros Alexston—Stormwind	Lady Katrana Prestor	Brotherhood's End	3750	
REWARD: 1 Seal of Wrynn									
You Have Served Us Well	Stormwind	Alliance	25	30	Zardeth of the Black Claw—Stormwind	Zggi	A Noble Brew	250	
REWARD: 1 Dread Mage Hat									
Humble Beginnings	Stormwind	Alliance	10	15	Baros Alexston—Stormwind	Baros Alexston		1050	7●
The Attack!	Stormwind	Alliance	16	31		Elling Trias	Items of Some Consequence	1900	
Southshore	Stormwind	Alliance	20	38	Milton Sheaf—Stormwind	Loremaster Dibbs	An Old History Book	700	
The Perenolde Tiara	Stormwind	Alliance	30	40	Count Remington Ridgewell—Stormwind	Count Remington Ridgewell		4700	1● 50●
Stormwind Library	Stormwind	Both	1	1		Donyal Tovald			
CHOICE OF: 1 The Story of Morgan Ladimore or 1 Legends of the Gurubashi, Volume 3									
The New Frontier	Stormwind	Alliance	54	55	Crier Goodman—Stormwind	Arch Druid Fandral Staghelm		550	
Down the Scarlet Path	Stormwind	Alliance	34	40	Brother Anton—Desolace Nijel's Point	Raleigh the Devout	Down the Scarlet Path	1550	
In the Name of the Light	Stormwind	Alliance	34	40	Raleigh the Devout—Hillsbrad Southshore	Raleigh the Devout	Down the Scarlet Path	4700	
CHOICE OF: 1 Sword of Serenity or 1 Bonebiter or 1 Black Menace or 1 Orb of Lorica									
Elmore's Task	Stormwind	Alliance	9	15	Verner Osgood—Redridge Lakeshire	Grimand Elmore	Stormpike's Delivery	110	
The Missing Diplomat	Stormwind	Alliance	28	28	Bishop DeLavey—Stormwind	Jorgen	The Missing Diplomat	230	
The Missing Diplomat	Stormwind	Alliance	28	28	Jorgen—Stormwind	Elling Trias	The Missing Diplomat	230	
The Missing Diplomat	Stormwind	Alliance	28	28	Elling Trias—Stormwind	Watcher Backus	The Missing Diplomat	230	
The Missing Diplomat	Stormwind	Alliance	28	30	Watcher Backus—Duskwood	Watcher Backus	The Missing Diplomat	2450	
The Missing Diplomat	Stormwind	Alliance	28	30	Watcher Backus—Duskwood	Elling Trias	The Missing Diplomat	250	
The Missing Diplomat	Stormwind	Alliance	28	31	Elling Trias—Stormwind	Dashel Stonefist	The Missing Diplomat	250	
The Missing Diplomat	Stormwind	Alliance	28	31	Dashel Stonefist—Stormwind	Elling Trias	The Missing Diplomat	250	
The Missing Diplomat	Stormwind	Alliance	28	33	Elling Trias—Stormwind	Mikhail	The Missing Diplomat	650	
The Missing Diplomat	Stormwind	Alliance	28	33	Mikhail—Wetlands Menethil	Mikhail	The Missing Diplomat	1300	
The Missing Diplomat	Stormwind	Alliance	28	33	Tapoke "Slim" Jahn—Wetlands Menethil	Mikhail	The Missing Diplomat	270	
The Missing Diplomat	Stormwind	Alliance	28	33	Mikhail—Wetlands Menethil	Commander Samaul	The Missing Diplomat	1300	
The Missing Diplomat	Stormwind	Alliance	28	35	Commander Samaul—Dustwallow Marsh Theramore	Archmage Tervosh	The Missing Diplomat	280	
The Missing Diplomat	Stormwind	Alliance	28	36	Archmage Tervosh—Dustwallow Marsh Theramore	Private Hendel	The Missing Diplomat	700	
The Missing Diplomat	Stormwind	Alliance	28	38		Lady Jaina Proudmoore	The Missing Diplomat	4300	1● 30●
REWARD: 1 Jaina's Signet Ring									
The Missing Diplomat	Stormwind	Alliance	28	28		Bishop DeLavey		230	
The Missing Diplomat	Stormwind	Alliance	28	38	Private Hendel—Dustwallow Marsh	Archmage Tervosh	The Missing Diplomat	2150	
Mazen's Behest	Stormwind	Alliance	37	41	Mazen Mac'Nadir—Stormwind	Acolyte Dellis		330	
Mazen's Behest	Stormwind	Alliance	37	41	Acolyte Dellis—Stormwind	Watcher Mahar Ba	Mazen's Behest	3300	
CHOICE OF: 1 Teacher's Sash or 1 Wanderlust Boots									
The Missing Diplomat	Stormwind	Alliance	28	31	Dashel Stonefist—Stormwind	Dashel Stonefist	The Missing Diplomat	1250	
In Search of The Temple	Stormwind	Alliance	38	43	Brohann Caskbelly—Stormwind	Brohann Caskbelly		3600	
To The Hinterlands	Stormwind	Alliance	38	43	Brohann Caskbelly—Stormwind	Falstad Wildhammer	In Search of The Temple	1800	
Gryphon Master Talonaxe	Stormwind	Alliance	38	43	Falstad Wildhammer—Hinterlands Aerie Peak	Gryphon Master Talonaxe	To The Hinterlands	900	

Title	Location	Faction	Min Level	Con Level	Starter Location	Finisher	Prerequisite	Max XP	Cash Reward
Rhapsody Shindigger	Stormwind	Alliance	38	43	Gryphon Master Talonaxe—Hinterlands	Rhapsody Shindigger	Gryphon Master Talonaxe	1800	
Rhapsody's Kalimdor Kocktail	Stormwind	Alliance	38	43	Rhapsody Shindigger—Hinterlands Dwarf	Rhapsody Shindigger	Rhapsody Shindigger	3600	
Children's Week	Stormwind	Alliance	10	60		Human Orphan			
Rhapsody's Tale	Stormwind	Alliance	38	43	Rhapsody Shindigger—Hinterlands Dwarf	Brohann Caskbelly	Rhapsody's Kalimdor Kocktail	2700	
Into The Temple of Atal'Hakkar	Stormwind	Alliance	38	50	Brohann Caskbelly—Stormwind	Brohann Caskbelly	Rhapsody's Tale	7100	
REWARD: 1 Guardian Talisman									
The Tome of Valor	Stormwind	Alliance	20	20	Tome of Valor	Duthorian Rall		390	
The Tome of Valor	Stormwind	Alliance	20	23	Duthorian Rall—Stormwind	Daphne Stilwell	The Tome of Valor	1850	
The Tome of Valor	Stormwind	Alliance	20	25	Daphne Stilwell—Westfall	Daphne Stilwell	The Tome of Valor	1000	
The Tome of Valor	Stormwind	Alliance	20	25	Daphne Stilwell—Westfall	Duthorian Rall	The Tome of Valor	2550	
REWARD: 1 Bastion of Stormwind									
The Tome of Nobility	Stormwind	Alliance	40	40	Duthorian Rall—Stormwind	Duthorian Rall			
Surena Caledon	Stormwind	Alliance	10	10	Gakin the Darkbinder—Stormwind	Gakin the Darkbinder		625	
The Binding	Stormwind	Alliance	10	10	Gakin the Darkbinder—Stormwind	Gakin the Darkbinder	Surena Caledon	625	
Devourer of Souls	Stormwind	Alliance	20	20	Gakin the Darkbinder—Stormwind	Takar the Seer	Devourer of Souls	775	
Heartswood	Stormwind	Alliance	20	20	Takar the Seer—Barrens Southern Barrens	Gakin the Darkbinder	Devourer of Souls	1550	
The Binding	Stormwind	Alliance	20	20	Gakin the Darkbinder—Stormwind	Gakin the Darkbinder	Heartswood	1150	
REWARD: 1 Small Soul Pouch									
The Tome of Valor	Stormwind	Alliance	20	20		Duthorian Rall	The Tome of Valor		
REWARD: 1 Tome of Valor									
Seeking Strahad	Stormwind	Alliance	30	30	Lago Blackwrench—Ironforge	Strahad Farsan		600	
Underground Assault	Stormwind	Alliance	15	20	Shoni the Shilent—Stormwind	Shoni the Shilent		1550	
CHOICE OF: 1 Polar Gauntlets or 1 Sable Wand									
Snatch and Grab	Stormwind	Alliance	10	10	Master Mathias Shaw—Stormwind	Master Mathias Shaw	Seek out SI: 7	850	
REWARD: 1 Blade of Cunning									
Mathias and the Defias	Stormwind	Alliance	20	20	Master Mathias Shaw—Stormwind	Agent Kearnen		390	
The Touch of Zanzil	Stormwind	Alliance	20	20	Master Mathias Shaw—Stormwind	Doc Mixilpixil	Klaven's Tower		
The Touch of Zanzil	Stormwind	Alliance	20	20	Doc Mixilpixil—Stormwind	Doc Mixilpixil	The Touch of Zanzil	160	
The Touch of Zanzil	Stormwind	Alliance	20	20	Doc Mixilpixil—Stormwind	Doc Mixilpixil	The Touch of Zanzil	1150	
REWARD: 1 Eau de Mixilpixil									
Infiltrating the Castle	Stormwind	Alliance	16	31	Elling Trias—Stormwind	Tyrion	Look to an Old Friend	250	
Items of Some Consequence	Stormwind	Alliance	16	31		Tyrion	Infiltrating the Castle	626	
The Origins of Smithing	Stormwind	Alliance	40	40	Hank the Hammer—Stormwind	Hank the Hammer		3150	
REWARD: 1 Plans: Golden Scale Gauntlets									
In Search of Galvan	Stormwind	Alliance	40	40	Hank the Hammer—Stormwind	McGavan	The Origins of Smithing	1550	
Gyrodrillmatic Excavationators	Stormwind	Alliance	20	30	Shoni the Shilent—Stormwind	Shoni the Shilent		2450	
CHOICE OF: 1 Shoni's Disarming Tool or 1 Shilly Mitts									
Goblin Engineering	Stormwind	Alliance	30	47	Lilliam Sparkspindle—Stormwind	Nixx Sprocketspring	The Pledge of Secrecy	420	
Gnome Engineering	Stormwind	Alliance	30	47	Lilliam Sparkspindle—Stormwind	Tinkmaster Overspark	The Pledge of Secrecy	420	
Bring the Light	Stormwind	Alliance	39	42	Archbishop Benedictus—Stormwind Cathedral of Light	Archbishop Benedictus		4300	
REWARD: 1 Vanquisher's Sword, 1Amberglow Talisman									
The Corruption Abroad	Stormwind	Alliance	18	24	Argos Nightwhisper—Stormwind	Gershala Nightwhisper		1450	13
Jonespyre's Request	Stormwind	Alliance	47	50	Tannysa—Stormwind	Quintis Jonespyre	Morrowgrain Research	1200	
Assisting Arch Druid Staghelm	Stormwind	Alliance	47	50	Innkeeper Allison—Stormwind	Arch Druid Fandral Staghelm		470	
The True Masters	Stormwind	Alliance	48	54	Highlord Bolvar Fordragon—Stormwind	Highlord Bolvar Fordragon	The True Masters	550	
The True Masters	Stormwind	Alliance	48	54	Highlord Bolvar Fordragon—Stormwind	Magistrate Solomon	The True Masters	5450	
The Tome of Nobility	Stormwind	Alliance	40	40	Tiza Battleforge—Ironforge	Duthorian Rall		320	
The Tome of Nobility	Stormwind	Alliance	40	40	Brandur Ironhammer—Ironforge	Duthorian Rall		320	
Good Natured Emma	Stormwind	Alliance	50	52	Royal Factor Bathrilor—Elwynn Stormwind	Ol' Emma	Better Late Than Never	5100	
A Call to Arms: The Plaguelands!	Stormwind	Alliance	50	50	Crier Goodman—Stormwind	Commander Ashlam Valorfist		470	
Desperate Prayer	Stormwind	Alliance	10	10		High Priestess Laurena			
Desperate Prayer	Stormwind	Alliance	10	10	Priestess Josetta—Elwynn Goldshire	High Priestess Laurena		210	
Desperate Prayer	Stormwind	Alliance	10	10	Laurna Morninglight—Teldrassil Dolanaar	High Priestess Laurena		210	
Desperate Prayer	Stormwind	Alliance	10	10	Maxan Anvol—Dun Morogh Kharanos	High Priestess Laurena		210	
Desperate Prayer	Stormwind	Alliance	10	10	Nara Meideros—Stormwind	High Priestess Laurena		210	
Desperate Prayer	Stormwind	Alliance	10	10	High Priest Rohan—Ironforge	High Priestess Laurena			
Desperate Prayer	Stormwind	Alliance	10	10	Priestess Alathea—Darnassus	High Priestess Laurena		210	
Arcane Feedback	Stormwind	Alliance	20	20		High Priestess Laurena			
Arcane Feedback	Stormwind	Alliance	20	20	High Priest Rohan—Ironforge	High Priestess Laurena		390	
Arcane Feedback	Stormwind	Alliance	20	20	Priestess Alathea—Darnassus	High Priestess Laurena		390	
Heeding the Call	Stormwind	Alliance	10	10	Theridran—Stormwind	Mathrengyl Bearwalker		85	
The First and the Last	Stormwind	Alliance	56	60	Highlord Bolvar Fordragon—Stormwind	Master Mathias Shaw		650	
Honor the Dead	Stormwind	Alliance	56	60	Master Mathias Shaw—Stormwind	Master Mathias Shaw	The First and the Last	660	
Flint Shadowmore	Stormwind	Alliance	56	60	Master Mathias Shaw—Stormwind	Flint Shadowmore	Honor the Dead	4950	
Order Must Be Restored	Stormwind	Alliance	56	60	Highlord Bolvar Fordragon—Stormwind	Highlord Bolvar Fordragon	The Blightcaller Cometh	9950	
CHOICE OF: 1 Gorewood Bow or 1 Stormrager or 1 Sacred Protector									
The Great Masquerade	Stormwind	Alliance	50	60		Highlord Bolvar Fordragon	Stormwind Rendezvous	9950	
The Dragon's Eye	Stormwind	Alliance	50	60	Highlord Bolvar Fordragon—Stormwind	Haleh	The Great Masquerade	6600	
Drakefire Amulet	Stormwind	Alliance	50	60	Haleh—Winterspring Mazthoril	Haleh	The Dragon's Eye	8300	
REWARD: 1 Drakefire Amulet									
Greatfather Winter is Here!	Stormwind	Alliance	10	60	Khole Jinglepocket—Stormwind Trade District	Greatfather Winter		650	
Victory for the Alliance	Stormwind	Alliance	60	60	Head of Onyxia	Highlord Bolvar Fordragon		9950	
Celebrating Good Times	Stormwind	Alliance	60	60	Highlord Bolvar Fordragon—Stormwind	Major Mattingly	Victory for the Alliance	9950	
CHOICE OF: 1 Onyxia Blood Talisman or 1 Dragonslayer's Signet or 1 Onyxia Tooth Pendant									
The Journey Has Just Begun	Stormwind	Alliance	60	60		Major Mattingly	Celebrating Good Times		
Emphasis on Sacrifice	Stormwind	Alliance	60	60	Lord Grayson Shadowbreaker—Stormwind	High Priest Rohan	Lord Grayson Shadowbreaker	650	
Lord Grayson Shadowbreaker	Stormwind	Alliance	60	60	Duthorian Rall—Stormwind	Lord Grayson Shadowbreaker		650	
Exorcising Terrordale	Stormwind	Alliance	60	60	Lord Grayson Shadowbreaker—Stormwind	Lord Grayson Shadowbreaker	To Show Due Judgment	6600	
The Work of Grimand Elmore	Stormwind	Alliance	60	60	Lord Grayson Shadowbreaker—Stormwind	Grimand Elmore	Lord Grayson Shadowbreaker	650	
Collection of Goods	Stormwind	Alliance	60	60	Grimand Elmore—Stormwind	Grimand Elmore	The Work of Grimand Elmore	1650	
Ancient Equine Spirit	Stormwind	Alliance	60	60	Lord Grayson Shadowbreaker—Stormwind	Ancient Equine Spirit	Grimand's Finest Work	4950	
The Divination Scryer	Stormwind	Alliance	60	60	Lord Grayson Shadowbreaker—Stormwind	Lord Grayson Shadowbreaker	Blessed Arcanite Barding	3300	
Judgment and Redemption	Stormwind	Alliance	60	60	Lord Grayson Shadowbreaker—Stormwind	Darkreaver's Fallen Charger	The Divination Scryer	9950	
Grimand's Finest Work	Stormwind	Alliance	60	60	Grimand Elmore—Stormwind	Lord Grayson Shadowbreaker	Collection of Goods	6600	
Again Into the Great Ossuary	Stormwind	Alliance	60	60		Lord Grayson Shadowbreaker	Judgment and Redemption		
REWARD: 1 Divination Scryer									
The Lord of Blackrock	Stormwind	Alliance	60	60	Head of Nefarian	Highlord Bolvar Fordragon		9950	
The Lord of Blackrock	Stormwind	Alliance	60	60	Highlord Bolvar Fordragon—Stormwind	Field Marshal Afrasiabi	The Lord of Blackrock	9950	
CHOICE OF: 1 Master Dragonslayer's Medallion or 1 Master Dragonslayer's Orb or 1 Master Dragonslayer's Ring									
A Donation of Wool	Stormwind	Alliance	12	60		Clavicus Knavingham		650	
A Donation of Silk	Stormwind	Alliance	26	60		Clavicus Knavingham		1650	
A Donation of Mageweave	Stormwind	Alliance	40	60		Clavicus Knavingham		3300	
A Donation of Runecloth	Stormwind	Alliance	50	60		Clavicus Knavingham	A Donation of Wool	6600	
Additional Runecloth	Stormwind	Alliance	50	60		Clavicus Knavingham	A Donation of Runecloth		
Hallow's End Treats for Jesper!	Stormwind	Alliance	10	60	Jesper—Stormwind	Jesper		1650	
REWARD: 30 Hallow's End Pumpkin Treat									
Flexing for Nougat	Stormwind	Alliance	10	60	Innkeeper Allison—Stormwind	Innkeeper Allison			

Title	Location	Faction	Min Level	Con Level	Starter Location	Finisher	Prerequisite	Max XP	Cash Reward
REWARD: 1 Stormwind Nougat									
The Lunar Festival	Stormwind	Alliance	1	60		Lunar Festival Harbinger			
Tiger Mastery	Stranglethorn Vale	Both	28	31	Ajeck Rouack—Stranglethorn	Ajeck Rouack	Welcome to the Jungle	1250	
Tiger Mastery	Stranglethorn Vale	Both	28	33	Ajeck Rouack—Stranglethorn	Ajeck Rouack	Tiger Mastery	1300	
Tiger Mastery	Stranglethorn Vale	Both	28	35	Ajeck Rouack—Stranglethorn	Ajeck Rouack	Tiger Mastery	2050	
Tiger Mastery	Stranglethorn Vale	Both	28	37	Ajeck Rouack—Stranglethorn	Ajeck Rouack	Tiger Mastery	2850	
REWARD: 1 Tiger Hunter Gloves									
Bloodscalp Ears	Stranglethorn Vale	Both	30	35	Kebok—Stranglethorn Booty Bay	Kebok		2050	35
REWARD: 8 Goblin Fishing Pole									
Panther Mastery	Stranglethorn Vale	Both	28	31	Sir S. J. Erlgadin—Stranglethorn	Sir S. J. Erlgadin	Welcome to the Jungle	1250	
Panther Mastery	Stranglethorn Vale	Both	28	33	Sir S. J. Erlgadin—Stranglethorn	Sir S. J. Erlgadin	Panther Mastery	1300	
Panther Mastery	Stranglethorn Vale	Both	28	38	Sir S. J. Erlgadin—Stranglethorn	Sir S. J. Erlgadin	Panther Mastery	2150	
Panther Mastery	Stranglethorn Vale	Both	28	40	Sir S. J. Erlgadin—Stranglethorn	Sir S. J. Erlgadin	Panther Mastery	3150	
REWARD: 1 Panther Hunter Leggings									
Raptor Mastery	Stranglethorn Vale	Both	28	34	Hemet Nesingwary—Stranglethorn	Hemet Nesingwary	Welcome to the Jungle	1350	
Raptor Mastery	Stranglethorn Vale	Both	28	36	Hemet Nesingwary—Stranglethorn	Hemet Nesingwary	Raptor Mastery	1400	
Raptor Mastery	Stranglethorn Vale	Both	28	41	Hemet Nesingwary—Stranglethorn	Hemet Nesingwary	Raptor Mastery	2450	
Raptor Mastery	Stranglethorn Vale	Both	28	43	Hemet Nesingwary—Stranglethorn	Hemet Nesingwary	Raptor Mastery	3600	
REWARD: 1 Raptor Hunter Tunic									
Supplies to Private Thorsen	Stranglethorn Vale	Alliance	30	32	Krazek—Stranglethorn Booty Bay	Private Thorsen		650	16
Bookie Herod	Stranglethorn Vale	Alliance	30	35	Lieutenant Doren—Stranglethorn	Bookie Herod's Records	Jungle Secrets	1350	
Investigate the Camp	Stranglethorn Vale	Both	28	32	Krazek—Stranglethorn Booty Bay	Krazek		260	16
Colonel Kurzen	Stranglethorn Vale	Alliance	30	40	Lieutenant Doren—Stranglethorn	Lieutenant Doren	Special Forces	3150	
REWARD: 1 Shrapnel Blaster									
The Second Rebellion	Stranglethorn Vale	Alliance	30	33	Sergeant Yohwa—Stranglethorn	Sergeant Yohwa		1950	
Bad Medicine	Stranglethorn Vale	Alliance	30	34	Sergeant Yohwa—Stranglethorn	Sergeant Yohwa		2700	
CHOICE OF: 1 Palm Frond Mantle or 1 Guerrilla Cleaver									
Troll Witchery	Stranglethorn Vale	Alliance	30	40	Brother Nimetz—Stranglethorn	Brother Nimetz	Kurzen's Mystery	3150	
Mai'Zoth	Stranglethorn Vale	Alliance	30	46	Brother Nimetz—Stranglethorn	Brother Nimetz	Colonel Kurzen	5050	
REWARD: 1 Tranquil Orb									
Kurzen's Mystery	Stranglethorn Vale	Alliance	30	38	Brother Nimetz—Stranglethorn	Brother Nimetz	The Second Rebellion	3550	
Big Game Hunter	Stranglethorn Vale	Both	28	43	Hemet Nesingwary—Stranglethorn	Hemet Nesingwary	Raptor Mastery	5350	
CHOICE OF: 1 Master Hunter's Bow or 1 Master Hunter's Rifle									
Skullsplitter Tusks	Stranglethorn Vale	Both	37	42	Kebok—Stranglethorn Booty Bay	Kebok	Bloodscalp Ears	3450	55
Krazek's Cookery	Stranglethorn Vale	Alliance	32	37	Corporal Kaleb—Stranglethorn	Krazek		1400	
Hostile Takeover	Stranglethorn Vale	Both	31	36	Kebok—Stranglethorn Booty Bay	Kebok		2800	
REWARD: 1 Gemmed Gloves									
Jungle Secrets	Stranglethorn Vale	Alliance	30	33		Lieutenant Doren		1300	
The Hidden Key	Stranglethorn Vale	Alliance	30	37	Bookie Herod's Records—Stranglethorn	Bookie Herod's Strongbox	Bookie Herod	1400	
REWARD: 1 Bookmaker's Scepter									
The Spy Revealed!	Stranglethorn Vale	Alliance	30	37	Bookie Herod's Strongbox—Stranglethorn	Lieutenant Doren	The Hidden Key	1400	
Patrol Schedules	Stranglethorn Vale	Alliance	30	37	Lieutenant Doren—Stranglethorn	Corporal Sethman	The Spy Revealed!	290	
Report to Doren	Stranglethorn Vale	Alliance	30	37	Corporal Sethman—Stranglethorn	Lieutenant Doren	Patrol Schedules	2850	
CHOICE OF: 1 Junglewalker Sandals or 1 Frost Metal Pauldrons									
The Green Hills of Stranglethorn	Stranglethorn Vale	Both	30	40	Barnil Stonepot—Stranglethorn	Barnil Stonepot	Welcome to the Jungle	4700	
REWARD: 1 Jungle Boots, 2Thick Armor Kit, 3Superior Healing Potion									
Chapter I	Stranglethorn Vale	Both	30	40	Barnil Stonepot—Stranglethorn	Barnil Stonepot		775	
REWARD: 1 Green Hills of Stranglethorn - Chapter I									
Chapter II	Stranglethorn Vale	Both	30	40	Barnil Stonepot—Stranglethorn	Barnil Stonepot		775	
REWARD: 1 Green Hills of Stranglethorn - Chapter II									
Chapter III	Stranglethorn Vale	Both	30	40	Barnil Stonepot—Stranglethorn	Barnil Stonepot		775	
REWARD: 1 Green Hills of Stranglethorn - Chapter III									
Chapter IV	Stranglethorn Vale	Both	30	40	Barnil Stonepot—Stranglethorn	Barnil Stonepot		775	
REWARD: 1 Green Hills of Stranglethorn - Chapter IV									
Stranglethorn Fever	Stranglethorn Vale	Both	40	45	Fin Fizracket—Stranglethorn Booty Bay	Fin Fizracket		5850	
REWARD: 1 Medicine Blanket									
Stranglethorn Fever	Stranglethorn Vale	Both	32	35		Witch Doctor Unbagwa			
The Defense of Grom'gol	Stranglethorn Vale	Horde	33	36	Commander Aggro'gosh—Stranglethorn Grom'gol Orc	Commander Aggro'gosh		2800	40
The Defense of Grom'gol	Stranglethorn Vale	Horde	33	37	Commander Aggro'gosh—Stranglethorn Grom'gol Orc	Commander Aggro'gosh	The Defense of Grom'gol	2850	
REWARD: 1 Grom'gol Buckler									
Mok'thardin's Enchantment	Stranglethorn Vale	Horde	33	38	Far Seer Mok'thardin—Stranglethorn Grom'gol Orc	Far Seer Mok'thardin		2150	
Mok'thardin's Enchantment	Stranglethorn Vale	Horde	33	41	Far Seer Mok'thardin—Stranglethorn Grom'gol Orc	Far Seer Mok'thardin	Mok'thardin's Enchantment	2450	
Mok'thardin's Enchantment	Stranglethorn Vale	Horde	33	41	Far Seer Mok'thardin—Stranglethorn Grom'gol Orc	Far Seer Mok'thardin	Mok'thardin's Enchantment	2450	
Mok'thardin's Enchantment	Stranglethorn Vale	Horde	33	44	Far Seer Mok'thardin—Stranglethorn Grom'gol Orc	Far Seer Mok'thardin	Mok'thardin's Enchantment	4650	
REWARD: 1 Choker of the High Shaman									
Special Forces	Stranglethorn Vale	Alliance	30	38	Sergeant Yohwa—Stranglethorn	Lieutenant Doren	The Second Rebellion	2850	
Supply and Demand	Stranglethorn Vale	Both	26	31	Drizzlik—Stranglethorn Booty Bay	Drizzlik		1250	22
Keep An Eye Out	Stranglethorn Vale	Both	37	42	Dizzy One-Eye—Stranglethorn Booty Bay	Dizzy One-Eye	The Bloodsail Buccaneers	2550	
REWARD: 1 Darktide Cape									
Some Assembly Required	Stranglethorn Vale	Both	31	36	Drizzlik—Stranglethorn Booty Bay	Drizzlik	Supply and Demand	1400	30
The Stone of the Tides	Stranglethorn Vale	Alliance	32	37	Baron Revilgaz—Stranglethorn Booty Bay	Baron Revilgaz	The Haunted Isle	2850	40
Whiskey Slim's Lost Grog	Stranglethorn Vale	Both	40	50	Whiskey Slim—Stranglethorn Booty Bay	Whiskey Slim		4700	
REWARD: 5 Rumsey Rum									
Hunt for Yenniku	Stranglethorn Vale	Horde	30	34	Nimboya—Stranglethorn Grom'gol	Nimboya		2000	
Headhunting	Stranglethorn Vale	Horde	30	37	Nimboya—Stranglethorn Grom'gol	Nimboya	Hunt for Yenniku	2100	
CHOICE OF: 1 Darkspear Cuffs or 1 Darkspear Armsplints									
Welcome to the Jungle	Stranglethorn Vale	Both	28	30	Barnil Stonepot—Stranglethorn	Hemet Nesingwary		250	
Bloodscalp Clan Heads	Stranglethorn Vale	Horde	30	41	Nimboya—Stranglethorn Grom'gol	Bubbling Cauldron	Headhunting	3300	
Speaking with Nezzliok	Stranglethorn Vale	Horde	30	40	Bubbling Cauldron—Stranglethorn Grom'gol	Bubbling Cauldron	Bloodscalp Clan Heads	2350	
Speaking with Gan'zulah	Stranglethorn Vale	Horde	30	46	Bubbling Cauldron—Stranglethorn Grom'gol	Bubbling Cauldron	Bloodscalp Clan Heads	4050	
Up to Snuff	Stranglethorn Vale	Both	37	41	Deeg—Stranglethorn Booty Bay	Deeg	The Bloodsail Buccaneers	1650	
The Fate of Yenniku	Stranglethorn Vale	Horde	30	45	Bubbling Cauldron—Stranglethorn Grom'gol	Kin'weelay	Speaking with Nezzliok	390	
The Singing Crystals	Stranglethorn Vale	Horde	30	45	Kin'weelay—Stranglethorn Grom'Gol	Kin'weelay	The Fate of Yenniku	3900	
The Mind's Eye	Stranglethorn Vale	Horde	30	46	Kin'weelay—Stranglethorn Grom'Gol	Kin'weelay	The Singing Crystals	5050	
Saving Yenniku	Stranglethorn Vale	Horde	30	46	Kin'weelay—Stranglethorn Grom'Gol	Nimboya	The Mind's Eye	5050	
CHOICE OF: 1 Nimboya's Mystical Staff or 1 Medal of Courage									
Filling the Soul Gem	Stranglethorn Vale	Horde	1	46		Yenniku			
REWARD: 1 Filled Soul Gem									
Message in a Bottle	Stranglethorn Vale	Both	45	45	Carefully Folded Note	Princess Poobah		2900	
The Bloodsail Buccaneers	Stranglethorn Vale	Both	37	41	First Mate Crazz—Stranglethorn Booty Bay	Bloodsail Correspondence		2450	40
Bloody Bone Necklaces	Stranglethorn Vale	Horde	30	37	Kin'weelay—Stranglethorn Grom'Gol	Kin'weelay		2100	
REWARD: 1 Bloodbone Band									
The Bloodsail Buccaneers	Stranglethorn Vale	Both	37	41	Bloodsail Correspondence—Stranglethorn	First Mate Crazz	The Bloodsail Buccaneers	2450	
Split Bone Necklace	Stranglethorn Vale	Horde	30	42	Kin'weelay—Stranglethorn Grom'Gol	Kin'weelay	Bloody Bone Necklaces	3450	
CHOICE OF: 1 Darkspear Shoes or 1 Darkspear Boots									
The Bloodsail Buccaneers	Stranglethorn Vale	Both	37	41	First Mate Crazz—Stranglethorn Booty Bay	Fleet Master Seahorn	The Bloodsail Buccaneers	825	
Venture Company Mining	Stranglethorn Vale	Both	30	41	Crank Fizzlebub—Stranglethorn Booty Bay	Crank Fizzlebub	Singing Blue Shards	3300	
CHOICE OF: 1 Goblin Igniter or 1 Silver Spade									

Stranglethorn Vale cont'd

Title	Location	Faction	Min Level	Con Level	Starter Location	Finisher	Prerequisite	Max XP	Cash Reward
Water Elementals	Stranglethorn Vale	Alliance	32	37	Baron Revilgaz—Stranglethorn Booty Bay	Baron Revilgaz	The Stone of the Tides	2850	40●
Magical Analysis	Stranglethorn Vale	Alliance	32	37	Baron Revilgaz—Stranglethorn Booty Bay	Archmage Ansirem Runeweaver	Water Elementals	1400	
Ansirem's Key	Stranglethorn Vale	Alliance	32	37	Archmage Ansirem Runeweaver—Alterac Mountains Dalaran	Catelyn the Blade	Magical Analysis	1400	
The Bloodsail Buccaneers	Stranglethorn Vale	Both	37	43	Fleet Master Seahorn—Stranglethorn Booty Bay	Fleet Master Seahorn	The Bloodsail Buccaneers	3600	
Singing Blue Shards	Stranglethorn Vale	Both	30	35	Crank Fizzlebub—Stranglethorn Booty Bay	Crank Fizzlebub		2750	35●
Scaring Shaky	Stranglethorn Vale	Both	30	41	"Sea Wolf" MacKinley—Stranglethorn Booty Bay	"Shaky" Phillipe		825	
Return to MacKinley	Stranglethorn Vale	Both	30	41	"Shaky" Phillipe—Stranglethorn Booty Bay	"Sea Wolf" MacKinley	Scaring Shaky	2450	40●
The Bloodsail Buccaneers	Stranglethorn Vale	Both	37	45	Fleet Master Seahorn—Stranglethorn Booty Bay	Fleet Master Seahorn	The Bloodsail Buccaneers	4850	
REWARD: 1 Blackwater Tunic									
Voodoo Dues	Stranglethorn Vale	Both	30	44	"Sea Wolf" MacKinley—Stranglethorn Booty Bay	"Sea Wolf" MacKinley	Return to MacKinley	3750	65●
"Pretty Boy" Duncan	Stranglethorn Vale	Alliance	32	39	Catelyn the Blade—Stranglethorn Booty Bay	Catelyn the Blade	Ansirem's Key	2250	
The Curse of the Tides	Stranglethorn Vale	Alliance	32	40	Catelyn the Blade—Stranglethorn Booty Bay	Baron Revilgaz	"Pretty Boy" Duncan	3150	
REWARD: 1 Robe of Crystal Waters									
Cracking Maury's Foot	Stranglethorn Vale	Both	30	44	"Sea Wolf" MacKinley—Stranglethorn Booty Bay	"Sea Wolf" MacKinley	Voodoo Dues	4650	
REWARD: 1 Collection Plate									
The Haunted Isle	Stranglethorn Vale	Alliance	32	37	Krazek—Stranglethorn Booty Bay	Baron Revilgaz		290	
Akiris by the Bundle	Stranglethorn Vale	Both	38	43	Privateer Bloods—Stranglethorn Booty Bay	Privateer Bloods		3600	60●
REWARD: 1 Scorching Sash									
Enticing Negolash	Stranglethorn Vale	Both	1	52		Ruined Lifeboat			
Zanzil's Secret	Stranglethorn Vale	Both	35	44	Crank Fizzlebub—Stranglethorn Booty Bay	Crank Fizzlebub		3750	
REWARD: 1 Belt of Corruption									
Return to Corporal Kaleb	Stranglethorn Vale	Alliance	32	37	Krazek—Stranglethorn Booty Bay	Corporal Kaleb	Favor for Krazek	2850	
REWARD: 1 Cap of Harmony									
Akiris by the Bundle	Stranglethorn Vale	Alliance	38	43	Privateer Bloods—Stranglethorn Booty Bay	Privateer Groy	Akiris by the Bundle	2700	45●
Cortello's Riddle	Stranglethorn Vale	Both	35	43	Cortello's Riddle	A Soggy Scroll		3600	
Cortello's Riddle	Stranglethorn Vale	Both	35	43	A Soggy Scroll—Swamp of Sorrows	Musty Scroll	Cortello's Riddle	3600	
Cortello's Riddle	Stranglethorn Vale	Both	35	51	Musty Scroll—Swamp of Sorrows	Cortello's Treasure	Cortello's Riddle	6100	
REWARD: 1 Explorer's Knapsack									
Favor for Krazek	Stranglethorn Vale	Alliance	32	37	Krazek—Stranglethorn Booty Bay	Krazek	Krazek's Cookery	2100	30●
Excelsior	Stranglethorn Vale	Both	31	38	Drizzlik—Stranglethorn Booty Bay	Drizzlik	Some Assembly Required	2850	
REWARD: 1 Excelsior Boots									
The Vile Reef	Stranglethorn Vale	Horde	30	37	Kin'weelay—Stranglethorn Grom'Gol	Kin'weelay		2850	
Message in a Bottle	Stranglethorn Vale	Both	45	51	Princess Poobah—Stranglethorn	Princess Poobah	Message in a Bottle	7350	
REWARD: 1 Poobah's Nose Ring									
Trollbane	Stranglethorn Vale	Horde	32	37	Nimboya—Stranglethorn Grom'gol	Zengu	Trollbane	700	
Avast Ye, Scallywag	Stranglethorn Vale	Both	55	60	"Pretty Boy" Duncan—Stranglethorn	Fleet Master Firallon		650	
The Caravan Road	Stranglethorn Vale	Alliance	25	30	Caravaneer Ruzzgot—Stranglethorn Booty Bay	Clerk Daltry	Passage to Booty Bay	1200	
Goblin Sponsorship	Stranglethorn Vale	Both	29	37	Wharfmaster Lozgil—Stranglehtorn Booty Bay	Baron Revilgaz	Goblin Sponsorship	290	
Goblin Sponsorship	Stranglethorn Vale	Both	29	37	Baron Revilgaz—Stranglethorn Booty Bay	Baron Revilgaz	Goblin Sponsorship	2850	
Goblin Sponsorship	Stranglethorn Vale	Both	29	37	Baron Revilgaz—Stranglethorn Booty Bay	Pozzik	Goblin Sponsorship	700	
The Mithril Order	Stranglethorn Vale	Both	40	40	McGavan—Strangelthorn Booty Bay	Galvan the Ancient	In Search of Galvan	3150	
Smelt On, Smelt Off	Stranglethorn Vale	Both	40	45	Galvan the Ancient—Stranglethorn	Galvan the Ancient	The Mithril Order	3900	
REWARD: 1 Plans: nate Mithril Pants									
The Great Silver Deceiver	Stranglethorn Vale	Both	40	45	Galvan the Ancient—Stranglethorn	Galvan the Ancient	The Mithril Order	3900	
REWARD: 1 Plans: nate Mithril Gloves									
The Art of the Imbue	Stranglethorn Vale	Both	40	45	Galvan the Ancient—Stranglethorn	Galvan the Ancient	The Mithril Order	3900	
REWARD: 1 Plans: nate Mithril Shoulder									
Galvan's Finest Pupil	Stranglethorn Vale	Both	40	45	Galvan the Ancient—Stranglethorn	Trenton Lighthammer	Smelt On, Smelt Off	2900	
Expert Blacksmith!	Stranglethorn Vale	Both	40	45	Galvan the Ancient—Stranglethorn	Galvan the Ancient	Smelt On, Smelt Off	3900	
REWARD: 1 Signet of Expertise									
Gnomer-gooooone!	Stranglethorn Vale	Horde	20	35	Scooty—Stranglethorn Booty Bay	Scooty	Chief Engineer Scooty		
REWARD: 1 Goblin Transponder									
The Pledge of Secrecy	Stranglethorn Vale	Horde	30	47	Oglethorpe Obnoticus—Stranglethorn Booty Bay	Oglethorpe Obnoticus	Gnome Engineering	420	
Show Your Work	Stranglethorn Vale	Horde	30	47	Oglethorpe Obnoticus—Stranglethorn Booty Bay	Oglethorpe Obnoticus	The Pledge of Secrecy	3150	
REWARD: 1 Gnome Engineer Membership Card									
Membership Card Renewal	Stranglethorn Vale	Both	30	47		Oglethorpe Obnoticus	Show Your Work		
REWARD: 1 Gnome Engineer Membership Card									
An OOX of Your Own	Stranglethorn Vale	Both	40	50		Oglethorpe Obnoticus	Rescue OOX-17/TN!	7100	
REWARD: 1 Mechanical Chicken									
Avast Ye, Admiral!	Stranglethorn Vale	Both	55	60	Fleet Master Firallon—Stranglethorn Monster Human Pirate Unique	Fleet Master Firallon		9950	
REWARD: 1 Bloodsail Admiral's Hat									
Tribal Leatherworking	Stranglethorn Vale	Horde	40	55	Se'Jib—Stranglethorn	Se'Jib	Master of the Wild Leather	4200	
Arena Master	Stranglethorn Vale	Both	1	55	Arena Master	Short John Mithril		550	
Arena Grandmaster	Stranglethorn Vale	Both	1	55		Short John Mithril	Arena Master		
REWARD: 1 Arena Grand Master									
The Captain's Chest	Stranglethorn Vale	Both	40	47	Captain Hecklebury Smotts—Stranglethorn	Captain Hecklebury Smotts		3150	
REWARD: 1 Bloodband Bracers									
The Monogrammed Sash	Stranglethorn Vale	Both	40	50	Monogrammed Sash	Captain Hecklebury Smotts		2350	
The Captain's Cutlass	Stranglethorn Vale	Both	40	50	Captain Hecklebury Smotts—Stranglethorn	Sprogger	The Monogrammed Sash	470	
Facing Negolash	Stranglethorn Vale	Both	40	50	Sprogger—Stranglethorn Booty Bay	Captain Hecklebury Smotts	The Captain's Cutlass	7100	
REWARD: 1 Smotts' Compass									
Dressing the Part	Stranglethorn Vale	Both	49	55		Fleet Master Firallon			
REWARD: 1 Buccaneer's Uniform									
Traitor to the Bloodsail	Stranglethorn Vale	Both	30	60		Bloodsail Traitor			

Swamp of Sorrows

Title	Location	Faction	Min Level	Con Level	Starter Location	Finisher	Prerequisite	Max XP	Cash Reward
Lack of Surplus	Swamp of Sorrows	Horde	35	40	Dar—Swamp of Sorrows Stonard	Tok'Kar		3150	
Lack of Surplus	Swamp of Sorrows	Horde	35	42	Tok'Kar—Swamp of Sorrows Misty Reed Post	Tok'Kar	Lack of Surplus	3450	
Draenethyst Crystals	Swamp of Sorrows	Both	30	35	Magtoor—Swamp of Sorrows	Magtoor		2750	
Noboru the Cudgel	Swamp of Sorrows	Both	29	39	Noboru's Cudgel	Magtoor		2250	
Galen's Escape	Swamp of Sorrows	Both	30	38	Galen Goodward—Swamp of Sorrows	Galen's Strongbox		2850	85●
REWARD: 1 Visionary Buckler									
Encroaching Wildlife	Swamp of Sorrows	Alliance	30	37	Watcher Biggs—Swamp	Watcher Biggs		2850	
Driftwood	Swamp of Sorrows	Alliance	30	42	Watcher Biggs—Swamp	Watcher Biggs	The Lost Caravan	3450	
Neeka Bloodscar	Swamp of Sorrows	Horde	30	35	Helgrum the Swift—Swamp of Sorrows Stonard	Neeka Bloodscar	Report to Helgrum	1350	
Coyote Thieves	Swamp of Sorrows	Horde	30	40	Neeka Bloodscar—Badlands	Neeka Bloodscar		3150	
Report to Helgrum	Swamp of Sorrows	Horde	30	40	Neeka Bloodscar—Badlands	Helgrum the Swift		2350	
The Lost Caravan	Swamp of Sorrows	Alliance	30	35	Watcher Biggs—Swamp	Watcher Biggs	Encroaching Wildlife	2750	
Threat From the Sea	Swamp of Sorrows	Horde	35	45	Tok'Kar—Swamp of Sorrows Misty Reed Post	Katar	Lack of Surplus		
The Lost Supplies	Swamp of Sorrows	Alliance	30	40	Lost Supplies	Quartermaster Lungertz		25	
REWARD: 1 Box of Supplies									
Pool of Tears	Swamp of Sorrows	Horde	38	43	Fel'zerul—Swamp of Sorrows Stonard	Fel'zerul		4450	1● 20●
Deliver the Shipment	Swamp of Sorrows	Alliance	30	42	Watcher Biggs—Swamp	Quartermaster Lungertz	Driftwood	2550	
Threat From the Sea	Swamp of Sorrows	Horde	35	43	Katar—Swamp of Sorrows Misty Reed Strand	Katar	Threat From the Sea	4450	
Threat From the Sea	Swamp of Sorrows	Horde	35	43	Katar—Swamp of Sorrows Misty Reed Strand	Tok'Kar	Threat From the Sea	3600	
CHOICE OF: 1 Tok'kar's Murloc Shanker or 1 Tok'kar's Murloc Basher or 1 Tok'kar's Murloc Chopper									
Continued Threat	Swamp of Sorrows	Horde	35	45	Katar—Swamp of Sorrows Misty Reed Strand	Katar	Threat From the Sea	3900	
The Atal'ai Exile	Swamp of Sorrows	Horde	38	44	Fel'zerul—Swamp of Sorrows Stonard	Atal'ai Exile	Pool of Tears	3750	
Fresh Meat	Swamp of Sorrows	Horde	35	44	Dar—Swamp of Sorrows Stonard	Dar		3750	
REWARD: 10 Grilled King Crawler Legs, 1Leather Chef's Belt									

Title	Location	Faction	Min Level	Con Level	Starter Location	Finisher	Prerequisite	Max XP	Cash Reward
Return to Fel'Zerul	Swamp of Sorrows	Horde	38	44	Atal'ai Exile—Hinterlands	Fel'zerul	The Atal'ai Exile	3750	
The Temple of Atal'Hakkar	Swamp of Sorrows	Horde	38	50	Fel'zerul—Swamp of Sorrows Stonard	Fel'zerul	Return to Fel'Zerul	5900	
REWARD: 1 Guardian Talisman									
The Essence of Eranikus	Swamp of Sorrows	Both	48	55	Oathstone of Ysera's Dragonflight	Itharius	The Essence of Eranikus	550	
In Eranikus' Own Words	Swamp of Sorrows	Both	48	55	Itharius—Swamp of Sorrows Itharius's Cave	Umbranse the Spiritspeaker	The Essence of Eranikus	4200	
The Prison's Bindings	Tainted Scar	Both	60	60	Daio the Decrepit—Blasted Lands Tainted Scar	Daio the Decrepit		6600	
The Prison's Casing	Tainted Scar	Both	60	60	Daio the Decrepit—Blasted Lands Tainted Scar	Daio the Decrepit		6600	
Suppression	Tainted Scar	Both	60	60	Daio the Decrepit—Blasted Lands Tainted Scar	Daio the Decrepit	The Prison's Bindings	6600	
REWARD: 1 Tome of Sacrifice									
The Scrimshank Redemption	Tanaris	Both	39	48	Senior Surveyor Fizzledowser—Tanaris Gadgetzan	Senior Surveyor Fizzledowser	Noxious Lair Investigation	4400	
Rise of the Silithid	Tanaris	Horde	39	48	Senior Surveyor Fizzledowser—Tanaris Gadgetzan	Zilzibin Drumlore	Insect Part Analysis	5450	
Noxious Lair Investigation	Tanaris	Alliance	39	47	Placeholder - Darkhollow Mine—Quest test pnagle	Alchemist Pestlezugg	Gadgetzan Water Survey	3150	50●
Insect Part Analysis	Tanaris	Both	39	48	Senior Surveyor Fizzledowser—Tanaris Gadgetzan	Alchemist Pestlezugg	The Scrimshank Redemption	440	
Insect Part Analysis	Tanaris	Both	39	48	Alchemist Pestlezugg—Tanaris Gadgetzan	Senior Surveyor Fizzledowser	Insect Part Analysis	440	70●
Rise of the Silithid	Tanaris	Alliance	39	49	Senior Surveyor Fizzledowser—Tanaris Gadgetzan	Gracina Spiritmight	Insect Part Analysis	5700	
Find OOX-17/TN!	Tanaris	Both	43	48	OOX-17/TN Distress Beacon	Homing Robot OOX-17/TN		4400	
Slake That Thirst	Tanaris	Horde	38	46	Chief Engineer Bilgewhizzle—Tanaris Gadgetzan	Chief Engineer Bilgewhizzle	Into the Field	3050	
REWARD: 1 Model 4711-FTZ Power Source									
Rescue OOX-17/TN!	Tanaris	Both	43	48	Homing Robot OOX-17/TN—Rescue the Robot (Tanaris)	Oglethorpe Obnoticus	Find OOX-17/TN!	5450	
CHOICE OF: 1 Optomatic Deflector or 1 Thermotastic Egg Timer									
Tanaris Field Sampling	Tanaris	Horde	38	46	Model 4711-FTZ Power Source	Chief Engineer Bilgewhizzle	Slake That Thirst	4050	
Another Power Source?	Tanaris	Horde	38	46	Chief Engineer Bilgewhizzle—Tanaris Gadgetzan	Chief Engineer Bilgewhizzle	Slake That Thirst		
REWARD: 1 Model 4711-FTZ Power Source									
Return to Apothecary Zinge	Tanaris	Horde	38	46	Chief Engineer Bilgewhizzle—Tanaris Gadgetzan	Apothecary Zinge	Tanaris Field Sampling	5050	1● 30●
CHOICE OF: 1 Skilled Handling Gloves or 1 Master Apothecary Cape or 1 Loreskin Shoulders									
Gadgetzan Water Survey	Tanaris	Both	38	46	Senior Surveyor Fizzledowser—Tanaris Gadgetzan	Senior Surveyor Fizzledowser		3050	35●
Tooga's Quest	Tanaris	Both	40	50	Tooga—Tanaris	Torta		5900	
CHOICE OF: 1 Chelonian Cuffs or 1 Band of the Great Tortoise									
Wastewander Justice	Tanaris	Both	40	43	Chief Engineer Bilgewhizzle—Tanaris Gadgetzan	Chief Engineer Bilgewhizzle		3600	60●
More Wastewander Justice	Tanaris	Both	40	44	Chief Engineer Bilgewhizzle—Tanaris Gadgetzan	Chief Engineer Bilgewhizzle	Wastewander Justice	3750	65●
Water Pouch Bounty	Tanaris	Both	40	44	Spigot Operator Luglunket—Tanaris Gadgetzan	Spigot Operator Luglunket		2800	
REWARD: 1 Gadgetzan Water Co. Care Package									
Water Pouch Bounty	Tanaris	Both	40	44		Spigot Operator Luglunket	Water Pouch Bounty	380	
REWARD: 1 Gadgetzan Water Co. Care Package									
The Thirsty Goblin	Tanaris	Both	44	49	Marin Noggenfogger—Tanaris Gadgetzan	Marin Noggenfogger		4550	70●
In Good Taste	Tanaris	Both	44	49	Marin Noggenfogger—Tanaris Gadgetzan	Sprinkle	The Thirsty Goblin	460	
Sprinkle's Secret Ingredient	Tanaris	Both	44	49	Sprinkle—Tanaris Gadgetzan	Sprinkle	In Good Taste	4550	
Delivery for Marin	Tanaris	Both	44	49	Sprinkle—Tanaris Gadgetzan	Marin Noggenfogger	Sprinkle's Secret Ingredient	460	
Noggenfogger Elixir	Tanaris	Both	44	49	Marin Noggenfogger—Tanaris Gadgetzan	Marin Noggenfogger	Delivery for Marin		70●
REWARD: 5 Noggenfogger Elixir									
The Super Egg-O-Matic	Tanaris	Both	42	47		Egg-O-Matic			
REWARD: 1 Egg Crate									
An Extraordinary Egg	Tanaris	Both	42	60		Curgle Cranklehop	The Super Egg-O-Matic		
REWARD: 1 Box of Goodies									
A Fine Egg	Tanaris	Both	42	60		Curgle Cranklehop	The Super Egg-O-Matic		
REWARD: 1 Box of Spells									
An Ordinary Egg	Tanaris	Both	42	60		Curgle Cranklehop	The Super Egg-O-Matic		
REWARD: 1 Box of Rations									
A Bad Egg	Tanaris	Both	42	60		Curgle Cranklehop	The Super Egg-O-Matic		7●
A Good Head On Your Shoulders	Tanaris	Both	40	45	Trenton Lighthammer—Tanaris Gadgetzan	Trenton Lighthammer	Galvan's Finest Pupil	3900	
The World At Your Feet	Tanaris	Both	40	45	Trenton Lighthammer—Tanaris Gadgetzan	Trenton Lighthammer	Galvan's Finest Pupil	3900	
The Mithril Kid	Tanaris	Both	40	45	Trenton Lighthammer—Tanaris Gadgetzan	Trenton Lighthammer	Galvan's Finest Pupil	3900	
WANTED: Caliph Scorpidsting	Tanaris	Both	39	46	Wanted Poster—Tanaris	Chief Engineer Bilgewhizzle		5050	1● 30●
Stoley's Debt	Tanaris	Both	40	45	"Sea Wolf" MacKinley—Stranglethorn Booty Bay	Stoley	Stoley's Shipment	390	
Stoley's Shipment	Tanaris	Both	40	45	Stoley—Tanaris Steamwheedle Port	Stoley		3900	50●
Deliver to MacKinley	Tanaris	Both	40	45	Stoley—Tanaris Steamwheedle Port	"Sea Wolf" MacKinley	Stoley's Shipment	3900	50●
CHOICE OF: 1 Swashbuckler Sash or 1 Shinkicker Boots									
WANTED: Andre Firebeard	Tanaris	Both	40	45	Wanted Poster—Tanaris	Security Chief Bilgewhizzle		3900	1● 30●
Ship Schedules	Tanaris	Both	40	45	Ship Schedule	Security Chief Bilgewhizzle		4850	1● 30●
Cuergo's Gold	Tanaris	Both	40	45	Cuergo's Treasure Map	Pirate's Treasure!			
REWARD: 1 Cuergo's Hidden Treasure									
The Stone Watcher	Tanaris	Both	45	50	Uldum Pedestal—Tanaris	Uldum Pedestal	Seeing What Happens	4700	
A Future Task	Tanaris	Alliance	45	50	Historian Karnik—Ironforge	High Explorer Magellas	Return to Ironforge	4700	2● 20●
Return to Thunder Bluff	Tanaris	Horde	45	50	Uldum Pedestal—Tanaris	Nara Wildmane	The Stone Watcher	470	
A Future Task	Tanaris	Horde	45	50	Nara Wildmane—Thunder Bluff	Sage Truthseeker	Return to Thunder Bluff	4700	2● 20●
Return to Ironforge	Tanaris	Alliance	45	50	Uldum Pedestal—Tanaris	Historian Karnik	The Stone Watcher	470	
Handle With Care	Tanaris	Alliance	42	47	Curgle Cranklehop—Tanaris Gadgetzan	Erelas Ambersky		2100	50●
Gahz'ridian	Tanaris	Both	43	48	Marvon Rivetseeker—Tanaris Broken Pillar	Marvon Rivetseeker		4400	
CHOICE OF: 1 Surveyor's Tunic or 1 Staff of Lore									
Did You Lose This?	Tanaris	Both	40	50	Trenton Lighthammer—Tanaris Gadgetzan	Trenton Lighthammer	A Good Head On Your Shoulders	7100	
REWARD: 1 Glimmering Mithril Insignia									
Thistleshrub Valley	Tanaris	Both	45	50	Tran'rek—Tanaris Gadgetzan	Tran'rek		4700	75●
Screecher Spirits	Tanaris	Both	40	44	Yeh'kinya—Tanaris Steamwheedle Port	Yeh'kinya		3750	
The Prophecy of Mosh'aru	Tanaris	Both	40	47	Yeh'kinya—Tanaris Steamwheedle Port	Yeh'kinya	Screecher Spirits	5250	
The God Hakkar	Tanaris	Both	40	53	Yeh'kinya—Tanaris Steamwheedle Port	Yeh'kinya	The Ancient Egg	7900	2● 40●
CHOICE OF: 1 Avenguard Helm or 1 Lifeforce Dirk or 1 Gemburst Circlet									
The Pledge of Secrecy	Tanaris	Both	30	47	Nixx Sprocketspring—Tanaris Gadgetzan	Nixx Sprocketspring	The Pledge of Secrecy	420	
Show Your Work	Tanaris	Both	30	47	Nixx Sprocketspring—Tanaris Gadgetzan	Nixx Sprocketspring	Show Your Work	3150	
REWARD: 1 Goblin Engineer Membership Card									
Membership Card Renewal	Tanaris	Both	30	47		Nixx Sprocketspring	Show Your Work		
REWARD: 1 Goblin Engineer Membership Card									
Bungle in the Jungle	Tanaris	Both	50	53	Alchemist Pestlezugg—Tanaris Gadgetzan	Alchemist Pestlezugg	March of the Silithid	5250	
Super Sticky	Tanaris	Both	48	54	Tran'rek—Tanaris Gadgetzan	Tran'rek		5450	1● 65●
Pawn Captures Queen	Tanaris	Both	50	54	Alchemist Pestlezugg—Tanaris Gadgetzan	Alchemist Pestlezugg	Bungle in the Jungle	5450	
Calm Before the Storm	Tanaris	Alliance	50	54	Alchemist Pestlezugg—Tanaris Gadgetzan	Gracina Spiritmight	Pawn Captures Queen	550	
Calm Before the Storm	Tanaris	Horde	50	54	Alchemist Pestlezugg—Tanaris Gadgetzan	Zilzibin Drumlore	Pawn Captures Queen	550	
The Ancient Egg	Tanaris	Both	40	50	Yeh'kinya—Tanaris Steamwheedle Port	Yeh'kinya	The Prophecy of Mosh'aru	5900	
The Final Tablets	Tanaris	Both	40	58	Prospector Ironboot—Tanaris Steamwheedle Port	Prospector Ironboot	The Lost Tablets of Mosh'aru	7750	
The Lost Tablets of Mosh'aru	Tanaris	Both	40	58	Prospector Ironboot—Tanaris Steamwheedle Port	Prospector Ironboot	The God Hakkar	7750	
Fire Plume Forged	Tanaris	Alliance	55	57	Krinkle Goodsteel—Tanaris Gadgetzan	Alchemist Arbington	Mold Rhymes With...	4500	
Fire Plume Forged	Tanaris	Horde	55	57	Krinkle Goodsteel—Tanaris Gadgetzan	Apothecary Dithers	Mold Rhymes With...	4500	
The Dunemaul Compound	Tanaris	Both	44	49	Andi Lynn—Tanaris Gadgetzan	Andi Lynn		4550	
CHOICE OF: 1 Witherseed Gloves or 1 Rugwood Mantle									
Clamlette Surprise	Tanaris	Both	35	45	Dirge Quikcleave—Tanaris Gadgetzan	Dirge Quikcleave		3900	
REWARD: 20 Clamlette Surprise									
Confront Yeh'kinya	Tanaris	Both	40	58	Prospector Ironboot—Tanaris Steamwheedle Port	Yeh'kinya	The Final Tablets	6200	
CHOICE OF: 1 Faded Hakkari Cloak or 1 Tattered Hakkari Cape									
The Hand of Rastakhan	Tanaris	Both	40	58	Prospector Ironboot—Tanaris Steamwheedle Port	Molthor	Confront Yeh'kinya	9300	

Tanaris cont'd

Title	Location	Faction	Min Level	Con Level	Starter Location	Finisher	Prerequisite	Max XP	Cash Reward
Pirate Hats Ahoy!	Tanaris	Both	40	45	Haughty Modiste—Tanaris Steamwheedle Port	Haughty Modiste		3900	
Southsea Shakedown	Tanaris	Both	40	45	Security Chief Bilgewhizzle—Tanaris Steamwheedle Port	Security Chief Bilgewhizzle		3900	65
CHOICE OF: 1 Southsea Head Bucket or 1 Southsea Mojo Boots									
The Path of the Protector	Tanaris	Both	60	60		Anachronos	The Path of the Conqueror	6600	
REWARD: 1 Signet Ring of the Bronze Dragonflight									
The Path of the Protector	Tanaris	Both	60	60		Anachronos	The Path of the Protector	6600	
REWARD: 1 Signet Ring of the Bronze Dragonflight									
The Path of the Protector	Tanaris	Both	60	60		Anachronos	The Path of the Protector	6600	
REWARD: 1 Signet Ring of the Bronze Dragonflight									
The Path of the Protector	Tanaris	Both	60	60		Anachronos	The Path of the Protector	6600	
REWARD: 1 Signet Ring of the Bronze Dragonflight									
The Protector of Kalimdor	Tanaris	Both	60	60		Anachronos	The Path of the Protector	9950	
REWARD: 1 Signet Ring of the Bronze Dragonflight									
The Path of the Conqueror	Tanaris	Both	60	60		Anachronos	The Path of the Invoker	6600	
REWARD: 1 Signet Ring of the Bronze Dragonflight									
The Path of the Conqueror	Tanaris	Both	60	60		Anachronos	The Path of the Conqueror	6600	
REWARD: 1 Signet Ring of the Bronze Dragonflight									
The Path of the Conqueror	Tanaris	Both	60	60		Anachronos	The Path of the Conqueror	6600	
REWARD: 1 Signet Ring of the Bronze Dragonflight									
The Path of the Conqueror	Tanaris	Both	60	60		Anachronos	The Path of the Conqueror	6600	
REWARD: 1 Signet Ring of the Bronze Dragonflight									
The Qiraji Conqueror	Tanaris	Both	60	60		Anachronos	The Path of the Conqueror	9950	
REWARD: 1 Signet Ring of the Bronze Dragonflight									
The Path of the Invoker	Tanaris	Both	60	60		Anachronos	The Path of the Protector	6600	
REWARD: 1 Signet Ring of the Bronze Dragonflight									
The Path of the Invoker	Tanaris	Both	60	60		Anachronos	The Path of the Invoker	6600	
REWARD: 1 Signet Ring of the Bronze Dragonflight									
The Path of the Invoker	Tanaris	Both	60	60		Anachronos	The Path of the Invoker	6600	
REWARD: 1 Signet Ring of the Bronze Dragonflight									
The Path of the Invoker	Tanaris	Both	60	60		Anachronos	The Path of the Invoker	6600	
REWARD: 1 Signet Ring of the Bronze Dragonflight									
The Grand Invoker	Tanaris	Both	60	60		Anachronos	The Path of the Invoker	9950	
REWARD: 1 Signet Ring of the Bronze Dragonflight									
The Changing of Paths - Protector No More	Tanaris	Both	60	60		Anachronos	The Protector of Kalimdor		
CHOICE OF: 1 Signet Ring of the Bronze Dragonflight or 1 Signet Ring of the Bronze Dragonflight									
The Changing of Paths - Invoker No More	Tanaris	Both	60	60		Anachronos	The Protector of Kalimdor		
CHOICE OF: 1 Signet Ring of the Bronze Dragonflight or 1 Signet Ring of the Bronze Dragonflight									
The Changing of Paths - Conqueror No More	Tanaris	Both	60	60		Anachronos	The Protector of Kalimdor		
CHOICE OF: 1 Signet Ring of the Bronze Dragonflight or 1 Signet Ring of the Bronze Dragonflight									
The Super Egg-O-Matic	Tanaris	Both	42	47		Egg-O-Matic	The Super Egg-O-Matic		
REWARD: 1 Egg Crate									
War at Sea	Tanaris	Both	40	60		Rumsen Fizzlebrack			

Teldrassil

Title	Location	Faction	Min Level	Con Level	Starter Location	Finisher	Prerequisite	Max XP	Cash Reward
A Troubling Breeze	Teldrassil	Alliance	4	6	Athridas Bearmantle—Teldrassil Dolanaar	Gaerolas Talvethren		270	
Gnarlpine Corruption	Teldrassil	Alliance	4	6	Gaerolas Talvethren—Teldrassil	Athridas Bearmantle	A Troubling Breeze	550	1 25
The Relics of Wakening	Teldrassil	Alliance	4	9	Athridas Bearmantle—Teldrassil Dolanaar	Athridas Bearmantle	Gnarlpine Corruption	775	
CHOICE OF: 1 Barkmail Leggings or 1 Gritroot Staff									
Ursal the Mauler	Teldrassil	Alliance	4	12	Athridas Bearmantle—Teldrassil Dolanaar	Athridas Bearmantle	The Relics of Wakening	1150	
CHOICE OF: 1 Defender Axe or 1 Thornroot Club									
The Road to Darnassus	Teldrassil	Alliance	5	8	Moon Priestess Amara—Teldrassil	Moon Priestess Amara		700	2 25
Zenn's Bidding	Teldrassil	Alliance	4	5	Zenn Foulhoof—Teldrassil	Zenn Foulhoof		450	
REWARD: 5 Severed Voodoo Claw									
Seek Redemption!	Teldrassil	Alliance	4	7	Sentinel Kyra Starsong—Teldrassil Dolanaar	Zenn Foulhoof	Zenn's Bidding	625	1 75
Timberling Seeds	Teldrassil	Alliance	4	7	Denalan—Teldrassil Dolanaar	Denalan		625	
REWARD: 10 Forest Mushroom Cap									
Timberling Sprouts	Teldrassil	Alliance	4	7	Denalan—Teldrassil Dolanaar	Denalan		800	3 50
CHOICE OF: 1 Gardening Gloves or 1 Graystone Bracers									
Rellian Greenspyre	Teldrassil	Alliance	4	7	Denalan—Teldrassil Dolanaar	Rellian Greenspyre	Timberling Seeds	320	
The Moss-twined Heart	Teldrassil	Alliance	5	12	Moss-twined Heart	Denalan		460	
Crown of the Earth	Teldrassil	Alliance	1	5	Corithras Moonrage—Teldrassil Dolanaar	Corithras Moonrage	Crown of the Earth	340	
The Glowing Fruit	Teldrassil	Alliance	4	10	Strange Fruited Plant—Teldrassil	Denalan	Timberling Seeds	850	3 50
The Shimmering Frond	Teldrassil	Alliance	4	10	Strange Fronded Plant—Teldrassil	Denalan	Timberling Seeds	850	3 50
Twisted Hatred	Teldrassil	Alliance	4	7	Tallonkai Swiftroot—Teldrassil Dolanaar	Tallonkai Swiftroot		625	
CHOICE OF: 1 Feral Bracers or 1 Viny Wrappings									
Crown of the Earth	Teldrassil	Alliance	1	9	Corithras Moonrage—Teldrassil Dolanaar	Corithras Moonrage	Crown of the Earth	775	
Crown of the Earth	Teldrassil	Alliance	1	11	Corithras Moonrage—Teldrassil Dolanaar	Arch Druid Fandral Staghelm	Crown of the Earth	1100	
CHOICE OF: 1 Ashwood Bow or 1 Thicket Hammer									
The Enchanted Glade	Teldrassil	Alliance	6	11	Sentinel Arynia Cloudsbreak—Teldrassil	Sentinel Arynia Cloudsbreak		440	
CHOICE OF: 1 Shackled Girdle or 1 Rain-spotted Cape									
Mist	Teldrassil	Alliance	7	12	Mist—Teldrassil	Sentinel Arynia Cloudsbreak		900	
CHOICE OF: 1 Cord Bracers or 1 Crag Buckler or 1 Scout's Cloak									
Teldrassil	Teldrassil	Alliance	6	11		Arch Druid Fandral Staghelm	The Enchanted Glade	440	
Planting the Heart	Teldrassil	Alliance	9	12	Denalan—Teldrassil Dolanaar	Denalan's Planter	The Moss-twined Heart	900	
REWARD: 1 Cleansed Timberling Heart									
Grove of the Ancients	Teldrassil	Alliance	6	11	Arch Druid Fandral Staghelm—Darnassus	Onu	Teldrassil	875	
Denalan's Earth	Teldrassil	Alliance	4	5	Syral Bladeleaf—Teldrassil Dolanaar	Denalan		230	50
Elixirs for the Bladeleafs	Teldrassil	Alliance	4	8	Syral Bladeleaf—Teldrassil Dolanaar	Syral Bladeleaf		700	
REWARD: 6 Earthroot, 6Mageroyal									
Dolanaar Delivery	Teldrassil	Alliance	1	5	Porthannius—Teldrassil Shadowglen	Innkeeper Keldamyr		110	
CHOICE OF: 5 Darnassian Bleu or 5 Refreshing Spring Water									
The Apple Falls	Teldrassil	Alliance	10	10	Jannok Breezesong—Teldrassil Dolanaar	Syurna		420	
Destiny Calls	Teldrassil	Alliance	10	10	Syurna—Night Elf	Syurna	The Apple Falls	850	
REWARD: 1 Blade of Cunning									
Erion Shadewhisper	Teldrassil	Alliance	16	16	Jannok Breezesong—Teldrassil Dolanaar	Erion Shadewhisper	Redridge Rendezvous	120	
The Sprouted Fronds	Teldrassil	Alliance	4	10		Sprouted Frond	The Shimmering Frond	85	
REWARD: 5 Sprouted Frond									
The Emerald Dreamcatcher	Teldrassil	Alliance	1	6	Tallonkai Swiftroot—Teldrassil Dolanaar	Tallonkai Swiftroot		410	1
Ferocitas the Dream Eater	Teldrassil	Alliance	1	8	Tallonkai Swiftroot—Teldrassil Dolanaar	Tallonkai Swiftroot	The Emerald Dreamcatcher	875	4 50
Return to Denalan	Teldrassil	Alliance	4	9	Rellian Greenspyre—Darnassus	Denalan	Tumors	80	
Oakenscowl	Teldrassil	Alliance	4	9	Denalan—Teldrassil Dolanaar	Denalan	Return to Denalan	975	6
CHOICE OF: 1 Dirtwood Belt or 1 Moss-covered Gauntlets									
Tears of the Moon	Teldrassil	Alliance	5	12	Priestess A'moora—Darnassus	Priestess A'moora		1150	10
The Temple of the Moon	Teldrassil	Alliance	5	10	Sister Aquinne—Darnassus	Priestess A'moora	Sathrah's Sacrifice	85	
Sathrah's Sacrifice	Teldrassil	Alliance	5	12	Priestess A'moora—Darnassus	Priestess A'moora	Tears of the Moon	900	
CHOICE OF: 1 Lace Pants or 1 Cushioned Boots									
The Sleeping Druid	Teldrassil	Alliance	3	8	Oben Rageclaw—Teldrassil	Oben Rageclaw		700	
Druid of the Claw	Teldrassil	Alliance	3	10	Oben Rageclaw—Teldrassil	Oben Rageclaw	The Sleeping Druid	1050	
CHOICE OF: 1 Sleeping Robes or 1 Brushwood Blade									
A Friend in Need	Teldrassil	Alliance	2	4	Iverron—Teldrassil Shadowglen	Dirania Silvershine	A Good Friend	90	

Title	Location	Faction	Min Level	Con Level	Starter Location	Finisher	Prerequisite	Max XP	Cash Reward
Iverron's Antidote	Teldrassil	Alliance	2	4	Dirania Silvershine—Teldrassil Shadowglen	Dirania Silvershine	A Friend in Need	360	
Iverron's Antidote	Teldrassil	Alliance	2	4	Dirania Silvershine—Teldrassil Shadowglen	Iverron	Iverron's Antidote	450	
CHOICE OF: 1 Sedgeweed Britches or 1 Barkmail Vest									
Recipe of the Kaldorei	Teldrassil	Alliance	1	7	Zarrin—Teldrassil Dolanaar	Zarrin		625	85
REWARD: 1 Recipe: Kaldorei Spider Kabob, 3Kaldorei Spider Kabob									
Garments of the Moon	Teldrassil	Alliance	5	4	Laurna Morninglight—Teldrassil Dolanaar	Laurna Morninglight		270	
REWARD: 1 Moon Robes of Elune									
In Favor of Elune	Teldrassil	Alliance	5	4	Shando—Teldrassil Shadowglen	Laurna Morninglight		90	
Heeding the Call	Teldrassil	Alliance	10	10	Kal—Teldrassil Dolanaar	Mathrengyl Bearwalker		85	
Taming the Beast	Teldrassil	Alliance	10	10	Dazalar—Teldrassil Dolanaar	Dazalar		850	
The Hunter's Path	Teldrassil	Alliance	10	10	Jocaste—Darnassus	Dazalar		85	
The Hunter's Path	Teldrassil	Alliance	10	10	Terenthis—Darkshore Auberdine	Dazalar		85	
The Hunter's Path	Teldrassil	Alliance	10	10	Einris Brightspear—Stormwind Dwarven District	Dazalar		85	
Taming the Beast	Teldrassil	Alliance	10	10	Dazalar—Teldrassil Dolanaar	Dazalar	Taming the Beast	850	
Taming the Beast	Teldrassil	Alliance	10	10	Dazalar—Teldrassil Dolanaar	Dazalar	Taming the Beast	850	
Training the Beast	Teldrassil	Alliance	10	10	Dazalar—Teldrassil Dolanaar	Jocaste	Taming the Beast	420	
The Hunter's Path	Teldrassil	Alliance	10	10	Olmin Burningbeard—Ironforge Hall of Arms	Dazalar		85	
The Hunter's Path	Teldrassil	Alliance	10	10	Grif Wildheart—Dun Morogh Kharanos	Dazalar		85	
Crown of the Earth	Teldrassil	Alliance	1	11	Corithras Moonrage—Teldrassil Dolanaar	Corithras Moonrage	Crown of the Earth	650	
Triage	Theramore	Alliance	35	45	Doctor Gustaf VanHowzen—Dustwallow Marsh	Doctor Gustaf VanHowzen		3900	
Lonebrow's Journal	Thousand Needles	Alliance	29	34	Henrig Lonebrow's Journal	Falfindel Waywarder		1350	
The Crone of the Kraul	Thousand Needles	Alliance	29	34	Falfindel Waywarder—Feralas Thalanaar	Falfindel Waywarder	Lonebrow's Journal	3350	
CHOICE OF: 1 Berylline Pads or 1 Stonefist Girdle or 1 Marbled Buckler REWARD: 1 "Mage-Eye" Blunderbuss									
Salt Flat Venom	Thousand Needles	Both	28	30	Fizzle Brassbolts—Thousand Needles Mirage Raceway	Fizzle Brassbolts		1850	25
Hardened Shells	Thousand Needles	Both	28	30	Wizzle Brassbolts—Thousand Needles Mirage Raceway	Wizzle Brassbolts		2450	25
Martek the Exiled	Thousand Needles	Both	26	35	Fizzle Brassbolts—Thousand Needles Mirage Raceway	Martek the Exiled	Salt Flat Venom	1350	
Encrusted Tail Fins	Thousand Needles	Both	28	35	Wizzle Brassbolts—Thousand Needles Mirage Raceway	Wizzle Brassbolts	Salt Flat Venom	3450	75
Indurium	Thousand Needles	Both	28	39	Martek the Exiled—Badlands Valley of Fangs	Martek the Exiled	Martek the Exiled	3000	
Rocket Car Parts	Thousand Needles	Both	28	31	Kravel Koalbeard—Thousand Needles Mirage Raceway	Kravel Koalbeard		2500	30
Wharfmaster Dizzywig	Thousand Needles	Both	30	36	Kravel Koalbeard—Thousand Needles Mirage Raceway	Wharfmaster Dizzywig		1400	
Parts for Kravel	Thousand Needles	Both	30	36	Wharfmaster Dizzywig—Barrens Ratchet	Kravel Koalbeard	Wharfmaster Dizzywig	1400	20
Delivery to the Gnomes	Thousand Needles	Both	30	36	Kravel Koalbeard—Thousand Needles Mirage Raceway	Fizzle Brassbolts	Parts for Kravel	700	10
The Rumormonger	Thousand Needles	Both	30	36	Kravel Koalbeard—Thousand Needles Mirage Raceway	Krazek	Delivery to the Gnomes	1400	
Dream Dust in the Swamp	Thousand Needles	Both	30	36	Krazek—Stranglethorn Booty Bay	Krazek	The Rumormonger	3500	
Rumors for Kravel	Thousand Needles	Both	30	36	Krazek—Stranglethorn Booty Bay	Kravel Koalbeard	Dream Dust in the Swamp	3500	75
Back to Booty Bay	Thousand Needles	Both	35	43	Kravel Koalbeard—Thousand Needles Mirage Raceway	Crank Fizzlebub	Rumors for Kravel	900	
Zanzil's Mixture and a Fool's Stout	Thousand Needles	Both	35	44	Crank Fizzlebub—Stranglethorn Booty Bay	Kravel Koalbeard	Zanzil's Secret	3750	
Get the Gnomes Drunk	Thousand Needles	Both	35	44	Kravel Koalbeard—Thousand Needles Mirage Raceway	Gnome Pit Boss	Zanzil's Mixture and a Fool's Stout	380	
Get the Goblins Drunk	Thousand Needles	Both	35	44	Kravel Koalbeard—Thousand Needles Mirage Raceway	Goblin Pit Boss	Zanzil's Mixture and a Fool's Stout	380	
Report Back to Fizzlebub	Thousand Needles	Both	35	44	Kravel Koalbeard—Thousand Needles Mirage Raceway	Crank Fizzlebub	Get the Gnomes Drunk	1850	
Melor Sends Word	Thousand Needles	Horde	20	30	Jorn Skyseer—Barrens Camp Taurajo	Melor Stonehoof	Steelsnap		
Steelsnap	Thousand Needles	Horde	20	30	Melor Stonehoof—Thunder Bluff	Melor Stonehoof		2450	
Fiora Longears	Thousand Needles	Alliance	18	20	Red Jack Flint—Wetlands Menethil	Fiora Longears	Journey to Astranaar	775	
Journey to Astranaar	Thousand Needles	Alliance	18	20	Fiora Longears—Dustwallow Marsh Theramore Isle	Shindrell Swiftfire			
Highperch Venom	Thousand Needles	Alliance	25	30	Fiora Longears—Dustwallow Marsh Theramore Isle	Fiora Longears		3650	
REWARD: 1 Windborne Belt									
News for Fizzle	Thousand Needles	Both	28	38	Martek the Exiled—Badlands Valley of Fangs	Fizzle Brassbolts	Indurium	1450	
CHOICE OF: 1 Fizzle's Zippy Lighter or 1 Gnomish Mechanic's Gloves									
The Swarm Grows	Thousand Needles	Horde	29	33	Korran—Barrens Crossroads	Belgrom Rockmaul		1300	
The Swarm Grows	Thousand Needles	Horde	29	33	Belgrom Rockmaul—Orgrimmar	Moktar Krin	The Swarm Grows	1950	
The Swarm Grows	Thousand Needles	Horde	29	35	Moktar Krin—Thousand Needles	Moktar Krin	The Swarm Grows	2750	35
Parts of the Swarm	Thousand Needles	Horde	28	35	Cracked Silithid Carapace	Korran		2750	
Test of Faith	Thousand Needles	Horde	25	26	Dorn Plainstalker—Thousand Needles The Weathered Nook	Dorn Plainstalker		1050	
Test of Endurance	Thousand Needles	Horde	25	30	Dorn Plainstalker—Thousand Needles The Weathered Nook	Dorn Plainstalker	Test of Faith	2450	
Test of Strength	Thousand Needles	Horde	25	30	Dorn Plainstalker—Thousand Needles The Weathered Nook	Dorn Plainstalker	Test of Endurance	3050	
Test of Lore	Thousand Needles	Horde	25	30	Dorn Plainstalker—Thousand Needles The Weathered Nook	Braug Dimspirit	Test of Strength	1200	
A New Ore Sample	Thousand Needles	Horde	25	29	Tatternack Steelforge—Barrens Camp Taurajo	Tatternack Steelforge	Weapons of CHOICE	2350	25
REWARD: 1 Orcish War Sword									
Test of Lore	Thousand Needles	Horde	25	30	Braug Dimspirit—Stonetalon The Talondeep Path	Braug Dimspirit	Test of Lore	1850	
Test of Lore	Thousand Needles	Horde	25	30	Braug Dimspirit—Stonetalon The Talondeep Path	Parqual Fintallas	Test of Lore	1200	
Test of Lore	Thousand Needles	Horde	25	36	Parqual Fintallas—Undercity	Parqual Fintallas	Test of Lore	2100	
A Bump in the Road	Thousand Needles	Both	28	33	Trackmaster Zherin—Thousand Needles Mirage Raceway	Trackmaster Zherin		2650	35
Load Lightening	Thousand Needles	Both	29	30	Pozzik—Thousand Needles Mirage Raceway	Pozzik		1850	25
Goblin Sponsorship	Thousand Needles	Both	29	37	Pozzik—Thousand Needles Mirage Raceway	Gazlowe	Load Lightening	700	
The Brassbolts Brothers	Thousand Needles	Alliance	28	30	Pilot Longbeard—Ironforge	Wizzle Brassbolts		2450	
Parts of the Swarm	Thousand Needles	Horde	28	35	Korran—Barrens Crossroads	Belgrom Rockmaul	Parts of the Swarm	1350	18
CHOICE OF: 1 Dryleaf Pants or 1 Bleeding Crescent									
The Eighteenth Pilot	Thousand Needles	Both	29	37	Pozzik—Thousand Needles Mirage Raceway	Razzeric	Goblin Sponsorship	290	
Razzeric's Tweaking	Thousand Needles	Both	29	41	Razzeric—Thousand Needles Mirage Raceway	Razzeric	The Eighteenth Pilot	3300	
Safety First	Thousand Needles	Both	29	41	Razzeric—Thousand Needles Mirage Raceway	Shreev	Razzeric's Tweaking	825	24
Safety First	Thousand Needles	Both	29	41	Shreev—Tanaris Gadgetzan	Razzeric	Safety First	825	
CHOICE OF: 1 Razzeric's Customized Seatbelt or 1 Razzeric's Racing Grips									
Keeping Pace	Thousand Needles	Both	29	41	Pozzik—Thousand Needles Mirage Raceway	Rizzle's Unguarded Plans	News for Fizzle	1650	
Zamek's Distraction	Thousand Needles	Both	29	41		Zamek	News for Fizzle		
Indurium Ore	Thousand Needles	Both	29	42		Pozzik	Rizzle's Schematics		6
Rizzle's Schematics	Thousand Needles	Both	29	41	Rizzle's Guarded Plans—Thousand Needles	Pozzik	Keeping Pace	1650	
The Sacred Flame	Thousand Needles	Horde	20	29	Rau Cliffrunner—Thousand Needles Freewind Post	Rau Cliffrunner	The Sacred Flame	2350	
CHOICE OF: 1 Cliffrunner's Aim or 1 Azure Sash									
Final Passage	Thousand Needles	Horde	25	36	Parqual Fintallas—Undercity	Dorn Plainstalker	Test of Lore	4200	
CHOICE OF: 1 Windstorm Hammer or 1 Dancing Flame									
Call of Air	Thousand Needles	Horde	30	30	Searn Fi	REWARDer—Orgrimmar	Prate Cloudseer	2450	
REWARD: 1 Air Totem									
Call of Air	Thousand Needles	Horde	30	30	Xanis Flameweaver—Thunder Bluff	Prate Cloudseer		2450	
REWARD: 1 Air Totem									
Gahz'rilla	Thousand Needles	Alliance	40	50	Wizzle Brassbolts—Thousand Needles Mirage Raceway	Wizzle Brassbolts		7100	75
REWARD: 1 Carrot on a Stick									
Message to Freewind Post	Thousand Needles	Horde	23	25	Brave Moonhorn—Thousand Needles The Great Lift	Cliffwatcher Longhorn	Pacify the Centaur	500	1 75
Wind Rider	Thousand Needles	Horde	25	29	Elu—Thousand Needles Freewind Post	Elu		1750	19
REWARD: 2 Heavy Armor Kit									
Homeward Bound	Thousand Needles	Horde	25	29	Pao'ka Swiftmountain—Thousand Needles Highperch	Motega Firemane		2350	19
Alien Egg	Thousand Needles	Horde	24	26	Hagar Lightninghoof—Thousand Needles Freewind Post	Hagar Lightninghoof		2100	15
Pacify the Centaur	Thousand Needles	Horde	23	25	Cliffwatcher Longhorn—Thousand Needles Freewind Post	Cliffwatcher Longhorn		2000	18
Serpent Wild	Thousand Needles	Horde	24	26		Motega Firemane	Alien Egg	1050	15
Assassination Plot	Thousand Needles	Horde	23	28	Assassination Note	Kanati Greycloud		2300	
Free at Last	Thousand Needles	Horde	25	29		Thalia Amberhide		2350	
CHOICE OF: 1 Windsong Cinch or 1 Windsong Drape									
Protect Kanati Greycloud	Thousand Needles	Horde	23	28	Kanati Greycloud—Thousand Needles Whitereach Post	Kanati Greycloud	Assassination Plot	2300	
CHOICE OF: 1 Lightheel Boots or 1 Loamflake Bracers or 1 Palestrider Gloves									

Thousand Needles cont'd

Title	Location	Faction	Min Level	Con Level	Starter Location	Finisher	Prerequisite	Max XP	Cash Reward
Sacred Fire	Thousand Needles	Horde	24	27	Motega Firemane—Thousand Needles Whitereach Post	Magatha Grimtotem	Serpent Wild	2200	22●
Grimtotem Spying	Thousand Needles	Horde	24	28		Cliffwatcher Longhorn	Pacify the Centaur	2300	
CHOICE OF: 1 Desert Shoulders or 1 Tundra Boots or 1 Grimtoll Wristguards									
Arikara	Thousand Needles	Horde	24	28	Magatha Grimtotem—Thunder Bluff	Motega Firemane	Sacred Fire	2300	
CHOICE OF: 1 Brute Hammer or 1 Stingshot Wand or 1 Clink Shield									
Wanted - Arnak Grimtotem	Thousand Needles	Horde	25	29	Wanted Poster - Arnak Grimtotem—Thousand Needles	Cliffwatcher Longhorn		2350	25●
CHOICE OF: 1 Brawnhide Armor or 1 Plainsguard Leggings									
Hypercapacitor Gizmo	Thousand Needles	Horde	24	30	Wizlo Bearingshiner—Thousand Needles Whitereach Post	Wizlo Bearingshiner		3050	
REWARD: 1 Inventor's League Ring									
Family Tree	Thousand Needles	Horde	32	35	Cliffwatcher Longhorn—Thousand Needles Freewind Post	Nataka Longhorn		2050	25●
Hemet Nesingwary	Thousand Needles	Both	28	31	Kravel Koalbeard—Thousand Needles Mirage Raceway	Hemet Nesingwary		1250	30●
Test of Lore	Thousand Needles	Horde	25	30	Braug Dimspirit—Stonetalon The Talondeep Path	Braug Dimspirit	Test of Lore	250	
Test of Lore	Thousand Needles	Horde	25	30	Parqual Fintallas—Undercity	Parqual Fintallas	Test of Lore	250	

Thunder Bluff

Title	Location	Faction	Min Level	Con Level	Starter Location	Finisher	Prerequisite	Max XP	Cash Reward
A Lesson to Learn	Thunder Bluff	Horde	16	16	Turak Runetotem—Thunder Bluff	Dendrite Starblaze		120	
Until Death Do Us Part	Thunder Bluff	Horde	12	15	Clarice Foster—Thunder Bluff	Yuriv's Tombstone		550	
The Ashenvale Hunt	Thunder Bluff	Horde	20	20	Bluff Runner Windstrider—Thunder Bluff	Senani Thunderheart		160	
Preparation for Ceremony	Thunder Bluff	Horde	7	11	Eyahn Eagletalon—Thunder Bluff	Eyahn Eagletalon		875	
CHOICE OF: 1 Bound Harness or 1 Tribal Warrior's Shield									
Gathering Leather	Thunder Bluff	Horde	4	8	Veren Tallstrider—Thunder Bluff	Veren Tallstrider		875	
CHOICE OF: 1 Animal Skin Belt or 1 Double-layered Gloves									
Kodo Hide Bag	Thunder Bluff	Horde	4	10	Veren Tallstrider—Thunder Bluff	Veren Tallstrider		420	
REWARD: 1 Pattern: Kodo Hide Bag									
Sergra Darkthorn	Thunder Bluff	Horde	10	10	Melor Stonehoof—Thunder Bluff	Sergra Darkthorn	The Hunter's Way	85	
The Barrens Oases	Thunder Bluff	Horde	10	10	Arch Druid Hamuul Runetotem—Thunder Bluff	Tonga Runetotem	The Forgotten Pools	85	
Serpentbloom	Thunder Bluff	Horde	14	18	Apothecary Zamah—Thunder Bluff	Apothecary Zamah		1700	20●
REWARD: 1 Apothecary Gloves									
The New Frontier	Thunder Bluff	Horde	54	55	Bluff Runner Windstrider—Thunder Bluff	Arch Druid Hamuul Runetotem		550	
Compendium of the Fallen	Thunder Bluff	Horde	28	38	Sage Truthseeker—Thunder Bluff	Sage Truthseeker		3550	
CHOICE OF: 1 Vile Protector or 1 Forcestone Buckler or 1 Omega Orb									
Forsaken Aid	Thunder Bluff	Horde	13	18	Magatha Grimtotem—Thunder Bluff	Apothecary Zamah	The Elder Crone	340	
Journey to Tarren Mill	Thunder Bluff	Horde	13	18	Apothecary Zamah—Thunder Bluff	Apothecary Lydon	Forsaken Aid	1350	
A Vengeful Fate	Thunder Bluff	Horde	29	34	Auld Stonespire—Thunder Bluff	Auld Stonespire		4050	
CHOICE OF: 1 Berylline Pads or 1 Stonefist Girdle or 1 Marbled Buckler									
Rabine Saturna	Thunder Bluff	Horde	54	55	Arch Druid Hamuul Runetotem—Thunder Bluff	Rabine Saturna	The New Frontier	1400	
The Sacred Flame	Thunder Bluff	Horde	20	25	Zangen Stonehoof—Thunder Bluff	Zangen Stonehoof		2550	35●
The Sacred Flame	Thunder Bluff	Horde	20	29	Zangen Stonehoof—Thunder Bluff	Rau Cliffrunner	The Sacred Flame	600	
The Platinum Discs	Thunder Bluff	Horde	40	47	Sage Truthseeker—Thunder Bluff	Bena Winterhoof	The Platinum Discs	420	
CHOICE OF: 5 Superior Healing Potion or 5 Greater Mana Potion REWARD: 1 Thawpelt Sack									
Portents of Uldum	Thunder Bluff	Horde	45	50	Sage Truthseeker—Thunder Bluff	Nara Wildmane	The Platinum Discs	470	
Seeing What Happens	Thunder Bluff	Horde	45	50	Nara Wildmane—Thunder Bluff	Uldum Pedestal	Portents of Uldum	4700	
Un'Goro Soil	Thunder Bluff	Horde	47	50	Arch Druid Hamuul Runetotem—Thunder Bluff	Ghede		4700	1●45●
Assisting Arch Druid Runetotem	Thunder Bluff	Horde	47	50	Innkeeper Pala—Thunder Bluff	Arch Druid Hamuul Runetotem		470	
Morrowgrain Research	Thunder Bluff	Horde	47	50	Arch Druid Hamuul Runetotem—Thunder Bluff	Bashana Runetotem	Un'Goro Soil	470	
REWARD: 20 Packet of Tharlendris Seeds									
Morrowgrain Research	Thunder Bluff	Horde	47	50	Bashana Runetotem—Thunder Bluff	Bashana Runetotem	Morrowgrain Research	4700	
REWARD: 1 Cenarion Circle Cache									
Morrowgrain to Thunder Bluff	Thunder Bluff	Horde	47	55		Bashana Runetotem	Morrowgrain Research	550	
REWARD: 1 Cenarion Circle Cache									
A Call to Arms: The Plaguelands!	Thunder Bluff	Horde	50	50	Bluff Runner Windstrider—Thunder Bluff	High Executor Derrington		470	
Searching for the Lost Satchel	Thunder Bluff	Horde	9	16	Rahauro—Thunder Bluff	Maur Grimtotem		875	
Testing an Enemy's Strength	Thunder Bluff	Horde	9	15	Rahauro—Thunder Bluff	Rahauro		1050	
Returning the Lost Satchel	Thunder Bluff	Horde	9	16	Maur Grimtotem—Ragefire Chasm	Rahauro	Searching for the Lost Satchel	1450	
CHOICE OF: 1 Featherbead Bracers or 1 Savannah Bracers									
Moonglade	Thunder Bluff	Horde	10	10	Turak Runetotem—Thunder Bluff	Dendrite Starblaze		210	
Heeding the Call	Thunder Bluff	Horde	10	10	Innkeeper Pala—Thunder Bluff	Turak Runetotem		85	
Body and Heart	Thunder Bluff	Horde	10	10	Turak Runetotem—Thunder Bluff	Turak Runetotem	Back to Thunder Bluff	850	
Lessons Anew	Thunder Bluff	Horde	14	14	Turak Runetotem—Thunder Bluff	Dendrite Starblaze		100	
Great-father Winter is Here!	Thunder Bluff	Horde	10	60	Whulwert Copperpinch—Thunder Bluff Low Rise	Great-father Winter		650	
A Donation of Wool	Thunder Bluff	Horde	12	60		Rumstag Proudstrider		650	
A Donation of Silk	Thunder Bluff	Horde	26	60		Rumstag Proudstrider		1650	
A Donation of Mageweave	Thunder Bluff	Horde	40	60		Rumstag Proudstrider		3300	
A Donation of Runecloth	Thunder Bluff	Horde	50	60		Rumstag Proudstrider	A Donation of Wool	6600	
Additional Runecloth	Thunder Bluff	Horde	50	60		Rumstag Proudstrider	A Donation of Runecloth		
Dancing for Marzipan	Thunder Bluff	Horde	10	60	Innkeeper Pala—Thunder Bluff	Innkeeper Pala			
REWARD: 1 Thunder Bluff Marzipan									
The Lunar Festival	Thunder Bluff	Horde	1	60		Lunar Festival Harbinger			

TH

Title	Location	Faction	Min Level	Con Level	Starter Location	Finisher	Prerequisite	Max XP	Cash Reward
Runecloth	Timbermaw Hold	Both	50	55	Meilosh—Timbermaw Monster Furbolg Common	Meilosh		5650	
CHOICE OF: 1 Shadowskin Spaulders or 1 Bricksteel Gauntlets									
Sacred Cloth	Timbermaw Hold	Both	50	55	Meilosh—Timbermaw Monster Furbolg Common	Meilosh		5650	
The Root of All Evil	Timbermaw Hold	Both	45	60	Gorn One Eye—Timbermaw Monster Furbolg Common	Gorn One Eye		6600	
REWARD: 1 Defender of the Timbermaw									
The Brokering of Peace	Timbermaw Hold	Alliance	45	60	Gorn One Eye—Timbermaw Monster Furbolg Common	King Magni Bronzebeard	The Root of All Evil	9950	
The Brokering of Peace	Timbermaw Hold	Horde	45	60	Gorn One Eye—Timbermaw Monster Furbolg Common	Thrall	The Root of All Evil	9950	

Tirisfal Glades

Title	Location	Faction	Min Level	Con Level	Starter Location	Finisher	Prerequisite	Max XP	Cash Reward
Deaths in the Family	Tirisfal Glades	Horde	7	11	Coleman Farthing—Tirisfal Glades	Coleman Farthing		875	4●
Speak with Sevren	Tirisfal Glades	Horde	7	10	Coleman Farthing—Tirisfal Glades	Magistrate Sevren	Deaths in the Family	85	
Rear Guard Patrol	Tirisfal Glades	Horde	6	11	Deathguard Linnea—Tirisfal Glades	Deathguard Linnea		650	3●
Graverobbers	Tirisfal Glades	Horde	4	8	Magistrate Sevren—Tirisfal Glades Brill	Magistrate Sevren		700	2●25●
CHOICE OF: 1 Cold Steel Gauntlets or 1 Zombie Skin Boots									
Forsaken Duties	Tirisfal Glades	Horde	6	9	Magistrate Sevren—Tirisfal Glades Brill	Deathguard Linnea	Graverobbers	200	
Return to the Magistrate	Tirisfal Glades	Horde	6	9	Deathguard Linnea—Tirisfal Glades	Magistrate Sevren	Forsaken Duties	390	1●50●
A Letter Undelivered	Tirisfal Glades	Horde	4	7	A Letter to Yvette	Yvette Farthing		480	
The Haunted Mills	Tirisfal Glades	Horde	7	10	Coleman Farthing—Tirisfal Glades	Coleman Farthing		420	
Fields of Grief	Tirisfal Glades	Horde	4	7	Deathguard Simmer—Tirisfal Glades	Apothecary Johaan		625	1●75●
A New Plague	Tirisfal Glades	Horde	6	6	Apothecary Johaan—Tirisfal Glades	Apothecary Johaan		550	1●25●
REWARD: 3 Weak Troll's Blood Potion									
A New Plague	Tirisfal Glades	Horde	6	9	Apothecary Johaan—Tirisfal Glades	Apothecary Johaan	A New Plague	775	3●
REWARD: 5 Slumber Sand									
A New Plague	Tirisfal Glades	Horde	6	11	Apothecary Johaan—Tirisfal Glades	Apothecary Johaan	A New Plague	220	
REWARD: 1 Apprentice Sash									
At War With The Scarlet Crusade	Tirisfal Glades	Horde	5	9	Executor Zygand—Tirisfal Glades Brill	Executor Zygand	At War With The Scarlet Crusade	775	3●
At War With The Scarlet Crusade	Tirisfal Glades	Horde	5	10	Executor Zygand—Tirisfal Glades Brill	Executor Zygand	At War With The Scarlet Crusade	850	3●50●
At War With The Scarlet Crusade	Tirisfal Glades	Horde	5	12	Executor Zygand—Tirisfal Glades Brill	Executor Zygand	At War With The Scarlet Crusade	900	
CHOICE OF: 1 Ceremonial Knife or 1 Striking Hatchet									
Proof of Demise	Tirisfal Glades	Horde	5	7	Deathguard Burgess—Tirisfal Glades Brill	Deathguard Burgess	At War With The Scarlet Crusade	625	1●75●
CHOICE OF: 1 Zombie Skin Bracers or 1 Clasped Belt or 1 Netted Gloves									
The Chill of Death	Tirisfal Glades	Horde	7	8	Gretchen Dedmar—Tirisfal Glades Brill	Gretchen Dedmar		700	2●25●
CHOICE OF: 1 Adept's Cloak or 1 Sewing Gloves									
Wanted: Maggot Eye	Tirisfal Glades	Horde	6	10	Wanted Poster—Tirisfal Glades	Executor Zygand		850	3●50●

Title	Location	Faction	Min Level	Con Level	Starter Location	Finisher	Prerequisite	Max XP	Cash Reward
CHOICE OF: 1 Brass Scale Pants or 1 Tiller's Vest									
A Putrid Task	Tirisfal Glades	Horde	4	6	Deathguard Dillinger—Tirisfal Glades Brill	Deathguard Dillinger		410	1●
The Prodigal Lich	Tirisfal Glades	Horde	5	8	Magistrate Sevren—Tirisfal Glades Brill	Bethor Iceshard	Graverobbers	180	
Fields of Grief	Tirisfal Glades	Horde	4	7	Apothecary Johaan—Tirisfal Glades	Captured Scarlet Zealot	Fields of Grief	160	
The Family Crypt	Tirisfal Glades	Horde	7	13	Magistrate Sevren—Tirisfal Glades Brill	Magistrate Sevren	Speak with Sevren	900	
CHOICE OF: 1 Darkwood Staff or 1 Bonecracker									
Proving Allegiance	Tirisfal Glades	Horde	5	12	Gunther Arcanus—Tirisfal Glades	Gunther Arcanus	Return the Book	675	
The Dormant Shade	Tirisfal Glades	Horde	5	10		Lillith's Dinner Table			
The Prodigal Lich Returns	Tirisfal Glades	Horde	5	12	Gunther Arcanus—Tirisfal Glades	Bethor Iceshard	Proving Allegiance	900	
REWARD: 1 Bone Buckler									
The Mills Overrun	Tirisfal Glades	Horde	6	8	Deathguard Dillinger—Tirisfal Glades Brill	Deathguard Dillinger	A Putrid Task	875	4● 50●
CHOICE OF: 1 Cryptwalker Boots or 1 Sturdy Cloth Trousers									
At War With The Scarlet Crusade	Tirisfal Glades	Horde	5	8	Executor Zygand—Tirisfal Glades Brill	Executor Zygand		700	2● 25●
Candles of Beckoning	Tirisfal Glades	Horde	5	10		Crate of Candles			
REWARD: 1 Candle of Beckoning									
Delivery to Silverpine Forest	Tirisfal Glades	Horde	9	10	Apothecary Johaan—Tirisfal Glades	Apothecary Renferrel		625	2● 50●
A New Plague	Tirisfal Glades	Horde	6	11	Apothecary Johaan—Tirisfal Glades	Captured Mountaineer	A New Plague	875	
Halgar's Summons	Tirisfal Glades	Horde	10	10	Ageron Kargal—Tirisfal Glades Brill	Carendin Halgar	Creature of the Void	210	
Stinking Up Southshore	Tirisfal Glades	Horde	25	60	Darkcaller Yanka—Tirisfal Glades	Darkcaller Yanka		1650	
REWARD: 15 Hallow's End Pumpkin Treat									
Mennet Carkad	Tirisfal Glades	Horde	10	10	Marion Call—Tirisfal Glades Brill	Mennet Carkad	The Deathstalkers	210	
Gordo's Task	Tirisfal Glades	Horde	5	5	Gordo—Tirisfal Glades	Junior Apothecary Holland		230	
Doom Weed	Tirisfal Glades	Horde	5	6	Junior Apothecary Holland—Tirisfal Glades	Junior Apothecary Holland	Gordo's Task	550	1● 25●
Garments of Darkness	Tirisfal Glades	Horde	5	4	Dark Cleric Beryl—Tirisfal Glades Brill	Dark Cleric Beryl		270	
REWARD: 1 Acolyte's Sacrificial Robes									
In Favor of Darkness	Tirisfal Glades	Horde	5	4	Dark Cleric Duesten—Tirisfal Glades Deathknell	Dark Cleric Beryl		90	
Rotten Eggs	Tirisfal Glades	Horde	30	60	Darkcaller Yanka—Tirisfal Glades	Keg		1650	
Ruined Kegs	Tirisfal Glades	Horde	25	60	Beer Keg—Hillsbrad	Darkcaller Yanka	Rotten Eggs	1650	
REWARD: 15 Hallow's End Pumpkin Treat									
Errand for Apothecary Zinge	Undercity	Horde	38	45	Apothecary Zinge—Undercity	Alessandro Luca		390	
Errand for Apothecary Zinge	Undercity	Horde	38	45	Alessandro Luca—Undercity	Apothecary Zinge	Errand for Apothecary Zinge	390	
Into the Field	Undercity	Horde	38	46	Apothecary Zinge—Undercity	Chief Engineer Bilgewhizzle	Errand for Apothecary Zinge	2000	
The Lich's Identity	Undercity	Horde	5	8	Bethor Iceshard—Undercity	Bethor Iceshard	The Prodigal Lich	525	1● 75●
Return the Book	Undercity	Horde	5	8	Bethor Iceshard—Undercity	Gunther Arcanus	The Lich's Identity	350	
The Crown of Will	Undercity	Horde	34	39	Sharlindra—Undercity	Melisara	The Crown of Will	300	
A Husband's Revenge	Undercity	Horde	10	20	Raleigh Andrean—Undercity	Raleigh Andrean	Raleigh and the Undercity	1550	12●
REWARD: 1 Ring of Scorn									
The Star, the Hand and the Heart	Undercity	Horde	30	44	Keeper Bel'dugur—Undercity	Keeper Bel'dugur	To the Undercity for Yogyin's Digest	5600	
The New Frontier	Undercity	Horde	54	55	Harbinger Balthazad—Undercity	Arch Druid Hamuul Runetotem		550	
Into The Scarlet Monastery	Undercity	Horde	33	42	Varimathras—Undercity	Varimathras		5150	
CHOICE OF: 1 Sword of Omen or 1 Prophetic Cane or 1 Dragon's Blood Necklace									
Going, Going, Guano!	Undercity	Horde	30	33	Master Apothecary Faranell—Undercity	Master Apothecary Faranell		3300	
Hearts of Zeal	Undercity	Horde	30	33	Master Apothecary Faranell—Undercity	Master Apothecary Faranell	Going, Going, Guano!	3300	
To Steal From Thieves	Undercity	Horde	27	36	Genavie Callow—Undercity	Genavie Callow		2800	
CHOICE OF: 1 Grim Pauldrons or 1 Gallan Cuffs									
The Binding	Undercity	Horde	10	10	Carendin Halgar—Undercity	Carendin Halgar	Creature of the Void	625	
Devourer of Souls	Undercity	Horde	20	20	Carendin Halgar—Undercity	Godrick Farsan	Devourer of Souls	160	
Creature of the Void	Undercity	Horde	10	10	Carendin Halgar—Undercity	Carendin Halgar	Creature of the Void	625	
The Binding	Undercity	Horde	20	20	Carendin Halgar—Undercity	Carendin Halgar	Hearts of the Pure	1550	
REWARD: 1 Small Soul Pouch									
Hearts of the Pure	Undercity	Horde	20	20	Godrick Farsan—Undercity	Carendin Halgar	Devourer of Souls	1550	
Tome of the Cabal	Undercity	Horde	30	30	Jorah Annison—Undercity	Jorah Annison	Tome of the Cabal	600	
Tome of the Cabal	Undercity	Horde	30	30	Jorah Annison—Undercity	Strahad Farsan	Tome of the Cabal	2450	
The Deathstalkers	Undercity	Horde	10	13	Mennet Carkad—Undercity	Mennet Carkad		675	
The Deathstalkers	Undercity	Horde	10	13	Mennet Carkad—Undercity	Andron Gant	The Deathstalkers	230	
The Deathstalkers	Undercity	Horde	10	13	Andron Gant—Undercity	Mennet Carkad	The Deathstalkers	230	
The Deathstalkers	Undercity	Horde	10	13	Mennet Carkad—Undercity	Varimathras	The Deathstalkers	900	
REWARD: 1 Blade of Cunning									
Fenwick Thatros	Undercity	Horde	16	16	Mennet Carkad—Undercity	Mennet Carkad		875	
Tools of the Trade	Undercity	Horde	16	20	Mennet Carkad—Undercity	Mennet Carkad	Fenwick Thatros	1550	
Reclaimed Treasures	Undercity	Horde	33	43	Patrick Garrett—Undercity	Patrick Garrett		3600	60●
Find the Shattered Hand	Undercity	Horde	16	16	Mennet Carkad—Undercity	Shenthul	To Orgrimmar!	120	
Lines of Communication	Undercity	Horde	42	47	Oran Snakewrithe—Undercity	Oran Snakewrithe		3150	70●
Seeking Strahad	Undercity	Horde	30	30	Carendin Halgar—Undercity	Strahad Farsan		600	
Bring the End	Undercity	Horde	37	42	Andrew Brownell—Undercity	Andrew Brownell		4300	
REWARD: 1 Vanquisher's Sword, 1Amberglow Talisman									
Goblin Engineering	Undercity	Horde	30	47	Graham Van Talen—Undercity	Nixx Sprocketspring	The Pledge of Secrecy	420	
Seeping Corruption	Undercity	Horde	45	52	Chemist Cuely—Undercity	Chemist Cuely		2550	40●
Seeping Corruption	Undercity	Horde	45	52	Chemist Cuely—Undercity	Thersa Windsong	Seeping Corruption	500	
Seeping Corruption	Undercity	Horde	45	52		Chemist Cuely	Seeping Corruption	5100	75●
Gnome Engineering	Undercity	Horde	30	47	Graham Van Talen—Undercity	Oglethorpe Obnoticus	The Pledge of Secrecy	420	
Assisting Arch Druid Runetotem	Undercity	Horde	47	50	Innkeeper Norman—Undercity	Arch Druid Hamuul Runetotem		470	
A Sample of Slime...	Undercity	Horde	48	52	Chemist Fuely—Undercity	Chemist Fuely		5100	60●
... and a Batch of Ooze	Undercity	Horde	48	56	Chemist Fuely—Undercity	Chemist Fuely		5800	65●
Testing for Impurities - Un'Goro Crater	Undercity	Horde	48	52		Testing Equipment			
REWARD: 1 Un'Goro Tested Sample									
Melding of Influences	Undercity	Horde	48	55	Chemist Fuely—Undercity	Chemist Fuely	A Sample of Slime...	7050	
CHOICE OF: 1 Chemist's Ring or 1 Chemist's Smock									
Testing for Corruption - Felwood	Undercity	Horde	48	52		Testing Equipment			
REWARD: 1 Corrupt Tested Sample									
The Jeremiah Blues	Undercity	Horde	50	52	Royal Overseer Bauhaus—Undercity	Jeremiah Payson	Better Late Than Never	5100	
A Call to Arms: The Plaguelands!	Undercity	Horde	50	50	Harbinger Balthazad—Undercity	High Executor Derrington		470	
Devouring Plague	Undercity	Horde	20	20	Miles Welsh—Thunder Bluff	Aelthalyste		390	
Devouring Plague	Undercity	Horde	20	20	Ur'kyo—Orgrimmar	Aelthalyste		390	
Touch of Weakness	Undercity	Horde	10	10		Aelthalyste			
Touch of Weakness	Undercity	Horde	10	10	Tai'jin—Durotar Razor Hill	Aelthalyste		210	
Touch of Weakness	Undercity	Horde	10	10	Var'jun—Mulgore Bloodhoof Village	Aelthalyste		210	
Touch of Weakness	Undercity	Horde	10	10	Ur'kyo—Orgrimmar	Aelthalyste		210	
Touch of Weakness	Undercity	Horde	10	10	Miles Welsh—Thunder Bluff	Aelthalyste		210	
Devouring Plague	Undercity	Horde	20	20		Aelthalyste			
The Power to Destroy...	Undercity	Horde	9	16	Varimathras—Undercity	Varimathras		1450	5● 33●
CHOICE OF: 1 Ghastly Trousers or 1 Dredgemire Leggings or 1 Gargoyle Leggings									
The Champion of the Banshee Queen	Undercity	Horde	54	56	Lady Sylvanas Windrunner—Undercity	Nathanos Blightcaller		1450	
Great-father Winter is Here!	Undercity	Horde	10	60	Nardstrum Copperpinch—Undercity Trade Quarter	Great-father Winter		650	
A Donation of Wool	Undercity	Horde	12	60		Ralston Farnsley		650	
A Donation of Silk	Undercity	Horde	26	60		Ralston Farnsley		1650	
A Donation of Mageweave	Undercity	Horde	40	60		Ralston Farnsley		3300	
A Donation of Runecloth	Undercity	Horde	50	60		Ralston Farnsley	A Donation of Wool	6600	

Undercity

Title	Location	Faction	Min Level	Con Level	Starter Location	Finisher	Prerequisite	Max XP	Cash Reward
Additional Runecloth	Undercity	Horde	50	60		Ralston Farnsley	A Donation of Runecloth		
Oran's Gratitude	Undercity	Horde	42	47		Oran Snakewrithe	Rin'ji's Secret	4200	70
CHOICE OF: 1 Undercity Reservist's Cap or 1 Antiquated Nobleman's Tunic									
Chicken Clucking for a Mint	Undercity	Horde	10	60	Innkeeper Norman—Undercity	Innkeeper Norman			
REWARD: 1 Undercity Mint									
The Lunar Festival	Undercity	Horde	1	60		Lunar Festival Harbinger			

Un'Goro Crater

Title	Location	Faction	Min Level	Con Level	Starter Location	Finisher	Prerequisite	Max XP	Cash Reward
Finding the Source	Un'Goro Crater	Both	51	55	Krakle—Un'Goro Crater Golakka Hot Springs	Krakle		5650	
The New Springs	Un'Goro Crater	Both	51	55	Krakle—Un'Goro Crater Golakka Hot Springs	Donova Snowden	Finding the Source	2800	
It's a Secret to Everybody	Un'Goro Crater	Both	47	52	A Wrecked Raft—Un'Goro Crater	A Small Pack		1250	
It's a Secret to Everybody	Un'Goro Crater	Both	47	52	A Small Pack—Un'Goro Crater	Linken	It's a Secret to Everybody	5100	
Expedition Salvation	Un'Goro Crater	Both	48	53	Williden Marshal—Un'Goro Crater Marshal's Refuge	Williden Marshal		4200	40
Roll the Bones	Un'Goro Crater	Both	49	51	Spark Nilminer—Un'Goro Crater Marshal's Refuge	Spark Nilminer		4900	
CHOICE OF: 1 Archaeologist's Quarry Boots or 1 Excavator's Utility Belt									
Alien Ecology	Un'Goro Crater	Both	48	52	Hol'anyee Marshal—Un'Goro Crater Marshal's Refuge	Hol'anyee Marshal		3050	40
Williden's Journal	Un'Goro Crater	Both	48	50	A Mangled Journal	Williden Marshal		3550	
It's a Secret to Everybody	Un'Goro Crater	Both	47	52	Linken—Un'Goro Crater Marshal's Refuge	Donova Snowden	It's a Secret to Everybody	5100	
The Videre Elixir	Un'Goro Crater	Both	47	52	Donova Snowden—Winterspring	Donova Snowden	It's a Secret to Everybody	5100	
Meet at the Grave	Un'Goro Crater	Both	47	52	Donova Snowden—Winterspring	Gaeriyan	The Videre Elixir	5100	
A Grave Situation	Un'Goro Crater	Both	47	52	Gaeriyan—Tanaris	A Conspicuous Gravestone	Meet at the Grave	2550	
Linken's Sword	Un'Goro Crater	Both	47	52	A Conspicuous Gravestone—Tanaris	Linken	A Grave Situation	5100	75
A Gnome's Assistance	Un'Goro Crater	Both	47	52	Linken—Un'Goro Crater Marshal's Refuge	J.D. Collie	Linken's Sword	1250	
Linken's Memory	Un'Goro Crater	Both	47	54	J.D. Collie—Un'Goro Crater Fire Plume Ridge	Eridan Bluewind	A Gnome's Assistance	5450	
Linken's Adventure	Un'Goro Crater	Both	47	54	J.D. Collie—Un'Goro Crater Fire Plume Ridge	Linken	Aquementas	2700	
It's Dangerous to Go Alone	Un'Goro Crater	Both	47	56	Linken—Un'Goro Crater Marshal's Refuge	Linken	Linken's Adventure	7300	
CHOICE OF: 1 Linken's Sword of Mastery or 1 Spirit of Aquementas REWARD: 1 Linken's Boomerang									
Aquementas	Un'Goro Crater	Both	47	54	Eridan Bluewind—Felwood Emerald Sanctuary	J.D. Collie	Silver Heart	5450	
Silver Heart	Un'Goro Crater	Both	47	54	Eridan Bluewind—Felwood Emerald Sanctuary	Eridan Bluewind	Linken's Memory	5450	
Muigin and Larion	Un'Goro Crater	Alliance	47	52	Muigin—Un'Goro Crater Marshal's Refuge	Muigin		5100	
A Visit to Gregan	Un'Goro Crater	Alliance	47	52	Muigin—Un'Goro Crater Marshal's Refuge	Gregan Brewspewer	Muigin and Larion	3800	
Haze of Evil	Un'Goro Crater	Alliance	47	52	Gregan Brewspewer—Feralas	Muigin	A Visit to Gregan	5100	75
Bloodpetal Sprouts	Un'Goro Crater	Alliance	47	53		Muigin	Haze of Evil	3950	
Larion and Muigin	Un'Goro Crater	Horde	47	52	Larion—Un'Goro Crater Marshal's Refuge	Larion		5100	75
Zapper Fuel	Un'Goro Crater	Horde	47	52	Liv Rizzlefix—Barrens Ratchet	Larion	Marvon's Workshop	5100	
Marvon's Workshop	Un'Goro Crater	Horde	47	52	Larion—Un'Goro Crater Marshal's Refuge	Liv Rizzlefix	Larion and Muigin	2550	
Bloodpetal Zapper	Un'Goro Crater	Horde	47	53		Larion	Zapper Fuel	3950	1 60
REWARD: 1 Bloodpetal Zapper									
Chasing A-Me 01	Un'Goro Crater	Both	48	53	Karna Remtravel—Un'Goro Crater Lakkari Tar Pits	A-Me 01		2650	
Chasing A-Me 01	Un'Goro Crater	Both	48	53	A-Me 01—Un'Goro Crater Monster Gorilla Common	A-Me 01	Chasing A-Me 01	3950	
Chasing A-Me 01	Un'Goro Crater	Both	48	53	A-Me 01—Un'Goro Crater Monster Gorilla Common	Karna Remtravel	Chasing A-Me 01	6550	1 60
Crystals of Power	Un'Goro Crater	Both	47	53	J.D. Collie—Un'Goro Crater Fire Plume Ridge	J.D. Collie		5250	80
The Northern Pylon	Un'Goro Crater	Both	47	53	J.D. Collie—Un'Goro Crater Fire Plume Ridge	J.D. Collie	Crystals of Power	3950	
The Eastern Pylon	Un'Goro Crater	Both	47	53	J.D. Collie—Un'Goro Crater Fire Plume Ridge	J.D. Collie	Crystals of Power	3950	
The Western Pylon	Un'Goro Crater	Both	47	53	J.D. Collie—Un'Goro Crater Fire Plume Ridge	J.D. Collie	Crystals of Power	3950	
The Apes of Un'Goro	Un'Goro Crater	Both	47	55	Torwa Pathfinder—Un'Goro Crater	Torwa Pathfinder		5650	85
The Fare of Lar'korwi	Un'Goro Crater	Both	48	53	Torwa Pathfinder—Un'Goro Crater	Torwa Pathfinder		5250	
The Scent of Lar'korwi	Un'Goro Crater	Both	48	53	Torwa Pathfinder—Un'Goro Crater	Torwa Pathfinder	The Fare of Lar'korwi	5250	
The Bait for Lar'korwi	Un'Goro Crater	Both	48	56	Torwa Pathfinder—Un'Goro Crater	Torwa Pathfinder	The Scent of Lar'korwi	7300	
CHOICE OF: 1 Plainstalker Tunic or 1 Outrider Leggings									
The Mighty U'cha	Un'Goro Crater	Both	50	55	Torwa Pathfinder—Un'Goro Crater	Torwa Pathfinder	The Apes of Un'Goro	5650	
CHOICE OF: 1 Beastsmasher or 1 Beastslayer									
Making Sense of It	Un'Goro Crater	Both	47	53	J.D. Collie—Un'Goro Crater Fire Plume Ridge	J.D. Collie	The Northern Pylon	525	
REWARD: 1 Crystal Pylon User's Manual									
Crystal Restore	Un'Goro Crater	Both	47	53		Northern Crystal Pylon	Making Sense of It		
REWARD: 6 Crystal Restore									
Crystal Force	Un'Goro Crater	Both	47	53		Eastern Crystal Pylon	Making Sense of It		
REWARD: 6 Crystal Force									
Crystal Ward	Un'Goro Crater	Both	47	53		Western Crystal Pylon	Making Sense of It		
REWARD: 6 Crystal Ward									
Crystal Yield	Un'Goro Crater	Both	47	53		Western Crystal Pylon	Making Sense of It		
REWARD: 6 Crystal Yield									
Crystal Charge	Un'Goro Crater	Both	47	53		Northern Crystal Pylon	Making Sense of It		
REWARD: 6 Crystal Charge									
Crystal Spire	Un'Goro Crater	Both	47	53		Eastern Crystal Pylon	Making Sense of It		
REWARD: 6 Crystal Spire									
A Little Help From My Friends	Un'Goro Crater	Both	50	55	Ringo—Un'Goro Crater Fire Plume Ridge	Spraggle Frock	Lost!	5650	
CHOICE OF: 1 Bejeweled Legguards or 1 Treetop Leggings or 1 Clayridge Helm									
Lost!	Un'Goro Crater	Both	50	55	Spraggle Frock—Un'Goro Crater Marshal's Refuge	Ringo		2800	
Beware of Pterrordax	Un'Goro Crater	Both	49	55	Wanted Poster—Un'Goro Crater	Spraggle Frock		5650	
CHOICE OF: 1 Grotslab Gloves or 1 Cragplate Greaves									
Shizzle's Flyer	Un'Goro Crater	Both	49	51	Shizzle—Un'Goro Crater Marshal's Refuge	Shizzle		4900	
CHOICE OF: 1 Shizzle's Drizzle Blocker or 1 Shizzle's Muzzle or 1 Shizzle's Nozzle Wiper									
Dadanga is Hungry!	Un'Goro Crater	Both	47	55		Dadanga			
REWARD: 1 Small Brown-wrapped Package									
Toxic Test	Un'Goro Crater	Both	50	52	Torwa Pathfinder—Un'Goro Crater	Torwa Pathfinder	Bloodpetal Poison	5100	
Bloodpetal Poison	Un'Goro Crater	Both	50	52	Torwa Pathfinder—Un'Goro Crater	Torwa Pathfinder		5100	
REWARD: 2 Major Healing Potion									
A Better Ingredient	Un'Goro Crater	Both	50	52	Torwa Pathfinder—Un'Goro Crater	Torwa Pathfinder	Toxic Test	6350	
CHOICE OF: 1 Grizzled Pelt or 1 Forest's Embrace or 1 Moonshadow Stave									

Valley of Trials

Title	Location	Faction	Min Level	Con Level	Starter Location	Finisher	Prerequisite	Max XP	Cash Reward
Cutting Teeth	Valley of Trials	Horde	1	2	Gornek—Durotar Valley of Trials	Gornek		170	
CHOICE OF: 1 Soft Wool Boots or 1 Battleworn Leather Gloves									
Sting of the Scorpid	Valley of Trials	Horde	1	3	Gornek—Durotar Valley of Trials	Gornek	Cutting Teeth	250	
CHOICE OF: 1 Soft Wool Belt or 1 Battleworn Cape									
Sarkoth	Valley of Trials	Horde	1	5	Hana'zua—Durotar Valley of Trials	Hana'zua		450	
Vile Familiars	Valley of Trials	Horde	2	4	Zureetha Fargaze—Durotar Valley of Trials	Zureetha Fargaze		450	
CHOICE OF: 1 Primitive Club or 1 Primitive Hand Blade or 1 Primitive Hatchet or 1 Primitive Walking Stick									
Burning Blade Medallion	Valley of Trials	Horde	1	5	Zureetha Fargaze—Durotar Valley of Trials	Zureetha Fargaze	Vile Familiars	675	
CHOICE OF: 1 Dust-covered Leggings or 1 Jagged Chain Vest or 1 Ripped Pants REWARD: 1 Minor Healing Potion									
Sarkoth	Valley of Trials	Horde	1	5	Hana'zua—Durotar Valley of Trials	Gornek	Sarkoth	110	
CHOICE OF: 1 Soft Wool Vest or 1 Battleworn Chain Leggings									
Report to Sen'jin Village	Valley of Trials	Horde	1	5	Zureetha Fargaze—Durotar Valley of Trials	Master Gadrin	Burning Blade Medallion	230	
Earth Sapta	Valley of Trials	Horde	4	4		Canaga Earthcaller	Call of Earth		
REWARD: 1 Earth Sapta									
Vile Familiars	Valley of Trials	Horde	1	4	Ruzan—Durotar Valley of Trials	Ruzan		360	
Vile Familiars	Valley of Trials	Horde	1	4	Ruzan—Durotar Valley of Trials	Zureetha Fargaze	Vile Familiars	35	
CHOICE OF: 1 Primitive Hand Blade or 1 Primitive Walking Stick									
Call of Earth	Valley of Trials	Horde	4	4	Canaga Earthcaller—Durotar Valley of Trials	Canaga Earthcaller	Call of Earth	270	
Call of Earth	Valley of Trials	Horde	4	4	Canaga Earthcaller—Durotar Valley of Trials	Minor Manifestation of Earth	Call of Earth	270	
Call of Earth	Valley of Trials	Horde	4	4	Minor Manifestation of Earth—Durotar Mulgore	Canaga Earthcaller	Call of Earth	450	

Title	Location	Faction	Min Level	Con Level	Starter Location	Finisher	Prerequisite	Max XP	Cash Reward
REWARD: 1 Earth Totem									
Simple Parchment	Valley of Trials	Horde	1	1	Gornek—Durotar Valley of Trials	Frang	Cutting Teeth	40	
Simple Tablet	Valley of Trials	Horde	1	1	Gornek—Durotar Valley of Trials	Frang	Cutting Teeth	40	
Etched Tablet	Valley of Trials	Horde	1	1	Gornek—Durotar Valley of Trials	Jen'shan	Cutting Teeth	40	
Encrypted Tablet	Valley of Trials	Horde	1	1	Gornek—Durotar Valley of Trials	Rwag	Cutting Teeth	40	
Rune-Inscribed Tablet	Valley of Trials	Horde	1	1	Gornek—Durotar Valley of Trials	Shikrik	Cutting Teeth	40	
Hallowed Tablet	Valley of Trials	Horde	1	1	Gornek—Durotar Valley of Trials	Ken'jai	Cutting Teeth	40	
Glyphic Tablet	Valley of Trials	Horde	1	1	Gornek—Durotar Valley of Trials	Mai'ah	Cutting Teeth	40	
Etched Parchment	Valley of Trials	Horde	1	1	Gornek—Durotar Valley of Trials	Jen'shan	Cutting Teeth	40	
Encrypted Parchment	Valley of Trials	Horde	1	1	Gornek—Durotar Valley of Trials	Rwag	Cutting Teeth	40	
Rune-Inscribed Parchment	Valley of Trials	Horde	1	1	Gornek—Durotar Valley of Trials	Shikrik	Cutting Teeth	40	
Tainted Parchment	Valley of Trials	Horde	1	1	Gornek—Durotar Valley of Trials	Nartok	Cutting Teeth	40	
Galgar's Cactus Apple Surprise	Valley of Trials	Horde	1	3	Galgar—Durotar Valley of Trials	Galgar	Cutting Teeth	380	50●
REWARD: 10 Cactus Apple Surprise									
Lazy Peons	Valley of Trials	Horde	3	4	Foreman Thazz'ril—Durotar Valley of Trials	Foreman Thazz'ril		450	
Welcome!	Valley of Trials	Horde	1	1	Valley of Trials Gift Voucher	Magga			
CHOICE OF: 1 Diablo Stone or 1 Panda Collar or 1 Zergling Leash									
Thazz'ril's Pick	Valley of Trials	Horde	3	4	Foreman Thazz'ril—Durotar Valley of Trials	Foreman Thazz'ril	Lazy Peons	450	1●50●
Alas, Andorhal	Western Plaguelands	Horde	50	60	High Executor Derrington—Western Plaguelands The Bulwark	High Executor Derrington	All Along the Watchtowers	8300	
REWARD: 1 Mark of Resolution									
Alas, Andorhal	Western Plaguelands	Alliance	50	60	Commander Ashlam Valorfist—Western Plaguelands Chillwind Point	Commander Ashlam Valorfist	All Along the Watchtowers	8300	
REWARD: 1 Mark of Resolution									
Scholomance	Western Plaguelands	Horde	55	55	High Executor Derrington—Western Plaguelands The Bulwark	Apothecary Dithers	All Along the Watchtowers		
Skeletal Fragments	Western Plaguelands	Horde	55	57	Apothecary Dithers—Western Plaguelands The Bulwark	Apothecary Dithers	Scholomance	4500	
A Matter of Time	Western Plaguelands	Both	53	56	Chromie—Western Plaguelands Ruins of Anderhol	Chromie		5800	
CHOICE OF: 1 Orchid Amice or 1 Gold Link Belt									
Counting Out Time	Western Plaguelands	Both	53	56	Chromie—Western Plaguelands Ruins of Anderhol	Chromie	A Matter of Time	5800	
REWARD: 1 Attuned Dampener									
Counting Out Time	Western Plaguelands	Both	53	56	Chromie—Western Plaguelands Ruins of Anderhol	Chromie	Counting Out Time	575	
REWARD: 1 Attuned Dampener									
The Wildlife Suffers Too	Western Plaguelands	Both	51	54	Mulgris Deepriver—Western Plaguelands The Writhing Haunt	Mulgris Deepriver		4100	
The Wildlife Suffers Too	Western Plaguelands	Both	51	56	Mulgris Deepriver—Western Plaguelands The Writhing Haunt	Mulgris Deepriver	The Wildlife Suffers Too	4350	
Glyphed Oaken Branch	Western Plaguelands	Alliance	51	56	Mulgris Deepriver—Western Plaguelands The Writhing Haunt	Mathrengyl Bearwalker	The Wildlife Suffers Too	5800	
REWARD: 1 Cerise Drape									
Glyphed Oaken Branch	Western Plaguelands	Horde	51	56	Mulgris Deepriver—Western Plaguelands The Writhing Haunt	Nara Wildmane	The Wildlife Suffers Too	5800	
REWARD: 1 Cerise Drape									
Better Late Than Never	Western Plaguelands	Both	50	52	Janice Felstone—Western Plaguelands	Janice's Parcel		2550	
Better Late Than Never	Western Plaguelands	Alliance	50	52	Janice's Parcel—Western Plaguelands	Royal Factor Bathrilor	Better Late Than Never	2550	
Better Late Than Never	Western Plaguelands	Horde	50	52	Janice's Parcel—Western Plaguelands	Royal Overseer Bauhaus	Better Late Than Never	2550	
Good Luck Charm	Western Plaguelands	Alliance	50	52	Ol' Emma—Stormwind	Janice Felstone	Good Natured Emma	2550	
Two Halves Become One	Western Plaguelands	Both	50	54	Janice Felstone—Western Plaguelands	Janice Felstone	Good Luck Charm	5450	
REWARD: 1 Felstone Good Luck Charm									
Mrs. Dalson's Diary	Western Plaguelands	Both	52	55		Mrs. Dalson's Diary			
Locked Away	Western Plaguelands	Both	52	55		Outhouse			
Locked Away	Western Plaguelands	Both	52	55		Locked Cabinet		7050	2●50●
REWARD: 1 Farmer Dalson's Shotgun, 1Dalson Family Wedding Ring									
Clear the Way	Western Plaguelands	Alliance	50	52	Commander Ashlam Valorfist—Western Plaguelands Chillwind Point	Commander Ashlam Valorfist		5100	75●
Scarlet Diversions	Western Plaguelands	Horde	50	53	High Executor Derrington—Western Plaguelands The Bulwark	High Executor Derrington		5250	80●
All Along the Watchtowers	Western Plaguelands	Alliance	50	56	Commander Ashlam Valorfist—Western Plaguelands Chillwind Point	Commander Ashlam Valorfist	Clear the Way	5800	85●
All Along the Watchtowers	Western Plaguelands	Horde	50	56	High Executor Derrington—Western Plaguelands The Bulwark	High Executor Derrington	Scarlet Diversions	5800	85●
Catalogue of the Wayward	Western Plaguelands	Both	57	60	Jeziba—Western Plaguelands Ruins of Anderhol	Catalogue of the Wayward	Wrath of the Blue Flight	700	
Breastplate of the Chromatic Flight	Western Plaguelands	Both	57	60	Catalogue of the Wayward—Western Plaguelands	Jeziba	Catalogue of the Wayward	9950	
REWARD: 1 Breastplate of the Chromatic Flight									
Legplates of the Chromatic Defier	Western Plaguelands	Both	57	60	Catalogue of the Wayward—Western Plaguelands	Jeziba	Catalogue of the Wayward	9950	
CHOICE OF: 1 Legguards of the Chromatic Defier or 1 Legplates of the Chromatic Defier									
The Scourge Cauldrons	Western Plaguelands	Alliance	50	53	Commander Ashlam Valorfist—Western Plaguelands Chillwind Point	High Priestess MacDonnell	Clear the Way	525	
Target: Felstone Field	Western Plaguelands	Alliance	50	53	High Priestess MacDonnell—Western Plaguelands Chillwind Point	Scourge Cauldron	The Scourge Cauldrons	5250	
Return to Chillwind Camp	Western Plaguelands	Alliance	50	53	Scourge Cauldron—Western Plaguelands	High Priestess MacDonnell	Target: Felstone Field	2650	80●
Felstone Field Cauldron	Western Plaguelands	Both	50	53		Scourge Cauldron	Return to Chillwind Camp	525	
Target: Dalson's Tears	Western Plaguelands	Alliance	50	55	High Priestess MacDonnell—Western Plaguelands Chillwind Point	Scourge Cauldron	Return to Chillwind Camp	5650	
Return to Chillwind Camp	Western Plaguelands	Alliance	50	55	Scourge Cauldron—Western Plaguelands	High Priestess MacDonnell	Target: Dalson's Tears	2800	80●
Dalson's Tears Cauldron	Western Plaguelands	Both	50	55		Scourge Cauldron	Return to Chillwind Camp	550	
Target: Writhing Haunt	Western Plaguelands	Alliance	50	55	High Priestess MacDonnell—Western Plaguelands Chillwind Point	Scourge Cauldron	Return to Chillwind Camp	5650	
Return to Chillwind Camp	Western Plaguelands	Alliance	50	55	Scourge Cauldron—Western Plaguelands	High Priestess MacDonnell	Target: Writhing Haunt	2800	85●
Writhing Haunt Cauldron	Western Plaguelands	Both	50	55		Scourge Cauldron	Return to Chillwind Camp	550	
Target: Gahrron's Withering	Western Plaguelands	Alliance	50	58	High Priestess MacDonnell—Western Plaguelands Chillwind Point	Scourge Cauldron	Return to Chillwind Camp	6200	
Return to Chillwind Camp	Western Plaguelands	Alliance	50	58	Scourge Cauldron—Western Plaguelands	High Priestess MacDonnell	Target: Gahrron's Withering	3100	90●
Gahrron's Withering Cauldron	Western Plaguelands	Both	50	58		Scourge Cauldron	Return to Chillwind Camp	625	
The Scourge Cauldrons	Western Plaguelands	Horde	50	53	High Executor Derrington—Western Plaguelands The Bulwark	Shadow Priestess Vandis	Scarlet Diversions	525	
Target: Felstone Field	Western Plaguelands	Horde	50	53	Shadow Priestess Vandis—Western Plaguelands The Bulwark	Scourge Cauldron	The Scourge Cauldrons	5250	
Return to the Bulwark	Western Plaguelands	Horde	50	53	Scourge Cauldron—Western Plaguelands	Shadow Priestess Vandis	Target: Felstone Field	2650	80●
Target: Dalson's Tears	Western Plaguelands	Horde	50	55	Shadow Priestess Vandis—Western Plaguelands The Bulwark	Scourge Cauldron	Return to the Bulwark	5650	
Return to the Bulwark	Western Plaguelands	Horde	50	55	Scourge Cauldron—Western Plaguelands	Shadow Priestess Vandis	Target: Dalson's Tears	2800	85●
Target: Writhing Haunt	Western Plaguelands	Horde	50	55	Shadow Priestess Vandis—Western Plaguelands The Bulwark	Scourge Cauldron	Return to the Bulwark	5650	
Return to the Bulwark	Western Plaguelands	Horde	50	55	Scourge Cauldron—Western Plaguelands	Shadow Priestess Vandis	Target: Writhing Haunt	2800	85●
Target: Gahrron's Withering	Western Plaguelands	Horde	50	58	Shadow Priestess Vandis—Western Plaguelands The Bulwark	Scourge Cauldron	Return to the Bulwark	6200	
Return to the Bulwark	Western Plaguelands	Horde	50	58	Scourge Cauldron—Western Plaguelands	Shadow Priestess Vandis	Target: Gahrron's Withering	3100	90●
Mission Accomplished!	Western Plaguelands	Alliance	50	58		Commander Ashlam Valorfist	Return to Chillwind Camp	9300	
CHOICE OF: 1 Valiant Shortsword or 1 Intrepid Shortsword REWARD: 1 Heroic Commendation Medal									
Mission Accomplished!	Western Plaguelands	Horde	50	58		High Executor Derrington	Return to the Bulwark	9300	
CHOICE OF: 1 Valiant Shortsword or 1 Intrepid Shortsword REWARD: 1 Heroic Commendation Medal									
Barov Family Fortune	Western Plaguelands	Horde	52	60	Alexi Barov—Western Plaguelands The Bulwark	Alexi Barov		6600	1●80●
The Last Barov	Western Plaguelands	Horde	52	60	Alexi Barov—Western Plaguelands The Bulwark	Alexi Barov	Barov Family Fortune	8800	1●85●
REWARD: 1 Barov Peasant Caller									
Barov Family Fortune	Western Plaguelands	Alliance	52	60	Weldon Barov—Western Plaguelands Chillwind Point	Weldon Barov		6600	1●80●
The Last Barov	Western Plaguelands	Alliance	52	60	Weldon Barov—Western Plaguelands Chillwind Point	Weldon Barov	Barov Family Fortune	8800	1●85●
REWARD: 1 Barov Peasant Caller									
Doctor Theolen Krastinov, the Butcher	Western Plaguelands	Both	55	60	Eva Sarkhoff—Western Plaguelands Caer Darrow	Eva Sarkhoff		6600	
Kirtonos the Herald	Western Plaguelands	Both	55	60	Eva Sarkhoff—Western Plaguelands Caer Darrow	Eva Sarkhoff	Krastinov's Bag of Horrors	8300	
CHOICE OF: 1 Penelope's Rose or 1 Mirah's Song REWARD: 1 Spectral Essence									
Argent Dawn Commission	Western Plaguelands	Both	50	55		Argent Officer Pureheart		550	
REWARD: 1 Argent Dawn Commission									
Minion's Scourgestones	Western Plaguelands	Both	50	55		Argent Officer Pureheart	Argent Dawn Commission	550	
REWARD: 1 Argent Dawn Valor Token									
Invader's Scourgestones	Western Plaguelands	Both	50	55		Argent Officer Pureheart	Argent Dawn Commission	550	
REWARD: 1 Argent Dawn Valor Token									
Corruptor's Scourgestones	Western Plaguelands	Both	50	55		Argent Officer Pureheart	Argent Dawn Commission	550	

Western Plaguelands cont'd

Title	Location	Faction	Min Level	Con Level	Starter Location	Finisher	Prerequisite	Max XP	Cash Reward
REWARD: 1 Argent Dawn Valor Token									
Argent Dawn Commission	Western Plaguelands	Both	50	55		Argent Officer Garush		550	
REWARD: 1 Argent Dawn Commission									
Corruptor's Scourgestones	Western Plaguelands	Both	50	55		Argent Officer Garush	Argent Dawn Commission	550	
REWARD: 1 Argent Dawn Valor Token									
Invader's Scourgestones	Western Plaguelands	Both	50	55		Argent Officer Garush	Argent Dawn Commission	550	
REWARD: 1 Argent Dawn Valor Token									
Minion's Scourgestones	Western Plaguelands	Both	50	55		Argent Officer Garush	Argent Dawn Commission	550	
REWARD: 1 Argent Dawn Valor Token									
The Human, Ras Frostwhisper	Western Plaguelands	Both	57	60	Magistrate Marduke—Western Plaguelands Caer Darrow	Magistrate Marduke	Kirtonos the Herald	6600	
The Dying, Ras Frostwhisper	Western Plaguelands	Both	57	60	Magistrate Marduke—Western Plaguelands Caer Darrow	Leonid Borthalomew the Revered	The Human, Ras Frostwhisper	4950	
The Lich, Ras Frostwhisper	Western Plaguelands	Both	57	60	Magistrate Marduke—Western Plaguelands Caer Darrow	Magistrate Marduke	Soulbound Keepsake	9950	
CHOICE OF: 1 Warblade of Caer Darrow or 1 Crown of Caer Darrow or 1 Darrowspike REWARD: 1 Darrowshire Strongguard									
Mantles of the Dawn	Western Plaguelands	Horde	55	60	Argent Quartermaster Hasana—Western Plaguelands The Bulwark	Argent Quartermaster Hasana	Argent Dawn Commission	6600	
The Key to Scholomance	Western Plaguelands	Alliance	55	60		Alchemist Arbington	Araj's Scarab	9950	
REWARD: 1 Skeleton Key									
Mantles of the Dawn	Western Plaguelands	Alliance	55	60	Argent Quartermaster Lightspark—Western Plaguelands Chillwind Point	Argent Quartermaster Lightspark	Argent Dawn Commission	6600	
The Key to Scholomance	Western Plaguelands	Horde	55	60		Apothecary Dithers	Araj's Scarab	9950	
REWARD: 1 Skeleton Key									
Mold Rhymes With...	Western Plaguelands	Horde	55	57	Apothecary Dithers—Western Plaguelands The Bulwark	Krinkle Goodsteel	Skeletal Fragments	600	
Krastinov's Bag of Horrors	Western Plaguelands	Both	55	60	Eva Sarkhoff—Western Plaguelands Caer Darrow	Eva Sarkhoff	Doctor Theolen Krastinov, the Butcher	6600	
Chromatic Mantle of the Dawn	Western Plaguelands	Alliance	55	60	Argent Quartermaster Lightspark—Western Plaguelands Chillwind Point	Argent Quartermaster Lightspark	Mantles of the Dawn	8300	
REWARD: 1 Chromatic Mantle of the Dawn									
Chromatic Mantle of the Dawn	Western Plaguelands	Horde	55	60	Argent Quartermaster Hasana—Western Plaguelands The Bulwark	Argent Quartermaster Hasana	Mantles of the Dawn	8300	
REWARD: 1 Chromatic Mantle of the Dawn									
Scholomance	Western Plaguelands	Alliance	55	55	Commander Ashlam Valorfist—Western Plaguelands Chillwind Point	Alchemist Arbington	All Along the Watchtowers	550	
Skeletal Fragments	Western Plaguelands	Alliance	55	57	Alchemist Arbington—Western Plaguelands Chillwind Point	Alchemist Arbington	Scholomance	4500	
Mold Rhymes With...	Western Plaguelands	Alliance	55	57	Alchemist Arbington—Western Plaguelands Chillwind Point	Krinkle Goodsteel	Skeletal Fragments	600	
Demon Dogs	Western Plaguelands	Both	52	56	Tirion Fordring—Eastern Plaguelands Monster Human Unique	Tirion Fordring		5800	
Blood Tinged Skies	Western Plaguelands	Both	52	56	Tirion Fordring—Eastern Plaguelands Monster Human Unique	Tirion Fordring		5800	
Carrion Grubbage	Western Plaguelands	Both	52	56	Tirion Fordring—Eastern Plaguelands Monster Human Unique	Tirion Fordring		5800	
Redemption	Western Plaguelands	Both	52	56	Tirion Fordring—Eastern Plaguelands Monster Human Unique	Tirion Fordring	Demon Dogs	575	
Of Forgotten Memories	Western Plaguelands	Both	52	57	Tirion Fordring—Eastern Plaguelands Monster Human Unique	Tirion Fordring	Redemption	6000	
Araj's Scarab	Western Plaguelands	Alliance	55	60	Alchemist Arbington—Western Plaguelands Chillwind Point	Alchemist Arbington	Fire Plume Forged	4950	
Araj's Scarab	Western Plaguelands	Horde	55	60	Apothecary Dithers—Western Plaguelands The Bulwark	Apothecary Dithers	Fire Plume Forged	4950	
Of Lost Honor	Western Plaguelands	Both	52	58	Tirion Fordring—Eastern Plaguelands Monster Human Unique	Tirion Fordring	Of Forgotten Memories	6200	
Of Love and Family	Western Plaguelands	Both	52	58	Tirion Fordring—Eastern Plaguelands Monster Human Unique	Artist Renfray	Of Lost Honor	6200	
Of Love and Family	Western Plaguelands	Both	52	60	Artist Renfray—Western Plaguelands	Tirion Fordring	Of Love and Family	6600	
Find Myranda	Western Plaguelands	Both	52	60	Tirion Fordring—Eastern Plaguelands Monster Human Unique	Myranda the Hag	Of Love and Family	4950	
Scarlet Subterfuge	Western Plaguelands	Both	52	60	Myranda the Hag—Western Plaguelands	Highlord Taelan Fordring	Find Myranda	6600	
In Dreams	Western Plaguelands	Both	52	60	Highlord Taelan Fordring—Western Plaguelands Monster Human Elite	Lord Tirion Fordring	Scarlet Subterfuge	10900	
CHOICE OF: 1 Mark of Fordring or 1 Ornate Adamantium Breastplate or 1 Shimmering Platinum Warhammer or 1 Shroud of the Exile or 1 Fordring's Seal									
Unfinished Business	Western Plaguelands	Both	50	56	Kirsta Deepshadow—Western Plaguelands	Kirsta Deepshadow		5800	
Unfinished Business	Western Plaguelands	Both	50	57	Kirsta Deepshadow—Western Plaguelands	Kirsta Deepshadow	Unfinished Business	6000	65●
Unfinished Business	Western Plaguelands	Both	50	58	Kirsta Deepshadow—Western Plaguelands	Kirsta Deepshadow	Unfinished Business	6200	1●75●
The Eastern Plagues	Western Plaguelands	Alliance	56	60	Flint Shadowmore—Eastern Plaguelands	Flint Shadowmore	Flint Shadowmore	8300	
The Blightcaller Cometh	Western Plaguelands	Alliance	56	60	Flint Shadowmore—Eastern Plaguelands	Highlord Bolvar Fordragon	The Eastern Plagues	6600	
Oculus Illusions	Western Plaguelands	Horde	55	60	Myranda the Hag—Western Plaguelands	Myranda the Hag	The Testament of Rexxar	6600	
Emberstrife	Western Plaguelands	Horde	55	60	Myranda the Hag—Western Plaguelands	Emberstrife	Oculus Illusions	4950	
Dispelling Evil	Western Plaguelands	Alliance	50	52	Commander Ashlam Valorfist—Western Plaguelands Chillwind Point	High Priest Thel'danis		5100	
Inert Scourgestones	Western Plaguelands	Alliance	50	52	High Priest Thel'danis—Western Plaguelands Uther's Tomb Monster Night Elf Unique	Commander Ashlam Valorfist	Dispelling Evil	2550	
Forging the Mightstone	Western Plaguelands	Alliance	50	52	Commander Ashlam Valorfist—Western Plaguelands Chillwind Point	Commander Ashlam Valorfist	Inert Scourgestones	6350	
CHOICE OF: 1 Lightforged Blade or 1 Sanctified Orb or 1 Chivalrous Signet REWARD: 1 Holy Mightstone									

Westfall

Title	Location	Faction	Min Level	Con Level	Starter Location	Finisher	Prerequisite	Max XP	Cash Reward
The Killing Fields	Westfall	Alliance	8	15	Farmer Saldean—Westfall	Farmer Saldean		1050	
CHOICE OF: 1 Harvester's Pants or 1 Harvester's Robe									
The People's Militia	Westfall	Alliance	9	12	Gryan Stoutmantle—Westfall	Gryan Stoutmantle		900	5●
The People's Militia	Westfall	Alliance	9	14	Gryan Stoutmantle—Westfall	Gryan Stoutmantle	The People's Militia	975	6●
The People's Militia	Westfall	Alliance	9	17	Gryan Stoutmantle—Westfall	Gryan Stoutmantle	The People's Militia	1600	
CHOICE OF: 1 Edge of the People's Militia or 1 Fist of the People's Militia or 1 Spark of the People's Militia									
Goretusk Liver Pie	Westfall	Alliance	9	12	Salma Saldean—Westfall	Salma Saldean		900	
REWARD: 3 Goretusk Liver Pie, 1Recipe: Goretusk Liver Pie									
Westfall Stew	Westfall	Alliance	9	10	Verna Furlbrow—Westfall	Salma Saldean		420	
Westfall Stew	Westfall	Alliance	9	13	Salma Saldean—Westfall	Salma Saldean	Westfall Stew	900	
REWARD: 3 Westfall Stew, 1Recipe: Westfall Stew, 1Salma's Oven Mitts, 12225									
Sweet Amber	Westfall	Alliance	40	44	Grimbooze Thunderbrew—Westfall	Grimbooze Thunderbrew		3750	65●
Sweet Amber	Westfall	Alliance	40	44	Grimbooze Thunderbrew—Westfall	Grimbooze Thunderbrew	Sweet Amber	4650	1●25●
Sweet Amber	Westfall	Alliance	40	44	Grimbooze Thunderbrew—Westfall	Grimbooze Thunderbrew	Sweet Amber	4650	1●25●
Sweet Amber	Westfall	Alliance	40	44	Grimbooze Thunderbrew—Westfall	Grimbooze Thunderbrew	Sweet Amber	4650	1●25●
Sweet Amber	Westfall	Alliance	40	44	Grimbooze Thunderbrew—Westfall	Grimbooze Thunderbrew	Sweet Amber	5600	
REWARD: 1 Thunderbrew's Boot Flask									
The Forgotten Heirloom	Westfall	Alliance	9	12	Farmer Furlbrow—Westfall	Farmer Furlbrow		900	
REWARD: 10 Freshly Baked Bread, 10Ice Cold Milk									
The Defias Brotherhood	Westfall	Alliance	14	18	Gryan Stoutmantle—Westfall	Wiley the Black		1350	
Patrolling Westfall	Westfall	Alliance	8	14	Captain Danuvin—Westfall	Captain Danuvin		975	
CHOICE OF: 1 Belt of the People's Militia or 1 Bracers of the People's Militia									
Keeper of the Flame	Westfall	Both	10	16	Captain Grayson—Westfall	Captain Grayson		1150	
CHOICE OF: 3 Minor Mana Potion or 3 Minor Healing Potion REWARD: 1 Scroll of Intellect, 1Scroll of Stamina									
The Coastal Menace	Westfall	Both	15	20	Captain Grayson—Westfall	Captain Grayson		1550	
CHOICE OF: 1 Grayson's Torch or 1 Buckler of the Seas or 1 Torchlight Wand									
Thunderbrew Lager	Westfall	Alliance	0	15	Grimbooze Thunderbrew—Westfall	Grimbooze Thunderbrew			
REWARD: 1 Keg of Thunderbrew Lager									
The Defias Brotherhood	Westfall	Alliance	14	18	Wiley the Black—Redridge Lakeshire	Gryan Stoutmantle	The Defias Brotherhood	675	
The Defias Brotherhood	Westfall	Alliance	14	18	Gryan Stoutmantle—Westfall	Master Mathias Shaw	The Defias Brotherhood	675	
Captain Sander's Hidden Treasure	Westfall	Both	10	16	Captain Sander's Treasure Map	Captain's Footlocker		575	
Captain Sander's Hidden Treasure	Westfall	Both	10	16	Captain's Footlocker—Westfall	Broken Barrel	Captain Sander's Hidden Treasure	575	
Captain Sander's Hidden Treasure	Westfall	Both	10	16	Broken Barrel—Westfall	Old Jug	Captain Sander's Hidden Treasure	575	
Captain Sander's Hidden Treasure	Westfall	Both	10	16	Old Jug—Westfall	Locked Chest	Captain Sander's Hidden Treasure	1150	8●
REWARD: 1 Silver Bar, 1Captain Sander's Shirt, 1Captain Sander's Sash, 13343									
The Defias Brotherhood	Westfall	Alliance	14	18	Master Mathias Shaw—Stormwind	Gryan Stoutmantle	The Defias Brotherhood	340	
The Defias Brotherhood	Westfall	Alliance	14	18	Gryan Stoutmantle—Westfall	Gryan Stoutmantle	The Defias Brotherhood	1350	
Poor Old Blanchy	Westfall	Alliance	9	14	Verna Furlbrow—Westfall	Verna Furlbrow		1250	
REWARD: 1 Old Blanchy's Blanket, 1Old Blanchy's Feed Pouch									
The Coast Isn't Clear	Westfall	Both	10	19	Captain Grayson—Westfall	Captain Grayson		1450	11●
Red Leather Bandanas	Westfall	Alliance	10	15	Scout Galiaan—Westfall	Scout Galiaan		1050	
CHOICE OF: 1 Cloak of the People's Militia or 1 Greaves of the People's Militia or 1 Leggings of the People's Militia									
The Defias Brotherhood	Westfall	Alliance	14	18	The Defias Traitor—Westfall	Gryan Stoutmantle	The Defias Brotherhood	1700	
The Defias Brotherhood	Westfall	Alliance	14	22	Gryan Stoutmantle—Westfall	Gryan Stoutmantle	The Defias Brotherhood	2600	

Title	Location	Faction	Min Level	Con Level	Starter Location	Finisher	Prerequisite	Max XP	Cash Reward
CHOICE OF: 1 Chausses of Westfall or 1 Tunic of Westfall or 1 Staff of Westfall									
Red Silk Bandanas	Westfall	Alliance	14	17	Scout Riell—Westfall	Scout Riell	The Defias Brotherhood	1250	
CHOICE OF: 1 Solid Shortblade or 1 Scrimshaw Dagger or 1 Piercing Axe									
Klaven's Tower	Westfall	Alliance	20	24	Agent Kearnen—Westfall	Master Mathias Shaw	Mathias and the Defias	1950	
REWARD: 1 Recipe: Thistle Tea									
A Swift Message	Westfall	Alliance	10	10	Quartermaster Lewis—Westfall	Thor		210	
Dungar Longdrink	Westfall	Alliance	10	10	Osric Strang—Stormwind	Dungar Longdrink	Continue to Stormwind	210	
Continue to Stormwind	Westfall	Alliance	10	10	Thor—Westfall	Osric Strang	A Swift Message	420	1 75
Return to Lewis	Westfall	Alliance	10	10	Dungar Longdrink—Stormwind	Quartermaster Lewis	Dungar Longdrink	1050	3 50
Sully Balloo's Letter	Thandol Span	Alliance	25	30	Waterlogged Envelope	Sara Balloo		2450	
MacKreel's Moonshine	Thandol Span	Alliance	28	30	Foggy MacKreel—Wetlands Thandol Span	Brewmeister Bilger		3050	55
Blisters on The Land	Wetlands	Alliance	20	26	Rethiel the Greenwarden—Wetlands	Rethiel the Greenwarden	Fire Taboo	2650	
CHOICE OF: 1 Fen Keeper Robe or 1 Forest Chain or 1 Phytoblade									
Tramping Paws	Wetlands	Alliance	20	21	Rethiel the Greenwarden—Wetlands	Rethiel the Greenwarden		1250	
Fire Taboo	Wetlands	Alliance	20	23	Rethiel the Greenwarden—Wetlands	Rethiel the Greenwarden	Tramping Paws	1850	
REWARD: 10 Spongy Morel									
Claws from the Deep	Wetlands	Alliance	20	22	Karl Boran—Wetlands	Karl Boran		1750	14
Reclaiming Goods	Wetlands	Alliance	20	25	Karl Boran—Wetlands	Damaged Crate	Claws from the Deep	500	
REWARD: 5 Healing Potion									
The Search Continues	Wetlands	Alliance	20	25	Damaged Crate—Wetlands	Sealed Barrel	Reclaiming Goods	500	
REWARD: 10 Dwarven Mild									
Search More Hovels	Wetlands	Alliance	20	25	Sealed Barrel—Wetlands	Half-buried Barrel	The Search Continues	1000	
Return the Statuette	Wetlands	Alliance	20	25	Half-buried Barrel—Wetlands	Karl Boran	Search More Hovels	1500	
CHOICE OF: 1 Icicle Rod or 1 Mariner Boots									
The Third Fleet	Wetlands	Alliance	22	27	First Mate Fitzsimmons—Wetlands	First Mate Fitzsimmons		220	
The Cursed Crew	Wetlands	Alliance	22	29	First Mate Fitzsimmons—Wetlands	First Mate Fitzsimmons	The Third Fleet	1750	19
Lifting the Curse	Wetlands	Alliance	22	30	First Mate Fitzsimmons—Wetlands	Intrepid's Locked Strongbox	The Cursed Crew	1200	
The Eye of Paleth	Wetlands	Alliance	22	30	Intrepid's Locked Strongbox—Wetlands	Glorin Steelbrow	Lifting the Curse	1200	
Cleansing the Eye	Wetlands	Alliance	22	30	Glorin Steelbrow—Wetlands	Archbishop Benedictus	The Eye of Paleth	2450	
REWARD: 1 Eye of Paleth									
Ormer's Revenge	Wetlands	Alliance	22	24	Ormer Ironbraid—Wetlands	Ormer Ironbraid		1950	17
Ormer's Revenge	Wetlands	Alliance	22	27	Ormer Ironbraid—Wetlands	Ormer Ironbraid	Ormer's Revenge	2200	22
Ormer's Revenge	Wetlands	Alliance	22	29	Ormer Ironbraid—Wetlands	Ormer Ironbraid	Ormer's Revenge	2950	
CHOICE OF: 1 Raptor's End or 1 Raptorbane Armor or 1 Excavation Rod REWARD: 1 Recipe: Curiously Tasty Omelet									
Uncovering the Past	Wetlands	Alliance	25	28	Prospector Whelgar—Wetlands	Prospector Whelgar		2300	25
REWARD: 1 Silk Mantle of Gamn									
The Dark Iron War	Wetlands	Alliance	25	30	Motley Garmason—Wetlands	Motley Garmason		2450	25
A Grim Task	Wetlands	Alliance	26	34	Longbraid the Grim—Wetlands	Longbraid the Grim		3350	
CHOICE OF: 1 Gold Lion Shield or 1 Tranquil Ring									
In Search of The Excavation Team	Wetlands	Alliance	21	24	Tarrel Rockweaver—Wetlands	Merrin Rockweaver		975	
In Search of The Excavation Team	Wetlands	Alliance	21	24	Merrin Rockweaver—Wetlands	Tarrel Rockweaver	In Search of The Excavation Team	490	
Lightforge Iron	Wetlands	Alliance	20	29	Glorin Steelbrow—Wetlands	Waterlogged Chest	The Doomed Fleet	600	
REWARD: 1 Lightforge Ingot									
Blessed Arm	Wetlands	Alliance	20	29	Glorin Steelbrow—Wetlands	Grimand Elmore	The Lost Ingots	1200	
The Lost Ingots	Wetlands	Alliance	20	29	Waterlogged Chest—Wetlands	Glorin Steelbrow	Lightforge Iron	1750	
The Fury Runs Deep	Wetlands	Alliance	22	27	Motley Garmason—Wetlands	Motley Garmason	The Dark Iron War	2750	
CHOICE OF: 1 Belt of Vindication or 1 Headbasher									
The Algaz Gauntlet	Wetlands	Alliance	19	21	Mountaineer Rockgar—Loch Modan	Valstag Ironjaw		1250	10
The Greenwarden	Wetlands	Alliance	20	21	First Mate Fitzsimmons—Wetlands	Rethiel the Greenwarden	Tramping Paws	825	
War Banners	Wetlands	Alliance	23	28	Captain Stoutfist—Wetlands	Captain Stoutfist		2300	25
Nek'rosh's Gambit	Wetlands	Alliance	23	31	Captain Stoutfist—Wetlands	Dragonmaw Catapult	War Banners	1900	
Search for Incendicite	Wetlands	Alliance	20	22	Pilot Stonegear—Dun Morogh Kharanos	Pilot Stonegear		1750	
REWARD: 1 Beerstained Gloves									
Report to Mountaineer Rockgar	Wetlands	Alliance	19	21	Mountaineer Kadrell—Loch Modan Thelsamar	Mountaineer Rockgar	The Algaz Gauntlet	170	
Daily Delivery	Wetlands	Alliance	18	21	Einar Stonegrip—Wetlands	James Halloran		825	7
Digging Through the Ooze	Wetlands	Alliance	19	24	Sida—Wetlands	Sida		2400	35
REWARD: 1 Ooze-covered Bag									
Apprentice's Duties	Wetlands	Alliance	18	26	James Halloran—Wetlands	James Halloran	Young Crocolisk Skins	2100	
CHOICE OF: 1 Malleable Chain Leggings or 1 Resilient Poncho REWARD: 1 Recipe: Crocolisk Gumbo									
Fall of Dun Modr	Wetlands	Alliance	25	25	Harlo Barnaby—Wetlands Menethil	Longbraid the Grim		1000	
Report to Captain Stoutfist	Wetlands	Alliance	23	28	Valstag Ironjaw—Wetlands Menethil	Captain Stoutfist	The Algaz Gauntlet	230	
Defeat Nek'rosh	Wetlands	Alliance	23	32	Dragonmaw Catapult—Wetlands	Captain Stoutfist	Nek'rosh's Gambit	2550	
CHOICE OF: 1 Ancient War Sword or 1 Barreling Reaper									
Young Crocolisk Skins	Wetlands	Alliance	18	22	James Halloran—Wetlands	James Halloran		1750	14
Lightforge Ingots	Wetlands	Alliance	20	29	Glorin Steelbrow—Wetlands	Glorin Steelbrow	Lightforge Iron	1750	
The Thandol Span	Wetlands	Alliance	28	31	Rhag Garmason—Wetlands	Ebenezer Rustlocke's Corpse		2500	
The Thandol Span	Wetlands	Alliance	28	31	Ebenezer Rustlocke's Corpse—Arathi Highlands	Rhag Garmason	The Thandol Span	2500	
The Thandol Span	Wetlands	Alliance	28	31	Rhag Garmason—Wetlands	Rhag Garmason	The Thandol Span	2500	
CHOICE OF: 1 Dwarven Guard Cloak or 1 Swampland Trousers									
Plea To The Alliance	Wetlands	Alliance	28	31	Rhag Garmason—Wetlands	Captain Nials	The Thandol Span	1250	
Trouble in Winterspring!	Everlook	Both	52	56	Meggi Peppinrocker—Winterspring Everlook	Donova Snowden		575	
Luck Be With You	Winterspring	Horde	55	60	Witch Doctor Mau'ari—Everlook	Witch Doctor Mau'ari		6600	90
Cache of Mau'ari	Winterspring	Horde	55	60	Witch Doctor Mau'ari—Everlook	Witch Doctor Mau'ari	Luck Be With You		
REWARD: 1 Cache of Mau'ari									
Are We There, Yeti?	Winterspring	Both	52	58	Umi Rumplesnicker—Winterspring Everlook	Umi Rumplesnicker	Are We There, Yeti?	4650	
Moontouched Wildkin	Winterspring	Alliance	52	55	Erelas Ambersky—Teldrassil Rut'theran Village	Erelas Ambersky	Favored of Elune?	5650	
Find Ranshalla	Winterspring	Alliance	52	57	Erelas Ambersky—Teldrassil Rut'theran Village	Ranshalla	Moontouched Wildkin	3000	
Are We There, Yeti?	Winterspring	Both	52	56	Umi Rumplesnicker—Winterspring Everlook	Umi Rumplesnicker		4350	
Wild Guardians	Winterspring	Horde	52	56	Trull Failbane—Felwood Bloodvenom Post	Trull Failbane		5800	
Wild Guardians	Winterspring	Horde	52	59	Trull Failbane—Felwood Bloodvenom Post	Trull Failbane	Wild Guardians	6400	
Wild Guardians	Winterspring	Horde	52	58	Trull Failbane—Felwood Bloodvenom Post	Trull Failbane	Wild Guardians	6200	
Frostsaber E'ko	Winterspring	Horde	55	60		Witch Doctor Mau'ari	Cache of Mau'ari		
REWARD: 3 Juju Flurry									
Winterfall E'ko	Winterspring	Horde	55	60		Witch Doctor Mau'ari	Cache of Mau'ari		
REWARD: 3 Juju Power									
Shardtooth E'ko	Winterspring	Horde	55	60		Witch Doctor Mau'ari	Cache of Mau'ari		
REWARD: 3 Juju Ember									
Chillwind E'ko	Winterspring	Horde	55	60		Witch Doctor Mau'ari	Cache of Mau'ari		
REWARD: 3 Juju Chill									
Ice Thistle E'ko	Winterspring	Horde	55	60		Witch Doctor Mau'ari	Cache of Mau'ari		
REWARD: 3 Juju Escape									
Frostmaul E'ko	Winterspring	Horde	55	60		Witch Doctor Mau'ari	Cache of Mau'ari		
REWARD: 3 Juju Might									
Wildkin E'ko	Winterspring	Horde	55	60		Witch Doctor Mau'ari	Cache of Mau'ari		
REWARD: 3 Juju Guile									
Strange Sources	Winterspring	Both	51	56	Donova Snowden—Winterspring	Donova Snowden	The New Springs	5800	
REWARD: 1 Deep River Cloak									
Enraged Wildkin	Winterspring	Alliance	53	59	Jaron Stoneshaper—Winterspring Starfall Village	Damaged Crate		3200	

Winterspring cont'd

Title	Location	Faction	Min Level	Con Level	Starter Location	Finisher	Prerequisite	Max XP	Cash Reward
Enraged Wildkin	Winterspring	Alliance	53	59	Damaged Crate—Winterspring	Jaron's Wagon	Enraged Wildkin	3200	
Enraged Wildkin	Winterspring	Alliance	53	59	Jaron's Wagon—Winterspring	Jaron Stoneshaper	Enraged Wildkin	6400	90
Guarding Secrets	Winterspring	Horde	52	59	Blue-feathered Necklace	Trull Failbane		3200	
Guarding Secrets	Winterspring	Horde	52	59	Trull Failbane—Felwood Bloodvenom Post	Nara Wildmane	Guarding Secrets	6400	
CHOICE OF: 1 Seaspray Bracers or 1 Shining Armplates									
Guardians of the Altar	Winterspring	Alliance	52	59	Ranshalla—Winterspring Owl Wing Thicket	Erelas Ambersky	Find Ranshalla	4800	
Wildkin of Elune	Winterspring	Alliance	52	57	Erelas Ambersky—Teldrassil Rut'theran Village	Arch Druid Fandral Staghelm	Guardians of the Altar	6000	
CHOICE OF: 1 Thornflinger or 1 Opaline Medallion									
Frostsaber Provisions	Winterspring	Alliance	58	60	Rivern Frostwind—Winterspring Frostsaber Rock	Rivern Frostwind			
Ursius of the Shardtooth	Winterspring	Horde	53	56	Storm Shadowhoof—Felwood Bloodvenom Post	Storm Shadowhoof		5800	
Brumeran of the Chillwind	Winterspring	Horde	53	58	Storm Shadowhoof—Felwood Bloodvenom Post	Storm Shadowhoof	Ursius of the Shardtooth	6200	
Shy-Rotam	Winterspring	Horde	53	60	Storm Shadowhoof—Felwood Bloodvenom Post	Storm Shadowhoof	Brumeran of the Chillwind	8300	
CHOICE OF: 1 Beasthunter Dagger or 1 Beaststalker Blade									
Past Endeavors	Winterspring	Horde	53	60		Storm Shadowhoof	Shy-Rotam	3300	
REWARD: 1 Hunter's Insignia Medal									
Cap of the Scarlet Savant	Winterspring	Both	57	60	Malyfous's Catalogue—Winterspring	Malyfous Darkhammer	Finkle Einhorn, At Your Service!		
REWARD: 1 Cap of the Scarlet Savant									
Leggings of Arcana	Winterspring	Both	57	60	Malyfous's Catalogue—Winterspring	Malyfous Darkhammer	Finkle Einhorn, At Your Service!		
REWARD: 1 Leggings of Arcana									
Breastplate of Bloodthirst	Winterspring	Both	57	60	Malyfous's Catalogue—Winterspring	Malyfous Darkhammer	Finkle Einhorn, At Your Service!		
REWARD: 1 Breastplate of Bloodthirst									
Threat of the Winterfall	Winterspring	Both	52	56	Donova Snowden—Winterspring	Donova Snowden		5800	
Winterfall Firewater	Winterspring	Both	52	56	Empty Firewater Flask	Donova Snowden		2900	
Falling to Corruption	Winterspring	Both	52	56	Donova Snowden—Winterspring	Deadwood Cauldron	Winterfall Firewater	4350	
Mystery Goo	Winterspring	Both	52	56	Deadwood Cauldron—Felwood	Donova Snowden	Falling to Corruption	4350	
Toxic Horrors	Winterspring	Both	52	56	Donova Snowden—Winterspring	Donova Snowden	Mystery Goo	5800	
Winterfall Runners	Winterspring	Both	52	57	Donova Snowden—Winterspring	Donova Snowden	Toxic Horrors	6000	
High Chief Winterfall	Winterspring	Both	52	59	Donova Snowden—Winterspring	Donova Snowden	Winterfall Runners	6400	
CHOICE OF: 1 Crystal Breeze Mantle or 1 Fernpulse Jerkin or 1 Willow Band Hauberk									
The Final Piece	Winterspring	Both	52	59	Crudely-written Log	Donova Snowden		3200	
Fiery Plate Gauntlets	Winterspring	Both	55	60	Malyfous Darkhammer—Winterspring Everlook	Malyfous Darkhammer	Hot Fiery Death	8300	
REWARD: 1 Plans: Fiery Plate Gauntlets, 1Fiery Plate Gauntlets									
Lorax's Tale	Winterspring	Both	55	60	Lorax—Winterspring	Lorax		650	
The Demon Forge	Winterspring	Both	55	60	Lorax—Winterspring	Lorax	Lorax's Tale	8300	
REWARD: 1 Plans: Demon Forged Breastplate, 5Elixir of Demonslaying, 1Demon Kissed Sack									
Words of the High Chief	Winterspring	Both	52	59	Donova Snowden—Winterspring	Kelek Skykeeper	The Final Piece	6400	
Wrath of the Blue Flight	Winterspring	Both	57	60	Haleh—Winterspring Mazthoril	Haleh	The Matron Protectorate	650	
Wrath of the Blue Flight	Winterspring	Both	57	60	Haleh—Winterspring Mazthoril	Jeziba	Wrath of the Blue Flight	7050	
Are We There, Yeti?	Winterspring	Both	52	58	Umi Rumplesnicker—Winterspring Everlook	Umi Rumplesnicker	Are We There, Yeti?	7750	
REWARD: 1 Mechanical Yeti									
Winterfall Intrusion	Winterspring	Alliance	58	60	Rivern Frostwind—Winterspring Frostsaber Rock	Rivern Frostwind	Frostsaber Provisions		
The Ruins of Kel'Theril	Winterspring	Alliance	53	56	Wynd Nightchaser—Winterspring Starfall Village	Jaron Stoneshaper		575	
Troubled Spirits of Kel'Theril	Winterspring	Alliance	53	56	Jaron Stoneshaper—Winterspring Starfall Village	Aurora Skycaller	The Ruins of Kel'Theril	5800	
Fragments of the Past	Winterspring	Alliance	53	56	Aurora Skycaller—Eastern Plaguelands Northpass Tower	Aurora Skycaller	Troubled Spirits of Kel'Theril	5800	
Fragments of the Past	Winterspring	Alliance	53	57	Aurora Skycaller—Eastern Plaguelands Northpass Tower	Aurora Skycaller	Fragments of the Past	6000	
Tormented By the Past	Winterspring	Alliance	53	58	Aurora Skycaller—Eastern Plaguelands Northpass Tower	Remorseful Highborne	Fragments of the Past	4650	
To Winterspring!	Winterspring	Alliance	53	56	Ivy Leafrunner—Felwood Emerald Sanctuary	Wynd Nightchaser		575	
Starfall	Winterspring	Alliance	53	56	Daryn Lightwind—Teldrassil Rut'theran Village	Wynd Nightchaser		575	
Remorseful Highborne	Winterspring	Alliance	53	58	Remorseful Highborne—Winterspring	Wynd Nightchaser	Tormented By the Past	4650	
The Crystal of Zin-Malor	Winterspring	Alliance	53	58	Wynd Nightchaser—Winterspring Starfall Village	Arch Druid Fandral Staghelm	Remorseful Highborne	6200	
CHOICE OF: 1 Turquoise Sash or 1 Plow Wood Spaulders or 1 Emerald Mist Gauntlets									
Sweet Serenity	Winterspring	Both	50	60	Lilith the Lithe—Winterspring Everlook	Lilith the Lithe	The Way of the Weaponsmith	8300	
REWARD: 1 Plans: Enchanted Battlehammer									
Snakestone of the Shadow Huntress	Winterspring	Both	50	60	Kilram—Winterspring Everlook	Kilram	The Way of the Weaponsmith	8550	
REWARD: 1 Plans: Dawn's Edge									
Corruption	Winterspring	Both	50	60	Seril Scourgebane—Winterspring Everlook	Seril Scourgebane	The Way of the Weaponsmith	8550	
REWARD: 1 Plans: Blazing Rapier									
Rampaging Giants	Winterspring	Alliance	58	60	Rivern Frostwind—Winterspring Frostsaber Rock	Rivern Frostwind	Frostsaber Provisions		
The Everlook Report	Winterspring	Alliance	50	52	Gregor Greystone—Winterspring Everlook	Argent Officer Pureheart		2550	
The Everlook Report	Winterspring	Horde	50	52	Gregor Greystone—Winterspring Everlook	Argent Officer Garush		2550	40
Duke Nicholas Zverenhoff	Winterspring	Both	50	52	Gregor Greystone—Winterspring Everlook	Duke Nicholas Zverenhoff		2550	
Enraged Wildkin	Winterspring	Alliance	53	59	Harlo Wigglesworth—Winterspring Everlook	Jaron Stoneshaper		650	
A Strange One	Winterspring	Horde	49	54	Harlo Wigglesworth—Winterspring Everlook	Winna Hazzard		550	
A Blue Light Bargain	Winterspring	Both	50	60		Derotain Mudsipper			
Imperial Plate Belt	Winterspring	Both	50	60		Derotain Mudsipper	A Blue Light Bargain		
REWARD: 1 Plans: Imperial Plate Belt									
Imperial Plate Boots	Winterspring	Both	50	60		Derotain Mudsipper	A Blue Light Bargain		
REWARD: 1 Plans: Imperial Plate Boots									
Imperial Plate Bracer	Winterspring	Both	50	60		Derotain Mudsipper	A Blue Light Bargain		
REWARD: 1 Plans: Imperial Plate Bracers									
Imperial Plate Chest	Winterspring	Both	50	60		Derotain Mudsipper	A Blue Light Bargain		
REWARD: 1 Plans: Imperial Plate Chest									
Imperial Plate Helm	Winterspring	Both	50	60		Derotain Mudsipper	A Blue Light Bargain		
REWARD: 1 Plans: Imperial Plate Helm									
Imperial Plate Leggings	Winterspring	Both	50	60		Derotain Mudsipper	A Blue Light Bargain		
REWARD: 1 Plans: Imperial Plate Leggings									
Imperial Plate Shoulders	Winterspring	Both	50	60		Derotain Mudsipper	A Blue Light Bargain		
REWARD: 1 Plans: Imperial Plate Shoulders									
Winterfall Activity	Winterspring	Both	45	58	Salfa—Winterspring Timbermaw Monster Furbolg Common SFC	Salfa		6200	
CHOICE OF: 1 Earth Warder's Gloves or 1 Gloves of the Pathfinder or 1 Vest of the Den Watcher or 1 Ursa's Embrace									
Beads for Salfa	Winterspring	Both	50	56		Salfa	Winterfall Activity	575	
Winterfall Ritual Totem	Winterspring	Both	50	56	Winterfall Ritual Totem	Kernda		5800	
REWARD: 3 Major Healing Potion, 3Major Mana Potion									
A Yeti of Your Own	Winterspring	Both	55	60		Umi Rumplesnicker	Are We There, Yeti?		
Making Amends	Winterspring	Both	40	60		Bronn Fitzwrench			

Global

Title	Location	Faction	Min Level	Con Level	Starter Location	Finisher	Prerequisite	Max XP	Cash Reward
CLUCK!	Global	Alliance	1	1		Chicken			
Azuregos's Magical Ledger	Global	Both	60	60	Magical Ledger	Narain Soothfancy	The Charge of the Dragonflights	6600	
Translating the Ledger	Global	Both	60	60		Narain Soothfancy	Azuregos's Magical Ledger	650	
Stewvul, Ex-B.F.F.	Global	Both	60	60	Narain Soothfancy—Tanaris	Inconspicuous Crate	Translating the Ledger	6600	
Scrying Goggles? No Problem!	Global	Both	60	60	Stewvul—Silverpine Forest	Narain Soothfancy	Stewvul, Ex-B.F.F.	8300	
REWARD: 3 Major Rejuvenation Potion									
Never Ask Me About My Business	Global	Both	60	60	Narain Soothfancy—Tanaris	Dirge Quikcleave	Translating the Ledger	650	
The Isle of Dread!	Global	Both	60	60	Dirge Quikcleave—Tanaris Gadgetzan	Dirge Quikcleave	Never Ask Me About My Business	6600	
Dirge's Kickin' Chimaerok Chops	Global	Both	60	60	Dirge Quikcleave—Tanaris Gadgetzan	Dirge Quikcleave	The Isle of Dread!	6600	2 70
REWARD: 1 Recipe: Dirge's Kickin' Chimaerok Chops, 20Dirge's Kickin' Chimaerok Chops									
Return to Narain	Global	Both	60	60	Dirge Quikcleave—Tanaris Gadgetzan	Narain Soothfancy	Dirge's Kickin' Chimaerok Chops	6600	
Draconic for Dummies	Global	Both	60	60	Narain Soothfancy—Tanaris	Freshly Dug Dirt	Translating the Ledger	6600	
rAnSOm	Global	Both	60	60	Freshly Dug Dirt—Tanaris	Narain Soothfancy	Draconic for Dummies	3300	

Title	Location	Faction	Min Level	Con Level	Starter Location	Finisher	Prerequisite	Max XP	Cash Reward
Love Song for Narain	Global	Both	60	60	Meridith the Mermaiden—Tanaris	Narain Soothfancy	Translating the Ledger	3300	
Decoy!	Global	Both	60	60	Narain Soothfancy—Tanaris	Narain Soothfancy	rAnS0m	6600	
The Only Prescription	Global	Both	60	60	Narain Soothfancy—Tanaris	Narain Soothfancy	Decoy!	6600	
REWARD: 1 Gnomish Turban of Psychic Might									
The Good News and The Bad News	Global	Both	60	60	Narain Soothfancy—Tanaris	Narain Soothfancy	The Only Prescription	6600	
The Wrath of Neptulon	Global	Both	60	60	Narain Soothfancy—Tanaris	Anachronos	The Good News and The Bad News	9950	
CHOICE OF: 1 Band of Icy Depths or 1 Darkwater Robes									
Nefarius's Corruption	Global	Both	60	60	Vaelastrasz the Corrupt—Blackwings Lair Monster Dragon Unique Elite	Anachronos	The Charge of the Dragonflights	9950	
CHOICE OF: 1 Onyx Embedded Leggings or 1 Amulet of Shadow Shielding									
Eranikus, Tyrant of the Dream	Global	Both	60	60		Forest Wisp	The Charge of the Dragonflights	6600	
Tyrande and Remulos	Global	Both	60	60	Forest Wisp—Teldrassil	Keeper Remulos	Eranikus, Tyrant of the Dream	1650	
The Nightmare's Corruption	Global	Both	60	60	Keeper Remulos—Moonglade	Keeper Remulos	Tyrande and Remulos	6600	
The Nightmare Manifests	Global	Both	60	60	Keeper Remulos—Moonglade	Keeper Remulos	The Nightmare's Corruption	9950	
CHOICE OF: 1 Drake Tooth Necklace or 1 Drudge Boots									
The Champion Returns	Global	Both	60	60	Keeper Remulos—Moonglade	Anachronos	The Nightmare Manifests	6600	
The Might of Kalimdor	Global	Both	60	60		Anachronos	The Champion Returns	9950	
Bang a Gong!	Global	Both	60	60		The Scarab Gong	The Might of Kalimdor		
REWARD: 1 Black Qiraji Resonating Crystal									
Treasure of the Timeless One	Global	Both	60	60		Jonathan the Revelator	The Might of Kalimdor	6600	
CHOICE OF: 1 Fang of Korialstrasz or 1 Shadowsong's Sorrow or 1 Runesword of the Red or 1 Ravencrest's Legacy									
Veteran Uzzek	World	Horde	10	10	Tarshaw Jaggedscar—Durotar Razor Hill	Uzzek	Path of Defense	85	
The Stonewrought Dam	World	Alliance	10	60	Human Orphan—World Orgrimmar	Human Orphan	Children's Week	650	
A Warrior's Training	World	Alliance	10	10	Lyria Du Lac—Elwynn Goldshire	Harry Burlguard	Bartleby the Drunk	85	
Bartleby the Drunk	World	Alliance	10	10	Harry Burlguard—Stormwind	Bartleby		85	
Beat Bartleby	World	Alliance	10	10	Bartleby—Stormwind Unique	Bartleby	Bartleby the Drunk	210	
Bartleby's Mug	World	Alliance	10	10	Bartleby—Stormwind Unique	Harry Burlguard	Beat Bartleby	420	
Marshal Haggard	World	Alliance	10	10	Harry Burlguard—Stormwind	Marshal Haggard	Bartleby's Mug	420	
Dead-tooth Jack	World	Alliance	10	10	Marshal Haggard—Elwynn	Marshal Haggard	Marshal Haggard	850	
CHOICE OF: 1 Haggard's Axe or 1 Haggard's Hammer or 1 Haggard's Dagger or 1 Haggard's Sword									
Vejrek	World	Alliance	10	11	Muren Stormpike—Ironforge	Muren Stormpike		1100	
Muren Stormpike	World	Alliance	10	10	Granis Swiftaxe—Dun Morogh Kharanos	Muren Stormpike	Vejrek	85	
Tormus Deepforge	World	Alliance	10	11	Muren Stormpike—Ironforge	Tormus Deepforge	Vejrek	90	
Ironband's Compound	World	Alliance	10	11	Tormus Deepforge—Ironforge	Tormus Deepforge	Vejrek	650	
Grey Iron Weapons	World	Alliance	10	10		Tormus Deepforge	Ironband's Compound	625	
CHOICE OF: 1 Umbral Axe or 1 Umbral Mace or 1 Umbral Dagger or 1 Umbral Sword									
Vorlus Vilehoof	World	Alliance	10	10	Elanaria—Night Elf	Elanaria		850	
Elanaria	World	Alliance	10	10	Sentinel Elissa Starbreeze—Darkshore Auberdine	Elanaria	Vorlus Vilehoof	85	
The Shade of Elura	World	Alliance	10	10	Elanaria—Night Elf	Elanaria	Vorlus Vilehoof	850	
Spooky Lighthouse	World	Alliance	10	60	Human Orphan—World Orgrimmar	Human Orphan	Children's Week	650	
Smith Mathiel	World	Alliance	10	10	Elanaria—Night Elf	Mathiel	The Shade of Elura	420	
Weapons of Elunite	World	Alliance	10	10		Mathiel	Smith Mathiel	625	
CHOICE OF: 1 Elunite Axe or 1 Elunite Hammer or 1 Elunite Dagger or 1 Elunite Sword									
Yorus Barleybrew	World	Alliance	20	20	Kelv Sternhammer—Ironforge	Yorus Barleybrew	The Rethban Gauntlet	160	
The Rethban Gauntlet	World	Alliance	20	22	Yorus Barleybrew—Redridge Lakeshire	Yorus Barleybrew		1300	
Grimand Elmore	World	Alliance	20	28	Furen Longbeard—Stormwind	Grimand Elmore	Furen's Armor	575	
Fire Hardened Mail	World	Alliance	20	28	Furen Longbeard—Stormwind	Furen Longbeard	The Shieldsmith	2300	
The Shieldsmith	World	Alliance	20	22	Yorus Barleybrew—Redridge Lakeshire	Furen Longbeard	The Rethban Gauntlet	440	
REWARD: 1 Furen's Favor									
Mathiel	World	Alliance	20	28	Furen Longbeard—Stormwind	Mathiel	Furen's Armor	1150	
Klockmort Spannerspan	World	Alliance	20	28	Furen Longbeard—Stormwind	Klockmort Spannerspan	Furen's Armor	575	
Burning Blood	World	Alliance	20	28	Grimand Elmore—Stormwind	Grimand Elmore	Furen's Armor	2300	
Grimand's Armor	World	Alliance	20	30		Grimand Elmore	Burning Blood	3050	
REWARD: 1 Fire Hardened Coif									
Iron Coral	World	Alliance	20	29	Klockmort Spannerspan—Ironforge	Klockmort Spannerspan	Furen's Armor	1750	
Klockmort's Creation	World	Alliance	20	30		Klockmort Spannerspan	Iron Coral	3050	
REWARD: 1 Fire Hardened Gauntlets									
Sunscorched Shells	World	Alliance	20	30	Mathiel—Darnassus	Mathiel	Furen's Armor	1850	
Mathiel's Armor	World	Alliance	20	30		Mathiel	Sunscorched Shells	3050	
REWARD: 1 Fire Hardened Leggings									
Cyclonian	World	Both	30	40	Bath'rah the Windwatcher—Alterac Mountains Chillwind Point	Bath'rah the Windwatcher		2350	
The Summoning	World	Both	30	40	Bath'rah the Windwatcher—Alterac Mountains Chillwind Point	Bath'rah the Windwatcher	Cyclonian	2350	
Essence of the Exile	World	Both	30	37		Bath'rah's Cauldron			
REWARD: 1 Essence of the Exile									
The Islander	World	Alliance	30	30	Kelv Sternhammer—Ironforge	Klannoc Macleod	The Affray	600	
The Affray	World	Both	30	30	Klannoc Macleod—Barrens	Klannoc Macleod		2450	
Furen's Armor	World	Alliance	20	28		Furen Longbeard	Fire Hardened Mail	3400	
REWARD: 1 Fire Hardened Hauberk									
The Windwatcher	World	Both	30	30	Klannoc Macleod—Barrens	Bath'rah the Windwatcher	The Affray	250	
Whirlwind Weapon	World	Both	30	40		Bath'rah the Windwatcher	The Summoning	3900	
CHOICE OF: 1 Whirlwind Axe or 1 Whirlwind Sword or 1 Whirlwind Warhammer									
Lordaeron Throne Room	World	Horde	10	60	Orcish Orphan—World Orgrimmar	Orcish Orphan	Children's Week	650	
Speak with Dillinger	World	Horde	10	10	Austil de Mon—Tirisfal Glades Brill	Deathguard Dillinger	Ulag the Cleaver	85	
Ulag the Cleaver	World	Horde	10	10	Deathguard Dillinger—Tirisfal Glades Brill	Deathguard Dillinger		850	
Speak with Coleman	World	Horde	10	10	Deathguard Dillinger—Tirisfal Glades Brill	Coleman Farthing	Ulag the Cleaver	210	
Agamand Heirlooms	World	Horde	10	11	Coleman Farthing—Tirisfal Glades	Coleman Farthing	Ulag the Cleaver	650	3
Heirloom Weapon	World	Horde	10	11		Coleman Farthing	Agamand Heirlooms	875	
CHOICE OF: 1 Heirloom Axe or 1 Heirloom Hammer or 1 Heirloom Dagger or 1 Heirloom Sword									
Speak with Ruga	World	Horde	20	20	Tarshaw Jaggedscar—Durotar Razor Hill	Ruga Ragetotem	Trial at the Field of Giants	160	
Trial at the Field of Giants	World	Horde	20	20	Ruga Ragetotem—Barrens Camp Taurajo	Ruga Ragetotem		1550	
REWARD: 1 Ruga's Bulwark									
Speak with Thun'grim	World	Horde	20	20	Ruga Ragetotem—Barrens Camp Taurajo	Thun'grim Firegaze	Trial at the Field of Giants	775	
Brutal Armor	World	Horde	20	30	Thun'grim Firegaze—Barrens Unique	Thun'grim Firegaze	Trial at the Field of Giants	3650	
Ula'elek and the Brutal Gauntlets	World	Horde	20	30	Thun'grim Firegaze—Barrens Unique	Ula'elek	Brutal Hauberk	1200	
Orm Stonehoof and the Brutal Helm	World	Horde	20	30	Thun'grim Firegaze—Barrens Unique	Orm Stonehoof	Brutal Hauberk	1200	
Velora Nitely and the Brutal Legguards	World	Horde	20	30	Thun'grim Firegaze—Barrens Unique	Velora Nitely	Brutal Hauberk	1200	
Satyr Hooves	World	Horde	20	30	Ula'elek—Durotar Sen'jin Village	Ula'elek	Brutal Hauberk	1200	
Brutal Gauntlets	World	Horde	20	30		Ula'elek	Satyr Hooves	1850	
REWARD: 1 Brutal Gauntlets									
Chimaeric Horn	World	Horde	20	30	Orm Stonehoof—Thunder Bluff	Orm Stonehoof	Brutal Hauberk	1200	
Brutal Helm	World	Horde	20	30		Orm Stonehoof	Chimaeric Horn	1850	
REWARD: 1 Brutal Helm									
Dragonmaw Shinbones	World	Horde	20	30	Velora Nitely—Undercity	Velora Nitely	Brutal Hauberk	1200	
Brutal Legguards	World	Horde	20	30		Velora Nitely	Dragonmaw Shinbones	1850	
REWARD: 1 Brutal Legguards									
Brutal Hauberk	World	Horde	20	30		Thun'grim Firegaze	Brutal Armor	3050	
REWARD: 1 Brutal Hauberk									
Speak with Jennea	World	Alliance	10	10	Zaldimar Wefhellt—Elwynn Goldshire	Jennea Cannon	Mirror Lake	420	
Mirror Lake	World	Alliance	10	10	Jennea Cannon—Stormwind	Jennea Cannon	Mage-tastic Gizmonitor	850	

Title	Location	Faction	Min Level	Con Level	Starter Location	Finisher	Prerequisite	Max XP	Cash Reward
CHOICE OF: 1 Ley Orb or 1 Ley Staff									
Speak with Bink	World	Alliance	10	10	Magis Sparkmantle—Dun Morogh Kharanos	Bink	Mage-tastic Gizmonitor	85	
Mage-tastic Gizmonitor	World	Alliance	10	10	Bink—Ironforge	Bink		850	
CHOICE OF: 1 Arcane Orb or 1 Arcane Staff									
Speak with Anastasia	World	Horde	10	10	Cain Firesong—Tirisfal Glades Brill	Anastasia Hartwell	The Balnir Farmstead	85	
The Balnir Farmstead	World	Horde	10	10	Anastasia Hartwell—Undercity	Anastasia Hartwell	Ju-Ju Heaps	850	
CHOICE OF: 1 Arcane Orb or 1 Arcane Staff									
Speak with Un'thuwa	World	Horde	10	10	Uthel'nay—Orgrimmar	Un'Thuwa		85	
Ju-Ju Heaps	World	Horde	10	10	Un'Thuwa—Durotar Sen'jin Village	Un'Thuwa		850	
CHOICE OF: 1 Ley Orb or 1 Ley Staff									
Report to Jennea	World	Alliance	15	15	Dink—Ironforge	Jennea Cannon	Investigate the Blue Recluse	110	
Investigate the Blue Recluse	World	Alliance	15	16		Jennea Cannon		1150	
Gathering Materials	World	Alliance	15	15	Jennea Cannon—Stormwind	Wynne Larson	Investigate the Blue Recluse	800	
Ur's Treatise on Shadow Magic	World	Alliance	26	28	High Sorcerer Andromath—Stormwind	High Sorcerer Andromath		2300	
High Sorcerer Andromath	World	Alliance	26	26	Bink—Ironforge	High Sorcerer Andromath	Ur's Treatise on Shadow Magic	1050	
Pristine Spider Silk	World	Alliance	26	26	High Sorcerer Andromath—Stormwind	Wynne Larson	Ur's Treatise on Shadow Magic	1600	
Manaweave Robe	World	Alliance	15	15		Wynne Larson	Gathering Materials	1050	
REWARD: 1 Manaweave Robe									
Astral Knot Garment	World	Alliance	26	26		Wynne Larson	Pristine Spider Silk	2100	
CHOICE OF: 1 Astral Knot Robe or 1 Astral Knot Blouse									
Speak with Deino	World	Horde	26	26	Anastasia Hartwell—Undercity	Deino	Waters of Xavian	210	
Waters of Xavian	World	Horde	26	26	Deino—Orgrimmar	Deino		2100	
Laughing Sisters	World	Horde	26	26	Deino—Orgrimmar	Kil'hala	Waters of Xavian	1600	
Nether-lace Garment	World	Horde	26	26		Kil'hala	Laughing Sisters	2100	
CHOICE OF: 1 Nether-lace Robe or 1 Nether-lace Tunic									
Journey to the Marsh	World	Horde	30	38	Ursyn Ghull—Thunder Bluff	Tabetha		290	
Items of Power	World	Both	30	40	Tabetha—Dustwallow Marsh The Quagmire	Tabetha	Journey to the Marsh	3150	
Hidden Secrets	World	Both	30	38	Tabetha—Dustwallow Marsh The Quagmire	Magus Tirth	Journey to the Marsh	1450	
Get the Scoop	World	Both	30	30	Magus Tirth—Thousand Needles Mirage Raceway	Magus Tirth	Hidden Secrets	1850	
Rituals of Power	World	Both	30	40	Magus Tirth—Thousand Needles Mirage Raceway	Tabetha	Get the Scoop	3150	
Mage's Wand	World	Both	30	40	Tabetha—Dustwallow Marsh The Quagmire	Tabetha	Rituals of Power	3150	
CHOICE OF: 1 Icefury Wand or 1 Nether Force Wand or 1 Ragefire Wand									
Return to the Marsh	World	Both	35	40		Tabetha	The Infernal Orb	320	
The Infernal Orb	World	Both	35	40	Tabetha—Dustwallow Marsh The Quagmire	Tabetha		2350	
The Exorcism	World	Both	35	40	Tabetha—Dustwallow Marsh The Quagmire	Tabetha	The Infernal Orb	2350	
Power in Uldaman	World	Both	35	40	Tabetha—Dustwallow Marsh The Quagmire	Tabetha	The Exorcism	3900	
Mana Surges	World	Both	35	40	Tabetha—Dustwallow Marsh The Quagmire	Tabetha	Power in Uldaman	2350	
Celestial Power	World	Both	35	40		Tabetha	Mana Surges	3150	
CHOICE OF: 1 Celestial Orb or 1 Celestial Stave									
Report to Anastasia	World	Horde	15	15	Cain Firesong—Tirisfal Glades Brill	Anastasia Hartwell	Investigate the Alchemist Shop	110	
Investigate the Alchemist Shop	World	Horde	15	16	Anastasia Hartwell—Undercity	Anastasia Hartwell		1150	
Gathering Materials	World	Horde	15	15	Anastasia Hartwell—Undercity	Josef Gregorian	Investigate the Alchemist Shop	800	
Spellfire Robes	World	Horde	15	15		Josef Gregorian	Gathering Materials	1050	
REWARD: 1 Lesser Spellfire Robes									
You Scream, I Scream...	World	Alliance	10	60	Human Orphan—World Orgrimmar	Human Orphan	The Bough of the Eternals	650	
A Warden of the Horde	World	Horde	10	60	Orcish Orphan—World Orgrimmar	Orphan Matron Battlewail	You Scream, I Scream...	1650	
CHOICE OF: 1 Piglet's Collar or 1 Rat Cage or 1 Turtle Box or 1 Curmudgeon's Payoff									
Honoring a Hero	World	Alliance	30	60	Wagner Hammerstrike—Dun Morogh Gates of Ironforge	Wagner Hammerstrike		6600	
REWARD: 1 For the Light!									
Honoring a Hero	World	Horde	30	60	Javnir Nashak—Durotar	Javnir Nashak		6600	
REWARD: 1 The Horde's Hellscream									
The Hunter's Charm	World	Horde	50	52	Holt Thunderhorn—Thunder Bluff Hunter Rise	Ogtinc		500	
A Simple Request	World	Horde	50	52	Ormok—Orgrimmar	Lord Jorach Ravenholdt		500	
Magecraft	World	Alliance	50	52	Maginor Dumas—Stormwind	Sanath Lim-yo		500	
Cenarion Aid	World	Alliance	50	52	Brother Joshua—Stormwind	Ogtinc		500	
For Great Honor	World	Horde	51	60	Horde Warbringer—World	Horde Warbringer		8300	2●70●
Battle of Warsong Gulch	World	Horde	10	19	Horde Warbringer—World	Horde Warbringer		1450	11●
Invaders of Alterac Valley	World	Horde	51	60	Horde Warbringer—World	Horde Warbringer		8300	2●70●
Conquering Arathi Basin	World	Horde	20	29	Horde Warbringer—World	Horde Warbringer		2350	
Concerted Efforts	World	Alliance	51	60	Alliance Brigadier General—World	Alliance Brigadier General		8300	2●70●
Fight for Warsong Gulch	World	Alliance	10	19	Alliance Brigadier General—World	Alliance Brigadier General		1450	11●
Claiming Arathi Basin	World	Alliance	20	29	Alliance Brigadier General—World	Alliance Brigadier General		2350	25●
Remember Alterac Valley!	World	Alliance	51	60	Alliance Brigadier General—World	Alliance Brigadier General		8300	1●80●
Remember Alterac Valley!	World	Alliance	51	60		Alliance Brigadier General	Remember Alterac Valley!	3300	
Claiming Arathi Basin	World	Alliance	20	29		Alliance Brigadier General	Claiming Arathi Basin	1200	
Concerted Efforts	World	Alliance	51	60		Alliance Brigadier General	Concerted Efforts	6600	90●
Fight for Warsong Gulch	World	Alliance	10	19		Alliance Brigadier General	Fight for Warsong Gulch	725	
Invaders of Alterac Valley	World	Horde	51	60		Horde Warbringer	Invaders of Alterac Valley	3300	
For Great Honor	World	Horde	51	60		Horde Warbringer	For Great Honor	6600	90●
Battle of Warsong Gulch	World	Horde	10	19		Horde Warbringer	Battle of Warsong Gulch	725	
Conquering Arathi Basin	World	Horde	20	29		Horde Warbringer	Conquering Arathi Basin	1200	
Claiming Arathi Basin	World	Alliance	30	39		Alliance Brigadier General	Claiming Arathi Basin	1500	
Claiming Arathi Basin	World	Alliance	40	49		Alliance Brigadier General	Claiming Arathi Basin	2250	
Claiming Arathi Basin	World	Alliance	30	39	Alliance Brigadier General—World	Alliance Brigadier General		3000	45●
Claiming Arathi Basin	World	Alliance	40	49	Alliance Brigadier General—World	Alliance Brigadier General		4550	70●
Claiming Arathi Basin	World	Alliance	50	59	Alliance Brigadier General—World	Alliance Brigadier General		6400	90●
Claiming Arathi Basin	World	Alliance	60	60	Alliance Brigadier General—World	Alliance Brigadier General		6600	90●
Claiming Arathi Basin	World	Alliance	50	59		Alliance Brigadier General	Claiming Arathi Basin	3200	
Claiming Arathi Basin	World	Alliance	60	60		Alliance Brigadier General	Claiming Arathi Basin	3300	
Fight for Warsong Gulch	World	Alliance	20	29	Alliance Brigadier General—World	Alliance Brigadier General		2350	25●
Fight for Warsong Gulch	World	Alliance	30	39	Alliance Brigadier General—World	Alliance Brigadier General		3000	45●
Fight for Warsong Gulch	World	Alliance	40	49	Alliance Brigadier General—World	Alliance Brigadier General		4550	70●
Fight for Warsong Gulch	World	Alliance	50	59	Alliance Brigadier General—World	Alliance Brigadier General		6400	90●
Fight for Warsong Gulch	World	Alliance	60	60	Alliance Brigadier General—World	Alliance Brigadier General		6600	90●
Fight for Warsong Gulch	World	Alliance	20	29		Alliance Brigadier General	Fight for Warsong Gulch	1200	
Fight for Warsong Gulch	World	Alliance	30	39		Alliance Brigadier General	Fight for Warsong Gulch	1500	
Fight for Warsong Gulch	World	Alliance	40	49		Alliance Brigadier General	Fight for Warsong Gulch	2250	
Fight for Warsong Gulch	World	Alliance	50	59		Alliance Brigadier General	Fight for Warsong Gulch	3300	
Fight for Warsong Gulch	World	Alliance	60	60		Alliance Brigadier General	Fight for Warsong Gulch	3300	
Elemental Mastery	World	Horde	50	50	Beram Skychaser—Thunder Bluff	Bath'rah the Windwatcher	Mastering the Elements	3800	
Chillwind Point	World	Alliance	50	50	Lord Grayson Shadowbreaker—Stormwind	Commander Ashlam Valorfist		500	
A Troubled Spirit	World	Horde	50	50	Christoph Walker—Undercity	Fallen Hero of the Horde		500	
An Imp's Request	World	Both	50	52	Warlock only—4 Quest Givers	Impsy	Hot and Itchy	3800	
Battle of Warsong Gulch	World	Horde	20	29	Horde Warbringer—World	Horde Warbringer		2350	25●
Battle of Warsong Gulch	World	Horde	30	39	Horde Warbringer—World	Horde Warbringer		3000	45●
Battle of Warsong Gulch	World	Horde	40	49	Horde Warbringer—World	Horde Warbringer		4550	
Battle of Warsong Gulch	World	Horde	50	59	Horde Warbringer—World	Horde Warbringer		6400	
Battle of Warsong Gulch	World	Horde	60	60	Horde Warbringer—World	Horde Warbringer		6600	

Title	Location	Faction	Min Level	Con Level	Starter Location	Finisher	Prerequisite	Max XP	Cash Reward
Battle of Warsong Gulch	World	Horde	20	29		Horde Warbringer	Battle of Warsong Gulch	1200	
Battle of Warsong Gulch	World	Horde	30	39		Horde Warbringer	Battle of Warsong Gulch	1500	
Battle of Warsong Gulch	World	Horde	40	49		Horde Warbringer	Battle of Warsong Gulch	2250	
Battle of Warsong Gulch	World	Horde	50	59		Horde Warbringer	Battle of Warsong Gulch	3200	
Battle of Warsong Gulch	World	Horde	60	60		Horde Warbringer	Battle of Warsong Gulch	3300	
Conquering Arathi Basin	World	Horde	30	39	Horde Warbringer—World	Horde Warbringer		3000	45
Conquering Arathi Basin	World	Horde	40	49	Horde Warbringer—World	Horde Warbringer		4550	70
Conquering Arathi Basin	World	Horde	50	59	Horde Warbringer—World	Horde Warbringer		6400	90
Conquering Arathi Basin	World	Horde	60	60	Horde Warbringer—World	Horde Warbringer		6600	90
Conquering Arathi Basin	World	Horde	30	39		Horde Warbringer	Conquering Arathi Basin	1500	
Conquering Arathi Basin	World	Horde	40	49		Horde Warbringer	Conquering Arathi Basin	2250	
Conquering Arathi Basin	World	Horde	50	59		Horde Warbringer	Conquering Arathi Basin	3200	
Conquering Arathi Basin	World	Horde	60	60		Horde Warbringer	Conquering Arathi Basin	3200	
Shrouded in Nightmare	World	Both	60	60	Nightmare Engulfed Object	Keeper Remulos		9950	
Waking Legends	World	Both	60	60	Keeper Remulos—Moonglade	Keeper Remulos	Shrouded in Nightmare		
REWARD: 1 Malfurion's Signet Ring									
Past Victories in Arathi	World	Alliance	1	1		Alliance Brigadier General			
REWARD: 3 Arathi Basin Mark of Honor									
Past Victories in Arathi	World	Horde	1	1		Horde Warbringer			
REWARD: 3 Arathi Basin Mark of Honor									
Past Victories in Warsong Gulch	World	Alliance	1	1		Alliance Brigadier General			
REWARD: 3 Warsong Gulch Mark of Honor									
Past Victories in Warsong Gulch	World	Horde	1	1		Horde Warbringer			
REWARD: 3 Warsong Gulch Mark of Honor									
Past Efforts in Warsong Gulch	World	Alliance	1	1		Alliance Brigadier General			
REWARD: 1 Warsong Gulch Mark of Honor									
Past Efforts in Warsong Gulch	World	Horde	1	1		Horde Warbringer			
REWARD: 1 Warsong Gulch Mark of Honor									
Morndeep the Elder	World	Both	1	60		Elder Morndeep			
REWARD: 1 Coin of Ancestry									
Splitrock the Elder	World	Both	1	60		Elder Splitrock			
REWARD: 1 Coin of Ancestry									
Rumblerock the Elder	World	Both	1	60		Elder Rumblerock			
REWARD: 1 Coin of Ancestry									
Silvervein the Elder	World	Both	1	60		Elder Silvervein			
REWARD: 1 Coin of Ancestry									
Highpeak the Elder	World	Both	1	60		Elder Highpeak			
REWARD: 1 Coin of Ancestry									
Stonefort the Elder	World	Both	1	60		Elder Stonefort			
REWARD: 1 Coin of Ancestry									
Obsidian the Elder	World	Both	1	60		Elder Obsidian			
REWARD: 1 Coin of Ancestry									
Hammershout the Elder	World	Both	1	60		Elder Hammershout			
REWARD: 1 Coin of Ancestry									
Bellowrage the Elder	World	Both	1	60		Elder Bellowrage			
REWARD: 1 Coin of Ancestry									
Darkcore the Elder	World	Both	1	60		Elder Darkcore			
REWARD: 1 Coin of Ancestry									
Stormbrow the Elder	World	Both	1	60		Elder Stormbrow			
REWARD: 1 Coin of Ancestry									
Snowcrown the Elder	World	Both	1	60		Elder Snowcrown			
REWARD: 1 Coin of Ancestry									
Ironband the Elder	World	Both	1	60		Elder Ironband			
REWARD: 1 Coin of Ancestry									
Graveborn the Elder	World	Both	1	60		Elder Graveborn			
REWARD: 1 Coin of Ancestry									
Goldwell the Elder	World	Both	1	60		Elder Goldwell			
REWARD: 1 Coin of Ancestry									
Primestone the Elder	World	Both	1	60		Elder Primestone			
REWARD: 1 Coin of Ancestry									
Runetotem the Elder	World	Both	1	60		Elder Runetotem			
REWARD: 1 Coin of Ancestry									
Ragetotem the Elder	World	Both	1	60		Elder Ragetotem			
REWARD: 1 Coin of Ancestry									
Stonespire the Elder	World	Both	1	60		Elder Ragetotem			
REWARD: 1 Coin of Ancestry									
Bloodhoof the Elder	World	Both	1	60		Elder Bloodhoof			
REWARD: 1 Coin of Ancestry									
Winterhoof the Elder	World	Both	1	60		Elder Winterhoof			
REWARD: 1 Coin of Ancestry									
Skychaser the Elder	World	Both	1	60		Elder Skychaser			
REWARD: 1 Coin of Ancestry									
Wildmane the Elder	World	Both	1	60		Elder Wildmane			
REWARD: 1 Coin of Ancestry									
Darkhorn the Elder	World	Both	1	60		Elder Darkhorn			
REWARD: 1 Coin of Ancestry									
Proudhorn the Elder	World	Both	1	60		Elder Proudhorn			
REWARD: 1 Coin of Ancestry									
Grimtotem the Elder	World	Both	1	60		Elder Grimtotem			
REWARD: 1 Coin of Ancestry									
Windtotem the Elder	World	Both	1	60		Elder Windtotem			
REWARD: 1 Coin of Ancestry									
Thunderhorn the Elder	World	Both	1	60		Elder Thunderhorn			
REWARD: 1 Coin of Ancestry									
Skyseer the Elder	World	Both	1	60		Elder Skyseer			
REWARD: 1 Coin of Ancestry									
Dawnstrider the Elder	World	Both	1	60		Elder Dawnstrider			
REWARD: 1 Coin of Ancestry									
Dreamseer the Elder	World	Both	1	60		Elder Dreamseer			
REWARD: 1 Coin of Ancestry									
Mistwalker the Elder	World	Both	1	60		Elder Mistwalker			
REWARD: 1 Coin of Ancestry									
High Mountain the Elder	World	Both	1	60		Elder High Mountain			
REWARD: 1 Coin of Ancestry									
Windrun the Elder	World	Both	1	60		Elder Windrun			
REWARD: 1 Coin of Ancestry									
Starsong the Elder	World	Both	1	60		Elder Starsong			
REWARD: 1 Coin of Ancestry									

Title	Location	Faction	Min Level	Con Level	Starter Location	Finisher	Prerequisite	Max XP	Cash Reward
Moonstrike the Elder	World	Both	1	60		Elder Moonstrike			
REWARD: 1 Coin of Ancestry									
Bladeleaf the Elder	World	Both	1	60		Elder Bladeleaf			
REWARD: 1 Coin of Ancestry									
Starglade the Elder	World	Both	1	60		Elder Starglade			
REWARD: 1 Coin of Ancestry									
Moonwarden the Elder	World	Both	1	60		Elder Moonwarden			
REWARD: 1 Coin of Ancestry									
Bladeswift the Elder	World	Both	1	60		Elder Bladeswift			
REWARD: 1 Coin of Ancestry									
Bladesing the Elder	World	Both	1	60		Elder Bladesing			
REWARD: 1 Coin of Ancestry									
Skygleam the Elder	World	Both	1	60		Elder Skygleam			
REWARD: 1 Coin of Ancestry									
Starweave the Elder	World	Both	1	60		Elder Starsong			
REWARD: 1 Coin of Ancestry									
Meadowrun the Elder	World	Both	1	60		Elder Meadowrun			
REWARD: 1 Coin of Ancestry									
Nightwind the Elder	World	Both	1	60		Elder Nightwind			
REWARD: 1 Coin of Ancestry									
Morningdew the Elder	World	Both	1	60		Elder Morningdew			
REWARD: 1 Coin of Ancestry									
Riversong the Elder	World	Both	1	60		Elder Riversong			
REWARD: 1 Coin of Ancestry									
Brightspear the Elder	World	Both	1	60		Elder Brightspear			
REWARD: 1 Coin of Ancestry									
Farwhisper the Elder	World	Both	1	60		Elder Farwhisper			
REWARD: 1 Coin of Ancestry									
A Carefully Wrapped Present	World	Both	1	1		Carefully Wrapped Present			
REWARD: 1 Carefully Wrapped Present									
A Gently Shaken Gift	World	Both	1	1		Gently Shaken Gift			
REWARD: 1 Gently Shaken Gift									
A Gaily Wrapped Present	World	Both	20	20		Gaily Wrapped Present			
REWARD: 1 Gaily Wrapped Present									
A Ticking Present	World	Both	40	40		Ticking Present			
REWARD: 1 Ticking Present									
A Gently Shaken Gift	World	Both	1	1		Gently Shaken Gift			
REWARD: 1 Gently Shaken Gift									
A Festive Gift	World	Both	10	10		Festive Gift			
REWARD: 1 Festive Gift									
One Commendation Signet	World	Alliance	1	60		Darnassus Commendation Officer			
One Commendation Signet	World	Alliance	1	60		Gnomeregan Commendation Officer			
One Commendation Signet	World	Alliance	1	60		Ironforge Commendation Officer			
One Commendation Signet	World	Alliance	1	60		Stormwind Commendation Officer			
One Commendation Signet	World	Horde	1	60		Orgrimmar Commendation Officer			
One Commendation Signet	World	Horde	1	60		Darkspear Commendation Officer			
One Commendation Signet	World	Horde	1	60		Undercity Commendation Officer			
One Commendation Signet	World	Horde	1	60		Thunder Bluff Commendation Officer			
Ten Commendation Signets	World	Alliance	1	60		Darnassus Commendation Officer			
Ten Commendation Signets	World	Alliance	1	60		Gnomeregan Commendation Officer			
Ten Commendation Signets	World	Alliance	1	60		Ironforge Commendation Officer			
Ten Commendation Signets	World	Alliance	1	60		Stormwind Commendation Officer			
Ten Commendation Signets	World	Horde	1	60		Orgrimmar Commendation Officer			

Title	Location	Faction	Min Level	Con Level	Starter Location	Finisher	Prerequisite	Max XP	Cash Reward
Ten Commendation Signets	World	Horde	1	60		Darkspear Commendation Officer			
Ten Commendation Signets	World	Horde	1	60		Thunder Bluff Commendation Officer			
Ten Commendation Signets	World	Horde	1	60		Undercity Commendation Officer			
Winter's Presents	World	Alliance	1	1		Greatfather Winter		10	
Winter's Presents	World	Horde	1	1		Great-father Winter		10	
One Commendation Signet	World	Alliance	1	60		Officer Lunalight			
Ten Commendation Signets	World	Alliance	1	60		Officer Lunalight			
One Commendation Signet	World	Horde	1	60		Officer Gothena			
Ten Commendation Signets	World	Horde	1	60		Officer Gothena			
One Commendation Signet	World	Alliance	1	60		Officer Ironbeard			
Ten Commendation Signets	World	Alliance	1	60		Officer Ironbeard			
One Commendation Signet	World	Alliance	1	60		Officer Maloof			
Ten Commendation Signets	World	Alliance	1	60		Officer Maloof			
One Commendation Signet	World	Alliance	1	60		Officer Porterhouse			
Ten Commendation Signets	World	Alliance	1	60		Officer Porterhouse			
One Commendation Signet	World	Horde	1	60		Officer Redblade			
Ten Commendation Signets	World	Horde	1	60		Officer Redblade			
One Commendation Signet	World	Horde	1	60		Officer Thunderstrider			
Ten Commendation Signets	World	Horde	1	60		Officer Thunderstrider			
One Commendation Signet	World	Horde	1	60		Officer Vu'Shalay			
Ten Commendation Signets	World	Horde	1	60		Officer Vu'Shalay			
Five Signets for War Supplies	World	Alliance	10	19		Field Marshal Snowfall			
REWARD: 1 Ahn'Qiraj War Effort Supplies									
Ten Signets for War Supplies	World	Alliance	20	29		Field Marshal Snowfall			
REWARD: 1 Ahn'Qiraj War Effort Supplies									
Fifteen Signets for War Supplies	World	Alliance	30	39		Field Marshal Snowfall			
REWARD: 1 Ahn'Qiraj War Effort Supplies									
Twenty Signets for War Supplies	World	Alliance	40	49		Field Marshal Snowfall			
REWARD: 1 Ahn'Qiraj War Effort Supplies									
Thirty Signets for War Supplies	World	Alliance	50	60		Field Marshal Snowfall			
REWARD: 1 Ahn'Qiraj War Effort Supplies									
Five Signets for War Supplies	World	Horde	10	19		Warlord Gorchuk			
REWARD: 1 Ahn'Qiraj War Effort Supplies									
Ten Signets for War Supplies	World	Horde	20	29		Warlord Gorchuk			
REWARD: 1 Ahn'Qiraj War Effort Supplies									
Fifteen Signets for War Supplies	World	Horde	30	39		Warlord Gorchuk			
REWARD: 1 Ahn'Qiraj War Effort Supplies									
Twenty Signets for War Supplies	World	Horde	40	49		Warlord Gorchuk			
REWARD: 1 Ahn'Qiraj War Effort Supplies									
Thirty Signets for War Supplies	World	Horde	50	60		Warlord Gorchuk			
REWARD: 1 Ahn'Qiraj War Effort Supplies									
Bronzebeard the Elder	World	Both	1	60		Elder Bronzebeard			
REWARD: 1 Coin of Ancestry									
Lunar Fireworks	World	Both	1	60	Lunar Festival Harbinger—World	Lunar Festival Harbinger			
REWARD: 1 Lunar Festival Invitation									
Valadar Starsong	World	Both	1	60	Lunar Festival Harbinger—World	Valadar Starsong	Lunar Fireworks	650	
Torwa Pathfinder	World	Both	50	52	Loganaar—Moonglade	Torwa Pathfinder		500	
Redeem iCoke Prize Voucher	World	Alliance				She number one			
REWARD: 1 Polar Bear Collar									
Redeem iCoke Gift Box Voucher	World	Alliance				She number two			
REWARD: 1 Summer Gift Package									
NYI - Establishing New Outposts	World PvP	Alliance	55	60	Establishing New Outposts				

Equipment & Item Tables

Equipment Statistics

There are a number of item modifiers that are useful to understand in World of Warcraft. Learning these gives you a fast idea what certain items are going to improve even before you look specifically at their stats. This is especially true with Uncommon (Green) items, which often have an animal name appended to their primary one. This section explains what these various terms imply.

Table of Random Item Suffixes

Term	Attributes/Statistics Improved
Agility	Agility Only
Arcane Wrath	+Arcane Spell Damage
Bear	Strength and Stamina
Boar	Strength and Spirit
Defense	Defense
Eagle	Intellect and Stamina
Falcon	Agility and Intellect
Fiery Wrath	+Fire Spell Damage
Frozen Wrath	+Frost Spell Damage
Gorilla	Intellect and Strength
Healing	+Healing Spell Effectiveness
Intellect	Intellect Only
Monkey	Agility and Stamina
Nature's Wrath	+Nature Spell Damage
Owl	Intellect and Spirit
Power	Attack Power (Melee *and Ranged)*
Shadow Wrath	+Shadow Spell Damage
Spirit	Spirit Only
Stamina	Stamina Only
Strength	Strength Only
Tiger	Agility and Strength
Whale	Spirit and Stamina
Wolf	Spirit and Agility

Table of Attribute/Statistic Functions

Term	Game Function
Agility	More Criticals From Physical Attacks, Higher Dodge, Hunters, Rogues, and Druids in Cat Form
Arcane	Some Mage and Druid Damage Spells
Attack Power	Increases Damage Done by Physical Attacks
Defense	Reduces Chance of Hit and Enemy Critical Hits, Raises Dodge, Block, and Parry
Fire	Warlock and Mage Damage Spells, Some Shaman Attacks
Frost	Mage Damage Spells, Some Shaman Attacks
Healing	Improves Amount of Health Restored per Healing Spell
Intellect	Provides More Mana, Raises Soekk Crit Rate
Nature	Druid and Shaman Spells, Some Hunter Attacks
Shadow	Warlock and Priest Spells, Fear Effects
Spirit	Better Regeneration of Health and Mana
Stamina	Provides More Health
Strength	Higher Melee Damage, More Damage Blocked by Shields

Armor

CLOTH

Epic Cloth Chest Armor

Lvl	Name	Binding	Armor	Vendor Purchase Value
42	Robes of Insight	Bind on Equip	74	1 25 66
PROPERTIES: Reduces the cost of your next spell cast within 10 sec by up to 500 mana				
50	Embrace of the Wind Serpent	Bind on Pickup	86	2 2 74
PROPERTIES: Nature Resist +12				
57	Alanna's Embrace	Bind on Pickup	96	3 2 22
PROPERTIES: Increases damage and healing done by magical spells and effects by up to 20				
57	Robe of the Archmage	Bind on Pickup	96	2 88 15
PROPERTIES: Increases damage and healing done by magical spells and effects by up to 40, Improves your chance to get a critical strike with spells by 1%, Restores 375 to 625 mana				
57	Robe of the Void	Bind on Pickup	96	2 89 20
PROPERTIES: Increases damage and healing done by magical spells and effects by up to 46, Heal your pet for 450 to 750				
57	Truefaith Vestments	Bind on Pickup	96	2 90 28
PROPERTIES: Increases healing done by spells and effects by up to 73, Restores 6 mana per 5 sec, Reduces the cooldown of your Fade ability by 2 sec				
60	Arcanist Robes	Bind on Pickup	102	3 42 53
PROPERTIES: Fire Resist +10, Increases damage and healing done by magical spells and effects by up to 23				
60	Black Ash Robe	Bind on Pickup	114	5 35 41
PROPERTIES: Fire Resist +30				
60	Crystal Webbed Robe	Bind on Pickup	128	8 92 70
PROPERTIES: Increases damage and healing done by magical spells and effects by up to 53				
60	Darkwater Robes	Bind on Pickup	117	6 8 72
PROPERTIES: Fire Resist +30, Increases damage done by Frost spells and effects by up to 39				
60	Doomcaller's Robes	Bind on Pickup	133	10 14 7
PROPERTIES: Increases damage and healing done by magical spells and effects by up to 41, Improves your chance to get a critical strike with spells by 1%, Decreases the magical resistances of your spell targets by 20				
60	Enigma Robes	Bind on Pickup	133	10 48 50
PROPERTIES: Increases damage and healing done by magical spells and effects by up to 39, Improves your chance to get a critical strike with spells by 1%, Decreases the magical resistances of your spell targets by 20				
60	Felheart Robes	Bind on Pickup	102	3 56 90
PROPERTIES: Fire Resist +10, Increases damage and healing done by magical spells and effects by up to 13, Improves your chance to hit with spells by 1%				
60	Field Marshal's Dreadweave Robe	Bind on Pickup	113	2 64 65
PROPERTIES: Increases damage and healing done by magical spells and effects by up to 32				
60	Field Marshal's Satin Vestments	Bind on Pickup	113	2 75 44
PROPERTIES: Increases damage and healing done by magical spells and effects by up to 33, Restores 4 mana per 5 sec				
60	Field Marshal's Silk Vestments	Bind on Pickup	113	2 56 92
PROPERTIES: Improves your chance to get a critical strike with spells by 1%, Increases damage and healing done by magical spells and effects by up to 33				
60	Flarecore Robe	Bind on Equip	102	3 49 11
PROPERTIES: Fire Resist +15, Increases damage and healing done by magical spells and effects by up to 23				
60	Flowing Ritual Robes	Bind on Pickup	100	3 22 57
PROPERTIES: Increases damage and healing done by magical spells and effects by up to 22				
60	Frostfire Robe	Bind on Pickup	138	13 21 73
PROPERTIES: Increases damage and healing done by magical spells and effects by up to 47, Improves your chance to hit with spells by 1%, Improves your chance to get a critical strike with spells by 1%, Decreases the magical resistances of your spell targets by 13,				
60	Garb of Royal Ascension	Bind on Pickup	109	4 74 33
PROPERTIES: Shadow Resist +25, Increases damage and healing done by magical spells and effects by up to 30, Improves your chance to hit with spells by 2%				
60	Jade Inlaid Vestments	Bind on Pickup	109	4 74 24
PROPERTIES: Increases damage and healing done by magical spells and effects by up to 44				

Epic Cloth Chest Armor

Lvl	Name	Binding	Armor	Vendor Purchase Value
60	Necro-Knight's Garb	Bind on Pickup	128	8 99 53
PROPERTIES: Increases damage and healing done by magical spells and effects by up to 37				
60	Nemesis Robes	Bind on Pickup	116	5 57 90
PROPERTIES: Fire Resist +10, Nature Resist +10, Improves your chance to get a critical strike with spells by 1%, Increases damage and healing done by magical spells and effects by up to 32				
60	Netherwind Robes	Bind on Pickup	116	5 68 61
PROPERTIES: Fire Resist +10, Nature Resist +10, Improves your chance to get a critical strike with spells by 1%, Increases damage and healing done by magical spells and effects by up to 32				
60	Plagueheart Robe	Bind on Pickup	138	12 65 86
PROPERTIES: Improves your chance to hit with spells by 1%, Increases damage and healing done by magical spells and effects by up to 51, Improves your chance to get a critical strike with spells by 1%				
60	Robe of Faith	Bind on Pickup	138	13 2 90
PROPERTIES: Increases healing done by spells and effects by up to 64, Restores 5 mana per 5 sec				
60	Robe of Volatile Power	Bind on Pickup	102	3 70 33
PROPERTIES: Improves your chance to get a critical strike with spells by 2%, Increases damage and healing done by magical spells and effects by up to 23				
60	Robes of Prophecy	Bind on Pickup	102	3 38 55
PROPERTIES: Fire Resist +10, Increases healing done by spells and effects by up to 22				
60	Robes of the Battleguard	Bind on Pickup	116	5 60 44
PROPERTIES: Increases damage and healing done by magical spells and effects by up to 36, Decreases the magical resistances of your spell targets by 20				
60	Robes of the Guardian Saint	Bind on Pickup	117	6 15 34
PROPERTIES: Increases healing done by spells and effects by up to 70, Restores 7 mana per 5 sec				
60	Robes of the Triumvirate	Bind on Pickup	114	5 43 79
PROPERTIES: Nature Resist +30, Restores 7 mana per 5 sec				
60	Robes of Transcendence	Bind on Pickup	116	5 83 49
PROPERTIES: Fire Resist +10, Nature Resist +10, Increases healing done by spells and effects by up to 57				
60	Vestments of the Oracle	Bind on Pickup	133	10 2 53
PROPERTIES: Increases damage and healing done by magical spells and effects by up to 36, Improves your chance to get a critical strike with spells by 1%, Decreases the magical resistances of your spell targets by 10				
60	Vestments of the Shifting Sands	Bind on Pickup	102	3 71 65
PROPERTIES: Increases damage and healing done by magical spells and effects by up to 32, Improves your chance to get a critical strike with spells by 1%				
60	Warlord's Dreadweave Robe	Bind on Pickup	113	2 55 93
PROPERTIES: Increases damage and healing done by magical spells and effects by up to 32				
60	Warlord's Satin Robes	Bind on Pickup	113	2 74 44
PROPERTIES: Increases damage and healing done by magical spells and effects by up to 33, Restores 4 mana per 5 sec				
60	Warlord's Silk Raiment	Bind on Pickup	113	2 75 33
PROPERTIES: Improves your chance to get a critical strike with spells by 1%, Increases damage and healing done by magical spells and effects by up to 33				
60	Deathmist Robe	Bind on Pickup	93	2 68 52
PROPERTIES: Increases damage and healing done by magical spells and effects by up to 12, Improves your chance to get a critical strike with spells by 1%				
60	Sorcerer's Robes	Bind on Pickup	93	2 62 69
PROPERTIES: Increases damage and healing done by magical spells and effects by up to 16, Decreases the magical resistances of your spell targets by 20				
60	Virtuous Robe	Bind on Pickup	93	2 76 32
PROPERTIES: Increases damage and healing done by magical spells and effects by up to 14, Restores 6 mana per 5 sec				
60	Zandalar Demoniac's Robe	Bind on Pickup	100	
PROPERTIES: Improves your chance to hit with spells by 1%, Increases damage and healing done by magical spells and effects by up to 27				
60	Zandalar Illusionist's Robe	Bind on Pickup	100	
PROPERTIES: Improves your chance to hit with spells by 1%, Increases damage and healing done by magical spells and effects by up to 27				
60	Glacial Vest	Bind on Equip	121	6 91 71
PROPERTIES: Frost Resist +40, Increases damage and healing done by magical spells and effects by up to 21				

Superior Cloth Chest Armor

Lvl	Name	Binding	Armor	Vendor Purchase Value
19	Corsair's Overshirt	Bind on Pickup	42	11 47
19	Tree Bark Jacket	Bind on Equip	42	12 2
20	Necrology Robes	Bind on Equip	43	13 34
PROPERTIES: Shadow Resist +5				
21	Black Velvet Robes	Bind on Equip	44	15 25
24	Robes of Arugal	Bind on Pickup	46	18 92
26	Mechbuilder's Overalls	Bind on Equip	48	23 52
PROPERTIES: Arcane Resist +5				
29	Beguiler Robes	Bind on Equip	50	32 23
33	Robe of Power	Bind on Pickup	55	47
PROPERTIES: Increases damage and healing done by magical spells and effects by up to 14				
35	Robe of the Magi	Bind on Equip	58	50 67
PROPERTIES: Increases damage and healing done by magical spells and effects by up to 22				
35	Death's Head Vestment	Bind on Equip	58	53 10
35	Civinad Robes	Bind on Pickup	54	41 98
36	Elemental Raiment	Bind on Equip	59	56 48
PROPERTIES: Fire Resist +5, Nature Resist +5, Frost Resist +5, Shadow Resist +5, Arcane Resist +5, Increases damage and healing done by magical spells and effects by up to 21				
38	Enchanted Gold Bloodrobe	Bind on Pickup	55	46 85
39	Robes of the Lich	Bind on Pickup	64	69 3
40	Dreamweave Vest	Bind on Equip	65	79 46
PROPERTIES: Increases damage and healing done by magical spells and effects by up to 18				
42	Grimlok's Tribal Vestments	Bind on Pickup	68	89 97
46	Funeral Pyre Vestment	Bind on Equip	73	1 23 56
PROPERTIES: Fire Resist +10				
46	Nature's Embrace	Bind on Pickup	73	1 14 47
PROPERTIES: Increases damage done by Holy spells and effects by up to 29, Restores 8 mana per 5 sec				
47	Chan's Imperial Robes	Bind on Equip	75	1 25 36
PROPERTIES: Nature Resist +5				
50	Robes of Servitude	Bind on Pickup	75	1 27 35
PROPERTIES: Increases damage done by Fire spells and effects by up to 23, Increases damage done by Shadow spells and effects by up to 23				
50	Vestments of the Atal'ai Prophet	Bind on Pickup	78	1 51 46
52	Robe of Winter Night	Bind on Equip	81	1 70 25
PROPERTIES: Increases damage done by Shadow spells and effects by up to 40, Increases damage done by Frost spells and effects by up to 40				
55	Robes of the Royal Crown	Bind on Pickup	85	2 4 75
PROPERTIES: Increases damage and healing done by magical spells and effects by up to 18				
55	Mooncloth Vest	Bind on Equip	85	2
56	Mooncloth Robe	Bind on Equip	87	2 16 83
56	Necropile Robe	Bind on Pickup	87	2 7 32
PROPERTIES: Increases damage and healing done by magical spells and effects by up to 8				
56	Polychromatic Visionwrap	Bind on Pickup	87	2 4 98
PROPERTIES: Fire Resist +20, Nature Resist +20, Frost Resist +20, Shadow Resist +20, Arcane Resist +20				
56	The Postmaster's Tunic	Bind on Pickup	87	2 11 17
PROPERTIES: Increases damage and healing done by magical spells and effects by up to 15				
57	Freezing Lich Robes	Bind on Pickup	88	2 17 78
PROPERTIES: Increases damage done by Frost spells and effects by up to 43				
57	Mindsurge Robe	Bind on Pickup	88	2 16 29
PROPERTIES: Restores 10 mana per 5 sec				
57	Robe of Everlasting Night	Bind on Pickup	88	2 15 36
PROPERTIES: Increases damage and healing done by magical spells and effects by up to 27				
58	Devout Robe	Bind on Pickup	89	2 26 16
58	Dreadmist Robe	Bind on Pickup	89	2 40 71
58	Ironweave Robe	Bind on Pickup	89	2 33 14
58	Knight-Captain's Dreadweave Robe	Bind on Pickup	89	1 10 54
PROPERTIES: Increases damage and healing done by magical spells and effects by up to 16				
58	Knight-Captain's Satin Robes	Bind on Pickup	89	1 18 66
PROPERTIES: Increases damage and healing done by magical spells and effects by up to 16				
58	Knight-Captain's Silk Raiment	Bind on Pickup	89	1 16 92
PROPERTIES: Improves your chance to get a critical strike with spells by 1%				

Superior Cloth Chest Armor

Lvl	Name	Binding	Armor	Vendor Purchase Value
58	Legionnaire's Dreadweave Robe	Bind on Pickup	89	1 12 23
PROPERTIES: Increases damage and healing done by magical spells and effects by up to 16				
58	Legionnaire's Satin Vestments	Bind on Pickup	89	1 12 21
PROPERTIES: Increases damage and healing done by magical spells and effects by up to 16				
58	Legionnaire's Silk Robes	Bind on Pickup	89	1 19 6
PROPERTIES: Improves your chance to get a critical strike with spells by 1%				
58	Magister's Robes	Bind on Pickup	89	2 24 45
58	Robe of Undead Cleansing	Bind on Pickup	89	2 27 22
PROPERTIES: Increases damage done to Undead by magical spells and effects by up to 48				
58	Robes of the Exalted	Bind on Pickup	89	2 31 18
PROPERTIES: Increases healing done by spells and effects by up to 68				
58	Widow's Clutch	Bind on Pickup	89	2 25 12
PROPERTIES: Arcane Resist +13				
60	Knight-Captain's Dreadweave Tunic	Bind on Pickup	96	1 48 26
PROPERTIES: Increases damage and healing done by magical spells and effects by up to 25				
60	Knight-Captain's Satin Tunic	Bind on Pickup	96	1 51 49
PROPERTIES: Increases damage and healing done by magical spells and effects by up to 21, Restores 6 mana per 5 sec				
60	Knight-Captain's Silk Tunic	Bind on Pickup	96	1 52 58
PROPERTIES: Improves your chance to get a critical strike with spells by 1%, Increases damage and healing done by magical spells and effects by up to 21				
60	Legionnaire's Dreadweave Tunic	Bind on Pickup	96	1 47 68
PROPERTIES: Increases damage and healing done by magical spells and effects by up to 25				
60	Legionnaire's Satin Tunic	Bind on Pickup	96	1 48 21
PROPERTIES: Increases damage and healing done by magical spells and effects by up to 21, Restores 6 mana per 5 sec				
60	Legionnaire's Silk Tunic	Bind on Pickup	96	1 48 76
PROPERTIES: Improves your chance to get a critical strike with spells by 1%, Increases damage and healing done by magical spells and effects by up to 21				
60	Bloodvine Vest	Bind on Equip	92	2 50 35
PROPERTIES: Improves your chance to hit with spells by 2%, Increases damage and healing done by magical spells and effects by up to 27				
60	Sylvan Vest	Bind on Equip	98	3 31 64
PROPERTIES: Nature Resist +30, Increases damage and healing done by magical spells and effects by up to 12				
60	Earthpower Vest	Bind on Pickup	93	2 54 95
PROPERTIES: Improves your chance to get a critical strike with spells by 1%, Increases damage and healing done by magical spells and effects by up to 25				

Epic Cloth Feet Armor

Lvl	Name	Binding	Armor	Vendor Purchase Value
60	Arcanist Boots	Bind on Pickup	70	2 58 85
PROPERTIES: Shadow Resist +10, Improves your chance to get a critical strike with spells by 1%, Increases damage and healing done by magical spells and effects by up to 11				
60	Betrayer's Boots	Bind on Pickup	69	2 58 78
PROPERTIES: Increases damage and healing done by magical spells and effects by up to 30				
60	Boots of Epiphany	Bind on Pickup	84	5 40 40
PROPERTIES: Increases damage and healing done by magical spells and effects by up to 34				
60	Boots of Prophecy	Bind on Pickup	70	2 69 62
PROPERTIES: Shadow Resist +7, Increases healing done by spells and effects by up to 18				
60	Boots of Pure Thought	Bind on Pickup	74	3 20 75
PROPERTIES: Increases healing done by spells and effects by up to 62				
60	Boots of Transcendence	Bind on Pickup	80	4 31 23
PROPERTIES: Fire Resist +10, Increases healing done by spells and effects by up to 35				
60	Doomcaller's Footwraps	Bind on Pickup	82	4 73 95
PROPERTIES: Increases damage and healing done by magical spells and effects by up to 28, Decreases the magical resistances of your spell targets by 10				
60	Enigma Boots	Bind on Pickup	82	4 84 53
PROPERTIES: Increases damage and healing done by magical spells and effects by up to 28, Improves your chance to hit with spells by 1%, Restores 4 mana per 5 sec				
60	Felheart Slippers	Bind on Pickup	70	2 61 81
PROPERTIES: Shadow Resist +7, Increases damage and healing done by magical spells and effects by up to 18				
60	Footwraps of the Oracle	Bind on Pickup	82	4 58 5
PROPERTIES: Increases damage and healing done by magical spells and effects by up to 21, Restores 3 mana per 5 sec				

Epic Cloth Feet Armor

Lvl	Name	Binding	Armor	Vendor Purchase Value
60	Frostfire Sandals	Bind on Pickup	89	6 79 30
PROPERTIES: Improves your chance to get a critical strike with spells by 1%, Increases damage and healing done by magical spells and effects by up to 28				
60	General's Dreadweave Boots	Bind on Pickup	75	1 62 6
PROPERTIES: Increases damage and healing done by magical spells and effects by up to 26				
60	General's Satin Boots	Bind on Pickup	75	1 74 4
PROPERTIES: Increases damage and healing done by magical spells and effects by up to 23				
60	General's Silk Boots	Bind on Pickup	75	1 68 36
PROPERTIES: Increases damage and healing done by magical spells and effects by up to 21, Improves your chance to hit with spells by 1%				
60	Marshal's Dreadweave Boots	Bind on Pickup	75	1 72 70
PROPERTIES: Increases damage and healing done by magical spells and effects by up to 26				
60	Marshal's Satin Sandals	Bind on Pickup	75	1 62 66
PROPERTIES: Increases damage and healing done by magical spells and effects by up to 23				
60	Marshal's Silk Footwraps	Bind on Pickup	75	1 75 23
PROPERTIES: Increases damage and healing done by magical spells and effects by up to 21, Improves your chance to hit with spells by 1%				
60	Mendicant's Slippers	Bind on Pickup	75	3 50 68
PROPERTIES: Restores 10 mana per 5 sec				
60	Nemesis Boots	Bind on Pickup	80	4 55 51
PROPERTIES: Fire Resist +10, Increases damage and healing done by magical spells and effects by up to 23				
60	Netherwind Boots	Bind on Pickup	80	4 20 7
PROPERTIES: Fire Resist +10, Increases damage and healing done by magical spells and effects by up to 27				
60	Plagueheart Sandals	Bind on Pickup	89	7 18 78
PROPERTIES: Increases damage and healing done by magical spells and effects by up to 32, Improves your chance to get a critical strike with spells by 1%				
60	Recomposed Boots	Bind on Pickup	80	4 47 56
PROPERTIES: Nature Resist +20, Increases damage and healing done by magical spells and effects by up to 20				
60	Ringo's Blizzard Boots	Bind on Pickup	75	3 38 5
PROPERTIES: Increases damage done by Frost spells and effects by up to 40, Improves your chance to hit with spells by 1%				
60	Sandals of Faith	Bind on Pickup	89	7 39 58
PROPERTIES: Restores 6 mana per 5 sec, Increases healing done by spells and effects by up to 44				
60	Shimmering Geta	Bind on Pickup	81	4 74 96
PROPERTIES: Restores 12 mana per 5 sec				
60	Snowblind Shoes	Bind on Pickup	73	2 97 46
PROPERTIES: Increases damage and healing done by magical spells and effects by up to 32, Restores 5 mana per 5 sec				
60	Deathmist Sandals	Bind on Pickup	64	2 2 13
PROPERTIES: Increases damage and healing done by magical spells and effects by up to 12				
60	Sorcerer's Boots	Bind on Pickup	64	2 8
PROPERTIES: Increases damage and healing done by magical spells and effects by up to 21				
60	Virtuous Sandals	Bind on Pickup	64	1 93 33
PROPERTIES: Increases damage and healing done by magical spells and effects by up to 12, Restores 7 mana per 5 sec				

Superior Cloth Feet Armor

Lvl	Name	Binding	Armor	Vendor Purchase Value
20	Spidersilk Boots	Bind on Equip	29	9 79
24	Moccasins of the White Hare	Bind on Equip	32	14 31
27	Acidic Walkers	Bind on Pickup	34	19 84
PROPERTIES: Nature Resist +5, Increases damage and healing done by magical spells and effects by up to 5				
28	Defiler's Cloth Boots	Bind on Pickup	34	22 42
PROPERTIES: Run speed increased slightly, Increases damage and healing done by magical spells and effects by up to 7				
28	Highlander's Cloth Boots	Bind on Pickup	34	21 38
PROPERTIES: Run speed increased slightly, Increases damage and healing done by magical spells and effects by up to 7				
33	Thoughtcast Boots	Bind on Equip	38	33 77
38	Defiler's Cloth Boots	Bind on Pickup	43	51 91
PROPERTIES: Run speed increased slightly, Increases damage and healing done by magical spells and effects by up to 8				
38	Highlander's Cloth Boots	Bind on Pickup	43	49 49
PROPERTIES: Run speed increased slightly, Increases damage and healing done by magical spells and effects by up to 8				
39	Furen's Boots	Bind on Equip	44	54 21
45	Mistwalker Boots	Bind on Equip	49	80 66
46	Vinerot Sandals	Bind on Pickup	50	91 7
PROPERTIES: Nature Resist +12				

Superior Cloth Feet Armor

Lvl	Name	Binding	Armor	Vendor Purchase Value
48	Defiler's Cloth Boots	Bind on Pickup	52	1 4 61
PROPERTIES: Run speed increased slightly, Increases damage and healing done by magical spells and effects by up to 9				
48	Highlander's Cloth Boots	Bind on Pickup	52	99 74
PROPERTIES: Run speed increased slightly, Increases damage and healing done by magical spells and effects by up to 9				
50	Coldstone Slippers	Bind on Equip	54	1 8 67
PROPERTIES: Restores 4 mana per 5 sec				
50	Phasing Boots	Bind on Equip	54	1 15 82
51	Mooncloth Boots	Bind on Equip	55	1 16 48
51	Soot Encrusted Footwear	Bind on Pickup	55	1 23 75
PROPERTIES: Increases healing done by spells and effects by up to 20				
53	Argent Boots	Bind on Equip	57	1 29 41
PROPERTIES: Shadow Resist +4				
54	Devout Sandals	Bind on Pickup	58	1 40 5
54	Dreadmist Sandals	Bind on Pickup	58	1 36 39
54	High Priestess Boots	Bind on Pickup	58	1 43 17
PROPERTIES: Shadow Resist +10				
54	Magister's Boots	Bind on Pickup	58	1 45 82
54	Ogreseer Tower Boots	Bind on Pickup	58	1 36 84
54	Omnicast Boots	Bind on Pickup	58	1 41 53
PROPERTIES: Increases damage and healing done by magical spells and effects by up to 22				
54	Wolfrunner Shoes	Bind on Equip	58	1 43 18
PROPERTIES: Increases damage and healing done by magical spells and effects by up to 13				
56	Ironweave Boots	Bind on Pickup	60	1 49 44
56	Kayser's Boots of Precision	Bind on Pickup	60	1 64 44
PROPERTIES: Improves your chance to hit with spells by 1%				
56	Necropile Boots	Bind on Pickup	60	1 62 51
PROPERTIES: Increases damage and healing done by magical spells and effects by up to 11				
56	The Postmaster's Treads	Bind on Pickup	60	1 64 25
PROPERTIES: Increases damage and healing done by magical spells and effects by up to 7				
57	Boots of the Full Moon	Bind on Pickup	60	1 56 92
PROPERTIES: Increases healing done by spells and effects by up to 26				
57	Maleki's Footwraps	Bind on Pickup	60	1 72 53
PROPERTIES: Increases damage done by Shadow spells and effects by up to 27				
58	Blood Guard's Dreadweave Boots	Bind on Pickup	61	85 44
PROPERTIES: Increases damage and healing done by magical spells and effects by up to 12				
58	Blood Guard's Satin Boots	Bind on Pickup	61	87 72
PROPERTIES: Increases damage and healing done by magical spells and effects by up to 12				
58	Blood Guard's Silk Footwraps	Bind on Pickup	61	85 11
PROPERTIES: Increases damage and healing done by magical spells and effects by up to 12				
58	Defiler's Cloth Boots	Bind on Pickup	61	1 78 3
PROPERTIES: Run speed increased slightly, Increases damage and healing done by magical spells and effects by up to 12				
58	Dragonrider Boots	Bind on Pickup	61	1 71 58
PROPERTIES: Fire Resist +10, Increases damage and healing done by magical spells and effects by up to 18				
58	Faith Healer's Boots	Bind on Pickup	61	1 78 74
PROPERTIES: Increases healing done by spells and effects by up to 26				
58	Fire Striders	Bind on Pickup	61	1 75 26
PROPERTIES: Fire Resist +15, Increases damage done by Fire spells and effects by up to 29				
58	Highlander's Cloth Boots	Bind on Pickup	61	1 65 82
PROPERTIES: Run speed increased slightly, Increases damage and healing done by magical spells and effects by up to 12				
58	Knight-Lieutenant's Dreadweave Boots	Bind on Pickup	61	87 36
PROPERTIES: Increases damage and healing done by magical spells and effects by up to 19				
58	Knight-Lieutenant's Satin Boots	Bind on Pickup	61	84 81
PROPERTIES: Increases damage and healing done by magical spells and effects by up to 12				
58	Knight-Lieutenant's Silk Boots	Bind on Pickup	61	84 16
PROPERTIES: Increases damage and healing done by magical spells and effects by up to 12				
58	Runed Stygian Boots	Bind on Equip	61	1 77 36
PROPERTIES: Shadow Resist +20, Restores 4 mana per 5 sec				
60	Blood Guard's Dreadweave Walkers	Bind on Pickup	64	95 36
PROPERTIES: Increases damage and healing done by magical spells and effects by up to 18				
60	Blood Guard's Satin Walkers	Bind on Pickup	64	95 36
PROPERTIES: Increases damage and healing done by magical spells and effects by up to 14				

Superior Cloth Feet Armor

Lvl	Name	Binding	Armor	Vendor Purchase Value
60	Blood Guard's Silk Walkers	Bind on Pickup	64	99
PROPERTIES: Increases damage and healing done by magical spells and effects by up to 15, Improves your chance to hit with spells by 1%				
60	Bloodvine Boots	Bind on Equip	63	1 89 15
PROPERTIES: Improves your chance to hit with spells by 1%, Increases damage and healing done by magical spells and effects by up to 19				
60	Knight-Lieutenant's Dreadweave Walkers	Bind on Pickup	64	1 3 7
PROPERTIES: Increases damage and healing done by magical spells and effects by up to 18				
60	Knight-Lieutenant's Satin Walkers	Bind on Pickup	64	95 26
PROPERTIES: Increases damage and healing done by magical spells and effects by up to 14				
60	Knight-Lieutenant's Silk Walkers	Bind on Pickup	64	98 65
PROPERTIES: Increases damage and healing done by magical spells and effects by up to 15, Improves your chance to hit with spells by 1%				
60	Quicksand Waders	Bind on Pickup	70	2 76 37
PROPERTIES: Increases damage and healing done by magical spells and effects by up to 16				
60	Treads of the Wandering Nomad	Bind on Pickup	69	2 52 59
PROPERTIES: Increases healing done by spells and effects by up to 37				

Epic Cloth Hand Armor

Lvl	Name	Binding	Armor	Vendor Purchase Value
57	Flarecore Gloves	Bind on Equip	60	1 49 2
PROPERTIES: Fire Resist +25				
57	Gloves of Spell Mastery	Bind on Equip	60	1 40 84
PROPERTIES: Improves your chance to get a critical strike with spells by 2%				
60	Arcanist Gloves	Bind on Pickup	63	1 73 22
PROPERTIES: Fire Resist +7, Restores 4 mana per 5 sec, Increases damage and healing done by magical spells and effects by up to 14				
60	Dark Storm Gauntlets	Bind on Pickup	83	5 16 55
PROPERTIES: Increases damage and healing done by magical spells and effects by up to 37, Improves your chance to hit with spells by 1%				
60	Doomcaller's Handwraps [PH]	Bind on Pickup	74	3 17 15
60	Ebony Flame Gloves	Bind on Pickup	72	2 83 12
PROPERTIES: Increases damage done by Shadow spells and effects by up to 43				
60	Felheart Gloves	Bind on Pickup	63	1 75 83
PROPERTIES: Fire Resist +7, Improves your chance to get a critical strike with spells by 1%, Increases damage and healing done by magical spells and effects by up to 9				
60	Frostfire Gloves	Bind on Pickup	83	5 1 16
PROPERTIES: Increases damage and healing done by magical spells and effects by up to 36				
60	General's Dreadweave Gloves	Bind on Pickup	68	1 8 87
PROPERTIES: Gives you a 50% chance to avoid interruption caused by damage while casting Searing Pain, Increases damage and healing done by magical spells and effects by up to 30				
60	General's Satin Gloves	Bind on Pickup	68	1 16 87
PROPERTIES: Gives you a 50% chance to avoid interruption caused by damage while casting Mind Blast, Increases damage and healing done by magical spells and effects by up to 23				
60	General's Silk Handguards	Bind on Pickup	68	1 12 65
PROPERTIES: Increases the damage absorbed by your Mana Shield by 285, Increases damage and healing done by magical spells and effects by up to 27				
60	Glacial Gloves	Bind on Equip	76	3 48 46
PROPERTIES: Frost Resist +30, Increases damage and healing done by magical spells and effects by up to 15				
60	Gloves of Dark Wisdom	Bind on Pickup	69	2 27 87
PROPERTIES: Increases healing done by spells and effects by up to 35, Restores 5 mana per 5 sec				
60	Gloves of Delusional Power	Bind on Pickup	69	2 27 77
PROPERTIES: Restores 5 mana per 5 sec, Increases damage and healing done by magical spells and effects by up to 27				
60	Gloves of Faith	Bind on Pickup	83	5 45 51
PROPERTIES: Increases healing done by spells and effects by up to 40, Restores 4 mana per 5 sec				
60	Gloves of Prophecy	Bind on Pickup	63	1 80 40
PROPERTIES: Fire Resist +7, Restores 6 mana per 5 sec, Increases healing done by spells and effects by up to 18				
60	Gloves of Rapid Evolution	Bind on Pickup	70	2 58 70
60	Gloves of the Hypnotic Flame	Bind on Pickup	67	2 26 65
PROPERTIES: Increases damage done by Fire spells and effects by up to 23, Increases damage and healing done by magical spells and effects by up to 9				

Epic Cloth Hand Armor

Lvl	Name	Binding	Armor	Vendor Purchase Value
60	Gloves of the Immortal	Bind on Pickup	68	2 28 75
60	Gloves of the Messiah	Bind on Pickup	74	3 18 46
PROPERTIES: Increases healing done by spells and effects by up to 26, Restores 10 mana per 5 sec				
60	Handguards of Transcendence	Bind on Pickup	72	2 88 56
PROPERTIES: Shadow Resist +10, Improves your chance to get a critical strike with spells by 1%, Increases healing done by spells and effects by up to 29				
60	Marshal's Dreadweave Gloves	Bind on Pickup	68	1 18 56
PROPERTIES: Gives you a 50% chance to avoid interruption caused by damage while casting Searing Pain, Increases damage and healing done by magical spells and effects by up to 30				
60	Marshal's Satin Gloves	Bind on Pickup	68	1 8 86
PROPERTIES: Increases damage and healing done by magical spells and effects by up to 23, Gives you a 50% chance to avoid interruption caused by damage while casting Mind Blast				
60	Marshal's Silk Gloves	Bind on Pickup	68	1 18 7
PROPERTIES: Increases damage and healing done by magical spells and effects by up to 27, Increases the damage absorbed by your Mana Shield by 285				
60	Nemesis Gloves	Bind on Pickup	72	2 75 73
PROPERTIES: Shadow Resist +10, Restores 4 health per 5 sec, Increases damage and healing done by magical spells and effects by up to 15, Improves your chance to get a critical strike with spells by 1%				
60	Netherwind Gloves	Bind on Pickup	72	2 81 9
PROPERTIES: Shadow Resist +10, Improves your chance to get a critical strike with spells by 1%, Increases damage and healing done by magical spells and effects by up to 20				
60	Plagueheart Gloves	Bind on Pickup	83	5 30 23
PROPERTIES: Improves your chance to get a critical strike with spells by 1%, Increases damage and healing done by magical spells and effects by up to 26				
60	Deathmist Wraps	Bind on Pickup	54	1 2 99
PROPERTIES: Increases damage and healing done by magical spells and effects by up to 13, Improves your chance to hit with spells by 1%				
60	Sorcerer's Gloves	Bind on Pickup	54	96 23
PROPERTIES: Increases damage and healing done by magical spells and effects by up to 12, Improves your chance to hit with spells by 1%				
60	Virtuous Gloves	Bind on Pickup	54	1 4 48
PROPERTIES: Increases damage and healing done by magical spells and effects by up to 11				

Superior Cloth Hand Armor

Lvl	Name	Binding	Armor	Vendor Purchase Value
15	Magefist Gloves	Bind on Equip	23	3 55
27	Hotshot Pilot's Gloves	Bind on Equip	31	13 8
29	Gloves of Old	Bind on Equip	32	15 65
40	Dreamweave Gloves	Bind on Equip	41	39 44
PROPERTIES: Increases damage and healing done by magical spells and effects by up to 18				
42	Jumanza Grips	Bind on Pickup	42	45 22
47	Atal'ai Gloves	Bind on Pickup	47	63 82
PROPERTIES: Increases damage and healing done by magical spells and effects by up to 9				
49	Silkweb Gloves	Bind on Pickup	48	70 63
PROPERTIES: Restores 3 mana per 5 sec				
50	Gloves of the Atal'ai Prophet	Bind on Pickup	49	76 29
52	Demonskin Gloves	Bind on Pickup	51	87 97
52	Mana Shaping Handwraps	Bind on Pickup	51	82 36
PROPERTIES: Increases damage and healing done by magical spells and effects by up to 16				
54	Devout Gloves	Bind on Equip	52	93 72
54	Dreadmist Wraps	Bind on Equip	52	91 27
54	Hands of the Exalted Herald	Bind on Pickup	52	94 74
PROPERTIES: Increases healing done by spells and effects by up to 33				
54	Magister's Gloves	Bind on Equip	52	90 93
55	Brightspark Gloves	Bind on Pickup	53	94 88
PROPERTIES: Improves your chance to get a critical strike with spells by 1%				
55	Hands of Power	Bind on Pickup	53	99 83
PROPERTIES: Increases damage and healing done by magical spells and effects by up to 26				
55	Shadowy Laced Handwraps	Bind on Pickup	53	1 2 50
PROPERTIES: Shadow Resist +12, Restores 5 mana per 5 sec				
56	Ironweave Gloves	Bind on Pickup	54	1 6 89
57	Darkshade Gloves	Bind on Pickup	55	1 4 78
PROPERTIES: Shadow Resist +10, Arcane Resist +15				

Superior Cloth Hand Armor

Lvl	Name	Binding	Armor	Vendor Purchase Value
57	Felcloth Gloves	Bind on Equip	55	1 11 39
PROPERTIES: Increases damage done by Shadow spells and effects by up to 33				
57	Inferno Gloves	Bind on Equip	55	1 11 78
PROPERTIES: Increases damage done by Fire spells and effects by up to 33				
57	Mooncloth Gloves	Bind on Equip	55	1 12 19
57	Shivery Handwraps	Bind on Pickup	55	1 14 25
PROPERTIES: Increases damage done by Frost spells and effects by up to 17				
57	The Shadow's Grasp	Bind on Pickup	55	1 4 61
PROPERTIES: Increases damage done by Shadow spells and effects by up to 20				
58	Blood Guard's Dreadweave Gloves	Bind on Pickup	56	57 17
PROPERTIES: Gives you a 50% chance to avoid interruption caused by damage while casting Searing Pain, Increases damage and healing done by magical spells and effects by up to 21				
58	Blood Guard's Satin Gloves	Bind on Pickup	56	58 68
PROPERTIES: Gives you a 50% chance to avoid interruption caused by damage while casting Mind Blast, Increases damage and healing done by magical spells and effects by up to 21				
58	Blood Guard's Silk Gloves	Bind on Pickup	56	57 16
PROPERTIES: Increases the damage absorbed by your Mana Shield by 285, Increases damage and healing done by magical spells and effects by up to 21				
58	Knight-Lieutenant's Dreadweave Gloves	Bind on Pickup	56	58 66
PROPERTIES: Gives you a 50% chance to avoid interruption caused by damage while casting Searing Pain				
58	Knight-Lieutenant's Satin Gloves	Bind on Pickup	56	56 96
PROPERTIES: Gives you a 50% chance to avoid interruption caused by damage while casting Mind Blast, Increases damage and healing done by magical spells and effects by up to 21				
58	Knight-Lieutenant's Silk Gloves	Bind on Pickup	56	56 52
PROPERTIES: Increases the damage absorbed by your Mana Shield by 285, Increases damage and healing done by magical spells and effects by up to 21				
60	Blood Guard's Dreadweave Handwraps	Bind on Pickup	58	67 23
PROPERTIES: Gives you a 50% chance to avoid interruption caused by damage while casting Searing Pain, Increases damage and healing done by magical spells and effects by up to 21				
60	Blood Guard's Satin Handwraps	Bind on Pickup	58	68 21
PROPERTIES: Gives you a 50% chance to avoid interruption caused by damage while casting Mind Blast, Increases damage and healing done by magical spells and effects by up to 21				
60	Blood Guard's Silk Handwraps	Bind on Pickup	58	68 45
PROPERTIES: Increases the damage absorbed by your Mana Shield by 285, Increases damage and healing done by magical spells and effects by up to 18				
60	Bloodtinged Gloves	Bind on Pickup	62	1 68 34
PROPERTIES: Increases damage and healing done by magical spells and effects by up to 19, Improves your chance to hit with spells by 1%				
60	Knight-Lieutenant's Dreadweave Handwraps	Bind on Pickup	58	68 47
PROPERTIES: Gives you a 50% chance to avoid interruption caused by damage while casting Searing Pain, Increases damage and healing done by magical spells and effects by up to 21				
60	Knight-Lieutenant's Satin Handwraps	Bind on Pickup	58	69 93
PROPERTIES: Gives you a 50% chance to avoid interruption caused by damage while casting Mind Blast, Increases damage and healing done by magical spells and effects by up to 21				
60	Knight-Lieutenant's Silk Handwraps	Bind on Pickup	58	65 52
PROPERTIES: Increases the damage absorbed by your Mana Shield by 285, Increases damage and healing done by magical spells and effects by up to 18				
60	Desert Bloom Gloves	Bind on Pickup	56	1 9 84
PROPERTIES: Increases healing done by spells and effects by up to 51				
60	Gloves of Undead Cleansing	Bind on Pickup	56	1 13 18
PROPERTIES: Increases damage done to Undead by magical spells and effects by up to 35				
60	Gordok's Handwraps	Bind on Pickup	53	99 15
PROPERTIES: Improves your chance to get a critical strike with spells by 1%				
60	Sandworm Skin Gloves	Bind on Pickup	56	1 12 25
PROPERTIES: Increases damage and healing done by magical spells and effects by up to 27				

Epic Cloth Head Armor

Lvl	Name	Binding	Armor	Vendor Purchase Value
49	Eye of Flame	Bind on Equip	70	1 50 73
PROPERTIES: Fire Resist +15, Increases damage done by Fire spells and effects by up to 43				
54	Circle of Flame	Bind on Pickup	74	1 92 92
PROPERTIES: Fire Resist +15, Channels 75 health into mana every 1 sec for 10 sec				

Epic Cloth Head Armor

Lvl	Name	Binding	Armor	Vendor Purchase Value
60	Arcanist Crown	Bind on Pickup	83	2 73 59
PROPERTIES: Fire Resist +10, Increases damage and healing done by magical spells and effects by up to 20, Improves your chance to hit with spells by 1%				
60	Circlet of Faith	Bind on Pickup	108	8 9 69
PROPERTIES: Increases healing done by spells and effects by up to 75, Restores 5 mana per 5 sec				
60	Circlet of Prophecy	Bind on Pickup	83	2 78 66
PROPERTIES: Fire Resist +10, Increases damage and healing done by magical spells and effects by up to 12				
60	Crystal Adorned Crown	Bind on Pickup	85	2 84 38
PROPERTIES: Increases healing done by spells and effects by up to 92				
60	Don Rigoberto's Lost Hat	Bind on Pickup	100	5 30 14
PROPERTIES: Increases healing done by spells and effects by up to 64, Restores 11 mana per 5 sec				
60	Doomcaller's Circlet	Bind on Pickup	100	5 46 61
PROPERTIES: Increases damage and healing done by magical spells and effects by up to 33, Improves your chance to get a critical strike with spells by 1%, Improves your chance to hit with spells by 1%				
60	Dustwind Turban	Bind on Pickup	86	3 6 62
PROPERTIES: Increases healing done by spells and effects by up to 31, Improves your chance to get a critical strike with spells by 1%				
60	Enigma Circlet	Bind on Pickup	100	5 81 70
PROPERTIES: Increases damage and healing done by magical spells and effects by up to 33, Improves your chance to get a critical strike with spells by 1%, Improves your chance to hit with spells by 1%				
60	Felheart Horns	Bind on Pickup	83	2 66 68
PROPERTIES: Fire Resist +10, Increases damage and healing done by magical spells and effects by up to 20				
60	Field Marshal's Coronal	Bind on Pickup	92	1 96 32
PROPERTIES: Increases damage and healing done by magical spells and effects by up to 32				
60	Field Marshal's Coronet	Bind on Pickup	92	2 5 75
PROPERTIES: Improves your chance to get a critical strike with spells by 1%, Increases damage and healing done by magical spells and effects by up to 33				
60	Field Marshal's Headdress	Bind on Pickup	92	2 4 39
PROPERTIES: Increases damage and healing done by magical spells and effects by up to 33, Restores 4 mana per 5 sec				
60	Frostfire Circlet	Bind on Pickup	108	7 43 16
PROPERTIES: Increases damage and healing done by magical spells and effects by up to 35, Improves your chance to hit with spells by 1%, Improves your chance to get a critical strike with spells by 2%				
60	Glacial Headdress	Bind on Pickup	102	6 2 64
PROPERTIES: Frost Resist +40, Increases damage and healing done by magical spells and effects by up to 18				
60	Gnomish Turban of Psychic Might	Bind on Pickup	93	4 29 35
PROPERTIES: Restores 9 mana per 5 sec, Increases your resistance to silence effects by 10%				
60	Halo of Transcendence	Bind on Pickup	94	4 34 40
PROPERTIES: Fire Resist +10,Frost Resist +10, Increases healing done by spells and effects by up to 48				
60	Mish'undare, Circlet of the Mind Flayer	Bind on Pickup	102	5 84 42
PROPERTIES: Increases damage and healing done by magical spells and effects by up to 35, Improves your chance to get a critical strike with spells by 2%				
60	Nemesis Skullcap	Bind on Pickup	94	4 15 21
PROPERTIES: Frost Resist +10, Shadow Resist +10, Restores 4 health per 5 sec, Increases damage and healing done by magical spells and effects by up to 32				
60	Netherwind Crown	Bind on Pickup	94	4 23 24
PROPERTIES: Frost Resist +10, Shadow Resist +10, Restores 4 mana per 5 sec, Increases damage and healing done by magical spells and effects by up to 32				
60	Plagueheart Circlet	Bind on Pickup	108	7 86 76
PROPERTIES: Increases damage and healing done by magical spells and effects by up to 33, Improves your chance to get a critical strike with spells by 2%, Improves your chance to hit with spells by 1%				
60	Preceptor's Hat	Bind on Pickup	102	6 25 61
PROPERTIES: Increases damage and healing done by magical spells and effects by up to 51				
60	Tiara of the Oracle	Bind on Pickup	100	5 28 26
PROPERTIES: Increases damage and healing done by magical spells and effects by up to 28, Restores 7 mana per 5 sec, Improves your chance to hit with spells by 1%				
60	Warlord's Dreadweave Hood	Bind on Pickup	92	1 91 21
PROPERTIES: Increases damage and healing done by magical spells and effects by up to 32				
60	Warlord's Satin Cowl	Bind on Pickup	92	2 5 10
PROPERTIES: Increases damage and healing done by magical spells and effects by up to 33, Restores 4 mana per 5 sec				
60	Warlord's Silk Cowl	Bind on Pickup	92	2 5 4
PROPERTIES: Improves your chance to get a critical strike with spells by 1%, Increases damage and healing done by magical spells and effects by up to 33				
60	Cap of the Scarlet Savant	Bind on Pickup	78	2 29 7
PROPERTIES: Improves your chance to get a critical strike with spells by 2%				

Epic Cloth Head Armor

Lvl	Name	Binding	Armor	Vendor Purchase Value
60	Deathmist Mask	Bind on Pickup	75	2
PROPERTIES: Increases damage and healing done by magical spells and effects by up to 16, Improves your chance to hit with spells by 1%				
60	Sorcerer's Crown	Bind on Pickup	75	2 8 73
PROPERTIES: Increases damage and healing done by magical spells and effects by up to 11, Improves your chance to get a critical strike with spells by 1%				
60	Virtuous Crown	Bind on Pickup	75	2 5 5
PROPERTIES: Increases damage and healing done by magical spells and effects by up to 11, Restores 6 mana per 5 sec, Improves your chance to get a critical strike with spells by 1%				

Superior Cloth Head Armor

Lvl	Name	Binding	Armor	Vendor Purchase Value
27	Holy Shroud	Bind on Equip	40	19 82
PROPERTIES: Increases healing done by spells and effects by up to 33				
30	Embalmed Shroud	Bind on Pickup	42	26 89
32	Electromagnetic Gigaflux Reactivator	Bind on Pickup	44	31 72
PROPERTIES: Channels a bolt of lightning and hurls it towards all enemies in front of the caster causing 147 to 167 Nature damage. The caster is then surrounded by a barrier of electricity for 10 min				
35	Corpseshroud	Bind on Equip	47	37 75
38	Papal Fez	Bind on Equip	51	48 85
PROPERTIES: Increases healing done by spells and effects by up to 22				
39	Miner's Hat of the Deep	Bind on Equip	52	52 36
39	Whitemane's Chapeau	Bind on Pickup	52	53 56
42	Cassandra's Grace	Bind on Equip	55	68 79
PROPERTIES: Increases healing done by spells and effects by up to 44				
44	Bad Mojo Mask	Bind on Pickup	57	78 58
PROPERTIES: Increases damage done by Shadow spells and effects by up to 14				
45	Dreamweave Circlet	Bind on Equip	58	85 93
PROPERTIES: Increases damage and healing done by magical spells and effects by up to 21				
46	Soulcatcher Halo	Bind on Equip	59	86 64
49	Eye of Theradras	Bind on Pickup	63	1 2 25
50	Chief Architect's Monocle	Bind on Pickup	64	1 11 91
53	Gemburst Circlet	Bind on Pickup	63	1 6 34
54	Crimson Felt Hat	Bind on Pickup	68	1 44 87
PROPERTIES: Increases damage and healing done by magical spells and effects by up to 30				
55	Dragonskin Cowl	Bind on Pickup	69	1 49 37
PROPERTIES: Increases damage and healing done by magical spells and effects by up to 18				
55	Starfire Tiara	Bind on Pickup	69	1 43 68
PROPERTIES: Fire Resist +10				
56	The Postmaster's Band	Bind on Pickup	70	1 63 67
PROPERTIES: Increases damage and healing done by magical spells and effects by up to 14				
57	Devout Crown	Bind on Pickup	71	1 63 35
57	Dreadmist Mask	Bind on Pickup	71	1 66 36
57	Magister's Crown	Bind on Pickup	71	1 59 12
57	Mooncloth Circlet	Bind on Equip	71	1 66 93
58	Champion's Dreadweave Hood	Bind on Pickup	73	83 54
PROPERTIES: Increases damage and healing done by magical spells and effects by up to 16				
58	Champion's Satin Cowl	Bind on Pickup	73	83 52
PROPERTIES: Increases damage and healing done by magical spells and effects by up to 16				
58	Champion's Silk Hood	Bind on Pickup	73	86 38
PROPERTIES: Improves your chance to get a critical strike with spells by 1%				
58	Crown of the Ogre King	Bind on Pickup	73	1 79 24
PROPERTIES: Improves your chance to get a critical strike with spells by 1%				
58	Ironweave Cowl	Bind on Pickup	73	1 75 49
58	Lieutenant Commander's Crown	Bind on Pickup	73	88 64
PROPERTIES: Improves your chance to get a critical strike with spells by 1%				
58	Lieutenant Commander's Diadem	Bind on Pickup	73	86 7
PROPERTIES: Increases damage and healing done by magical spells and effects by up to 16				
58	Lieutenant Commander's Headguard	Bind on Pickup	73	88 63
PROPERTIES: Increases damage and healing done by magical spells and effects by up to 16				
60	Bloodvine Goggles	Bind on Equip	75	1 86 39

Superior Cloth Head Armor

Lvl	Name	Binding	Armor	Vendor Purchase Value
PROPERTIES: Improves your chance to hit with spells by 2%, Improves your chance to get a critical strike with spells by 1%, Restores 9 mana per 5 sec				
60	Champion's Dreadweave Cowl	Bind on Pickup	81	1 24 43
PROPERTIES: Increases damage and healing done by magical spells and effects by up to 21, Improves your chance to get a critical strike with spells by 1%				
60	Champion's Satin Hood	Bind on Pickup	81	1 30 62
PROPERTIES: Increases damage and healing done by magical spells and effects by up to 21, Restores 6 mana per 5 sec				
60	Champion's Silk Cowl	Bind on Pickup	81	1 31 56
PROPERTIES: Improves your chance to get a critical strike with spells by 1%, Increases damage and healing done by magical spells and effects by up to 21				
60	Lieutenant Commander's Dreadweave Cowl	Bind on Pickup	81	1 25 41
PROPERTIES: Increases damage and healing done by magical spells and effects by up to 21, Improves your chance to get a critical strike with spells by 1%				
60	Lieutenant Commander's Satin Hood	Bind on Pickup	81	1 28 23
PROPERTIES: Increases damage and healing done by magical spells and effects by up to 21, Restores 6 mana per 5 sec				
60	Lieutenant Commander's Silk Cowl	Bind on Pickup	81	1 29 17
PROPERTIES: Improves your chance to get a critical strike with spells by 1%, Increases damage and healing done by magical spells and effects by up to 21				
60	Spellweaver's Turban	Bind on Pickup	73	1 78 70
PROPERTIES: Increases damage and healing done by magical spells and effects by up to 36, Improves your chance to hit with spells by 1%				
60	Sylvan Crown	Bind on Equip	80	2 49 61
PROPERTIES: Nature Resist +30, Increases damage and healing done by magical spells and effects by up to 18				
60	The Hexxer's Cover	Bind on Pickup	81	2 49 79
PROPERTIES: Increases damage and healing done by magical spells and effects by up to 41				
60	Zulian Headdress	Bind on Pickup	78	2 28 89
PROPERTIES: Increases healing done by spells and effects by up to 55				
60	Crown of Caer Darrow	Bind on Pickup	73	1 74 69
PROPERTIES: Frost Resist +15				
NA	Green Lens	Bind on Equip	57	77 70

Epic Cloth Leg Armor

Lvl	Name	Binding	Armor	Vendor Purchase Value
58	Manastorm Leggings	Bind on Pickup	85	3 3 94
PROPERTIES: Restores 14 mana per 5 sec				
60	Arcanist Leggings	Bind on Pickup	89	3 39 90
PROPERTIES: Shadow Resist +10, Improves your chance to get a critical strike with spells by 1%, Increases damage and healing done by magical spells and effects by up to 20				
60	Doomcaller's Trousers	Bind on Pickup	107	7 26 15
PROPERTIES: Increases damage and healing done by magical spells and effects by up to 34, Improves your chance to get a critical strike with spells by 1%				
60	Empowered Leggings	Bind on Pickup	103	6 19 90
PROPERTIES: Increases healing done by spells and effects by up to 77, Improves your chance to get a critical strike with spells by 1%				
60	Enigma Leggings	Bind on Pickup	107	7 72 86
PROPERTIES: Increases damage and healing done by magical spells and effects by up to 34, Improves your chance to get a critical strike with spells by 1%, Restores 5 mana per 5 sec				
60	Fel Infused Leggings	Bind on Pickup	95	4 32 77
PROPERTIES: Increases damage done by Shadow spells and effects by up to 64				
60	Felheart Pants	Bind on Pickup	89	3 58 21
PROPERTIES: Shadow Resist +10, Increases damage and healing done by magical spells and effects by up to 30				
60	Flarecore Leggings	Bind on Equip	94	4 50 6
PROPERTIES: Fire Resist +16, Increases damage and healing done by magical spells and effects by up to 43				
60	Frostfire Leggings	Bind on Pickup	116	10 91 14
PROPERTIES: Improves your chance to hit with spells by 1%, Increases damage and healing done by magical spells and effects by up to 46				
60	General's Dreadweave Pants	Bind on Pickup	95	2 21 92
PROPERTIES: Increases damage and healing done by magical spells and effects by up to 37				
60	General's Satin Leggings	Bind on Pickup	95	2 37 89
PROPERTIES: Increases damage and healing done by magical spells and effects by up to 32, Restores 4 mana per 5 sec				
60	General's Silk Trousers	Bind on Pickup	95	2 37
PROPERTIES: Increases damage and healing done by magical spells and effects by up to 30, Improves your chance to get a critical strike with spells by 1%				
60	Leggings of Arcane Supremacy	Bind on Pickup	93	4 25 46
PROPERTIES: Frost Resist +10,Arcane Resist +10, Increases damage done by Arcane spells and effects by up to 36				
60	Leggings of Faith	Bind on Pickup	116	10 75 74
PROPERTIES: Increases healing done by spells and effects by up to 66				
60	Leggings of Polarity	Bind on Pickup	112	9 2 86
PROPERTIES: Increases damage and healing done by magical spells and effects by up to 44, Improves your chance to get a critical strike with spells by 2%				
60	Leggings of the Black Blizzard	Bind on Pickup	97	4 54 3
PROPERTIES: Increases damage and healing done by magical spells and effects by up to 41, Improves your chance to get a critical strike with spells by 1%				
60	Leggings of the Festering Swarm	Bind on Pickup	101	5 71 4
PROPERTIES: Increases damage done by Fire spells and effects by up to 57				
60	Leggings of Transcendence	Bind on Pickup	101	5 81 35
PROPERTIES: Shadow Resist +10, Arcane Resist +10, Increases healing done by spells and effects by up to 46, Restores 7 mana per 5 sec				
60	Marshal's Dreadweave Leggings	Bind on Pickup	95	2 26 95
PROPERTIES: Increases damage and healing done by magical spells and effects by up to 37				
60	Marshal's Satin Pants	Bind on Pickup	95	2 36 26
PROPERTIES: Increases damage and healing done by magical spells and effects by up to 32, Restores 4 mana per 5 sec				
60	Marshal's Silk Leggings	Bind on Pickup	95	2 37 80
PROPERTIES: Increases damage and healing done by magical spells and effects by up to 30, Improves your chance to get a critical strike with spells by 1%				
60	Nemesis Leggings	Bind on Pickup	101	5 55 75
PROPERTIES: Fire Resist +10,Arcane Resist +10, Increases damage and healing done by magical spells and effects by up to 39				
60	Netherwind Pants	Bind on Pickup	101	5 66 47
PROPERTIES: Fire Resist +10,Arcane Resist +10, Increases damage and healing done by magical spells and effects by up to 30, Improves your chance to get a critical strike with spells by 1%				
60	Outrider's Silk Leggings	Bind on Pickup	88	3 35 26
PROPERTIES: Increases damage and healing done by magical spells and effects by up to 28				
60	Pants of Prophecy	Bind on Pickup	89	3 72 86
PROPERTIES: Shadow Resist +10, Restores 6 mana per 5 sec, Increases healing done by spells and effects by up to 22				
60	Plagueheart Leggings	Bind on Pickup	116	10 45 17
PROPERTIES: Improves your chance to get a critical strike with spells by 1%, Increases damage and healing done by magical spells and effects by up to 37, Decreases the magical resistances of your spell targets by 10				
60	Sentinel's Silk Leggings	Bind on Pickup	88	3 41 49
PROPERTIES: Increases damage and healing done by magical spells and effects by up to 28				
60	Trousers of the Oracle	Bind on Pickup	107	7 15 14
PROPERTIES: Increases damage and healing done by magical spells and effects by up to 33, Restores 6 mana per 5 sec				
60	Glacial Leggings	Bind on Pickup	106	7 30 85
PROPERTIES: Frost Resist +40, Increases damage and healing done by magical spells and effects by up to 18				

Superior Cloth Leg Armor

Lvl	Name	Binding	Armor	Vendor Purchase Value
17	Darkweave Breeches	Bind on Equip	35	9 6
20	Abomination Skin Leggings	Bind on Pickup	37	12 43
PROPERTIES: Increases damage and healing done by magical spells and effects by up to 9				
26	Leech Pants	Bind on Pickup	42	22 98
30	Blighted Leggings	Bind on Pickup	45	35 59
PROPERTIES: Increases damage done by Shadow spells and effects by up to 10				
30	Necromancer Leggings	Bind on Equip	45	36 20
PROPERTIES: Increases damage done by Shadow spells and effects by up to 10				
35	Stoneweaver Leggings	Bind on Pickup	51	50 94
45	Spellshock Leggings	Bind on Equip	63	1 9 62
PROPERTIES: Increases damage and healing done by magical spells and effects by up to 23				
47	Dalewind Trousers	Bind on Equip	65	1 28 15
50	Kilt of the Atal'ai Prophet	Bind on Pickup	69	1 52 2
50	Senior Designer's Pantaloons	Bind on Pickup	69	1 50 32
PROPERTIES: Increases healing done by spells and effects by up to 40				
52	Haunting Specter Leggings	Bind on Pickup	71	1 65 81
52	Sacred Cloth Leggings	Bind on Equip	71	1 72 28
PROPERTIES: Increases damage and healing done by magical spells and effects by up to 14				

Superior Cloth Leg Armor

Lvl	Name	Binding	Armor	Vendor Purchase Value
53	Mooncloth Leggings	Bind on Equip	72	1 81 13
53	Rainstrider Leggings	Bind on Pickup	69	1 50 37
55	Skyshroud Leggings	Bind on Pickup	75	1 92 30
PROPERTIES: Increases damage and healing done by magical spells and effects by up to 34				
56	Devout Skirt	Bind on Pickup	76	2 8 20
56	Dreadmist Leggings	Bind on Pickup	76	2 12 2
56	Magister's Leggings	Bind on Pickup	76	2 2 81
56	Necropile Leggings	Bind on Pickup	76	2 17 46
56	Padre's Trousers	Bind on Pickup	76	2 5 88
PROPERTIES: Restores 6 mana per 5 sec, Increases healing done by spells and effects by up to 42				
56	Skullsmoke Pants	Bind on Pickup	76	2 15 85
PROPERTIES: Fire Resist +10, Shadow Resist +5				
56	The Postmaster's Trousers	Bind on Pickup	76	2 17 46
56	Wolfshear Leggings	Bind on Pickup	76	1 98 80
PROPERTIES: Nature Resist +10, Increases healing done by spells and effects by up to 26				
57	Abyssal Cloth Pants	Bind on Equip	77	2 12 27
PROPERTIES: Improves your chance to get a critical strike with spells by 1%				
57	Ironweave Pants	Bind on Pickup	77	2 23 66
58	Knight-Captain's Dreadweave Leggings	Bind on Pickup	78	1 18 60
PROPERTIES: Increases damage and healing done by magical spells and effects by up to 16				
58	Knight-Captain's Satin Leggings	Bind on Pickup	78	1 15 18
PROPERTIES: Increases damage and healing done by magical spells and effects by up to 19				
58	Knight-Captain's Silk Leggings	Bind on Pickup	78	1 17 35
PROPERTIES: Increases damage and healing done by magical spells and effects by up to 19				
58	Leggings of Torment	Bind on Pickup	78	2 19 68
PROPERTIES: Increases damage done by Shadow spells and effects by up to 34				
58	Legionnaire's Dreadweave Leggings	Bind on Pickup	78	1 11 82
PROPERTIES: Increases damage and healing done by magical spells and effects by up to 28				
58	Legionnaire's Satin Trousers	Bind on Pickup	78	1 11 79
PROPERTIES: Increases damage and healing done by magical spells and effects by up to 19				
58	Legionnaire's Silk Pants	Bind on Pickup	78	1 15 60
PROPERTIES: Increases damage and healing done by magical spells and effects by up to 19				
58	Runed Stygian Leggings	Bind on Equip	78	2 37 33
PROPERTIES: Shadow Resist +25, Restores 6 mana per 5 sec				
58	Spiritshroud Leggings	Bind on Pickup	78	2 23 44
PROPERTIES: Increases damage and healing done by magical spells and effects by up to 19				
60	Bloodtinged Kilt	Bind on Pickup	87	3 44 28
PROPERTIES: Increases damage and healing done by magical spells and effects by up to 28				
60	Bloodvine Leggings	Bind on Equip	80	2 51 29
PROPERTIES: Improves your chance to hit with spells by 1%, Increases damage and healing done by magical spells and effects by up to 37				
60	Knight-Captain's Dreadweave Legguards	Bind on Pickup	84	1 47 71
PROPERTIES: Increases damage and healing done by magical spells and effects by up to 28				
60	Knight-Captain's Satin Legguards	Bind on Pickup	84	1 50 96
PROPERTIES: Increases damage and healing done by magical spells and effects by up to 21, Restores 6 mana per 5 sec				
60	Knight-Captain's Silk Legguards	Bind on Pickup	84	1 52 3
PROPERTIES: Increases damage and healing done by magical spells and effects by up to 21, Improves your chance to get a critical strike with spells by 1%				
60	Legionnaire's Dreadweave Legguards	Bind on Pickup	84	1 46 5
PROPERTIES: Increases damage and healing done by magical spells and effects by up to 28				
60	Legionnaire's Satin Legguards	Bind on Pickup	84	1 46 60
PROPERTIES: Increases damage and healing done by magical spells and effects by up to 21, Restores 6 mana per 5 sec				
60	Legionnaire's Silk Legguards	Bind on Pickup	84	1 47 14
PROPERTIES: Increases damage and healing done by magical spells and effects by up to 21, Improves your chance to get a critical strike with spells by 1%				
60	Ritualistic Legguards	Bind on Pickup	84	2 80 9
PROPERTIES: Increases healing done by spells and effects by up to 37				
60	Cenarion Reservist's Pants	Bind on Pickup	78	2 19 68
PROPERTIES: Nature Resist +25, Increases damage and healing done by magical spells and effects by up to 15				
60	Cenarion Reservist's Pants	Bind on Pickup	78	2 19 68
PROPERTIES: Nature Resist +25, Increases healing done by spells and effects by up to 29				

Superior Cloth Leg Armor

Lvl	Name	Binding	Armor	Vendor Purchase Value
60	Deathmist Leggings	Bind on Pickup	81	2 66 95
PROPERTIES: Increases damage and healing done by magical spells and effects by up to 16				
60	Sorcerer's Leggings	Bind on Pickup	81	2 55 1
PROPERTIES: Increases damage and healing done by magical spells and effects by up to 16				
60	Virtuous Skirt	Bind on Pickup	81	2 60 7
PROPERTIES: Increases damage and healing done by magical spells and effects by up to 16, Restores 6 mana per 5 sec				

Epic Cloth Shoulder Armor

Lvl	Name	Binding	Armor	Vendor Purchase Value
56	Flarecore Mantle	Bind on Equip	71	2 13 65
PROPERTIES: Fire Resist +24				
60	Arcanist Mantle	Bind on Pickup	76	2 55 91
PROPERTIES: Shadow Resist +7, Restores 4 mana per 5 sec, Increases damage and healing done by magical spells and effects by up to 14				
60	Defiler's Epaulets	Bind on Pickup	75	2 58 89
PROPERTIES: Increases damage and healing done by magical spells and effects by up to 12, Restores 4 mana per 5 sec				
60	Doomcaller's Mantle	Bind on Pickup	89	4 68 68
PROPERTIES: Increases damage and healing done by magical spells and effects by up to 28, Decreases the magical resistances of your spell targets by 10, Improves your chance to hit with spells by 1%				
60	Enigma Shoulderpads	Bind on Pickup	89	4 98 95
PROPERTIES: Increases damage and healing done by magical spells and effects by up to 30, Decreases the magical resistances of your spell targets by 10, Restores 4 mana per 5 sec				
60	Felheart Shoulder Pads	Bind on Pickup	76	2 65 72
PROPERTIES: Shadow Resist +7, Increases damage and healing done by magical spells and effects by up to 9				
60	Field Marshal's Dreadweave Shoulders	Bind on Pickup	85	1 97 75
PROPERTIES: Increases damage and healing done by magical spells and effects by up to 25				
60	Field Marshal's Satin Mantle	Bind on Pickup	85	2 5 85
PROPERTIES: Increases damage and healing done by magical spells and effects by up to 25				
60	Field Marshal's Silk Spaulders	Bind on Pickup	85	1 93 42
PROPERTIES: Increases damage and healing done by magical spells and effects by up to 25, Decreases the magical resistances of your spell targets by 10				
60	Frostfire Shoulderpads	Bind on Pickup	97	6 76 69
PROPERTIES: Increases damage and healing done by magical spells and effects by up to 36				
60	Highlander's Epaulets	Bind on Pickup	75	2 57 1
PROPERTIES: Increases damage and healing done by magical spells and effects by up to 12, Restores 4 mana per 5 sec				
60	Mantle of Phrenic Power	Bind on Pickup	87	4 55 77
PROPERTIES: Increases damage done by Fire spells and effects by up to 33				
60	Mantle of Prophecy	Bind on Pickup	76	2 54 90
PROPERTIES: Shadow Resist +7, Increases damage and healing done by magical spells and effects by up to 9				
60	Mantle of the Blackwing Cabal	Bind on Pickup	84	3 89 44
PROPERTIES: Increases damage and healing done by magical spells and effects by up to 34				
60	Mantle of the Oracle	Bind on Pickup	89	4 59 83
PROPERTIES: Increases damage and healing done by magical spells and effects by up to 20, Restores 3 mana per 5 sec, Decreases the magical resistances of your spell targets by 10				
60	Nemesis Spaulders	Bind on Pickup	87	4 19 98
PROPERTIES: Fire Resist +10, Restores 4 health per 5 sec, Increases damage and healing done by magical spells and effects by up to 23				
60	Netherwind Mantle	Bind on Pickup	87	4 28 2
PROPERTIES: Fire Resist +10, Restores 4 mana per 5 sec, Increases damage and healing done by magical spells and effects by up to 21				
60	Pauldrons of Transcendence	Bind on Pickup	87	4 39 18
PROPERTIES: Fire Resist +10, Increases healing done by spells and effects by up to 26				
60	Plagueheart Shoulderpads	Bind on Pickup	97	7 16 23
PROPERTIES: Improves your chance to hit with spells by 1%, Increases damage and healing done by magical spells and effects by up to 36				
60	Rime Covered Mantle	Bind on Pickup	94	6 27 57
PROPERTIES: Increases damage and healing done by magical spells and effects by up to 39, Improves your chance to get a critical strike with spells by 1%				
60	Shoulderpads of Faith	Bind on Pickup	97	7 37 3
PROPERTIES: Increases healing done by spells and effects by up to 51, Restores 3 mana per 5 sec				
60	Ternary Mantle	Bind on Pickup	86	4 4 82
PROPERTIES: Increases healing done by spells and effects by up to 44				

Epic Cloth Shoulder Armor

Lvl	Name	Binding	Armor	Vendor Purchase Value
60	Warlord's Dreadweave Mantle	Bind on Pickup	85	1 90 51
PROPERTIES: Increases damage and healing done by magical spells and effects by up to 25				
60	Warlord's Satin Mantle	Bind on Pickup	85	2 4 37
PROPERTIES: Increases damage and healing done by magical spells and effects by up to 25				
60	Warlord's Silk Amice	Bind on Pickup	85	1 87 51
PROPERTIES: Increases damage and healing done by magical spells and effects by up to 25, Decreases the magical resistances of your spell targets by 10				
60	Glacial Mantle	Bind on Pickup	94	5 93 90
PROPERTIES: Frost Resist +33, Increases damage and healing done by magical spells and effects by up to 16				
60	Zandalar Confessor's Mantle	Bind on Pickup	78	
PROPERTIES: Increases healing done by spells and effects by up to 22				
60	Zandalar Demoniac's Mantle	Bind on Pickup	71	
PROPERTIES: Increases damage and healing done by magical spells and effects by up to 12				
60	Zandalar Illusionist's Mantle	Bind on Pickup	71	
PROPERTIES: Increases damage and healing done by magical spells and effects by up to 12				

Superior Cloth Shoulder Armor

Lvl	Name	Binding	Armor	Vendor Purchase Value
20	Magician's Mantle	Bind on Equip	32	10 20
PROPERTIES: Increases damage and healing done by magical spells and effects by up to 5				
22	Slime-encrusted Pads	Bind on Pickup	34	11 90
PROPERTIES: Restores 3 health every 4 sec				
23	Feline Mantle	Bind on Pickup	34	13 4
27	Batwing Mantle	Bind on Pickup	37	20 41
33	Pads of the Venom Spider	Bind on Equip	41	34 53
PROPERTIES: Nature Resist +5				
34	Beryline Pads	Bind on Pickup	39	27 65
42	Flameseer Mantle	Bind on Pickup	51	65 98
PROPERTIES: Increases damage done by Fire spells and effects by up to 14				
47	Kentic Amice	Bind on Pickup	56	90 79
PROPERTIES: Increases damage and healing done by magical spells and effects by up to 14				
48	Mantle of Lost Hope	Bind on Pickup	57	97 13
PROPERTIES: Increases healing done by spells and effects by up to 26, Restores 3 mana per 5 sec				
48	Rotgrip Mantle	Bind on Pickup	57	1 3 83
51	Elder Wizard's Mantle	Bind on Equip	60	1 23 55
PROPERTIES: Increases damage and healing done by magical spells and effects by up to 11				
52	Boreal Mantle	Bind on Pickup	61	1 27 20
PROPERTIES: Increases damage done by Frost spells and effects by up to 29				
55	Devout Mantle	Bind on Pickup	64	1 49 25
55	Dreadmist Mantle	Bind on Pickup	64	1 56 50
55	Magister's Mantle	Bind on Pickup	64	1 45 97
55	Soulstealer Mantle	Bind on Pickup	64	1 43 15
56	Burial Shawl	Bind on Pickup	65	1 52 15
PROPERTIES: Increases damage and healing done by magical spells and effects by up to 20				
56	Ironweave Mantle	Bind on Pickup	65	1 60 90
56	Mantle of the Scarlet Crusade	Bind on Pickup	65	1 49 44
PROPERTIES: Increases healing done by spells and effects by up to 20				
56	Mooncloth Shoulders	Bind on Equip	65	1 58 40
56	Necropile Mantle	Bind on Pickup	65	1 63 67
56	Sunderseer Mantle	Bind on Pickup	65	1 64 22
PROPERTIES: Increases damage and healing done by magical spells and effects by up to 8				
57	Deadwalker Mantle	Bind on Pickup	66	1 70 62
PROPERTIES: Increases damage done by Shadow spells and effects by up to 13				
57	Diabolic Mantle	Bind on Pickup	66	1 61 62
PROPERTIES: Restores 8 mana per 5 sec				
58	Champion's Dreadweave Shoulders	Bind on Pickup	67	84 49
PROPERTIES: Increases damage and healing done by magical spells and effects by up to 12				
58	Champion's Satin Shoulderpads	Bind on Pickup	67	84 47
PROPERTIES: Increases damage and healing done by magical spells and effects by up to 12				
58	Champion's Silk Shoulderpads	Bind on Pickup	67	89 62
PROPERTIES: Increases damage and healing done by magical spells and effects by up to 12				

Superior Cloth Shoulder Armor

Lvl	Name	Binding	Armor	Vendor Purchase Value
58	Lieutenant Commander's Dreadweave Mantle	Bind on Pickup	67	83 22
PROPERTIES: Increases damage and healing done by magical spells and effects by up to 12				
58	Lieutenant Commander's Satin Amice	Bind on Pickup	67	89 31
PROPERTIES: Increases damage and healing done by magical spells and effects by up to 12				
58	Lieutenant Commander's Silk Spaulders	Bind on Pickup	67	88 33
PROPERTIES: Increases damage and healing done by magical spells and effects by up to 12				
58	Shroud of the Nathrezim	Bind on Pickup	67	1 67 6
PROPERTIES: Improves your chance to get a critical strike with spells by 1%				
58	Thuzadin Mantle	Bind on Pickup	67	1 64 76
PROPERTIES: Increases damage and healing done by magical spells and effects by up to 12				
59	Argent Shoulders	Bind on Equip	68	1 75 41
PROPERTIES: Shadow Resist +5				
59	Mantle of the Timbermaw	Bind on Equip	68	1 87 58
PROPERTIES: Restores 6 mana per 5 sec				
60	Abyssal Cloth Amice	Bind on Pickup	72	2 10 28
PROPERTIES: Improves your chance to hit with spells by 1%				
60	Champion's Dreadweave Spaulders	Bind on Pickup	75	1 24 90
PROPERTIES: Increases damage and healing done by magical spells and effects by up to 12, Improves your chance to get a critical strike with spells by 1%				
60	Champion's Satin Mantle	Bind on Pickup	75	1 31 9
PROPERTIES: Increases damage and healing done by magical spells and effects by up to 16, Restores 6 mana per 5 sec				
60	Champion's Silk Mantle	Bind on Pickup	75	1 32 4
PROPERTIES: Increases damage and healing done by magical spells and effects by up to 15, Improves your chance to get a critical strike with spells by 1%				
60	Lieutenant Commander's Dreadweave Spaulders	Bind on Pickup	75	1 25 89
PROPERTIES: Increases damage and healing done by magical spells and effects by up to 12, Improves your chance to get a critical strike with spells by 1%				
60	Lieutenant Commander's Satin Mantle	Bind on Pickup	75	1 28 71
PROPERTIES: Increases damage and healing done by magical spells and effects by up to 16, Restores 6 mana per 5 sec				
60	Lieutenant Commander's Silk Mantle	Bind on Pickup	75	1 29 64
PROPERTIES: Increases damage and healing done by magical spells and effects by up to 15, Improves your chance to get a critical strike with spells by 1%				
60	Mantle of Maz'Nadir	Bind on Pickup	78	2 89 16
PROPERTIES: Increases damage and healing done by magical spells and effects by up to 21				
60	Sylvan Shoulders	Bind on Equip	74	2 50 51
PROPERTIES: Nature Resist +20, Increases damage and healing done by magical spells and effects by up to 7				
60	Deathmist Mantle	Bind on Pickup	69	1 91 38
PROPERTIES: Increases damage and healing done by magical spells and effects by up to 12				
60	Sorcerer's Mantle	Bind on Pickup	69	1 87 88
PROPERTIES: Increases damage and healing done by magical spells and effects by up to 9				
60	Virtuous Mantle	Bind on Pickup	69	1 97 69
PROPERTIES: Increases damage and healing done by magical spells and effects by up to 12				

Epic Cloth Waist Armor

Lvl	Name	Binding	Armor	Vendor Purchase Value
57	Belt of the Archmage	Bind on Equip	54	1 47 44
PROPERTIES: Improves your chance to get a critical strike with spells by 1%				
60	Angelista's Grasp	Bind on Pickup	66	3 13 29
PROPERTIES: Improves your chance to hit with spells by 2%				
60	Arcanist Belt	Bind on Equip	57	1 73 88
PROPERTIES: Fire Resist +10, Increases damage and healing done by magical spells and effects by up to 14				
60	Belt of Faith	Bind on Pickup	75	5 9 17
PROPERTIES: Increases healing done by spells and effects by up to 48				
60	Belt of the Dark Bog	Bind on Pickup	61	2 28 79
PROPERTIES: Nature Resist +25, Increases damage and healing done by magical spells and effects by up to 14				
60	Belt of Transcendence	Bind on Pickup	65	3 1 53
PROPERTIES: Shadow Resist +10, Increases healing done by spells and effects by up to 26				
60	Eyestalk Waist Cord	Bind on Pickup	75	4 95 96
PROPERTIES: Improves your chance to get a critical strike with spells by 1%, Increases damage and healing done by magical spells and effects by up to 41				
60	Felheart Belt	Bind on Equip	57	1 76 49

Epic Cloth Waist Armor

Lvl	Name	Binding	Armor	Vendor Purchase Value
PROPERTIES: Fire Resist +7, Increases damage and healing done by magical spells and effects by up to 20				
60	Firemaw's Clutch	Bind on Pickup	64	2 76 3
PROPERTIES: Increases damage and healing done by magical spells and effects by up to 35, Restores 5 mana per 5 sec				
60	Frostfire Belt	Bind on Pickup	75	5 16 86
PROPERTIES: Increases damage and healing done by magical spells and effects by up to 28, Improves your chance to hit with spells by 1%				
60	Girdle of Prophecy	Bind on Equip	57	1 70 59
PROPERTIES: Fire Resist +7, Restores 4 mana per 5 sec, Increases damage and healing done by magical spells and effects by up to 9				
60	Grasp of the Old God	Bind on Pickup	75	5 10 78
PROPERTIES: Increases healing done by spells and effects by up to 59, Restores 7 mana per 5 sec				
60	Mana Igniting Cord	Bind on Pickup	61	2 22 80
PROPERTIES: Increases damage and healing done by magical spells and effects by up to 25, Improves your chance to get a critical strike with spells by 1%				
60	Nemesis Belt	Bind on Pickup	65	2 81 6
PROPERTIES: Shadow Resist +10, Improves your chance to get a critical strike with spells by 1%, Increases damage and healing done by magical spells and effects by up to 25				
60	Netherwind Belt	Bind on Pickup	65	2 78 95
PROPERTIES: Shadow Resist +10, Increases damage and healing done by magical spells and effects by up to 23				
60	Plagueheart Belt	Bind on Pickup	75	5 32 15
PROPERTIES: Increases damage and healing done by magical spells and effects by up to 34, Improves your chance to get a critical strike with spells by 1%				
60	Sash of Whispered Secrets	Bind on Pickup	61	2 16 11
PROPERTIES: Increases damage done by Shadow spells and effects by up to 33, Restores 6 health per 5 sec				
60	Zandalar Confessor's Bindings	Bind on Pickup	53	
PROPERTIES: Increases healing done by spells and effects by up to 26				

Superior Cloth Waist Armor

Lvl	Name	Binding	Armor	Vendor Purchase Value
18	Keller's Girdle	Bind on Equip	23	5 24
24	Belt of Arugal	Bind on Pickup	26	10
27	Warsong Sash	Bind on Pickup	25	8 13
28	Defiler's Cloth Girdle	Bind on Pickup	28	15 5
PROPERTIES: Increases damage and healing done by magical spells and effects by up to 11				
28	Highlander's Cloth Girdle	Bind on Pickup	28	14 41
PROPERTIES: Increases damage and healing done by magical spells and effects by up to 11				
32	Sutarn's Ring	Bind on Equip	30	21 47
36	Deathmage Sash	Bind on Pickup	33	29 10
38	Defiler's Cloth Girdle	Bind on Pickup	35	31 87
PROPERTIES: Increases damage and healing done by magical spells and effects by up to 14				
38	Highlander's Cloth Girdle	Bind on Pickup	35	33 36
PROPERTIES: Increases damage and healing done by magical spells and effects by up to 14				
45	Satyrmane Sash	Bind on Pickup	40	58 18
PROPERTIES: Shadow Resist +10				
48	Dawnspire Cord	Bind on Pickup	43	68 65
48	Defiler's Cloth Girdle	Bind on Pickup	43	64 23
PROPERTIES: Improves your chance to get a critical strike with spells by 1%, Increases damage and healing done by magical spells and effects by up to 9				
48	Highlander's Cloth Girdle	Bind on Pickup	43	67 23
PROPERTIES: Improves your chance to get a critical strike with spells by 1%, Increases damage and healing done by magical spells and effects by up to 9				
48	Serenity Belt	Bind on Equip	43	68 65
49	Ban'thok Sash	Bind on Pickup	43	74 62
PROPERTIES: Improves your chance to hit with spells by 1%, Increases damage and healing done by magical spells and effects by up to 12				
53	Devout Belt	Bind on Equip	46	90 58
53	Dreadmist Belt	Bind on Equip	46	85 92
53	Magister's Belt	Bind on Equip	46	86 94
53	Sash of the Burning Heart	Bind on Pickup	46	91 53
PROPERTIES: Increases damage done by Fire spells and effects by up to 14				
53	Wisdom of the Timbermaw	Bind on Equip	46	92 32
PROPERTIES: Restores 4 mana per 5 sec				

Superior Cloth Waist Armor

Lvl	Name	Binding	Armor	Vendor Purchase Value
54	Grimgore Noose	Bind on Pickup	47	94 1
54	Whipvine Cord	Bind on Pickup	47	93 76
PROPERTIES: Restores 6 mana per 5 sec, Increases healing done by spells and effects by up to 31				
55	Frostwolf Cloth Belt	Bind on Pickup	48	1 2 85
PROPERTIES: Frost Resist +5, Increases damage and healing done by magical spells and effects by up to 18				
55	Stormpike Cloth Girdle	Bind on Pickup	48	94 88
PROPERTIES: Frost Resist +5, Increases damage and healing done by magical spells and effects by up to 18				
55	Waistband of Balzaphon	Bind on Pickup	48	94 88
PROPERTIES: Increases damage done by Frost spells and effects by up to 20				
56	Clutch of Andros	Bind on Pickup	49	1 9 50
PROPERTIES: Improves your chance to hit with spells by 1%				
56	Dustfeather Sash	Bind on Pickup	49	1 2 51
PROPERTIES: Increases damage and healing done by magical spells and effects by up to 9				
56	Ironweave Belt	Bind on Pickup	49	99 63
56	Thuzadin Sash	Bind on Pickup	49	1 1 1
PROPERTIES: Increases damage and healing done by magical spells and effects by up to 11				
58	Defiler's Cloth Girdle	Bind on Pickup	50	1 20 38
PROPERTIES: Improves your chance to get a critical strike with spells by 1%, Increases damage and healing done by magical spells and effects by up to 14				
58	Highlander's Cloth Girdle	Bind on Pickup	50	1 19 11
PROPERTIES: Improves your chance to get a critical strike with spells by 1%, Increases damage and healing done by magical spells and effects by up to 14				
58	Runed Stygian Belt	Bind on Equip	50	1 19 8
PROPERTIES: Shadow Resist +20, Restores 3 mana per 5 sec				
60	Belt of the Inquisition	Bind on Pickup	56	1 78 50
PROPERTIES: Increases healing done by spells and effects by up to 24, Restores 4 mana per 5 sec				
60	Belt of Untapped Power	Bind on Pickup	54	1 50 43
PROPERTIES: Increases damage and healing done by magical spells and effects by up to 29				
60	Belt of Tiny Heads	Bind on Pickup	55	1 65 75
PROPERTIES: Restores 7 mana per 5 sec				
60	Deathmist Belt	Bind on Pickup	52	1 26 19
PROPERTIES: Increases damage and healing done by magical spells and effects by up to 12				
60	Sorcerer's Belt	Bind on Pickup	52	1 31 80
PROPERTIES: Increases damage and healing done by magical spells and effects by up to 14				
60	Virtuous Belt	Bind on Pickup	52	1 29 92
PROPERTIES: Increases damage and healing done by magical spells and effects by up to 12				

Epic Cloth Wrist Armor

Lvl	Name	Binding	Armor	Vendor Purchase Value
40	Dryad's Wrist Bindings	Bind on Pickup	31	54 1
PROPERTIES: Increases damage and healing done by magical spells and effects by up to 16				
50	Dryad's Wrist Bindings	Bind on Pickup	37	1 4 85
PROPERTIES: Increases damage and healing done by magical spells and effects by up to 20				
60	Arcanist Bindings	Bind on Equip	44	1 71 92
PROPERTIES: Increases damage and healing done by magical spells and effects by up to 12, Restores 3 mana per 5 sec				
60	Bindings of Faith	Bind on Pickup	58	5 11 9
PROPERTIES: Increases healing done by spells and effects by up to 40				
60	Bindings of Transcendence	Bind on Pickup	51	3 2 60
PROPERTIES: Increases healing done by spells and effects by up to 33				
60	Black Bark Wristbands	Bind on Pickup	48	2 16 38
PROPERTIES: Increases damage and healing done by magical spells and effects by up to 25				
60	Blacklight Bracer	Bind on Pickup	44	1 69 54
PROPERTIES: Improves your chance to get a critical strike with spells by 1%				
60	Bracelets of Royal Redemption	Bind on Pickup	54	3 75 49
PROPERTIES: Increases healing done by spells and effects by up to 53				
60	Bracers of Arcane Accuracy	Bind on Pickup	50	2 62 68
PROPERTIES: Improves your chance to hit with spells by 1%, Increases damage and healing done by magical spells and effects by up to 21				
60	Burrower Bracers	Bind on Pickup	54	3 84 99
PROPERTIES: Increases damage and healing done by magical spells and effects by up to 28				

Epic Cloth Wrist Armor

Lvl	Name	Binding	Armor	Vendor Purchase Value
60	Dryad's Wrist Bindings	Bind on Pickup	44	1 75 9
PROPERTIES: Increases damage and healing done by magical spells and effects by up to 22				
60	Felheart Bracers	Bind on Equip	44	1 75 17
PROPERTIES: Increases damage and healing done by magical spells and effects by up to 13				
60	Flarecore Wraps	Bind on Equip	43	1 69 11
PROPERTIES: Fire Resist +7, Restores 9 mana per 5 sec				
60	Frostfire Bindings	Bind on Pickup	58	5 18 79
PROPERTIES: Decreases the magical resistances of your spell targets by 10, Increases damage and healing done by magical spells and effects by up to 27				
60	Glacial Wrists	Bind on Equip	53	3 49 73
PROPERTIES: Frost Resist +20, Increases damage and healing done by magical spells and effects by up to 12				
60	Nemesis Bracers	Bind on Pickup	51	2 82 13
PROPERTIES: Increases damage and healing done by magical spells and effects by up to 15				
60	Netherwind Bindings	Bind on Pickup	51	2 86 42
PROPERTIES: Increases damage and healing done by magical spells and effects by up to 19, Restores 4 mana per 5 sec				
60	Plagueheart Bindings	Bind on Pickup	58	5 34 7
PROPERTIES: Increases damage and healing done by magical spells and effects by up to 23				
60	Shackles of the Unscarred	Bind on Pickup	48	2 29 63
PROPERTIES: Increases damage and healing done by magical spells and effects by up to 21, Decreases the magical resistances of your spell targets by 10				
60	The Soul Harvester's Bindings	Bind on Pickup	55	4 26 8
PROPERTIES: Improves your chance to get a critical strike with spells by 1%, Increases damage and healing done by magical spells and effects by up to 21				
60	Vambraces of Prophecy	Bind on Equip	44	1 71 89
PROPERTIES: Restores 2 mana per 5 sec, Increases healing done by spells and effects by up to 24				
60	Bracers of Hope	Bind on Pickup	41	1 27 89
PROPERTIES: Increases healing done by spells and effects by up to 18				
60	Rockfury Bracers	Bind on Pickup	42	1 45 33
PROPERTIES: Increases damage and healing done by magical spells and effects by up to 27, Improves your chance to hit with spells by 1%				
60	Zandalar Confessor's Wraps	Bind on Pickup	41	
PROPERTIES: Increases healing done by spells and effects by up to 24				
60	Zandalar Demoniac's Wraps	Bind on Pickup	41	
PROPERTIES: Increases damage and healing done by magical spells and effects by up to 16				
60	Zandalar Illusionist's Wraps	Bind on Pickup	41	
PROPERTIES: Increases damage and healing done by magical spells and effects by up to 14				

Superior Cloth Wrist Armor

Lvl	Name	Binding	Armor	Vendor Purchase Value
17	Mindthrust Bracers	Bind on Equip	17	4 64
26	Glowing Magical Bracelets	Bind on Equip	21	12 16
41	Forgotten Wraps	Bind on Equip	29	41 33
45	Arena Wristguards	Bind on Equip	31	57 58
PROPERTIES: Improves your chance to get a critical strike with spells by 1%				
45	First Sergeant's Silk Cuffs	Bind on Pickup	31	27 44
45	Sergeant Major's Silk Cuffs	Bind on Pickup	31	26 74
49	Aristocratic Cuffs	Bind on Equip	34	74 63
52	Devout Bracers	Bind on Equip	35	85 77
52	Dreadmist Bracers	Bind on Equip	35	81 38
52	Flameweave Cuffs	Bind on Pickup	35	86 6
PROPERTIES: Fire Resist +10				
52	Magister's Bindings	Bind on Equip	35	87 65
52	Tearfall Bracers	Bind on Pickup	35	81 19
54	Funeral Cuffs	Bind on Pickup	37	91 91
PROPERTIES: Shadow Resist +10				
54	Manacle Cuffs	Bind on Pickup	34	79 39
55	Sublime Wristguards	Bind on Pickup	37	94 88
PROPERTIES: Increases damage and healing done by magical spells and effects by up to 12				
56	Ironweave Bracers	Bind on Pickup	38	99 63
56	Necropile Cuffs	Bind on Pickup	38	1 7 58
57	Bracers of Mending	Bind on Pickup	38	1 12 69
PROPERTIES: Increases healing done by spells and effects by up to 18				

Superior Cloth Wrist Armor

Lvl	Name	Binding	Armor	Vendor Purchase Value
57	Magiskull Cuffs	Bind on Equip	38	1 12 91
58	Bracers of Undead Cleansing	Bind on Equip	39	1 16 15
PROPERTIES: Increases damage done to Undead by magical spells and effects by up to 26				
58	First Sergeant's Silk Cuffs	Bind on Pickup	39	56 95
58	Sergeant Major's Silk Cuffs	Bind on Pickup	39	56 13
60	Abyssal Cloth Wristbands	Bind on Pickup	42	1 40 4
60	Bracers of Qiraji Command	Bind on Pickup	44	1 76
PROPERTIES: Restores 4 mana per 5 sec				
60	Deathmist Bracers	Bind on Pickup	40	1 26 66
PROPERTIES: Increases damage and healing done by magical spells and effects by up to 8				
60	Sorcerer's Bindings	Bind on Pickup	40	1 32 27
PROPERTIES: Increases damage and healing done by magical spells and effects by up to 8				
60	Virtuous Bracers	Bind on Pickup	40	1 30 38
PROPERTIES: Increases damage and healing done by magical spells and effects by up to 9, Restores 2 mana per 5 sec				
60	Wyrmthalak's Shackles	Bind on Pickup	37	95 5

LEATHER

Epic Leather Chest Armor

Lvl	Name	Binding	Armor	Vendor Purchase Value
60	Bloodfang Chestpiece	Bind on Pickup	225	7 34 80
PROPERTIES: Fire Resist +10, Nature Resist +10, Improves your chance to get a critical strike by 1%, Improves your chance to hit by 2%				
60	Bonescythe Breastplate	Bind on Pickup	262	16 52 32
PROPERTIES: Improves your chance to get a critical strike by 2%, +80 Attack Power, Improves your chance to hit by 1%				
60	Deathdealer's Vest	Bind on Pickup	253	13 49 62
PROPERTIES: Improves your chance to get a critical strike by 1%, Improves your chance to hit by 1%				
60	Dreamwalker Tunic	Bind on Pickup	262	16 5 71
PROPERTIES: Increases healing done by spells and effects by up to 66, Restores 8 mana per 5 sec				
60	Field Marshal's Dragonhide Breastplate	Bind on Pickup	220	3 32 2
PROPERTIES: Increases damage and healing done by magical spells and effects by up to 21, Improves your chance to get a critical strike by 1%				
60	Field Marshal's Leather Chestpiece	Bind on Pickup	220	3 33 24
PROPERTIES: Improves your chance to get a critical strike by 1%, Improves your chance to hit by 1%				
60	Genesis Vest	Bind on Pickup	253	12 81 76
PROPERTIES: Increases damage and healing done by magical spells and effects by up to 28, Improves your chance to get a critical strike with spells by 1%, Improves your chance to get a critical strike by 1%				
60	Ghoul Skin Tunic	Bind on Pickup	241	9 71 50
PROPERTIES: Improves your chance to get a critical strike by 2%				
60	Interlaced Shadow Jerkin	Bind on Pickup	212	5 65 52
PROPERTIES: Shadow Resist +30, +28 Attack Power				
60	Malfurion's Blessed Bulwark	Bind on Pickup	222	7 2 77
60	Nightslayer Chestpiece	Bind on Pickup	200	4 31 37
PROPERTIES: Fire Resist +10, Improves your chance to get a critical strike by 1%				
60	Polar Tunic	Bind on Equip	234	8 93 77
PROPERTIES: Frost Resist +40				
60	Stormrage Chestguard	Bind on Pickup	225	7 13 51
PROPERTIES: Fire Resist +10, Nature Resist +10, Improves your chance to get a critical strike with spells by 1%, Increases healing done by spells and effects by up to 42				
60	Thick Silithid Chestguard	Bind on Pickup	208	5 1 58
PROPERTIES: Fire Resist +5, Nature Resist +5, Frost Resist +5, Shadow Resist +5, Arcane Resist +5				
60	Vest of Swift Execution	Bind on Pickup	229	7 98 70
60	Warlord's Dragonhide Hauberk	Bind on Pickup	220	3 36 88
PROPERTIES: Increases damage and healing done by magical spells and effects by up to 21, Improves your chance to get a critical strike by 1%				
60	Warlord's Leather Breastplate	Bind on Pickup	220	3 29 59
PROPERTIES: Improves your chance to hit by 1%, Improves your chance to get a critical strike by 1%				
60	Breastplate of Bloodthirst	Bind on Pickup	190	3 51 92
PROPERTIES: Improves your chance to get a critical strike by 2%, Increases your chance to dodge an attack by 1%				
60	Darkmantle Tunic	Bind on Pickup	185	3 19 70
PROPERTIES: Improves your chance to hit by 2%				

Epic Leather Chest Armor

Lvl	Name	Binding	Armor	Vendor Purchase Value
60	Feralheart Vest	Bind on Pickup	185	3 33 13
PROPERTIES: Increases damage and healing done by magical spells and effects by up to 12, Restores 4 mana per 5 sec				
60	Zandalar Haruspex's Tunic	Bind on Pickup	197	
PROPERTIES: Increases healing done by spells and effects by up to 33				
60	Zandalar Madcap's Tunic	Bind on Pickup	197	
PROPERTIES: Improves your chance to get a critical strike by 2%, +44 Attack Power				
60	Cenarion Vestments	Bind on Pickup	200	4 64 39
PROPERTIES: Fire Resist +10, Restores 3 mana per 5 sec, Increases healing done by spells and effects by up to 22				

Superior Leather Chest Armor

Lvl	Name	Binding	Armor	Vendor Purchase Value
17	Starsight Tunic	Bind on Equip	89	11 37
19	Blackened Defias Armor	Bind on Pickup	92	14 67
20	Gloomshroud Armor	Bind on Equip	94	15 53
22	Tunic of Westfall	Bind on Pickup	92	14 12
30	Spirewind Fetter	Bind on Equip	112	41 61
31	Wolffear Harness	Bind on Equip	113	49 68
34	Quillward Harness	Bind on Equip	120	61 91
44	Jinxed Hoodoo Skin	Bind on Pickup	144	1 32 41
45	Feathered Breastplate	Bind on Equip	146	1 44 78
46	Cow King's Hide	Bind on Equip	148	1 51 67
PROPERTIES: Fire Resist +10, Nature Resist +10, Frost Resist +10, Shadow Resist +10, Arcane Resist +10				
46	Fungus Shroud Armor	Bind on Pickup	148	1 44 50
48	Flamestrider Robes	Bind on Pickup	153	1 66 59
PROPERTIES: Fire Resist +10, Increases damage and healing done by magical spells and effects by up to 20				
50	Mixologist's Tunic	Bind on Pickup	158	1 98 46
50	Warbear Harness	Bind on Equip	158	1 97 17
52	Stormshroud Armor	Bind on Equip	163	2 9 66
PROPERTIES: Improves your chance to get a critical strike by 2%, Increases your chance to dodge an attack by 1%				
52	Forest's Embrace	Bind on Pickup	151	1 51 52
PROPERTIES: Increases healing done by spells and effects by up to 55				
52	Grizzled Pelt	Bind on Pickup	151	1 52 70
53	Ironfeather Breastplate	Bind on Equip	165	2 36 50
53	Songbird Blouse	Bind on Pickup	165	2 19 72
55	Living Breastplate	Bind on Equip	169	2 47 76
PROPERTIES: Nature Resist +5, Increases healing done by spells and effects by up to 26				
56	Cadaverous Armor	Bind on Pickup	172	2 50 48
PROPERTIES: +60 Attack Power				
56	Nightbrace Tunic	Bind on Pickup	172	2 50 48
PROPERTIES: Fire Resist +10, Shadow Resist +10, +50 Attack Power				
57	Chestplate of Tranquility	Bind on Pickup	174	2 84 59
PROPERTIES: Increases damage and healing done by magical spells and effects by up to 23				
57	Tombstone Breastplate	Bind on Pickup	174	2 68 8
PROPERTIES: Improves your chance to get a critical strike by 2%				
58	Knight-Captain's Dragonhide Tunic	Bind on Pickup	176	1 50 39
PROPERTIES: Increases damage and healing done by magical spells and effects by up to 16, Improves your chance to get a critical strike by 1%				
58	Knight-Captain's Leather Armor	Bind on Pickup	176	1 48 27
PROPERTIES: Improves your chance to get a critical strike by 1%				
58	Legionnaire's Dragonhide Breastplate	Bind on Pickup	176	1 41 30
PROPERTIES: Improves your chance to get a critical strike by 1%, Increases damage and healing done by magical spells and effects by up to 16				
58	Legionnaire's Leather Hauberk	Bind on Pickup	176	1 41 84
PROPERTIES: Improves your chance to get a critical strike by 1%				
58	Shadowcraft Tunic	Bind on Pickup	176	3 1 90
58	Tunic of the Crescent Moon	Bind on Pickup	176	2 74 61
PROPERTIES: Increases damage and healing done by magical spells and effects by up to 15, Improves your chance to get a critical strike with spells by 1%				
58	Tunic of Undead Slaying	Bind on Pickup	176	2 88 25
PROPERTIES: +81 Attack Power when fighting Undead				

Superior Leather Chest Armor

Lvl	Name	Binding	Armor	Vendor Purchase Value
58	Wildheart Vest	Bind on Pickup	176	2 78 41
60	Blood Tiger Breastplate	Bind on Equip	181	3 19 93
60	Knight-Captain's Dragonhide Chestpiece	Bind on Pickup	188	1 83 30
PROPERTIES: Improves your chance to get a critical strike by 1%, Increases damage and healing done by magical spells and effects by up to 15				
60	Knight-Captain's Leather Chestpiece	Bind on Pickup	188	1 86
PROPERTIES: Improves your chance to get a critical strike by 1%, Improves your chance to hit by 1%, +34 Attack Power				
60	Legionnaire's Dragonhide Chestpiece	Bind on Pickup	188	1 79 87
PROPERTIES: Improves your chance to get a critical strike by 1%, Increases damage and healing done by magical spells and effects by up to 15				
60	Legionnaire's Leather Chestpiece	Bind on Pickup	188	1 81 23
PROPERTIES: Improves your chance to get a critical strike by 1%, Improves your chance to hit by 1%, +34 Attack Power				
60	Primal Batskin Jerkin	Bind on Equip	181	3 16 44
PROPERTIES: Improves your chance to hit by 1%				

Epic Leather Feet Armor

Lvl	Name	Binding	Armor	Vendor Purchase Value
54	Corehound Boots	Bind on Equip	126	2 43 97
PROPERTIES: Fire Resist +24				
60	Bloodfang Boots	Bind on Pickup	154	5 53 5
PROPERTIES: Fire Resist +10, Increases your chance to dodge an attack by 1%				
60	Bonescythe Sabatons	Bind on Pickup	171	8 49 22
PROPERTIES: Improves your chance to hit by 1%, Improves your chance to get a critical strike by 1%, +64 Attack Power				
60	Boots of Displacement	Bind on Pickup	166	7 76 14
PROPERTIES: Increases your effective stealth level				
60	Boots of Fright	Bind on Pickup	148	4 65 18
PROPERTIES: Increases damage and healing done by magical spells and effects by up to 34				
60	Boots of the Shadow Flame	Bind on Pickup	166	7 47 34
PROPERTIES: +44 Attack Power, Improves your chance to hit by 2%				
60	Boots of the Vanguard	Bind on Pickup	138	3 41 9
60	Cenarion Boots	Bind on Pickup	138	3 43 39
PROPERTIES: Shadow Resist +7, Restores 3 mana per 5 sec, Increases healing done by spells and effects by up to 18				
60	Deathdealer's Boots	Bind on Pickup	158	5 94 59
PROPERTIES: Improves your chance to hit by 1%				
60	Dreamwalker Boots	Bind on Pickup	171	9 11 65
PROPERTIES: Increases healing done by spells and effects by up to 46, Restores 5 mana per 5 sec				
60	Drudge Boots	Bind on Pickup	156	5 81 16
PROPERTIES: Nature Resist +20				
60	General's Dragonhide Boots	Bind on Pickup	146	2 22 17
PROPERTIES: Increases damage and healing done by magical spells and effects by up to 16				
60	General's Leather Treads	Bind on Pickup	146	2 9 64
PROPERTIES: Increases the duration of your Sprint ability by 3 sec				
60	Genesis Boots	Bind on Pickup	158	5 85 80
PROPERTIES: Increases damage and healing done by magical spells and effects by up to 20, Restores 4 mana per 5 sec, Decreases the magical resistances of your spell targets by 10				
60	Hive Tunneler's Boots	Bind on Pickup	156	5 81 16
60	Marshal's Dragonhide Boots	Bind on Pickup	146	2 4 92
PROPERTIES: Increases damage and healing done by magical spells and effects by up to 16				
60	Marshal's Leather Footguards	Bind on Pickup	146	2 10 41
PROPERTIES: Increases the duration of your Sprint ability by 3 sec				
60	Nightslayer Boots	Bind on Pickup	138	3 28 42
PROPERTIES: Shadow Resist +7				
60	Stormrage Boots	Bind on Pickup	154	5 37 9
PROPERTIES: Fire Resist +10, Improves your chance to get a critical strike with spells by 1%, Increases healing done by spells and effects by up to 26				
60	Darkmantle Boots	Bind on Pickup	127	2 52 61
PROPERTIES: Increases your effective stealth level				
60	Feralheart Boots	Bind on Pickup	127	2 44 38
PROPERTIES: Increases damage and healing done by magical spells and effects by up to 11, Restores 2 mana per 5 sec				

Superior Leather Feet Armor

Lvl	Name	Binding	Armor	Vendor Purchase Value
19	Feet of the Lynx	Bind on Equip	63	10 75
25	Harbinger Boots	Bind on Equip	71	19 59
27	Warsong Boots	Bind on Pickup	67	14 48
28	Defiler's Chain Greaves	Bind on Pickup	74	27 53
PROPERTIES: Run speed increased slightly				
28	Defiler's Leather Boots	Bind on Pickup	74	26 63
PROPERTIES: Run speed increased slightly				
28	Defiler's Lizardhide Boots	Bind on Pickup	74	26 2
PROPERTIES: Run speed increased slightly				
28	Defiler's Mail Greaves	Bind on Pickup	74	27 92
PROPERTIES: Run speed increased slightly				
28	Highlander's Chain Greaves	Bind on Pickup	74	26 43
PROPERTIES: Run speed increased slightly				
28	Highlander's Leather Boots	Bind on Pickup	74	26 52
PROPERTIES: Run speed increased slightly				
28	Highlander's Lizardhide Boots	Bind on Pickup	74	27 32
PROPERTIES: Run speed increased slightly				
28	Highlander's Mail Greaves	Bind on Pickup	74	27 42
PROPERTIES: Run speed increased slightly				
31	Briar Tredders	Bind on Equip	78	36 6
32	Swampwalker Boots	Bind on Equip	79	40 93
38	Defiler's Leather Boots	Bind on Pickup	89	59 99
PROPERTIES: Run speed increased slightly, +6 Attack Power				
38	Defiler's Lizardhide Boots	Bind on Pickup	89	60 23
PROPERTIES: Run speed increased slightly, +6 Attack Power				
38	Highlander's Leather Boots	Bind on Pickup	89	61 41
PROPERTIES: Run speed increased slightly, +6 Attack Power				
38	Highlander's Lizardhide Boots	Bind on Pickup	89	63 25
PROPERTIES: Run speed increased slightly, +6 Attack Power				
42	Sandstalker Ankleguards	Bind on Pickup	95	87 84
47	Slitherscale Boots	Bind on Pickup	104	1 17 4
48	Albino Crocscale Boots	Bind on Pickup	105	1 24 58
PROPERTIES: Nature Resist +5				
48	Defiler's Leather Boots	Bind on Pickup	105	1 25 61
PROPERTIES: Run speed increased slightly, +12 Attack Power				
48	Defiler's Lizardhide Boots	Bind on Pickup	105	1 22 74
PROPERTIES: Run speed increased slightly, +12 Attack Power				
48	Highlander's Leather Boots	Bind on Pickup	105	1 23 73
PROPERTIES: Run speed increased slightly, +12 Attack Power				
48	Highlander's Lizardhide Boots	Bind on Pickup	105	1 27 46
PROPERTIES: Run speed increased slightly, +12 Attack Power				
49	Sandals of the Insurgent	Bind on Equip	107	1 39 93
50	Shadefiend Boots	Bind on Pickup	109	1 44 64
52	Coal Miner Boots	Bind on Pickup	112	1 54 95
PROPERTIES: Fire Resist +10				
52	Firemoss Boots	Bind on Pickup	112	1 53 83
PROPERTIES: Increases healing done by spells and effects by up to 20				
52	Whisperwalk Boots	Bind on Pickup	104	1 24 25
PROPERTIES: Increases your effective stealth level by 1				
53	Dawn Treaders	Bind on Equip	114	1 76 21
PROPERTIES: Increases your chance to dodge an attack by 1%				
53	Waterspout Boots	Bind on Pickup	114	1 61 37
PROPERTIES: Increases damage and healing done by magical spells and effects by up to 25				
54	Shadowcraft Boots	Bind on Pickup	115	1 75 5
54	Swiftwalker Boots	Bind on Pickup	115	1 76 99
54	Wildheart Boots	Bind on Pickup	115	1 77 66
55	Pads of the Dread Wolf	Bind on Pickup	116	1 80 24
PROPERTIES: +40 Attack Power				
56	Ash Covered Boots	Bind on Pickup	118	1 86 55
PROPERTIES: Increases your chance to dodge an attack by 1%				
56	Boots of Ferocity	Bind on Pickup	118	2 1 93
56	Cadaverous Walkers	Bind on Pickup	118	1 90 74
PROPERTIES: +24 Attack Power				
56	Verdant Footpads	Bind on Pickup	118	2 3 86
PROPERTIES: Increases healing done by spells and effects by up to 37, Increases damage done by Nature spells and effects by up to 24				
57	Boots of the Shrieker	Bind on Pickup	120	2
PROPERTIES: Shadow Resist +10, Increases damage and healing done by magical spells and effects by up to 12				
57	Mongoose Boots	Bind on Equip	120	2 13 40
58	Blood Guard's Dragonhide Boots	Bind on Pickup	121	1 12 82
PROPERTIES: Increases damage and healing done by magical spells and effects by up to 14				
58	Blood Guard's Leather Treads	Bind on Pickup	121	1 3 60
PROPERTIES: Increases the duration of your Sprint ability by 3 sec				
58	Defiler's Leather Boots	Bind on Pickup	121	2 6 45
PROPERTIES: Run speed increased slightly, +16 Attack Power				
58	Defiler's Lizardhide Boots	Bind on Pickup	121	2 7 27
PROPERTIES: Run speed increased slightly, +16 Attack Power				
58	Highlander's Leather Boots	Bind on Pickup	121	2 5 69
PROPERTIES: Run speed increased slightly, +16 Attack Power				
58	Highlander's Lizardhide Boots	Bind on Pickup	121	2 6 47
PROPERTIES: Run speed increased slightly, +16 Attack Power				
58	Knight-Lieutenant's Dragonhide Footwraps	Bind on Pickup	121	1 6 76
PROPERTIES: Increases damage and healing done by magical spells and effects by up to 14				
58	Knight-Lieutenant's Leather Boots	Bind on Pickup	121	1 6 38
PROPERTIES: Increases the duration of your Sprint ability by 3 sec				
60	Animist's Boots	Bind on Pickup	134	3 19 25
PROPERTIES: Increases healing done by spells and effects by up to 29				
60	Blood Guard's Dragonhide Treads	Bind on Pickup	126	1 19 21
PROPERTIES: Increases damage and healing done by magical spells and effects by up to 14				
60	Blood Guard's Leather Walkers	Bind on Pickup	126	1 21 92
PROPERTIES: Increases the duration of your Sprint ability by 3 sec, +28 Attack Power				
60	Blooddrenched Footpads	Bind on Pickup	129	2 69 69
PROPERTIES: Improves your chance to hit by 1%				
60	Bramblewood Boots	Bind on Equip	132	2 93 2
PROPERTIES: Nature Resist +25				
60	Knight-Lieutenant's Dragonhide Treads	Bind on Pickup	126	1 27 92
PROPERTIES: Increases damage and healing done by magical spells and effects by up to 14				
60	Knight-Lieutenant's Leather Walkers	Bind on Pickup	126	1 29 76
PROPERTIES: Increases the duration of your Sprint ability by 3 sec, +28 Attack Power				
60	Dunestalker's Boots	Bind on Pickup	121	2 9 69
60	Sandstorm Boots	Bind on Pickup	121	2 5 95
PROPERTIES: Increases damage and healing done by magical spells and effects by up to 14, Restores 4 mana per 5 sec				
60	Sedge Boots	Bind on Pickup	121	2 5 95
PROPERTIES: Nature Resist +5,Shadow Resist +5				

Epic Leather Hand Armor

Lvl	Name	Binding	Armor	Vendor Purchase Value
37	Gloves of Holy Might	Bind on Equip	86	53 44
PROPERTIES: Improves your chance to get a critical strike by 1%, +20 Attack Power, +30 Attack Power when fighting Undead				
60	Aged Core Leather Gloves	Bind on Pickup	130	2 65 6
PROPERTIES: Fire Resist +8, Shadow Resist +5, Improves your chance to get a critical strike by 1%, Increased Daggers +5				
60	Bile-Covered Gauntlets	Bind on Pickup	143	4 2 30
PROPERTIES: Nature Resist +20				
60	Bloodfang Gloves	Bind on Pickup	140	3 70 4
PROPERTIES: Shadow Resist +10, Immune to Disarm				
60	Bonescythe Gauntlets	Bind on Pickup	158	6 26 58
PROPERTIES: Improves your chance to hit by 1%, +66 Attack Power, Improves your chance to get a critical strike by 1%				
60	Cenarion Gloves	Bind on Pickup	125	2 30 55
PROPERTIES: Fire Resist +7, Increases healing done by spells and effects by up to 18				

Epic Leather Hand Armor

Lvl	Name	Binding	Armor	Vendor Purchase Value
60	Doomhide Gauntlets	Bind on Pickup	133	2 92 12
PROPERTIES: Fire Resist +8, Shadow Resist +8, +42 Attack Power				
60	Dreamwalker Handguards	Bind on Pickup	158	6 72 40
PROPERTIES: Increases healing done by spells and effects by up to 53				
60	Gauntlets of New Life	Bind on Pickup	134	3 10 27
PROPERTIES: Increases healing done by spells and effects by up to 26, Restores 4 mana per 5 sec				
60	General's Dragonhide Gloves	Bind on Pickup	133	1 38 19
PROPERTIES: Slightly increases your stealth detection, Increases damage and healing done by magical spells and effects by up to 12				
60	General's Leather Mitts	Bind on Pickup	133	1 40 80
PROPERTIES: Improves your chance to get a critical strike by 1%				
60	Gloves of Ebru	Bind on Pickup	139	3 31 1
PROPERTIES: Increases damage and healing done by magical spells and effects by up to 27, Improves your chance to get a critical strike with spells by 1%				
60	Gloves of Enforcement	Bind on Pickup	140	3 51 58
PROPERTIES: Improves your chance to hit by 1%				
60	Gloves of the Hidden Temple	Bind on Pickup	148	4 71 3
PROPERTIES: Shadow Resist +6				
60	Marshal's Dragonhide Gauntlets	Bind on Pickup	133	1 41 32
PROPERTIES: Slightly increases your stealth detection, Increases damage and healing done by magical spells and effects by up to 12				
60	Marshal's Leather Handgrips	Bind on Pickup	133	1 44 44
PROPERTIES: Improves your chance to get a critical strike by 1%				
60	Nightslayer Gloves	Bind on Pickup	125	2 20 57
PROPERTIES: Fire Resist +7, Improves your chance to hit by 1%				
60	Polar Gloves	Bind on Equip	146	4 48 51
PROPERTIES: Frost Resist +30				
60	Stormrage Handguards	Bind on Pickup	140	3 59 40
PROPERTIES: Shadow Resist +10, Increases healing done by spells and effects by up to 42				
60	Taut Dragonhide Gloves	Bind on Pickup	142	3 94 43
PROPERTIES: Improves your chance to get a critical strike with spells by 1%, Restores 6 mana per 5 sec				
60	Wasphide Gauntlets	Bind on Pickup	143	3 84 54
PROPERTIES: Increases healing done by spells and effects by up to 53				
60	Darkmantle Gloves	Bind on Pickup	108	1 20 34
60	Feralheart Gloves	Bind on Pickup	108	1 25 46
PROPERTIES: Increases damage and healing done by magical spells and effects by up to 11				

Superior Leather Hand Armor

Lvl	Name	Binding	Armor	Vendor Purchase Value
22	Naga Battle Gloves	Bind on Pickup	61	9 80
22	Toughened Leather Gloves	Bind on Equip	61	9 62
22	Wolfclaw Gloves	Bind on Equip	61	9 80
23	Brawler Gloves	Bind on Equip	62	10 70
30	Ebon Vise	Bind on Pickup	70	22 32
35	Shadowskin Gloves	Bind on Equip	76	33 21
PROPERTIES: Improves your chance to get a critical strike by 1%				
37	Arachnid Gloves	Bind on Pickup	79	40 14
PROPERTIES: Nature Resist +10				
41	Gauntlets of the Sea	Bind on Equip	85	53 63
PROPERTIES: Heal friendly target for 300 to 500				
45	Elven Spirit Claws	Bind on Equip	91	68 17
PROPERTIES: Increases damage done by Nature spells and effects by up to 21				
48	Bloodfire Talons	Bind on Pickup	96	85 20
PROPERTIES: Fire Resist +10, Increases damage and healing done by magical spells and effects by up to 18				
49	Ogreseer Fists	Bind on Pickup	97	85 32
PROPERTIES: Increases damage and healing done by magical spells and effects by up to 13				
51	Mar Alom's Grip	Bind on Equip	100	1 5 19
PROPERTIES: Increases healing done by spells and effects by up to 22				
53	Devilsaur Gauntlets	Bind on Equip	103	1 17 1
PROPERTIES: +28 Attack Power, Improves your chance to get a critical strike by 1%				
53	Plaguebat Fur Gloves	Bind on Equip	103	1 13 71
PROPERTIES: Shadow Resist +10				

Superior Leather Hand Armor

Lvl	Name	Binding	Armor	Vendor Purchase Value
54	Gloves of Restoration	Bind on Pickup	105	1 12 96
PROPERTIES: Increases healing done by spells and effects by up to 37				
54	Shadowcraft Gloves	Bind on Equip	105	1 17 14
54	Skul's Fingerbone Claws	Bind on Pickup	105	1 14 3
PROPERTIES: +40 Attack Power				
54	Stonebark Gauntlets	Bind on Equip	105	1 15 87
PROPERTIES: Nature Resist +16				
54	Wildheart Gloves	Bind on Equip	105	1 22 44
56	Cadaverous Gloves	Bind on Pickup	107	1 26 68
PROPERTIES: +44 Attack Power				
56	Fallbrush Handgrips	Bind on Pickup	107	1 36 38
PROPERTIES: Increases healing done by spells and effects by up to 20				
56	Gargoyle Slashers	Bind on Pickup	107	1 24 27
PROPERTIES: Improves your chance to get a critical strike by 1%				
56	Slaghide Gauntlets	Bind on Pickup	107	1 33 43
57	Quickdraw Gloves	Bind on Pickup	109	1 30 76
PROPERTIES: Increases your chance to dodge an attack by 1%				
57	Stormshroud Gloves	Bind on Equip	109	1 32 12
PROPERTIES: Improves your chance to get a critical strike by 1%, Improves your chance to hit by 1%				
58	Blood Guard's Dragonhide Gauntlets	Bind on Pickup	110	68 53
PROPERTIES: Slightly increases your stealth detection				
58	Blood Guard's Leather Vices	Bind on Pickup	110	69 32
PROPERTIES: +32 Attack Power				
58	Knight-Lieutenant's Dragonhide Gloves	Bind on Pickup	110	74 14
PROPERTIES: Slightly increases your stealth detection				
58	Knight-Lieutenant's Leather Gauntlets	Bind on Pickup	110	73 88
PROPERTIES: +32 Attack Power				
59	Timbermaw Brawlers	Bind on Equip	112	1 55 76
60	Blood Guard's Dragonhide Grips	Bind on Pickup	115	79 47
PROPERTIES: Slightly increases your stealth detection				
60	Blood Guard's Leather Grips	Bind on Pickup	115	83 73
PROPERTIES: +20 Attack Power, Improves your chance to get a critical strike by 1%				
60	Blooddrenched Grips	Bind on Pickup	122	2 10 51
PROPERTIES: +34 Attack Power, Improves your chance to get a critical strike by 1%				
60	Gauntlets of Southwind	Bind on Pickup	126	2 41 85
PROPERTIES: Increases damage and healing done by magical spells and effects by up to 25				
60	Knight-Lieutenant's Dragonhide Grips	Bind on Pickup	115	84 97
PROPERTIES: Slightly increases your stealth detection				
60	Knight-Lieutenant's Leather Grips	Bind on Pickup	115	86 19
PROPERTIES: +20 Attack Power, Improves your chance to get a critical strike by 1%				
60	Primal Batskin Gloves	Bind on Equip	113	1 58 80
PROPERTIES: Improves your chance to hit by 2%				
60	Shadow Panther Hide Gloves	Bind on Equip	113	1 51 79
PROPERTIES: Improves your chance to get a critical strike by 1%				
60	Toughened Silithid Hide Gloves	Bind on Pickup	122	2 2 62
60	Gloves of Earthen Power	Bind on Pickup	109	1 42 31
PROPERTIES: Increases damage and healing done by magical spells and effects by up to 27				
60	Gordok's Gloves	Bind on Pickup	106	1 23 48
PROPERTIES: Improves your chance to get a critical strike with spells by 1%				
60	Handwraps of Undead Slaying	Bind on Pickup	110	1 39 89
PROPERTIES: +60 Attack Power when fighting Undead				

Epic Leather Head Armor

Lvl	Name	Binding	Armor	Vendor Purchase Value
55	Molten Helm	Bind on Equip	150	2 57 9
PROPERTIES: Fire Resist +29, Increases your chance to dodge an attack by 1%				
60	Bloodfang Hood	Bind on Pickup	183	5 57 7
PROPERTIES: Frost Resist +10, Shadow Resist +10, Improves your chance to get a critical strike by 1%				
60	Bonescythe Helmet	Bind on Pickup	205	9 29 5
PROPERTIES: Improves your chance to hit by 1%, Improves your chance to get a critical strike by 2%				

Epic Leather Head Armor

Lvl	Name	Binding	Armor	Vendor Purchase Value
60	Cenarion Helm	Bind on Pickup	163	3 49 49
PROPERTIES: Fire Resist +10, Increases damage and healing done by magical spells and effects by up to 12				
60	Circlet of Restless Dreams	Bind on Pickup	175	4 47 13
PROPERTIES: Increased Daggers +6				
60	Creeping Vine Helm	Bind on Pickup	183	5 21 40
PROPERTIES: Increases healing done by spells and effects by up to 59				
60	Deathdealer's Helm	Bind on Pickup	192	6 90 81
PROPERTIES: Improves your chance to get a critical strike by 1%, Improves your chance to hit by 1%				
60	Deviate Growth Cap	Bind on Pickup	175	4 55 35
PROPERTIES: Increases healing done by spells and effects by up to 64, Restores 8 mana per 5 sec, Improves your chance to get a critical strike with spells by 1%				
60	Dreamwalker Headpiece	Bind on Pickup	205	9 97 88
PROPERTIES: Increases healing done by spells and effects by up to 66				
60	Field Marshal's Dragonhide Helmet	Bind on Pickup	179	2 48 11
PROPERTIES: Improves your chance to get a critical strike by 1%, Increases damage and healing done by magical spells and effects by up to 18				
60	Field Marshal's Leather Mask	Bind on Pickup	179	2 51 72
PROPERTIES: Improves your chance to get a critical strike by 1%, Improves your chance to hit by 1%				
60	Foror's Eyepatch	Bind on Pickup	160	3 9 36
PROPERTIES: Improves your chance to get a critical strike by 2%, +44 Attack Power				
60	Genesis Helm	Bind on Pickup	192	6 73 1
PROPERTIES: Increases damage and healing done by magical spells and effects by up to 27, Improves your chance to get a critical strike by 1%				
60	Guise of the Devourer	Bind on Pickup	180	5 4 12
PROPERTIES: Increases your chance to dodge an attack by 1%				
60	Nightslayer Cover	Bind on Pickup	163	3 24 76
PROPERTIES: Fire Resist +10, Improves your chance to get a critical strike by 2%				
60	Polar Helmet	Bind on Pickup	196	7 96 7
PROPERTIES: Frost Resist +44				
60	Stormrage Cover	Bind on Pickup	183	5 41 11
PROPERTIES: Frost Resist +10, Shadow Resist +10, Restores 6 mana per 5 sec, Increases healing done by spells and effects by up to 29				
60	Warlord's Dragonhide Helmet	Bind on Pickup	179	2 53 57
PROPERTIES: Increases damage and healing done by magical spells and effects by up to 18, Improves your chance to get a critical strike by 1%				
60	Warlord's Leather Helm	Bind on Pickup	179	2 45 40
PROPERTIES: Improves your chance to hit by 1%, Improves your chance to get a critical strike by 1%				
60	Darkmantle Cap	Bind on Pickup	150	2 61 2
PROPERTIES: Improves your chance to get a critical strike by 1%				
60	Feralheart Cowl	Bind on Pickup	150	2 46 19
PROPERTIES: Increases damage and healing done by magical spells and effects by up to 16				

Superior Leather Head Armor

Lvl	Name	Binding	Armor	Vendor Purchase Value
28	Enduring Cap	Bind on Equip	88	26 55
32	Adventurer's Pith Helmet	Bind on Equip	94	40 83
33	Expert Goldminer's Helmet	Bind on Equip	95	42 20
PROPERTIES: Increased Axes +7				
40	Wolfshead Helm	Bind on Equip	109	74 21
PROPERTIES: When shapeshifting into Cat form the Druid gains 20 energy, when shapeshifting into Bear form the Druid gains 5 rage				
43	Winged Helm	Bind on Equip	115	96 24
45	Embrace of the Lycan	Bind on Pickup	118	1 8 58
PROPERTIES: +32 Attack Power				
45	Helm of Fire	Bind on Equip	118	1 8 19
PROPERTIES: Fire Resist +5, Hurls a fiery ball that causes 286 to 376 Fire damage and an additional 40 damage over 8 sec				
47	Soothsayer's Headdress	Bind on Pickup	122	1 14 1
47	Engineer's Guild Headpiece	Bind on Pickup	113	88 47
51	Tattered Leather Hood	Bind on Equip	130	1 44 54
PROPERTIES: Improves your chance to hit by 1%				

Superior Leather Head Armor

Lvl	Name	Binding	Armor	Vendor Purchase Value
52	Ghostshroud	Bind on Pickup	132	1 64 84
PROPERTIES: Shadow Resist +5				
52	Mask of the Unforgiven	Bind on Pickup	132	1 58 95
PROPERTIES: Improves your chance to hit by 2%, Improves your chance to get a critical strike by 1%				
52	Ragefury Eyepatch	Bind on Pickup	132	1 66 69
PROPERTIES: Improves your chance to get a critical strike by 2%				
52	Ebon Mask	Bind on Pickup	122	1 18 93
PROPERTIES: Improves your chance to get a critical strike by 1%, +36 Attack Power				
53	Felhide Cap	Bind on Pickup	134	1 61 37
PROPERTIES: Fire Resist +8, Shadow Resist +8				
55	Tribal War Feathers	Bind on Pickup	137	1 77 52
PROPERTIES: Increases healing done by spells and effects by up to 33				
56	Helm of the New Moon	Bind on Pickup	139	1 86 81
PROPERTIES: Increases damage and healing done by magical spells and effects by up to 23				
56	Insightful Hood	Bind on Pickup	139	1 86 55
PROPERTIES: Improves your chance to get a critical strike with spells by 1%, Increases healing done by spells and effects by up to 33				
57	Bone Ring Helm	Bind on Pickup	141	2 14 4
57	Shadowcraft Cap	Bind on Pickup	141	1 99 62
57	Wildheart Cowl	Bind on Pickup	141	2 14 90
58	Champion's Dragonhide Helm	Bind on Pickup	143	1 5 58
PROPERTIES: +16 Attack Power, Increases damage and healing done by magical spells and effects by up to 13				
58	Champion's Leather Headguard	Bind on Pickup	143	1 6 76
PROPERTIES: Increases your chance to dodge an attack by 1%, Improves your chance to hit by 1%, +12 Attack Power				
58	Eye of Rend	Bind on Pickup	143	2 10 31
PROPERTIES: Improves your chance to get a critical strike by 2%				
58	Feathermoon Headdress	Bind on Equip	143	2 5 46
58	Lieutenant Commander's Dragonhide Shroud	Bind on Pickup	143	1 3 17
PROPERTIES: +16 Attack Power, Increases damage and healing done by magical spells and effects by up to 13				
58	Lieutenant Commander's Leather Veil	Bind on Pickup	143	1 11 60
PROPERTIES: Increases your chance to dodge an attack by 1%, +12 Attack Power, Improves your chance to hit by 1%				
60	Blooddrenched Mask	Bind on Pickup	153	2 84 10
PROPERTIES: Improves your chance to hit by 2%				
60	Bloodvine Lens	Bind on Equip	147	2 32 11
PROPERTIES: Improves your chance to get a critical strike by 2%, Slightly increases your stealth detection				
60	Bramblewood Helm	Bind on Equip	156	2 91 90
PROPERTIES: Nature Resist +30				
60	Champion's Dragonhide Headguard	Bind on Pickup	158	1 54 38
PROPERTIES: Increases damage and healing done by magical spells and effects by up to 18				
60	Champion's Leather Helm	Bind on Pickup	158	1 56 72
PROPERTIES: Improves your chance to get a critical strike by 1%, Improves your chance to hit by 1%, +36 Attack Power				
60	Helm of Regrowth	Bind on Pickup	162	3 39
PROPERTIES: Increases healing done by spells and effects by up to 22				
60	Lieutenant Commander's Dragonhide Headguard	Bind on Pickup	158	1 55 60
PROPERTIES: Increases damage and healing done by magical spells and effects by up to 18				
60	Lieutenant Commander's Leather Helm	Bind on Pickup	158	1 57 95
PROPERTIES: Improves your chance to get a critical strike by 1%, Improves your chance to hit by 1%, +36 Attack Power				
60	Southwind Helm	Bind on Pickup	164	3 70 98
PROPERTIES: Improves your chance to hit by 1%				
60	Sanctified Leather Helm	Bind on Pickup	149	2 42 82
PROPERTIES: Increases healing done by spells and effects by up to 40				
??	Moonshadow Hood	Bind on Pickup	122	1 14 8
PROPERTIES: Increases damage and healing done by magical spells and effects by up to 18, Improves your chance to get a critical strike with spells by 1%				
??	Pirate's Eye Patch	Bind on Pickup	122	1 13 76
PROPERTIES: Increases your chance to resist Fear effects by 4%				

Epic Leather Leg Armor

Lvl	Name	Binding	Armor	Vendor Purchase Value
59	Salamander Scale Pants	Bind on Pickup	171	3 84 45
PROPERTIES: Fire Resist +10, Increases healing done by spells and effects by up to 51, Restores 9 mana per 5 sec				

Epic Leather Leg Armor

Lvl	Name	Binding	Armor	Vendor Purchase Value
60	Bloodfang Pants	Bind on Pickup	197	6 92 9
PROPERTIES: Fire Resist +10,Arcane Resist +10, Improves your chance to get a critical strike by 1%				
60	Bonescythe Legplates	Bind on Pickup	221	13 64 18
PROPERTIES: Improves your chance to get a critical strike by 1%, Improves your chance to hit by 1%				
60	Cenarion Leggings	Bind on Pickup	175	4 23 15
PROPERTIES: Shadow Resist +10, Improves your chance to get a critical strike with spells by 1%, Restores 4 mana per 5 sec, Increases healing done by spells and effects by up to 22				
60	Dark Heart Pants	Bind on Pickup	186	5 76 13
PROPERTIES: Improves your chance to get a critical strike by 2%, +48 Attack Power				
60	Deathdealer's Leggings	Bind on Pickup	207	9 52 40
PROPERTIES: Improves your chance to get a critical strike by 1%				
60	Dreamwalker Legguards	Bind on Pickup	221	13 25 83
PROPERTIES: Increases healing done by spells and effects by up to 66, Restores 8 mana per 5 sec				
60	General's Dragonhide Leggings	Bind on Pickup	186	2 94 13
PROPERTIES: Improves your chance to get a critical strike by 1%				
60	General's Leather Legguards	Bind on Pickup	186	2 85 76
PROPERTIES: Improves your chance to hit by 2%, Improves your chance to get a critical strike by 1%				
60	Genesis Trousers	Bind on Pickup	207	9 7 51
PROPERTIES: Increases damage and healing done by magical spells and effects by up to 27, Improves your chance to get a critical strike by 1%, Restores 4 mana per 5 sec				
60	Leggings of Apocalypse	Bind on Pickup	211	10 27 41
PROPERTIES: Improves your chance to get a critical strike by 2%				
60	Leggings of Immersion	Bind on Pickup	190	6 21 17
PROPERTIES: Increases damage and healing done by magical spells and effects by up to 39, Restores 6 mana per 5 sec				
60	Marshal's Dragonhide Legguards	Bind on Pickup	186	2 84 72
PROPERTIES: Improves your chance to get a critical strike by 1%				
60	Marshal's Leather Leggings	Bind on Pickup	186	2 90 98
PROPERTIES: Improves your chance to hit by 2%, Improves your chance to get a critical strike by 1%				
60	Nightslayer Pants	Bind on Pickup	175	4 34 66
PROPERTIES: Shadow Resist +10, Improves your chance to get a critical strike by 1%				
60	Outrider's Leather Pants	Bind on Pickup	173	4 39 35
PROPERTIES: Improves your chance to get a critical strike by 1%				
60	Outrider's Lizardhide Pants	Bind on Pickup	173	4 40 92
PROPERTIES: Increases damage and healing done by magical spells and effects by up to 11				
60	Sentinel's Leather Pants	Bind on Pickup	173	4 22 17
PROPERTIES: Improves your chance to get a critical strike by 1%				
60	Sentinel's Lizardhide Pants	Bind on Pickup	173	4 23 73
PROPERTIES: Increases damage and healing done by magical spells and effects by up to 11				
60	Stormrage Legguards	Bind on Pickup	197	7 24 15
PROPERTIES: Fire Resist +10,Arcane Resist +10, Increases healing done by spells and effects by up to 48, Restores 6 mana per 5 sec				
60	Leggings of Arcana	Bind on Pickup	166	3 50 57
PROPERTIES: Increases damage and healing done by magical spells and effects by up to 18				
60	Polar Leggings	Bind on Pickup	205	9 16 82
PROPERTIES: Frost Resist +40				

Superior Leather Leg Armor

Lvl	Name	Binding	Armor	Vendor Purchase Value
18	Leggings of the Fang	Bind on Pickup	79	12 56
25	Petrolspill Leggings	Bind on Equip	90	26 83
PROPERTIES: Fire Resist +-10				
25	Troll's Bane Leggings	Bind on Equip	90	25 74
34	Warchief Kilt	Bind on Equip	105	60 74
35	Triprunner Dungarees	Bind on Pickup	101	52 67
38	Basilisk Hide Pants	Bind on Equip	113	80 40
44	Jinxed Hoodoo Kilt	Bind on Pickup	126	1 32 90
49	Windscale Sarong	Bind on Pickup	136	1 75 95
50	Stormshroud Pants	Bind on Equip	138	1 87 28
PROPERTIES: Improves your chance to get a critical strike by 2%, Increases your chance to dodge an attack by 1%				
50	Shadowhide Leggings	Bind on Pickup	132	1 51 46
PROPERTIES: Shadow Resist +6				

Superior Leather Leg Armor

Lvl	Name	Binding	Armor	Vendor Purchase Value
51	Unbridled Leggings	Bind on Equip	140	2 6 85
PROPERTIES: Restores 7 health per 5 sec				
52	Leggings of Frenzied Magic	Bind on Pickup	142	2 23 28
PROPERTIES: Increases damage and healing done by magical spells and effects by up to 16, Restores 5 mana per 5 sec				
52	Living Leggings	Bind on Equip	142	2 12 77
PROPERTIES: Nature Resist +5, Increases healing done by spells and effects by up to 26				
52	Warbear Woolies	Bind on Equip	142	2 22 33
53	Warstrife Leggings	Bind on Pickup	144	2 23 84
PROPERTIES: Increases your chance to dodge an attack by 2%				
54	Luminary Kilt	Bind on Pickup	147	2 36 77
PROPERTIES: Increases damage and healing done by magical spells and effects by up to 22				
55	Devilsaur Leggings	Bind on Equip	148	2 57 9
PROPERTIES: +46 Attack Power, Improves your chance to get a critical strike by 1%				
55	Earthborn Kilt	Bind on Equip	148	2 53 8
55	Tressermane Leggings	Bind on Pickup	148	2 39 48
PROPERTIES: Increases damage and healing done by magical spells and effects by up to 19				
56	Cadaverous Leggings	Bind on Pickup	150	2 51 45
PROPERTIES: +52 Attack Power				
56	Ghoul Skin Leggings	Bind on Pickup	150	2 54 56
PROPERTIES: Increases healing done by spells and effects by up to 44				
56	Shadowcraft Pants	Bind on Pickup	150	2 55 42
56	Wildheart Kilt	Bind on Pickup	150	2 71 92
57	Abyssal Leather Leggings	Bind on Equip	152	2 76 45
PROPERTIES: Improves your chance to get a critical strike by 1%				
57	Ghostloom Leggings	Bind on Pickup	152	2 63 97
PROPERTIES: Restores 6 mana per 5 sec				
57	Plaguehound Leggings	Bind on Equip	152	2 61 12
PROPERTIES: Improves your chance to hit by 1%				
57	Tanglemoss Leggings	Bind on Pickup	150	2 68 11
PROPERTIES: Improves your chance to get a critical strike with spells by 1%				
58	Blademaster Leggings	Bind on Pickup	154	2 77 17
PROPERTIES: Improves your chance to hit by 1%, Improves your chance to get a critical strike by 1%, Increases your chance to dodge an attack by 2%				
58	Knight-Captain's Dragonhide Leggings	Bind on Pickup	154	1 50 92
PROPERTIES: Increases your chance to dodge an attack by 1%, +18 Attack Power				
58	Knight-Captain's Leather Legguards	Bind on Pickup	154	1 49 34
PROPERTIES: Improves your chance to get a critical strike by 2%				
58	Legionnaire's Dragonhide Trousers	Bind on Pickup	154	1 40 25
PROPERTIES: Increases your chance to dodge an attack by 1%, +18 Attack Power				
58	Legionnaire's Leather Leggings	Bind on Pickup	154	1 47 23
PROPERTIES: Improves your chance to get a critical strike by 2%				
60	Animist's Leggings	Bind on Pickup	170	4 33 54
PROPERTIES: Increases healing done by spells and effects by up to 35				
60	Blooddrenched Leggings	Bind on Pickup	170	4 20 99
60	Knight-Captain's Dragonhide Leggings	Bind on Pickup	165	1 83 96
PROPERTIES: Improves your chance to get a critical strike with spells by 1%, Increases damage and healing done by magical spells and effects by up to 14				
60	Knight-Captain's Leather Legguards	Bind on Pickup	165	1 86 66
PROPERTIES: Improves your chance to get a critical strike by 1%, Improves your chance to hit by 1%, +34 Attack Power				
60	Legionnaire's Dragonhide Leggings	Bind on Pickup	165	1 80 55
PROPERTIES: Improves your chance to get a critical strike with spells by 1%, Increases damage and healing done by magical spells and effects by up to 14				
60	Legionnaire's Leather Legguards	Bind on Pickup	165	1 81 91
PROPERTIES: Improves your chance to get a critical strike by 1%, Improves your chance to hit by 1%, +34 Attack Power				
60	Cenarion Reservist's Leggings	Bind on Pickup	154	2 95 71
PROPERTIES: Nature Resist +25, +26 Attack Power				
60	Cenarion Reservist's Leggings	Bind on Pickup	154	2 74 61
PROPERTIES: Nature Resist +25, Increases healing done by spells and effects by up to 29				
60	Darkmantle Pants	Bind on Pickup	160	3 18 89
60	Feralheart Kilt	Bind on Pickup	160	3 32 39
PROPERTIES: Increases damage and healing done by magical spells and effects by up to 9				

Epic Leather Shoulder Armor

Lvl	Name	Binding	Armor	Vendor Purchase Value
60	Bloodfang Spaulders	Bind on Pickup	169	5 65 32
PROPERTIES: Fire Resist +10, Increases your chance to dodge an attack by 1%				
60	Bonescythe Pauldrons	Bind on Pickup	186	8 45 95
PROPERTIES: Improves your chance to get a critical strike by 1%, Improves your chance to hit by 1%				
60	Cenarion Spaulders	Bind on Pickup	150	3 18 59
PROPERTIES: Shadow Resist +7, Restores 4 mana per 5 sec, Increases healing done by spells and effects by up to 18				
60	Deathdealer's Spaulders	Bind on Pickup	172	6 14 83
PROPERTIES: Improves your chance to hit by 1%				
60	Defiler's Leather Shoulders	Bind on Pickup	148	3 21 23
PROPERTIES: +30 Attack Power				
60	Defiler's Lizardhide Shoulders	Bind on Pickup	148	3 22 43
PROPERTIES: +30 Attack Power				
60	Dreamwalker Spaulders	Bind on Pickup	186	9 8 38
PROPERTIES: Restores 5 mana per 5 sec, Increases healing done by spells and effects by up to 48				
60	Field Marshal's Dragonhide Spaulders	Bind on Pickup	165	2 46 31
PROPERTIES: Increases damage and healing done by magical spells and effects by up to 18				
60	Field Marshal's Leather Epaulets	Bind on Pickup	165	2 53 52
PROPERTIES: Improves your chance to hit by 1%				
60	Fireguard Shoulders	Bind on Pickup	159	4 22 44
PROPERTIES: Fire Resist +22				
60	Genesis Shoulderpads	Bind on Pickup	172	5 83 58
PROPERTIES: Increases damage and healing done by magical spells and effects by up to 20, Restores 3 mana per 5 sec				
60	Highlander's Leather Shoulders	Bind on Pickup	148	3 18 94
PROPERTIES: +30 Attack Power				
60	Highlander's Lizardhide Shoulders	Bind on Pickup	148	3 20 12
PROPERTIES: +30 Attack Power				
60	Mantle of Wicked Revenge	Bind on Pickup	170	5 81 4
60	Nightslayer Shoulder Pads	Bind on Pickup	150	3 27 19
PROPERTIES: Shadow Resist +7, Improves your chance to hit by 1%				
60	Polar Shoulder Pads	Bind on Pickup	181	7 79 4
PROPERTIES: Frost Resist +33				
60	Stormrage Pauldrons	Bind on Pickup	169	5 45 7
PROPERTIES: Fire Resist +10, Increases healing done by spells and effects by up to 29, Restores 4 mana per 5 sec				
60	Taut Dragonhide Shoulderpads	Bind on Pickup	170	5 89 54
PROPERTIES: +46 Attack Power				
60	Unnatural Leather Spaulders	Bind on Pickup	161	4 63 53
PROPERTIES: Nature Resist +25, +18 Attack Power				
60	Warlord's Dragonhide Epaulets	Bind on Pickup	165	2 54 48
PROPERTIES: Increases damage and healing done by magical spells and effects by up to 18				
60	Warlord's Leather Spaulders	Bind on Pickup	165	2 46 31
PROPERTIES: Improves your chance to hit by 1%				
60	Wild Growth Spaulders	Bind on Pickup	159	4 6 78
PROPERTIES: Increases healing done by spells and effects by up to 62				
60	Zandalar Madcap's Mantle	Bind on Pickup	140	
PROPERTIES: Improves your chance to hit by 1%				

Superior Leather Shoulder Armor

Lvl	Name	Binding	Armor	Vendor Purchase Value
25	Feathered Mantle	Bind on Equip	77	19 44
25	Mantle of Thieves	Bind on Equip	77	19 57
26	Forest Tracker Epaulets	Bind on Equip	78	23 26
27	Watchman Pauldrons	Bind on Equip	80	24 88
33	Flintrock Shoulders	Bind on Equip	88	41 40
37	Fleshhide Shoulders	Bind on Pickup	95	59 57
40	Sheepshear Mantle	Bind on Equip	100	69 90
46	Phytoskin Spaulders	Bind on Pickup	111	1 14 25
PROPERTIES: Nature Resist +10				
47	Atal'ai Spaulders	Bind on Pickup	113	1 14 76
49	Ironfeather Shoulders	Bind on Equip	117	1 27 58
49	Living Shoulders	Bind on Equip	117	1 38 3
PROPERTIES: Nature Resist +3, Increases healing done by spells and effects by up to 31				

Superior Leather Shoulder Armor

Lvl	Name	Binding	Armor	Vendor Purchase Value
50	Splinthide Shoulders	Bind on Pickup	118	1 39 41
PROPERTIES: Increases damage and healing done by magical spells and effects by up to 9				
52	Dark Warder's Pauldrons	Bind on Pickup	122	1 57 39
52	Icy Tomb Spaulders	Bind on Equip	122	1 53 80
PROPERTIES: Frost Resist +10, Shadow Resist +10				
54	Demonic Runed Spaulders	Bind on Pickup	126	1 80 88
54	Stormshroud Shoulders	Bind on Equip	126	1 76 31
PROPERTIES: Improves your chance to get a critical strike by 1%, Increases your chance to dodge an attack by 1%				
55	Shadowcraft Spaulders	Bind on Pickup	127	1 81 75
55	Wildheart Spaulders	Bind on Pickup	127	1 93 54
56	Cyclone Spaulders	Bind on Pickup	129	2 4 65
PROPERTIES: Increases damage and healing done by magical spells and effects by up to 14				
56	Spaulders of the Unseen	Bind on Equip	129	1 93 70
56	Truestrike Shoulders	Bind on Pickup	129	1 91 49
PROPERTIES: Improves your chance to hit by 2%, +24 Attack Power				
57	Death's Clutch	Bind on Pickup	131	1 96 52
57	Flamescarred Shoulders	Bind on Pickup	131	2 14 18
PROPERTIES: Fire Resist +10				
58	Champion's Dragonhide Spaulders	Bind on Pickup	132	1 4 79
PROPERTIES: Increases damage and healing done by magical spells and effects by up to 8				
58	Champion's Leather Mantle	Bind on Pickup	132	1 10 2
PROPERTIES: +12 Attack Power				
58	Lieutenant Commander's Dragonhide Epaulets	Bind on Pickup	132	1 2 78
PROPERTIES: Increases damage and healing done by magical spells and effects by up to 8				
58	Lieutenant Commander's Leather Spaulders	Bind on Pickup	132	1 12 39
PROPERTIES: +12 Attack Power				
58	Wyrmtongue Shoulders	Bind on Pickup	132	2 10 36
59	Golden Mantle of the Dawn	Bind on Equip	134	2 18 45
PROPERTIES: Increases your chance to dodge an attack by 1%				
60	Abyssal Leather Shoulders	Bind on Pickup	141	2 62 86
PROPERTIES: Improves your chance to hit by 1%				
60	Animist's Spaulders	Bind on Pickup	141	2 71 68
PROPERTIES: Increases healing done by spells and effects by up to 37				
60	Blood Tiger Shoulders	Bind on Equip	136	2 40 82
60	Champion's Dragonhide Shoulders	Bind on Pickup	146	1 54 95
PROPERTIES: Increases damage and healing done by magical spells and effects by up to 14				
60	Champion's Leather Shoulders	Bind on Pickup	146	1 61 52
PROPERTIES: +22 Attack Power, Improves your chance to get a critical strike by 1%, Improves your chance to hit by 1%				
60	Chitinous Shoulderguards	Bind on Pickup	151	3 79 36
60	Lieutenant Commander's Dragonhide Shoulders	Bind on Pickup	146	1 56 19
PROPERTIES: Increases damage and healing done by magical spells and effects by up to 14				
60	Lieutenant Commander's Leather Shoulders	Bind on Pickup	146	1 58 54
PROPERTIES: +22 Attack Power, Improves your chance to get a critical strike by 1%, Improves your chance to hit by 1%				
60	Darkmantle Spaulders	Bind on Pickup	136	2 28 64
60	Feralheart Spaulders	Bind on Pickup	136	2 38 30
PROPERTIES: Increases damage and healing done by magical spells and effects by up to 6, Restores 2 mana per 5 sec				
60	Halycon's Muzzle	Bind on Pickup	127	1 80 28
PROPERTIES: Arcane Resist +10				

Epic Leather Waist Armor

Lvl	Name	Binding	Armor	Vendor Purchase Value
56	Sash of Mercy	Bind on Equip	105	1 77 33
PROPERTIES: Increases healing done by spells and effects by up to 53				
60	Belt of Never-ending Agony	Bind on Pickup	142	6 65 25
PROPERTIES: +64 Attack Power, Improves your chance to get a critical strike by 1%, Improves your chance to hit by 1%				
60	Bloodfang Belt	Bind on Pickup	126	3 47 38
PROPERTIES: Shadow Resist +10, Improves your chance to get a critical strike by 1%				
60	Bonescythe Waistguard	Bind on Pickup	142	6 28 92
PROPERTIES: , Improves your chance to get a critical strike by 1%				
60	Cenarion Belt	Bind on Equip	113	2 22 21
PROPERTIES: Fire Resist +7, Restores 4 mana per 5 sec, Increases damage and healing done by magical spells and effects by up to 9				

Epic Leather Waist Armor

Lvl	Name	Binding	Armor	Vendor Purchase Value
60	Corehound Belt	Bind on Equip	118	2 78 31
PROPERTIES: Fire Resist +12, Increases healing done by spells and effects by up to 62				
60	Dreamwalker Girdle	Bind on Pickup	142	6 74 81
PROPERTIES: Increases healing done by spells and effects by up to 51, Restores 4 mana per 5 sec				
60	Flayed Doomguard Belt	Bind on Pickup	115	2 33 65
PROPERTIES: Improves your chance to get a critical strike with spells by 1%, Increases damage and healing done by magical spells and effects by up to 14				
60	Lava Belt	Bind on Equip	113	2 12 48
PROPERTIES: Fire Resist +26				
60	Molten Belt	Bind on Equip	118	2 79 31
PROPERTIES: Fire Resist +12				
60	Nightslayer Belt	Bind on Equip	113	2 21 39
PROPERTIES: Fire Resist +7, Improves your chance to get a critical strike by 1%				
60	Regenerating Belt of Vek'nilash	Bind on Pickup	133	4 77 82
PROPERTIES: Increases healing done by spells and effects by up to 55				
60	Stormrage Belt	Bind on Pickup	126	3 64 72
PROPERTIES: Shadow Resist +10, Increases healing done by spells and effects by up to 26, Restores 4 mana per 5 sec				
60	Taut Dragonhide Belt	Bind on Pickup	125	3 30 84
PROPERTIES: +60 Attack Power, Increases your chance to dodge an attack by 1%				
60	Thick Qirajihide Belt	Bind on Pickup	126	3 55 60
PROPERTIES: Increases your chance to parry an attack by 1%				
60	Zandalar Haruspex's Belt	Bind on Pickup	105	
PROPERTIES: Increases healing done by spells and effects by up to 15				

Superior Leather Waist Armor

Lvl	Name	Binding	Armor	Vendor Purchase Value
18	Deviate Scale Belt	Bind on Equip	51	6 58
22	Silver-lined Belt	Bind on Equip	55	10 31
26	Moss Cinch	Bind on Pickup	59	14 42
28	Defiler's Chain Girdle	Bind on Pickup	61	17 54
PROPERTIES: +24 Attack Power				
28	Defiler's Leather Girdle	Bind on Pickup	61	17 95
PROPERTIES: +24 Attack Power				
28	Defiler's Lizardhide Girdle	Bind on Pickup	61	18 2
28	Defiler's Mail Girdle	Bind on Pickup	61	18 34
28	Highlander's Chain Girdle	Bind on Pickup	61	18 74
PROPERTIES: +24 Attack Power				
28	Highlander's Leather Girdle	Bind on Pickup	61	17 88
PROPERTIES: +24 Attack Power				
28	Highlander's Lizardhide Girdle	Bind on Pickup	61	18 41
28	Highlander's Mail Girdle	Bind on Pickup	61	18 8
32	Gem-studded Leather Belt	Bind on Equip	65	26 52
PROPERTIES: Heal yourself for 225 to 375				
37	Ogron's Sash	Bind on Equip	71	38 30
38	Defiler's Leather Girdle	Bind on Pickup	73	41 87
PROPERTIES: +30 Attack Power				
38	Defiler's Lizardhide Girdle	Bind on Pickup	73	42 2
38	Highlander's Leather Girdle	Bind on Pickup	73	41 39
PROPERTIES: +30 Attack Power				
38	Highlander's Lizardhide Girdle	Bind on Pickup	73	42 62
48	Defiler's Leather Girdle	Bind on Pickup	86	84 98
PROPERTIES: Improves your chance to get a critical strike by 1%, +20 Attack Power				
48	Defiler's Lizardhide Girdle	Bind on Pickup	86	85 30
PROPERTIES: Improves your chance to get a critical strike with spells by 1%				
48	Highlander's Leather Girdle	Bind on Pickup	86	83 41
PROPERTIES: Improves your chance to get a critical strike by 1%, +20 Attack Power				
48	Highlander's Lizardhide Girdle	Bind on Pickup	86	85 90
PROPERTIES: Improves your chance to get a critical strike with spells by 1%				
50	Girdle of Beastial Fury	Bind on Pickup	89	93 29
PROPERTIES: +30 Attack Power				

Superior Leather Waist Armor

Lvl	Name	Binding	Armor	Vendor Purchase Value
52	Serpentine Sash	Bind on Equip	92	1 6 1
53	Might of the Timbermaw	Bind on Equip	93	1 11 16
53	Shadowcraft Belt	Bind on Equip	93	1 11 96
53	Wildheart Belt	Bind on Equip	93	1 16 20
54	Nagmara's Whipping Belt	Bind on Pickup	89	98 19
55	Cloudrunner Girdle	Bind on Pickup	95	1 24 34
55	Frostwolf Leather Belt	Bind on Pickup	95	1 18 60
PROPERTIES: Frost Resist +5				
55	Stormpike Leather Girdle	Bind on Pickup	95	1 18 60
PROPERTIES: Frost Resist +5				
56	Belt of the Trickster	Bind on Pickup	97	1 24 46
56	Cadaverous Belt	Bind on Pickup	97	1 24 76
PROPERTIES: +40 Attack Power				
56	Crystallized Girdle	Bind on Pickup	97	1 26 68
PROPERTIES: Increases damage and healing done by magical spells and effects by up to 9				
57	Eyestalk Cord	Bind on Pickup	98	1 30 76
PROPERTIES: Increases healing done by spells and effects by up to 35				
57	Frostbite Girdle	Bind on Pickup	98	1 30 51
PROPERTIES: Frost Resist +10				
57	Girdle of Insight	Bind on Equip	98	1 41 26
57	Mugger's Belt	Bind on Pickup	98	1 30 76
PROPERTIES: Improves your chance to get a critical strike by 1%, Increased Daggers +5				
58	Defiler's Leather Girdle	Bind on Pickup	99	1 43 56
PROPERTIES: Improves your chance to get a critical strike by 1%, +34 Attack Power				
58	Defiler's Lizardhide Girdle	Bind on Pickup	99	1 40 29
PROPERTIES: Improves your chance to get a critical strike with spells by 1%				
58	Highlander's Leather Girdle	Bind on Pickup	99	1 47 84
PROPERTIES: Improves your chance to get a critical strike by 1%, +34 Attack Power				
58	Highlander's Lizardhide Girdle	Bind on Pickup	99	1 48 36
PROPERTIES: Improves your chance to get a critical strike with spells by 1%				
60	Bramblewood Belt	Bind on Equip	108	1 96 7
PROPERTIES: Nature Resist +15				
60	Shadow Panther Hide Belt	Bind on Equip	102	1 52 95
PROPERTIES: Increases your chance to dodge an attack by 1%				
60	Southwind's Grasp	Bind on Pickup	110	2 18 45
PROPERTIES: Increases damage and healing done by magical spells and effects by up to 16, Improves your chance to get a critical strike with spells by 1%				
60	Belt of Preserved Heads	Bind on Pickup	108	2 6 45
PROPERTIES: Improves your chance to hit by 1%				
60	Darkmantle Belt	Bind on Pickup	102	1 60 61
60	Feralheart Belt	Bind on Pickup	102	1 55 36
PROPERTIES: Increases damage and healing done by magical spells and effects by up to 7				
60	Vosh'gajin's Strand	Bind on Pickup	95	1 20 64
PROPERTIES: Improves your chance to get a critical strike by 1%, Increases your chance to dodge an attack by 1%				

Epic Leather Wrist Armor

Lvl	Name	Binding	Armor	Vendor Purchase Value
40	Forest Stalker's Bracers	Bind on Pickup	64	61 81
44	Bladebane Armguards	Bind on Equip	69	88 2
50	Forest Stalker's Bracers	Bind on Pickup	75	1 20 43
60	Beetle Scaled Wristguards	Bind on Pickup	95	2 99 5
PROPERTIES: Nature Resist +15, +18 Attack Power				
60	Bloodfang Bracers	Bind on Pickup	98	3 48 72
PROPERTIES: Improves your chance to hit by 1%				
60	Bonescythe Bracers	Bind on Pickup	111	6 31 32
PROPERTIES: Improves your chance to get a critical strike by 1%				
60	Cenarion Bracers	Bind on Equip	88	2 29 72
PROPERTIES: Increases damage and healing done by magical spells and effects by up to 6				
60	Dragonspur Wraps	Bind on Pickup	93	2 96 43
PROPERTIES: Fire Resist +4, Nature Resist +4, Frost Resist +4, Shadow Resist +4, Arcane Resist +4, +32 Attack Power				

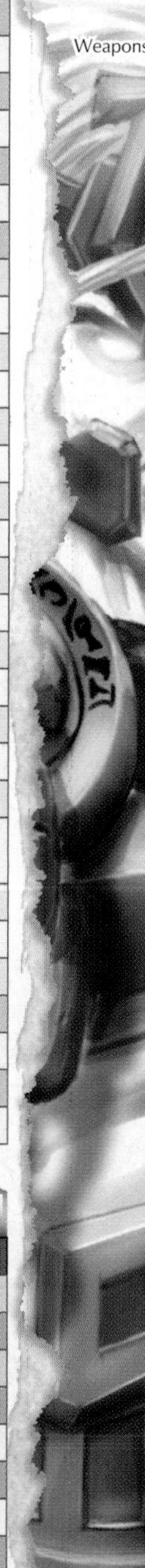

Epic Leather Wrist Armor

Lvl	Name	Binding	Armor	Vendor Purchase Value
60	Dreamwalker Wristguards	Bind on Pickup	111	6 77 21
PROPERTIES: Increases healing done by spells and effects by up to 40, Restores 5 mana per 5 sec				
60	Forest Stalker's Bracers	Bind on Pickup	86	2 1 83
60	Nightslayer Bracelets	Bind on Equip	88	2 19 77
60	Polar Bracers	Bind on Equip	102	4 61 75
PROPERTIES: Frost Resist +20				
60	Qiraji Execution Bracers	Bind on Pickup	103	4 65 95
PROPERTIES: Improves your chance to hit by 1%				
60	Stormrage Bracers	Bind on Pickup	98	3 66 6
PROPERTIES: Increases healing done by spells and effects by up to 33				
60	Wristguards of Stability	Bind on Pickup	86	2 1 83
60	Bracers of Subterfuge	Bind on Pickup	81	1 60 48
60	Zandalar Haruspex's Bracers	Bind on Pickup	82	
PROPERTIES: Increases healing done by spells and effects by up to 24				
60	Zandalar Madcap's Bracers	Bind on Pickup	82	

Superior Leather Wrist Armor

Lvl	Name	Binding	Armor	Vendor Purchase Value
20	Drakewing Bands	Bind on Equip	41	8 53
27	Barbaric Bracers	Bind on Equip	47	15 89
28	Emissary Cuffs	Bind on Pickup	47	18 25
PROPERTIES: Arcane Resist +5				
30	Unearthed Bands	Bind on Equip	49	20 96
PROPERTIES: +8 Attack Power				
34	Enchanted Kodo Bracers	Bind on Equip	52	30 63
45	Arena Bracers	Bind on Equip	64	72 24
45	First Sergeant's Dragonhide Armguards	Bind on Pickup	64	34 17
45	First Sergeant's Leather Armguards	Bind on Pickup	64	36 62
45	Sergeant Major's Dragonhide Armsplints	Bind on Pickup	64	34 4
45	Sergeant Major's Leather Armsplints	Bind on Pickup	64	33 78
47	Darkwater Bracers	Bind on Pickup	66	75 62
PROPERTIES: Shadow Resist +7				
50	Deepfury Bracers	Bind on Equip	69	95 5
52	Cinderhide Armsplints	Bind on Pickup	71	1 3 98
PROPERTIES: Fire Resist +10				
52	Shadowcraft Bracers	Bind on Equip	71	1 4 46
52	Wildheart Bracers	Bind on Equip	71	1 6 2
53	Malefic Bracers	Bind on Equip	72	1 9 10
54	Magistrate's Cuffs	Bind on Pickup	73	1 12 96
PROPERTIES: Restores 4 mana per 5 sec				
55	Wristguards of Renown	Bind on Pickup	74	1 24 3
56	Bleak Howler Armguards	Bind on Pickup	75	1 25 20
PROPERTIES: Increases healing done by spells and effects by up to 15				
57	Bracers of the Eclipse	Bind on Pickup	76	1 43 29
PROPERTIES: +24 Attack Power				
58	Blackmist Armguards	Bind on Pickup	77	1 40 18
PROPERTIES: Shadow Resist +10, Improves your chance to hit by 1%				
58	Bracers of Prosperity	Bind on Pickup	77	1 37 30
PROPERTIES: Increases healing done by spells and effects by up to 22				
58	First Sergeant's Dragonhide Armguards	Bind on Pickup	77	74 93
58	First Sergeant's Leather Armguards	Bind on Pickup	77	68 80
58	Sergeant Major's Dragonhide Armsplints	Bind on Pickup	77	69 63
58	Sergeant Major's Leather Armsplints	Bind on Pickup	77	69 10
58	Wristwraps of Undead Slaying	Bind on Equip	77	1 46 24
PROPERTIES: +45 Attack Power when fighting Undead				
60	Abyssal Leather Bracers	Bind on Pickup	82	1 82 51
60	Primal Batskin Bracers	Bind on Equip	79	1 59 39
PROPERTIES: Improves your chance to hit by 1%				
60	Scaled Bracers of the Gorger	Bind on Pickup	87	2 38 26
60	Darkmantle Bracers	Bind on Pickup	79	1 65 98

Superior Leather Wrist Armor

Lvl	Name	Binding	Armor	Vendor Purchase Value
60	Feralheart Bracers	Bind on Pickup	79	1 56 53
PROPERTIES: Increases damage and healing done by magical spells and effects by up to 5				

MAIL

Epic Mail Chest Armor

Lvl	Name	Binding	Armor	Vendor Purchase Value
39	Icemail Jerkin	Bind on Equip	294	1 41 13
PROPERTIES: Frost Resist +10				
52	Savage Gladiator Chain	Bind on Pickup	369	3 35 33
PROPERTIES: , Improves your chance to get a critical strike by 2%				
57	Invulnerable Mail	Bind on Equip	404	4 38 36
PROPERTIES: When struck in combat has a 5% chance to make you invulnerable to melee damage for 3 sec. This effect can only occur once every 30 sec. Increased Defense +13				
57	Onyxia Scale Breastplate	Bind on Equip	398	4 19 37
PROPERTIES: Fire Resist +9, , Improves your chance to get a critical strike by 1%				
60	Breastplate of Ten Storms	Bind on Pickup	482	8 33 55
PROPERTIES: Fire Resist +10, Nature Resist +10, Increases damage and healing done by magical spells and effects by up to 23				
60	Cryptstalker Tunic	Bind on Pickup	576	19 33 11
PROPERTIES: Improves your chance to hit by 1%, Improves your chance to get a critical strike by 1%, Restores 4 mana per 5 sec				
60	Dragonstalker's Breastplate	Bind on Pickup	482	8 94 96
PROPERTIES: Fire Resist +10, Nature Resist +10, Improves your chance to get a critical strike by 1%				
60	Dreamscale Breastplate	Bind on Equip	434	5 79 58
PROPERTIES: Nature Resist +30, Restores 4 mana per 5 sec				
60	Earthshatter Tunic	Bind on Pickup	576	18 48 92
PROPERTIES: Increases healing done by spells and effects by up to 59, Restores 12 mana per 5 sec				
60	Field Marshal's Chain Breastplate	Bind on Pickup	470	3 89 68
PROPERTIES: , Improves your chance to get a critical strike by 1%				
60	Giantstalker's Breastplate	Bind on Pickup	422	5 41 48
PROPERTIES: Fire Resist +10, Improves your chance to get a critical strike by 1%				
60	Icy Scale Breastplate	Bind on Equip	506	10 6 42
PROPERTIES: Frost Resist +40, +40 Attack Power				
60	Obsidian Mail Tunic	Bind on Equip	458	7 31 28
PROPERTIES: +76 Attack Power, Improves your chance to get a critical strike by 1%, Spell Damage received is reduced by 10				
60	Runed Bloodstained Hauberk	Bind on Pickup	416	4 93 25
PROPERTIES: +58 Attack Power, Improves your chance to get a critical strike by 1%				
60	Stormcaller's Hauberk	Bind on Pickup	553	15 20 80
PROPERTIES: Increases damage and healing done by magical spells and effects by up to 32, Improves your chance to get a critical strike by 1%, Improves your chance to get a critical strike with spells by 1%				
60	Striker's Hauberk	Bind on Pickup	553	14 97 87
PROPERTIES: Improves your chance to get a critical strike by 1%, Increases damage and healing done by magical spells and effects by up to 9				
60	Earthfury Vestments	Bind on Pickup	422	5 19 56
PROPERTIES: Fire Resist +10, Improves your chance to get a critical strike with spells by 1%, Increases healing done by spells and effects by up to 22				
60	Warlord's Chain Chestpiece	Bind on Pickup	470	3 98 43
PROPERTIES: , Improves your chance to get a critical strike by 1%				
60	Warlord's Mail Armor	Bind on Pickup	470	3 86 81
PROPERTIES: Improves your chance to get a critical strike by 1%, Improves your chance to get a critical strike with spells by 1%, Increases damage and healing done by magical spells and effects by up to 9				
60	Beastmaster's Tunic	Bind on Pickup	387	4 10 15
PROPERTIES: Increases your pet's armor by 10%, Improves your chance to get a critical strike by 1%				
60	Vest of The Five Thunders	Bind on Pickup	387	3 83 68
PROPERTIES: Improves your chance to get a critical strike with spells by 1%, Increases damage and healing done by magical spells and effects by up to 14				
60	Zandalar Augur's Hauberk	Bind on Pickup	416	
PROPERTIES: Increases damage and healing done by magical spells and effects by up to 34, Improves your chance to get a critical strike with spells by 1%				

Superior Mail Chest Armor

Lvl	Name	Binding	Armor	Vendor Purchase Value
20	Phantom Armor	Bind on Pickup	201	18 80
20	Tortoise Armor	Bind on Pickup	201	18 72
21	Martyr's Chain	Bind on Equip	204	22 13
23	Mutant Scale Breastplate	Bind on Pickup	211	26 20
24	Shining Silver Breastplate	Bind on Equip	214	29 35
25	Double Link Tunic	Bind on Equip	218	31 8
PROPERTIES: , Increased Defense +9				
26	Avenger's Armor	Bind on Equip	221	33 79
28	Fire Hardened Hauberk	Bind on Pickup	218	32 42
PROPERTIES: Increase Rage by 30				
30	Ironspine's Ribcage	Bind on Pickup	235	53 20
30	Brutal Hauberk	Bind on Pickup	218	30 98
PROPERTIES: Increase Rage by 30				
31	Green Iron Hauberk	Bind on Equip	238	56 58
33	Archon Chestpiece	Bind on Equip	245	67 23
34	Scarlet Chestpiece	Bind on Equip	250	69 92
39	Deathchill Armor	Bind on Pickup	270	1 4 34
39	Polished Jazeraint Armor	Bind on Equip	270	1 3 1
43	Gahz'rilla Scale Armor	Bind on Pickup	290	1 46 34
46	Dragonscale Breastplate	Bind on Equip	306	1 84 55
PROPERTIES: Fire Resist +13,Frost Resist +13, Shadow Resist +12, Absorbs 600 magical damage.Lasts 2 min Buff				
47	Atal'ai Breastplate	Bind on Pickup	311	1 84 32
PROPERTIES: +22 Attack Power				
47	Green Dragonscale Breastplate	Bind on Equip	311	1 99 38
PROPERTIES: Nature Resist +11				
49	Wildthorn Mail	Bind on Equip	322	2 6 42
PROPERTIES: Increases damage done by Nature spells and effects by up to 34				
52	Blue Dragonscale Breastplate	Bind on Equip	338	2 44 9
PROPERTIES: Arcane Resist +8				
52	Deathdealer Breastplate	Bind on Pickup	338	2 45 90
PROPERTIES: Improves your chance to get a critical strike by 2%				
53	Black Dragonscale Breastplate	Bind on Equip	344	2 60 71
PROPERTIES: Fire Resist +12, +50 Attack Power				
53	Royal Decorated Armor	Bind on Pickup	344	2 67 61
56	Bloodmail Hauberk	Bind on Pickup	360	3 25 9
PROPERTIES: Increases your chance to dodge an attack by 1%				
56	Bonebrace Hauberk	Bind on Equip	360	3 22 71
PROPERTIES: +56 Attack Power				
56	Red Dragonscale Breastplate	Bind on Equip	360	2 98 36
PROPERTIES: Fire Resist +12, Increases healing done by spells and effects by up to 66				
57	Dreamwalker Armor	Bind on Equip	365	3 33 87
57	Ogre Forged Hauberk	Bind on Pickup	365	3 13 31
PROPERTIES: Improves your chance to get a critical strike by 1%				
57	Sandstalker Breastplate	Bind on Equip	365	3 39 17
PROPERTIES: Nature Resist +25				
57	Spitfire Breastplate	Bind on Equip	365	3 40 36
PROPERTIES: Restores 6 mana per 5 sec, Increases damage and healing done by magical spells and effects by up to 15				
58	Beaststalker's Tunic	Bind on Pickup	370	3 44 35
58	Breastplate of the Chosen	Bind on Pickup	370	3 59 55
58	Chestguard of Undead Slaying	Bind on Pickup	370	3 44 63
PROPERTIES: +81 Attack Power when fighting Undead				
58	Knight-Captain's Chain Hauberk	Bind on Pickup	370	1 65 71
PROPERTIES: +26 Attack Power, Improves your chance to get a critical strike by 1%				
58	Legionnaire's Chain Breastplate	Bind on Pickup	370	1 74 75
PROPERTIES: +26 Attack Power, Improves your chance to get a critical strike by 1%				
58	Legionnaire's Mail Chestpiece	Bind on Pickup	370	1 68 27
PROPERTIES: Improves your chance to get a critical strike by 1%				
58	Vest of Elements	Bind on Pickup	370	3 59 62
60	Bloodsoul Breastplate	Bind on Equip	381	3 96 83
PROPERTIES: Improves your chance to get a critical strike by 2%				
60	Knight-Captain's Chain Hauberk	Bind on Pickup	398	2 18 33

Superior Mail Chest Armor

Lvl	Name	Binding	Armor	Vendor Purchase Value
PROPERTIES: Improves your chance to get a critical strike by 2%				
60	Legionnaire's Chain Hauberk	Bind on Pickup	398	2 13 41
PROPERTIES: Improves your chance to get a critical strike by 2%				
60	Legionnaire's Mail Hauberk	Bind on Pickup	398	2 15 5
PROPERTIES: Improves your chance to get a critical strike by 1%				

Epic Mail Foot Armor

Lvl	Name	Binding	Armor	Vendor Purchase Value
56	Black Dragonscale Boots	Bind on Equip	270	3 26 53
PROPERTIES: Fire Resist +24, +28 Attack Power				
60	Boots of the Endless Moor	Bind on Pickup	311	4 95 95
PROPERTIES: Nature Resist +25, Restores 3 mana per 5 sec				
60	Boots of the Fallen Prophet	Bind on Pickup	319	5 91 5
PROPERTIES: Increases damage and healing done by magical spells and effects by up to 20				
60	Cryptstalker Boots	Bind on Pickup	372	10 23 91
PROPERTIES: Improves your chance to hit by 1%				
60	Dragonstalker's Greaves	Bind on Pickup	332	6 71 78
PROPERTIES: Fire Resist +10				
60	Earthfury Boots	Bind on Pickup	290	3 85 50
PROPERTIES: Shadow Resist +7, Increases healing done by spells and effects by up to 18				
60	Earthshatter Boots	Bind on Pickup	372	10 55 4
PROPERTIES: Increases healing done by spells and effects by up to 37, Restores 6 mana per 5 sec				
60	General's Chain Boots	Bind on Pickup	311	2 63 5
PROPERTIES: Improves your chance to hit by 1%				
60	General's Mail Boots	Bind on Pickup	311	2 47 95
PROPERTIES: Increases the speed of your Ghost Wolf ability by 15%, Increases damage and healing done by magical spells and effects by up to 20, Restores 5 mana per 5 sec				
60	Giantstalker's Boots	Bind on Pickup	290	4 13 82
PROPERTIES: Shadow Resist +7				
60	Greaves of Ten Storms	Bind on Pickup	332	6 25 52
PROPERTIES: Fire Resist +10, Increases damage and healing done by magical spells and effects by up to 20				
60	Malignant Footguards	Bind on Pickup	315	5 50 79
PROPERTIES: Increases damage and healing done by magical spells and effects by up to 27				
60	Marshal's Chain Boots	Bind on Pickup	311	2 49 82
PROPERTIES: Improves your chance to hit by 1%				
60	Sabatons of the Flamewalker	Bind on Pickup	298	4 59 73
PROPERTIES: +30 Attack Power				
60	Stormcaller's Footguards	Bind on Pickup	340	7
PROPERTIES: Increases damage and healing done by magical spells and effects by up to 22, Decreases the magical resistances of your spell targets by 10, Restores 4 mana per 5 sec				
60	Striker's Footguards	Bind on Pickup	340	7 51 68
PROPERTIES: Increases damage and healing done by magical spells and effects by up to 6				
60	Beastmaster's Boots	Bind on Pickup	266	3 10 9
PROPERTIES: Increases damage dealt by your pet by 3%				
60	Boots of The Five Thunders	Bind on Pickup	266	3 4 51
PROPERTIES: Increases damage and healing done by magical spells and effects by up to 12, Restores 4 mana per 5 sec				

Superior Mail Foot Armor

Lvl	Name	Binding	Armor	Vendor Purchase Value
16	Silver-linked Footguards	Bind on Equip	129	8 50
27	Coverndeep Trudgers	Bind on Equip	154	29 45
28	Defiler's Lamellar Greaves	Bind on Pickup	157	33 77
PROPERTIES: Run speed increased slightly				
28	Defiler's Plate Greaves	Bind on Pickup	157	32 34
PROPERTIES: Run speed increased slightly				
28	Highlander's Lamellar Greaves	Bind on Pickup	157	31 62
PROPERTIES: Run speed increased slightly				
28	Highlander's Plate Greaves	Bind on Pickup	157	31 37
PROPERTIES: Run speed increased slightly				

Superior Mail Foot Armor

Lvl	Name	Binding	Armor	Vendor Purchase Value
30	Ravasaur Scale Boots	Bind on Equip	161	39 96
30	Scarlet Boots	Bind on Equip	161	37 90
32	Black Ogre Kickers	Bind on Equip	166	45 81
40	Defiler's Chain Greaves	Bind on Pickup	183	76 82
PROPERTIES: Run speed increased slightly				
40	Defiler's Mail Greaves	Bind on Pickup	183	77 90
PROPERTIES: Run speed increased slightly				
40	Highlander's Chain Greaves	Bind on Pickup	183	73 75
PROPERTIES: Run speed increased slightly				
40	Highlander's Mail Greaves	Bind on Pickup	183	76 50
PROPERTIES: Run speed increased slightly				
45	Elven Chain Boots	Bind on Equip	206	1 29 54
48	Defiler's Chain Greaves	Bind on Pickup	218	1 50 77
PROPERTIES: Run speed increased slightly				
48	Defiler's Mail Greaves	Bind on Pickup	218	1 58 69
PROPERTIES: Run speed increased slightly				
48	Fleetfoot Greaves	Bind on Pickup	218	1 46 68
48	Greaves of Withering Despair	Bind on Pickup	218	1 49 72
PROPERTIES: Increases damage and healing done by magical spells and effects by up to 11, Improves your chance to hit with spells by 1%				
48	Highlander's Chain Greaves	Bind on Pickup	218	1 48 59
PROPERTIES: Run speed increased slightly				
48	Highlander's Mail Greaves	Bind on Pickup	218	1 54 17
PROPERTIES: Run speed increased slightly				
49	Bloodshot Greaves	Bind on Pickup	221	1 61 43
52	Savage Gladiator Greaves	Bind on Pickup	233	1 93
53	Swiftdart Battleboots	Bind on Pickup	236	1 97 85
54	Beaststalker's Boots	Bind on Pickup	240	2 14 21
54	Boots of Elements	Bind on Pickup	240	2 10 27
54	Merciful Greaves	Bind on Pickup	240	2 20 57
PROPERTIES: Increases healing done by spells and effects by up to 20				
54	Timmy's Galoshes	Bind on Pickup	240	2 11 68
56	Bloodmail Boots	Bind on Pickup	247	2 25 59
PROPERTIES: Improves your chance to hit by 1%				
56	Wind Dancer Boots	Bind on Equip	247	2 25 61
PROPERTIES: Increases your chance to dodge an attack by 1%				
56	Windreaver Greaves	Bind on Pickup	247	2 33 38
PROPERTIES: Improves your chance to hit by 1%				
57	Flame Walkers	Bind on Pickup	251	2 44 28
PROPERTIES: Fire Resist +18, Increases your chance to dodge an attack by 1%				
57	Odious Greaves	Bind on Pickup	251	2 37 91
PROPERTIES: +22 Attack Power				
57	Shadowy Mail Greaves	Bind on Pickup	251	2 59 10
PROPERTIES: Shadow Resist +10				
58	Blood Guard's Chain Boots	Bind on Pickup	255	1 34 52
PROPERTIES: Increases your chance to dodge an attack by 1%				
58	Blood Guard's Mail Walkers	Bind on Pickup	255	1 24 85
PROPERTIES: Increases damage and healing done by magical spells and effects by up to 14, Increases the speed of your Ghost Wolf ability by 15%				
58	Defiler's Chain Greaves	Bind on Pickup	255	2 56 57
PROPERTIES: Run speed increased slightly				
58	Defiler's Mail Greaves	Bind on Pickup	255	2 68 18
PROPERTIES: Run speed increased slightly				
58	Highlander's Chain Greaves	Bind on Pickup	255	2 72 6
PROPERTIES: Run speed increased slightly				
58	Highlander's Mail Greaves	Bind on Pickup	255	2 73 2
PROPERTIES: Run speed increased slightly				
58	Knight-Lieutenant's Chain Boots	Bind on Pickup	255	1 35 96
PROPERTIES: Increases your chance to dodge an attack by 1%				
59	Heavy Timbermaw Boots	Bind on Equip	258	2 80 61
PROPERTIES: +20 Attack Power				

Superior Mail Foot Armor

Lvl	Name	Binding	Armor	Vendor Purchase Value
60	Blood Guard's Chain Greaves	Bind on Pickup	266	1 50 84
60	Blood Guard's Mail Greaves	Bind on Pickup	266	1 47 51
PROPERTIES: , Increases the speed of your Ghost Wolf ability by 15%				
60	Bloodstained Greaves	Bind on Pickup	274	3 16 46
60	Boots of the Fiery Sands	Bind on Pickup	293	4 5 51
PROPERTIES: Restores 4 mana per 5 sec, Increases damage and healing done by magical spells and effects by up to 12				
60	Boots of the Qiraji General	Bind on Pickup	285	3 99 19
60	Knight-Lieutenant's Chain Greaves	Bind on Pickup	266	1 52 53
60	Seafury Boots	Bind on Pickup	274	3 21 35
PROPERTIES: Increases damage and healing done by magical spells and effects by up to 12, Restores 5 mana per 5 sec				

Epic Mail Hand Armor

Lvl	Name	Binding	Armor	Vendor Purchase Value
44	Edgemaster's Handguards	Bind on Equip	201	1 6 1
PROPERTIES: Increased Axes +7, Increased Daggers +7, Increased Swords +7				
46	Stonerender Gauntlets	Bind on Equip	209	1 14 47
PROPERTIES: Nature Resist +10				
60	Black Grasp of the Destroyer	Bind on Equip	279	3 35 21
PROPERTIES: +28 Attack Power, Improves your chance to get a critical strike by 1%, On successful melee or ranged attack gain 8 mana and if possible drain 8 mana from the target				
60	Chromatic Gauntlets	Bind on Equip	279	3 19 43
PROPERTIES: Fire Resist +5, Nature Resist +5, Frost Resist +5, Shadow Resist +5, +44 Attack Power, Improves your chance to get a critical strike by 1%, Improves your chance to get a critical strike with spells by 1%				
60	Cryptstalker Handguards	Bind on Pickup	346	7 52 5
PROPERTIES: Improves your chance to get a critical strike by 1%, Restores 4 mana per 5 sec				
60	Dragonstalker's Gauntlets	Bind on Pickup	301	4 32 75
PROPERTIES: Shadow Resist +10, Improves your chance to get a critical strike by 1%				
60	Earthfury Gauntlets	Bind on Pickup	264	2 57 81
PROPERTIES: Fire Resist +7, Improves your chance to get a critical strike with spells by 1%, Increases damage and healing done by magical spells and effects by up to 9				
60	Earthshatter Handguards	Bind on Pickup	346	7 74 91
PROPERTIES: Increases healing done by spells and effects by up to 35, Restores 6 mana per 5 sec				
60	Gauntlets of Kalimdor	Bind on Pickup	309	4 86 45
PROPERTIES: Increases damage and healing done by magical spells and effects by up to 20, Improves your chance to get a critical strike with spells by 1%				
60	Gauntlets of Ten Storms	Bind on Pickup	301	4 13 56
PROPERTIES: Shadow Resist +10, Restores 6 mana per 5 sec, Increases damage and healing done by magical spells and effects by up to 8, Increases healing done by spells and effects by up to 15				
60	General's Chain Gloves	Bind on Pickup	283	1 63 31
PROPERTIES: Increases the damage done by your Multi-Shot by 4%, Improves your chance to get a critical strike by 1%				
60	General's Mail Gauntlets	Bind on Pickup	283	1 65 18
PROPERTIES: Improves your chance to get a critical strike by 1%				
60	Giantstalker's Gloves	Bind on Pickup	264	2 77 62
PROPERTIES: Fire Resist +7, Improves your chance to hit by 2%				
60	Gloves of the Fallen Prophet	Bind on Pickup	298	4 20 13
PROPERTIES: Increases healing done by spells and effects by up to 44				
60	Icy Scale Gauntlets	Bind on Equip	316	5 7 12
PROPERTIES: Frost Resist +30, +22 Attack Power				
60	Marshal's Chain Grips	Bind on Pickup	283	1 66 44
PROPERTIES: Increases the damage done by your Multi-Shot by 4%, Improves your chance to get a critical strike by 1%				
60	Seafury Gauntlets	Bind on Pickup	271	3 8 40
PROPERTIES: Improves your chance to get a critical strike by 1%, Improves your chance to get a critical strike with spells by 1%, Restores 7 mana per 5 sec				
60	Slimy Scaled Gauntlets	Bind on Pickup	271	2 86 58
PROPERTIES: Increases damage and healing done by magical spells and effects by up to 12, Improves your chance to get a critical strike with spells by 1%				
60	Vek'lor's Gloves of Devastation	Bind on Pickup	320	5 38 35
PROPERTIES: Improves your chance to get a critical strike by 1%				
60	Beastmaster's Gloves	Bind on Pickup	223	1 49 41
PROPERTIES: Increases your pet's critical strike chance by 2%				
60	Gauntlets of The Five Thunders	Bind on Pickup	223	1 55 58
PROPERTIES: Restores 4 mana per 5 sec, Increases damage and healing done by magical spells and effects by up to 12				

Superior Mail Hand Armor

Lvl	Name	Binding	Armor	Vendor Purchase Value
18	Thorbia's Gauntlets	Bind on Equip	122	7 87
22	Warsong Gauntlets	Bind on Pickup	130	11 58
23	Algae Fists	Bind on Pickup	132	12 75
29	Grubbis Paws	Bind on Pickup	144	22 60
30	The Frozen Clutch	Bind on Pickup	147	26 84
PROPERTIES: +20 Attack Power				
31	Reticulated Bone Gauntlets	Bind on Equip	149	29 16
31	Stormgale Fists	Bind on Equip	149	29 5
39	Gauntlets of Divinity	Bind on Pickup	168	54 36
PROPERTIES: +32 Attack Power				
40	Dragonscale Gauntlets	Bind on Equip	171	59 79
PROPERTIES: Improves your chance to get a critical strike by 1%				
41	Murkwater Gauntlets	Bind on Equip	174	60 86
48	Battlecaller Gauntlets	Bind on Equip	198	1 3 74
48	Rockgrip Gauntlets	Bind on Pickup	198	96 46
PROPERTIES: +28 Attack Power				
50	Azurite Fists	Bind on Pickup	195	99 75
PROPERTIES: Improves your chance to get a critical strike with spells by 1%				
51	Green Dragonscale Gauntlets	Bind on Equip	208	1 25 90
PROPERTIES: Nature Resist +9				
52	Savage Gladiator Grips	Bind on Pickup	211	1 27 62
53	Molten Fists	Bind on Pickup	215	1 30 83
PROPERTIES: Fire Resist +10				
54	Beaststalker's Gloves	Bind on Equip	218	1 42 68
54	Gauntlets of Elements	Bind on Equip	218	1 40 59
54	Storm Gauntlets	Bind on Equip	218	1 40 99
PROPERTIES: Fire Resist +10, Adds 3 Lightning damage to your melee attacks, Increases damage done by Nature spells and effects by up to 21				
54	Trueaim Gauntlets	Bind on Pickup	218	1 43 66
PROPERTIES: Increased Bows +8, Improves your chance to hit by 1%, Increased Guns +8, Increased Crossbows +8,				
55	Gilded Gauntlets	Bind on Pickup	221	1 44 82
PROPERTIES: Restores 4 mana per 5 sec				
56	Bloodmail Gauntlets	Bind on Pickup	225	1 49 16
PROPERTIES: Improves your chance to get a critical strike by 1%				
57	Sandstalker Gauntlets	Bind on Equip	228	1 68 98
PROPERTIES: Nature Resist +20				
57	Spitfire Gauntlets	Bind on Equip	228	1 70 78
PROPERTIES: Restores 5 mana per 5 sec, Increases damage and healing done by magical spells and effects by up to 11				
58	Blood Guard's Chain Gauntlets	Bind on Pickup	231	88 96
PROPERTIES: Reduces the mana cost of your Arcane Shot by 15				
58	Blood Guard's Mail Grips	Bind on Pickup	231	83 18
PROPERTIES: Increases damage and healing done by magical spells and effects by up to 19				
58	Dracorian Gauntlets	Bind on Pickup	231	1 72 10
PROPERTIES: Increases damage and healing done by magical spells and effects by up to 16				
58	Gauntlets of Deftness	Bind on Pickup	231	1 72 31
58	Handguards of Savagery	Bind on Pickup	231	1 64 76
PROPERTIES: +38 Attack Power				
58	Harmonious Gauntlets	Bind on Pickup	231	1 79 88
PROPERTIES: Increases healing done by spells and effects by up to 51				
58	Knight-Lieutenant's Chain Gauntlets	Bind on Pickup	231	82 23
PROPERTIES: Reduces the mana cost of your Arcane Shot by 15				
60	Blood Guard's Chain Vices	Bind on Pickup	242	99 73
PROPERTIES: Increases the damage done by your Multi-Shot by 4%				
60	Blood Guard's Mail Vices	Bind on Pickup	242	1 1 57
PROPERTIES: Improves your chance to get a critical strike with spells by 1%, Increases damage and healing done by magical spells and effects by up to 13				
60	Bloodsoul Gauntlets	Bind on Equip	238	1 99 80
PROPERTIES: Improves your chance to get a critical strike by 1%				
60	Gloves of the Tormented	Bind on Pickup	249	2 24 84
PROPERTIES: Improves your chance to get a critical strike by 1%				
60	Knight-Lieutenant's Chain Vices	Bind on Pickup	242	1 1 60
PROPERTIES: Increases the damage done by your Multi-Shot by 4%				

Superior Mail Hand Armor

Lvl	Name	Binding	Armor	Vendor Purchase Value
60	Scaled Silithid Gauntlets	Bind on Pickup	266	2 95 23
60	Desertstalkers's Gauntlets	Bind on Pickup	231	1 66 47
60	Gordok's Gauntlets	Bind on Pickup	221	1 47 62
PROPERTIES: Improves your chance to get a critical strike with spells by 1%				
60	Handguards of Undead Slaying	Bind on Pickup	231	1 68 51
PROPERTIES: +60 Attack Power when fighting Undead				
60	Voone's Vice Grips	Bind on Pickup	221	1 45 33
PROPERTIES: Improves your chance to hit by 2%				
60	Wastewalker's Gauntlets	Bind on Pickup	231	1 65 83

Epic Mail Head Armor

Lvl	Name	Binding	Armor	Vendor Purchase Value
54	Helm of Narv	Bind on Equip	309	2 76 36
57	Helm of the Lifegiver	Bind on Pickup	324	3 13 84
PROPERTIES: Increases healing done by spells and effects by up to 42				
60	Crown of Destruction	Bind on Pickup	392	6 39 75
PROPERTIES: Fire Resist +10, Improves your chance to get a critical strike by 2%, +44 Attack Power				
60	Cryptstalker Headpiece	Bind on Pickup	449	11 15 21
PROPERTIES: Improves your chance to get a critical strike by 2%, Restores 3 mana per 5 sec				
60	Dragonstalker's Helm	Bind on Pickup	392	6 46 72
PROPERTIES: Frost Resist +10, Shadow Resist +10, Improves your chance to get a critical strike by 1%				
60	Earthfury Helmet	Bind on Pickup	343	3 91 11
PROPERTIES: Fire Resist +10, Restores 6 mana per 5 sec, Increases healing done by spells and effects by up to 22				
60	Earthshatter Headpiece	Bind on Pickup	449	11 49 49
PROPERTIES: Increases healing done by spells and effects by up to 68, Restores 8 mana per 5 sec				
60	Field Marshal's Chain Helm	Bind on Pickup	382	2 91 17
PROPERTIES: Improves your chance to get a critical strike by 1%				
60	Giantstalker's Helmet	Bind on Pickup	343	4 7 59
PROPERTIES: Fire Resist +10, Improves your chance to get a critical strike by 1%				
60	Helmet of Ten Storms	Bind on Pickup	392	6 83 14
PROPERTIES: Frost Resist +10, Shadow Resist +10, Improves your chance to get a critical strike with spells by 1%, Increases damage and healing done by magical spells and effects by up to 9, Increases healing done by spells and effects by up to 18				
60	Icy Scale Coif	Bind on Pickup	425	9 31 64
PROPERTIES: Frost Resist +44				
60	Infernal Headcage	Bind on Pickup	358	4 80 35
PROPERTIES: Fire Resist +10, Shadow Resist +10, Increases damage and healing done by magical spells and effects by up to 16				
60	Stormcaller's Diadem	Bind on Pickup	416	8 4 45
PROPERTIES: Increases damage and healing done by magical spells and effects by up to 32, Improves your chance to get a critical strike with spells by 1%				
60	Striker's Diadem	Bind on Pickup	416	8 69 39
PROPERTIES: Improves your chance to get a critical strike by 1%, Increases damage and healing done by magical spells and effects by up to 12				
60	Warlord's Chain Helmet	Bind on Pickup	382	2 99 91
PROPERTIES: Improves your chance to get a critical strike by 1%				
60	Warlord's Mail Helm	Bind on Pickup	382	2 91 17
PROPERTIES: Improves your chance to get a critical strike by 1%, Improves your chance to get a critical strike with spells by 1%, Increases damage and healing done by magical spells and effects by up to 9				
60	Beastmaster's Cap	Bind on Pickup	314	2 92 12
PROPERTIES: Improves your chance to hit by 1%, Increases your pet's maximum health by 3%				
60	Coif of The Five Thunders	Bind on Pickup	314	3 4 27
PROPERTIES: Increases damage and healing done by magical spells and effects by up to 14, Improves your chance to get a critical strike with spells by 1%				
60	Skyfury Helm	Bind on Pickup	324	3 24 40
PROPERTIES: Improves your chance to get a critical strike with spells by 2%, Improves your chance to get a critical strike by 1%				

Superior Mail Head Armor

Lvl	Name	Binding	Armor	Vendor Purchase Value
27	Frostreaver Crown	Bind on Equip	182	30 21
28	Sunblaze Coif	Bind on Equip	185	32 1
PROPERTIES: Fire Resist +10				

Superior Mail Head Armor

Lvl	Name	Binding	Armor	Vendor Purchase Value
37	Raging Berserker's Helm	Bind on Pickup	213	68 63
PROPERTIES: Improves your chance to get a critical strike by 1%				
42	High Bergg Helm	Bind on Equip	231	1 5 43
46	Bloomsprout Headpiece	Bind on Pickup	249	1 36 10
PROPERTIES: Nature Resist +10, +36 Attack Power				
47	Braincage	Bind on Equip	253	1 36 69
51	Horns of Eranikus	Bind on Pickup	271	85 97
52	Savage Gladiator Helm	Bind on Pickup	275	1 90 73
53	Fervent Helm	Bind on Pickup	279	2 9 89
PROPERTIES: Restores 7 health per 5 sec				
53	Helm of Exile	Bind on Pickup	266	1 69 80
55	Dragoneye Coif	Bind on Pickup	288	2 23 74
PROPERTIES: +38 Attack Power				
56	Helm of the Great Chief	Bind on Equip	292	2 42 85
57	Beaststalker's Cap	Bind on Pickup	297	2 48 68
57	Coif of Elements	Bind on Pickup	297	2 57 78
58	Champion's Chain Headguard	Bind on Pickup	301	1 31 54
PROPERTIES: +12 Attack Power				
58	Champion's Mail Helm	Bind on Pickup	301	1 25 72
PROPERTIES: Improves your chance to get a critical strike by 1%				
58	Crown of Tyranny	Bind on Pickup	301	2 53 36
PROPERTIES: +40 Attack Power, Improves your chance to get a critical strike by 1%				
58	Lieutenant Commander's Chain Helmet	Bind on Pickup	301	1 29 14
PROPERTIES: +12 Attack Power				
60	Bloodstained Coif	Bind on Pickup	337	3 87 39
PROPERTIES: Improves your chance to get a critical strike by 2%, +28 Attack Power				
60	Champion's Chain Helm	Bind on Pickup	337	1 83 84
PROPERTIES: Improves your chance to get a critical strike by 2%				
60	Champion's Mail Headguard	Bind on Pickup	337	1 94 54
PROPERTIES: Improves your chance to get a critical strike by 1%, Improves your chance to get a critical strike with spells by 1%				
60	Coif of Elemental Fury	Bind on Equip	323	3 19 99
PROPERTIES: Improves your chance to get a critical strike with spells by 1%, Increases damage and healing done by magical spells and effects by up to 20				
60	Lieutenant Commander's Chain Helm	Bind on Pickup	337	1 85 33
PROPERTIES: Improves your chance to get a critical strike by 2%				
60	Backwood Helm	Bind on Pickup	301	2 57 41
PROPERTIES: Improves your chance to get a critical strike by 1%				
60	Helm of Latent Power	Bind on Pickup	297	2 57 96
PROPERTIES: Improves your chance to get a critical strike with spells by 1%, Increases damage and healing done by magical spells and effects by up to 14				

Epic Mail Leg Armor

Lvl	Name	Binding	Armor	Vendor Purchase Price
60	Ancient Corroded Leggings	Bind on Pickup	401	6 80 76
60	Cryptstalker Legguards	Bind on Pickup	484	15 95 99
PROPERTIES: Improves your chance to get a critical strike by 1%, Restores 6 mana per 5 sec				
60	Dragonstalker's Legguards	Bind on Pickup	422	8 59 17
PROPERTIES: Fire Resist +10,Arcane Resist +10, Improves your chance to hit by 1%, Improves your chance to get a critical strike by 1%				
60	Earthfury Legguards	Bind on Pickup	369	5 23 46
PROPERTIES: Shadow Resist +10, Restores 6 mana per 5 sec, Increases damage and healing done by magical spells and effects by up to 12				
60	Earthshatter Legguards	Bind on Pickup	484	15 26 88
PROPERTIES: Increases healing done by spells and effects by up to 59, Restores 9 mana per 5 sec				
60	Emberweave Leggings	Bind on Pickup	417	8 6 59
PROPERTIES: Fire Resist +35				
60	General's Chain Legguards	Bind on Pickup	396	3 46 66
PROPERTIES: Improves your chance to get a critical strike by 1%				
60	General's Mail Leggings	Bind on Pickup	396	3 36 62
PROPERTIES: Increases damage and healing done by magical spells and effects by up to 27, Improves your chance to get a critical strike with spells by 1%, Improves your chance to get a critical strike by 1%				
60	Giantstalker's Leggings	Bind on Pickup	369	5 45 43
PROPERTIES: Shadow Resist +10, Improves your chance to get a critical strike by 1%				
60	Leggings of Elemental Fury	Bind on Pickup	468	12 85 29
PROPERTIES: Increases damage and healing done by magical spells and effects by up to 32, Improves your chance to get a critical strike with spells by 2%				
60	Leggings of the Demented Mind	Bind on Pickup	401	7 2 20
PROPERTIES: Increases healing done by spells and effects by up to 40				
60	Legplates of Ten Storms	Bind on Pickup	422	9 7 73
PROPERTIES: Fire Resist +10,Arcane Resist +10, Improves your chance to get a critical strike with spells by 1%, Increases damage and healing done by magical spells and effects by up to 29				
60	Marshal's Chain Legguards	Bind on Pickup	396	3 37 88
PROPERTIES: Improves your chance to get a critical strike by 1%				
60	Onyx Embedded Leggings	Bind on Pickup	427	9 23 11
PROPERTIES: Shadow Resist +30				
60	Outrider's Chain Leggings	Bind on Pickup	364	5
PROPERTIES: Improves your chance to get a critical strike by 1%, Improves your chance to hit by 1%				
60	Outrider's Mail Leggings	Bind on Pickup	364	5 6 50
PROPERTIES: Improves your chance to get a critical strike by 1%, Improves your chance to get a critical strike with spells by 1%, Restores 6 mana per 5 sec				
60	Primalist's Linked Legguards	Bind on Pickup	417	8 31 16
PROPERTIES: Improves your chance to get a critical strike with spells by 2%, Improves your chance to hit with spells by 1%				
60	Scaled Leggings of Qiraji Fury	Bind on Pickup	422	8 31 11
PROPERTIES: Increases damage and healing done by magical spells and effects by up to 36, Improves your chance to get a critical strike with spells by 1%				
60	Scaled Sand Reaver Leggings	Bind on Pickup	427	8 82 79
PROPERTIES: +62 Attack Power, Improves your chance to get a critical strike by 2%				
60	Sentinel's Chain Leggings	Bind on Pickup	364	4 84 41
PROPERTIES: Improves your chance to get a critical strike by 1%, Improves your chance to hit by 1%				
60	Slime-coated Leggings	Bind on Pickup	432	9 79 99
PROPERTIES: Nature Resist +28, Increases damage and healing done by magical spells and effects by up to 11, +40 Attack Power				
60	Stormcaller's Leggings	Bind on Pickup	448	10 84 79
PROPERTIES: Increases damage and healing done by magical spells and effects by up to 29, Improves your chance to get a critical strike with spells by 1%, Restores 4 mana per 5 sec				
60	Striker's Leggings	Bind on Pickup	448	10 56 30
PROPERTIES: Improves your chance to get a critical strike by 1%, Increases damage and healing done by magical spells and effects by up to 9				
60	Icy Scale Leggings	Bind on Pickup	443	11 4 9
PROPERTIES: Frost Resist +40				
60	Legguards of the Chromatic Defier	Bind on Pickup	349	4 54 82
PROPERTIES: Fire Resist +5, Nature Resist +5, Frost Resist +5, Shadow Resist +5, Arcane Resist +5				
60	Legplates of the Chromatic Defier	Bind on Pickup	349	4 25 65
PROPERTIES: Fire Resist +5, Nature Resist +5, Frost Resist +5, Shadow Resist +5, Arcane Resist +5				

Superior Mail Leg Armor

Lvl	Name	Binding	Armor	Vendor Purchase Value
21	Dreamsinger Legguards	Bind on Equip	179	22 41
22	Chausses of Westfall	Bind on Pickup	173	17 27
34	Firemane Leggings	Bind on Equip	218	76 21
PROPERTIES: Fire Resist +10				
34	Legguards of the Vault	Bind on Equip	218	73 19
35	Dual Reinforced Leggings	Bind on Pickup	211	63 44
PROPERTIES: , Increased Defense +5				
38	Scarlet Leggings	Bind on Pickup	233	95 87
45	Infernal Trickster Leggings	Bind on Pickup	263	1 73 94
PROPERTIES: Increased Bows +4				
48	Searingscale Leggings	Bind on Pickup	277	2 1 41
PROPERTIES: Fire Resist +10				
49	Green Dragonscale Leggings	Bind on Equip	282	2 24 82
PROPERTIES: Nature Resist +11				
51	Windrunner Legguards	Bind on Equip	291	2 50 65
52	Savage Gladiator Leggings	Bind on Pickup	296	2 53 36
53	Woollies of the Prancing Minstrel	Bind on Pickup	301	2 68 64
PROPERTIES: Restores 10 mana per 5 sec				

Superior Mail Leg Armor

Lvl	Name	Binding	Armor	Vendor Purchase Value
55	Blue Dragonscale Leggings	Bind on Equip	310	3g 10s 83c
PROPERTIES: Arcane Resist +12				
56	Beaststalker's Pants	Bind on Pickup	315	3g 16s 94c
56	Bloodmail Legguards	Bind on Pickup	315	3g 26s 22c
56	Kilt of Elements	Bind on Pickup	315	3g 5s 41c
57	Abyssal Mail Legguards	Bind on Equip	320	3g 35s 36c
PROPERTIES: Improves your chance to get a critical strike by 1%				
57	Black Dragonscale Leggings	Bind on Equip	320	3g 19s 33c
PROPERTIES: Fire Resist +13, +54 Attack Power				
57	Maelstrom Leggings	Bind on Pickup	320	3g 13s 18c
PROPERTIES: Increases healing done by spells and effects by up to 13				
57	Silvermoon Leggings	Bind on Pickup	320	3g 13s 84c
PROPERTIES: Increases damage and healing done by magical spells and effects by up to 18				
58	Knight-Captain's Chain Leggings	Bind on Pickup	324	1g 66s 35c
PROPERTIES: Improves your chance to get a critical strike by 1%, Increases your chance to dodge an attack by 1%				
58	Leggings of Destruction	Bind on Pickup	324	3g 55s 96c
PROPERTIES: Improves your chance to get a critical strike by 1%				
58	Legionnaire's Chain Leggings	Bind on Pickup	324	1g 76s 3c
PROPERTIES: Improves your chance to get a critical strike by 1%, Increases your chance to dodge an attack by 1%				
58	Legionnaire's Mail Leggings	Bind on Pickup	324	1g 73s 49c
PROPERTIES: Increases damage and healing done by magical spells and effects by up to 25				
58	Tristam Legguards	Bind on Pickup	324	3g 33s 88c
PROPERTIES: +34 Attack Power, Increases your chance to dodge an attack by 2%				
60	Bloodstained Legplates	Bind on Pickup	363	5g 1s 47c
PROPERTIES: Improves your chance to get a critical strike by 1%				
60	Knight-Captain's Chain Legguards	Bind on Pickup	348	2g 19s 15c
PROPERTIES: Improves your chance to get a critical strike by 2%				
60	Legionnaire's Chain Legguards	Bind on Pickup	348	2g 14s 23c
PROPERTIES: Improves your chance to get a critical strike by 2%				
60	Legionnaire's Mail Legguards	Bind on Pickup	348	2g 23s 95c
PROPERTIES: Increases damage and healing done by magical spells and effects by up to 21, Improves your chance to get a critical strike with spells by 1%				
60	Obsidian Scaled Leggings	Bind on Pickup	377	6g 11s 36c
PROPERTIES: Increases damage and healing done by magical spells and effects by up to 19				
60	Seafury Leggings	Bind on Pickup	348	4g 23s 31c
PROPERTIES: Increases damage and healing done by magical spells and effects by up to 16				
60	Beastmaster's Pants	Bind on Pickup	339	3g 97s 35c
60	Cenarion Reservist's Legguards	Bind on Pickup	324	3g 43s 14c
PROPERTIES: Nature Resist +25				
60	Cenarion Reservist's Legguards	Bind on Pickup	324	3g 53s 58c
PROPERTIES: Nature Resist +25				
60	Kilt of The Five Thunders	Bind on Pickup	339	3g 82s 71c
PROPERTIES: Increases damage and healing done by magical spells and effects by up to 11				
60	Leggings of the Plague Hunter	Bind on Pickup	339	3g 81s 47c
PROPERTIES: Improves your chance to get a critical strike by 1%				

Epic Mail Shoulder Armor

Lvl	Name	Binding	Armor	Vendor Purchase Value
57	Fiery Chain Shoulders	Bind on Equip	299	3g 14s 60c
PROPERTIES: Fire Resist +25				
60	Barrage Shoulders	Bind on Pickup	348	5g 78s 56c
60	Black Brood Pauldrons	Bind on Pickup	357	6g 53s 75c
PROPERTIES: Restores 9 mana per 5 sec				
60	Cryptstalker Spaulders	Bind on Pickup	406	10g 19s 97c
PROPERTIES: Improves your chance to get a critical strike by 1%				
60	Deep Earth Spaulders	Bind on Pickup	339	4g 88s 36c
PROPERTIES: Increases damage done by Nature spells and effects by up to 40				
60	Defiler's Chain Pauldrons	Bind on Pickup	312	3g 92s 93c
60	Defiler's Mail Pauldrons	Bind on Pickup	312	3g 99s 85c
PROPERTIES: Restores 4 mana per 5 sec				
60	Dragonstalker's Spaulders	Bind on Pickup	362	6g 44s 82c
PROPERTIES: Fire Resist +10, Improves your chance to hit by 1%				

Epic Mail Shoulder Armor

Lvl	Name	Binding	Armor	Vendor Purchase Value
60	Earthfury Epaulets	Bind on Pickup	317	3g 95s 82c
PROPERTIES: Shadow Resist +7, Restores 4 mana per 5 sec, Increases healing done by spells and effects by up to 18				
60	Earthshatter Spaulders	Bind on Pickup	406	10g 51s 9c
PROPERTIES: Increases healing done by spells and effects by up to 42, Restores 6 mana per 5 sec				
60	Epaulets of Ten Storms	Bind on Pickup	362	6g 81s 40c
PROPERTIES: Fire Resist +10, Improves your chance to get a critical strike with spells by 1%				
60	Field Marshal's Chain Spaulders	Bind on Pickup	353	2g 95s 76c
PROPERTIES: Improves your chance to hit by 1%				
60	Giantstalker's Epaulets	Bind on Pickup	317	4g 12s 37c
PROPERTIES: Shadow Resist +7, Improves your chance to hit by 1%				
60	Highlander's Chain Pauldrons	Bind on Pickup	312	3g 68s 67c
60	Highlander's Mail Pauldrons	Bind on Pickup	312	3g 70s 9c
PROPERTIES: Restores 4 mana per 5 sec				
60	Mantle of the Desert's Fury	Bind on Pickup	362	6g 81s 86c
PROPERTIES: Increases damage and healing done by magical spells and effects by up to 28				
60	Pauldrons of Elemental Fury	Bind on Pickup	401	9g 68s 25c
PROPERTIES: Increases damage and healing done by magical spells and effects by up to 26, Improves your chance to get a critical strike with spells by 1%, Improves your chance to hit with spells by 1%				
60	Runic Stone Shoulders	Bind on Pickup	344	5g 38s 78c
PROPERTIES: Increases damage and healing done by magical spells and effects by up to 14				
60	Stormcaller's Pauldrons	Bind on Pickup	371	7g 8s 61c
PROPERTIES: Increases damage and healing done by magical spells and effects by up to 28, Restores 3 mana per 5 sec				
60	Striker's Pauldrons	Bind on Pickup	384	8g 76s 26c
PROPERTIES: Increases damage and healing done by magical spells and effects by up to 6				
60	Warlord's Chain Shoulders	Bind on Pickup	353	3g 3s 41c
PROPERTIES: Improves your chance to hit by 1%				
60	Warlord's Mail Spaulders	Bind on Pickup	353	2g 94s 66c
PROPERTIES: Increases damage and healing done by magical spells and effects by up to 16				
60	Icy Scale Spaulders	Bind on Pickup	393	9g 59s 26c
PROPERTIES: Frost Resist +33				
60	Zandalar Predator's Mantle	Bind on Pickup	326	
PROPERTIES: Restores 4 mana per 5 sec				

Superior Mail Shoulder Armor

Lvl	Name	Binding	Armor	Vendor Purchase Value
24	Sparkleshell Mantle	Bind on Equip	161	23s 12c
37	Herod's Shoulder	Bind on Pickup	196	68s 67c
38	Skeletal Shoulders	Bind on Equip	199	73s 40c
40	Spaulders of a Lost Age	Bind on Equip	205	85s 53c
50	Dregmetal Spaulders	Bind on Pickup	246	1g 66s 10c
50	Lead Surveyor's Mantle	Bind on Pickup	246	1g 70s 50c
PROPERTIES: Increases damage and healing done by magical spells and effects by up to 15				
51	Golem Fitted Pauldrons	Bind on Pickup	250	1g 73s 11c
53	Demonheart Spaulders	Bind on Pickup	258	2g 11s 57c
54	Blue Dragonscale Shoulders	Bind on Equip	262	2g 5s 43c
PROPERTIES: Arcane Resist +6				
55	Beaststalker's Mantle	Bind on Pickup	266	2g 28s 22c
55	Black Dragonscale Shoulders	Bind on Equip	266	2g 17s 36c
PROPERTIES: Fire Resist +6, +40 Attack Power				
55	Denwatcher's Shoulders	Bind on Pickup	266	2g 14s 44c
PROPERTIES: Increases damage and healing done by magical spells and effects by up to 18				
55	Pauldrons of Elements	Bind on Pickup	266	2g 19s 95c
55	Stratholme Militia Shoulderguard	Bind on Equip	266	2g 25s 3c
56	Drakesfire Epaulets	Bind on Equip	270	2g 30s 83c
PROPERTIES: Fire Resist +10				
57	Bone Golem Shoulders	Bind on Pickup	274	2g 45s 27c
57	Royal Cap Spaulders	Bind on Pickup	274	2g 47s 92c
PROPERTIES: Increases healing done by spells and effects by up to 26				
58	Bonespike Shoulder	Bind on Pickup	278	2g 54s 46c
PROPERTIES: Deals 60 to 90 damage when you are the victim of a critical melee strike				

Superior Mail Shoulder Armor

Lvl	Name	Binding	Armor	Vendor Purchase Value
58	Champion's Chain Pauldrons	Bind on Pickup	278	1 33 9
PROPERTIES: +12 Attack Power				
58	Champion's Mail Shoulders	Bind on Pickup	278	1 31 17
PROPERTIES: Increases damage and healing done by magical spells and effects by up to 6				
58	Lieutenant Commander's Chain Pauldrons	Bind on Pickup	278	1 29 23
PROPERTIES: +12 Attack Power				
60	Abyssal Mail Pauldrons	Bind on Pickup	298	3 16 83
PROPERTIES: Improves your chance to hit by 1%				
60	Bloodsoul Shoulders	Bind on Equip	286	3
60	Champion's Chain Shoulders	Bind on Pickup	311	1 85 36
PROPERTIES: Improves your chance to get a critical strike by 1%				
60	Champion's Mail Pauldrons	Bind on Pickup	311	1 96 11
PROPERTIES: Increases damage and healing done by magical spells and effects by up to 15, Improves your chance to get a critical strike with spells by 1%				
60	Lieutenant Commander's Chain Shoulders	Bind on Pickup	311	1 86 84
PROPERTIES: Improves your chance to get a critical strike by 1%				
60	Beastmaster's Mantle	Bind on Pickup	286	2 84 2
60	Pauldrons of The Five Thunders	Bind on Pickup	286	2 75 64
PROPERTIES: Increases damage and healing done by magical spells and effects by up to 12				

Epic Mail Waist Armor

Lvl	Name	Binding	Armor	Vendor Purchase Value
54	Fiery Chain Girdle	Bind on Equip	214	1 86 10
PROPERTIES: Fire Resist +24				
60	Belt of Ten Storms	Bind on Pickup	271	4 50 65
PROPERTIES: Shadow Resist +10, Improves your chance to get a critical strike with spells by 1%, Increases healing done by spells and effects by up to 26				
60	Cryptstalker Girdle	Bind on Pickup	311	7 54 94
PROPERTIES: Improves your chance to hit by 1%, Improves your chance to get a critical strike by 1%, Restores 3 mana per 5 sec				
60	Dragonstalker's Belt	Bind on Pickup	271	4 26 37
PROPERTIES: Shadow Resist +10, Improves your chance to get a critical strike by 1%				
60	Earthfury Belt	Bind on Equip	237	2 56 82
PROPERTIES: Fire Resist +7, Restores 4 mana per 5 sec, Increases healing done by spells and effects by up to 18				
60	Earthshatter Girdle	Bind on Pickup	311	7 98 46
PROPERTIES: Restores 7 mana per 5 sec, Increases healing done by spells and effects by up to 42				
60	Giantstalker's Belt	Bind on Equip	237	2 76 63
PROPERTIES: Fire Resist +7, Improves your chance to get a critical strike by 1%				
60	Girdle of Elemental Fury	Bind on Pickup	301	6 42 64
PROPERTIES: Increases damage and healing done by magical spells and effects by up to 29, Restores 5 mana per 5 sec				
60	Grasp of the Fallen Emperor	Bind on Pickup	288	5 69 33
PROPERTIES: Increases damage and healing done by magical spells and effects by up to 19, Restores 5 mana per 5 sec				
60	Ossirian's Binding	Bind on Pickup	258	3 43 13
PROPERTIES: Improves your chance to get a critical strike by 1%, Improves your chance to hit by 1%				
60	Primalist's Linked Waistguard	Bind on Pickup	275	4 78 33
PROPERTIES: Increases damage and healing done by magical spells and effects by up to 20				
60	Therazane's Link	Bind on Pickup	295	5 95 61
PROPERTIES: +44 Attack Power, Improves your chance to get a critical strike by 1%				
60	Zandalar Augur's Belt	Bind on Pickup	221	
PROPERTIES: Increases damage and healing done by magical spells and effects by up to 12, Restores 4 mana per 5 sec				
60	Zandalar Predator's Belt	Bind on Pickup	221	
PROPERTIES: Improves your chance to hit by 1%				

Superior Mail Waist Armor

Lvl	Name	Binding	Armor	Vendor Purchase Value
15	Stormbringer Belt	Bind on Equip	104	5 34
19	Cobrahn's Grasp	Bind on Pickup	111	8 44
28	Defiler's Lamellar Girdle	Bind on Pickup	128	22 10
28	Defiler's Plate Girdle	Bind on Pickup	128	21 22
28	Girdle of Golem Strength	Bind on Equip	128	20 55
PROPERTIES: Increased Defense +3				

Superior Mail Waist Armor

Lvl	Name	Binding	Armor	Vendor Purchase Value
28	Highlander's Lamellar Girdle	Bind on Pickup	128	20 75
28	Highlander's Plate Girdle	Bind on Pickup	128	20 58
34	Stonefist Girdle	Bind on Pickup	134	28 30
37	Boar Champion's Belt	Bind on Pickup	147	45 41
40	Defiler's Chain Girdle	Bind on Pickup	149	49 11
PROPERTIES: Improves your chance to get a critical strike by 1%, +8 Attack Power				
40	Defiler's Mail Girdle	Bind on Pickup	149	51 34
40	Highlander's Chain Girdle	Bind on Pickup	149	52 8
PROPERTIES: Improves your chance to get a critical strike by 1%, +8 Attack Power				
40	Highlander's Mail Girdle	Bind on Pickup	149	50 22
44	Belt of the Gladiator	Bind on Equip	166	77 16
48	Defiler's Chain Girdle	Bind on Pickup	178	98 58
PROPERTIES: Improves your chance to get a critical strike by 1%, +20 Attack Power				
48	Defiler's Mail Girdle	Bind on Pickup	178	1 3 9
PROPERTIES: Improves your chance to get a critical strike with spells by 1%				
48	Highlander's Chain Girdle	Bind on Pickup	178	1 4 95
PROPERTIES: Improves your chance to get a critical strike by 1%, +20 Attack Power				
48	Highlander's Mail Girdle	Bind on Pickup	178	1 1 21
PROPERTIES: Improves your chance to get a critical strike with spells by 1%				
51	Verek's Leash	Bind on Pickup	187	1 14 89
PROPERTIES: Increases damage and healing done by magical spells and effects by up to 11				
52	Chillsteel Girdle	Bind on Pickup	190	1 27 67
PROPERTIES: Frost Resist +10				
53	Beaststalker's Belt	Bind on Equip	193	1 37 88
53	Cord of Elements	Bind on Equip	193	1 34 40
53	Heavy Timbermaw Belt	Bind on Equip	193	1 32 91
PROPERTIES: +42 Attack Power				
55	Chiselbrand Girdle	Bind on Pickup	199	1 53 10
PROPERTIES: +44 Attack Power				
55	Frostwolf Mail Belt	Bind on Pickup	199	1 53 19
PROPERTIES: Frost Resist +5				
55	Sash of the Grand Hunt	Bind on Pickup	199	1 42 33
PROPERTIES: Increased Bows +2, Increased Guns +2, Increased Crossbows +2				
55	Stormpike Mail Girdle	Bind on Pickup	199	1 42 33
PROPERTIES: Frost Resist +5				
56	Barrage Girdle	Bind on Pickup	202	1 49 44
PROPERTIES: Increases damage and healing done by magical spells and effects by up to 23				
56	Bloodmail Belt	Bind on Pickup	202	1 64 27
56	Foresight Girdle	Bind on Pickup	202	1 57 79
PROPERTIES: Restores 5 health per 5 sec				
56	Marksman's Girdle	Bind on Pickup	202	1 49 33
PROPERTIES: Improves your chance to hit by 1%				
56	Sash of the Windreaver	Bind on Equip	202	1 60 80
PROPERTIES: Increases damage done by Nature spells and effects by up to 29				
56	Warpwood Binding	Bind on Pickup	202	1 49 44
PROPERTIES: Improves your chance to get a critical strike by 1%				
57	Detention Strap	Bind on Pickup	205	1 64 47
58	Defiler's Chain Girdle	Bind on Pickup	208	1 67 75
PROPERTIES: Improves your chance to get a critical strike by 1%, +34 Attack Power				
58	Defiler's Mail Girdle	Bind on Pickup	208	1 75 45
PROPERTIES: Improves your chance to get a critical strike with spells by 1%				
58	Feralsurge Girdle	Bind on Pickup	208	1 72 85
PROPERTIES: , Restores 8 mana per 5 sec				
58	Highlander's Chain Girdle	Bind on Pickup	208	1 76 13
PROPERTIES: Improves your chance to get a critical strike by 1%, +34 Attack Power				
58	Highlander's Mail Girdle	Bind on Pickup	208	1 76 77
PROPERTIES: Improves your chance to get a critical strike with spells by 1%				
60	Light Obsidian Belt	Bind on Equip	224	2 28 85
PROPERTIES: +32 Attack Power, Improves your chance to get a critical strike by 1%, +5 All Resistances				
60	Beastmaster's Belt	Bind on Pickup	214	1 84 32
60	Belt of Shriveled Heads	Bind on Pickup	230	2 46 84

Superior Mail Waist Armor

Lvl	Name	Binding	Armor	Vendor Purchase Value
60	Cord of The Five Thunders	Bind on Pickup	214	1 94 85
PROPERTIES: Increases damage and healing done by magical spells and effects by up to 12, Restores 4 mana per 5 sec				

Epic Mail Wrist Armor

Lvl	Name	Binding	Armor	Vendor Purchase Value
40	Windtalker's Wristguards	Bind on Pickup	130	74 18
PROPERTIES: +28 Attack Power				
50	Windtalker's Wristguards	Bind on Pickup	156	1 44 52
PROPERTIES: +34 Attack Power				
60	Bracers of Ten Storms	Bind on Pickup	211	4 49 4
PROPERTIES: Restores 6 mana per 5 sec				
60	Cryptstalker Wristguards	Bind on Pickup	242	7 57 82
PROPERTIES: Improves your chance to hit by 1%				
60	Dragonstalker's Bracers	Bind on Pickup	211	4 24 81
60	Earthfury Bracers	Bind on Equip	185	2 58 79
PROPERTIES: Increases damage and healing done by magical spells and effects by up to 6				
60	Earthshatter Wristguards	Bind on Pickup	242	8 1 27
PROPERTIES: Increases healing done by spells and effects by up to 33, Restores 4 mana per 5 sec				
60	Giantstalker's Bracers	Bind on Equip	185	2 75 64
60	Icy Scale Bracers	Bind on Equip	221	5 5 16
PROPERTIES: Frost Resist +20, +32 Attack Power				
60	Windtalker's Wristguards	Bind on Pickup	182	2 42 20
PROPERTIES: +38 Attack Power				
60	Wristguards of True Flight	Bind on Pickup	198	3 24 58
PROPERTIES: Improves your chance to hit by 1%				
60	Zandalar Augur's Bracers	Bind on Pickup	172	
PROPERTIES: Increases damage and healing done by magical spells and effects by up to 13, Restores 4 mana per 5 sec				
60	Zandalar Predator's Bracers	Bind on Pickup	172	
PROPERTIES: +34 ranged Attack Power, Restores 4 mana per 5 sec				

Superior Mail Wrist Armor

Lvl	Name	Binding	Armor	Vendor Purchase Value
21	Jimmied Handcuffs	Bind on Pickup	89	10 98
22	Yorgen Bracers	Bind on Equip	91	12 41
25	Pugilist Bracers	Bind on Equip	95	16 92
36	Crushridge Bindings	Bind on Equip	113	43 98
37	Ironaya's Bracers	Bind on Pickup	115	44 90
44	Slimescale Bracers	Bind on Equip	129	76 24
45	Arena Bands	Bind on Equip	131	87
PROPERTIES: +28 Attack Power				
45	First Sergeant's Mail Wristguards	Bind on Pickup	131	43 48
45	Sergeant Major's Chain Armguards	Bind on Pickup	131	43 1
49	Bracers of the Stone Princess	Bind on Pickup	141	1 2 25
PROPERTIES: +30 Attack Power				
50	Rubicund Armguards	Bind on Pickup	143	1 17 38
51	Marksman Bands	Bind on Equip	146	1 23 22
PROPERTIES: Increased Bows +2, Increased Crossbows +2, Increased Guns +2				
52	Beaststalker's Bindings	Bind on Equip	148	1 30 55
52	Bindings of Elements	Bind on Equip	148	1 25 86
52	Pyremail Wristguards	Bind on Pickup	148	1 25 25
PROPERTIES: Fire Resist +10				
54	Lordly Armguards	Bind on Equip	153	1 40 1
55	Brazecore Armguards	Bind on Pickup	155	1 49 16
PROPERTIES: Restores 3 mana per 5 sec				
55	Slashclaw Bracers	Bind on Pickup	155	1 44 74
PROPERTIES: Improves your chance to hit by 1%				
56	Loomguard Armbraces	Bind on Pickup	157	1 60 19
PROPERTIES: Increases healing done by spells and effects by up to 33				

Superior Mail Wrist Armor

Lvl	Name	Binding	Armor	Vendor Purchase Value
57	Demon Howl Wristguards	Bind on Pickup	160	1 71 33
PROPERTIES: +14 Attack Power				
57	Sandstalker Bracers	Bind on Equip	160	1 64 1
PROPERTIES: Nature Resist +15				
57	Spitfire Bracers	Bind on Equip	160	1 71 39
PROPERTIES: Restores 4 mana per 5 sec, Increases damage and healing done by magical spells and effects by up to 8				
57	Swift Flight Bracers	Bind on Equip	160	1 71 94
PROPERTIES: +41 ranged Attack Power				
58	First Sergeant's Mail Wristguards	Bind on Pickup	162	89 60
58	Sergeant Major's Chain Armguards	Bind on Pickup	162	88 1
58	Wristguards of Undead Slaying	Bind on Equip	162	1 64 76
PROPERTIES: +45 Attack Power when fighting Undead				
60	Abyssal Mail Armguards	Bind on Pickup	174	2 10 28
60	Sand Reaver Wristguards	Bind on Pickup	181	2 44 9
60	Beastmaster's Bindings	Bind on Pickup	167	1 85
60	Bindings of The Five Thunders	Bind on Pickup	167	1 92 75
PROPERTIES: Increases damage and healing done by magical spells and effects by up to 8				

PLATE

Epic Plate Chest Armor

Lvl	Name	Binding	Armor	Vendor Purchase Value
60	Avenger's Breastplate	Bind on Pickup	985	9 94 63
PROPERTIES: Increases damage and healing done by magical spells and effects by up to 18, Improves your chance to get a critical strike with spells by 1%, Improves your chance to get a critical strike by 1%				
60	Breastplate of Annihilation	Bind on Pickup	824	5 15 70
PROPERTIES: Improves your chance to get a critical strike by 1%, Improves your chance to hit by 1%				
60	Breastplate of Might	Bind on Pickup	749	3 60 95
PROPERTIES: Fire Resist +10, Increases your chance to block attacks with a shield by 3%, Increased Defense +7				
60	Breastplate of Wrath	Bind on Pickup	857	6 5 3
PROPERTIES: Fire Resist +10, Nature Resist +10, Increased Defense +11				
60	Conqueror's Breastplate	Bind on Pickup	985	10 2 63
PROPERTIES: Increased Defense +6				
60	Dreadnaught Breastplate	Bind on Pickup	1027	12 88 87
PROPERTIES: Increased Defense +13, Increases your chance to dodge an attack by 1%, Improves your chance to hit by 2%				
60	Field Marshal's Lamellar Chestplate	Bind on Pickup	835	2 66 54
PROPERTIES: Improves your chance to get a critical strike by 1%, Increases damage and healing done by magical spells and effects by up to 25, Restores 5 mana per 5 sec				
60	Field Marshal's Plate Armor	Bind on Pickup	835	2 51 7
PROPERTIES: Improves your chance to get a critical strike by 1%				
60	Icebane Breastplate	Bind on Equip	899	6 83 90
PROPERTIES: Frost Resist +42, Increased Defense +8				
60	Judgement Breastplate	Bind on Pickup	857	5 88 1
PROPERTIES: Fire Resist +10, Nature Resist +10, Restores 5 mana per 5 sec, Increases damage and healing done by magical spells and effects by up to 25				
60	Lawbringer Chestguard	Bind on Pickup	749	3 71 44
PROPERTIES: Fire Resist +10, Increases healing done by spells and effects by up to 22				
60	Plated Abomination Ribcage	Bind on Pickup	953	9 12 56
PROPERTIES: Improves your chance to get a critical strike by 1%, Improves your chance to hit by 1%				
60	Redemption Tunic	Bind on Pickup	1027	12 37 67
PROPERTIES: Increases healing done by spells and effects by up to 59, Improves your chance to get a critical strike with spells by 1%, Restores 10 mana per 5 sec				
60	Silithid Carapace Chestguard	Bind on Pickup	867	5 90 78
PROPERTIES: Nature Resist +35				
60	Thick Obsidian Breastplate	Bind on Equip	814	4 96 24
PROPERTIES: When struck by a non-periodic damage spell you have a 30% chance of getting a 6 sec spell shield that absorbs 300 to 500 of that school of damage				
60	Warlord's Plate Armor	Bind on Pickup	835	2 61 78
PROPERTIES: Improves your chance to get a critical strike by 1%				
60	Breastplate of Heroism	Bind on Pickup	684	2 63 59
PROPERTIES: Improves your chance to hit by 1%				

Epic Plate Chest Armor

Lvl	Name	Binding	Armor	Vendor Purchase Value
60	Breastplate of the Chromatic Flight	Bind on Pickup	706	2 94 61
PROPERTIES: Fire Resist +15				
60	Soulforge Breastplate	Bind on Pickup	684	2 62 66
PROPERTIES: Increases damage and healing done by magical spells and effects by up to 14, Improves your chance to get a critical strike by 1%				
60	Zandalar Freethinker's Breastplate	Bind on Pickup	738	
PROPERTIES: Improves your chance to get a critical strike by 1%				
60	Zandalar Vindicator's Breastplate	Bind on Pickup	738	
PROPERTIES: Increased Defense +4				

Superior Plate Chest Armor

Lvl	Name	Binding	Armor	Vendor Purchase Value
40	Carapace of Tuten'kash	Bind on Pickup	373	63 77
44	Truesilver Breastplate	Bind on Equip	519	1 8 99
PROPERTIES: When struck in combat has a 3% chance to heal you for 60 to 100				
49	Hydralick Armor	Bind on Equip	567	1 43 41
PROPERTIES: Fire Resist +10				
49	Spiderfang Carapace	Bind on Pickup	567	1 40 76
PROPERTIES: Increases damage and healing done by magical spells and effects by up to 13				
49	Warrior's Embrace	Bind on Pickup	567	1 42 33
PROPERTIES: Increases your chance to dodge an attack by 2%				
50	Carapace of Anub'shiah	Bind on Pickup	577	1 55 96
52	Demon Forged Breastplate	Bind on Equip	597	1 66 40
PROPERTIES: When struck has a 3% chance of stealing 120 life from the attacker over 4 sec.\n				
54	Dark Iron Plate	Bind on Pickup	617	1 94 28
PROPERTIES: Fire Resist +19				
54	Energized Chestplate	Bind on Pickup	617	1 80 73
PROPERTIES: Restores 5 mana per 5 sec				
54	Skul's Cold Embrace	Bind on Pickup	617	1 81 76
PROPERTIES: Frost Resist +10, Increased Defense +6				
55	Plate of the Shaman King	Bind on Pickup	627	1 90 85
PROPERTIES: Increases damage and healing done by magical spells and effects by up to 18				
56	Deathbone Chestplate	Bind on Pickup	637	2 5 78
PROPERTIES: Increased Defense +17, Restores 5 mana per 5 sec				
57	Kromcrush's Chestplate	Bind on Pickup	647	2 25 21
PROPERTIES: Increased Defense +10				
58	Breastplate of Undead Slaying	Bind on Pickup	657	2 28 92
PROPERTIES: +81 Attack Power when fighting Undead				
58	Breastplate of Valor	Bind on Pickup	657	2 26 9
58	Darkrune Breastplate	Bind on Equip	657	2 30 51
PROPERTIES: Shadow Resist +25, Increases your chance to dodge an attack by 1%				
58	Enchanted Thorium Breastplate	Bind on Equip	657	2 39 72
PROPERTIES: Increased Defense +9				
58	Knight-Captain's Lamellar Breastplate	Bind on Pickup	657	1 16 91
PROPERTIES: Improves your chance to get a critical strike by 1%				
58	Knight-Captain's Plate Chestguard	Bind on Pickup	657	1 15 64
PROPERTIES: Improves your chance to get a critical strike by 1%				
58	Legionnaire's Plate Armor	Bind on Pickup	657	1 19 91
PROPERTIES: Improves your chance to get a critical strike by 1%				
58	Lightforge Breastplate	Bind on Pickup	657	2 22 70
60	Darksoul Breastplate	Bind on Equip	676	2 41 92
PROPERTIES: Improves your chance to hit by 1%				
60	Ironvine Breastplate	Bind on Equip	726	3 14 92
PROPERTIES: Nature Resist +30, Increased Defense +7				
60	Knight-Captain's Lamellar Breastplate	Bind on Pickup	706	1 41 69
PROPERTIES: Increases damage and healing done by magical spells and effects by up to 25				
60	Knight-Captain's Plate Hauberk	Bind on Pickup	706	1 49 87
PROPERTIES: Improves your chance to get a critical strike by 1%				
60	Legionnaire's Plate Hauberk	Bind on Pickup	706	1 41 20
PROPERTIES: Improves your chance to get a critical strike by 1%				
60	Ornate Adamantium Breastplate	Bind on Pickup	657	2 25 19
PROPERTIES: Increased Defense +10				

Epic Plate Foot Armor

Lvl	Name	Binding	Armor	Vendor Purchase Value
40	Boots of Avoidance	Bind on Equip	360	78 7
PROPERTIES: Increases your chance to dodge an attack by 2%				
60	Acid Inscribed Greaves	Bind on Pickup	559	3 42 98
PROPERTIES: Nature Resist +25, Increased Defense +6				
60	Avenger's Greaves	Bind on Pickup	604	4 56 19
PROPERTIES: Increases damage and healing done by magical spells and effects by up to 14, Restores 4 mana per 5 sec				
60	Boots of the Fallen Hero	Bind on Pickup	581	3 95 68
PROPERTIES: Improves your chance to hit by 1%				
60	Boots of the Redeemed Prophecy	Bind on Pickup	567	3 90 90
PROPERTIES: Increases healing done by spells and effects by up to 33				
60	Boots of the Unwavering Will	Bind on Pickup	567	3 93 64
PROPERTIES: Increased Defense +5				
60	Chromatic Boots	Bind on Pickup	596	4 68 26
PROPERTIES: Improves your chance to hit by 1%				
60	Conqueror's Greaves	Bind on Pickup	604	4 65 19
PROPERTIES: Increased Defense +4				
60	Core Forged Greaves	Bind on Pickup	544	3 37 61
PROPERTIES: Fire Resist +12, Shadow Resist +8, Increased Defense +4				
60	Dark Iron Boots	Bind on Equip	544	3 17 9
PROPERTIES: Fire Resist +28				
60	Dreadnaught Sabatons	Bind on Pickup	662	7 31 73
PROPERTIES: Increased Defense +9, Increases your chance to dodge an attack by 1%				
60	General's Plate Boots	Bind on Pickup	552	1 72 10
PROPERTIES: Improves your chance to hit by 1%				
60	Judgement Sabatons	Bind on Pickup	589	4 39 44
PROPERTIES: Fire Resist +10, Increases damage and healing done by magical spells and effects by up to 18				
60	Lawbringer Boots	Bind on Pickup	515	2 57 78
PROPERTIES: Shadow Resist +7, Restores 2 mana per 5 sec, Increases healing done by spells and effects by up to 18				
60	Magma Tempered Boots	Bind on Pickup	544	3 35 18
PROPERTIES: Fire Resist +8, Increases healing done by spells and effects by up to 18				
60	Marshal's Lamellar Boots	Bind on Pickup	552	1 72 5
PROPERTIES: Increases damage and healing done by magical spells and effects by up to 18, Restores 6 mana per 5 sec				
60	Marshal's Plate Boots	Bind on Pickup	552	1 66 42
PROPERTIES: Improves your chance to hit by 1%				
60	Redemption Boots	Bind on Pickup	662	7 5 62
PROPERTIES: Increases healing done by spells and effects by up to 42, Improves your chance to get a critical strike with spells by 1%, Restores 5 mana per 5 sec				
60	Sabatons of Might	Bind on Pickup	515	2 67 78
PROPERTIES: Shadow Resist +7, Increased Defense +5				
60	Sabatons of Wrath	Bind on Pickup	589	4 52 21
PROPERTIES: Fire Resist +10, Increases the block value of your shield by 14, Increased Defense +7				
60	Boots of Heroism	Bind on Pickup	470	1 96 24
PROPERTIES: Improves your chance to hit by 1%				
60	Soulforge Boots	Bind on Pickup	470	1 95 52
PROPERTIES: Increases damage and healing done by magical spells and effects by up to 12, Restores 4 mana per 5 sec				

Superior Plate Foot Armor

Lvl	Name	Binding	Armor	Vendor Purchase Value
40	Defiler's Lamellar Greaves	Bind on Pickup	289	52 27
PROPERTIES: Run speed increased slightly				
40	Defiler's Plate Greaves	Bind on Pickup	289	49 68
PROPERTIES: Run speed increased slightly				
40	Highlander's Lamellar Greaves	Bind on Pickup	289	48 57
PROPERTIES: Run speed increased slightly				
40	Highlander's Plate Greaves	Bind on Pickup	289	48 20
PROPERTIES: Run speed increased slightly				
40	Obsidian Greaves	Bind on Equip	257	47 85
48	Defiler's Lamellar Greaves	Bind on Pickup	383	96 32
PROPERTIES: Run speed increased slightly				
48	Defiler's Plate Greaves	Bind on Pickup	383	1 1 22
PROPERTIES: Run speed increased slightly				

Equipment
Armor
Weapons

Superior Plate Foot Armor

Lvl	Name	Binding	Armor	Vendor Purchase Value
48	Highlander's Lamellar Greaves	Bind on Pickup	383	97 87
PROPERTIES: Run speed increased slightly				
48	Highlander's Plate Greaves	Bind on Pickup	383	97 11
PROPERTIES: Run speed increased slightly				
50	Battlechaser's Greaves	Bind on Equip	397	1 14 6
50	Entrenching Boots	Bind on Pickup	397	1 18 82
PROPERTIES: Increases damage and healing done by magical spells and effects by up to 7				
53	Sapphiron's Scale Boots	Bind on Equip	417	1 40 87
53	Shalehusk Boots	Bind on Pickup	417	1 37 32
PROPERTIES: Increases your chance to dodge an attack by 2%				
54	Boots of Valor	Bind on Pickup	424	1 45 36
54	Death Knight Sabatons	Bind on Pickup	424	1 43 75
54	Lightforge Boots	Bind on Pickup	424	1 36 88
56	Deathbone Sabatons	Bind on Pickup	438	1 52 61
PROPERTIES: Restores 6 mana per 5 sec, Increased Defense +10				
56	Master Cannoneer Boots	Bind on Pickup	438	1 54 33
56	Ribsteel Footguards	Bind on Pickup	438	1 60 69
57	Corpselight Greaves	Bind on Pickup	445	1 70 1
PROPERTIES: Shadow Resist +10				
58	Blood Guard's Plate Boots	Bind on Pickup	452	88 66
58	Defiler's Lamellar Greaves	Bind on Pickup	452	1 79 27
PROPERTIES: Run speed increased slightly				
58	Defiler's Plate Greaves	Bind on Pickup	452	1 70 98
PROPERTIES: Run speed increased slightly				
58	Grimy Metal Boots	Bind on Pickup	452	1 76 6
PROPERTIES: Increases your chance to dodge an attack by 1%				
58	Highlander's Lamellar Greaves	Bind on Pickup	452	1 79 95
PROPERTIES: Run speed increased slightly				
58	Highlander's Plate Greaves	Bind on Pickup	452	1 79 31
PROPERTIES: Run speed increased slightly				
58	Knight-Lieutenant's Lamellar Sabatons	Bind on Pickup	452	84 13
58	Knight-Lieutenant's Plate Boots	Bind on Pickup	452	82 86
60	Blood Guard's Plate Greaves	Bind on Pickup	472	98 27
60	Bloodsoaked Greaves	Bind on Pickup	486	2 21 42
PROPERTIES: Increased Defense +5				
60	Boots of the Desert Protector	Bind on Pickup	519	2 68 10
PROPERTIES: Restores 4 mana per 5 sec				
60	Knight-Lieutenant's Lamellar Sabatons	Bind on Pickup	472	1
PROPERTIES: Increases damage and healing done by magical spells and effects by up to 15				
60	Knight-Lieutenant's Plate Greaves	Bind on Pickup	472	1 4 54
60	Peacekeeper Boots	Bind on Pickup	486	2 15 71
PROPERTIES: Restores 6 mana per 5 sec, Increases healing done by spells and effects by up to 22				
60	Slime Kickers	Bind on Pickup	519	2 84 87
PROPERTIES: Improves your chance to hit by 1%				
60	Crystal Encrusted Greaves	Bind on Pickup	452	1 64 57
PROPERTIES: Increased Defense +5				
60	Crystal Lined Greaves	Bind on Pickup	452	1 65 21
PROPERTIES: Increases healing done by spells and effects by up to 15				

Epic Plate Hand Armor

Lvl	Name	Binding	Armor	Vendor Purchase Value
57	Stronghold Gauntlets	Bind on Equip	441	1 52 71
PROPERTIES: Immune to Disarm, Increases your chance to parry an attack by 1%, Improves your chance to get a critical strike by 1%				
60	Dark Iron Gauntlets	Bind on Equip	495	2 24 25
PROPERTIES: Fire Resist +28				
60	Dreadnaught Gauntlets	Bind on Pickup	615	5 39 74
PROPERTIES: Increased Defense +9, Increases your chance to block attacks with a shield by 3%, Increases the block value of your shield by 21				
60	Fists of the Unrelenting	Bind on Pickup	629	5 80 39
PROPERTIES: Immune to Disarm, Improves your chance to get a critical strike by 1%, Improves your chance to hit by 1%				

Epic Plate Hand Armor

Lvl	Name	Binding	Armor	Vendor Purchase Value
60	Flameguard Gauntlets	Bind on Pickup	488	2 12 83
PROPERTIES: Improves your chance to get a critical strike by 1%, +54 Attack Power				
60	Gauntlets of Annihilation	Bind on Pickup	615	5 8 91
PROPERTIES: Improves your chance to get a critical strike by 1%, Improves your chance to hit by 1%				
60	Gauntlets of Might	Bind on Pickup	468	1 79 17
PROPERTIES: Fire Resist +7, Improves your chance to hit by 1%, Increased Defense +5				
60	Gauntlets of Steadfast Determination	Bind on Pickup	535	2 83 40
PROPERTIES: Increased Defense +9				
60	Gauntlets of the Immovable	Bind on Pickup	482	2 4 91
PROPERTIES: Increases your chance to parry an attack by 1%, Increased Defense +5				
60	Gauntlets of the Righteous Champion	Bind on Pickup	549	3 23 15
PROPERTIES: Increases damage and healing done by magical spells and effects by up to 16, Improves your chance to get a critical strike by 1%				
60	Gauntlets of the Shining Light	Bind on Pickup	509	2 44 59
PROPERTIES: Increases healing done by spells and effects by up to 22				
60	Gauntlets of Wrath	Bind on Pickup	535	3
PROPERTIES: Shadow Resist +10, Increases your chance to parry an attack by 1%, Increased Defense +7				
60	General's Plate Gauntlets	Bind on Pickup	502	1 15 98
PROPERTIES: Hamstring Rage cost reduced by 3, Improves your chance to get a critical strike by 1%				
60	Gloves of the Redeemed Prophecy	Bind on Pickup	529	2 79 6
PROPERTIES: Increases healing done by spells and effects by up to 37				
60	Gloves of the Swarm	Bind on Pickup	482	1 90 33
PROPERTIES: Increases damage and healing done by magical spells and effects by up to 12				
60	Icebane Gauntlets	Bind on Equip	562	3 43 21
PROPERTIES: Frost Resist +32, Increased Defense +5				
60	Judgement Gauntlets	Bind on Pickup	535	2 84 22
PROPERTIES: Shadow Resist +10, Restores 6 mana per 5 sec, Increases damage and healing done by magical spells and effects by up to 15				
60	Lawbringer Gauntlets	Bind on Pickup	468	1 72 49
PROPERTIES: Fire Resist +7, Increases healing done by spells and effects by up to 18				
60	Marshal's Lamellar Gloves	Bind on Pickup	502	1 14 29
PROPERTIES: Increases the Holy damage bonus of your Judgement of the Crusader by 20, Improves your chance to get a critical strike by 1%				
60	Marshal's Plate Gauntlets	Bind on Pickup	502	1 11 35
PROPERTIES: Hamstring Rage cost reduced by 3, Improves your chance to get a critical strike by 1%				
60	Ooze-ridden Gauntlets	Bind on Pickup	529	2 66 82
PROPERTIES: Nature Resist +25				
60	Peacekeeper Gauntlets	Bind on Pickup	482	1 91 1
PROPERTIES: Increases healing done by spells and effects by up to 59, Restores 4 mana per 5 sec				
60	Redemption Handguards	Bind on Pickup	615	5 10 99
PROPERTIES: Restores 8 mana per 5 sec, Increases healing done by spells and effects by up to 33				
60	Gauntlets of Heroism	Bind on Pickup	393	1
PROPERTIES: Improves your chance to get a critical strike by 1%				
60	Soulforge Gauntlets	Bind on Pickup	393	1
PROPERTIES: Increases damage and healing done by magical spells and effects by up to 11, Improves your chance to get a critical strike by 1%				

Superior Plate Hand Armor

Lvl	Name	Binding	Armor	Vendor Purchase Value
40	Cragfists	Bind on Pickup	300	37 85
PROPERTIES: Increased Defense +5				
40	Plated Fist of Hakoo	Bind on Equip	300	40 61
40	Truesilver Gauntlets	Bind on Equip	300	40 28
43	Vice Grips	Bind on Pickup	318	48 40
PROPERTIES: +14 Attack Power				
51	Fists of Phalanx	Bind on Pickup	367	78 78
53	Fiery Plate Gauntlets	Bind on Equip	379	89 19
PROPERTIES: Fire Resist +10, Adds 4 fire damage to your weapon attack				
54	Gauntlets of Valor	Bind on Equip	386	97 94
54	Lightforge Gauntlets	Bind on Equip	386	90 91
54	Razor Gauntlets	Bind on Pickup	386	90 36
PROPERTIES: When struck in combat inflicts 3 Arcane damage to the attacker				

Superior Plate Hand Armor

Lvl	Name	Binding	Armor	Vendor Purchase Value
55	Backusarian Gauntlets	Bind on Pickup	392	1 3 16
PROPERTIES: Restores 4 mana per 5 sec				
55	Stonegrip Gauntlets	Bind on Equip	392	1 4 26
PROPERTIES: Increased Defense +10				
56	Deathbone Gauntlets	Bind on Pickup	398	1 2 12
PROPERTIES: Increased Defense +10, Restores 4 mana per 5 sec				
56	Force Imbued Gauntlets	Bind on Pickup	398	1 1 79
PROPERTIES: Increased Defense +7				
56	Reiver Claws	Bind on Pickup	398	1 5 58
PROPERTIES: Improves your chance to get a critical strike by 1%				
57	Boneclenched Gauntlets	Bind on Pickup	404	1 5 61
PROPERTIES: Increased Defense +7				
57	Death Grips	Bind on Pickup	404	1 6 88
PROPERTIES: Immune to Disarm				
58	Blood Guard's Plate Gloves	Bind on Pickup	410	59 31
PROPERTIES: Hamstring Rage cost reduced by 3				
58	Darkrune Gauntlets	Bind on Equip	410	1 14 84
PROPERTIES: Shadow Resist +20, Increases your chance to block attacks with a shield by 2%				
58	Knight-Lieutenant's Lamellar Gauntlets	Bind on Pickup	410	56 30
PROPERTIES: Increases the Holy damage bonus of your Judgement of the Crusader by 20				
58	Knight-Lieutenant's Plate Gauntlets	Bind on Pickup	410	55 45
PROPERTIES: Hamstring Rage cost reduced by 3				
59	Gloves of the Dawn	Bind on Equip	417	1 16 6
60	Blood Guard's Plate Gauntlets	Bind on Pickup	429	63 57
PROPERTIES: Hamstring Rage cost reduced by 3				
60	Bloodsoaked Gauntlets	Bind on Pickup	460	1 71 52
PROPERTIES: Increased Defense +5, Increases your chance to dodge an attack by 1%				
60	Ironvine Gloves	Bind on Equip	454	1 58 6
PROPERTIES: Nature Resist +20, Increased Defense +10				
60	Knight-Lieutenant's Lamellar Gauntlets	Bind on Pickup	429	66 51
PROPERTIES: Increases the Holy damage bonus of your Judgement of the Crusader by 20, Improves your chance to get a critical strike by 1%				
60	Knight-Lieutenant's Plate Gauntlets	Bind on Pickup	429	69 45
PROPERTIES: Hamstring Rage cost reduced by 3				
60	Sacrificial Gauntlets	Bind on Pickup	441	1 49 36
PROPERTIES: Improves your chance to get a critical strike by 1%, Improves your chance to hit by 1%				
60	Gauntlets of Undead Slaying	Bind on Pickup	410	1 19 12
PROPERTIES: +60 Attack Power when fighting Undead				
60	Gordok's Handguards	Bind on Pickup	392	98 5
PROPERTIES: Improves your chance to get a critical strike by 1%				

Epic Plate Head Armor

Lvl	Name	Binding	Armor	Vendor Purchase Value
56	Lionheart Helm	Bind on Equip	565	2 18 94
PROPERTIES: Improves your chance to get a critical strike by 2%, Improves your chance to hit by 2%				
60	Avenger's Crown	Bind on Pickup	739	5 81 53
PROPERTIES: Increases damage and healing done by magical spells and effects by up to 23, Improves your chance to get a critical strike by 1%				
60	Conqueror's Crown	Bind on Pickup	739	5 30 37
PROPERTIES: Increased Defense +6				
60	Dark Iron Helm	Bind on Equip	608	2 53 99
PROPERTIES: Fire Resist +35				
60	Dreadnaught Helmet	Bind on Pickup	800	8
PROPERTIES: Increases your chance to dodge an attack by 1%, Increased Defense +14				
60	Field Marshal's Lamellar Faceguard	Bind on Pickup	679	2
PROPERTIES: Improves your chance to get a critical strike by 1%, Increases damage and healing done by magical spells and effects by up to 25, Restores 5 mana per 5 sec				
60	Field Marshal's Plate Helm	Bind on Pickup	679	1 89 3
PROPERTIES: Improves your chance to get a critical strike by 1%				
60	Helm of Domination	Bind on Pickup	661	3 74 96
PROPERTIES: Increases your chance to parry an attack by 1%, Increased Defense +7				

Epic Plate Head Armor

Lvl	Name	Binding	Armor	Vendor Purchase Value
60	Helm of Endless Rage	Bind on Pickup	679	4 11 78
60	Helm of Might	Bind on Pickup	608	2 71 70
PROPERTIES: Fire Resist +10, Increases your chance to dodge an attack by 1%, Increased Defense +7				
60	Helm of Wrath	Bind on Pickup	696	4 49
PROPERTIES: Frost Resist +10, Shadow Resist +10, Increased Defense +11				
60	Icebane Helmet	Bind on Pickup	757	6 34 66
PROPERTIES: Frost Resist +44, Increased Defense +8				
60	Judgement Crown	Bind on Pickup	696	4 24 72
PROPERTIES: Frost Resist +10, Shadow Resist +10, Increases damage and healing done by magical spells and effects by up to 32				
60	Lawbringer Helm	Bind on Pickup	608	2 79 56
PROPERTIES: Fire Resist +10, Restores 4 mana per 5 sec, Increases healing done by spells and effects by up to 22				
60	Redemption Headpiece	Bind on Pickup	800	7 72 25
PROPERTIES: Increases healing done by spells and effects by up to 64, Improves your chance to get a critical strike with spells by 1%, Restores 8 mana per 5 sec				
60	Warlord's Plate Headpiece	Bind on Pickup	679	1 97 7
PROPERTIES: Improves your chance to get a critical strike by 1%				
60	Helm of Heroism	Bind on Pickup	556	1 99 16
PROPERTIES: Improves your chance to get a critical strike by 1%				
60	Soulforge Helm	Bind on Pickup	556	1 98 45
PROPERTIES: Increases damage and healing done by magical spells and effects by up to 14, Improves your chance to get a critical strike with spells by 1%				

Superior Plate Head Armor

Lvl	Name	Binding	Armor	Vendor Purchase Value
40	Horned Viking Helmet	Bind on Pickup	303	13 72
PROPERTIES: Charge an enemy, knocking it silly for 30 seconds. Also knocks you down, stunning you for a short period of time. Any damage caused will revive the target				
40	Icemetal Barbute	Bind on Pickup	383	51 97
PROPERTIES: Frost Resist +10				
47	Mugthol's Helm	Bind on Equip	445	90 80
48	Helm of the Mountain	Bind on Pickup	453	1 4 57
PROPERTIES: Nature Resist +10, Increased Defense +7				
50	Foreman's Head Protector	Bind on Pickup	469	1 12 91
PROPERTIES: Increases damage and healing done by magical spells and effects by up to 13				
51	Golem Skull Helm	Bind on Pickup	477	1 18 61
PROPERTIES: Increased Defense +7				
52	Fury Visor	Bind on Pickup	445	99 37
PROPERTIES: Improves your chance to get a critical strike by 1%, Improves your chance to hit by 1%				
53	Helm of Awareness	Bind on Pickup	493	1 36 94
PROPERTIES: Increases your chance to dodge an attack by 2%				
53	Avenguard Helm	Bind on Pickup	461	1 5 54
55	Gyth's Skull	Bind on Pickup	509	1 48 61
PROPERTIES: Increased Defense +9				
55	Whitesoul Helm	Bind on Equip	509	1 48 59
PROPERTIES: , Increases healing done by spells and effects by up to 35				
57	Enchanted Thorium Helm	Bind on Equip	526	1 72 45
PROPERTIES: Increased Defense +9				
57	Helm of Valor	Bind on Pickup	526	1 62 10
57	Lightforge Helm	Bind on Pickup	526	1 59 68
58	Champion's Plate Headguard	Bind on Pickup	534	90 24
58	Darkrune Helm	Bind on Equip	534	1 73 52
PROPERTIES: Shadow Resist +25, Improves your chance to get a critical strike by 1%				
58	Grand Crusader's Helm	Bind on Pickup	534	1 65 80
PROPERTIES: Shadow Resist +15				
58	Helm of the Executioner	Bind on Pickup	534	1 64 76
PROPERTIES: Improves your chance to hit by 2%				
58	Lieutenant Commander's Lamellar Headguard	Bind on Pickup	534	88
58	Lieutenant Commander's Plate Helm	Bind on Pickup	534	86 41
60	Champion's Plate Helm	Bind on Pickup	598	1 32 5
PROPERTIES: Improves your chance to get a critical strike by 1%, Improves your chance to hit by 1%				

Superior Plate Head Armor

Lvl	Name	Binding	Armor	Vendor Purchase Value
60	Gurubashi Helm	Bind on Equip	549	1 84 95
60	Helm of the Holy Avenger	Bind on Equip	574	2 12 53
PROPERTIES: Increases damage and healing done by magical spells and effects by up to 20, Improves your chance to get a critical strike by 1%				
60	Lieutenant Commander's Lamellar Headguard	Bind on Pickup	598	1 28 26
PROPERTIES: Increases damage and healing done by magical spells and effects by up to 26				
60	Lieutenant Commander's Plate Helm	Bind on Pickup	598	1 27 29
PROPERTIES: Improves your chance to get a critical strike by 1%, Improves your chance to hit by 1%				

Epic Plate Leg Armor

Lvl	Name	Binding	Armor	Vendor Purchase Value
55	Dark Iron Leggings	Bind on Equip	598	2 64 41
PROPERTIES: Fire Resist +30				
55	Titanic Leggings	Bind on Equip	598	2 52 76
PROPERTIES: Improves your chance to hit by 2%, Improves your chance to get a critical strike by 1%				
56	Flamewaker Legplates	Bind on Pickup	608	2 84 93
PROPERTIES: Fire Resist +11, Shadow Resist +11, Increases your chance to dodge an attack by 1%				
57	Cloudkeeper Legplates	Bind on Equip	617	2 99
PROPERTIES: Increases Attack Power by 100 for 30 sec				
60	Avenger's Legguards	Bind on Pickup	796	7 9 52
PROPERTIES: Increases damage and healing done by magical spells and effects by up to 16, Improves your chance to get a critical strike by 1%, Restores 4 mana per 5 sec				
60	Bloodsoaked Legplates	Bind on Pickup	674	3 96 65
PROPERTIES: Increased Defense +10				
60	Conqueror's Legguards	Bind on Pickup	796	7 15 29
PROPERTIES: Increased Defense +6, Improves your chance to hit by 1%				
60	Dreadnaught Legplates	Bind on Pickup	861	10 64 20
PROPERTIES: Increased Defense +13, Increases your chance to dodge an attack by 1%, Increases the block value of your shield by 32				
60	General's Plate Leggings	Bind on Pickup	703	2 27 82
PROPERTIES: Improves your chance to get a critical strike by 2%, Improves your chance to hit by 1%				
60	Judgement Legplates	Bind on Pickup	749	5 64 15
PROPERTIES: Fire Resist +10,Arcane Resist +10, Increases damage and healing done by magical spells and effects by up to 20, Restores 4 mana per 5 sec				
60	Lawbringer Legplates	Bind on Pickup	655	3 38 48
PROPERTIES: Shadow Resist +10, Restores 3 mana per 5 sec, Increases healing done by spells and effects by up to 22				
60	Leggings of the Grand Crusader	Bind on Pickup	833	8 79 50
PROPERTIES: Increases damage and healing done by magical spells and effects by up to 26, Improves your chance to get a critical strike by 2%				
60	Legguards of the Fallen Crusader	Bind on Pickup	740	5 56 9
60	Legplates of Blazing Light	Bind on Pickup	749	5 51 93
PROPERTIES: Increases healing done by spells and effects by up to 68, Improves your chance to get a critical strike with spells by 1%				
60	Legplates of Carnage	Bind on Pickup	815	8 12 97
PROPERTIES: Improves your chance to get a critical strike by 2%				
60	Legplates of Might	Bind on Pickup	655	3 63 58
PROPERTIES: Shadow Resist +10, Increases your chance to parry an attack by 1%, Increased Defense +7				
60	Legplates of Wrath	Bind on Pickup	749	5 96 52
PROPERTIES: Fire Resist +10,Arcane Resist +10, Increases your chance to dodge an attack by 2%, Increased Defense +11				
60	Marshal's Lamellar Legplates	Bind on Pickup	703	2 37 93
PROPERTIES: Increases damage and healing done by magical spells and effects by up to 27, Improves your chance to get a critical strike by 1%				
60	Marshal's Plate Legguards	Bind on Pickup	703	2 18 56
PROPERTIES: Improves your chance to get a critical strike by 2%, Improves your chance to hit by 1%				
60	Outrider's Plate Legguards	Bind on Pickup	646	3 31 47
PROPERTIES: Improves your chance to get a critical strike by 1%, Improves your chance to hit by 1%				
60	Redemption Legguards	Bind on Pickup	861	10 25 83
PROPERTIES: Improves your chance to get a critical strike with spells by 1%, Increases healing done by spells and effects by up to 42, Restores 8 mana per 5 sec				
60	Sentinel's Lamellar Legguards	Bind on Pickup	646	3 42 71
PROPERTIES: Improves your chance to get a critical strike by 1%, Improves your chance to hit by 1%, Increases damage and healing done by magical spells and effects by up to 25				

Epic Plate Leg Armor

Lvl	Name	Binding	Armor	Vendor Purchase Value
60	Sentinel's Plate Legguards	Bind on Pickup	646	3 32 69
PROPERTIES: Improves your chance to get a critical strike by 1%, Improves your chance to hit by 1%				
60	Strangely Glyphed Legplates	Bind on Pickup	712	4 69 89
PROPERTIES: Increases healing done by spells and effects by up to 29				
60	Icebane Leggings	Bind on Pickup	787	7 28 32
PROPERTIES: Frost Resist +40, Increased Defense +6				

Superior Plate Leg Armor

Lvl	Name	Binding	Armor	Vendor Purchase Value
41	Golem Shard Leggings	Bind on Equip	429	80 24
PROPERTIES: Increased Defense +6				
46	Silvershell Leggings	Bind on Equip	470	1 16 84
49	Elemental Rockridge Leggings	Bind on Pickup	496	1 42 44
PROPERTIES: Nature Resist +10				
52	Legplates of the Eternal Guardian	Bind on Pickup	522	1 64 56
PROPERTIES: , Increased Defense +15				
53	Lavacrest Leggings	Bind on Pickup	531	1 79 76
55	Handcrafted Mastersmith Leggings	Bind on Pickup	548	1 98 90
56	Chitinous Plate Legguards	Bind on Pickup	557	2 1 24
PROPERTIES: Restores 5 mana per 5 sec				
56	Deathbone Legguards	Bind on Pickup	557	2 5 3
PROPERTIES: Restores 5 mana per 5 sec, Increased Defense +13				
56	Legplates of Valor	Bind on Pickup	557	2 12 13
56	Lightforge Legplates	Bind on Pickup	557	2 3 54
57	Abyssal Plate Legplates	Bind on Equip	566	2 9 84
PROPERTIES: Improves your chance to get a critical strike by 1%				
57	Eldritch Reinforced Legplates	Bind on Pickup	566	2 11 35
PROPERTIES: Improves your chance to get a critical strike by 1%				
57	Wraithplate Leggings	Bind on Pickup	566	2 20 26
PROPERTIES: Increases your chance to parry an attack by 1%				
58	Direwing Legguards	Bind on Equip	575	2 20 90
58	Enchanted Thorium Leggings	Bind on Equip	575	2 40 58
PROPERTIES: Increased Defense +8				
58	Knight-Captain's Lamellar Leggings	Bind on Pickup	575	1 17 75
PROPERTIES: Improves your chance to get a critical strike by 2%				
58	Knight-Captain's Plate Leggings	Bind on Pickup	575	1 16 6
PROPERTIES: Improves your chance to get a critical strike by 2%				
58	Legionnaire's Plate Legguards	Bind on Pickup	575	1 20 75
PROPERTIES: Improves your chance to get a critical strike by 2%				
58	Legplates of Vigilance	Bind on Pickup	575	2 22 8
PROPERTIES: , Increased Defense +15				
58	Warmaster Legguards	Bind on Pickup	575	2 31 96
PROPERTIES: Increases your chance to dodge an attack by 2%				
60	Darksoul Leggings	Bind on Equip	592	2 42 86
PROPERTIES: Improves your chance to hit by 2%				
60	Knight-Captain's Lamellar Leggings	Bind on Pickup	618	1 42 22
PROPERTIES: Increases damage and healing done by magical spells and effects by up to 25				
60	Knight-Captain's Plate Leggings	Bind on Pickup	618	1 50 42
PROPERTIES: Improves your chance to get a critical strike by 2%				
60	Legionnaire's Plate Leggings	Bind on Pickup	618	1 41 75
PROPERTIES: Improves your chance to get a critical strike by 2%				
60	Legplates of the Destroyer	Bind on Pickup	670	4 6 11
PROPERTIES: Increases damage and healing done by magical spells and effects by up to 12				
60	Legplates of the Qiraji Command	Bind on Pickup	644	3 50 75
PROPERTIES: Improves your chance to get a critical strike by 2%				
60	Peacekeeper Leggings	Bind on Pickup	618	2 88 70
PROPERTIES: Increases healing done by spells and effects by up to 37, Restores 7 mana per 5 sec				
60	Cenarion Reservist's Legplates	Bind on Pickup	575	2 27 8
PROPERTIES: Nature Resist +25, Increased Defense +9				
60	Cenarion Reservist's Legplates	Bind on Pickup	575	2 19 68
PROPERTIES: Nature Resist +25				

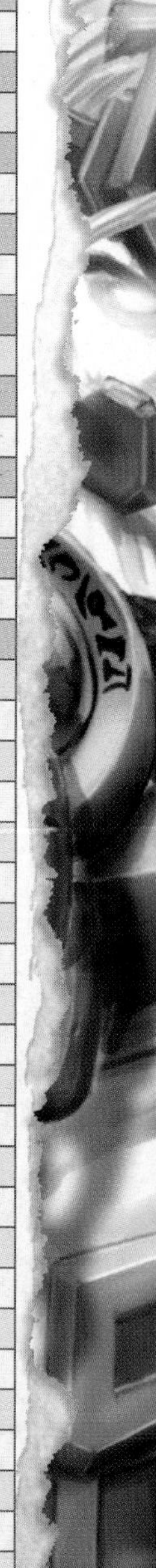

Superior Plate Leg Armor

Lvl	Name	Binding	Armor	Vendor Purchase Value
60	Legplates of Heroism	Bind on Pickup	601	2 67 86
PROPERTIES: Increased Defense +5				
60	Soulforge Legplates	Bind on Pickup	601	2 66 92
PROPERTIES: Increases damage and healing done by magical spells and effects by up to 11				

Epic Plate Shoulder Armor

Lvl	Name	Binding	Armor	Vendor Purchase Value
50	Stockade Pauldrons	Bind on Equip	472	1 53 78
PROPERTIES: Increased Defense +10				
60	Acid Inscribed Pauldrons	Bind on Pickup	610	3 40 30
PROPERTIES: Nature Resist +25, Increased Defense +6				
60	Avenger's Pauldrons	Bind on Pickup	659	4 61 45
PROPERTIES: Increases damage and healing done by magical spells and effects by up to 14, Restores 3 mana per 5 sec				
60	Conqueror's Spaulders	Bind on Pickup	659	4 59 87
PROPERTIES: Increased Defense +4, Improves your chance to hit by 1%				
60	Defiler's Lamellar Spaulders	Bind on Pickup	553	2 66 35
60	Defiler's Plate Spaulders	Bind on Pickup	553	2 55 8
60	Drake Talon Pauldrons	Bind on Pickup	634	3 93 95
PROPERTIES: Increases your chance to dodge an attack by 1%				
60	Dreadnaught Pauldrons	Bind on Pickup	722	7 29 11
PROPERTIES: Improves your chance to hit by 1%, Increases the block value of your shield by 21, Increased Defense +9				
60	Field Marshal's Lamellar Pauldrons	Bind on Pickup	626	1 87 57
PROPERTIES: Increases damage and healing done by magical spells and effects by up to 19, Restores 6 mana per 5 sec				
60	Field Marshal's Plate Shoulderguards	Bind on Pickup	626	1 90 47
PROPERTIES: Improves your chance to hit by 1%				
60	Highlander's Lamellar Spaulders	Bind on Pickup	553	2 47 48
60	Highlander's Plate Spaulders	Bind on Pickup	553	2 46 54
60	Icebane Pauldrons	Bind on Pickup	698	6 21 3
PROPERTIES: Frost Resist +33, Increased Defense +7				
60	Judgement Spaulders	Bind on Pickup	642	4 21 55
PROPERTIES: Fire Resist +10, Restores 5 mana per 5 sec, Increases damage and healing done by magical spells and effects by up to 13				
60	Lawbringer Spaulders	Bind on Pickup	562	2 54 85
PROPERTIES: Shadow Resist +7, Increases healing done by spells and effects by up to 18				
60	Mantle of the Desert Crusade	Bind on Pickup	642	4 51
PROPERTIES: Increases healing done by spells and effects by up to 44				
60	Mantle of the Horusath	Bind on Pickup	610	3 56 31
PROPERTIES: Increases damage and healing done by magical spells and effects by up to 14				
60	Pauldrons of Might	Bind on Pickup	562	2 73 64
PROPERTIES: Shadow Resist +7, Increases your chance to block attacks with a shield by 2%, Increased Defense +5				
60	Pauldrons of the Unrelenting	Bind on Pickup	650	4 54 85
PROPERTIES: Increased Defense +9, Increases your chance to dodge an attack by 1%				
60	Pauldrons of Wrath	Bind on Pickup	642	4 45 83
PROPERTIES: Fire Resist +10, Increases the block value of your shield by 27, Increased Defense +7				
60	Redemption Spaulders	Bind on Pickup	722	7 3
PROPERTIES: Improves your chance to get a critical strike with spells by 1%, Increases healing done by spells and effects by up to 40, Restores 4 mana per 5 sec				
60	Spaulders of the Grand Crusader	Bind on Pickup	714	6 57 20
PROPERTIES: Restores 4 mana per 5 sec, Improves your chance to get a critical strike by 1%, Increases damage and healing done by magical spells and effects by up to 20				
60	Warlord's Plate Shoulders	Bind on Pickup	626	1 98 50
PROPERTIES: Improves your chance to hit by 1%				

Superior Plate Shoulder Armor

Lvl	Name	Binding	Armor	Vendor Purchase Value
45	Big Bad Pauldrons	Bind on Pickup	396	85 93
46	Wyrmslayer Spaulders	Bind on Equip	403	89 97
47	Earthslag Shoulders	Bind on Pickup	410	93 60
PROPERTIES: Increases damage and healing done by magical spells and effects by up to 9				
52	Wailing Nightbane Pauldrons	Bind on Pickup	448	1 31 2
PROPERTIES: Shadow Resist +10, Increased Defense +3				

Superior Plate Shoulder Armor

Lvl	Name	Binding	Armor	Vendor Purchase Value
52	Razorsteel Shoulders	Bind on Pickup	410	97 97
PROPERTIES: Improves your chance to hit by 1%				
53	Dawnbringer Shoulders	Bind on Equip	455	1 30 80
PROPERTIES: Increases healing done by spells and effects by up to 44				
54	Ebonsteel Spaulders	Bind on Pickup	463	1 43 68
55	Bulky Iron Spaulders	Bind on Pickup	470	1 42 33
PROPERTIES: Increased Defense +6				
55	Lightforge Spaulders	Bind on Pickup	470	1 45 92
55	Slamshot Shoulders	Bind on Pickup	470	1 42 4
PROPERTIES: +20 Attack Power				
55	Spaulders of Valor	Bind on Pickup	470	1 52 7
56	Stoneform Shoulders	Bind on Pickup	478	1 63 67
PROPERTIES: , Increased Defense +7				
57	Bile-etched Spaulders	Bind on Pickup	485	1 60 93
PROPERTIES: Increased Defense +7				
58	Champion's Plate Pauldrons	Bind on Pickup	493	82 23
58	Lieutenant Commander's Lamellar Shoulders	Bind on Pickup	493	88 63
58	Lieutenant Commander's Plate Pauldrons	Bind on Pickup	493	87 36
60	Abyssal Plate Epaulets	Bind on Pickup	530	2 10 28
PROPERTIES: Improves your chance to hit by 1%				
60	Bloodsoaked Pauldrons	Bind on Pickup	552	2 61 7
PROPERTIES: Increased Defense +3				
60	Champion's Plate Shoulders	Bind on Pickup	552	1 31 58
PROPERTIES: Improves your chance to get a critical strike by 1%				
60	Darksoul Shoulders	Bind on Equip	507	1 82 85
PROPERTIES: Improves your chance to hit by 1%				
60	Lieutenant Commander's Lamellar Shoulders	Bind on Pickup	552	1 28 73
PROPERTIES: Increases damage and healing done by magical spells and effects by up to 20				
60	Lieutenant Commander's Plate Shoulders	Bind on Pickup	552	1 27 76
PROPERTIES: Improves your chance to get a critical strike by 1%				
60	Polished Obsidian Pauldrons	Bind on Equip	530	2 14 14
PROPERTIES: Increased Defense +7				
60	Soulforge Spaulders	Bind on Pickup	507	1 91 36
PROPERTIES: Increases damage and healing done by magical spells and effects by up to 12, Restores 4 mana per 5 sec				
60	Spaulders of Heroism	Bind on Pickup	507	1 92 3

Epic Plate Waist Armor

Lvl	Name	Binding	Armor	Vendor Purchase Value
60	Belt of Might	Bind on Equip	421	1 79 81
PROPERTIES: Fire Resist +7, Increases your chance to dodge an attack by 1%, Increased Defense +5				
60	Belt of the Fallen Emperor	Bind on Pickup	512	3 78 19
PROPERTIES: Increases healing done by spells and effects by up to 35				
60	Belt of the Grand Crusader	Bind on Pickup	536	4 36 47
PROPERTIES: Increases damage and healing done by magical spells and effects by up to 21, Restores 7 mana per 5 sec				
60	Dreadnaught Waistguard	Bind on Pickup	554	5 3 34
PROPERTIES: Increases the block value of your shield by 18, Increases your chance to block attacks with a shield by 3%, Increased Defense +9				
60	Girdle of the Fallen Crusader	Bind on Pickup	488	3 17 76
60	Girdle of the Mentor	Bind on Pickup	536	4 44 73
PROPERTIES: Improves your chance to get a critical strike by 1%, Improves your chance to hit by 1%				
60	Judgement Belt	Bind on Pickup	482	2 79 96
PROPERTIES: Shadow Resist +10, Increases damage and healing done by magical spells and effects by up to 23				
60	Lawbringer Belt	Bind on Equip	421	1 71 19
PROPERTIES: Fire Resist +7, Increases healing done by spells and effects by up to 18				
60	Onslaught Girdle	Bind on Pickup	494	3 14 69
PROPERTIES: Improves your chance to get a critical strike by 1%, Improves your chance to hit by 1%				
60	Redemption Girdle	Bind on Pickup	554	5 20 55
PROPERTIES: Increases healing done by spells and effects by up to 40, Restores 5 mana per 5 sec				
60	Royal Qiraji Belt	Bind on Pickup	512	3 57 53
PROPERTIES: Increases your chance to parry an attack by 1%, Increased Defense +8				
60	Triad Girdle	Bind on Pickup	476	2 67 84
60	Unmelting Ice Girdle	Bind on Pickup	452	2 36 19
PROPERTIES: Frost Resist +16, Increased Defense +8				

Epic Plate Waist Armor

Lvl	Name	Binding	Armor	Vendor Purchase Value
60	Waistband of Wrath	Bind on Pickup	482	2 96 14
PROPERTIES: Shadow Resist +10, Increases your chance to block attacks with a shield by 3%, Increased Defense +7				
60	Zandalar Freethinker's Belt	Bind on Pickup	391	
PROPERTIES: Increases healing done by spells and effects by up to 26				
60	Zandalar Vindicator's Belt	Bind on Pickup	391	
PROPERTIES: Improves your chance to get a critical strike by 1%				

Superior Plate Waist Armor

Lvl	Name	Binding	Armor	Vendor Purchase Value
40	Defiler's Lamellar Girdle	Bind on Pickup	236	34 48
40	Defiler's Plate Girdle	Bind on Pickup	236	32 75
40	Enormous Ogre Belt	Bind on Equip	164	27 4
40	Highlander's Lamellar Girdle	Bind on Pickup	236	32 1
40	Highlander's Plate Girdle	Bind on Pickup	236	31 76
46	Atal'alarion's Tusk Ring	Bind on Pickup	302	62 63
48	Defiler's Lamellar Girdle	Bind on Pickup	313	69 48
PROPERTIES: Improves your chance to get a critical strike by 1%				
48	Defiler's Plate Girdle	Bind on Pickup	313	65 99
PROPERTIES: Improves your chance to get a critical strike by 1%				
48	Highlander's Lamellar Girdle	Bind on Pickup	313	69 46
PROPERTIES: Improves your chance to get a critical strike by 1%				
48	Highlander's Plate Girdle	Bind on Pickup	313	70 75
PROPERTIES: Improves your chance to get a critical strike by 1%				
50	Stonewall Girdle	Bind on Pickup	324	73 78
52	Girdle of Uther	Bind on Equip	336	82 26
53	Belt of Valor	Bind on Equip	341	92 95
53	Girdle of the Dawn	Bind on Equip	341	93 65
53	Lightforge Belt	Bind on Equip	341	86 25
53	Rainbow Girdle	Bind on Pickup	341	89 88
55	Belt of the Ordained	Bind on Equip	353	96 95
PROPERTIES: Increases healing done by spells and effects by up to 42				
55	Frostwolf Plate Belt	Bind on Pickup	353	1 1 76
PROPERTIES: Frost Resist +5				
55	Stormpike Plate Girdle	Bind on Pickup	353	94 88
PROPERTIES: Frost Resist +5				
56	Deathbone Girdle	Bind on Pickup	358	1 1 35
PROPERTIES: Increased Defense +9, Restores 4 mana per 5 sec				
56	Elemental Plate Girdle	Bind on Pickup	358	99 63
58	Brigam Girdle	Bind on Pickup	369	1 16 42
PROPERTIES: Improves your chance to hit by 1%				
58	Defiler's Lamellar Girdle	Bind on Pickup	369	1 17 83
PROPERTIES: Improves your chance to get a critical strike by 1%				
58	Defiler's Plate Girdle	Bind on Pickup	369	1 12 29
PROPERTIES: Improves your chance to get a critical strike by 1%				
58	Handcrafted Mastersmith Girdle	Bind on Pickup	369	1 19 87
58	Highlander's Lamellar Girdle	Bind on Pickup	369	1 13 94
PROPERTIES: Improves your chance to get a critical strike by 1%				
58	Highlander's Plate Girdle	Bind on Pickup	369	1 13 52
PROPERTIES: Improves your chance to get a critical strike by 1%				
60	Belt of the Sand Reaver	Bind on Pickup	414	1 63 34
PROPERTIES: Increased Defense +5				
60	Heavy Obsidian Belt	Bind on Equip	397	1 42 82
PROPERTIES: +5 All Resistances				
60	Ironvine Belt	Bind on Equip	408	1 58 64
PROPERTIES: Nature Resist +15, Increased Defense +3				
60	Belt of Heroism	Bind on Pickup	380	1 24 76
PROPERTIES: Increased Defense +7				
60	Belt of Shrunken Heads	Bind on Pickup	408	1 63 37
60	Omokk's Girth Restrainer	Bind on Pickup	353	95 42
PROPERTIES: Improves your chance to get a critical strike by 1%				
60	Soulforge Belt	Bind on Pickup	380	1 24 31
PROPERTIES: Increases damage and healing done by magical spells and effects by up to 12, Restores 4 mana per 5 sec				

Epic Plate Wrist Armor

Lvl	Name	Binding	Armor	Vendor Purchase Value
40	Berserker Bracers	Bind on Pickup	229	49 45
50	Berserker Bracers	Bind on Pickup	275	96 35
54	Dark Iron Bracers	Bind on Equip	294	1 26 37
PROPERTIES: Fire Resist +18				
60	Berserker Bracers	Bind on Pickup	323	1 76 99
60	Bracelets of Wrath	Bind on Pickup	375	2 95 7
60	Bracers of Brutality	Bind on Pickup	356	2 41 4
60	Bracers of Might	Bind on Equip	328	1 77 86
60	Dragonbone Wristguards	Bind on Pickup	351	2 16 38
PROPERTIES: Increases your chance to parry an attack by 1%				
60	Dreadnaught Bracers	Bind on Pickup	431	5 5 27
PROPERTIES: Increased Defense +5				
60	Hive Defiler Wristguards	Bind on Pickup	384	3 17 27
60	Icebane Bracers	Bind on Equip	393	3 44 52
PROPERTIES: Frost Resist +24, Increased Defense +5				
60	Judgement Bindings	Bind on Pickup	375	2 78 89
PROPERTIES: Increases damage and healing done by magical spells and effects by up to 7				
60	Lawbringer Bracers	Bind on Equip	328	1 70 54
PROPERTIES: Restores 4 mana per 5 sec				
60	Redemption Wristguards	Bind on Pickup	431	5 7 19
PROPERTIES: Increases healing done by spells and effects by up to 31, Restores 4 mana per 5 sec				
60	Wristguards of Vengeance	Bind on Pickup	407	4 8 3
PROPERTIES: Improves your chance to get a critical strike by 1%				
60	Deeprock Bracers	Bind on Pickup	309	1 44 25
60	Zandalar Freethinker's Armguards	Bind on Pickup	304	
PROPERTIES: Increases healing done by spells and effects by up to 11				
60	Zandalar Vindicator's Armguards	Bind on Pickup	304	

Superior Plate Wrist Armor

Lvl	Name	Binding	Armor	Vendor Purchase Value
40	Skullplate Bracers	Bind on Equip	163	30 27
43	Giantslayer Bracers	Bind on Equip	223	47 15
45	Arena Vambraces	Bind on Equip	231	58 21
45	First Sergeant's Plate Bracers	Bind on Pickup	231	28 78
45	Sergeant Major's Plate Wristguards	Bind on Pickup	231	28 47
46	Noxxion's Shackles	Bind on Pickup	235	57 23
PROPERTIES: Nature Resist +15				
48	Runed Golem Shackles	Bind on Equip	244	64 64
PROPERTIES: Increased Defense +4				
52	Black Steel Bindings	Bind on Pickup	261	85 22
52	Bracers of Valor	Bind on Equip	261	87 38
52	Emberplate Armguards	Bind on Pickup	261	86 37
PROPERTIES: Fire Resist +10				
52	Lightforge Bracers	Bind on Equip	261	81 5
54	Vambraces of the Sadist	Bind on Pickup	270	92 96
PROPERTIES: Improves your chance to get a critical strike by 1%				
56	Morlune's Bracer	Bind on Equip	279	1 4 16
57	Fel Hardened Bracers	Bind on Pickup	283	1 4 61
PROPERTIES: Increased Defense +3				
57	Vigorsteel Vambraces	Bind on Pickup	283	1 10 5
58	Battleborn Armbraces	Bind on Pickup	287	1 16 40
PROPERTIES: Improves your chance to hit by 1%, Improves your chance to get a critical strike by 1%				
58	Bracers of Undead Slaying	Bind on Equip	287	1 15 72
PROPERTIES: +45 Attack Power when fighting Undead				
58	First Sergeant's Plate Bracers	Bind on Pickup	287	58 89
58	Gordok Bracers of Power	Bind on Pickup	287	1 9 84
58	Sergeant Major's Plate Wristguards	Bind on Pickup	287	58 4
60	Abyssal Plate Vambraces	Bind on Pickup	309	1 40 19
60	Bracers of Heroism	Bind on Pickup	296	1 25 68
PROPERTIES: Increased Defense +3				
60	Soulforge Bracers	Bind on Pickup	296	1 25 24
PROPERTIES: Increases damage and healing done by magical spells and effects by up to 8				

SHIELD

Epic Shields

Lvl	Name	Binding	Armor	Vendor Purchase Value
36	The Green Tower	Bind on Equip	1308	1 25 77
PROPERTIES: When struck in combat has a 1% chance of raising a thorny shield that inflicts 3 Nature damage to attackers when hit and increases Nature resistance by 50 for 30 sec.\n				
41	Blackskull Shield	Bind on Equip	1795	1 88 15
PROPERTIES: Shadow Resist +10				
45	Wall of the Dead	Bind on Equip	1937	2 32 73
PROPERTIES: When struck in combat has a 3% chance to encase the caster in bone, increasing armor by 150 for 20 sec				
54	Skullflame Shield	Bind on Equip	2256	4 22 96
PROPERTIES: Fire Resist +10, Shadow Resist +10, When struck in combat has a 3% chance of stealing 35 life from target enemy, When struck in combat has a 1% chance of dealing 75 to 125 Fire damage to all targets around you				
60	Aegis of the Blood God	Bind on Pickup	2575	6 50 77
PROPERTIES: Increases the block value of your shield by 30, Increased Defense +7, Increases your chance to block attacks with a shield by 2%				
60	Blessed Qiraji Bulwark	Bind on Pickup	2964	11 5 63
PROPERTIES: Increases your chance to block attacks with a shield by 3%, Increases the block value of your shield by 15, Increased Defense +8				
60	Buru's Skull Fragment	Bind on Pickup	2575	6 6 74
PROPERTIES: Increased Defense +6				
60	Death's Bargain	Bind on Pickup	3106	13 34 26
PROPERTIES: Improves your chance to get a critical strike with spells by 1%, Increases healing done by spells and effects by up to 29, Restores 4 mana per 5 sec				
60	Drillborer Disk	Bind on Pickup	2539	5 79 70
PROPERTIES: When struck in combat inflicts 3 Arcane damage to the attacker, Increases your chance to block attacks with a shield by 2%, Increases the block value of your shield by 23				
60	Earthen Guard	Bind on Pickup	2468	5 66 44
PROPERTIES: Increased Defense +7, Increases the block value of your shield by 12				
60	Elementium Reinforced Bulwark	Bind on Pickup	2893	9 80 56
PROPERTIES: Increases the block value of your shield by 19, Increased Defense +7				
60	Force Reactive Disk	Bind on Equip	2468	5 64 16
PROPERTIES: When the shield blocks it releases an electrical charge that damages all nearby enemies. This also has a chance of damaging the shield, 0				
60	Grand Marshal's Aegis	Bind on Pickup	2929	3 18 7
PROPERTIES: When struck in combat has a 5% chance of inflicting 35 to 65 Nature damage to the attacker				
60	High Warlord's Shield Wall	Bind on Pickup	2929	3 19 17
PROPERTIES: When struck in combat has a 5% chance of inflicting 35 to 65 Nature damage to the attacker				
60	Jagged Obsidian Shield	Bind on Equip	2645	6 74 40
PROPERTIES: Increases your chance to block attacks with a shield by 2%, +5 All Resistances, When struck by a harmful spell, the caster of that spell has a 5% chance to be silenced for 3 sec				
60	Malistar's Defender	Bind on Pickup	2822	8 79 60
PROPERTIES: Restores 9 mana per 5 sec				
60	Red Dragonscale Protector	Bind on Pickup	2787	8 44 2
PROPERTIES: Increases healing done by spells and effects by up to 37				
60	Shield of Condemnation	Bind on Pickup	3425	19 42 25
PROPERTIES: Restores 6 mana per 5 sec, Increases healing done by spells and effects by up to 59				
60	Stygian Buckler	Bind on Pickup	3106	12 85 89
PROPERTIES: When struck has a 15% chance of reducing the attacker's movement speed by 50% for 5 secs				
60	The Face of Death	Bind on Pickup	3354	17 48 10
PROPERTIES: Increases your chance to block attacks with a shield by 3%, Increases the block value of your shield by 21				
60	The Immovable Object	Bind on Pickup	2468	15 90 59
PROPERTIES: Increases the block value of your shield by 27				
60	The Plague Bearer	Bind on Pickup	3106	12 47 17
PROPERTIES: Frost Resist +15, Increased Defense +9				
60	Wormscale Blocker	Bind on Pickup	3035	12 27 59
PROPERTIES: Increases healing done by spells and effects by up to 35, Restores 6 mana per 5 sec				

Superior Shields

Lvl	Name	Binding	Armor	Vendor Purchase Value
15	Gold-plated Buckler	Bind on Pickup	471	10 67
15	Kresh's Back	Bind on Pickup	471	10 64
PROPERTIES: Increased Defense +4				
19	Redbeard Crest	Bind on Equip	547	19 20
20	Seedcloud Buckler	Bind on Pickup	566	20 67
23	Commander's Crest	Bind on Pickup	623	27 11
25	Shield of Thorsen	Bind on Equip	661	33 59
26	Resplendent Guardian	Bind on Equip	680	39 60
PROPERTIES: Increases your chance to block attacks with a shield by 1%				
27	Arctic Buckler	Bind on Pickup	642	30 28
PROPERTIES: Frost Resist +5				
31	Heart of Agamaggan	Bind on Pickup	776	63 9
32	Thermaplugg's Central Core	Bind on Pickup	795	69 17
PROPERTIES: When struck in combat has a 5% chance of inflicting 35 to 65 Nature damage to the attacker				
33	Skullance Shield	Bind on Equip	814	71 23
34	Marbled Buckler	Bind on Pickup	776	61 5
37	Olaf's All Purpose Shield	Bind on Pickup	1287	28 19
PROPERTIES: Reduces your fall speed for 10 sec				
37	Savage Boar's Guard	Bind on Pickup	1287	96 52
39	Aegis of the Scarlet Commander	Bind on Pickup	1548	1 16 81
41	Mountainside Buckler	Bind on Equip	1612	1 32 35
43	Troll Protector	Bind on Equip	1676	1 52 96
PROPERTIES: Increases your chance to block attacks with a shield by 2%				
47	Stoneshell Guard	Bind on Pickup	1803	1 98 93
48	Gizlock's Hypertech Buckler	Bind on Pickup	1835	2 26 30
PROPERTIES: Restores 4 mana per 5 sec				
49	Aegis of Stormwind	Bind on Equip	1867	2 35 5
51	Astral Guard	Bind on Pickup	1930	2 58 83
51	Crest of Supremacy	Bind on Pickup	1930	2 46 45
53	Rock Golem Bulwark	Bind on Pickup	1994	2 90 83
PROPERTIES: Nature Resist +10, Arcane Resist +10				
54	Avalanchion's Stony Hide	Bind on Equip	2026	2 89 18
PROPERTIES: Increases the block value of your shield by 10				
54	Quel'dorai Guard	Bind on Equip	2026	2 94 42
PROPERTIES: Arcane Resist +11, Increases your chance to dodge an attack by 1%				
55	Crest of Retribution	Bind on Pickup	2057	3 6 56
PROPERTIES: Deals 5 to 35 damage every time you block				
56	Husk of Nerub'enkan	Bind on Pickup	2089	3 23 3
PROPERTIES: Nature Resist +15				
56	Observer's Shield	Bind on Pickup	2089	3 45 69
56	Rhombeard Protector	Bind on Pickup	2089	3 50 31
57	Barrier Shield	Bind on Pickup	2121	3 45 89
PROPERTIES: Increases your chance to block attacks with a shield by 2%, Increases the block value of your shield by 18				
57	Dreadguard's Protector	Bind on Pickup	2121	3 34 20
57	Garrett Family Crest	Bind on Equip	2121	3 46 94
57	Intricately Runed Shield	Bind on Pickup	2121	3 34 76
PROPERTIES: Increases the block value of your shield by 24				
57	Lord Blackwood's Buckler	Bind on Pickup	2121	3 38 37
PROPERTIES: Increases the block value of your shield by 27				
57	Rattlecage Buckler	Bind on Pickup	2121	3 41 81
PROPERTIES: Shadow Resist +7				
58	Draconian Aegis of the Legion	Bind on Pickup	2153	3 51 50
PROPERTIES: Increases damage and healing done by magical spells and effects by up to 20				
58	Draconian Deflector	Bind on Pickup	2153	3 52 12
PROPERTIES: Fire Resist +10, Increased Defense +10				
60	Zulian Defender	Bind on Pickup	2312	4 88 26
60	Argent Defender	Bind on Pickup	2121	3 65 15
PROPERTIES: Has a 1% chance when struck in combat of increasing chance to block by 50% for 10 sec				
60	Darrowshire Strongguard	Bind on Pickup	2153	3 67 20
PROPERTIES: Nature Resist +10, Frost Resist +10				
60	Milli's Shield	Bind on Pickup	2026	3 2 31
PROPERTIES: Restores 4 health per 5 sec				
60	Sacred Protector	Bind on Pickup	2121	3 56 31
??	Ironbark Shield	Bind on Pickup	1803	2 12 77
PROPERTIES: Improves your chance to get a critical strike with Nature spells by 1%				

CLOAK

Epic Cloaks

Lvl	Name	Binding	Armor	Vendor Purchase Value
57	Chromatic Cloak	Bind on Equip	48	2 30 6
PROPERTIES: Fire Resist +9, Shadow Resist +9, Improves your chance to get a critical strike with spells by 1%				
57	Hide of the Wild	Bind on Equip	48	2 8 89
PROPERTIES: Increases healing done by spells and effects by up to 42				
57	Shifting Cloak	Bind on Equip	48	2 9 71
PROPERTIES: Increases your chance to dodge an attack by 1%				
60	Cape of Eternal Justice	Bind on Pickup	52	
PROPERTIES: Restores 5 mana per 5 sec				
60	Cape of the Trinity	Bind on Pickup	57	4 9 37
PROPERTIES: Increases damage and healing done by magical spells and effects by up to 21				
60	Cloak of Clarity	Bind on Pickup	66	7 69 6
PROPERTIES: Increases healing done by spells and effects by up to 40, Restores 8 mana per 5 sec				
60	Cloak of Concentrated Hatred	Bind on Pickup	56	3 86 77
PROPERTIES: Improves your chance to hit by 1%				
60	Cloak of Consumption	Bind on Pickup	52	2 99 66
PROPERTIES: Increases damage and healing done by magical spells and effects by up to 23, Improves your chance to hit with spells by 1%				
60	Cloak of Draconic Might	Bind on Pickup	54	3 19 56
60	Cloak of Firemaw	Bind on Pickup	57	4
PROPERTIES: +50 Attack Power				
60	Cloak of Flames	Bind on Equip	50	2 60 18
PROPERTIES: Fire Resist +15, Deals 5 Fire damage to anyone who strikes you with a melee attack				
60	Cloak of Suturing	Bind on Pickup	63	6 20 91
PROPERTIES: Increases healing done by spells and effects by up to 48, Restores 5 mana per 5 sec				
60	Cloak of the Brood Lord	Bind on Pickup	63	5 91 15
PROPERTIES: Increases damage and healing done by magical spells and effects by up to 28				
60	Cloak of the Devoured	Bind on Pickup	66	7 43 94
PROPERTIES: Increases damage and healing done by magical spells and effects by up to 30, Improves your chance to hit with spells by 1%				
60	Cloak of the Fallen God	Bind on Pickup	66	7 51 74
60	Cloak of the Gathering Storm	Bind on Pickup	52	
PROPERTIES: Increases damage and healing done by magical spells and effects by up to 14				
60	Cloak of the Golden Hive	Bind on Pickup	59	4 81 18
PROPERTIES: Increased Defense +6				
60	Cloak of the Honor Guard	Bind on Pickup	50	2 42 79
PROPERTIES: +34 Attack Power				
60	Cloak of the Necropolis	Bind on Pickup	68	8 64 39
PROPERTIES: Increases damage and healing done by magical spells and effects by up to 26, Improves your chance to get a critical strike with spells by 1%, Improves your chance to hit with spells by 1%				
60	Cloak of the Scourge	Bind on Pickup	63	5 98 17
PROPERTIES: +30 Attack Power, Improves your chance to hit by 1%				
60	Cloak of the Shrouded Mists	Bind on Pickup	57	3 86 89
PROPERTIES: Fire Resist +6, Nature Resist +6				
60	Cloak of the Unseen Path	Bind on Pickup	52	
PROPERTIES: Improves your chance to hit by 1%				
60	Cloak of Unending Life	Bind on Pickup	52	
PROPERTIES: Increases damage and healing done by magical spells and effects by up to 11				
60	Cloak of Untold Secrets	Bind on Pickup	59	4 68 30
PROPERTIES: Shadow Resist +20				
60	Cloak of Veiled Shadows	Bind on Pickup	52	
PROPERTIES: Improves your chance to hit by 1%				
60	Cryptfiend Silk Cloak	Bind on Pickup	63	6 16 51
PROPERTIES: Increased Defense +7, Increases your chance to dodge an attack by 1%, Improves your chance to hit by 1%				
60	Deathguard's Cloak	Bind on Pickup	50	2 63 53
PROPERTIES: +34 Attack Power				
60	Dragon's Blood Cape	Bind on Pickup	56	3 75 37
PROPERTIES: Fire Resist +5, Shadow Resist +5, Arcane Resist +5				
60	Drape of Benediction	Bind on Pickup	52	2 91 47
PROPERTIES: Increases healing done by spells and effects by up to 31				

Epic Cloaks

Lvl	Name	Binding	Armor	Vendor Purchase Value
60	Drape of Unyielding Strength	Bind on Pickup	52	
PROPERTIES: Improves your chance to hit by 1%				
60	Drape of Vaulted Secrets	Bind on Pickup	52	
PROPERTIES: Increases damage and healing done by magical spells and effects by up to 18				
60	Elementium Threaded Cloak	Bind on Pickup	59	4 66 61
PROPERTIES: Increases your chance to dodge an attack by 2%				
60	Eskhandar's Pelt	Bind on Pickup	51	2 73 70
PROPERTIES: Improves your chance to get a critical strike by 1%				
60	Fireproof Cloak	Bind on Pickup	54	3 26 65
PROPERTIES: Fire Resist +18				
60	Glacial Cloak	Bind on Equip	61	5 30 45
PROPERTIES: Frost Resist +24				
60	Green Dragonskin Cloak	Bind on Pickup	54	3 26 75
PROPERTIES: Nature Resist +20, Restores 4 health per 5 sec				
60	Puissant Cape	Bind on Pickup	54	3 30 28
PROPERTIES: +40 Attack Power, Improves your chance to hit by 1%				
60	Sandstorm Cloak	Bind on Pickup	55	3 60 24
PROPERTIES: Increases your chance to dodge an attack by 1%, Increased Defense +6				
60	Sapphiron Drape	Bind on Pickup	55	3 72 3
PROPERTIES: Frost Resist +6,Arcane Resist +6, Increases damage and healing done by magical spells and effects by up to 14				
60	Shroud of Dominion	Bind on Pickup	68	8 25 78
PROPERTIES: Improves your chance to get a critical strike by 1%, +50 Attack Power				
60	Shroud of Infinite Wisdom	Bind on Pickup	52	
PROPERTIES: Increases healing done by spells and effects by up to 24				
60	Shroud of Pure Thought	Bind on Pickup	57	4 29 19
PROPERTIES: Increases healing done by spells and effects by up to 33, Restores 6 mana per 5 sec				
60	Shroud of Unspoken Names	Bind on Pickup	52	
PROPERTIES: Increases damage and healing done by magical spells and effects by up to 18				
60	Veil of Eclipse	Bind on Pickup	63	6 30 14
PROPERTIES: Increases damage and healing done by magical spells and effects by up to 28, Decreases the magical resistances of your spell targets by 10				
60	Windshear Cape	Bind on Pickup	50	2 42 89

Superior Cloaks

Lvl	Name	Binding	Armor	Vendor Purchase Value
16	Firebane Cloak	Bind on Equip	19	6 17
PROPERTIES: Fire Resist +5				
17	Glowing Lizardscale Cloak	Bind on Pickup	20	7 1
18	Battle Healer's Cloak	Bind on Pickup	20	7 30
PROPERTIES: Increases healing done by spells and effects by up to 9				
18	Caretaker's Cape	Bind on Pickup	20	7 30
PROPERTIES: Increases healing done by spells and effects by up to 9				
19	Sentry Cloak	Bind on Equip	21	8 63
20	Cape of the Brotherhood	Bind on Pickup	21	9 40
23	Amy's Blanket	Bind on Equip	23	13 31
24	Glowing Thresher Cape	Bind on Pickup	23	15 23
28	Battle Healer's Cloak	Bind on Pickup	25	21 22
PROPERTIES: Increases healing done by spells and effects by up to 13				
28	Caretaker's Cape	Bind on Pickup	25	21 54
PROPERTIES: Increases healing done by spells and effects by up to 13				
29	Tigerstrike Mantle	Bind on Equip	25	24 46
30	Sergeant's Cape	Bind on Pickup	26	12 88
30	Sergeant's Cloak	Bind on Pickup	26	13 22
32	Dark Hooded Cape	Bind on Equip	27	31 59
33	Wing of the Whelpling	Bind on Equip	28	34 28
34	Energy Cloak	Bind on Equip	28	36 72
PROPERTIES: Restores 375 to 425 mana				
35	Icy Cloak	Bind on Equip	29	37 88
PROPERTIES: Frost Resist +11				

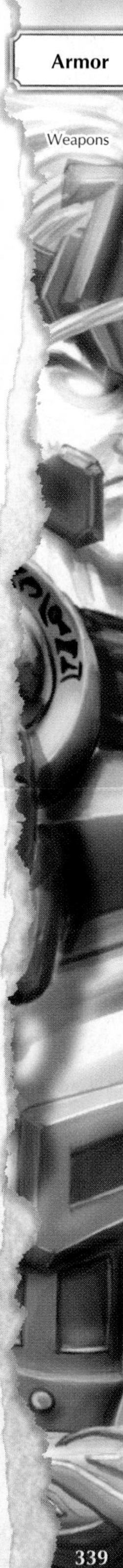

Superior Cloaks

Lvl	Name	Binding	Armor	Vendor Purchase Value
35	Silky Spider Cape	Bind on Pickup	30	47 99
36	Mantle of Lady Falther'ess	Bind on Pickup	30	40 89
PROPERTIES: Increases damage and healing done by magical spells and effects by up to 9				
38	Battle Healer's Cloak	Bind on Pickup	31	47 80
PROPERTIES: Increases healing done by spells and effects by up to 18				
38	Caretaker's Cape	Bind on Pickup	31	49 86
PROPERTIES: Increases healing done by spells and effects by up to 18				
41	Blackmetal Cape	Bind on Equip	33	63 41
44	Blackflame Cape	Bind on Equip	35	81 52
PROPERTIES: Fire Resist +5, Shadow Resist +5				
45	Sergeant's Cape	Bind on Pickup	36	41 78
45	Sergeant's Cloak	Bind on Pickup	36	42 85
47	Grovekeeper's Drape	Bind on Pickup	37	91
PROPERTIES: Nature Resist +10				
47	Spritecaster Cape	Bind on Pickup	37	99 99
PROPERTIES: Increases damage and healing done by magical spells and effects by up to 14				
48	Battle Healer's Cloak	Bind on Pickup	38	96 31
PROPERTIES: Increases healing done by spells and effects by up to 22				
48	Blackveil Cape	Bind on Pickup	38	96 98
48	Caretaker's Cape	Bind on Pickup	38	1
PROPERTIES: Increases healing done by spells and effects by up to 22				
48	Nightfall Drape	Bind on Pickup	38	1 2 61
49	Featherskin Cape	Bind on Pickup	39	1 5 95
50	Blisterbane Wrap	Bind on Equip	39	1 9 80
PROPERTIES: Shadow Resist +6				
50	Cloak of Fire	Bind on Equip	39	1 12 80
PROPERTIES: Fire Resist +6, Deals 25 Fire damage every 5 sec to all nearby enemies for 15 sec				
50	Dark Phantom Cape	Bind on Equip	39	1 14 89
50	Graverot Cape	Bind on Pickup	39	1 16 55
51	Stoneshield Cloak	Bind on Equip	40	1 15 94
51	Deep Woodlands Cloak	Bind on Pickup	37	85 85
PROPERTIES: Increases damage and healing done by magical spells and effects by up to 12				
52	Duskbat Drape	Bind on Pickup	37	94 44
PROPERTIES: Reduces damage from falling				
53	Butcher's Apron	Bind on Pickup	41	1 32 32
53	Cape of the Fire Salamander	Bind on Pickup	41	1 39 79
PROPERTIES: Fire Resist +12				
53	Juno's Shadow	Bind on Equip	41	1 28 88
PROPERTIES: Shadow Resist +15				
53	Mageflame Cloak	Bind on Equip	41	1 35 85
PROPERTIES: Fire Resist +10, Increases damage done by Fire spells and effects by up to 21				
54	Gracious Cape	Bind on Equip	42	1 42 75
PROPERTIES: Restores 6 mana per 5 sec				
54	Royal Tribunal Cloak	Bind on Pickup	42	1 37 38
54	Shadewood Cloak	Bind on Pickup	42	1 41 16
PROPERTIES: Nature Resist +7				
55	Armswake Cloak	Bind on Pickup	43	1 55 29
PROPERTIES: +16 Attack Power				
55	Frostwolf Advisor's Cloak	Bind on Pickup	43	1 51 55
PROPERTIES: Frost Resist +5, Increases damage and healing done by magical spells and effects by up to 14				
55	Frostwolf Legionnaire's Cloak	Bind on Pickup	43	1 50 44
PROPERTIES: Frost Resist +5, +24 Attack Power				
55	Heliotrope Cloak	Bind on Pickup	43	1 42 33
PROPERTIES: Improves your chance to get a critical strike with spells by 1%				
55	Onyxia Scale Cloak	Bind on Equip	43	1 51 98
PROPERTIES: Fire Resist +16, Protects the wearer from being fully engulfed by Shadow Flame				
55	Stormpike Sage's Cloak	Bind on Pickup	43	1 52 9
PROPERTIES: Frost Resist +5, Increases damage and healing done by magical spells and effects by up to 14				
55	Stormpike Soldier's Cloak	Bind on Pickup	43	1 51
PROPERTIES: Frost Resist +5, +24 Attack Power				

Superior Cloaks

Lvl	Name	Binding	Armor	Vendor Purchase Value
55	The Emperor's New Cape	Bind on Pickup	43	1 45 88
56	Archivist Cape	Bind on Pickup	43	1 57 22
PROPERTIES: Restores 4 mana per 5 sec				
56	Shroud of Arcane Mastery	Bind on Pickup	43	1 52 23
PROPERTIES: Improves your chance to hit with spells by 1%				
56	Stoneskin Gargoyle Cape	Bind on Pickup	43	1 52 1
56	Wildfire Cape	Bind on Pickup	43	1 63 59
PROPERTIES: Fire Resist +20				
57	Cloak of the Cosmos	Bind on Pickup	44	1 68 30
PROPERTIES: Increases healing done by spells and effects by up to 26				
57	Cloak of Warding	Bind on Equip	44	1 70 70
PROPERTIES: Increased Defense +5				
57	Fluctuating Cloak	Bind on Pickup	44	1 59 71
PROPERTIES: Restores 4 health per 5 sec				
57	Pale Moon Cloak	Bind on Pickup	44	1 71 94
PROPERTIES: Shadow Resist +10				
57	Phantasmal Cloak	Bind on Pickup	44	1 64 60
58	Battle Healer's Cloak	Bind on Pickup	45	1 81 16
PROPERTIES: Increases healing done by spells and effects by up to 26				
58	Bloodmoon Cloak	Bind on Pickup	45	1 68 84
PROPERTIES: Arcane Resist +7				
58	Cape of the Black Baron	Bind on Pickup	45	1 64 98
PROPERTIES: +20 Attack Power				
58	Caretaker's Cape	Bind on Pickup	45	1 70 98
PROPERTIES: Increases healing done by spells and effects by up to 26				
58	Cloak of Revanchion	Bind on Pickup	45	1 64 76
58	Crystalline Threaded Cape	Bind on Equip	45	1 69 3
PROPERTIES: Increases damage and healing done by magical spells and effects by up to 20				
58	Frostweaver Cape	Bind on Pickup	45	1 69 48
PROPERTIES: Frost Resist +10				
58	Redoubt Cloak	Bind on Pickup	45	1 67 70
PROPERTIES: Increased Defense +7				
58	Sergeant's Cape	Bind on Pickup	45	88 30
58	Sergeant's Cloak	Bind on Pickup	45	85 77
58	Shadow Prowler's Cloak	Bind on Pickup	45	1 64 76
58	Shroud of Domination	Bind on Pickup	45	1 64 76
58	Faded Hakkari Cloak	Bind on Pickup	42	1 45 90
PROPERTIES: Restores 6 mana per 5 sec				
58	Tattered Hakkari Cape	Bind on Pickup	42	1 46 41
PROPERTIES: Restores 6 health per 5 sec				
60	Cloak of the Hakkari Worshipers	Bind on Pickup	48	2 21 62
PROPERTIES: Increases damage and healing done by magical spells and effects by up to 23				
60	Cloak of the Savior	Bind on Pickup	52	2 91 32
PROPERTIES: Increases healing done by spells and effects by up to 22				
60	Gaea's Embrace	Bind on Equip	49	2 46 1
PROPERTIES: Nature Resist +20				
60	Hakkari Loa Cloak	Bind on Pickup	50	2 53 56
PROPERTIES: Increases healing done by spells and effects by up to 33				
60	Might of the Tribe	Bind on Pickup	48	2 22 41
PROPERTIES: +28 Attack Power				
60	Overlord's Embrace	Bind on Pickup	50	2 51 65
PROPERTIES: Increased Defense +7, Increases your chance to block attacks with a shield by 1%				
60	Zulian Tigerhide Cloak	Bind on Pickup	48	2 16 55
PROPERTIES: Improves your chance to hit by 1%				
60	Earthweave Cloak	Bind on Pickup	44	1 64 9
PROPERTIES: Improves your chance to hit by 1%				
60	Shroud of the Exile	Bind on Pickup	45	1 78 55

Weapons

AXES

Epic One-Hand Axes

Lvl	Name	Binding	DPS	Damage	Speed	Vendor Purchase Value
42	Flurry Axe	Bind On Pickup	35.3	Physical 37—69	1.5	2 96 27
PROPERTIES: Grants 1 extra attack on your next swing						
52	Axe of the Deep Woods	Bind On Pickup	41.5	Physical 78—146	2.7	5 41 23
PROPERTIES: Blasts a target for 90 to 126 Nature damage, Main hand Weapon						
60	Ancient Hakkari Manslayer	Bind On Acquire	49.8	Physical 69—130	2	9 80 86
PROPERTIES: Steals 48 to 54 life from target enemy						
60	Blessed Qiraji War Axe	Bind On Acquire	60.6	Physical 110—205	2.6	16 40 24
PROPERTIES: Improves your chance to get a critical strike by 1%, +14 Attack Power						
60	Crul'shorukh, Edge of Chaos	Bind On Acquire	62.8	Physical 101—188	2.3	18 21 48
PROPERTIES: +36 Attack Power						
60	Deathbringer	Bind On Acquire	56.4	Physical 114—213	2.9	13 48 32
PROPERTIES: Sends a shadowy bolt at the enemy causing 110 to 140 Shadow damage						
60	Doom's Edge	Bind On Acquire	51.5	Physical 83—154	2.3	10 60 98
60	Grand Marshal's Handaxe	Bind On Acquire	59.5	Physical 138—207	2.9	5
PROPERTIES: Improves your chance to get a critical strike by 1%, +28 Attack Power						
60	Hatchet of Sundered Bone	Bind On Acquire	65.4	Physical 119—221	2.6	21 37 75
PROPERTIES: +36 Attack Power, Improves your chance to get a critical strike by 1%						
60	High Warlord's Cleaver	Bind On Acquire	59.5	Physical 138—207	2.9	5 2 25
PROPERTIES: Improves your chance to get a critical strike by 1%, +28 Attack Power						
60	Scythe of the Unseen Path	Bind On Acquire	51.5	Physical 86—161	2.4	
PROPERTIES: Restores 3 mana per 5 sec						
60	Sickle of Unyielding Strength	Bind On Acquire	51.4	Physical 75—141	2.1	
PROPERTIES: Increased Defense +4						

Superior One-Hand Axes

Lvl	Name	Binding	DPS	Damage	Speed	Vendor Purchase Value
15	Serpent's Kiss	Bind On Pickup	13.4	Physical 23—44	2.5	16 86
PROPERTIES: Poisons target for 7 Nature damage every 3 sec for 15 sec						
18	Guillotine Axe	Bind On Pickup	15	Physical 28—53	2.7	24 52
PROPERTIES: Main Hand Weapon						
18	Razor's Edge	Bind On Pickup	15.2	Physical 25—48	2.4	25 89
20	Butcher's Cleaver	Bind On Acquire	16.2	Physical 23—32	1.7	33
20	Grimclaw	Bind On Pickup	16	Physical 22—42	2	33 37
PROPERTIES: Sends a shadowy bolt at the enemy causing 30 Shadow damage						
22	Axe of the Enforcer	Bind On Pickup	17.1	Physical 31—58	2.6	39 37
25	Bearded Boneaxe	Bind On Pickup	18.9	Physical 25—47	1.9	51 43
PROPERTIES: Main Hand Weapon						
25	Headsplitter	Bind On Pickup	18.9	Physical 30—57	2.3	56 5
25	Vibroblade	Bind On Pickup	19.1	Physical 21—40	1.6	52 88
PROPERTIES: Punctures target's armor lowering it by 100						
31	Pronged Reaver	Bind On Acquire	24	Physical 40—75	2.4	97 88
32	Stalvan's Reaper	Bind On Pickup	24.8	Physical 50—94	2.9	1 6 82
PROPERTIES: Lowers all attributes of target by 2 for 1 min						
33	Steelclaw Reaver	Bind On Pickup	25.8	Physical 32—61	1.8	1 12 90
PROPERTIES: Main Hand Weapon						
33	Shovelphlange's Mining Axe	Bind On Pickup	25.7	Physical 50—94	2.8	1 13 80
PROPERTIES: +10 Attack Power						
34	Sickle Axe	Bind On Pickup	26.5	Physical 48—90	2.6	1 16 85
40	Curve-bladed Ripper	Bind On Pickup	30.3	Physical 40—75	1.9	1 97 78
PROPERTIES: Main Hand Weapon						
40	Digmaster 5000	Bind On Pickup	30.3	Physical 38—71	1.8	1 85 60
PROPERTIES: , Punctures target's armor lowering it by 100						
43	Winter's Bite	Bind On Pickup	32.1	Physical 47—88	2.1	2 47 48
PROPERTIES: Launches a bolt of frost at the enemy causing 20 to 30 Frost damage and slowing movement speed by 50% for 5 sec, Main Hand Weapon						
45	Ripsaw	Bind On Acquire	33.3	Physical 63—117	2.7	2 88 53
PROPERTIES: Wounds the target for 75 damage, Main Hand Weapon						
48	Ribsplitter	Bind On Pickup	35.2	Physical 66—124	2.7	3 53 32
PROPERTIES: +10 Attack Power, Main Hand Weapon						
48	Axe of Rin'ji	Bind On Pickup	35	Physical 46—87	1.9	3 47 5
50	Grizzle's Skinner	Bind On Acquire	36.5	Physical 61—114	2.4	3 67 52
PROPERTIES: Main Hand Weapon						
50	Dawn's Edge	Bind On Pickup	36.4	Physical 53—100	2.1	3 60 44
PROPERTIES: Improves your chance to get a critical strike by 1%						
51	Tooth of Eranikus	Bind On Acquire	37.1	Physical 62—116	2.4	3 88 1
PROPERTIES: Improves your chance to hit by 1%, Main Hand Weapon						
51	Wraith Scythe	Bind On Acquire	37	Physical 57—106	2.2	4 7 32
PROPERTIES: Steals 45 life from target enemy, Main Hand Weapon						
52	Soul Breaker	Bind On Acquire	37.5	Physical 42—78	1.6	4 41 42
PROPERTIES: Target enemy loses 12 health and mana every 3 sec for 30 sec, Main Hand Weapon						
53	Rivenspike	Bind On Acquire	38.1	Physical 77—144	2.9	4 41 6
PROPERTIES: Punctures target's armor lowering it by 200. Can be applied up to 3 times						
54	Demonfork	Bind On Acquire	38.9	Physical 76—142	2.8	4 50 85
PROPERTIES: Transfers 10 health every 5 seconds from the target to the caster for 25 sec, Main Hand Weapon						
55	Hedgecutter	Bind On Acquire	39.5	Physical 60—90	1.9	4 74 43
56	Serathil	Bind On Pickup	40	Physical 53—99	1.9	5 39 57
PROPERTIES: Armor 100						
57	Iceblade Hacker	Bind On Acquire	40.8	Physical 57—106, Frost 1—5	2	5 66 83
PROPERTIES: Main Hand Weapon						
57	Bone Slicing Hatchet	Bind On Acquire	40.6	Physical 48—90	1.7	5 24 27
57	Soulrender	Bind On Acquire	40.8	Physical 71—133	2.5	5 23 6
PROPERTIES: +28 Attack Power						
58	Annihilator	Bind On Pickup	41.5	Physical 49—92	1.7	5 71 50
PROPERTIES: Reduces an enemy's armor by 200.Stacks up to 3 times, Main Hand Weapon						
60	Dark Iron Destroyer	Bind On Pickup	42.7	Physical 71—134	2.4	6 39 73
PROPERTIES: Fire Resist +6, Main Hand Weapon						
60	Frostbite	Bind On Acquire	42.6	Physical 80—150	2.7	6 39 99
60	Zulian Hacker	Bind On Pickup	42.7	Physical 71—134	2.4	6 9 51
PROPERTIES: Increased Axes +2						
60	Windreaper	Bind On Acquire	39.3	Physical 63—118	2.3	5 14 18
PROPERTIES: Inflicts Nature damage every 2 sec for 20 sec						

Epic Two-Hand Axes

Lvl	Name	Binding	DPS	Damage	Speed	Vendor Purchase Value
35	Fiery War Axe	Bind On Pickup	40.3	Physical 93—141	2.9	2 15 28
PROPERTIES: Hurls a fiery ball that causes 155 to 197 Fire damage and an additional 24 damage over 6 sec						
44	Kang the Decapitator	Bind On Pickup	47.4	Physical 136—205	3.6	4 45 80
PROPERTIES: Wounds the target causing them to bleed for 560 damage over 30 sec						
55	Brain Hacker	Bind On Pickup	56.7	Physical 95—143	2.1	7 90 64
PROPERTIES: Wounds the target for 200 to 300 damage and lowers Intellect of target by 25 for 30 sec						
58	Treant's Bane	Bind On Acquire	59.4	Physical 128—193	2.7	9 67 48
PROPERTIES: Improves your chance to get a critical strike by 2%						
60	Dark Edge of Insanity	Bind On Acquire	86.6	Physical 242—364	3.5	26 65 69
PROPERTIES: Disorients the target, causing it to wander aimlessly for up to 3 sec						

Epic Two-Hand Axes

Lvl	Name	Binding	DPS	Damage	Speed	Vendor Purchase Value
60	Draconic Avenger	Bind On Acquire	68.1	Physical 174—262	3.2	13 50 86
PROPERTIES: Increases your chance to parry an attack by 2%						
60	Drake Talon Cleaver	Bind On Acquire	73.4	Physical 199—300	3.4	18 8 12
PROPERTIES: Delivers a fatal wound for 240 damage						
60	Grand Marshal's Sunderer	Bind On Acquire	77.4	Physical 235—353	3.8	5 72 27
PROPERTIES: Improves your chance to get a critical strike by 1%						
60	High Warlord's Battle Axe	Bind On Acquire	77.4	Physical 235—353	3.8	5 74 48
PROPERTIES: Improves your chance to get a critical strike by 1%						
60	Neretzek, The Blood Drinker	Bind On Acquire	68.2	Physical 202—303	3.7	14 71 80
PROPERTIES: Steals 141 to 163 life from target enemy						
60	Nightfall	Bind On Pickup	67	Physical 187—282	3.5	12 91 12
PROPERTIES: Spell damage taken by target increased by 15% for 5 sec						
60	Severance	Bind On Acquire	81.8	Physical 235—354	3.6	24 15 20
PROPERTIES: Improves your chance to get a critical strike by 2%						
60	Spinal Reaper	Bind On Acquire	74.7	Physical 203—305	3.4	17 90 67
PROPERTIES: Restores 150 mana or 20 rage when you kill a target that gives experience; this effect cannot occur more than once every 10 seconds, +34 Attack Power						

Superior Two-Hand Axes

Lvl	Name	Binding	DPS	Damage	Speed	Vendor Purchase Value
15	Boahn's Fang	Bind On Pickup	17.6	Physical 35—53	2.5	20 84
15	Prospector Axe	Bind On Pickup	17.5	Physical 33—51	2.4	22 5
18	Night Reaver	Bind On Pickup	19.7	Physical 52—78, Shadow 1—5	3.3	30 66
PROPERTIES: Sends a shadowy bolt at the enemy causing 60 to 90 Shadow damage						
18	Taskmaster Axe	Bind On Acquire	19.6	Physical 42—64	2.7	30 79
20	The Axe of Severing	Bind On Acquire	21	Physical 50—76	3	42 13
21	Killmaim	Bind On Pickup	21.7	Physical 55—84	3.2	47 71
PROPERTIES: Wounds the target causing them to bleed for 100 damage over 30 sec						
23	Supercharger Battle Axe	Bind On Pickup	23	Physical 51—78	2.8	54 83
PROPERTIES: Blasts a target for 80 to 100 Nature damage						
27	Bloodspiller	Bind On Pickup	26.7	Physical 57—87	2.7	78 74
PROPERTIES: Wounds the target causing them to bleed for 130 damage over 30 sec						
28	Burning War Axe	Bind On Pickup	27.7	Physical 73—110	3.3	87 56
PROPERTIES: Hurls a fiery ball that causes 86 to 110 Fire damage and an additional 18 damage over 6 sec						
29	Corpsemaker	Bind On Acquire	28.9	Physical 88—132	3.8	99 30
32	Thermaplugg's Left Arm	Bind On Acquire	32.6	Physical 70—106	2.7	1 35 60
34	Manslayer	Bind On Pickup	34.5	Physical 88—133	3.2	1 58 75
PROPERTIES: +38 Attack Power						
35	Hellslayer Battle Axe	Bind On Pickup	34.5	Physical 82—124	2.9	1 72 9
PROPERTIES: +66 Attack Power when fighting Undead						
35	Obsidian Cleaver	Bind On Pickup	35.6	Physical 94—141	3.3	1 68 95
37	Ravager	Bind On Acquire	37.3	Physical 104—157	3.5	1 89 23
PROPERTIES: You attack all nearby enemies for 9 sec causing weapon damage plus an additional 5 every 3 sec						
39	Pendulum of Doom	Bind On Pickup	38.9	Physical 124—187	4	2 14 89
PROPERTIES: Delivers a fatal wound for 250 to 350 damage						
40	Bonebiter	Bind On Acquire	38.8	Physical 105—159	3.4	2 34 76
40	Whirlwind Axe	Bind On Acquire	35.6	Physical 102—154	3.6	1 67 66
43	Executioner's Cleaver	Bind On Pickup	41.8	Physical 127—191	3.8	3 19 67
PROPERTIES: Improves your chance to hit by 1%						
44	The Minotaur	Bind On Pickup	42.7	Physical 109—164	3.2	3 40 67
48	Gatorbite Axe	Bind On Acquire	45.8	Physical 117—176	3.2	4 29 51
PROPERTIES: Wounds the target causing them to bleed for 230 damage over 30 sec						
49	Bleakwood Hew	Bind On Pickup	46.5	Physical 100—151	2.7	4 61 54
PROPERTIES: Enemy is inflicted with the Bleakwood Curse that reduces their magic resistances by 25.Can be applied up to 3 times						

Superior Two-Hand Axes

Lvl	Name	Binding	DPS	Damage	Speed	Vendor Purchase Value
51	Angerforge's Battle Axe	Bind On Acquire	48.1	Physical 100—150	2.6	4 88 82
51	Lord Alexander's Battle Axe	Bind On Pickup	48.1	Physical 123—185	3.2	4 96 40
52	Dark Iron Sunderer	Bind On Pickup	48.8	Physical 101—153	2.6	5 12 25
PROPERTIES: Reduces targets armor by 300 for 20 sec						
53	The Nicker	Bind On Acquire	49.8	Physical 159—239	4	5 49 24
PROPERTIES: Wounds the target for 50 to 150 damage and deals an additional 6 damage every 1 sec for 25 sec						
53	Waveslicer	Bind On Acquire	49.7	Physical 123—185	3.1	5 51 89
PROPERTIES: Improves your chance to get a critical strike by 1%						
54	Dreadforge Retaliator	Bind On Acquire	50.5	Physical 149—225	3.7	5 81 3
PROPERTIES: Increases your chance to parry an attack by 1%, Improves your chance to get a critical strike by 1%, +30 Attack Power						
57	Gravestone War Axe	Bind On Acquire	53.1	Physical 144—217	3.4	6 67 54
PROPERTIES: Diseases target enemy for 55 Nature damage every 3 sec for 15 sec						
57	Malicious Axe	Bind On Acquire	52.9	Physical 131—197	3.1	6 78 44
PROPERTIES: +26 Attack Power						
58	Arcanite Reaper	Bind On Pickup	53.8	Physical 153—256	3.8	7 30 36
PROPERTIES: +62 Attack Power						
60	Gri'lek's Carver	Bind On Acquire	58.5	Physical 182—274	3.9	8 85 11
PROPERTIES: +117 Attack Power when fighting Dragonkin						
60	Zulian Stone Axe	Bind On Acquire	58.6	Physical 131—197	2.8	8 78 68
PROPERTIES: +44 Attack Power, Improves your chance to get a critical strike by 1%						

BOWS

Epic Bows

Lvl	Name	Binding	DPS	Damage	Speed	Vendor Purchase Value
37	Bow of Searing Arrows	Bind On Pickup	25	Physical 47—88	2.7	1 47 22
PROPERTIES: Chance to strike your ranged target with a Searing Arrow for 18 to 26 Fire damage						
48	Hurricane	Bind On Pickup	30.3	Physical 34—63	1.6	3 20 32
PROPERTIES: Chance to strike your target with a Frost Arrow for 31 to 45 Frost damage						
60	Bow of Taut Sinew	Bind On Acquire	38.6	Physical 59—111	2.2	7 65 70
PROPERTIES: Nature Resist +8, +22 Attack Power						
60	Grand Marshal's Bullseye	Bind On Acquire	46.1	Physical 66—100	1.8	3 47 31
PROPERTIES: +36 ranged Attack Power						
60	Heartstriker	Bind On Acquire	44	Physical 80—149	2.6	10 46 9
PROPERTIES: +24 Attack Power						
60	High Warlord's Recurve	Bind On Acquire	46.1	Physical 66—100	1.8	3 49 97
PROPERTIES: +36 ranged Attack Power						
60	Huhuran's Stinger	Bind On Acquire	46.3	Physical 87—163	2.7	11 49 21
60	Mandokir's Sting	Bind On Acquire	37.5	Physical 68—127	2.6	6 49 72
60	Rhok'delar, Longbow of the Ancient Keepers	Bind On Acquire	44	Physical 89—166	2.9	
PROPERTIES: , Improves your chance to get a critical strike by 1%, +17 ranged Attack Power						
60	Soulstring	Bind On Acquire	50.9	Physical 103—192	2.9	15 75 20
PROPERTIES: Improves your chance to get a critical strike by 1%, +16 Attack Power						
60	Striker's Mark	Bind On Acquire	39.6	Physical 69—129	2.5	7 57 46
PROPERTIES: +22 Attack Power, Improves your chance to hit by 1%						

Superior Bows

Lvl	Name	Binding	DPS	Damage	Speed	Vendor Purchase Value
18	Outrider's Bow	Bind On Acquire	11.7	Physical 19—37	2.4	18 25
18	Outrunner's Bow	Bind On Acquire	11.7	Physical 19—37	2.4	18 25
20	Ranger Bow	Bind On Pickup	12.6	Physical 23—45	2.7	24 21
27	Harpyclaw Short Bow	Bind On Pickup	16.1	Physical 20—38	1.8	47 65
27	Nightstalker Bow	Bind On Acquire	16.2	Physical 19—36	1.7	50 86
28	Outrider's Bow	Bind On Acquire	16.7	Physical 28—52	2.4	51 32

Superior Bows

Lvl	Name	Binding	DPS	Damage	Speed	Vendor Purchase Value
28	Outrunner's Bow	Bind On Acquire	16.7	Physical 28—52	2.4	51 32
34	Skystriker Bow	Bind On Pickup	20.7	Physical 30—57	2.1	89 85
36	Monolithic Bow	Bind On Pickup	21.9	Physical 41—77	2.7	1 2 75
38	Outrider's Bow	Bind On Acquire	22.7	Physical 38—71	2.4	1 19 24
38	Outrunner's Bow	Bind On Acquire	22.7	Physical 38—71	2.4	1 19 24
42	Needle Threader	Bind On Pickup	24.5	Physical 34—64	2	1 66 94
42	Stinging Bow	Bind On Pickup	24.5	Physical 36—67	2.1	1 72 49
PROPERTIES: +14 Attack Power						
48	Houndmaster's Bow	Bind On Acquire	27.2	Physical 34—64	1.8	2 44 33
PROPERTIES: Attack Power increased by 24 when fighting Beasts						
48	Outrider's Bow	Bind On Acquire	27.5	Physical 46—86	2.4	2 41 17
48	Outrunner's Bow	Bind On Acquire	27.5	Physical 46—86	2.4	2 41 17
50	Gryphonwing Long Bow	Bind On Pickup	28.3	Physical 53—100	2.7	2 79 90
51	Verdant Keeper's Aim	Bind On Acquire	27.3	Physical 53—100	2.8	2 60 46
PROPERTIES: Chance to strike your ranged target with Keeper's Sting for 15 to 21 Nature damage						
53	Satyr's Bow	Bind On Acquire	29.8	Physical 50—93	2.4	3 29 88
PROPERTIES: Improves your chance to hit by 1%						
54	Riphook	Bind On Acquire	30.2	Physical 46—87	2.2	3 63 18
PROPERTIES: +22 Attack Power						
55	Deep Strike Bow	Bind On Acquire	30.7	Physical 58—108	2.7	3 73 36
55	Screeching Bow	Bind On Acquire	30.7	Physical 70—71	2.3	3 83 2
PROPERTIES: Shadow Resist +10						
56	Ancient Bone Bow	Bind On Acquire	31.3	Physical 61—114	2.8	3 78 94
56	Malgen's Long Bow	Bind On Acquire	31.2	Physical 63—118	2.9	3 73 62
PROPERTIES: +20 Attack Power						
58	Eaglehorn Long Bow	Bind On Pickup	32.2	Physical 40—76	1.8	4 27 3
58	Outrider's Bow	Bind On Acquire	32.3	Physical 54—101	2.4	4 40 11
58	Outrunner's Bow	Bind On Acquire	32.3	Physical 54—101	2.4	4 11 91
60	Hoodoo Hunting Bow	Bind On Acquire	35	Physical 68—128	2.8	5 67 83
60	Gorewood Bow	Bind On Acquire	31.8	Physical 55—104	2.5	4 14 51

CROSSBOWS

Epic Crossbows

Lvl	Name	Binding	DPS	Damage	Speed	Vendor Purchase Value
60	Ashjre'thul, Crossbow of Smiting	Bind On Acquire	45.6	Physical 124—186	3.4	11 15 46
PROPERTIES: +36 ranged Attack Power						
60	Crossbow of Imminent Doom	Bind On Acquire	41.6	Physical 103—155	3.1	9 34 11
PROPERTIES: Improves your chance to hit by 1%						
60	Grand Marshal's Repeater	Bind On Acquire	46.4	Physical 107—162	2.9	3 51 30
PROPERTIES: +36 ranged Attack Power						
60	High Warlord's Crossbow	Bind On Acquire	46.4	Physical 107—162	2.9	3 52 59
PROPERTIES: +36 ranged Attack Power						
60	Nerubian Slavemaker	Bind On Acquire	57.2	Physical 128—238	3.2	21 18 49
PROPERTIES: +24 Attack Power, Improves your chance to get a critical strike by 1%						
60	Polished Ironwood Crossbow	Bind On Acquire	41	Physical 101—153	3.1	8 16 72
PROPERTIES: Nature Resist +7, +24 Attack Power						

Superior Crossbows

Lvl	Name	Binding	DPS	Damage	Speed	Vendor Purchase Value
27	Crystalpine Stinger	Bind On Pickup	15.9	Physical 35—54	2.8	47 29
35	Swiftwind	Bind On Pickup	21.3	Physical 34—51	2	96 30
43	Skull Splitting Crossbow	Bind On Pickup	25.2	Physical 52—79	2.6	1 78 92
PROPERTIES: +14 Attack Power						

Superior Crossbows

Lvl	Name	Binding	DPS	Damage	Speed	Vendor Purchase Value
51	Heartseeking Crossbow	Bind On Pickup	28.9	Physical 71—108	3.1	2 94 44
PROPERTIES: Chance to strike your ranged target with a Shadowbolt for 13 to 19 Shadow damage						
54	Blackcrow	Bind On Acquire	30.3	Physical 77—117	3.2	3 60 55
PROPERTIES: Improves your chance to hit by 1%						
56	Carapace Spine Crossbow	Bind On Acquire	31.2	Physical 82—124	3.3	3 75 93
57	Stoneshatter	Bind On Acquire	31.7	Physical 73—111	2.9	4 19 28
PROPERTIES: Increased Crossbows +4						
60	Bloodseeker	Bind On Acquire	32.3	Physical 85—128	3.3	4 41 71
60	Fahrad's Reloading Repeater	Bind On Acquire	33.3	Physical 85—128	3.2	4 57 28
PROPERTIES: Improves your chance to hit by 1%						

DAGGERS

Epic Daggers

Lvl	Name	Binding	DPS	Damage	Speed	Vendor Purchase Value
40	Gut Ripper	Bind On Pickup	33.9	Physical 42—80	1.8	2 70 31
PROPERTIES: Wounds the target for 95 to 121 damage						
48	Shadowblade	Bind On Pickup	38.9	Physical 38—71	1.4	4 67 10
PROPERTIES: Sends a shadowy bolt at the enemy causing 110 to 140 Shadow damage						
58	Alcor's Sunrazor	Bind On Pickup	45.4	Physical 41—77	1.3	7 87 72
PROPERTIES: Fire Resist +10, Blasts a target for 75 to 105 Fire damage						
58	Felstriker	Bind On Acquire	45.6	Physical 54—101	1.7	7 56 24
PROPERTIES: All attacks are guaranteed to land and will be critical strikes for the next 3 sec						
60	Black Amnesty	Bind On Pickup	47.8	Physical 53—100	1.6	9 28 96
PROPERTIES: Reduce your threat to the current target making them less likely to attack you						
60	Blessed Qiraji Pugio	Bind On Acquire	60.6	Physical 72—134	1.7	16 52 47
PROPERTIES: Improves your chance to get a critical strike by 1%, Improves your chance to hit by 1%, +18 Attack Power						
60	Claw of Chromaggus	Bind On Acquire	58.3	Physical 61—114	1.5	15 21 4
PROPERTIES: Increases damage and healing done by magical spells and effects by up to 64, Restores 4 mana per 5 sec						
60	Core Hound Tooth	Bind On Acquire	51.3	Physical 57—107	1.6	10 92 75
PROPERTIES: Improves your chance to get a critical strike by 1%, +20 Attack Power						
60	Dagger of Veiled Shadows	Bind On Acquire	51.7	Physical 65—121	1.8	
PROPERTIES: Improves your chance to hit by 1%						
60	Death's Sting	Bind On Acquire	66.4	Physical 95—144	1.8	20 69 67
PROPERTIES: +38 Attack Power, Increased Daggers +3						
60	Dragonfang Blade	Bind On Acquire	55.3	Physical 69—130	1.8	13 9 7
60	Emerald Dragonfang	Bind On Acquire	52.5	Physical 66—123	1.8	10 84 99
PROPERTIES: Blasts the enemy with acid for 87 to 105 Nature damage						
60	Fang of the Faceless	Bind On Acquire	49.7	Physical 66—123	1.9	10 6 5
PROPERTIES: Improves your chance to get a critical strike by 1%, +28 Attack Power						
60	Fang of the Mystics	Bind On Acquire	51.7	Physical 54—101	1.5	10 93 7
PROPERTIES: Improves your chance to get a critical strike with spells by 1%, Restores 4 mana per 5 sec, Increases damage and healing done by magical spells and effects by up to 40						
60	Grand Marshal's Dirk	Bind On Acquire	59.5	Physical 95—143	2	4 84 58
PROPERTIES: Improves your chance to get a critical strike by 1%, +28 Attack Power						
60	Grand Marshal's Mageblade	Bind On Acquire	59.5	Physical 95—143	2	4 56 71
PROPERTIES: Increases damage and healing done by magical spells and effects by up to 72, Improves your chance to get a critical strike with spells by 1%						
60	Gutgore Ripper	Bind On Acquire	50.6	Physical 63—119	1.8	10 44 72
PROPERTIES: Sends a shadowy bolt at the enemy causing 75 Shadow damage and lowering all stats by 25 for 30 sec						
60	Harbinger of Doom	Bind On Acquire	65.3	Physical 83—126	1.6	19 48 70
PROPERTIES: Improves your chance to get a critical strike by 1%, Improves your chance to hit by 1%						
60	High Warlord's Razor	Bind On Acquire	59.5	Physical 95—143	2	4 88 12
PROPERTIES: Improves your chance to get a critical strike by 1%, +28 Attack Power						

Epic Daggers

Lvl	Name	Binding	DPS	Damage	Speed	Vendor Purchase Value
60	High Warlord's Spellblade	Bind On Acquire	59.5	Physical 95—143	2	4 56 71
PROPERTIES: Increases damage and healing done by magical spells and effects by up to 72, Improves your chance to get a critical strike with spells by 1%						
60	Kingsfall	Bind On Acquire	73.1	Physical 105—158	1.8	26 51 85
PROPERTIES: , Improves your chance to get a critical strike by 1%, Improves your chance to hit by 1%						
60	Kris of Unspoken Names	Bind On Acquire	51.7	Physical 54—101	1.5	
PROPERTIES: Increases damage and healing done by magical spells and effects by up to 59						
60	Maexxna's Fang	Bind On Acquire	65.3	Physical 94—141	1.8	19 93 92
PROPERTIES: +36 Attack Power, Improves your chance to hit by 1%						
60	Midnight Haze	Bind On Acquire	62.8	Physical 90—136	1.8	18 1 71
PROPERTIES: Increases damage and healing done by magical spells and effects by up to 85						
60	Mindfang	Bind On Acquire	47.4	Physical 56—105	1.7	8 56 53
PROPERTIES: Increases damage and healing done by magical spells and effects by up to 30, Improves your chance to get a critical strike with spells by 1%. Armor 40						
60	Perdition's Blade	Bind On Acquire	58.3	Physical 73—137	1.8	14 87 14
PROPERTIES: Blasts a target for 40 to 56 Fire damage						
60	Qiraji Sacrificial Dagger	Bind On Acquire	48.2	Physical 64—119	1.9	9 25 93
PROPERTIES: +20 Attack Power						
60	Sageclaw	Bind On Acquire	47.4	Physical 56—105	1.7	8 84 72
PROPERTIES: Increases damage and healing done by magical spells and effects by up to 30, Improves your chance to get a critical strike with spells by 1%. Armor 40						
60	Shadowsong's Sorrow	Bind On Acquire	57.4	Physical 68—127	1.7	14 22 69
60	The Lobotomizer	Bind On Acquire	47.2	Physical 59—111	1.8	25 13 23
PROPERTIES: Wounds the target for 200 to 300 damage and lowers Intellect of target by 25 for 30 sec						
49	Blade of Eternal Darkness	Bind On Acquire	39.3	Physical 41—77	1.5	4 67 96
PROPERTIES: Chance on landing a damaging spell to deal 100 Shadow damage and restore 100 mana to you, Main Hand Weapon						
60	Fang of Korialstrasz	Bind On Acquire	57.5	Physical 72—135	1.8	14 28 5
PROPERTIES: Increases healing done by spells and effects by up to 121, Main Hand Weapon						
60	Fang of Venoxis	Bind On Acquire	47.3	Physical 43—80	1.3	8 18 95
PROPERTIES: Increases damage and healing done by magical spells and effects by up to 24, Restores 6 mana per 5 sec, Main Hand Weapon						
60	Sorcerous Dagger	Bind On Acquire	47.1	Physical 46—86	1.4	8 56 45
PROPERTIES: Increases damage and healing done by magical spells and effects by up to 20, Main Hand Weapon						

Superior Daggers

Lvl	Name	Binding	DPS	Damage	Speed	Vendor Purchase Value
18	Evocator's Blade	Bind On Pickup	15.3	Physical 17—32	1.6	25 9
18	Scout's Blade	Bind On Acquire	15.3	Physical 18—34	1.7	24 33
18	Sentinel's Blade	Bind On Acquire	15.3	Physical 18—34	1.7	26 10
19	Assassin's Blade	Bind On Pickup	15.5	Physical 20—39	1.9	29 74
20	Blackfang	Bind On Pickup	16.3	Physical 17—32	1.5	33 86
PROPERTIES: Shadow Resist +5						
20	Doomspike	Bind On Pickup	16.3	Physical 17—32	1.5	32 29
21	Blackvenom Blade	Bind On Pickup	16.7	Physical 21—39, Shadow 1—7	1.8	35 94
PROPERTIES: Poisons target for 5 Nature damage every 3 sec for 15 sec						
21	Prison Shank	Bind On Acquire	16.7	Physical 21—39	1.8	35 52
21	Talon of Vultros	Bind On Pickup	16.8	Physical 23—44	2	38
23	Bite of Serra'kis	Bind On Acquire	17.7	Physical 16—30	1.3	46 65
PROPERTIES: Poisons target for 4 Nature damage every 2 sec for 20 sec						
24	Meteor Shard	Bind On Acquire	18.3	Physical 23—43	1.8	48 93
PROPERTIES: Blasts a target for 35 Fire damage						
26	Vendetta	Bind On Pickup	19.2	Physical 17—33	1.3	57 65
27	Claw of the Shadowmancer	Bind On Pickup	20.5	Physical 27—51	1.9	67 31
PROPERTIES: Sends a shadowy bolt at the enemy causing 35 Shadow damage						
27	Toxic Revenger	Bind On Acquire	20.5	Physical 27—51	1.9	65 92
PROPERTIES: Deals 5 Nature damage every 5 sec to any enemy in an 8 yard radius around the caster for 15 sec						

Superior Daggers

Lvl	Name	Binding	DPS	Damage	Speed	Vendor Purchase Value
28	Scout's Blade	Bind On Acquire	21.2	Physical 25—47	1.7	69 69
28	Sentinel's Blade	Bind On Acquire	21.2	Physical 25—47	1.7	70 74
30	Scorn's Focal Dagger	Bind On Acquire	22.9	Physical 22—42	1.4	26 65
PROPERTIES: Increases damage and healing done by magical spells and effects by up to 9						
30	Swinetusk Shank	Bind On Acquire	23	Physical 24—45	1.5	88 66
31	Howling Blade	Bind On Pickup	23.9	Physical 23—44	1.4	94 66
PROPERTIES: Reduces target's attack power by 30 for 30 sec						
31	Stonevault Shiv	Bind On Pickup	24	Physical 25—47	1.5	97 89
32	Sliverblade	Bind On Pickup	25	Physical 24—46	1.4	1
PROPERTIES: Blasts a target for 45 Frost damage						
34	Hypnotic Blade	Bind On Acquire	26.8	Physical 26—49	1.4	38 35
PROPERTIES: Increases damage and healing done by magical spells and effects by up to 9						
34	The Ziggler	Bind On Pickup	26.5	Physical 31—59	1.7	1 24 72
PROPERTIES: Blasts a target for 10 to 20 Nature damage						
38	Scout's Blade	Bind On Acquire	29.1	Physical 34—65	1.7	1 73 58
38	Sentinel's Blade	Bind On Acquire	29.1	Physical 34—65	1.7	1 63 76
39	Coldrage Dagger	Bind On Acquire	29.7	Physical 31—58	1.5	1 71 93
PROPERTIES: Launches a bolt of frost at the enemy causing 20 to 30 Frost damage and slowing movement speed by 50% for 5 sec						
40	Black Menace	Bind On Acquire	29.7	Physical 31—58	1.5	1 75 22
PROPERTIES: Sends a shadowy bolt at the enemy causing 30 Shadow damage						
42	Gutwrencher	Bind On Pickup	31.6	Physical 35—66	1.6	2 27 38
PROPERTIES: Wounds the target causing them to bleed for 80 damage over 30 sec						
42	Widowmaker	Bind On Pickup	31.6	Physical 42—78	1.9	2 24 79
44	Stealthblade	Bind On Pickup	32.9	Physical 32—60	1.4	2 73 66
PROPERTIES: Reduces threat level on all enemies by a small amount for 10 sec						
45	Satyr's Lash	Bind On Acquire	33.2	Physical 39—74	1.7	2 87 85
PROPERTIES: Sends a shadowy bolt at the enemy causing 55 to 85 Shadow damage						
46	Searing Needle	Bind On Pickup	33.9	Physical 42—80	1.8	2 88 83
PROPERTIES: Blasts a target for 60 Fire damage and increases damage done to target by Fire damage by 10 for 30 sec						
48	Scout's Blade	Bind On Acquire	35	Physical 41—78	1.7	3 49 82
48	Sentinel's Blade	Bind On Acquire	35	Physical 41—78	1.7	3 29 96
49	Hookfang Shanker	Bind On Acquire	35.7	Physical 35—65	1.4	3 54 51
PROPERTIES: Corrosive acid that deals 7 Nature damage every 3 sec and lowers target's armor by 50 for 30 sec						
49	Charstone Dirk	Bind On Acquire	35.9	Physical 40—75	1.6	3 54 83
PROPERTIES: Restores 2 mana per 5 sec, Main Hand Weapon						
50	Julie's Dagger	Bind On Pickup	36.5	Physical 33—62	1.3	3 61 57
PROPERTIES: Heals wielder of 78 damage over 12 sec						
50	Barman Shanker	Bind On Acquire	36.5	Physical 51—95	2	3 94 11
PROPERTIES: Wounds the target causing them to bleed for 100 damage over 30 sec, Main Hand Weapon						
51	Dire Nail	Bind On Acquire	36.7	Physical 38—72	1.5	4 4 27
PROPERTIES: Shadow Resist +5						
52	Blood-etched Blade	Bind On Acquire	37.7	Physical 39—74	1.5	4 34 91
PROPERTIES: Increases damage and healing done by magical spells and effects by up to 6						
52	Flarethorn	Bind On Acquire	37.5	Physical 47—88	1.8	4 38 78
PROPERTIES: Increases damage done by Fire spells and effects by up to 17						
52	The Shadowfoot Stabber	Bind On Pickup	37.5	Physical 47—88	1.8	4 42 10
PROPERTIES: +18 Attack Power						
52	Glacial Spike	Bind On Acquire	34.6	Physical 31—59	1.3	3 6 51
PROPERTIES: Your Frostbolt spells have a 6% chance to restore 50 mana when cast						
53	Lifeforce Dirk	Bind On Acquire	35.9	Physical 40—75	1.6	3 53 15
55	Crystal Tipped Stiletto	Bind On Acquire	39.5	Physical 52—98	1.9	4 74 43
PROPERTIES: +24 Attack Power						
55	Keris of Zul'Serak	Bind On Acquire	39.4	Physical 49—93	1.8	5 11 99
PROPERTIES: Inflicts numbing pain that deals 10 Nature damage every 2 sec and increases time between target's attacks by 10% for 10 sec						
56	Fang of the Crystal Spider	Bind On Acquire	40.3	Physical 45—84	1.6	5 33 88
PROPERTIES: Slows target enemy's casting speed and increases the time between melee and ranged attacks by 10% for 10 sec						
56	Frightalon	Bind On Acquire	40	Physical 39—73	1.4	5 24 22
PROPERTIES: Lowers all attributes of target by 10 for 1 min						

Superior Daggers

Lvl	Name	Binding	DPS	Damage	Speed	Vendor Purchase Value
57	Bonescraper	Bind On Acquire	40.7	Physical 40—74	1.4	5 54 38
PROPERTIES: +30 Attack Power						
57	Specter's Blade	Bind On Acquire	40.8	Physical 51—96	1.8	5 40 72
PROPERTIES: +45 Attack Power when fighting Undead						
57	Witchblade	Bind On Acquire	40.6	Physical 45—85	1.6	5 36 12
PROPERTIES: Increases damage and healing done by magical spells and effects by up to 14						
57	Blade of the New Moon	Bind On Acquire	40.7	Physical 40—74	1.4	5 67 16
PROPERTIES: Increases damage done by Shadow spells and effects by up to 19, Main Hand Weapon						
57	Lorespinner	Bind On Acquire	37.7	Physical 45—68	1.5	4 6 95
PROPERTIES: Restores 3 mana per 5 sec, Main Hand Weapon						
57	Distracting Dagger	Bind On Acquire	40.8	Physical 42—64	1.3	5 67 10
PROPERTIES: Increased Daggers +6, Off Hand Weapon						
58	Gift of the Elven Magi	Bind On Acquire	41.3	Physical 43—81	1.5	5 65 17
58	Heartseeker	Bind On Pickup	41.5	Physical 49—92	1.7	5 82 15
PROPERTIES: Improves your chance to get a critical strike by 1%						
58	Scarlet Kris	Bind On Pickup	41.3	Physical 43—81	1.5	5 98 51
58	Scout's Blade	Bind On Acquire	41.5	Physical 49—92	1.7	5 95 34
58	Sentinel's Blade	Bind On Acquire	41.5	Physical 49—92	1.7	5 61 43
58	Finkle's Skinner	Bind On Acquire	41.2	Physical 37—70	1.3	5 79 91
PROPERTIES: Skinning +10, +45 Attack Power when fighting Beasts, Main Hand Weapon						
60	Electrified Dagger	Bind On Acquire	42.5	Physical 53—100	1.8	6 33
PROPERTIES: Blasts a target for 45 Nature damage						
60	Glacial Blade	Bind On Acquire	42.5	Physical 53—100	1.8	6 30 65
PROPERTIES: Blasts a target for 45 Frost damage						
60	Darrowspike	Bind On Acquire	41.3	Physical 43—81	1.5	5 78 6
PROPERTIES: Blasts a target for 90 Frost damage						
60	The Thunderwood Poker	Bind On Acquire	42.5	Physical 53—100	1.8	6 49 76
60	Dark Whisper Blade	Bind On Pickup	42.5	Physical 41—78	1.4	6 5 51
PROPERTIES: Increases damage and healing done by magical spells and effects by up to 19, Main Hand Weapon						
60	The Lost Kris of Zedd	Bind On Pickup	45	Physical 47—88	1.5	7 5 73
PROPERTIES: Improves your chance to get a critical strike with spells by 1%, Increases damage and healing done by magical spells and effects by up to 14, Main Hand Weapon						
60	Wushoolay's Poker	Bind On Acquire	45	Physical 50—94	1.6	7 35 65
PROPERTIES: Increases healing done by spells and effects by up to 31, Restores 6 mana per 5 sec, Main Hand Weapon						
60	Shivsprocket's Shiv	Bind On Acquire	42.7	Physical 44—84	1.5	6 54 46
PROPERTIES: Increases damage and healing done by magical spells and effects by up to 13, Main Hand Weapon						
60	Verimonde's Last Resort	Bind On Acquire	43.2	Physical 42—79	1.4	6 45 12
PROPERTIES: Increases damage and healing done by magical spells and effects by up to 19, Main Hand Weapon						

FIST

Epic Fist Weapons

Lvl	Name	Binding	DPS	Damage	Speed	Vendor Purchase Value
60	Claw of the Black Drake	Bind On Acquire	56.3	Physical 102—191	2.6	13 69 28
PROPERTIES: Improves your chance to get a critical strike by 1%, Main Hand Weapon						
60	Eskhandar's Right Claw	Bind On Acquire	48	Physical 50—94	1.5	9 9 5
PROPERTIES: Increases your attack speed by 30% for 5 sec, Main Hand Weapon						
60	Grand Marshal's Right Hand Blade	Bind On Acquire	59.5	Physical 138—207	2.9	4 93 39
PROPERTIES: Improves your chance to get a critical strike by 1%, +28 Attack Power, Main Hand Weapon						
60	High Warlord's Right Claw	Bind On Acquire	59.5	Physical 138—207	2.9	4 95 16
PROPERTIES: Improves your chance to get a critical strike by 1%, +28 Attack Power, Main Hand Weapon						
60	Silithid Claw	Bind On Acquire	57.5	Physical 64—120	1.6	14 11 69
PROPERTIES: Improves your chance to get a critical strike by 1%, +30 Attack Power, Main Hand Weapon						

Epic Fist Weapons

Lvl	Name	Binding	DPS	Damage	Speed	Vendor Purchase Value
60	Thekal's Grasp	Bind On Acquire	47	Physical 72—135	2.2	8 59 49
PROPERTIES: Improves your chance to get a critical strike by 1%, Main Hand Weapon						
60	Arlokk's Grasp	Bind On Acquire	47	Physical 49—92	1.5	8 40 70
PROPERTIES: Sends a shadowy bolt at the enemy causing 55 to 85 Shadow damage, Off Hand Weapon						
60	Claw of the Frost Wyrm	Bind On Acquire	71.7	Physical 75—140	1.5	26 71 43
PROPERTIES: Improves your chance to get a critical strike by 1%, Improves your chance to hit by 1%, +22 Attack Power, Off Hand Weapon						
60	Eskhandar's Left Claw	Bind On Acquire	48	Physical 50—94	1.5	9 5 76
PROPERTIES: Slows enemy's movement by 60% and causes them to bleed for 150 damage over 30 sec, Off Hand Weapon						
60	Grand Marshal's Left Hand Blade	Bind On Acquire	59.5	Physical 138—207	2.9	5
PROPERTIES: Improves your chance to get a critical strike by 1%, +28 Attack Power, Off Hand Weapon						
60	High Warlord's Left Claw	Bind On Acquire	59.5	Physical 138—207	2.9	5 2 15
PROPERTIES: Improves your chance to get a critical strike by 1%, +28 Attack Power, Off Hand Weapon						

Superior Fist Weapons

Lvl	Name	Binding	DPS	Damage	Speed	Vendor Purchase Value
21	Iron Knuckles	Bind On Acquire	16.5	Physical 19—37	1.7	36 63
PROPERTIES: Pummel the target for 4 damage and interrupt the spell being cast for 5 sec						
46	Vilerend Slicer	Bind On Pickup	33.9	Physical 33—62	1.4	3 6 56
PROPERTIES: Wounds the target for 75 damage, Main Hand Weapon						
47	Claw of Celebras	Bind On Acquire	34.4	Physical 43—81	1.8	3 33 51
PROPERTIES: Poisons target for 9 Nature damage every 2 sec for 20 sec, Off Hand Weapon						
51	Bloodfist	Bind On Acquire	36.7	Physical 38—72	1.5	3 92 42
PROPERTIES: Wounds the target for 20 damage						
54	Gargoyle Shredder Talons	Bind On Acquire	38.9	Physical 49—91	1.8	4 63 12
PROPERTIES: Wounds the target causing them to bleed for 110 damage over 30 sec, Off Hand Weapon						
55	Hurd Smasher	Bind On Acquire	39.4	Physical 49—93	1.8	5 8 51
PROPERTIES: Knocks target silly for 2 sec						
55	Blood Talon	Bind On Acquire	39.2	Physical 35—67	1.3	4 88 21
PROPERTIES: Wounds the target causing them to bleed for 100 damage over 30 sec, Main Hand Weapon						
56	Willey's Back Scratcher	Bind On Acquire	40.2	Physical 73—136	2.6	5 47 93
PROPERTIES: +10 Attack Power, Main Hand Weapon						
56	Lefty's Brass Knuckle	Bind On Acquire	40	Physical 42—78	1.5	5 20 93

GUNS

Epic Guns

Lvl	Name	Binding	DPS	Damage	Speed	Vendor Purchase Value
43	Precisely Calibrated Boomstick	Bind On Pickup	2707	Physical 38—45	1.5	2 45 39
53	Dwarven Hand Cannon	Bind On Pickup	32.8	Physical 66—124	2.9	4 50 40
PROPERTIES: Chance to strike your ranged target with a Flaming Cannonball for 33 to 49 Fire damage						
60	Blastershot Launcher	Bind On Acquire	40.2	Physical 73—136	2.6	8 25 72
PROPERTIES: Improves your chance to get a critical strike by 1%						
60	Blessed Qiraji Musket	Bind On Acquire	47.3	Physical 86—160	2.6	13 9 49
PROPERTIES: +31 ranged Attack Power						
60	Core Marksman Rifle	Bind On Pickup	36.8	Physical 64—120	2.5	6 63 47
PROPERTIES: +22 ranged Attack Power, Improves your chance to hit by 1%						
60	Dragonbreath Hand Cannon	Bind On Acquire	43.9	Physical 86—160	2.8	10 65 74
60	Grand Marshal's Hand Cannon	Bind On Acquire	46.4	Physical 107—162	2.9	3 59 45
PROPERTIES: +36 ranged Attack Power						

Epic Guns

Lvl	Name	Binding	DPS	Damage	Speed	Vendor Purchase Value
60	Gurubashi Dwarf Destroyer	Bind On Acquire	38.9	Physical 76—142	2.8	7 38 37
PROPERTIES: +30 Attack Power						
60	High Warlord's Street Sweeper	Bind On Acquire	46.4	Physical 107—162	2.9	3 66 2
PROPERTIES: +36 ranged Attack Power						
60	Larvae of the Great Worm	Bind On Acquire	49.2	Physical 103—192	3	13 21 77
PROPERTIES: Improves your chance to get a critical strike by 1%, +18 Attack Power						
60	Toxin Injector	Bind On Acquire	49	Physical 68—128	2	14 23 62
PROPERTIES: +28 Attack Power						
60	The Purifier	Bind On Acquire	33.8	Physical 71—132	3	4 74 43
PROPERTIES: Improves your chance to get a critical strike by 1%						

Superior Guns

Lvl	Name	Binding	DPS	Damage	Speed	Vendor Purchase Value
16	Lil Timmy's Peashooter	Bind On Pickup	11	Physical 20—37	2.6	14 56
22	Double-barreled Shotgun	Bind On Pickup	13.3	Physical 21—40	2.3	30 20
24	Hi-tech Supergun	Bind On Pickup	14.3	Physical 23—43	2.3	36 32
28	Chesterfall Musket	Bind On Pickup	16.5	Physical 26—50	2.3	55 14
29	Ironweaver	Bind On Pickup	17.3	Physical 31—59	2.6	58 74
30	Glass Shooter	Bind On Acquire	17.9	Physical 36—68	2.9	66 52
37	The Silencer	Bind On Pickup	22.3	Physical 43—82	2.8	1 15 32
PROPERTIES: +14 Attack Power						
38	Shadowforge Bushmaster	Bind On Pickup	22.8	Physical 46—86	2.9	1 30 52
PROPERTIES: Shadow Resist +7						
42	Galgann's Fireblaster	Bind On Acquire	24.6	Physical 44—84	2.6	1 66 81
PROPERTIES: Chance to strike your ranged target with a Fire Blast for 12 to 18 Fire damage						
45	Guttbuster	Bind On Pickup	26.1	Physical 49—92	2.7	2 10 29
48	Houndmaster's Rifle	Bind On Acquire	27.4	Physical 44—82	2.3	2 45 27
PROPERTIES: Attack Power increased by 24 when fighting Beasts						
48	Megashot Rifle	Bind On Acquire	27.4	Physical 32—61	1.7	2 64 25
PROPERTIES: Arcane Resist +5, +19 ranged Attack Power						
50	Dark Iron Rifle	Bind On Pickup	28.3	Physical 53—100	2.7	2 91 52
PROPERTIES: Chance to strike your ranged target with Shadow Shot for 18 to 26 Shadow damage						
51	Burstshot Harquebus	Bind On Acquire	28.8	Physical 52—98	2.6	2 96 70
PROPERTIES: +10 Attack Power						
53	Shell Launcher Shotgun	Bind On Pickup	29.8	Physical 48—89	2.3	3 47 4
PROPERTIES: Chance to strike your ranged target with a Flaming Shell for 18 to 26 Fire damage						
56	Flawless Arcanite Rifle	Bind On Pickup	31.2	Physical 65—122	3	4 6 25
PROPERTIES: Increased Guns +4, +10 ranged Attack Power						
56	Willey's Portable Howitzer	Bind On Acquire	31.2	Physical 63—118	2.9	3 84 43
PROPERTIES: +8 Attack Power						
57	Xorothian Firestick	Bind On Acquire	31.7	Physical 57—108	2.6	4 31 29
PROPERTIES: Shadow Resist +6						
60	Crystal Slugthrower	Bind On Pickup	33.4	Physical 65—122	2.8	4 54 13
PROPERTIES: +20 Attack Power						
60	Silithid Husked Launcher	Bind On Pickup	35	Physical 68—128	2.8	5 25 22

MACES

Epic One-Hand Maces

Lvl	Name	Binding	DPS	Damage	Speed	Vendor Purchase Value
38	Ardent Custodian	Bind On Pickup	32.9	Physical 48—90	2.1	2 15 32
PROPERTIES: Increased Defense +5, Main Hand Weapon, Armor 100						
40	Hammer of Expertise	Bind On Acquire	36.9	Physical 54—101	2.1	
PROPERTIES: Main Hand Weapon						
49	Hammer of the Northern Wind	Bind On Pickup	39.5	Physical 58—108	2.1	4 52 67
PROPERTIES: Launches a bolt of frost at the enemy causing 20 to 30 Frost damage and slowing movement speed by 50% for 5 sec, Main Hand Weapon						
55	Ironfoe	Bind On Acquire	43.5	Physical 73—136	2.4	6 30 86
PROPERTIES: Grants 2 extra attacks on your next swing, Main Hand Weapon						
57	Hand of Edward the Odd	Bind On Pickup	45	Physical 50—94	1.6	7 5 54
PROPERTIES: Next spell cast within 4 sec will cast instantly						
58	Persuader	Bind On Pickup	45.7	Physical 86—161	2.7	8 5 54
PROPERTIES: Improves your chance to hit by 1%, Improves your chance to get a critical strike by 1%, Main Hand Weapon						
60	Empyrean Demolisher	Bind On Acquire	48	Physical 94—175	2.8	9 5 58
PROPERTIES: Increases your attack speed by 20% for 10 sec, Main Hand Weapon						
60	Gavel of Infinite Wisdom	Bind On Acquire	51.5	Physical 97—181	2.7	
PROPERTIES: Restores 4 mana per 5 sec, Increases healing done by spells and effects by up to 90, Main Hand Weapon						
60	Hammer of Bestial Fury	Bind On Acquire	52.4	Physical 69—130	1.9	10 93 27
PROPERTIES: +154 Attack Power in Cat, Bear, and Dire Bear forms only, Main Hand Weapon, Armor 90						
60	Hammer of the Gathering Storm	Bind On Acquire	51.5	Physical 86—161	2.4	
PROPERTIES: Increases damage and healing done by magical spells and effects by up to 53, Main Hand Weapon						
60	Jin'do's Hexxer	Bind On Acquire	47.9	Physical 80—150	2.4	8 82 92
PROPERTIES: Increases healing done by spells and effects by up to 51, Improves your chance to get a critical strike with spells by 1%, Main Hand Weapon						
60	Lok'amir il Romathis	Bind On Acquire	62.9	Physical 92—172	2.1	18 1 16
PROPERTIES: Increases damage and healing done by magical spells and effects by up to 84, Main Hand Weapon						
60	Mace of Unending Life	Bind On Acquire	51.5	Physical 93—175	2.6	
PROPERTIES: Increases damage and healing done by magical spells and effects by up to 40, +140 Attack Power in Cat, Bear, and Dire Bear forms only, Main Hand Weapon						
60	Scepter of the False Prophet	Bind On Acquire	66.4	Physical 83—156	1.8	22 43 99
PROPERTIES: Increases healing done by spells and effects by up to 187, Restores 3 mana per 5 sec, Main Hand Weapon						
60	Spineshatter	Bind On Acquire	54.4	Physical 99—184	2.6	12 88 25
PROPERTIES: Increased Defense +5, Main Hand Weapon						
60	Stinger of Ayamiss	Bind On Acquire	50.6	Physical 85—158	2.4	9 99 35
PROPERTIES: Improves your chance to get a critical strike with spells by 1%, Increases damage and healing done by magical spells and effects by up to 36, Main Hand Weapon						
60	Anubisath Warhammer	Bind On Acquire	52.5	Physical 66—123	1.8	11 81 75
PROPERTIES: Increased Maces +4, +32 Attack Power						
60	Aurastone Hammer	Bind On Acquire	50.6	Physical 95—178	2.7	10 21 78
PROPERTIES: Restores 5 mana per 5 sec, Increases damage and healing done by magical spells and effects by up to 25						
60	Blessed Qiraji War Hammer	Bind On Acquire	60.7	Physical 89—166	2.1	17 21 35
PROPERTIES: +280 Attack Power in Cat, Bear, and Dire Bear forms only, Increased Defense +8, Armor 70						
60	Ebon Hand	Bind On Pickup	51.6	Physical 90—168	2.5	10 36 89
PROPERTIES: Fire Resist +7, Sends a shadowy bolt at the enemy causing 125 to 275 Shadow damage						
60	Grand Marshal's Punisher	Bind On Acquire	59.5	Physical 138—207	2.9	4 96 84
PROPERTIES: Improves your chance to get a critical strike by 1%, +28 Attack Power						
60	Grand Marshal's Warhammer	Bind On Acquire	59.5	Physical 138—207	2.9	4 56 71
PROPERTIES: Increases healing done by spells and effects by up to 134, Restores 6 mana per 5 sec						
60	Hammer of the Twisting Nether	Bind On Acquire	73.2	Physical 97—181	1.9	28 4 18

Epic One-Hand Maces

Lvl	Name	Binding	DPS	Damage	Speed	Vendor Purchase Value
PROPERTIES: Increases healing done by spells and effects by up to 238, Restores 8 mana per 5 sec						
60	High Warlord's Battle Mace	Bind On Acquire	59.5	Physical 138—207	2.9	4 56 71
PROPERTIES: Increases healing done by spells and effects by up to 134, Restores 6 mana per 5 sec						
60	High Warlord's Bludgeon	Bind On Acquire	59.5	Physical 138—207	2.9	4 98 61
PROPERTIES: Improves your chance to get a critical strike by 1%, +28 Attack Power						
60	Misplaced Servo Arm	Bind On Acquire	65.4	Physical 128—238	2.8	20 31 82
PROPERTIES: Chance to discharge electricity causing 100 to 150 Nature damage to your target						
60	Sand Polished Hammer	Bind On Acquire	53.5	Physical 97—181	2.6	12 1 42
PROPERTIES: Improves your chance to get a critical strike by 1%, +20 Attack Power						
60	The Castigator	Bind On Acquire	65.4	Physical 119—221	2.6	20 77 85
PROPERTIES: Improves your chance to get a critical strike by 1%, Improves your chance to hit by 1%, +16 Attack Power						
60	The End of Dreams	Bind On Acquire	65.3	Physical 86—162	1.9	19 79 46
PROPERTIES: Increases damage and healing done by magical spells and effects by up to 95, +305 Attack Power in Cat, Bear, and Dire Bear forms only, Restores 5 mana per 5 sec						
60	The Widow's Embrace	Bind On Acquire	62.9	Physical 83—156	1.9	18 91 14
PROPERTIES: Increases healing done by spells and effects by up to 161						

Superior One-Hand Maces

Lvl	Name	Binding	DPS	Damage	Speed	Vendor Purchase Value
16	Face Smasher	Bind On Pickup	14	Physical 25—48	2.6	20 25
19	Skeletal Club	Bind On Pickup	15.6	Physical 28—53	2.6	29 96
PROPERTIES: Sends a shadowy bolt at the enemy causing 30 Shadow damage, Main Hand Weapon						
19	Stinging Viper	Bind On Acquire	15.5	Physical 30—57	2.8	30 18
PROPERTIES: Poisons target for 7 Nature damage every 3 sec for 15 sec						
20	Diamond Hammer	Bind On Pickup	16.2	Physical 28—53	2.5	32 76
22	Crested Scepter	Bind On Pickup	17.1	Physical 31—58	2.6	40 28
PROPERTIES: Main Hand Weapon						
23	Oscillating Power Hammer	Bind On Pickup	17.5	Physical 24—46	2	44 19
24	Beazel's Basher	Bind On Pickup	18.4	Physical 32—60	2.5	48 63
PROPERTIES: Main Hand Weapon						
26	Looming Gavel	Bind On Pickup	19.8	Physical 33—62	2.4	59 71
PROPERTIES: Main Hand Weapon						
28	Dreamslayer	Bind On Pickup	21.4	Physical 31—59	2.1	69 2
PROPERTIES: Main Hand Weapon						
30	Ironspine's Fist	Bind On Acquire	22.9	Physical 38—72	2.4	88 36
30	Royal Diplomatic Scepter	Bind On Acquire	23	Physical 37—69	2.3	89 2
31	Excavator's Brand	Bind On Pickup	24	Physical 43—82	2.6	98 59
PROPERTIES: Hurls a fiery ball that causes 40 Fire damage and an additional 9 damage over 6 sec						
32	Deadwood Sledge	Bind On Pickup	25	Physical 33—62	1.9	1 4 64
PROPERTIES: Main Hand Weapon						
32	Ebony Boneclub	Bind On Pickup	25	Physical 31—59	1.8	1 9 27
PROPERTIES: Shadow Resist +5						
33	Midnight Mace	Bind On Pickup	25.8	Physical 45—84, Shadow 1—10	2.5	1 16 20
PROPERTIES: Shadow Resist +10						
34	Fight Club	Bind On Pickup	26.6	Physical 41—76	2.2	1 19 70
37	Stonevault Bonebreaker	Bind On Pickup	28.7	Physical 54—101	2.7	1 48 53
39	Hand of Righteousness	Bind On Acquire	29.8	Physical 56—105	2.7	1 79 22
PROPERTIES: Increases healing done by spells and effects by up to 15, Main Hand Weapon						
40	Heaven's Light	Bind On Pickup	30.4	Physical 57—107	2.7	1 94 41
PROPERTIES: Main Hand Weapon						
40	Wirt's Third Leg	Bind On Pickup	30.4	Physical 49—91	2.3	1 95 77
41	Mug O' Hurt	Bind On Pickup	31.2	Physical 37—69	1.7	2 7 36
PROPERTIES: Slows the target's movement by 50% for 10 sec						

Superior One-Hand Maces

Lvl	Name	Binding	DPS	Damage	Speed	Vendor Purchase Value
42	The Shatterer	Bind On Pickup	31.7	Physical 53—99	2.4	2 31 59
PROPERTIES: Disarm target's weapon for 10 sec, Main Hand Weapon						
43	The Hand of Antu'sul	Bind On Acquire	32.2	Physical 61—113	2.7	2 41 11
PROPERTIES: Blasts nearby enemies with thunder increasing the time between their attacks by 11% for 10 sec and doing 7 Nature damage to them. Will affect up to 4 targets, Main Hand Weapon						
45	Changuk Smasher	Bind On Pickup	33.4	Physical 44—83	1.9	2 67 47
48	Bonesnapper	Bind On Pickup	35.2	Physical 66—124	2.7	3 38 32
PROPERTIES: Main Hand Weapon						
48	Fist of Stone	Bind On Acquire	35.3	Physical 44—83	1.8	3 47 35
PROPERTIES: Restores 50 mana, Main Hand Weapon						
48	Fist of Stone	Bind On Acquire	35.3	Physical 44—83	1.8	3 21 56
PROPERTIES: Restores 50 mana, Main Hand Weapon						
49	Might of Hakkar	Bind On Acquire	35.8	Physical 60—112	2.4	3 46 65
PROPERTIES: Main Hand Weapon						
49	Viking Warhammer	Bind On Pickup	35.8	Physical 60—112	2.4	3 58 15
PROPERTIES: Main Hand Weapon						
51	Rubidium Hammer	Bind On Acquire	36.8	Physical 51—96	2	4 4 39
PROPERTIES: Main Hand Weapon. Armor 120						
52	Hurley's Tankard	Bind On Acquire	37.6	Physical 71—132	2.7	4 14 78
PROPERTIES: Main Hand Weapon						
52	Serenity	Bind On Pickup	37.5	Physical 52—98	2	4 27 21
PROPERTIES: Dispels a magic effect on the current foe, Main Hand Weapon						
52	The Hammer of Grace	Bind On Acquire	37.6	Physical 71—132	2.7	4 36 48
PROPERTIES: Increases healing done by spells and effects by up to 31, Main Hand Weapon						
54	Baron Charr's Sceptre	Bind On Pickup	38.8	Physical 70—132	2.6	4 51 84
PROPERTIES: Blasts a target for 35 Fire damage, Main Hand Weapon						
54	Energetic Rod	Bind On Acquire	38.7	Physical 71—107	2.3	4 93 20
PROPERTIES: Increases damage and healing done by magical spells and effects by up to 14, Main Hand Weapon						
55	Mastersmith's Hammer	Bind On Acquire	39.4	Physical 66—123	2.4	4 92 4
PROPERTIES: Increases damage and healing done by magical spells and effects by up to 14, Main Hand Weapon						
55	Bashguuder	Bind On Acquire	39.4	Physical 49—93	1.8	5 19 45
PROPERTIES: Punctures target's armor lowering it by 200. Can be applied up to 3 times						
55	Venomspitter	Bind On Acquire	39.5	Physical 52—98	1.9	5 17 71
PROPERTIES: Poisons target for 7 Nature damage every 2 sec for 30 sec						
56	Bludstone Hammer	Bind On Pickup	40.2	Physical 59—110	2.1	5 26 5
PROPERTIES: Main Hand Weapon						
56	Hammer of Revitalization	Bind On Acquire	40	Physical 75—141	2.7	4 98 16
PROPERTIES: Increases healing done by spells and effects by up to 26, Main Hand Weapon						
56	Hammer of the Vesper	Bind On Acquire	40.2	Physical 70—131	2.5	5 11
56	The Cruel Hand of Timmy	Bind On Acquire	40	Physical 50—94	1.8	5 14 40
PROPERTIES: Lowers all attributes of target by 15 for 1 min						
56	The Jaw Breaker	Bind On Acquire	40.3	Physical 45—84	1.6	5 30 54
PROPERTIES: Improves your chance to get a critical strike by 1%						
57	Mass of McGowan	Bind On Pickup	40.9	Physical 80—149	2.8	5 48 40
PROPERTIES: Main Hand Weapon						
57	Masterwork Stormhammer	Bind On Pickup	41.5	Physical 58—108	2	5 63 4
PROPERTIES: Blasts up to 3 targets for 105 to 145 Nature damage, Main Hand Weapon						
57	Bonechill Hammer	Bind On Acquire	40.6	Physical 68—127	2.4	5 32 22
PROPERTIES: Blasts a target for 90 Frost damage						
57	Hardened Steel Warhammer	Bind On Acquire	40.8	Physical 74—138	2.6	5 23 6
PROPERTIES: Increases healing done by spells and effects by up to 11						
57	Timeworn Mace	Bind On Acquire	40.7	Physical 62—117	2.2	5 23 6
PROPERTIES: Armor 120						
58	Scepter of the Unholy	Bind On Acquire	41.3	Physical 69—129	2.4	5 84 29
PROPERTIES: Increases damage done by Shadow spells and effects by up to 19, Main Hand Weapon						
60	Cold Forged Hammer	Bind On Acquire	41.4	Physical 72—135	2.5	5 86 93
PROPERTIES: Restores 3 mana per 5 sec, Main Hand Weapon						

Superior One-Hand Maces

Lvl	Name	Binding	DPS	Damage	Speed	Vendor Purchase Value
60	Simone's Cultivating Hammer	Bind On Acquire	42.5	Physical 53—100	1.8	6 56 75
PROPERTIES: Increases healing done by spells and effects by up to 37, Main Hand Weapon						
60	Gri'lek's Grinder	Bind On Acquire	44.8	Physical 75—140	2.4	7 5 37
PROPERTIES: +48 Attack Power when fighting Dragonkin						
60	Sceptre of Smiting	Bind On Acquire	42.7	Physical 77—145	2.6	6 25 89
PROPERTIES: Increased Maces +2, Blasts the enemy with poison for 63 to 93 Nature damage						
60	Stormstrike Hammer	Bind On Acquire	42.6	Physical 80—150	2.7	6 42 27
60	Zulian Scepter of Rites	Bind On Acquire	44.8	Physical 81—152	2.6	7 44 10
PROPERTIES: Increases healing done by spells and effects by up to 26, Restores 4 mana per 5 sec						

Legendary Two-Hand Maces

Lvl	Name	Binding	DPS	Damage	Speed	Vendor Purchase Value
60	Sulfuras, Hand of Ragnaros	Bind On Acquire	80.4	Physical 223—372	3.7	33 26 23
PROPERTIES: Fire Resist +30, , Hurls a fiery ball that causes 273 to 333 Fire damage and an additional 75 damage over 10 sec, Deals 5 Fire damage to anyone who strikes you with a melee attack						

Epic Two-Hand Maces

Lvl	Name	Binding	DPS	Damage	Speed	Vendor Purchase Value
47	Taran Icebreaker	Bind On Pickup	49.6	Physical 91—137	2.3	5 52 89
PROPERTIES: Hurls a fiery ball that causes 180 to 220 Fire damage and an additional 36 damage over 8 sec						
60	Draconic Maul	Bind On Acquire	67	Physical 187—282	3.5	13 6 38
PROPERTIES: Improves your chance to get a critical strike by 2%						
60	Earthshaker	Bind On Acquire	62.6	Physical 175—263	3.5	11 36 31
PROPERTIES: Knocks down all nearby enemies for 3 sec, +22 Attack Power						
60	Finkle's Lava Dredger	Bind On Acquire	67.1	Physical 155—234	2.9	13 55 94
PROPERTIES: Fire Resist +15, Restores 9 mana per 5 sec						
60	Fist of Cenarius	Bind On Acquire	62.6	Physical 175—263	3.5	11 12 20
PROPERTIES: Increases damage and healing done by magical spells and effects by up to 40, Improves your chance to get a critical strike with spells by 2%						
60	Grand Marshal's Battle Hammer	Bind On Acquire	77.4	Physical 235—353	3.8	6 25 42
PROPERTIES: Improves your chance to get a critical strike by 1%						
60	Grand Marshal's Demolisher	Bind On Acquire	77.4	Physical 235—353	3.8	5 70 53
PROPERTIES: Restores 7 mana per 5 sec, Increases damage and healing done by magical spells and effects by up to 27						
60	Hammer of Ji'zhi	Bind On Acquire	70.7	Physical 198—297	3.5	16 22 98
PROPERTIES: Increases damage and healing done by magical spells and effects by up to 30						
60	Herald of Woe	Bind On Acquire	73.4	Physical 199—300	3.4	16 60 93
60	High Warlord's Destroyer	Bind On Acquire	77.4	Physical 235—353	3.8	5 70 89
PROPERTIES: Restores 7 mana per 5 sec, Increases damage and healing done by magical spells and effects by up to 27						
60	High Warlord's Pulverizer	Bind On Acquire	77.4	Physical 235—353	3.8	6 27 63
PROPERTIES: Improves your chance to get a critical strike by 1%						
60	Jeklik's Crusher	Bind On Acquire	61.5	Physical 177—266	3.6	11 10 3
PROPERTIES: Wounds the target for 200 to 220 damage						
60	Maul of the Redeemed Crusader	Bind On Acquire	84.9	Physical 244—367	3.6	26 6 74
PROPERTIES: Restores 8 mana per 5 sec, Increases damage and healing done by magical spells and effects by up to 35						
60	Might of Menethil	Bind On Acquire	95.3	Physical 289—435	3.8	32 64 65
PROPERTIES: , Improves your chance to get a critical strike by 2%						
60	Sulfuron Hammer	Bind On Pickup	63.6	Physical 176—295	3.7	12 23 11
PROPERTIES: Hurls a fiery ball that causes 83 to 101 Fire damage and an additional 16 damage over 8 sec						
60	The Unstoppable Force	Bind On Acquire	61.4	Physical 175—292	3.8	31 29 80
PROPERTIES: Improves your chance to get a critical strike by 2%, Stuns target for 1 sec						

Superior Two-Hand Maces

Lvl	Name	Binding	DPS	Damage	Speed	Vendor Purchase Value
16	Black Malice	Bind On Pickup	18.3	Physical 48—73, Shadow 1—6	3.3	24 95
PROPERTIES: Sends a shadowy bolt at the enemy causing 55 to 85 Shadow damage						
16	Rakzur Club	Bind On Pickup	18.3	Physical 38—57	2.6	23 62
18	Smite's Mighty Hammer	Bind On Acquire	19.7	Physical 55—83	3.5	31 3
22	Verigan's Fist	Bind On Acquire	25.6	Physical 65—99	3.2	74 59
23	Dense Triangle Mace	Bind On Pickup	22.9	Physical 44—66	2.4	54 36
24	Slaghammer	Bind On Pickup	23.8	Physical 53—80	2.8	63 40
29	Cobalt Crusher	Bind On Pickup	28.9	Physical 74—111, Frost 5	3.2	1 1 46
PROPERTIES: Blasts a target for 110 to 120 Frost damage						
29	Manual Crowd Pummeler	Bind On Acquire	29	Physical 46—70	2	95 64
PROPERTIES: Increases your attack speed by 50% for 30 sec						
30	Viscous Hammer	Bind On Pickup	30.2	Physical 70—105	2.9	1 8 9
PROPERTIES: +34 Attack Power						
32	The Pacifier	Bind On Pickup	32.5	Physical 104—156	4	1 28 23
32	The Shoveler	Bind On Pickup	32.5	Physical 88—133	3.4	1 28 31
PROPERTIES: +20 Attack Power						
37	Thornstone Sledgehammer	Bind On Pickup	37.2	Physical 95—143	3.2	1 94 7
PROPERTIES: Nature Resist +10						
39	Mograine's Might	Bind On Acquire	38.9	Physical 87—131	2.8	2 25 67
40	The Jackhammer	Bind On Pickup	39.6	Physical 79—119	2.5	2 54 63
PROPERTIES: Increases your attack speed by 30% for 10 sec						
40	Whirlwind Warhammer	Bind On Acquire	35.7	Physical 97—146	3.4	1 72 64
44	The Rockpounder	Bind On Acquire	42.7	Physical 126—190	3.7	3 22 48
PROPERTIES: Improves your chance to get a critical strike by 2%						
45	Blanchard's Stout	Bind On Pickup	43.4	Physical 107—162	3.1	3 50 42
PROPERTIES: Fire Resist +5						
45	Ragehammer	Bind On Pickup	43.4	Physical 128—193	3.7	3 67 32
PROPERTIES: Increases damage done by 20 and attack speed by 5% for 15 sec						
47	The Judge's Gavel	Bind On Pickup	45	Physical 122—184	3.4	3 78 33
PROPERTIES: Stuns target for 3 sec						
49	Princess Theradras' Scepter	Bind On Acquire	46.5	Physical 126—190	3.4	4 48 63
PROPERTIES: Wounds the target for 160 damage and lowers their armor by 100						
50	Dark Iron Pulverizer	Bind On Pickup	47.4	Physical 140—211	3.7	4 57 60
PROPERTIES: Stuns target for 8 sec						
51	Enchanted Battlehammer	Bind On Pickup	48.1	Physical 100—150	2.6	4 81 24
PROPERTIES: Increases your chance to parry an attack by 1%, Improves your chance to hit by 2%						
51	Force of Magma	Bind On Acquire	48.1	Physical 123—185	3.2	5 1 77
PROPERTIES: Blasts a target for 150 Fire damage						
52	Impervious Giant	Bind On Acquire	48.9	Physical 105—159	2.7	5 41 67
PROPERTIES: Improves your chance to hit by 1%, Improves your chance to get a critical strike by 2%. Armor 30						
53	Lavastone Hammer	Bind On Acquire	49.7	Physical 135—203	3.4	5 70 79
PROPERTIES: Increases damage and healing done by magical spells and effects by up to 20						
53	Twig of the World Tree	Bind On Pickup	49.7	Physical 147—221	3.7	5 65 88
54	Frightskull Shaft	Bind On Acquire	50.4	Physical 137—206	3.4	5 98 91
PROPERTIES: Deals 8 Shadow damage every 2 sec for 30 sec and lowers their Strength for the duration of the disease						
55	Fist of Omokk	Bind On Acquire	51.4	Physical 135—204	3.3	5 94 10
56	Malown's Slam	Bind On Acquire	52.1	Physical 158—238	3.8	6 23 80
PROPERTIES: Knocks target silly for 2 sec and increases Strength by 50 for 30 sec						
57	Hammer of Divine Might	Bind On Acquire	53.1	Physical 89—134	2.1	6 53 83
PROPERTIES: Increases damage and healing done by magical spells and effects by up to 27						
57	Unyielding Maul	Bind On Acquire	53	Physical 135—204	3.2	6 53 83
PROPERTIES: Increased Defense +8. Armor 250						
58	Crystal Spiked Maul	Bind On Pickup	53.8	Physical 168—252	3.9	7 1 71
PROPERTIES: Improves your chance to get a critical strike by 2%						

Superior Two-Hand Maces

Lvl	Name	Binding	DPS	Damage	Speed	Vendor Purchase Value
58	Hammer of the Grand Crusader	Bind On Acquire	53.9	Physical 116—175	2.7	6 88 18
PROPERTIES: Increases healing done by spells and effects by up to 22						
58	Hammer of the Titans	Bind On Pickup	53.8	Physical 163—246	3.8	7 9 12
PROPERTIES: Stuns target for 3 sec						
58	Seeping Willow	Bind On Acquire	53.9	Physical 155—233	3.6	7 8 84
PROPERTIES: Lowers all stats by 20 and deals 20 Nature damage every 3 sec to all enemies within an 8 yard radius of the caster for 30 sec						
60	Gavel of Qiraji Authority	Bind On Acquire	61.4	Physical 108—162	2.2	10 36 86
PROPERTIES: Increases damage and healing done by magical spells and effects by up to 19, Restores 6 mana per 5 sec						
60	Bonecrusher	Bind On Acquire	53.8	Physical 129—194	3	7 12 36
PROPERTIES: Improves your chance to get a critical strike by 1%						
60	Doomulus Prime	Bind On Acquire	55.7	Physical 158—265	3.8	7 65 7
PROPERTIES: Improves your chance to hit by 1%						
60	Shimmering Platinum Warhammer	Bind On Acquire	53.9	Physical 142—192	3.1	7 35 97
PROPERTIES: Blasts a target for 180 to 250 Nature damage						

POLEARMS

Epic Polearms

Lvl	Name	Binding	DPS	Damage	Speed	Vendor Purchase Value
58	Shadowstrike	Bind On Acquire	59.4	Physical 147—221	3.1	9 85 14
PROPERTIES: Steals 100 to 180 life from target enemy, Transforms Shadowstrike into Thunderstrike						
58	Thunderstrike	Bind On Acquire	59.4	Physical 147—221	3.1	9 70 74
PROPERTIES: Blasts up to 3 targets for 150 to 250 Nature damage. Each target after the first takes less damage, Transforms Thunderstrike into Shadowstrike						
60	Barb of the Sand Reaver	Bind On Acquire	76.1	Physical 225—338	3.7	18 67 28
60	Blackfury	Bind On Pickup	62.6	Physical 105—158	2.1	11 65 31
PROPERTIES: Fire Resist +10, Improves your chance to get a critical strike by 1%						
60	Grand Marshal's Glaive	Bind On Acquire	77.4	Physical 235—353	3.8	5 69 93
PROPERTIES: Improves your chance to get a critical strike by 1%						
60	Halberd of Smiting	Bind On Acquire	62.6	Physical 175—263	3.5	11 20 9
PROPERTIES: Chance to decapitate the target on a melee swing, causing 452 to 676 damage						
60	High Warlord's Pig Sticker	Bind On Acquire	77.4	Physical 235—353	3.8	5 90 17
PROPERTIES: Improves your chance to get a critical strike by 1%						
60	The Eye of Nerub	Bind On Acquire	85	Physical 251—378	3.7	26 43 92
PROPERTIES: Increased Bows +4, Increased Crossbows +4, Increased Guns +4						

Superior Polearms

Lvl	Name	Binding	DPS	Damage	Speed	Vendor Purchase Value
20	Gargoyle's Bite	Bind On Pickup	19	Physical 44—66	2.9	28 54
PROPERTIES: Armor 60						
23	Bloodpike	Bind On Pickup	23.1	Physical 59—89	3.2	53 82
PROPERTIES: Wounds the target causing them to bleed for 110 damage over 30 sec						
31	Poison-tipped Bone Spear	Bind On Pickup	31.3	Physical 57—87	2.3	1 21 83
PROPERTIES: Poisons target for 30 Nature damage every 6 sec for 30 sec						
34	Ruthless Shiv	Bind On Pickup	34.8	Physical 75—113	2.7	1 50 74
35	Grim Reaper	Bind On Pickup	35.6	Physical 88—133	3.1	1 58 5
PROPERTIES: Wounds the target for 130 damage						
39	Khoo's Point	Bind On Pickup	38.8	Physical 77—117	2.5	2 18 33
42	Grimlok's Charge	Bind On Acquire	40.9	Physical 88—133	2.7	2 82 18
43	Bonechewer	Bind On Pickup	42	Physical 94—141	2.8	2 93 67
43	Eyegouger	Bind On Pickup	41.8	Physical 100—151	3	3 17 25
44	Diabolic Skiver	Bind On Acquire	42.8	Physical 99—149	2.9	3 33 46
PROPERTIES: Delivers a fatal wound for 160 to 180 damage						

Superior Polearms

Lvl	Name	Binding	DPS	Damage	Speed	Vendor Purchase Value
45	Blight	Bind On Pickup	43.3	Physical 93—141	2.7	3 38 57
PROPERTIES: Diseases a target for 50 Nature damage and an additional 180 damage over 1 min						
46	Headspike	Bind On Acquire	44.2	Physical 106—159	3	3 92 88
47	Stoneraven	Bind On Pickup	44.8	Physical 118—178	3.3	3 87 19
49	Smoldering Claw	Bind On Acquire		Physical 108—162	2.9	4 59 80
PROPERTIES: Fire Resist +10, Hurls a fiery ball that causes 135 Fire damage and an additional 15 damage over 6 sec						
51	Flame Wrath	Bind On Acquire	46.6	Physical 127—191	3.3	5 12 87
PROPERTIES: Envelops the caster with a Fire shield for 15 sec and shoots a ring of fire dealing 130 to 170 damage to all nearby enemies						
51	Frenzied Striker	Bind On Pickup	48.2	Physical 108—162	2.8	4 83 30
PROPERTIES: Increases your chance to parry an attack by 1%, Improves your chance to hit by 2%						
54	Peacemaker	Bind On Acquire	50.4	Physical 137—206	3.4	5 99 27
PROPERTIES: Improves your chance to get a critical strike by 1%, +56 Attack Power						
55	Darkspear	Bind On Pickup	51.3	Physical 131—197	3.2	6 26 25
PROPERTIES: Party members have chance to crit increased by 4%.Lasts for 20 sec						
55	Stonecutting Glaive	Bind On Acquire	51.4	Physical 152—228	3.7	6 15 43
55	The Needler	Bind On Pickup	51.4	Physical 90—136	2.2	6 7 84
PROPERTIES: Wounds the target for 75 damage						
56	Chillpike	Bind On Acquire	52.3	Physical 117—176	2.8	6 26 29
PROPERTIES: Blasts a target for 160 to 250 Frost damage						
56	Huntsman's Harpoon	Bind On Acquire	52.2	Physical 150—226	3.6	6 43 98
57	Monstrous Glaive	Bind On Acquire	53.1	Physical 123—185	2.9	7 1 27
PROPERTIES: Increases your chance to parry an attack by 1%, Increased Defense +7						
58	Blackhand Doomsaw	Bind On Acquire	54	Physical 151—227	3.5	7 43 46
PROPERTIES: Wounds the target for 324 to 540 damage						
60	Pitchfork of Madness	Bind On Acquire	58.4	Physical 163—246	3.5	9 12 76
PROPERTIES: +117 Attack Power when fighting Demons						
60	Tigule's Harpoon	Bind On Acquire	58.5	Physical 154—232	3.3	8 98 71
PROPERTIES: Improves your chance to hit by 2%, +60 Attack Power when fighting Beasts						
52	Hunting Spear	Bind On Acquire	45	Physical 111—168	3.1	4 5 24
PROPERTIES: Improves your chance to get a critical strike by 1%, Restores 5 mana per 5 sec						
60	Ice Barbed Spear	Bind On Acquire	53.9	Physical 155—233	3.6	7 33 53

STAVES

Legendary Staves

Lvl	Name	Binding	DPS	Damage	Speed	Vendor Purchase Value
60	Atiesh, Greatstaff of the Guardian	Bind On Acquire	97.1	Physical 225—338	2.9	52 62 76
PROPERTIES: Increases healing done by magical spells and effects of all party members within 30 yards by up to 62. , Increases your spell damage by up to 120 and your healing by up to 300. Creates a portal, teleporting group members that use it to Karazhan—Priest only						
60	Atiesh, Greatstaff of the Guardian	Bind On Acquire	97.1	Physical 225—338	2.9	56 20 16
PROPERTIES: Improves your chance to hit with spells by 2%, Increases damage and healing done by magical spells and effects by up to 150, Increases the spell critical chance of all party members within 30 yards by 2%, Creates a portal, teleporting group members that use it to Karazhan—Mage only						
60	Atiesh, Greatstaff of the Guardian	Bind On Acquire	97.1	Physical 225—338	2.9	56 38 44
PROPERTIES: Improves your chance to get a critical strike with spells by 2%, Increases damage and healing done by magical spells and effects by up to 150, Increases damage and healing done by magical spells and effects of all party members within 30 yards by up to 33—Warlock only						
60	Atiesh, Greatstaff of the Guardian	Bind On Acquire	97.1	Physical 225—338	2.9	52 82 64
PROPERTIES: Restores 11 mana per 5 seconds to all party members within 30 yards, Increases healing done by spells and effects by up to 300, +420 Attack Power in Cat, Bear, and Dire Bear forms only, Creates a portal, teleporting group members that use it to Karazhan—Druid only						

Epic Staves

Lvl	Name	Binding	DPS	Damage	Speed	Vendor Purchase Value
35	Staff of Jordan	Bind On Pickup	40.4	Physical 119—180	3.7	2 17 70
PROPERTIES: Increases damage and healing done by magical spells and effects by up to 26						

Epic Staves

Lvl	Name	Binding	DPS	Damage	Speed	Vendor Purchase Value
43	Warden Staff	Bind On Pickup	46.5	Physical 89—134	2.4	4 28 63
PROPERTIES: Increased Defense +10. Armor 260						
49	Glowing Brightwood Staff	Bind On Pickup	51.3	Physical 127—191	3.1	5 70 18
PROPERTIES: Nature Resist +15						
56	Elemental Mage Staff	Bind On Pickup	57.5	Physical 147—221	3.2	8 30
PROPERTIES: Fire Resist +20,Frost Resist +20, Increases damage done by Fire spells and effects by up to 36, Increases damage done by Frost spells and effects by up to 36						
57	Headmaster's Charge	Bind On Acquire	58.4	Physical 135—204	2.9	8 70 13
PROPERTIES: Gives 20 additional intellect to party members within 30 yards						
60	Amberseal Keeper	Bind On Acquire	63.6	Physical 168—252	3.3	11 92 78
PROPERTIES: Fire Resist +5, Nature Resist +5, Frost Resist +5, Shadow Resist +5, Arcane Resist +5, Restores 12 mana per 5 sec, Increases damage and healing done by magical spells and effects by up to 44						
60	Anathema	Bind On Acquire	73.3	Physical 176—264	3	
PROPERTIES: Shadow Resist +20, Calls forth Benediction, Restores 7 mana per 5 sec, Increases damage done by Shadow spells and effects by up to 69						
60	Benediction	Bind On Acquire	73.3	Physical 176—264	3	
PROPERTIES: Shadow Resist +20, Calls forth Anathema, Increases the critical effect chance of your Holy spells by 2%, Increases healing done by spells and effects by up to 106						
60	Blessed Qiraji Acolyte Staff	Bind On Acquire	78.8	Physical 189—284	3	21 90 3
PROPERTIES: Increases damage and healing done by magical spells and effects by up to 76, Improves your chance to hit with spells by 2%, Improves your chance to get a critical strike with spells by 1%						
60	Blessed Qiraji Augur Staff	Bind On Acquire	78.8	Physical 189—284	3	19 95 83
PROPERTIES: Increases healing done by spells and effects by up to 143, Restores 15 mana per 5 sec						
60	Brimstone Staff	Bind On Acquire	85	Physical 217—327	3.2	24 54 98
PROPERTIES: Improves your chance to hit with spells by 2%, Increases damage and healing done by magical spells and effects by up to 113, Improves your chance to get a critical strike with spells by 1%						
60	Grand Marshal's Stave	Bind On Acquire	77.3	Physical 185—279	3	5 94 59
PROPERTIES: Increases damage and healing done by magical spells and effects by up to 71						
60	High Warlord's War Staff	Bind On Acquire	77.3	Physical 185—279	3	5 96 81
PROPERTIES: Increases damage and healing done by magical spells and effects by up to 71						
60	Ironbark Staff	Bind On Acquire	61.5	Physical 156—262	3.4	11 1 99
PROPERTIES: Improves your chance to get a critical strike with spells by 2%, Increases damage and healing done by magical spells and effects by up to 41. Armor 100						
60	Ironbark Staff	Bind On Acquire	61.5	Physical 156—262	3.4	10 9 19
PROPERTIES: Improves your chance to get a critical strike with spells by 2%, Increases damage and healing done by magical spells and effects by up to 41. Armor 100						
60	Jin'do's Judgement	Bind On Acquire	62.6	Physical 165—248	3.3	10 79 9
PROPERTIES: Improves your chance to hit with spells by 2%, Restores 14 mana per 5 sec, Increases damage and healing done by magical spells and effects by up to 27						
60	Lok'delar, Stave of the Ancient Keepers	Bind On Acquire	73.3	Physical 187—282	3.2	
PROPERTIES: Nature Resist +10, , Improves your chance to get a critical strike by 2%, +45 Attack Power when fighting Demons						
60	Nat Pagle's Fish Terminator	Bind On Acquire	61.4	Physical 172—258	3.5	10 27 29
60	Shadow Wing Focus Staff	Bind On Acquire	73.3	Physical 187—282	3.2	16 48 35
PROPERTIES: Increases damage and healing done by magical spells and effects by up to 56						
60	Soulseeker	Bind On Acquire	95.2	Physical 243—366	3.2	32 77 28
PROPERTIES: Increases damage and healing done by magical spells and effects by up to 126, Improves your chance to get a critical strike with spells by 2%, Decreases the magical resistances of your spell targets by 25						
60	Spire of Twilight	Bind On Acquire	85	Physical 217—327	3.2	24 64 40
PROPERTIES: Restores 10 mana per 5 sec, Increases healing done by spells and effects by up to 178						
60	Staff of Dominance	Bind On Acquire	67.1	Physical 155—234	2.9	13 86 46
PROPERTIES: Improves your chance to get a critical strike with spells by 1%, Increases damage and healing done by magical spells and effects by up to 40						
60	Staff of Rampant Growth	Bind On Acquire	68.3	Physical 142—213	2.6	13 71 84
PROPERTIES: Nature Resist +20, Increases healing done by spells and effects by up to 84, Restores 11 mana per 5 sec						

Epic Staves

Lvl	Name	Binding	DPS	Damage	Speed	Vendor Purchase Value
60	Staff of the Qiraji Prophets	Bind On Acquire	73.3	Physical 170—255	2.9	16 80 41
PROPERTIES: Fire Resist +10, Nature Resist +10, Frost Resist +10, Shadow Resist +10, Arcane Resist +10, Increases damage and healing done by magical spells and effects by up to 56, Gives a chance when your harmful spells land to reduce the magical resista						
60	Staff of the Ruins	Bind On Acquire	69.6	Physical 189—284	3.4	14 79 14
PROPERTIES: Increases damage and healing done by magical spells and effects by up to 60, Improves your chance to get a critical strike with spells by 1%, Improves your chance to hit with spells by 1%						
60	Staff of the Shadow Flame	Bind On Acquire	81.9	Physical 209—315	3.2	22 17 50
PROPERTIES: Improves your chance to get a critical strike with spells by 2%, Increases damage and healing done by magical spells and effects by up to 84						
60	Will of Arlokk	Bind On Acquire	61.5	Physical 147—222	3	10 47 7
PROPERTIES: Increases healing done by spells and effects by up to 46						

Superior Staves

Lvl	Name	Binding	DPS	Damage	Speed	Vendor Purchase Value
17	Witching Stave	Bind On Pickup	19.2	Physical 55—83	3.6	29 22
PROPERTIES: Increases damage done by Shadow spells and effects by up to 11						
18	Advisor's Gnarled Staff	Bind On Acquire	19.7	Physical 45—69	2.9	30 42
PROPERTIES: Restores 3 mana per 5 sec						
18	Emberstone Staff	Bind On Acquire	19.7	Physical 47—71	3	31 61
18	Lorekeeper's Staff	Bind On Acquire	19.7	Physical 45—69	2.9	30 42
PROPERTIES: Restores 3 mana per 5 sec						
18	Staff of the Blessed Seer	Bind On Pickup	19.7	Physical 47—71	3	32 55
PROPERTIES: Increases healing done by spells and effects by up to 24						
19	Staff of the Friar	Bind On Pickup	20.4	Physical 42—64	2.6	35 98
19	Twisted Chanter's Staff	Bind On Pickup	20.4	Physical 55—84	3.4	35 17
20	Living Root	Bind On Acquire	21.2	Physical 49—74	2.9	40 53
PROPERTIES: Nature Resist +5						
21	Odo's Ley Staff	Bind On Acquire	21.7	Physical 50—76	2.9	48 2
22	Staff of the Shade	Bind On Pickup	22.3	Physical 46—70	2.6	50 16
PROPERTIES: Increases damage done by Shadow spells and effects by up to 21						
22	Crescent Staff	Bind On Acquire	20.3	Physical 47—71	2.9	36 80
22	Staff of Westfall	Bind On Acquire	20.5	Physical 49—74	3	36 39
24	Rod of the Sleepwalker	Bind On Acquire	23.8	Physical 53—80	2.8	59 54
26	Gnarled Ash Staff	Bind On Pickup	25.6	Physical 65—99	3.2	70 69
27	Wind Spirit Staff	Bind On Acquire	26.7	Physical 70—106	3.3	82 67
28	Advisor's Gnarled Staff	Bind On Acquire	27.8	Physical 64—97	2.9	85 54
PROPERTIES: Restores 4 mana per 5 sec						
28	Lorekeeper's Staff	Bind On Acquire	27.8	Physical 64—97	2.9	89 74
PROPERTIES: Restores 4 mana per 5 sec						
31	Loksey's Training Stick	Bind On Acquire	31.3	Physical 77—117	3.1	1 22 79
PROPERTIES: +60 Attack Power when fighting Beasts						
32	Windweaver Staff	Bind On Pickup	32.4	Physical 80—121	3.1	1 28 74
PROPERTIES: Increases damage done by Arcane spells and effects by up to 14						
33	Black Duskwood Staff	Bind On Pickup	33.6	Physical 75—113	2.8	1 45 77
PROPERTIES: Sends a shadowy bolt at the enemy causing 110 to 140 Shadow damage						
34	Illusionary Rod	Bind On Acquire	34.7	Physical 94—142	3.4	47 77
37	Ironshod Bludgeon	Bind On Acquire	37.2	Physical 74—112	2.5	1 86 39
38	Advisor's Gnarled Staff	Bind On Acquire	38.1	Physical 88—133	2.9	1 98 74
PROPERTIES: Restores 6 mana per 5 sec						
38	Lorekeeper's Staff	Bind On Acquire	38.1	Physical 88—133	2.9	2 7 72
PROPERTIES: Restores 6 mana per 5 sec						
40	Celestial Stave	Bind On Acquire	35.7	Physical 85—129	3	1 57 37
PROPERTIES: Increases damage and healing done by magical spells and effects by up to 22						

Superior Staves

Lvl	Name	Binding	DPS	Damage	Speed	Vendor Purchase Value
41	Tanglewood Staff	Bind On Pickup	40.3	Physical 109—165	3.4	2 62 9
PROPERTIES: Increases damage done by Nature spells and effects by up to 14						
42	Bludgeon of the Grinning Dog	Bind On Pickup	41.2	Physical 112—168	3.4	2 69 74
PROPERTIES: Stuns target for 3 sec						
42	Witch Doctor's Cane	Bind On Pickup	41.1	Physical 75—114	2.3	2 95 85
PROPERTIES: Increases damage done by Nature spells and effects by up to 33						
42	Zum'rah's Vexing Cane	Bind On Acquire	40.9	Physical 88—133	2.7	2 81 61
PROPERTIES: Increases damage and healing done by magical spells and effects by up to 21						
45	The Chief's Enforcer	Bind On Acquire	43.5	Physical 118—178	3.4	3 59 36
PROPERTIES: Stuns target for 3 sec						
48	Advisor's Gnarled Staff	Bind On Acquire	45.9	Physical 106—160	2.9	4 1 95
PROPERTIES: Restores 7 mana per 5 sec						
48	Kindling Stave	Bind On Acquire	45.9	Physical 106—160	2.9	4 32 34
PROPERTIES: Fire Resist +10, Improves your chance to get a critical strike with spells by 1%						
48	Lorekeeper's Staff	Bind On Acquire	45.9	Physical 106—160	2.9	4 18 56
PROPERTIES: Restores 7 mana per 5 sec						
49	Soulkeeper	Bind On Pickup	46.6	Physical 141—213	3.8	4 34 20
49	Spire of Hakkar	Bind On Acquire	46.5	Physical 126—190	3.4	4 43 14
PROPERTIES: Increases damage and healing done by magical spells and effects by up to 18						
51	Spire of the Stoneshaper	Bind On Pickup	48.2	Physical 131—197	3.4	4 85 1
PROPERTIES: Increases armor by 1000 for 10 sec but cannot cast spells or attack for the duration of the spell						
51	Resurgence Rod	Bind On Acquire	45.8	Physical 139—209	3.8	4 7 47
PROPERTIES: Restores 8 mana per 5 sec, Restores 5 health every 5 sec						
52	Moonshadow Stave	Bind On Acquire	45	Physical 133—200	3.7	3 78 92
PROPERTIES: Increases damage and healing done by magical spells and effects by up to 18, Restores 7 mana per 5 sec, Improves your chance to get a critical strike with spells by 1%						
52	Soul Harvester	Bind On Acquire	44.8	Physical 118—178	3.3	4 6 71
PROPERTIES: Improves your chance to hit with spells by 1%, Increases damage done by Shadow spells and effects by up to 24						
52	Wildstaff	Bind On Acquire	45	Physical 90—135	2.5	4 6 67
PROPERTIES: Improves your chance to hit by 1%, Improves your chance to get a critical strike by 1%						
53	Quel'dorai Channeling Rod	Bind On Acquire	49.6	Physical 111—167	2.8	5 66 44
PROPERTIES: Restores 8 mana per 5 sec						
54	Guiding Stave of Wisdom	Bind On Acquire	50.5	Physical 133—200	3.3	5 83 22
PROPERTIES: Frost Resist +10, Increases healing done by spells and effects by up to 53						
55	Amethyst War Staff	Bind On Acquire	51.4	Physical 119—179	2.9	6 1 75
PROPERTIES: Increases damage and healing done by magical spells and effects by up to 34						
55	Slavedriver's Cane	Bind On Acquire	51.4	Physical 160—241	3.9	6 37 69
55	Staff of Balzaphon	Bind On Acquire	51.4	Physical 160—241	3.9	5 93 4
PROPERTIES: Increases damage and healing done by magical spells and effects by up to 29, Improves your chance to get a critical strike with spells by 1%						
56	Redemption	Bind On Acquire	52.1	Physical 87—132	2.1	6 22 70
PROPERTIES: Increases healing done by spells and effects by up to 66						
56	Trindlehaven Staff	Bind On Acquire	52.1	Physical 87—132	2.1	6 57 49
PROPERTIES: Increases damage and healing done by magical spells and effects by up to 14						
57	Staff of Hale Magefire	Bind On Pickup	53	Physical 140—210	3.3	6 52 25
57	Staff of Metanoia	Bind On Acquire	53.1	Physical 89—134	2.1	6 94
PROPERTIES: Increases healing done by spells and effects by up to 35						
58	Advisor's Gnarled Staff	Bind On Acquire	54	Physical 125—188	2.9	7 1 71
PROPERTIES: Restores 8 mana per 5 sec						
58	Lord Valthalak's Staff of Command	Bind On Acquire	53.8	Physical 90—136	2.1	7 12 51
PROPERTIES: Increases damage and healing done by magical spells and effects by up to 30, Improves your chance to hit with spells by 1%						
58	Lorekeeper's Staff	Bind On Acquire	54	Physical 125—188	2.9	7 12 29
PROPERTIES: Restores 8 mana per 5 sec						

Superior Staves

Lvl	Name	Binding	DPS	Damage	Speed	Vendor Purchase Value
58	Rod of the Ogre Magi	Bind On Acquire	53.9	Physical 116—175	2.7	7 15 3
PROPERTIES: Improves your chance to get a critical strike with spells by 1%, Increases damage and healing done by magical spells and effects by up to 23						
60	Crackling Staff	Bind On Acquire	55.6	Physical 138—207	3.1	7 97 5
PROPERTIES: Increases damage and healing done by magical spells and effects by up to 15						
60	Whiteout Staff	Bind On Acquire	55.6	Physical 138—207	3.1	7 94 11
PROPERTIES: Increases damage and healing done by magical spells and effects by up to 15						
60	Zulian Ceremonial Staff	Bind On Pickup	55.6	Physical 115—174	2.6	7 56 2
PROPERTIES: Increases damage and healing done by magical spells and effects by up to 32						
60	Argent Crusader	Bind On Acquire	53	Physical 127—191	3	6 77 82
60	Dancing Sliver	Bind On Acquire	51.3	Physical 98—148	2.4	6 45 2

SWORDS

Legendary One-Hand Swords

Lvl	Name	Binding	DPS	Damage	Speed	Vendor Purchase Value
60	Thunderfury, Blessed Blade of the Windseeker	Bind On Acquire	61.8	Physical 82—153, Nature 16 30	1.9	25 53 55
PROPERTIES: Fire Resist +8, Nature Resist +9, Blasts your enemy with lightning, dealing 300 Nature damage and then jumping to additional nearby enemies.Each jump reduces that victim's Nature resistance by 25. Affects 5 targets.						

Epic One-Hand Sword

Lvl	Name	Binding	DPS	Damage	Speed	Vendor Purchase Value
36	Dazzling Longsword	Bind On Pickup	31.5	Physical 37—70	1.7	1 85 29
PROPERTIES: Decrease the armor of the target by 100 for 30 sec.While affected, the target cannot stealth or turn invisible, Main Hand Weapon						
45	Bloodrazor	Bind On Pickup	37	Physical 70—130	2.7	3 91 25
PROPERTIES: Wounds the target causing them to bleed for 120 damage over 30 sec, Main Hand Weapon						
51	Krol Blade	Bind On Pickup	40.9	Physical 80—149	2.8	5 18 57
PROPERTIES: Improves your chance to get a critical strike by 1%, Main Hand Weapon						
52	Dragon's Call	Bind On Acquire	41.4	Physical 72—135	2.5	5 69 21
PROPERTIES: Calls forth an Emerald Dragon Whelp to protect you in battle for a short period of time						
58	Elemental Attuned Blade	Bind On Pickup	45.7	Physical 67—125	2.1	7 54 10
PROPERTIES: Increases damage and healing done by magical spells and effects by up to 32, Restores 3 mana per 5 sec, Main Hand Weapon						
59	Sageblade	Bind On Pickup	46.4	Physical 58—109	1.8	8 42 91
PROPERTIES: Increases damage and healing done by magical spells and effects by up to 20, Decreases the magical resistances of your spell targets by 10, Main Hand Weapon						
60	Ancient Qiraji Ripper	Bind On Acquire	58.4	Physical 114—213	2.8	14 65 70
PROPERTIES: Improves your chance to get a critical strike by 1%, +20 Attack Power						
60	Blackguard	Bind On Pickup	51.7	Physical 65—121	1.8	10 28 90
PROPERTIES: Increases your chance to parry an attack by 1%						
60	Brutality Blade	Bind On Acquire	51.6	Physical 90—168	2.5	10 40 89
PROPERTIES: Improves your chance to get a critical strike by 1%						
60	Chromatically Tempered Sword	Bind On Acquire	58.5	Physical 106—198	2.6	15 89 29
60	Grand Marshal's Longsword	Bind On Acquire	59.5	Physical 138—207	2.9	4 96 36
PROPERTIES: Improves your chance to get a critical strike by 1%, +28 Attack Power						
60	Grand Marshal's Swiftblade	Bind On Acquire	59.4	Physical 85—129	1.8	4 56 71
PROPERTIES: Improves your chance to get a critical strike by 1%, +28 Attack Power						
60	Gressil, Dawn of Ruin	Bind On Acquire	73.1	Physical 138—257	2.7	27 83 98
PROPERTIES: +40 Attack Power						
60	High Warlord's Blade	Bind On Acquire	59.5	Physical 138—207	2.9	4 94 83
PROPERTIES: Improves your chance to get a critical strike by 1%, +28 Attack Power						

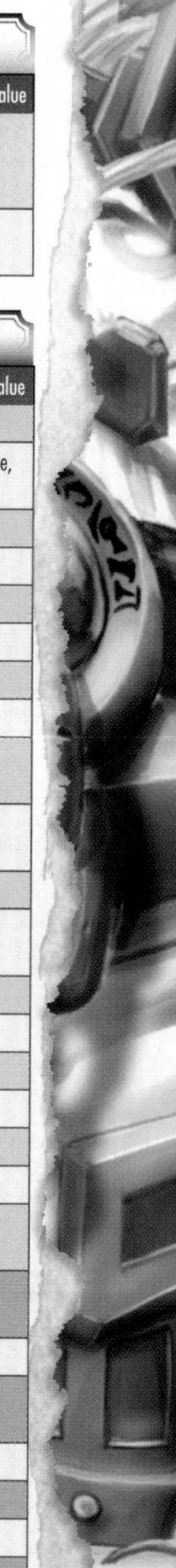

Epic One-Hand Sword

Lvl	Name	Binding	DPS	Damage	Speed	Vendor Purchase Value
60	High Warlord's Quickblade	Bind On Acquire	59.4	Physical 85—129	1.8	4 56 71
PROPERTIES: Improves your chance to get a critical strike by 1%, +28 Attack Power						
60	Iblis, Blade of the Fallen Seraph	Bind On Acquire	62.8	Physical 70—131	1.6	18 35 89
PROPERTIES: Improves your chance to get a critical strike by 1%, Improves your chance to hit by 1%, +26 Attack Power						
60	Maladath, Runed Blade of the Black Flight	Bind On Acquire	56.4	Physical 86—162	2.2	13 99 89
PROPERTIES: Increases your chance to parry an attack by 1%, Increased Swords +4						
60	Nightmare Blade	Bind On Acquire	52.6	Physical 99—185	2.7	10 80 80
PROPERTIES: +32 Attack Power. Armor 70						
60	Ravencrest's Legacy	Bind On Acquire	57.4	Physical 84—157	2.1	15 18 68
60	The Hungering Cold	Bind On Acquire	73	Physical 76—143	1.5	26 92 53
PROPERTIES: Increased Swords +6. Armor 140						
60	Vis'kag the Bloodletter	Bind On Acquire	55.2	Physical 100—187	2.6	13 52 66
PROPERTIES: Delivers a fatal wound for 240 damage						
60	Widow's Remorse	Bind On Acquire	62.8	Physical 70—131	1.6	18 22 4
PROPERTIES: Improves your chance to hit by 1%. Armor 100						
60	Wraith Blade	Bind On Acquire	65.3	Physical 82—153	1.8	20 16 33
PROPERTIES: Increases damage and healing done by magical spells and effects by up to 95, Improves your chance to hit with spells by 1%, Improves your chance to get a critical strike with spells by 1%						
60	Azuresong Mageblade	Bind On Acquire	52.5	Physical 88—164	2.4	11 18 23
PROPERTIES: Improves your chance to get a critical strike with spells by 1%, Increases damage and healing done by magical spells and effects by up to 40, Main Hand Weapon						
60	Blade of Eternal Justice	Bind On Acquire	51.5	Physical 83—154	2.3	
PROPERTIES: Restores 4 mana per 5 sec, Main Hand Weapon						
60	Blade of Vaulted Secrets	Bind On Acquire	51.5	Physical 83—154	2.3	
PROPERTIES: Improves your chance to hit with spells by 1%, Increases damage and healing done by magical spells and effects by up to 40, Main Hand Weapon						
60	Bloodcaller	Bind On Acquire	49.8	Physical 69—130	2	10 24 8
PROPERTIES: Increases damage and healing done by magical spells and effects by up to 33, Main Hand Weapon						
60	Bloodlord's Defender	Bind On Acquire	48.2	Physical 64—119	1.9	8 73 23
PROPERTIES: Increased Defense +4, Main Hand Weapon. Armor 80						
60	Quel'Serrar	Bind On Acquire	52.5	Physical 84—126	2	11 26 51
PROPERTIES: When active, grants the wielder 13 defense and 300 armor for 10 sec, Main Hand Weapon						
60	Runesword of the Red	Bind On Acquire	57.3	Physical 88—164	2.2	13 79 11
PROPERTIES: Increases damage and healing done by magical spells and effects by up to 64, Main Hand Weapon						
60	Sharpened Silithid Femur	Bind On Acquire	59.3	Physical 95—178	2.3	16 9 86
PROPERTIES: Increases damage and healing done by magical spells and effects by up to 72, Improves your chance to get a critical strike with spells by 1%, Main Hand Weapon						
60	Teebu's Blazing Longsword	Bind On Pickup	47.2	Physical 96—178	2.9	8 70 8
PROPERTIES: Blasts a target for 150 Fire damage, Main Hand Weapon						
60	Warblade of the Hakkari	Bind On Acquire	49.7	Physical 59—110	1.7	10 27 60
PROPERTIES: +28 Attack Power, Improves your chance to get a critical strike by 1%, Main Hand Weapon						
60	Warblade of the Hakkari	Bind On Acquire	47.9	Physical 57—106	1.7	8 69 94
PROPERTIES: +40 Attack Power, Off Hand Weapon						

Superior One-Hand Swords

Lvl	Name	Binding	DPS	Damage	Speed	Vendor Purchase Value
15	Ironpatch Blade	Bind On Pickup	13.5	Physical 24—46	2.6	17 70
15	Night Watch Shortsword	Bind On Pickup	13.5	Physical 24—46	2.6	17 42
18	Legionnaire's Sword	Bind On Acquire	15	Physical 28—53	2.7	24 33
18	Protector's Sword	Bind On Acquire	15	Physical 28—53	2.7	25 82
19	Shadowfang	Bind On Pickup	15.6	Physical 29—55, Shadow 4 8	2.7	29 64
PROPERTIES: Sends a shadowy bolt at the enemy causing 30 Shadow damage, Main Hand Weapon						
19	Cruel Barb	Bind On Acquire	15.5	Physical 30—57	2.8	29 64
PROPERTIES: +12 Attack Power						
21	Twisted Sabre	Bind On Pickup	16.7	Physical 21—39	1.8	38 40
PROPERTIES: Main Hand Weapon						
22	Heavy Marauder Scimitar	Bind On Pickup	17.1	Physical 28—54	2.4	39 22
PROPERTIES: Main Hand Weapon						
22	Wingblade	Bind On Acquire	15.7	Physical 24—45	2.2	29 33
PROPERTIES: Main Hand Weapon						
22	Sword of Corruption	Bind On Pickup	17.1	Physical 25—47	2.1	41 38
PROPERTIES: Corrupts the target, causing 30 damage over 3 sec						
23	Sword of Decay	Bind On Pickup	17.6	Physical 33—62	2.7	45 62
PROPERTIES: Reduces target's Strength by 10 for 30 sec, Main Hand Weapon						
26	The Black Knight	Bind On Pickup	19.7	Physical 26—49	1.9	61 5
PROPERTIES: Sends a shadowy bolt at the enemy causing 35 to 45 Shadow damage, Main Hand Weapon						
26	The Butcher	Bind On Pickup	19.6	Physical 38—72	2.8	57 47
PROPERTIES: Main Hand Weapon						
28	Legionnaire's Sword	Bind On Acquire	21.3	Physical 40—75	2.7	68 43
28	Protector's Sword	Bind On Acquire	21.3	Physical 40—75	2.7	72 85
29	Electrocutioner Leg	Bind On Acquire	22.1	Physical 26—49	1.7	75 64
PROPERTIES: Blasts a target for 10 to 20 Nature damage, Main Hand Weapon						
29	Zealot Blade	Bind On Pickup	22.1	Physical 43—81	2.8	80 94
30	Outlaw Sabre	Bind On Acquire	18.9	Physical 35—67	2.7	54 92
PROPERTIES: +15 Attack Power						
31	Tainted Pierce	Bind On Pickup	24.2	Physical 32—60	1.9	92 22
PROPERTIES: Corrupts the target, causing 45 damage over 3 sec						
32	Blade of the Basilisk	Bind On Pickup	25	Physical 33—62	1.9	1
PROPERTIES: Defense +33 for 5 sec						
34	Scorpion Sting	Bind On Pickup	26.5	Physical 44—83	2.4	1 17 74
PROPERTIES: Poisons target for 13 Nature damage every 5 sec for 25 sec						
35	Annealed Blade	Bind On Pickup	27.2	Physical 34—64	1.8	1 29 80
36	Ginn-su Sword	Bind On Pickup	27.9	Physical 33—62	1.7	1 35 94
36	Speedsteel Rapier	Bind On Pickup	28.1	Physical 35—66	1.8	1 47 10
38	Legionnaire's Sword	Bind On Acquire	29.3	Physical 55—103	2.7	1 58 99
38	Nordic Longshank	Bind On Acquire	29.3	Physical 45—84	2.2	50 70
38	Protector's Sword	Bind On Acquire	29.3	Physical 55—103	2.7	1 58 99
40	Sword of Serenity	Bind On Acquire	30	Physical 46—86	2.2	1 87 14
41	Bloodletter Scalpel	Bind On Pickup	31.1	Physical 39—73	1.8	2 10 60
PROPERTIES: Wounds the target for 60 to 70 damage						
42	Shortsword of Vengeance	Bind On Pickup	31.7	Physical 53—99	2.4	2 35 56
PROPERTIES: Smites an enemy for 30 Holy damage						
42	Sword of Omen	Bind On Acquire	29.7	Physical 39—74	1.9	1 82 55
42	Vanquisher's Sword	Bind On Acquire	30	Physical 46—86	2.2	1 77 96
PROPERTIES: +28 Attack Power						
44	Phantom Blade	Bind On Pickup	32.7	Physical 59—111	2.6	2 55 8
PROPERTIES: Decrease the armor of the target by 100 for 20 sec.While affected, the target cannot stealth or turn invisible, Main Hand Weapon						
44	Serpent Slicer	Bind On Pickup	32.8	Physical 57—107	2.5	2 51 41
PROPERTIES: Poisons target for 8 Nature damage every 2 sec for 20 sec						
45	Jang'thraze the Protector	Bind On Acquire	33.4	Physical 44—83	1.9	2 74 3
PROPERTIES: Combines Jang'thraze and Sang'thraze to form the mighty sword, Sul'thraze, Shields the wielder from physical damage, absorbing 55 to 85 damage. Lasts 20 sec, Main Hand Weapon						

Superior One-Hand Swords

Lvl	Name	Binding	DPS	Damage	Speed	Vendor Purchase Value
45	Jang'thraze the Protector	Bind On Acquire	33.4	Physical 44—83	1.9	2 83 34
PROPERTIES: Combines Jang'thraze and Sang'thraze to form the mighty sword, Sul'thraze, Shields the wielder from physical damage, absorbing 55 to 85 damage. Lasts 20 sec						
45	Joonho's Mercy	Bind On Pickup	33.3	Physical 49—91	2.1	2 87 88
PROPERTIES: Blasts a target for 70 Arcane damage						
48	Arbiter's Blade	Bind On Acquire	35.2	Physical 59—110	2.4	3 38 35
PROPERTIES: Increases damage and healing done by magical spells and effects by up to 8, Main Hand Weapon						
48	Firebreather	Bind On Acquire	35.2	Physical 54—101	2.2	3 50 69
PROPERTIES: Hurls a fiery ball that causes 70 Fire damage and an additional 9 damage over 6 sec						
48	Inventor's Focal Sword	Bind On Acquire	35.2	Physical 54—101	2.2	3 21 6
PROPERTIES: Improves your chance to get a critical strike with spells by 1%						
48	Legionnaire's Sword	Bind On Acquire	35.2	Physical 66—124	2.7	3 21 56
48	Protector's Sword	Bind On Acquire	35.2	Physical 66—124	2.7	3 21 56
49	Doomforged Straightedge	Bind On Pickup	35.8	Physical 47—89	1.9	3 49 25
PROPERTIES: +12 Attack Power						
50	Hanzo Sword	Bind On Pickup	36.3	Physical 38—71	1.5	3 72 86
PROPERTIES: Wounds the target for 75 damage						
51	Lord General's Sword	Bind On Acquire	36.9	Physical 67—125	2.6	3 92 54
PROPERTIES: Increases attack power by 50 for 30 sec, Main Hand Weapon						
51	Blazing Rapier	Bind On Pickup	37.1	Physical 44—82	1.7	3 86 48
PROPERTIES: Burns the enemy for 100 damage over 30 sec						
51	Thrash Blade	Bind On Acquire	35.2	Physical 66—124	2.7	3 28 54
PROPERTIES: Grants an extra attack on your next swing						
52	Assassination Blade	Bind On Pickup	37.6	Physical 71—132	2.7	4 9 88
PROPERTIES: Improves your chance to get a critical strike by 1%						
52	Phase Blade	Bind On Acquire	37.6	Physical 55—103	2.1	4 41 42
54	Ebon Hilt of Marduk	Bind On Acquire	38.9	Physical 73—137	2.7	4 87 70
PROPERTIES: Corrupts the target, causing 210 damage over 3 sec, Main Hand Weapon						
54	Fiendish Machete	Bind On Acquire	38.8	Physical 74—112	2.4	4 74 6
PROPERTIES: +36 Attack Power when fighting Elementals						
56	Cho'Rush's Blade	Bind On Acquire	40	Physical 67—125	2.4	5 38 22
PROPERTIES: +28 Attack Power						
57	Blade of Necromancy	Bind On Acquire	40.7	Physical 42—80	1.5	5 36 83
PROPERTIES: Improves your chance to get a critical strike with spells by 1%, Main Hand Weapon						
57	Mind Carver	Bind On Acquire	40.8	Physical 57—106	2	5 75 16
PROPERTIES: Increases damage and healing done by magical spells and effects by up to 12, Main Hand Weapon						
57	Silent Fang	Bind On Acquire	40.6	Physical 45—85	1.6	5 68 80
PROPERTIES: Silences an enemy preventing it from casting spells for 6 sec, Main Hand Weapon						
57	Lord Blackwood's Blade	Bind On Acquire	40.7	Physical 42—80	1.5	5 69 51
PROPERTIES: Armor 60						
58	Dal'Rend's Sacred Charge	Bind On Acquire	41.4	Physical 81—151	2.8	5 48 12
PROPERTIES: Improves your chance to get a critical strike by 1%, Main Hand Weapon						
58	Frostguard	Bind On Pickup	41.3	Physical 66—124	2.3	5 69 43
PROPERTIES: Target's movement slowed by 30% and increasing the time between attacks by 25% for 5 sec, Main Hand Weapon						
58	Sword of Zeal	Bind On Pickup	41.4	Physical 81—151	2.8	5 54
PROPERTIES: A burst of energy fills the caster, increasing his damage by 10 and armor by 150 for 15 sec, Main Hand Weapon						
58	Dal'Rend's Tribal Guardian	Bind On Acquire	41.4	Physical 52—97	1.8	6 3 63
PROPERTIES: Increased Defense +7, Off Hand Weapon. Armor 100						
58	Legionnaire's Sword	Bind On Acquire	41.5	Physical 78—146	2.7	5 49 22
58	Protector's Sword	Bind On Acquire	41.5	Physical 78—146	2.7	5 49 22
58	Skullforge Reaver	Bind On Acquire	41.4	Physical 72—135	2.5	5 67 30
PROPERTIES: Drains target for 2 Shadow damage every 1 sec and transfers it to the caster. Lasts for 30 sec						
60	Dark Iron Reaver	Bind On Pickup	42.7	Physical 71—134	2.4	6 37 38
PROPERTIES: Fire Resist +6, Main Hand Weapon						

Superior One-Hand Swords

Lvl	Name	Binding	DPS	Damage	Speed	Vendor Purchase Value
60	Fiery Retributer	Bind On Acquire	44.7	Physical 56—105	1.8	7 43 73
PROPERTIES: Increased Defense +5, Adds 2 fire damage to your melee attacks, Main Hand Weapon. Armor 60						
60	Renataki's Soul Conduit	Bind On Acquire	45	Physical 66—123	2.1	7 32 93
PROPERTIES: Increases damage and healing done by magical spells and effects by up to 16, Restores 6 mana per 5 sec, Main Hand Weapon						
60	Zulian Slicer	Bind On Acquire	44.8	Physical 78—146	2.5	7 5 66
PROPERTIES: Slices the enemy for 72 to 96 Nature damage, +12 Attack Power, Skinning +10						
60	Argent Avenger	Bind On Acquire	40.7	Physical 71—108	2.2	5 36 22
PROPERTIES: Increases Attack Power against Undead by 200 for 10 sec						
60	Mirah's Song	Bind On Acquire	40	Physical 57—87	1.8	5 12 73
60	Ravenholdt Slicer	Bind On Acquire	42.7	Physical 83—156	2.8	6 52 11
PROPERTIES: +26 Attack Power						

Legendary Two-Hand Swords

Lvl	Name	Binding	DPS	Damage	Speed	Vendor Purchase Value
60	Ashbringer	Bind On Acquire	88	Physical 201—247, Holy 30—50	3	26 14 7
PROPERTIES: Blasts a target for 700 Fire damage						

Epic Two-Hand Swords

Lvl	Name	Binding	DPS	Damage	Speed	Vendor Purchase Value
39	Nightblade	Bind On Pickup	43.4	Physical 97—146	2.8	2 95 13
PROPERTIES: Sends a shadowy bolt at the enemy causing 125 to 275 Shadow damage						
50	Sul'thraze the Lasher	Bind On Acquire	52.1	Physical 108—163	2.6	6 19 36
PROPERTIES: Strikes an enemy with the rage of Sul'thraze. Lowers target's strength by 15 and deals 90 to 210 Shadow damage with an additional 125 damage over 15 sec						
52	Destiny	Bind On Pickup	53.8	Physical 112—168	2.6	7
PROPERTIES: Increases Strength by 200 for 10 sec						
58	Blackblade of Shahram	Bind On Acquire	59.4	Physical 166—250	3.5	9 52 41
PROPERTIES: Summons the infernal spirit of Shahram						
58	Runeblade of Baron Rivendare	Bind On Acquire	59.4	Physical 171—257	3.6	9 13 45
PROPERTIES: Increases movement speed and life regeneration rate						
59	Blade of Hanna	Bind On Pickup	60.2	Physical 101—152	2.1	10 47 29
60	Ashkandi, Greatsword of the Brotherhood	Bind On Acquire	81.9	Physical 229—344	3.5	22 85 17
PROPERTIES: +86 Attack Power						
60	Bonereaver's Edge	Bind On Acquire	75.9	Physical 206—310	3.4	19 64 38
PROPERTIES: Your attacks ignore 700 of your enemies' armor for 10 sec. This effect stacks up to 3 times, Improves your chance to get a critical strike by 1%						
60	Claymore of Unholy Might	Bind On Acquire	81.8	Physical 235—354	3.6	23 98 11
PROPERTIES: +98 Attack Power						
60	Corrupted Ashbringer	Bind On Acquire	90	Physical 259—389	3.6	28 85 27
PROPERTIES: Inflicts the will of the Ashbringer upon the wielder, Improves your chance to get a critical strike by 2%, Improves your chance to hit by 1%, Steals 185 to 215 life from target enemy						
60	Grand Marshal's Claymore	Bind On Acquire	77.4	Physical 235—353	3.8	6 1 18
PROPERTIES: Improves your chance to get a critical strike by 1%						
60	High Warlord's Greatsword	Bind On Acquire	77.4	Physical 235—353	3.8	6 3 39
PROPERTIES: Improves your chance to get a critical strike by 1%						
60	Kalimdor's Revenge	Bind On Acquire	81.9	Physical 209—315	3.2	23 3 18
PROPERTIES: Instantly lightning shocks the target for 239 to 277 Nature damage						
60	Manslayer of the Qiraji	Bind On Acquire	62.5	Physical 180—270	3.6	11 32 87
60	Obsidian Edged Blade	Bind On Acquire	64.7	Physical 176—264	3.4	12 57 68
PROPERTIES: Increased Two-handed Swords +8						
60	The Untamed Blade	Bind On Acquire	70.7	Physical 192—289	3.4	16 4 53
PROPERTIES: Increases Strength by 300 for 8 sec						

Epic Two-Hand Swords

Lvl	Name	Binding	DPS	Damage	Speed	Vendor Purchase Value
60	Typhoon	Bind On Acquire	64.7	Physical 150—225	2.9	12 52 78
PROPERTIES: Increases your chance to parry an attack by 1%						
60	Zin'rokh, Destroyer of Worlds	Bind On Acquire	64.6	Physical 196—295	3.8	12 35 2
PROPERTIES: +72 Attack Power						

Superior Two-Hand Swords

Lvl	Name	Binding	DPS	Damage	Speed	Vendor Purchase Value
18	Searing Blade	Bind On Pickup	19.6	Physical 39—59	2.5	32 60
PROPERTIES: Hurls a fiery ball that causes 70 Fire damage and an additional 9 damage over 6 sec						
20	Duskbringer	Bind On Pickup	21	Physical 57—86	3.4	39 61
PROPERTIES: Sends a shadowy bolt at the enemy causing 60 to 100 Shadow damage						
21	Guardian Blade	Bind On Pickup	21.7	Physical 50—76	2.9	45 16
PROPERTIES: Increased Defense +9. Armor 40						
21	Onyx Claymore	Bind On Pickup	21.6	Physical 48—73	2.8	46 29
23	Pysan's Old Greatsword	Bind On Pickup	22.9	Physical 60—91	3.3	57 44
24	Gizmotron Megachopper	Bind On Pickup	23.9	Physical 61—92	3.2	61 21
26	Deanship Claymore	Bind On Pickup	23.8	Physical 53—80	2.8	61 91
PROPERTIES: Increased Defense +10						
26	Strike of the Hydra	Bind On Acquire	25.6	Physical 67—102	3.3	71 55
PROPERTIES: Corrosive acid that deals 7 Nature damage every 3 sec and lowers target's armor by 50 for 30 sec						
28	Combatant Claymore	Bind On Pickup	27.8	Physical 64—97	2.9	85 24
30	Morbid Dawn	Bind On Acquire	30.2	Physical 70—105	2.9	1 11 24
31	Archaic Defender	Bind On Pickup	31.3	Physical 77—117	3.1	1 22 80
PROPERTIES: Increased Defense +10. Armor 100						
32	Boneslasher	Bind On Pickup	32.6	Physical 70—106	2.7	1 37 54
35	X'caliboar	Bind On Acquire	37.3	Physical 98—148	3.3	2 1 44
36	Sword of the Magistrate	Bind On Pickup	36.5	Physical 96—145	3.3	1 75 96
39	Witchfury	Bind On Pickup	38.9	Physical 87—131	2.8	2 29 11
PROPERTIES: Sends a shadowy bolt at the enemy causing 150 Shadow damage						
40	Whirlwind Sword	Bind On Acquire	35.5	Physical 82—124	2.9	1 73 25
42	Mutilator	Bind On Acquire	41.2	Physical 82—124	2.5	2 91 79
PROPERTIES: Increases damage done to target by physical attacks by 5 for 1 min. Stacks up to 5 times						
43	Deathblow	Bind On Pickup	42	Physical 94—141	2.8	2 92 45
PROPERTIES: Delivers a fatal wound for 160 damage						
44	Blade of the Titans	Bind On Pickup	42.6	Physical 112—169	3.3	3 23 89
44	Stoneslayer	Bind On Acquire	42.7	Physical 133—200	3.9	3 28 51
PROPERTIES: Increases damage by 10 for 8 sec						
47	Lightforged Blade	Bind On Acquire	44.8	Physical 118—178	3.3	3 78 73
PROPERTIES: Fire Resist +10,Frost Resist +10, Shadow Resist +10, Increases damage done by Holy spells and effects by up to 16						
47	Truesilver Champion	Bind On Pickup	45	Physical 108—162	3	3 85 48
PROPERTIES: Protects the caster with a holy shield						
47	Warmonger	Bind On Pickup	45	Physical 108—162	3	4 16 77
PROPERTIES: Improves your chance to hit by 3%						
48	Drakefang Butcher	Bind On Acquire	45.9	Physical 99—149	2.7	4 24 46
PROPERTIES: Wounds the target causing them to bleed for 150 damage over 30 sec						
51	Stone of the Earth	Bind On Acquire	48.1	Physical 123—185	3.2	5 7 39
PROPERTIES: Armor 280						
52	Demonslayer	Bind On Pickup	48.9	Physical 121—182	3.1	5 28
PROPERTIES: +99 Attack Power when fighting Demons						
52	Ta'Kierthan Songblade	Bind On Pickup	48.9	Physical 129—194, Arcane 1—20	3.3	5 35 98
53	Corruption	Bind On Acquire	49.7	Physical 119—179	3	5 68 8
55	Doombringer	Bind On Pickup	51.4	Physical 115—173	2.8	5 91 86
PROPERTIES: Sends a shadowy bolt at the enemy causing 125 to 275 Shadow damage						
56	Barovian Family Sword	Bind On Acquire	52.1	Physical 87—132	2.1	6 84 26
PROPERTIES: Deals 30 Shadow damage every 3 sec for 15 sec. All damage done is then transferred to the caster						

Superior Two-Hand Swords

Lvl	Name	Binding	DPS	Damage	Speed	Vendor Purchase Value
57	Darkstone Claymore	Bind On Acquire	52.9	Physical 152—229	3.6	7 1 20
PROPERTIES: +54 Attack Power						
57	Relentless Scythe	Bind On Acquire	53	Physical 140—210	3.3	6 95 37
PROPERTIES: Increases your chance to parry an attack by 1%						
58	Arcanite Champion	Bind On Pickup	53.8	Physical 129—194	3	7 46 19
PROPERTIES: Heal self for 270 to 450 and Increases Strength by 120 for 30 sec						
58	Barbarous Blade	Bind On Acquire	53.9	Physical 138—207	3.2	7 31 1
PROPERTIES: Improves your chance to get a critical strike by 1%, +60 Attack Power						
58	Demonshear	Bind On Acquire	53.8	Physical 163—246	3.8	7 27 70
PROPERTIES: Sends a shadowy bolt at the enemy causing 150 Shadow damage and dealing 40 damage every 2 sec for 6 sec						
60	Warblade of Caer Darrow	Bind On Acquire	53.9	Physical 142—214, Frost 1—22	3.3	6 98 26

THROWN WEAPONS

Superior Thrown Weapons

Lvl	Name	Binding	DPS	Damage	Speed	Vendor Purchase Value
55	Flightblade Throwing Axe	Bind On Acquire	35.5	Physical 54—102	2.2	11

WANDS

Epic Wands

Lvl	Name	Binding	DPS	Damage	Speed	Vendor Purchase Value
58	Crimson Shocker	Bind On Acquire	73.3	Fire 102—191	2	5 97 41
PROPERTIES: Fire Resist +10						
60	Cold Snap	Bind On Acquire	85.3	Frost 101—189	1.7	7 77 91
PROPERTIES: Increases damage done by Frost spells and effects by up to 20						
60	Doomfinger	Bind On Acquire	139	Shadow 146—271	1.5	22 93 38
PROPERTIES: Improves your chance to get a critical strike with spells by 1%, Increases damage and healing done by magical spells and effects by up to 16						
60	Dragon's Touch	Bind On Acquire	95.6	Fire 107—199	1.6	10 34 61
PROPERTIES: Increases damage and healing done by magical spells and effects by up to 6						
60	Essence Gatherer	Bind On Acquire	85.4	Arcane 83—156	1.4	7 95 98
PROPERTIES: Restores 5 mana per 5 sec						
60	Mar'li's Touch	Bind On Acquire	76.8	Nature 91—170	1.7	6 23 48
60	Touch of Chaos	Bind On Acquire	82	Shadow 86—160	1.5	7 59 90
PROPERTIES: Increases damage and healing done by magical spells and effects by up to 18						
60	Wand of Fates	Bind On Acquire	113.7	Shadow 119—222	1.5	14 72 83
PROPERTIES: Increases damage and healing done by magical spells and effects by up to 12, Improves your chance to hit with spells by 1%						
60	Wand of Qiraji Nobility	Bind On Acquire	102.2	Shadow 114—213	1.6	12 11 94
PROPERTIES: Increases damage and healing done by magical spells and effects by up to 19						
60	Wand of the Whispering Dead	Bind On Acquire	113.7	Shadow 119—222	1.5	14 89 94
PROPERTIES: Increases healing done by spells and effects by up to 22						

Superior Wands

Lvl	Name	Binding	DPS	Damage	Speed	Vendor Purchase Value
15	Firebelcher	Bind On Acquire	20.3	Fire 24—45	1.7	13 12
16	Skycaller	Bind On Pickup	21.6	Arcane 24—45	1.6	14 23
17	Cookie's Stirring Rod	Bind On Acquire	22.3	Arcane 20—38	1.3	16 60
22	Thunderwood	Bind On Pickup	27.1	Nature 36—67	1.9	29 91
27	Gravestone Scepter	Bind On Acquire	29	Shadow 30—57	1.5	35 35
PROPERTIES: Shadow Resist +5						

Superior Wands

Lvl	Name	Binding	DPS	Damage	Speed	Vendor Purchase Value
29	Starfaller	Bind On Pickup	32.9	Arcane 32—60	1.4	58 51
30	Necrotic Wand	Bind On Acquire	33.2	Shadow 32—61	1.4	66 49
33	Earthen Rod	Bind On Pickup	35.6W	Nature 42—79	1.7	86 28
34	Freezing Shard	Bind On Pickup	35.8	Frost 32—61	1.3	95 92
PROPERTIES: Increases damage done by Frost spells and effects by up to 10						
35	Plaguerot Sprig	Bind On Acquire	37.2	Nature 41—78	1.6	96 60
PROPERTIES: Shadow Resist +7						
36	Lady Falther'ess' Finger	Bind On Acquire	38.1	Shadow 34—65	1.3	1 5 36
PROPERTIES: Increases damage done by Shadow spells and effects by up to 10						
37	Jaina's Firestarter	Bind On Pickup	39.4	Fire 44—82	1.6	1 14 87
40	Icefury Wand	Bind On Acquire	37.2	Frost 41—78	1.6	98 42
PROPERTIES: Increases damage done by Frost spells and effects by up to 9						
40	Nether Force Wand	Bind On Acquire	37.3	Arcane 39—73	1.5	1 1 3
PROPERTIES: Increases damage done by Arcane spells and effects by up to 9						
40	Ragefire Wand	Bind On Acquire	37.1	Fire 36—68	1.4	98 5
PROPERTIES: Increases damage done by Fire spells and effects by up to 9						
44	Flaming Incinerator	Bind On Pickup	47.2	Fire 59—111	1.8	1 91 39
PROPERTIES: Fire Resist +8						
45	Wand of Allistarj	Bind On Pickup	48.4	Arcane 64—120	1.9	2 9 45
PROPERTIES: Arcane Resist +9						
46	Noxious Shooter	Bind On Acquire	50	Nature 56—104	1.6	2 25 19
PROPERTIES: Nature Resist +5						
48	Pyric Caduceus	Bind On Acquire	52.5	Fire 66—123	1.8	2 50 83
PROPERTIES: Increases damage done by Fire spells and effects by up to 13						
51	Rod of Corrosion	Bind On Acquire	55	Nature 50—93	1.3	2 89 89
PROPERTIES: Nature Resist +10						
51	Serpentine Skuller	Bind On Acquire	54.6	Shadow 53—100	1.4	2 91 6
PROPERTIES: Shadow Resist +10						
52	Skul's Ghastly Touch	Bind On Acquire	55.8	Shadow 70—131	1.8	3 8 53
PROPERTIES: Increases damage done by Shadow spells and effects by up to 14						
52	Wand of Eternal Light	Bind On Acquire	55.7	Holy 58—109	1.5	3 6 55
PROPERTIES: Restores 2 mana per 5 sec, Increases healing done by spells and effects by up to 9						
52	Woestave	Bind On Acquire	51.3	Shadow 68—127	1.9	2 42 29
PROPERTIES: Increases damage done by Shadow spells and effects by up to 11						
53	Torch of Austen	Bind On Pickup	56.8	Fire 55—104	1.4	3 35 90
PROPERTIES: Fire Resist +10						
54	Wand of Arcane Potency	Bind On Pickup	58.4	Arcane 65—122	1.6	3 65 95
PROPERTIES: Increases damage done by Arcane spells and effects by up to 16						
55	Banshee Finger	Bind On Acquire	59.7	Frost 79—148	1.9	3 77 27
PROPERTIES: Frost Resist +10						
56	Mana Channeling Wand	Bind On Acquire	60.9	Frost 68—127	1.6	3 73 62
PROPERTIES: Restores 4 mana per 5 sec						
57	Bonecreeper Stylus	Bind On Acquire	62.6	Arcane 83—155	1.9	3 93 4
PROPERTIES: Increases damage and healing done by magical spells and effects by up to 11						
57	Oblivion's Touch	Bind On Acquire	62.5	Shadow 78—147	1.8	4 10 11
57	Sparkling Crystal Wand	Bind On Acquire	62.3	Nature 65—122	1.5	3 94 97
PROPERTIES: Increases damage and healing done by magical spells and effects by up to 5						
58	Ritssyn's Wand of Bad Mojo	Bind On Acquire	63.8	Shadow 58—108	1.3	4 27 63
PROPERTIES: Increases damage and healing done by magical spells and effects by up to 11						
60	Antenna of Invigoration	Bind On Pickup	71.6	Nature 80—149	1.6	5 27 26
PROPERTIES: Restores 3 mana per 5 sec, Increases healing done by spells and effects by up to 13						
60	Thoughtblighter	Bind On Acquire	62.7	Shadow 90—168	1.8	5 55 76
PROPERTIES: Restores 5 mana per 5 sec						
60	Stormrager	Bind On Acquire	71.7	Nature 57—106	1.3	4 16 3
60	Wand of Biting Cold	Bind On Acquire	64	Frost 67—125	1.5	4 43 27
PROPERTIES: Increases damage done by Frost spells and effects by up to 16						

These are some of the rare mobs you can find in Azeroth. This can be cross-referenced with the "Rare Mobs" section of BradyGames' World of Warcraft Atlas for zone, and map grid locations. They are presented in alphabetical order for easier use.

Accursed Slitherblade

LEVEL 35

FACTION	AGGRO	CLASS
Naga	Social	Warrior

Hit Points	Armor
1342	1387

SPELL RESIST

—

ABILITIES

—

Alshirr Banebreath

LEVEL 54

FACTION	AGGRO	CLASS
Demon	Social	Warrior

Hit Points	Armor
3292	3237

SPELL RESIST

—

ABILITIES

—

Achellios the Banished

LEVEL 31

FACTION	AGGRO	CLASS
Centaur, Galak	Social	Warrior

Hit Points	Armor
1307	1247

SPELL RESIST

—

ABILITIES

Battle Shout

Ambassador Bloodrage

LEVEL 36

FACTION	AGGRO	CLASS
Quilboar, Razorfen	Social	Paladin

Hit Points	Armor
3150	1234

SPELL RESIST

—

ABILITIES

Shadow Bolt, Cripple, Call of the Grave

Akkrilus

LEVEL 26

FACTION	AGGRO	CLASS
Demon	Social	Paladin

Hit Points	Armor
683	887

SPELL RESIST

—

ABILITIES

Rain of Fire, Fire Shield II

Anathemus

LEVEL 45

FACTION	AGGRO	CLASS
Giant	Social	Warrior

Hit Points	Armor
8316	2742

SPELL RESIST

—

ABILITIES

—

Akubar the Seer

LEVEL 54

FACTION	AGGRO	CLASS
Lost Ones	Social	Paladin

Hit Points	Armor
2633	2610

SPELL RESIST

—

ABILITIES

Lightning Bolt, Slow, Chain Lightning

Antilos

LEVEL 50

FACTION	AGGRO	CLASS
Monster	Social	Warrior

Hit Points	Armor
2768	3018

SPELL RESIST

—

ABILITIES

Swoop, Rend, Cleave

Apothecary Falthis
LEVEL 22

FACTION	AGGRO	CLASS
Undead, Forsaken	Aggressive, Social	Mage

HIT POINTS	ARMOR
472	499

SPELL RESIST
—

ABILITIES
Summon Voidwalker, Shadow Bolt

Azzere the Skyblade
LEVEL 25

FACTION	AGGRO	CLASS
Monster	Monster	Paladin

HIT POINTS	ARMOR
622	858

SPELL RESIST
—

ABILITIES
Fireball, Flame Spike

Araga
LEVEL 35

FACTION	AGGRO	CLASS
Monster	Monster	Warrior

HIT POINTS	ARMOR
1342	1387

SPELL RESIST
—

ABILITIES
—

Barnabus
LEVEL 38

FACTION	AGGRO	CLASS
Wolf	Social, Predator	Warrior

HIT POINTS	ARMOR
1046	1724

SPELL RESIST
—

ABILITIES
—

Arash-ethis
LEVEL 49

FACTION	AGGRO	CLASS
Monster	Monster	Warrior

HIT POINTS	ARMOR
2672	2963

SPELL RESIST
—

ABILITIES
Chain Lightning, Shock

Bayne
LEVEL 10

FACTION	AGGRO	CLASS
Wolf	Social, Predator	Warrior

HIT POINTS	ARMOR
198	518

SPELL RESIST
—

ABILITIES
Rend, Tendon Rip

Azurous
LEVEL 59

FACTION	AGGRO	CLASS
Dragonflight - Black	Social	Warrior

HIT POINTS	ARMOR
8883	3512

SPELL RESIST
Frost +295

ABILITIES
Freezing Breath, Thrash

Big Samras
LEVEL 27

FACTION	AGGRO	CLASS
Bear	Social	Warrior

HIT POINTS	ARMOR
1080	1108

SPELL RESIST
—

ABILITIES
—

Bjarn
LEVEL 12

FACTION	AGGRO	CLASS
Bear	Social	Warrior

Hit Points	Armor
247	580

SPELL RESIST
—

ABILITIES
Ice Claw, Rend Flesh

Blackmoss the Fetid
LEVEL 13

FACTION	AGGRO	CLASS
Monster	Monster	Warrior

Hit Points	Armor
273	615

SPELL RESIST
—

ABILITIES
—

Blind Hunter
LEVEL 32

FACTION	AGGRO	CLASS
Monster	Social	Warrior

Hit Points	Armor
5285	1283

SPELL RESIST
—

ABILITIES
—

Boss Galgosh
LEVEL 22

FACTION	AGGRO	CLASS
Trogg	Social	Warrior

Hit Points	Armor
573	932

SPELL RESIST
—

ABILITIES
Dual Wield, Enrage

Boulderheart
LEVEL 25

FACTION	AGGRO	CLASS
Monster	Monster	Warrior

Hit Points	Armor
699	1037

SPELL RESIST
—

ABILITIES
—

Brack
LEVEL 19

FACTION	AGGRO	CLASS
Murloc	Social	Warrior

Hit Points	Armor
449	826

SPELL RESIST
—

ABILITIES
Pierce Armor, hamstring, Strike

Broken Tooth
LEVEL 37

FACTION	AGGRO	CLASS
Monster	Social	Warrior

Hit Points	Armor
1603	1607

SPELL RESIST
—

ABILITIES
—

Brokespear
LEVEL 17

FACTION	AGGRO	CLASS
Kolkar	Social	Warrior

Hit Points	Armor
386	756

SPELL RESIST
—

ABILITIES
Throw, Slowing Poison

Bruegal Ironknuckle
LEVEL 26

FACTION	AGGRO	CLASS
Defias	Social	Warrior

Hit Points 2250 **Armor** 1072

SPELL RESIST
—

ABILITIES
—

Captain Gerogg Hammertoe
LEVEL 27

FACTION	AGGRO	CLASS
Dwarf, Ironforge	Aggressive, Social	Warrior

Hit Points 2400 **Armor** 1108

SPELL RESIST
—

ABILITIES
Defensive Stance, Improved Blocking, Shield Bash, Shield Wall

Burgle Eye
LEVEL 38

FACTION	AGGRO	CLASS
Murloc	Social	Paladin

Hit Points 1305 **Armor** 1418

SPELL RESIST
—

ABILITIES
—

Carnivous the Breaker
LEVEL 16

FACTION	AGGRO	CLASS
Furbolg	Social	Warrior

Hit Points 356 **Armor** 721

SPELL RESIST
—

ABILITIES
Pierce Armor, Thrash

Captain Beld
LEVEL 11

FACTION	AGGRO	CLASS
Dwarf, Dark Iron	Social	Warrior

Hit Points 222 **Armor** 545

SPELL RESIST
—

ABILITIES
—

Chatter
LEVEL 23

FACTION	AGGRO	CLASS
Spider	Non Social	Warrior

Hit Points 617 **Armor** 967

SPELL RESIST
—

ABILITIES
Paralyzing Poison, Poison

Captain Flat Tusk
LEVEL 11

FACTION	AGGRO	CLASS
Quilboar, Razormane	Social	Warrior

Hit Points 666 **Armor** 545

SPELL RESIST
—

ABILITIES
Heroic Strike

Clack the Reaver
LEVEL 53

FACTION	AGGRO	CLASS
Scorpid	Social	Warrior

Hit Points 3188 **Armor** 3183

SPELL RESIST
—

ABILITIES
Venom Sting, Knockdown

Clutchmother Zavas
LEVEL 54

FACTION	AGGRO	CLASS
Silithid	Social	Warrior

Hit Points	Armor
3292	3237

SPELL RESIST
—

ABILITIES
Pierce Armor, Cleave

Commander Felstrom
LEVEL 32

FACTION	AGGRO	CLASS
Undead, Scourge	Social	Warrior

Hit Points	Armor
1162	1283

SPELL RESIST
—

ABILITIES
—

Crystal Fang
LEVEL 60

FACTION	AGGRO	CLASS
Monster	Social	Warrior

Hit Points	Armor
9156	3566

SPELL RESIST
—

ABILITIES
—

Cyclok the Mad
LEVEL 48

FACTION	AGGRO	CLASS
Ogre	Social	Mage

Hit Points	Armor
1803	1462

SPELL RESIST
—

ABILITIES
Bloodlust, Arcane Explosion, Arcane Bolt

Darbel Montrose
LEVEL 39

FACTION	AGGRO	CLASS
Monster	Social	Paladin

Hit Points	Armor
5900	1517

SPELL RESIST
—

ABILITIES
Summon Succubus, Curse of Weakness, Shadow Bolt, Banish

Darkmist Widow
LEVEL 40

FACTION	AGGRO	CLASS
Spider	Social	Warrior

Hit Points	Armor
1752	1980

SPELL RESIST
—

ABILITIES
—

Dart
LEVEL 38

FACTION	AGGRO	CLASS
Raptor	Social	Warrior

Hit Points	Armor
1604	1724

SPELL RESIST
—

ABILITIES
—

Death Flayer
LEVEL 11

FACTION	AGGRO	CLASS
Scorpid	Social	Warrior

Hit Points	Armor
222	545

SPELL RESIST
—

ABILITIES
Venom Sting

Death Howl
LEVEL 49

FACTION	AGGRO	CLASS
Wolf	Social, Predator	Warrior

HIT POINTS	ARMOR
2672	2963

SPELL RESIST
—

ABILITIES
—

Deathsworn Captain
LEVEL 25

FACTION	AGGRO	CLASS
Worgen	Social	Warrior

HIT POINTS	ARMOR
2097	1037

SPELL RESIST
—

ABILITIES
Cleave, Battle Stance, Hamstring

Deatheye
LEVEL 49

FACTION	AGGRO	CLASS
Basilisk	Basilisk	Warrior

HIT POINTS	ARMOR
2672	2963

SPELL RESIST
Fire +100

ABILITIES
Call of the Grave, Crystal Gaze

Deeb
LEVEL 12

FACTION	AGGRO	CLASS
Murloc	Social	Paladin

HIT POINTS	ARMOR
230	479

SPELL RESIST
—

ABILITIES
Shock

Deathmaw
LEVEL 53

FACTION	AGGRO	CLASS
Wolf	Social, Predator	Warrior

HIT POINTS	ARMOR
3188	3183

SPELL RESIST
—

ABILITIES
Tendon Rip

Dessecus
LEVEL 56

FACTION	AGGRO	CLASS
Monster	Social	Paladin

HIT POINTS	ARMOR
6477	2699

SPELL RESIST
—

ABILITIES
Lightning Cloud

Deathspeaker Selendre
LEVEL 56

FACTION	AGGRO	CLASS
Undead, Scourge	Social	Mage

HIT POINTS	ARMOR
2550	1686

SPELL RESIST
Shadow +56

ABILITIES
Shadow Bolt, Curse of Tongues, Drain Life

Diamond Head
LEVEL 45

FACTION	AGGRO	CLASS
Makrura	Social	Warrior

HIT POINTS	ARMOR
2217	2742

SPELL RESIST
—

ABILITIES
Knockdown

Digmaster Shovelphlange

LEVEL 38

FACTION	AGGRO	CLASS
Monster	Monster	Warrior

Hit Points	Armor
6975	1724

SPELL RESIST
—

ABILITIES
Dual Wield, Sunder Armor, Defensive Stance

Drogoth the Roamer

LEVEL 37

FACTION	AGGRO	CLASS
Monster	Monster	Warrior

Hit Points	Armor
1536	1607

SPELL RESIST
—

ABILITIES
—

Dishu

LEVEL 13

FACTION	AGGRO	CLASS
Monster	Social	Warrior

Hit Points	Armor
273	615

SPELL RESIST
—

ABILITIES
Summon Savannah Cubs

Duggan Wildhammer

LEVEL 55

FACTION	AGGRO	CLASS
Dwarf, Wildhammer	Aggressive, Social	Warrior

Hit Points	Armor
3398	3292

SPELL RESIST
—

ABILITIES
Cleave, Shoot

Dreadscorn

LEVEL 57

FACTION	AGGRO	CLASS
Demon	Social	Warrior

Hit Points	Armor
3758	3402

SPELL RESIST
—

ABILITIES
Bloodlust, Strike, Backhand

Duskstalker

LEVEL 9

FACTION	AGGRO	CLASS
Leopard	Predator	Warrior

Hit Points	Armor
176	412

SPELL RESIST
—

ABILITIES
Tendon Rip

Dreadwhisper

LEVEL 58

FACTION	AGGRO	CLASS
Undead, Scourge	Social	Warrior

Hit Points	Armor
3875	3457

SPELL RESIST
—

ABILITIES
Veil of Shadow, Shadow Bolt Volley, Cripple

Eck'alom

LEVEL 27

FACTION	AGGRO	CLASS
Elemental	Elemental	Paladin

Hit Points	Armor
724	917

SPELL RESIST
Frost +75

ABILITIES
Freeze, Frost Shock

Edan the Howler

LEVEL 9

FACTION	AGGRO	CLASS
Worgen	Social	Warrior

Hit Points	Armor
176	412

SPELL RESIST

—

ABILITIES

Frost Breath

Faulty War Golem

LEVEL 46

FACTION	AGGRO	CLASS
Monster	Monster	Warrior

Hit Points	Armor
2398	2798

SPELL RESIST

—

ABILITIES

Malfunction Proc (10%)

Elder Mystic Razorsnout

LEVEL 15

FACTION	AGGRO	CLASS
Quilboar, Razormane	Social	Paladin

Hit Points	Armor
903	566

SPELL RESIST

—

ABILITIES

Healing Ward, Earthbind Totem, Searing Totem, Healing Wave

Fedfennel

LEVEL 12

FACTION	AGGRO	CLASS
Gnoll, Riverpaw	Social	Warrior

Hit Points	Armor
247	580

SPELL RESIST

—

ABILITIES

Demoralizing Shout, Nimble Reflexes

Engineer Whirleygig

LEVEL 19

FACTION	AGGRO	CLASS
Monster	Social	Warrior

Hit Points	Armor
449	826

SPELL RESIST

—

ABILITIES

Summon Explosive Sheep, Compact Harvest Reaper

Fellicent's Shade

LEVEL 12

FACTION	AGGRO	CLASS
Monster	Social	Paladin

Hit Points	Armor
230	479

SPELL RESIST

—

ABILITIES

Veil of Shadow, Arcane Bolt, Arcane Explosion

Farmer Solliden

LEVEL 8

FACTION	AGGRO	CLASS
Scarlet Crusade	Social	Warrior

Hit Points	Armor
156	322

SPELL RESIST

—

ABILITIES

Strike

Fenros

LEVEL 32

FACTION	AGGRO	CLASS
Worgen	Social	Mage

Hit Points	Armor
1403	694

SPELL RESIST

—

ABILITIES

Frost Nova, Frost Armor, Flame Spike

Fingat
LEVEL 43

FACTION	AGGRO	CLASS
Murloc	Social	Warrior

Hit Points	Armor
2059	2414

SPELL RESIST
—

ABILITIES
Thrash

Foreman Grills
LEVEL 19

FACTION	AGGRO	CLASS
Monster	Social	Warrior

Hit Points	Armor
314	826

SPELL RESIST
—

ABILITIES
Dual Wield, Battle Stance, Hamstring

Firecaller Radison
LEVEL 19

FACTION	AGGRO	CLASS
Monster	Social	Mage

Hit Points	Armor
379	442

SPELL RESIST
—

ABILITIES
Fireball, Fire Nova

Foreman Jerris
LEVEL 62

FACTION	AGGRO	CLASS
Scarlet Crusade	Social	Warrior

Hit Points	Armor
9711	3677

SPELL RESIST
—

ABILITIES
Dual Wield, Snap Kick, Thrash

Flagglemurk the Cruel
LEVEL 16

FACTION	AGGRO	CLASS
Murloc	Social	Warrior

Hit Points	Armor
356	721

SPELL RESIST
—

ABILITIES
Knockdown, Strike

Foreman Marcrid
LEVEL 58

FACTION	AGGRO	CLASS
Scarlet Crusade	Social	Warrior

Hit Points	Armor
3875	3457

SPELL RESIST
—

ABILITIES
Cleave, Strike

Foe Reaper 4000
LEVEL 20

FACTION	AGGRO	CLASS
Monster	Monster	Warrior

Hit Points	Armor
484	861

SPELL RESIST
—

ABILITIES
Trample

Foreman Rigger
LEVEL 24

FACTION	AGGRO	CLASS
Monster	Social	Warrior

Hit Points	Armor
1953	1002

SPELL RESIST
—

ABILITIES
Pierce Armor, Net

Foulbelly
LEVEL 42

FACTION	AGGRO	CLASS
Ogre	Social	Paladin

HIT POINTS	ARMOR
6605	1841

SPELL RESIST
—

ABILITIES
Plague Cloud, Aura of Rot, Deadly Poison, Slowing Poison

Gatekeeper Rageroar
LEVEL 50

FACTION	AGGRO	CLASS
Furbolg, Timbermaw	Social	Warrior

HIT POINTS	ARMOR
2768	3018

SPELL RESIST
—

ABILITIES
Entangling Roots

Foulmane
LEVEL 52

FACTION	AGGRO	CLASS
Undead, Scourge	Social	Warrior

HIT POINTS	ARMOR
3082	3128

SPELL RESIST
—

ABILITIES
Rend, Thrash, Infected Wound

General Colbatann
LEVEL 57

FACTION	AGGRO	CLASS
Dragonflight - Black	Social	Warrior

HIT POINTS	ARMOR
8352	3402

SPELL RESIST
—

ABILITIES
Sunder Armor, Battle Shout, Demoralizing Shout

Fury Shelda
LEVEL 8

FACTION	AGGRO	CLASS
Harpy	Social	Warrior

HIT POINTS	ARMOR
156	322

SPELL RESIST
—

ABILITIES
Deafening Screech

General Fangferror
LEVEL 51

FACTION	AGGRO	CLASS
Naga	Social	Warrior

HIT POINTS	ARMOR
2979	3072

SPELL RESIST
—

ABILITIES
Strike, Cleave, Knockdown

Garneg Charskull
LEVEL 29

FACTION	AGGRO	CLASS
Orc, Dragonmaw	Orc, Dragonmaw	Paladin

HIT POINTS	ARMOR
811	975

SPELL RESIST
—

ABILITIES
Flame Spike, Fire Shield II, Flame Shock

Geolord Mottle
LEVEL 9

FACTION	AGGRO	CLASS
Quilboar, Razormane	Social	Paladin

HIT POINTS	ARMOR
166	342

SPELL RESIST
—

ABILITIES
Healing Wave, Lightning Shield

Geopriest Gukk'rok
LEVEL 19

FACTION	AGGRO	CLASS
Quilboar, Bristleback	Social	Paladin

HIT POINTS	ARMOR
404	684

SPELL RESIST
—

ABILITIES
Power Word: Shield, Renew, heal

Gibblewilt
LEVEL 11

FACTION	AGGRO	CLASS
Gnome, Leper	Social	Mage

HIT POINTS	ARMOR
199	286

SPELL RESIST
—

ABILITIES
Fireball

Gesharahan
LEVEL 20

FACTION	AGGRO	CLASS
Monster	Social	Warrior

HIT POINTS	ARMOR
1452	861

SPELL RESIST
—

ABILITIES
Thrash, Deadly Poison

Giggler
LEVEL 34

FACTION	AGGRO	CLASS
Wolf	Social, Predator	Warrior

HIT POINTS	ARMOR
1279	1353

SPELL RESIST
—

ABILITIES
—

Ghok Bashguud
LEVEL 59

FACTION	AGGRO	CLASS
Orc, Blackrock	Social	Warrior

HIT POINTS	ARMOR
8883	3512

SPELL RESIST
—

ABILITIES
—

Gilmorian
LEVEL 43

FACTION	AGGRO	CLASS
Murloc	Social	Warrior

HIT POINTS	ARMOR
2059	2414

SPELL RESIST
—

ABILITIES
Gouge, Sinister Strike

Gibblesnik
LEVEL 28

FACTION	AGGRO	CLASS
Kobold	Social	Warrior

HIT POINTS	ARMOR
895	1142

SPELL RESIST
—

ABILITIES
Sunder Armor

Gish the Unmoving
LEVEL 56

FACTION	AGGRO	CLASS
Undead, Scourge	Social	Warrior

HIT POINTS	ARMOR
3643	3348

SPELL RESIST
—

ABILITIES
Gargoyle Strike, Rend

Gluggle
LEVEL 37

FACTION	AGGRO	CLASS
Murloc	Social	Mage

Hit Points 1115 **Armor** 858

SPELL RESIST
—

ABILITIES
Acid Splash

Grandpa Vishas
LEVEL 34

FACTION	AGGRO	CLASS
Monster	Social	Warrior

Hit Points 3489 **Armor** 1353

SPELL RESIST
—

ABILITIES
—

Gnawbone
LEVEL 24

FACTION	AGGRO	CLASS
Gnoll, Mosshide	Social	Warrior

Hit Points 664 **Armor** 1002

SPELL RESIST
—

ABILITIES
Dual Wield, Rend

Great Father Arctikus
LEVEL 11

FACTION	AGGRO	CLASS
Troll, Frostmane	Social	Paladin

Hit Points 208 **Armor** 450

SPELL RESIST
—

ABILITIES
Devotion Aura, Renew, Lesser Heal

Gorefang
LEVEL 13

FACTION	AGGRO	CLASS
Wolf	Social, Predator	Warrior

Hit Points 273 **Armor** 615

SPELL RESIST
—

ABILITIES
Rend

Greater Firebird
LEVEL 46

FACTION	AGGRO	CLASS
Beast - Carrion Bird	Social	Warrior

Hit Points 2398 **Armor** 2798

SPELL RESIST
Fire +110

ABILITIES
Crimson Fury, Fire Nova

Gorgon'och
LEVEL 54

FACTION	AGGRO	CLASS
Ogre	Social	Paladin

Hit Points 2633 **Armor** 2610

SPELL RESIST
—

ABILITIES
Torch, Bloodlust, Fireball

Gretheer
LEVEL 57

FACTION	AGGRO	CLASS
Spider	Non Social	Warrior

Hit Points 3758 **Armor** 3402

SPELL RESIST
—

ABILITIES
Deadly Poison, Web

Grimmaw
LEVEL 11

FACTION	AGGRO	CLASS
Furbolg	Social	Warrior

Hit Points	Armor
222	545

SPELL RESIST
—

ABILITIES
Vicious Bite

Grubthor
LEVEL 58

FACTION	AGGRO	CLASS
Monster	Monster	Warrior

Hit Points	Armor
3875	3457

SPELL RESIST
—

ABILITIES
Trample

Grimungous
LEVEL 50

FACTION	AGGRO	CLASS
Giant	Social	Warrior

Hit Points	Armor
6645	3018

SPELL RESIST
—

ABILITIES
War Stomp, Trample

Gruff Swiftbite
LEVEL 12

FACTION	AGGRO	CLASS
Gnoll, Riverpaw	Social	Warrior

Hit Points	Armor
247	580

SPELL RESIST
—

ABILITIES
Thrash

Grizlak
LEVEL 15

FACTION	AGGRO	CLASS
Kobold	Social	Paladin

Hit Points	Armor
301	566

SPELL RESIST
—

ABILITIES
Renew, Power Word: Fortitude

Gruklash
LEVEL 59

FACTION	AGGRO	CLASS
Orc, Blackrock	Social	Warrior

Hit Points	Armor
3997	3512

SPELL RESIST
—

ABILITIES
Backhand, Pummel

Grizzle Snowpaw
LEVEL 59

FACTION	AGGRO	CLASS
Furbolg	Social	Paladin

Hit Points	Armor
3198	2832

SPELL RESIST
—

ABILITIES
Blizzard, Maul, Frost Shock

Grunter
LEVEL 50

FACTION	AGGRO	CLASS
Monster	Monster	Warrior

Hit Points	Armor
2768	3018

SPELL RESIST
—

ABILITIES
Rushing Charge, Berserker Charge, Tendon Rip

Haarka the Ravenous

LEVEL 50

FACTION	AGGRO	CLASS
Silithid	Social	Warrior

Hit Points	Armor
2768	3018

SPELL RESIST

—

ABILITIES

Thrash, Sunder Armor

Harb Foulmountain

LEVEL 27

FACTION	AGGRO	CLASS
Monster	Social	Warrior

Hit Points	Armor
920	1108

SPELL RESIST

Nature +65

ABILITIES

War Stomp, Thrash

Hagg Taurenbane

LEVEL 26

FACTION	AGGRO	CLASS
Quilboar, Razormane	Social	Warrior

Hit Points	Armor
2250	1072

SPELL RESIST

—

ABILITIES

Battle Stance, Cleave, Hamstring, Demoralizing Shout

Hed'mush the Rotting

LEVEL 57

FACTION	AGGRO	CLASS
Undead, Scourge	Social	Warrior

Hit Points	Armor
3758	3402

SPELL RESIST

—

ABILITIES

Mighty Blow, Disease Cloud

Hahk'Zor

LEVEL 54

FACTION	AGGRO	CLASS
Ogre	Social	Warrior

Hit Points	Armor
3292	3237

SPELL RESIST

—

ABILITIES

—

Heggin Stonewhisker

LEVEL 24

FACTION	AGGRO	CLASS
Dwarf, Ironforge	Aggressive, Social	Warrior

Hit Points	Armor
585	1002

SPELL RESIST

—

ABILITIES

Shoot, Fire Shot

Hammerspine

LEVEL 12

FACTION	AGGRO	CLASS
Trogg	Social	Warrior

Hit Points	Armor
321	580

SPELL RESIST

—

ABILITIES

Thrash

Hematos

LEVEL 60

FACTION	AGGRO	CLASS
Dragonflight - Black	Social	Warrior

Hit Points	Armor
15260	3566

SPELL RESIST

—

ABILITIES

Flame Breath

High General Abbendis

LEVEL 59

FACTION	AGGRO	CLASS
Scarlet Crusade	Social	Paladin

Hit Points	Armor
8291	2832

SPELL RESIST

—

ABILITIES

Battle Shout, Demoralizing Shout, Holy Strike

Huricanian

LEVEL 58

FACTION	AGGRO	CLASS
Elemental	Elemental	Paladin

Hit Points	Armor
3100	2788

SPELL RESIST

—

ABILITIES

Chain Lightning

High Priestess Hai'watna

LEVEL 57

FACTION	AGGRO	CLASS
Troll, Bloodscalp	Social	Mage

Hit Points	Armor
8770	1714

SPELL RESIST

—

ABILITIES

Heal, Shadow Bolt Volley, Hex

Immolatus

LEVEL 56

FACTION	AGGRO	CLASS
Demon	Social	Warrior

Hit Points	Armor
8097	3348

SPELL RESIST

—

ABILITIES

Knock Away, Fire Shield

Highlord Mastrogonde

LEVEL 51

FACTION	AGGRO	CLASS
Blackfathom	Social	Paladin

Hit Points	Armor
5502	2477

SPELL RESIST

—

ABILITIES

Polymorph, Power Word: Shield, Shadow Bolt, Shadow Word: Pain

Ironback

LEVEL 51

FACTION	AGGRO	CLASS
Monster	Monster	Warrior

Hit Points	Armor
2979	3072

SPELL RESIST

—

ABILITIES

Spikes

Hissperak

LEVEL 37

FACTION	AGGRO	CLASS
Basilisk	Basilisk	Warrior

Hit Points	Armor
1603	1607

SPELL RESIST

—

ABILITIES

—

Jade

LEVEL 47

FACTION	AGGRO	CLASS
Dragonflight - Green	Social	Warrior

Hit Points	Armor
6467	2853

SPELL RESIST

—

ABILITIES

Acid Breath

Jalinde Summerdrake

LEVEL 49

FACTION	AGGRO	CLASS
High Elf, Silvermoon Remnant	Aggressive, Social	Warrior

HIT POINTS	ARMOR
2672	2963

SPELL RESIST

—

ABILITIES

Shoot, Poisoned Shot, Explosive Shot

Kaskk

LEVEL 40

FACTION	AGGRO	CLASS
Demon	Social	Warrior

HIT POINTS	ARMOR
1752	1980

SPELL RESIST

Fire +95

ABILITIES

—

Jed Runewatcher

LEVEL 59

FACTION	AGGRO	CLASS
Orc, Blackrock	Social	Warrior

HIT POINTS	ARMOR
8883	3512

SPELL RESIST

—

ABILITIES

Shield Charge, Shield Bash, Strike

Kazon

LEVEL 27

FACTION	AGGRO	CLASS
Orc, Blackrock	Social	Warrior

HIT POINTS	ARMOR
840	1108

SPELL RESIST

—

ABILITIES

Backhand

Jimmy the Bleeder

LEVEL 23

FACTION	AGGRO	CLASS
Syndicate	Social	Warrior

HIT POINTS	ARMOR
617	967

SPELL RESIST

—

ABILITIES

—

Kovork

LEVEL 36

FACTION	AGGRO	CLASS
Ogre	Social	Warrior

HIT POINTS	ARMOR
1468	1494

SPELL RESIST

—

ABILITIES

—

Kashoch the Reaver

LEVEL 60

FACTION	AGGRO	CLASS
Giant	Social	Warrior

HIT POINTS	ARMOR
9156	3566

SPELL RESIST

—

ABILITIES

Cleave, Thrash

Kregg Keelhaul

LEVEL 47

FACTION	AGGRO	CLASS
Monster	Social	Warrior

HIT POINTS	ARMOR
2487	2853

SPELL RESIST

—

ABILITIES

Cleave

Krellack
LEVEL 56

FACTION	AGGRO	CLASS
Scorpid	Social	Warrior

Hit Points	Armor
3508	3348

SPELL RESIST
—

ABILITIES
Fatal Sting

Lady Hederine
LEVEL 61

FACTION	AGGRO	CLASS
Demon	Social	Paladin

Hit Points	Armor
27665	2921

SPELL RESIST
Shadow +60

ABILITIES
Dominate Mind, Shadow Word: Pain, Lash of Pain, Fear

Krethis Shadowspinner
LEVEL 15

FACTION	AGGRO	CLASS
Spider	Non Social	Paladin

Hit Points	Armor
301	566

SPELL RESIST
—

ABILITIES
Shadow Shock

Lady Sesspira
LEVEL 51

FACTION	AGGRO	CLASS
Naga	Social	Paladin

Hit Points	Armor
2384	2477

SPELL RESIST
—

ABILITIES
Forked Lightning, Explosive Shot, Shoot

Krom'Grul
LEVEL 54

FACTION	AGGRO	CLASS
Ogre	Social	Paladin

Hit Points	Armor
2633	2610

SPELL RESIST
—

ABILITIES
Torch

Lady Szallah
LEVEL 46

FACTION	AGGRO	CLASS
Naga	Social	Paladin

Hit Points	Armor
1918	2255

SPELL RESIST
—

ABILITIES
Forked Lightning, Enveloping Winds, Lightning Bolt

Kurmokk
LEVEL 42

FACTION	AGGRO	CLASS
Gorilla	Social	Warrior

Hit Points	Armor
1981	2262

SPELL RESIST
—

ABILITIES
—

Lady Vespia
LEVEL 22

FACTION	AGGRO	CLASS
Naga	Social	Paladin

Hit Points	Armor
507	771

SPELL RESIST
—

ABILITIES
Aqua Jet, Frostbolt Volley, Quick Frost Ward, Forked Lightning, Knockdown

Lady Zephris
LEVEL 33

FACTION	AGGRO	CLASS
Naga	Social	Mage

Hit Points	Armor
918	712

SPELL RESIST
—

ABILITIES
—

Leprithus
LEVEL 19

FACTION	AGGRO	CLASS
Undead, Scourge	Social	Paladin

Hit Points	Armor
404	684

SPELL RESIST
—

ABILITIES
Wither Touch, Poison

Lapress
LEVEL 60

FACTION	AGGRO	CLASS
Silithid	Social	Warrior

Hit Points	Armor
12208	3566

SPELL RESIST
—

ABILITIES
Rend

Licillin
LEVEL 14

FACTION	AGGRO	CLASS
Grell	Social	Mage

Hit Points	Armor
263	344

SPELL RESIST
—

ABILITIES
Curse of Weakness, Shadow Bolt

Leech Widow
LEVEL 24

FACTION	AGGRO	CLASS
Spider	Non Social	Warrior

Hit Points	Armor
664	1002

SPELL RESIST
—

ABILITIES
Deadly Leech

Lo'Grosh
LEVEL 39

FACTION	AGGRO	CLASS
Ogre	Social	Mage

Hit Points	Armor
1196	974

SPELL RESIST
—

ABILITIES
Bloodlust, Fire Shield III, Flame Spike

Lord Angler
LEVEL 44

FACTION	AGGRO	CLASS
Makrura	Social	Warrior

Hit Points	Armor
2138	2574

SPELL RESIST
—

ABILITIES
—

Lord Malathrom
LEVEL 31

FACTION	AGGRO	CLASS
Undead, Scourge	Social	Paladin

Hit Points	Armor
935	1033

SPELL RESIST
—

ABILITIES
Minions of Malathrom, Shadow Word: Pain

Lord Captain Wyrmak
LEVEL 45

FACTION	AGGRO	CLASS
Dragonflight - Green	Social	Warrior

Hit Points	Armor
6468	2742

SPELL RESIST
Nature +100

ABILITIES
Cleave, Acid Breath

Lord Maldazzar
LEVEL 56

FACTION	AGGRO	CLASS
Undead, Scourge	Social	Paladin

Hit Points	Armor
2914	2699

SPELL RESIST
—

ABILITIES
Summon Skeleton, Shadow Bolt, Drain Life

Lord Condar
LEVEL 16

FACTION	AGGRO	CLASS
Monster	Monster	Warrior

Hit Points	Armor
356	721

SPELL RESIST
—

ABILITIES
—

Lord Roccor
LEVEL 51

FACTION	AGGRO	CLASS
Elemental	Elemental	Warrior

Hit Points	Armor
11460	3072

SPELL RESIST
Fire +153, Nature +153

ABILITIES
Ground Tremor, Earth Shock, Flame Shock

Lord Darkscythe
LEVEL 57

FACTION	AGGRO	CLASS
Undead, Scourge	Social	Warrior

Hit Points	Armor
3758	3402

SPELL RESIST
—

ABILITIES
Cleave, Sunder Armor

Lord Sakrasis
LEVEL 45

FACTION	AGGRO	CLASS
Naga	Social	Warrior

Hit Points	Armor
1848	2742

SPELL RESIST
—

ABILITIES
Cleave Execute 3

Lord Sinslayer
LEVEL 16

FACTION	AGGRO	CLASS
Naga	Social	Warrior

HIT POINTS	ARMOR
356	721

SPELL RESIST
—

ABILITIES
Aqua Jet, Strike

Magister Hawkhelm
LEVEL 52

FACTION	AGGRO	CLASS
Naga	Social	Warrior

HIT POINTS	ARMOR
3082	3128

SPELL RESIST
—

ABILITIES
Shoot, Multi-Shot

Lost One Chieftain
LEVEL 39

FACTION	AGGRO	CLASS
Lost Ones	Social	Warrior

HIT POINTS	ARMOR
1677	1849

SPELL RESIST
—

ABILITIES
—

Magosh
LEVEL 21

FACTION	AGGRO	CLASS
Trogg	Social	Paladin

HIT POINTS	ARMOR
473	741

SPELL RESIST
—

ABILITIES
Lightning Bolt, Shock, Healing Wave

Lost One Cook
LEVEL 37

FACTION	AGGRO	CLASS
Lost Ones	Social	Paladin

HIT POINTS	ARMOR
1256	1325

SPELL RESIST
—

ABILITIES
Immolate, Knockdown

Magronos the Unyielding
LEVEL 56

FACTION	AGGRO	CLASS
Ogre	Social	Warrior

HIT POINTS	ARMOR
3643	3348

SPELL RESIST
—

ABILITIES
Cleave, Hamstring

Lupos
LEVEL 23

FACTION	AGGRO	CLASS
Wolf	Social, Predator	Warrior

HIT POINTS	ARMOR
617	967

SPELL RESIST
—

ABILITIES
—

Malfunctioning Reaver
LEVEL 56

FACTION	AGGRO	CLASS
Dwarf, Dark Iron	Social	Warrior

HIT POINTS	ARMOR
3643	3348

SPELL RESIST
—

ABILITIES
Thrash, Uppercut

Ma'ruk Wyrmscale
LEVEL 23

FACTION	AGGRO	CLASS
Orc, Dragonmaw	Orc, Dragonmaw	Warrior

Hit Points	Armor
617	967

SPELL RESIST
—

ABILITIES
Battle Shout, Improved Blocking

Mezzir the Howler
LEVEL 55

FACTION	AGGRO	CLASS
Monster	Social	Warrior

Hit Points	Armor
3398	3292

SPELL RESIST
—

ABILITIES
Terrifying Roar, Demoralizing Roar, Frost Breath

Master Digger
LEVEL 15

FACTION	AGGRO	CLASS
Kobold	Social	Warrior

Hit Points	Armor
328	685

SPELL RESIST
—

ABILITIES
Rend, Battle Stance, Heroic Strike

Mirelow
LEVEL 25

FACTION	AGGRO	CLASS
Monster	Monster	Warrior

Hit Points	Armor
733	1037

SPELL RESIST
Nature +50

ABILITIES
Entangling Roots

Master Feardred
LEVEL 52

FACTION	AGGRO	CLASS
Demon	Social	Warrior

Hit Points	Armor
3082	3128

SPELL RESIST
—

ABILITIES
Arcane Explosion

Mist Howler
LEVEL 22

FACTION	AGGRO	CLASS
Wolf	Social, Predator	Warrior

Hit Points	Armor
573	932

SPELL RESIST
—

ABILITIES
Terrifying Howl, Rend, Tendon Rip

Meshlok the Harvester
LEVEL 48

FACTION	AGGRO	CLASS
Elemental	Social	Warrior

Hit Points	Armor
6186	2907

SPELL RESIST
—

ABILITIES
War Stomp

Mith'rethis the Enchanter
LEVEL 52

FACTION	AGGRO	CLASS
Troll, Vilebranch	Social	Paladin

Hit Points	Armor
5691	2522

SPELL RESIST
—

ABILITIES
Enchanted Quickness, Slow, Shadow Word: Pain

Mojo the Twisted
LEVEL 48

FACTION	AGGRO	CLASS
Ogre	Social	Mage

Hit Points 1803
Armor 1462

SPELL RESIST
—

ABILITIES
Shadow Bolt, Shadow Bolt Volley

Monnos the Elder
LEVEL 54

FACTION	AGGRO	CLASS
Giant	Social	Warrior

Hit Points 7599
Armor 3237

SPELL RESIST
—

ABILITIES
War Stomp, Trample, Knock Away

Molok the Crusher
LEVEL 39

FACTION	AGGRO	CLASS
Ogre	Social	Warrior

Hit Points 1677
Armor 1849

SPELL RESIST
—

ABILITIES
Backhand

Morgaine the Sly
LEVEL 10

FACTION	AGGRO	CLASS
Defias	Social	Warrior

Hit Points 198
Armor 518

SPELL RESIST
—

ABILITIES
Gouge, Backstab

Molt Thorn
LEVEL 42

FACTION	AGGRO	CLASS
Monster	Monster	Warrior

Hit Points 2476
Armor 2262

SPELL RESIST
—

ABILITIES
Thorn Volley

Muad
LEVEL 10

FACTION	AGGRO	CLASS
Murloc	Social	Paladin

Hit Points 186
Armor 426

SPELL RESIST
—

ABILITIES
Shock, Healing Wave

Mongress
LEVEL 50

FACTION	AGGRO	CLASS
Bear	Social	Warrior

Hit Points 3322
Armor 3018

SPELL RESIST
—

ABILITIES
—

Mugglefin
LEVEL 23

FACTION	AGGRO	CLASS
Murloc	Social	Warrior

Hit Points 907
Armor 967

SPELL RESIST
—

ABILITIES
Volatile Infection

Murderous Blisterpaw

LEVEL 43

FACTION	AGGRO	CLASS
Wolf	Social, Predator	Warrior

Hit Points 2059 | **Armor** 2414

SPELL RESIST
—

ABILITIES
Fatal Bite, Rend, Thrash

Narillasanz

LEVEL 44

FACTION	AGGRO	CLASS
Dragonflight - Red	Social	Paladin

Hit Points 12121 | **Armor** 2082

SPELL RESIST
—

ABILITIES
Flame Breath, Renew

Mushgog

LEVEL 60

FACTION	AGGRO	CLASS
Monster	Monster	Warrior

Hit Points 61040 | **Armor** 3566

SPELL RESIST
—

ABILITIES
Thorn Volley, Entangling Roots, Spore Cloud

Nefaru

LEVEL 34

FACTION	AGGRO	CLASS
Worgen	Social	Warrior

Hit Points 1279 | **Armor** 1353

SPELL RESIST
—

ABILITIES
Terrifying Howl, Tendon Rip

Naraxis

LEVEL 27

FACTION	AGGRO	CLASS
Spider	Non Social	Warrior

Hit Points 840 | **Armor** 1108

SPELL RESIST
—

ABILITIES
Deadly Poison Naraxis Web

Nimar the Slayer

LEVEL 37

FACTION	AGGRO	CLASS
Troll, Witherbark	Social	Warrior

Hit Points 1536 | **Armor** 1607

SPELL RESIST
—

ABILITIES
Whirlwind, Cleave, Berserker Stance, Execute

Narg the Taskmaster

LEVEL 10

FACTION	AGGRO	CLASS
Kobold	Social	Warrior

Hit Points 257 | **Armor** 518

SPELL RESIST
—

ABILITIES
Battle Shout

Oakpaw

LEVEL 27

FACTION	AGGRO	CLASS
Furbolg	Social	Paladin

Hit Points 862 | **Armor** 917

SPELL RESIST
Nature +79

ABILITIES
Corrupted Strength, Corrupted Stamina, Corrupted Agility, Rejuvenation

Old Cliff Jumper
LEVEL 42

FACTION	AGGRO	CLASS
Wolf	Social, Predator	Warrior

Hit Points	Armor
1981	2262

SPELL RESIST
—

ABILITIES
Blood Howl, Tendon Rip

Oozeworm
LEVEL 42

FACTION	AGGRO	CLASS
Monster	Monster	Warrior

Hit Points	Armor
1981	2262

SPELL RESIST
—

ABILITIES
—

Old Grizzlegut
LEVEL 43

FACTION	AGGRO	CLASS
Bear	Social	Warrior

Hit Points	Armor
2574	2414

SPELL RESIST
—

ABILITIES
—

Panzor the Invincible
LEVEL 57

FACTION	AGGRO	CLASS
Dwarf, Dark Iron	Social	Warrior

Hit Points	Armor
13920	3402

SPELL RESIST
Fire +153, Nature +153, Frost +153, Shadow +153, Arcane +153

ABILITIES
—

Old Vicejaw
LEVEL 14

FACTION	AGGRO	CLASS
Bear	Social	Warrior

Hit Points	Armor
375	650

SPELL RESIST
—

ABILITIES
Strike

Pridewing Patriarch
LEVEL 25

FACTION	AGGRO	CLASS
Monster	Social	Warrior

Hit Points	Armor
712	1037

SPELL RESIST
—

ABILITIES
Poison

Omgorn the Lost
LEVEL 50

FACTION	AGGRO	CLASS
Ogre	Social	Warrior

Hit Points	Armor
2768	3018

SPELL RESIST
—

ABILITIES
Mortal Strike

Prince Kellen
LEVEL 33

FACTION	AGGRO	CLASS
Demon	Social	Warrior

Hit Points	Armor
1221	1317

SPELL RESIST
—

ABILITIES
—

Prince Nazjak
LEVEL 41

FACTION	AGGRO	CLASS
Naga	Social	Warrior

HIT POINTS	ARMOR
1902	2117

SPELL RESIST
—

ABILITIES
—

Quartermaster Zigris
LEVEL 59

FACTION	AGGRO	CLASS
Orc, Blackrock	Social	Warrior

HIT POINTS	ARMOR
23688	3512

SPELL RESIST
—

ABILITIES
Hooked Net, Shoot, Stun Bomb

Prince Raze
LEVEL 32

FACTION	AGGRO	CLASS
Demon	Social	Paladin

HIT POINTS	ARMOR
1332	1063

SPELL RESIST
—

ABILITIES
Fire Nova, Fireball, Charged Arcane Bolt

Ragepaw
LEVEL 51

FACTION	AGGRO	CLASS
Furbolg	Social	Warrior

HIT POINTS	ARMOR
2865	3072

SPELL RESIST
—

ABILITIES
—

Putridius
LEVEL 58

FACTION	AGGRO	CLASS
Undead, Scourge	Social	Warrior

HIT POINTS	ARMOR
3588	3457

SPELL RESIST
—

ABILITIES
Putrid Stench, Knock Away, Uppercut

Rak'shiri
LEVEL 57

FACTION	AGGRO	CLASS
Monster	Social	Warrior

HIT POINTS	ARMOR
3758	3402

SPELL RESIST
—

ABILITIES
Terrify

Qirot
LEVEL 47

FACTION	AGGRO	CLASS
Silithid	Social	Warrior

HIT POINTS	ARMOR
2487	2853

SPELL RESIST
—

ABILITIES
Poison

Ranger Lord Hawkspear
LEVEL 60

FACTION	AGGRO	CLASS
High Elf, Silvermoon Remnant	Aggressive, Social	Warrior

HIT POINTS	ARMOR
4120	3566

SPELL RESIST
—

ABILITIES
Shoot, Dual Wield, Strike, Kick

RATHORIAN
LEVEL 15

FACTION	AGGRO	CLASS
Monster	Social	Warrior

HIT POINTS	ARMOR
328	685

SPELL RESIST
—

ABILITIES
—

RAZORTALON
LEVEL 44

FACTION	AGGRO	CLASS
Monster	Monster	Warrior

HIT POINTS	ARMOR
2138	2574

SPELL RESIST
—

ABILITIES
Rend, Tendon Rip, Strike

RAVAGE
LEVEL 51

FACTION	AGGRO	CLASS
Wolf	Social, Predator	Warrior

HIT POINTS	ARMOR
2979	3072

SPELL RESIST
—

ABILITIES
Infected Bite, Poison

REKK'TILAC
LEVEL 48

FACTION	AGGRO	CLASS
Spider	Non Social	Warrior

HIT POINTS	ARMOR
2577	2907

SPELL RESIST
Fire +125

ABILITIES
Fire Shield, Deadly Poison

RAVENCLAW REGENT
LEVEL 22

FACTION	AGGRO	CLASS
Undead, Scourge	Social	Paladin

HIT POINTS	ARMOR
507	771

SPELL RESIST
—

ABILITIES
Shadow Word: Pain, Dominate Mind

RESSAN THE NEEDLER
LEVEL 11

FACTION	AGGRO	CLASS
Monster	Social	Warrior

HIT POINTS	ARMOR
277	545

SPELL RESIST
—

ABILITIES
Sonic Burst

RAZORMAW MATRIARCH
LEVEL 31

FACTION	AGGRO	CLASS
Raptor	Social	Warrior

HIT POINTS	ARMOR
1106	1247

SPELL RESIST
—

ABILITIES
Rend Flesh, Fatal Bite

RETHEROKK THE BERSERKER
LEVEL 48

FACTION	AGGRO	CLASS
Troll, Vilebranch	Social	Warrior

HIT POINTS	ARMOR
2577	2907

SPELL RESIST
—

ABILITIES
Thrash, Dual Wield

Rex Ashil
LEVEL 57

FACTION	AGGRO	CLASS
Silithid	Social	Warrior

Hit Points	Armor
8352	3402

SPELL RESIST
—

ABILITIES
Pierce Armor

Ribchaser
LEVEL 17

FACTION	AGGRO	CLASS
Gnoll, Redridge	Social	Warrior

Hit Points	Armor
386	756

SPELL RESIST
—

ABILITIES
—

Rippa
LEVEL 44

FACTION	AGGRO	CLASS
Monster	Social	Warrior

Hit Points	Armor
2316	2574

SPELL RESIST
—

ABILITIES
—

Ripscale
LEVEL 39

FACTION	AGGRO	CLASS
Monster	Social	Warrior

Hit Points	Armor
1750	1849

SPELL RESIST
—

ABILITIES
—

Ro'Bark
LEVEL 28

FACTION	AGGRO	CLASS
Gnoll, Mudsnout	Social	Warrior

Hit Points	Armor
895	1142

SPELL RESIST
—

ABILITIES
—

Rohh the Silent
LEVEL 26

FACTION	AGGRO	CLASS
Gnoll, Shadowhide	Social	Warrior

Hit Points	Armor
787	1072

SPELL RESIST
—

ABILITIES
Backstab, Sneak, Poison, Dual Wield

Roloch
LEVEL 38

FACTION	AGGRO	CLASS
Ogre	Social	Warrior

Hit Points	Armor
1604	1724

SPELL RESIST
—

ABILITIES
Cleave

Rorgish Jowl
LEVEL 25

FACTION	AGGRO	CLASS
Furbolg	Social	Warrior

Hit Points	Armor
712	1037

SPELL RESIST
—

ABILITIES
Thrash

Rumbler
LEVEL 45

FACTION	AGGRO	CLASS
Elemental	Elemental	Warrior

HIT POINTS	ARMOR
2217	2742

SPELL RESIST
Nature +70

ABILITIES
Ground Tremor, Trample

Scargil
LEVEL 30

FACTION	AGGRO	CLASS
Murloc	Social	Warrior

HIT POINTS	ARMOR
1002	1212

SPELL RESIST
—

ABILITIES
—

Ruul Onestone
LEVEL 39

FACTION	AGGRO	CLASS
Ogre	Social	Paladin

HIT POINTS	ARMOR
3540	1517

SPELL RESIST
—

ABILITIES
Bloodlust, Lightning Bolt, Rain of Fire

Scarlet Executioner
LEVEL 60

FACTION	AGGRO	CLASS
Scarlet Crusade	Social	Warrior

HIT POINTS	ARMOR
9156	3566

SPELL RESIST
—

ABILITIES
Execute, Mortal Strike, Cleave

Scald
LEVEL 49

FACTION	AGGRO	CLASS
Elemental	Elemental	Warrior

HIT POINTS	ARMOR
2672	2963

SPELL RESIST
—

ABILITIES
Immolate

Scarlet High Clerist
LEVEL 63

FACTION	AGGRO	CLASS
Scarlet Crusade	Social	Paladin

HIT POINTS	ARMOR
7995	3009

SPELL RESIST
—

ABILITIES
Power Word: Shield, Heal, Prayer of Healing, Holy Fire

Scale Belly
LEVEL 45

FACTION	AGGRO	CLASS
Basilisk	Basilisk	Warrior

HIT POINTS	ARMOR
2217	2742

SPELL RESIST
—

ABILITIES
Crystal Flash

Scarlet Interrogator
LEVEL 61

FACTION	AGGRO	CLASS
Scarlet Crusade	Social	Warrior

HIT POINTS	ARMOR
9432	3622

SPELL RESIST
—

ABILITIES
Dual Wield, Immolate

Scarlet Judge
LEVEL 60

FACTION	AGGRO	CLASS
Scarlet Crusade	Social	Paladin

Hit Points	Armor
7326	2876

SPELL RESIST
—

ABILITIES
Hammer of Justice, Holy Strike, Crusader Strike

Setis
LEVEL 61

FACTION	AGGRO	CLASS
Elemental	Elemental	Warrior

Hit Points	Armor
31440	3622

SPELL RESIST
—

ABILITIES
War Stomp, Crowd Pummel

Scarlet Smith
LEVEL 59

FACTION	AGGRO	CLASS
Scarlet Crusade	Social	Warrior

Hit Points	Armor
8883	3512

SPELL RESIST
Fire +177

ABILITIES
Strike, Knockdown

Shadowclaw
LEVEL 13

FACTION	AGGRO	CLASS
Monster	Monster	Warrior

Hit Points	Armor
204	615

SPELL RESIST
—

ABILITIES
Sneak, Curse of Weakness

Seeker Aqualon
LEVEL 21

FACTION	AGGRO	CLASS
Elemental	Elemental	Warrior

Hit Points	Armor
521	897

SPELL RESIST
—

ABILITIES
—

Shadowforge Commander
LEVEL 40

FACTION	AGGRO	CLASS
Dwarf, Dark Iron	Social	Warrior

Hit Points	Armor
1752	1980

SPELL RESIST
—

ABILITIES
Devotion Aura

Sergeant Brashclaw
LEVEL 18

FACTION	AGGRO	CLASS
Gnoll, Riverpaw	Social	Warrior

Hit Points	Armor
417	791

SPELL RESIST
—

ABILITIES
Frenzied Command, Knockdown

Shleipnarr
LEVEL 47

FACTION	AGGRO	CLASS
Monster	Monster	Warrior

Hit Points	Armor
2487	2853

SPELL RESIST
Fire +95, Shadow +95

ABILITIES
Mana Burn, Terrify

Siege Golem
LEVEL 40

FACTION	AGGRO	CLASS
Dwarf, Dark Iron	Social	Warrior

HIT POINTS	ARMOR
5334	1980

SPELL RESIST
—

ABILITIES
Fireball

Skhowl
LEVEL 36

FACTION	AGGRO	CLASS
Monster	Social	Warrior

HIT POINTS	ARMOR
1468	1494

SPELL RESIST
—

ABILITIES
Intimidating Roar, Backhand, Demoralizing Roar

Singer
LEVEL 34

FACTION	AGGRO	CLASS
Monster	Social	Paladin

HIT POINTS	ARMOR
1063	1121

SPELL RESIST
—

ABILITIES
Dual Wield, Dominate Mind, Demoralizing Shout

Skul
LEVEL 58

FACTION	AGGRO	CLASS
Undead, Scourge	Social	Mage

HIT POINTS	ARMOR
13065	1742

SPELL RESIST
—

ABILITIES
Frostbolt, Frost Shock, Frost Armor, Arcane Bolt, Blizzard

Sister Hatelash
LEVEL 11

FACTION	AGGRO	CLASS
Harpy	Social	Paladin

HIT POINTS	ARMOR
416	450

SPELL RESIST
—

ABILITIES
Lightning Bolt, Lightning Barrier

Slark
LEVEL 15

FACTION	AGGRO	CLASS
Murloc	Social	Warrior

HIT POINTS	ARMOR
328	685

SPELL RESIST
—

ABILITIES
Thrash

Skarr the Unbreakable
LEVEL 58

FACTION	AGGRO	CLASS
Ogre	Social	Warrior

HIT POINTS	ARMOR
57420	3457

SPELL RESIST
—

ABILITIES
Cleave, Knockdown, Mortal Strike

Slave Master Blackheart
LEVEL 50

FACTION	AGGRO	CLASS
Dwarf, Dark Iron	Social	Warrior

HIT POINTS	ARMOR
2768	3018

SPELL RESIST
—

ABILITIES
Throw Net, Shoot

Sludge Beast
LEVEL 19

FACTION	AGGRO	CLASS
Monster	Monster	Warrior

Hit Points	Armor
449	826

SPELL RESIST
—

ABILITIES
Black Sludge

Snarler
LEVEL 42

FACTION	AGGRO	CLASS
Wolf	Social, Predator	Warrior

Hit Points	Armor
1981	2262

SPELL RESIST
Fire +100, Nature +100, Frost +100, Shadow +100, Arcane +100

ABILITIES
Fade Out

Sludginn
LEVEL 30

FACTION	AGGRO	CLASS
Monster	Monster	Warrior

Hit Points	Armor
974	1212

SPELL RESIST
—

ABILITIES
Dark Sludge, Leech Poison

Snarlmane
LEVEL 23

FACTION	AGGRO	CLASS
Gnoll, Rothide	Social	Warrior

Hit Points	Armor
726	967

SPELL RESIST
—

ABILITIES
Rage of Thule

Smoldar
LEVEL 50

FACTION	AGGRO	CLASS
Elemental	Elemental	Warrior

Hit Points	Armor
2768	3018

SPELL RESIST
Fire +170, Nature +170

ABILITIES
Molten Metal

Snort the Heckler
LEVEL 17

FACTION	AGGRO	CLASS
Wolf	Social, Predator	Warrior

Hit Points	Armor
386	756

SPELL RESIST
—

ABILITIES
Toxic Spit, Tendon Rip

Snagglespear
LEVEL 9

FACTION	AGGRO	CLASS
Gnoll, Shadowhide	Social	Warrior

Hit Points	Armor
176	412

SPELL RESIST
—

ABILITIES
Throw Net

Soriid the Devourer
LEVEL 50

FACTION	AGGRO	CLASS
Silithid	Social	Warrior

Hit Points	Armor
2768	3018

SPELL RESIST
—

ABILITIES
Pierce Armor, Rend

Spirestone Battle Lord
LEVEL 58

FACTION	AGGRO	CLASS
Orc, Blackrock	Social	Warrior

Hit Points	Armor
17226	3457

SPELL RESIST
—

ABILITIES
—

Stonespine
LEVEL 60

FACTION	AGGRO	CLASS
Undead, Scourge	Social	Warrior

Hit Points	Armor
15260	3566

SPELL RESIST
—

ABILITIES
Vicious Rend

Spiteflayer
LEVEL 52

FACTION	AGGRO	CLASS
Beast - Carrion Bird	Social	Warrior

Hit Points	Armor
3082	3128

SPELL RESIST
—

ABILITIES
Curse of Blood, Thrash

Takk the Leaper
LEVEL 19

FACTION	AGGRO	CLASS
Raptor	Social	Warrior

Hit Points	Armor
1347	826

SPELL RESIST
—

ABILITIES
Battle Stance, Charge

Squiddic
LEVEL 19

FACTION	AGGRO	CLASS
Murloc	Social	Warrior

Hit Points	Armor
449	826

SPELL RESIST
—

ABILITIES
—

Terrorspark
LEVEL 55

FACTION	AGGRO	CLASS
Demon	Social	Paladin

Hit Points	Armor
2718	2654

SPELL RESIST
—

ABILITIES
Fireball, Fire Shield, Summon Flamekin Torcher, Summon Flamekin Rager

Sri'skulk
LEVEL 13

FACTION	AGGRO	CLASS
Spider	Non Social	Warrior

Hit Points	Armor
341	615

SPELL RESIST
—

ABILITIES
Deadly Poison

Terrowulf Packlord
LEVEL 32

FACTION	AGGRO	CLASS
Monster	Social	Warrior

Hit Points	Armor
1162	1283

SPELL RESIST
—

ABILITIES
Intimidating Growl, Battle Roar

Thauris Balgarr

LEVEL 57

FACTION	AGGRO	CLASS
Dwarf, Dark Iron	Social	Warrior

HIT POINTS	ARMOR
3758	3402

SPELL RESIST

—

ABILITIES

Summon Dark Iron Land Mine, Shoot, Net

The Razza

LEVEL 60

FACTION	AGGRO	CLASS
Monster	Monster	Paladin

HIT POINTS	ARMOR
73260	2876

SPELL RESIST

—

ABILITIES

Chain Lightning, Poison Bolt

The Evalcharr

LEVEL 48

FACTION	AGGRO	CLASS
Monster	Social	Warrior

HIT POINTS	ARMOR
2577	2907

SPELL RESIST

—

ABILITIES

Fireball, Lightning Breath

The Reak

LEVEL 49

FACTION	AGGRO	CLASS
Monster	Monster	Warrior

HIT POINTS	ARMOR
2672	2963

SPELL RESIST

Nature +240

ABILITIES

Black Sludge, Putrid Breath

The Husk

LEVEL 62

FACTION	AGGRO	CLASS
Monster	Monster	Warrior

HIT POINTS	ARMOR
4369	3677

SPELL RESIST

—

ABILITIES

Infected Wound, Tendon Rip

The Rot

LEVEL 43

FACTION	AGGRO	CLASS
Monster	Monster	Warrior

HIT POINTS	ARMOR
2059	2414

SPELL RESIST

—

ABILITIES

—

The Ongar

LEVEL 51

FACTION	AGGRO	CLASS
Monster	Monster	Warrior

HIT POINTS	ARMOR
2979	3072

SPELL RESIST

—

ABILITIES

—

Threggil

LEVEL 6

FACTION	AGGRO	CLASS
Demon	Social	Paladin

HIT POINTS	ARMOR
115	150

SPELL RESIST

—

ABILITIES

Strike

Thunderstomp
LEVEL 24

FACTION	AGGRO	CLASS
Monster	Monster	Warrior

Hit Points 664 **Armor** 1002

SPELL RESIST
—

ABILITIES
Chained Bolt, Thunderclap

Thuros Lightfingers
LEVEL 11

FACTION	AGGRO	CLASS
Defias	Social	Warrior

Hit Points 222 **Armor** 545

SPELL RESIST
—

ABILITIES
Backstab, Dual Wield

Timber
LEVEL 10

FACTION	AGGRO	CLASS
Wolf	Social, Predator	Warrior

Hit Points 198 **Armor** 518

SPELL RESIST
—

ABILITIES
Rabies

Tsu'zee
LEVEL 59

FACTION	AGGRO	CLASS
Monster	Social	Warrior

Hit Points 17766 **Armor** 3512

SPELL RESIST
—

ABILITIES
Dual Wield, Gouge, Sinister Strike, Blind, Backstab

Twilight Lord Everun
LEVEL 60

FACTION	AGGRO	CLASS
Monster	Social	Paladin

Hit Points 3296 **Armor** 2876

SPELL RESIST
—

ABILITIES
Shadow Shock, Fireball

Uhk'loc
LEVEL 53

FACTION	AGGRO	CLASS
Gorilla	Social	Warrior

Hit Points 3188 **Armor** 3183

SPELL RESIST
—

ABILITIES
Battle Shout, Uppercut, Pummel

Ursol'lok
LEVEL 31

FACTION	AGGRO	CLASS
Bear	Social	Warrior

Hit Points 1257 **Armor** 1247

SPELL RESIST
—

ABILITIES
Maul

Uruson
LEVEL 7

FACTION	AGGRO	CLASS
Furbolg	Social	Warrior

Hit Points 137 **Armor** 245

SPELL RESIST
—

ABILITIES
Demoralizing Roar

Varo'then's Ghost
LEVEL 48

FACTION	AGGRO	CLASS
Undead, Scourge	Social	Warrior

Hit Points	Armor
2577	2907

SPELL RESIST
—

ABILITIES
Curse of Weakness

Volchan
LEVEL 60

FACTION	AGGRO	CLASS
Giant	Social	Paladin

Hit Points	Armor
12210	2876

SPELL RESIST
—

ABILITIES
Fire Shield, Flamecrack, Fire Nova

Vengeful Ancient
LEVEL 30

FACTION	AGGRO	CLASS
Elemental	Elemental	Warrior

Hit Points	Armor
1002	1212

SPELL RESIST
—

ABILITIES
Curse of Thorns

Vultros
LEVEL 26

FACTION	AGGRO	CLASS
Beast - Carrion Bird	Social	Warrior

Hit Points	Armor
787	1072

SPELL RESIST
—

ABILITIES
Swoop

Verifonix
LEVEL 42

FACTION	AGGRO	CLASS
Venture Company	Social	Warrior

Hit Points	Armor
1981	2262

SPELL RESIST
—

ABILITIES
Pierce Armor

War Golem
LEVEL 36

FACTION	AGGRO	CLASS
Dwarf, Dark Iron	Social	Warrior

Hit Points	Armor
1468	1494

SPELL RESIST
—

ABILITIES
Lock Down

Veyzhak the Cannibal
LEVEL 48

FACTION	AGGRO	CLASS
Troll, Frostmane	Social	Warrior

Hit Points	Armor
6186	2907

SPELL RESIST
—

ABILITIES
Dual Wield, Rend

Warlord Kolkanis
LEVEL 9

FACTION	AGGRO	CLASS
Kolkar	Social	Warrior

Hit Points	Armor
176	412

SPELL RESIST
—

ABILITIES
Pummel, Thunderclap

Warlord Thresh'jin
LEVEL 58

FACTION	AGGRO	CLASS
Troll, Frostmane	Social	Warrior

HIT POINTS	ARMOR
3875	3457

SPELL RESIST
—

ABILITIES
Whirlwind, Sunder Armor, Hamstring

Zora
LEVEL 59

FACTION	AGGRO	CLASS
Silithid	Social	Warrior

HIT POINTS	ARMOR
8883	3512

SPELL RESIST
—

ABILITIES
Poison Bolt

Witherheart the Stalker
LEVEL 45

FACTION	AGGRO	CLASS
Troll, Vilebranch	Social	Warrior

HIT POINTS	ARMOR
2217	2742

SPELL RESIST
—

ABILITIES
Dual Wield, Sneak, Backstab

Zul'arek Hatefowler
LEVEL 43

FACTION	AGGRO	CLASS
Troll, Vilebranch	Social	Warrior

HIT POINTS	ARMOR
2059	2414

SPELL RESIST
—

ABILITIES
Silence, Shadow Bolt Volley

Zalas Witherbark
LEVEL 40

FACTION	AGGRO	CLASS
Troll, Witherbark	Social	Paladin

HIT POINTS	ARMOR
1409	1619

SPELL RESIST
—

ABILITIES
Polymorph, Chains of Ice, Wither Touch, Shadow Bolt Volley, Dual Wield

Zul'Brin Warpbranch
LEVEL 59

FACTION	AGGRO	CLASS
Troll, Frostmane	Social	Mage

HIT POINTS	ARMOR
2798	1770

SPELL RESIST
—

ABILITIES
Hex, Healing Wave, Chain Lightning, Flame Shock

Zerillis
LEVEL 45

FACTION	AGGRO	CLASS
Troll, Frostmane	Social	Warrior

HIT POINTS	ARMOR
5544	2742

SPELL RESIST
—

ABILITIES
Frost Shot, Shoot, Net

ADDITIONAL CONTENT

Vendor Pets

Pet Name	Zone	NPC Name	Price
Ancona Chicken	Thousand Needles	Magus Tirith	1
Black Kingsnake	Orgrimmar	Xan'tish	50
Brown Snake	Orgrimmar	Xan'tish	50
Cat Carrier - Bombay	Elwynn Forest	Donni Anthania	40
Cat Carrier - Cornish Rex	Elwynn Forest	Donni Anthania	40
Cat Carrier - Orange Tabby	Elwynn Forest	Donni Anthania	40
Cat Carrier - Silver Tabby	Elwynn Forest	Donni Anthania	40
Cat Carrier - White Kitten	Stormwind	Lil Timmy (rare)	60
Cockroach	Undercity	Jeremiah Payson	50
Crimson Snake	Orgrimmar	Xan'tish	50
Great Horned Owl	Darnassus	Shylenai	50
Hawk Owl	Darnassus	Shylenai	50
Parrot Cage - Cockatiel	Stranglethorn Vale	Narkk	40
Parrot Cage - Senegal	Stranglethorn Vale	Narkk	40
Prairie Dog Whistle	Thunder Bluff	Halpa	50
Rabbit Crate - Snowshoe	Dun Morogh	Yarlyn Amberstill	20
Tree Frog Box	Darkmoon Faire	Flik	1
Wood Frog Box	Darkmoon Faire	Flik	1

Dropped Pets

Pet Name	Zone	NPC Name
Cat Carrier - Black Tabby	Alterac Mountains	Multiple Dalaran mobs.
	Silverpine Forest	Dalaran Spellscribe (rare)
Cat Carrier - Siamese	The Deadmines	Cookie
Dark Whelpling	Badlands	Scalding Whelp
	Dustwallow Marsh	Searing Whelp
Disgusting Oozeling	Eastern Plaguelands	Rotting Sludge
	Felwood	Tainted Ooze
	The Temple of Atal'Hakkar	Oozeling
	Western Plaguelands	Devouring Ooze, Oozeling
Parrot Cage - Green Wing Macaw	The Deadmines	Defias Pirate
Parrot Cage - Hyacinth Macaw	Stranglethorn Vale	Multiple Bloodsail mobs.
Tiny Crimson Whelpling	Wetlands	Multiple Whelp Mobs
Tiny Emerald Whelpling	Swamp of Sorrows	Dreaming Whelp

Crafted Pets

Pet Name	Skill Required
Lifelike Mechanical Toad	Engineering - 265
Mechanical Squirrel Box	Engineering - 75
Pet Bombling	Engineering – 205

Special Pets

Pet Name	Requirements
Blue Murloc Egg	Requires Blizzcon Trade Show Key
Diablo Stone	WoW Collectors Edition required
Green Helper Box	Found in gifts during the Greatfather Winter's Festival.
Panda Collar	WoW Collectors Edition/Korea Invitational Key required.
Red Helper Box	Found in gifts during the Greatfather Winter's Festival.
Zergling Leash	WoW Collectors Edition required
Hippogyrph Hatchling	WoW Trading Card Game Key

Quest Reward Pets

Pet Name	Quest Starting Zone	Quest NPC Name
Mechanical Chicken	Stranglethorn Vale	Oglethorpe Obnoticus
QUEST INFO-You must complete the Robo-chicken quest series Rescue OOX-09/HL!, Rescue OOX-17/TN!, and Rescue OOX-22/FE! in the Hinterlands, Tanaris and Feralas before you can get the Mechanical Chicken.		
Smolderweb Carrier	Burning Steppes	Kibler
QUEST INFO-The quest is called "En-Ay-Es-Tee-Why" where Kibler would like you to go into Blackrock Spire and bring out 15 Spire Spider Eggs.		
Sprite Darter Egg	Feralas	Agnar Beastamer
QUEST INFO-Alliance only. Must complete this quest chain - "Freedom for All Creatures" "Doling Justice" "An Orphan Looking For a Home" "A Short Incubation" "The Newest Member of the Family" "Food for Baby" and "Becoming a Parent."		
Worg Carrier	Burning Steppes	Kibler
QUEST INFO-The quest is called "Kibler's Exotic Pet's" where he would like you to go into Blackrock Spire and cage some Worg pups.		
Human Orphan Whistle	Stormwind	Orphan Matron Nightingale
Orcish Orphan Whistle	Orgrimmar	Orphan Matron Battlewail
QUEST INFO-Once a year, there comes a yearly event called Children's Week. During this time the Orphan Matrons will let you take a small child around to see the sights, eat some ice cream, and have an all around good time. It is also known that through the hardships of war, growing up an orphan has made the children a rather tough breed, and they will not come to any harm from running through the most dangerous areas of Azeroth, drowning, jumping from high cliffs, or being outrun by your fastest mount. As the Horde will tell you…they've tried and failed…all week long.		
Chicken Egg	Westfall - Saldean's Farm	Chicken/Farmer Saldean
QUEST INFO-Alliance only. Go to Westfall, talk to Farmer Saldean and purchase some of his "Special Chicken Feed" Next, walk to the first chicken you see, and start using the emote /cluck. Do this over and over until the chicken looks at you quizzically, give it the "Special Chicken Feed" and it will lay an egg. Grab the egg and you will have your very own chicken.		

EXCLUSIVE WORLD MAP

- **LARGE 36" X 48" DIMENSIONS**
  2-sided, full-color poster fits standard poster frame

- **A PERFECT ADDITION FOR YOUR WORLD OF WARCRAFT™ COLLECTION!**

- **SIDE 1:**
  The Azeroth map with all flight paths, dungeons, cities and regions

- **SIDE 2:**
  The Azeroth map, unfettered — shows a clear view of the topography of the continents

ONLY AVAILABLE AT
bradygames.com*

bradygames.com / wow

*For sale only at bradygames.com and its online affiliate partners.

www.bradygames.com

www.worldofwarcraft.com

THE ULTIMATE RESOURCE

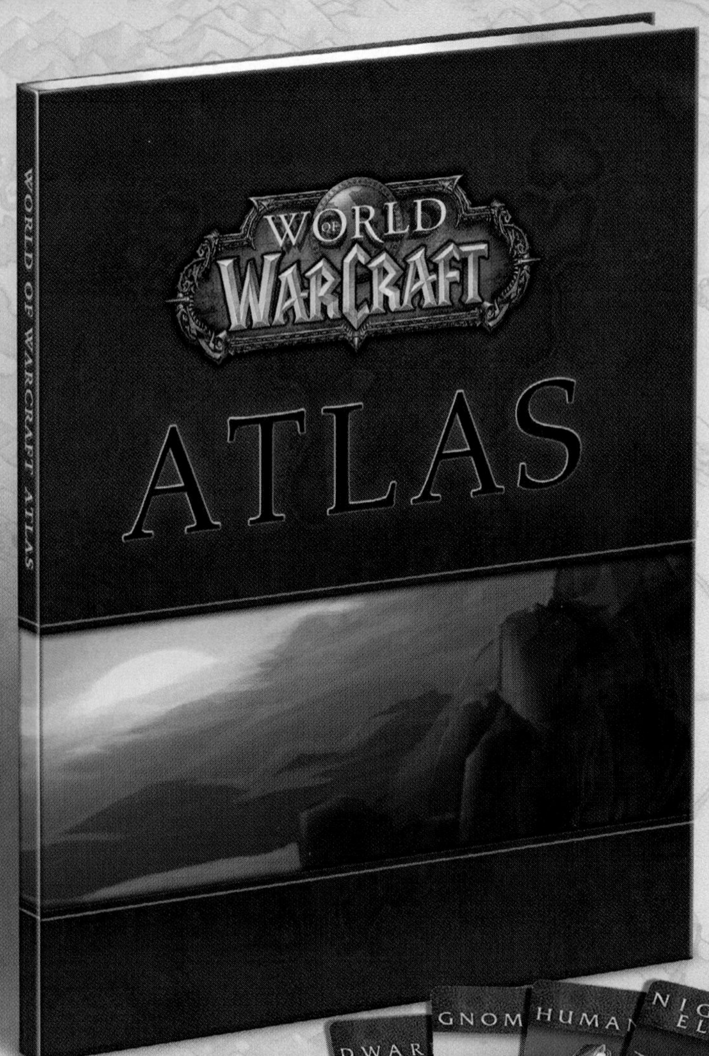

MAPS FOR EVERY AREA—
including All Regions and Major Cities. Special "lay-flat" binding showcases maps in their full glory.

EXHAUSTIVE INDEX—
includes a Complete Listing of all NPCs, Named Enemies, and Beasts—along with their locations on map grids for easy use.

EXCLUSIVE TOWN MAPS—
hand-drawn maps include callouts for everyone in the towns.

WORLD MAP—
marks flight paths, main cities, instance dungeons, and battleground locations.

COLLECTIBLE BOOKMARKS INCLUDED—
this special collection representing each race, their race emblem, and their storyline makes the perfect addition to this beautiful Atlas.

bradygames.com / wow

www.bradygames.com

www.worldofwarcraft.com

MASTER GUIDE

SECOND EDITION

BradyGAMES® Publishing

An Imprint of DK Publishing Inc.
800 East 96th Street, Third Floor
Indianapolis, Indiana 46240

ISBN: 0-7440-0819-0

Printing Code: The rightmost double-digit number is the year of the book's printing; the rightmost single-digit number is the number of the book's printing. For example, 05-1 shows that the first printing of the book occurred in 2005.

09 08 07 06 4 3 2 1

Manufactured in the United States of America.

BRADYGAMES STAFF

Publisher
David Waybright

Editor-In-Chief
H. Leigh Davis

Director of Marketing
Steve Escalante

Creative Director
Robin Lasek

Licensing Manager
Mike Degler

CREDITS

Development Editor
Brian Shotton

Screenshot Editor
Michael Owen

Lead Designer
Brent Gann

Layout Designers
Dan Caparo
Areva
Bob Klunder

KAYAL

Author
Michael Lummis
Kirin Tor-Dovrani

SUMBA

Author
Ed Kern
Kirin Tor-Dovrani

ADELHEID

H. Leigh Davis
Dethroc-Wyrd

HEWN

Brian Shotton
Dethroc-Wyrd

KEJEK

Chris Hausermann
Dethroc-Wyrd

MOOSETRAX

Dan Caparo
Dethroc-Wyrd

BIRK

Ken Schmidt
Perenolde-Blame the Mage

SHADOWSTORM

Christian Sumner
Dethroc-Wyrd

LUMMIS'S ACKNOWLEDGEMENTS

I normally say that I would "like to thank" various people for their assistance with a project. For this guide, it is probably more appropriate to say that I "darn well better thank various people." There is no way that any single person could make it through such an amazing game and writing project without immense help from the Blizzard, Brady's editors and designers, personal friends, fellow players, and so forth. Before saying anything else, I'll bow to each and all. "Thank you so very much!" Now, on to the specifics.

Many thanks to Blizzard for their support for the guide. Getting data for our tables is a brutal task. Some of it we do alone. Plenty of it we do with help, and the data provided to us was a gift from the heavens.

I can't praise enough people at Brady for getting this elegant mammoth of a guide together. Christian Sumner and Brian Shotton did the editing work for the guide, and Christian also flew out to do both hard work at Blizzard HQ and make some good buddies there as well! And to Brady's design team, I'll just leave my hat off, since I've been impressed since day one of the FIRST WoW guide. I can't wait to have the new book on my coffee table and my computer desk. Give it to me now! J

Slaps on the back and cigars all around for our home team. To Edwin Kern, a soldier of war on and off of the e-battlefield, I again smile and thank for standing at my side. Without his knowledge of dungeons, group dynamics, and so forth, I would rarely venture too far from the Battlegrounds or the outdoor zones.

To Kurt, Katie, Dave, Burton, Jesse, and Christy, I give a fine /wave. It was nice to have some real life friends in game to play with while making the guide. We had some pretty great times (again).

To Maim on Kirin Tor, I give my /salute. This PvP guild was one of the best that I've had the honor to serve with. Its leading members contributed suggestions for certain portions of the text, collected the entire pet table for the pet store (thanks Jason), helped write quite a portion of the guild section (thanks to you too, Lady Zakota, you crazy Moonkin), and made rank grinding into a darn good time.

To Kirin Tor, my first RP WoW server, I also give a fair shout. After leveling fully on a standard server and on a PvP one, it was nice to get into my character for a while. Kayal made a number of friends out there, and despite many battles with the Alliance, I don't think I made many enemies. Good fortune to both the Horde and Alliance players that I met there.

BRIAN'S ACKNOWLEDGEMENTS

This little guide, and by little I mean gigantic, was put in my lap many moons ago. During that time, I have come to realize what it means to completely trust those people you are working with to succeed. Not only was this trust well placed, I have been humbled by the amount of time and work others spent to make this something more than Brady or I dared to dream.

There is no doubt; I wanted this to be special. I love playing World of Warcraft. In this job, you seldom get to do a guide on a game you love. Often we learn to love the games we are doing, but rarely, if ever, do we get to revisit a game of this magnitude.

From the beginning, I wanted to make a book that was eminently useful. Although we certainly stumbled a few times, never did we, as a team, lose site of the goal. What we were after, from the beginning, rests in your hands. And, as you read my paltry thanks, know that behind each acknowledgement is an individual who by choice sacrificed more than words can express:

To Blizzard, you have created a world of wonder. From the game to the resources you so diligently provide, nothing would have been done if you had not taken the first step.

To Michael Lummis and Ed Kern, you have put forth the standard. When others use the WoW guide as an example on what they want done, know it is you who placed that bar so high. Everything is measured in relation to your work.

To Brent Gann, a freakin awesome design dude! You and I had some long hours and even longer meetings, but man does this book look sweet. You win the internet.

To Dan, Areva, Brad, Tracy, and Bob, thanks for the eleventh hour help. Even with all the extra hours we would have been doomed without you guys picking us up.

To SC, in every project there is an MVP. I cannot express my gratitude enough for the help you provided Xian, myself, and all of Brady. In the span of two days, you took us from the pit of destruction to the lofty pinnacle of success. Without you this guide would in no way be what is was envisioned. Thank you.

To Leigh, thanks for the opportunity. I hope you are as pleased with the product as I.

To Xian, this thing started with you and owes much of its focus and direction to your forward thinking.

To my group on Dethroc, you guys make this all worth while. Vanya, Cyrddin, Kelek, Scarie, and Adelheid, no better mates can an undead Rogue ask for.

And to you, thanks for purchasing the second coming of the OSG. Enjoy.

KERN'S ACKNOWLEDGEMENTS

Even with a guide of this size and complexity, the acknowledgement section seems to be the hardest to write. There are so many people that have aided this guide in one way or another that it would be impossible to list them all, even if I could remember all the names. There is so much to learn in a game this size that even Mages that insist on pulling with Pyroblast or Priests that pull with Mind Blast teach me how to play a healer or tank even better.

/cheer to Blizzard for both an amazing game and for making the time to help us make an amazing guide. World of Warcraft is a game that I enjoy nearly to the point of stupidity. Thanks for the legal crack that is WoW ←

The Brady staff deserves a week off. I have decreed this and so it shall be! Well, maybe I don't have that kind of power, but the extra work that was put in by Christian Sumner, Brian Shotton, and the design team is worth a paid week off and more. This guide would never have gotten anywhere without everyone pulling their weight and more.

I've played the game so long that half of the guilds I'd like to thank no longer exist. Storm on Elune, Redxx in particular, taught me to master the Hunter class and how to work in large raids. With them I saw the beginning of the end-game. Maim and its sister-guild Nightsong Clan on Kirin Tor showed me how to heal teammates, hinder enemies, and run the flag at the same time. These guilds were nearly unstoppable at any small-group challenge, be it in the battlegrounds or an instance. I wasn't in Lost Heroes on Kirin Tor for long, but they treated me with respect and kindness. They also showed me how to play an effective healer in a raid environment and many of the end-game zones. There are many other guilds that have come and gone. Each has taught me something and I'm glad to have met all of them.

Few guilds can offer what a circle of close friends can. I've enjoyed playing with close friends so much that it's hard to imagine WoW without them. Whether it was snaring enemies in Warsong Gulch, tearing dwarves off me in Blackrock Depths, blasting the annoying rats off me in Stratholme or listening to me whine about another group wipe in guild chat, my friends have always been there. Dave, Katie, Jesse, Christy, Kurt, and Burton also deserve a week of paid vacation!

No one can single-handedly produce a guide this size. Keeping me sane, the guide on track, and the deadlines at bay was Mike Lummis. The man can take any game and say how long each section will take and which sections we should do first. With his guidance, I was able to contribute to something that is much bigger than myself.

BLIZZARD ENTERTAINMENT

Creative Development Manager
Shawn Carnes

Director of Global Licensing
Cory Jones

Producer
Gloria Soto

Art Approvals
Joanna Cleland-Jolly

QA Approvals
Daniel Polcari
Andrew Rowe
John Lynch

Additional Support
Jason Weng
Joseph Magdalena

QA Feedback
Joseph Ryan
Timothy Ismay
Asher Litwin
Morgan Day
Dan Kramer
Sean Reyes
Foster Elmendorf
Art Peshkov
Jason Weng
Joseph Magdalena
Robert Boxeth

Licensing Specialist
Brian Hsieh

Blizzard Special Thanks
Chris Metzen
Ben Brode
Michael Gilmartin
Shane Cargilo